MORRIS AUTOMATED INFORMATION NETWORK

0 1021 0138129 5

ON LINE

Twentieth-Century
Literary Criticism

Guide to Gale Literary Criticism Series

For criticism on	Consult these Gale series
Authors now living or who died after December 31, 1999	*CONTEMPORARY LITERARY CRITICISM (CLC)*
Authors who died between 1900 and 1999	*TWENTIETH-CENTURY LITERARY CRITICISM (TCLC)*
Authors who died between 1800 and 1899	*NINETEENTH-CENTURY LITERATURE CRITICISM (NCLC)*
Authors who died between 1400 and 1799	*LITERATURE CRITICISM FROM 1400 TO 1800 (LC)* *SHAKESPEAREAN CRITICISM (SC)*
Authors who died before 1400	*CLASSICAL AND MEDIEVAL LITERATURE CRITICISM (CMLC)*
Authors of books for children and young adults	*CHILDREN'S LITERATURE REVIEW (CLR)*
Dramatists	*DRAMA CRITICISM (DC)*
Poets	*POETRY CRITICISM (PC)*
Short story writers	*SHORT STORY CRITICISM (SSC)*
Black writers of the past two hundred years	*BLACK LITERATURE CRITICISM (BLC)* *BLACK LITERATURE CRITICISM SUPPLEMENT (BLCS)*
Hispanic writers of the late nineteenth and twentieth centuries	*HISPANIC LITERATURE CRITICISM (HLC)* *HISPANIC LITERATURE CRITICISM SUPPLEMENT (HLCS)*
Native North American writers and orators of the eighteenth, nineteenth, and twentieth centuries	*NATIVE NORTH AMERICAN LITERATURE (NNAL)*
Major authors from the Renaissance to the present	*WORLD LITERATURE CRITICISM, 1500 TO THE PRESENT (WLC)* *WORLD LITERATURE CRITICISM SUPPLEMENT (WLCS)*

ISSN 0276-8178

Volume 103

Twentieth-Century Literary Criticism

**Criticism of the
Works of Novelists, Poets, Playwrights,
Short Story Writers, and Other Creative Writers
Who Lived between 1900 and 1999,
from the First Published Critical
Appraisals to Current Evaluations**

Linda Pavlovski
Editor

GALE GROUP

Detroit
New York
San Francisco
London
Boston
Woodbridge, CT

STAFF

Lynn M. Spampinato, Janet Witalec, *Managing Editors, Literature Product*
Kathy D. Darrow, *Product Liaison*
Linda Pavlovski, *Editor*
Mark W. Scott, *Publisher, Literature Product*

Jennifer Baise, Jenny Cromie, Ellen McGeagh, *Editors*
Thomas Ligotti, *Associate Editor*
Scott Darga, *Assistant Editor*
Mary Ruby, *Technical Training Specialist*
Deborah J. Morad, Kathleen Lopez Nolan, *Managing Editors*
Susan M. Trosky, *Director, Literature Content*

Maria L. Franklin, *Permissions Manager*
Edna Hedblad, *Permissions Specialist*

Victoria B. Cariappa, *Research Manager*
Tracie A. Richardson, *Project Coordinator*
Tamara C. Nott, *Research Associate*
Nicodemus Ford, Sarah Genik, Timothy Lehnerer, Ron Morelli, *Research Assistants*

Dorothy Maki, *Manufacturing Manager*
Stacy L. Melson, *Buyer*

Mary Beth Trimper, *Manager, Composition and Electronic Prepress*
Gary Leach, *Composition Specialist*

Michael Logusz, *Graphic Artist*
Randy Bassett, *Imaging Supervisor*
Robert Duncan, Dan Newell, *Imaging Specialists*
Pamela A. Reed, *Imaging Coordinator*
Kelly A. Quin, *Editor, Image and Multimedia Content*

Library of Congress Catalog Card Number 76-46132
ISBN 0-7876-4563-x
ISSN 0276-8178
Printed in the United States of America

10 9 8 7 6 5 4 3 2 1

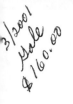

Contents

Preface

Since its inception more than fifteen years ago, *Twentieth-Century Literary Criticism* (*TCLC*) has been purchased and used by nearly 10,000 school, public, and college or university libraries. *TCLC* has covered more than 500 authors, representing 58 nationalities and over 25,000 titles. No other reference source has surveyed the critical response to twentieth-century authors and literature as thoroughly as *TCLC*. In the words of one reviewer, "there is nothing comparable available." *TCLC* "is a gold mine of information—dates, pseudonyms, biographical information, and criticism from books and periodicals—which many librarians would have difficulty assembling on their own."

Scope of the Series

TCLC is designed to serve as an introduction to authors who died between 1900 and 1999 and to the most significant interpretations of these author's works. Volumes published from 1978 through 1999 included authors who died between 1900 and 1960. The great poets, novelists, short story writers, playwrights, and philosophers of the period are frequently studied in high school and college literature courses. In organizing and reprinting the vast amount of critical material written on these authors, *TCLC* helps students develop valuable insight into literary history, promotes a better understanding of the texts, and sparks ideas for papers and assignments. Each entry in *TCLC* presents a comprehensive survey on an author's career or an individual work of literature and provides the user with a multiplicity of interpretations and assessments. Such variety allows students to pursue their own interests; furthermore, it fosters an awareness that literature is dynamic and responsive to many different opinions.

Every fourth volume of *TCLC* is devoted to literary topics. These topics widen the focus of the series from the individual authors to such broader subjects as literary movements, prominent themes in twentieth-century literature, literary reaction to political and historical events, significant eras in literary history, prominent literary anniversaries, and the literatures of cultures that are often overlooked by English-speaking readers.

TCLC is designed as a companion series to Gale's *Contemporary Literary Criticism,* (*CLC*) which reprints commentary on authors who died after 1999. Because of the different time periods under consideration, there is no duplication of material between *CLC* and *TCLC*.

Organization of the Book

A *TCLC* entry consists of the following elements:

■   The **Author Heading** cites the name under which the author most commonly wrote, followed by birth and death dates. Also located here are any name variations under which an author wrote, including transliterated forms for authors whose native languages use nonroman alphabets. If the author wrote consistently under a pseudonym, the pseudonym will be listed in the author heading and the author's actual name given in parenthesis on the first line of the biographical and critical information. Uncertain birth or death dates are indicated by question marks. Single-work entries are preceded by a heading that consists of the most common form of the title in English translation (if applicable) and the original date of composition.

■   A **Portrait of the Author** is included when available.

■   The **Introduction** contains background information that introduces the reader to the author, work, or topic that is the subject of the entry.

■   The list of **Principal Works** is ordered chronologically by date of first publication and lists the most important works by the author. The genre and publication date of each work is given. In the case of foreign authors whose works have been translated into English, the English-language version of the title follows in brackets. Unless otherwise indicated, dramas are dated by first performance, not first publication.

■ Reprinted **Criticism** is arranged chronologically in each entry to provide a useful perspective on changes in critical evaluation over time. The critic's name and the date of composition or publication of the critical work are given at the beginning of each piece of criticism. Unsigned criticism is preceded by the title of the source in which it appeared. All titles by the author featured in the text are printed in boldface type. Footnotes are reprinted at the end of each essay or excerpt. In the case of excerpted criticism, only those footnotes that pertain to the excerpted texts are included.

■ A complete **Bibliographical Citation** of the original essay or book precedes each piece of criticism.

■ Critical essays are prefaced by brief **Annotations** explicating each piece.

■ An annotated bibliography of **Further Reading** appears at the end of each entry and suggests resources for additional study. In some cases, significant essays for which the editors could not obtain reprint rights are included here. Boxed material following the further reading list provides references to other biographical and critical sources on the author in series published by Gale.

Indexes

A **Cumulative Author Index** lists all of the authors that appear in a wide variety of reference sources published by the Gale Group, including *TCLC*. A complete list of these sources is found facing the first page of the Author Index. The index also includes birth and death dates and cross references between pseudonyms and actual names.

A **Cumulative Nationality Index** lists all authors featured in *TCLC* by nationality, followed by the number of the *TCLC* volume in which their entry appears.

A **Cumulative Topic Index** lists the literary themes and topics treated in the series as well as in *Classical and Medieval Literature Criticism, Literature Criticism from 1400 to 1800, Nineteenth-Century Literature Criticism,* and the *Contemporary Literary Criticism* Yearbook, which was discontinued in 1998.

An alphabetical **Title Index** accompanies each volume of *TCLC*. Listings of titles by authors covered in the given volume are followed by the author's name and the corresponding page numbers where the titles are discussed. English translations of foreign titles and variations of titles are cross-referenced to the title under which a work was originally published. Titles of novels, dramas, nonfiction books, and poetry, short story, or essay collections are printed in italics, while individual poems, short stories, and essays are printed in roman type within quotation marks.

In response to numerous suggestions from librarians, Gale also produces an annual paperbound edition of the *TCLC* cumulative title index. This annual cumulation, which alphabetically lists all titles reviewed in the series, is available to all customers. Additional copies of this index are available upon request. Librarians and patrons will welcome this separate index; it saves shelf space, is easy to use, and is recyclable upon receipt of the next edition.

Citing *Twentieth-Century Literary Criticism*

When writing papers, students who quote directly from any volume in the Literary Criticism Series may use the following general format to footnote reprinted criticism. The first example pertains to material drawn from periodicals, the second to material reprinted from books.

George Orwell, "Reflections on Gandhi," *Partisan Review* 6 (Winter 1949): 85-92; reprinted in *Twentieth-Century Literary Criticism,* vol. 59, ed. Jennifer Gariepy (Detroit: The Gale Group, 1995), 40-3.

William H. Slavick, "Going to School to DuBose Heyward," *The Harlem Renaissance Re-examined,* ed. Victor A. Kramer (AMS, 1987), 65- 91; reprinted in *Twentieth-Century Literary Criticism,* vol. 59, ed. Jennifer Gariepy (Detroit: The Gale Group, 1995), 94-105.

Suggestions are Welcome

Readers who wish to suggest new features, topics, or authors to appear in future volumes, or who have other suggestions or comments are cordially invited to call, write, or fax the Managing Editor:

Managing Editor, Literary Criticism Series
The Gale Group
27500 Drake Road
Farmington Hills, MI 48331-3535
1-800-347-4253 (GALE)
Fax: 248-699-8054

Acknowledgments

The editors wish to thank the copyright holders of the excerpted criticism included in this volume and the permissions managers of many book and magazine publishing companies for assisting us in securing reproduction rights. We are also grateful to the staffs of the Detroit Public Library, the Library of Congress, the University of Detroit Mercy Library, Wayne State University Purdy/Kresge Library Complex, and the University of Michigan Libraries for making their resources available to us. Following is a list of the copyright holders who have granted us permission to reproduce material in this volume of *TCLC*. Every effort has been made to trace copyright, but if omissions have been made, please let us know.

COPYRIGHTED EXCERPTS IN *TCLC*, VOLUME 103, WERE REPRODUCED FROM THE FOLLOWING PERIODICALS:

American Literature, v. 53, May, 1981. Copyright © 1981 by Duke University Press. Reproduced by permission.—*American Quarterly,* v. VI, Summer, 1954. Copyright 1954, renewed 1982 American Studies Association. Reproduced by permission of The Johns Hopkins University Press.—*American Studies,* v. XIV, Spring, 1973 for "Making the Sublime Mechanical: Henry Blake Fuller's 'Chicago'" by Guy Szuberla. Copyright © Mid-American Studies Association, 1973. Reprinted by permission of the publisher and the author.—*Art in America,* v. 73, October, 1985 for "The Postmodern Museum" by John Rajchman. Copyright © 1985 by John Rajchman. Reproduced by permission of the author.—*Artforum,* v. XXIV, September, 1985 for "A Reflection on Post-Modernism" by Kate Linker. Copyright © 1985 Artforum International Magazine, Inc. All rights reserved. Reproduced by permission of the publisher and the author.—*Canadian Journal of Italian Studies,* v. 10, 1987. Reproduced by permission of The Desoto Press Inc.—*The Centennial Review,* v. XXXII, Fall, 1988 for "Postmodernity, Narratives, Sexual Politics: Reflections on Jean-Francois Lyotard" by John R. Leo. Copyright © *The Centennial Review,* 1988. Reproduced by permission of the publisher and the author.—*Chicago Review,* v. 35, Spring, 1987. Copyright © 1987 by *Chicago Review.* All rights reserved. Reproduced by permission.—*Commentary,* v. 43, April, 1967 for "John Peale Bishop & the Other Thirties" by Leslie A. Fiedler. Copyright © Leslie Fiedler 1967. All rights reserved. Reproduced by permission of the publisher and the author.—*Diacritics,* v. 9, Summer, 1979; v. 14, Fall, 1984; v. 19, Fall-Winter, 1989; v. 24, Spring, 1994. Copyright © 1979, 1984, 1989, 1994 The Johns Hopkins University Press. All rights reserved. All reproduced by permission.—*Education Week,* v. 12, November 4, 1992 for "What If Montessori Education Is Part of the Answer?" by Dennis Schapiro. Reproduced by permission of the author. v. 9, December 13, 1989. Reproduced by permission from *Education Week.*—*History of Education Quarterly,* v. 19, Spring, 1979 for a review of "Maria Montessori" by Joan N. Burstyn. Reproduced by permission of the author.—*Italian Americana,* v. VII, Fall-Winter, 1981. Copyright © 1982 by Ruth Falbo and Richard Gambino. Reproduced by permission.—*The Journal of Aesthetics and Art Criticism,* v. 48, Winter, 1990. Copyright © 1990 by The American Society for Aesthetics. Reproduced by permission.—*The Journal of Religion,* v. 71, April, 1991. © 1991 by The University of Chicago. All rights reserved. Reproduced by permission of The University of Chicago Press.—*New German Critique,* n. 33, Fall, 1984. Copyright © New German Critique, Inc., 1985. All rights reserved. Reproduced by permission.—*The New York Times Book Review,* August 9, 1998 for "Seven Types of Ambiguity" by Joel Conarroe. Copyright © 1998 by The New York Times Company. Reproduced by permission of the author.—*Philosophy and Literature,* v. 13, April, 1989. Copyright © The Johns Hopkins University Press 1989. All rights reserved. Reproduced by permission.—*Philosophy & Social Criticism,* v. 16, 1990. Reproduced by permission of Sage Publications, Ltd.—*The Review of Metaphysics,* v. XLII, September, 1988. Copyright © 1988 by *The Review of Metaphysics.* Reproduced by permission.—*Rocky Mountain Review of Language and Literature,* v. 50, 1996. Reproduced by permission.—*The Sewanee Review,* v. XC, Summer, 1982 for "The Sorrows of John Peale Bishop" by Lewis P. Simpson. Copyright © 1982 by The University of the South. Reproduced with permission of the editor and the author.—*The South Atlantic Quarterly,* v. LII, July, 1953. Copyright © 1953, renewed 1981 by Duke University Press, Durham, NC. Reproduced by permission.—*Southern Humanities Review,* v. XIX, Fall, 1985. Copyright © 1985 by Auburn University. All rights reserved. Reproduced by permission.—*The Southern Journal of Philosophy,* v. XXVIII, Winter, 1990. Copyright 1990 by the Department of Philosophy, Memphis State University. Reproduced by permission.—*The Southern Literary Journal,* v. VII, Spring, 1975. Copyright 1975 by the Department of English, University of North Carolina at Chapel Hill. Reproduced by permission.—*Sub-Stance,* v. VIII, 1979. Copyright © 1980 Sub-Stance Inc., 1980. Reproduced by permission.—*Substance,* v. 15, 1986; v. XXV, 1996. © 1986, 1996 by the Board of Regents of the University of Wisconsin System. Both reproduced by permission.—*Telos,* n. 83, Spring, 1990. © 1990, Telos Press Ltd. Reproduced by permission.—*Times Literary Supplement,* n. 4681, December 18, 1992. © The Times Supplements Limited 1992. Reproduced from *The Times Literary Supplement* by permission.—*Women's Studies: An Interdisciplinary Journal,* v. 20, March, 1992. © 1992 Gordon and Breach Science Publishers SA. All rights reserved. Reproduced by permission.

John Peale Bishop
1892-1944

American poet, short story writer, novelist, critic, essayist, and editor.

INTRODUCTION

Bishop's literary reputation rests upon a small body of sparse and painstakingly crafted poems, as well as his short stories "Resurrection" (1922) and "Many Thousands Gone" (1931), and his novel *Act of Darkness* (1935). These works readily reveal Bishop's influences: Archibald Mac-Leish in his poetry and William Faulkner in his fiction. Despite the seemingly derived style of much of his body of work, Bishop is admired for his depictions of romantic and sexual love in his poetry, and his renderings of sexual and spiritual awakening in his fiction. A Princeton class-mate of Edmund Wilson and F. Scott Fitzgerald, Bishop probably is remembered most as a friend of these men, as well as a longtime friend of writers Allen Tate and Mac-Leish.

BIOGRAPHICAL INFORMATION

Bishop was born in what is now Charles Town, West Virgina, into an affluent and cultured family. His father was a doctor who taught his son how to paint, beginning Bish-op's lifelong affinity with the visual arts. Bishop's literary talents were also encouraged. When his father died, Bishop was ten years old, and he believed this event and his moth-er's eventual remarriage to have precipitated a long bout of illness that caused him to miss two years of school. He attended Washington County High School in Hagerstown, Maryland, for four years, and attended Mercersburg Acad-emy, a preparatory school, before enrolling at Princeton in 1913. Having already published his first poem in *Har-per's Weekly* in 1912, Bishop immediately immersed him-self in the school's literary milieu as a contributor to and later editor of the school's *Nassau Literary Magazine*. At Princeton, he met Edmund Wilson and F. Scott Fitzgerald, who fictionalized Bishop as Thomas Parke D'Invilliers, the poet character in his novels *This Side of Paradise* and *The Great Gatsby*. Bishop continued to publish his poetry, winning many undergraduate awards for his efforts. Many of these works appeared in his inaugural volume of verse, *Green Fruit* (1917). Graduating in 1917, Bishop enlisted as a lieutenant in the infantry during World War I. He traveled to France, but did not engage in battle. Instead he served as an escort for prisoners-of-war and, later, worked on the disinterment and reburial of American soldiers. This last experience served as inspiration for the graphic

short story "Resurrection," considered among his finest pieces of fiction. Following his military service, Bishop accepted a staff position at *Vanity Fair,* where he became managing editor. During this period, he collaborated on *The Undertaker's Garland* (1922) with Edmund Wilson, a collection of short stories and poems that presented sar-donic accounts of death. Bishop married in 1922 and moved with his wife to Europe, where he met and became close friends with MacLeish. In 1924, the Bishops re-turned to New York. He worked at Paramount Pictures during this time and continued work on his unfinished and unpublished novel, *The Huntsmen Are up in America,* an endeavor that he eventually abandoned when his publisher lost interest. Bishop and his wife moved back to France, purchased a chateau outside Paris, and lived in near-seclusion. Later, Bishop and his wife moved back to the United States, lived for awhile in his father's native state of Connecticut, spent a year in New Orleans, then built a house, Sea Change, on Cape Cod. In 1940, Bishop became chief poetry editor for the *Nation* magazine. MacLeish ar-ranged for U. S. government appointments for his friend, including Director of Publications of the Bureau of Cultural Relations of the Council of National Defense and Resident Fellow in Comparative Literature at the Library of Congress during World War II, but Bishop had to abandon both posts because of his failing health. He suffered a heart attack in 1944, and died two weeks later.

MAJOR WORKS

Bishop wrote much of his most mature work while residing in France. The poems collected in *Now with His Love* (1933) are romantic and erotic odes to his wife that display the influence of MacLeish, Ezra Pound, and T. S. Eliot. *Minute Particulars* (1935), another collection of poems, contains such critically admired pieces as "Southern Pines," "An Interlude," and "A Frieze." Before he died, Bishop published his *Selected Poems* (1941), which was expanded by Allen Tate for the posthumous *The Collected Poems of John Peale Bishop* (1948). *Many Thousands Gone* (1931), often considered Bishop's most successful fiction, is a cycle of stories set in a fictional Southern town that inspired critical comparisons to Faulkner's Yoknapatawpha County. His autobiographical novel, *Act of Darkness,* contains many passages admired by critics, but many commentators considered the work's shifting narrative perspectives unstructured and undisciplined. Much of Bishop's nonfiction is contained the posthumous collection *The Collected Essays of John Peale Bishop* (1948), edited by Edmund White, and *The Republic of Letters in America: The Correspondence of John Peale Bishop and Allen Tate* (1981).

PRINCIPAL WORKS

Green Fruit (poetry) 1917
The Undertaker's Garland [with Edmund Wilson] (poetry and short stories) 1922
Many Thousands Gone (short stories) 1931
Now with His Love (poetry) 1933
Act of Darkness (novel) 1935
Minute Particulars (poetry) 1935
Selected Poems (poetry) 1941
The Collected Essays of John Peale Bishop (essays) 1948
The Collected Poems of John Peale Bishop (poetry) 1948
Selected Poems of John Peale Bishop (poetry) 1960
The Republic of Letters in America: The Correspondence of John Peale Bishop and Allen Tate (letters) 1981

CRITICISM

Robert Wooster Stallman (essay date 1953)

SOURCE: "The Poetry of John Peale Bishop," in *Southern Renascence,* edited by Louis D. Rubin and Robert D. Jacobs, The Johns Hopkins Press, 1953, pp. 368-91.

[*In the following essay, Stallman examines the contemporary influences of Ezra Pound, Archibald MacLeish, T. S. Eliot, and others on Bishop's poetry.*]

> He who would do good to another
> Must do it in minute particulars
>
> —*Minute Particulars*

I

Paul Valéry, remarking on Poe's far reaching influence (from Baudelaire to Valéry himself), contends that the surest criterion of the value of poetic genius is a long descent of prolific influence, not the production of masterpieces. As late as 1936, T. S. Eliot was rejecting Milton on the grounds that "Milton's poetry could *only* be an influence for the worse, upon any poet whatever." Reversing this stand in his recent British Academy lecture, Eliot no longer impugns Milton on grounds of influence: "The only relation in which the question of influence good and bad is significant, is the relation to the immediate future." As T. Sturge Moore first pointed out (in the *Criterion*, 1926), Valéry's notion of influence is a scientific or historical standard but not an aesthetic one. The question we should ask of any poet is: what are the masterpieces he has produced? Not influence, but achievement in terms of achieved poems should be the basis of critical assessment.

The problem of influence in terms of what the poet has borrowed from other poets is raised by Bishop's poetry more than by any other poetry of our time. Bishop's poetry is the collective catch-all of the chief fashions which his age made current. His derivations and echoes, as other critics have pointed out,[1] constitute a catalogue of contemporary poets:—Pound, Eliot, Yeats, Tate, MacLeish, Cummings, W. C. Williams, Wallace Stevens, Paul Valéry; even perhaps Edith Sitwell and Hart Crane.[2] Pound and Eliot predominate in *Now With His Love* (1933), Yeats and Tate more especially in *Minute Particulars* (1935). While the influence of Eliot and Pound diminishes in the later poems, that of Yeats persists beyond *Selected Poems* (1941). (For instance: **"Ghoul's Wharf,"** which is Yeats-like in form and seems likely to have had Yeats' "What Then?" as model.) What Oscar Wilde says of Mrs. Cheveley in *An Ideal Husband* applies to many of Bishop's poems: "A work of art, on the whole, but showing the influence of too many schools."

In tracing a poet's sources we chronicle his poetic development, but the critical question is whether the derived convention, idiom or tone, has been transformed so that what has been borrowed is now integrated anew. It is not without symbolic significance that the name he gave to his place on a stretch of salt-marsh at Cape Cod was "Sea Change." (Cf. "Full Fathom Five" in *The Tempest*.) Bishop succeeded again and again in transforming his borrowings, transforming them not necessarily into "something rich and strange," but into something that survives as his own. The paradox of his "originality" is illustrated, for one example, by **"Young Men Dead:"**

Bernard Peyton is dead
It is thirteen years:
Son of a decayed house
He might have made his roof
Less contumelious
Had there been time enough
Before they buried his bed;
Now it is thirteen years
At seventeen years old.
And Mooch of the bull-red
Hair who had so many dears
Enjoyed to the core
And Newlin who hadn't one
To answer his shy desire
Are blanketed in the mould
Dead in the long war.
And I who have most reason
Remember them only when the sun
Is at his dullest season.

(In *Now With His Love*, 1933)

"Only the best of Yeats" (to quote Tate) is better than this.

The worst that can be said of derivative writing is that it is an admission of failure in self-discovery. "My imitation of other poets," Bishop admits, "is in part a desire not to be myself." Mr. Ransom once remarked to me, though not in reference to Bishop's poetry, that a poet ought not permit himself more than two or three voices, three at most. Bishop expresses himself by over a half-dozen; and his style, even when it is not a borrowed idiom, is impersonal and neutral, as neutral as the style of Robert Bridges. His poetry lacks the signature of a personal idiom, an identifying voice or tone.

The Gregory-Zaturenska *History of American Poetry* scorches Bishop with the easy verdict that his ***Selected Poems*** "could be used as a textbook illustrating changes in poetic taste from 1916 to 1940—and no single poem, no matter how polished it may have seemed at first reading, has the distinction of an individually formed taste and imagination." But this criticism is rather unjust and requires some qualification. Bishop readapted current techniques, but he readapted them from their originals, employing the same attitudes (to paraphrase Warren) from which these techniques were developed. What Bishop wrote of Edna St. Vincent Millay applies equally to his own poetry: "Many of her images seem to come to her from other poets; actually she has taken them out of the public domain and by long familiarity made them her own" (***Collected Essays***, 1948, page 325).

Edmund Wilson's prejudiced notion that Bishop's poetry evidences "the finest poetic instrument that we have had in the United States since Pound and Eliot" (in *We Moderns*) can scarcely be taken literally. For a "poetic instrument" means, for one thing, an original idiom or style. The individuality that Bishop attained he attained only at rare intervals. Frost is often dull, but there is no mistaking his speech for another's. In MacLeish of the *Conquistadors* the identifying idiom is a mechanical mannerism of syntax and voice; in Cummings, a forced eccentricity of typogra-

phy and prosody; the signature of Ransom is unmistakable—his witty, ironic tone. Originality, as Frost defines it, "consists in wagging the mind in one's art differently." Of course a style of unmistakable identity produces as many bad poems as it does good poems—in Cummings, for example. The critical determinant is not solely originality.

Bishop's concessions to modernity spoil no small number of his poems, yet there remain two groups of about a dozen poems each: (1) the poems in which these influences have been successfully transformed, reintegrated into structural wholes; and (2) the poems which show no traces of influence and are entirely Bishop's own. A third group consists of his translations; notably his renderings from the French of two Rimbaud sonnets and his superb translations from the Greek anthology—*To A Swallow and Epitaph,* which have been rated the best translations of these poems ever written.

Bishop studied and absorbed into his poetry practically the whole range of Western literature and art: Greek and Latin, French, British and American. Music he knew intimately, and painting he knew from first-hand practice. The influence of painting upon his poetry and critical writings is seen in such poems as **"Riviera"** and in **"Still Life: Carrots."** **"Ballet"** imitates Giorgio de Chirico, and **"Fiametta"** the Fiametta of Boccaccio. **"Perspectives Are Precipices"** is the poem as a Dali painting. His concern with painting in relationship to literature is found in such critical pieces as **"The Passion of Pablo Picasso," "The Infanta's Ribbon,"** and **"Poetry and Painting."** This last is especially interesting in relation to his poem **"Paolo Uccello's Battle Horses."** As for his literary echoes, they extend beyond his contemporaries to Chaucer and Wyatt; Shakespeare and Elizabethan dramatists; Jonson, Donne, and Dryden; Blake, Shelley, Emily Dickinson, Dante Gabriel Rossetti, Swinburne, and Ernest Dowson. Emily Dickinson is deliberately echoed in **"A Subject of Sea Change:"** "Death greets us without civilities." Rossetti and Keats appear in **"And When the Net Was Unwound Venus Was Found Ravelled With Mars,"** a poem that imitates chiefly the manner of Pound: "In black silk her bosom seemed / Taking flight for heaven in heaviest breath." Frost himself might have written:

> You'd think that he would cause a shock
> The scorpion with his double cock,
> Both sides erect, but not at all.
> The scorpion is a liberal.
>
> One thrusts to right, one sticks to left
> As he advances toward the cleft
> And then presents in copulation
> The New Republic of the Nation.

(This poem, untitled except by its first line, was first published in the ***Collected Poems***, 1948.) Though Bishop did not care much for Frost's poetry, the influence of Frost is noticeable in Bishop's landscape poems such as **"Moving Landscape With Rain." "The Dream,"** posthumously published in 1945, is done somewhat in the manner of

Mark Van Doren. And **"A Spare Quilt,"** having perhaps its model in the poems of Mark Van Doren, can be read as in effect a criticism by Bishop of his New England fellow craftsman.

II

Bishop's poetic output (approximately one hundred and twenty-five poems, the same in volume as Yvor Winters's) is slight by comparison with the fecundity of Frost or Mark Van Doren. It would be absurd to label a poet "minor" on that account. A "major" poet is not a major poet by virtue of his bulky output. Frost and Van Doren are certainly bulky, but not at their best. The labels "minor" and "major" defy definition (Eliot's attempts notwithstanding), but if the perfections of poets were weighed one against another the critic would have a more accurate measurement of poetic stature than now prevails. It takes no pair of scales to decide that Bishop is a minor poet, yet his achieved poems surprise in number. Very few poets, however bulky their output, produce more than a dozen first-rate poems. There is a distinction to be made, of course, between poems that are perfectly contrived wholes and poems that are triumphs. Triumphs occur only now and then.

Bishop's elected best are **"The Return"** and **"Perspectives are Precipices."** From *Now With His Love* (1933) I would also single out **"Speaking of Poetry," "Young Men Dead," "Fiametta," "Behavior of the Sun,"** and **"This Dim and Ptolemaic Man."** From *Minute Particulars* (1935) I would single out as best **"Southern Pines," "An Interlude," "A Recollection," "Your Chase Had a Beast in View," "A Frieze,"** and possibly **"Apparition."** From *Selected Poems:* **"The Yankee Trader,"** perhaps also **"John Donne's Statue"** and **"The Statue of Shadow,"** but superior to all these is **"Colloquy With A King-Crab."** The less said about Bishop's first volume, *Green Fruit* (1917) the better. And the same holds true for most of his uncollected and unpublished early poems reproduced in *Collected Poems* (1948). The best of his uncollected later poems seem to me **"The Submarine Bed," "The Paralle," "The Spare Quilt,"** and **"The Dream;"** of the unpublished later poems reproduced in *Collected Poems* the only one worth singling out is **"This Critic."** A formidable list indeed; not many poets do much better!

His poetry belongs to that classification which Hopkins designated as *Parnassian,* a derivative poetry or a poetry representing one stage in the evolution of a poetic style. In Bishop it is the style of the Symbolists, almost exclusively. The Metaphysicals influenced him scarcely at all; the one exception is **"The Submarine Bed,"** a late poem.

It is Eliot rather than Donne that Bishop leans upon in **"John Donne's Statue:"**

> Proud Donne was one did not believe
> In heirs presumptive to a bone . . .

In style Bishop inclines more to Jonson or Dryden than to Donne. Dryden, whom Eliot taught us to admire, models at least one passage from this same poem:

> Proud Donne was one did not believe
> In heirs presumptive to a bone
> Or boys' pursuit of love, their leave
> To sensual oblivion.
> Come dying then! Too fine a joy
> And too intrinsic for a boy:
> Sustain that ecstasy in stone!

"The Submarine Bed" is metaphysical *and* symbolic. His other poems dealing with lovers or with women are, however, simply imagistic—not witty in tone, not ironical but purely sensual. The sensual characterizes Bishop's poetry almost as much as Keats' or Marlowe's: musically patterned, visually plastic, concrete and richly connotative.

"A Recollection," one of Bishop's perfections, epitomizes the primary defining quality of Bishop's poetry as a whole—its tactile quality. Here is the craftsmanship of a master:

> Famously she descended, her red hair
> Unbound and bronzed by sea-reflections, caught
> Crinkled with sea-pearls. The fine slender taut
> Knees that let down her feet upon the air,
>
> Young breasts, slim flanks and golden quarries were
> Odder than when the young distraught
> Unknown Venetian, painting her portrait, thought
> He'd not imagined what he painted there,
>
> And I too commerced with that golden cloud:
> Lipped her delicious hands and had my ease
> Faring fantastically, perversely proud.
>
> All loveliness demands our courtesies.
> Since she was dead I praised her as I could
> Silently, among the Barberini bees.

The woman is remembered as she was in life, that is, before "the young distraught / Unknown Venetian" painted her portrait. The opening stanzas of the sonnet depict her also as she is in the painting, transposed here on the fresco with the intensity and impact of life itself. Perhaps no such woman existed and the painter but "thought / He'd not imagined what he'd painted there." Where does beauty exist—in fact or in imagination? It was perhaps that very question that caused the painter to be "distraught." Has the painter reproduced the beauty he knew in the flesh or solely the beauty he imagined? Like the painter, the poet too has "commerced with that golden cloud:"—that perfection of beauty which all men seek.

His poem is a painting, but like the fresco the poem is far more than merely a faithful rendering of the original. Art, far from being no more than an imitation of reality, is an imaginative recreation possessing a life all its own. Neither the poet nor the painter has been merely copyistic. The poem implies questions about the relationship of life to art. Its fluid syntax functions to impart an ambiguity of time past and present, the one melting into the other, and simultaneously an ambiguity between fact and fiction. The ambiguity is thematic.

"Commerced" prepares for the final phrase—"the Barberini bees," by which the recollection of the poet returns him from the realms of "golden cloud" to the noisy world of fact:

> Since she was dead I praised her as I could
> *Silently*, among the Barberini bees.

"Since she was dead" transfers to the poet's vision, which is extinguished as his poem glides back to the noisy world of actuality signalized by "the Barberini bees." This vision dies away, but yet the world to which he is returned by "Barberini bees" is not without its beauty too, for the very phrase is beautiful in itself. The painter fulfilled his vision in the painting, and the poet in his poem. He is furthermore compensated by an enrichment of manner, thought, and speech—his life and ours are thus enriched. It is permissable to make one further inference: the poet, like the painter, was "distraught" during the process of composition.

In technique Bishop belongs to his own age, but in his endorsement of passionate flesh he harks back to Shakespeare's *Antony and Cleopatra*, Marlowe's "Hero and Leander," the Elizabethan love-lyric, and Wyatt's "They Flee From Me:"

> I was the first to nakedness. Suddenly she
> Left her dress and her feet were on the floor.

This is from **"And When the Net Was Unwound Venus Was Found Ravelled With Mars,"** a poem about a soldier's momentary "Farewell to Arms" in time of war. (Another piece suggesting Hemingway is **In the Dordogne:"** "the leaves fell / And were blown away; the young men rotted / Under the shadow of the tower.") Whereas the lovers in **"The Submarine Bed"** are troubled by a sense of guilt arising from their union, in **"Metamorphosis"** the lovers are unashamed:

> There was no shame in that
> Consuming nakedness
> For we were one; and a disparate
> Skin is love's own dress.
> But our division of air
> Was burned between ecstasies.

In **"The Spare Quilt,"** obversely, the lovers—frigid New Englanders—lack all passion. Poems "realistically" depicting the sex-act are rather scarce. In modern poetry among the best in this kind are Yeats' "Leda and the Swan" and W. R. Rodgers's "The Net" (in *Botteghe Oscure,* VIII); but both of these poems are symbolic as well as realistic, and Yeats' "Leda and the Swan" is also mythical. The love lyrics of E. E. Cummings, like the lewd poems of Rochester, are witty; they differ from Bishop's poems also in their lack of realistic delineation of object or act. In Bishop's **"Les Balcons Qui Rêvent,"** for instance:

> The lovers sleep, their dreams increased
> By shudders from the night before.

> His breath upon his parted lips,
> Sleeping he flows into her sleep.
> Her belly slumbers, but the tips
> of both dusk breasts are bright awake.

Here the lovers are discovered at dawn; in **"Speaking of Poetry"** the lovers—Desdemona and the Moor—"meet, naked, at dead of night," while "the torches deaden at the bedroom door." **"October Tragedy"**—another "bitter tale of love / And violations on a summer night"—vulgarly describes "The unwilling struggle and the willing fall." Bishop's realism descends to vulgarity again in **"Metamorphosis of M"** (Margaret, his wife), in **"And When the Net Was Unwound,"** and in **"Venus Anadyomene."** In **"To Helen,"** a poem which echoes Pound, the motto used is from Tourneur's *Atheist Tragedie:* "I salute you in the spirit of copulation." That motto applies equally to almost a dozen Bishop poems. Tupping is their subject, the disrobing of the mistress, the caressed body. Bishop's love poems share with a painter the predilection for naked flesh. Their unabashed sensuality seems almost unprecedented in American poetry. Bishop, unlike Auden and Whitman, does not exploit love *as* a doctine. What he celebrates is the experience of love; not a doctrine of love, but an act of love in the sensual moment now. In his affirmation of passion one is reminded of Blake. It is from Blake that Bishop took the title of **Minute Particulars:**

> He who would do good to another
> Must do it in minute particulars.

And from Chaucer he took the title of *Now With His Love:*

> What is this world? What asketh man to have?
> Now with his love, now in his colde grave
> Allone, with-outen any companye.

The love-and-war poems of *Now With His Love*, as Joseph Frank observes, remind us irresistibly "of the early Hemingway, also obsessed with death, also seeking for a source of positive value in naked sensuous experience."

III

"The aim of all the arts," Bishop states in his essay **"The Discipline of Poetry,"** "is to present the conflict of man with time. . . . And the famous release which the arts afford is essentially a release from time." Triumphs over time! But how shall the artist achieve them? How fix the flux of temporal experience, which is without form, into formed structures of meaning? Didacticism is not the answer. "The poem comes inevitably to its end, but the poet does not reach a logical conclusion." Almost without exception, the poems attempting to reach "a logical conclusion" fail—*viz.,* **"Hunger and Thirst," "Counsel of Grief," "Trinity of Crime," "The Tree,"** and **"The Saint."** (My opinion here runs counter to that of M. D. Zabel, who listed these last three poems, in 1941, as among Bishop's best.) These poems substitute statement for symbol, and I think they fail by their didactic resolution of theme.

Bishop is at his best in the poems that *discover* their own theme, their own form, rather than in the poems that directly state their theme. He is a technician of the first order (as Louise Bogan remarked), "incapable of falling into any mawkishness or sentimentality."[3] On the other hand, he is capable of falling into banality (as in **"And When the Net was Unwound"**), vulgarity (as in **"October Tragedy"**), and downright bad taste, as in **"Epithalamium."** The instance Warren singles out, where Bishop's taste fails him flagrantly, is the ending of the **"Ode:"**

> But he is dead,
> Christ is dead. And in a grave
> Dark as a sightless skull He lies
> And of His bones are charnels made.

Bishop's poetry of statement—the finest pure statement poem being **"Young Men Dead"**—is not the pure poetry of statement found in Dryden or in certain poems of the later Yeats. The difference is that Bishop's poetry of statement incorporates also symbolism, as in **"A Defense."** His poetry is mainly a poetry of obliquity, and it is in poems oblique in meaning that he scores his major successes.

Almost none of his poems, not even brief lyrics like **"Green Centuries"** or **"Colloquy in a Garden,"** delivers its meaning at once. And each poem poses a new technical problem and attempts to solve it anew—not by formula. As his critical essays testify, Bishop was preoccupied with problems of form and methods of achieving formal structures. In **"Aphorisms and Notes"** he writes: "A poem has unity of form when, after arousing in the reader a desire to have something happen (in the poem), it satisfies that desire in such a way that the reader is surprised but not resentful." Here Bishop is not exactly original. His definition derives from Kenneth Burke's *Counter-Statement* and reads like a paraphrase. Important is the definition appearing in **"Poetry and Painting:"**—"The ultimate question concerning any work of art is out of how deep a life does it come. But the question that must first be asked is whether it has a life of its own. And the life of art is in its form."

The problem of form Bishop mastered in a significant number of perfectly executed poems, and it is this primary and all-saving virtue of structural achievement that counters and largely cancels Bishop's censorable defects of eclecticism and anonymity. His poetry and criticism, as Hyman says, are substantially of a piece, each reinforcing the other.

Bishop's characteristic structure is a two-part structure of contrasted symbols: the first part being a landscape, portrait, or action by which the theme is initiated, and the second part a symbolic or mythical image contriving the resolution of theme. It is where the second part is symbolic that Bishop's poems are more likely to succeed, whether they begin in statement or in symbol. **"Your Chase Had a Beast in View,"** for example, pictures the hunting of leopards, whose slaughter makes the exultant hunter "A moment young." The literal situation, the hunt,

described in the first part is transposed in the final stanza into symbolic significance:

> Only in singing it might be
> Supported by the sense alone,
> One syllable of ecstasy
> Confusing shame, confounding bone.

The slaughter of the beasts is an event of no duration *until* that event is recreated into art-form, where alone the actual event becomes justified. Among the hunters: "The youngest sang a stranger love." It is his singing that redeems the slaughter. The youngest hunter is, as it were, the poet whose poetic rendering of the bestial contest is the saving thing that makes "sense" of the senseless conquest of the hunted by the hunters. ("At times it seemed they hunted us.") The triumph of art over time is signified also in **"A Frieze,"** while **"Speaking of Poetry"** and **"Colloquy With a King-Crab"** symbolize the methods by which such triumphs are attained.

"Speaking of Poetry" provides the answer: Some mythos, some ceremony or ritual of meaning must be found. This poem, which itself achieves its own prescribed dictum, uses the form-symbols of Othello and Desdemona for the opposition of Life and Art. Set down in ironic contrast, Life is huge and foreign and barbarous, emotionally crude; Art is restrained and delicate, sophisticated and aristocratic. Unions of no spiritual value may deceive the Senator (the critic) or "outwit his disapproval; honest Iago / Can manage that: it is not enough." Life and Art, Emotion and Intellect, how shall they be aesthetically united?

> O, it is not enough
> That they should meet, naked at dead of night
> In a small inn on a dark canal.

They must be wed in magnificent architectures, structures rich with the forms of convention, rich in myth and fable. They must be clothed in textures rich with the symbols of tradition. Their union must be a ritual of timeless imagination, *traditional in ceremony* with antiquities of language strange—symbolic and strange "with never before heard music." Poetry is neither naked emotion nor naked intellect but the perfect fusion of the two. Didacticism—in Tate's canon too *that* is the poet's greatest evil—will not suffice.

> Procurers
> Less expert than Iago can arrange as much.
> The Ceremony must be found
> Traditional, with all its symbols
> Ancient as the metaphors in dreams;
> Strange, with never before heard music; continuous
> Until the torches deaden at the bedroom door.

There the music ends: in the union of Emotion and Intellect.

The best artist is the one who constructs his poems in such a way as to admit of no interpretation but the one intended, the intended meaning being determined by evidence of the poem itself. Bishop's poems are not readily exhaustible in meaning and in no instance are they incoherent at their core, ambiguous or obscure in their dominant intention. Much of the so-called Obscurity in Modern Poetry exists, I believe, chiefly in critical discussions about it. **"Speaking of Poetry"** leaves room for variant readings of its minute particulars, and the same may be said of Bishop's most difficult poem, **"Colloquy With a King-Crab,"** but the overall intention of both poems can scarcely be disputed. The Desdemona needlework of Bishop in **"Speaking of Poetry,"** for all "the subtlety of the stitches," is clearly enough speaking primarily about poetry. Other allegories are not authorized by this one. The present brief reading by no means exhausts the poem. The marriage ceremony in **"Speaking of Poetry"** symbolizes, to add Joseph Frank's reading, tradition; but only a Marxian critic would be inclined to force a reduction of the poem to a sociological tract.

IV

The difficulty of being a poet without a mythos troubles Bishop not only in **"Speaking of Poetry"** but again in **"Behavior of the Sun."** **"Behavior of the Sun"** is Bishop's lament, as artist, for the loss of myth in our scientific civilization. In **"O Let Not Virtue Seek"** the sunward-soaring aviator, Icarus, represents the triumph of science over time and space, science and myth being equated and their "triumphs" obliquely compared. Identical imagery and symbolism recur throughout Bishop's poetry. The dominant imagery is of cloud, wind, sun and shadow, sand and sea. An overlapping of theme likewise links poem to poem. The theme is obversely treated in **"This Dim and Ptolemaic Man:"**

> For forty years, for forty-one,
> Sparing the profits of the sun,
> This farmer piled his meagre hoard
> To buy at last a rattly Ford.
>
> Now crouched on a scared smile he feels
> Motion spurt beneath his heels,
> Rheumatically intent shifts gears,
> Unloosing joints of rustic years.
>
> Morning light obscures the stars,
> He swerves avoiding other cars,
> Wheels with the road, does not discern
> He eastward goes at every turn.
>
> Nor how his aged limbs are hurled
> Through all the motions of the world,
> How wild past farms, past ricks, past trees,
> He perishes toward Hercules.

Modern man has misused "the profits of the sun" and sacrificed himself for the god Science, whose token is that rattly contrivance of our cheap tin age, the Ford.[4] In the motion he feels "spurt beneath his heels," the farmer—like Icarus—seems to possess power over time and space. But his power is an illusion. And science, for all its Herculean labors to conquer nature, can no more triumph over space

than Hercules could do so over time. Death *was* his match. The poet's reduction of Copernican man to Ptolemaic man and again of Science to the Gates of Hercules points to his cynicism:—the one myth is no more valid than the other.

Myth provides the poet with forms of meaning amidst a world confronting him as meaningless or without absolute spiritual values. **"A Divine Nativity"** and **"The Saints"** attempt to establish, by a sensual mingling of Greek and Christian myths, an integration of values, but they fail (I think) in their rendering of the supernatural. These poems are attempts to reinstate a set of beliefs in which the poet himself does not believe. Neither Bishop nor Tate commits himself to the Christian legend. It is by Greek myth rather than by Christian myth that Bishop measures his disbelieving world. Science has stripped the modern world of the possibility for belief, of the possibility for imaginative belief in myth, and it has discredited art as but itself a form of myth. Bishop's position squares with the defense of Myths made by I. A. Richards: "Without his mythologies man is only a cruel animal without a soul . . . a congeries of possibilities without order and aim" (In *Coleridge on the Imagination*). Bishop's major theme is the loss of myth, the loss of belief, the loss of traditional values public and private.

In **"Behavior of the Sun,"** as in **"Colloquy With a King-Crab,"** the fascination of what's difficult is at its pithiest.

The artist, as if to insist upon the validity of his own aesthetic viewpoint, ironically discourses on science in terms of pictures. He embodies his theme in visual images—"the sunlight came in flashes." (We are blinded too much by the light of scrutinizing reason.) Instead of presenting a rational argument, the artist contrarily presents a poem—a piece of symbolism.

The same symbolism of sun and shadow, and with similar meaning, reappears in **"Perspectives Are Precipices"** and in **"The Mothers,"** and here again the theme is the loss of myth. And the tone is similarly one of despair: "After revolt, what triumph and what deaths?" The mothers, older myths whose heritage of religous beliefs our age of science denies, appear, distant and improbable as "vast shadows on the rocks." "And in their eyes are myths conceived." But shadows have no credible substance, no truth of existence; and "We are their sons."

> Over their eyelids, in ethereal bronze
> Deploy, Icarus! For among their rocks
> Are depths where a man might drown.

The sons of these mothers are Icarian sons, Icarus figuring as the new generation of modern science. In personifying our scientific age in the mythical personage of Icarus the poet employs irony, inasmuch as our present-day faith in science is but another myth—the modern myth. "Our course is, I think, nearer to the sun." But as our course is "nearer to the sun," so too is our destiny an Icarian one.

V

The poems in Part VIII of *Selected Poems*—including **"The Saints," "Trinity of Crime," "Divine Nativity,"** and **"The Tree"**—are the result of Bishop's experiment "to make more and more statements, without giving up all that we have gained from Rimbaud." None of them seems to me successful wholes. **"The Saints"** is quite as much a "poetry of the will" (Tate's term) as anything of Shelley, at least in this portion:

> Dilate
> Our loves beyond
> All loves that age
> Or lust consumes,
> O thirst and rage
> For the lost kingdoms!

Bishop is at his best where he is, like Keats, a painting poet. Many of his very best poems are poems *as* paintings. His perfection in this kind is **"Perspectives Are Precipices:"**

> *Sister Anne, Sister Anne,*
> *Do you see anybody coming?*
>> I see a distance of black yews
>> Long as the history of the Jews
>
>> I see a road sunned with white sand
>> Wide plains surrounding silence. And
>
>> Far off, a broken colonnade
>> That overthrows the sun in shade.
> *Sister Anne, Sister Anne,*
> *Do you see nobody coming?*
>
>> A man
>> Upon that road a man who goes
>> Dragging a shadow by its toes.
>
>> Diminishing he goes, head bare
>> Of any covering even hair.
>
>> A pitcher depending from one hand
>> Goes mouth down. And dry is sand.
> *Sister Anne, Sister Anne,*
> *What do you see?*
>> His dwindling stride. And he seems blind
>> Or worse to the prone man behind.
> *Sister Anne! Sister Anne!*
>
>> I see a road. Beyond nowhere
>> Defined by cirrus and blue air.
>
>> I saw a man but he is gone
>> His shadow gone into the sun.

This is the Dali desert of Eliot's "Waste Land." Both poems, like MacLeish's "You Andrew Marvell," convert time into space-images. In his essay on **"Poetry and Painting"** Bishop cites, as an example of a poem situated in space, that passage of "The Waste Land" which begins:

> Here is no water but only rock
> Rock and no water and the sandy road

Bishop points out that "the dry rocks and the sandy road winding toward the mountain where there is still no water are but symbols of a spiritual drought, due to the disappearance of faith in the truth of Christianity, which is itself a disaster of time." These perceptions transpose into an explication of Bishop's own Dali painting. Here the symbols of that spiritual drought are the dry sand and the dry pitcher (replacing the rock in Eliot's landscape). Sister Anne's perspective of history is a perspective of broken colonnades (cultures and beliefs destroyed by the anti-religious attitude) and of a road—once the road of religious faith, now the road of scientific reason—down which man and his civilizations disappear. "Beyond nowhere" is Sister Anne's single image of hope and consolation. The road of scientific reason ends ultimately in realms of the supernatural. Yet her image defines a vacuum: The world of faith is as empty as the world of reason is desolate. Hence Sister Anne's discourse echoes with doubt (*"Do you see nobody coming?"*), of despair (*"What do you see?"*), and of fear (*"Sister Anne! Sister Anne!"*). Questioner and Answerer personify the theme of the poem, and its dialogue form is thus determined. Ironically, it is Science (or Reason) questioning; it is Religion (or Faith) answering. Bishop is using here the French fairy tale of Bluebeard (as Hyman has noted). Though the poem and the fairy tale do not bear point for point relationship, the fact of discrepancies in their literal situation does not constitute, it seems to me, necessarily a flaw in the poem. As in **"Behavior of the Sun,"** the poet discourses in pictures, in images rather than in statements. Tate, in his essay on Bishop (reprinted in *On the Limits of Poetry*), points out that the plastic method of the poem, its method of concretion, is violated by the Metaphysical wit of "long as the history of the Jews," but that blemish is a minor one. Except for this instance of Metaphysical wit, the poem is wholly an aesthetic discourse in terms of pictures, as distinguished from a scientific discourse in terms of statements.

Bishop's **"Perspectives Are Precipices"** is Eliot's Waste Land in miniature. The temporal is converted into images of space not only in these poems but also in Eliot's Sweeney "Among the Nightingales" and in MacLeish's "You, Andrew Marvell." Keats' sonnet, "On First Looking Into Chapman's Homer," presents two consecutive images of space to define simultaneously a single moment. The time-span symbolized by the space-images in Bishop's **"Perspectives"** is extended from Keats' moment to Spengler's history of man. The consecutive images of space in **"Perspectives"** occur successively and not, as they would in a Dali painting, simultaneously. They define a disaster of time, present-past-future: Man's present spiritual drought (the pitcher is its emblem) is the resultant disaster of his tragic past ("a distance of black yews") and images his future wasteland in the present one. **"The Statue of Shadow"** repeats the symbolism of **"Perspectives,"** expressing the same mood of fear and the same theme of history as the lengthened shadow of man.

"The Return," as Bishop himself explains, is a simile with one term of the comparison omitted. The two-part structure of the poem unites fact and myth. As the form of Roman civilization was destroyed by that materialism which created it, so the form of modern civilization is threatened by the same sea of materialism. Though the poem is about the loss of form, it is (to quote Cleanth Brooks) "perfectly 'formed' itself—even the fluid grammar is functioning as 'form' in terms of the poem." The temples of the seagod become the sea itself. "Form is overwhelmed. . . . The movement of the invading sea dominates the rhythm of the stanza, overwhelms the syntax."

Time as fate pitted against man, his art and his civilizations—that is Bishop's commonplace, the obsessive motif of whole poems or of their particulars. Except in **"Riviera,"** where the sea manifests space, the time-motif is symbolized by the sea. **"Beyond Connecticut, Beyond the Sea,"** in which poem Bishop catalogues his forbears, opens and closes upon the sea-symbol—the same as in **"Farewell to Many Cities."** The sequence of ancestral images is thus framed in circle-form. The sea is the emblem most frequently manipulated into an expanding or a contracting spatial image (as in "Vast cities of Atlantis discovered in a skull"); it is chiefly by this device that Bishop achieves his effects of painting.

The problem of the poet centers in his choice of theme and the appropriate symbols by which to form it. This is the problem-theme of **"Colloquy With A King-Crab"** and **"Speaking of Poetry."** In **"Colloquy With a King-Crab"** the poet finds his symbols in nature. Will the horseshoe crab suffice as symbol "To say what I have sought?" The answer, which constitutes one of the obliquities of the poem, is probed out of the crab-symbol phrase by phrase, line by line. There is a second obliquity in the deftly indirect comparison of the crab with the poet. Each derives from the sea of time past. But observe their differences: "This crab is no abstraction"—"His head all belly and his sword all tail, / But to the imagination is suspect. / Reject him? Why?" Well, the poet is a complex of head and heart, one part of him *abstract,* one part *concrete;* his senses reject all abstractions, and his mind suspects all sense-perceptions. As for the crab, he is "no abstraction." But he is the symbol of an abstraction. The crab thus represents these two aspects of art and philosophy: the concrete and the abstract. *That* precisely is "To say what I have sought." For the poet the major problem of his art is to establish and evoke relationships between imagery and theme, between the concrete and the abstract.

VI

"There was not one of the great Symbolist poets," writes Bishop in reviewing Mark Van Doren's poetry, "who might not have declared, as the last of them did, that his aim was to write of his race and reality." This is also Bishop's aim: not to escape from life but to report on his world, to explore, as the Symbolists did before him, the effects of a decayed civilization on modern sensibility. The province of his vision is not an imaginary Shropshire or Celtic twilight-land but a reality of time past and present, the province of his vision extending across seas of historic generations from Virginia and Connecticut to Troy and Rome. The predicament of modern civilization arises from the glorification of the scientific vision at the expense of the aesthetic vision. The resultant disruption of sensibility is the problem-theme underlying much of the poetry of Bishop and the Southern poets.

Bishop is a Southern poet[5] by regional and personal ties with Ransom, Tate, and Warren, but more fundamentally by affinities in his later poems with their moral and traditional problems—the issues of our scientific civilization with its industrial economy. His closest affinity is with Tate. They are alike in their search for a historic religion, in their inquiry into the metaphysics of time and space and the nature of the *elan vital,* in their perspectives of history—time-past juxtaposed with time-present under contexts of mythological and historical symbols—and in their personal definitions of the relationship of the artist to his society and to his forbears. The influence of Tate upon Bishop's **Minute Particulars** is chiefly the influence of this philosophical bias. Again, Bishop is a Southern poet by virtue of his Southern heritage (prior to the Civil War), even as he is a New England poet by virtue of his New England residence. But though he shared Connecticut with Mark Van Doren, he has not made New England his poetic property as Van Doren has done. Nor is he "a Southern regionalist" (as one reviewer labels him). Both his Southern lyrics (only **"Apparition"** is specifically localized) and his New England lyrics (Part IV of the **Selected Poems**) transcend their regional material to unite with other poems on the same theme: the loss of tradition.

"Another Acteon" presents the personal plight of Bishop as the exiled poet returning from a sterile Europe to begin his apprenticeship with domestic traditions, Southern and New England. This poem is an apt occasion for critical judgment in terms of Eliot's criterion of the Objective Correlative. The predicaments of Acteon and the poet do not provide an adequate solution for the emotion expressed by the poet in his plight. That solution (the meaning of his personal plight) is located, not in **"Another Acteon,"** but in companion-poems which answer the questions here asked and upon which our full understanding of this poem depends. **"The Ancestors"** reiterates the same mood of self-questioning fear and objectifies in a single expanded image the reason for that fear. Again, the plight of **"Another Acteon"** is restated in the less oblique **"Return to Connecticut."** What the poet seeks is sustenance in his ancestral land; but his quest ends in disillusionment. The reason for his disillusionment is located in **"Moving Landscape With Falling Rain,"** or again in **"Conquest of the Wind."** Time-past is severed from time-present.

Time, **"The Burning Wheel,"** is personified in the poem by that name in Aeneas and Anchises. As before in flight from disastrous Troy, Aeneas on his shoulders bore Anchises, so

> They, too, the stalwart conquerors of space
> Each on his shoulders wore a wise delirium

> Of memory and age: ghostly embrace
> Of fathers slanted toward a western tomb.

Each cycle of civilization bears on its back the death of its former triumphs, each repeating cycle ending in oblivion. The modern Aeneases, pioneers who conquered the West to found new Romes, "They saw the west, a sky of falling flame". The always pioneering course of mankind toward the West, symbolically, is toward the land of the dead (so the West was identified by the classical poets). The plight of Aeneas, in **"The Burning Wheel,"** fleeing from old worlds lost to new worlds unconquered, is also the plight of **"Another Acteon."**

In **"The Yankee Trader,"** the question of **"Another Acteon"** ("What do I ask for?") is again answered, here by the symbol of an old abandoned sofa. The sofa represents the Puritan tradition of New England: faded in pattern, worn-out in form, abandoned. The sofa-symbol speaks for those values enduring in all patterns, all forms, all traditions. Their loss is the burden of the poem.

What has gone out of New England, since Emily Dickinson defined it in "The Missing All," is the soul sufficient to itself, whose loss Bishop sets down in his essay of that title, and again in his poem **"The Spare Quilt."** Sterile even in Emily's day, Puritanism (the New England Idea, which to the post-war writers of Bishop's generation was the enemy) no longer nurtures the artist.

What history has made of the South is epitomized in the acid etching **"Southern Pines."** (**"Collapse of Time"** develops the same theme, the loss of tradition, and echoes in images of fear the devastated landscape of **"Southern Pines."**) **"Southern Pines"** echoes no other poet. Masefield's "Cargoes" has a similar structural ordering inasmuch as each stanza frames a portrait of an age, the progression defining by contrast a decline. In both poems the method is symbolic. Obliquities of symbol unite with theme: the loss of cultural and spiritual values. Here is the history of our spiritual degeneration:

> White pine, yellow pine
> The first man fearing the forest
> Felled trees, afraid of shadow,
> His own shade in the shadow of pinewoods.
>
> Slash pine, loblolly,
> The second man wore tarheels,
> Slashed pine, gashed pine,
> The silent land changed to a sea-charge.
>
> Short leaf, long leaf,
> The third man had aching pockets.
> Mill town, lumber mill,
> And buzzards sailed the piney barrens.
> Cut pine, burnt pine,
> The fourth man's eyes burned in starvation.
> Bone-back cattle, razor-back hogs
> Achieve the seedlings, end the pinewoods.

"Achieve" keynotes the irony. Stripped of spiritual values, without traditions (those pines to shadow him), man thirsts in starvation. But he no longer has a heart to ache, only "aching pockets." His spiritual death, announced by the starved hogs who alone remain to achieve for him the final devastation, is foretold by the buzzards sailing "the piney barrens." What man has destroyed is his belief in a world of values outside himself ("the first man fearing the forest") and his belief in a world of values within ("afraid of shadow, / His own shade"). What the hogs, symbolizing four generations of progress, achieve is the ultimate triumph of civilization over culture: the destruction of Southern tradition and of her hopes of spiritual growth. They "end the pinewoods." All shadow of belief is gone. Those pines, the symbol of man's source of spiritual beauty and power, once towered over man and held him in awe. That awe—his respect for a power beyond himself—is connoted in the silent "f" alliteration of lines 2-3. The silent land of "white pine" (the beauty of the forest) becomes a noisy land—"changed to a sea-charge"—by the noisy vowels in the harsher refrain of "Slashed pine, gashed pine" (the ugliness of the forest). Stripped of pines, the forest is again silent in the "l's" of "Short leaf, long leaf" and of "Mill town, lumber town." The silence, which was first broken by the "s" alliteration (lines 3-8), is replaced by the noise of "buzzards" sailing "the piney barrens," and by the "b" alliteration and repeated harsh vowels in the last stanza. Together with the refrain on "pines," these four key consonants carry the burden of the poem, define its shifts of moods, and link the four parts. Twice this refrain is broken (lines 11 and 15), the breaking of this pattern emphasizing the two intended symbols of opposition (mills and hogs) to the symbolic pines.

Notes

1. The following checklist of writings on Bishop's poetry supplements "John Peale Bishop: A Checklist," which J. Max Patrick and I compiled for *The Princeton University Library Chronicle,* 7 (Feb., 1946), 62-79. The PULC checklist provides a full bibliographical account of Bishop's books; his contributions to anthologies; poems, essays, short stories, editorial comments, and reviews appearing in periodicals. (It does not include writings on Bishop.) The starred items represent essays or reviews containing critical discussion of the poems and cataloguing some of the influences on Bishop's poetry, echoes from his contemporaries.

Christian Gauss in *Princeton Alumni Weekly,* 18 (Apr. 17, 1918), 608-609; Gilbert Seldes, *Dial;* 73 (Nov., 1922), 574-578; R. Holden, *New Republic,* 33 (Feb. 14, 1923), 329; Horace Gregory*, NYHT-*Books,* Dec. 10, 1933, p. 8; in NYTBR, Dec. 17, 1933, p. 9; R. P. Blackmur*, *American Mercury,* 31 (Feb., 1934), 244-246; Eda Lou Walton*, *Nation,* 138 (Feb. 7, 1934), 162-163; Allen Tate, *New Republic,* 78 (Feb. 21, 1934), 52-53; R. P. Warren, *Poetry,* 43 (Mar., 1934), 342-346; R. P. Warren, *American Review,* 3 (Apr., 1934), 22-28; Babette Deutsch, *Virginia Quarterly Review,* 10 (April, 1934), 298-302; Allen Tate*, *Southern Review,* 1 (Autumn, 1935), 357-364 (reprinted in *Reactionary*

Essays, 1936); T. C. Wilson*, NYHT-*Books,* Mar. 15, 1936, p. 23; R. E. F. Larsson, *New Republic,* 87 (June 10, 1936), 138; John Holmes, *Virginia Quarterly Review,* 12 (April, 1936), 288-295; H. G. Leach, *Forum,* 96 (Aug., 1936), 96; F. C. Flint*, *Southern Review,* 1 (Winter, 1936), 650-672; Conrad Aiken*, *New Republic,* 102 (Apr. 22, 1940), 540-541; Louise Bogan, **New Yorker,* 17 (Mar. 1, 1941), 57; M. D. Zabel*, *Nation,* 152 (Apr. 12, 1941), 447-448; Lloyd Frankenberg, *NYHT-*Books,* Apr. 13, 1941, p. 4; Dudley Fitts, **Saturday Review of Literature,* 24 (Apr. 26, 1941), 13; Thomas Howells, **Poetry,* 58 (May, 1941), 96-99; in *Booklist,* 37 (May 1, 1941), 404; in *Bookmark,* 2 (May, 1941), 7; Conrad Aiken*, *New Republic,* 104 (June 16, 1941), 830-832; John L. Sweeney, *Yale Review,* 30 (June, 1941), 817-822; Ben Bellitt, **Virginia Quarterly Review,* 17 (Summer, 1941), 460-465; R. P. Blackmur*, *Southern Review,* 7, (Summer, 1941), 187-213; W. R. Moses, *Accent,* 1 (Summer, 1941), 250; Babette Deutsch*, *Decision,* 2 (Aug., 1941), 59-61; in *Springfield Republican,* Dec. 28, 1941, p. 7e; Peter Munro Jack, *NYTBR, Jan. 4, 1942, p. 5; Harry Brown, *Vice Versa,* 1 (Jan., 1942), 69-72; Cleanth Brooks, **Kenyon Review,* 4 (Spring, 1942), 242-247; B. Alsterlund, *Wilson Library Bulletin,* 18 (Feb., 1944), 424 (biographical sketch); Christian Gauss, *Princeton University Library Chronicle,* 5 (Feb., 1944), 41-50; R. W. Stallman, **Western Review,* 11 (Autumn, 1946), 4-19; Joseph Frank, **Sewanee Review,* 55 (Winter, 1947), 71-107; Allen Tate, *Western Review,* 12 (Winter, 1948), 67-71 (memoir, reprinted in *Collected Poems,* 1948, pp. xi-xvi); F. C. Flint, *Kenyon Review,* 11 (Winter, 1949), 165-171; Stanley Edgar Hyman*, *Accent,* 9 (Winter, 1949), 102-113.

The Collected Poems of John Peale Bishop, edited with a Preface and a Personal Memoir by Allen Tate, and *The Collected Essays,* edited by Edmund Wilson, were published in 1948 by Charles Scribner's Sons. A notable tribute to Bishop is Tate's poem *Seasons of the Soul, in The Winter Sea* (1945).

I wish to acknowledge the kind permission of Charles Scribner's Sons to reproduce a number of Bishop's poems in this essay. They are reprinted from *The Collected Poems of John Peale Bishop;* copyright 1917, 1922, 1948.

Portions of this essay are reprinted from "The Poetry of John Peale Bishop," which appeared in *The Western Review,* 11 (1946), and from *The Explicator* (1946), by permission of the Editors. The present essay considerably extends my earlier version and represents almost a complete revision of it.

2. The above list of influences is not exhaustive. The points of reference between Bishop and F. Scott Fitzgerald, for instance, are considerable enough to

justify a rather lengthy note, particularly between Bishop's poetry and *The Great Gatsby.*

3. In the *New Yorker* for March 1, 1941. Bishop is not mentioned in Miss Bogan's *Achievement in American Poetry,* 1951.

4. The Ford of the 1920's, that is; not certainly the modern Ford!

5. Bishop was born in Charles Town, West Virginia, on May 21, 1892; he died on April 4, 1944. At Princeton he was the editor of the Lit, the class poet, and the colleague of Scott Fitzgerald and Edmund Wilson. In 1917, during his senior year at Princeton, he published a volume of verse, *Green Fruit;* after the war, in which he served as First Lieutenant in the Infantry, he became managing editor of *Vanity Fair.* He is described in the character of Tom D'Invilliers in Scott Fitzgerald's *This Side of Paradise* (1920). With Edmund Wilson he published *The Undertaker's Garland* (1922), a collection of sketches and poems. It was not until 1930, however, that his poetry and literary criticism began to appear in the major critical journals. He published two books of Southern fiction: *Many Thousands Gone* (1931) and *Act of Darkness* (1935). From 1922 to 1933 he and his wife lived in France, and upon returning to America in 1933 he settled first at Westport, Connecticut, and then at South Harwich on Cape Cod, producing then the poems about his ancestors—as in *Beyond Connecticut, Beyond the Sea.* In the *Princeton University Library Chronicle* for February, 1944, Christian Gauss has provided a portrait of Bishop during his Princeton days.

Cecil D. Elby, Jr. (essay date 1962)

SOURCE: "The Fiction of John Peale Bishop," in *Twentieth Century Literature,* Vol. 7, No. 1, April, 1962, pp. 3-9.

[*In the following essay, Elby traces the influence of American Southern culture in Bishop's* Act of Darkness *and the short story collection* Many Thousands Gone.]

For a time it seemed that John Peale Bishop (1892-1944) would be remembered largely as a secondary character in the history of American expatriation during the 1920's, as an obscure figure pushed occasionally into the foreground by his friends Hemingway and Fitzgerald. Admirers of his poetry felt that he deserved more than a footnote linking him with Fitzgerald's Thomas Parke D'Invilliers and more than was implied by R. P. Blackmur's phrase "a superlative amateur" or Joseph Frank's "perfect minor achievement."[1] During the evaluation of the "Lost Generation," Bishop was overlooked for various reasons: his "lostness" was primarily inconspicuous and undramatic; his poetry was "eclectic, derivative, anonymous";[2] and his fiction had somehow been forgotten altogether. In short, Bishop entered the 1940's with decreasing stature and seemed destined for that oblivion reserved for the "minor" writer. But oblivion has been averted by a reawakened interest in his poetry and his criticism since the Second World War. The **Collected Poetry**, edited in 1947 by Allen Tate, and the **Collected Essays**, edited in the following year by Edmund Wilson, have ushered in a period during which Bishop's reputation has steadily gained ground. Few anthologies now omit samples of his poems, and his essays—particularly **"The Sorrows of Thomas Wolfe"** and **"Homage to Hemingway"**—turn up in critical miscellanies and textbooks. Yet little has been written about his fiction, except now and then a passing reference to it in connection with his other work.

Bishop's best fiction is found in two books, **Many Thousands Gone** (1931), a collection of short stories, and **Act of Darkness** (1935), a novel. These constitute a moral exploration of the Upper South between 1850 and 1910. The eclecticism of his poetry is replaced in his fiction by a severe regionalism as Bishop focuses upon the culture which had, as he had remarked elsewhere, "produced a manner of living somewhat more amiable than any other that has been known on this continent."[3] Distrusting the industrialization, urbanization, and collectivism which were uprooting traditional values in the twentieth century, Bishop, like the Nashville Agrarians, sought to find in the South the remnants of a civilization that could provide the framework for a revitalized national tradition or, failing this, at least a place of refuge from the dehumanized anarchy of his time. But unlike the Agrarians, he found only a "country of moribund customs dating from another age"[4] with little in it to salvage or to emulate. If the grand manner of living had ever really existed in the South, it had long ago been buried by a complex and irrelevant ritual which trapped, not released, the human will. Mordington, the West Virginia village of his fiction, evokes associations of death and is for Bishop the microcosm of the modern South.[5]

The key to Bishop's fiction is found in his conception of the conflict between human impulse and social tradition. When his characters, like George Cochran or the Sabine ladies, sacrifice themselves upon the sacred altar of their tradition, they perish from within; on the other hand, when others, like Charlie Marston or Cecily Burwell, yield to impulse, they are isolated and lost. Bishop hoped to find the ceremony that would unite social control with individual force. But he concluded that if this ceremony ever existed in the South it occurred in the eighteenth, not in the nineteenth, century. The popular myth held that the Civil War was the locus of Southern experience, and most modern writers of the South have worked within this myth. But for Bishop a return to Gettysburg or to Shiloh was not enough. He saw that the Civil War was a culmination of forces generating long before, and his fiction pictures a South that was sterile and decadent long before the Confederacy existed. The Virginia he describes dropped its fruit before Mississippi bloomed. Independently of Faulkner, Bishop broke away from the nostalgic mood and

the "lost-cause" manner of the Southern literary tradition as he showed the corroded values of the Old South.

II

According to Allen Tate, parts of **Many Thousands Gone** were in manuscript as early as 1928, one year before the publication of *The Sound and the Fury* and *Sartoris*. Bishop, then, is not another of the many imitators of William Faulkner. While each of his stories has an independent structure, each is related broadly to an underlying theme—the moral and social disorder in Mordington between 1850 and 1900. Historical or chronological time is less significant than a general continuum of consciousness in which different characters, suffering from similar maladies caused by the oppressive conditions of Mordington, play their individual roles without specific relation to each other. Images of death and burial are found in all the stories (as even their titles indicate), but the author's tone is coolly objective. Each story evokes moods of moribundity, stagnation, and death.

"The Corpse in the House—1852" dramatizes Bishop's awareness of how passion and individuality have been undermined by the fossilized obligations of the Southern code of honor. George Cochran, a reactionary politician who drinks too much in private, returns to Mordington when he hears that his fiancée, Rose, has been freed by the death of her guardian, Mrs. Doyne. For eight years the lovers have been kept apart by Rose's passive obligation to the old woman and by George's dutiful acquiescence. Born under George III, Mrs. Doyne embodied all the vitality, the earthiness, and the rude strength of an eighteenth-century patrician. For her the individual will was everything, the code nothing. During her life, George detested this snuff-dipping relic who, by mere force of will, kept him from marrying Rose. Yet secretly he admired and even envied her careless force. She was, after all, "a last link with the past," and with her death it seemed to him that a virile generation came to its end. It is ironical that George, who has retained only the superfical mannerisms of the Southern tradition, has been chosen by his political party to run on the platform, "where Virginia stood in 1787." He contrasts Mrs. Doyne with Rose, who filters all emotion through the code, and he senses for the first time that his fiancée is emotionally dead. Her hair smells like "dead leaves" and during their walk to the private burying ground Rose says, "It would be frightfully disconcerting to rise up in the Judgment Day and find nothing but strangers around you." Surrounded by the ghosts of their ancestral dead, the Virginian lovers cringe from the unfamiliar experiences that threaten them from the outside world. Moreover, although George finds that his love for Rose has disappeared, he knows that he will respond to the obligations of the social code and that they will be married in course. For such as he, tradition has been a destructive rather than a liberating force.

"The Cellar—1860-1863" strains the first-person point of view in which it is told, for the narrator could not have possessed all the details he relates, but the careful control of the violent denouement makes the story perhaps the most dramatic one in the collection. Charlie Ambler, who is publicly regarded as a week-willed skulker, has been kept from joining the Confederate Army by his abnormal loyalty to his mother. During the first two years of the war he cares for her devotedly, resigns himself of her sarcasm, and submits to the indignities of the Union soldiers who pass back and forth through the region. After her death, he buries her in the family plot and drowns his sorrows among the gambling and drinking set in Mordington. Returning to his farm one afternoon he finds four Yankees looting the place. In digging for the family plate, they have accidentally disinterred Mrs. Ambler and left her body exposed on the ground. With cold deliberation Charlie seals up the soldiers in the cellar, slaughters them one by one, and thereby purges himself of his year of frustration and servitude. Yet the violent conclusion to the story is less important to the story than its irony, for Bishop seems less concerned with what happened than with why it happened. Charlie's sense of values has been based upon idealization of the mother-figure, and when his sacred image is defiled, a destructive impulse is loosed. By his violent act Charlie breaks through the code and becomes at last a human being with a will of his own. Yet the murder of these soldiers, which would have been commendable upon the battlefield, becomes the stigmata of his disgrace among other Virginians. Both within and without the ring of tradition he finds only rejection.

"Young Death and Desire—1862" consists of sharp contrasts between life and death, day and night, emotion and tradition. Having exhausted herself in a futile effort to save the life of a dying soldier, Cecily Burwell, the daughter of Mordington's physician, gives herself to a living soldier. Her dilemma is that of a Southern woman who is powerless to fight the enemy or to assist the dying, and her hysteria finds its release in the single act of womanhood which can give her at least the illusion of functioning. The war has uprooted the conventional rituals of her tradition. "Byron failed her as Scott had done;" neither love nor war conforms to the romanticism of her books. Since the code of gentility has no provision for a delirious soldier bleeding to death in her kitchen, Cecily resorts, through terror of death, to an act of sex that involves her own, not the social, will. Her lover is an anonymous male beneath her own rank. In the darkened room she experiences a pain that is at least proof that she lives. The present moment overcomes the past and the future. More than any other character in the bleak galleries of *Many Thousands Gone,* Cecily Burwell confirms her existence and repudiates her tradition, even though she knows that in the morning there will be guilt. emptiness, and revulsion:

> She would regret what she had done, but not now, now she did not regret it. In the window she was aware of a faint light; morning was near. But still for a little while she could hold this happiness, hold it against the very turning of the earth that turned them toward the sun. They were not dead.

Although **"Many Thousands Gone—1864"** is the most ambitious story in Bishop's book and its subject—the spoilation of Mordington by the Yankees—is the dramatic center of the stories, it lacks the structural tightness of the others. Twenty-odd shifting scenes and as many characters prevent clear focus upon Mordington's day of humiliation. While it has some value as a realistic reconstruction of an historical event, **"Many Thousands Gone"** is nevertheless too much a potpourri consisting of indeterminate fragments to merit much attention as art. Its relation to the preceding stories is, however, clear. Having weighed the imperfections and limitations of the Virginia tradition, Bishop now destroys it utterly as he shows Mordington helpless and vanquished by the hated Yankees. Colonel Strother, born a Virginian, is the Union commander whose sardonic contempt doubtless echoes Bishop's own: "They are all alike—shiftless and pretentious. Virginians! And to think, by God, I was born one!" The rape of Mordington symbolizes the ultimate desecration of the South as both country and culture and ends forever its claim to moral and political superiority. The victors, rapacious, uncouth, and sensual, embody the powerful but amoral forces of the America-to-be. Mordington, unable to resist, goes under. And the greatest irony is that only a Negro servant, by castrating the soldier who seduced his wife, makes any significant gesture of resistance or retaliation. The slave destroys his liberator.

The last story, **"If Only—1867-1900,"** is the high point of Bishop's fiction and deserves more detailed discussion. The central characters inherit from the Virginia past only liabilities—the memory of the defunct grand tradition and the necessity for believing it still exists. The fatherless Sabine ladies, Lou and Ellen, naively believe that had the South won the war, life would have been different. But since the Confederacy has failed them, they will build an illusion of the grand style which will compare favorably with that of "before-the-war." The narrative level of the story is deceptively simple. In an era of undependable servants, they discover in their kitchen Bones, a black Chesterfield with an undiscoverable past, who attaches himself without invitation to their household as chef, butler, housekeeper, and gardener. Through the threadbare elegance of the Reconstruction period, only Bones seems able to preserve the aristocratic proprieties of the prewar Virginia tradition. All the savors of the old South revive in their kitchen, Victorian bric-a-brac is removed to make way for a "discomfort that was almost colonial," and it was, as the ladies say, "as though the war had never been fought." The sound of a man in the big house at night, trying locks and sliding bolts, provides the ladies with a sense of security, but their security gives way to terror when Lou discovers Bones naked in her bathroom. Although he is dismissed, he soon returns and reestablishes himself without their consent, and the ladies permit him to stay. After all, they dare not publicize their anxiety to Mordington for fear of scandal; moreover, only Bones can provide them with their prewar comforts. "With him they lived in terror, but in tradition. Their digestions were destroyed, their nerves frayed, but their pride sustained." Bones seems to be insane, but except for his single offensive defection, he remains quiet and good-humored. The story has no conclusion, for the ladies live with Bones until the end of their lives. Ironically, the Negro has inadvertently enslaved them by their social weakness.

Beyond this literal reading of the story there are some ambiguous and suggestive meanings. We can never be certain, for example, that Lou actually saw Bones in her bathroom. She is susceptible to occasional hallucinations, and Ellen must insist, "You're sure you saw him?" and her reply is evasive, "I saw everything. I even saw the threads in the carpet. It was so clear." Her father is dead, her brother was killed in the war, and George Hite, her aging lover of the chivalric tradition, never presses her to "hard and male possession." The white men about her are either ghosts or relics of the past; none of them have or had any relation to her as males. Lou is pursued by phantoms, among which are the great Lee, "his eyes not on her but fixed afar in the very ecstasy of battle. She saw him . . . with drawn sword, naked steel; he did not see her, but she saw that his eyes were pale and the lashes frozen." In contrast to the dead, there is the living—Bones. Whether she saw or whether she but wished to see him as a naked male, Bishop does not explicitly say. So there is a Freudian implication in his story that gives it another dimension. Not only does Bones, an elusive spectre from the past and a shadow without a future, confront the ladies with the complex social problem of the Negro, but also he terrifies them with the implications of sexuality itself.

"If Only" is a story which is set in the subjunctive mood. Bishop presents a credible drama in which the domestic comedy is endowed with overtones of horror without recourse to a flood of violence. (These Sabine women, after all, undergo a fate far worse than rape.) Since the story has no termination, the precarious balance between Bones and the ladies continues, by implication, until the present century. As symbolic stories of the post-war South "A Rose for Emily" and "If Only" deserve high places, but Bishop, unlike Faulkner, resolved his action without recourse to melodrama or shock. In posing an ambiguity and in relying upon a plausible situation, Bishop worked within the realistic tradition of James rather than the romantic tradition of Poe. Moveover, he concluded *Many Thousands Gone* with the theme that initiated it—the plight of those who are encumbered by a defunct ritual and manner of life that represses emotion and denies individuality. The Sabine ladies feel that the loss of the war caused their peculiar troubles; they know nothing of George Cochran's emotional strangulation long before it.

III

Despite its uneven style and its superabundance of undeveloped characters, Bishop's only novel, *Act of Darkness,* is impressive for its treatment of the ramifications of evil, its insights into the agony of adolescence, and its continued exploration of the Southern tradition. There can be little doubt that relying upon his own recollections of a boyhood in the South, Bishop was too close to his subject to achieve the detachment that characterized his stories. It is clear, further, that in trying to manage the larger bulk of the novel he was involved with a process as hazardous as a lyric poet attempting an epic. But within the novel can be seen his evolution as a novelist: the narcissistic impressionism of the early chapters gives way gradually to a more literal prose and to more objective characterization.

Mordington is here unchanged, although a little older. The brittle outlines of the prewar South still remain, and a local poet has accurately summarized the emotional climate in his lines: "The land where dreams are dying / And the heart's not yet awake."[6] The most enduring legacy from the past has been pride, which still separates class from class and person from person. Virginia Crannock, who inherits the cultivated tradition of the older gentry, lives vicariously upon Shelley and the Greek poets; Charle Martson, a degenerate aristocrat, relieves his boredom by violence and his self-hatred by brutality; Judge Marston, once a promising statesman, fritters away his life in a vain effort to solve the riddle of the West Virginia debt; Aunt Maria passes in and out of the novel en route to the Virginia Springs, visited in the off-season in order to avoid contacts with "foreigners." Within this intimate circle John, the narrator, must confront his own adolescent loneliness and must fabricate his own patchwork of values.

John's evolution from innocence to experience forms the plot of the novel. Virginia Crannock, the embodiment of romantic sensibility and cloistered virtue, is raped by Charlie Marston, the embodiment of anarchic force. John, painfully caught between his loyalty for both of them, discovers that the assault was not the result of sexual passion but rather the outburst of Charlie's perverse hatred. The flower of Southern womanhood is violated by a man whose worse quality is his inability to find a constructive outlet for his physical energy. But during the trial an unsolved problem arises: how much did Virginia resist and how much did she encourage this perverse violation? John learns, however, that evil exists and that it invariably dominates. Of one thing he is certain: there is no force or love in Mordington sufficient to hold him there. In the final scene of the novel, he boards the train that will take him to college at Princeton and turns his back upon the South forever. Isolation lies ahead, but better this involvement with one's own individuality than with a destructive tradition:

> The train was rumbling toward an alien land. There I should be alone. So much I know, but also that, when I looked on it, day, returning from the east, would have filled it with light.

Act of Darkness ends where Bishop's own personal involvement with the South ended. The novel reflects, like his short stories, the conflict between tradition and impulse. Charlie Marston, who denied his tradition, destroyed Virginia Crannock because she represented for him the superficial commitments of this tradition. And Virginia may have really acquiesced in her destruction. John, of course, never finds out what really happened, but he learns something of the complex ramifications of human evil. Bishop explored the myth of the south and found one conclusion inescapable: the burden of twentieth-century existence was too great to rest upon the frail skeleton of a bygone "amiable manner." A return to the past would yield only the burial rites of a civilization long dead.

Notes

1. J. Max Patrick and Robert Wooster Stallman, "John Peale Bishop: A Checklist," *Princeton University Library Chronicle,* VII (February, 1946), 62; Joseph Frank, "Force and Form: A study of John Peale Bishop," *Sewanee Review,* LV (Winter, 1947), 107.

2. Patrick and Stallman, p. 62.

3. "The South and Tradition," *The Collected Essays of John Peale Bishop* (New York, 1948), p. 3.

4. "How Brakespeare Fell in Love," *ibid.,* p. 479.

5. Mordington is Bishop's name for Charles Town, which until recent times regarded itself as a Virginian, not a West Virginian, town. Significantly, it is the place where the Civil War began, since John brown was executed there in 1859.

6. Bishop intended a burlesque of Daniel B. Lucas' "The Land Where We Were Dreaming," one of the more "unreconstructed" and nostalgic Southern poems of the 1860's.

Joseph Frank (essay date 1963)

SOURCE: "The Achievement of John Peale Bishop," in *The Widening Gyre: Crisis and Mastery in Modern Literature,* Rutgers University Press, 1963, pp. 203-28.

[*In the following essay, originally published in the Spring 1962 issue of* The Minnesota Review, *Frank places Bishop among the best poets and fiction writers of the "Lost Generation."*]

John Peale Bishop, who died in 1944, was one of the most gifted and sensitive talents among the American writers who came to maturity after the First World War. A classmate of Edmund Wilson and F. Scott Fitzgerald at Princeton, Bishop was the third member of a triumvirate destined to take a prominent place in modern American letters; but his own work never won him the fame of his collegiate friends. Bishop was an exacting rather than a powerful writer, and his limited production, perfect though much of it was, never imposed itself on the American literary scene with the impact necessary to make a lasting impression. Even the posthumous publication in 1948 of his *Collected Poems* and his *Collected Essays* did little to remedy this unjust situation.[1]

One of the criticisms most frequently made of Bishop during his lifetime was that his work lacked unity—that it was fragmentary and peripheral, destitute of any serious focus. R. P. Blackmur once neatly summarized the prevalent impression by calling Bishop a "superlative amateur," who gave the sense of writing poetry as an "avocation" rather than out of whole-souled dedication and passionate purpose.[2] Such an impression can hardly persist, however, if one reads Bishop's work as a whole—both his creative and critical prose as well as his poetry; for what then strikes one most forcefully is the constancy of Bishop's preoccupation with the spiritual dilemma of his generation.

Bishop defined this dilemma himself in a much-quoted article called **"The Missing All"** (the phrase is from a poem by Emily Dickinson); it is the dilemma familiar to all readers of Hemingway—the breakdown of values as an aftermath of the First World War. All of Bishop's work is a response to this breakdown, which formed the existential horizon of his generation; but Bishop's own evolution is quite unique, and it is impossible to place him in any convenient and familiar category. His feeling for tradition and for formal values in literature, his sense that man needed some ultimate metaphysical justification, linked him with the followers of T. S. Eliot; and he was allied by sympathy and personal friendship with Allen Tate and the Southern Agrarians. Yet the sense of life in his later work reminds one more of D. H. Lawrence than of any other contemporary writer. And his achievement is precisely to have created an original and very appealing synthesis—small in scale though impressive in quality—of these two major antagonistic traditions of modern Anglo-American literature.

I

John Peale Bishop's début in the turbulent literary world of the twenties was not particularly auspicious. His first book of poems, published in 1917, bears the modest title **Green Fruit;** and the suggestion of immaturity is indicative both of Bishop's modesty and of his critical intelligence. For the poems are indeed filled with youthful echoes of *fin-de-siècle* decadence, obviously garnered from the pages of Swinburne and *The Yellow Book*—the favorite reading of literary undergraduates of Bishop's generation.

By the time Bishop published his second book, however, written in collaboration with Edmund Wilson, he had gone through the archetypal war experience of his generation. And the very title of the work—a curious potpourri of prose and verse in celebration of death called **The Undertaker's Garland** (1922)—reveals its typical orientation. **The Undertaker's Garland** unmistakably bears the stamp of its time—a time when Edna St. Vincent Millay was burning the candle at both ends in Greenwich Village, when the revolt against Puritanism was in full swing, and when the contributors to *Civilization in the United States* were jubilantly declaring that no such thing existed. Both young writers, after their contact with war and Europe, found the Puritan materialism of their homeland intolerable. And in a book defiantly dedicated to death, they set out to *épater les Américains* as best they could.

Much the most important of Bishop's contributions to this high-spirited volume is a short story called **"Resurrection."** Here we feel the naked impact of Bishop's war experience for the first time, uncluttered by the pseudo-macabre bric-à-brac marring his other efforts. Little more than an anecdote, the story pictures the disinterment of a dead American soldier for reburial. A young lieutenant almost faints at the sight of the decaying, putrescent corpse, and he returns to his tent haunted by "the pervasive odor of decay; the blanketed mass he had just seen, with its poor upturned face, had broken down within him some last wall of resisting flesh." It is the contrast between this feeling and the images ordinarily evoked by the word "resurrection" on which the story plays; the result is a grim, unspoken irony similar to the minor poems of Hardy. And here is the first groping statement of what was to become Bishop's perennial theme—the bare and brutal facts of physical reality in conflict with the values by which man tries to dignify his brief existence.

The Undertaker's Garland marks the end of Bishop's juvenilia and the beginning of a period of literary stock-taking that lasted for almost a decade. During this time Bishop printed an occasional review or poem; but it was only in 1931 that he brought out a volume of stories, *Many Thousands Gone,* and this was followed in 1932 by a volume of poetry, *Now With His Love.* These books initiate Bishop's mature work; and to follow his development we may start most conveniently with the volume of poetry. This contains work written over the intervening period, and it will allow us to trace the evolution of Bishop's themes from the immediate reflection of his war trauma to the search for a tradition and a metaphysical order that would exorcise its effects.

II

Bishop's poetry, in *The Undertaker's Garland,* had still been filled with the vestiges of late nineteenth-century mannerisms; but in the interval his poetic style had considerably matured. Now the sensuous clarity of Eliot and Pound are noticeable influences, along with the taut symbolic lyricism of Yeats and the Valéry of *Charmes.* Bishop, indeed, experiments in this volume with a variety of poetic styles, as he was to continue to do all through his life. But as Allen Tate has argued, a good poem in a period style is still a good poem;[3] and *Now With His Love* is filled with good poems that have an unmistakably personal note. Moreover, as the title from Chaucer indicates, the book has a good deal of thematic unity as well. For the experience of **"Resurrection"** has by no means been forgotten; and it is only love that the poet finds to obliterate the horror.

In reading the love-and-war poems of *Now With His Love* we are irresistibly reminded of the early Hemingway, also obsessed with death, also seeking for a source of positive value in naked sensuous experience. It is no accident that Bishop returned again and again to Hemingway in his critical writings, and that his **"Homage to Hemingway"** is

one of the finest studies of that writer. "His vision of life," Bishop writes, "is one of perpetual annihilation. Since the will can do nothing against circumstance, choice is precluded; those things are good which the senses report good; and beyond their brief record there is only the remorseless devaluation of nature, which, like the vast blue flowing of the Gulf Stream beyond Havana, bears away of our great hopes, emotions and ambitions only a few and soon disintegrating trifles." Bishop here is not only analyzing Hemingway; he is defining one essential aspect of his own work.

But this vision of life does not lead Bishop—as it led Hemingway or, to mention a poet of Bishop's generation, Archibald MacLeish—into a glorification of the primitive. It is a fact of particular significance that Bishop's images of sensuous beauty are invariably expressed in terms of art, the art of the Mediterranean world, of Greece and the Italian Renaissance. Bishop, indeed, is one of the few modern writers in English (the early Ezra Pound and D. H. Lawrence are others) who have been able to write genuinely erotic love poetry without falling into either vulgarity or platitude; and the reason lies in the classical purity of his feeling for the body and the senses. The following stanza from his beautiful **"Metamorphoses of M,"** for example, illustrates the precise elegance of his refined and filtered sensuality. Nor should one fail to note the casual complexity of the controlling paradox, with its imagery as from an early Renaissance tapestry playfully reproducing some monkish bestiary of the Middle Ages:

> Your beauty is not used. Though you have lain
> A thousand nights upon my bed, you rise
> Always so splendidly renewed that I have thought,
> Seeing the sweet continence of your breast,
> Mole-spotted, your small waist, and long slim thigh,
> That even the unicorn that savage beast
> If he should startle on you fresh from light
> Would be so marvelled by virginity
> That he would come, trotting and mild,
> To lay his head upon your fragrant lap
> And be surprised.

This is the world of love (real and yet ideal) that Bishop posed against the nihilistic experience of death shared by his generation. "All loveliness demands our courtesies," he writes in a later poem (**"Recollection"**), which sums up this phase of his work. And the word "courtesy" (the troubadour *cortezia*) could not have been better chosen. For Bishop's attitude toward loveliness is precisely that of a stately formal obeisance, controlled by a discipline for which the senses, like the Platonic Eros, are valuable only as an avenue to a higher realm of the spirit.

III

Bishop knew too much history, however, to believe that such an avenue could be simply the personal construction of an isolated individual. It is culture that mediates between the senses and the spirit in Bishop's poetry; and culture implies tradition. A number of poems in *Now With*

His Love deal with the breakdown of such traditions—not only that of Christianity, but those of classical antiquity and of the eclectic modern world as well. **"The Return"** vividly evokes the despairing torpor of vanquished Rome waiting for the arrival of the conqueror. And in **"Ballet"**—obviously inspired by the painting of Dali and Chirico, as well as by the poetry of Cocteau—the chaos of the contemporary world is depicted in a frightening *mise en scène*. The best embodiment of this theme, however, is **"Perspectives are Precipices,"** one of the most widely known of Bishop's poems. Allen Tate has sensitively analyzed the manner in which this work achieves the effects of painting;[4] but it also contains a number of Bishop's key symbols and has far more than merely a formal significance.

Bishop uses an incident from the conclusion of the Bluebeard story in Perrault's *Fairy Tales* as a framework for the poem. Bluebeard is about to kill his most recent wife for having looked into the room where his other victims are hanging; but he gives her a few minutes' grace to say her prayers. During this time she calls her Sister Anne, and asks the latter to mount to the tower and see if their brothers are riding to the rescue. Bishop discards all the incidents of the Bluebeard story, but he keeps the question-and-answer refrain of the dialogue between the wife and Sister Anne; and he turns the rescue motif into a symbolic comment on the fate of modern culture. For while in the tale the brothers arrive to confound Bluebeard and save their sisters, the erstwhile rescuer in Bishop's poem recedes rather than approaches and finally vanishes altogether.

What Sister Anne spies when she goes to the tower is a road running through a harshly sunlit desert landscape; and this would appear to be the track of abstract time starting in the past and continuing into the future ("I see a distance of black yews / Long as the history of the Jews"). On the road is "a man who goes / Dragging a shadow by its toes"; in his hand is an empty pitcher, mouth down:

> Sister Anne, Sister Anne,
> What do you see?
>
>   His dwindling stride. And he seems blind
>   Or worse to the prone man behind.
> Sister Anne! Sister Anne!
>
>   I see a road. Beyond nowhere
>   Defined by cirrus and blue air.
>
>   I saw a man but he is gone
>   His shadow gone into the sun.

Man's shadow would appear to refer to his past, to history and to time as human continuity (perhaps there is an implied reference here to the sundial). But he is "blind or worse" to his past and pursues his path "beyond nowhere" till he vanishes completely into nature. Typical for Bishop is the sun-baked landscape, the symbolic importance of "shadow," and, as Mr. Tate has noted, the "spatial" quality of the imagery ("Wide plains surrounding silence"). The use of such imagery clearly is linked with the theme of time's obliteration.

To counterbalance such a future, only the birth of a new cultural tradition will suffice; and this need furnishes the inspiration for **"Speaking of Poetry."** The problem of the poet, of course, is the age-old one of maintaining the proper equilibrium between inspiration and discipline, passion and reason. But for Bishop this is the problem of culture as well; and, using symbolism drawn from *Othello,* he takes this as his theme. How can the delicate Desdemona, the flower of Venetian culture, be truly united with the dark and passionate Moor? Othello is still an inchoate force of nature, powerful but undisciplined; any irregular union between the two will lead to disaster;

> O, it is not enough
> that they should meet, naked, at dead of night
> in a small inn on a dark canal. Procurers
> less expert than Iago can arrange as much.
>
> The ceremony must be found.
>
> Traditional, with all its symbols
> ancient as the metaphors in dreams;
> strange, with never before heard music; continuous
> until the torches deaden at the bedroom door.

The ceremony must be found. And Bishop's book of short stories, **Many Thousands Gone** (1931), indicates where he thought it might be discovered—or at least where an American could requicken his sense of what such a ceremony had meant in his own past. The stories of **Many Thousands Gone,** all of which deal with incidents occurring in Virginia during the Civil War, are in effect a condensed moral history of the South; and they should be read in conjunction with Bishop's article **"The South and Tradition"** (1933). Bishop was himself of mixed New England and Virginia stock; but his boyhood had been spent in West Virginia, and he easily identified himself in feeling with the Southern Agrarians. His relation to the Agrarians, however, should not be overstressed; for he always remained his own man, and what he took from his Agrarian friends was immediately transformed into his own personal terms.

Like the Agrarians, Bishop disliked the world of science, mechanization, and the machine that had dehumanized modern life. What attracted him to the myth of the South—and he had no hesitation in calling it a myth—was the sense of moral certainty that he felt had once existed at the heart of Southern life. This moral certainty had enabled his Southern great-uncles to ride off to war heroically, while his own generation of Americans had gone to face their ordeal by fire with no real beliefs to sustain them. What Hemingway was seeking in the Spanish bull ring at about the same time—a moral code that would enable one to face death unflinchingly—Bishop sought in the image of a society that had seemed to provide such a code, and, moreover, could not be held responsible for the bleak materialism and Puritanical hypocrisy of American life that he had already castigated in *The Undertaker's Garland.*

But, while Bishop might persuade himself intellectually that such a tradition had existed in the South, he was too honest a writer to force his feelings. What he had experienced, as a member of the Lost Generation, was the breakdown of tradition; and when he came to write his stories of the South he chose to portray what he could feel. For he takes the Southern tradition at a moment when it had already hardened into a lifeless and moribund convention or was collapsing under the impact of war and invasion. All the stories reinforce the same theme of a society in bondage to the past, a society whose conventions are no longer adequate to cope with reality. And in one story, **"If Only,"** he produces a little masterpiece.

All that remains of the Southern tradition here is a pitiful and morbid nostalgia; it has become a dream world of wish and desire, a world of fantasy which is well conveyed in the slightly Kafkaesque quality of detail. The action concerns two Southern gentlewomen, pathetically living on their memories, who hire a miraculous Negro cook named Bones. As if by magic, Bones turns dream into reality: "With this one tall, black, jovial Negro in the house it was as though the War had never been fought or, having been fought, had turned into a triumph for the South." Bones' extravagances soon drive them to the brink of penury; and they finally discover that he is literally mad. But they find themselves unable to drive him away. "With him they lived in terror, but in the tradition. . . . They would keep him, as it were a dear obsession, till they were dead." The unforced symbolism of Bishop's story, which focuses in a microcosm the tragic white-Negro relationship in the South, has the inevitable rightness of a completely realized achievement.

IV

Despite Bishop's volume of stories, American themes had shown up in only one or two of the poems in *Now With His Love.* But in his next volume, *Minute Particulars* (1935), we find one sequence of five poems devoted to New England, and another, called **"Experience in the West,"** dealing with the theme of the American pioneer. The New England group is personal—the poet's return to the land of his ancestors, where he finds abandoned, "dishonored houses" and a countryside scarred by the defacements of industrialism. "There is no sustenance in this ground," he concludes.

"Experience in the West" is more ambitious, and on the whole more successful, in conveying a complex historical experience in Bishop's carefully wrought pictorial symbols. These poems, with their sensuously compelling visual surfaces, appear vivid enough on first reading though somewhat obscure. But just as his fellow Symbolist Yeats provided glosses on his poetry in *A Vision* and other prose works, so Bishop was in the habit of explaining his symbols in his criticism; and the best way to read **"Experience in the West"** is to see what he says about the American pioneer in his articles of the mid-thirties.

In his brilliant and moving study of the Lost Generation, **"The Missing All,"** Bishop remarks that Puritanism—the New England idea—had gone bad in the Midwest. Puritanism originally had been based on a hatred of nature, and the ordeal of the wilderness had only increased that hatred; but the original transcendental meaning of this emotion was lost in being transplanted. "The meaning of Puritanism is a contempt for mortality; in the Midwest it was forgotten." When the pioneer came out of the forest onto the prairies, he had been toughened physically but emptied spiritually; he had sloughed off all his traditional values and was left with only a hatred-of-life that had lost its religious rationale. This theme begins in Bishop's **"The Burning Wheel,"** which describes the pioneer carrying his culture on his back as Aeneas carried Anchises:

> They, too, the stalwart conquerors of space
> Each on his shoulders wore a wise delirium
> Of memory and age: ghostly embrace
> Of Fathers slanted toward a western tomb.

These burdens stayed "Aloft, until they were as light as autumn / Shells of locusts"; and were finally deposited in some "Wilderness oblivion."

"Green Centuries" then evokes an image of the forest in which the pioneer lost his soul. "In green no soul was found, / In that green savage clime / Such ignorance of time." Time—which is always Bishop's word for history, continuity, tradition, for the ebb and flow of human experience—comes to a stop "when every day dawned Now." And time is replaced by space, quality by quantity: "Time dreams eternity / Their nights were starred with space." But the end of the poem finds the pioneer's "death-set face" assuming "an idle frown"; his task is done, his virtues superfluous. This is a preparation for **"Loss in the West,"** whose gloss may be found in some remarks Bishop made about the Idaho novelist Vardis Fisher. "The heroic age is past," he writes. "Courage and hope, those two most admirable virtues of the frontiersman, have become in this late and unpromising land [Idaho, the last frontier] cruelly meaningless."

"Cast out of the fray / The man in the coonskin cap." The pioneer no longer has a place in modern life ("What have we to do with a fear that stalked / In a savage unlit wood?"). But the world that the pioneer created still continues its restless and never-ending expansion:

> Yet gaunt—bone, gut, sinews—
> Something like man pursued
> And still pursues
> What? Wheel of the sun
> In Heaven? The west wind? Or only a will
> To his own destruction?

And this pursuit is presented in the fourth and final poem—ironically entitled **"O Pioneers"**—under the guise of a pioneer party that has lost its way in search of gold and perishes in the desert. Thematically, at least, these poems seem to me to stand by themselves in American literature as a direct rejection of the myth of the frontier. And to feel their full force they should be read against the background of those works of Whitman, Hart Crane, and Archibald MacLeish that celebrate the pioneer *mystique.*

It was part of Bishop's cosmopolitanism that, despite his preoccupation with America, he never shared the cultural nationalism that led to the belief in American "uniqueness." As he explains in his important article on **"The Golden Bough,"** the blind forward surge of the American pioneer is merely one aspect of the scientific conquest of nature—the conquest of space—begun in the Renaissance. And this whole movement has had the same effect on Western culture as the pioneer ethos had on American life. It has destroyed all traditional standards of man, without replacing them by anything equally viable. This is the theme of **"O Let Not Virtue Seek,"** one of Bishop's most ambitious poems but not among his most successful; it suffers from the attempt to combine Symbolist obliquity and Shakespearean declamation. But it is instructive to see how he juxtaposes the quantitative universe of science against the qualitative uniqueness of human experience. Astronomy has now given us "unavailable millenniums" but "we stifle for a second / When desire bends our knees above our love." The two orders are incommensurate; and even worse, as he remarks in the same article, "we have reached the skeptical point where we see the scientific universe as a projection of our own immortal desire for order, yet realize that it leaves all our desires, even that desire, unsatisfied."

V

If Bishop's poetry had done nothing more than dramatize this dilemma, it would be difficult, despite individual successes, to accord him any higher rank than that of a gifted epigone. But Bishop's most original poetry attempts to go beyond despair in an entirely independent direction, and to communicate a sense of a cosmic order in which modern man can believe. "For," he writes, "it is only by perceiving order in those external forces on which his continuance depends, that man can hope to bring his own being into accord with them." In his *Selected Poems* (1941), the last book to appear in his lifetime, Bishop took three poems from *Minute Particulars* and grouped them together. These compose his first answer to the dichotomy of modern culture; and it is regrettable that when these poems have been noticed at all their true impact has been either overlooked or misunderstood.

Even Allen Tate, who has done more than anyone else to keep Bishop's reputation alive, went wide of the mark in commenting on this phase of his friend's work. For Mr. Tate speaks of one of these poems, **"Divine Nativity,"** as attempting "to use the Christian myth" and then collapsing "with a final glance at anthropology." But there is a collapse only if we believe the two are incompatible and that

Bishop, as Mr. Tate writes, was attempting "to replace our secular philosophy, in which he does not believe, with a vision of the divine, in which he tries to believe."[5] Bishop's "vision of the divine" is one in which the opposition between Christianity and anthropology has ceased to exist; and the great merit of these poems is precisely that of creating a world in which this antagonism is nullified.

Once again it is illuminating to turn to Bishop's **"Golden Bough"** article for a commentary. "In Sir James Frazer's pages," Bishop writes, "there is revealed what one may in all simplicity call the true religion of mankind." Bishop argues that Frazer's researches in anthropology, far from destroying Christianity (as the nineteenth century believed), have on the contrary given it a new authenticity. For if we take "religion as a revelation of human destiny, we must see that He is not less divine because of the company of Adonis, Osiris and Thammuz. His divinity is to be found in precisely those attributes which He shares with these other and older incarnate gods." The central mystery of Christianity is the Mass, which "turns out to be a symbolic presentation of the eternal relation of man to a living and sustaining earth." The Mass derives from the immemorial worship of the Vegetable God; but it transforms "what was originally a form of expressing physical concerns to spiritual ends." Religion, we now see, arose out of the fear that life might cease; it succeeds in giving death and disintegration a positive meaning, and endows the elemental lusts and passions with human significance.

From this point of view, the role of death in authentic religion—or at least in Bishop's "true religion of mankind"—must be carefully distinguished from the death-longing of asceticism, "the belief in dying as an escape from time and change into the unchanging and timeless." Bishop argues that the ascetic element in Christianity, its "peculiar taint of death," is closer "to the collapse of the State than to the rise of the Church." In other words, it is not an essential component of that part of Christianity explored by Frazer. For the worship of the Vegetable God, the true religion of mankind, is based on "knowledge of the revolving year and the memory of the season's return"; it is "coeval with the conception of time." Asceticism is an escape from time and change, a residual vestige of the earliest ages when man lived "in a savage jungle of fear . . . and there [were] no gods and no time."

These reflections throw a good deal of light on what Bishop was trying to do in the poems in question. **"The Saints,"** for example, shows us a group of starvelings staggering through a landscape of "bright waste of sands" and "desert rock." These are certainly the ascetics trying to escape from time:

> Subduing time
> In naked trance,
> Construe as crime
> Continuance,
> All that changes
> Confound with scorn.
> So each man avenges
> A child born.

The saints renounce life in the hope of triumphing over death:

> O concreate
> And never abandoned
> Longing! Dilate
> Our loves beyond
> All loves that age
> Or lust consumes,
> O thirst and rage
> For the lost kingdoms!

But this attempt to capture divinity outside of time is futile: "Whoever says / Divine has said / Dying."

Life and death cannot be separated: this is the theme of **"The Tree,"** whose details are taken from the Adam and Eve myth. Once the first man and woman have eaten what they receive "from a serpent clasp of cold coils," they lose their status as demigods in timeless Eden; they become aware of each other's sex, and "a sudden light" borders the tree with "a bright burnish of desire." Now, like the incarnate god, they have become human; the woman has been "embraced by the lips with death's taste." Debased to the human status, they are drawn into the process of nature:

> From the living stem
> Such sustenance
> Draws into their dance
> Stars follow them.
> Clasping they control
> The coursing light from pole to pole.

And, as with all life, the act of love and the act of death are inseparable. "All delight of leaf and sun / Dreams of dissolution."

Bishop's own idea of true divinity is the subject of **"Divine Nativity."** This poem plays with the idea of incarnation, the birth of the gods:

> O fabled truth:
> Did the god's bride
> Know an armored youth
> His bronze cast aside?

The Incarnation is both truth and fable, divine and human, flesh and spirit. The arrival of the gods is always linked with an outburst of sexual passion ("Adoring Leda leaned upon / A bright encumbrance of wild swan"). But, in whatever form they appear, the gods bring joy, hope, and rejuvenescence; and in this moment the animal, the human, and the divine are inextricably intermingled:

> Eagle, swan or dove
> White bull or cloud
> Incarnate love
> Alone is proud.
> The arrogant know
> In the bestial part
> Overflow
> Of the elated heart.

These poems compose Bishop's answer to the problem first posed to modern culture in *The Waste Land,* a work which also, it will be recalled, took its departure from Frazer and his pupil Jessie Weston. Eliot too uses the pattern of the vegetation myths as the controlling principle of order in his poem, but he already accentuates the Christian element—the idea of the self-sacrifice of the Dying God—as the source of the restoration of fertility. Bishop, on the other hand, takes a direction similar to D. H. Lawrence's in his emphasis on sexuality and his rejection of asceticism. But just as he had spiritualized the mindless sensationalism of the Lost Generation, so now he does not simply surrender to the deification of the primitive and chthonic powers. He refuses to abandon either the physical ("the bestial part") or the spiritual ("the elated heart"), either to abstract man from nature or to submerge him in its tug. And the fine balance of Bishop's humanism, expressed in the firm control of these masterly poems, seems to me to entitle them to a distinguished place in contemporary poetry.

The same balance is maintained in Bishop's only published novel, *Act of Darkness* (1935), which takes on its full significance only in the context of the poems we have just discussed. As a novel, *Act of Darkness* suffers from an annoying technical flaw—an unexplained alternation between a first-person and a third-person narrator. But aside from this minor defect it is a vivid and memorable little work, written with a fine, fresh lyricism lacking in Bishop's earlier prose. At first sight it may seem merely another example of the American discovery-of-life genre, the awakening of an adolescent to the reality of evil (which, as in Sherwood Anderson's "I Want to Know Why," is usually given a sexual guise). Bishop's originality, however, lies in his dissociation of sexuality and evil; it is rather the attempt to escape from sexuality, to evade the inevitable *rites de passage* into manhood and life, which here, as in the poetry, becomes the true evil.

The "act of darkness" referred to in the title (taken from *Othello*) is a rape, committed by the narrator's uncle. The action is seen largely through the eyes of the adolescent narrator, John; and this fateful outbreak of sexual dynamism—a dynamism that John also had felt stirring in himself—brings on a grave psychic crisis in the boy. John stifles his vitality and falls ill, unwilling to face the fact that life and manhood carry the possibility of both suffering and inflicting evil. But one day he finds himself wishing to die physically, rather than continue to linger in a twilight zone of death-in-life; and the spell of fear is broken. "Having accepted death, I returned to life." And he seals his recovery by a visit to a brothel, where he himself experiences the ritual act of darkness—the initiation rites into the true religion of mankind—which prepares for the perils of manhood. But this experience also coincides with the discovery of Shakespeare, who teaches John that art can "impose a sensuous order on the moral disorder of the world." Here again we find Bishop's acute awareness of the primitive roots of life going hand in hand with a sense of its need for aesthetic and human sublimation. Order and vitality belong together, else we get barbarism or desiccation.

VI

Bishop's *Selected Poems* contains a number of new items either written after *Minute Particulars* or, for some reason, not included in that volume. On the whole, however, these poems do not reveal any significant development in Bishop's work; only his accustomed mastery in familiar themes and styles. Bishop wrote little poetry between 1936 and 1940, but beginning in the latter year he had a remarkable spurt which produced some new poems of striking breadth and power and with a significant extension of thematic range. The death of his old friend F. Scott Fitzgerald in 1940 resulted in a moving threnody; and the events of the following years, particularly the fall of France, filled him with foreboding.

"The fall of France was a terrible shock to him; one was astonished at the violence of his reaction to it," writes Edmund Wilson, whose own political isolationism presumably made him impervious to the catastrophe.[6] But Bishop felt himself a son of Western culture to his very fingertips; and for him that culture was inconceivable without France. "I am dismayed," he said in a speech delivered in 1941, "by the dangerous changes that may come to Western civilization and in the end destroy its continuity." He enjoined the American artist, now that France was silent, to take up the French task of preserving this continuity. "We must find a way to reconcile our own past with the vast past of Western civilization." With his own injunction as a guide, Bishop's last poetry meditates on the rise and fall of cultures, on destruction but also on rebirth. And its imagery, derived from the classical Mediterranean world he had always loved, reveals his own effort to fulfill the obligation he had laid on American art.

These meditations compose a group of poems, **"The Statues,"** unpublished in Bishop's lifetime and only made available in Allen Tate's edition of his poetry. Mr. Tate places their composition in 1940, but with no conclusive evidence; in any case, they obviously take up the theme of **"The Divine Nativity"** group. But instead of replacing the gods in the life-cycle of nature, as he had done earlier, Bishop now explores their relationship with human order and civilization. The sequence is based on a contrast between desert-imagery of space, drought, and barrenness (familiar from **"The Saints"**) and sea-imagery of time and destruction, but also of fecundation and reimmersion in the waters of life.

It is from the sea that the gods are born; but in the first poem they are **"The Uneaten Gods,"** cast up broken and drowned on a shore which is that of modernity. And so the sea, as it were, becomes desacralized ("Only the waves are seen . . . / Not the force under the waves, / Nor the forces above the waves"). Once the gods had been "embodiments of time"; and this was the birth of Greek civilization. In a

magnificent passage, which recalls the neo-Hellenism of Schiller and Hölderlin, Bishop pictures this event:

> Imaginings of order
> Rose, beyond the lucent headlands,
> Above the marble stairs. And columns rose,
> Voluptuous doves among the capitals,
> Supporting and overcoming azure.
> The gods stood. Men saw their simulacra
> Display immortal visions. So let the wild
>   white horses
> Rise from the bay, and run, bestriding spindrift,
> To rock the shores with stormier tramplings!
> The gods stood. And while they stood, the state
> And every sea-gaze circled to the same horizon,
> All speech proclaimed one tongue of praise.

The following two poems, **"Dunes on the March"** and **"Sojourn in the Desert,"** show what occurs when the gods remain uneaten. The flowering shore of the sea becomes barren sand dunes "burning the vision / In excess of space." But the sojourn in this desert could not give rise to any new flowering ("Ascetic drought was there . . . / But the saint's secret was not there"). Orpheus could not be reborn in this desolation, nor did "the haggard John / In his wild cloak of camel's hair" hear the Word in this desert. Only in **"Return of the Sea"** does life come again to the parched landscape—"Rushing as though water were the word / Death made flesh / The Word death / and the Word made flesh!"/

The poem **"Statue of Shadow"** is the most enigmatic of all: a vision of "that mystery of clearest light," the shadow cast by the body at high noon on a coast of "burning sand." In **"Perspectives are Precipices,"** Bishop had used "shadow" to symbolize human history and continuity. And what "shadow" seems to indicate here, following the rebirth of the return of the sea, is a recovery of the past and hence of the possibility of creating the future. "The shade of all those centuries / Whose death is longing and fate a crime / Lay long / But no longer / Than the statue of shadow / The sun at its silent noon laid at my feet." And the last two poems, **"The Great Statues"** and **"The Archipelagoes,"** resolve the sequence in a recovery of serenity arising from this contemplation of past beauty and harmony and the conviction of its restoration in the future:

> The day returns, but not the day
> Of these gods. Yet the dawn resumes the amazed
> Smile of a brute Apollo,
> Dazzling in bronze of sea-encrusted blue-green.

"The Statues" still sees the rise and fall of cultures primarily in the perspective of the primordial rhythms of the "true religion of mankind." But while the earlier poetry, inspired by the revolt against Puritanism, had concentrated on the incarnation of spirit, **"The Statues"** emphasizes, as it were, the spiritualization of nature and the flesh. Nature may now have only the lineaments of a "brute Apollo," but total brutishness had forever been exorcised for those who preserve the continuity of Western culture. Nor are all cultures any longer dissolved into one; it is the culture and the gods of Greek humanism that have become the pattern for man. "The time-adorning monuments / Restore the secrets of eternity." Considering the historical background of these poems—the rise and triumph of nazism, with its obscene worship of the fearsome gods of blood, race, and soil—it is hardly surprising that Bishop should have shifted his accents in this fashion.

And this new anthropocentrism is expressed even more clearly in his last important poem, **"A Subject of Sea Change."** Here again we find the predominant sea-imagery of this last period. But the sea is now no longer simply the source of life; it has also become the paradoxical, ambiguous, Janus-faced image of history itself. The spectacle of the sea, writes the poet, allowed him "To hold in instant contemplation / The shifting flow of human history / That seaward sets even as it shoreward moves."

In this poem Bishop directly expresses his trepidations about the fate of Western culture as he hears "the great bombs drop"; and he reminds his readers "That every ordered change of form / Brings mind's disorder and destroying storm." But in face of the all-destroying flux, characteristically felt as a breakdown of manners ("Death greets us all without civility / And every color of the sea is cold"), a man must never fall below the noble image of himself immortalized by the Greeks. As with Oedipus, there is no escape from the responsibility of the tragic role in which he has been cast; but he must uphold human dignity to the end:

> I must learn again the great part of Man—
> Though the lines are scant that any man can speak—
> Proclaiming with such passion as I can
> The part first played, and nobly, by a Greek.
> Time is man's tragic responsibility
> And on his back he bears
> Both the prolific and destroying years.
> And so, I swear, he must surround each act
> With scruples that will hold intact
> Not merely his own, but human dignity.

These were John Peale Bishop's last words.

Notes

1. *The Collected Poems of John Peale Bishop,* ed. by Allen Tate (New York: Charles Scribner's Sons, 1948); *The Collected Essays of John Peale Bishop,* ed. by Edmund Wilson (New York: Charles Scribner's Sons, 1948). All the poems and articles by Bishop cited in this essay are included in these two volumes.

2. R. P. Blackmur, "Twelve Poets," *The Southern Review* VIII, 1 (Summer, 1941), 198.

3. Allen Tate, "John Peale Bishop," *The Man of Letters in the Modern World* (New York: Meridian, 1955), p. 271.

4. *Ibid.,* p. 275.

5. *Ibid.,* p. 276.

6. Edmund Wilson, Introduction, *The Collected Essays of John Peale Bishop,* p. xiii.

Eugene Haun (essay date 1964)

SOURCE: "John Peale Bishop: A Celebration," in *Reality and Myth: Essays in American Literature in Memory of Richmond Croom Beatty,* edited by William E. Walker and Robert L. Welker, Vanderbilt University Press, 1964, pp. 80-97.

[*In the following excerpt, Haun asserts that Bishop is a lesser-known writer than such contemporaries as F. Scott Fitzgerald and Ernest Hemingway because he wrote about a wider variety of subject matter in different genres.*]

During the nineteen-twenties, when I was a small boy, one of the last full-scale Confederate reunions took place in our town. The town put the big pot into the little one because the reunion had not been held there for almost twenty years, and we realized that there would never be another. My mother and my grandmother wept as the old men, too old even to carry their own banners, marched for the last time down Main Street. It was a brave sight.

Our house was filled with old people: One of my great-grandfathers was there, with his surviving brothers and sisters, all in their eighties or late seventies. I would not venture among them, where they sat in their cane-bottom chairs on the front porch, until my grandmother took me by the hand and said, "Come and say hello to Grandpaw."

I protested that I didn't know what to say to them.

"You always have to make your manners to your old people or you won't feel right about yourself later on," she explained. "Now you be sure you show your raising."

Fame and reputation are not always sought by those who deserve them. Sometimes they are even shunned. If one is to become a famous literary figure, ability is not always enough, nor talent, nor even genius. Becoming famous is a career in itself. One must work tirelessly to place poems and essays. Even such fame as one achieves by these methods will be qualified: One comes to be known only by other people who are trying to do the same thing.

Now, if the writer has no interest in fame or reputation, if he wilfully limits an edition of a book of verse to one hundred and fifty copies, if he refuses to do any of the back-scratching or log-rolling or cocktail throwing, in short, if he does not cultivate his own cult, he may never have a very wide readership.[1] Even if he writes novels, he must consent to have his picture printed on the dust jacket of the novel, with his hair aflying and his collar open. He must bustle about in the world. He must, in short, accomplish something worthy of note besides the writing of literature, or he will have no legend, therefore no following, therefore no fame. He may be soon forgotten. Good work alone will seldom turn the trick.

Nothing in the printed record indicates that John Peale Bishop took much thought for the historiographical morrow. He wrote in such a variety of forms that he cannot be pinned down like F. Scott Fitzgerald as a novelist, or like Edmund Wilson as a critic, or like E. E. Cummings as a poet. He must be regarded as a man of letters, even though his principal achievement was poetry. During his lifetime there were published five volumes of his verse,[2] including one in which he shared honors with Mr. Wilson,[3] two volumes of fiction, and a great variety of fugitive pieces. One of these volumes of poetry was actually limited to one hundred and fifty copies. Many of his uncollected poems were brought together, along with those that he had seen published himself, by Allen Tate after Bishop's death.[4] Mr. Wilson during the same year edited the collected essays.[5] The two books of fiction[6] published in the nineteen-thirties remain available in libraries. That is the corpus of his published work.[7]

Though this output was small, it was uniform in quality, and the quality was very high. However, Bishop suffered to a certain extent the same fate as his friend, F. Scott Fitzgerald: He was a man of the nineteen-twenties who lived through the nineteen-thirties, and his literary attitudes and intentions were unpopular with the critics of the latter decade.

His death, April 4, 1944, was noted in some literary periodicals and in the working press, but he has received little attention since that time. It may well be that younger critics have been intimidated by the excellence of the commentary, however short, of Mr. Wilson in his introduction to the essays and of Mr. Tate in his memoir which was published with the poems.[8] Joseph Frank has done the best study to date on Bishop's work, but it is short.[9] Robert Wooster Stallman has published a piece in which he presented his own exegesis of certain of Bishop's poems.[10] There have been other notices,[11] but Bishop has yet to receive the major study which his life and work merit. He is certainly among the more interesting personalities in the history of American literature; his work is distinguished by its variety, its erudition, its skill, and its elegance.

The bare biographical data are easy to come by. Mr. Wilson, Mr. Tate, and Mr. Stallman have set them forth. However, the development of his personality and of his art as it might be demonstrated in the more intimate life records which must be extant has yet to be accorded deep consideration. The over-all achievement has not been assayed. The place which he might occupy as a member of his literary generation has not been firmly established.

The readiest approach to Bishop's work is through the essays. These are not personal essays, and they could not by any stretch of the vernacular be called familiar. They are, like everything else that he wrote, art objects. The speech of these pieces is easy and fluent, but it is the discourse of a man of parts talking objectively to equals; he does not unbosom himself to his audience. As he once remarked, the use of good manners is to keep other people at a distance. A perusal of the essays, however, will introduce the reader to an intelligence which had examined its environment from large to small. Bishop was too well balanced to wheel off into metaphysics; he did not essay the cosmic. He was at home in this world, but only during the proper hours. When he concerned himself with larger aspects of experience, he was more apt to think of living human beings. When he presented his understanding of the essence of religion, it was in terms of the larger relationships of religion to politics. He was capable of considering the effect of the collapse of the Puritan ethic upon American life; but he presented the reflections of this collapse as they appeared in the work of Fitzgerald and of Hemingway. When he meditated upon the relationship of the artist to society, it was in an essay in which he considered the benefits, paltry though he thought them, conferred upon the poets of the nineteen-thirties by the Federal Projects. During that same period, when the American artists began their retreat from Moscow, he considered this phenomenon in a study of the work of Cummings.

The essays also established Bishop as one of the more acute critics of his generation. In offering this opinion, I am not suggesting that Bishop initiated any new theory of criticism. I doubt that he had any interest in doing such a thing. He did not adumbrate any theory then current. He set up no creaking mechanisms. He did not persistently ferret out symbols. He did not worry the text. If he saw beauties in the text, he mentioned them; if he saw failures, he was merciless but not vindictive. Consider this passage from **"The Discipline of Poetry,"** when he is measuring the difference between poetry and verse:

> For when the requirements of the verse are met at the expense of the poetry, the result is apt to be precious.
>
> · · · · ·
>
> But where the poetry overcomes the resistance of the verse, what we get is Whitman or something not nearly so good as Whitman. Where the importance of what is to be said surpasses everything else, we get the later poems of D. H. Lawrence. It would be hard to find a case in which the value of craft is more clearly shown by its absence. Lawrence to every appearance was born to be a poet; he had every gift and only lacked the knowledge. He is the perfect instance of the bitter fact that the man who looks only for expression never succeeds in finding it. When his spirit was with him, he could accomplish a prose as beautiful and moving as any our time has known; but Lawrence died as he had lived, a poet thwarted in what he had to say. "Any poet who does not know exactly what rhymes each word allows," said Baudelaire, "is incapable of expressing any idea whatever." He knew. And Lawrence did not. It was a knowledge of which he was, I should guess, contemptuous. All he knew was that he had not at his death succeeded in saying what he was born to say.
>
> Where there is no conflict between the poet and his verse, we get neither verse nor poetry. We get *The People, Yes,* which claims our attention only as communication.[12]

In this brief passage, much of the artistic contribution of three important poets is summed up.

He was interested in most of the arts. He wrote little about music, but he had an intense, limited interest in it. He was very much aware of architecture. He took the medium of the motion picture seriously enough to be angry with it long before it was regarded as an art form by most people. He epitomized the appeal of Chaplin, of Mary Pickford, and of Rudolph Valentino in a few sentences, and in doing so, he exposed the essential childishness of an art form that must appeal to the masses in order to survive.

In all his criticism—of literature, of visual art, of the art of living—there was little of the specialization which one finds in current criticism. This was a whole man passing judgment. He had not isolated the art object from its environment, and he was not himself isolated. He was in his place, and he knew where that place was. If the things around him were not in their places, they very soon would be, for he would put them there. There was even a place for the abyss. This was not a petty man fussing about in a carrel. Overhead, the night expanded dark and enormous, and he was quite aware that hell might open up under foot at any moment. He could get the horrors along with the most sensitive souls, but he did not intend to write only about the horrors any more than he intended to ignore them.

What one may observe in this mind is the classical balance of the eighteenth century, a balance which he achieved not without torment, not without sadness, not without loss, but a balance. At least a part of this balance may be attributed to Bishop's countrified background: the feeling of place and rank and order in society which prevailed in his childhood. If this attitude is not strictly Southern, it at least obtains in societies which live long in one place. Mr. Wilson tells us of a "little treatise" composed by Bishop concerning one of his ancestors, replete with the genealogy of his mother's family. This feeling of knowing something of the people from whom he came, from having seen as a child the houses and the lands where his forebears lived—these awarenesses contributed to the achievement of his identity. Furthermore, the countryman is more apt to be aware of the fundamental realities of birth and death. "Tupping is still tupping." This countrified aspect of Bishop's nature, noted by Wilson, gave him a firm purchase on reality, from which he was not to be moved by any of his later school experience or by his expatriation in France. Though he was noted for the elegance of his living and the refinement of his manners, he retained—to borrow words written about another poet—that peculiar "combination of aristocratic and backwoodsy tendencies that social historians still find it difficult to understand in persons of Southern antecedents."[13] Both as a collegian and as an adult, he would fall into the directness of speech and the bluntness of vocabulary which are characteristic of the well-bred Southerner when he is talking with other men.

He seems to have been deeply committed to a number of ideas which he regarded as permanent, but he showed little interest in intellectual fads, and he was moved not at all by the tintamar of contemporaneous political opinion. Perhaps this lack of interest indicates belief that discussion was vain.

> Do what? Add my name to a Trotsky faction
> To bury more revolutions:
> Make integers of an improper fraction,
> Distribute soup, or Salvation buns?
> Assault the police in a fit of distraction,
> From an office desk assail the Huns?
> Declare the Black Shirt has a sexual attraction?
> Rush over the border and rape some nuns?
>   . . . . .
> Present evils are for men of action,
> Art has the irremediable ones.[14]

The feeling of place and rank and order in society may well be a great desire rather than an awareness of actuality. Doubtless, such desire would carry over somewhat into actuality. The feeling may also be a memory of previous order, witness to social arrangements which once existed but which have now passed from all except memory. Bishop himself was certainly well aware that the social order out of which he came had effactually passed away thirty years before he was born. With a New England father and a Southern mother, he was a living talisman of the conflict which left the old order of the South in shards. The stubborn insistence of the upper ranks of Southern society that nothing essential was really changed by the Civil War could not face down the fact of poverty, nor could it erase the memory of violation. All the while that the North was attempting to reconstruct the Union, the South was attempting to reconstruct the South.

The two books of fiction written by Bishop testify to his ability to distinguish the dream which the South remembered from the reality through which it had passed. The first of these books, *Many Thousands Gone,* is a novel only by courtesy. Actually, it is a series of five short stories in which some of the characters appear more than once. It is the depiction of a civilization in collapse, with all that such a state could mean to people who immediately thought they remembered only stability, repose, and order. A stirring of new life in the ashes, however, may be seen in the brilliant story, **"Young Death and Desire,"** in which the Southern doctor's virgin daughter takes a wandering country soldier as her lover for one night while another soldier dies down cellar. Even while her lover was with her, she knew she would regret her act, "but not now. . . . They were not dead."

The beginnings of the compromise by which Southern society perpetuated its old image if not its old actualities are also drawn in masterfully. In the title story, two women are featured. The bedridden Miss Hester sternly reads the Bible to the invaders as they turn her out of her bed to search for hidden valuables. Under the mattress they discover the general's uniform (dating from the Mexican War) which belonged to Miss Cary's father. This younger woman stands to one side. Having led the soldiers to her cousin's room to prove that the invalid was bedridden and could not be moved, she is hoping that they will not burn down her house. As she struggles to maintain her composure before these intruders,

> [it] was in her mind that they were playing a joke on her, a heartless joke that would presently end. But that would not take away from its cruelty or lessen her terror at being hurt. "I must not let them know," she thought, "the only thing is not to let them know."

Other works of fiction which might serve as points of comparison came immediately to mind in considering *Many Thousands Gone—So Red the Rose* and *Gone with the Wind.* Both of these novels have more bulk than the stories of Bishop; neither has more substance. Neither presents the causes and consequences of the collapse of Southern culture in a fashion more memorable. In the work of Bishop is none of the sentimentality which mars both the other novels. The novels of Stark Young and Margaret Mitchell are panoramas, whereas the stories of Bishop are made up of swift, sharp, single scenes. Bishop did by implication what the other two novelists did in explicit detail.

Bishop's second book of fiction, *Act of Darkness,* may take as its point of comparison Allen Tate's masterful story, *The Fathers.* Both of these novels are basically concerned with the shift in cultural patterns brought on by the Civil War. (It is no discourtesy to Bishop's memory to pronounce Tate's novel the better of the two: I can think of no compliment greater, since there is no other novel on the same subject which will bear comparison.) Young John, who narrates *Act of Darkness,* is a figure of traditional innocence, readily comparable to Lacy Buchan in *The Fathers.* Both are confronted by the disestablishment of all they thought permanent and the degradation of all they thought noble. Both have already seized enough of their tradition to enable them to survive, however imperfectly. "Tradition is all the learning life which men receive from their fathers and which, having tried it in their own experience, they consent to pass on to their sons."[15]

Both of Bishop's works of fiction are concerned with the loss of tradition. That Bishop recognized the loss as inevitable from the outset is obvious in the opening story of *Many Thousands Gone,* "A Corpse in the House," which is dated 1852. As many cultures had done before them, the South took the loss and made a new tradition of that. The loss of the tradition came to be the tradition. Out of this latter-day memory, Bishop wrote.

No phoenix is wingless.

Bishop's poems, which take up about two hundred and fifty printed pages, were written between his twentieth year and the time of his death, if we include the epitaph he dictated to his wife.[16] These poems epitomize his work, and they were the most carefully tended of all his literary efforts.

It has been said that Bishop was a follower of Yeats and Eliot. Tate had the final word on that subject, however, some years before Bishop's death:

It has been said that Bishop has imitated all the chief modern poets. He has virtually conducted his poetical education in public. But the observation is double-edged. In our age of personal expression the poet gets credit for what is "his own": the art is not the thing, but rather the information conveyed about a unique personality. Applauding a poet only for what is uniquely his own, we lose thereby much that is good. If a poem in Yeats' manner appears in Bishop's book, and is as good as Yeats, it is as good there as it is anywhere else.[17]

As Tate has pointed out, the central aspect of Bishop's work is the aspect of form. Bishop wrote in a great variety of stanza forms; oftentimes, he wrote free verse; sometimes he wrote irregular blank verse. Occasionally he even wrote sonnets. There are two-line epigrams and four-line aphorisms. There are narratives. There are poems in which the verse form is used expressionistically. It might be noted that each of these poems achieves its own form, which is always related to the subject.

In all the poems of Bishop, there is the same quality of polite detachment as there is in the essays. He was not interested in displaying a unique personality; he was obviously interested in the poem as an art object, more as a conveyance of public feeling than of private emotion. Expression of private feelings in public he permitted himself only on rare occasions. Bishop was not the sort of poet to feel that everything he wrote he must spin out of his own navel like a spider weaving a web. What he sought to express was the quality of the emotion rather than the origin of it. He sought also accuracy and elegance. In this search, he achieved a high style. Even in those poems in which he has, consciously or not, imitated Eliot and Yeats, he achieved a form, a complete statement, a statement not vitiated by similarities to the work of other poets. Occasionally, there will be a poem in which the influences come together, as in **"Twelfth Night"**:

> All night I thought on those wise men who took
> A midnight leave of towers and came peering
> Pyramidally down to the dark guards
> And stared apart, each with a mad, hid look
> Twitching his mummied beard
>   while the night swords
> Conferred and chains fell and the unwieldy bar
> Slid and swung back
>   then wandered out to name
> The living demon of an unnamed star.

The poem at once calls to mind Eliot's poem beginning, "A cold coming we had of it." The subject was certainly used by Eliot, but the vocabulary and syntax are those of Yeats.

One remembers Yeats's less familiar poem, "The Magi":

> Now as at all times I can see in the mind's eye,
> In their stiff, painted clothes, the pale unsatisfied ones
> Appear and disappear in the blue depth of the sky
> With all their ancient faces like rain-beaten stones,
> And all their helms of silver hovering side by side,

And all their eyes still fixed, hoping to find once more,
Being by Calvary's turbulence unsatisfied,
The uncontrollable mystery on the bestial floor.

Are we to assume that Eliot was imitating Yeats also?

The beginnings of Bishop's "poetical education" are apparent in his earliest writings. His readings are reflected in his verse. "Give me your hand. She was lovely. Mine eyes blind."[18] Surely this is an echo from *The Duchess of Malfi:* "Cover her face. Mine eyes dazzle. She died young."

Resonances from Browning and the pre-Raphaelites commingle in this early work, as in **"Filippo's Wife":**

> *A serving woman speaks:*
> Black velvet trails its folds over the day;
> White tapers dripping in their silver frames
> Wave their thin flames and shadows in the wind.
>
> *Pia, Pompia, Bella Cunizza, come—come away!*
> We will not touch her till the end of day.
> Her cheeks are clear as tapers tipped with flames,
> Her lips like red leaves frightened in the wind.
>
> *Pia, Pompia, Bella Cunizza, come—come away!*
> Her toes are stiffened like a stork's in flight.
> She's laid upon her bed, on the white sheets,
> Her hands pressed on her smooth bust like a saint.

Among a number of others, the poem called **"In the Beginning"** reflects the manner of the Imagists:

> I had dreamed that Love would come under broad
>   pennons of gold.
> With rumbling of ponderous drums and conches braying
> Straying of crimson,
> Bickering of banners blown to vermilion and gold,
> With brown-burnt faces under barbaric turbans,
> And a tumult of hoofs upon stony pavements.

Compare this passage with the following from John Gould Fletcher:

> Whirlpools of purple and gold,
> Winds from the mountains of cinnabar,
> Lacquered mandarin moments, palanquins swaying
>   and balancing
> Amid the vermilion pavilions, against the jade
>   balustrades.[19]

Dowson and *The Yellow Book* are heard in such a poem as **"Interior."**

> The divine languor of souls beyond surprise
> Lives in the cold curve of her lip; her eyes
> Are calm as with a deep desire foregone.
> Her jewelled ears drip threaded pearls upon
> The fragile laces of her flaring ruff;
> Her bosom sighs in crimson, and a rich stuff
> Tumbles in crimson folds about her feet.

The Roman images which Bishop was to develop later are first seen in *Green Fruit,* as in **"Messalina Prepares a Festival."** There is even some folk material in the section of the book called "Poems Out of Jersey and Virginia."

Over all this early work broods the languid *fin de siècle* shade of Aubrey Beardsley, moving in a resplendent milieu of *art nouveau,* glittering with Tiffany, Lalique, and Daum, the whiplash line revealed in every curve of the Thonet furnishings, as in **"The Death of a Dandy"** from *The Undertaker's Garland:*

> The exquisite banality of rose and ivory:
> Shadows of ivory carved into panels, stained
> And decayed in the moulding; rose-colour looped
> Casting a shadow of mauve; blown cherubs
> Bulging in silver,
> Lift six tapers to the lighted mirror.
>   . . . . .
> The chamfered fall of silken rose—
> Muffling London and the autumn rain—
> Lifts and recurves,
> A beautiful young man,
> Naked, but for a superb white tiewig,
> Moves in with slow pacings of a cardinal
> Dreaming on his cane.

There is little in the later work which cannot be found in this early writing; but, as his talent matured, Bishop found his own voice. The sonnet, **"A Recollection,"** admired by Stallman, is certainly an individual achievement:

> Famously she descended, her red hair
> Unbound and bronzed by sea-reflections, caught
> Crinkled with sea-pearls. The fine slender taut
> Knees that let down her feet upon the air,
> Young breasts, slim flanks and golden quarries were
> Odder than when the young distraught
> Unknown Venetian, painting her portrait, thought
> He'd not imagined what he painted there.
>
> And I too commerced with that golden cloud:
> Lipped her delicious hands and had my ease
> Faring fantastically, perversely proud.
>
> All loveliness demands our courtesies.
> Since she was dead I praised her as I could
> Silently, among the Barberini bees.

Perhaps it is not mere coincidence that Bishop achieves the sound of his own voice most definitely when he is speaking in dramatic monologue. A dramatic monologue, he pointed out, was one-half of a metaphor, the other half of which was not stated. In **"An Interlude"** and **"No More the Senator,"** he was speaking as a Roman, regarding the collapse of the empire. What the other half of the metaphor might be, he left to the reader. Bishop was not unaware of the tides of events in his times. Perhaps he thought his own civilization was in a state of collapse similar to that experienced by the Romans at the time of the fall of the Empire. Both of these poems are spoken by members of the patrician class. The speaker in **"An Interlude"** is a dispassionate observer, ironical and resigned:

> Our indolence was despair. We were still at times
>   struck

When morning attained the deiformed emperors
Where they stood, gaudy in armor, with laurels
    crowned,
One arm uplifted among the columns.
             There was never
Of course, any lack of statues to instruct us
In the aspect of virtue: magnanimous brows
Sterner than marble; in the sun's silence
Aquiline stares.

He is thoroughly aware of the traditions of Rome from the most ancient times, although he never says so directly; he is in a position to have observed the personal behavior of the emperor in crisis:

          Deliberate
Even in the worst disease of his defeat,
The infecting tumult, he found time
Before morning to consult with others
On their causes for our long decline from greatness.

He recognizes clearly that the Empire is surrounded by barbarians who must be held off by tribute:

In the meantime, the barbarians are back in the passes.
Nothing is left but to stay devastation by tribute.

He knows the Empire has still a long course to run, but it has suffered its first major military defeat, and the course is set downwards.[20]

The senator in the poem which mentions this office is an old man living at the end of all:

For the Caesars have long been extinct: the eyebrows
Concise upon seeing eyes and the whole face
Stern upon conquest. I have seen them only in stone.
         The name
Snatched up by barbarians and worn with a swagger
Is on bearded faces and a burst of vacant eyeballs.
It is so long we have known our divinities only
         through Ovid
And mentioned their names only on official occasions.

He is a monk, now that he is an old man, possibly an abbot or a prior, a man who has received the best education. His concern is to record the literature of the classical period, a task to which he has set the monks in his charge. The speaker is a man who is "convinced in the mind" of the truth of Christianity, but his heart is with his classical tradition, and he exhorts his monks to copy his manuscripts of Seneca and Euripides:

We'll keep no fasts if fasting blurs your eyes.
Whatever else is lost, O them
Whom God did not, Caesar will not, slaves cannot,
Save!

When reading these poems, I find it impossible not to meditate upon the analogies between the Romans and ourselves.

The language in these two monologues is a strongly individualized utterance. Bishop's style and vocabulary are el-

evated, but there are sinew and strength in the language. At the same time, it is quite idiomatic and follows the basic rhythms. The length of the lines is irregular, but the whole moves from within; it has a rhythm of its own which catches the ear, which delights it, without calling attention to itself.

The rhythm of another of Bishop's monologues is even more persuasive, that of the **"Portrait of Mrs. C: *Aetatis suae* 75,"** because it is the rhythm of the speech that Bishop must have heard in his childhood. One can hear the "murmuring distillation of old Virginia times now dead and gone"[21] in this poem:

Where I was born
The gardens were all terraces and the grapevines
Ran everywhere; that shrivelled and turned brown
At the first frost, were raked
And burned in piles: the dead leaves.
The river bottoms drifted like smoke
And the woods, the woods, were yellow as bonfires
In the fall—in the hunting season
When even the slaves fed upon partridge.
The mornings were cold. I used to run
Down to the nearest cabin and climb into bed
With my nigger mammy. It was warm there.
But this place falls to rack and ruin;
What can I do with these rapscallion blacks
That want three dollars just to clean the yard.
I am alone. No one. Not even a negro girl
To bring the wood in and to fix the fires.

Perhaps this poem is no better known than it is because the reading audience is not aware of the actual cadence of Southern speech and cannot hear the explanatory emphasis on the word "dead" in the fifth line; cannot hear the lyrical lift when "the woods" is repeated in the seventh line; cannot hear the sudden shift in rhythm to accompany a change of subject.

Throughout the poem there is rapid extrapolation from one subject to another, in the manner of many old women. The old lady plays the part of everyone she mentions, but this was a common conversational practice among women of her place and class, who considered conversation a chief social grace. Leading restricted lives in a provincial environment, they learned to interest themselves in the commonplace and to endow it with some humor and significance. In her conversation, the old lady draws upon her long familial memory, stored up over several generations of residence in one place. She recollects the wildness of her brothers, the prodigality of her ancestors, the long association with the Negro. She quotes two Negro songs in her musings, "Many Thousands Gone" and "Nebuchadnezzar," the latter also quoted in *Act of Darkness.* She considers with bewilderment, distaste, and dismay a recent visit from her granddaughter, who came to borrow her wedding garments. She is perfectly well aware of the decay of her family and quite well aware that there is nothing that she can do about it:

It does not matter that she thinks me
A foolish old woman, half-daft, fit only

For a modest funeral. I do <u>not</u> care.
I said I do not care. And yet, at times,
She fills me with more cold
Than all the creaking of this lonely house.

The theme of this poem is the survival of personal integrity based on cultural values. This monologue will certainly bear comparison with the famous telephone speech of Estelle Wingfield in *The Glass Menagerie* of Tennessee Williams. There is not a trace of decadence in this old woman, however. Everything around her has decayed, including her young people, but she is furiously intact:

Ah, no! There's something I have no more lost
Than I have lost (although I've given my pew up)
Faith in God! But when I die, she'll say,
It is too far to come. She took
The veil. The slippers were too small.

Old, somewhat deaf, vague, but her own woman yet. Furthermore, she has style, and she has irony.

The reading of a dramatic monologue is not a lyrical effort; it is a public occasion. The writer of a dramatic monologue intends that some other character should mediate between himself and the audience. He has put on the buskins or the *cothurni*. The poet cannot honorably conceal himself, however, when the occasion of the poem is really public, as in **"A Subject of Sea Change,"** which was the Phi Beta Kappa poem at Columbia University, June 1, 1942. This poem is not one of Bishop's most individual, but it is one of the most typical, and it does offer him an opportunity for several magnificent pronouncements, worthy of inscription in stone:

I've had no sadder thing to bear than change,
No darker thing than night,
No more dread sight
Than warriors to whom honor is strange.

The theme is the same one as in **"Portrait of Mrs. C,"** a survival of personal integrity based on cultural values, even though all the values have suffered sea change.

An elegy is also a public occasion. Certainly among the great elegies in the language is that written by Bishop upon the death of his classmate and lifelong friend, F. Scott Fitzgerald. The poem is noble. Like the Phi Beta Kappa poem, it is replete with classical allusions, but they fall into the pattern without affectation or distortion. The poem is in the first person; it is a public utterance of private feelings; and the decorum of the elegist is superb. This is not eulogy, this is lament, but it is as formal as a state funeral:

All day, knowing you dead,
I have sat in this long-windowed room,
Looking upon the sea and, dismayed
By mortal sadness, though without thought to resume
Those hours which you and I have known—
Hours when youth like an insurgent sun
Showered ambition on an aimless air,

Hours foreboding disillusion,
Hours which now there is none to share.
Since you are dead, I leave them all alone.

Again, one is reminded of Yeats:

I have walked and prayed for this young child an
    hour
And heard the sea-wind scream upon the tower,
And under the arches of the bridge, and scream
In the elms above the flooded stream;
Imagining in excited reverie
That the future years had come,
Dancing to a frenzied drum,
Out of the murderous innocence of the sea.[22]
All day in the one chair
From dream to dream and rhyme to rhyme I have
    ranged
In rambling talk with an image of air:
Vague memories, nothing but memories.[23]

Nothing of grief is withheld; nothing of the feeling of loss, or worse, the feeling of waste, is withheld; but all of the drunken horror of Fitzgerald's misspent years is set forth in language which redeems the whole by its honesty, its elevation, and its intensity:

When the dissipation of the night is past,
Hour of the outcast and the outworn whore,
That is past three and not yet four—
When the old blackmailer waits beyond the door
And from the gutter with unpitying hands
Demands the same sad guiltiness as before,
The hour of utter destitution
When the soul knows the horror of its loss
And knows the world too poor
For restitution,
                                Past three o'clock
And not yet four—
                                When not pity, pride,
Or being brave,
Fortune, friendship, forgetfulness of drudgery
Or of drug avails, for all has been tried,
And nothing avails to save
The soul from recognition of its night.

This is an elegy which is fit for the company of *Adonais and Lycidas*. It is called **"The Hours"** and is based upon Fitzgerald's statement, "In the real dark night of the soul it is always three o'clock in the morning." The symbols are drawn from nature, from mythology, from the private life of Fitzgerald, though they never become private symbols. This poem is surely one of the saddest poems written in our time, confronting, as it does, all aspects of mortality.

The dark has come. I cannot pluck you bays,
Though here the bay grows wild. For fugitive
As surpassed fame the leaves this sea-wind frays.
Why should I promise what I cannot give?

The title of this essay was not drawn up without thought. I make no pretense that I have examined the works of John Peale Bishop properly, but I hope that I have stirred other people to do so. He is neglected, and he is rewarding.

Criticism is surely among the most presumptuous of all undertakings.

Notes

1. "He had a queer way of hiding his work or of preventing it from being known. . . . [One of his volumes of verse] was published in a limited edition of one hundred and fifty copies, so that few people except his friends ever saw it." Edmund Wilson, Introduction to *The Collected Essays of John Peale Bishop* (New York: Charles Scribner's Sons, 1948), pp. xi-xii.

2. *Green Fruit* (Boston: Sherman, French and Co., 1917); *Now with His Love* (New York: Charles Scribner's Sons, 1933); *Minute Particulars* (New York: Alcestis Press, 1936); *Selected Poems* (New York: Charles Scribner's Sons, 1941).

3. *The Undertaker's Garland* (New York: Alfred A. Knopf, 1922). Boris Artzybasheff did black-and-white illustrations for this book.

4. *The Collected Poems of John Peale Bishop* (New York: Charles Scribner's Sons, 1948).

5. *Collected Essays. Cf.* William Arrowsmith, "An Artist's Estate," *Hudson Review*, II (Spring 1949), 118-127, a review of this volume and the poems.

6. *Many Thousands Gone* (New York: Charles Scribner's Sons, 1931); *Act of Darkness* (New York: Charles Scribner's Sons, 1935).

7. *Vide* J. M. Patrick and R. W. Stallman, "John Peale Bishop: A Checklist," *Princeton University Library Chronicle*, VII (February 1946), 62-79.

8. *Cf.* Allen Tate's essay on Bishop in *Reactionary Essays on Poetry and Ideas* (New York: Charles Scribner's Sons, 1936), pp. 52-63.

9. "Force and Form: A Study of John Peale Bishop," *Sewanee Review*, LV (Winter 1947), 71-107.

10. "Examination of Modern Poets: 1. John Peale Bishop," *The Western Review*, XI (Autumn 1946), 5-19.

11. For instance, *vide* S. E. Hyman, "Notes on the Organic Unity of John Peale Bishop," *Accent*, IX (Winter 1949), 102-113.

12. *Collected Essays*, pp.103-104.

13. Donald Davidson, "In Memory of John Gould Fletcher," *Poetry*, LXXVII (October 1950-March 1951), 157-158.

14. "Art and Action," *Collected Poems*, p.150.

15. "The South and Tradition," *Collected Essays*, p.8.

16. *Collected Poems*, p.xvi.

17. Tate, *op. cit.*, p.56.

18. *Collected Poems*, p.202.

19. John Gould Fletcher, *Irradiations—Sand and Spray* (Boston: Houghton Mifflin Company, 1915), V.

20. I am unable to discover any actual event on which Bishop based this poem. Perhaps it refers to the destruction of the three legions under Quintilius Varus at Saltus Teutoburgiensis during the reign of Augustus. Suetonius wrote about this disaster. The emperors did not go on campaign frequently.

21. Donald Davidson, "Lee in the Mountains," *Lee in the Mountains and Other Poems* (New York: Houghton Mifflin Company, 1938).

22. William Butler Yeats, "A Prayer for My Daughter," *The Variorum Edition of the Poems of William Butler Yeats,* edited by Peter Allt and Russell K. Alspach (New York: The Macmillan Company, 1957), p.403.

23. "Broken Dreams," *ibid.*, p.357.

Leslie A. Fielder (essay date 1967)

SOURCE: "John Peale Bishop and the Other Thirties," in *Commentary*, April, 1967, pp. 74-82.

[*In the following essay, Fielder claims that Bishop was the best Southern novelist of the 1930s despite the fact that he published only one novel.*]

The revival of the literature of the 30's through which we have recently been living—the republication of novels long out of print, the redemption of reputations long lapsed, the compilation of anthologies long overdue—has been oddly one-sided, a revival of one half only of the literary record of that dark decade: the urban, Marxist, predominantly Jewish half, whose leading journal was the *New Masses* and whose monster-in-chief was Joseph Stalin. And this skewed emphasis, though somewhat misleading, is comprehensible enough; for we live at a moment when a large reading public, educated by a second generation of urban Jewish writers (ex-Marxists, this time around), begins by identifying with certain contemporary literary heroes, like Moses Herzog, whose minds were made by this 30's tradition, and ends by wanting to read the books they read: the fiction of Nathanael West and Daniel Fuchs and Henry Roth, even Mike Gold's *Jews Without Money*.

Some writers, however, who move us just now at least as strongly as Saul Bellow, writers ranging all the way from neo-Gothic journalists like Truman Capote to latter-day prophets like Marshall McLuhan, were nurtured on another, rival tradition which also flourished in the 30's: a provincial, Agrarian, primarily WASP tradition, whose chief journal was the *Southern Review* and whose monster-in-chief was Huey Long. We are less likely to know the basic manifesto of that tradition, a compilation of paeans to the old South called *I'll Take My Stand* by "Twelve Southerners," than such Marxist equivalents as Malcom Cowley's *Exile's Return* or Edmund Wilson's *American Jitters*.

Yet the former is no more dated, no more alien in its aspirations than the two latter, which, indeed, have been drastically rewritten in later editions, as their authors have changed with the times. All three books are exemplary, useful both for illuminating their own age and tempering our enthusiasm for the unguarded goals and hopes of our own. Just as we find it therapeutic to recall that Cowley and Wilson once looked to the Soviet Union for salvation, we may find it equally so to remember that Robert Penn Warren could once write of the Southern Negro that he "is likely to find in agricultural and domestic pursuits the happiness that his good nature and easy ways incline him to as an ordinary function of his being."

And it is well, too, to come to terms with the hopes for literature which the Southern Conservatives, like the Eastern Radicals, attached to their social and political programs—in order to savor the full irony of the fact that both movements did, indeed, produce literary revivals; though in each case, the most moving books arose out of tension and delusion rather than allegiance and simple faith. The great writer of the South was already on the scene when the 30's began, but he remained as invisible to the doctrinaire advocates of Southern Agrarianism as Nathanael West or Henry Roth were to be to the doctrinaire Marxist critics. Not until 1939 did George Marion O'Donnell give full recognition to Faulkner in the *Kenyon Review,* successor to the *Southern Review.* In 1939, when *I'll Take My Stand* appeared, Donald Davidson, who was entrusted with commenting on the arts, did not even mention him—concentrating instead on Ellen Glasgow and James Branch Cabell, the latter his leading contender for the laureateship of the South. Yet some of Faulkner's very best work had already been published; though, indeed, so embattled and bleak a novel as *The Sound and the Fury* provides little of that "repose" and "continuity" which Davidson hoped for from the Old Dominion; part of his problem being, of course, that it was Virginia and not Mississippi which he had in mind when he spoke generally about the South. Madness, stylistic improvisation, and a radical dislocation of the tradition are what Faulkner was then prepared to offer; and that, Davidson thought, was already being supplied in sufficient quantities by certain despised writers from New York and Chicago.

From our present vantage-point, it is easy to see that Glasgow and Cabell, addressing the past as they did in hushed and genteel voices (for all Cabell's vaunted pornography), could evoke from it no promise of a renaissance of letters; and that Faulkner alone was capable of providing models for the literature to come which was to celebrate the terrible and elegant death of the South. Not, let us recall, the Faulkner of post-Nobel Prize banalities about dignity and endurance, but the shrill and despairing Faulkner, who mocked the world of the mid-30's with *Sanctuary,* and was able still to write as late as 1944 (in the course of asserting that his real subject matter had never been the South at all): ". . . life is a phenomenon but not a novelty, the same frantic steeplechase toward nothing everywhere, and man stinks the same stink no matter where in time."

Before any other Southern writer of distinction, John Peale Bishop seems to have sensed the value and significance of what this Faulkner was doing—not merely going on record in praise of his double vision, his capacity to appreciate simultaneously the myth of the Sartorises and the fact of the Snopeses; but imitating his techniques as well in, for instance, a story called **"Toadstools Are Poison,"** which he published in 1932 in emulation of Faulkner's "That Evening Sun." We are more likely to be aware of such later heirs of the dark Faulkner as Robert Penn Warren and Eudora Welty, Carson McCullers and Truman Capote, even so belated a continuer of the line as Flannery O'Connor. Yet Bishop was there first in picking up the cues for a fiction Gothic, as the fiction of the South has always been since the days of Edgar Poe, but fully aware at last of what before had only been hinted: that the blackness of darkness which haunts it is not merely embodied in the Negro, but quite simply *is* the Negro—that nightmare creature born of the contempt for manual labor and the fear of the sexuality of their own women which had so paradoxically made the white masters of the South heroes but not quite men.

Such a fiction is by definition even further from the possibility of "repose" than that of the industrial North and East; for if the latter is torn between the terrible fact of the present and the dream of a barely possible pure future, the latter is pulled apart between an equally dismal actuality and the dream of a manifestly unreal pure past. Nonetheless, the manifestos of the Agrarians tell the kind of lie which illuminates the truth of the fiction of Faulkner and Warren and Bishop, even as the Marxist manifestos tell the kind of lie which illuminates the truth of the novels of Nathanael West and Henry Roth. If we would recapture the past of three decades ago, we need to relive both the elation of the beautiful lies which nurtured it, and the discomfiture of the grim truths spoken from the heart of those lies. It would, therefore, be a special shame if Bishop's single completed novel, **Act of Darkness,** remained unavailable a moment longer, since in it one committed by birth and temperament to the myth of the South both rehearses it and—passionately as well as tenderly—gives it the lie.

We must, then, if we are to understand Bishop and his age, learn to think of him as perhaps the most important Southern novelist of the 30's[1] despite the slimness of his production. Yet if we bring him to mind at all these days, we are likely to associate him with a different genre, a different decade, even a different region. Certainly we tend to remember him first as a poet, second as a critic—and only last, if at all, as a writer of fiction. And though this emphasis is, on the one hand, a function of the way in which his influential friends (Scott Fitzgerald, Edmund Wilson, Allen Tate, among others) have chosen to mythicize and preserve him; on the other, it is a result of how his writing career actually developed.

True enough, Bishop may have first captured the imagination of a large audience as the semi-fictional highbrow poet, Tom D'Invilliers, who moves through the pages of Fitzgerald's *This Side of Paradise;* but his verse had already appeared in print under his own name even before the publication of that novel in 1920—in fact, three years before the start of World War I, which is to say, a year before the initiation of Harriet Monroe's *Poetry* and the official beginnings of modernism in American verse. And he continued to write poems until his death in 1944, publishing four volumes in his lifetime and leaving enough uncollected poetry to justify Tate's putting together a **Collected Poems** in 1948, as well as a special selection for English readers in 1960.

In his preface to the latter volume, Tate celebrated Bishop's achievement as a poet, paid a passing compliment to his fiction, then went on to give the highest praise to his criticism—recording a belief that his dead friend had been "one of the best literary critics of the 20's and 30's." And in this opinion, Edmund Wilson (perhaps even better qualified to judge) had seemed to concur, when he had earlier gathered Bishop's scattered criticism into book form for the first time. But Bishop's critical writing, collected in a single volume, disconcertingly adds up to less than one would have expected from the impressions created by individual pieces; just as his verse, however elegant and accomplished, now seems too much a fading echo of styles already obsolescent before he had perfected his skills.

No, it is only in Bishop's fiction that I, at any rate, hear an authentic and original voice, only in his one successful novel and a handful of short stories that I come on rhythms and phrases, images and myths that live on in my head. But he does not seem at first glance a 30's writer even in this area of his greatest achievement; for he began to write fiction, too, long before the collapse of post-World War I prosperity had made the 30's possible—publishing his very first stories when the 20's had barely started: one of them, characteristically elegant and unconnected with things to come, in **The Undertaker's Garland,** a volume on which he had collaborated with Edmund Wilson.

Wilson and Fitzgerald, Fitzgerald and Wilson; how inextricably Bishop's life as a writer is involved with theirs, and how inevitably we are tempted to see him through what we know more securely about them. But the clues they seem to offer are likely to lead us astray, suggesting that Bishop's spiritual home was Princeton (where he had met his two friends); that not *The Sound and the Fury* but *The Great Gatsby* provided him with a model for his fiction; and, finally, that he is a 20's writer in his deepest heart. Wilson, to be sure, who began as a true child of that earlier decade, was reborn as a leading spokesman for the radical 30's and survived to become a kind of elder statesman to the generation of the 40's and 50's; but Fitzgerald we think of as having belonged so utterly to the era which learned in large part its very life-style from him that he could not survive its disappearance. And Bishop seems, after all, much more like the latter than the former.

Why not, then, regard him simply as a 20's writer, who, living too long without accommodating to a new era, found

himself quite out of fashion? Certain of his allegiances, surely, like a great deal of his rhetoric, he shared with those older writers, who—having barely found their voices before World War I—were bereft by that war of subjects appropriate to those voices; and insisted forever after on regarding its horrors as a personal affront rather than a universal catastrophe. Like many of his contemporaries, too, Bishop subscribed with equal fervor to the cult of self-pity and the religion of art, which seemed for a while—until the coming of more fashionable political faiths—to fill quite satisfactorily the vacuum left by the vanishing of older pieties. And like most of them, he espoused a righteous contempt for the vulgarities of American culture and a yearning for Old World charm which, combined with a favorable exchange rate, led to expatriation in the Holy City of Paris.

It was the war which took him to France for the first time; and returning briefly to America, he did not cease to remember it, writing at the close of an essay on his alma mater, which he published in 1921: "If I had a son who was an ordinarily healthy, not too intelligent youth I should certainly send him to Princeton. But if ever I find myself the father of an extraordinary youth I shall not send him to college at all. I shall lock him up in a library until he is old enough to go to Paris." Shortly thereafter, he made his first postwar removal to Europe, then a second much longer one, which lasted until 1933, and during which three sons were born to him on the continent to which he dreamed of sending them if they proved themselves "extraordinary" enough.

And what does all this shuttling between Princeton and New York and Paris have to do with the 30's, which turned from New York and Princeton, as well as Detroit or Sauk City or Newark, New Jersey toward the Holy City of Moscow (to which only a few were foolish enough to venture in fact)—or alternatively, to the Holy Anti-City of Jefferson's Monticello (to which none, however foolish, could manage to return)? Little enough in fact; indeed, so little that we are not surprised when Bishop, in quest of a setting for his one finished novel, moves backward in time, out of the mid-30's which saw the publication of the book to the pre-World War I years of his own childhood. And in that relatively remote era, he rehearses—or rather lets his boy hero with whom he shares the almost anonymous name of John rehearse—a familiar tale, not less indebted to certain prevailing modes of the 20's for being so palpably autobiographical. The commonplace which reminds us that life often imitates art does not make sufficiently clear that it is inevitably yesterday's art, outmoded art, i.e., a cliché, which today's life is likely to repeat.

In *Act of Darkness,* at any rate, we find Bishop, though apparently convinced he is recreating his own early experience, recreating instead fictional patterns already well established by his predecessors and contemporaries at home and abroad. On the one hand, we encounter such standard American plots as the belated flight from mama; or the boy vicariously inducted into maturity by witnessing the fall to woman of an older man on whom he has a homo-sexual crush. On the other, we are confronted by such fashionable European imports as the direct initiation into manhood at the hands of a whore (fumbled the first time, achieved the second); and especially the fable of conversion popularized by Joyce's *Portrait of the Arist as a Young Man,* in which a baffled youngster—realizing after many wrong turnings that only Art gives meaning to Life—goes forth to write his first novel.

All this familiar stuff is transformed in *Act of Darkness,* however, not only by the subtlety of language and delicacy of cadence which Bishop somehow redeemed from mere elegance by transferring it from verse to prose; but also by the typical 30's tone and voice in which he renders it. It is not finally a social message which gives to the fiction of the Depression years its special character, though the critics of that age once liked to think so. Horace Gregory, who was willing to hail Bishop's book when it first appeared as "one of the few memorable novels of the decade . . . ," hastened to add, almost apologetically, that it had "no pretensions of being a 'social document.'" No matter, since the hallmark of the 30's is rather a certain panic shrillness, a sense of apocalypse, yearning to become religious but held by the mode to secular metaphors.

This we find everywhere in the period: in those atypical novels produced then by writers out of another decade—in Faulkner's *Sanctuary,* for instance, or Hemingway's *To Have and Have Not,* or James Gould Cozzens's *Castaway;* as well as in the most characteristic work of writers who belong entirely to that dark decade—in Nathanael West's *Miss Lonely-hearts,* say, or Henry Roth's *Call It Sleep.* They are *mad* books, all of them, even more disturbingly than they are crypto-religious ones: sometimes actual projections of madness, sometimes accounts of long flirtations with insanity, ending in not quite credible escapes back into reason and peace—as if the political debates which occupied the age were finally mere analogues, leftover 19th-century metaphors called on to express a crisis of consciousness for which the times had not yet found a new language.

And of all the books of the period, *Act of Darkness* (along with *Call It Sleep*) comes closest to revealing that not-quite secret. How different its panic mood is from the more theatrical despair typical of the 20's (think of Fitzgerald's *All the Sad Young Men*), which, after all, was never incompatible with euphoria. A comparison of the two types of book reveals how—though the Great War may have been felt chiefly as a personal affront—the Great Depression seemed Armageddon itself, a kind of end of the world. It is odd and maybe even a little degrading to realize how we Americans (not only our writers, finally, but all of us) were driven to ultimate despair not by contemplating the destruction of fabled cities abroad or even the prospect of our own deaths in foreign lands, but by a confrontation at home with the Crash, the end of prosperity and fun and games. The colloquial phrase says it exactly: the Depression struck *home* to us as the war had not; and the image

of the desolated American city seemed an image also of our own devastated souls, whereas that of the ravaged European capital had signified only the death of that culture with which we had never been quite at ease.

Most Depression novels, therefore, played out their fables against the background of the ruined American city, making the native urban landscape for the first time the chief symbolic setting for our kind of Gothic. Not so in Bishop's case, however, despite his commitment after his college years to the Princeton-New York-Paris circuit, despite his father's Northern city origins, despite his own final retreat to New England to die. Faulkner himself may have been driven in the Depression years from Jefferson to Memphis, out of whose back-alleys Popeye emerges to stalk the pages of *Sanctuary,* that other inverted parable of rape and the Southern Lady. But Bishop turns back, in the midst of the general panic that was possessing the land, to where his own personal panic had begun, to precisely the sort of small Southern community in a farm setting which the Agrarians celebrated; but which for him (despite the kind things he had to say of the South in his more abstract commentary) is the place of horror from which, at the end of his book, he is escaping, even as he escapes the "soft torture" of his mother's love and the temptation to madness.

His poems, on the other hand, do have a kind of urban setting; since in them he imagined himself and his friends (Edmund Wilson, for example, turned not so improbably into an antique senator) moving through an imaginary city clearly intended to remind us of Rome. But his is *not* the Rome—however much Allen Tate would like us to believe it—created in the fantasy of Southern neo-Classicists like George Washington Custis, delivering his annual Fourth of July oration dressed in a toga, or Thomas Jefferson dreaming the University of Virginia. Bishop's is rather a doomed and decadent city—much like the "unreal City" of T. S. Eliot's *The Waste Land,* or even more like Cavafy's Alexandria: an imperial capitol whose great Caesars are all dead, and which is assailed from without by barbarians and Christians, from within, by doubt; a city whose inhabitants are waiting—as so many so variously but so nearly unanimously waited in the 30's—for the End:

> We did not know the end was
>   coming: nor why
> It came; only that long before
>   the end
> Were many wanted to die. . . .

So, too, his first and unfinished novel, *The Huntsmen are Up in America,* is set in legendary dying cities—this time called Venice and New York. But that novel stutters away before its intended close in the most legendary part of New York (doubly strange and wonderful for the Southerner), which is to say, in Harlem, where Bishop tries to bring to the surface the underground theme that obsessed him: the idyll which turns nightmare of a sacred union of white and Negro, the pale virgin and the black stud. The idyllic names for the partners in that union are

Venetian, of course, Desdemona and Othello; but to do justice to its nightmare aspects, Bishop had to take it back to where, in his troubled mind, it really belongs: back to his own birthplace of Charles Town, West Virginia, called in his fiction "Mordington"; though its actual name is distributed between the two leading characters of his completed novel, to the Charlie and Virginia, who were for him the prototypes of Othello and Desdemona.

"Mordington" is, at any rate, the background not only for *Act of Darkness,* which he published in 1935, but also for the collection of stories called *Many Thousands Gone,* which had appeared four years earlier. It was apparently Bishop's aim in the five stories which make up the book, as well as in the novel, to create a mythical equivalent of the small town he knew best: his own Yoknapatawpha County, which is to say, a microcosm of the South, true both to its sociological facts and its legendary meanings. Sociologically, Bishop is not nearly so successful as Faulkner; for despite his patent determination to write the sort of "realistic" book his age had convinced itself it admired, his data keep incandescing (at best) into poetry, or dissolving (at worst) into self-conscious symbolism. Yet in the course of his failed attempt at recording history, he does succeed in releasing from himself and from whatever of the past lives on in his memory, their essential myth.

In an extraordinary little story called **"If Only,"** a pair of genteel Southern spinsters known as "the Sabine Sisters," who have survived the Civil War only to confront indigence, find themselves one day possessed of a Negro servant called "Bones." The allegorical import of the names is not less important for being self-evident: the evocation of Rome and rape in the first, of death and the Minstrel Show in the second. Bones, at any rate, almost miraculously restores the decayed household of the sisters to an elegance which they perhaps only dreamed of having had before; but simultaneously begins to appear before them in darkly sinister, though inconclusively sexual manifestations—winking out at them in naked insolence from their bathtub, asleep on one of their beds, "terrible and tall . . . and very black." Dismayed and horrified, the two women find themselves incapable of telling whether their ambiguous servant is a madman, or a figment of their own madness; and they cannot, in any event, disengage themselves from their "nigger," since "with him they lived in terror, but in the tradition."

Act of Darkness, which is concerned with the escape from both the terror and the tradition, is less perfectly achieved; but by the same token, it seems richer, less a bare parable. And we are finally more deeply moved and illuminated by it, for all its obtrusive faults: its two halves which fall apart in tone and tempo, its point of view which shifts without clear motivation or redeeming grace, etc. etc. Any teacher of composition could tick off its flaws; yet the tale it tells survives its technical ineptitude: the story of a boy early bereft of his father, almost swallowed up by his mother's love and dogged through his lonely house by a Negro homosexual of his own age, who at last finds a kind

of salvation by attaching himself, purely and passionately, to his young Uncle Charlie. Uncle Charlie, however, first seduces a young farm girl whom the boy is prepared to love though not possess; then takes him to a whorehouse in an unsuccessful attempt at inducting him into guilt and manhood; finally rapes a not-so-young Southern lady, a friend of and surrogate for the boy's mother, called by the twice symbolic name of Virginia.

The climax of the book's action and the heart of its meaning is contained in a long courtroom scene, during which Charlie is, at the lady's instigation, tried for having assaulted her; and ends by claiming that not he—dandy and bully and restless seducer—but the woman herself—intellectual and freethinker and virgin—had been the effective rapist: that "he shamelessly allowed her to complete his animal rapture," maintaining the while "only a passive prowess." And young John is undone by the confession, pushed over the brink of a breakdown by what seems to him the ultimate affront to his own dubious masculinity: "What I could not forgive was his denying his domination over what had been done in the darkness of the woods. . . ." But John is not alone in his dismay at this comic-tragic denouement; for the reader finds himself shaken as he is shaken only when some inadequate but long-lived archetypal version of the way things are is inverted and extended, an ulterior, and uncomfortable, significance made clear.

I should suppose that the Southern reader especially would be discomfited; for though rape is the subject *par excellence* of Southern literature in the 19th and 20th centuries—a concern as obsessive as that with seduction in 18th-century England—it is typically the rape of a white woman by a black man, real or fancied, which lies at the center of the plot. Bishop's novel, however, tells no nightmare tale of a black man grossly offending or falsely accused; though there is an attenuated and dislocated echo of the standard fable in the sub-plot of the black fairy with whom the white boy narrator flirts in horrified attraction, and who is finally killed off-scene by being pushed out of a window by somebody else. In the main action, a white man, a gentleman—in fact, just such a gentleman farmer as the Agrarians were then making the focus of their hopes for social reform—is responsible, at least passively, for the act of darkness which the color of his skin seems to belie.

But *why,* the book insists that we ask, why such a total inversion of the archetype? Surely not just because it happens to have happened so in some series of actual events from which Bishop may have made his fiction. So easy an answer the novel itself will not let us accept, evoking as a clue toward its close the pair of ill-fated Shakespearean lovers who had already begun to haunt Bishop, as we have seen. Desdemona and Othello appear again and again during the 30's in all of Bishop's work, whether in verse or prose, the first explicit reference, as we might expect, in the book whose protagonist is called. "Brakespeare," *The Huntsmen are Up in America.* Describing the city of Venice, Bishop writes, as if by the way, "it was only there, I am sure, that the ceremony could have been found that would have wed Desdemona to her black Moor." And a gloss on the metaphor is to be found in one of his best poems, a kind of epigraph to the body of his work, which he called **"Speaking of Poetry"**:

> The ceremony must be found
> that will wed Desdemona to the
> huge Moor.
>   It is not enough—
> to win the approval of the Sena-
> tor . . .
>   For then,
> though she may pant again in his
> black arms
> (his weight resilient as a Barbary
> stallion's)
> She will be found
> when the ambassadors of the Ve-
> netian state arrive
> again smothered . . .
>   (Tupping is still tupping
> though that particular word is
> obsolete . . .)

The allegorical meanings are clear enough: elegance must be married to force, art to magic, the mind to the body— *married,* not merely yielded up to the kind of unceremonious possession which turns inevitably into destruction. It is ritual, "ceremony," which makes of passionate attachment a true marriage, as it makes of passionate perception a true poem: which is to say, the marriage of Desdemona and Othello becomes a metaphor for the poetic act. Equally clear is the nature of the appeal of that metaphor to the race-obsessed, sexually queasy Southern mind: the image of black "tupping" white, a miscegenation, which—lacking appropriate ceremonials—is no more than a rape.

Fair enough, then, that after Charlie's trial and conviction, his unnerved nephew—who had earlier found satisfaction in simpler boys' books, idyllic like Audubon or sinister like *Oliver Twist*—should have turned to Bishop's favorite play to learn for himself how the poet can confer order and beauty and significance on what otherwise must remain heartbreakingly chaotic and sordid and meaningless. "Had the actual murderer of Desdemona . . ." Bishop reports him as thinking, "been brought into a Venetian court, his trial would have made no more sense than Charlie's had done in the Mordington courthouse."

But there is no "huge Moor" in the Mordington affair, we want to cry out at this point, no black man at all, only Uncle Charlie. To which Bishop responds through his narrator, evoking for the first time relevant Shakespearean criticism as well as the text: *neither was Othello a "huge Moor" really—only a Venetian nobleman, neither blacker nor whiter than the farmer from West Virginia.* "The Venetian gentleman," Bishop's John explains to us, "who wore mulberries on his shield, since his name was Il Moro, had, in the repetition of the story of the murder of his wife, been mistaken for a Moor. In time, passing to the North, he had become a blackskinned barbarian, Othello."

The blackness of Othello is, then, *Act of Darkness* insists, a misconception, a mistake; or more precisely, the rapist of white women is black only as the dream of revenge against their emasculating Ladies is black inside the darkness of the white heads of Southern males. The prosecuting attorney, pressing for Charlie's conviction, underlines this when he so oddly repeats in his own language the burden of the scholarship on *Othello:* ". . . once more the cry of rape is heard in the land and . . . this heinous and horrible crime, has been committed, not by a man of the colored race . . . but is imputed to one whose former education, training, and fair tradition should have predisposed him to a career of honor and worthy actions."

There is another turn of the screw beyond this, however, as we already know; a second and even more terrifying inversion implicit in Charlie's plea that it was he who had been raped, that the true Othello is Desdemona: the pale virgin dreaming her own dark violation, and projecting that dream outward upon the white male who resents her—at the cost of his manhood and honor, and at the risk of his life. But the end of the illusion which concealed this truth from a defeated nation, which survived only by imagining itself the last home of chivalry, means the beginning of the end of that nation's myth and its very existence. Intuiting this, *Act of Darkness* becomes a work of prophecy, a parable of that death of the South which all of us are living through in agony right now.

Its protagonist, at any rate, having been deprived of that illusion by his uncle and Shakespeare, is preparing at the book's end to leave not only the small lies of his mother, but the larger lies of the sweet land which seemed for a while to sustain them, to go North. First, however, he has to return to the whorehouse to which his uncle had earlier taken him in vain, where, this time, he musters up enough "passive power" to accomplish his own deflowering. "It was when her hands were on me," he tells us, "that I knew what was again being accomplished was the act in the woods, that all its gestures must be repeated and forever repeated, the rape of the mind by the body."

But at this point, we are no longer sure (and how did we ever deceive ourselves that we were, even in deepest Dixie?) about which is mind, which body, which White, which Black, who Desdemona, who Othello, who the virgin and who the whore. The mythical marriage which Bishop imagined in his verse has, in fact, been accomplished, the archetypal opposites united in a confusion that begins in madness and ends in poetry.

Note

1. Carson McCullers is his chief rival; but though her first and best book, *The Heart Is A Lonely Hunter,* which appeared in 1936, is a true 30's book, adapting the terror of the Depression to a world of freaks reflected in a child's eye, her reputation belongs to the 40's through which she lived, and to which she provided a bridge.

Simone Vauthier (essay date 1975)

SOURCE: "The Meaning of Structure: Toward a New Reading of John Peale Bishop's *Act of Darkness*," in *The Southern Literary Journal*, Vol. VII, No. 2, Spring, 1975, pp. 50-76.

[*In the following excerpt, Vauthier defends Bishop's use of shifting points of view in his novel* Act of Darkness.]

The critics of John Peale Bishop's *Act of Darkness* seem to have been compelled strangely to qualify their praise of the story by cavilling at its technique. Relying on the old dichotomy between form and content, Leslie Fiedler, for instance, confidently asserts: "Any teacher of composition could tick off its flaws; yet the tale it tells survives its technical ineptitude."[1] The two major flaws to which even well-disposed critics take exception relate to the handling of the point of view and the structure. In fact, Bishop's manipulation of viewpoints appears quite justified when, instead of looking for possible psychological motivation one examines its effects on the narration.[2] One of these already touches upon matters of structure. For the shift in focus emphasizes the absence of the act of darkness from the narration and its replacement by another scene—a substitution of great significance in a novel conspicuously concerned with desire and its displacements. But it is necessary to take a longer and closer look at the structuration of *Act of Darkness.*

The structural feature of the novel which has drawn the greatest critical fire is what Robert White calls "the collapse of the novel into two disjointed parts." If Leslie Fiedler mentions only in passing "its two halves which fall apart in tone and tempo," Mr. White deals less cursorily with this failing and his comments deserve to be quoted at length:

> The first half deals, in rather diffuse fashion with the death of John's father and with John's adolescent delights and misgivings. This section reports upon his relations with members of his family and with various citizens of Mordington, his boyhood readings, his companionship with other boys of the town, and the pangs and doubts attendant upon the first stirrings of his sexual urges. The second half focuses upon the "act of darkness" which gives the novel its title, and upon the consequences of that act: the denunciation of Charlie as a rapist, Charlie's trial and eventual imprisonment, and John's sickening after he has witnessed the shattering of the ideal he had imagined Charlie to be.[3]

"To a certain extent," Mr. White adds in all fairness, "these halves of the novel are not unrelated." But such connections as may exist seem in the end too weak to the critic:

> Ultimately (. . .) the first portion of the book fails to link up with the second half. Although the trial and shame of his uncle lead directly to John's illness, and are therefore bound up with his youthful fears and hopes, Charlie's trial is not consequent upon most of what goes on in the first half of the book. Charlie's

trial is a public drama, but the opening half deals with the private world of John's adolescence. In the second half, until after the close of the trial, John's thoughts and actions are minimized. At the novel's close Bishop attempts to link up the two parts, but large fragments of the varied material of the first part refuse to lend themselves to such a fusion—and contribute little to what becomes the dominant concern of the book.[4]

The lack of unity of *Act of Darkness* is therefore to be explained by Bishop's failure to "weld into a coherent whole" his "two separate ends"—conveying the joys and terrors of John's adolescence and "establishing in firm outline the character of the community which finally brings Charlie Marston to trial."[5]

On the whole this interpretation of *Act of Darkness* seems to rest on a misconception of what the novel attempts to do. (As to what the novelist intended to do, only Bishop's notes and correspondence would enable one to advance a theory, and I can only work here on the evidence provided by the text of the Avon edition.) Certainly Charlie's trial is "not consequent upon most of what goes on" before, and neither is Rush's death, to give another example, because the unity of the book does not lie in *the plot,* understood as a causal sequence of events. Granted that horizontally, in the causal-chronological chain, Charlie's trial can be traced back only to the act in the woods; vertically, the scene in which he doubly violates the code of the Southern gentleman by denouncing the lady in the case and denying "his own domination as a male," is related on the one hand to all his former transgressions, actual or verbal, his adultery with Ardista, his debunking of the Southern Woman, and on the other hand to the transgressions of other characters, including those of Rush, the dark homosexual double. The "passion for destruction" that moves Charlie in the court-room is to be correlated to the destructiveness that inspired some of his earlier actions; his loss of control before the jury when he is "exalted by rage" is to be linked to earlier manifestations of his recklessness and wildness. In this way the scene enters into vertical relation with many other scenes with which it forms paradigms of greater or lesser extensions. Because they also add to the credibility of the character (who is then *seen* as 'true to his self') such links are immediately perceived by the reader as part of the psychological web of the narration and their place in more abstract patterns is obscured.

But if, in the same trial scene, we isolate yet another node of signification, the paradigmatic layering of the narration will appear more distinctly. What is at stake throughout is the life of Charlie. On being made to admit that it was on his mind to make propositions to Virginia, Charlie asserts: "No man was ever hanged for that" (243). But the point of the whole spectacle is that he *can* be hanged for rape. Now the possibility, indeed the likelihood, of Charlie's being sentenced to death intermeshes with the other deaths in the novel: Ardista's, the two babies', Aunt Maria's and, singularly, the narrator's father's. (This death occurs in the wings so to speak, in one of the ellipses of the narration. But, needless to say, the father's absence is an important element of John's development.) Charlie, of course, does not die. But once sentenced to jail, he too becomes the absent father. John believes that no one could "save" him "unless it were Charlie. And Charlie was in prison" (283). John's feeling after his father's death that "in his dying, I was punished" (31) becomes in effect when his uncle is in jail, something like: in his punishment, I was dying. This unconscious feeling is acted out and originates the sickness sequence culminating in the death-rebirth scene of Book III, chapter 2.[6] More layers yet can be observed to the paradigm. For death—and guns and blood—is associated to Charlie from the opening of the novel, when, his canvas jacket "wet" with "stains," he hands over a bag of dead partridges to his nephew (8). Later his playing with guns is made to appear ominous.

The fact that the trial turns potential slayer into potential slain, far from annulling, enhances the relationship between such scenes. Nor is Charlie's destructiveness, contrary to the impressions which John's unconscious fear of him may create, simply directed against others, since he once, in his despair and denied guilt over Ardista's death, wants to commit suicide, and, by claiming that he was seduced by Virginia, he provokes the jury and courts death. Furthermore, death is not shown as purely a private matter. On one occasion it is clearly presented as the punishment meted out to the man who transgresses the community's laws. Interestingly, it is Virginia who, while walking with Charlie to the fateful woods, initiates a conversation on John Brown, of all people. She recalls that "when they took John Brown out on his coffin to hang him, he looked up as though he had seen [the countryside] for the first time and said—'This is beautiful country!'—" (162). The reference to John Brown's hanging—further taken up by Charlie—is utterly useless as far as causation is concerned. To use the concepts established by Roland Barthes,[7] the narrative unit is not a *fonction* (function) but an *indice* (token) or rather it is a nexus of *indices*. At the same time as it illuminates Virginia's mind, it generally suggests the dangers of flirting with such a girl; and more particularly it foreshadows the peculiar risk implied in a transgression which violates the Southern tradition and mores, thus discreetly fusing the major themes of the novel, death, desire and the law. In addition, the allusion to hanging links proleptically this narrative unit both to Charlie's trial and to Rush's death; for this—possibly, probably murder at the hands of young whites—may well have been brought about by defenestration, yet it looks curiously like hanging, hence its astonishing effect on the narrator:

> I was not sorry to know Rush dead. But I *stifled* when I heard how the body had been found. Only for a moment did the oppression last. *His neck was broken.* . . . He had been pitched head long, since one leg had been caught in the *wire* of a *pile of crates and boxes,* which tumbled on him when he fell. *One foot was held high* from the pavement (297, italics added).

The radical exclusion from society which Charlie, the heterosexual transgressor, barely escapes, is accidentally (or

with premeditation) imposed on the doubly errant Rush, a mulatto homosexual courting the friendship of whites. Therefore although there is no horizontal relation between John Brown's hanging, Charlie's trial and Rush's fate, they enter into a vertical relationship as aspects of the death paradigm. To sum up, weak as the causal concatenation may be in *Act of Darkness,* there are marked patterns which unite the various episodes, even those that may be regarded as belonging to different subplots. Indeed because of these patterns to which we shall return later, the "two separate ends," the social chronicle and the personal adventure, combine into a neat patchwork of complex design.

On the other hand Robert White may have been looking for—and failing to find—unity of structure in the treatment of the narrator-hero's evolution, since he tells us that John's growth, at first dealt with in "rather diffuse fashion," is "minimized" in the second half when the "public drama" of Charlie's trial takes precedence over John's private world. In fact, even if one assumes that the main interest of *Act of Darkness* is the *character* of John, because the story is roughly shaped by what Scholes and Kellogg call the "autobiographical plot of self-discovery and assumption of a vocation,"[8] it does not follow that the novel should be structured like the traditional Bildungsroman. Here the question arises of the nature of the hero's quest. Unlike many earlier—and later—heroes, John is not so much in search of identity, asking "what am I?," as he is engaged in "self-process." A literary prototype of Robert Jay Lipton's "Protean man," he is exploring, experimenting in a pattern which in many ways resembles what Erik Erikson has called "identity diffusion" or "identity confusion."[9] Just as "the impaired psychological functioning which these terms suggest" can be very much present in the Protean style, so impairment is once manifested in John's case when the youth, out of his inner confusion, withdraws from the world into psychosomatic illness, "simply living as little" as he can (290).

This is not the place to analyse John's personality; but relevant to the structure is his attitude to himself and to the world: John is trying on *roles,* looking to others for images of possible roles, as he himself realizes. At the close of the drama he has the impression that he has found no valid image: "I saw around me *all the possibilities of my life:* I have *told their names* in the course of this story; none of them all could now have saved me, unless it were Charlie. And Charlie was in prison" (283, italics added). The "superabundance of undeveloped characters" (in Cecil Eby's phrase)[10] must be seen as the metaphorical range of possibilities and impossibilities under John's observation. John stands among these characters, "enlivened by their living," and yet since what he searches for is his own self he is sometimes confused by the multiplicity of the potential self-images which the world offers him. An episode is a metaphor for this particular confusion: in the Hall of Mirrors John is bewildered: "Myself came at me, from as many as seven directions. I turned a corner and as many mirrorings of myself moved at new angles. The light was dim and the reflections in the glass not very clear. . . . I was lost. Wherever I went, I met only myself. It seemed to me strange that I should be alone among these wandering mirrors . . ." (105). His salvation will be his discovery that by assuming the vocation of poet he himself will become a mirror encompassing others, will become a very Proteus. Just as there is no strong synthetizing self to face the outside world, so the narration cannot be organized along straightforward lines of causal development. It needs must be splintered, fragmented into character sketches, bits of Mordington chronicle, reported dialogues, narrated monologues and the apparently unrelated incidents which make up *Act of Darkness.*

Together with this quest for roles (which implying identification cannot of course shortcircuit the Oedipal situation), another quest goes on, unrecognized by the hero and therefore still pursued by the narrator through and in his narration. The obscure quest for the unaccessible origins of the subject originates a story which predictably does not lead to recuperation of the self at the place of origins, but ends with the decision to leave the mother and the native land after the hero has delivered himself of a new self literally *inter faeces et urinas.* In this light it is the evidence of disorganization in the narration which becomes significant and must be evaluated by the reader—the surprising collocations of episodes, the ruptures, the ellipses riddling the text, and notably the elimination of the father from his own death-scene and most of the novel, the shadowiness of the mother, strong as she yet is, and the contrasting relief into which the figures of Charlie and Virginia, the desiring couple, are thrown, as a narrative metaphor for the central metonymy of the novel.

Under the circumstances, to look for a principle of *unity* in the personality of the narrator-hero can only lead to the foregone conclusion that the novel, for all its sensitivity and beauty, is "diffuse" and "falls apart" when the narration turns to the lengthy account of Charlie's trial. But if, bearing in mind Bishop's deep concern for form, his belief that "the meaning of a novel should be in its structure" (*CE* 131), one reverses the procedure and starts questioning the structural systems of *Act of Darkness* rather than evaluating them by critical standards evolved from different fictional practices,[11] one can then be brought to make altogether different assessments, while coming perhaps closer to the meaning of the novel.

That a polarity magnetizes the structural systems seems evident. Yet any attempt to summarize what each "half" of the novel is *about* reveals that neither half is really a *thematic* unit. What in fact cleaves the book is something which is missing in the narration. The unnarrated act of darkness is the invisible fault separating two stages of life, before and after the act, two phases of narration which are not so much joined as *disjoined* in order to be brought into correlation by the global act of writing/reading. Before, John may believe that he lives in a world of law since he does not apprehend the signification of the transgressions which do occur; after, he is aware that he lives in a world

of violation, notwithstanding the emphasis which the social discourse puts on law. Prelapsarian or postlapsarian, it is the same time, suddenly seen as out of joint, with "the masks [falling] from the countenance and form of all." And the narration is born to set it right. By insisting on the difference, it obfuscates the resemblance. But what is repressed is all the better seen, and darkness is indeed made visible.

Thus, on either side of the fault, we find an alignment of narrative units which I will call *"parallels."* Whatever their link—causal or chronological, if any—in the syntagmatic chain, and whatever their thematic importance, these parallels or doublets have in common the basic action, positive or negative, which they unfold. The two visits of John to the whorehouse, before the act and after, come readily to mind but they are only the most obvious instances of parallelism; the character of the action makes them perhaps more conspicuous; certainly, too, they stand out because they more closely amount to a repetition than other instances, since agent, action, object of action and place are the same. Yet in other cases as well the same agent may be involved in the action. John turns to Charlie after his father has just died (29), later searches for his father when Charlie in prison can no longer "save" him (289). Following his failure with the prostitute, he thinks, "I am sick. I must die," while acutely conscious that he wants to water (146); following Charlie's failure to dominate Virginia, he falls sick, and, one night, suffering from dysentery and passing blood, he thinks "I'm dying" (219). Sometimes the agent changes while the action remains similar: Charlie calls on Dr. Passmore to assuage his inner anguish and his guilt at having seduced Ardista (117*ff.*). Virginia calls on the same Dr. Passmore to accuse Charlie of rape (189), thus divesting herself of her guilt. Impotent with the prostitute, John as he rides home goes back in imagination to her room: his fantasies, which mingle the actuality of the symbol-laden sights he sees along the busy street and the dream of conquest he pursues "undaunted" (146), announce the more expanded surrealistic sequence of Virginia's own fantasies. In a time-confused delirium which inextricably mixes the storm outside and the chaos inside her, the thunder and lightning and the deflowering, Virginia hysterically relives her (as she believes) unwanted sexual initiation. More rarely, both the action and the object of it are similar while the agents differ. Strikingly, two persons are puzzled by the relationship of Virginia to another woman. Aunt Maria asks John, "'Is she a special friend of Sally's?' 'I don't think so,' I said" (22), and later Miss Sadie, observing Virginia's behavior to Caroline after the act in the woods (of which both Sadie and Caroline are at that time unaware), inquires:

> "Is she a special friend of yours?"
> "No," said Caroline. "I've known Virginia a long time. I'm very fond of her. But I wouldn't say she was a special friend. Why?" (172)

As the example above shows, the parallel may extend to the verbal form, though in my definition what constitutes a doublet is the similarity in action.

This similarity, however, can imply a change of sign: on crossing the invisible line, the same action can become inverted. Often the inversion is from positive to negative. Virginia gives a copy of Shelley to John, later takes back her books and her friendship (75, 178). Whereas at the carnival John, looking at his fellow townsmen, could feel "enlivened by their living," at the time of his uncle's trial and his trials Mordington offers him the spectacle of "purposeless" activities, of "dull and mean" faces, offers him only images of death, "nameless old men saving nothing out of a long life," which could "scarcely have been worth the pain" (283). The dark, passionate look which Charlie sends to Virginia at the beginning of the novel fills John with trembling expectancy and the sense of "the unutterable beauty of being alive" (27); later the same feeling of being "included in whatever had happened" between Charlie and Virginia is a "corrupting" consciousness: "at the act in the woods I was *horribly thrilled*" (italics added, 227). But sometimes the parallels show a reversal, in the sense of greater life. Before the act of darkness, having failed in the rites of sexual initiation, John, humiliated and desolate, sees only ugliness in Hagerstown; having asserted his potency, he feels "light and free" and walks about the same town, now the scene of his success, as "if [he] were air" (300).

Another significant reversal concerns a parallel that is less conspicuous, because what is correlated is not the overt action of the scene but the symbolic action it entails. In the bathing pool interlude, when John's body runs "with a liquid motion" and he is so pleasantly "lost in the water," one can read a fantasm of return to the matricial waters, of regression to the womb. A moment of peace and innocence, it nevertheless has ego-destroying potentialities. In the death scene, when, wallowing in blood and excrement, John believes himself to be dying and sends his mother away, one can read on the contrary a rebirth scene: "Having accepted death, I returned to life" (292). In the contrast between these two parallels is implied the major theme, and indeed the whole movement of the novel.

Just as significant and more immediately perceived is the opposition that unites the opening and the closing narrative units. The novel starts as John thinks of going to his mother while dusk deepens and the withered leaves run colorless from the raked piles, and as he opens the door to Charlie who, as his mother's brother and a model of manly behavior, is doubly a parental image. It ends with John's going away from mother and the South, *not* thinking of Charlie at Ruddimont, of his father in his grave, or of his grandfather "pacing in his vehement age," thinking still of his mother, but conscious of "the soft torture of [her] love," riding in "the night unknown" yet aware of the coming dawn:

> Now it was with *expectant wonder* of that world to which I, sleepless and inert, hurried on rushing rails. The train was rumbling toward an *alien land*. There should I be *alone*. So much I knew, but also that, when I looked on it, *day returning from the east, would have filled with light* (italics added).

With the last sentence is closed a narrative chain which began with "When I saw it was growing *dark,* I thought of *going to my mother. . . .*" The parallel is clear; so is the reversal which shows the hero, his apron-strings at last cut, facing darkness alone in the expectation of solitude *and* light.

Such parallels—and my list does not pretend to be exhaustive[12]—constitute strong links between the two halves of the novel, at the same time as they mark clearly its binary articulation. A similar effect is obtained by the overall relation which exists between the two parts. The second, in fact, can be taken as a refraction of the first. Undoubtedly there is a disjunction between the "private world" and the "public drama," which is precisely a major element in the novel's thematic scheme. In a sense, it is a disjunction of this kind which *in the diegesis* the judicial processes try to eliminate, attempting as they do to throw public light on private darkness and to reduce private evil to socially-coded wrong. Since we are concerned with the narration, we must observe that *on the narrative level* we are given the same material to scrutinize in both parts. With the exception of the imported counsel, most of the actors who appear in the court room scenes have put in one appearance, or more, before. Above all, what is brought into the limelight, together with the act in the woods, is the very stuff of the Marstons' everyday life, the familiar activities, and the patterns of habits with which we have been made conversant before. But in the frame of the legal investigation, this material is verbalized or re-verbalized in a different way, so that the Same becomes the Other. Conversely, what is new, i.e., the lawyers' presentation of the case, cannot be understood independently from the context of Mordington, or independently, for instance, from the community's concept of a "good woman" which early incidents have indirectly elaborated. In fact, the attorneys' speeches weave into either a defence or denunciation of Charlie innumerable fragments of former speeches—utterances of the many actors and witnesses, statements of "their learned friends," together with snatches of the Bible and Shakespeare, proverbs, clichés and other bits of folk wisdom. Because many swift touches and dialogues have created in Part I a believable community with its deeply-held, albeit conflicting, set of values, the lawyers' speeches in Part II are perceived as the ritual bringing to focus of communal ethics, whose discordance is thus dramatized in the opposition between prosecution and defence. Retroactively the legal discourses throw light, *not* on the act of darkness as they claim to, but on the town's never-ceasing collective discourse set forth in Part I, while Mordington's fragmentary but inclusive discourse lays in advance the foundations for the forensic logics of the disjunctive presentations of the case.

But on becoming public drama, the events of the private world seem to lose some of their reality. "What struck me," says John, "was the meticulous dullness of the proceedings, the lifelessness of the law" (235). This sense of deflation, of a letting down was felt by Scott Fitzgerald; and he considered it a flaw in the structure of the book:

The first half of your book [he wrote to Bishop] is so heavy with stimuli and promises, that the later catastrophe of the rape is minimized—both in itself and in its consequences. . . . You had put out so many leads by that time that the reader was practically expecting the World War, and the actual fact that Charlie violated a spinster is anticlimactical as is her ensuing denunciation of him.[13]

As a closer look shows, however, we have been deceived into taking as "promises" of the narration what are, in fact, simply an adolescent's expectations. Aggrandizing Charlie to fit the needs of his imagination, John turns him into a sort of Byronic hero who would combine quintessential evil and fundamental goodness: he is like one "damned" or "possessed" but he is also all that is "sound" (see in particular pages 132-133). Because we see him through John's eyes for a long time, we mistakenly tend to expect something on the grand scale from Charlie. But the lesson of the novel is that heroes belong to the chivalrous past of Robert E. Lee, or the even more glorious days of General Charles Lee. In the postbellum South, life is less heroic and more humdrum.[14] Charlie's sins are very ordinary sins—adultery with his servant, visits to the brothel, sexual intercourse with his wife's old maidish friend. Ordinary sins, to be sure . . . but sins nonetheless. Transgressions of a code to which Southern society clings all the more as the code is its claim to moral superiority—violations of the other, or of the self's and the body's integrity. Charlie admits to John: *Maybe that is all we can do to other people—violate them. I loved Ardista. And you know what came of that. It was wrong. It was wrong*" and later, "And Virginia, I went with her. But I never wanted her. And that was wrong. Do you understand? Wrong" (203, italics added). Anticlimactic as the rape may first appear to the reader, evil is not minimized: "the evil remains more inexplicable than ever" (284), and it is shown up as an inescapable fact of life. "I could not but identify [Charlie's] evil with his inordinate desires for living," says John (286), who later learns to accept "even the irremediable evil of [his] own existence" (297). Nor can the infinite complexities of evil, its far-spreading consequences, be measured or sanctioned by society's justice. When the conflict that has been acted out between Charlie and Virginia, each wanting to dominate the other, Charlie with an assertion of phallic power, Virginia with a display of her "masculine" intelligence, then, in betrayal of her own self, with a resort to the Southern myth of womanhood—when this conflict is made the matter of a public spectacle, the dramatic nature of their confrontation may be diluted in technical procedures and forensic rhetoric, but paradoxically the inner quality of the drama comes out more clearly. It glimmers in Charlie's ambiguous moment of truth, in Virginia's dark persistence, in all that slips through the inadequate net of the court proceedings. (One of the strengths of the novel is to show how an act that might seem to involve two, or perhaps three, individuals if one includes the wronged wife, is at the convergence of the private and public worlds: sex is nature *and* culture.

Furthermore, the act is far from appearing anticlimactic to John, since it precipitates a crisis in his life. The publicity around the act in the woods turns him into what he unconsciously wanted to be—a *voyeur* who consciously aspires to "take now one, now the other part, or even . . . be both Charlie and Virginia" (262), yearning, that is to say, to be the combined parent and the *tertium aliud* at the place of origins. During the trial, moreover, John discovers that the dichotomy is not, as he thought, between dominating male and dominated female. Charlie "destroy[s] his own manhood" when he swears that "he had maintained only a passive prowess," that he had been "ravished instead of ravishing" (246-247). If woman can be the dominating partner, role choice becomes all the more difficult, sexual encounter all the more dangerous. The spectre of castration, which has been haunting the novel, now looms more distinctly. Indeed, Charlie is punished for whatever he did to Virginia of the symbolic name. As for John, although what he has done remains "quite unknown" to him, his sense of guilt is overwhelming (and suggests that through vicarious participation in the act of darkness, he has not only assumed his uncle's actual or alleged crime, but reactivated the phantasy of a much darker act, incest). So he punishes himself. He attempts to "untie those knots of desire," "suppressing all activity of his body" as far as possible, until he comes to death's door. Only when he later accepts the life of desire again will he understand his dead father, who in renouncing his painting—and perhaps in renouncing living—"had denied his desire." In fact, before the hero can come into his own, two fathers must "die" symbolically, the real one in the first part of the narration from which he is almost entirely eliminated, the surrogate father in the second half which seen from this angle can no longer be regarded as an anticlimax. The repetition of the pattern, moreover, stresses that both are destroyed, to a certain extent, for opposite reasons, Charlie for "his inordinate desire for living," the father for his denial of desire. (But is it not because it is Charlie, his mother's brother, to whom the hero feels at the end "very close," that he has the strength to survive, to get out of his double bind?) Beyond the difference between the two men, there also runs more secretly the filigree of the similarity in their relation to women, since both tangle with Virginia ladies convinced of their superiority to men. Here the non-sequitur between John's description of his father's paintings and his subsequent allusion to his mother's having married beneath her becomes deeply significant (see 288).

Far from "collapsing" into two, therefore, the novel relies on a binary structure which bodies forth a fundamental duality (signally manifested in the polarities male/female, activity/passivity, mind/body, life-impulse/death-impulse, self/other, order/disorder) and the basic process of duplication which is at the root of the desiring activity.[15] In other words, on the thematic level, the act of darkness is the razor's edge where male and female, the self and the other join in the transient unity of coition, mind ravishes body and body mind, Eros becomes undistinguishable from Thanatos; it marks the absent place of the fantasmatic wish for incest which secretly stage-directs John's dramatizings of himself and of the world. On the level of the narration, the act is the caesura that functions as the paradigmatic line of the novel's full scheme of narrative declension and emphasizes the basic dichotomy which generates the story.

In the complex network of the narration, however, the basic polarity of the structure is partly masked by a number of formal characteristics, which, different as they may be, all work toward the blurring of duality. *The handling of the point of view* is one: the impersonal focus of narration being reserved to the second third of the novel, the middle section with its shifting visions and voices stands in contrast to, and serves as a hinge between, the two others which are told entirely in the first person. From this angle, a ternary distribution of the text is possible. In the second place, within the gross structure, a series of *thematic oscillations and alternations* atomize and modulate the fundamental dichotomy. In the larger sequence of the father's death, for instance, smaller narrative units introduce the contrasts of Charlie's "animal pride" and vitality, the stirrings of John's sexuality and his confused identification to both Charlie and Virginia, the sudden ecstasies of being alive. Or between sequences that are apparently unrelated, patterns of similarity and difference can be traced: the conversation in which Charlie petulantly comments on "the Southern Woman" (55-57) is juxtaposed with a scene in which Rush makes homosexual advances to John in his bedroom (58-59); this in turn is followed by a scene which gathers the two strains:

> I was aware of waking and of a dark chill beyond the comfort of the bed. Shook my shoulder. All that was me cowered into sleep. And again the hand and in a huge grip the covers went. I sat up in terror of the darkness.
>
> "Did I scare you?" It was Charlie. Not Rush with the importunities of his hands (59).

John's confusion of persons and the possibility of a confusion of roles do not last. Soon Charlie is back at the familiar complaint about women, how "they want to drain you" and do not leave one alone, as nephew and uncle ride towards the mountains. The obstacle to peace is now female, now male—but what strange appeal lies beyond the importunity of women, and of Rush? The chapter ends on a provisional resolution as, in the mountains, John meets with Ardista, his first object of heterosexual love—for whom he is unwittingly destined to be his uncle's unsuccessful, because too innocent, competitor. (Such are again the devious ways of the Oedipus complex.) This and similar patterns evincing "continuity in the midst of change"[16] or change in the midst of continuity create a rhythm which, cutting across the basic structural duality, pervades the whole novel and gives it a pulsating unity.

Similarly, all the parts of *Act of Darkness* are linked through a complex system of *echoes* or recurring clusters of motifs. The death paradigm examined above is composed of such echoes. The device contributes so importantly to the unity of Bishop's novel that it must be studied further. Charlie's frequently voiced opinions on women in general and Virginia in particular, delivered freely at

various moments, enter into ironic relation with one another, with his behavior toward Virginia, and with the advice his father gives to John. "Never seduce a virgin. Never go with a common whore" (80). If the discussions on Woman may seem a privileged example, less obtrusive motifs also acquire significance through repetition. Although she passes as somewhat stingy, Aunt Maria unexpectedly loads her orphaned grand nephew with Christmas gifts (34 *ff*.); later, while making John her heir, she leaves surprising legacies to charitable institutions, not bequeathing to her niece the furniture the latter had looked forward to inheriting someday. Her unpredictable generosity is to be correlated to the largess of Virginia, who is known in Mordington for her good works (32, 33). In the course of the action, she makes a present of her father's precious Shelley to John (75) and of a fine linen handkerchief to Charlie (160). Yet Virginia, it appears, has kept among the antiques of her own house a sword given to a Negro servant, in the days of John Brown (111); and she abruptly recalls her gift to John. So many instances of giving and keeping cannot be simply coincidental; nor do they function merely as clues to the characters of both women. They have a bearing to one another and to the crux of the novel, to Virginia's giving—or not giving—of herself, and her later wish to deny that something has been given, and/or taken. Obviously too there are links, one of them ironical, between the business of the bloody handkerchief and what is to transpire later:

> But he took her handkerchief and wiped away the smears of blood from his arm.
> "I'm sorry. I oughtn't to have taken it."
> "I gave it to you." Virginia rose.
> "But look! It's all bloody."
> For some moments they were motionless, while Charlie stared at her (160).

The introduction of the "tiny web of linen" may also be taken as an early allusion to *Othello,* the play which will later provide John with a measuring-test of the tragedy in his life. Read together, these minute incidents build up a muted counterpoint to the major thematic nexus of the novel. They establish donation as exchange, cession and *demande* from both donor and donee, extended invitation to further exchange—and perhaps seduction. At the same time they show that the circulation of gifts can be abruptly blocked, for instance by being reversed in violation of the tacit rules of giving. What is in question here is possession, the right and the rites of possession; what is symbolically asserted is again the need for the "ceremony"[17] that will order the erratic give-and-take of human relationships, the "ceremony" whose absence makes for the chaos of the act of darkness. Taken by itself the gift cluster acts as a generator of movement within the text. And since it is characterized by predictability/unpredictability, it never limits the possibilities that are open to the action or the ambiguities that are left for the characters to act out or ponder on. (Aunt Maria's strange legacies are no less ambiguous for being in character. Virginia's denial that she gave her consent comes both as a surprise and as a reaction that one might have expected. That she does not take back her accusation but clings to her version of the facts throughout the trial when the issue is the *taking* of Charlie's life, is again both unexpected, in particular by Charlie himself, and likely.)

Such functioning of the main patterns contributes to the creation of "verbal movement"—a feature which Bishop praised in James Joyce's writing.[18] Such shifts of course influence the reader's response and upset his facile assignation of right and wrong, leaving him uncertain of which is the violator and which the violated, "which . . . mind and which body, who Desdemona and who Othello,"[19] unsure even of what is the deepest transgression. More examples could be adduced of a patterning which is at once poetical in that it depends on reiterated returns, and ideological in that the units are manifestations of the same idea, or rather polarity. Lack of space prevents me from doing justice to the most quintessential echo in *Act of Darkness,* the mirror motif, itself an inner metaphor for the narrative phenomenon of reiteration, which would deserve a study of its own. The intricacy of all these patterns requires an attentive reader. Just as for Bishop, "the intellectual labor of the artist is properly confined to the perception of relations" (*CE,* 134), so must the reader be ready to perceive the multiple relations that intermesh horizontally and vertically into the total web of the novel.

Needless to say, every narration is engendered by the interplay of the same and the other and grounded in the law of repetition. Where *Act of Darkness* makes a significant departure is in exhibiting rather than attempting to efface its groundwork. In the conventional novel, causal concatenation, to mention but one method of obliteration, blurs the repetitions which appear to have been socially or psychologically determined, in other words, to belong to the diegesis and not to the narration. In *Act of Darkness,* on the contrary, the loose chronological consecution incites the reader to look for linkages between the narrative units and to find them in repeated motifs and/or contrasts and similarities. Thus meaning is seen to be dependent on the narration, on the shaping and interweaving of patterns. To adapt a familiar analogy, rather than a mirror held up along the street, in which we watch the moving pageant of life as it goes by, aware perhaps of the frame of our fictive looking-glass but hardly of its surface, the metaphor for *Act of Darkness* is the hall of mirrors[20] in which John gets lost, alive with reflections and glances, dim glimmers and bright flashes. The fascination proceeds less from the sights which are reflected than from the distortions, the blurring, darkening or effulgent effects due to the process of multiple refractions—and hence too from our awareness of the mirrors themselves, their number, size, color, purity or murkiness, and of the very purpose that has so conveniently arranged their angles. In this way *Act of Darkness* can "give us not the illusion of life, but the reality of the imagination" (*CE,* 65).

Lest the realistic-minded reader should remain engrossed in the representation of "life" and miss the point, the narration constantly draws attention to its real nature by the frequent insertion of *inner duplications*[21] which underline the fundamental duplicity of the fiction. These would need a more detailed analysis than is possible here and I shall merely note a few points. Interior duplications range from mere quotations (e.g., the Shelley lines: Thus on the way / Mask after mask fell from the countenance / And form of all . . . ," 178), through the story of a rape and murder case within the trial to a full discussion of *Othello,* to cite but a few. Beyond creating new perspectives, the *mises en abyme* are a small-scale model of the global action, or of a major aspect of it. In *Oliver Twist,* "a terrible book," "a lovely book," young John perceives the joys and terrors of his adolescence; Fagin "fascinate(s)" him because he empathizes with Oliver's homosexual fears of his tormentor, without being conscious of their sexual root, and more consciously, because Fagin arouses anxiety at the deceptive ambiguity of appearances ("He was at his worst when he seemed most kind," 45). When John *reads* about Oliver *reading* presumably safe in Mr. Brownlow's house and looking up to see "at the window the peering Jew," this sends us back to a previous experience of John, who once was "bewildered" to see Dumb Peter peering at him through the kitchen window (18), and seems to foreshadow an action which, though he fears it, does not however come to pass: while John is immersed in Oliver's tremors, Charlie's steps are heard across the porch and John is "in dismay" lest his uncle may "come to the window and peer in" (46), thereby revealing the sexual ambivalence of his adolescent hero-worshipping.

Othello provides a much more complex model. But since its thematic relevance to the story has been brilliantly analyzed by Leslie Fiedler and its critical significance stressed by Robert White, the reader can be referred to these critics. I shall simply underline that whereas *Othello* is for John an *analogon a posteriori* of the action, for the reader it is a formal *analogon,* contemporaneous with at least part of the reading experience. It therefore exerts its heuristic function at two levels, intra and extradiegetic. Indeed, both the *Oliver Twist* and the *Othello* units are riddled, significantly and dizzyingly, with duplications within duplications. For instance, the narration shows John reading and reacting to *Othello* twice, and despite the fact that in fictional time the second reading follows immediately upon the first, the narration separates the two accounts by a passage of summary that tells about Aunt Maria's death, her legacy and the educational opportunity it offers to John, his decision not to go to the University of Virginia but "to escape to the East" (293-94). Thus discontinuity again emphasizes duplication and the significant deviation between repetitions: "I could not repeat the experience I had had the first time I encountered Othello. For that had been what may properly be called an illumination, a conscious escape from time, a seeing beyond space, from which it is scarcely possible to return unchanged" (294). (Not surprisingly, we find here again the image of the mirror: "the whole tragic action [of *Othello*] seemed to be taking place before a huge golden mirror." [292])

If in the diegesis, the characters do suffer from "the loss of form, the loss of myth, the loss of a pattern,"[22] the narration itself, far from lacking form, might almost seem contrived to the reader who would not enjoy along with the surface thrills of a good story the more intellectual fascination of its narrative games and stratagems.[23] Duplication—here taken in a general sense—is the conspicuous strategy of John Peale Bishop's novel, mirroring and shaping its theme which is disjunction. Disjunction implying union, the story can only exist because there are moments of conjunction—the sexual act, the creative act, madness (whose temptation is very real to John) and, less drastically, phantasms and daydreams. Nevertheless, in the main action, duality does not *resolve* dialectically into unity. Although the jury chooses one, and we may prefer the other, two contradictory versions of the act of darkness remain in presence. The antagonists never acknowledge each other but as adversaries; their deepest desire in any case has all along been destruction, not intercourse, and this desire they never really renounce. In the story there is no reconciliation of opposites and, symbolically, no child is born out of all Charlie's matings, despite the hopes or fears to the contrary. Nor is there any transcendental goodness to which the suffering, sinning characters could relate and which would make whole, if only in another world, what has been sundered by evil. "I had no father," says John, "either in heaven or on earth" (283). And indeed, Creator or Redeemer, God is absent from the universe of *Act of Darkness.*

True, John forgives Charlie for denying his own manhood and therefore his youthful worshipper's. John learns, through suffering and the catharsis of reading Shakespeare and Ecclesiastes, to "look on evil" in himself and in the world. His renunciation of Charlie as a mediator of his desire implies a reduction of his ambivalence toward his uncle; but it is gained at the price of learning that "every soul is irremediably itself," that there is no merging of the self and the other. However he may have endeavoured to escape polarization and to subsume male and female in himself, John has to give up one sexual role. Besides, he can only complete his initiation insofar too as he has accepted to live out the divorce between mind and body: "I asked only not to think. I had thought already too much about what I was going to do. I knew I could trust my body, provided no conscience intervened to destroy my honor" (300). In this sense and to this degree, his experience with the prostitute is a re-enactment of the act in the woods:

> It was when her hands were on me that I knew what was being accomplished was the act in the woods, that all its gestures must be repeated and forever repeated, the rape of the mind by the body. But that rape had now gone so far, I had so far ravished my mind, that I acquiesced in it. I was not afraid, I was no longer ashamed. And in the darkness with which we were now surrounded I knew that I had lost more than my virginity (300).

Whatever unity is achieved at the end of the novel is an indirect assertion of duality. In the deepest intimacy, male and female can only meet as separate beings. "The body

and spirit are not one but two that move along parallel lines, supplementing each other to form a track."[24] What is more, there is within the self a radical, i.e., an ineradicable heteronomy between that which knows and that which is known, a gaping discontinuity which can never be bridged in life, simply be displaced: "But what I sought was really not so much to know myself—which is, I suspect a vain quest and one which if it succeeded could only be quit by suicide, since what is completely understood has accomplished its changes and is complete in death—as to know those conditions within which I had uncomprehendingly to live" (285). In fact, this discontinuity is life, since full integration means death—the death of desire reflecting the desire of death.

But the inescapable duality which is one of the conditions of man's life, increased perhaps by what Robert Penn Warren calls "the division of the age,"[25] can nonetheless find resolution through art, and art only.[26] Art it is that in *Othello* "makes a conscious harmony of discordant emotions" (296). For "it is the privilege of literature to propose its own formal solutions for problems which in life have none" (*CE*, 44). In this sense, the diegesis of *Act of Darkness* opens onto the possibility of a kind of reconciliation, an integration of roles, to be achieved in the future of John's poetry. (It must be remembered in this connection that Bishop regarded the poet as able to assume a bisexual role.[27]) More importantly still, the narration interweaves the discordant elements of the story into a harmonious composition. It fixes and arrests the fluid "reality of the imagination" in which the narrator-hero can be both himself and the other, both Charlie *and* Virginia. Mediating between oppositions it creates a non-disjunctive space where the act of darkness is neither rape nor notrape.

Drawing the parallel between the "moral disorder" which lies at the root of both *Othello* and his uncle's case, John comments on the difference between art and reality: "Had the actual murderer of Desdemona, or whatever her historical name was, been brought into a Venetian court, his trial, I suspect, would have made no more sense than Charlie's had done in the Mordington courthouse" (296). If what John is brought to perceive is the difference between life and the aesthetic "way of seeing the world," the narration for its part both disguises the difference by claiming to reproduce life and reasserts it, triumphantly through its very organization, slyly through the many allusions to literary characters and authors which annul the distinction they pretend either to blunt or stress, and through what Scott Fitzgerald called "traces of other people," which, whether conscious or unconscious, affirm the literarity of the work.[28] The reader in any case approaches both play and novel as literature. Without claiming for *Act of Darkness* the greatness of *Othello*—a claim which in any case would be irrelevant—we must grant Bishop's novel the same nature of artistic order. My contention throughout has been that *Act of Darkness* is, in one of Bishop's metaphors, a successful "ceremony":

> Traditional with all its symbols

ancient as the metaphors in dreams
strange with never before heard music . . .

("Speaking of Poetry")

In a strongly patterned structure and in a sensuous, flexible and measured style, it weds the antitheses of violation and law, human cruelty and love, the vital animality of man and his struggling mind, the inherent ambivalence and endless transferability of desire itself.

Notes

1. Leslie Fiedler, "Afterword." *Act of Darkness* by John Peale Bishop (Avon paperback: New York, 1967), p. 315. All references will be to this edition and will be identified in the text. Page references to *The Collected Essays of John Peale Bishop,* ed. with an introd. by Edmund Wilson (New York: C. Scribner's, 1948) will also be given parenthetically, preceded by *CE.*

2. I argue this in an article I am preparing, "Perspectives are Precipices, Points of View in John Peale Bishop's *Act of Darkness.*"

3. Robert L. White, *John Peale Bishop* (New York: Twayne Publishers, 1966), p. 81. Although I do not share Mr. White's views of Bishop's technique, I am greatly indebted to his book, the only full-length study of Bishop.

4. *Ibid.*

5. *Ibid.,* p. 82.

6. *Act of Darkness* may be read as a story of initiation into adulthood with, in this order, two failed rites (the first visit to the prostitute, the homoerotic scene at the bathing pool) and two successful ones, the agony scene when the hero accepts death and separation from the mother, and the sexual encounter with the prostitute.

   Scott Fitzgerald seemed to think that Charlie was the "heroic figure" in the novel; see his letter to Bishop on *Act of Darkness* in *Letters of F. Scott Fitzgerald,* ed. Andrew Turnball (London: Bodley Head, 1964), 364-66.

7. See Roland Barthes, "Introduction à l'analyse structurale des récits," *Communications,* VIII, 1966. ". . . La sanction des Indices est 'plus haut,' parfois même virtuelle, hors du syntagme explicite . . . c'est une sanction paradigmatique; au contraire, la sanction des "Fonctions" n'est jamais que "plus loin," c'est une sanction syntagmatique. *Fonctions et Indices* recouvrent donc une autre distinction classique; les Fonctions impliquent des relata métonymiques, les Indices des relata métaphoriques; les unes correspondent à une fonctionnalité du faire, les autres à une fonctionnalité de l'être" (p. 9).

   One more word about the general terminology of this paper. In order to avoid all confusion between what is narrated and the narration, I use the word *diegesis* to refer to the space-time universe of the novel, *diegetic* therefore being applied to what belongs, and *extradiegetic* to what does not belong, to this universe. (For an explication and amplification of these concepts, see Gérard Genette, *Figures II,* [Paris: Editions du Seuil, 1969] and *Figures III,* [Paris: Editions du Seuil, 1972].)

8. Robert Scholes and Robert Kellogg, *The Nature of Narrative* (London: Oxford Univ. Press, 1966), 237.

9. Robert Jay Lipton, "Protean Man," *Partisan Review,* XXXV (Winter, 1968), 17.

10. Cecil D. Eby, Jr., "The Fiction of John Peale Bishop," *Twentieth Century Literature,* VII (Apr., 1961), 8.

11. *Act of Darkness* has been judged as a traditional novel—and found wanting. Without going into the problem of influences, it would have been more to the purpose to see it as a successor of, i.e., written after, such novels as *Portrait of the Artist, The Great Gatsby,* and *The Sound and the Fury.* In his "Aphorisms" Bishop pointed to the importance in postwar style of "non-logical associations. Freud and the automobile. *Les Lauriers sont coupés,* Joyce" (*CE,* 383).

12. Sometimes attention is drawn in the text to such parallels. See "My mother almost never mentioned Charlie's name. And now I remembered she had scarcely spoken of my father since she died . . ." (285). The narrator hardly needs to remind us of the fact, which had been made clear in the earlier narration, e.g., "she could forget now and never did she mention this to me again" (47), etc.

13. Fitzgerald, p. 365.

14. *Act of Darkness* illustrates Ellington White's contention that the South "is witnessing the deterioration both of the family and of the capacity it (the region) once had for heroic action." "The View from the Picture Window," *The Lasting South,* ed. Louis D. Rubin, Jr., and James J. Kilpatrick (Chicago: H. Regnery, 1967), p. 169.

15. See Marie Cariou, *Freud et le désir* (Paris: Presses universitaires, 1973). "Le désir: toujours pris dans le piège d'un double" (p. 80).

16. "Continuity in the midst of change" (*CE,* 105) was a major concern of Bishop's thought (see White, ch. II).

17. Bishop uses the metaphor in the poem "Speaking of Poetry," which "uses the form-symbols of Othello and Desdemona for the opposition of life and art" and proclaims that "some mythos, some ceremony or ritual of meaning must be found" to wed the two (Robert W. Stallman, "The Poetry of John Peale Bishop" in *Southern Renascence,* ed. Louis D. Rubin, Jr., and Robert D. Jacobs [Baltimore: Johns Hopkins Press, 1953], 378).

18. Apropos of *Ulysses,* Bishop wrote: "In a sense the story is after the story. Yet the book is full of verbal

movement. Collision of atoms. Like a table seen by a modern physicist. A table moved from one side of room to another. The room will never be quite the same. In the meanwhile the most intense activity goes on" (*CE,* 386).

19. Fiedler, p. 319.

20. In its use of the hall of mirrors, *Act of Darkness* is linked on the one hand to Joyce's "Araby" and on the other to John Barth's *Lost in the Fun House.*

21. I have borrowed the term from Bruce Morrissette's important essay "Un héritage d'André Gide: la duplication intérieure," *Comparative Literature Studies,* VIII (1964), 125-142. The *mise en abyme* (inescutcheon) of French critics is more suggestive than the term proposed by Morrissette, which moreover raised special problems in an essay concerning duplication in a larger sense, but inner duplication has the merit of being immediately clear.

22. "Bishop's basic theme is the loss of form, the loss of myth, the loss of a pattern" Cleanth Brooks wrote of Bishop's poetry, "Form and Content," *Kenyon Review,* IV (Spring, 1942), 244; reprinted in Dorothy Nyren, ed., *A Library of Literary Criticism* (New York: F. Ungar, 1960), p. 59.

23. Bishop seems to have regretted the loss of organic form and wrote: "The sense of plastic form, the obsession of unity (which Mozart had) has that not disappeared from everything? Our structures are intellectually and deliberately imposed" ("Bishop Papers," quoted by White, p. 48).

24. Fred T. Marsh, *New York Times,* March 17, 1935, quoted in Dorothy Nyren.

25. In the drastic foreshortening which a study such as this entails, I have had to omit all reference to the social aspects of *Act of Darkness.* Insofar as it also embodies a myth of the South (and a criticism of the myth) the novel is of course also concerned with the gap between reality and myth, actuality and dream.

26. The reader must be referred here to the essays of Bishop, to the chapter which Robert White devoted to Bishop's criticism and to S. C. Moore's essay "The Criticism of John Peale Bishop," *Twentieth Century Literature,* XII (July, 1966).

27. "The vigor and daring of the poet should be employed at the moment of conception. The elaboration should be carried out with delicacy. The male should engender, the female complete, the poem" (*CE,* 373). This is the reason why Apollo has, in Bishop's eye, a "bisexual countenance."

28. The manipulation of viewpoints is another way to signal the fictional status of the story. Another such wink at the reader may be found in the name of the narrator. Insofar as John is so common as to make the narrator almost anonymous, it is an invitation to read the novel as fiction, e.g., as a symbolic story of

initiation, as a myth of the modern South, etc. Insofar as it is also the Christian name of the author, it is an invitation to read the book as autobiography. The lack of a defining name exerts a disruptive influence. One might well apply to Bishop's narrator what Roland Barthes wrote of Proust's: "Toute subversion, ou toute soumission romanesque commence donc par le Nom Propre; si précise—si bien précisée—que soit la situation sociale du narrateur proustien, son absence de nom, périlleusement entretenue, provoque une déflation capitale de l'illusion réaliste." *S/Z* (Paris: Editions du Seuil, 1970), 102.

Thomas Daniel Young and John J. Hingle (essay date 1981)

SOURCE: An introduction to *The Republic of Letters in America: The Correspondence of John Peale Bishop and Allen Tate,* edited by Thomas Daniel Young and John J. Hindle, The University Press of Kentucky, 1981, pp. 1-10.

[*In the following excerpt from the introduction to* The Republic of Letters: The Correspondence of John Peale Bishop and Allen Tate, *Young and Hingle discuss the friendship of Tate and Bishop, and their critical contributions to each other's writings.*]

Few writers of the twentieth century have been so profoundly dedicated to the vocation of letters as was Allen Tate. A young English poet publishing his first poem in an obscure little magazine received from Tate a few days after the poem appeared a letter of commendation and detailed comment on the strengths and weaknesses of the poem. Moved that an established man of letters would devote so much attention to the work of a novice, this young poet (Geoffrey Hill) pursued his craft with increased diligence and confidence. It is clear, as Lewis P. Simpson has pointed out, that Tate felt that one of the responsibilities of the man of letters was the restoration of an age of faith at a time when science was becoming a dominant force in every area of human thought and activity. Quite early in his carreer he realized that the artist in the materialistic economic pattern of the American system was working against society, not with it, so he endeavored to set up a literary community, what Simpson calls "an idealized community of alienation." To accomplish this purpose Tate deliberately set about a campaign to establish a "Republic of Letters in the Modern World" by unifying writers and would-be writers around the concept that they composed a community set against an alien world. The unceasing and ever-important task of the artist, he reiterated, following the leadership of T. S. Eliot, one of his acknowledged "masters"—the other was John Crowe Ransom—was that of confronting the "dissociation of sensibility" as the dominant cultural phenomenon of his age. The poetic community had the dual function, he argued, of making the world aware of the cultural crisis it faces and of preserving the health and vitality of the language.

In an attempt to establish and maintain a vocation of letters, Tate undertook a voluminous correspondence with a broad range of writers—some virtually unknown, some well established—in England, America, and France. Among the persons with whom he corresponded regularly over long periods were T. S. Eliot, John Crowe Ransom, Donald Davidson, Robert Penn Warren, Cleanth Brooks, Herbert Read, Andrew Lytle, and Robert Lowell. Less frequently he exchanged letters with Peter Taylor, Geoffrey Hill, Kenneth Burke, Howard Nemerov, Randall Jarrell, Ernest Hemingway, Archibald MacLeish, Malcolm Cowley, Edmund Wilson, and many others. As Radcliffe Squires has observed, however, the tone of Tate's correspondence with John Peale Bishop is different from that of all the others. Although there are exceptions—particularly in letters to Andrew Lytle—Tate's letters to his other correspondents tend to form a definite pattern: those to Donald Davidson, on the plight of the artist in the modern world and on their shared interest in Agrarianism; those to John Crowe Ransom (though few of these survive), on the details of operating a literary quarterly and on the development of a theory of literature as a means of cognition; those to Edmund Wilson, on interpretations of individual works of art and on the functions of literature in a democratic society. The letters to Bishop were more personal, and, as Squires has noted, to both men they were a source of strength:

> To look through their correspondence is to discover how fully each trusted the other, and how fresh their friendship stayed. Their criticism of each other's work was never the usual harmless compliments which old friends seem to deliver almost as a reflex action. It was careful criticism; they often suggested specific emendations of words or lines to each other. Upon occasion they wrote "companion pieces," poems which were variations on one of the other's poems and themes.

Tate was introduced to Bishop in a New York speakeasy by Kenneth Burke in September 1925. Three years later, while Tate was in Paris on a Guggenheim fellowship, Robert Penn Warren came over from Oxford, where he was a Rhodes Scholar, and Bishop joined the two for a night on the town, coming in from his home in Orgeval, about twenty kilometers outside the French capital. The three had a memorable evening together, sampling the wine in some of Bishop's favorite cafes and concluding the celebration over a bottle of Scotch in Tate's apartment. Sometime around midnight, Bishop responded to a request that he read some of his poetry. Although Bishop had been writing verse for many years—he published one volume, **Green Fruit,** shortly after his graduation from Princeton, and collaborated with Edmund Wilson on another, **The Undertaker's Garland**—and although he was a close friend of Ernest Hemingway, F. Scott Fitzgerald, Archibald MacLeish, and Edmund Wilson, his literary career had come to a standstill. His literary friends often asked him to read and comment on their work, but they apparently regarded him as a man with an assured income (his wife's family apparently was fairly wealthy) who merely dabbled in the arts. The incisive and complimentary commentary on Bishop's poems by Tate and Warren had a stimulating effect. About five years later he wrote Tate that "it was from that evening" that he decided he was talented enough to pursue a career in the arts.

Not only was there a noticeable increase in Bishop's output in poetry but in fiction as well. Almost immediately he published a poem in *the New Republic,* a short story in *Vanity Fair,* and won the 1930 Scribner's short story prize of $5,000 for **"Many Thousands Gone."** In 1931 a collection of his short stories appeared. His letters to Tate, after they began corresponding regularly in 1929, reflect Bishop's increased confidence in his abilities as an artist, almost in direct ratio to the serious, careful, and helpful commentary that were always accorded the poems or stories he had sent to Tate.

What proved tonic for Bishop, however, proved even more salutary for Tate. Although Tate was deeply engrossed in the Agrarian movement, and his letters to his friends in Nashville were filled with details of this movement—projects proposed and rejected, comments of various critics weighed and analyzed—his letters to Bishop barely mention Agrarianism and never in any detail. The verses he sent Bishop were always perceptively and wisely scrutinized. Bishop gave detailed criticism of meter, rhyme, diction, and structure. Comparison of the versions of the poems Tate sent Bishop with those published demonstrates quite clearly how much Tate profited from Bishop's suggestions. Bishop never achieved Tate's literary stature or reputation because his work was too uneven and his productivity too sporadic. Although there is no indication that the friendship was adversely affected by this fact, the correspondence shows that both men considered Tate the superior artist. But in many respects Bishop supplemented Donald Davidson's criticism, and the two of them gave Tate the most useful commentary his poetry ever received. When Bishop died on April 4, 1944, most of Tate's best poetry had been written.

Time after time in these letters Tate refers to the helpfulness of Bishop's honest, practical criticism. In 1931 Tate wrote: "I rewrote the *Ode to Fear,* adopting most of your suggestions. I hope you are getting as much out of our correspondence as I am." In dedicating one of his finest and most evenly sustained poems, "Seasons of the Soul," to Bishop, Tate insisted that he had "reason apart from sentiment" because some of Bishop's suggestions were incorporated verbatim into the poem. A letter Bishop wrote Tate very early in the correspondence illustrates the kind of detailed and technical criticism, as well as the helpful encouragement, Tate always received from Bishop:

> Your own two poems are very fine, particularly the Anabasis, which is noble and grave and pure. At first, I was inclined to think that the rhythm halted in one or two places. Now, I am not so sure. But I will put down my comments for what they are worth. Line 2—Dash instead of comma. 1. 3—Substitute 0 for A or qualify "woman" with an adjective of direct address. 1. 5—for, 1. 8, "unstudiously" for "unstudiedly"; 1. 12 for, 1. 13; avoid accent on "that" (it shall—. that shall, possibly) 1. 19: is "The" right? 1. 22, 23, 24 Obscure.

Although a careful study of Tate's poetry written in the thirties and early forties demonstrates quite clearly the seriousness with which he always received Bishop's perceptive criticism (many of the suggested changes affected the final form of the poem), Bishop's most profound assistance, perhaps, came in connection with "Picnic at Cassis," later retitled, at Bishop's suggestion, "The Mediterranean." On October 31, 1932, Tate wrote to Bishop: "I enclose one which is not one of my best, but it has a few nice phrases. I've tried to keep it direct and classical, suppressing the dramatic irony that usually I try to put in." Bishop's response was immediate and enthusiastic: "You're wrong. 'Picnic at Cassis' is not one of your best poems. It is the best. . . . It is—I hesitate, but it is—a great poem. Never I think, has the feeling of the Mediterranean from one of Northern blood (which you are) been so well expressed. Maybe The Mediterranean or something vague like that would be [a] better [title]." Bishop then listed a series of specific changes, many of which, after careful consideration, Tate rejected. But he did adopt Bishop's title, and Bishop's unqualified praise of the poem changed Tate's attitude toward it. For the remainder of his life it remained one of the three or four of his poems that he valued most highly. ("Ode to the Confederate Dead" was not among these.)

Tate replied, thanking Bishop for his praise, and although he was deeply engrossed in a biography of Robert E. Lee, which he was finding difficult to conclude, he put that manuscript aside and attempted to alter the poem in the manner Bishop had suggested. Again Bishop responded promptly, asserting that the revised version of the poem was not as good as the first. As always he expressed his objection in specific terms:

> I may seem to be wrong in condemning your shift in time. But I can't think so. You describe in your poem a place—the shore of the Mediterranean. The time is continuous with the progress of the verse. But behind this time is the arrival of Aeneas on these same or similar shores and this carries you to another arrival on other shores. You make the reader aware of Trojan time. I don't think you need devote a stanza to it. The information contained in it . . . had better be put in your motto. What that should be is the Latin for your first motto, or perhaps better, your translation of the Virgil.

Bishop concluded by indicating rightly that "Aeneas at Washington," which Tate had written as a companion piece to "The Mediterranean" was "vastly inferior to the earlier poem."

Bishop was the author of a prize-winning book of short stories, and was working on his much-underrated novel, *Act of Darkness,* when Tate hesitantly and abashedly submitted for Bishop's reaction his first attempt at fiction. It was in late 1933, when Tate took another respite from the troublesome book on Lee, that he attempted his first short story—called "The Immortal Woman" (1933). He sent it to Bishop and asked him not to be "too severe with it." As usual Bishop's comments were detailed and helpful:

I think the story has decided possibilities: As I see it your story takes place on three planes: The narrator's mind (his reminiscences and comment), his eyes (what he sees of the old lady), his ears (what he overhears Mrs. Dulany saying). There is, therefore, a great deal to be said for putting it all in one scene. That is, begin say with description of the old lady in the street (street or lady first as you choose), present her as seen: then as remembered, giving along with the recollection as much of the narrator's character and surrounding as necessary to understand, then place Mrs. Dulany.

Tate replies: "Your analysis of my so-called story is penetrating and exhaustive. . . . I'm not sure yet whether I will try to rewrite it or will go on with something else. If I do I will adopt your radical suggestion about making the whole action in two present scenes." Two days after Bishop received this letter, he wrote: "You really ought to finish it if only for the sake of discipline and technique." There is ample evidence to support the contention that Tate took Bishop's advice seriously and worked hard on the story trying to make its basic action less obscure. Realizing that most readers were not able to determine "what happened" in the story because of his inexpert handling of point of view, Tate worked hard on mastering this fundamental of fictional technique. As a consequence, although the story remains unnecessarily ambiguous and obscure (worse than even Henry James would allow, Donald Davidson wrote Tate), the labor accomplished much. One of the great strengths of Tate's only novel, *The Fathers* (1938) is his use of Lacy Buchan as the point of view, a retired doctor relating events fifty years in the past and reporting simultaneously his feelings about those events when they occurred and his feelings about them fifty years later.

After completing *Stonewall Jackson: The Good Soldier* (1928) and *Jefferson Davis: His Rise and Fall* (1929), Tate worked diligently for three or four years on a biography of Robert E. Lee. Finally in October 1932, he concluded he could not complete the biography. His reasons for reaching this decision are summarized in a letter to Bishop:

> The whole Southern incapacity for action since 1865 is rationalized in the popular conception of Lee. . . . Lee did not love power; my thesis about him, stated in these terms, is that he didn't love it because he was profoundly cynical of all action for the public good. He could not see beyond the needs of his own salvation, and he was not generous enough to risk soiling his military cloak for the doubtful salvation of others. . . . This is what I feel about Lee. Yet is it true? That is what keeps me awake at night. I can't "prove" a word of it. Of course, the facts do not in the least prove the current notion of him.

Bishop's response to Tate's determination to abandon a project that had consumed a major portion of his time for four or five years was most emphatic. "Proceed with your Lee," he wrote in mid-October, 1932; "if it is not true to the facts of Lee's life, it will be true to you. And that is more important. . . . So if you write the life of the Southerner (yourself, myself, all of us) in terms of Lee, so much more it will be than a life of Lee. I feel this now as a moral problem, and I urge you forward."

Tate had tired of Lee, however, and had his mind fixed on another project, a work more frankly autobiographical and fictional. He proposed to write of his own ancestry, bringing forward to the present the story of Robert Read who came to Virginia in 1638, and attempting to explain how two persons so much unlike as his brother Ben and he, each epitomizing a different kind of American, could belong to the same family. He designed the book to include one person representing each of the two contrasting types in each generation from the seventeenth to the twentieth century. In essence what he conceived was to trace the development of his father's bloodline and that of his mother, and thereby to demonstrate the development of two prominent American character types—that of the pioneer, with his restlessness and his chaotic energies and that of the Virginia Tidewater aristocrat with his cultural roots in tradition, stability, and order. Although he thought through this project sufficiently to outline it in detail, chapter by chapter, and to write a segment of it, he finally abandoned it too. He wrote Bishop on October 30, 1933: "I've been in a crisis. I have out of heroism or cowardice (take your choice) thrown over the ancestry book forever. The agony was great, but the peace of mind is greater. It was a simple problem that I could not solve. The discrepancy between the outward significance and the private was so enormous that I decided that I could not handle the material in that form at all, without either faking the significance or the material."

The effort that Tate had put into this autobiographical novel and into the biography of Lee was not wasted, however, for much of the thought and planning that had gone into these two projects were reflected in Tate's second short story, "The Migration" (1934), in the "Sonnets of the Blood" (1931), and most significantly in Tate's only novel, *The Fathers* (1938), which resembles in many ways Bishop's novel *Act of Darkness* (1935). Through this series of letters, too, one can follow clearly Tate's search for an authoritative source to give order, direction, and meaning to his personal life, from his early hope for the traditional society of the antebellum South to the dogma, doctrine, and the discipline of the Roman Catholic Church.

If this exchange of letters is important for the extent to which it reveals the intellectual and spiritual development of Allen Tate during a crucial period of his life, it is equally important for its effect on John Peale Bishop. By his own admission it resurrected his literary career and maybe saved his life. "You are a grand person, Allen," Bishop once wrote Tate, "and but for you I should probably have committed suicide more than three years ago. If not in the flesh, still in the spirit. I only hope I can keep to the level you are generous enough to accord me." Bishop dated the beginning of his career from the evening Tate and Warren first read his poems. *Green Fruit* (1917), which he wrote while a student at Princeton and published just before leaving for the Army in World War I, he classified as apprentice work, calling it "my attempt to swallow and digest . . . the French Symbolistes." Although since the end of the war he had been almost constantly in the circle of important English and American writers who had settled in France, literary aspirations were no longer a moving force in his life. In December 1933, several years after their meeting in Paris, he wrote Tate:

> Do you remember the evening in the Rue Mignard which you and Warren spent with me over a bottle of Scotch? Well, it was pleasant enough and casual enough for you both. But it was from that evening, from the comment you two made on the verses I most shyly showed you that I conceived it might still be possible for me to make a place for myself as a poet. I do not think even you, who have been so much in my intimacy since, can know upon what despair and forlorness your words came. The confidence I had in youth was gone with youth. I saw myself with little done and that little had not only had no recognition that I was aware of, but I had almost convinced myself that it deserved none . . . always I have known that but for that evening, . . . I should not now in any real sense exist.

Tate responded to this letter, with its extravagant praise and its almost embarrassingly frank relevation, in an uncharacteristically impersonal manner:

> Yes, I remember the evening in the rue Mignard, but I could not understand all of its implications at the time, though I must confess that something in your response to what Warren and I said led me to reflect, a little later, on the kind of friendships with which you seemed to surround yourself. In fact, I became a little impatient though secretly with your suicidal disinterestedness. . . . I decided that your generosity and real love of craft had permitted you to surround yourself with the most unmerciful crew of bloodsuckers it had been my luck to observe. The really bad part of it was that they were nearly all highly gifted people, who in a sense deserved the attention you gave them; but because you clamored for little or no attention yourself you got none.

Tate ends his comment by saying that he deserves no praise for what he had done because he merely saw "some fine work, said it was fine, and thereby only did my simple duty by the republic of letters."

In the years following that "evening in the rue Mignard" Tate was unstinting, perhaps at times extravagant, in his praise of Bishop's work. "Your poem is splendid," he wrote on April 17, 1931. "I feel no need of being severe. I envy your power of setting the emotional tone so clearly that you don't have to keep telling us about it." Tate was also impressed by Bishop's fiction, commenting once about *Many Thousands Gone:* "There are few books in our day that are written out of a full and settled view of human nature. Yours is one of them." And even when he found serious technical flaws in Bishop's fiction, Tate nonetheless found room to praise it by seizing on its overriding virtues. While reading proofs of Bishop's novel *Act of Darkness* in the fall of 1934, for example, Tate wrote that he "became a little alarmed" at Bishop's shift of viewpoint for a crucial scene, adding that while he understood the reasons for the change, he wished "it could be done less violently where the scene is not so conspicuous." Later in the same letter, however, he adds that "the amount of social and human insight that you've put into this book vastly exceeds anything else I've seen from the South."

In spite of the high quality of Bishop's prose, however, Tate was convinced that his natural mode of expression was poetry. Tate wrote on November 5, 1931, "Perhaps your poetry is better than your prose for this reason: You have a *feeling for rhythm by phrases,* but not sentences, and your whole interest is in *emotion not action.*" So that Bishop would not think his praise of the poetry too effusive, Tate reminded him: "I never flatter anybody but women, so you must be aware that what I say about your poetry is the truth." Then he moved on to make specific technical comments about a poem Bishop had just sent him.

Perhaps posterity is justified in not finding as much artistic merit in Bishop's creations as Tate accorded them. One conclusion, however, is inevitable. Except for Tate's well intended and genuinely felt praise, the world of letters would not have two dozen or so highly original and structurally superior poems, a book of excellent short stories, an undeservedly neglected novel, and nearly a dozen perceptive and illuminating critical essays. Not a large quantity of work to be sure, but some of it is of a quality to merit more attention than it is currently receiving.

It is hard to believe that two men so obviously fond of each other, with so many perceptions, observations, and impressions they wished to share, were able to spend so little time together. For a while after their first meeting, they lived on two continents, but Tate spent almost two years in France on Guggenheim fellowships and the two friends had some time together. Later there was a memorable week in New Orleans, some of it shared with Andrew Lytle and the Robert Penn Warrens, and an occasional meeting at a writers' conference. A few times, while Bishop was living in South Chatham, Massachusetts, and Tate in Princeton, the two had a convivial weekend in New York, and Tate arranged for Bishop to give a lecture early in 1940 to the students in the Creative Arts Program at Princeton. During Bishop's visit he and Tate spent much time going over manuscripts of Bishop's poetry, editing and choosing for Bishop's 1941 **Selected Poems.** Time after time, however, these letters refer to missed connections, after weeks of careful planning for a brief reunion, or to misunderstood directions. For whatever reasons, Tate was not able to spend as much time with Bishop as he did with his other friends—Ransom or Warren, for example—or Bishop with Edmund Wilson or E. E. Cummings. Both men were always, it seems, trying to arrange a meeting—a speaking engagement at the same place at the same time, or one near enough the other's home for them to have some time together. When Tate was a member of the panel that presented the radio program "Invitation to Learning," he tried desperately to have Bishop join him on the panel, but instead Bishop became Tate's replacement. In November 1943, Tate, who had become consultant in poetry at the Library of Congress in September, persuaded Archibald MacLeish to create the position of resident fellow in comparative literature and to appoint

Bishop to fill it. After two weeks in office, however, Bishop suffered a severe heart attack, from which he died a few months later. Tate's last communication informed Bishop that financial arrangements associated with their only cooperative literary venture, the anthology *American Harvest,* had been settled and that they could expect a royalty payment within a few weeks. Bishop did not live to receive his share.

Lewis P. Simpson (essay date 1982)

SOURCE: "The Sorrows of John Peale Bishop," in *The Sewanee Review,* Vol. XC, No. 3, Summer, 1982, pp. 480-84.

[*In the following excerpted review of* The Republic of Letters in America, *Simpson finds that Bishop's fiction displays more of an affinity to the writings of Thomas Wolfe than to the writing of Allen Tate.*]

The Donald Davidson-Allen Tate letters (edited by John Tyree Fain and Thomas Daniel Young, University of Georgia Press, 1974) and the John Peale Bishop-Tate letters [***The Republic of Letters in America: The Correspondence of John Peale Bishop & Allen Tate,*** edited by Thomas Daniel Young and John J. Hindle. University Press of Kentucky, 1981, 232 pages]. . . have one striking aspect in common. In both exchanges Tate was corresponding with a man older than himself (by six years in the case of Davidson, seven in that of Bishop), who, unlike Tate, had seen service in France in World War I; yet in each set of letters Tate is the presiding intelligence. This is partly because Tate is the more aggressive and the more incisive writer. But there is a deeper reason: Tate's self-conscious dedication to the concept of the literary vocation as subsistent in the polity of writers. Inherent in his dedication was the assumption that he had a mission to maintain the literary order; this demanded that he exercise a certain leadership in his literary relationships.

Bishop and Tate first met casually in 1925, when Kenneth Burke introduced them in a New York speakeasy. Fresh from the Fugitive group in Nashville, the Tennessean Tate had come to the metropolis seeking his literary fortune. Bishop, who had been born in Charles Town, West Virginia, to a father from New England and a mother from Virginia, had already had a various career. After attending Princeton, where he had become the friend of Edmund Wilson and F. Scott Fitzgerald, he had served as an infantry officer in France, married Margaret Grosvenor Hutchins (according to Tate in his *Memoirs and Opinions,* a woman of "the *haut monde,* or near to it"), gone back to France for three years, and then returned again to work for *Vanity Fair.* When he met Tate he was on the verge of going back to France to settle in the Château du Petit Tressancourt in the village of Orgèval near Paris. Here and in the city, where he maintained an apartment, Bishop, now more or less committed to permanent expatriation in the name of literature and art, lived in the midst of an entertaining circle of writers and artists. Overly deferential to his acquaintances, he masked his own literary aspirations in dandyism and hedonism and allowed his very genuine talent to languish. In the memoir of Bishop that prefaces the posthumous collection of his poems (1948) Tate quotes a "wit" of the Bishop circle: "John is like a man lying in a warm bath who faintly hears the telephone ringing downstairs." That Bishop ever answered the phone again—that he did not commit suicide, at least spiritually—was largely because of Tate, who in 1928 came to live in France for two years and was frequently in Bishop's company. Five years later Bishop—now engaged in the composition of poems and in the writing of his novel, *Act of Darkness*—wrote to Tate expressing his gratitude for an evening in 1929 when Tate had listened to him read some of his poems and he had "conceived that it might still be possible for me to make a place for myself as poet." Entering into a sympathetic correspondence with Bishop after he left France, Tate continued to be a constructive, to be sure a redemptive, influence on Bishop. Yet, as Tate explained in a response to Bishop's expression of thanks, it was an impersonal service he had rendered to him: "I saw some fine work, said it was fine, and thereby only did my simple duty by the republic of letters (which is the only kind of republic I believe in, a kind of republic that can't exist in a political republic)."

The fifteen-year correspondence of Bishop and Tate records not the story of the fulfillment of Tate's act on behalf of the literary republic but its frustration and defeat. Ironically it is a story strangely dominated by the weaker rather than the stronger correspondent.

Essentially what Tate offered Bishop was a vision of the place of their nativity, the American South, as both home sweet home and, conceived symbolically, the preservation, even the renaissance, of the humanistic tradition, or the high culture, of the West—as the last refuge of the modern, secular realm of letters that had its inception in Dante and Petrarch. Profoundly disturbed by feelings of displacement and homelessness, Bishop tried hard to associate himself with Tate's South. The documents of this effort include *Act of Darkness,* a novel about the South, and a provocative essay entitled "The South and Tradition." The more tangible evidence of Bishop's desire to associate himself with the South includes his residency in New Orleans for a year after he returned from France in the mid-1930s, his attendance at the writers' conference in Baton Rouge in 1935, and his interest in the *Southern Review* and other such enterprises.

Bishop's outlook was scarcely compatible with the spirit of cultural renewal that motivated Tate and other southern writers. Devising a program for a "Southern movement" in 1929, Tate said in a letter to Donald Davidson (as he had said earlier in a letter to Robert Penn Warren), "We must be the last Europeans—there being no Europeans left in Europe at present." About a year after the publication of *I'll Take My Stand* (1930) Bishop wrote to Tate: "The Russians may well survive, for they are the beginning of something non-European; we are the end of all that is European. With us Western civilization ends." There is a

subtle yet distinct difference between these assertions. Tate implies that the South could take the initiative in a recovery of the literary and artistic—the intellectual and spiritual—community of the high culture. Bishop indicates that the South (and for that matter America) is the apocalypse of this order. He was obsessed with a withering conviction of the irredeemable decay of the classical-Christian civilization. In *A Second Flowering* Malcolm Cowley argues that the young American writers of the twenties should not be called "lost" but "lucky." While Cowley's view corrects a tendency to deform the creative impulse of the twenties and thirties, we cannot discount the recognition on the part of writers during the age between the great wars that they were the recorders of irreparable cultural loss, nor fail to recognize their awareness—acute in some instances—that they were the living emblems of this loss. Tate belonged to the lucky, Bishop to the lost. He dreamed Tate's dream of the American South as the cultural resurrection of western civilization only because Tate embodied for him what he longed to represent yet could not will to represent, the authority and continuity of the man of letters and the literary mind. How desperately Bishop lived in Tate's image becomes transparent in two letters written late in his career. Toward the end of 1942 Tate, always aware of his implication in literary history, suggested to Bishop that they might shortly deposit their correspondence of the past several years in the Princeton library. Refusing to part with the letters Tate had sent him, Bishop replied that he liked to get them out from time to time "and peruse them, not only for the virtues they contain, but for the magic in them to give me myself again." Two or three months later Bishop—now living in New England, where he settled for good after his New Orleans year—confessed to Tate that "wherever you are is, I have no doubt, as much the South as I shall ever find."

To some degree Bishop's anxious dependence on Tate for his identity may be related to his perception of France. Like other American writers in the twenties he had more than halfway believed that by living in France, the bastion of the high culture, he could simply assume his identity as a writer. But historical events shattered his image of this stronghold. The first blow was the election of the Blum government. When he returned to France briefly in 1937 to sell Tressancourt, Bishop informed Tate that socialist France is like a house "the day after the funeral." In 1940 came the German capture of Paris. In one letter of this period Bishop describes to Tate a recurrent dream: wandering alone for hours through the deserted streets of the city, he eventually discovers its sole life to be a contingent of German soldiers surrounding the Arc de Triomphe.

By this time Bishop was no longer attempting to maintain himself in Tate's image. Almost in defiance of Tate he had discovered an empathy with Thomas Wolfe, a novelist Tate dismissed as unreadable because he had nothing to offer but a boring "personal philosophy." The year after Wolfe's death Bishop published **"The Sorrows of Thomas Wolfe"** in the first number of John Crowe Ransom's *Kenyon Review.* A sensitive meditation on the failure of Wolfe as an artist, this essay turns on its author's deliberate neglect of a salient fact about the novelist—that he was of the South. Wolfe, Bishop intimates, was a writer from the South who was so far gone in the solipsism of modernity that he had completely lost his heritage. For Wolfe the "rewards of experience were always such that he turned back upon himself." Alone in "his sensations," he "sought for a door, and there was really none, or only one, the door to death." Describing himself as much as Wolfe, Bishop even so tacitly asserts a distinction between his situation and Wolfe's. While Wolfe had lost the connection with tradition (was no longer aware of being the last of Europe), Bishop the man of letters knew with Tate what had been lost in the closure of the being in the autonomous self: nothing less than the supporting structure of the mind—that is to say, instinctive spiritual being, the soul. "We must live from the instincts," Bishop had observed earlier in **"The South and Tradition,"** "for the mind unsupported not only cannot tell us how to behave, it cannot give any very satisfactory reasons for living at all."

Although Bishop shared this knowledge with Tate, he had given up his futile attempts to act on it. He now sought an image of his despair. When his precise contemporary, Fitzgerald, died in 1940, Bishop composed an elegy called **"The Hours."** In this work—which Tate was moved to call one of his best poems—Bishop recalls, in a way celebrates, his communion with his longtime friend, which reached its nadir in the hour when the soul not only knows its "utter destitution" but "knows the world too poor / For restitution." In his conviction of the soul's depletion in a decayed culture incapable of offering any hope of its renewal, Bishop experienced a far darker night of the soul than the medieval mystics. Ironically his portrayal of Fitzgerald as a fellow sufferer is more fanciful than real. As unhappy as his life became, Fitzgerald was among the lucky, one who believed in the capacity of the literary talent to transcend the modern fragmentation of culture. As with Wolfe, Bishop made him an emblem of his own sorrows.

The final irony of the Bishop-Tate relationship, and of Bishop's career as a whole, is not recorded in his correspondence with Tate. It is, however, set forth in Tate's memoir. Tate tells how his friend roused from the unconscious state in which he lay after the heart attack in 1944 that would soon claim his life and dictated his epitaph to his wife.

Long did I live
Consistent, lonely, proud.
Not death, but the fear of death,
Restores us to the crowd.

Tate makes no comment on these lines, although he must have had no doubt about their implication. After a fashion a deathbed confession to the gravest of sins, pride in intellect, they are a repudiation of Bishop's long agonizing struggle to identify himself as a man of letters and to find a community with other men of letters. Incapable of believing in the high culture's interpretation of the traditional, or instinctive, community as Tate did, he was incapable of believing in the restoration of the literary order, and thus of achieving a restoring faith in letters. At the last his weary mind, unsupported, willed its oblivion, and Bishop was restored to the only instinctive community available to him—the universal, inarticulate, traditional democracy of our most common fear. At least he said so, but he said it in the ironic voice of the modern poet.

FURTHER READING

Criticism

Hyman, Stanley Edgar. *The Promised End.* Cleveland and New York: The World Publishing Company, 1963, 380 pp.
> Includes a lengthy 1949 review of Bishop's *Collected Poems.*

Tate, Allen, ed. *The Collected Poems of John Peale Bishop.* New York: Charles Scribner's Sons. 1948, 277 pp.
> Includes a preface and personal memoir of Bishop by Tate.

White, Robert L. "Some Unpublished Poems of John Peale Bishop." *Sewanee Review* 71, No. 4 (October-December 1963): 527-37.
> Includes two of Bishop's poems of which Allen Tate had no knowledge, as well as an introduction by White asserting that Bishop deserves recognition as a major poet.

———. *John Peale Bishop.* New York: Twayne Publishers, 1966, 176 pp.
> The only book-length consideration of Bishop's fiction, criticism, and poetry.

Additional coverage of Bishop's life and career is contained in the following sources published by the Gale Group: *Contemporary Authors*, Vols. 107, 155; *Dictionary of Literary Biography*, Vols. 4, 9, 45.

Henry Blake Fuller
1857-1929

(Also wrote under the pseudonym Stanton Page) American novelist, playwright, essayist, and short story writer.

INTRODUCTION

Best-known for his novels focusing on turn-of-the-century Chicago, Fuller is remembered as one of the pioneers of realism in American literature. His novels and short stories often explored the differences between America and Europe. As a result, his work was frequently compared to that of authors such as Henry James and William Dean Howells.

BIOGRAPHICAL INFORMATION

Fuller was born on 9 January, 1857, in Chicago, Illinois. His family was a proud, old New England family. As a young man he disliked the commercial aspect of Chicago and when he was old enough, he attended the Allison Classical Academy in Oconomowoc, Wisconsin. By 1875 he returned to Chicago and worked in a crockery store and a bank. In 1879 he made a pilgrimage to Europe, traveling for a year before returning to Chicago. Returning to Europe in 1883, he began to compose sketches, stories, and essays exploring the differences between America and Europe, which would become a recurring theme in his work. When his father died in 1885, Fuller was forced to return to Chicago. While managing his father's business investments, he wrote *The Chevalier of Pensieri-Vani* (1891), which garnered commercial and critical success. He continued to write novels, essays, sketches, and stories set in Chicago and Italy. He died on 28 July 1929.

MAJOR WORKS

The Cliff-Dwellers (1893) and *With the Procession* (1895) are Fuller's most highly regarded novels. Set in Chicago, both stories explore the empty lives of several characters that strive for material success and ignore art, beauty, and culture. In *The Cliff-Dwellers,* George Ogden, an ambitious young banker, rises through the ranks to achieve economic prosperity and social acceptance. Unfortunately, the pressure of this life prompts him to steal money from his bank, thereby precipitating his ultimate downfall. *With the Procession* chronicles the unsuccessful attempt of the once-proud Marshall family as they struggle to regain social prominence. As several characters scheme to become more socially acceptable or maintain their elite position in Chicago society, they lose their souls, spirituality, and individuality. Both of these novels are considered prime examples of American realism because they focus on the lives of ordinary characters and provide an unsparing look at the conditions and repercussions of life in industrial-age Chicago.

CRITICAL RECEPTION

Fuller is often praised for his skill as a realist and a satirist, especially with his best-known novels, *The Cliff-Dwellers* and *With the Procession.* He is viewed as a pioneer of the realist movement in America. Many critics view his unsparing depiction of socially ambitious people striving for material success at the expense of art and culture as the author's protest against the lack of beauty and spiritual life in industrialized Chicago. Yet he is also derided as a snob for his harsh indictment of life in turn-of-the-century Chicago. Fuller is compared to Henry James for his novels and short stories featuring materialistic American characters traveling in cultured, sophisticated Europe. As Fuller's work has fallen into relative obscurity, a few scholars have unfavorably compared his work with that of his contemporaries, such as Hamlin Garland, William Dean Howells, Theodore Dreiser, and Frank Norris.

PRINCIPAL WORKS

The Chevalier of Pensieri-Vani [as Stanton Page] (novel) 1891
The Châtelaine of La Trinité (novel) 1892
The Cliff-Dwellers (novel) 1893
With the Procession (novel) 1895
The Puppet-Booth (sketches) 1896
From the Other Side (short stories) 1898
The Last Refuge (short stories) 1900
Under the Skylights (short stories) 1901
Waldo Trench and Others (short stories) 1908
Lines Long and Short (poetry) 1917
On the Stairs (novel) 1918
Bertram Cope's Year (novel) 1919
Gardens of This World (novel) 1930

Not on the Screen (novel) 1930

CRITICISM

Agnes Repplier (essay date 1892)

SOURCE: "A By-Way in Fiction," in *Essays in Miniature,* Charles L. Webster & Co., 1892, pp. 87-103.

[*In the following mixed review of* The Chevalier of Pensieri-Vani, *Repplier regards the novel as "a series of detached episodes" that "rambles backward and forward in such a bewildering fashion that the chapters might be all rearranged without materially disturbing its slender thread of continuity."*]

Now and then the wearied and worn novel-reader, sick unto death of books about people's beliefs and disbeliefs, their conscientious scruples and prejudices, their unique aspirations and misgivings, their cumbersome vices and virtues, is recompensed for much suffering by an hour of placid but genuine enjoyment. He picks up rather dubiously a little, unknown volume, and, behold! the writer thereof takes him gently by the hand, and leads him straightway into a fair country, where the sun is shining, and men and women smile kindly on him, and nobody talks unorthodox theology, and everybody seems disposed to allow everybody else the privilege of being happy in his own way. When to these admirable qualities are added humor and an atmosphere of appreciative cultivation, the novel-reader feels indeed that his lines have been cast in pleasant places, and he is disposed to linger along in a very contented and uncritical frame of mind.

There has come to us recently a new and beautiful edition of such a little book, published in America, but born of Italian soil and sunshine. It has for a title *The Chevalier of Pensieri-Vani, together with Frequent Allusions to the Prorege of Arcopia,* which is rather an unmerciful string of words to describe so gay and easy-going a narrative. It is the first full-fledged literary venture of its author, Mr. Henry Fuller, also known as Stanton Page, whose New England grandfather was a cousin of Margaret Fuller's. The story, which is not really a story at all, but a series of detached episodes, rambles backward and forward in such a bewildering fashion that the chapters might be all rearranged without materially disturbing its slender thread of continuity. It is equally guiltless of plot or purpose, of dramatic incidents or realistic details. The Chevalier may be found now in Pisa, now in Venice, now in Ostia or Ravenna, never driven by the vulgar spur of necessity, always wandering of his own free and idle will. He is accompanied sometimes by his friend Hors-Concours, an Italianized Frenchman from Savoy, and sometimes by the Prorege of Arcopia, the delightful Prorege, who gives to the book its best and most distinctive flavor. At once dig-

nified and urbane, conscious of his exalted position, and convinced that he fills it with equal grace and correctness, this superb official moves through the tale in an atmosphere of autocratic reserve, tempered with the most delicate courtesy. His ministerial views are as unalterable as the rocks, and as sound; but he listens to the democratic ravings of his young American *protégé,* Occident, with the good-humored indulgence one accords to a beloved and precocious child. It must be confessed that Occident fails to make his arguments very convincing, or to impress his own personality with any degree of clearness upon the reader's mind. He is at best only a convenient listener to the Prorege's delicious theories; he is of real value only because the Prorege condescends to talk to him. When he ventures upon a truly American remark about trying "to find the time" for something, his august friend reminds him, with dignity, that "the only man to be envied was the man whose time was in some degree his own, and the most pitiable object that civilization could offer was the rich man a slave to his chronometer. Too much had been said about the dignity of labor, and not enough about the preciousness of leisure. Civilization in its last outcome was heavily in the debt of leisure, and the success of any society worth considering was to be estimated largely by the use to which its *fortunati* had put their spare moments. He wrung from Occident the confession that, in the great land of which Shelby County may be called the centre, activity, considered of itself and quite apart from its objects and its results, was regarded as a very meritorious thing; and he learned that the bare figure of leisure, when exposed to the public gaze, was expected to be decorously draped in the garment of strenuous endeavor. People were supposed to appear busy, even if they were not. This gave the Prorege a text for a little disquisition on the difference between leisure and idleness."

In fact, a beautiful, cultivated, polished, unmarred, well-spent inactivity is the keynote of this serene little book; and to understand its charm and meaning we have but to follow the Chevalier, in the second chapter, to Pisa—to Pisa the restful, where "life is not strongly accentuated by positive happenings, where incident is unusual, and drama quite unknown." The Chevalier's windows, we are told, faced the north, and he sat and looked out of them rather more than active persons would deem pleasant or profitable. It even happened that the Prorege remarked this comfortable habit, and demanded of his friend what it was he looked at, inasmuch as there seemed to be no appreciable change from day to day. To which the Chevalier, in whom "Quietism was pretty successfully secularized; who knew how to sit still, and occasionally enjoyed doing so," replied with great acumen that what *had* gone on was quite as interesting to him as what was going on, and that nothing was more gratifying, from his point of view, than that very absence of change which had taken his Excellency's attention—since any change would be a change for the worse.

He is destined, as it chances, to prove the truth of his own theories, for it is in Pisa, of all places, that he is tempted to throw aside for once his *rôle* of contemplative philosopher, and to assume that of an active philanthropist, with very disastrous results. There is an admirable satire in the description of the two friends, Pensieri-Vani and Hors-Concours, gravely plotting to insure the success of an operatic *débutante,* to bring her out in the sunshine of their generous patronage, and with the direct approval of the Prorege himself, who kindly consents to sit in the front of a middle box, and to wear a round half-dozen of his most esteemed decorations. Unhappily, an Italian audience does not like to have its enthusiasm expressed for it, even by such noble and consummate critics. As each well-arranged device of flowers or love-birds in a gilded cage is handed decorously forward, the house grows colder and more quizzical, until the *débutante* sees herself on the extreme verge of failure, and, putting forth all her powers in one appealing effort, she triumphs by dint of sheer pluck and ability over the fatal kindness of her friends. The poor Chevalier, who has in the meantime left the theatre with many bitter self-communings, receives his lesson in a spirit of touching humility, recognizing at once his manifest limitations. "He perceived that he was less fitted to play the part of special providence than he had previously supposed; and he brought from this experience the immeasurable consolation that comes from knowing that very frequently in this sadly twisted world, things, if only left to their own courses, have a way of coming out right in the end."

The Pisan episode, the delicious journey of the Prorege and Pensieri-Vani in search of the "Madonna Incognita," a mysterious and illusive Perugino which turns out, after all, to be a Sodoma, and the memorable excursion to Ostia, are the finest and best-told incidents in the book. The story of the Iron Pot is too broadly farcical, too Pickwickian in its character, to be in harmony with the rest of the narrative; the Contessa's fête at Tusculum is so lightly sketched as to be absolutely tantalizing; and the practical jokes which that lady and the Prorege delight in playing upon one another are hardly as subtle and acute as we would like to find them. Indeed, the Prorege's conduct on board his own yacht is so deeply objectionable that I, for one, positively refuse to believe he was ever guilty of such raw rudeness. It is not kind or right in Mr. Fuller to wickedly calumniate this charming and highbred gentleman whom he has given us for a friend. Neither is the battle of the Aldines as thrilling as might be expected, probably because it is impossible to accept the Duke of Avon and Severn upon any terms whatever. Occident, the American, is misty and ill-defined; but he does not lack proportion, only vitality. The English duke is a mistake throughout, a false note that disturbs the atmosphere of serene good temper which is the principal attraction of the book; an effort on the author's part to be severe and cynical, just when we were congratulating ourselves that severity and cynicism were things far, far remote from his tolerant and kindly spirit.

The excursion to Ostia, however, is enough to redeem the whole volume from any charge of ill-nature; for if the Contessa does seize this opportunity to play one of her du-

bious tricks upon the Prorege, it is not until the little group of friends have proved themselves gentle, and sympathetic, and full of fine and generous instincts. It is a delicious bit of description throughout. La Nullaniuna has been crowned the day before at her Tusculum fête as "the new Corinne," and naturally feels that her proper cue is that of "genius-blasted fragility," overpowered and shattered by her own impassioned burst of song. With her is the widowed Princess Altissimi, her cherished friend and foil, a sombre beauty of a grave and chastened demeanor, against whose dark background the Contessa, "who was fully as flighty, and capricious, and *théâtrale* as a woman of semi-genius usually finds it necessary to be, posed and fidgeted to her heart's content." The Prorege, sublimely affable as ever, Pensieri-Vani, and young Occident, eager and radiant, make up the party; and after the little inn has furnished them with a noonday meal of unusual profusion and elegance, they visit the adjoining church at the instigation of the Princess Altissimi, who is anxious to see what this solitary and humble temple is like. All that follows is so exquisite that I must quote it as it stands, in proof of the author's faculty for delicate and sympathetic delineation:

"They were met on the threshold by the single priest in charge, a dark and sallow young man of peasant extraction, whose lonely battle with midsummer malaria had left him wholly gaunt and enervate. He saluted them with the deference which the Church sometimes shows to the World, though he was too true an Italian to be awed, or even embarrassed by their rank; and he brightened up into something almost like eagerness as he offered to do the honors of his charge. The Prorege indulgently praised the wretched frescoes which he exhibited so proudly, and the Contessa called up a flickering smile of pleasure in his emaciated face as she feigned an enthusiasm for the paltry fripperies of the high altar. This appreciative interest emboldened him to suggest their ascent to the gallery, where, from his manner, the great treasure of the church was to be revealed. The great treasure was a small cabinet organ, and Occident—triumphing in the ubiquity of the Western genius, yet somewhat taken back by this new illustration of the incongruities it sometimes precipitated—read upon it a name familiar to his earliest years. The priest, who evidently conceived it an impossibility for his beloved instrument to be guilty of a discord of any kind whatever, pleaded with a mute but unmistakable pathos that its long silence might now be ended; and the Princess, motioning Pensieri-Vani to the keyboard, sang this poor solitary a churchly little air, with such a noble seriousness and such a gracious simplicity as to move, not only him, but all the others too. Occident, in particular, who kept within him quite unimpaired his full share of that fund of sensibility which is one of the best products of Shelby County, and who would have given half his millions just then to have been able to sit down and play the simplest tune, implored Pensieri-Vani in looks, if not in words, to do for him what he himself was so powerless to compass; and the Cavaliere, who, like a good and true musician, preferred support from the lowest quarter to indifference in the highest, kept his place until their poor host, charmed, warmed through and through, attached again to the great body of humanity, could scarcely trust himself to voice his thanks. But the Princess whispered in the Cavaliere's ear, as his series of plain and simple little tunes came to an end, that he had not lost since she last heard him."

There is nothing finer in the story than this, perhaps nothing quite so good, though all of Pensieri-Vani's journeys are fruitful in minute incidents of a pleasant and picturesque quality. It is curious, too, to see how the Chevalier, who, except for that catlike scratching about the Aldines, is the gentlest and least hurtful of men, manifests at times a positive impatience of his own refined and peaceful civilization, a breathless envy of sterner races and of stormier days. When he discovers the tomb of the old Etrurian warrior, he is abashed and humbled at the thought of that fierce spirit summoned from thirty centuries of darkness to see the light of this invertebrate and sentimental age; requested to forget his deep draughts of blood and iron, and to contentedly "munch the dipped toast of a flabby humanitarianism, and sip the weak tea of brotherly love." When he stands in the dim cathedral of Anagni, and contemplates the tombs of the illustrious Gaetani family, and the mosaics which blazon forth their former splendors, he shrinks with sudden shame from the contrast between his feeble, forceless will and the rough daring of that mighty clan. "The stippling technique of his own day seemed immeasurably poor and paltry compared with the broad, free, sketchy touch with which these men dashed off their stirring lives; and he stood confounded before that fiery and robust intensity which, so gloriously indifferent to the subtilties of the grammarian, the niceties of the manicure, and the torments of the supersensitive self-analyst, could fix its intent upon some definite desire, and move forward unswervingly to its attainment. Poor moderns! he sighed, who with all our wishing never reach our end, and with all our thinking never know what we really think."

These unprofitable musings of the Chevalier's seem to reflect some recurring discontent, some restless, unchastened yearnings on the part of the author himself; but they find no echo in the serene breast of the Prorege. He at least is as remote from envying the hostilities of the past as he is innocent of aspiring to the progressiveness of the future. He is fully alive to the merits of his own thrice-favored land, where the evil devices of a wrong-headed generation have never been suffered to penetrate: "Arcopia, the gods be praised, was exempt from the modern curse of bigness. One chimney was not offensive; but a million made a London. One refuse-heap could be tolerated; but accumulated thousands produced a New York. A hundred weavers in their own cottages meant peaceful industry and home content; a hundred hundred, massed in one great factory, meant vice and squalor and disorder. Society had never courted failure or bid for misery more ardently than when it had accepted an urban industrialism for a basis. . . . Happily the Arcopian population, except a fraction that followed the arts and another fraction that followed the sea, was largely agricultural, and exhibited in high union

the chief virtue and the chief grace of civilized society— order and picturesqueness. The disturbing and ungracious catch-word, 'Égalité,' had never crossed the Arcopian sea; if the Prorege had not been tolerably sure that his mild sway was to be undisturbed by the clangor of cantankerous boiler-makers and the bickerings of a bumptious, shop-keeping *bourgeoisie,* he would never have undertaken the task at all. He regarded himself as a just, humane, and sympathetic ruler, but he believed that every man should have his own proper place and fill it."

Such are the views smilingly detailed to the puzzled and outraged Occident, who, having been nourished in boyhood on the discourses of rustic theologians, and the forensics of Shelbyville advocates, finds it difficult to assimilate his own theories of life with a civilization he so imperfectly understands. He doubts his ability to take the European attitude, he doubts the propriety of the attitude when taken, and the struggle ends in the usual manner by his marrying a wife, and going back to Shelby County to be a good citizen for the rest of his days. Hors-Concours, mindful of the duties entailed on the proprietor of a small patrimony and an ancient name, espouses with becoming gravity and deliberation the Princess Altissimi. The Prorege retires to Arcopia the blessed, whither we would fain follow him if we could; and Pensieri-Vani, left desolate and alone, consoles himself with the reflection that life has many sides, and that Italy has not yet given up to him all she has to give: "Others might falter; but he was still sufficient unto himself, still master of his own time and his own actions, and enamored only of that delightful land whose beauty age cannot wither, and whose infinite variety custom can never stale."

Floyd Dell (essay date 1913)

SOURCE: "Chicago in Fiction," in *The Bookman,* Vol. XXXVIII, November 3, 1913, pp. 270-77.

[*In the following essay, Dell contrasts Fuller's Chicago novels with those of Frank Norris and Robert Herrick.*]

I

"Chicago," wrote Frank Norris scornfully in one of his early tales, "is not a place where stories happen." San Francisco was still large enough for his imagination—San Francisco, and the bay, and the ocean of piracy and adventure beyond, and on the other side of the city the great wheat fields of California. But the wheat, capturing his imagination, led him to Chicago, and in *The Pit* he undertook to prove himself wrong. He tried to show that stories could happen in Chicago.

He came, and saw, and wrote his novel. An astonishing capacity for seeing, he had, too. In him the reporting instinct amounted to genius. He sketched the city in broad, powerful strokes, taking in with his amateur vision aspects of its life that veteran Chicagoans had felt without being able to express. Never, surely was a city "done" so well. Better than in any book written by a real Chicagoan, he gives us in his novel a sense of Chicago's streets and buildings and business—its objective, localised existence.

So much must be said for *The Pit*—it is the best fictional guide-book to Chicago in existence. Intrinsically, of course, as a picture of Chicago life, it simply doesn't stand up beside any of the books written about Chicago by Chicagoans. For Frank Norris, who had the gift of seeing the outside of things, did not penetrate with his imagination to the heart of the city, to discover there the pretences, at once shallow and cruel, which Chicago's own writers have made it their main business to show up. Is Chicago ever called nowadays the Windy City? It was the Windy City in the nineties, a city of vast and immitigable bluff. The feverish straining of the eighties, with its few flashes of beautiful and futile idealism, culminating in the World's Fair, had passed. Chicago had arrived, commercially and industrially. Its pride in itself, in its bigness, its hardness, and its success, knew no bounds. It was an uncritical pride that led directly into the mire of fatuous self-deception, from which Chicago's novelists have ever since, not without some success, been trying to pull it. No lie was too egregious to tell about the new-world, western glory that was Chicago. And Frank Norris, it seems, believed it all.

He really knew better. He had already in *The Octopus* exposed the windy shams of the commerce and politics of his native State. But he fell into a curious attitude of unthinking admiration before Jadwin, the wheat speculator, the typical Chicago hero of the period, and his insane way of doing business on the Board of Trade. The Board of Trade building, standing there in the middle of La Salle Street, appeared to him romantically as "crouching on its foundations like a monstrous sphinx with blind eyes." It would have been impossible for a Chicago writer to take so much trouble in making up a phrase about the Board of Trade, without saying something more to the point.

As one walks north on State Street out of the "loop" district, one passes South Water Street, one of the real and characteristic sights of the town—a narrow street filled with horses and wagons backed up to the doors of commission houses, the sidewalks packed with boxes and crates and barrels, with greenstuffs and vegetables and fruit from all over the United States, and from all over the world. One remembers how Frank Norris wrote about it. "It was the Mouth of the City, and drawn from all directions, over a territory of immense area, this glut of crude subsistence was sucked in, as if into a rapacious gullet, to feed the sinews and to nourish the fibres of an immeasurable colossus."

He is enthusiastic, as Chicago was enthusiastic, over the town's being a colossus. But colossus is as colossus does. Only the other day this same colossus, after a quarrel with a garbage-reducing company which had been exploiting it past all enduring, faced the problem of seizing and operating this reducing plant, or else letting the wastage of this "glut of crude subsistence" rot at the back doors of its citizens. And, colossus though it was, it dared not take the bolder move. Instead, like any little prairie village, it bought a big hole to dump it in. One is reminded of the phrase which seems to be the net result of the Balkan wars—"les Grandes Impuissances d'Europe."

But, putting sociological reflections aside, one walks across the State Street bridge, and sees the Chicago River, much the same as it was in Frank Norris's day, though not quite so alive with fleets of tugs, lake steamers, lumber barges, grain boats, coal scows, produce steamers and grimy rowboats. A little farther north, at the corner of Huron and Cass Streets, opposite St. James's Chruch, is an odd little house of an ecclesiastic style of architecture, standing back in a small yard. It is the house where Laura Dearborn, the heroine of Frank Norris's novel, lived with her sister, Page. They wouldn't live there now, of course. They might possibly live somewhere on Sheridan Road. But as one looks at the house one has a feeling that not merely a few years, but at least a century, has elapsed since the wooing of Laura Dearborn by Jadwin in that little house there on the corner. It was a wooing so different from modern wooings, at least from those which gain the attention of modern novelists. It was at once brutal and romantic, a wooing in which crude masculine insistence rather than feminine preference had the chief part.

> "I thought all the time that you'd told him you wouldn't have him," said Page wonderingly to her elder sister.
>
> "I did," said Laura. "I told him I did not love him. Only last week I told him so."
>
> "Well, then, why did you promise?"
>
> "My goodness!" exclaimed Laura. "You don't realise what it's been. Do you suppose you can say 'no' to that man?"
>
> "Of course not, of course not," declared Mrs. Cressler joyfully. "That's 'J.' all over. I might have known he'd have you if he set out to do it."
>
> "Morning, noon and night," Laura continued, "He seemed willing to wait as long as I wasn't definite; but one day I wrote to him and gave him a square 'No,' so as he couldn't mistake, and just as soon as I'd said that he—he—began. I didn't have any peace until I'd promised him, and the moment I had promised he had a ring on my finger. He'd had it ready in his pocket for weeks, it seems."

The secret of the girl's complaisance is, of course, the fact that like all Chicago she was bluffing. She was making the bluff of being cold and unapproachable. She explains her idea of love somewhere in the book. "A man ought to love a woman more than she loves him. It ought to be enough for him if she lets him give her everything she wants in the world. He ought to serve her like the old knights—give up his whole life to satisfy some whim of hers; and it's her part, if she likes, to be cold and distant. That's my idea of love."

Standing there in front of the decaying house on the corner, and thinking of that curious attitude, so almost unthinkable in these days of feminine frankness, independence and exploit, one can only shake one's head and say, "Well, well! How manners have changed!"

For one thing, Laura was brought up on *Idyls of the King* and Ruskin's *Queen's Gardens.* The Laura of today would be more likely to read *Man and Superman.* And her sister Page would never take the trouble to say, when accused of having a liking for a certain young man: "I won't have you insinuate that I would run after any man, or care in the least whether he's in love or not. I just guess I've got some self-respect. . . . As if I hadn't yet to see the man I'd so much as look at a second time." She wouldn't say it, for no one would believe her, and she would only get laughed at for her futile bluff. The atmosphere has cleared since then for girls in Chicago, and Chicago novelists, along with the rest of the world of writers, have had something to do with the clearing of it.

II

Robert Herrick, in particular, has not been imposed upon by his town. If anything, he has been too harsh in his dislike of those very features of Chicago life which Frank Norris so naïvely admired. All periods, from the early eighties down to the present time, have been dealt with in Mr. Herrick's novels, but it is that early period, the period of the striving eighties, which has remained to him most significant, and it has dominated his conception of the whole history of the city. It is in his *Memoirs of an American Citizen* that he sets forth this idea of Chicago, through the medium of a pseudo-autobiography of E. V. Harrington, the stockyards magnate. Of this striving Mr. Herrick sees for the most part only the more sordid side, and he even considers sordid what to most people has a nobler side. There is Ambition, which even if it be directed to purely commercial ends yet retains a certain human dignity, if not a romantic beauty. But Mr. Herrick declines emphatically to respect, as he declines to romanticise Ambition—the ambition, that is to say, of the business man. It is to him a dirty affair.

One walks along West Van Buren Street, looking for, and at last finding, the three story and basement house where E. V. Harrington roomed and boarded when he first came, in 1876, to Chicago, a boy fresh from an Indiana farm, an impressionable boy, ready to be whatever Chicago chose to make of him. And of the Chicago which was to mould this boy into a successful pork-packer and politician, the Pierson boarding-house stands in Mr. Herrick's pages as a symbol. It is run by a pale slave of a woman whose husband, coming to the city to get rich, has failed and become a slovenly loafer. About her table in the little basement dining-room are grouped Harrington and his fellows— "strugglers on the outside of prosperity, trying hard to climb up somewhere in the bread-and-butter order of life, and to hold on tight," he says, "to what we had got." No one ever came to Chicago, at least in these days, "without

a hope in his pocket of landing at the head of his game sometime. Even Ma Pierson cherished a secret dream of a rich marriage for one or other of her girls."

All they think about, the Chicagoans of this period, is getting on. When they go to church, it is to a fashionable church, where they can look at the rich people and talk about them. It occupies their days and their dreams. They talk of nothing else. When a girl at the Pierson boardinghouse at last protests against this perpetual topic, she is rebuked by one of the "hustlers" at the table.

> "What else are we here for, except to make money?" Slocum demanded more bitterly than usual.
>
> He raised his long arm in explanation, and swept it to and fro over the struggling prairie city, with its rough, patched look. I didn't see what there was in the city to object to: it was just a place like any other, to work, eat and sleep in. Later, however, when I saw the little towns back East, the pleasant hills, the old homes in the valleys, and the red brick house on the elm-shaded street in Portland, then I knew what Slocum meant.
>
> Whatever was there in Chicago in 1877 to live for except Success?

That is Mr. Herrick's indictment of Chicago—or rather, that is part of it—that it makes people desire Success. The other part of his indictment is that when they occasionally do not desire Success, when they desire something finer and greater, then Chicago crushes them to death. In *The Web of Life* he tells the story of a rebel against the convention of "hustling"—a doctor who objects to working up a fashionable practice, and all that sort of thing. What happens to him is that he is beaten down in the mud, mashed in misery until he is ready to crawl back and surrender. One remembers the picture of the desolate region on the south side, amid the ruins of the World's Fair, where he and a woman, an unsuccessful rebel like himself, walk and talk, with the consciousness of their defeat pressing upon their minds, and some presentiment of the impending final tragedy subduing their mood to consonance with the wreck and ruin of the Dream City that lies about them—while to the south the flare from the blast furnaces of the steel works, lurid and scornful sign of the heedless triumph of industry, lights up the evening sky.

Most of Mr. Herrick's novels, in fact, including *The Common Lot, The Healer,* and even his latest serious novel, *One Woman's Life,* deal with the tragedy of the defeated idealist. Incidentally, he holds woman, her education, her ideals and her conception of love and marriage, pretty much to blame for the downfall of the idealist; but that, for our present purposes, is neither here nor there. The point is that Mr. Herrick believes that Chicago warps and degrades the finest instincts of her people—and he hates Chicago for it. And accordingly in writing stories of Chicago life he is concerned not so much with the objective character of that life as with the inward process in which natural and beautiful aspirations are corroded and destroyed. The Chicago with which he deals is a pervasive influence—a condition and not a place.

One looks almost in vain in his novels for pictures of Chicago. He never gives a picture for its own sake, as one enchanted with a suddenly beautiful or impressive aspect of a familiar spot, the miraculous strangeness of the known. Nor in general do the places in which his characters are more or less vaguely placed, the special environment in which his action takes place, have any real significance to him. Mr. Herrick cannot be said to have any sense of place. And this is curiously true of most of the Chicago novelists.

They do not stake off a part of Chicago, as Frank Norris in *McTeague* staked off a part of San Francisco, and stay within its limits, content with its materials, finding infinite riches in a little room. It is not that the opportunity does not exist. Halsted Street is sufficient unto itself, and so is Hyde Park, where the University of Chicago is situated. The Wilson Avenue district ought to content any one who has the novelist's sense of place, the sense which stimulates him as the limitations of the sonnet stimulate a poet. A dozen streets have their own specific character, their own peculiar savour, their own definite kind of life. But Chicago writers have been obsessed with Chicago. It has appealed to them as a problem rather than as a vast and splendid collection of fictional materials. And so they have not written about any place in particular, they have written about Chicago in general. During the next generation we may expect the novels laid in Chicago to take Chicago more for granted, and to settle down to the business of conveying whatever aspect of its life has excited the novelist to the writing-point. When there cease to be novels "about" Chicago, then Chicago will really have its novels.

III

Henry B. Fuller, who is the author of two Chicago novels, is less of a sociologist and more of an observer than Mr. Herrick. He is a satirist, but in a very quiet way. *The Cliff Dwellers* was something of an attempt to envisage the life of the city as such, but his other story, *With the Procession,* had a less ambitious theme, and is more penetrating. Like Frank Norris's novel, it deals with the Chicago of the nineties, but with a difference. He is always conscious, in his account of the belated struggle of an old family to keep up with the procession, of the futility of the whole proceeding. Not that he lashes them savagely for their ambition, as Mr. Herrick would have done. He never loses his sympathy for the Marshalls—in their decision to move out of their "sedate, decorous old homestead" on Michigan Avenue—soon to be swept out of existence by the tides of business—to a more promising place three miles south, and in all the manuvres by which Jane, groomed out of her ungainliness, is finally pushed into "society." It is not a case of the vulgarity of the newly rich; it is the pathetic effort of a family which has fallen behind the times to catch up again. But Mr. Fuller keeps in mind the figure of old Dave Marshall, stooped over his desk in his tea and coffee supply house, straining his worn-out nerves in the effort to finance all this achievement. When it is accom-

plished he collapses, and at his funeral for the first time his family have time to think of him and his part in the whole affair.

But Mr. Fuller does not over-emphasise this struggle for social recognition, nor attribute to it a wholly unworthy motive. To him it is merely a part of the whole tragi-comedy which went on in Chicago in the nineties, when Chicago undertook to prove herself a great city. Not content with bluff, Chicago determined to make her bluff good. What does a great city need? Tell us and we'll get it! That was the spirit in which Chicago rose to such an undertaking as the founding of the Theodore Thomas orchestra. One remembers hearing old-timers tell of the way Chicago went to the first concerts, not understanding for the most part nor caring, but determined to do their duty by Chicago; and in that heroic endeavour stifling their yawns and striving desperately to keep awake—not by any means successfully, as witness the whole rows and tiers of sleepers in the middle of a symphony, waking up at the end to applaud vigorously, as their duty bade them.

From the point of view of a sophisticated person, Chicago was hopeless. Truesdale Marshall, son of old Dave Marshall, home from four years at the Beaux Arts and elsewhere, views the town with quiet despair. "The great town in fact sprawled and coiled about him like a hideous monster—piteous, floundering monster, too. It almost called for tears. Nowhere a more tireless activity, nowhere a more profuse expenditure, nowhere a more determined striving after the ornate, nowhere a more undaunted endeavour toward the monumental expression of success, yet nowhere a result more pitifully grotesque, gruesome, appalling. 'So little taste,' sighed Truesdale, 'so little training, so little education, so total an absence of any collective sense of the fit and proper.'"

Truesdale finds no promenade—except the meagre stretch of Michigan Avenue; while as for the café, "that crowning gem in the coronet of civilisation," the name was everywhere, the thing nowhere. Truesdale sums it up, from his continental point of view: "No journals, no demi-tasse, no clientele, no leisure. No, nor any excursions; nor any general market; nor any lottery, nor even any morgue. And five francs for a cab."

But Chicago was not hopeless, for Chicago was willing to learn. Chicago went to school desperately to find out what was good and what was bad in music, art, architecture and social intercourse. When Jane makes her first call on a stately society woman, she learns that her hostess belongs to three or four classes. She is "studying and learning right along."

"What do you suppose happened to me last winter?" the older woman asks. "I had the greatest setback of my life. I asked to join the Amateur Musical Club. They wouldn't let me in. Well, I played before their committee, and then the secretary wrote me a note. It was a nice enough note, of course, but I knew what it meant. I see now well enough that my fingers were stiffer than I realised, and that my Twinkling Sprays and Fluttering Zephyrs were not quite up to date. They wanted Grieg and Lassen and Chopin. Very well, I said, just wait. Now, I never knuckle under. I never give up. So I sent right out for a teacher. I practised scales an hour a day for weeks and months. I tackled Grieg and Lassen and Chopin—yes, and Tschaikowsky, too. I'm going to play for that committee next month. Let me see if they dare to vote me out again."

Behold in her the Chicago of the nineties. "Just you wait!" Chicago would have an orchestra—and she did. She would have pictures, and books, and beautiful buildings. Well, it is not an ignoble striving that Mr. Fuller has depicted. She would have a real "society," too, with footmen and butlers—as the astonished Jane said, on her first sight of one of them, "only eighty years from the massacre and hardly eight hundred feet from the Monument." This monument, it should perhaps be explained, is a bronze group which appears to represent a friendly Indian chief rescuing by moral suasion—he is certainly not using any effective kind of force,—a white woman from the tomahawk of a redskin, and is supposed to commemorate the Fort Dearborn Massacre; and may serve to remind us, in case we feel uncharitable toward Chicago's still existing cultural defects, that a hundred years ago Chicago did not exist.

One writer who is always definite about places is Theodore Dreiser, whose novel, *Sister Carrie,* is in part laid in Chicago. There is no difficulty about finding the place where Carrie lived with Drouet, nor the little theatre, only a few blocks away, where she made her first appearance on the stage. To one who is interested in "placing" the scenes of his favourite novels, this trait of Mr. Dreiser's comes as an enormous relief, after the vagueness of certain other writers. Mr. Dreiser is as alive as anybody to the spiritual drama, but he never forgets that the external conditions are a part of that spiritual drama. One stands on Ogden Avenue looking up at that grey stone-faced house fronting on Union Park, or a little farther east at Madison and Throop Streets, at the Waverley Theatre, now turned into a livery stable—and the life of Sister Carrie, that life with its curious twists and turns and the gradually revealed hardness of the girl's soul by which she copes with it, become vivid realities.

The Bookman (essay date 1924)

SOURCE: "The Literary Spotlight, XXVII: Henry Blake Fuller," in *The Bookman,* Vol. LVIII, No. 6, February, 1924, pp. 645-49.

[*In the following essay, the anonymous critic surveys the reasons for Fuller's virtual obscurity amongst the American reading public.*]

In a brilliant sentence wherein he gives us the character and temperament of the hero of his *Chevalier of Pensieri-*

Vani Henry Blake Fuller also thus partly describes himself: "He was sufficient unto himself, exempt from the burdens of wealth, the chafings of domestic relations, the chains of affairs, the martyrdom of great ambition and the dwarfing provincialism that comes from a settled home."

So sufficient is he unto himself that it is only with the greatest difficulty that one can unearth anything about him. Those who have known him for a great number of years as intimately as Mr. Fuller can be known, can tell you very little except that he is a charming gentleman. He is exempt from the burdens of wealth, though he has an income from some property in Chicago which suffices amply for his needs. Far from being chafed by domestic relations, he hasn't even a permanent residence. His address is set down in "Who's Who" simply as "Chicago". He is constantly changing his lodgings, whose location he keeps not only from acquaintances he would avoid but from his closest associates. He receives his mail ordinarily at the office of *Poetry: A Magazine of Verse* That he does not suffer the martyrdom of great ambition is evidenced by the dilettante character of his whole career. He spent a great part of his youth abroad and seems rather to have yearned wistfully for Italy all his life. That he is utterly lacking in the provincialism that comes from a settled home is perhaps one reason why his excellent novels shoot over the hearts and heads of the public: he is in life but not of it, and that aloofness of the author which gives so great an air of artistic detachment to his work is, in the last analysis, the elusiveness of personality in a man whose zest is very tepid.

It is all very well to declaim bitterly against the general reader's neglect of an artist, but it is an eminently sensible procedure now and then to take pains to discover to what extent the artist himself is responsible for this neglect. Mr. Fuller's first great literary master, Stendhal, is hard put to it even at this late day to muster that handful of appreciative readers who, he said, would not only understand his work but would cherish it as being unique. Irony and satire, especially if they are refined over subtly, have never a general appeal; and the irony and satire of Mr. Fuller's novels are not ensanguined by any passion whatever. Stendhal, literary caviar as he is, had animated and driving emotions: he worshiped Napoleon, and his Julien Sorel is the first great avatar of the Nietzschean superman. Mr. Fuller has, apparently, not even any inclinations, to say nothing of worship, concerning any person or thing. There is no palpable idea in his work; there is only a pervading and gentlemanly diffidence. And diffidence is the last thing in the world to excite the general reader. What it all comes down to, I am afraid, is that Mr. Fuller is deficient in vitality, that vitality which makes pages glow with human warmth and animates the reader with sympathy or distaste. Critics will never quarrel over Mr. Fuller's merits; they will either acknowledge them without passion or remain indifferent to them. And the public, I suspect, will continue to exist in happy ignorance of the dozen books with which he has honored American literature.

Within the last year I have observed a phenomenon which gives credence to my impression that Mr. Fuller's shyness and self isolation is that of a disappointed man. He has begun of a sudden to appear as a prolific reviewer; his analyses and estimates of books appear simultaneously in a half dozen publications; at sixty four years of age he seems to have decided belatedly to impress his name, if only by repetition, upon the minds of American readers. Throughout his career as a writer he has been an occasional contributor of reviews and papers to the literary magazines; but these appearances were so few and far between that the cumulative effect was never great enough to keep an audience aware of his existence. Every once in a while he would be referred to by some critic as the "late H. B. Fuller": and his achievements were somehow thought of as belonging to the last century, even though his last novel, *Bertram Cope's Year,* was published as late as 1919.

I believe that if Mr. Fuller had had his present urge to be useful in the literary scene when he was a younger man he would not only have been much better known as a writer but would have endowed his novels with just that animation which they lack. He had no need ever to struggle for a living; he prepared himself for a profession only in a dilettante way by studying music and architecture and wrote his first novel without any bread and butter urgency. He has never held any job except that as an honorary advisory editor of *Poetry: A Magazine of Verse.* In this capacity, Harriet Monroe tells me, he is faithful, punctual, and efficient: he is at his desk several mornings out of a week, reading poetry in manuscript, dictating letters of rejection, discussing with the other editors the verse which is to be used in the forthcoming issue of the magazine. But this again is a sort of make believe employment; there is no suggestion of professionalism in his editing, his journalism, his criticism, or, indeed, in his fiction making. He has had, in fine, no real work to do in his life. Possessed, like his Chevalier, of a temperament opposed to all restrictions upon his freedom, scouting the obligations imposed by great ambition, domestic life, augmented wealth, and a permanent home, he practically cut himself free from life altogether. He has not even had his Chevalier's flair for adventurous activity. His career in the flesh no less than in fiction seems to be characterized entirely by an austerely passionless curiosity.

In person Mr. Fuller is a furtive little fellow with a neatly trimmed white beard and white hair; his skin is smooth and white; his voice is soft and hesitant; his eyes gleam with amused inquisitiveness; and he is always perfectly shod and tailored. He is neat, gracious, charming, excessively quiet. At any gathering, at tea or dinner, he never takes part in general discussion; at best, if he says anything, it is to one or two people whom he has withdrawn or who have withdrawn him into a corner. He chuckles, rather one suspects from nervousness and shyness than from actual mirth; he chuckles a great deal when there is nothing particularly to chuckle about. In any discussion he is much more concerned with drawing out the other fellow than with expressing any opinion himself. When he does

express an opinion orally he circumscribes it with reservations and puts it forth, as it were, tentatively, as though ready to withdraw it on second thought.

He is deeply interested in young people, and for a bachelor and recluse he has an extraordinary habit of keeping in touch with the children and grandchildren of his friends. If there is a boy or girl in the family of his circle of acquaintance who is being graduated at high school or college, Mr. Fuller somehow learns of it and, on graduation night, is always to be found in the first row, beaming in a sort of proprietary or parental pride. He follows the activities of the literary youngsters with a sympathy and understanding which is unusual among men past middle age. He has, so far as I know, never uttered a deprecatory, admonitory, or shocked word against the younger generation. So alive is he to what is being done by the younger men that not long ago he wrote a highly appreciative article pointing out the peculiar merits of a dozen or so of the most eccentric and revolutionary of the young modern poets.

II

Mr. Fuller's first novel, *The Chevalier of Pensieri-Vani,* was written as long ago as 1886. It did not find a publisher until 1890, when it came out anonymously. When the second edition of the book was issued he attached his name to it. A year later appeared his *Chatelaine of La Trinité,* which, like the first novel, was a romantic comedy, with a touch of the gentlest raillery, the scene laid in Italy. In his next two novels, *The Cliff Dwellers* (1893) and *With the Procession* (1895), he took up the realistic manner and applied it to stories of contemporary life in Chicago. In these books no less than in his earlier ones, however, a tincture of Stendhalian irony, heightened perhaps by Mr. Fuller's instinctive repugnance for the crudeness and garishness of the Chicago of those days, gave his books, if not a bite, at least a nip. In the books he published between 1895 and the advent of the world war— *From the Other Side, The Last Refuge, Under the Skylights,* and *Waldo Trench and Others*—there is the same exquisite design, the same polished style, the same quiet humor and delicate irony which distinguish all his work, and the same absence of any glow that would give his work force and character. Then there was a period of nine years when nothing, except a few articles here and there, appeared under his name. In 1917 he brought out a book of humorous and experimental verse, parodies and adaptations of the manner of the free verse writers. The book, many items of which had already appeared in Bert Leston Taylor's "Line-o-Type" column in the Chicago *Tribune,* was called *Lines Long and Short.* Then in 1918 he wrote a novel in strict conformity to his theory that no novel should exceed 60,000 words in length, wherein he developed two contrasting figures of equal importance to his story, one of them the vital and successful, though crude, man of action and the other an artist in temperament, unassertive, withdrawn from life. In this novel there seems to have dawned upon him the first realization of what I believe to be the failure of his own career—the failure to make a choice between two roads. If he was to stay in Chicago and use the fiction material at hand in such a way as to give it great significance and meaning, it would have been necessary for him to accept Chicago with fewer regrets that it was not Florence or Milan. If he was to expatriate himself it would have been necessary to do it as thoroughly as did Henry James. In *On the Stairs* he showed for the first time his understanding that vitality and driving purpose, however crude, is naturally more admirable than ineffectiveness, however cultured and beautifully mannered.

It may be said that *Bertram Cope's Year,* in so far as it was read and understood at all, shocked Mr. Fuller's friends so painfully that they silenced it into limbo. It is a story, delicately done with the most exquisite taste, of a sublimated irregular affection. It received scant and unintelligent notice from the reviewers and, though it was filled with dynamite scrupulously packed, it fell as harmless as a dud, only to be whispered about here and there by grave people who wondered why Mr. Fuller should choose such a theme. Since then he has written no novels or, if he has written some, he has not published them. Diffidence again and disappointment have conspired to keep his name only a name in our contemporary literature. He has the sensibility and intelligence, the subtlety and delicacy, to produce artistic masterpieces but he lacks temper and gusto—vitality. This is all the more lamentable in that we have in our American literature an abundance of vitality, but not enough of the qualities which Mr. Fuller possesses in a high degree.

Charles C. Baldwin (essay date 1925)

SOURCE: "Henry Blake Fuller," in *The Men Who Make Our Novels,* revised edition, Dodd, Mead and Company, 1925, pp. 190-94.

[*In the following brief essay, Baldwin deems Fuller as "an amateur, a lover and appreciator of the beautiful rather than a craftsman with rolling eye and a passion for creation."*]

Were I the editor of a weekly review looking for the perfect reviewer to take charge of my literary department I should know that my quest was ended once Mr. Fuller had consented to act for me, for he is, in my opinion, as a man of letters, easily among the first of living Americans. He has scholarship and the best of good taste, charm and grace of style, wide reading and instant sympathy. He is at home with Mary Stuart and the Maid of Orleans, with the sages of Concord and Camden and the Lake Country. He realizes that Carlyle does not need to be right to be moving and profound. He would not improve upon Jane Welch or Mrs. Wharton. He is familiar with Marlowe's mighty lines and the terrific tragedies of Kyd. He knows the farces in which Garrick played and the comedies of Molière. He has read Vanburgh and Hebbel, Corneille, Goldoni, Eu-

gene Field, D'Annunzio and Mathilde Serao. He can quote from Lessing, Diderot, Strachey, Menander, Firdusi and Franklin. I read him recently on the loves of Sarah Bernhardt and he was all attention. He would be as considerate of the platonism of Dante or the grave passion of Abelard, the lechery of Villon and the hopeless adoration of Keats. And, to top it all, he is a gentleman.

He is a gentleman! Those words proclaim at once his weakness and his strength. Yet they mean more than any casual reading done while running would lead the unobservant to believe; for your writer is by ordinary a bounder. Your writer takes, he says, all life for his province—or, at any rate, so much of it as he can see and understand; and it still remains true, as it was when Wilde wrote his *De Profundis,* that of two men in prison one will look out upon the stars and the other on the filthy pavements of the prison yard.

II

A generation ago Mr. Fuller wrote his *Chevalier of Pensieri-Vani* and in his first sentence he told us how the Chevalier halted his traveling-coach on the brow of the Ciminian Forest to look down upon the wide-spread Campagna di Roma. The Chevalier was a dilettante cut to the measure of Mr. Fuller's mild æstheticism and he dabbled in archæology and the lesser improprieties of minor poets. He would naturally make a sentimental journey through Italy. But his journey was bound to end, in a lodging above the Arno, in a fit of despondency. It had meant nothing, with his doubtful Madonna and his all too genuine Contessa. He was forced, as Mr. Fuller has at times been forced, to write himself down a failure.

Twenty-seven years went by and Mr. Fuller published *On The Stairs*; and there, in a sentence, he explained that failure. It is impossible, you see, to be an artist and give yourself out; to be a gentleman and hold yourself in; you end by being nothing.

III

Mr. Fuller is, in Rossetti's use of the word, an amateur, a lover and appreciator of the beautiful rather than a craftsman with rolling eye and a passion for creation. There have been long periods when he has written nothing and published nothing, 1901-1908, 1908-1917; and in those periods, so short is memory, he seems to have completely disappeared and to have been more or less forgotten, his name misspelled—as in William Archer's *The American Language,* 1899, where he is referred to as Henry Y. Puller. Only Mencken and Huneker were loyal—or Mr. Hamlin Garland in whose *Son of the Middle Border* he appears again and again, and always vividly, suggestive and stimulating.

IV

He was born in Chicago, January 9th, 1857. His family had been well established in the city for two generations—

his grandfather, Henry Fuller, being one of the first to settle around Fort Dearborn. On both sides of the house he is English; his father's people landing in New England soon after the Mayflower; and his mother's immediately after the War of 1812.

He started life intending to become a composer; and since he had some notion about the freedom of the arts and both his father and his grandfather were merchants, wealthy and well-respected, he decided that first he must make himself independent. So he took a job as bookkeeper, saving his money and finally leaving home for a two years' sojourn in Italy. There the idea of the *Chevalier of Pensieri-Vani* was born; there the book was written at odd moments, stuffed away in a trunk, a jumble of notes, to be rescued and copied and started on a dreary round of the publishers' offices, to be invariably returned unwanted, and finally to be brought out at the author's expense, to win some praise, enjoy a short success, and go the way of forgetfulness.

Then followed *The Chatelaine of La Trinité* wherein Mr. Fuller joins his realist-romancer Fin de Siècle, in a search for the soul enshrined in woman's body.

A little later he came under the influence of William Dean Howells and began to discover Chicago and to write about Chicago and, for the first time, to produce real flesh and blood women in Camelia McDodd and Cecelia Ingalls of *The Cliff-Dwellers.*

Followed stories of Chicago art-life, *Under the Skylights,* and of Americans traveling in Europe, *From the Other Side.*

V

"As may be gathered," he says, "I am as much concerned with form and technique as with any of the other elements involved in fiction; all because these two features seem to be increasingly disregarded by the ordinary reader. I have been helping my friend, Miss Harriet Monroe, of *Poetry,* as one of her advisory committee; and during the earlier days I helped her on proofs and looked after some of the routine of her printing. The atmosphere of free verse prompted me to try some free verse myself, as applied to the short story; hence *Lines Long and Short,* 1917. Then the vogue of the long and amorphous novel led me to revive my novel-writing (after a lapse of some years) in a briefer, compacter form; hence *On the Stairs,* 1918, together with my discussions of the matter in *The Dial.*"

"I was in Europe in 1879-80, in '83, '92, '94 and '97. These trips supplemented some schooling in Chicago and in a Wisconsin Academy. During these later years I have had to keep in America and almost altogether in Chicago, where practical concerns have often been unfavorable to literary production. This circumscribed locus—together with changes naturally brought by time itself—will account, I suppose, for certain alterations in field and in themes."

Victor Schultz (essay date 1929)

SOURCE: "Henry Blake Fuller: Civilized Chicagoan," in *The Bookman,* Vol. LXX, No. 1, September, 1929, pp. 34-8.

[*In the following essay, Schultz discusses the defining characteristics of Fuller's novels.*]

There was in Chicago until this year an old man, born there in 1857, who was hailed by Huneker as his master, who was described by another as among the first of living American men of letters, who wrote one recognized masterpiece and influenced a whole school of modern writers. And yet when he died at the end of July his books were out of print, they are to be found only on the older shelves of the public libraries, and few people know anything about him or them. How does this happen, in a country where advertising and publicity have made all things of merit known to our people everywhere?

It is true Henry Blake Fuller has not been altogether unrecognized. In every group there is likely to be one who knows his books and who speaks enthusiastically of him. James Gibbons Huneker both spoke and wrote. In *Unicorns* he said, "Our other felicitous example of cosmopolitanism is Henry Blake Fuller". The critic valued Fuller's praise more than that of others. And Carl Van Vechten has published an essay in which he says that the Chicagoan combines "the fortunate moment and the felicitous hand". Note the repetition of the word "felicitous"; it describes the man's style better than any other. Agnes Repplier, reviewing his book, spoke of his "faculty for delicate and sympathetic delineation". Professor Norton showed the volume to Lowell, who praised it. Howells, discussing one of the women of a Fuller novel in his *Heroines of Fiction,* declared that "among western novelists we must go to the pages of Henry Blake Fuller, apparently more sensitive to eastern influences or the western advances of feminization, for a heroine of fit proportions".

Mr. Fuller wrote two kinds of books, Italian tales and novels of modern Chicago. He was born of a family that settled on the shores of Lake Michigan shortly after an Indian massacre had failed to wipe out an indomitable village. He lived his life there, except for a few years of his youth spent in Europe. Italy was the chief attraction, and there he studied music and architecture. It is to these, perhaps, that we can attribute the sense of form shown in his books, and it is not altogether misleading to recall that Hardy was also trained as an architect. Fuller returned to Chicago, and turned to writing of the turbulent commercial life of the city. It was fruitful material. Perhaps his idea of it is shown in a few words he wrote two or three years ago on the Bromfield saga, in The Bookman: "The modern developments of industrial Ohio are, as compared with related manifestations in Chicago, but as moonlight to sunlight, and as hard cider to corrosive sublimate. Yet somehow one contrives to extract needed good from necessary evil. This evil is not so much local as modern."

The influence of his Chicago novels is to be seen in many of those which deal with our modern business world. (Theodore Dreiser, in fact, has said that they started him on his career. It is a pity that Mr. Dreiser did not also follow Mr. Fuller in the matter of style, but perhaps it is too much to ask for both power and form in one man, and thank heaven when he appears.) These books about his home city were written with the advantage of foreign travel, and those about Italy have a mildly western viewpoint. But in treating Chicago Mr. Fuller did not make comparisons between it and European cities, as a cruder artist would have tried to do. However well done, these would have been entirely outside the Fuller method. He avoided entirely anything so obvious, and even suggested contempt for those of his characters who condemn Chicago because it is not like eastern American cities. He allowed Chicago to make its own criticism of itself. And in his delightful sketches of Italy he brought in the American point of view very deftly by means of an American traveller, Mr. George W. Occident, who is not at all uncomfortably out of place among the restful Europeans.

As a matter of fact, the manner of Mr. Fuller's two kinds of books does not change except as their subjects differ. There is the same quiet irony and mild humor in each. Mr. Van Vechten has summed up the style well enough: "His contribution to American fiction is a certain calm, a repose of manner, a decorative irony, exquisite in its not too completely hidden implications, a humor which is informed with abundant subtlety, a study of human nature abroad and at home as searching as it is careful, and above all, a delicate, abiding charm".

His first book, *The Chevalier of Pensieri-Vani,* will be liked best by the average reader, and it is the one praised most by the critics who know anything about him. Agnes Repplier, at the time of its publication, described it as a series of detached episodes, without particular order, "with the keynote a beautiful, cultivated, polished, unmarred, well-spent inactivity". Unforgettable is the picture of the Cavaliere sitting at his window, looking out upon an empty plain, telling his friend the Prorege that what had gone on was quite as interesting as what was going on, and that nothing was more gratifying, from his point of view, than the very absence of change—since any change would be a change for the worse. That is typical of the charm of the book. Huneker declared that not even Fuller could repeat this excursion into Arcadia. Perhaps he came as near it as anyone in the next, *The Châtelaine of La Trinité,* similar in method and style. It is possibly the best description of these volumes to say that Thornton Wilder shows their influence on every page, particularly in *The Cabala.* It is like Fuller's world to come to know the master by avid reading of the pupil.

A later book *The Last Refuge,* was a favorite of its author and praised by Van Vechten as his best work: "a forerunner of *South Wind* and quite comparable to that book in its degree of glamour. It is the story of a pilgrimage to the City of Happiness, which the author locates in Sicily, land of other idyls. It is a fable of the pursuit of different desires, written by a man who came very near achieving an avoidance of all desire. The chief personage of the book, a traveller who has reached forty, looks about for a youth to furnish the eyes through which he will recall the ecstasies caused by these scenes years before. This is a familiar theme in Fuller. He always had, even in the writings of his younger days, a view of life as a moving scene. There are nearly always these two points of view—old and young— and a contrast of their reactions. Nearly always the author appears on the side of age. He seems to say that time takes from us our capacity for certain delights, that mostly we are engaged in trying to hold these, and the wiser man makes use of a sympathetic contact with those about him who are still young. Always his stories have the tone of age, of time, as if it were the chief fact of life."

The Chicago novels began in 1893, evidently under some stimulus from the World's Fair, with *The Cliff Dwellers.* There is pointed comment on pioneer cities in this book: "If you can only be big you don't mind being dirty". It contains an element of melodrama lacking in most of his books, and actually renounced openly in *On the Stairs,* one of his last. An example of his happy sentences is the description of the business man of early Chicago: "He towered and swayed like a rank plant that has sprung rapidly from the earth and has brought the slime and mold on its sheath and stalk". That is pointed summary for the rapid growth of a whole civilization. Similarly he analyzes our modern methods: "And now we are beginning to build on these foundations. We might have put up our buildings first and then put in the underpinning, afterwards. That is a common way, but ours will be found to have its advantages".

The book which followed *The Cliff Dwellers, With the Procession,* was another story of his home town. This was reviewed in The Bookman in 1895 with the regret that "so charming a book should be wholly a work of disintegration, of discontent, and despair". It does not seem that bad now, although none of Mr. Fuller's books preaches any particular happiness. But it is perhaps characteristic of criticism in those days that the same volume of The Bookman contains a review of *Jude the Obscure* which calls it a "novel of lubricity", and which denounces Hardy for "deliberate obscenity" in its writing. *With the Procession* contains one scene which several commentators have praised highly, in which the travelled scion of the Chicago family brushes aside their respectable fears of scandal. It is gentle exposition of the sophisticated view of the world, and an effective comparison of that view with the strait philosophy.

Under the Skylights is a collection of stories of artists' lives, laid in Chicago, which, Mr. Fuller used to say, it was fun to write, and which it is certainly fun to read. One of these characters, Abner Joyce, is as good as he ever did, and character delineation was his best accomplishment. Artists are favorite subjects in nearly all of his books. The spectacle of the artist in America interested Mr. Fuller as the statement of our whole problem as a growing society. Another of his occasional volumes is *The Puppet-Booth,* a series of dramatic sketches, and **"At St. Judas's"**, a psychological study, drew further praise from Huneker. *From the Other Side* and *Waldo Trench and Others* are collections of stories about Europe and Americans travelling abroad. The latter book was another of Mr. Blake's favorites. One of its best stories is that of the final and complete rejection of Americanization by an Italian community and its overlord: edifying reading for those who regard the rest of the world as waiting anxiously in the darkness for our message. *Lines Long and Short* is a volume of poetry—short biographies in free verse. Mr. Fuller was for a long time one of Harriet Monroe's advisers on *Poetry: a Magazine of Verse,* and he was in the thick of the battle for what was once the new movement. He advocated, in one of his magazine articles, the use of free verse for story telling, as the most economical form and the most suitable for modern reading habits.

One of Mr. Fuller's later novels, *On the Stairs,* is worth notice because it throws some light on his own life. It was written to prove his own theory, set forth in the *Dial* in 1918, that a novel should not exceed 60,000 words except under unusual circumstances, and that all description and conversation should be as short as possible. Two figures are developed, one of them a vital and successful, though crude, man of action, and the other an artist in temperament, unassertive and withdrawn from life. An anonymous writer in The Bookman, whose short sketch is reprinted in *The Literary Spotlight,* said "there seems to have dawned upon him the first realization of what I believe to be the failure of his own career—the failure to make a choice between two roads. He shows for the first time his understanding that vitality and driving purpose, however crude, are naturally more admirable than ineffectiveness, however cultured and beautifully mannered". Let us suggest gently that if Mr. Fuller came to any such decision as that vitality is admirable for itself, even when crude, it was because of some one of those strange delusions that swept the country during the war, for his settled conviction and preference, shown by both earlier and later works, are the other way.

Huneker liked *On the Stairs,* which he humorously subtitled "the dilettante as slacker". He called it a sardonic masterpiece, and wrote its author: "Dilettantism is dead . . . Seven devils of war and woe and misery and cruelty, hatred, murder, and rapine, have driven forth the gentle arts from the House of Life". The war is gone now, and the reaction against it is so complete that it must be reassuring to those who love these gentle arts, however much they were disillusioned when it came. But reaction after disillusionment, wisdom without new illusions, these made Mr. Fuller's view of the world.

It will not do to get the notion that Mr. Fuller's taste was mere primness. He proved that it was not in *Bertram Cope's Year,* his latest—and, he declared at the time, his last—novel, which was published obscurely the year after the war. It is a masterful handling of a dangerous theme,

so subtle that if the reader is not wise he can miss it altogether. The anonymous Bookman writer said his friends were shocked by the book, but no one else will be—only profoundly moved.

There was nothing cosmic about Fuller. He was no Melville, no Hawthorne. Huneker liked *The Chevalier of Pensieri-Vani* because, for one thing, the author did not try to prove anything. He cannot easily be classed as a pessimist, although he confessed he himself had tired of the clamorous optimism "which for the past two generations has been the chronic atmosphere of this town". But his notion of the world was surely more completely pessimistic than that of those who write bitterly about it. He said nothing of reform: there was for him no amelioration save the few pleasures of the civilized man who knows where to find beauty and how to enjoy it in quietness. What he said was that the world is a place of certain limited happinesses. These he pointed out, and the rest he put aside as uninteresting, or unprofitable.

Mr. Fuller was allowed to remain comparatively unknown because of what the annoyed critics call diffidence. "His work lacks temper, gusto, vitality", observe those who have these qualities. For the average man there are two possible reactions to a world of Chicagos. One may rail at it, or one may flee from it. But Mr. Fuller remained, and he did not rail. He turned it back upon itself with a mirror of irony, and a mirror, of course, is not an active weapon. He stayed in Chicago, he used to say, because he and his family belonged there. He evidently felt, or he learned in Europe to feel, the necessity of a permanent background. If he did not assume a passionate attitude toward the world, it was because he did not choose to. There are those who denounce the world intemperately: Mr. Fuller declined to have a great deal of interest in it, and this was surely criticism, a most civilized criticism. One feels that this was a deliberate choice; that in all of his writing he was in complete command of his attitude. If he did not write a thing, it was not from careless omission. What he refrained from writing is what made him less than popular. No American can understand any withholding of action. Our muscular civilization makes a fetish of exercise: resources are to be used, stories are to be told to the last detail, even if the author does wallow about for eight hundred pages in the telling of them. But that was not Mr. Fuller's method. In *The Last Refuge* he put this line: "There are times when one may work one's will by simply staying one's hand".

His books did not fail. Any man likes praise, but if it come from a few it is sufficient for the wise. Mr. Fuller had that. The failure, as Oscar Wilde said and as Mr. Fuller would not have said, has been the public's. But surely he had assurances of his influence, and extravagant compliments came from a few of respectable discernment. Considering his temperament, it is safe to hold that this is all he really desired. Since he had no delusions of ordinary success, it cannot be said that he was disappointed. As early as 1899 he wrote in The Bookman, on **"Art in America",** an essay which proved that any welcome for art in this country is exceedingly unlikely. We are too much under the Anglo-Saxon influence, he concluded, and this "feels the irksomeness of form and resents its tyranny, while it is the Latin who asks for clarity, proportion, and clean cut contour". He pointed out that our interest in biography is the result of our occupation of a new, bare, empty country. "We have no traditions, no accumulations of interests from the past; like little Dombey, we have 'taken life unfurnished'. Thus our great interest is the human interest—our interest in each other." And more significant still: "Our climate is against us. Ethnologists call our continent the graveyard of nations; its air has stimulated race after race into their graves. Too much of our work in art is the direct product of mere nervous irritation". He started his career with that conviction. Can it be doubted that he was prepared for neglect?

Besides, he was always aware of his tastes. The confession of the writer in **The Last Refuge** might be his own. "I have succeeded," this man explained. "I have established myself, and have position, recognition, a following. But my position is only about so high; my recognition not completely general; my following, to confess the truth, rather limited. I ask myself why. I have almost found the answer. My participation in life has been, after all, but partial. I have always felt a slight reluctance about committing myself—a touch of dread about letting myself go. I have lived, in fact, by the seashore without ever venturing into the water. Others have gone in before my eyes, and I have recorded, to the best of my endeavor, the exhilaration they appeared to feel, the dangers they appeared to brave. But as soon as the waves have stolen up to my own toes, I have always stepped back upon the dry sands."

"There are other elements beside water," observed the Freiherr. "The sea hath its pearls, true; but no less has the land its diamonds. . . . And there is air. . . . A little whiff of air, rightly directed, may compass all the weal or woe that our poor flesh is capable of enduring."

Mr. Fuller used the air; it is light, but refreshing, invigorating, and for those who love civilized writing—what ought to be called suggestive writing, with varied turns and overtones—it is more meaningful than most of the cyclones that blow over our land.

Harriet Monroe (essay date 1929)

SOURCE: "Comment: Henry B. Fuller," in *Poetry,* Vol. 35, No. 1, October, 1929, pp. 34-41.

[*In the following essay, Monroe offers personal reminiscences of Fuller and an assessment of his literary career.*]

The editor's return in early August, just in time to prepare our seventeenth-birthday number, was saddened by news of the passing of Henry B. Fuller, who died on Sunday, July 28th, in the seventy-third year of his age. Poetry has always been deeply indebted to this distinguished member of its advisory committee, who shrank from any acknowledgment of his loyal service.

Urbanity, gentleness, politeness, humor both searching and kind, sensitiveness, keen wisdom, modesty, scholarship—these and other old-fashioned words rise out of one's inner consciousness with memories of the fine spirit who has slipped out of his quiet place on earth. My memories go back to his youth in our neighborhood, when my sister used to tell of this strange retiring boy who didn't fit in with the rather boisterous group that laughed and danced and rode horseback up and down Michigan Avenue in those days of wide lawns and gardens, of fast trotters and sleigh-rides, of looking back to the Chicago Fire and forward to the Columbian Exposition, both the greatest of their kind. I didn't fit in either, because I was younger than the dominant crowd, and always longing in vain to break through their impenetrable tyrannous barriers and be recognized as an equal among my elders and betters.

In those days I saw Harry Fuller only a few times and afar off. A shy little girl myself, this shy youth was remotely out of my orbit—we never passed near enough to exchange a word. And for years, while my sister and his other contemporaries were getting married and going into business, I heard no more of him.

Then one day—it must have been in 1890—his friend and ours, Mrs. Charles Edward Cheney, brought to my sister a little poorly printed paper covered volume written and put out into the cold world by the man she had known in his sensitive shrinking boyhood. For this book she bespoke our favor, telling us what a lonely lot was its author's, how he was different from everybody around him, and had written his first book in the intervals of clerking in some forlorn and poorly paid pursuit. He had little hope, she said, of anyone's noticing so slight a thing—anyone who counted; it would mean much to him if we liked it—though heaven knows we counted for nothing in the literary world of those days.

I have inherited this book, a precious copy of the first edition of **The Chevalier of Pensieri-Vani**—that cheaply made, badly printed first edition which was afterwards revised and corrected by the author, and put through stricter, more graceful paces by the Century Company. Charles Eliot Norton somehow got hold of a copy and sent other copies to his influential friends; until the down-east literary world rang and re-echoed and resounded with praises, and an obscure young Chicagoan awoke one morning and found himself famous. Incidentally his fame carried his native city on its wings—could a thing so perfect come out of Chicago!—could a work of such exquisite and accomplished art have been begun and carried on and finished among stock-yards and mowing-machines and other unmentionable vulgarities!

I think it was a disappointment to the author, certainly to his business-trained father and family, that this extraordinary *succès d'estime* failed to translate itself into dollars.

The book, in spite of the enthusiasm of the elect, never had a great sale. And it was a disappointment to the elect when, after one more essay in the same vein—the less brilliant *Chatelaine of La Trinité*—Mr. Fuller turned to modern realism.

This right-about-face to a new direction was the first evidence of Henry Fuller's love of literary experiment and variety. He refused to be labeled or to walk in his own footsteps. Catalogued as a romanticist by his first two books—a delicately satirical romanticist if you will—he set out, in his next two, to prove himself a modern realist of as stern a mood as Norris or Dreiser could be capable of; and his satirical weapon, a sheathed rapier in *Pensieri-Vani,* became a bludgeon in *The Cliff-dwellers.* Mr. Robert Morss Lovett, in the *New Republic,* thinks that Fuller was not instinctively a satirist, but that the Spanish War and its Philippine consequences embittered him and dried up his creative energy. But I feel that the satiric quality of his humor was evident from the first, long before the Spanish war, and that political events had a merely superficial effect on his serenity. The truth lay nearer home, in that love and hatred of his native city which was a fundamental motive in a life singularly aloof from passionate experience. His youth had been starved and beaten to the earth by Chicago's preoccupation with "business"; he had escaped to Italy in the flesh for brief travels, and his imagination, taking refuge in "that lovely land" after his return, had consoled itself by writing a masterpiece to celebrate its beauty. Now he turned another facet of his mind upon the city which had tried to make a commercial slave of him, and proceeded to punish its materialistic ideals.

No doubt he overdid the punishment. The very summer when *The Cliff-dwellers* was running serially in *Harper's Weekly,* the Columbian Exposition was providing for the whole country a new and highly provocative inspiration toward beauty. Still, the city deserved his arraignment, as any modern city deserves it for that matter, and *The Cliff-dwellers,* re-read today after thirty-five years, seems unexpectedly enduring—it holds its place as a true and uncompromising revelation of certain dominant forces in modern life. And its people are to me more alive and convincing than those of *With the Procession,* the later Chicago novel in which its author tried to soften his blows. George Ogden and old Erastus Brainard and his family are true to type in action and speech, but Susan Bates is a theoretic lay-figure rather than a real person, representing the author's idea of what a substantial and magnanimous middle-western society leader, who had come up from the ranks, so to speak, would be and do and say. Her shy and retiring creator romanticized her, and she escaped him in the process.

After these two essays in realism, Mr. Fuller tried another form in *The Puppet-Booth,* following the fashion of more or less mystical one-act plays which had been set by Maurice Maeterlinck a few years before. In these and *The Last Refuge,* which followed in 1900, we have a return to the romantic mood—romance delicately veiled in satire, as in *Pensieri-Vani.* The former deals figuratively with certain

lapses and omissions in our claims to civilization, carrying them out usually, with merciless logic, to some catastrophic end. The latter is pure whim and fantasy, the effort of a modern very international group to find Arcadia and disport themselves fitly therein—a delicious and penetrating study of human illusions and disillusions.

Through all the years represented by these and later volumes Henry Fuller never quite took the plunge into life. For him human passion was impossible as a personal experience—he stood outside its arena, looking on at its frantic action with an amused and indulgent—indeed a somewhat wistful—tolerance. The wisdom of a keen observer combined with an ever-present sense of humor to make him instinctively a satirist, a satirist not bitter but sympathetic and benign. Such portrait sketches as those of Chicagoans in *Under the Skylights,* and of travelling Americans in *From the Other Side* and *Waldo Trench and Others,* were slight and unpretentious indulgences of this mood—very true and trenchant outline of familiar types, with just a touch of caricature. And his later brief novels—*On the Stairs* and *Bertram Cope's Year*—were little more.

Through all these years of fitful literary activity I used to see him often and value his friendship, but our closer intercourse began and continued with Poetry. In that hazardous enterprise he showed a kindly interest from my first mention of it, and consented at whatever threatening risk to his reputation as a man of taste and letters, to give it the high authority of his name as a member of its advisory committee. I remember gratefully how eager he was that the new magazine should be progressive and not stodgy, how he welcomed the cooperation of Ezra Pound and other revolutionists, how quickly he recognized original talent as we steered our way through those first experimental months. Also he was an accomplished proof-reader, and if our early issues were not full of *errata* it was because he sat up nights to eliminate them and see the sheets through the press.

I felt that we had a right to claim his sympathetic help because, though not technically a poet by actual practice, he had a poet's imagination and keen feeling for rhythm and beauty of style, and his scholarship and critical acumen in the art were beyond praise. But he used to laugh at himself for intruding in a province where, as he put it, he "didn't belong"; and even when, five years later, he tried his hand at free verse, and published his volume of *Lines Long and Short,* he would have been the last to class these clever satirical portraits as poems. Perhaps however, they belong to the art as much as certain more long-winded satires done two centuries ago in the "heroic couplets" of Queen Anne's time.

From the beginning of the magazine in 1912 even to the last week of his life, Henry Fuller was a frequent and most welcome visitor at the Poetry office. Sometimes he would read manuscripts and write brief incisive comments on the envelopes. Sometimes he would look over our foreign exchanges, for he knew French and Italian and could make a dash at Spanish and German. Again he loved to read the pending proof, taking a hunter's delight in the chase of uninvited words and furtive commas. And always his literary experience and taste were most helpful, and his talk of men and events and books was full of kindly humor and mellow wisdom. He was the only member of Poetry's staff who has companioned its editor through all these seventeen years, and now without him the advisory committee seems sadly incomplete.

During this progress of a friendship both personal and professional I discovered gradually the unselfish sweetness of a spirit that could not, however endowed with a gift for beautiful utterance, reveal its true quality to the world. There was in its deepest recesses an unconquerable reticence—Henry Fuller found it impossible to tell his whole story. He could not give himself away, and therefore it may be that the greatest book of which his genius was capable was never written, the book which would have brought the world to his feet in complete accord.

A few years ago he told us lightly that he would write no more, that no one was less interested in the Quest than he; reviews and other articles in various weeklies would be his only concession to the muse. Yet quite recently she dropped another seed, to the surprise of her reluctant votary; and Alfred A. Knopf will soon put out the result of it in two posthumous books. May this autumnal bloom, springing up before the final frost, give us the perfect flower!

Meantime let us go back to *Pensieri-Vani,* which is already a classic, and renew our delight in its exquisite prose. I wish we had room to quote those long beautifully modulated sentences about the hero's organ-playing in the cathedral of Orvieto. This passage is famous—we shall find it between pages 62 and 68, and it will remind us that its author was also an organ-*improvisatore* in his youth, and that he even composed words and music for an opera which never reached the stage.

Donald M. Murray (essay date 1953)

SOURCE: "Henry B. Fuller: Friend of Howells," in *The South Atlantic Quarterly,* Vol. LII, 1953, pp. 431-44.

[*In the following essay, Murray unfavorably compares Fuller's literary career to that of William Dean Howells.*]

One of the pleasantest ways to absorb American literary history in the barren stretch from 1865 to the turn of the century is to read the letters of William Dean Howells. The man was keenly alive to literary and social forces; as editor and novelist he was himself shaping American writing. His letters have charm, not the cool elegance of James or the rowdy virility of Mark Twain, but a warm, human urbanity and an admirable sanity. Above all, he is inclusive. He knew his Ohio, and he had lived in Italy; he was

accepted by the literati under the Cambridge elms and by the busy penmen of New York City. He wrote constantly and to everyone—poets, presidents, and publishers—and his correspondence, which extends from 1857 to 1920, shows that—with due consideration for the natural toll of age—he grew with his times. His literary taste, in spite of certain well-known limitations, was broad. During his later years Zolaism made him blush, but he was able to appreciate on the one hand Henry James, about whom he was enthusiastic as early as 1866, and Sam Clemens on the other. He spoke often of his admiration for James's close, firm texture. To Mark Twain he once wrote:

> I wish you could understand how unshaken you are, you old tower, in every way; your foundations are struck so deep that you will catch the sunshine of immortal years, and bask in the same light as Cervantes and Shakespeare.

What seems chiefly interesting about Howells is his adjustment to a culturally divided America, an adjustment grounded on his solid faith in the utility of democratic society as a basis for art. Here he stands with Emerson and Whitman as a monument against the belief that the standardized commonplaceness of middle-class society lacks poetry and kills the creative spirit. "Mobocracy," said Frank Lloyd Wright in a recent book, demoralizes the artist. We hear this now, and we have heard it before. In Howells's time it was the belief of his young Chicago friend Henry Blake Fuller.

Fuller as a writer is small beer compared with Howells, James, and Mark Twain. Few people now even read his best books, the realistic Chicago novels *The Cliff-Dwellers* and *With the Procession.* But even though Fuller and Howells are of unequal stature as novelists, and despite the fact that Fuller was twenty years Howells's junior, it illuminates certain basic cultural trends to look at them together for a moment. Their most richly productive periods coincide; by comparing them we can see opposite reactions to these trends. Where one succeeded, the other failed.

The younger man was an unhappy Midwesterner, a thwarted cosmopolite, an aesthete in Porkopolis. Between 1890 and 1929 he wrote eight novels, some romantic and escapist like *The Chevalier of Pensieri-Vani* and *The Chatelaine of La Trinite,* and others, realistic stories of Chicago life such as the two I have called his best. His career touched Howells's at several points; Howells consistently aided and encouraged him and thought well enough of the "plain" heroine of *With the Procession* to include her in his *Heroines of Fiction* gallery. Fuller acknowledged having learned much from Howells's earlier novels, and at first his career paralleled roughly that of the older man. Like Howells he got an initial push forward from Lowell; like Howells he had the Italian experience; and like Howells he wrote his first (and last) novels of distinction when dealing with the American scene.

But Fuller responded differently to this scene. In his earliest book, *The Chevalier of Pensieri-Vani,* he wistfully imagined a society called Arcopia, where "the disturbing and ungracious word *égalité*" had never crossed the sea; he made a character say that "self-government on any but a small scale and in any but a young and simple society was a ludicrous and hideous fallacy." A member of Chicago's Old Settler group, he identified himself with the "Anglo-Saxon" elite of society and came to fear the newcomers that swarmed off the immigrant trains as much as ever Thomas Bailey Aldrich feared those who came through the unguarded gates at Ellis Island. Like David Marshall in his second Chicago novel, he apparently thought that "a man's best use for his own money was to protect himself and his interests from an alien and rabble populace." All his life he yearned for an Italy that was a sort of projection of his own fancy, "not the land that is, but the land that is not, and yet must and shall be and will not be denied." It was a beautiful place far from LaSalle Street, where "cloud and wave, and temple column and olive grove, and bell tower and scarlet sail, all joined together in one suave and alluring chorus: if you are of the kingdom, enter." Whereas Howells found cause for pride "in the loveliness of an apparently homely average," Fuller dreamed of a society where the warmhearted peasantry was sharply divided from the cognoscenti, with no dull in-between class to blur the contrast. Naturally, he could not be happy in Chicago during the Brown Decades. In an early poem he wrote:

> It was not meant that I should reach life's height,
> Or why was I not elsewhere born and reared?

In a late collection of ironic free-verse sketches, he must have been thinking of himself when he wrote, of **"Albert F. McComb"**:

> His continued hankering after the Old World
> Had made him a failure in the New . . .

Though he might have been content as a Bostonian, he was a Westerner when, as Mr. Canby has said, there was a great deal more difference than there is now between East and West. Whereas Howells successfully bridged the gap between the two halves of America, Fuller perished artistically because he was unable to do so.

Concerning these two halves, it is possible to simplify and say that by the nineties there were the beginnings of a Western "school" which showed virility and originality; there was in the East a long-established and still dominant group which tended toward academicism and imitation of past glories. Symbolically, we may use a picture of the young Mark Twain, busy making a book out of his Mississippi River experience, contrasted with a view of the aging Lowell, gazing out of his study windows toward Europe. Howells stands between, the admirer of Lowell but the first promoter of Mark Twain's Mississippi book. Whatever the truth in this simplification, it is certain that an interest in what James called "the soul aboundingly uncivilized" grew out of folklore and local color stories into a critical realism mainly Western. There was Edgar Watson Howe's *Story of a Country Town* in 1883, Joseph Kirk-

land's *Zury* in 1887, Hamlin Garland's *Main-Travelled Roads* in 1891, and Frank Norris's and Theodore Dreiser's work by 1900. Muckraking appeared in the next decade, Anderson's and Farrell's fiction in the twenties. Principally in the East, on the other hand, there was for a long time the heavy weight of traditionalism, which extended its dead hand over all of writing America. Emerson's "American Scholar" address of 1837 went unheeded. The prestige of Lowell, who lived till 1891, dazzled younger writers, Howells and Fuller included; Charles Eliot Norton pontificated from his study on matters of taste; standards of New England's Golden Day lasted on through the influential literary periodicals and through critics like Edmund Clarence Stedman. The giants of fiction had disappeared; poetry was dominated by genteelists, who hung "upon the wheel of time's advancement." They wrote of Bedouins and houris and wanderlovers and deplored Whitman. Romanticism seemed to side with traditionalism against a struggling school of native realism.

When in 1902 Howells wrote to Fuller for the names of the "Chicago group" of authors and was given the list, he exclaimed, "Not a group, but an army!" But, strong as it was, this army felt all along the disdain of the East. The idea of "choriambics from Chicago" made Stedman laugh when Harriet Monroe as a neophyte visited the great man in New York. "Poetry in Porkopolis" a Philadelphia paper entitled an editorial on her magazine, when she launched it in 1912. The East expected Chicago's Columbian Exposition to be a cattle show, and even the fair's own Committee on Ceremonies was hard to persuade that Miss Monroe should do the Exposition Ode. One of that body, James W. Ellsworth, wanted to substitute for the Chicago poetess the aging Whittier of Massachusetts.

The Chicago Uplift Movement itself had its conservatives and its radicals. There was the genteel element, which, imitating the Cambridge cognoscenti, set itself up as arbiter of taste and decorum; Fuller was consistently a member of this group. There were also rebellious spirits, among whom the young Garland was the most articulate. He denied the Easterners' right to supremacy, insisted that Boston and New York were too near London and Paris to be genuinely American, and cried out for "veritism"—truth to locality as well as truth to life. The Garland program more than the Fuller genteelism became generally identified with the area and led to the work of Norris, Dreiser, and Sandburg. When he declared that the new literature of America must be essentially democratic in spirit, Garland was in line with the theory and practice of Howells and opposed to the main tendency exhibited in the work of Fuller.

Fuller came to literary maturity in the midst of these conflicting currents and was a friend of both Garland and Howells. But though he contributed two novels to the new school of fiction and raised his polite voice occasionally in conservative judgment on Chicago's burgeoning culture, he was not actually a standard-bearer. He made his position known, but eschewed squabbles. The reciprocal relationship between artist and environment is a puzzle not to be solved here, but it seems clear that, compared to Howells and Garland, Fuller was more acted upon than acting; the cultural waves tumbled him about, often leaving him stranded on his little island. Though Dreiser called him "the father of American realism" and though his first Chicago novels have linked him with "the Chicago school of fiction" in the genealogical line of Dreiser and Farrell, Fuller was essentially something quite different. The terms "escapist," "traditionalist," "romanticist" come as near as labels can to pigeonholing him. "Can't you see it your duty to write, hereafter, my novels for me?" Howells generously complimented him at the close of a letter in 1909. But Fuller, I suspect, would rather have written Lowell's books or have delivered Norton's lectures.

The Fullers, like the Marshall Fields, had established themselves in Chicago before the great fire of 1871; the novelist's grandfather (cousin to Margaret Fuller) had prospered in banking and in the building of street railways. By Henry Blake's time, however, the family was not among the wealthy. Young Fuller went to the city schools and had a happy year at Allison Classical Academy in Oconomowoc, but he did not go to college. Instead, he educated himself strenuously and continuously, filling his notebooks with eager jottings on Ruskin, Spanish phrases, and the chronology of French literature, while he earned wages at Ovington's or the Home National Bank. When at twenty-two he first went to Europe, he went as a passionate pilgrim and kept extensive journals of determined sightseeing. *The Chevalier of Pensieri-Vani* is a result of his trip.

This is a plotless, discursive "novel" compounded of the mild adventures of a young Italian connoisseur-nobleman who takes his leisurely way through thirteen chapters of landscapes, cathedrals, tombs, and towns. It is Fuller's travel notes on Italy, some based on experience and some on reading, all fictionized in the full tide of a youthful, uncritical infatuation with an older culture. The characters are not human beings; the geography is not of guidebook usefulness; the art criticism is merely dilute Ruskin; and there is no historicity, since the Cavaliere's Italy is politically and economically nonexistent. The only positive quality in the novel is an air of refinement. I find it dull. Yet dozens of readers have had a good word for it, from the ardent Italianists, Lowell and Norton, who praised it in 1890, through the critics Harriet Monroe and Burton Rascoe up to Van Wyck Brooks. To know of the book and like it is taken as a sort of touchstone of taste, though few critics go further than to say it is urbane and sophisticated. One wonders whether they all read it through. These adjectives apply, indeed, but the thin substance renders stylistic excellencies pointless. Its chief interest is extrinsic: the book is an example of genteel taste rather than creative vigor; in its speculative passages it presents clearly a deep dissatisfaction with mobocracy. Once, coming home from a journey, the Cavaliere looks out of his window and remarks that the most charming thing about his village is that nothing has changed since he last saw it. Fuller, looking out of his own window in a Chicago office building, saw everywhere a noisy flux and the materialistic triumph of the middle class. In his book, therefore, he pictured Arcopia as a static society divided into landowning cognoscenti and peasants; no bourgeoisie. The American Fuller could probably no more have accommodated himself permanently to an actual Arcopia than could the American character in the book. Yet the pictured Arcopia glows splendidly, a sort of ideal, unattainable but infinitely desirable.

Fuller's next book, *The Chatelaine of La Trinite,* was of much the same sort. Then in 1893 came his brilliant excursion into realistic localism, *The Cliff-Dwellers,* a story tracing the interlocked lives and fortunes of the tenants of a large Chicago office building. The first thing that strikes a reader who leaves the *Chatelaine* to enter this new world is that it is inhabited by real people whom Fuller knows living in a city with which he is familiar. In the basement of the Clifton is the Underground National Bank headed by Erastus Brainard (A real one turned up and protested about the coincidental use of the name), a self-made millionaire who is hard, unscrupulous, completely materialistic. He is a forerunner of Herrick's Jackson Powers, Norris's Curtis Jadwin, Dreiser's Frank Cowperwood. Influencing the lives of all the personae is Mrs. Cecilia Ingles, first lady of society, probably suggested by Mrs. Potter Palmer, whom Fuller knew. All the men want to succeed in the manner of Brainard; all the women want to climb to Mrs. Ingles's heights. Into this setting is dropped George Ogden, a New Englander come west to make his fortune. He is an average young man, as Dreiser's Clyde Griffiths was to be. He takes a job in the bank and marries spendthrift Jessie Bradley, whose passion for social climbing ruins him. The novel has a melodramatic ending, which rescues Ogden financially and matrimonially; Fuller was not yet as good a student of Howells and James as he was to become. But on the whole the tale is convincing, the characters being accidentally thrown together in the economically motivated life of a great city. It is a respectable contribution to the realistic writing that was having its birth in America at the time.

With the Procession (1895) is an even better book; it has less melodrama, richer characterization (including the heroine Howells ranked with his favorites), and keener insights into society and business. Its outlines are softer, and it lacks a tendency toward caricature present in the preceding novel. It concerns a family who, like the Fullers, are Old Settlers. The Marshalls cannot keep up with the rapidly changing mores of the city, partly because they refuse to adopt the sharp business practices of the newer entrepreneurs. David Marshall, in fact, adopts an attitude toward social climbing and conspicuous waste resembling that of the first Marshall Field. Newcomers in business and society are represented by the Beldens, a set of scrambling *arrivistes*. The dilettante Cavaliere is here metamorphosed into the recognizably human Truesdale Marshall, a son of David, who has been playing at art study in Paris. Truesdale comes home to make whimsically cutting remarks on the ugly monotony of the metropolitan scene: he finds near Chicago no ruined abbeys to paint.

As Fuller here presents the city it is far from monotonous; it is alive. There is interesting discussion of the new architecture; the architects A. B. and I. K. Pond were Fuller's close friends, and he must have met the great Sullivan. There is a sort of recreation establishment for working girls; Jane Addams's settlement house had been on the scene since 1889. There are the Marshall Field type, the Potter Palmer type, the immigrants. The *Dial* was right in calling the book a document as well as a good story. Howells, who pushed the novel, went so far as to say that no New Yorker had done so much for his city, no Bostonian for Boston. It is a pity that Fuller dropped realism here; with his consciousness of style he might have surpassed Dreiser.

His next book was a collection of playlets in the manner of Maeterlinck and Ibsen; some of them were performed in the Fine Arts Building in the studios of his friend, the dramatic coach Anna Morgan, who received an actual bouquet from Maeterlinck, a figurative one from Shaw. After the plays came a collection of Jamesian international stories. In 1899 Fuller paused in his literary experiments to lambast McKinley imperialism: ***The New Flag*** is a curious show of involvement in a contemporary issue, expressed in bad verse. In 1900 he fled to Italy again, figuratively speaking, with ***The Last Refuge.*** He revived the Freiherr, a personage created for the ***Chevalier*** and never actually very much alive. Now grown old, the Freiherr attempts to recapture the joys of Italian travel in company with a young man, just as Fuller himself was to do in 1924 with a young university student from Urbana. It is a weak and thin book. Howells, writing in "The Easy Chair," generously said as much as can be said in recognition of the "delicate pleasure" provided by this "pensive *capriccio*," but added that if Fuller's next book were to be about Chicago instead of Sicily he would not be sorry.

Thus by 1900 Fuller had come full circle; one wonders whether some single event had altered his course after the realistic phase so bravely started. The biographical facts available do not reveal one. They do, however, give a picture of Fuller during the Uplift, that extraordinarily self-conscious movement in the nineties by which the city of Chicago attempted to raise itself by its bootstraps to aesthetic and moral heights on a level with Boston. The movement is a fascinating phenomenon in itself; it embraced contrasting aims and is difficult to evaluate as a whole. As Mr. Bernard Duffey, of Michigan State College, points out in an unpublished paper, the effort had its highly beneficial effects: it gave Chicago its orchestra, its university, some great libraries, and the Art Institute, all permanent features; happily, the Great White City of the Exposition quickly disappeared. On the other hand, there was something farcical about it as well, namely, the assumption that Culture could be in a few short years captured and enshrined at the foot of Lake Michigan. Eugene Field justifiably drew a garland of sausages "in the similitude of a laurel wreath" for presentation to the giant pork-packing industrial capital now suddenly overorganized into Shelley clubs. Finally, though the individual artistic nodes of the Uplift gave to the artists some status in the community, they were infected with the blight of New England genteelism. The Little Room, an important though informal club for artists and writers, was an exclusive circle, not so much calculated to encourage what was original as to imitate the taste and tone of Brahmin Boston.

This group, Chicago's Saturday Club that met on Fridays, flourished in the decades before and after the turn of the century. It met in various places—for a time in the studio of the artist Ralph Clarkson in the Fine Arts Building—and was mainly a tea-party social affair with a very high *ton*. Though Garland was a member and characteristically a pusher of the organization while he was in Chicago—he also started the Cliff-Dwellers Club, named after Fuller's book—Fuller was its spiritual leader. Anna Morgan in her chatty memoirs tells us of the parties, plays, and conversations enjoyed by the members, of the distinguished guests from the East who gathered around the samovar and peppermint plate. There exists a photograph, probably taken in Clarkson's studio, showing the painter, tall and darkly elegant, standing with Mrs. Clarkson at one end of a carved wooden settee, while at the other end, distant and rather dwarfed by furniture and companions, sits a little man shyly clutching his bowler—Henry Blake Fuller. The outstanding member of the club is dapper, reserved in mien.

In addition to painters and writers, the club included architects like the Pond brothers; sculptors such as Lorado Taft; publishers (Ralph Fletcher Seymour still has an office in the Fine Arts Building); the cartoonist McCutcheon and the *Graustark* McCutcheon; even the head of an art bindery, Mrs. Hobart Chatfield Chatfield-Taylor. They had great larks, giving vaudeville skits in funny costumes or enjoying feasts of reason, as when Fuller spoke on some literary topic. Mostly they drank tea, and, it appears, congratulated themselves on their exclusiveness. Of the talent represented, however, outside of Fuller, Garland, and Harriet Monroe (then just getting a start), there was little above the second-rate. The feeble Bohemian poetry of Wallace Rice, the romantic-traditionalist sculpture of Taft, and the mild books of Hobart Chatfield-Taylor will never rank among the great achievements of American art. The *Contributors' Club Magazine,* privately and expensively printed in 1893-94, contains some of the Little Roomers' work. It is thin and effete. In fact, it is inferior to that produced by the New York circle composed of Stedman's friends, to whom Harriet Monroe paid court in the eighties.

In **"The Downfall of Abner Joyce"** Fuller himself has given an amusing insight into Little Room life. The story is particularly valuable in focusing on the differing characters and aims of the author and Garland, who appear as Adrian Bond and Abner Joyce respectively. Abner is a heavy-handed young writer fresh from the farm and seething with veritism and Henry Georgeism: "sweaty, panting, begrimed, hopeful, indignant, sincere, self-confident." He is vital but not *comme il faut.* Bond, on the other hand, is the "futile spinner of sophistications" who says: "My things so far, I know (none better) *are* slight, flimsy, exotic, factitious." The ironic self-criticism is much to Fuller's credit, but the adjectives do stick—to both Fuller and the Little Room. They were flimsy, and the supercilious view of native, original art in America had now become a fundamental part of Fuller's thinking. In an essay for the *Bookman* in 1899 he had expanded the thesis that art has such a poor chance of growing in the barren soil of this country that we would do better to let it entirely alone for a time and consolidate our gains in politics, finance, and invention.

> The young student of the arts—he grows more numerous daily—fills one with sympathetic dread. For his equipment he has his initial enthusiasm and a certain measure of academic training. But there are no springs in the national life to feed his reservoir, and in a few years he will run dry.

Our inartistic Anglo-Saxon ancestry, our lack of traditions, the spread of "common school education"—all militate against the growth of an indigenous art.

Thus Fuller was both the personification of the more genteel aspects of the Uplift and the prophet of hopelessness for American art. Naturally, then, he was the satirist of the immoderately optimistic promoters of culture, as in **"Dr. Gowdy and the Squash,"** an hilarious farce based on the efforts of Dr. Frank Gunsaulus and others to spread interest in painting to the hinterland. A farm boy does a vulgarly realistic picture of a squash (a native growth, like veritism), and makes the whole effort look ridiculous. The culture boom was, of course, fair game, but back of Fuller's ironies was always a defeatism and an approach to the matter as from Parnassian regions. Compare the more indigenous funmaking by Eugene Field, who wrote for "Sharps and Flats" in 1891 a mock program for the reception of E. C. Stedman in Chicago. The eminent critic was to be met at the station by a wonderful parade, composed of many eager devotees of Culture. Interspersed among police officers, brass bands, and the advertising car of Armour and Co. would be the Robert Browning Clubs in Parmelee busses; the Homer Clubs afoot preceded by a fife-and-drum corps and a Real Greek Philosopher, attired in a tunic; a gilded chariot bearing Charles F. Gunther's Shakespeare autograph; the Fishbladder Brigade; the Blue Island Avenue Shelley Club; and two hundred Chicago poets afoot.

The squib illustrates, as Fuller's stories do not, the subservience of the Uplift to the East. Incidentally, it seems more in line with native American humor, for is not the wild exaggeration, the assumed provincial bedazzlement with culture, like the work of Mark Twain and Artemus Ward? The Innocent Abroad had, in 1869, made just such fun of European art and literature.

Fuller never wrote in this vein, though he continued to produce, experimenting with various forms until his death

in 1929. He possessed always a little court of admirers, mainly from the Little Room, who urged him to repeat the **Chevalier**, just as Howells continually requested another **With the Procession**; but by the twenties he considered himself an "old old-writer" in contrast to, say, the "young young-writer," Thornton Wilder. Certainly the "famous revolt of the Younger Generation," as Stuart Sherman called it, was outside his ken. Dell, Masters, Lindsay, Sandburg, and Anderson were no Little Roomers and were propelled by forces unknown to that group. Although, as Fuller tells us himself, he was once ejected from the Public Library for having a too audible literary discussion with Theodore Dreiser, he had ceased early to swim in the fictional stream Dreiser made famous. When in 1921 Professor Sherman asked him what novel he considered the best of the year, Fuller was emphatic that it was not *Main Street.* In a long article for the *Freeman* he expounded upon Lewis's lack of artistry, insisting that the new novelist was not "significant," as Sherman had contended.

The last year of Fuller's life saw the production of two novels, **Gardens of this World** and **Not on the Screen.** The first is ample evidence that he was still a would-be Cavaliere. *"C'etait un livre selon son coeur"*—he quoted from a biography of Stendhal in the epigraph; it is again travel notation suffused with nostalgia for Italy. It has a verbal glossiness but no substance. **Not on the Screen,** by contrast, shows some interesting pictures of Chicago, but it is pale compared to the earlier Chicago books and is obviously a potboiler. The pattern of Fuller's literary life remains that of a genteel writer dissatisfied with the democratic scene, who was basically an escapist, and a realist only temporarily and tangentially. Perhaps nothing "happened" to him to cause his defection from the realistic school after 1893; temperamentally and intellectually and artistically he was the same all along.

Contrast the literary life of Howells, who made an adjustment to both cultural halves of America, who felt artistically at home in a middle-class society, who, though older by twenty years, kept up astonishingly well with the rapidly changing American procession. He turned East; he worshiped Lowell; he went to Italy. But somehow he did not lose his grip on his Ohio values or apply for admission into the Brahmin tribe. When he went to Europe it was more as the innocent than as the passionate pilgrim: "Our people are manlier and purer," he wrote back to his sister. In his Italian novels, early and late, he showed more interest in manners than intoxication with the older culture. The last part of *The Lady of the Aroostook* reveals Old World marriage custom in a hard light; *A Foregone Conclusion* plays out its comedy in Venetian salons around an American girl and an American consul much like Howells himself. That genuinely sophisticated novel *Indian Summer* has for its core the hearts of real human beings. There is a pretty Italian background, but when Howells does a love scene in the Boboli Gardens the participants come alive. Colville himself, the middle-aged American "hero," is a great creation, perhaps the best Howells ever did, certainly the wittiest. Here is urbanity with some "body," sophisticated talk that is about something. Howells simply saw more of life than Fuller ever did, loved ordinary human beings more, and put down what he saw and understood.

When he was a resident literary man in Cambridge he did not, like Aldrich, become "Boston-plated," though he moved among the Brahmins. He once told James that he could not draw upper-class Boston the way the author of "A New England Winter" could; but his touch was sure, nevertheless, in characterizations like Bromfield Corey of *Silas Lapham*. Especially interesting is the irony in the picture of this ineffectual gentleman, who peeled his oranges in the Neapolitan manner and made *bons mots* at dinner; we are not allowed to forget that an earlier Corey sailed the clipper ships which made the family fortune and that Bromfield is as useless as he is charming.

Living in the citadel of the Coreys, Howells did not lose touch with the rest of changing America. His letters, especially those to his father in Ohio, tell a story of social awareness and sympathy for men completely absent in Fuller. For instance, in 1887 he made a bold effort in the face of strong criticism to secure a fair trial for the Chicago anarchists. Though he called himself at one time a "theoretical socialist," he was neither political propagandist nor, actually, doctrinaire theorist. His attitude was the result of interest and compassion.

In literature, however, he did have a theory, one as consistently and devotedly held as was Fuller's allegiance to the Little Room or Arcopia. He was the champion of realism, a theory and a technique formed of his affection for the commonplace America he knew and from the study of the European realists. A frequently quoted declaration of 1891 explains his position; he is speaking about a kind of literary revolution:

> Nevertheless, I am in hopes that . . . it will occur within the lives of men now overawed by the foolish old superstition that literature and art are anything but the expression of life, and are to be judged by any other test than that of their fidelity to it.

His encouragement of younger talents—especially the realists—is well known. He launched Mark Twain, continually supported James, gave heart to Garland, Norris, Crane. Once, when Fuller miserably credited his unproductiveness to "no great liking for the environment I must depict, and no great zest for life as it is lived," Howells replied with high praise for Fuller's work and—to convey some "zest"—reported a recent breakfast with the ebullient Theodore Roosevelt. It has often been pointed out that Howells could not stomach Zolaism, that he was squeamish over books like Herrick's *Together*. Nevertheless, seen in his time, he appears as a sturdy progressive. Compare him with Fuller.

These two contemporary practitioners in the art of fiction represent conflicting intellectual currents in the Gilded Age. Fuller was a man temperamentally unable to feel at home in a middle-class society, an artist who felt the East-West tension and was unable to withstand it. Howells was an artist who made a successful adjustment to the two area-attitudes and whose faith in democracy as a basis for art never wavered. Not one of the greatest artists America has produced, he was, nevertheless, an original and creative spirit, who built purposefully in the midst of what many found an arid cultural climate.

The East-West dichotomy has disappeared from the American scene, though Chicagoans still proudly display "bigger" monuments to visiting New Yorkers; but the attitude which deprecates our leveled society as a matrix for artistic creation is still with us, an element in a familiar pattern of antidemocratic thought. As the editors of *Harper's* said in a recent number of that magazine, there have always been Europeans (one could add, Americans) who lament the lack,

> in middle-class industrial society, of the dramatic contrasts and rich variety characteristic of societies in which the color and sturdy charm of peasant crafts existed side-by-side with the elaborate, idiosyncratic subtlety and splendor produced for (or by) a privileged few. To them the new middle class inevitably . . . seemed to be all of one gray and monotonous hue, intellectually, morally, and aesthetically.

Fuller's story is one of lament and withdrawal; Howells's is one of faith and constructive participation.

Elwood P. Lawrence (essay date 1954)

SOURCE: "Fuller of Chicago: A Study in Frustration," in *American Quarterly*, Vol. VI, No. 2, Summer, 1954, pp. 137-46.

[*In the following essay, Lawrence explores autobiographical aspects of Fuller's life, in particular his personal and professional frustrations.*]

Henry B. Fuller who died in 1929, is now only a footnote in the history of American writing, but in the 1890's, on the strength of *The Cliff-Dwellers* and *With the Procession,* he was hailed by critics as the rising star of Midwestern realism. The decline of his reputation was even more spectacular than this suggests, for by 1900 he was already being referred to by some critics as "the late Mr. Fuller."[1] A reading of Fuller's writing after 1900 will bear out the justice of this verdict.

An explanation of Fuller's eclipse can be found in the biographical details that have come down to us, in Fuller's own pronouncements on his craft, and most of all in his writing about Chicago. The evidence shows that he was the victim of a severe and chronic case of frustration. He was a charter member of the "lost generation" before that term was invented, but unlike the young writers of the 1920's he was unable to escape to Europe; that is, in mind and spirit. Actually he was able to make seven journeys abroad, but he was always drawn back into the irritations of Chicago life. Caught in an uncongenial environment, he took his revenge by attacking and ridiculing this environment.

There can be no question that for a moment Fuller burned brightly on the literary horizon. Hamlin Garland declared that in *The Cliff-Dwellers* Fuller had "beaten the realists at their own game."[2] Howells found in this novel the style of James and the methods and principles of the art of Zola, with the additional merit that the author "has kept scrupulously to the Anglo-Saxon decencies." No writer had done as much for New York or Boston, Howells thought, as had Fuller for Chicago, yet the work was not narrowly provincial; the characters "are of New York as much as they are of Chicago; perhaps nine-tenths of the whole city life of America can find itself glassed in this unflattering mirror."[3]

In a *Cosmopolitan* review of 1894, H. H. Boyesen cried up *The Cliff-Dwellers* as the "first serious study of the western metropolis," and declared that "to the lover of wholesome realism it is of absorbing interest."[4] Three years later the *Critic* hailed Fuller as

> one of our rising novelists, whose Chicago novels are a complete refutation of the theory . . . that this country cannot furnish inspiration to its writers.

He was again called the literary discoverer of Chicago, and was urged to exploit further this vast field so full of "truly heroic material."[5]

Fuller did not justify these critical expectations, for the reason that frustration by itself is not a lasting creative impulse. Evidence of this frustration runs through the facts that are known of Fuller's life. He was acutely unhappy in Chicago, and once declared to Hamlin Garland: "Why stay in this town if you can get out of it? . . . If I could get away I would go to Italy and never return." He blamed his immolation on "my damned New England conscience."[6] Harriet Monroe ascribed his dissatisfaction to the fact that Chicago "had tried to make a commercial slave of him," and to what she called his "starved" boyhood.[7]

Fuller's failure to find a popular reception for his writing was also advanced as a cause for his distress. He confessed once, "with a chuckle which concealed his chagrin," that the poor sale of his books "amounts to being privately printed."[8] Theodore Dreiser reported that Fuller's career as a novelist was checked because:

> he was most vociferously and outrageously assailed by a puritan or romantic and mentally undernourished band of critics, who had proceeded to shout that his contributions were not only libels on life but worthless as reading matter. In his own Chicago world and circle of friends he had been met with not only personal disapproval, but contumely. Sensitive to, as well as fond of, the society of which he was a part, as he explained to

me, and finding himself facing social as well as literary ostracism, he desisted.[9]

If this be true, Fuller's inability to surmount difficulties no greater than those encountered by Dreiser is further evidence of temperamental weakness.

Evidence of Fuller's unhappiness is borne out by the phrases used to describe him; they consistently point to his temperamental maladjustment. He was "a strange, elusive, homeless being," "he stood outside its human passion's arena," he was "subject to moods of measureless despondency" and showed "at times a bitter distaste for social inter-course," he was "a furtive little fellow," at tea or dinner "he never takes part in any general discussion. . . . He chuckles . . . from nervousness and shyness . . . he chuckles a great deal when there is nothing in particular to chuckle about."

Further evidence of his conflict is revealed in the various idiosyncracies attributed to him. He ate in cheap restaurants and sat in cheap seats at the opera, though he was not poor.[10] In 1907 he refused to assist Garland in the formation of an artists' club, though he became a member;[11] later, when the name was changed to "Cliff Dwellers" in his honor, he resigned.[12] He had no permanent residence: in *Who's Who* he gave his address simply as "Chicago." He changed his lodgings frequently and would not tell his closest friends where he lived; he received his mail at the editorial address of *Poetry*[13] In his personal copy of Anna Morgan's *My Chicago,* the leaves containing an appreciation of his work were pasted together.[14] He often failed to turn up at a gathering to which he had been invited: "Sometimes when bored by our talk, he disappeared for weeks altogether, and no questioning when he reappeared afforded any clue to his whereabouts."[15]

The frustration evident in these biographical details is enforced by Fuller's own remarks about his writings. When Garland applauded the realism of *The Cliff-Dwellers,* Fuller rejoined coolly: "There are a good many ways to skin a cat, and the realistic way, I dare say, is as good as any."[16] This is more than modesty; it is acute embarrassment born of extreme self-consciousness. Why? Probably because realism was to Fuller not creation but a contrivance for revenge. For, as he confessed in a self-conscious, third-person style in a letter to Garland, he was really interested in something else than a realistic portrayal of life in Chicago:

> The only thing H. B. F. really enjoys . . . is "to take pen in hand," to write (strictly and simply)—to string words together. He gets enough of the crudities, vulgarities, and asperities right where he is; he wants to bust forth, and break away and scoot through the blue air of heaven.[17]

Here again is the condition suggested by the biographical details.

The same conclusion can be drawn from the variety of literary forms that Fuller practiced—translation, short story, free verse, criticism, naturalistic fiction—and from the fact that he did not practice any one of these consistently. Harriet Monroe puts her finger on this aspect of Fuller's problem when she writes: "Fuller had to try each new literary mode, never content to live out or write out the whole truth about himself."[18]

Evidence of this conflict in Fuller is substantiated so neatly by his writings as to suggest that he was consciously psychoanalyzing himself. We meet a statement of conflict in his first work, *The Chevalier of Pensieri-Vani.* The hero of this novel (perhaps "morality" would be a closer designation) is George W. Occident, young son of a middle western businessman who

> resolved to flee the general awfulness of Shelby County to see for himself if life were not better worth living than he could make it seem in the region where he had the misfortune to be born.

But he found, as a consequence of his cultural baptism in Italy, that:

> He was between two fires, both of which scorched him, between two stools, neither of which offered him a comfortable seat; between the two horns of a dilemma, each of which seemed more cruelly sharp than the other.[19]

This quotation states Fuller's life-long problem clearly. In George W. Occident we see Fuller, himself the son of a Chicago banker. He was never able to adjust to life in the Middlewest or to escape from it. The mark of the conflict is on all his writings dealing with Chicago and with literature. *The Cliff-Dwellers*[20] and *With the Procession*[21] are themselves products of discontent, and the tone of subsequent Chicago writings and of his critical articles shows first, that the metropolitan scene was a source of irritation to him; second, that any advance of realism beyond the limits imposed by Howells was repugnant to him; and third, that his was a critical, not a creative talent.

Chicago, because it was his home town, cast a spell over Fuller and directly or indirectly was the preoccupation of many of his writings. When he looked at Chicago, what did he see? Not the essentially romantic vision which Carl Sandburg detected through the smoke of its mills and factories. Fuller saw only a mushrooming metropolis dominated by the business and social activities of its commercial class. He had no faith in the moral or intellectual fiber of his class nor of the civilization he thought it was creating, and he spent his creative life painting its ugly features.

The foundation of Fuller's resentment of Chicago is set forth in the two previously mentioned novels, *The Cliff-Dwellers* and *With the Procession.* In the first of these his theme is that Chicago is a

> community where prosperity has drugged patriotism into unconsciousness and where the bare scaffoldings

of materialism felt themselves quite independent of the graces and draperies of culture.[22]

He substantiates this criticism by citing the record of Erastas M. Brainard, president of the Underground National Bank, a boom town financial mushroom. Brainard has been in jail, he is a former Methodist camp exhorter, he is suspected of manipulating city councilors and state legislators. His favorite practice is to repurchase, at less than two-thirds of its value, stock he has originally sold to widowed and unprotected women. He is ruthless to his employees and to his family. He uses the minor peculations of a bank messenger to blackmail the boy's father into the purchase of some worthless property held by the bank. He browbeats his wife, ostracizes a daughter who has married a bigamist, and ruins his son Marcus because the boy would rather paint than figure interest on mortgages. At the end of the novel, Marcus, a sodden misfit, stabs his father with a paper knife and commits suicide. It is evident that to Fuller big business is not a subject for epic treatment, as in Frank Norris' novel of Chicago grain dealings, *The Pit.* At best it is only sordid and mock heroic.

Fuller refuses to find any redeeming quality in metropolitan life. George Ogden, an employee of Brainard, and the son of honest, hard-working New Englanders, is morally flabby. By a combination of circumstances which include a brother-in-law who causes Ogden's inheritance to sink out of sight in a swampy subdivision, and a "delicate" wife whose health and social position force him to live beyond his means, he is tempted to embezzle money from Brainard's bank. Only the banker's death saves him from jail.

In the second novel about Chicago, *With the Procession,* Fuller shifts his attack from big business and the men who run it to their socially pretentious wives and daughters. This theme was foreshadowed near the close of *The Cliff-Dwellers,* when George Ogden sees at the theatre a "radiant, magnificent creature, splendid, like all her mates, with a new and eager splendor of long opportunity." Ogden, speaking with Fuller's voice, reflects:

> He knew perfectly well who she was. She was Cecilia Ingles, and his heart was constricted by the sight of her. It is for such a woman that one man builds a skyscraper and that a hundred others are martyred in it.[23]

In other words, Fuller is saying that big business exists to keep the wives of business men in fur coats and diamonds!

The "procession" in *With the Procession* is social, and in the wealthy Sue Bates, Fuller attacks the entire group of social climbers in Chicago. She is newly rich, and her house is a vulgar and ostentatious symbol of her class. A catalog of the establishment includes: a footman in knee breeches, a music room stocked with scores of the German classics and the "usual French and Italian operas" (never played), a library whose standard sets of the classics symbolize solid learning (unfortunately the key to the bookcases has been lost), a grand salon in Louis XV style, and a room to impress "princes, counts, and notables," called the Sala de los Embajadores. It had the misfortune of being baroque rather than Moorish.[24] Backed by such impressive evidence of her importance, Mrs. Bates bears her banner aggressively at the head of the social procession. She cries ". . . keep up with the procession is my motto, and head it if you can."[25] She sets the social standard for the mushrooming commercial society: the Beldens try in vain to eclipse her in grandeur; she unwittingly contributes to David Marshall's troubles by urging his daughter Rosy into the social melee, and by inciting Marshall himself to live up to his income. She even corrupts a young socialist, Brower, by enticing him to attend a charity ball as her guest.

It was on the evidence of these two novels that critics encouraged Fuller to expand his treatment of the Chicago scene, and that Huneker and Dreiser recognized him as a kind of midwife to a new realism. Fuller's subsequent writings fail to warrant the critical hope. What may have attracted Huneker and Dreiser—the crudity of the material and the absence of any of the pleasanter hues of life—is not the result of conscious art, but of irritation and distaste.

Fuller's lack of sympathy with civilization in Chicago extended beyond his dislike for big business. In the two novels already mentioned he makes a passing attack on the state of culture in the middle western metropolis. The chief desire of Marcus Brainard in *The Cliff-Dwellers* was to be an artist; instead he ended as a drunkard and a suicide. Truesdale Marshall in *With the Procession* has traveled in Europe, and is continually sighing for the boulevard society of Paris. It seems to have been Fuller's belief that the materialism rampant in Chicago in the 1890's stifled any desire on the part of its inhabitants for what are sometimes called "the finer things in life."

To declare that art suffers in a society dominated by materialism is consistent with a condemnation of big business. But having scored with two realistic novels, Fuller proceeded to repudiate realism; having demonstrated that big business is bad because it suppresses culture, he heaps ridicule on Chicago's art colony. It was the conflict of George W. Occident all over again.

This further evidence of Fuller's frustration is found in *Under the Skylights.*[26] Two of the three sketches in this work are attacks on "veritism," the title given by Hamlin Garland to the kind of realism he was attempting to create in his short stories. In "The Downfall of Abner Joyce" the central character, Joyce, is Garland himself. What Fuller objects to in Garland's picture of life in the Middlewest is his grim outlook. The poor, says Garland in effect, lead lives of utter privation, on about the animal level.

Fuller ridicules the idea by showing how Abner's view of life is mellowed by popular success and the blandishments of wealth. The distortion of truth in Garland's veritistic portrayal of rural life is exposed when Abner visits an Illinois farm and discovers that the parents of his fiancée

> had their books and magazines, they have a pair of good trotters and a capacious carry-all, with all other like aids to locomotion in reserve; they had a telephone; they had a pianola, with a change of rolls once a month; they had neighbors of their own sort and were indomitable in keeping up neighborly relations.[27]

Fuller carried on the same attack in "Dr. Gowdy and the Squash," the second story in the volume. Here he shows how a starry-eyed young farmer, Jared Stiles, learns from a book of sermons that beauty is truth, sees an exhibition of veritistic art, and decides on a career of painting squashes. Jared is so successful as a realistic painter that his paintings are indistinguishable from the real squashes exhibited alongside for comparison.

The repudiation of realism remained an obsession of Fuller's to the end of his life, but was, however, no resolution of his conflict; it was rather a further development of it. What he condemned in others he was never able to escape himself, returning again and again to the superficialities of the Chicago scene. He criticized D. H. Lawrence and Marcel Proust for their attempts to explore the subconscious, a preoccupation which he regarded as in bad taste.[28] And in writing of Chekov he maintained that "no work can be well conditioned, primarily, on a fragmental and realistic production of actuality."[29]

One of the clearest pieces of evidence of the conflict inherent in Fuller is connected with his denunciation of realism. In 1917 he wrote "The Plea for Shorter Novels,"[30] an attack on the form of the naturalistic novel. Here he claims that 50,000 words are sufficient to "cover long periods of time" and to "handle adequately a large number of individuals and family groups." He then wrote *On the Stairs* to exemplify this technique.

But, perversely, *On the Stairs* is neither realism nor fiction; it is a satire on methods employed by popular novelists, to which the story plays second fiddle. For instance, Fuller makes a fuss about the choice of a name for his central character. Finally Oliver W. Ormsby is chosen, but later the name turns out to be George W. Waite. In the same vein he breaks off a dramatic scene to write:

> Pardon me, dear reader. The simple fact is, I have suddenly been struck by my lack of drama. You see how awkwardly I provide it, when I try. What bank robbers, I ask you, would undertake such an adventure at half-past four in the afternoon? I cannot compete with the films. As a matter of fact, the vault stood locked, the tellers were gone, even the office boy had stolen away, and Johnny and I were left alone together, exchanging rather feebly and with increasing feebleness, some faint and unimportant boyhood reminiscences. . . . I feel abysmally abashed; let us open a new section.[31]

Fuller employed the last sketch in *Under the Skylights* to take a slap at both art and big business. "Little O'Grady

and the Grindstone" pits the Chicago art group—Lorado Taft, Ralph Clarkson, Bessie Porter, Charles Francis Browne, and Herman MacNeil, according to Hamlin Garland—against the directors of the Grindstone National Bank. Fuller heaps ridicule on both factions. The theme of the story is the decoration of the new bank building, and how the artists try unsuccessfully to impose historical and symbolical motifs on the directors. The directors in turn are suspicious of art generally; what they want is something they can understand. When the artists submit the finished plans the president brings the contest to a conclusion with the exasperated declaration: "To hell with art! What I wanted to do was to advertise my business."[32] Art wins a hollow victory over business when, a short time after the new building is occupied, the Grindstone fails.

Proof that Fuller's frustration would rise to the surface no matter what literary form he tried will be found in ***Lines Long and Short.***[33] The volume consists of free verse poems, each a description of a frustrated middle western character whose struggle to escape the mediocrity of life in Chicago lampoons both the desire and the fulfillment. He describes a poet who has exhausted the thin vein of his inspiration, the struggles of a society matron to infuse culture into the life of the city, the rise of the beautiful daughter of a patent-medicine king to the dizzy triumph of marriage to a titled Englishman.

Just as ***The Chevalier of Pensieri-Vani*** introduces the conflict in Fuller's character, so ***Lines Long and Short*** provides what may be taken as a final comment on it in the poem **"Tobias Holt, Bachelor."** The parallel lies not in the fact that Fuller himself was unmarried, but in the character's situation and in Fuller's treatment of this situation. Holt is a man who has spent his life remembering the anniversaries of his friends and their children. The climax of the poem is a sickbed scene in which Fuller playfully discusses all the possible outcomes of the illness—realistic or sentimental, depressing or cheerful. Here is the situation of the stools; Fuller is unable to make a choice. Then he concludes:

> Yes, perhaps he did
> Come through all right—
> With much or little sympathy—
> To take up, with what zest he could,
> the frantic rôle
> Of buying favors from a cooling world.
> Spend as you will,
> It's sad to be old, and alone.
> (Fudge! That's the very thing
> I tried hard not to say!)[34]

This parenthetical coyness and hesitancy suggests Fuller's lifelong inability to face up to personal and literary problems. He yearned for Italy, yet he remained in Chicago. As a writer he desired to "scoot through the blue air of heaven," yet he was earthbound by his irritation at the crudities of middle western civilization and his inability to settle on a satisfactory form of expression. As a consequence he was not a magnificent failure, but only a frustrated one.

Notes

1. "Henry Blake Fuller," *Bookman*, LVIII (February 1924), 646.

2. Hamlin Garland, *Roadside Meetings of A Literary Nomad* (New York: Macmillan Co., 1913), p. 257.

3. W. D. Howells, "The Cliff-Dwellers," *Harper's Bazar*, XXVI (October 28, 1893), 883.

4. "The Cliff-Dwellers," XVL (January 1894), 373.

5. Roger Riordan, "Henry B. Fuller," *Critic*, XXX (March 27, 1897), 221-22.

6. Hamlin Garland, *My Friendly Contemporaries* (New York: Macmillan Co., 1932), p. 25.

7. Harriet Monroe, *A Poet's Life* (New York: Macmillan Co., 1938), p. 37.

8. Hamlin Garland, *Companions on the Trail* (New York: Macmillan Co., 1931), p. 99.

9. Theodore Dreiser, "The Great American Novel," *American Spectator*, I (December 1932), 1.

10. Hamlin Garland, *Roadside Meetings*, p. 272.

11. Hamlin Garland, *Companions on the Trail*, p. 323.

12. R. M. Lovett, "Fuller of Chicago," *New Republic*, LX (August 21, 1929), 18.

13. "Henry Blake Fuller," *Bookman*, LVIII (February 1924), 645.

14. C. M. Griffin, *Henry Blake Fuller* (Philadelphia: University of Pennsylvania Press, 1939), pp. 72-73.

15. Hamlin Garland, *Roadside Meetings*, p. 270.

16. *Ibid.*, p. 257.

17. Hamlin Garland, *Companions on the Trail*, p. 59.

18. Harriet Monroe, *A Poet's Life*, p. 198.

19. H. B. Fuller, *The Chevalier of Pensieri-Vani* (New York: Century Co., 1892), p. 177.

20. H. B. Fuller, *The Cliff-Dwellers* (New York: Harper and Bros., 1893).

21. H. B. Fuller, *With the Procession* (New York: Harper and Bros., 1895).

22. H. B. Fuller, *The Cliff-Dwellers*, p. 50.

23. *Ibid.*, p. 324.

24. H. B. Fuller, *With The Procession*, pp. 49-66.

25. *Ibid.*, p. 72.

26. H. B. Fuller, *Under the Skylights* (New York: D. Appleton and Co., 1901).

27. *Ibid.*, p. 49.

28. H. B. Fuller, "Embracing the Realities," *Dial*, LXII (March 22, 1917), 237-38.

29. H. B. Fuller, "Anton Chekov," *New Republic*, XXXVIII (March 26, 1924), 129-30.

30. H. B. Fuller, "The Plea for Shorter Novels," *Dial*, LXIII (August 3, 1917), 139-41.

31. H. B. Fuller, *On the Stairs* (Boston: Houghton Mifflin, 1919), pp. 82-83.

32. H. B. Fuller, *Under the Skylights*, p. 289.

33. H. B. Fuller, *Lines Long and Short* (Boston: Houghton Mifflin, 1917).

34. *Ibid.*, pp. 7-8.

Darrel Abel with Henry Fuller (essay date 1957)

SOURCE: "Howells or James?" edited by Darrel Abel, in *Modern Fiction Studies*, Vol. III, No. 2, Summer, 1957, pp. 159-64.

[*In the following essay, Abel introduces Fuller's essay, maintaining that it documents Fuller's early inclination toward realism.*]

The paper by Henry Blake Fuller which is here published for the first time[1] was apparently completed in 1885.[2] By this date William Dean Howells, who at the outset of his fictional career had been classified as an "idyllist" and romancer, was now explicitly committed to realism, and had acknowledged Henry James to be the leader of a new American school of realistic novelists. Howells called realism "almost the only literary movement of our time that has vitality in it,"[3] and praised James as the leader of the new movement in the United States:

> The art of fiction has in fact become a finer art in our day than it was with Dickens and Thackeray. . . . The new school derives from Hawthorne and George Eliot rather than any others; but it studies human nature much more in its wonted aspect, and finds its ethical and dramatic examples in the operation of lighter but not really less vital motives. . . . This school, which is so largely of the future as well as the present, finds its chief exemplar in Mr. James; it is he who is shaping and directing American fiction, at least.[4]

While Howells was thus praising James as the chief exemplar of the new realism, who was shaping and directing American fiction, Fuller was venturing to doubt both James's realism and his Americanism. Fuller cannot have failed to understand what Howells was saying about James, but he thought Howells' praise was too generous. He thought Howells' realism was more realistic than James's, and his Americanism more American; and thought Howells himself ought to be acknowledged as the shaper and director of American fiction.

Fuller's paper is of interest not only as a pioneer comparative criticism of Howells and James, but also as documentary evidence of Fuller's own early inclination toward realism. Fuller's first book, *The Chevalier of Pensieri-Vani*, was not published until 1890, but it was mostly written during 1886.[5] Both *The Chevalier* and his second book, *The Chatelaine of La Trinite* (1892), were hailed as "charming excursions into fancy" and praised for their ro-

mantic treatment of exotic materials. Apparently Fuller's earliest books, written soon after his explicit declaration in favor of realism and of the treatment of materials from ordinary American life, were in technique and content directly contrary to his own theory. But only apparently: *The Chevalier* and *The Chatelaine* are essentially literary utilizations of Fuller's European (mostly Italian) travel journals of 1879-80 and 1883.[6] These journals contain a record of romanticized rather than romantic travel. Before Fuller used them as the substance of his first two books he became convinced that the realistic treatment of native materials was the proper work for an American novelist, evidently being persuaded of this by the critical theories and fictional practice of Howells. Fuller's fictional contrivance for utilizing the substance of his early travel journals is manifestly, if considered by itself, almost entirely an addition of realism. A hitherto unnoted fact, which "Howells or James?" helps to establish,[7] is that from the beginning of his fictional career Fuller was in practice, so far as his data and his capabilities permitted, as well as in theory, a realist.[8]

HOWELLS OR JAMES?

The literary gossip of the last ten years, whether of tongue or type, has perhaps employed no phrase with more assiduity or gusto than that of **"Howells and James."** The language, in its printed form, at least, has even been enriched with a doubly hyphenated adjective which seems to express more fully and exactly than any less modern phrase a certain sort of hero and heroine, a certain sort of plot, and a certain set of ideas with regard to the methods and ends of fiction. Such being the case, one may well justify himself in the intimation that this particular expression has perhaps been a trifle overworked, and allow himself the suggestion that so well worn a collocation of words now give way to the related but dissimilar one of "Howells *or* James?" Substituting, then, for the complacent period the restless mark of interrogation, let us now consider points of difference instead of points of similarity,—asking ourselves which of these two representative writers is to be pronounced most instrumental in the shaping of American fiction,[9] and which of them will ultimately come to be recognized as most firmly and completely a factor in an historical American literature. Mr. Howells, it is true, generously conceded, a year or so ago, the first place to Mr. James.[10] But the vigorous and dextrous opening of his own new serial in the November *Century*[11] clearly indicates that his hand has lost none of its mastery, and his prompt and authoritative welcome lately extended to certain newcomers in the ranks of Realism[12] unmistakably shows that he does not consider his own position that of a subordinate; so he will perhaps tolerate the hint that to him and not to his friend is entrusted the direction of our contemporary novel-writing, and that he, rather than any one else, may be allowed by the opinion of another generation, the place of undisputed chief. It is worthwhile, on this point, to note the attitude of each toward life and society in general, and toward American life and society in particular.

We may say, in general, and for the purpose of a direct comparison, that Howells is a realist, and James an idealist. Few, perhaps, who have in mind Mr. James' first and most famous "international" effort will regard the creator of Daisy Miller—least of all, the perpetrator of Daisy Miller's little brother—as an idealizer. But a man has a right to ask that we judge him by his highest and best, by the nature of that whose representation is to him most congenial and self-satisfying. If, then, Mr. James' most finished and elaborate portraits of persons are marked with exceptional attributes of wit, polish, beauty, culture, wealth, intellect,—and if his most careful and ambitious portraits of places (the phrase is his own) result, after his own peculiar process of selection, rejection, and combination, in a whole of unblemished picturesqueness and unbroken harmony, his claim to the title of idealist seems placed beyond dispute. That he deals, ultimately, in realities, is true enough; but a realism made up of select actualities is pretty apt to come out idealistically in the end.

Now we, in these days of democracy, take a very frank and undisguised interest in ourselves; we are a good deal concerned with our own day and generation—in our art as well as elsewhere. Literature, monopolized for a great many long centuries by fortune, beauty, splendor, and general heroics, has at length descended to the common level of general humanity, and has consented to take an interest in plain every day people and plain every day happiness. Flora, goddess of flowers, is no longer the airy, radiant, lily-crowned nymph of the Renaissance; a clever young Parisian has shown her to be simply a plain old peasant woman in sabots and frilled cap with a big basket of astors [sic] and geraniums at her side. We are not ashamed to confess that at the present time we take but a limited interest in, for example, an Achilles or a Beatrice, while we vehemently discuss, *con amore,* the character of a Bartley Hubbard or the doings of a Lydia Blood.[13] It may be safely said that this state of things has come to stay; such an interest in ourselves, once aroused, is pretty apt to be permanent. We shall not so greatly care to hear about other things when we can hear so much and so minutely about ourselves. Realism seems coincident with modern democracy, and the advance of the one will doubtless be accompanied by the spread of the other. Realism as Mr. Howells himself has lately said, is but a phase of humanity;[14] and the writer who is most thoroughly permeated with the realistic spirit may confidently expect the widest hearing and the securest place.

Again: Mr. Howells' attitude toward life is sympathetic; Mr. James' is rather the reverse. James has, of course, his own peculiar sympathies and predilections, but they are of a very exclusive and circumscribed character. He regards life as a superficies; Howells looks at it as a substance. James makes a survey of it; Howells gives us a cross-section of it. The one is satisfied with the cultivation of the mere top-dressing; the other has a healthy liking for the honest clay and gravel of the great middle stratum. James has, of course, his due liking for virtue, truth, justice, and the rest, but he does not always appear to appreciate them at their full value when unlinked with fortunate circumstances and the culture of a refined society.[15] Howells, on the other hand, can interest himself sympathetically in all the qualities—not the good, merely; but the doubtful and the bad as well—which may present themselves to him in his actual contact with society in any of its forms. He himself declares that the study of human life, if close, is sure to be kindly.[16] And a hearty sympathy with the general life of the community has never met with a readier recognition and response than it meets with today.

The present attitude of these two authors, respectively, with regard to our own particular life and society, assuredly need not be made matter for formal exposition. But it is interesting to note that within the last few years the attitude of the one has materially changed, while that of the other has become, if anything, more statuesquely immovable. The time is not far back when both Howells and James were stationed at the far end of that transatlantic bridge which it is the chief boast and distinction of the latter to have constructed between the Old World and the New. Howells, with a clear perception of the direction in which the cat—to use the common phrase—was about to jump, crossed over a few years back (pausing in the middle for the "Foregone Conclusion" and the "Lady of the Aroostook") and has steadfastly remained with us ever since. James, with a perception less clear, or from preferences not easily to be overcome, has held to the same remote standpoint that he occupied when his striking figure was first discerned by the modern novel-reader. A year back, indeed, he sent Lady Barberina over to us; but she didn't stay long.[17] That each is now permanently established on his own ground, and fully fixed as to his own point of view, the fall announcements of the publishers made yet more sure. Mr. Howells, in the "Rise of Silas Lapham" will still farther extend the field of sympathetic realism which he first entered in the "Modern Instance." Mr. James, in the "Princess Casamassima" (in whom we may confidently recognize the striking figure of an old acquaintance)[18] will bring to a still higher degree of perfection his own particular little garden of exotic culture which has already blossomed with "Roderick Hudson" and the *Portrait of a Lady.*

A common complaint against the novels of both Howells and James—how easily the phrase runs off!—has been that most of them have been unduly taken up with various small and insignificant questions of social manners and usages that ruffle the mere surface of society without by any means stirring its depths. But there are now indications that the depths are to be stirred, after all. The stratification of our society has undeniably begun, and symptoms of the movement are coming to appear in print. Now the novel in our day has become the great universal medium. New theories in philosophy, new ideas in art, new phases in religion, politics, and what not, now hasten to enclose themselves within the covers of a "fiction." And if all these, why not sociology, as well? May we not reasonably look for the formulation of American society in the pages of the *Atlantic* or the *Century?* And such a process—to whom would we most willingly entrust it, to Howells or to James? Who would do it most kindly, most sympathetically—he who deals with the normal earning of money at home, or he who prefers to deal with the exceptional and privileged spending of money abroad? He who lives amongst us and knows us intimately and treats us all with the fullest measure of good will; or he who alienates himself from us, knows us, in general, none too perfectly, and doesn't feel sure but that we are a big mistake, after all? With the strong intimation that Mr. Howells has just given of his design to bring order out of our social chaos, I am glad to remember that he is an "Ohio man," and it was toward Ohio, let us recollect, that Mr. Matthew Arnold directed his gaze when searching for the "average American."

Mr. James, no doubt, would be glad to like us, if he could; perhaps he has even conscientiously endeavored to do so. But an undue insistence upon agreeable externals has worked to prevent his becoming acquainted with us as we really are. He leaves us in no doubt that he prefers, for instance, weather-stained stucco to freshly-painted clapboarding; and a pair of sabots strikes in him a responsive chord that a pair of plain cowhide boots quite fails to affect.[19] The boots and the clapboarding repel him; so he stays over there with his sabots and his stucco. Mr. Howells' organs of aesthetic digestion are much more healthy and vigorous. He approaches boldly all the various externals of American life—grotesque though they be, and ugly, and irritating, and distressing—which so often cause us to quail before the gaze of our European censors, and subdues them instead of letting them subdue him. He can print the word "buggy" without the help of quotation marks, and writes "guess" with an unconscious freedom that Mr. James has never attained.

Howells, in fine, has come to the mountain: James seems to expect that he can bring the mountain to him. A few loose stones and boulders, it is true, have rolled his way; but the general form and outline of the mountain have not been materially changed, and its firm base is probably quite as immovable as it ever was. There is a strong probability that Mr. James, notwithstanding his very exceptional gifts and his score of delightful qualities, will sometime come to find himself a "thing apart" in a sense and to an extent that he does not now foresee. From his isolated position he may come to regard, with a feeling approximating envy, the comfortable position of a competitor who, believing that there's no place like home, has made himself the leader and centre of a school whose members, working in fields however scattered, have an aim and a method that should render them worthy of an appreciative hearing and the objects of an affectionate pride.

Notes

1. The manuscript is in the Henry B. Fuller Collection in the Newberry Library, Chicago. It is here published by kind permission of the Librarian, Mr. Stanley Pargellis.

2. The decisive indication is Fuller's statement that James's "Lady Barberina" had appeared in the U. S.

"a year back": "Lady Barberina" was serialized in the *Century* in May, June, and July of 1884. Also, Fuller recognized in *The Princess Casamassima* "the striking figure of an old acquaintance"; since *The Princess* ran serially in the *Atlantic* from September, 1885, through October, 1886, Fuller could hardly have recognized his old acquaintance earlier than September, 1885.

3. "Two Notable Novels," *Century,* XXVIII (Aug., 1884), 632.

4. "Henry James, Jr.," *Century,* XXV (Nov., 1882), 28. The English quarterlies were incensed at Howells' opinion that the future of the novel lay with continental realism rather than with the discursive subjectivism of Dickens and Thackeray, and also by his suggestion that American novelists, especially James, were making more significant advances than British writers. For an account of the ensuing hubbub, see Edwin H. Cady's *The Road to Realism* (Syracuse University Press, 1956), pp. 218-221.

5. According to an unpublished ms. in the Newberry, "My Early Books."

6. Fuller's voluminous journals, never published, are in the Newberry Library collection.

7. Another unpublished article in the Newberry collection, "The American School of Fiction," develops further Fuller's early opinions about the future of American fiction. It was written soon after "Howells or James?", and its general conclusions are the same. It does, however, agree that European materials are more "interesting" to the writer because of the richness of an old and complex society and scene.

8. This thesis needs detailed demonstration which it would not be appropriate to undertake here, but which I will supply in a forthcoming study of Fuller which examines at length the question of his realism and his relation to the development of naturalistic fiction in the U. S.

9. An apparent reference to the Howells passage quoted above; see fn. 4.

10. In "Henry James, Jr."; see fn. 4 above.

11. *The Rise of Silas Lapham.* This reference, suggesting that the publication of the first instalment of *Lapham* (Nov., 1884), was current or very recent, seems inconsistent with the dating I have argued for in fn. 2, but it is more likely that Fuller *completed* the paper in 1885 than in 1884.

12. See Howells' "Two Notable Novels," *Century,* XXVIII (August, 1884), 632-634. In this review of Howe's *Story of a Country Town* and Bellamy's *Miss Ludington's Sister,* Howells wrote: "Not the least interesting thing about them was the witness they bore of the prevalence of realism in the artistic atmosphere to such degree that two very differently gifted writers, having really something to say in the way of fiction, could not help giving it the realistic character."

13. Characters, respectively, in Howells' novels *A Modern Instance* (1882) and *The Lady of the Aroostook* (1879).

14. See "Two Notable Novels," p. 633.

15. Howells permitted himself to hint a similar criticism of James in "Henry James, Jr." (p. 25): "He had from the start all those advantages which, when they go too far, become limitations."

16. "Two Notable Novels," p. 633.

17. For a serial story, "Lady Barberina" was unusually brief—three monthly instalments.

18. The Princess is Christina Light of *Roderick Hudson.*

19. Probably Fuller had in mind the famous paragraphs in James's *Hawthorne* (New York, 1879) remarking the "thinness" of "the crude and simple society" of America, as material for a novelist, in contrast to "the denser, richer, warmer European spectacle," (pp. 41-43).

Mark Harris (essay date 1965)

SOURCE: An introduction to *With the Procession,* by Henry B. Fuller, The University of Chicago Press, 1965, pp. v-xiv.

[*In the following introduction to* With the Procession, *Harris considers the role of the American dream in Fuller's novel.*]

Shall we be consoled by the idea that the luxurious misery of the principal persons of **With the Procession** is the continuing misery of American society—was and will be with us forever—or shall we renew our indignation that such a country was ever begun? The events which pained Henry Blake Fuller, seeming to motivate the composition of this novel, pain us now. His lament is ours.

On the other hand, our dilemma is deepened by our paradox, for we too celebrate this Procession; this *march,* as Fuller also calls it; this *caravan,* he says—the very word of Henry Adams in the very connection.

Where will this Procession lead? For one Irish family it has led to the White House. Perhaps that family is related to the Irish cop we meet in Chapter I. The Procession is a dream of that sort of success, and our expectation may be, as we read, that it marches the right way toward the best of history's alternatives.

The Procession is that principle of American freedom promising opportunity for men formerly without hope, political power for men formerly voiceless; wealth, of course; ascension in a single generation to that social class next above one's own. Give us your tired, your poor, yearning to be . . .

And yet if we can almost see justice, equality, human dignity, and more sweet abundance than any men ever consumed we see also conspicuous anxiety. Tyrannized by mediocrity, something within us may question democracy, making us sound a little snobbish when we ask whether a less flexible society might not improve our anxieties.

Whichever way we stand, we must know at least that the opposite idea exists before we approach **With the Procession,** for Fuller may be engaging us in a cause not quite our own. Perhaps he has been somewhere we have not—has had his own experience of the Procession, been tempted to join it, detected its dangers to the independence of his art, rescued himself. He was at mid-career, in age near forty, and he had remained alert, observing that increasing powers of workmanship do not necessarily excite popular admiration. His business honestly transacted along the lines of the old ethic—the old art—he nevertheless saw his trade diverted to practitioners who, like the spiritual enemies of his hero, David Marshall, speculated in quick returns.

The year of the novel is sometime in the early 1890s. The place is Chicago, called by Fuller a "great and complex city," but still sometimes referred to by his characters as "the town," so youthful is it: its population is two million; twenty years earlier it had been only 300,000.

The action of the novel begins with David Marshall, to whom Fuller gives an extended paragraph, then drops with a line—"But this is no way to begin." Perhaps this pretense at a false beginning was an afterthought. No matter, the uncertainty warns us that Fuller had in mind another hero, not David. David, after all, is a merchant ("teas, coffees, spices, flour, sugar, baking-powder"). He and Fuller had neither wandered the same routes of the world nor followed similar trades. David was hardly an author's logical disguise.

Presumably, then, it is to David's son, Truesdale, whom we look for Fuller's statement, who ought to assert the meaning of the events through we shall live. Truesdale, we are told, is an artist; like Fuller, he has been enormously impressed by sights abroad. Our logical expectation is that it is he, not his father, who shall tell us our story.

It was also Fuller's logical procedure. But Truesdale, as either an artist in spirit or a painter in practice, fails to persuade. His response to his own outrage is too often limited to the ejaculation *Ouf!,* as if the author were reluctant to entrust to Truesdale a mature articulation which would have been incongruous against Fuller's fidelity to realism. Where Truesdale at last rises to coherent protest against esthetic chaos it is not in his own language at all, but with an interior monologue paraphrased by the author. Truesdale ironically views a respectable proposal for "a piece of actual architecture":

> Then he festooned it with telegraph wires, and draped it with fire-escapes, and girdled it with a stretch of elevated road, and hung it with signboards, and hedged it

in with fruit-stands, and swathed it in clouds of coal smoke, and then asked them to find it; that was the puzzle, he said.

Significantly, this passage is instantly followed by Fuller's recognition that father and son "were dangerously near to the common ground upon which they had never yet met." Why *dangerously?* The word is truly inexplicable at that point, and may in fact more accurately refer to the danger Fuller escaped in transferring his sympathies from Truesdale to David than to relationships within the novel.

The speculation is worth the risk, for unless the book is seen as David's we fail to appreciate some of the force of Fuller's dedication to the life of his characters, even at the expense of his own intention. His rescue of himself from his miscalculation is surely a first achievement of **With the Procession,** and a signal of Fuller's loyalty to craft. (We may also support the speculation by noting the shift of the designation *Marshall* from Truesdale to David, and the reduction, after the early pages, of *Marshall* to the boyish *Truesdale.*)

It is David whose decline and death span the book, and David who utters its cry and appeal, not in the author's voice but in the more difficult voice of a civilized merchant drawn to life. "To David Marshall, art in all its forms was an inexplicable thing. . . ." Yet it is David whose art is true.

David established, Fuller turns to the Procession itself, and to Truesdale Marshall. Truesdale, younger son of David, is returning at twenty-three from three years of "culture and adventure" abroad, "to catch up again . . . rejoin the great caravan." From Truesdale's viewpoint, as we re-enter the city we see an actual caravan suggesting the figurative:

> . . . a long line of waiting vehicles took up their interrupted course through the smoke and the stench . . . first a yellow streetcar; then a robust truck laden with rattling sheetiron, or piled high with fresh wooden pails and willow baskets; then a junk-cart bearing a pair of dwarfed and bearded Poles . . . then, perhaps, a bespattered buggy . . . then a butcher's cart loaded with the carcasses of calves . . . an express wagon with a yellow cur yelping from its rear; then, it may be, an insolently venturesome landau, with crested panel and top-booted coachman. Then drays and omnibuses and more street-cars; then, presently, somewhere in the line between the tail end of one truck and the menacing tongue of another, a family carry-all . . .

This carry-all belongs to the Marshall family, and it is likened to them, as a writer a generation after Fuller might liken a family automobile to its owners. But the carry-all personifies David, not his son. David persists in the language of the author's description of the carry-all, where the emphasis falls upon the relationship between virtue and fashion:

> It is very capable and comprehensive vehicle, as conveyances of that kind go. It is not new, it is not pre-

cisely in the mode; but it shows material and workmanship of the best grade, and it is washed, oiled, polished with scrupulous care. It advances with some deliberation, and one might fancy hearing in the rattle of its tires, or in the suppressed flapping of its rear curtain, a word of plaintive protest. "I am not of the great world," it seems to say; "I make no pretence to fashion. We are steady and solid, but we are not precisely in society, and we are far, very far indeed, from any attempt to cut a great figure. However, do not misunderstand our position; it is not that we are under, nor that we are exactly aside; perhaps we have been left just a little behind. Yes, that might express it—just a little behind."

Fuller's scene set, his materials felt, his workmanship is never less than the workmanship of the conscientious artisan who made the carry-all. Scornful of simplification, he creates both heroes and villains too real to bear if we indolently insist upon easy identification. The novel is purest for the impurities of its actors, heroes not purely good, villains never merely bad. Among the heroes, for example, Truesdale is a snob, and sister Jane is a plain girl without prospects. The character Paston, whom we ought not to like, wins a rich reward; Jane has no such luck; David dies; Roger endures. The Procession marches on.

Consider the villains! May we even call them that? Are Mrs. Granger Bates and Roger Marshall really so wicked, after all?

Mrs. Bates appears to us at first as only that passive Mrs. Jones we compel ourselves to keep up with. It was not Mrs. Bates who searched out Jane Marshall, to poison Jane's mind with restlessness; no, it was Jane who sought Mrs. Bates. "I declare, when I called on Mrs. Bates and went over the place and compared their house and their way of living with ours. . . . When I saw that magnificent style she lived in . . ." At Mrs. Bates's house the gayest chapters of the book occur. We are disarmed. We find ourselves witness to the first hour of a friendship likely to survive long beyond the period of the book itself.

How can this be bad? Mrs. Bates would be astonished that we name her a candidate for villain. She is certain that she has in mind no thought but Jane's advancement. She teaches Jane to develop much that is best in her, converts her plainness to something closer to her potential beauty, and guides her to the Charity Ball.

Jane's first "glimpse" of Mrs. Bates, and ours, was of "one of the big, the broad, the great, the triumphant; . . . one of a Roman amplitude and vigor, an Indian keenness and sagacity, an American ambition and determination . . . one of the conquerors, in short."

There is no dissimulation, no fraudulence, no misrepresentation on the part of Mrs. Bates. She knows where she has been and where she wants to go.

> ". . . We weren't so very stylish ourselves, but we had some awfully stylish neighbors . . . 'We'll get there,

too, some time,' I said to Granger. 'This is going to be a big town, and we have a good show to be big people in it. Don't let's start in life like beggars going to the back door for cold victuals.' . . . Well, we worked along fairly for a year or two, and finally I said to Granger: 'Now, what's the use of inventing things and taking them to those companies and making everybody rich but yourself? You pick out some one road, and get on the inside of that, and stick there . . .' We have fought the fight—a fair field and no favor—and we have come out ahead. And we shall stay there, too; keep up with the procession is my motto, and head it if you can. I *do* head it, and I feel that I'm where I belong. When I can't foot it with the rest, let me drop by the wayside and the crows have me."

There is nothing of subtlety to her except that subtlety which is worst of all because it remains unknown to Mrs. Bates herself: she lacks a knowledge not of her actions but of their implications. Not what she does, but what her doing means, remains inaccessible to her. How can she help but admire herself when all her activities are praised and publicized? To a vision so willingly obstructed what's good for one's own vanity takes on the aspect of beneficence.

Jane's initiative liberates Mrs. Bates's initiative, the innocent provoking the villain, though her villainy consists of nothing so patent as conspiracy with any forces except itself. Unconscious, subtlest of all, it characterizes not only Mrs. Bates but the entire Procession, shielding old settler and immigrant from the implications of their actions. With every best intention Mrs. Bates now goes to David Marshall to urge him to invest in a monument for himself:

> ". . . Imagine a man disposed to devote two or three hundred thousand dollars to the public, and giving it to help pay off the municipal debt. How many people would consider themselves benefited by the gift, or would care a cent for the name of the giver? Or fancy his giving it to clean up the streets of the city. The whole affair would be forgotten with the coming of the next rain-storm. . . . You drive out to the University campus this time next year, David, and you'll see Bates Hall—four stories high, with dormers and gables and things, and the name carved in gray-stone over the doorway, to stay there for the next century or two. I think I shall name it Susan Lathrop Bates Hall . . ."

It is Mrs. Bates, not Fuller, who places Mrs. Bates on record. In this same disciplined way Fuller presents the second villain, working always within the limits his craft has set for itself. Perhaps he yearned for a more expansive vocabulary, a wider viewpoint. If so, he refrained from indulgence. (Jane's use of the phrase "historical and sociological" is sufficiently extraordinary for Fuller to make a point of it.)

Roger Marshall had none of the liberal advantages of his younger brother, Truesdale.

> Roger was held by his family to be above all foibles and frailties; his aunt Lydia had once told him . . . that

he had too much head and not enough heart. It is certain that he had marked out a definite course for himself, and that nothing, so far, had had the power to divert him materially from it; and he had a far-reaching contempt for the man who permitted the gray matter of his brain to be demoralized by the red matter in his veins. . . . His severe face was smooth-shaven, as he thought the face of a lawyer ought to be, and he could address the higher courts with such a loud and brazen utterance as to cause the court-loungers almost to feel the judges shrinking and shriveling under their robes. His was a hot and vehement nature, but it burned with a flame blue rather than red.

Selected by his father to serve as the family's attorney, Roger's is the final act of the book—the assignment of a portion of David's estate to Jane, rather than, as had been stipulated, to a monument of the sort recommended by Mrs. Bates. If Roger's act is questionably legal it is undeniably brotherly, and we view him here at the last, as we saw him earlier, the defender, the protector, saving his sister from her own sentimentality.

Shall we complain of such a man? How is he a villain? At worst he may be one of the wreckers of civilization, but within the terms of Fuller's novel he is only dull and uninteresting. Every family has its practical son, proud of his own hard code, seldom aware that his assumptions are merely assumptions or that his motivations extend beyond superficial consciousness. Roger is "tough and technical and litigious; his was the hand to seize, not to soothe." He is the Procession's unconscious theorist.

It may be a weakness of **With the Procession** that Roger is sometimes indistinguishable from the other men who compose those younger forces surrounding David Marshall, who will carry on the business of business but who are incapable of inheriting David's style. The architect Bingham, whose ambition is in the mold of Roger, argues with David that "the noblest mountain in the world, when you come right down to details, is only a heap of dirt and rocks strewn over with sticks and stones. But if you will just step back far enough to get the proper point of view—well, you know what the painters can do with such things as these."

But David cannot be deceived: "I can't step back, Bingham. I started here; I've stayed here; I belong here. I'm living right *on* your mountain, and its sticks and stones are all about me. Don't ask me to see them for anything else; don't ask me to call them anything else."

> "Make your impression while you may," Bingham urges: "This is the time—this very year. The man who makes his mark here today will enjoy a fame which will spread as the fame of the city spreads and its power and prosperity increases. You know what we are destined to be—a hundred times greater than we are today. Fasten your name on the town, and your name will grow as the town itself does."

It is the ancient appeal to the artist to exploit, to reduce his vision, to barter his soul for name and fame "today."

But the merchant was unable to be less than he was. "To David Marshall, art in all its forms was an inexplicable thing . . ." He had no language for it, only a passion, a devotion:

> Why did he go to bed at half-past nine? In order that he might be at the store at half-past seven. Why must he be at the store by half-past seven? . . . because it was the only thing he wanted to do; because it was the only thing he could do; because it was the only thing he was pleased and proud to do; because it was the sole thing which enabled him to look upon himself as a useful, stable, honored member of society.

David, like Fuller—or Fuller, like David—worked within the limits of the material at hand. Neither felt himself responsible for social consequences beyond the work itself: well-made, the object created was its own morality and its own reward. "We have enough to bother us," says David, "without reporters coming around." That was the ideal.

As David declined, we are told, the "dismay" of his family "was now such as might occur at the Mint if the great stamp were suddenly and of its own accord to cease its coinage of double-eagles and to sink into a silence of supine idleness." He is Mint, he is carry-all, the conscience and the clarity of the Procession, set slightly apart.

Conceivably, the values of David Marshall never reigned except within the imagination of Henry Blake Fuller. Conceivably, the Procession is the best of all possible processions, neither so ominous nor so destructive as we may fear. All that is finally certain is that Fuller, having described the conflict of values for himself in his own decades, describes it as well for us in ours. Few literary restorations are more to the present point.

Edmund Wilson (essay date 1970)

SOURCE: "Two Neglected American Novelists: I—Henry B. Fuller, The Art of Making It Flat," in *The New Yorker,* May 23, 1970, pp. 112-39.

[*In the following essay, Wilson provides a thematic and stylistic analysis of Fuller's work.*]

The nineties and the early nineteen-hundreds, when looked at from the later decades, are likely to seem a dim period in American literature. The quality and the content of the fiction were mainly determined by the magazines that aimed to please a feminine public. There were writers of great reputation whom no one except the literary historian would think of looking into today. But there did exist also—outsold and outpublicized—a kind of underground of real social critics and conscientious artists who were hardly recognized or who were recognized only when one of them struck off some book that was daring or arresting enough to call special attention to its author. Harold Frederic's *The Damnation of Theron Ware,* which dealt in a

disturbing way with the contemporary problems of the clergy, was a book that was much read both in England and here; Stephen Crane's *The Red Badge of Courage* was so intensely conceived and written that, though poohpoohed by academics like Barrett Wendell, it could not be disregarded, and Crane himself became a public legend, although every effort was made to see that this legend was a disreputable one; George W. Cable, in the eighties, had had his success with a serious novel, *The Grandissimes,* but his treatment of situations created in the South by the mixture of white and black blood and his pamphleteering books on the Negro question became so repugnant to his editors and so outrageous to his Southern neighbors that he was forced to fall back on sentimental romance and exploitation of the then marketable "local color;" Kate Chopin, who wrote also of Louisiana, was also acceptable as a local-colorist, but she so scandalized the public in 1899 by her treatment of adultery in *The Awakening* that she is said to have been discouraged from writing any more novels; and, in spite of the championship of Howells, the New Englander John DeForest, in his Balzacian effort to cover his own era as well as parts of the historical past—the Revolution and the Salem witches, the Civil War and the corruption of the Grant Administration—in an objective and realistic way, was never accepted at all.

It has been only in quite recent years that this area has been gradually excavated. The first collection of Crane, who died in 1900, was brought out in 1925, in a very limited edition. DeForest's *Miss Ravenel's Conversion,*" his most notable Civil War novel, was reprinted only in 1939, *The Grandissimes* only in 1957. *The Damnation of Theron Ware* has suddenly been resuscitated in no less than three recent reprintings, and Frederic's stories of the Civil War have now for the first time been collected in one volume and brought out by the Syracuse University Press. The latest of these writers to be discovered and the one who has in general had least justice done him is Henry B. Fuller of Chicago, but now at last **With the Procession,** one of the best of his novels, has been reprinted by the Chicago University Press, and this provides an occasion to give some account of Fuller, a unique and distinguished writer who does not deserve to be dumped in the drawer devoted to regional novelists for a chapter in an academic literary history.

Henry Blake Fuller was born in Chicago (January 9, 1857), but his family on both sides had been New Englanders. His grandfather was a cousin of Margaret Fuller. This grandfather, following a frequent progression, had moved first to western New York, then to the Middle West. He was one of those Americans of the period who combined making money in business with a sense of public responsibility. He had been a dry-goods merchant in Albion, New York, a county judge in Michigan, and in still pioneering Chicago a railroad man and the entrepreneur of the laying of forty miles of water pipes. Henry was an only son. At school he was a brilliant student. He did not go to college but had all the New England will to self-improvement. He learned languages and studied music, composed, wrote poetry, kept a diary, and made lists of necessary reading. He led a protected and isolated life, saw little of other young people. Out of school, he worked at first in his father's bank, but when Henry was twenty-two, Judge Fuller died, and he probably left his grandson some money, for Henry sailed for Europe that summer. He travelled in Europe a year, and thereafter, through the eighties and nineties, continued every few years to return for six months or so.

The first result of these visits, published in 1890, under a pseudonym and at Fuller's own expense, was a short novel, *The Chevalier of Pensieri-Vani.* This book, which was called in its time a little classic and a minor masterpiece, became the object of a kind of cult, of which I believe the last representative was the late Carl Van Vechten. It is an account of the travels in Italy of a cultivated Italian gentleman, and is something of an actual travel book in the taste of the then frequent articles in the more serious magazines, with their drawings of Old Chester and Picturesque Tuscany, intended especially for ladies who were obliged to stay at home or who saved ap to and looked forward to eventual trips. But it is also something other than this. It is diversified by little adventures and flavored with demure humor. *The Chevalier*—which soon went into a better edition, published under Fuller's own name—was the first of a series of novels all preserving the same tone and dealing with the same group of characters. The names of these characters alone will convey Fuller's playful humor: besides the Cavaliere himself, there are his friend the French Seigneur of Hors-Concours; the Swiss Chatelaine of La Trinité and her companion Miss Aurelia West of Ohio, who later marries a Lyon manufacturer and becomes Mme. la Comtesse Aurélie de Feuillevolante; the Duke of Avon and Severn; Baron Zeitgeist and the Freiherr von Kaltenau; the Prorege of Arcopia and the Marquis of Tempo-Rubato; and Mr. Occident, also from Ohio. The second of these books, *The Chatelaine of La Trinité,* appeared in 1892, but Fuller did not follow these up till *The Last Refuge,* of 1900, and did not conclude the series till 1929, when, just before the end of his life, he published *Gardens of This World.* These books belong to a school that is nowadays of little interest. The then fashionable stories of Americans encountering sophisticated Europeans, usually embellished by titles, have today become rather embarrassing. They are one of the symptoms of the longing to get away from the ugly and crass society that flourished after the Civil War. Americans then had a mania for looking up their family trees and trying to establish connections with some noble house in England or elsewhere. Henry James had his Passionate Pilgrim, Mark Twain his American Claimant. At its gaudiest, this dream produced Graustark, the imaginary Balkan kingdom of glamour, dashing deeds, and gallant romance which was created by George Barr McCutcheon, originally a farm boy from Indiana.

A more alembicated product was the late fiction of Henry Harland, a coy kind of fairy tales—marvels of American snobbery and syrupy *fin-de-siècle* fine writing—which, so popular in the early nineteen-hundreds, are ridiculous,

though still readable, today. The enchanting young hero and heroine, conversing in well-bred banter, are either royal or of very high rank, which, in their willingness to fall in love with commoners, they implausibly manage to conceal till they are headed for the final embrace. Harland's *The Cardinal's Snuffbox,* once thought so utterly delightful and the author's greatest success, is actually so absurd that when the editor of *Punch,* Owen Seaman, attempted to parody it in his book *Borrowed Plumes,* he could only fall short of the original. Edgar Saltus, the New York "society" novelist, is also in this tradition, but, a man of real worldly experience, he is genuinely amusing and witty, and he cultivated a certain perversity which prevented him from becoming saccharine as it prevented him from being popular. The European novels of Fuller belong to this tradition, too, but though they are not so wicked as Saltus's, they are very much more intelligent and much better written than Harland's. And Fuller, who so loved his noble connoisseurs, with their self-assured Old World savoir-faire, is nevertheless drolly ironic about those Americans themselves who admired and exaggerated these qualities. The happiest episode in the series seems to me the account of the efforts of Miss West of Ohio to induce the Chatelaine of La Trinité to live up to her ancestry and social position, which she has always taken for granted and to which she has not given much thought, and to arrange matches for her with suitable men none of whom are much interested in her. The Chatelaine herself loses interest in the operation and retires to a house of retreat in Lausanne. In *Gardens of This World,* which is supposed to take place after the First World War, these characters, now grown old, are still wandering around Europe, still in search of charming quiet spots, but they everywhere encounter Americans—millionaire who wants to buy up ruins and works of art and transport them to the United States, but also two adventurous and energetic boys who are interested in flying and one of whom (he is half French, the son of Feuillevolante) eventually goes into his father's business.

For, in spite of Fuller's regret at the decline of Europe and his harsh or sad criticisms of his own country, there was a strong strain of patriotism in him, even a feeling of loyalty to Chicago. In the intervals between his trips abroad, he had always had to return to his native city, where, after his father's death, in 1885, he took over the responsibilities of the family's business affairs. In those of his books that take place in Europe, one is impressed by the thoroughness and exactitude of his knowledge of history, geography, literature, art, and architecture. He was equally well informed about Chicago. He seems always to have been up-to-date on the streets, the population, the buildings, on new developments and organizations. The objection sometimes made to Henry James that he knew nothing about American business is not at all in order in the case of the part-time expatriate Fuller. He knew everything about the interests which he had to administer—industry, real estate, finance, and the legal procedures entailed by these. In connection with the family properties, he collected rents and checked on the buildings; he could even himself mend the plumbing, and complained that this took up too much of his time. And he now began to write about Chicago. The results of this were rather surprising. The precision and elegance of Fuller's style—so unusual in the United States of the nineties—really make a better showing here, because they lend a distinction to often crude material, than they do in the European books, where they still leave a little arid, a little bleak with accurate fact, material which the author has labored to render graceful and alluring and foreign. In his travels, he is not very far from the tinted impressionism of Henry James, which seems to emanate from his mind like a vapor.

Fuller now writes two novels—*The Cliff-Dwellers* (1893) and *With the Procession* (1895)—about the life of the new, energetic city. The first of these dramatizes the organism of an eighteen-story office building, the Clifton—the man who built it and the people who work in it; the second the fortunes of a family of more or less simple Western origins (the father is a well-to-do wholesale grocer) who, as the city grows and prospers, are unable to adjust themselves to its more and more accelerated progress and, borne along by the money-driven tide which is symbolized in the first pages by the traffic of a Chicago street, become bewildered and broken in their efforts to keep up "with the procession." The general situation is embodied in the figure of the rich Mrs. Granger Bates, compelled by reason of her money to try to live up to a high position and to occupy a grand mansion but reduced by her homely tastes to reconstituting a kind of inner sanctuary in the image of the snug and vulgar home of her youth. The author has summed up in these novels both his intimate observation of Chicago and his half-alien criticism of it. There is the overpowering faith of the Chicagoans in the future of their new city: "Individually, we may be of a rather humble grade of atoms," he makes one of the men in *The Cliff-Dwellers* say, "but we are crystallizing into a compound that is going to exercise a tremendous force. . . . You may have seen the boiling of the kettle, but you have hardly seen the force that feeds the flame. The big buildings are all well enough, and the big crowds in the streets, and the reports of the banks and railways and the Board of Trade. But there is something, now, beyond and behind all that. . . . Does it seem unreasonable that the State which produced the two greatest figures of the greatest epoch in our history, and which has done most within the last ten years to check alien excesses and un-American ideas, should also be the State to give the country the final blend of the American character and its ultimate metropolis?" "His wife sat beside him silent, but with her hand on his," adds Fuller, "and when he answered, she pressed it meaningly; for to the Chicagoan—even the middle-aged female Chicagoan—the name of the town, in its formal, ceremonial use, has a power that no other word in the language quite possesses. It is a shibboleth, as regards its pronunciation; it is a trumpet call, as regards its effect. It has all the electrifying and unifying power of a college yell." And there is the social insecurity of Chicagoans: "Commercially, we feel our own footing; socially, we are rather abashed by the pretensions that any new ar-

rival chooses to make. We are a little afraid of him, and, to tell the truth, we are a little afraid of each other." Fuller is able, from his knowledge of Europe, to understand the beginnings of gangsterism, which, with the increase of immigrant workers, is already manifesting itself as an unruly and dangerous element: "The populations of Italy and Poland and Hungary," says one of the characters in *With the Procession,* "what view now do *they* take of the government—their government, all government? Isn't it an implacable and immemorial enemy—a great and cruel and dreadful monster to be evaded, hoodwinked, combated, stabbed in the dark if occasion offers? . . . Is it an easy matter, on their coming over here, to make them feel themselves a part of [the government], and to imbue them with a loyalty to it?" One of the features of both these books is the figure, which was to become so familiar in the American fiction of this period, of the extravagant and socially ambitious woman who drives and sometimes ruins her hard-working husband. In *The Cliff-Dwellers,* the power behind everything, the wife of the owner of the office building, "a radiant, magnificent young creature, splendid, like all her mates, with the new and eager splendor of a long-awaited opportunity," appears, at an opera performance, only at the end of the book. A newly married husband in the audience has never seen her before, but "he knew that she was Cecilia Ingles, and his heart was constricted at the sight of her. It is for such a woman that one man builds a Clifton and that a hundred others are martyred in it."

The Cliff-Dwellers, which takes for its subject the accidental modern unit of the office building, the diversity of human beings who have it in common that they are thrown together by working there, was perhaps suggested by Zola, and it anticipates such similar books as Waldo Frank's *City Block* and Dos Passos's *Manhattan Transfer. With the Procession,* a better novel, is closer to the tradition of Howells—the low-keyed, prosaic domestic chronicle. But, having done his duty by Chicago in these studies of a social organism, the author, still involved with his city, went on to pieces of lesser scope, in which he is more himself and more enjoyable today than in either of these solider novels or in his fantasies of leisured Europeans.

Fuller said that he hated Chicago and that if it were not for his family interests he would leave it and go to live in Italy, and he advised Hamlin Garland, a young writer from Wisconsin, since Garland did not have to stay there, to leave. But he was not entirely unmoved by the cultural ambitions of the city, which was ridiculed in the East for some Chicagoan's statement that Chicago was going to "make culture hum." Chicago was to have its Art Institute and its Opera, both genuinely superior institutions. An excellent literary review, the *Dial,* to which Fuller often contributed, had been started in Chicago in 1880 and was to remain there till 1916; the *Chap-Book,* in the *Yellow Book* tradition, which ran from 1894 to 1898, published Yeats and Henry James; and *Poetry,* which printed the early work of Eliot, Pound, and other then unknown but later famous poets and to which Fuller acted as adviser, was started in 1912. In 1890, the University of Chicago had been founded, with Rockefeller money. Its first president, William R. Harper, of Ohio, a leading Hebrew scholar who had been teaching at Yale, was a man full of enthusiasm and innovating ideas, and he brought to the West an extraordinary faculty, which included, on the side of the humanities (the scientific side was equally remarkable): in English—Robert M. Lovett of Massachusetts and Harvard, William Vaughn Moody, the poet and dramatist, of Indiana and Harvard, Robert Herrick, the novelist, of Cambridge and Harvard, and John M. Manly, the Chaucerian scholar, of Alabama and Harvard; in Classics—Paul Shorey of Iowa and Harvard; and in History—Ferdinand Schevill of Ohio and Yale, and the Baltic outlaw H. E. von Holst, who became an authority on American history. Thorstein Veblen spent fourteen years, and wrote "The Theory of the Leisure Class," at Chicago, and John Dewey was at one time director of the school of education. This group of scholars and writers combined the best of the East with the best of the Middle West who had been educated in the East. Some of them had studied in Europe, and many spent their vacations there. They equalled, if they did not surpass, the group that Woodrow Wilson not much later (1902) was able to recruit for Princeton. I have heard Robert Lovett tell of the high missionary spirit with which these young men set out to create from scratch, in what had lately been a swampy waste, a great emporium of learning and inspiration. Robert Herrick, so thorough a New Englander, fastidious and rather thin-skinned, was to remain in Chicago thirty years, and in his entertaining novel *Chimes,* though putting on record the crudity and disorder of the University's early days and its struggles with its backers and trustees, he brings out the bold aims of the president and the courage and good will of the pioneering teachers. The University did provide an intellectual center for the competitive scramble that Fuller described, and he followed its activities with much interest, as he did the artistic activities of the city. He established close relations with the academic people, and he responded with lively interest to any manifestations of talent on the part of young painters or writers. His spirit seems to have been pervasive, and the tributes collected after his death by Anna Morgan, the manager of a little theatre, are evidence of the gratitude of his colleagues, who felt the stimulus of the presence among them of a craftsman of very high standards who had put himself to school to the finest of the scholarship and art of the world. And the novelist, on his side, diverted himself by writing about these cultural exploits.

In 1901, Fuller published a group of three stories called **Under the Skylights.** Perhaps the best of these, **"The Downfall of Abner Joyce,"** is based on the career of Hamlin Garland. Abner Joyce, on coming to Chicago, writes stark and indignant stories about the rigors of life on the Western farms and affects to despise the activities of what he regards as an effete intelligentsia, but when he finds himself taken up by them and given an entrée into the social life of Chicago he develops an appetite for it and is obviously very much gratified at becoming a fashionable

figure. This characterization is amply confirmed by the four volumes of Garland's memoirs, in which he recounts at length his relations with many celebrities of the literary and political and moneyed worlds, whom he never missed a chance of seeing and whose kindness to and praise of himself he obviously loved to chronicle. He was always presiding at meetings of academies and getting up artists' clubs. When he organized such a club in Chicago and called it the Cliff-Dwellers, after Fuller's novel, Fuller—no doubt embarrassed—refused to become a member, or even, Garland says, so far as he knows, to accept in invitation to dine there. Yet it is evidence of Fuller's generosity where anyone of real talent was concerned that, in spite of his portrait of Garland as something of a bumpkinish climber, he should have remained on good terms with him all his life and that he did not forfeit Garland's respect. He was evidently, however, to return to the subject in another little comedy, called **"Addolorata's Intervention."** Here the character who represents Fuller and the character who represents Garland accidentally meet in Sicily. The former, a novelist who has never had much audience, cannot but feel that the latter, now a popular writer, is treating him with a cavalier condescension. He meets, also, a young lady fan of his own unpopular works, but he praises his rival to her, and she immediately attaches herself to the other, who eagerly snatches her up. The first writer, who is conscious of his superiority and really does not care about the girl, looks on at the whole comedy with a detachment not untinged by a certain disdainful envy.

It should be said at this point, in parenthesis, before we pass in review the more successful books of Fuller, that he was curiously unsuccessful and gave evidence of unexpectedly uncertain taste when he tried to work in any other form or vein than those of his ironic fiction. *The Puppet-Booth* (1896), which followed *With the Procession,* is a collection of little plays—with Maeterlinck somewhere in the background—that depart from the realistic without managing to achieve the poetic. And when the *Spoon River Anthology* of Edgar Lee Masters appeared, in 1915, Fuller was excited by it and thought that this kind of epitaph in vers libre or broken prose had interesting possibilities. Two years later, he published a book of such epitaphs called *Lines Long and Short,* but they lack the grim pathos of Masters. Fuller here is simply sketching the same kind of characters that appear in his novels, but with much less telling effect. In the meantime, in 1899, he had been provoked by the war with Spain and our occupation of the Philippines to a quite uncharacteristic outbreak—a satire in verse called *The New Flag.* He was unable to find a publisher for what was thought, in that imperialistic era, an anti-patriotic tirade, and had it printed at his own expense. *The New Flag* is ill-written as verse and even rather coarse in its violence. Robert Lovett, in an article in the *New Republic* at the time of Fuller's death, expressed the opinion that this blast had a bad effect on Fuller's career: it made him unpopular in Chicago, and, what was worse, it deranged and poisoned a temperament and a talent which were normally calm and aloof. McKinley's invasion of the Philippines, with its two years of war on the natives, was an act of gratuitous conquest that shocked men who had forgotten the Mexican War and accepted the Civil War—men such as Mark Twain and William Vaughn Moody, who protested with blistering bitterness. It is significant that the part-time expatriate Fuller, who ridiculed and deplored the tendencies of contemporary America, should still have retained enough of old-fashioned American idealism to flare up and give vent to such vituperation.

Under the Skylight was followed, in 1908, by *Waldo Trench and Others: Stories of Americans in Italy,* which exploits much more successfully the same materials as an earlier collection, of 1898, *From the Other Side: Stories of Transatlantic Travel.* The European figures of these earlier stories are the phantoms of a consolatory daydream, but the Americans abroad of *Waldo Trench* represent situations at home of which Fuller had had first-hand experience. In the story which gives the volume its title, a young man from Oklahoma is first seen much moved and excited at discovering, in downtown New York, a church which is a hundred and fifty years old. "How it brings back the old Revolutionary days!" he exclaims. "I expect to see few things more impressive than this." But he is on his way to Europe, and when he gets there he discovers the Renaissance, by which he is even more excited. He is infatuated with Van Dyck and Raphael, Brunelleschi and Isabella d'Este, till someone puts him on to the Middle Ages, and he decides that Isabella d'Este is inferior to Dante's Beatrice and that he must go at once to Assisi. But then he is told by someone that classical Rome is the thing if one wants "to get the foundations of a good solid education," and while he is doing Rome someone else tells him that "the Etruscans were the first schoolmasters of the Romans. They whipped those poor, uncouth creatures into shape and passed them on to the Greeks," so Trench goes to study the Etruscan cities. But, poking among their ruins, he runs into an Englishman who exclaims to him scornfully, "Why, they're only Etruscan!" "What did you expect them to be?" "'I'm after the Pelasgians,' [the Englishman] returned in the sourest tone imaginable; 'what is this modern world to *me*?'" The next step back into the European past would be to explore the remains of the early Sicilian rockdwellers, "called Sikelians or Sicanians." But a friend, with mischievous intent, explains at once to Waldo that these names belong to two different groups: "The distinction between them is an important one and well worthy of the best endeavors of an ambitious young *savant.*" In the meantime, he has met a rich girl from Ohio, whose aunt, also rich, is pulsing with the spirit of Western enterprise and discourages Waldo's researches. She thinks that he is headed in the wrong direction: "That young man," she declares. "Such amazing vigor, such exhaustless driving power, such astonishing singleness of purpose! And all, at present, so misapplied. Think what such qualities are going to effect for him on those farms and in the civic life of his new commonwealth!" He gives up his ambition to penetrate the past and marries the niece and returns to Oklahoma. Another of these stories, **"For the Faith,"** seems to me a comic masterpiece. It presents in a few pages a whole cultural shift in American life and might

well be included in the reading list of a course in American history. A young schoolteacher from Stoneham Falls, Connecticut, is taking, with a couple of other girls, a vacation trip to Europe and writing to a friend at home. She finds herself on the boat with a very well-known "plutocrat," to whom she always refers with a proper New England scorn both snobbish and moralistic. But the plutocrat has with him an agreeable nephew, who pays the young lady compliments and seems to feel a real interest in her. She, however, maintains her attitude and, when she meets them again on her travels, insists to him that he and his uncle only want to buy up European art treasures and take them back to America: "Oh, leave those poor things alone! Let the land that originated them keep them a little longer. They were born here and they belong here. Restrain yourself. I'd much rather you went back to America and learned to rob your fellow-citizens." But Philippa, as in those days they used to say, has set her cap for young Thorpe. She has at first been writing of her plans for doing England in the usual guidebook way—"Salisbury and Winchester and Wells"—but she afterward manages an itinerary which enables her to keep up her acquaintance with the plutocrat and his nephew. Eventually, she bags her prey. The young man, when he gets back to the States, is going to have a job in one of his uncle's companies in Colorado, and she looks forward to being founder and president of the first women's club in the town. The modulation from her original point of view into complete acceptance of the millionaire is accomplished by Fuller with much humorous subtlety. Though her tone remains equally priggish, she now has a rationalization for her approval of everything she condemned before: "We cannot have an omelet without breaking a few eggs; we cannot bring a vast new country under the plough without turning under, at the same time, a certain number of innocent flowers; nor can a man seat himself at the apex of an enormous fortune without the charge of many minor injustices from a chorus of outspoken enemies. The old gentleman—whom I at last view not as a sociological abstraction but as a human creature like the rest of us—has probably had his beliefs and convictions, after all, and has in some degree suffered and sacrificed himself for them." What puts everything on a perfectly sound basis is discovering that the millionaire was, like herself, a product of the Naugatuck Valley: "He had been born on a farm *near* Stoneham Falls and been carried over into Fairfield County at the age of one."

Fuller published in the *Dial* in 1917 **"A Plea for Shorter Novels,"** which is based, among other considerations, on the needlessness of writing descriptions of such places as everyone knows and of characters whom the reader will in any case identify with people he has seen. He "would sweep away . . . all laborious effort on stuff that is dragged in because someone will think it 'ought to be there'—clichés, conventional scenes and situations." In the next year, he published **On the Stairs,** which seems to me one of his best things. I used to amuse myself by telling foreign visitors that it was "the great American novel." (I find that James Huneker, in a letter to Fuller, calls it "the great Chicago novel.") *On the Stairs* deals with life in Chicago, but it dispenses with realistic trappings, and the author explains in a foreword that the book is an attempt at the kind of thing which he has recently been recommending. His device in this story is to tell it much as if he were an old Chicagoan recounting to another Chicagoan who takes the town and the milieu for granted the inside story of families that both of them have known. In the last quarter of the last century, two boys grow up in the city. One of them, Raymond Prince, is the son of a well-to-do family, who, like Fuller's, has come to the West, by way of New York State, from New England; the other, Johnny McComas, is the son of their stableman, who has lived with his family in the stable. Raymond breaks away, like Fuller, from the family background of banking and real estate, studies architecture and art, and spends a few years in Europe. In the meantime, Johnny has left school early, has worked hard, and soon becomes envied and admired as "the youngest bank-president in the 'Loop.'" We follow thereafter the progress of Johnny, as he grows more and more prosperous, and the gradual subsidence of Raymond, who has no interest in the family bank—it eventually goes into receivership—but never succeeds in doing anything of any worth in line with his artistic tastes. Raymond's discontented wife from the East, to his bitter humiliation, divorces him and marries Johnny, and Raymond is now so impoverished that he is obliged to let Johnny put his son through Yale. To make matters even worse from the point of view of Raymond, this son marries Johnny's daughter, a daughter by an earlier, very bourgeois wife. Now, in a story by Henry James, it would be made clear that Raymond had the finer values and that his frustration was not without nobility; in a story by Horatio Alger, Johnny would be a self-made hero who had achieved the kind of success that every American wants. But the point of Fuller's novel is that the two men are equally mediocre and that the social distinctions which originally divided them have in two generations disappeared. Raymond, to be sure, is pathetic, but we do not much sympathize with him. Johnny is relatively impressive by reason of his masculine vigor, and he behaves in a not ungenerous way, but he remains rather coarse and discomforting, and we do not like *him* much, either. Huneker compared *On the Stairs* to Flaubert's "Bouvard et Pécuchet."

The futility of the young man who comes back to Chicago from Europe with greater sophistication and polish but enfeebled qualifications for making himself a place in the world of his origin has already been illustrated by Fuller in Truesdale Marshall of *With the Procession*. This is, in fact, with Fuller a recurrent theme—a kind of caricature of one aspect of himself. But he was not, of course, himself an ineffectual dilettante. Continuing to live in his native city and, as he once told Garland, with "no expectation of seeing satisfactory improvement in this town during my lifetime," he remained nevertheless indefatigable in his attempts to encourage anyone who showed any sign of serious cultural ambition. He put himself at the service of young painters and writers; with the latter, he read and criticized their manuscripts and even corrected their proofs.

For years he conducted a book department in one of the daily papers. The volume of "Tributes to Henry B. from friends in whose minds and hearts he will always live" (the title on the cover is "Henry B. Fuller"), compiled by Anna Morgan, shows how many and what various people felt that they owed him a debt: Jane Addams, Louis Bromfield, Hamlin Garland, Lorado Taft, the sculptor; Bert Leston Taylor, the columnist; John T. McCutcheon, the cartoonist and illustrator; Harriet Monroe, the editor of *Poetry;* Thornton Wilder, Booth Tarkington, and other figures less well known. A good many of them seemed to feel that, less successful than some of them, he was somehow a little above them. At every gathering he was eagerly expected, though he did not always appear. Like many intelligent and affectionate born bachelors, he counted very much on his friends. He looked on sympathetically at their family relations and liked to amuse their children, with whom he was very popular and to whom he sometimes stood godfather; he would make the evenings gay by playing and enjoying old songs. But about his own life he was always guarded. He was supposed to have a room in his mother's house, but actually he seemed to live, says his biographer, Constance M. Griffin, "in a succession of rooming houses, where he could not be reached by telephone, and where no one would presume to call." No one ever knew his address, and he was regarded as something of a "mystery." This way of life is partly to be explained by his dislike of being disturbed, his scrupulous independence, and his resolute intention, so unaccountable in Chicago, not to have to make any money beyond his modest family income. In a society in which, as Fuller describes it, one's status depended on one's income and in which, as a consequence, this status was always precarious, he chose to maintain the cultural prestige to which he had been born in the city by accepting somewhat sordid conditions of living. Hamlin Garland complains of Fuller that he has "lived so long in restaurants that his table manners annoy me. He automatically polishes his coffee cup and wipes all the forks and knives on his napkin or on a corner of the tablecloth. He turns each piece of toast (looking for a possible fly) and peers into the milk or cream jug for a cockroach, all of which is funny for a time but comes to be an irritation at last—and yet he is the ablest, most distinctive, most intellectual of all our Western writers. He can be—and generally is—the most satisfactory of all my literary companions." Though Garland says in his memoirs that he was irked by Fuller's fault-finding, the adjective most often applied to him in the Morgan collection of tributes is "gentle." It is said of him that though his character was essentially steely, his manner in company was shy. Burton Rascoe thus described him in a "profile" of 1924: "In person Mr. Fuller is a furtive little fellow with a neatly trimmed white beard and white hair; his skin is smooth and white; his voice is soft and hesitant; his eyes gleam with amused inquisitiveness; and he is always perfectly shod and tailored. He is neat, gracious, charming, excessively quiet." In the photographs of Fuller in his later years one notes always a slight look of anxiety.

There was perhaps another reason for the secrecy of Fuller's habits. He was evidently homosexual. This seems obvious throughout his work, in which he prefers to dwell on the splendid physiques of his young male characters rather than on the attractions of the women. He has a tendency, as in **On the Stairs,** to favor his vigorous vulgarians at the expense of his effete *raffinés*. On the death of Rudolph Valentino, Fuller wrote, but did not publish, a eulogy of this "Sheik" of the movies, who was apparently, according to Mencken's account of his curious interview with him, a genuinely sensitive fellow. Though certain conventionally desirable matings do occur in Fuller's novels, the situations that involve the affections are likely to be those in which some older man—it was apparently Fuller's problem—is trying to find a sympathetic younger man to live or travel with him. In his **"Plea for Shorter Novels,"** he includes among elements to be eliminated "reluctant love passages" and "repellent sex discussions." But this emphasis was undoubtedly one of the reasons—together with his resolve to avoid "scenes of violence and bloodshed with which one may have no proper affinity" and "indelicate 'close-ups' which explore and exploit poor humanity beyond the just bounds of decorum"—for Fuller's lack of popularity. The novelists of that sentimental period—Owen Wister in *The Virginian* and George Cable in *The Cavalier*—were capable of glorifying virility in a way that probably flushed with pride their masculine readers as well as excited their large feminine audience, but Fuller was incapable of such specious romance: he is ironic about even his handsome young men. His books contain no sex interest of any kind. It is all the more startling, then, that he should suddenly, in **The Puppet-Booth**—in one of his short plays, called **"At Saint Judas's"**—have given such frank expression to that element of his personality. This rather absurd piece—Fuller is bad when he tries to be overtly dramatic—is concerned with the crisis that precedes a wedding, when the best man, the bridegroom's close friend, with whom he has been sharing rooms, turns up in the sacristy of the church in a state of hysterical emotion and tells the groom that he must not get married, that the prospective bride is a slut, that she has been going to bed with him, the best man. In this story, however, he soon breaks down, knowing well that the other will not believe it: "*I* am here. And *she* will never be. You may wait, but you shall wait in vain. (*He places his hand upon the other's shoulder.*) If she were to come, I should not let her have you. She shall not have you. Nobody shall have you." A horrible scene ensues—a scene too horrible for Fuller to handle. The friend attempts to bar the groom from entering the church. The groom says, "Stand aside. I hate you; I detest you; I despise you; I loathe you." "We have been friends always," the other replies. "I have loved you all my life. . . . The thought of *her* made me mad, made me desperate." He declares that one of the three shall die. The bride-groom invites him to "use your blade" (he evidently refers to a sword). The bride is coming up the aisle, and the groom enters the church. "*Upon the floor of the sacristy lies the body of a man in a pool of blood.*" The trouble here is that Fuller is incapable of imagining at all convincingly such an outbreak of naked passion—espe-

cially between characters who are carrying swords. I agree with Miss Griffin when she says that the middle-aged Freiherr von Kaltenau, as he appears in **The Last Refuge,** travelling with an adored young man, is to be identified with Fuller when this character, taking stock of his life, concludes that it "had been indeed too free—too free from ties, from duties, from obligations, from restraints; too free from guidance, too free from the kindly pressure of any ordering hand. . . . The book of life had been opened wide before him, but he had declined to make the usual advance that leads straight on from chapter to chapter; rather had he fluttered the leaves carelessly, glanced at the end before reaching the middle, and thoroughly thwarted the aims and intentions of the great Author." I agree that the author identifies himself also with another of the people in this book, a novelist whose "principal concern was the portrayal of his contemporaries in works of fiction," when he confesses that his "participation in life has been, after all, but partial. I have always felt a slight reluctance about committing myself—a touch of dread about letting myself go. I have lived, in fact, by the seashore without ever venturing into the water. Others have gone in before my eyes, and I have recorded, to the best of my endeavor, the exhilarations they appeared to feel, the dangers they appeared to brave. But as soon as the waves have stolen up to my own toes, I have always stepped back upon the dry sands."

"There was in its deepest recesses," writes Harriet Monroe of Fuller's character, without assigning a specific cause, "an unconquerable reticence—Henry Fuller found it impossible to tell his whole story. He could not give himself away, and therefore it may be that the greatest book of which his genius was capable was never written, the book which would have brought the world to his feet in complete accord and delight." But one cannot imagine Fuller's writing such a book, and when he did reveal his secret, so far from bringing the world to his feet, he made it look the other way. In 1919, when he was sixty-two, he took the audacious step of publishing a novel, **Bertram Cope's Year,** with homosexual characters. His attitude about this at first is quite unabashed and cool: "I wrote," he tells Henry Kitchell Webster, another Illinois novelist, "in complete reaction from the love flummery of Holworthy Hall, et al. [Holworthy Hall was a pseudonym, the name of one of the Harvard dormitories, used by Harold Everett Porter, a writer for *Collier's* and the *Saturday Evening Post.*] Those fellows tire me. Perhaps I've gone too far the other way. While doing the job, I *did* think, now and then, of some of your own aberrations and perversions (Olga, Helena, et cet.)—but these in latter-day society are getting almost too common to be termed 'abnormal.' Lots of people must have read you in unperturbed innocency, and I hope a good many will read me that way, too. Certainly we are both 'Innocent Kids' compared with Cabell in 'Jurgen.'" And **Bertram Cope's Year,** though it involves homosexual situations, is not really a book about homosexuality. It has a kind of philosophic theme, which seems to me to raise it well above the fiction of social surfaces of the school of William Dean Howells. The story is made to take place in a Middle Western university town, which derives, Fuller admits, to some extent from Evanston, Illinois. Bertram Cope is a young instructor who is working for an M.A. in English. He is very good-looking, with yellow hair, and not stupid, though not strikingly intelligent, and he is found attractive by a number of persons. There is, first, Mr. Basil Randolph, a "scholar manqué," who works in the family brokerage business but is far more interested in collecting jades and other objects d'art and in hovering around the male students, who are likely themselves to be hovering around the quadrangle that houses the girls. There is also Medora Phillips, a well-to-do widow, who likes to have young people around her and has living in the house with her a niece, a girl secretary, and a girl boarder. All these people become infatuated with Bertram, who does not become attached to any of them. He is said to be "an ebullient Puritan," with New England perhaps in the background, and he is interested only in making his way. The niece traps him into an engagement, from which he afterward manages to extricate himself; the more aggressive boarder, who is fearfully jealous of the niece, tries to ensnare him by painting his portrait; the secretary writes him sonnets which are considered by the older generation to go pretty far for a young girl. And Mrs. Phillips herself—though he regards her merely as a person to whose house he is glad to go—becomes much preoccupied with Bertram. The designs of Mr. Randolph are frustrated—he has taken new rooms, with an extra bedroom—when Bertram himself takes new rooms in order to accommodate a friend with whom he has been intimately corresponding and whom he brings on to keep him company. This friend, whose name is Arthur Lemoyne, Mr. Randolph does not at first want to meet and, when he does, immediately recognizes as the wrong kind of homosexual and resents as a dangerous rival: "His dark eyes were too liquid; his person was too plump," etc. Lemoyne, on his side, has brought pressure on Bertram to get out of his engagement with the niece, and he now pits himself against Randolph and all the ladies of the Phillips household. But nothing can dispel the enchantment which Bertram continues to exercise over all of them. When he tips over in a small sailboat, he is saved by his fiancée, who disentangles him from the mainsail and cordage, but he gets credit for having saved *her;* when the Philips cottage on the dunes is broken into by an escaped convict, Bertram merely wakes up with a shriek while another man grapples with the burglar, but it is Bertram who becomes the hero. When he passes out at a dinner as the result of drinking wine, to which he is not accustomed, on top of a day of excessive work and a more or less empty stomach, he becomes the object of everyone's attention and everyone's solicitude. Mrs. Phillips's rather sour brother-in-law, crippled and half-blind, who plays the role of the detached observer and is completely aware of what is going on, growls that it all reminds him of a religious festival he once attended in an Italian hill town near Florence: "There was a kind of grotto in the church, under the high altar; and in the grotto was a full-sized figure of a dead man, carved and painted—and covered with wounds; and round that figure half the women and girls of the town were collected, stroking, kissing. . . . Adonis all over again!"

This establishes the real point of the story, which is that Bertram's admirers all look to find in him a version of a semi-divine ideal that he makes no attempt to live up to; that he is quite unconscious that his beauty and charm, together with a hard, self-sufficient core of character, have caused them to endow him with qualities which he does not at all possess. In the end, he simply gets his degree and leaves. But in the meantime he had been separated from Arthur Lemoyne. The latter has taken a feminine role in a college musical comedy and has had a unique success as a female impersonator; after the play, he has disgraced himself behind the scenes by making advances to a boy who has been playing a male part. His connection with the college is tenuous—something arranged by Bertram, through Randolph—and the authorities let him go. Bertram appeals to Randolph, who refuses to be helpful, and Arthur, with his bad reputation, is now a nuisance, anyhow, to Bertram. Bertram goes East and gets a better job in a better university. Randolph and Mrs. Phillips talk about him after he has left. She believes that when Bertram is earning enough, he will marry her secretary, the only one of his friends to whom he has written, though in a quite noncommittal way; Randolph, on the contrary, believes that Bertram will set up housekeeping with Arthur. At no point has the reader been given any clue as to Bertram's sexual inclinations. Fuller's rather difficult problem here has been to make Bertram intrinsically uninteresting and even rather comic, but at the same time to dramatize convincingly the spell of enchantment he is supposed to cast. This is seen in his effect on the other characters, but the reader is not made to feel it: Bertram is represented as behaving in an agreeable enough way, but, in his self-centeredness, he never does anything that is made to seem really attractive. And the result, as in *On the Stairs,* is a kind of deliberate flatness.

This curious book, which is perhaps Fuller's best, seems never to have had adequate attention. The few people who have written about Fuller at any length have, so far as my reading goes, always treated it very gingerly. The only contemporary, so far as I know, who showed any real appreciation was James Huneker, who very much prided himself on his sophistication and lack of prudery and had previously applauded **"At Saint Judas's."** He wrote Fuller of *Bertram Cope's Year* that he had read it three times: "Its portraiture and psychological strokes fill me with envy and also joy. *Ça y est,* I said to myself. And Chicago! It is as desolate, your dissection, as a lunar landscape. We are like that, not like Whitman's Camerados and his joyful junk. Why do you speak of your last book! You are only beginning, you implacable Stendhal of the lake!" But otherwise the effect of the novel was a slighting reproof or a horrified silence. André Gide had then only the prestige of a very limited cult; Proust had not yet been translated. Burton Rascoe wrote, "It may be said that *Bertram Cope's Year,* in so far as it was read and understood at all, shocked Mr. Fuller's friends so painfully that they silenced it into limbo. It is a story, delicately done with the most exquisite taste, of a sublimated irregular affection. It received scant and unintelligent notice from the reviewers, and though it was filled with dynamite scrupulously packed, it fell as harmless as a dud, only to be whispered about here and there by grave people who wondered why Mr. Fuller should choose such a theme." But even this writer of the early twenties who wants to do justice to Fuller does not accurately describe the book. The central theme, as I have said above, is not "a sublimated irregular affection." Fuller has merely, in writing of the power exerted by a "charismic" personality, extended what was then the conventional range. The effect on poor Fuller himself of the reception of his book was terrible. He disparaged his own courage by saying that he wished he had never written it, and he burned up his manuscript and proofs. It was ten years before he ventured to publish another novel.

He returned in 1929, in *Gardens of This World*—of which I have already spoken—to his beloved group of Old World characters. "Such a goddam lovely little book," he says in a letter to one of his young friends. *Not on the Screen,* which was published in 1930, is the last of his Chicago novels and not only the most stripped but the palest of them; yet Fuller is always readable and always winning, through his dry sense of comedy. The book begins with a movie which a girl and a young man are watching. In the picture, there is a melodramatic situation. The rest of the novel is the story of the subsequent relations of the couple, which repeats the story of the film but is not at all melodramatic. The upstart young man from the country wins the hand of the rich young girl without any very stiff struggle. There are some rather disagreeable but not very dramatic encounters between this modest but successful young man and a socially well-situated and insolent young banker who is competing for the hand of the girl. The banker, who has power of attorney for the girl's widowed mother, resorts to unscrupulous practices in his efforts to gain his end, by threatening to ruin the family and attempting to send the young man to jail. But, although in the film the corresponding character is made to play the role of the villain, the character in the novel is not himself sent to jail. He is never melodramatically unmasked, but, in a quiet way, pressure is put upon him to restore the family fortunes. The mistress of the young banker, who would figure as the "vamp" in the picture, is a cheap and rather pathetic figure who, although she arouses suspicion by going out with the *jeune premier,* has never for a moment tempted him. The story is all told in terms of the social nuances of Chicago, of which Fuller was an amused observer, but the point of the whole thing is that in a Western city like Chicago—and perhaps, by implication, anywhere in the United States—these differences matter very little. You cannot get a thrilling drama out of them. This novel is another exercise in the art of making it flat—the quality of which art, of course, was appreciated little by the public and which accounts for the lessening interest in the books of Fuller's later years.

In this very late last burst of energy—Fuller was now seventy-two—he started still another novel, but he did not get far with this or see the publication of either *Not on the Screen* or *Gardens of This World.* He died alone in a rooming house in July, 1929. One is reminded of the ending of one of the character sketches in *Lines Long and Short,* the portrait of a familyless bachelor who has tried to make a life for himself by his attentions to the families of friends and who is left with little consolation:

> Yes, perhaps he did
> Come through all right—
> With much or little sympathy—
> To take up, with what zest he
>   could,
> The frantic role
> Of buying favors from a cooling
>   world.
> Spend as you will,
> It's sad to be old, and alone.
> (Fudge! that's the very thing
> I tried hard not to say!)

The literature on Fuller is extremely meagre. Besides the volume of tributes mentioned and a few other scattered memoirs, there is only the inadequate biography by Constance M. Griffin, published by the University of Pennsylvania Press—evidently one of those theses which the estimable Arthur H. Quinn of Pennsylvania, the author of comprehensive and useful books on American fiction and drama, induced his students to write on neglected American authors. We must be grateful to Mr. Quinn. If it had not been for him, we should have had nothing of value at all on such writers as Kate Chopin and Fuller. But something more searching and solid is needed, and now that the University of Chicago Press has reprinted *With the Procession,* I should like to suggest that it commission a life and letters of Fuller, as well as a volume of his uncollected pieces. He did a good deal of reviewing in his lifetime. I have just been through the articles he contributed to the *New Republic* during the twenties when he was not writing novels. They are always discriminating and conscientious, and it is interesting to know what he thought about Chekhov, Cabell, and Proust. Miss Griffin's selective bibliography includes many other items which awaken curiosity, as well as a long list of unpublished or uncollected stories. We know from those stories of Kate Chopin and Cable which were rejected by the conventional magazines of the nineties and the early nineteen-hundreds that some of these authors' most interesting things were inacceptable to the squeamish editors. Fuller's early humorous writings for *Life* should also be investigated. I have looked up "A Transcontinental Episode, or, Metamorphoses at Muggins' Misery: A Co-operative Novel by Bret James and Henry Harte" (published in 1884). It is juvenile but not unamusing. A Jamesian young man who has lived abroad and is always slipping into French arrives in one of Harte's tough California settlements. He falls in love with the local belle and she with him, as the result of which he tries to transform himself into the kind of man he thinks she admires. But she, on her side, during an absence of his, has schooled herself to be refined. Fuller supplies two alternative endings, by each of the collaborators. In Harte's version, when her lover returns in the garb of a rugged Westerner, she casts off her elegant clothes and with a whoop leaps into his arms. In James's, she preserves the "finer" manners and dress to which her contact with the travelled young Easterner has raised her, but the question of whether they can ever now get together is left, in the Jamesian fashion, completely up in the air. This little skit states already the theme of the constant conflict between the two states of American culture which was to occupy Fuller all his life.

Guy Szuberla (essay date 1973)

SOURCE: "Making the Sublime Mechanical: Henry Blake Fuller's Chicago," in *American Studies,* Vol. XIV, No. 1, Spring, 1973, pp. 83-93.

[*In the following essay, Szuberla examines Fuller's use of the urban modern landscape in* The Cliff-Dwellers *and* With the Procession.]

"We need Nature," Ralph Waldo Emerson once wrote in a journal entry, "and cities give the human senses not room enough."[1] That cities stifle the human senses has seemed a self-evident truth for a diverse number of American thinkers. This commonplace of agrarian thought, expressed by Jefferson, Henry Adams, Frederick Jackson Turner and others, reinforces the native notion that this country's open spaces and virgin land generate freedom and spiritual redemption. And so, Emerson's presumptive use of the all inclusive "we"—no less than Turner's famed frontier thesis—implicitly denies that writers, artists, or the ordinary city-dweller could experience the city as a place where the human senses are liberated or that anyone could see the urban landscape as a terrain without confining limits. Though America has built no walled cities, that old world image haunts the American imagination. It is, perhaps, not until the Chicago novelist Henry Blake Fuller articulates his vision of a cityscape that American literature reflects a new idea of urban space. For Fuller, the city, not Nature gives the human senses infinite room.

His transvaluation of the agrarian myth, with its concomitant image of the city's suffocating bounds, projects a discovery of the city's machine-made beauty. Fuller's Chicago novels, ***The Cliff-Dwellers*** (1893) and ***With the Procession*** (1895), celebrate an industrialized city, the mechanized anti-type of America's mythical garden. Like his contemporary, the Chicago architect Louis Sullivan, he shapes his spatial aesthetics out of the technological conditions of his time. Chicago's modern architecture, especially the towering skyscrapers built in the 1890s, created a new sense of urban space: urban vistas now pierced and fragmented Nature, obliterating the land that in terms of America's pastoral myth was boundless. By abandoning and subverting that myth, Fuller perceived that the city's infinite vistas evoked a pleasing terror—a modern, technological sublime.

Functionalist assumptions inform Fuller's reading of Chicago's architecture and the urban landscape. Fully conscious that Chicago, "of all the very large cities in the world, is the only one that has been built together under completely modern conditions," he nevertheless urged architects and city-planners to stamp Chicago with the impress of machine-made "new materials."[2] His weekly newspaper columns in the Chicago *Evening Post* bristled with attacks on architecture that "reeks with far-fetched picturesqueness and foolish illogical effectism" or that "revels in the falsification of construction and of material."[3] The modern city, his rejection of the picturesque suggests, could not be made over in the image of a garden or contained by time-worn architectural forms. In this embrace of modernism, he anticipates Hart Crane's contentious demand that literature "absorb the machine" and "surrender . . . temporarily, to the sensations of urban life."[4]

This is not to say Fuller willingly surrendered his sensibilities to every assault his city might mount. What he pleaded for and worked at in his fiction was the assimilation of the modern city into art. His novels, even today, teach the reader how to see the city's beauty and spatial form. To be sure, he had his doubts about using the city of Chicago as literary subject: "Who wants to read about this repellent town?" he once asked William Dean Howells.[5] No modern writer—one now assumes—asks himself, as Fuller certainly did, whether an urban landscape seemingly void of meaning and beauty is worthy of fictional treatment, whether its denatured surface might compose an aesthetically significant pattern. Fuller's vision of the city's chaos, unlike that of contemporary novelists such as Saul Bellow or Thomas Pynchon, springs from a consciousness of genteel aesthetics: that is, the belief that art should present a vision of *ideal* beauty and harmony.

In defining the spatial form of the city, Fuller traced the split along the line of cleavage between genteel notions of order and beauty and the new visual order he believed Chicago's modern landscape created. The genteel landscape—rhetorically beflowered by the sublime, the beautiful and the picturesque—placed premium value on "Nature" and the mossy architectural motifs of the past. Fuller's own ***The Chevalier of Pensieri-Vani*** (1886) distilled into exquisite prose "views" of picturesque old Italian villas and pastoral fêtes. That he parodies the genteel vocabulary in his city novels signals, to me, his discovery that the city inverts genteel values as well as the pastoral myth. Against an idealized pastoral landscape, his city novels reify the aesthetic values embodied in a landscape distinctively modern and machine-made.

I

Fuller's ***The Cliff-Dwellers*** demonstrated a novel appreciation of the beauty within the ugliness of the industrialized city. To many contemporary reviewers, it was a startling and displeasing view of the urban landscape; critics thought it delighted in "the loathsome and cruel" and dwelled on the "sordid."[6] An anonymous reviewer, writing in the October 7, 1893 issue of *The Critic,* advised the "judicious reader" to skip over Fuller's descriptions of skyscrapers to find those passages where the author confesses "Chicago stands in need of idealization." He ended his review by smugly counseling Fuller "to vary" his talk about "realities . . . with a vision of some Offenbachian Arcadia."[7] Wresting a meaning and aesthetic form out of the city's chaos seemed insignificant to a generation that, perhaps much like our own, wished to reclaim a lost Eden. To be told that the city, in spreading its boundaries toward the infinite, rivalled and often transcended Nature was to be shown a reality they found both disgusting and incredible.

William Dean Howells came closer to interpreting Fuller's intentions when he praised the work for "adopting Zola's principles of art." Moreover, he lauded Fuller's masterly skill in handling the "ugliness" of the city, saying that "perhaps nine-tenths of the whole city life in America can find itself glassed in this unflattering mirror."[8] H. H. Boyesen, praising the novel in *The Cosmopolitan,* agreed with Howells: "we breathe, from the first chapter to the last, the atmosphere of Chicago; we quiver and tingle with a perpetual sub-consciousness of its intense activity and tremendous metropolitan uproar. . . ."[9] What could not be denied, but what so many of Fuller's genteel critics overlooked, is that Chicago's "ugliness"—its force and sprawl and bluster—held genuine aesthetic and literary interest for Fuller.

The language that Fuller employs in the introductory chapter of *The Cliff-Dwellers* suggests the ambivalence of his attitude toward Chicago as well as the difficulties of hypostatizing an urban milieu. The opening lines set down the central metaphor:

> Between the former site of old Fort Dearborn and the present site of our newest Board of Trade there lies a restricted yet tumultuous territory through which, during the course of the last fifty years, the rushing streams of commerce have worn many a deep and rugged chasm. These great canyons . . . cross each other with a sort of systematic rectangularity, and in deference to the practical directness of local requirements they are in general called simply—streets. Each of these canyons is closed in by a long frontage of towering cliffs, and these soaring walls of brick and limestone and granite rise higher and higher with each succeeding year, according as the work of erosion at their bases goes onward—the work of that seething flood of carts, carriages, omnibuses, cars, messengers, shoppers, clerks, and capitalists, which surges with increasing violence. . . . (*CD,* 1)[10]

The extended metaphorical comparison of buildings and streets to canyons, natural objects, sets up an implied antithesis between them and natural scenery, yet never explicitly condemns the unnatural quality of so much masonry. We are later told that no "direct sunlight" (*CD,* 32) reached the lower floors of the Clifton, that this is a "treeless country" (*CD,* 3). Recording the obliteration and over-

shadowing of traditional and natural symbols of beauty, Fuller maintains the illusion of almost scientific impartiality in setting down details. While he echoes "Kubla Khan" in speaking of "a deep and rugged chasm," he does not extend the figure to the point where he exploits the sympathies the reader may carry over from romantic poetry. On the contrary, the reader, despite the reservations written into the passage, is enticed into admiring the power and movement of the scene, even the "violence" of it. Fuller does not describe a static scene, regardless of the fact that the salient objects in it are static. These buildings are "towering" and "soaring"; he dares to compare the wonder they inspire with marvels of Nature. In the next paragraph, the author asserts that "El Capitan is duplicated time and again both in bulk and in stature . . ." (*CD,* 2), and one marvels over the size and scale of the scene.

Fuller is playing on the reader's preconceived aesthetic values, values formed by romantic poetry. In mimicking nineteenth century poetic diction, he undercuts its spatial values, fitting this "mighty yet unprepossessing landscape" (*CD,* 4) into a novel aesthetic category. Romantic poetry disclosed the sublime feelings to be experienced in the presence of the natural landscape; Fuller lures the reader into transferring that response to an urban landscape. The antithesis of "mighty" and "unprepossessing" suggests the ambivalence of Fuller's attitude toward this scene—he is at once disgusted and fascinated by it. But in confessing to the "hideousness" (*CD,* 2) of the landscape, he continues to elaborate on the image and compile details—returning repeatedly to the central image of the skyscraper throughout the book—and in so doing confesses to his fascination with the power of this scene.

These buildings—or rather the forces symbolized by them—dominate the city and the people in it. The omniscient author views this scene from below, giving these architectural structures an emphasis and a prominence that reduces human beings to insignificance in the landscape. They are but particles in a stream flowing at the base of these skyscrapers. In this image, Fuller symbolizes man's relationship to the urban environment. He implicitly recognizes what architects now insist is true: a building defines and symbolizes spatial and temporal relationships, as well as social and psychological relationships among people. Within the Clifton skyscraper, the major and minor characters of the novel act out lives which are to a great extent controlled by the forces of economics and business housed within the building. For the first half of the novel, the Clifton, as an embodiment of the urban milieu, is a chief actor in the novel. Its impersonality and ubiquitous presence match the forces of the modern city.

Fuller stresses the modernity of this urban milieu by making his main character, George Ogden, reflect a sense of discovery. An Easterner, newly arrived from the old state of Massachusetts, George comes to a city possessing the newest architecture and no visible past. He has come to Chicago to make his fortune, but before learning to adapt to the urban environment he suffers an unhappy marriage and financial reverses that nearly put him into jail. The setting for George's struggles is the Clifton, which symbolizes the modern technological forces Chicago produced. It was in Chicago during the 1880s and nineties, Fuller reminds us, that the construction of skyscrapers was pioneered.

By using the medium of George's perceptions, Fuller indirectly suggests what is new about Chicago and his own mode of interpreting the urban landscape. To indicate the difference between the old and the new, Fuller exploits that eighteenth century exercise in nature poetry: the view from a prospect. In applying the convention first to a rural Wisconsin scene and then to a Chicago landscape, Fuller subverts the genre and also reveals his distaste for pastoral pleasures. The distaste for the country that prompted him to call the chirp of the robins a "yelp" is rather subtly inscribed into George's view of rural Wisconsin. From a bluff high above the shores of a lake, George emits these bland, conventional remarks: "'How it balances—how it composes!' he said of the view, as he recrossed the bridge. 'And how it's kept!' he said of the town. . . . 'Really'— with unconscious patronage—'it's the only thing West, so far, that has tone and finish'" (*CD,* 204). Composing the scene in painterly terms, George concocts a representative illustration of the picturesque. The result might well be framed as a "chromo" in a Victorian living room; so neatly, in fact, does the scene fit the frame, and so quietly does the composition rest before the eye that one begins to wonder if Fuller is not attributing a disturbing stasis to nature. George's response, besides being remarkable for the extremely genteel quality in the reference to "tone and finish," is revealing for what it does not include. He attributes no spiritual values to the landscape: though he is troubled over love, he does not in any perceptible way project his feelings into the scene. And the banality of George's "unconscious patronage" ironically quashes any notion the reader might have had that this was meant to be beautiful, aesthetically interesting or pleasing.

George's limitations are no less apparent in another view from a prospect a few pages later where he acts the part of a Chicago native. From the top of the Clifton he proudly shows Chicago to an elderly Wisconsin couple visiting a friend of his. Fuller invests the urban vista with an energy and fascination not present in the Wisconsin scene:

> Ogden waved his hand over the prospect—the mouth of the river with its elevators and its sprawling miles of railway track; the weakish blue of the lake, with the coming and going of schooners and propellers, and the "cribs" that stood on the faint horizon—"that's where our water comes from," George explained; the tower of the water-works itself, and the dull and distant green of Lincoln Park; the towering bulk of other great skyscrapers and the grimy spindling of a thousand surrounding chimneys; the lumber-laden brigs that were tugged slowly through the drawbridges, while long strings of drays and buggies and street-cars accumulated during the wait. "My! don't they look little!" cried Mrs. McNabb.
>
> George smiled with all the gratified vanity of a native. (*CD,* 210-11)

As Fuller notes, natural objects are obliterated by industrialism and urbanization; the scene, prismed through a dusty haze of smoke, discloses a "weakish blue lake," the "dull and distant green" of a park, an urbanized and bounded garden. This imputes not beauty nor moral significance to Nature, but shows its weakness and diminution. The machine, an extension of man and the city, even marks the horizon, a symbol of Nature's once infinite power.

Unlike the Wisconsin scene, we do not have pictorial framing of the vista. Instead of balance and composition, we have limitless sprawl. The catalogue of the city's features—machines and natural scenery; the railroads, the river, streetcars and the lake—is given in no apparent order; the passage is designed to make us see the city's chaos, its transcendence of Nature. At the same time, Fuller invites us to marvel over the activity, movement and diversity of this chaos. In so doing, he parodies and overthrows the aesthetic category of the picturesque so patently present in the static Wisconsin scene. In opening the city's vistas to distant horizons, Fuller has created a mock or modern version of the sublime.[11] In the eighteenth century, poets and artists looked at mountains and delighted in their own smallness in facing the infinite majesty and terror of God. Here the scale of a *man-made* setting, as in the opening scene of the novel, shrinks Nature and human beings to a frightening smallness. This inverts the neoclassical sublime, since here man delights in his ability to see the smallness of other human beings: "My! don't they look little!" The novelty of its impression on the simple farm folk from Wisconsin underscores the newness and interest of the scene.

Neither the McNabbs' pleasure over the smallness of the spectacle below nor George's agreement with them passes as an authoritative comment on the urbanization of Chicago; in satirically calling George's attitude "the gratified vanity of a native," Fuller undercuts the credit we give George's pride or the McNabbs' surprise over the "prospect." The omniscient author, who has outlined this awesome array of mechanical, industrial and urban force attacking Nature, does not prompt the reader to feel pleasure, pride, surprise or unmitigated disgust. I think, instead, that this passage is meant to evoke a feeling akin to that the eighteenth century felt in the presence of the sublime: that is, a pleasing terror. There is a feeling expressed here that some terrible force is destroying a natural landscape, that it is in fact threatening to diminish man to nothingness. Nevertheless, Fuller seizes out of this view the perception that, horrible as all this may be, there is in it a dramatic surge of power that when viewed from a distance holds a pleasure for him. That power, unlike the omnipotent God the eighteenth century located in the Alps and infinite vistas, is mechanical, social, urban. Cataloguing the effect of these forces, taking their animating power in the city as his theme, Fuller writes realistically, yet with a lyric intensity and energy that expresses wonder and awe.

Fuller thus displaces the aesthetic derived from America's pastoral ideal with one drawn from modern technology and a seemingly infinite urban space. The technological sublime that his characters experience atop the Clifton redefines the pastoral ideal. Once Nature seemed unbounded and infinite; here, it is the city that reaches out towards infinity and Nature that seems finite. From the height of the skyscraper, the city can no longer be measured against the pastoral ideal because it has, physically and symbolically, transcended it. The modern city, an unbounded and bewildering immense place, required an aesthetic that would give its sprawl order and meaning, and Fuller, in denying the myth of a boundless land, moved towards defining the city's sublime power, its subtle order and violent beauty.

II

With the Procession, Fuller's second city novel, resumes his parodic satire of the genteel landscape. As in **The Cliff-Dwellers,** his parody discloses why the city's beauty and visual order could never be revealed by measuring it against a pastoral ideal or the spatial aesthetics that ideal implied. He focuses his attack on what his newspaper column, some years later, was to call "far-fetched picturesqueness."[12] It does not, however, stretch analogy to the breaking point to suggest that Fuller's satiric view of a family bent on regaining Nature's picturesque pleasures anticipates the current flight to suburban split-shingled chateaus, ornamented by Mediterranean furniture, set, presumably, in Nature. The "picturesque" and the "natural" remain, in the mass mind, synonyms for beauty.

With the Procession recounts an old Chicago family's abandonment of their home for a more fashionable one. The Marshalls move because, among other reasons, their old neighborhood has changed radically in the thirty years they have lived there. That change is symbolized in the dust thrown off from a nearby railroad; the dust covers all their old furniture, all the pietistic curios Mrs. Marshall once thought to be beautiful. The dust kills their garden and the grass outside their home: "A locomotive was letting off steam opposite the house, and the noise and the vapor came across the hundred yards of dead grass together" (*WP,* 166). The locomotive here symbolizes all the intensive forces of industrialism and technology that pursued Thoreau to Walden. The locomotive in this context, however, does not invade the countryside, but the city. To escape this force, the Marshalls do not attempt to return to some simpler idyllic wilderness. They cannot return to the countryside, because they did not come from it. Instead they move to another part of Chicago, hoping half-heartedly to regain their lost social position. Despite the industrialization of the city, Mrs. Marshall continues to see Chicago as "an Arcadia still—bigger, noisier, richer" (*WP,* 10). The city is not, Fuller's satire of Mrs. Marshall makes clear, an Arcadia. He implies that defining Chicago through a pastoral ideal is fatuous, since it is a search for a non-existent mythical garden. The pastoral myth, which has served to define the America of the past, has lost its relevance in the modern city.

Her son Truesdale Marshall, a would-be artist and sometime cosmopolitan traveler, holds no illusions about the Arcadian quality of Chicago. Through him, however, Fuller ironically undercuts an equally conventional and equally distorted view of the urban landscape, the affected and genteel love of "the picturesque" and "the beautiful." Truesdale airs carefully acquired European tastes when he ridicules Chicago and its lack of beauty. He sets forth, for example, what he insinuates is a paradigm for the city's "architectural conditions": "He improvised an ornate and airy edifice of his own, which he allowed them to dedicate to art, to education, to charity, to what you will. Then he festooned it with telegraph wires, and draped it with fire-escapes, and girdled it with a stretch of elevated road, and hung it with signboards, and hedged it in with fruitstands, and swathed it in clouds of coal. . . ." (*WP,* 245). Chicago's architecture, Truesdale believes, was "too debased to justify one's serious endeavors towards improvement." What debased it, in his mind, is the industry and technology that have given it form. From the viewpoint of a lover of the picturesque ruins of Europe, modern city architecture in Chicago appears as the antithesis of beauty.

Truesdale's pretensions to artistry and avant-gardism rest on his self-conscious love of the foreign and the picturesque. He jokes about his taste for the picturesque early in the novel, when he plans a sketching trip in rustic Wisconsin: "No canoeing, of course, on the Lahn and the Moselle; I must fall back upon the historic Illinois, with its immemorial towns and villages and crumbling cathedrals, and the long line of ancient and picturesque chateâux between Ottawa and Peoria" (*WP,* 73). Yet, when his own ideal of architecture floats before him in a reverie, we see revealed an infatuation with the "picturesque":

> He saw before him a high-heaped assemblage of red-tiled roofs, and above them rose the fretwork of a soaring Gothic spire. A narrow river half encircled the town, and a battered old bridge, guarded by a round-towered gateway, led out into the open country towards a horizon bounded by a low range of blue hills. Trumpet-calls rang out from distant barrack-yards, and troops of dragoons clattered noisily over the rough pavement of the great square. . . . High towards stars towered the columns and pediments of a vast official structure, whose broken sky-line sawed the heavens, and whose varied cornices and ledges were disjointed by deep and perplexing shadows. On each side of the great portal which opened through the pillared arcade there was stationed a mounted cuirassier. . . . (*WP,* 192)

The "towers" and battlements, with the "deep and perplexing shadows" topped by the "soaring Gothic spire," bring into relief the irregular outlines of the picturesque. The scene exemplifies that quite eclectic Gothicism that swept through the United States in the 1880's, leaving behind such landmarks as the French Gothic chateau Richard Morris Hunt designed for Mrs. William K. Vanderbilt.

Truesdale's taste, despite his posture as an impressionist painter and decadent, reflects the old-fashioned perspective of a Claude glass, and his sketching tour through Wisconsin suggests that his vision has, most certainly, been formed by books like Robert Louis Stevenson's *Travels with a Donkey in the Cevennes* (1879) and F. Hopkinson Smith's *Gondola Days.*[13] These travel books had taught American travelers to view European scenes as though they were framed statically as pictures—ruins, moss, rot, decay, chasms and gorges, the principal elements of the scenery. No wonder, then, that Truesdale found Chicago "so pitifully grotesque, grewsome [*sic*], appalling . . . ," that it had "so little taste" (*WP,* 73). He would prefer, he says, to return to the "villeggiatura at Frascati or Fiesole" or to indulge a taste for "wild ravines and gorges" (*WP,* 73). His one moment of aesthetic delight in American scenery comes when he can paint water colors of the "picturesque" and "inexhaustible . . . beauties of nature" (*WP,* 237). He flaunts tastes patently derived from conventions of the picturesque, and expresses them in transparently pretentious cliches.

But Fuller is not Truesdale. Though his early fantasy-travel books, ***The Chevalier of Pensieri-Vani*** and ***The Chatelaine of La Trinite,*** might suggest he too indulged himself in the pleasures of the picturesque, Fuller has articulated Truesdale's precious disgust with Chicago's modernity so that he can explode it. Truesdale, no less than his mother, is seen as a victim of faulty vision who insists on viewing the city against a long since vanished pastoral ideal. Fuller satirizes his characters' affectations to show that the problem with modern technology was to assimilate it into the aesthetic, not to vainly look for ways to expunge it. The city, he argued, in his newspaper criticism of the picturesque, should treat "new materials" honestly.[14] If the Chicago landscape disclosed no glimpses of the ideal and framed no picturesque ruins, it still held a strange beauty and a power to evince the technological sublime.

In an opening scene of ***With the Procession*** Fuller expresses, through Truesdale's ingenuous sister Rosy Marshall, a powerfully impressionistic response to the city at night: "The evening lights doubled and trebled—long rows of them appeared overhead at incalculable altitudes. The gongs of the cable cars clanged more and more imperiously as the crowds surged in great numbers round grip and trailer. The night life of the town began to bestir itself, and little Rosy, from her conspicuous place, beamed with a bright intentness upon its motley spectacle. . . ." (*WP,* 9) From below, we see skyscrapers, or rather their lights "at incalculable altitudes," fixing a scale and perspective almost beyond imagination. If this is not—in Hart Crane's terms—"a surrender . . . to the sensations of urban life,"[15] it is, in any case, a vivid realization of the new spatial form of the city. The surge of mechanical vitality and movement, despite the ambivalence of the clinching epithet "motley," produces a cinematic effect, and suggests that Fuller has, temporarily, surrendered to the sensations and beauty of the city.

By covertly comparing the city's skyscrapers and mechanized landscapes to phantom pastoral gardens and picture book Gothic, Fuller comes close to seeing the city as a place of wondrous possibility, a modern and man-made Arcadia. His parodic strategy counters, overwhelms, and finally demolishes the genteel platitudes he places in Truesdale's mouth. The cult of ideality with the pastoral ideal fall before his satire. The novelty of his urban aesthetics stand in bold outline when it is remembered that not until 1908 did the Ash Can school of painters first begin to give visual form to the American city. Fuller does not precisely anticipate their imagery, though he, like John Sloan and George Bellows (who in 1913 titled a painting "Cliff Dwellers"), sees the city as possessing a peculiar beauty heretofore ignored or derided. He, thus, annexes and assimilates into the realm of the aesthetic the vast reality of the modern city, impressing its form with his own vision.

III

What Fuller saw in Chicago fit few of the established literary forms, yet he did not turn away or betray his impressions. Waking from the dream that America was a pastoral garden, the late nineteenth century found that their world was really a mechanized and industrialized city. The city landscape that emerges in Fuller's novels, nevertheless, reflects what few American writers of the nineteenth century had grasped or made vivid. That is, the artist who took the city for a subject had to abandon or modify a set of aesthetic values and a mode of perception based on a pastoral ideal. Fuller acknowledged that the city stood as the antitype of America's pastoral garden, and in confronting that face honestly freed himself to construct an aesthetic out of the forms and materials of the modern city.

The flight from the American city, in this half of the twentieth century, does not testify to the failure of Fuller's vision. What it means, among other things, is that Americans have felt alien in the city because they have seldom abandoned the values, the aesthetics and the sense of space rooted in the pastoral myth. Harmony with the city seems, for many, an impossibility, a surrender of freedom or a compromise with the forces and ugliness of a modern inferno. Americans have not yet found the image of the city that would symbolize man's place in the urban environment; we have not created an urban ideal to replace the pastoral ideal. To return to the garden has seemed, for much of this century, a far more compelling aim than building an urban civilization.

Only lately have students of American urban life, such as Alan Trachtenberg in his *Brooklyn Bridge,* begun to recognize that the pastoral myth, in fact, disguises a process of urbanization.[16] Man's transcendence of Nature—whether figured as a trek to the frontier or as the building of roads into the wilderness—makes for the inevitable extension of the city and the machine's annihilation of the pastoral landscape. Fuller, in parodying our vision of inexhaustible and unbounded Nature, disclosed that truth long ago.

Notes

1. Ralph Waldo Emerson, *The Journals of Ralph Waldo Emerson: V, 1835-1837,* ed. Merton Sealts (Cambridge, Mass., 1965), 372.

2. Henry Blake Fuller, "'Municipal Art' Substitute," Chicago *Evening Post,* 11 May 1901, 6.

3. Fuller, "New Study for the Clubs," Chicago *Evening Post,* 13 July 1901, 6.

4. Hart Crane, "Modern Poetry," in *The Complete Poems and Selected Letters of Hart Crane* (Garden City, N.Y., 1966), 261-62.

5. Fuller in a letter to William Dean Howells, as quoted by Bernard Bowron, *Henry Blake Fuller: A Critical Study,* unpublished dissertation (Harvard, 1948), 440.

6. Among Fuller's papers at the Newberry Library is one folder containing reviews of *The Cliff-Dwellers.* The passages below, which provide the sources for the language in my text, are representative of the genteel complaints found there: "There is almost everywhere a sense of power and almost everywhere a misuse of it, and something that reminds you of M. Zola's delight in what is loathsome and cruel."—anon., *The Times* (August 13, 1895).

"We are far from saying that any aspect of life should be untouched by the novelist; it is his privilege as an artist to select his own subject. But the writer who says, 'Lo! I will be realistic,' usually becomes trivial or merely disgusting. Life is not altogether sordid, however we look at it. . . . We are inclined to think that he [Fuller] had better stick to his chevaliers and chatelaines. . . ."—anon., Providence, R.I., *Daily Journal* (March 27, 1893).

7. "The Cliff-Dwellers," *The Critic,* XXIII (October 7, 1893), 221.

8. Howells, "The Cliff-Dwellers," *Harper's Bazaar,* XXVI (October 28, 1893), 883.

9. Hjalmar Hjorth Boyesen, "The Cliff-Dwellers," *The Cosmopolitan,* XVI (January, 1894), 373-74.

10. Future references to both *The Cliff-Dwellers* (CD) and *With the Procession* (WP) will be given parenthetically in the text. I have used the Gregg Press facsimile reprint of *The Cliff-Dwellers* (Ridgewood, N.J., 1968); the University of Chicago Press reprint of *With the Procession* (Chicago, 1965).

11. The critic Montgomery Schuyler, in "Last Words about the Fair," *Architectural Record* (January-March, 1894), speaks of his age's taste for the "artificial infinite" in architecture, defining it in part as "an effect that depends greatly upon magnitude." Discussing the architecture of the Chicago World's Fair of 1893, he links the desire for the "artificial infinite" to an American preference for "mere bigness." He finds, moreover, that "in Chicago, the citadel of the superlative degree, [bigness] counts for more, perhaps, than it counts for elsewhere in this country." I cite his comments to illustrate that architectural aesthetics in this period retained a notion of the sublime or infinite, secularized though it was.

The term "modern version of the sublime" is mine, but my indebtedness to William Empson's *Some Versions of the Pastoral* (Norfolk, Conn., n.d.) is self-evident.

12. Fuller, "New Study for the Clubs."

13. Willard Thorp, "Pilgrim's Return" in *Literary History of the United States,* ed. Robert Spiller *et al.* (New York, 1963), 832.

14. Fuller, "New Study For The Clubs."

15. Crane, "Modern Poetry."

16. Trachtenberg, *Brooklyn Bridge: Fact and Symbol* (New York, 1965), 20, says "Americans have always subscribed to Eden, and proceeded to transform it in the name of progress."

Park Dixon Goist (essay date 1977)

SOURCE: "The City as Noncommunity: Theodore Dreiser and Henry Blake Fuller," in *From Main Street to State Street: Town, City, and Community in America,* Kennikat Press, 1977, pp. 68-79.

[*In the following essay, Goist explores the ideas of community and individuality in the Chicago novels of Fuller and Theodore Dreiser.*]

Though he lived in cities and even wrote one "urban novel," Hamlin Garland remained essentially a writer of the frontier or middle border. But the locale of his one effort at city fiction has been the focal point of a good deal of novelistic effort. At the turn of the nineteenth century two of the outstanding novelists of Chicago were Theodore Dreiser (1871-1945) and Henry Blake Fuller (1857-1929). Their backgrounds were quite different, as were both their literary and life styles. Dreiser came from the hinterlands and spent a good portion of his career attempting to come to terms with America's largest cities, Chicago and New York. Fuller was born and lived all his life in Chicago, and after an initial effort to deal with his native city he turned largely to other kinds of work. Given these and other differences to be discussed in this chapter, it is interesting to note that both Dreiser and Fuller share a structure of feeling with Garland in regard to individualism and community in the city.

In her study *The American Urban Novel* (1954), Blanche Gelfant maintains that "with the publication of *Sister Carrie,* the twentieth-century American city novel came into being" (p. 63). It is significant to note that Theodore Dreiser, the author of this important urban novel, like his contemporaries Booth Tarkington, Zona Gale, Sherwood Anderson, and Sinclair Lewis, grew up in small town America. Like Tarkington he was from Indiana, and like Anderson he knew small town poverty at first hand. But unlike these members of his generation Dreiser became a novelist of the city, and in his books he attempted to define the meaning of large cities for American life.

Forty years after Dreiser's *Sister Carrie* appeared in 1900, the Chicago sociologist Louis Wirth wrote a now classic essay entitled "Urbanism as a Way of Life," in which he argued that the uniqueness of a big city lifestyle results from the interaction of the large size, diversity, and heterogeneity of its population. Theodore Dreiser was not a sociologist consciously measuring the relative weight of certain given variables, but he was a participant observer who, like Wirth, sought in his aesthetic rendering of the metropolis to explain what urbanism meant as a way of life.[1]

Before writing *Sister Carrie* Dreiser was a successful newspaper and free-lance magazine writer. Only reluctantly, at the urging of a close friend, did he take a hand at writing a novel. But once he set to work, he was able to complete the book in seven months (probably only four of which were actually spent on *Sister Carrie*). In that relatively short period he produced an American literary classic. Dreiser was able to achieve this feat in part because he had spent the preceding seven years writing prodigiously for newspapers and magazines, thus learning his craft. Also, when he turned to fiction he drew on his own personal encounters with the city. As the experiences of George Willard and Felix Fay in the towns of Ohio, Iowa, and Illinois encouraged them to look to Chicago as the next step in their ventures, so Dreiser and his fictional characters were drawn to that metropolis of the Midwest to find the meaning of life. The adventures of Carrie take up where the stories of George and Felix leave off: in her the meaning and impact of the city upon the half-formed small town youngster is traced. Dreiser's volume is an urban novel precisely because it reveals how the city environment shaped the lives of its individual characters.[2]

The book's plot revolves around the fortunes of three people and covers the period from August, 1889, to January, 1897. Caroline Meeber comes to Chicago from Columbia City, Wisconsin, and gets a physically exhausting, low-paying job in a cheap shoe factory. She lives with her sister and brother-in-law, whose pinched existence is determined largely by his menial job cleaning refrigerator cars at the city's stockyards. Following a short illness, Carrie loses her job and, without an income from which to pay the rent or buy clothes for the winter, accidentally runs into Charles Drouet, a flashy traveling salesman she had met on the train to Chicago. Disheartened by the restrictive life at her sister's flat, unable to secure a job, convinced of Drouet's concern for her, and desirous of the lifestyle he can provide, she accepts his offer and the two begin living together.

Soon thereafter Drouet introduces his "wife" to George Hurstwood, the suave manager of Fitzgerald and Moy's, a fashionable downtown bar. Hurstwood has a comfortable life, a substantial home, and a respectable wife who has conventional social ambitions for her two children. But he falls in love with Carrie, who does not yet know he is married, wins her away from Drouet, who, when he finds out what has been going on, tells her about Hurstwood's

marital status. As his own marriage collapses, Hurstwood, in a moment of wine-confused panic, takes almost $11,000 from his employer's safe, and by a ruse tricks Carrie into going to Montreal with him. He is forced to return most of the money; then he and Carrie, who has reconciled herself to the situation (she does not know about the theft of the money), change their name, get married, and go to New York. There Hurstwood experiences a decline of fortunes that eventually leads him to the Bowery where he resorts to panhandling. In contrast, his wife (now Carrie Medenda) launches a stage career which brings her wealth and prominence, abandoning Hurstwood in the process. At the end of the novel Hurstwood, now a completely defeated individual, crawls away into a flophouse, turns on the gas, and ends his life. Carrie, unfulfilled by her success, sits alone in her rocking-chair, amidst luxurious surroundings, unhappy, yearning for something she is unable to attain.[3]

The plot and characters in the novel were drawn largely from Dreiser's own family experiences. In 1885 his sister Emma began an affair with a man some fifteen years her senior who was a cashier at a swank Chicago bar. She soon learned that he was married and had three children. Nonetheless, she joined him and they went to Montreal; on the way he revealed that while drunk he had stolen money from his employers. He returned most of the $3,500, the employers did not prosecute, and he and Emma settled in New York as managers of a rather shady rooming house. In the novel Dreiser's sister becomes Sister Carrie and the Chicago cashier is Hurstwood. The figure of Drouet was based on a clever, popular, and well-dressed student Dreiser had envied at the University of Indiana, which he attended in 1889-90. More important than these close parallels between fiction and fact is the way the events and characters are recreated to reflect Dreiser's understanding of the meaning of city life.

The first thing one notices about Carrie is how little influence a small town background contributes in her adjustments to the metropolis. A reader learns almost nothing about her parents (except that her father works in a flour mill) and nothing at all about her eighteen years in Columbia City. When she leaves, "the threads which bound her so lightly to girlhood were irretrievably broken" (p. 1), and only rarely does she have "a far-off thought of Columbia City" (p. 58). When she does have a fleeting memory of her home town, it is because she is disturbed or confused over some moral and/or economic issue: as she begins living with Drouet (p. 86), as she contrasts North Shore Drive elegance with Drouet's Ogden Place rooms (p. 128), or just after she has left Drouet and learned that Hurstwood is married (p. 271). But even when she has lost her job in the shoe factory and her sister suggests that she return home, although Carrie agrees, this is never a real alternative. "Columbia City, what was there for her? She knew its dull, little round by heart." Like Rose Dutcher she has seen Chicago, and here she wants to stay and experience life. "Here was the great, mysterious city which was still a magnet for her. What she had seen only suggested its possibilities. Now to turn her back on it and live the little old life out there . . ." seemed impossible (pp. 73-74). In the next scene Carrie allows Drouet to buy her clothes and set her up in an apartment. The glittering possibilities of the city have overcome whatever moral hesitation still lingers "lightly" from her Columbia City girlhood.

As Carrie enters the city, although she is eighteen, her character is essentially unformed. Self-interest is her guiding characteristic; enjoying "the keener pleasures of life," she is "ambitious to gain in material things." She is "a fair example of the middle American class—two generations removed from the emigrant" (p. 2). What impact does the city have on this young, half-formed middle American? It impresses itself on Carrie, as it had on Dreiser himself, as a place of sharp contrasts between drudgery, poverty, and anonymity on the one hand, ease, wealth, and prominence on the other. Carrie quickly responds to the latter. The joyless, relentless, laboring, and humdrum existence of her sister and brother-in-law represent one urban reality. In contrast to this narrowness is the more luxurious life of Drouet, Hurstwood, and her female acquaintants Mrs. Hale and Mrs. Vance. That life revolves around fine clothes and jewelry, the fashion promenades in Chicago (and later in New York), social contacts, good restaurants, and the excitement of the theater—all made possible by money. "Money: something everybody else has and I must get . . ." (p. 70). If the city measures one's worth by what one has, then she intends to get. Carrie's capacity to understand what society values and her spirit in pursuing those goals are her inherited characteristics; the specific values she accepts are acquired from the city environment. Urbanism as a way of life for Carrie means attempting to achieve a lifestyle marked by prominence and wealth.

The irony is that Carrie does achieve success, as a noted actress, and yet she is unfulfilled. She seems as little responsible for her rise to stardom as Hurstwood is for his plunge from an upper class position ("the first grade below the luxuriously rich") to being a street beggar. At the end of the novel, as Hurstwood ends his life by his own hand, finally defeated by circumstances over which he has no control, Carrie sits idly rocking in her chair, successful according to the terms she has accepted but in her way also trapped, dreaming vaguely of something beyond her elegant surroundings. Carrie has recently been stirred by the urgings of Robert Ames of Indianapolis that she give up comedy and turn to serious drama. Ames argues that her face reflects a longing which many people feel and are struggling to express, and that she should (indeed, has an obligation to) use this genius on the stage so that people can express themselves through her. Carrie does not understand the import of what Ames is urging, and as the world represented by Drouet and Hurstwood loses its allure she is left confused and uncertain about life.

Dreiser's point here is important in understanding his interpretation of the city. When Carrie comes to Chicago, she has the imagination and capacity to respond to beauty, but her vague aesthetic yearnings have as yet no guiding principle or definite focal point for realization. The urban ideal of beauty held up so alluringly before her is one of glitter and show, and being an imaginative and impressionable person she responds accordingly and makes the city's goals her own. Dreiser is not criticizing Carrie for her choice, for it was a choice he had himself made when first encountering the city. But when she achieves the earthly success represented by Hurstwood and offered by the city, she senses that it somehow does not bring happiness. She is, Dreiser tells us, "an illustration of the devious ways by which one who feels, rather than reasons, may be led in the pursuit of beauty" (p. 557). The realization of the material success valued in Chicago and New York does not bring emotional and human fulfillment, but on the contrary leaves one emotionally drained and spiritually confused.

In his use of symbols and imagery, as in his manipulation of plot and characters, Dreiser's conception of the city is discerned. Carrie is seen as "a waif amid forces," "half-equipped little knight," "a soldier of fortune," "a pilgrim," "a wisp in the wind," and "a harp in the wind"—in other words, a wanderer at the mercy of arbitrary gods. As she is bounced hither and yon, her shifting identity is reflected in various names: Caroline Meeber becomes in the course of her wanderings "Sister Carrie," "Cad," "Mrs. Drouet," "Mrs. G. W. Murdock," "Mrs. Wheeler," and finally "Carrie Medenda." Her real entry into the cherished "walled city" (the world of wealth and luxury) is attained by her discovery of "the gate to the world," the theater. The stage, as so often in novels of this period, represents not only the show and glamour of city life, but is also pictured as providing a means for actors and audiences alike to play a role in life. It is a way, so Dreiser and other authors imply, for the many estranged urbanites to gain the illusion that they are a part of things, for a moment at least. For Carrie, then, her way of entering into the swirl of life around her means having a role to play. "Oh if she could only have such a part, how broad would be her life! She too could act appealing" (p. 345). In this "elfland" world of Aladdin her success is, arbitrarily, assured. A final recurring symbol, that of the rocking chair, captures this note of the ceaseless yet meaningless urban movement, a to-and-fro motion with no apparent direction: the rise and fall of individual lives has as much reason as the back-and-forth rocking of Carrie's chair.

If community involves, as recent sociologists argue, the meaningful interaction of people who share certain socially sanctioned norms and behavior, then there is no community in the city world of *Sister Carrie*. People in the novel live and die alone. Personal relationships are of only the most tenuous nature. Hurstwood leaves his family with startling ease, with no twinge of conscience. His wife's main concern over her husband's departure is of a strictly monetary nature. Hurstwood's "friends" at the bar are merely casual acquaintances, whose "hail fellow well met" élan is but a facade. Drouet is a man with no permanent home and no lasting relationships, a traveling salesman who flits easily from place to place, woman to woman. Carrie finds it only slightly more difficult to break family ties and intimate relationships with Drouet and Hurstwood.

Dreiser's city is a world where even the closest and most intimate relationships are easily abandoned. Here there is no hope of developing and maintaining the bonds which traditionally have held community together. The city of Theodore Dreiser is the epitome of noncommunity.

In 1928 Theodore Dreiser wrote of a little-known author, Henry B. Fuller, that he was "the man who led the van of realism in America." Dreiser praised Fuller's novel **With the Procession** (1895), calling it "as sound and agreeable a piece of American realism as that decade, or any since, produced."[4] Not widely known even in his own lifetime, though highly respected by a few style-conscious writers and critics, Fuller has recently been the focus of renewed interest, evidenced most clearly by the publication of a combined biography and critical study in 1974. Bernard Bowron, Jr.'s, *Henry B. Fuller of Chicago* carried the appropriate subtitle "The Ordeal of a Genteel Realist in Ungenteel America." Appropriate because Fuller, though a native Chicagoan whose grandfather had come to the city in 1849 and made a sizable fortune, was a recluse who did not share the booster attitude and aggressive business values which dominated his city. Yet Fuller did not flee America to become a literary expatriate, but sought in some of his early work to deal with the "formulation of American society" as exemplified in Chicago.[5]

With the Procession is the story of one of Chicago's Old Settler families, the Marshalls, whose commitment to the standards of a bygone day has left them "out of things," the social parade having passed them by. The novel involves the efforts of a younger generation of Marshalls to lift the family into "the procession."[6]

David Marshall, the father, has built up a successful grocery business through thirty-five years of steady work and conservative economic practices. He performs his role in life with "an air of patient, self-approving resignation" (p. 17). He works on from year to year at his business, with no particular goal in mind, because this is what he knows and what he does best. He has lost interest in "society," and he understands his obligation to be to his family and to his employees and their families, but not to the public at large. In his life and outlook David Marshall exemplifies an individualism and privatism which Fuller implies was more appropriate to an earlier day. A good part of the efforts on the part of other characters in the novel is aimed at persuading David Marshall of his duty to the broader society of Chicago.

The elder Marshall resists these overtures largely because the Chicago "public" he is becoming aware of is not at all the same "society" that his daughters wish to join. In the first place, it is eventually revealed that Marshall's business practices have not always been as decorous as he might have wished them to be. His partner Gilbert Belden

follows the more aggressive, extralegal practices of the day. How did such a man become an associate of the more staid and cautious Marshall? Belden was taken into the firm during the financial panic of 1873, just two years after the great Chicago fire, when Marshall & Co. was on the brink of ruin. Marshall is forced to resort to tactics "quite outside the lines of mercantile morality, and barely inside the lines of legality itself," and Belden is hired away from a rival firm to accomplish the maneuver (p. 100). Once established, he pushes ahead to become a full partner, eventually attempts to wrest control from Marshall and transform the business into a stock company. But Fuller is not simply attributing all good to the Old Settlers and all bad to the newcomers: there is obviously a closer relationship between the sharp practices of the new businessmen and the "conservatism" of the Old Settlers than David Marshall might at times like to admit to himself.

Near the end of the novel, with David on his deathbed, Marshall & Belden is in receivership. But the family fortune (some $3,000,000) is not lost. David's oldest son Roger has successfully invested his father's money in speculative real estate ventures, which represents another break with the professed practices of the past. Roger Marshall is a lawyer, also involved with the seamier aspects of the family business. In the process of these dealings he becomes familiar with the rapidly changing social character of the city.

Roger participates in one set of events, the details of which take place "offstage" and are revealed only piecemeal in snatches of conversation. They reflect the inescapable entanglement of the Marshalls with a newer Chicago. An immigrant woman, Mrs. Van Horn, has purchased goods from David and is reselling them from her residence, which is only two blocks from the Marshall home. A writ is issued to halt the practice, but the woman is alerted by a relative connected with the police court, and when the search takes place no goods are found. Her son is an alderman, her nephew a bailiff, and when the matter gets to court it is continued (delayed) three times. When Roger presses the issue in the lower court, two of the woman's nephews break into the Marshall stable and beat the coachman. When these ruffians go before the court, the alderman's son writes out a fictitious bail bond, then the two muggers jump bail and the bond is forfeited.

Roger's function in all this, and other such matters, is to act as an intermediary, a sort of buffer, between the Marshalls and the changing world of Chicago which is engulfing them. At the unsatisfactory conclusion of the Van Horn affair, Roger tells his father, who is gradually becoming aware of the implications of such incidents:

> You have lifted off the cover and looked in. Do you want to go deeper? You'll find a hell-broth—thieves, gamblers, prostitutes, pawnbrokers, saloon-keepers, aldermen, heelers, justices, bailiffs, policemen—all concocted for us within a short quarter of a century. . . . I never felt so cheap and filthy in my life. (P. 145)

David wonders if he himself isn't to blame as he sees his son coarsening under the impact of such activities. Again, the "new" Chicago is impinging forcefully upon David Marshall and his family. The survival of the family is due in no small part to its ability, in the person of Roger, to understand change and adapt to new conditions.

Eliza Marshall, David's wife, is initially even more immune to the changing world in which she lives than her husband. She is, the narrator tells us, "a kind of antiquated villager—a geological survival from an earlier age" (p. 7). Her Chicago is still the town of 1860 (a "town," incidentally, with a population of 190,000 in that year), "an Arcadia which, in some dim and inexplicable way, had remained for her an Arcadia still—bigger, noisier, richer, yet different only in degree, and not essentially in kind" (p. 10). The Marshall home had been built in 1860 in a sedate residential area on Michigan Avenue, but thirty years later the neighborhood has changed drastically. By 1893 the local church has moved and old neighbors gone to more fashionable areas. Hotels, business offices, boarding houses, even a cheap music hall, have replaced the former homes. A suburban railway which runs close by spews its smoke and cinders over the yard into the house. Finally the family experiences urban violence when the Van Horn ruffians break into the Marshall stable.

Eliza clings tenaciously to her aging possessions and old ways amidst all this hectic change. This trait is effectively symbolized in her annual jelly making, which takes place every July, despite the fact that the "smoke and cinders of metropolitan life" have killed all her currant bushes. She now cans store-bought currants. The urban smoke has also killed Eliza's cherry tree and the rest of the garden as well. Successful efforts to effect a move from this "dear old place" to a new, more fashionable house are one of the key indications that the Marshalls have indeed begun once again to march "with the procession."

Jane Marshall is the daughter responsible for bringing about the family's entrance into the mainstream of Chicago's upper class social procession. She is also the family member most marked by the Old Settler spirit. Jane, thirty-three and single, launches her younger sister Rosy into the social limelight, and even succeeds in pushing her reluctant father into the role of an after-dinner speaker. Once in society, Rosy becomes insufferable, marries a somewhat nebulous Englishman because his father has a title, and cuts her mother's old friends from the wedding list, making sure her new "society" acquaintances are invited. Jane is also successful in convincing the elder Marshall that a move "further out" is called for, and the new house is nearing completion as the novel ends (the old home to be knocked down and replaced by a warehouse). Jane has twinges of remorse: "If it hadn't been for me we should never have left our old home and given up our old life" (p. 261). But she is consoled by a proposal of marriage from Theodore Brower, a progressive, reform-minded insurance man.

Jane is forcefully assisted in her successful social maneuvers on behalf of the Marshall family by the wealthy and socially prominent Mrs. Granger Bates. The daughter of a "boss-carpenter," she and her husband have struggled up to a position of financial, cultural, and philanthropic leadership in Chicago. She is proud of this achievement and her position. "We have fought the fight—a fair field and no favor—and we have come out ahead. And we shall stay there too; keep up with the procession is my motto, and head it if you can. I *do* head it, and I feel that I'm where I belong" (p. 58). Years before, David Marshall was one of her favorite suitors, and though they have not seen one another in years she is now eager to help Jane with her plans.

Mrs. Bates has a strong streak of nostalgia for the earlier times and simpler ways of her childhood, but, as Bowron points out, she is not a sentimentalist (p. 156). She has a good sense of just how much of the procession is mere show and how much is of cultural value. If the dominant values of "privatism," of laissez-faire business enterprise, can give rise to socially valuable and culturally worthwhile creations, Fuller suggests that it will be due to people of the kind represented by Mrs. Granger Bates and Jane Marshall. They do not want to see the Old Settler spirit give way before the onslaught of the Beldens and other newcomers. Thus, Mrs. Bates is willing to help Jane, in whom she finds "one of *us.*"

In contrast to the artistic and social hopes for a business culture which Mrs. Bates represents, is the almost complete disdain for Chicago expressed by Truesdale, Jane's younger brother. Truesdale leaves Yale to study art and music in Europe, or more correctly, "on the Continent." He returns to Chicago, where he observes there is "so little taste . . . so little training, so little education, so total an absence of any collective sense of the fit and proper" (p. 73). In Chicago Truesdale deplores the lack of promenades, cafes, journals, and the absence of an atmosphere of leisure he believes conducive to art and culture. American cities are too big, too noisy, too dirty, and too confusing and disordered to serve as an environment in which a true culture could flourish. Truesdale's pretentious ridicule of Chicago is based on his self-consciously acquired appreciation of the picturesque Gothic in France and Italy. At the end of the novel Truesdale is on his way to Japan, after it has been discovered that while in Europe he had an affair with an Alsatian girl whose father is now working for Marshall & Belden. The resolution of this sordid matter by Roger (which includes buying off the girl's family by providing a willing husband for her) is just one more element driving David Marshall to his deathbed.

In sharp contrast to Truesdale stands the engineer-architect Tom Bingham, president of Bingham Construction Company. Bingham (who may have been based on Fuller's friend Daniel Burnham, a famous Chicago architect and city planner) thoroughly accepts Chicago values and gives them form in the ornate residences and steel-frame business towers which he builds. He is the architect and builder of the Marshalls' new home. Also in contrast to Truesdale, but from a different angle, is Theodore Brower, the man Jane chooses over Bingham as a husband. Brower's role in the novel is somewhat ambiguous. His is the one voice of near-dissent in the book, but his interesting reform suggestion of a legal-aid justice center for the poor is dropped. Instead it is decided to have a college building serve as a monument to David Marshall. In leading up to his original suggestion, Brower observes:

> This town of ours labors under one peculiar disadvantage: it is the only great city in the world to which all its citizens have come for one common, avowed object of making money. . . . In this Garden City of ours every man cultivates his own little bed and his neighbor his, but who looks after the paths between? . . . The thing to teach the public is this: the general good is a different thing from the sum of the individual goods. Over in the settlements we are trying to make these newcomers realize that they are a part of the body politic; perhaps we need another settlement to remind some of the original charter-members of the same fact. (Pp. 203-4)

What Brower is talking about is community and, as Larzer Ziff points out, Fuller seems to put more stock in this approach to Chicago's future than in the hopes many people placed in the transforming power of the example of planned orderliness represented by the buildings of the famous "White City" built for the Chicago World's Fair in 1893. This seems to be confirmed in Jane Marshall's choice of Brower as a husband rather than Bingham, an architect whose hopes for the future are akin to those of the City Beautiful advocate who designed the buildings and grounds for that famous fair.[7]

As far as Fuller would go with the reform theme was to suggest that in some vague way the Old Settler spirit of Mrs. Granger Bates would be melded with the liberal concerns of Brower. This was, at least, a step beyond the limitations of David Marshall's individualism, Eliza's nostalgic blindness, Truesdale's superciliousness, and Bingham's entrepreneurism. But Fuller, with one exception, dropped Chicago from his future literary subject matter, abandoning the difficult task of giving creative shape to a society he was so ambiguous toward. And yet, as Bowron has pointed out, "his inability to escape Chicago, both as fact and symbol, is, ironically, the essence of his art" (p. xxvii). What Fuller attempted and could not do was to cope with the contradictions, caused by rapid growth and change, which were so characteristic of Chicago in the 1890s and after.

Guy Szuberla, in his study of Fuller's vision of Chicago as a "city-scape," has indicated one important aspect of **With the Procession** as an urban novel. Szuberla argues that Fuller is probably the first American novelist to discard the agrarian myth as an adequate mode of perception for dealing with the modern machine-made city environment. In this interpretation Fuller's work "reflects a new idea of urban space" akin to Hart Crane's later directive that literature "absorb the machine" and "surrender . . . temporarily, to the sensations of urban life" (pp. 83-84).[8] What this means in **With the Procession** is that both the Arca-

dian perception of Mrs. Marshall and the pseudosophisticated view of the picturesque and pastoral held by her son Truesdale are rejected as ways of seeing the city. The lesson is clear: "The pastoral myth, which has served to define the America of the past, has lost its relevance in the modern city" (p. 90).

Szuberla's point is convincing, but in the context of the present discussion it needs to be supplemented by a further observation. Though the pastoral myth *had* been abandoned by Fuller as a way of seeing the city, he was unable to come to terms with the growing social contradictions of Chicago. He could not resolve the dilemma between his respect for the individualistic Old Settler spirit and the vague community consciousness of Brower. For an instant Brower becomes a spokesman for the immigrants and poor of the city. Fuller's awareness of the impact of social change is shown in the Van Horn affair and in Brower's response to it. But the author's inability to cope with the meaning of these events is reflected in the fact that the action of the Van Horn affair takes place offstage and is revealed to the reader only indirectly. Instead, Fuller emphasizes the more traditional literary motif of tension between an older established class, the Marshalls, and social parvenus like the Beldens. Thus, one of the final scenes is the put-down of Mrs. Belden by Eliza Marshall (who conveys the false impression that daughter Rosy has been "presented at court"). Fuller was, at the same time, aware of the much more important conflict between the immigrant poor and the Old Settlers. But by inclination and social position (he was manager of his family's business affairs after his father's death in 1885) he ultimately shied away from the issue. Clearly, however, for all the ambiguities he felt, his final vote was cast for the individualism of the Old Settlers.

The city of Theodore Dreiser lacks community in the sense that the word is being used in the present study. People in Dreiser's Chicago and New York lack the basic social interaction and sharing which are now so frequently understood to be primary characteristics of community. *Sister Carrie* suggests that such traits have always been lacking in the city. In Henry Blake Fuller's Chicago, on the other hand, an older "style" of upper class community is being challenged by significant social changes resulting from industrialization and immigration. This older way of living is also being shattered by a growing materialistically oriented effort to keep up with the procession, and by those new to the game who don't always follow the established rules. It is not suggested by Fuller that all was peace and harmony in the past, but among a certain stratum of society there was a distinct "us" feeling, a sense of belonging based on social and economic position. An exclusive community, the Old Settlers' Chicago involved social interaction and shared experiences among a class operating in a given geographic locale. But the locale was rapidly changing after 1860, in physical dimension, population size, and social composition. The older sense of community and the lifestyle it represented were being undermined both by the "immigrant hordes" and by aggressive middle class social climbers. If for Dreiser the city was just naturally always anticommunity, from Fuller's perspective it had become so by the 1890s.

Notes

1. Louis Wirth, "Urbanism as a Way of Life," *American Journal of Sociology* 44 (July 1938): 1-24; Blanche Housman Gelfant, *The American City Novel,* pp. 42-94.

2. Biographical material on Dreiser in this chapter is based on Robert H. Elias. *Theodore Dreiser;* W. A. Swanberg, *Dreiser;* Theodore Dreiser, *A Book about Myself,* and *Dawn.*

3. Theodore Dreiser, *Sister Carrie.*

4. Theodore Dreiser, introduction, Frank Norris, *McTeague* (New York, 1928), p. vii-xi; "The Great American Novel," *American Spectator* 1 (December 1932): 1.

5. Biographical material on Fuller in this chapter is based on Bernard R. Bowron, Jr., *Henry Blake Fuller of Chicago,* and John Pilkington, *Henry Blake Fuller.*

6. Henry Blake Fuller, *With the Procession.*

7. Larzer Ziff, *The American 1890s,* pp. 112-13. See also Thomas Hines, *Burnham of Chicago.*

8. Guy Szuberla, "Making the Sublime Mechanical." I would like to thank Professor Szuberla for his helpful suggestions in regard to this chapter.

Guy Szuberla (essay date 1981)

SOURCE: "Henry Blake Fuller and the 'New Immigrant'," in *American Literature,* Vol. 53, No. 2, May, 1981, pp. 246-65.

[*In the following essay, Szuberla traces Fuller's attitude toward immigration and the idea of the American "melting pot" in his life and work.*]

Like many of his contemporaries, Henry Blake Fuller (1857-1929) frequently paired his ideas and his fears of the "new immigrant" with the spectre of a declining or dispossessed "native American stock." Much like Henry James in *The American Scene,* he pondered what it meant, and what it would mean, "to share the sanctity of his American consciousness, the intimacy of his American patriotism, with the inconceivable alien. . . ." Though those words belong to James, the sense of "dispossession" they express belonged to Fuller too.[1] Over the course of his long career as a writer he shifted between the view that the immigrant might be assimilated into a "homogeneous" American race and a set of beliefs close to those that marked the strenuous nativism of his time. He feared the unmeltable and alien influence of the "new immigrant" (Eastern and Southern Europeans) and, on occasion, exag-

gerated the virtues of the "old immigrants" (the descendants of a vaguely defined Anglo-Saxon or American race).

Some of the typology of race and character historians have come to call the "nativism" of the American 1890s, then, flows into his first city novels. Present in crowds, in "gangs," or "swarming hordes," immigrants in these novels seem to possess but a half-life, a virtually nameless, subterranean existence. Their speech and manners mark them, in the eyes of many "Anglo-Saxon" characters, as "unclassifiable foreigners." They are almost uniformly associated with the chaos of the industrialized city.[2] Apart from a handful of minor figures—supernumeraries like the nameless Swedish maid in **The Cliff-Dwellers** (1893); the stage villain, Andreas Leppin of **With the Procession** (1895)—the immigrants inhabiting Fuller's cityscapes in the 1890s are sealed off to anonymnity, immured in what seems a brooding silence. To the "native" American characters who mediate between us and Fuller's point of view, the alien's strangeness looms as a threatening force, charged with an almost apocalyptic meaning.

Yet Fuller sometimes believed, or expressed the hope (in an 1897 *Atlantic* article), that the "gulf between . . . the native and the alien" might be bridged. In 1912 he wrote in *Century Magazine* that social centers like Hull-House and Chicago parks were promoting "the amalgamation of diverse racial elements into one homogeneous people."[3] During World War I he composed two poems, **"The Alien"** and **"Toward the New World,"** that expressed a highly sympathetic understanding of the immigrants' problems in the new world.[4] Still later, he would turn away from such sympathies. In 1924, in an essay for *The New York Times Book Review,* he denounced assimilationist notions as "speciousness" and attacked "our variegated new comers" for hastening the decline of Anglo-Saxon decency in American arts, letters, and politics. He summed up the premise of his article in the bluntly worded title: **"The Melting Pot Begins to Smell."**[5]

To understand his ambivalent sense of the new immigrant and the covalent image of the native Anglo-Saxon, it is necessary to read his work against a backdrop of nativist rhetoric and standard theories of uplift and assimilation. Fuller was attuned to both the progressive reformers' view of the immigrant and the nativist views that exercised Henry Cabot Lodge and the Immigration Restriction League in the 1890s and after. He was a Chicago novelist who studied the immigrant on city streets and in settlement house parlors.[6] Friend to the reform-minded I. K. Pond and A. B. Pond, the architects of Hull-House and other Chicago settlement houses, he was equally close to Hobart Chatfield-Taylor, the editor and publisher of *America,* a nativist journal (subtitled *For Americans: Devoted to Honest Politics and Good Literature*).[7]

This shifting and divided response to the immigrant has not been given sustained attention in readings of his urban fiction, perhaps because the immigrants' presence seems so transient there. So, while Fuller scholars like Bernard

Bowron and John Pilkington have noted the contrast between the "old" village of Chicago and the "new" industrialized city in *The Cliff-Dwellers* and *With the Procession,* they have given only passing attention to the corresponding and equally important contrast setting off the Anglo-Saxon from the immigrant, and they have overlooked altogether the implicit push and pull of assimilationist and restrictionist ideas in these novels.[8] Moreover, no one—neither Fuller scholars, nor historians of American nativism—has aligned the images of the immigrant and the Anglo-Saxon in his fiction with cognate ideas and images given in his poetry, his numerous editorials for Chicago papers, and his essays and reviews in national journals.

Historians of American nativism—John Higham and Barbara Solomon, principal among them—have defined the seminal role Prescott F. Hall, Henry Cabot Lodge, and other New England figures played in disseminating the myth of a superior and homogeneous native stock; but they have given little attention to a similar role exercised by the Chicago scholars, newspapermen, and social leaders who underwrote *America,* and none to Henry Blake Fuller's ambivalent response to nativism and the "new immigrant."[9] Fuller was not a polemicist: his voice was not a strong or dominating one in the heated debate over immigration restriction that swept the country at the turn of the century. Yet, to read his fiction, and to sample his steady stream of articles on the Anglo-Saxon and the immigrant, is to come to understand a large part of the history of nativism in the 1890s and early 1900s.

At the same time Fuller's writings reveal the mingled patterns of hope and fear and noble expectation that reformers and others wrought in the myth of the "melting pot." Attracted to the work of the settlement house movement from its inception in the 1890s, Fuller frequently championed settlement house programs for "social amelioration" and generally promoted their notions of "immigrant gifts." In short, his belief in the power of genteel culture to "uplift" those without culture made him an early supporter of those assimilationist ideals embodied in the symbol of the melting pot. Why, in late 1924, he abruptly rejected the myth of the melting pot and turned towards the nominally opposed myth of Anglo-Saxon superiority is a question that cannot be answered quickly. Charting such shifts in perspective through the various images of the immigrant and the "native" American he records—and defining the evolution of attitudes these shifts represent—will be the central purpose of this essay.

I.

Fuller was the last male descendant of a Dr. Samuel Fuller of the Mayflower Company (in the parlance of the 1890s and early 1900s, the "old immigrants"). On his mother's side, he could trace his line back to an ancestor who arrived in Massachusetts eleven years after the Mayflower. Though he was born in Chicago in 1857, he was in many ways a son of New England. For all the taunts and jibes Fuller hurled against New England narrowness and smug-

ness, colonial America and the early republic remained touchstones for his values.[10] The antebellum village of Chicago, which glows warmly in the Old Settlers' recollections given in *With the Procession,* seems more a New England village than a midwestern one, peopled as it is by transplanted New Englanders. Here, so Fuller's private legend runs, a simple but genuine community flourished; its politics, civic virtues, and commonweal, were blessed and buoyed up by a homogeneous spirit, tradition, and people.

The Cliff-Dwellers (1893), the first of his city novels, playfully and satirically expressed his ambivalent sense of Chicago in the 1890s. New England and industrialized Chicago are set off against each other, the old village and the burly, brawling city implicitly contrasted. Through the eyes of a transplanted New Englander, George Ogden of Boston, Fuller registers the shock and disorientation of a first encounter with Chicago's urban-industrial sprawl. Ogden has come to Chicago from Boston to repair his family's fortune and open up a career to his own modest talents. The novel's action turns on the rise and fall of his fortunes.

Fuller's young man Going West becomes acutely conscious of his New England lineage even as he ties himself inextricably closer to Chicago. He boasts of Anglo-Saxon descent, of blood manifestly destined to rule the world:

> "Oh, well," began George, with the air proper to a launching out into a broad and easy generalization, "aren't we New England Puritans the cream of the Anglo-Saxon race? And why does the Anglo-Saxon race rule the globe except because the individual Anglo-Saxon can rule himself?" (*CD,* p.224)

Ogden pours out this "broad and easy generalization" unimpeded and unopposed, almost as though Fuller can find no character or arguments to contest his nativist sentiments. Though George Ogden's values are not his, Fuller will only jab lightly at them, noting that they are "broad and easy." Ogden's roommate Theodore Brower, who in *With the Procession* would come to speak the settlement house workers' view of the immigrant, answers "discontentedly": "Oh, I know . . . that's all right, up to a certain point" (*CD,* p. 225). Ogden's rhetorical questions stand with a finality that seems to admit of no rebuttal.

Though nowhere else in the novel does Ogden state his assumptions of superiority so plainly, his view of the Eastern and Southern European immigrants in Chicago—like that of several other leading characters—regularly springs from his sense of Anglo-Saxon identity. The general reader of the 1890s, presumably, required few explicit reminders of Anglo-Saxon racial and cultural superiority to understand George's perceptions of the "new immigrant." When the young Bostonian observes during his first weeks in the city that the immigrants he sees belong to "a range of human types completely unknown to his past experience" (*CD,* pp. 53-54), Fuller relies on his audience to fill in the definition of what ordinary or normal humanity is assumed to be. The strangeness, the bewildering heterogeneity of the crowds of immigrants, fits no principle of order or sense of reality that Ogden's experience can command. The strange costumes, manners, and faces he first encounters dramatize the disorientation he feels in Chicago; they are, likewise, symbolic projections of the alienation he feels in this new and crowded urban landscape.

In a long passage given over to recording Ogden's confusion and disgust over "the town's swarming hordes" (*CD*, p. 53), Fuller catalogs the features of the immigrant that mark him as a stranger: "skulls, foreheads, gaits, odors, facial angles; ears, with their different shapes and sets; eyes, with their varying shapes and colors . . . ; dialects, brogues, patois, accents in all their palatal and labial varieties . . ." (*CD*, p. 54). In noting these differences, Ogden assumes for a time that these features and the ethnic types they represent "might be scheduled, classified, brought into a sort of *catalogue raisonné*" (*CD*, p. 54). But once he is thrown into face to face contact with a crowd of immigrants, he abandons even that halting and uneasy belief in order, and sees, as before, that the immigrant symbolizes or creates chaos in the city. He recalls that one afternoon, in the public library at City Hall, he was forced to spend an hour in the midst of a crowd of immigrants, where he was swallowed up in a "confused cataract of nationalities." With the windows closed to a storm outside, the atmosphere of the room becomes stifling. From the crowd, out of the mix of nationalities, comes a smell that "stunned him with a sudden and sickening surprise—the bogs of Kilkenny, the dung-heaps of the Black Forest, the miry ways of Transylvania and Little Russia had all contributed to it" (*CD*, p. 55). The images of the immigrant in this scene—a "human maelstrom," a crowd emitting noxious "fumes"—anticipate, by way of contrast and opposition, Israel Zangwill's all-too-famous metaphor of the melting pot: America as the cauldron of nations, purifying their dross metal into a precious alloy. The melding and mixing of nationalities Fuller seems to image here signals a process of pollution, not purification.

What the "final blend of the American character" will be, Fuller's novel does not directly predict. Fairchild, the city booster, argues that everything depends on checking "alien excesses and un-American ideas" (*CD*, p. 242). He believes that the newly arrived immigrants are of one uniformly cast temperament and mind, indiscrete parts of a single mass. They are grouped in "gangs of unclassifiable foreigners" (*CD*, p. 175), spoken of as muddish "peasant material" (*CD*, p. 250), as political radicals equally possessed by "half-baked notions" (*CD*, p. 66). The aristocratic Boston visitor, Winthrop C. Floyd, judges them all to be "a horrible rout of foreign peasantry." He adds that he'd never seen "such a beastly rabble" until he saw the crowds of immigrants in Chicago (*CD*, p. 236). Such hyperbolic flourishes suggest that Floyd, like Ogden, has forgotten or somehow ignored the crowds of immigrants back in Boston. In Chicago's sprawling chaos he sees their numbers multiplied and their presence magnified into an overpowering threat.

Only once in this novel does an individual immigrant step forward from this faceless crowd. In the penultimate chapter a nameless Swedish maid tells of the melodramatic death of a banker's son in a "primitive way . . . with a horrible and harrowing directness" (*CD*, p. 310). Fuller strongly implies that the emotionless, "super-civilized" (*CD*, p. 298) Anglo-Saxon characters would not, or could not, summon up such feeling.

II

Like *The Cliff-Dwellers*, Fuller's *With the Procession* (1895) chronicles the fear and loathing that the immigrant "invasion" provoked in old Chicagoans and more recently arrived "Anglo-Saxon" Americans. Corrupt Irish politicos, "dwarfed and bearded Poles" (*WP*, p. 4), a "sinister" Alsatian (*WP*, p. 196), and other aliens crowd forward to show what it means to live on "the edge of . . . Babel" (*WP*, p. 20). Through David Marshall, a wealthy wholesale grocer, we feel the sense of siege that the immigrants have inflicted upon the citizens of old Chicago. And the death of Marshall—a man "almost too Anglo-Saxon in his puremindedness" (*WP*, p. 213)—seems to signal the passing of an era in the city's history if not the waning or the end of a once great race. Yet, though this novel treats the fears of the old Americans with measured sympathy and satire, *With the Procession*—as opposed to *The Cliff-Dwellers*—accords a place to the settlement-house workers' belief that the "new-comers" (*WP*, p. 203) might be assimilated. While *With the Procession* dramatizes the city's multifarious fears of the immigrant and the nativists' vision of a dying Anglo-Saxon race, in the end it balances them against the meliorism of the settlement-house workers' view, here expressed by Theodore Brower. The novel, insofar as Brower speaks for Fuller, forecasts the increasingly sympathetic view of the immigrant his writings would reveal down through the end of World War I.

Fuller's novel, it appears, grows out of the fierce debates over the immigrant and immigration restriction that raged, in and outside Chicago, during the 1890s and for many years afterward. The prospect of assimilating the new immigrant—and the countervailing fear that the native Anglo-Saxon stock would be overwhelmed by the immigrants' increasing numbers—generated a variety of pressure groups and an almost incalculable number of notions about the origins and destiny of the Anglo-Saxon race. The idea of the Anglo-Saxon and its attendant ambiguities arose initially, John Higham has shown in *Strangers in the Land*, "out of political and literary speculation, not out of scientific inquiry. . . ."[11] What the idea of a "native Anglo-Saxon stock" meant to those polemicists in and outside the Immigration Restriction League who used it as a lever of attack against the new immigrant is not hard to say. But what the "Anglo-Saxon" signified to those who also sought to consecrate the myth of America's single national or racial origin is nearly impossible to fix with any final certainty, so various were the meanings given the term before 1900.

To read **With the Procession** and Fuller's ensuing writings against the background of *America* illuminates both the tangled history of the idea of the Anglo-Saxon and the particular meaning this idea held for Fuller. *America: A Journal for Americans: Devoted to Honest Politics and Good Literature* was a weekly published in Chicago between 1888 and 1891. Some of the city's leading merchants, writers, and scholars contributed to its pages, together with some rabidly anti-Catholic and anti-Irish labor union officers. Though Fuller did not contribute, he knew the journal; and he most certainly came to know of its principal policies during the 1890s, when Hobart Chatfield-Taylor, *America*'s financial angel, co-editor, and founder, became his close friend. The columns and articles appearing in *America* illuminate Fuller's ideas on the Anglo-Saxon and the new immigrant. They help define the local coloration given nativist ideas and thus light up Fuller's treatment of them in his writings.

Every week, for more than four years, *America* cried havoc, warning that "wave after wave of European degradation breaks upon our shores, and rushing far inland, obliterates the precious vestiges of American nationality."[12] Week after week the editors published their box score, with a wry joke or two, of the number of "alien arrivals" at Boston and Ellis Island. While statistics might vary with the season, and the definition of what groups made up the alien "horde" might change subtly from columnist to columnist, *America*'s editors remained steadfast in declaring their belief that "the race of native Americans—the descendants of the founders of this republic—is fast perishing as a victim of its own criminal folly" ("The American Race Tendency," 23 June 1888, p. 3). Chatfield-Taylor called upon Americans to "sedulously guard race characteristics" lest the alien "invasion . . . make of the American people a Babeltongued horde" or "a mongrel refuse breed" (14 July 1888, p. 4).

It was *America*'s role to propagate the nativist ideas that would soon spawn the Immigration Restriction League. The prominence *America* gave the Harvard intellectuals who promoted the League—Professor Nathaniel Shaler, Senator Lodge, and George W. Curtis (editor of *Harper*'s)—reflects the shared values and views of Chicago and New England nativists. Shaler's arguments against immigration, put forward in two early issues of *America* (25 October 1888 and 1 November 1888), illustrate the characteristically filial-pietistic stance the journal took toward the Anglo-Saxon and the New Englander. Shaler's two long, lead articles on "The Immigration Problem Historically Considered" define the links that joined the Chicago and the Harvard nativists. In them, he makes two general and rhetorically interdependent claims: (1) "the political and social instincts on which our social fabric rests are in the main those of one people," which he defined as "Anglo-Saxon and Teutonic"; (2) "the inheritances of a thousand years or more . . . remain in the descendants of Europeans and are more powerful for good or evil than any immediate impulses which our American conditions can bring upon the people." Thus, Shaler suc-

ceeded in articulating the "immigration problem"—and the values of American civilization—largely in terms of inheritance; he minimized or discounted altogether the assumption that democracy or the American environment could "uplift the peasant class" which, in increasing numbers, now threatened to overwhelm the "pure-blooded" New Englander and his descendants.

With the Procession and many later writings suggest that Fuller had listened closely to the arguments over immigrants and immigration restriction that *America* and its allies had initiated. Through the story of the Marshalls' fears and the adumbration of the problems that immigrants faced and created in Chicago, Fuller projects yet parodies the ideas *America* articulated. Before the Civil War, the Marshalls counted themselves among Chicago's leading families; but, long before the novel opens, they had fallen behind "the procession." Much of the novel's action turns on the eldest daughter Jane's determined efforts to recapture the family's high social standing. The city's *nouveaux riches* have far outstripped them. Their Michigan Avenue home and their once fashionable neighborhood are, by 1893 and 1894, the time of the novel, beset by industrial blight and the encroachment of immigrant families. To these mingled facts David Marshall, the old settler, responds, though wearily, in language as fierce as that of *America*. He, his family, his race and its values, stand "in a state of siege" (*WP*, p. 22).

In many ways, then, the novel dramatizes a popular belief that the immigrant would, through indifference or hereditary hostility to American values, undermine the country's politics and government and displace the native Anglo-Saxon stock. David Marshall articulates such fears when he complains that young toughs have broken into his stable, vandalized his coach, and beaten his coachmen: "The steerage-rats . . . have left their noisome holds to swarm into our houses, over them, through them, everywhere . . ." (*WP*, p. 133).[13] Though he cannot identify the culprits by nationality—"they are Poles, or Bohemians, or Jews—Heaven knows what" (*WP*, p. 134), he knows them as a threat. His son Roger discovers, when he tries to put the vandals in jail, that the police, the ward alderman, and the lawbreakers are all in league against law-abiding citizens like the Marshalls. Because the culprits are precinct workers and brothers to the ward's alderman, they seem immune to the ordinary processes of law. "Our ward," Roger cries, "hasn't elected anything but crime-brokers for the last ten years" (*WP*, p. 194). With the flood of immigrants the city has become "a hell-broth—thieves, gamblers, prostitutes, pawnbrokers, saloon-keepers, aldermen, heelers, justices, bailiffs, policemen—and all concocted for us within a short quarter of a century" (*WP*, pp. 194-95).

But if Fuller thus sets up the narrative structure of **With the Procession** to condemn immigrants, he stops short of espousing the nativism David and Roger Marshall and *America* represent. He takes his stand with the settlement house workers who argued that the "new immigrant" might be assimilated. His justification for this view—clearly intended to allay fears about the immigrant invasion—is stated forcefully, sometimes sententiously, in the speeches delivered by the settlement-house worker Theodore Brower. Though Fuller implicitly mocks the high Victorian seriousness of his rhetoric, Brower's discourses on political evolution are meant to win sympathy for the immigrants. Brower's speeches in effect plead for community among immigrants and "native" Americans: "Over in the Settlement we are trying to make those new-comers realize that they are a part of the body politic; perhaps we need another settlement to remind some of the original charter-members of the same fact" (*WP,* pp. 203-04). While Brower acknowledges that "heavy immigration from southeastern Europe" has "brought elements that have never been in our national life before," he confidently asserts that in time, as the immigrant comes to understand his political obligations in a democracy and as he escapes from feudal habits, he will join "our national life" (*WP,* p. 202).

III.

During the mid 1890s, in the years when he wrote *With the Procession,* Fuller's ideal of assimilation and his confidence in the powers of "uplift" seem generally to have matched Brower's. He too assumed that the immigrant would be happily absorbed into a homogeneous and dominantly Anglo-Saxon "national life." But this rather conventional definition of assimilation was shortly to change. The imperial excesses of the Spanish-American War with its loose talk about racial destiny stirred the usually soft-spoken Fuller to satirize the Anglo-Saxon myth of superiority. And, as his attacks on Anglo-Saxonism turned more scornful, he began to examine with increasing sympathy the role the immigrant might play in shaping America's culture and literature.

Fuller's assertions about assimilation in **"The Upward Movement in Chicago,"** an 1897 *Atlantic* article, measure his changing attitudes. Here Fuller speaks in rather booster-like tones about "the flood of foreign immigration" inundating Chicago: "How soon the vast body of newcomers may consciously achieve a national allegiance is a question; their civic allegiance, thanks to the compelling personality of the city itself, is instant and complete."[14] In talking of "newcomers" (rather than of "hordes of Immigrants," as certain magazine writers customarily did), Fuller relies on the language and sentiments he had placed in Brower's speeches. With this choice of settlement-house rhetoric runs the virtually untroubled assumption that the immigrant "newcomers" will forget their foreign allegiances, be uplifted and assimilated into the "national life."

With the onset of the Spanish-American war in 1898, Fuller moved into an anti-imperialistic position that compelled him to turn many of the standard prejudices about Anglo-Saxon superiority inside out. **"Art in America,"** published in *The Bookman* in 1899, attacks the inbred emotional sterility and the absence of art in Anglo-Saxon life. Invoking the current racial and cultural theories of na-

tivists like Henry Cabot Lodge, he plays upon the idea that America is "the graveyard of nations" and would, before long, be the death of the Anglo-Saxon race. That the Anglo-Saxons had evolved into "a race of rulers and administrators" points to their "poverty of temperament," a deadly inheritance from their English and New England forefathers.[15] Salvation and survival itself might be won through the steady dilution of such an Anglo-Saxon heritage. With heavy emphasis on that paradox, Fuller provocatively concludes: "The fusion of racial elements—we are not all Anglo-Saxons!—may bring us a shining aptitude for the arts, and a day . . . less devoted to grimy new facts . . . nervous tension and headlong speed."[16]

In the doggerel verse of *The New Flag* (1899), he attacks American involvement in the Spanish-American War and burlesques the idea of Anglo-Saxon manifest destiny:

> By swearing the principle's confined to
> Those whom McKinley has a mind to,
> That is to say the Anglo Saxon
> Who has the right to lay a tax on
> Whomso the March of Progress waylays—
> Just now it is the dusky Malays.
> Unless 'tis gain to let blind Destiny
> Worm eat our Constitution. . . .[17]

He smoothed and tempered his language but softened no conviction in **"Why is the Anglo-Saxon Disliked?,"** a short piece published in *The Saturday Evening Post* (6 January 1900). Once more, as in *The New Flag* and **"Art in America,"** he strikes out at the Anglo-Saxon myth: "The Anglo-Saxon may be looked upon as a specialist highly effective in his one department—the domain of the practical. The fair, all-round development on a general emotional basis he leaves to men of different blood."[18]

Fuller was never again to be so relentlessly belligerent in criticism of the received idea of the Anglo-Saxon as he was during the Spanish-American War years. But he continued for some time to charge that America's failure to create great art and great artists somehow grew out of the Puritan heritage and the thinned-out blood passed down to Americans from their Anglo-Saxon forebears. He pressed these arguments lightly in the short story **"Pilgrim Sons"** (1898), a satire on ancestor-hunting.[19] **"Alonzo Grout,"** a poem published many years later in *Lines Long and Short* (1917), makes a more somber point about the burden of Anglo-Saxon ancestry, even though Fuller makes it again in a serio-comic vein. Grout, descended from American ancestors "on both sides . . . for generations," like others of his "blood" finds himself "quite empty" of creative power. "The great things" in art and literature, Fuller tells us, will be done by poets "whose blood showed various mingled strains." The poem's embrace of a melting pot myth in such passages rests implicitly on a criticism of "our native stock." It looks, that is, to the infusion of "bright young foreigners" to invigorate and enrich American literature and culture.[20]

Even before Zangwill's play (of 1909) had indelibly stamped the idea of "The Melting Pot" on American thought, Fuller had shown a marked receptivity to this image of assimilation and the allied notion of "immigrant gifts." In 1903, in a review of a book on "the linguistic conditions of Chicago," he conceded that his city was a "modern Babel" but also asserted that "the compelling power of our civic life, the public school and the English language" would make Americans of the "newcomers" and their children. Implicit in these conclusions is his steadfast sense of Chicago as a melting pot—he speaks of the city as a "municipal crucible" that could transform "a diversity of human elements" into a "serviceable homogeneity." The review further shows that he was intuitively aware—more so than Zangwill and other popularizers—of the painful loss of identity that Americanization exacted. He recalls, in the same review, that he had once seen first hand how children ridiculed the foreign speech and manners of a ten-year-old "Russian Jewess" who desperately shouted back "I am an American; I am—I am."[21] Later, in a Chicago *Record-Herald* editorial titled **"Getting Americanized"** (16 October 1910), he acknowledged that in the process of melting down identities and stripping away national allegiances, pain and conflicts "within family groups" become inevitable. His editorial retold the story of an Americanized Italian whose success as a banker split him away from his "peasant" wife.[22] Such observations reflected his groping effort to see the individual and even the interior lives of those who had to suffer the experience of "getting Americanized."

These efforts led, more or less directly, to two World War I era poems, **"The Alien"** and **"Toward the New World,"** on balance, Fuller's most sustained and sympathetic treatments of the immigrant and the theme of alienation. **"The Alien,"** published in *Lines Long and Short* (1917), seems to grow directly out of the narrative lines of the editorial **"Getting Americanized."** That is, the poem tells almost sentimentally the story of an old woman who has come from an unnamed European country to America "impelled by hope, or misery, or courage." At the end of her life she finds herself intensely alone, separated from her family by her son's "quick success." This "good old soul" is now "a little in one world, / a little in another, / a good deal out of both."[23]

Though **"Toward the New World"** verges on the satiric (rather than the sentimental) the poem stands as a companion piece to **"The Alien,"** for it too takes up the price of separation and alienation from the old world as its theme. Told in the first person, it quite cleverly recreates the dreams a young Italian has of the new world. The speaker, though he has not yet left Italy, brashly talks as one who already feels Americanized: "I am ready for it all—/Know their language and should soon pick up their ways." The catalogue of complaints he has about "the cramped old life of a cramped old land" seems conventional and, on the surface, reasonable enough. They lead him to call out for "Room—room; an open way and a new start." But Fuller's attitude toward this pre-Americanized Italian sounds ambivalent in the end. This immigrant's energy and spirit are admirable, but his casual and sweeping rejection of the whole of the old world—including the picturesque, mediaeval landscape that Fuller, the author of *The Chevalier of Pensieri-Vani,* never ceased to value—suggests that his values are flawed. Similarly, his unquestioning acceptance of America's "crowded new cities" and "new speed" suggests that he will suffer some of the same disillusionment that **"The Alien"** recorded.[24]

"Toward the New World" (dated 1920, though never published) stands, finally, as an ambiguous marker in the evolution of Fuller's attitude toward the immigrant and assimilation. It is an interior monologue and, as such, moves Fuller closer than ever before to an examination of what he referred to elsewhere as the ideals, motives, and "impulses that propel a continental miscellany to our shores."[25] The speaker of the poem, who reveals himself to be a poet of a distinctly Whitman-like stripe, wants to be ". . . set quite free / From all those smooth conventions / stale and specious / that cloud the air of ancient lands. . . ." He wants "to aid and celebrate / a vast grand Newness in the making." He sounds, in short, like one of the bright young foreign poets that the poem **"Alonzo Grout"** implicitly welcomes to the new world.

Fuller's failure to publish **"Toward the New World"** suggests that, as the lost generation's scorn of convention began to make itself felt, he had many second thoughts. His writings in the 1920s make clear that he could not cut himself free from genteel literary conventions or values, much as poems like **"Alonzo Grout"** or **"Toward the New World"** might show that he deeply wanted to. Instead, the excesses of the "nervous generation" gradually led him to the suspicion that the massive force of immigration, and the dilution of the native stock, would finally corrupt American literature and culture.

"The Melting Pot Begins to Smell" (21 December 1924) announces Fuller's sharp turn away from many of the "cosmopolitan ideals" he had intermittently advocated for thirty years. The article, published in the *New York Times Book Review,* is a surprisingly severe, sweeping attack upon "a congeries of new arrivals," which he described as "rather irresponsible and . . . insolent beyond its own consciousness."[26] Just a few months earlier, he had, in reviewing Charles W. Eliot's *Late Harvest,* tacitly endorsed the claim that one of America's "five contributions to civilization" was "the welcoming of new-comers."[27] But here he seems disillusioned with the ideas and values he had poured into the "melting pot." He begins by recanting past beliefs: "To us the Melting Pot, notwithstanding the introduction of many miscellaneous elements, was to retain its primal purity; all such virtues and graces as we possessed—or thought we possessed—were to be passed along unimpaired to the new arrivals. . . ." "Zangwill's idea," which once "seemed . . . so humane," turns out to be mere "speciousness"—and more, a disguised threat to the manners and culture of "the American stock."

What caused Fuller to turn so abruptly against the notions of assimilation he had once championed? What moved him to attack the immigrant "new-comers" in the rhetoric he had in **With the Procession** and essays such as **"Art in America"** parodied or satirized? The question, perhaps, cannot be answered with precision or final certainty: his criticism of aliens and alien influences is so general—he deals, as he says, "with that intangible yet vital thing called atmosphere"—as to hamper analysis of the irritants provoking his attacks. Seeing Fuller's outrage as his resistance to the liberated spirit of the 1920s, rather than as an awakened nativism or xenophobia, however, helps to clarify the meaning of **"The Melting Pot Begins to Smell."** What he seems to fear most, that is, is not the immigrant but the way in which he threatens to liberate the native American from Anglo-Saxon scruples. He judges it "deplorable," for example, that now "the native American, hovering timidly under the shelter of the boardwalk, begins to borrow sanction from the bold aliens in the surf."

These lines, and the metaphor of a land-locked self-constraint embedded there, echo different but related fears, feelings of detachment similar to those he had expressed in his novel **The Last Refuge** (1900). In it he had said, through a surrogate character: "I have lived . . . by the seashore without ever venturing into the water." The writer-surrogate had gone on to say that he hoped and longed to be carried "in one great wave" into "this wonderful sea of life."[28] Bernard Bowron, in his seminal study of Fuller's life and work, examines this passage closely, showing that it reveals his "sense of isolation" and confesses to his feelings of "numbness and failure."[29] Which is to say, by way of analogy and the association Fuller strikes between the alien and the sea, that the immigrant simultaneously posed a threat and an attraction.

Such ambivalence toward the alien betokens the emotional liberation that Fuller both feared and desired. While he might complain about the constraints of American civilization or resist his own Anglo-Saxon heritage, he persistently found ways to cling to those inhibitions. This paradoxical attitude led him to project his half-suppressed desire for liberation on to the alien and the immigrant. Thus, in his short story **"New Wine,"** he characterizes Italian peasants as people who "live the natural hours of the natural man." He presents their violent attacks upon transplanted American enterprises as heroic opposition to the regimented chaos of modern life. In Italy, "grave peasants" can symbolize Fuller's idea of ignorant, emotional wholeness; at such safe removes they can represent a healthy antipathy to American practicality and the deadening routines of Anglo-Saxon order. But in America a "throng of dark-eyed" immigrants can become a threat to the psychic order and the inhibitions Fuller lived by.[30] He could not imagine, he could only fear, surrendering fully to the primitive freedom they seemed to embody. What was alien to his insular sense of identity had to be safely assimilated or kept at an unreachable distance, somewhere beyond an impassable Atlantic.

Though the immigrant symbolized liberation from Anglo-Saxon scruples and restraints, he threatened to destroy an identity and culture based on those same constraints. Despite the hesitant ventures toward the liberation that the foreign symbolized in **"Alonzo Grout,"** despite the attractions of the freedom and Whitmanic expansiveness the immigrant-poet expressed in **"Toward the New World,"** Fuller could not leave what he comes to call, in his "Melting Pot" essay, the "repressive shelter" of Anglo-Saxon decorum and modesty.

Shortly after Fuller wrote **"The Melting Pot Begins to Smell,"** he took on the editing of Chatfield-Taylor's memoirs, *Cities of Many Men* and was eventually left with the job of seeing the book to press in the summer of 1925. Chatfield-Taylor's nostalgic recreation of Chicago before the twin invasions of immigration and industrialization illuminates Fuller's essay in that it suggests a convergence of his views with those of the one-time editor of *America.* Chatfield-Taylor's correspondence with Fuller that summer seems to assume that they now share the same views on the decline of American culture and the destruction of its native character.[31] Chatfield-Taylor's book recalls *America* and its nativist philosophy, speaking of the magazine's virulent campaigns against "unrestricted immigration" as a noble but lost cause. Noting that "Chicago's greatness . . . came from an unusual and balanced combination of the best blood of New England and of the South," he laments the passing of the quiet New England village of his childhood. He finishes his elegy to this city of the past by deploring Chicago's present condition as "a smoke-ridden Babel where thirty tongues are spoken by as many alien races. . . ."[32] Together with others of their generation alive in the 1920s, Fuller and his life-long friend felt compelled to think of themselves as the last of a dying or disappearing race.

Fuller's transvaluation of the Melting Pot myth, his attacks upon the "new immigrant," and his apparent turn toward Anglo-Saxonism in 1924 speak finally of his sense of displacement and dispossession. The new and "homogeneous people" that he had eloquently welcomed in a score of articles between 1900 and 1920 came to seem either a less possible or a less desirable race. He had never, even in his most sympathetic renderings of the immigrant, envisioned an American culture or identity built upon the ever-swirling waters of pluralism. But by the mid 1920s he had come to feel that the "variegated newcomers" had "vitiated and polluted" the atmosphere of America; they threatened to absorb and assimilate a world he could not abandon.[33]

It gives one measure of the widening distance between Fuller and the generation of Fitzgerald and Hemingway to note that he now took with renewed seriousness the Anglo-Saxon mythology he had rejected in the late 1890s. Fitzgerald might burlesque Stoddard's *Rising Tide of Color* through Tom Buchanan's buffoonery; Hemingway, without compunction, could parody the apocalyptic warnings of Madison Grant's *The Passing of a Great Race* in the subtitle and plot of his *Torrents of Spring* (1926). But Fuller spoke solemnly of "the American stock": "Now, this stock, whatever outsiders may think, is not new and for that reason pliant. Essentially we come—over a long and varied road, it is true—from the forests of Northern Germany."[34] For him these battered ideas of a "native stock," the very notions of the Anglo-Saxon he had satirized at the turn of the century, came to be a tenuous link with an idealized past.

Notes

1. See Henry James, *The American Scene* (1907; rpt. Bloomington: Indiana Univ. Press, 1968), pp. 85-86.

   Author's note: I wish to thank the University of Toledo for the Summer Research Fellowship that made it possible for me to research the papers of the Immigration Restriction League (Widener Library, Harvard University) and the papers of Henry Blake Fuller. I owe thanks, as well, to the Newberry Library for the fellowship in the summer of 1978 that gave me access to the Fuller Papers and the rich resources of the Newberry. And I wish to thank my colleague, William U. McDonald, for his generous help in reading and criticizing a draft of this essay.

2. Henry Blake Fuller, *The Cliff-Dwellers* (New York: Harper & Brothers, 1893), pp. 53 and 175. All page references to *The Cliff-Dwellers* are to this edition and will be given parenthetically in the text. References to Fuller's *With the Procession* (published in 1895) will also be given in the text. I have used the University of Chicago reprint of *With the Procession* (Chicago, 1965).

3. "The Upward Movement in Chicago," *Atlantic Monthly,* 80 (Oct. 1897), 538; "Chicago," *Century Magazine,* 84 (May 1912), 28.

4. "The Alien" appears in *Lines Long and Short* (Boston: Houghton Mifflin, 1917), pp. 118-23. "Toward the New World," written about 1920, was not published; the manuscript may be found in the Henry Blake Fuller Papers, Newberry Library (Chicago).

5. "The Melting Pot Begins to Smell," *The New York Times Book Review* (21 Dec. 1924), 2.

6. See Robert Burns Peattie's sketch of Fuller in *Henry B. Fuller,* ed. Anna Morgan (Chicago: Ralph Fletcher Seymour, 1929), p. 71.

7. *America: A Journal for Americans: Devoted to Honest Politics and Good Literature* was published weekly in Chicago between 1888 and 1891. Chatfield-Taylor (1865-1945), one of the principal editors and the chief financial backer of the journal, knew Fuller from the early 1890s on.

8. Bernard Bowron, *Henry B. Fuller of Chicago: The Ordeal of a Genteel Realist in Ungenteel America* (Westport, Conn.: Greenwood Press, 1974), and John Pilkington, Jr., *Henry Blake Fuller* (New York: Twayne Publishers, 1970).

9. John Higham's *Strangers in the Land: Patterns of American Nativism, 1860-1925* (New York:

Atheneum, 1974) remains the principal work in this field. Barbara Solomon's *Ancestors and Immigrants* (Cambridge, Mass.: Harvard Univ. Press, 1956) stresses the New England sources for American nativism.

10. In *The Chevalier of Pensieri-Vani* (New York: The Century Co., 1899; republished by The Gregg Press, 1970), he sneers at the moral smugness of New England: "If you prefer a civilization that shall address exclusively the 'moral sense,' I must refer you to New England, with its clapboard school-houses and its Cotton Mathers" (p. 57).

11. Higham, p. 11.

12. Edward Gilpin Johnson, "The Vital Question," *America,* 1 (14 March 1889), 2. All future references to articles in *America* will be given parenthetically in the text.

13. David Marshall's rhetoric sounds much like *America*'s. For example, Chatfield-Taylor's editorial "The Rough and the Hoodlum" declared that "the rough class is almost exclusively composed of foreigners who emigrated at an early age and the American offspring of foreign parents" (*America,* 28 July 1888, p. 3).

14. "The Upward Movement in Chicago," p. 538.

15. "Art in America," *Bookman,* 10 (Nov. 1899), 221, 218, and 220.

16. See the penultimate paragraph of "Art in America," pp. 224 and 218.

17. Copies of Fuller's *The New Flag* (Chicago?, privately printed, 1899) are scarce: these lines (p. 24) come from a copy in the Chicago Historical Society. William M. Gibson points out—in "Mark Twain and Howells: Anti-Imerialists," *New England Quarterly,* 20 (Dec. 1947), 436—that Fuller's stance was close to the "anti-Imperialist" view taken by Howells, Twain, Charles Eliot Norton, William James, and other American writers.

18. "Why Is the Anglo-Saxon Disliked?," *Saturday Evening Post,* 172 (6 Jan. 1900), 590.

19. "Pilgrim Sons" appears in *From the Other Side* (Boston: Houghton Mifflin, 1898), a collection of Fuller's short fiction.

20. See "Alonzo Grout" in *Lines Long and Short* (Boston: Houghton Mifflin, 1917), pp. 86-91.

21. "Chicago's Varied Population Made Subject of Linguistic Study," *The Chicago Evening Post* (7 March 1903), "Book Section." From a clipping in the Henry Blake Fuller Papers, Newberry Library (Chicago).

22. "Getting Americanized," Chicago *Record-Herald* (16 Oct. 1910), 4. From a clipping in the Henry Blake Fuller Papers, Newberry Library (Chicago).

23. *Lines Long and Short,* pp. 118, 120, and 122-23.

24. Manuscript poem in the Henry Blake Fuller Papers, Newberry Library. Quoted by permission of the Newberry Library.

25. "Professor Pupin Becomes an American," *The New York Times Book Review,* 28 (14 Oct. 1923), 2.

26. "The Melting Pot Begins to Smell" is printed in full on page 2 of *The New York Times Book Review* (21 Dec. 1924).

27. "Dr. Eliot Examines the World," *New York Times Book Review* (30 March 1924), 24.

28. See *The Last Refuge* (Boston: Houghton Mifflin, 1900), pp. 98-101.

29. Bowron, pp. 191-93.

30. See "New Wine" in *Waldo Trench and Others* (New York: Charles Scribner's Sons, 1908), pp. 78, 91, and 93.

31. In thanking Fuller for his work on *Cities of Many Men* (Boston: Houghton Mifflin, 1925), he implies that Fuller had worked on the book in early 1925. See the letter from Hobart Chatfield-Taylor to Fuller, 10 Sept. 1925. Henry Blake Fuller Papers, Newberry Library (Chicago).

32. Chatfield-Taylor, *Cities of Many Men,* pp. 193, 222, and 283.

33. "The Melting Pot Begins to Smell," p. 2.

34. Ibid.

Sue Morton (essay date 1981)

SOURCE: "Italy as an Ideal: Henry B. Fuller's *The Chevalier of Pensieri-Vani*," in *Italian Americana,* Vol. VII, No. 1, Fall-Winter, 1981, pp. 75-88.

[*In the following essay, Morton discusses Fuller's conceptions of culture and civilization as evinced in* The Chevalier of Pensieri-Vani.]

Henry Blake Fuller, a talented writer from Chicago, initially gained recognition in the 1890s with his first book-length work, *The Chevalier of Pensieri-Vani.* This travel-fiction book set in Italy drew the praise of important Italianists like Charles Eliot Norton and James Russell Lowell, and their praise helped to secure a hearing for Fuller from American publishers and readers.

Fuller was born in Chicago on January 9, 1857. He could trace his ancestry back to the beginnings of New England through both his parents. His grandfather migrated westward from Massachusetts and ultimately settled in Chicago in 1849. While living in St. Joseph, Michigan, the grandfather became a county judge. In Chicago, Judge Henry Fuller involved himself in the construction of the local railroad system and the first city water development. Fuller's father, George Wood Fuller, was secretary of the Southside Railway Company, then cashier of the Home National Bank. At his death in 1885, he was also the bank's vice-president.

Henry B. Fuller was very conscious of himself as an American who had deep roots at the beginning and in the significant development of this country. He called himself one of the "charter members" of America.[1] He expressed pride in his New England ancestry and in his membership in one of Chicago's old families.[2] He was an excellent student, and he displayed an early interest in drama, books, and writing. On his own, he studied languages and culture. He developed a decided concern for architecture. He became very interested in visiting Europe in order to see for himself many of the things he had studied. He carefully planned and recorded his first trip to Europe between August 1879 and August 1880. While his family undoubtedly expected him to take his place in the Chicago business community, Fuller showed his preference for a world of culture and art with his studies, his writing, and his European travel. In an early essay, **"The American School of Fiction,"** he had recognized "that the Old World has still almost a practical monopoly of the scenery, the properties and the atmosphere that tempt the literary tyro on."[3] Much of his own literature would stem from his studies and his travel in Europe.

In *The Chevalier of Pensieri-Vani,* Fuller opposed the limitations of Puritan America to the richness of Italy: "The Italian civilization addresses itself primarily to the eye, but after, with immense reaches of depth and breadth, to the intellect. If you prefer a civilization that shall address exclusively the 'moral sense,' I must refer you to New England, with its clapboard school-houses and its Cotton Mathers."[4] In one of his European journals, Fuller had revealed: "Oh, this question that troubles me so much, what, after all, is civilization?"[5] The achievement of *The Chevalier of Pensieri-Vani* lies in its definition of civilization.

Fuller's feelings about culture and civilization are the focus of *The Chevalier of Pensieri-Vani.* The very writing of this book reflects his own necessity for disassociating himself from the American world of business. But Fuller always had a strong sense of himself as a part of his own society, and the Midwestern American characters in this work speak not so much of rejection as they do of cultural relativity. The strongest comment about American society emerges through the Chevalier, who is Fuller's model of a civilized man. An examination of the characterization of the Chevalier (Fuller calls him "the Cavaliere," because his title is Italian) indicates a close relationship between him and his creator. Fuller's self-education enabled him to escape the confines of the Chicago business world and to demonstrate what a young man from Chicago could do. What he could do, what he had taught himself to do, was to discuss with perfect ease and expertise the towns and the by-ways of Tuscany and indeed of all Italy. How far he had come from Chicago was described best perhaps by a review which exclaimed that "There is nothing in Chicago so unlike Chicago as 'The Chevalier of Pensieri-

Vani.'"[6] Fuller, however, included something of Chicago in his book through the character of George W. Occident, a Midwestern American. He also comes to Europe with a desire to learn and to understand the meaning of civilization.

In *The Chevalier of Pensieri-Vani,* Fuller presented an ideal atmosphere. The Chevalier and his circle of friends and acquaintances are appropriate to the atmosphere, and through them Fuller portrayed his ideal of civilization. The book tells about their life while it tells about their travels in Italy—in Etruria, Rome, Anagni, Ravenna, and Venice. Their life is one of leisure, and their interests are cultural and social. They are the *fortunati* as well as the *cognoscenti.* It is important to recognize—with Edmund Wilson—that Fuller displayed "the thoroughness and exactitude of his knowledge of history, geography, literature, art, and architecture" in his European books[7] as in his later Chicago books. His knowledge and observations here as in his Chicago books enabled him to include and to develop details and metaphors which often contained the implications of the whole work.

One of the Chevalier's circle is the Prorege of Arcopia, the vice-regent of a small Adriatic kingdom, reportedly a combination of Arcadia and Utopia. By virtue of his position and his personality, the Prorege is a good representative of a static, stratified society with a paternalistic, even despotic, government. Fuller gave the Prorege some of his own interests and characteristics. The Prorege is an aristocrat who is culturally inclined and socially refined. He has a deep appreciation of music and a definite interest in architecture, with considerable skill as an architect. Fuller said that architecture was a profession and an art he himself might have pursued except for his unwillingness or inability to cope with certain problems of structural design.[8] The Prorege shares Fuller's appreciation for architecture and his limitation in structural design: "He troubled himself very little about foundations, but was matchless when it came to façades. He reveled in theory, but in the matter of practice he was apt to fall back upon his bureau of construction" (p. 94). His achievement, however, was the very thing Fuller hoped for from architecture: "The Prorege's faculty with stone and mortar was, in fact, the one thing that as much as any other endeared him to his subjects; for the Arcopians gloried in a monumental expression of their civic greatness, and looked upon peoples who could not express their race and epoch in enduring marble as very poor creatures indeed" (p. 94). The Prorege is one of many characters in Fuller's fiction in whom he would project certain aspects of himself, almost to caricature at times. While Fuller actually was self-sufficient, the Prorege is self-indulgent; and the book gently but humorously mocks the vanity and the self-interest of this regal personage. As part of his attraction to young men ("One with the right look out of his eyes and the right slope to his shoulders seldom failed of the princely favor" [p. 95]), the Prorege takes under his guidance "a promising young barbarian," George W. Occident (p. 95). His interest in young men suggests Fuller, who—especially in his later years—culti-

vated the friendship of young men; and in his discussions with Occident, the Prorege expresses some of the convictions Fuller himself stated elsewhere.

The young man who stimulates the Prorege's instruction has come to Italy in search of a more congenial environment. His name and his description suggest the West. He is twenty-two years old, the same age Fuller was when he first went to Europe,[9] and Occident, too, felt dissatisfied in his culturally narrow Midwestern birthplace. While Occident appreciates the Prorege and his friends and while he feels a compatibility with life in Italy, he is absolutely unable to alter his deep commitment to a mobile society and a democratic government. If Occident represents Fuller's own commitment to America, he can represent only what Fuller might have become without his course of self-education. And he can represent the kind of young men Fuller might have seen around him in Chicago: "Occident, in his uninstructed state, really had no more business among the monuments that fill the valley of the Po or of the Arno than a deaf man has at a symphony concert, . . . and he could ramble about the streets of Verona or Siena or Vicenza,—almost every one of them a free gallery of masterpieces,—seeing nothing and quite unconscious that there was anything to see. If he happened to admire anything, it was sure to be the worst" (pp. 95-96). Earlier the reader had learned that, in spite of his lack of worldly possessions, one of the Chevalier's resources is "an almost unbounded fund of artistic and historical knowledge which enabled *him* to see clearly where others saw through a glass darkly, or saw not at all, or quite failed, indeed, to realize that there was anything whatever *to* see. The ability to perceive, to understand what one perceives, to extract the full measure of profit and enjoyment by so understanding,—this must be in great part the wealth of a pilgrim in Italy" (p. 57). The word "pilgrim" really applies much more to Fuller than to the Chevalier, and the meaning of the book rests in Fuller's ability to master an understanding of Italy. Like the Prorege, Fuller regarded Occident as an apt pupil: "Occident was extremely bright . . . a clever fellow, a handsome fellow" (p. 96). Again like the Prorege, Fuller was justified in considering himself a "master" (p. 90); his book was a testimony to his mastery of Italy. The book's success certainly encouraged Fuller to feel that he could be a model and a teacher to the Occidents of Midwestern America, and, of course, Occident plans to return to America at the close of the book.

The development of the relationship between the Prorege and Occident, between master and pupil, provides an ample opportunity for Fuller to express his feelings and convictions. In his later essay "Art in America," he expresses much the same conceptions that the Prorege does in this book about the differences between Latin and Anglo-Saxon civilizations. Latin civilizations, the Prorege explains to Occident, have a superstructure of art and culture which rests on a rather insecure political and financial foundation; Anglo-Saxon civilizations have a solid foundation of political and financial accomplishments with no head of artistic accomplishment to put upon it. His explanation concludes a discussion between the two about the value of their respective forms of government. Occident "delighted in the pictorial aspects of the Southern civilizations, but he was by no means blind to the merits of his own, and he felt that the more he defended the social scheme of which he was a part, the more he would be obliged to defend himself for having detached himself from it" (p. 105). The Prorege acknowledged that "a perfect ideal civilization" would possess the balance of a strong foundation under a strong superstructure of art (p. 104), but Occident and Fuller, unlike the Prorege, hoped to realize a perfect type of civilization in Chicago, and part of the importance of this book is its contribution toward a strong superstructure of art to put atop the strong foundation of politics and finance in America.

The Prorege also states some of Fuller's views about industrialization and about nature. In an indignant protest against the development of industry, which "brutal Progresso" has brought to Italy, the Prorege asks himself:

> Whose was the earth? . . . Was it the exclusive possession of those merely who were now living out their brief day upon it, or was it something more—the foothold and heritage of generations yet to come? Who could make good to those of the coming century the felled trees, the gashed and leveled hills, the polluted ponds and choked-up streams that signalized our present dealings with outraged and suffering Mother Nature? Who was to render back to them an earth as beautiful as that which we ourselves received as our right,—an earth whose possession and enjoyment is as much, as inalienably, their right as ours? More; what power could save us—us, full of small greeds and great irreverences—from the amaze and scorn and contempt and indignation of millions yet unborn? (pp. 163-164)

Although Fuller gives these words to the Prorege, behind them is partly a very American concern, a concern for our children and for the future which belongs to our children. Much of what the Prorege said about nature Fuller restated in an article **"The Modern Man and Nature,"** which appeared in *The Saturday Evening Post* on January 20, 1900. The indictment of industrial progress by the Prorege is aimed largely against America, as is shown by the development of the chapter in which it occurs. Here Fuller connects democracy with the problems brought about by widespread industrialism. The chapter involves a visit to Arcopia, and one of the Prorege's quests, the Duke of Avon and Severn, who had observed the processes of industry and democracy in England, supports the sentiments of the Prorege. Both the Duke and his host oppose an unbridled growth, and Winthrop Floyd in *The Cliff-Dwellers* later echoes their feelings in his observation about Chicago: "'I see,' said Winthrop. 'If you can only be big you don't mind being dirty.'"[10]

The Prorege's strongest statement, which almost causes him to break with Occident, is his objection to any man becoming "a mere money-machine" (p. 169). With this statement Fuller presented his own objection to American society: it forced its men to become mere tools for producing money. He would go on in his fictions to elaborate this aspect of American society, this reduction of its identity.

One of the significant techniques Fuller uses in this book is his narrator, who identifies himself as a friend of the Chevalier. He tells the whole book as if it were one long report or a tale with appropriate divisions. He is very much at home in the world of the Chevalier and his friends, and his knowledge of Italy, art, and culture is so like theirs that he even seems a part of the circle: "I ventured to question him on this point some time after" (p. 65) and "He, as far as I am aware, is the only being in the world who knows all that *might* be said" (p. 89) are the kind of comments he uses to indicate his connection with the Chevalier. The circumstances of the narrator, however, extend beyond the Chevalier's, because he is not so distinctly a European personality as his friend is. Shortly after he introduces the Chevalier, the narrator associates himself with his American readers: "Dost know the tombs of Castel d'Asso? The towers of San Gimignano? The outlooks from Montepulciano? The palaces of Pienza? The cloisters of Oliveto Maggiore? Hast ever penetrated the obscure renown of the Fanum Voltumnae,—or followed the fading frescos of the Grotta del Trinclinio,—or studied the lengthening shadows of the Val di Chiana,—or boated it across to the lonely isles of the Lago Trasimeno? No? Nor have I" (p. 2). His "Nor have I" is assuring to the readers who might now know Italy (potential Occidents); but his recital of places is enough to attract interest, the interest of those readers who do know Italy and that of those who might want to know it. His use of language, with its elegance and cadence, captures the spirit of the circle; and as the story progresses, his presence and the lack of dialogue are hardly noticeable. He is a variety of an omniscient narrator, and, like the narrators in many of Fuller's works, he is not far away from Fuller himself. The interjections which identify the teller of the story as the narrator also suggest his mobility. He travels in Italy, and seemingly his movement carries him to America, perhaps even to Chicago. Occident's return to his Midwestern American birthplace helps to prepare for this possibility.

The first chapter and its development indicate that the Chevalier is the central figure in the book. The atmosphere and activity of the book emerge from its first sentence: "It was the Chevalier of Pensieri-Vani who halted his traveling-carriage upon the brow of the Ciminian Forest to look down over the wide-spread Campagna di Roma" (p. 1). The beginning suggests the travel and leisure of the Chevalier and his interest in aesthetics. And soon we learn that he is traveling to meet his friends, to share with them his discovery of an Etruscan tomb. Culture and art are important to him and his circle. But the friends, in fact, come to meet the Chevalier; he is important, too.

With the Chevalier's discovery, Fuller presents an episode that would connect this hero with some of his later ones. The Chevalier takes the crown from the head of the ancient warrior lying on the bier in the tomb. He, of course, had no inclination to steal anything; he only wanted to substantiate his finding of a lifetime. But when he came to return the crown and to close the tomb:

> Old Lucumo had vanished. The crown had come back, but there was no head on which to place it. Only a handful of fine dust remained upon the bier, and served to index the mystery. The old warrior, after having triumphed for threescore years over the chances of war, and the dangers of fire and flood,—after sleeping calm and undisturbed through the tempests and earthquakes of three thousand years,—had crumbled pitifully away to nothing before the vagrant breezes of a summer day. The Cavaliere's friends—he had not told them of the old man whose crown he had presumed to sieze—showed the appreciative delight of true *cognoscenti* as they reviewed the frescos on the rock-hewn walls, and fingered the various objects that surrounded the vacant couch; but the Cavaliere's pleasure was sadly incomplete, and the Cavaliere's conscience began to make itself felt. He had done an evil thing. (pp. 8-9)

While his intentions were as close as possible to the best, he could not avoid complicity. Fuller partly attributes the act to the spirit of the modern age, and his statement of such an influence refers as much to himself as to the Chevalier: "I have more than once heard my hero rather disdainfully disclaim to represent the age; yet it may be that he misrepresents it in a less degree than he imagines" (p. 7). The comment ("He had done an evil thing" [p. 9]) and the act itself suggest the inextricable nature of good and evil in the modern world, and Fuller would return to face this inextricability which the Chevalier found in his great discovery, which was "his heart's dearest desire" (p. 5).

The Chevalier's title, the book tells us, "really was the most prized" of his possessions (p. 56). Indeed, there is as much validity as humor in a comment made by one of his visitors, who said that the Chevalier really "was as poor as a church mouse, and that the sum of his earthly belongings might easily be comprised in his title" (p. 56). And the title relates to life in America:

> Civilization is many-sided, but of all its facets none is more glittering than the one which may be called the power of formulation. We may appreciate genius; we may even give to our appreciation a casual and informal expression; but until we can formulate this expression and give its object an authoritative and widely accepted stamp we are far from an ideal polish and brilliancy. This grace the Latin civilization can claim; if one is a notable, the world may be so informed—one's notability is officialized. Pensieri-Vani was a notable; and a society which has at its bestowal such an amplitude of honor that even the meritorious alien may be cloaked by its generous folds dubbed him so. *This* is how the Cavaliere became a cavaliere, and I am really ashamed to have spent so much time over so simple a matter. (p. 68)

The comment about being "ashamed" to spend so much time over so "simple" a matter Fuller made with tongue-in-cheek, because he found the status of artists in America

a problem over which to spend a considerable amount of his thought and time. He wrote **"Art in America"** out of his strong feelings about the problems of the American artist. Some of his later fictions would deal specifically with American artists. The artistic Chevalier obtains his title when he plays the organ unusually well for a special High Mass at the Cathedral of Orvieto. Music had a special interest, along with architecture and literature, for Fuller. He had attempted to publish some of his own musical compositions, and, although he had not been successful in developing a career for himself in music, he did reflect his interest in it in much of his fiction.

Underlying Fuller's presentation of an ideal of civilization and adding to the complexity of this book is a novelistic structure in it involving the Chevalier and his friend Hors-Concours. In a private journal, which Fuller began in 1876, he wrote about his desire for a close, compatible friend: "It may seem incredible that I have paddled so far out into the sea of life without hailing a bosom friend. Such is the melancholy fact. I have never yet found a thoroughly congenial person whom I could make friend and confidante."[11] He thought about advertising for his friend and provided an outline of what he would insist upon in him:

> The youth must be—I am conscious that I expose myself in a most vulnerable point, and am certain that I shall receive a thrust from some moralizer—the youth must be handsome. I would pass by twenty beautiful women to look upon a handsome man. A man with a fine form, a beautiful head, and a handsome face is a feast for my eyes. Why could I not have lived with Sophocles? Why could I not have caught a glimpse of Byron's glorious head?
>
> Again, my youth must be of aesthetic tastes. He shall love literature, art, and music. Oh, to find a few in this rough and tumble squabble for dollars and cents, dollars and cents, who can find in books something better than bullion, and in culture something higher than cash.
>
> Third, my youth must be moral; I don't ask for religion, but for morality. He will be honest, conscientious. In our days, when the Almighty Dollar is the highest goal of man's ambition, it is a grand, a proud thing to be a man of truth and honor.[12]

The Chevalier, like Fuller, was attractive, cultured, honest, and talented; and he, too, desired a close friend. Even in its initiation, the relationship between the Chevalier and Hors-Concours is what Fuller longed for. The two young men meet on the steps of the Cathedral at Orvieto. The Chevalier had been seeking someone who could appreciate the church, "which received so little and yet deserved so much" (p. 58), and it was not until he met the "young Savoyard who was passing a few days at the Aquila, and with whom he was not slow in striking up an intimacy, that he found any one with whose views and feelings on this point his own seemed in exact accord" (p. 59). The Chevalier continues his close relationship to Hors-Concours through most of the activity in the book: "When he silently pressed the Seigneur's arm, or the Seigneur his, each one knew just what the other meant without any waste of words" (p. 14). His reaction in the final pages of the book to the marriage plans of Hors-Concours indicates the significance of his friend: "In the fit of despondency into which the nuptials of his friend threw him he was disposed to confound all nice distinctions, to dispense with all saving clauses, and to write the word *failure* against his whole life and career" (p. 184).

At Anagni, the Chevalier and Hors-Concours meet the German scholar Gregorianius. Like Fuller, the eminent German had "theorized the entire peninsula with the greatest zeal and ardor, and was perfectly acquainted with the frescos at Assisi and the mosaics at Ravenna years before" circumstances had allowed him to come to "the home of art" (p. 114). He began his career as a medievalist in Tuscany; but when he realized that his youthful years had passed, he turned to "classical antiquity at Rome" (p. 115), a study more in keeping with his mature years. When he began to consider himself old, he took another step back in the history of Italian civilizations to study the Etruscans; and finally at eighty years of age, he "betook himself" to study the Cyclopean towns (p. 117). "He had never been without the power of drawing young men about him, and when he took a modest little room in the palace at Anagni, his two youthful fellow-lodgers promptly and enthusiastically placed themselves at his disposal, and, after pretty largely despoiling their own quarters to make his a little less uncomfortable, they accompanied him in all the various excursions by which he taxed his failing strength" (p. 117). The Chevalier and Hors-Concours take care of him until he dies, and the Chevalier agrees to complete his erudite history of Italian civilizations. The narrator suggests that the German's death was somewhat of a warning to the Chevalier to "do as others do," as Fuller advised himself in one of his journals.[13] Neither Fuller nor the Chevalier very seriously considered changing his ways, which indeed would have meant changing his nature. "By this time he should have had a wife, a hearthstone, a family of children," the narrator had commented about Gregorianius (p. 115), but the scholar seemed no more inclined than the Chevalier to the usual domestic scene. The Chevalier "valued his freedom above all things, and felt that he could never assume the conjugal yoke without presently experiencing an irresistible disposition to cast it off. He sometimes thought he saw in the dim distance the coming of the day when the long-dominant and long taken-for-granted idea of Matrimony should go to meet, in the realm of the dispensable and the dismissed, the other idea, once equally dominant and equally taken for granted, of Monarchy" (pp. 54-55). The views on Monarchy seem more Fuller's than the Chevalier's, and the views on marriage, too, were those Fuller would voice again and again. The German scholar's ability to attract young men, his being able to die in the arms—so to speak—of two of them, and his success in convincing one of them to continue his work might be the very things Fuller would have chosen for himself. Certainly nothing in his later life, perhaps nothing in his life, pleased him more than having talented, young writers communicate with him or speak of him as their guide or example.[14] He knew that the pattern of the German's life was a warning, and he would use it as such in a later short story, **"Waldo Trench Regains His Youth."** He showed the same scholar, however, as influencing Raymond Prince away from the interests of ordinary boys in the autobiographical novel *On the Stairs.* Gregorianus and his life actually were very appealing to Fuller.

The last chapter in this book not only brings to the attention of the Chevalier the marriage plans of Hors-Concours but also the marriage of George Occident. He weds an American singer, whom Fuller never names, one who has made a career for herself in the Italian operatic world. Fuller resembles the singer as much as he does Occident. She goes to Europe not so much as a student of as a participant in its cultural scene; she is able to communicate with and even capture Italy on its own terms, She shares the interest in music of Fuller and of many of his characters, and in the second chapter, the Chevalier and Hors-Concours try to help make her debut in Pisa a success. When Occident tells the Chevalier of his marriage, the Chevalier identifies the singer with himself (and Fuller) as he expresses to himself his feeling that marriage almost always "was a weakness, and in this case it involved nothing less than a sacrifice" (p. 183). In his later fictions, Fuller also would represent himself or part of himself in feminine characters, and some of his comments in an early diary indicate how easily he thought of or accepted himself as having feminine tendencies.[15] In the marriage of the singer and Occident, he brings about a merger of culture and business as well as a reconciliation and a return to the American Midwest. He also effects a merger of some of the different aspects of himself and of America which appear in these two characters. Their marriage suggests Fuller's focus on a Midwestern setting, but at this point, he is too involved in his attraction to Europe. The Chevalier was not very concerned with "these Occidental doings" (p. 183), that is with these Western and American things. He recovers from the breakdown of his friendship with Hors-Concours and becomes himself again: "He could still congratulate himself on his exemption from the burdens of wealth, the chafings of domestic relations, the chains of affairs, the martyrdom of a great ambition, and the dwarfing provincialism that comes from one settled home" (p. 184). The Chevalier remained Fuller's ideal of a civilized man, and it is important to notice that if one could identify him "with any particular town, that town might be Florence" (p. 55). Among the things which would reappear in Fuller's work is his concept of Florence as an ideal city and a model for Chicago.

Before he returned his attention to Chicago, Fuller wrote another European travel-fiction book, *The Chatelaine of La Trinité* Both The Chevalier of Pensieri-Vani and The Chatelaine of La Trinité testified against a society in which business and materialism were ends in themselves and so dominated life that people lost their dignity and self-respect. In opposition to the widespread materialism and industrialism of America, Fuller's two European books successfully created an ideal of civilization. His ideal civilization was one which balanced political and financial accomplishment with artistic achievement, one which recognized art as a human value as necessary to humanity as any other human pursuit. A civilized society accorded a dignity to all people and apprehended the message of nature as—in Henry James' words—"not so much a 'Live upon me and thrive by me' as a 'Live *with* me, somehow, and let us make out together what we may do for each other.'"[16] An ideal society recognized that time given to aesthetic and social experience was as valuable as time given to business and industry. In both of these early European books, Fuller opposed American materialistic values with the freedom, the dignity, and the gaiety that emerged from the cultivation of imaginative values. The appeal of his fictional world, the elegance and authority of its language and experience, the sheer delight, especially of *The Chevalier of Pensieri-Vani* (which, as Larzer Ziff says, "breathes frivolity on almost every page"[17]) are all measures of Fuller's creative attainment.

Notes

1. Henry B. Fuller, "The Melting Pot Begins to Smell," *New York Times Book Review,* December 21, 1924, p. 2.

2. For examples see Henry B. Fuller, "The Bromfield Saga," *Bookman,* 65 (April 1927), 202; Hamlin Garland, *Roadside Meetings* (New York: Macmillan Co., 1930), pp. 268-270.

3. Henry Blake Fuller, "The American School of Fiction," ed. Darrel Abel, *American Literary Realism,* 3 (Summer 1970), 250.

4. Henry B. Fuller, *The Chevalier of Pensieri-Vani,* 5th ed. (New York: Century Co., 1899), p. 57. Subsequent references to this work will appear in the text and are to this edition.

5. "A Year in Europe," November 6, 1879, The Henry Blake Fuller Papers, The Newberry Library, Chicago.

6. *Boston Gazette,* September 13, 1891, quoted in John Pilkington, Jr., *Henry Blake Fuller* (New York: Twayne Publishers, 1970), p. 59; Bernard R. Bowron, Jr., *Henry B. Fuller of Chicago: The Ordeal of a Genteel Realist in Ungenteel America* (Westport, Conn.: Greenwood Press, 1974), p. 38.

7. Edmund Wilson, *The Devils and Canon Barham: Ten Essays on Poets, Novelists and Monsters,* with a Foreword by Leon Edel (New York: Farrar, Straus and Giroux, 1973), p. 23.

8. Henry B. Fuller, *The Cliff-Dwellers,* with an Introduction by Paul Rosenblatt (New York: Holt, Rinehart & Winston, 1973), p. ix.

9. Pilkington, p. 65.

10. *The Cliff-Dwellers,* p. 190.

11. "Journal: 1876" ('78; '79), The Henry Blake Fuller Papers, The Newberry Library, Chicago.

12. "Journal: 1876."

13. "Legacy to Posterity," The Henry Blake Fuller Papers, The Newberry Library, Chicago.

14. Anna Morgan, ed., *Henry B. Fuller* ([Chicago]: Ralph Fletcher Seymour, 1929), p. 106, pp. 113-114; Bowron, pp. xix-xx, pp. 228-229.

15. Bowron, p. 12.

16. Henry James, *The American Scene* (New York: Harper & Bros., 1907), p. 20.

17. Larzer Ziff, *The American 1890s: Life and Times of a Lost Generation* (New York: Viking Press, 1966), p. 109.

William D. Burns (essay date 1996)

SOURCE: "The Chevalier of Pensieri-Vani: Henry Fuller's Not-So-Elusive Anatomy," in *Rocky Mountain Review of Language and Literature,* Vol. 50, No. 2, 1996, pp. 147-63.

[*In the following essay, Burns underscores the ironic and satirical voice in Fuller's* The Chevalier of Pensieri-Vani.]

> *Satire is a sort of Glass, wherein beholders do generally discover everybody's Face but their Own; which is the chief reason for that kind Reception it meets in the world, and that so very few are offended with it.*
>
> *Jonathan Swift*

The Chevalier of Pensieri-Vani creates some interesting dilemmas for the student of literature. Although Fuller's first book enjoyed considerable success, generating four editions in the first two years following its initial publication, the response to it was as ambivalent in judgment of its form as it was appreciative of its aesthetic merit. In 1892, the year of the novel's fourth revised edition, Agnes Repplier discussed *The Chevalier* with admiration, but also mystification at its lack of identifiable characteristics:

> The story, which is not really a story at all, but a series of detached episodes, rambles backward and forward in such a bewildering fashion that the chapters might be all rearranged without materially disturbing its slender thread of continuity. It is equally guiltless of plot or purpose, of dramatic incidents or realistic details. (88)

Repplier makes no attempt to classify the book. Edmund Wilson, a modern critic who revived Fuller scholarship for a brief time in the late sixties, describes the novel as "something of an actual travel book in the taste of the then frequent articles in the more serious magazines . . ." (20). John Pilkington labels the book an "Italian romance" (*Fuller* 58), yet he notes its satiric elements and considers the work thematically as "an attack upon modern industrialism, modern bigness, and modern governmental corruption" (71). Darrel Abel comes somewhat closer to the real case; he notes the sentimentalism of the novel but points out more accurately the work's theme in his discussion of the only American in the book, the young Mr. Occident:

"[He] grows vividly aware of the difference between American innocence and rawness and European culture and decadence, between American energy and growth and European formality and sterility" (246).

Certainly, the book has romantic elements. The descriptions show the imagination and ideality typical of genteel writers of the day. However, as Abel notes, an ironic play runs through the entire work. The equivocal voice of the narrator, the treatment of the characters and the numerous hypocrisies in which they embroil themselves, and the ultimate depiction of a decrepit and decadent European aristocracy all undermine the notion of this book as a romance proper. To read this work as other than an anatomy or a satire constitutes a failure to recognize the overwhelming tone throughout the narrative as a whole.

Kenneth Scambray notes that Fuller's first novel comprises many of the author's personal recollections from travels in Europe. On his first trip, he began what developed into a three-part travel diary of his trip, **"A Year in Europe"** (36-37). He later used the material he recorded in his continental novels, ***The Chevalier of Pensieri-Vani, The Chatelaine of La Trinité, The Last Refuge,*** and ***Gardens of This World.*** Much of Fuller's early work demonstrates his penchant for satire. After his return from the continent, he worked at odd jobs and published two anonymous satirical poems, **"The Ballade of the Tourists"** and **"The Ballade of the Bank-Teller"** (49). He published his first story, entitled **"A Transcontinental Episode, Or, Metamorphoses at Muggins' Misery: A Co-Operative Novel by Bret James and Henry Harte"** in the January edition of *Life.* The story parodies Harte's sentimental western stories and James' transatlantic novels (55). Fuller became a regular contributor to *Life,* and his works were predominantly satiric pieces including a short poem entitled **"Some Day,"** which pokes fun at "the divorce-plagued status of contemporary marriage" (55). He also produced a number of other collections of stories, including satires on contemporary artistic figures and movements, one of which targeted Fuller's close friend Hamlin Garland. In 1886, Fuller began work on his first novel on the back of a discarded envelope that he pulled from a wastebasket. That work, ***The Chevalier of Pensieri-Vani, together with Frequent Allusions to the Prorege of Arcopia,*** was published at the author's expense in February 1890.

The Chevalier of Pensieri-Vani is not an easy work to summarize. As Repplier noted, the narrative recounts a series of episodes involving the cavaliere (the Italian form of the main character's title), the Prorege of Arcopia, the French noble the Seigneur des Hauts Rochers de Hors-Concours, the Contessa Nullaniuna, the English Duke of Avon and Severn, the American George Occident, and a number of other minor aristocratic characters. The first half of the novel deals with the prorege's attempts to track down and purchase what he believes to be a valuable Perugino entitled *Madonna Incognita* (the "Unknown Madonna"). After chasing through the picturesque back-

ground of mainland Italy, the prorege and his friends trace the painting back to Pisa, the very city where their investigation began. Much to the dismay of the vice regent, the painting turns out to be not a Perugino, but a Sodoma.

Other episodes include an explanation of the origination of the chevalier's title, reports on various practical jokes and devious deceptions that the characters play on each other, the story of the Margravine of Schwahlbach-Schreckenstein and her struggle to gain ownership of the Iron Pot of San Sabio, and the prorege's eventually successful attempt to add to the decorative architecture of the viceregal palace. The episodes center on themes about art, architecture, politics, industrialism, the value of leisure, and the contrast between American and European cultural values. The descriptions of the setting provide an ambience that recalls the sublime locales in works like Ann Radcliffe's *The Mysteries of Udolpho* and the romantic pastoral scenes in Hawthorne's *The Marble Faun.*

Considerable ambivalence appears in criticism about this novel. As mentioned previously, many critics have held firmly to the notion of its romantic qualities. Kenneth Scambray hedges not in the least, referring explicitly to ***The Chevalier*** as "the romance" (64) and noting that one review called the work "a sort of nineteenth-century *Sentimental Journey*" (169). But Scambray questions Fuller's belief that ***The Chevalier*** "evaded all the conventional categories of prose fiction," and he posits that the novel is merely "broadly eclectic, drawing upon many long-established conventional forms" (67). In *The Literature of the American People,* the work is called "[i]n no sense a novel," but a "mélange of travel, conversation, and narrative—half fanciful, half real" (Ghodes 747). Larzer Ziff, in his *The American 1890s: Life and Times of a Lost Generation,* gracefully bows out of the dialectical skirmish by stating simply, "It defies criticism. Although it breathes frivolity on almost every page, the book is nevertheless a feat of elegance and precision . . ."(109). For the most part, critics seem to vacillate between a number of possible categories for the work.

Darrel Abel notes the two extreme authorial characters that previous critics have identified as the "real" Fuller: "—romantic and realistic—and whichever side a critic prefers is to him the essential Fuller" (246). Abel disagrees with these extreme labels:

> The either/or approach to Fuller is bound to yield only half-truths about him, no matter which authorial character the critic prefers. In the last analysis Fuller was neither a realist nor romanticist, but an ironist, who saw both good and bad in either extreme position, and who used contrasting attitudes to criticize each other. (247)

Jeffrey Swanson supports some elements of Abel's assessment, but he also notes that Fuller himself proved to be ambivalent in his affirmation of the tenets of either realism or romanticism. Swanson cites two essays written by Fuller previous to his novel, **"Howells or James?"** and **"The**

American School of Fiction," both edited by Abel, that apparently contradict the approach the author took to the novel. He points out that Fuller's endorsement of "a How-ellsian realism" does not seem congruent with the author's first novel, which the critic claims "clearly owes much to the genteel genre of European travel literature." However, Swanson also notes that the author's later critique of realism came about while Fuller was writing his more realistic works, such as *The Cliff-Dwellers* and *With the Procession.* With this note, the critic adds, "[I]t is not much of an exaggeration to say that Fuller seemed to put himself outside the literary mainstream regardless of which way it was running" (196). Nonetheless, Swanson fails to address Abel's main contention of Fuller as ironist. Swanson, like earlier readers, gets caught in the same rhetorical snare, or as Abel put it: Fuller's "irony was a trap for critics, who identified themselves with whatever suited their own pre-dilections and dismissed the rest as unessential" (247). Certainly, Fuller owed quite a bit to the genteel tradition, much in the same way that Jane Austen was indebted to the works of Gothic romance as the "inspiration" for *Northanger Abbey.* But his main technique was not merely irony, as Abel suggests, but satire, which Fuller uses in the guise of travel literature, to evaluate not only American society but European culture as well.

Some attention to the nature and function of satire and irony will clarify Fuller's treatment of narrative in *The Chevalier of Pensieri-Vani.* According to the *Harper Handbook to Literature,* the word "satire" stems from the Latin *satura,* itself derivative of *satyra,* and means "a mixed dish or, metaphorically, a medley" (413). Satire posits a tone of antagonism between a writer and the material he or she deals with and, in this, is aligned with irony. The definition distinguishes the range of extremes in literary satire into the purely fantastic and the purely ironic, but notes that it is usually a combination of the two (414). As a genre, satire stems from the anatomy, or Mennipean satire, which focuses on "intellectual limitations and mental attitudes" ("Mennipean Satire" 282) and essentially dissects these attitudes ("Anatomy" 32). The *Handbook* offers Swift's *Gulliver's Travels,* Voltaire's *Candide,* and Aldous Huxley's *Brave New World* as examples of anatomy.

To what end, though, does an anatomy dissect its subject? In *English Satire,* James Sutherland discusses the function of satire and its rhetorical role. Sutherland distinguishes the satiric writer from the comic in that the writer of satire "cannot accept or refuses to tolerate" imbecility on the part of fellow humankind. "Confronted with the same human shortcomings as the writer of comedy," the critic states, "[the satirist] is driven to protest" (4). He notes that satire is "an art of persuasion," and that "persuasion is the chief function of rhetoric" (5). In addition, the satirist intends to "expose, deride, or condemn" (7); this feature distinguishes the satiric from the merely comic. In the introduction to his work on satire, H. James Jensen notes that "satire [is] bounded by an essentially rhetorical nature, a nature generically defined by the author's vision of reality

and his art" (xiv). The art of the satirist is, then, the art of persuasion; its aim, to expose; and its primary technique, irony.

As Abel suggests, *The Chevalier* seethes with irony, and Fuller provides numerous cues to mark his satiric intent. One of the strongest hints Fuller gives to his reader about how the novel should be read is the essentially equivocal voice of the narrator. Throughout the work, the narrative persona undermines its own authority, hedging and qualifying the actions of the characters, withholding information or hinting at deviance in the attitudes of the aristocratic personalities that the reader encounters in the text. The opening passage in *The Chevalier* immediately sets the tone of the entire work and suggests that something is not altogether trustworthy about our guide through this series of episodes:

> It was the Chevalier of Pensieri-Vani who halted his traveling-carriage upon the brow of the Ciminian Forest to look down over the wide-spread Campagna di Roma. Or, to be more accurate, the carriage was not his, but was merely hired by him from a certain vetturino of Viterbo. Or, again, to be accurate beyond any possibility of cavil or question, it was not a carriage, but simply a sort of little gig or chaise, a due posti, and was neither new, nor neat, nor overcomfortable. (1)

The repeated qualification of the state of the carriage— pardon, *chaise*— seems odd enough to cause the reader to wonder just what the narrator is up to. In addition, the syntactic arrangement of the first sentence suggests that the main element of concern is *who* sat in the gig. Yet the narrator continues in the following sentences to discuss the quality of the alleged carriage rather than to illuminate the main character's identity for the reader.

Finally, though, the narrator brings the focus back to the protagonist and elaborates: "The Chevalier, I now scarce need confess, was a 'poor gentleman'—one with much, perhaps, behind him, but very little by him, and not much before him" (2). Clearly, the narrator suggests the operant values here: it is not who one is but what one possesses that is important. In addition to the oddities of the first paragraph, the narrative voice employs a manner of locution that would ring archaic even to the late nineteenth-century ear, using the forms "dost" and "hast" and anachronistic interrogative syntax. This element, though, could simply be the narrator's attempt to wax poetic. However, the reader's trust, given the narrator's later irregularities, begins to wane.

The narrative's treatment of the characters also suggests more than a passing tinge of irony. The narrator describes the cavaliere's personality, his likes and dislikes, and, in doing so, adds an air of *hauteur* to the protagonist:

> If you had asked the Cavaliere . . . why he cared so much for old Etruria, I am not sure that his answer would have been as clean-cut as your question. Indeed, he might not have tried to frame an answer at all: he might have given up at once any idea of making him-

self, his tastes, his preferences, his actions, perfectly intelligible before the prying criticism of the utilitarian Philistine. (2-3)

The reader cannot help but notice the air of open condescension in the narrative voice. In the next paragraph, the narrator again reveals the protagonist's supercilious attitude toward the audience and his air of disdain for the self-abasement involved in appealing to the *obviously* bourgeois reader:

> And why he was on his way to Rome, I can perhaps contrive partly to tell without any great violation of secrecy. But the Cavaliere would hardly care to accept the gift of fame at the hands of the vulgar, and if I do tell, I need not look to him for thanks. (3)

The protagonist, at least from the perspective of the narrative, looks at audience and narrator alike with contempt. The speaker includes himself when he speaks of "the vulgar," and, from this passage, the reader must derive that the narrator should be regarded with suspicion; he is quite clearly a gossip.

The self-debasing voice of the speaker should set the reader *en garde,* and any statements offered as justification for the character's actions, thus, necessitate close observation. The audience learns that the cavaliere's sojourn into Etruria holds more import than the simple pleasures of the tourist. He comes to find the tomb of Lars of Lucumo, an ancient Etruscan warrior-king. At this point, the narrative goes on the offensive, albeit in a very subtle manner. The speaker informs the audience that the cavaliere intends to bring back a trophy to his friends, something from the tomb to prove his discovery—the king's crown of burnished gold. Yet the narrator goes to some lengths to explain that the cavaliere's intentions should arouse no suspicions of thievery:

> I have told you of the token that he carried; but let none accuse him, laden with such a serious ponderosity of time and story, of a light-minded frivolity, or an impertinent curiosity, or, above all, of a vulgar penchant for pilfering. How little he took compared with what he might have taken! (5)

The suspicions of the audience again become aroused when the narrator justifies the cavaliere's acts a second time, stating, "I repeat that he was not actuated by mere motives of idle curiosity, nor prompted by a morbid desire to probe after the cloaked and the forbidden" (5). For the rest of the paragraph, the speaker continues to elaborate on the honesty and uprightness of the protagonist's character. Our friendly cavaliere is no grave-robber, but simply an archaeologist. The cavaliere does eventually return the circlet, so why does the narrator qualify the protagonist's actions? The reader must suspect that the speaker protests too much.

In the fifth chapter, "Orvieto: How the Cavaliere Won His Title," the narrative provides even more proof positive of the suspect cavaliere. The protagonist and his new com-

panion, the Seigneur des Hauts Rochers de Hors-Concours, explore the rocky terrain of the country around Orvieto and find a dilapidated old church on a ridge overlooking the town. Inside the chapel, the two find a few remaining shreds of ancient frescoes still clinging to the walls. After closer scrutiny, they discover that one of the patches is a "Madonna of the *tre-cento,* Tuscan utterly, and as Giottesque as the sweet asceticism of her thin and sharply drawn features could make her" (61). The chevalier, who does not hold his title at this point of the narrative, has desired a Madonna for quite a while, and the following passage describes the thoughts running through the protagonist's mind:

> It was merely a bit of plaster a few inches square, and already half loosened from its hold; the building was dark and deserted; the sacristan was old, and feeble, and half blind—perhaps even venal. A few cuts with a penknife would detach the picture altogether; a cunningly folded coat or mantle would serve to transfer it, undetected, from the edifice; the train to Florence would be passing in an hour—But all this has nothing to do with Pensieri-Vani's title. He waited for a Madonna until he could obtain one without ignoring the Decalogue. . . . (61-2)

The narrative suggests that the cavaliere at least entertains the thought of bribing the sacristan and stealing the fresco. The speaker reveals the protagonist to be a petty criminal, or at least to have urgings in that direction. So far, though, the chevalier has not actively committed any actual deviations from the moral code.

The object of the cavaliere's desire in the previously mentioned chapter is a Madonna, and he eventually locates and purchases one. The section in which this occurs, "Tuscan Towns," helps illuminate the protagonist's character even more and also gives the reader a sense of the chevalier's quality as a purveyor of the *beaux-arts.* Originally, the cavaliere merely acts as a companion to the Prorege of Arcopia, who traipses around Tuscany trying to track down and purchase what he believes to be a painting by Perugino, the *Madonna Incognita.* When the party finally locates the painting, the prorege finds, to his dismay, that the work is not even related to the school of Perugino. The vice regent is not the only person disappointed by this discovery. The Margravine of Schwahlbach-Schreckenstein also comes to view the painting, believing it to be a Del Sarto, and is equally disgusted. The cavaliere, who fancies himself a connoisseur, recognizes the work's true origin, and imagines himself pulling a quick deception on his friend, the prorege, and the margravine:

> If the Margravine had a present craze for Del Sarto . . . and could just now discern the merits of no other painter; and if the Prorege had an equal craze for Perugino to the exclusion of all other masters, why should not he himself, taking advantage—a justifiable advantage—of so much narrowness and bigotry, improve the opportunity to possess himself of a gem whose beauty neither of the others had been able to perceive? (38)

The chevalier keeps the antiquarian art dealer from revealing the name of the artist in order to secure the painting for himself. He has recognized the real creator—Sodoma, a student of Leonardo da Vinci, and, as the narrator informs us, "Sodoma was his delight" (39). Aside from the questionable ethics of the cavaliere, this passage reveals a number of other interesting ironies.

Sodoma was indeed a student of Da Vinci's and not some imaginary persona with a contrived, metaphorical name from Fuller's imagination. The students of Da Vinci have a rather dubious reputation in the art world. Bernard Berenson, in *Italian Painters of the Renaissance,* evaluates their contribution without sympathy: "[L]ike mnemonic jingles, they flatter the most commonplace minds" (181). Of Sodoma, whom Berenson considers Da Vinci's most gifted student, he is equally severe:

> The bulk of his work is lamentable. No form, no serious movement, and, finally, not even lovely faces or pleasant color; and of his connexion with Leonardo no sign, unless the slapdash, unfunctional light and shade be a distorted consequence of the great master's purposeful chiaroscuro. (186)

Clearly, the cavaliere has a questionable eye for art. The name of the artist and its literal interpretation suggest an additional irony. The word *Sodoma* translates to Sodom or sodomy in English. Given the topic of the painting, the Madonna, this reader begins to suspect that Fuller is playing a game here—Sodom's "Unknown Madonna," or a "sodomized" Madonna. Whether or not Fuller chose this name out of the annals of artistic failures with the intention of crafting this anomaly cannot be affirmed. One idea, though, seems relatively clear in light of the painter's reputation and the pains to which the chevalier goes to secure the work: the protagonist cannot distinguish between the work of a master and an "unnatural" act.

The cavaliere's real nobility becomes even more questionable when the reader discovers how the title "Chevalier of Pensieri-Vani" has been earned. The audience learns that the cavaliere is given his title, which he considers his most valuable possession (56), for officiating in a high mass as an organist. This action also requires a deception on his part, due to his lay status, but he preserves "the proper decorum" by assuming "the vestments befitting the office" (62). Posing as a member of the vocation, Pensieri-Vani performs a tumultuous fantasia which sweeps the occupants of the cathedral off their feet. Oddly, though, no one can identify the piece he plays. Many of the listeners venture comparisons—Angelo's "Last Judgement"; Dante's "Inferno"; Signorelli's "Resurrection"; Kaulbach's "Destruction of Jerusalem." The narrator notes that his own attempts to draw out the origin of the piece from the chevalier merely result in an evasive answer. As the narrator himself describes the experience, "I cannot phrase it; nor could he" (65). With an American reader, unfamiliar with the merits of the orders of aristocracy, this reward for such a dubious performance seems rather exorbitant, frivolous. The cavaliere's nobility stems from a single incident, one of questionable import. The reader understands the narrator's expressed shame at the end of the chapter for having dwelled so long on such an apparently insignificant affair.

Certainly one reprehensible character in a novel does not constitute the designation "satire." Yet, with closer examination, nearly all of the characters appear just as ridiculous. The character of second-most importance is the Prorege of Arcopia, "whose good nature was proverbial" (18). The reader learns of the prorege's love for the opera and of his (con)descent to attend the performance of a debutante *prima donna.* The narrator then adds that such compliance on his part is no small matter: "He suffered from inferiority immensely, and from mediocrity hardly less; but he would take the chance for friendship's sake, and come—if proper accommodation could be made for him." The sacrifice becomes all the more obvious when the speaker notes that the prorege "furthermore agreed to smile from such a post as benignly as a man of his age could be expected to" (18). This meeting gives the reader a glimpse of the prorege's vanity, but the details of his exile and his activities provide a clearer conception of the vice regent.

The prorege rules the small kingdom of Arcopia which is, according to his Excellency, "no Arcadia, no Utopia; it was only the two combined" (169). The Arcopian prince, though, has exiled himself from the kingdom over a dispute about some minor changes he wanted to make, a mere embellishment of "the long façade of the viceregal residence in the Piazza Grande with a magnificent portico of twenty neo-Ionic columns" (31). The self-indulgence of the prorege makes itself painfully noticeable throughout the novel. The vice regent preoccupies himself by designing architecture for the capital city and makes numerous excursions to the mainland to search out suitable designs on which to base his own.

> It were ungracious, perhaps, to comment pointedly here upon the Prorege's motives and preferences; but it is useless to deny that he was somewhat prone to self-indulgence, or to blink the fact that if he were going back to Italy on an architectural excursion he would be merely going just where he wanted to go in order to do what he wanted to do. (93)

Although the kingdom is a virtual combination of Arcadian and Utopian qualities, the prorege rarely spends any time there. The execution of his duties also causes him considerable grief, as the narrator explains, because of the constitutional restrictions and limitations that harassed and embarrassed him. "It seemed to him," the narrator notes, "that a mild despotism was the only rational and practicable form of government" (32).

In the matter of the Perugino, the prince of Arcopia reveals his true Machiavellian instinct. He seems perfectly willing to cast all ethics to the wind in order to attain the painting, "for in a case like this the end amply justified the means" (37). In a later chapter, the prorege reveals his willingness to follow this scheme when he comes upon the Duke of Avon and Severn in Siena. When the viceroy's plans work to detain the duke, the narrative notes that the prorege "could not restrain a smile as the consciousness of his own Mephistophelean attitude grew upon him" (48). Although the reader continually faces examples of the vice regent's indulgence, the narrator smilingly excuses the prorege's greed and selfishness. His final practical joke on Contessa Nullaniuna in the penultimate chapter must convince the reader that "his Excellency" can be considered no better than petty, conniving, and selfish.

The two principal characters in this work turn out to be rather ludicrous examples of nobility. Very few of the other characters show themselves to be much better. The names and titles of these characters often attest to the personalities which they reveal. The cavaliere, who "fully appreciated his own modest little title" (12), shows his reasoning and moral stature to be as empty as his claim to the title. Kenneth Scambray translates the protagonist's name and title as "the Chevalier of Vain Thoughts" (70), but perhaps a more accurate translation would be "empty thoughts" (*van-o*). The Contessa Nullaniuna is literally, and in her lack of tact and social grace, "nothing connected." Princess Altissimi, who seems like the only decent one of the bunch, has both social rank and ethical stature; her name means "the Almighty." The Margravine of Schwahlbach-Schreckenstein lives up to her name in her confrontation over the iron pot of San Sabio. Literally, she governs a "torrential word stream" and a "fearsome rock"-like exterior. Her opponent, the Baron Joch von Hoch, is the German consul to Florence, a "yoke from above" joining the two countries. Seigneur des Hauts Rochers de Hors-Concours, who reveals very few traits with which to object, and who appears to be the only landed noble, is of "lofty prominence," but essentially "out of the competition." The names alone suggest that Fuller has more than a romantic agenda here.

By this point the purpose of this essay seems almost belabored. A reader unfamiliar with Fuller's first novel may be tempted to ask, "How could anyone read this book as anything *but* satire?" Regardless, the critical appraisal of *The Chevalier* leaned heavily toward a romantic reading of the work. This perception of the novel, though, may be due to the parties responsible for its promotion in the high circles of Boston society and to the genteel sensibility of the novelist's audience. As John Pilkington describes in an anthologized biography of Fuller, "The book might have gone entirely unnoticed had not someone sent a copy to Charles Eliot Norton. Norton immediately acclaimed it as a work of genius and sent a copy to James Russell Lowell, who also found the work impressive" ("Fuller" 193). Fuller's popularity in Boston grew overnight, and after three J. G. Cupples editions, the Century Company brought out the fourth edition, which included a dedication to Norton.

Irrespective of the book's success and Norton's acclaim for the work, as Pilkington notes, "Uniformly the critics failed to grasp the essential meaning of the book" (193). In *A Varied Harvest,* Scambray discusses contemporary reviews of the work, including one in the *Boston Evening Transcript* which "revealed Norton's enthusiastic endorsement of the romance and the special delight he took in Fuller's protagonist, the Cavaliere" (66). The review also pointed out Fuller's New England roots and bore an un-

mistakably condescending tone when referring to Fuller's hometown, Chicago. Other newspapers in Boston, Louisville, and New York also proclaimed their faith in the romance and questioned "Chicago's ability to appreciate such a refined work." Scambray also notes the inability of the reviewers to pin down the novel in a conventional class or genre:

> While [Fuller's] critics found the work charming and delightful, they often admitted that it defied classification as a travel book, romance, or novel. One reviewer wrote, "it is certainly not a novel, and yet it has characters and incidents. It is not an essay on painting, music and bric-a-brac in Italy, and yet that is what its pages are full of." (67)

Like the reviewers of the nineties, later critics also failed to see the true nature of the work. Those critics who have recognized the satiric element in the work, such as Jeffrey Swanson and John Pilkington, have emphasized the novel's attack on modern industrialism at the expense of perhaps the most notable features of *The Chevalier*'s critique. That the satire in *The Chevalier* has been largely misunderstood by its contemporary audience and by twentieth-century critics simply cannot be denied.

As Pilkington and Scambray both note, the book's success was due in large part to Charles Eliot Norton's endorsement of it. Norton, a renowned Italianist and Harvard professor of art, praised the work highly and even wrote to the author to congratulate him, claiming, "Every lover of Italy should like your book, for you have won from her her charm for your pages." He also offered some suggestions for the second edition because he "felt that the romance was 'worth more trouble'" (65). Given the rather dubious nature of this compliment, a reader may not be surprised that Fuller misunderstood the comment. Something else, though, does not settle well with Norton's appraisal of the work.

The professor was well known for his lecture-hall criticisms of America's cultural barrenness, and he constantly compared modern societies with the Classical and Renaissance periods. He viewed industrialism as an evil and contended that art represented a higher level of civilization. In essence, Norton's attitudes toward urban industrial America were quite similar to those of Fuller's prorege, who was certain the "iron-shod hoof" of the "brutal Progresso" would rebarbarize Italy, "but Arcopia never" (163). In the final chapter, the narrator reveals the prorege's disdain for democracy and industrialism, stating, "Society had never courted failure or bid misery more ardently than when it had accepted an urban industrialism as its basis" (168). Such a sentiment could have come straight from the lips of Norton. The indictment of industrialism in the penultimate chapter, the only chapter that makes any overt criticisms of American industrialism, would be of primary interest to Norton and to the higher circles of Boston society that looked upon Chicago and its urban industry as the epitome of philistinism. Given Norton's reception of the work and the genteel nature of New England society, it is quite possible that the work's criticism of European culture went entirely missed by the contemporary readers of **The Chevalier.** As Pilkington notes, "If there lurked beneath the humor and gentle satire a serious message, the critics of Boston and Chicago failed to discover it" (*Fuller* 61). Yet even Pilkington's criticism, though it recognizes the satiric content, fails to note the full range of Fuller's critique. In this work, there is not "flesh, fish or fowl; but there seems a fair promise of a liberal supply of good red herring" (qtd. in Abel 254).

One must grant to the prorege in Fuller's novel that he can offer a moving justification for curbing the wanton spread of industrialism. Given this chapter alone, a reader may actually find something with which to sympathize in the vice regent other than his fine taste for art and music:

> Whose was the earth? our indignant prince would ask himself when considerations of this kind rose up to irritate him. Was it the exclusive possession of those merely who were now living out their brief day upon it, or was it something more—the foothold and heritage of generations yet to come? Who could make good to those of the coming century the felled trees, the gashed and leveled hills, the polluted ponds and choked-up streams that signalized our present dealings with outraged and suffering Mother Nature? (164)

Such sentiment for nature and heritage seem to fit with the romantic ideal of European nobility. Yet these words come from the mouth of the character who proves himself to be a devious, selfish, and arrogant hedonist. Ironically, the very chapter in which the prorege reveals his ugliest side, "Siena: A Vain Abasement," is the chapter that Fuller added to the fourth edition of **The Chevalier,** the edition dedicated to Charles Eliot Norton. Perhaps Fuller felt he had not made the character of the prorege clear enough.

The inconsistent character of nobility shows itself in other characters as well. Agnes Repplier states her confusion with the episode about the margravine and the iron pot and its apparent inconsistencies compared to the other episodes: "The story of the Iron Pot is too broadly farcical, too Pickwickian in its character to be in harmony with the rest of the narrative" (94). The story relates the Margravine of Schwahlbach-Schreckenstein's attempts to obtain an iron pot unearthed at an abbey near Rome. The pot has been alternately identified by Gregorianius, a German scholar, as an ancient Etruscan artifact; by the Archaeologist-in-chief as a Teutonic piece; and finally by the cavaliere who declares it "a relic of the Garibaldian Era" dating back possibly to the mid-nineteenth century (80). The margravine, convinced of the Germanic origins of the pot, attains control of the relic, and she promptly impoverishes herself in order to pay the duties for the importation of the item. Yet to read this episode as a fluke, as an irrelevant farcical warp in the text, one would have to ignore that each and every episode of this text reports a character's attempts at attaining some *objet d'art* or some object of artistic pretension. The characters of the narrative continually debase themselves to attain whatever they

desire. If anything, the story of "the Margravine and the Iron Pot" simply shows overtly what the entire work shows more covertly—the nobility in this book lack *noblesse oblige.*

What reviewers, readers, and critics have all, with the exception of Darrel Abel, somehow missed is the presentation of the European nobility in this work, an exposé of an ossified fossil that no longer lives up to noble ideals nor functions in the interest of society as a whole. In the first chapter of the work, Fuller provides a handy comparison of the modern European nobility and the ancient warrior kings of Etruria. When the cavaliere returns to the tomb of Lucumo with his friends to return the gold crown, he finds that the desiccated corpse of the old warrior has turned to dust, and he senses he has committed an act of desecration:

> The stern old warrior-priest, who might have been wakened to a Nero, a Hildebrand, a Torquemada, a Napolean, had been invited to rest his blinking and startling gaze upon a Garrison, a Nightingale, a Peabody. Slumbering through the long ages wherein might made right, he had been called back to light to participate in an epoch of invertebrate sentimentalism. Drunk on deep draughts of blood and iron, his reviver now sought to force him to munch the dipped toast of a flabby humanitarianism, and to sip the weak tea of brotherly love. This refreshment he had loftily declined. (10)

The age of the chevalier promises nothing but decay and decadence to the noble Lucumo. The depiction of aristocracy in this novel corresponds well with the "invertebrate sentimentalism" of the time. By the final chapter of the novel, the reader can hardly sympathize with the pathetic cavaliere who "writes *failure* against his whole life and career" (184). One might sympathize, though, with Occident, the American representative in the work and an expatriate who recognizes his position with distaste: "He was between two fires, both of which scorched him; between two stools, neither of which offered him a comfortable seat; between the two horns of a dilemma, each of which seemed more cruelly sharp than the other" (177). With these two "bookend" episodes, the "yankee smile" (267) which Carl Van Doren attributes to this narrative voice hides a tinge of bitterness and contempt.

Such a misreading on the part of reviewers and critics seems highly unlikely, yet the preponderance of the critical response, which is rather sparse to begin with, has neglected to recognize this satiric attack on both the urban industrialism of America and the decadence of European culture. However unlikely, misreadings such as this have occurred before. Wayne Booth notes the duplicitous nature of satire in *A Rhetoric of Irony* in which he notes that "irony always presupposes such victims." He also cites James T. Boulton's assessment that an author who employs irony writes for two audiences, "those who will recognize the ironic intention and enjoy the joke, and those who are the object of the satire and are deceived by it" (105). Fuller dissects both cultural extremes in this satire, the European noble and the American industrialist. Naturally, the forces which romanticize the aristocratic European values must fall prey to the critique as well. Norton and the genteel readers of **The Chevalier** simply failed to see the implications that the satire sets up. Perhaps the key difference between this satire and others is its genteel influence. The polished language, the picturesque descriptions, and the apparent refinement take in the naive reader, unlike the less covert satires of Swift. However, the unmistakable irony, the equivocal narrator, the devious caricatures of European nobility, and the relatively frivolous adventures that the characters undertake all support the reading of this work as an anatomy or a satire, and a none-too-elusive one at that. Early readers and later critics alike have peered into Fuller's glass and have failed to recognize their own countenance looking back.

Works Cited

Abel, Darrel. "Expatriation and Realism in American Fiction in the 1880's: Henry Blake Fuller." *American Literary Realism* 3 (1969): 245-57.

"Anatomy." *Harper Handbook to Literature*. Ed. Northrop Frye, Sheridan Baker, and George Perkins. New York: Harper & Row, 1985.

Booth, Wayne C. *A Rhetoric of Irony*. Chicago: University of Chicago Press, 1974.

Berenson, Bernard. *The Italian Painters of the Renaissance*. London: Phaidon, 1952.

Fuller, Henry B. *The Chevalier of Pensieri-Vani*. 4th ed. New York: Century, 1892.

Ghodes, Clarence. "The Later Nineteenth Century." *The Literature of the American People: an Historical and Critical Survey*. Ed. Arthur Hobson Quinn. New York: Appleton-Century-Crofts, 1951. 569-809.

Jensen, H. James. Introduction. *The Satirist's Art*. Eds. H. James Jensen and Malvin R. Zirker. Bloomington: Indiana University Press, 1972.

"Mennipean Satire." *Harper Handbook to Literature*. Ed. Northrop Frye, Sheridan Baker, and George Perkins. New York: Harper & Row, 1985.

Pilkington, John. "Henry Blake Fuller." *American Realists and Naturalists: Dictionary of Literary Biography*, Vol. 12. Ed. Donald Pizer and Earl N. Harbert. Detroit: Gale Research, 1982.

————. *Henry Blake Fuller*. New York: Twayne, 1970.

Repplier, Agnes. "A By-Way in Fiction." *Essays in Miniature*. 1892. New York: AMS, 1982.

"Satire." *Harper Handbook to Literature*. Ed. Northrop Frye, Sheridan Baker, and George Perkins. New York: Harper & Row, 1985.

Scambray, Kenneth. *A Varied Harvest: the Life and Works of Henry Blake Fuller*. Pittsburgh: University of Pittsburgh Press, 1987.

Sutherland, James. *English Satire*. Cambridge: Cambridge University Press, 1962.

Swanson, Jeffrey. "'Flesh, Fish or Fowl': Henry Blake Fuller's Attitudes Toward Realism and Romanticism." *American Literary Realism* 7 (1974): 195-210.

Van Doren, Carl. *The American Novel 1789-1939*. 2nd ed. New York: Macmillan, 1940.

Wilson, Edmund. *The Devils and Canon Barham*. New York: Farrar, Straus and Giroux, 1973.

Ziff, Larzer. *The American 1890s: Life and Times of a Lost Generation*. New York: Viking, 1966.

Joel Conarroe (essay date 1998)

SOURCE: "Seven Types of Ambiguity," in *The New York Times Book Review,* August 9, 1998, p. 13.

[*In the following review of a new edition of* Bertram Cope's Year, *Conarroe deems Fuller's novel an entertaining and worthwhile read.*]

Nobody asks, and Bertram Cope certainly doesn't tell. The result? No fewer than six people, representing both sexes and various ages and backgrounds, make a Midwestern university's newly arrived instructor the object of their affection—or, more accurately, of their "longing admiration." This unwitting heartbreaker even manages an accidental engagement to one especially ardent member of the infatuated sextet, and nearly commits himself to a couple of others. Fortunately for all parties, no wedding bells ring.

Bertram Cope's Year is an entertaining satirical novel (set in a thinly camouflaged Evanston, Ill.) that was written and self-published nearly 80 years ago by a once well-regarded but now nearly forgotten Chicago novelist and poet, Henry Blake Fuller. Modern readers may be reminded of several novels and films its main themes foreshadow. *The Object of My Affection,* Stephen McCauley's account of a young woman who falls in love with a gay teacher; *Something for Everyone,* in which Michael York plays an amoral hustler who erotically manipulates an entire household; Pasolini's brilliant *Teorema,* featuring Terence Stamp as a seductive stranger who beds every member of a bourgeois household.

Despite being blessed with blond, blue-eyed good looks and a "glacial geniality," Bertram Cope is a young man who is extraordinary largely by virtue of being so very ordinary Aside from his leading-man appearance (he resembles in almost eerie detail that current favorite of star-struck adolescents, Leonardo DiCaprio), there is nothing at all remarkable about him. In fact, it is the very absence of a forthright, uncloseted identity that causes otherwise sensible people to project onto his essential blankness their own unsatisfied desires.

Thus it is that several lonely individuals manage, in a number of awkward ways, to behave foolishly over Bertram. This uncharmed circle includes three artistically minded women in their early 20's, a robust widow in her 40's and a confirmed bachelor who is 50-something. The young women, who remain clueless about their hero's lack of serious interest in them, don't quite come to life on the page. The widow, on the other hand, is an inspired comic creation. Mrs. Medora T. Phillips is a pretentious powerhouse whose approach to flirtation consists largely of bossy scolding. She would be right at home in a play by Congreve or Wilde.

In contrast, the story's urbane older bachelor, Basil Randolph, seems to have strolled in from a novel by Henry James. Carefully groomed and ambiguously wealthy, this scholar manqué is a collector of amusing objects who would gladly add Bertram to his collection; he even moves to larger quarters in hopes of attracting overnight visits. But his callous young acquaintance resists these subtle overtures.

Given his unsuccessful quests for intimate companionship (Cope is simply this season's sublimated affection), Randolph personifies to the letter James's idea of the unlived life. His only close friend, Joe Foster, a wheelchair-bound bachelor resigned to a passionless existence, speaks with controlled fury about the ingratitude of the young. As Andrew Solomon suggests in a perceptive afterword to the novel, Foster is the only character who recognizes the folly of pursuing young Mr. Cope, and his bitterness may afford us the clearest view of the author's own disillusionment.

For readers responsive to the uninhibited fiction of Edmund White Dale Peck, David Leavitt and others, Fuller's approach to sensuality will seem almost comically prim. Although at least four of the novel's characters are homosexual, the word does not appear anywhere in the narrative—and "gay," of course, is used only in its traditional sense. The closest Fuller comes to delineating intimacy is in describing a handshake that is held just a beat too long or, more explicitly, a hand placed lightly on another's shoulder. An unexpected scene in which Cope and Randolph take a nude swim in Lake Michigan includes no hint of surreptitious voyeurism.

Arthur Lemoyne, the "chum" with whom Cope cohabits, is the one character who is both relatively unconflicted about his orientation and somewhat flamboyant; he is described as having an "artistic temperament" and "light tenor tones." He is also the one character who comes to grief. His fate may well offer a clue to the author's restrained, indirect approach to erotic feelings and actions. Fuller was clearly not oblivious of the era's assumption (this was, after all, the Age of Howells) that any sort of "perversion" must necessarily be associated with guilt, disgrace and even punishment.

Performing with "mincing ways" a drag role in the university's all-male revue, Lemoyne, unable to "leave his part" after the curtain goes down, remains altogether too effectively in character. Endeavoring to "bestow a measure of upwelling femininity upon another performer . . . in the dress of his own sex," he receives, in response, a bashed forehead. "Such," Fuller observes, "are the risks run by the sincere, self-revealing artist."

However quaint his own risks now seem, Fuller did indeed court disapproval—and a symbolically bruised forehead—in this eminently readable work that is finally distinguished not so much by any prescient psychological probings as by its beautifully evoked period atmosphere, its sly humor and its picturesque diction. If his approach to eros seems excessively decorous by today's more tolerant standards, we should resist basking too smugly in the glow of our enlightenment. It is probable, after all, that 80 years in the future some of our own attitudes will strike our successors as no less benighted than Fuller's blinkered "self-revealing" prose does today.

Audacious for its time, ***Bertram Cope's Year*** was either ignored or misunderstood when it was first published, with few copies sold. Discouraged, Fuller burned both the original manuscript and the remaining unbound proofs. "There seems to be no way," he wrote his friend Hamlin Garland, "for one to get read or paid, so—Shutters up." It is a pleasure to have those shutters taken back down to reveal an engaging and quite undeservedly neglected comedy of bad manners.

FURTHER READING

Bibliographies

Silet, Charles L. P. *Henry B. Fuller and Hamlin Garland: A Reference Guide*. Boston: G. K. Hall & Co., 1976, pp. 1-53.
> Chronological listing of secondary writings about Fuller and his work.

Swanson, Jeffrey. "A Checklist of the Writings of Henry Blake Fuller (1857-1929)." *American Literary Realism* 7, No. 3 (Summer 1974): 211-43.
> Categorizes Fuller's writings by genre.

Criticism

Bowron, Bernard R., Jr. *Henry B. Fuller of Chicago: The Ordeal of a Genteel Realist in Ungenteel America*. Westport, Conn.: Greenwood Press, 1974, 278 p.
> Biographical and critical study of Fuller.

Duffey, Bernard. "Henry Fuller." In *The Chicago Renaissance in American Letters: A Critical History*. Wesport, Conn.: Greenwood Press, 1954, pp. 27-50.
> Defines Fuller's role in the "upward movement" in Chicago.

Garland, Hamlin. "Henry B. Fuller." In *Roadside Meetings*. New York: The Macmillan Co., 1930, pp. 262-75.
    Offers personal reminiscences of Fuller.

Quinn, Arthur Hobson. "The Urbane Note in American Fiction." In *American Fiction: An Historical and Critical Survey*. New York: D. Appleton-Century Co., 1936, pp. 408-32.
    Brief overview of Fuller's career.

Vechten, Carl van. "Henry Blake Fuller." In *Excavations: A Book of Advocacies*. New York: Alfred A. Knopf, 1926, pp. 129-47.

Notes the critical and commercial obscurity of Fuller and predicts "that this general neglect of Fuller is both temporary and artificial."

Ziff, Larzer. "Crushed Yet Complacent: Hamlin Garland and Henry Blake Fuller." In *American 1890s: Life and Times of a Lost Generation*. New York: The Viking Press, 1966, pp. 93-119.
    Compares the literary careers of Fuller and Hamlin Garland.

Additional coverage of Fuller's life and career is contained in the following sources published by the Gale Group: *Contemporary Authors,* **Vol. 108;** *Dictionary of Literary Biography,* **Vol. 12.**

Jean-François Lyotard
1924-1998

French philosopher.

INTRODUCTION

Lyotard was one of the seminal theoreticians of Postmodernism, a subversive and complex anti-systematic philosophy that challenges the belief that there can be an all- encompassing truth, categorical Idea, or defining "master narrative" as, historically, the dominant religious, political, economic, and philosophical systems have asserted there must be. Instead, Lyotard championed an open-ended philosophy of disagreement based on the existence of a multitude of small, sometimes irreconcilable "narratives." Furthermore, he stipulated that not everything that exists can be represented, but that the unrepresentable can be approached through the sublime, which he defined as an intense experience of the discrepancy between what we can apprehend and what we sense we cannot.

BIOGRAPHICAL INFORMATION

Born in Versailles, Lyotard attended the Sorbonne after twice failing the entrance exam for the prestigious École Normale Supérieure. In 1948, his essay "Nés en 1925" ("Born in 1925") was published in Jean Paul Sartre's journal, *Les Temps Modernes*. In 1950, he moved to Algeria, then a French colony on the verge of a struggle for independence, to teach high school philosophy. In 1954, he published his first major work, *La Phénomènologie* (*Phenomenology*.) Siding with the Algerian independence movement but wary of the value of a class analysis for the situation in Algeria and repelled by the Stalinism which had pemeated Marxism, he joined *Socialisme ou Barbarie* ("socialism or barbarism"), a group of radical, intellectual Marxists critical of the Soviet Union, and wrote analyses of the political situation for its journal. These were collected and published in 1989 in a volume called *La Guerre des Algériens* (*The Algerian War*). He returned to France in 1959 to teach philosophy at the University of Paris. In 1964 he was among a group who split off from *Socialisme ou Barbarie* to form *Pouvoir Ouvrier* ("worker power"). He left the movement entirely in 1966, and in that year began teaching at Nanterre in Paris where he was an active participant in the revolutionary uprising which spread throughout France in May 1968. The failure of the official communist party to support and understand the uprising, which was about liberation from the spirit of alienation rather than simply controlling a reorganized means of production, or obtaining higher wages inside an unchanged

society, drove him, as it did many others, away from Marxism. In 1973, his book *Dérive à partir de Marx et Freud* (*Adrift from Marx and Freud*) appeared, and in 1974, he published *Économie libidinale* (*Libidinal Economy*). These books signaled not only his break with Marxism, but his distrust of any unifying system of truth or analysis, which he defined as totalitarian because in its exclusionary practice it obliterates any other perspective. Lyotard continued to pursue this deconstruction of what he termed "master narratives" in his writing and teaching and, along with a number of rebel French academic intellectuals like Gilles Deleuze, Michel Foucault, and Jacques Derrida, promoted a philosophy called Postmodernism, a term for which Lyotard gained international recognition with his book *La condition postmoderne* (*The Postmodern Condition*) in 1979. Until his death in 1998, Lyotard continued his academic career, often as a visiting professor at universities throughout Europe and the Americas. He published more than forty books, numerous articles and was curator of an exhibition, *Les Immatériaux* (*Immaterials*), devoted to postmodernism, at the Pompidou Center in Paris in 1985.

MAJOR WORKS

Devoted as he was to subverting master narratives and committed to the idea that there are incommensurable language games between which meaning cannot be negotiated, Lyotard sought non-authoritarian ways of establishing the grounds for authenticity, legitimation, and justice. He was also concerned with analyzing the rhetorical strategies of Holocaust deniers, and in *Heidegger et "les juifs"* (*Heidegger and "the jews"*) (1988), with understanding the German philosopher's active support of Nazism. Building on the work of Kant, Nietzsche, Wittgenstein, and Freud, Lyotard constructed a philosophy which set language against figure, and both against a fundamental, prelinguistic human energy he called "intensity." In *Libidinal Economy, Discours/figure* (*Discourse/Figure*) (1971), *Au Juste* (*Just Gaming*) (1979), and *Le Différend* (*The Differend,*) (1983) Lyotard set forth a critique of language, philosophy, art, technology, and social institutions as vehicles for conveying the "master narratives" which have mobilized masses of people in catastrophic, single-minded enterprises. In *Instructions païennes* (*Pagan Instructions*) (1977) and *Peregrinations* (1988) he established an anarchic philosophy that privileged "drifting" over ideology, community stories over universal doctrines, and an appreciation of "incommensurables" as the democratic mechanism enabling peaceful and fertile human coexistence.

CRITICAL RECEPTION

Lyotard has been both esteemed and reviled, depending on his critics' regard or distaste for postmodernism. During the last quarter of the twentieth century, his work had a major influence on thinking about philosophy, literature, politics, technology, art, and science. Opposition to Lyotard's work from the Left has usually concerned what critics perceived as relativism in his philosophy and abandonment of the struggle for social change and economic justice. Opponents from the Right have cited him for undermining traditional values and distorting history. Critics have found his prose difficult and full of jargon and the expression of his ideas incoherent. Other readers, however, argued that this apparent incoherence reflects Lyotard's use of text to present thought figurally, rather than to represent it discursively. Moreover, his way of writing, they asserted, may be seen as reflecting Lyotard's commitment to undermining textual authority and the sovereignty of all-encompassing narratives.

PRINCIPAL WORKS

La Phénomènologie [*Phenomenology*] (philosophy) 1954
Discours/figure [*Discourse/Figure*] (philosophy) 1971
Dérive à partir de Marx et Freud [*Adrift from Marx and Freud*] (philosophy) 1973

Des dispositifs pulsionels [*Pulsating Processes*] (philosophy) 1973
Économie libidinale [*Libidinal Economy*] (philosophy) 1974
Instructions païennes [*Pagan Instructions*] (philosophy) 1977
Récits tremblants [*Unsteady Narratives*] (philosophy) 1977
Les Transformateurs Duchamp [*Duchamp's Trans/Formers*] (philosophy) 1977
La condition postmoderne [*The Postmodern Condition*] (philosophy) 1979
Au Juste [*Just Gaming*] (philosophy) 1979
Le Mur du pacifique [*Pacific Wall*] (philosophy) 1979
Le Différend [*The Differend*] (philosophy) 1983
Tombeau de l'intellectuel et autre papiers [*The Tomb of the Intellectual and Other Writings*] (philosophy) 1984
Driftworks (philosophy) 1984
Les Immatériaux [*Immaterials*] (exhibition) 1985
L'Enthousiasme: la critique kantienne de l'histoire [*Enthusiasm: the Kantian Critique of History*] (philosophy) 1986
Le postmoderne éxplique aux enfants [*The Postmodern Explained to Children*] (philosophy) 1986
Heidegger et "les juifs" [*Heidegger and "the Jews"*] (philosophy) 1988
L'Inhumain: causeries sur le temps [*The Inhuman: Reflections on Time*] (philosophy) 1988
Peregrinations: Law, Event, Form (philosophy) 1988
La Guerre des Algériens [*The Algerian War*] (philosophy) 1989
The Lyotard Reader (philosophy) 1989
Leçons sur l'analytique du sublime [*Lessons on the Analytic of Sublime*] 1991
Lectures d'enfance [*Lectures from Childhood*] (philosophy) 1991
Moralités postmodernes [*Postmodern Moralities*] (philosophy) 1993
Signé Malraux [*Signed Malraux*] (philosophy) 1996
La Chambre sourde [*The Deaf Chamber*] (philosophy) 1998
La Confession d'Augustin (philosophy) 1999

CRITICISM

Marc Blanchard (essay date 1979)

SOURCE: "Never Say Why?" in *Diacritics,* Vol. 9, No. 2, Summer, 1979, pp. 17-29.

[*In the following excerpt, Blanchard offers an exegesis critical of Lyotard's* Économie libidinale.]

If one were to go, one by one, over all the articles in *Diacritics* that deal with this or that manifestation of Continental philosophical and literary criticism, one would probably put the pile of issues back on the stack and sigh: what next? For it seems that, for the last ten years or so, much of structuralist criticism has been engaged in a constant game of brinkmanship and one-up-manship. Most of the linguistically oriented criticism, based on the work of Jakobson and Levi-Strauss, developed as a reaction against the school of psychological and historical criticism which had established itself in splendid isolation from all related disciplines, including a more recent existential psychology. This stage of structural criticism, which prevailed in France during the sixties and which, because of translation and communication problems, is only now and only partially available here, was soon to be left behind owing to the advent of Derrida and the Post-Structuralists. In America today, it seems that the last word on these and most any other critical revolutions can be found in *De la Grammatologie,* now translated after its original publication in French some twelve years ago. That Derrida has moved from a strict deconstruction of Saussurean linguistics to a more flexible enterprise of weaving that deconstruction into the flow of his own first person writing is apparently of little importance. Of equally little importance seems the fact that this Gargantuan enterprise of deconstruction, which has been received here with so much fanfare, is itself all but disseminated, floated, as it were, into the overall philosophical escapism now gripping Paris. It is as if, once the great metacritical enthusiasm had begun to be experienced as yet another in a long series of dogmatic thrusts, the Derridean enterprise itself, in spite of its cautionary demonstrations, its admonitions, could only be felt as the last struggle for conceptual power: how to transcend, or rather, to *supplement,* the closure imposed by a Saussurean/Jakobsonian philosophy of linguistic universals.

But the argument could be taken one step further. If, as more recent Derridean publications like *Glas* and *Eperons* have shown, there is now in Derrida and in many others an attempt to work an empirical praxis from the theoretical considerations presented as a reflection on the history of Western philosophy, then any escape out of this closure should not lead us into another closure, where we would only justify our logocentricity, by simply taking down each and every piece of model-simulacrum erected in its name. Escaping closure can only come with a radical transformation of the idea of escape itself. The escape should be a real one, not a reworking of historical parts of knowledge, but also and first of all, an escape. That is to say, it should include a rejection of theory as the process which keeps us imprisoned in our modes of linguistic modelization. Baudrillard, whom Lyotard criticizes for holding on to an ideology of closure in his obsessive search for new theories, thus represents rather well the last cliff-hanger trick in an ideology which must now be left behind: "the only thing left to us is theoretical violence. Speculating to death with only one strategy: to radicalize all hypotheses. Even *code, symbolic* are still coverup terms—if only they could be withdrawn from our discourse one by one" [*L'Echange symbolique et la mort* (Paris: Gallimard, 1976), p. 13].

Lyotard then already. It is only appropriate that his name should have been introduced here, even before a discus-

sion of his work had begun, since in his work he not only seeks to deny himself the privilege of a new theoretical posture, but he also fully rejects the mere possibility of any theory in general as well as the Cartesian-Saussurean trap of seeing only *des choses claires et distinctes* according to the dichotomy of a binary principle (black/white, I/you, here/there). In this sense also, any formal introduction to Lyotard's work where one attempts to deal, first, with the context of Post-Structuralism, only to restore later to the more frantic parts of Lyotard's discourse their logical and historical coherence, would appear to constitute just as much of a trap, because it requires that one elaborate a metatheoretical position from which to examine each and every move made by Lyotard to expose the prison-house of his language. To do justice then to the *Economie libidinale* would be to insist that it is a theoretical piece only *malgré soi,* in spite of itself: that is, if we insist that it be a testimony to the current Parisian impatience with dogmatic theory and the overreliance on the powers of conceptual language, it is, as such, representative of the general Post-Structuralist climate. But the *appearance* (not the Truth) is that Lyotard's piece advertizes itself as some sort of impossibility. It simply *rejects,* not only the possibility of any metacritical position, but also *possibility itself* as an expression of the will to structure with which we limit and shortchange our desire. To the objection that we do need signs to communicate and that our use of signs always standing in lieu of things makes the actualization of the libido contingent upon a conceptual game of possibilities, an alternation of presence and absence, the *Economie libidinale* responds in several oblique ways.

First, the book seeks to deny itself the privilege of serious philosophical knowledge. Attacking everyone by rejecting no specific position, it chooses the untenable posture of *drift* [*dérive*]. This drift is not in the form of a calculated distance from *words,* from *signs,* from appearances. It *happens* between levels of appearance: what Lyotard calls *theatricalization.* However, because he is fully aware that the posture of *drift* implies an origin, and even more certainly an end, and because the search for this origin and this end, inherent in the notion of any narrative, of any drifting, would eventually make it impossible for our desire simply to be there (that is, to continue being itself: unrestricted, unfinished and full of contradictions), Lyotard will not reject this theatricality. On the contrary, he will seek to bring it out for what it is: pure effect and fantasy. Better still, he will praise it and rejecting instead those who reject it, he will embark on his own narrative, treating History, and specifically the history of philosophy, as though they were the story of his own book.

The *Economie libidinale* thus presents itself as an act. It invites us to experience the pleasure that can be derived (*drifted*) from the creative practice of theatrics. The use of critical models is not absolutely banned and Lyotard insists that he too can use models, as he powerfully demonstrated earlier in *Discours/Figures,* when he used the Jakobsonian grille to show libidinal affects in the space opened by structural relations between linguistic functions: for example, the addresser/addressee relation; the code-message relation, where objects designated by our discourse are no longer linguistic objects, arbitrary, anonymous, but allow us the experience of meaning in a very specific, very personal mimesis. However, because using models implies using stable references (to a context, to a modelizing subject), the **Economie** seeks to appear as an invitation, if not a temptation, to fantasize the end of all overt or covert referencing practices. Indeed, if the need to use models and to structure is representative of our Western logocentricity, from Aristotle to Saussure to Derrida, this logocentricity cannot be broken so long as our desire to construct a critique of this representation is referred to, and signified by, a presence/absence of the subject responsible for this logocentricity. Lyotard's temptation then is to lure us into a fictional/critical narrative which, instead of rejecting structure and theory of structure as futile, uses structure to set the stage for the *sweeping operation* [*balayage*] of an anarchic, anonymous libido. That is to say, there must be no difference between critical and non-critical activity, between *showing* and *telling;* criticism is in itself an intensely libidinal activity in that it allows the subject to fantasize himself as both patient and agent of a text, while his discourse continues to maintain a barrier between the two:

> confusion is inevitable because language is not an isolated sphere; because it belongs, in patches, to the same surface as these loins of golden gray moving under your palms and these cheeks cuddling the cluster of your balls. Scream communication, that is the assertion it seeks, language as an extension of the libido, revolving upon itself, into the area of meaning and order, to the Logos, which the Western world and above all the philosopher have always wanted to protect from the monstrousness of impious lovers and politicians. [p. 102]

Only if one stops referring *mimesis* to a theory underpinning *mimesis* can reference-interpretation cease (be it a reference to the Other or to the image of one's own vacuous Self), and with reference-interpretation, the illusion that one must or can always criticize, explain. Moreover, to *show something* means to subvert the mechanisms of semiotic communication in the sense that, if something happens in the moment of that showing, to us, to our body, to our mind, this *something* cannot be explained, separated from the mimetic process activating it by a critical (Hegel/Derrida) or even creative (Proust/Joyce) investigation of those mechanisms. *It* must be left alone; and if anything, *it* must be protected from our critical consciousness: *dis-inserted, dis-inscribed* from rational discourse in the hope that *it* can be experienced without mediation, as appearance or phenomenon.

However, it would be wrong to infer from this that the Lyotardian approach is a phenomenological one, since for Lyotard, as for Derrida, albeit not for the same reasons, phenomenology is basically a hoax in its attempt to give substance to the theatricality involved in the semiotic game. Thus, to the phenomenologist, the sign stands for something else, which I as a subject immediately recognize and make mine by *temporalizing* (Heidegger) the absence of the thing implied by the sign and thus bringing myself in thought or in fantasy to that point (the locus of the object, of the Other) which I do not occupy. The appearance of which Lyotard speaks and which he calls *dissimulation* is not a negative of Truth, in the Hegelian sense that to dispel all obscurities one needs only the clarifying power of sign-consciousness; it is produced by the fact that the object of desire, and with it and through it, the *positive* reality of drives [*Triebe*], is negated in the very moment the subject actualizes them through his sign-system. Why?—That is the question never to ask. Because to say *why?* is to replace ourselves within a framework of semiotic construction and deconstruction which can only ascribe to a representation standing for the Truth (God/the Spirit), that is to say properly standing *for nothing,* the work of an irreducible libido. Instead, Lyotard sees this work carried out in terms of the unlikely, almost absurd conjunction of two systems or two kinds of *signs* (for lack of better words): one which manifests libido by being a part of it and intensifying it and the other which works it over into interpretive sets, thus reducing it to a mere fragment, a possibility. For every part of our bodies, of our minds, of the world, that would enjoy the thrusts of a sign-free libido—one beyond the fragmentation of our linguistic universe—there would be a thousand others equally anxious to enjoy themselves. Not only do we seek to possess the body, the mind of others, but in our own body, we also experience the impossibility of total and absolute gratification: it is as if the mouth were jealous of the ear; the ear, of the eye, *ad infinitum.* The fear of such libidinal turmoil quite naturally induces the ordering compulsion we have and which Freud ascribed to Eros: the force that keeps us alive, out of the chaos and death of impossible revolutions, by always leading us into more love dances, by always effecting more maneuvers to mask all too powerful libidinal thrusts with the rhetoric of a strict rational order.

The fact is, Lyotard's dissimulation is not new. In another, more symbolic context, I would like to suggest that the same problematics is already present in literary texts working through a representation and an emblematics of Eros in classical and medieval literature. In the Hellenistic romance of *Daphnis and Chloe,* for instance, the lead story, explaining and covering all the others, that of Eros pursuing (shooting his darts) and being pursued (by all humans), remains the generator of an overall narrative constantly disconnecting and reconnecting what remains till the end of the romance but the mere possibility of a shared enjoyment between two theoretical outsiders: the shepherds Daphnis and Chloe longing for total pastoraldom in the midst of a world full of interdicts. There, the pastoral quest for a safe (external/theoretical) position is carried out by means of the juxtaposition of unrelated tales of masking and substitution, themselves reflected into other, older tales from mythology, and the success of the romance is predicated on the possibility for the two heroes to adopt and to retain their status as outsiders. In the context of the ***Economie libidinale,*** Eros' never-ending pursuit would symbolize the force of a complex of pain and pleasure which cannot be withstood on either side (the pursuer/the pursued) precisely because the gratification expected is so overwhelming that it can only come with Death itself. This complex is exactly what Lyotard wants us to approach: not in the Freudian context of a dichotomy between Love and Death, but in the context of what he terms the *uncoiling of a section of the libidinal surface around us* [*un désenroulement de la bande libidinale*] and which represents the locus of all pleasure and pain conjoined. An unbearable locus, since, owing to our incapacity to fulfill all our desires at once (say, for instance, love and hate, fully and entirely without compromise), we have no choice but to live under the law of repression. In a veritably seminal analysis of *Beyond the Pleasure Principle,* Lyotard shows how Freud himself may have gone beyond what was later to be reduced to a simple opposition between two drives. The Freudian insight may have been that the metatheoretical division into two drives was necessary if we wanted to understand the pragmatic devices through which a person's psyche could eventually be returned to normalcy in the process of the cure. However, normalcy is but an expression of the fact that we must localize the world through semiotic forms which function metaphorically—in the very fact of their assignation: thus Freud assigns a positive (Eros) or negative sign to the libido—and metonymically—in the reference to an unconscious, albeit universal language in whose displacements the subject seeks refuge. Lyotard, for his part, suggests that this semiotization can be used to retrieve portions of desire obliterated in the coiling experience to avoid the potentially disastrous sweep of an unrestrained libido. And one of the ways to achieve this is to tap sign-systems *for the intensity,* not the structure, of their communication.

This is where the title ***Economie libidinale*** takes on its fullest meaning. That the human psyche attempts to regulate impulses it fears may take it over: nothing new in that. That this regulation allows only for a minimal part of the whole psychic process to reach our consciousness: nothing new in that either, as the Freudian delineation of regions and hierarchization of processes will show (the Unconscious appears as a vast *terra incognita* which the conscious mind penetrates only unwittingly and through the form of a dialogue with the Other). What is new, however, is the possibility that this regulation could now, through its own excesses, involve the whole energetic substratum (the libidinal surface) available through the individual; moreover, that it could be used to cause the deregulation of the regulating subject himself as an instance of power and launch an attack against all types of regulation, of interpretation: economic, religious, philosophical. Here, Lyotard uses Freud's analysis of Schreber's paranoia to show how the regulating system reconstructed by Freud on a principle already equivalent to that of Eros-containing-Death (a paranoiac reconstructs a world he must save, lest he die himself) is actually worked over by an overwhelming intensity (*incandescence*), as the body of the President

is involved in blocking all impulses which it fears may take it over. In Schreber's case, almost unbeknownst to the subject, to the patient, the various bodily functions are enlisted to serve various, not to say, opposite libidinal purposes. The effect is sheer pain and terror. Thus, since the President fears both defecation (because his defecation might please Dr. Flechsig, for whom Schreber feels homosexual love) and penetration by the organ of God (because this penetration would be an admission that he, Schreber, cannot be like anybody else and that Flechsig is right in treating him like a patient), the name of Dr. Flechsig works as a perfect primer to detonate an enormous quantity of libido in all directions. Schreber is not himself either to others or to himself. He has become the occasion, the locus and perhaps, the sign, of an incredible coiling of the libidinal surface. The libido is manifested in so many ways that he feels crucified: his mouth, his mind and his hands are used to perform a rhetorical function by investing parts of his libido into the writing of the *Denkwürdigkeiten;* his penis is used in an unconscious manner with Flechsig; his anus, to the same purpose, only the reverse; his supposedly castrated penis-vagina is ready to receive God's penis; to which must be added the innumerable references to other parts of his *feminine* body, helping him ensure the sweep of as many sections of the libidinal surface as possible. On the one hand, he is the occasion of an unbelievable repression designed to obviate an all-out libidinal satisfaction, and on the other hand, he is fully enjoying the chaos of this neurotic orgy: "and thus it is the supposed boundary of Schreber's body which finds itself violated by the name of Flechsig [. . .] this boundary is itself pulverized by a dizzying vertigo; the President's body is being undone and parts of it are being projected through libidinal space by getting mixed with other parts into an inextricable patchwork" [pp. 74-76]. Now one could give a simple, semiotic account of this passage by saying that the sign (here, the name of *Flechsig*) has not only been referring to something or someone else real (the Doctor), but that it has also been connoting its reference in a symbolic way (the Doctor is now Schreber's Tormentor). But this would be to forget that denotation and connotation are one and the same thing, that it is not possible to distinguish between them. They are hopelessly intricated: the sign regulating the symbol, and the symbol deregulating the sign, just as the Tormentor lurks beneath the Doctor. Taking a cue from the President, Lyotard suggests to us that now is the time to avail ourselves of this confusion—this dissimulation—to revel in it, to help spread it, so that we may with it experience more libido, more passion.

Here, Lyotard's philosophy of confusion and weakness of the sign must be understood in both a philosophical and a historical context. Philosophically speaking, that part of the dialectic process produced by the *Verneinung,* the negation, must be privileged, because it offers the opportunity to negate or rectify past assertions concerning the Truth. However, cautious not to place himself in a theoretical position again, Lyotard would argue that he does not wish to negate anything, but on the contrary, that he desires to extend assertion to everything. As he says: "the libido does not invest conditionally; it invests unconditionally" [p. 13]. In any case, and as was already clear from Hegel, the position of the negation of self-identity which is arrived at only in the second stage of the dialectic process [*The Phenomenology of Mind*, A,I], where in order for the Other to be fully constituted as Other, the specificity of my own consciousness must be negated, *this position, which is one of negation (anonymity) of the subject, is the most convenient locus for getting in touch with libidinal activity.* Not only is it *below,* in terms of a dialectic of power, and destined, therefore, to help the subject subvert the position of prominence now occupied by the object, the Other, but it is, in libidinal terms, the most enviable position. First, it does not require the creation and maintenance of the apparatus regulating the position *ober.* Second, because it happens to be the position where the struggle with regulation offers not only the possibility of asserting new rules to supplant those one seeks to abolish, but also the prospect of total freedom (for instance, the workers of the world have nothing to lose but their chains by uniting against their industrial masters), the subject *neben* can fully embrace the duplicity, the full dissimulation of what is the thrust of both Eros and Death, without ultimately fearing (i) a take-over of the regulating Eros function, (ii) a take-over of the deregulating Death function. Both can how be experienced without a (rational/guilty) sense that they are different from each other or that one is in any way restricting the other.

Some of these suggestions obviously take on a political connotation. Clearly the most obvious implication of the position *neben* is that it excludes all considerations of structural order and that it does not demand to be transformed into a position *ober* by forcing the subject to invent a structure, a rule which would justify this transformation and give it meaning: say, by calling a strike to push demands for higher wages and the restoration of a human dimension scrapped by automation. Thus, historically, a riot where workers break machines (the revolt of French weavers against Jaccard machines) and the subsequent blooming of industry-less communities based on craft and agriculture (Saint-Simon, Cabet and the early Fabians) means more than a simple set of demands within the dialectic structure of workers and bosses—in the fighting contest between human work, human values and capitalist profit; it also means a desire to break everything, to end all reigns and all dominations. To end organization itself: "it is not to reconquer their dignity that workers rebel, break machines, kidnap the bosses, bounce the leaders [. . .] there is no such thing as libidinal dignity; nor is there a libidinal fraternity; there are libidinal contacts without communication (due to lack of *message*)" [p. 138].

This desire, which is always ascribed to the mob, is irrepressible. It can only be channeled and controlled, but it always seeks to express itself, nonetheless. This may explain how, in practically every crisis, there occur strange alliances and maneuvers, which a Marxist will justify by inventing a sequence of cause and effect heretofore hidden from objective consciousness, but which, to someone like

Lyotard, merely point to an irritation, an *incandescence* of the libidinal surface beyond any rationalization. Thus today, the 1977-1978 miner's strike, which was variously attributed to the excessive profit search of the mining companies at a time when coal is, again, fast becoming the major staple of industrial production, to the former corruption and now current ineptitude of union bosses, and finally, to the independent and fiery character of Appalachian men *à la James Dickey,* can also be interpreted by substituting libidinal factors for economic or ideological considerations. It can be seen as a desire on the part of the miners to seek *pleasure (jouissance)* in the determination of their own life rhythm, while also asserting the right, almost *ex officio,* to shake down a work structure, which exploits them in the privacy of their body, their mind, but which has remained basically unchanged after the strike. The documentary film *Harlan County* made that quite clear a couple of years ago by showing how the particular set-up of the Kentucky strike actually left highly individualistic miners no choice but to go out on an indefinite strike in the face of organized scabbing by the management. In this context, the miners' failure to achieve practical objectives and their rejection of agreements worked out between their bosses and the management could only be read as indicating a desire simply not to be co-opted: *not to be read as anything in particular.* In this sense also, unionization and union politics carry the reverse of their ideological content: while seeking to develop bargaining clout, they also spawn a desire for unrestrained freedom, which expresses itself in what negotiators tend to view as mere obstructionism among the rank and file and which the union bosses find very difficult to deal with. Moreover, as other *libidinal investments* are made *laterally,* so to speak, the political situation can only get more complicated. One might recall, for instance, how the help given to the miners by independent farmers made Harlan appear as a symbol of defiance to the American tradition of organized bargaining. Now it could be argued that such occurrences only testify to a rise in the political consciousness of America's *Lumpen* (the down and out farmers side by side with the down and out miners). But it is more interesting, and Lyotard would probably argue, more *satisfying,* to view them in a new context, where the body-politic would constitute but one section of the libidinal surface seeking to escape policy itself: *politeia.*

That those various instances of Libido and Death may be related, at best, to the hippyism (the *Revolution for the Hell of it* syndrome) of the sixties, and at worst, to some form of anarchism, is evident. Whence the attacks to which *Lyotard-le menteur,* the ex-party member, the traitor, has sometimes been subjected by activists on the Left. If it is true that political alliances and options are decided without an understanding of a situation's libidinal components, because they are all determined by an allegiance to the ideology of the power system, then one might ask what kind of political action is indeed possible. Marx had predicated revolutionary failures on the lack of objective revolutionary consciousness. For instance, he had criticized the Second Republic or the Paris Commune for not having been able to analyze correctly the relation of socio-political structures to the economic components of a crisis where an impromptu alliance of immature left-leaning bourgeois intellectuals and vintage revolutionary craftsmen did not succeed in bringing off the dictatorship of the proletariat. He argued that in both cases the lack of generalized working class support for the *Aufhebung* of the position *neben* had been determined by the incapacity to define common meaningful objectives. In essence then, and although the *Capital* and the *Grundrisse* often read like a program of reconstructed sequences of cause and effect lying beyond the grasp of individual consciousness, and for this reason, perhaps, like a depressing account of the capacity of Capitalism to absorb schisms in its midst, Marx implied that the praxis of every political action is always dependent on theoretical and metatheoretical reflection. That is, it insists not only on the setting-up of a proper strategy of *Vemeinung* and *Aufhebung* in the given historical context, but also on setting up a position of exteriority and Otherness in the act of theorizing itself. So that, in the end, the actual political action for or against is merely an expanded metaphor of the action of the theorizing subject setting up his own exteriority. Whence the constant failure of a circular process which Lyotard sees as an intricate part of theatricality: the masquerade which provides the struggling subject with the illusory hope of attaining a position of dominance by investing his struggle with religious overtones (the Resurrection/the Rise of the Spirit/the victory of the Proletariat). To all this, the ***Economie*** responds, as usual, obliquely, by cutting across semiotics, history, economics—while always avoiding a deconstruction which would only solidify the theatricality therein. For my part, and instead of launching into a critique of the critique of present-day relations between Capitalism and Desire, I would like to examine those sweeps which make Lyotard's critique possible, in the sense that they help us understand how seemingly heterogeneous patches are actually contiguous parts in one huge libidinal surface.

By instancing a libidinal surface extending to all parts of the socio-economic, political system and containing them all (including the subject who structures them together) into a hypothetical body swept by the libido, Lyotard resolves, or rather, bypasses, the insoluble problem of mediation: the *Mitte. Mitte* between the one and the other; power of the assertion/negation complex, which attaches a circle of dominance to the activity and the relations of all consciousness. His great epidermic fantasy enables him to posit, behind a system of rational signs, albeit remaining an indissoluble part of it, another system of *tensor-signs* which, because its function is simply to localize and invest the flashing incandescence of the libido, must be voided of the discursive and referring characteristics of all sign-systems (for example, a sign is purely arbitrary and enters into a system where signs refer to other signs). It must take on, instead, a value which will be experienced as unique *without, however, being different,* as the instancing of one single difference would predicate a return to the power system of binarism and exclusion. These *tensor-signs* are not exactly signs, because they work under the

cover of a true system of commutative signs (language/ money); but also, and mostly, because they are more tensors than signs. They work in a non-semiotic fashion by instancing an intensity instead of a reference to other signs; by being on location, almost like indexes, they are already a part of the flashing surface of the libidinal body, of its membrane [*la pellicule*], and they cannot be said to constitute a mediation independent from both consciousness and/or the membrane. In other words, because of the displacement of the mediation, a system of *rational* signs will evolve and become a system where exchange and information has become moot, as all commutations turn into juxtapositions: when one section of the libidinal surface is incandescent, its tensor-sign does not exclude all others by contradistinction; but, on the contrary, all other tensors demand recognition as well. The *Mitte* as the power instance in the sign standing for that which is absent, as *Potenz,* has thus been transformed into *Vermittung;* the power of representation and exclusion, into one of infinite exchange. Now, because this transformation is concurrent with the development of an economic system where tensor-signs proliferate, allowing the greatest possible amount of libidinal material to circulate through an incessant preoccupation with money—particularly inflated money—and profit, the ***Economie*** ends up wending its way toward a coherent presentation of libidinal capitalism. What had, so far, been modulated only from a New-Hegelian perspective, by modifying the power of dominance inherent in the sign, now appears in yet another, albeit totally Lyotardian, perspective, where the *Potenz* has passed from a position of strict inhibition of desire, also inherent in the sign, to one where the sign itself is used, *not to stand in lieu of* (of work, of supply and demand, etc. . . .), *but to carry* vast quantities of monied energies. Capitalism, particularly through the institution of credit, lending and spending, is the system that makes this investment of new energies possible.

With this statement, we naturally move on to what makes Lyotard's book, one of economic purposes, end with a joint reflection on the combined values of economic and linguistic accumulation. Now, although Lyotard's main preoccupation is to avoid the pitfalls of a theoretical or meta-theoretical position, in order to free the libido from what he sees as a history of conceptual repression, he cannot avoid discussing concepts from a point of view which would be that of a historian of philosophy. Thus, he must, in his discussion of value and money, go back to the Aristotelian concept of *chreia* (*the need* fostering both consumption and trade of goods) as the basis for the measured production and exchange of goods around a civic *meson* (the center of the city, both economically and administratively). He must then demonstrate how the regulation of value and money is tied to a desire to exclude from this communal *chreia* in the *meson* any sort of immeasured gain: one not in relation to properly assessed economic needs; and how their deregulation is caused by the incapacity of the *meson* to take into account the obvious expansion of the *chreia* outside the network of the city, into the modern state and the multinational world of capitalism. But while he is thus obligated to some sort of historical perspective, this obligation is somehow voided by an argument with which he has managed to erase all traces of origin and beginning: the argument that there is no real history to be written, no class struggle to be reported, no progress or decadence against which to measure libidinal affects. In societies supposedly made of good savages, theorists from Marx to Baudrillard argue that accumulation of goods and alienation from work do not exist, because there is really no production nor mode of production, as everything is consumed right then and there; they see no division of labor either, because, without profit or disvaluation of work, there exists the possibility of an organic relationship between the body and Nature (Marx), or of a symbolic exchange between goods and the libido (Baudrillard). Lyotard attacks this notion of historical primitivity as representing the hope, the fantasy of an unalienated region. The fact is, all exchanges *must* be mediated in some fashion, even if this mediation can itself be modified and displaced. Thus Mauss's, Durkheim's or Lévi-Strauss's contention that all social systems originate in the non-convertible, unmediated structure of the *gift* and *counter-gift* is simply unwarranted. The gift and counter-gift, while apparently non-convertible and unmediated, are actually instances of libidinal intensities flashed by the tensors onto the socio-political scene. Now, because there is no primitive society, and no region considered unalienated, there is no region that should be considered fully alienated either. There is always room for intensities, even in the most structured, the most repressive of systems.

Having thus, paradoxically, resurrected the Marxian axiom that political structures are indeed irrelevant, Lyotard's book considers pell-mell such different regimes as the Athenian city, the absolute monarchy of Louis XIV and the capitalistic democracies of today, without allowing his considerations to imply any kind of political judgment or praxis. For better or for worse, the strategy of political action is completely discarded. What interests Lyotard is to show how the only strategy, the only praxis there is, is to increase the interaction between (dissimulated) tensor-signs and (dissimulating) rational signs. Now, the upshot of this ideology—from the displacement of the *Mitte* to the call for a praxis of ongoing dissimulation—is that History, in the Hegelian as well as in the Marxian sense, has disappeared: instead of the history of conflicts and dominations, we now have a certain *history* of dissimulation. This means that, far from being able to write an objective account or rely on a factual series organized through a system of linguistic and logical choices, one can only register instances where the libidinal patchwork has been made incandescent, that is, where the tensor-signs seem to have taken as much importance as the rational signs. Instead of constructing and organizing metacritical sequences, one will attempt to produce instances of dissimulation: to set up fictions and myths, for instance, so as to exploit their simulating potential. Thus, and as there is no difference between libidinal affects and the affects of a discourse made of flashes and escapes, the new historian's,

that is, the libidinal economist's task will be to mix a reasoned, theoretical presentation (the economy of the Greek city, the philosophy of value in the *Capital*) with a narrative allowing the representation of this theory in the form of an address to the reader:

> the pain bears no relation to the little suffering resulting from castration, which is suffering in the concept, flaw and scar always made anew [*Lyotard means that the pain resulting from the impossibility of satisfying all our drives has nothing to do with the theoretical loss implied in a linguistic theory of the Unconscious such as Lacan's, where a signified always points to an occulted signifier*]. Here, then, is how to picture it, Perfumed Mane. You take this bar separating the this and the non-this, That is to say, any segment. You place it in a neutral space—let us say: a tri-dimensional space, in order to facilitate the imagination's very rustic intuition. You apply to it a rotating motion around a point belonging to that segment—a motion with the three following properties: rotation occurs on every conceivable axis without exception; the point in the center itself moves along the segment in an unpredictable way; finally, it moves in the neutral space above. In this way is generated a surface, which is no other but the libidinal surface in question: this surface always uses a width equal to the length of the segment. [p. 24]

Each discussion which could pass for theoretical is thus presented in the form of a story. However, as if to emphasize the fact that whole, well rounded narratives do not exist, these stories are never more than eclectic fragments, culled from books of macro-economics, opera libretti, chronicles of colonial wars or, even, Marx's own correspondence. Since the *Economie* is thus only a patchwork itself, one could decide that any account of it should only be made in the form of a libidinal narrative itself: something resembling Lyotard's recent experiment with the painter Monory [*Récits tremblants* (Paris: Galilée, 1977)], where only a visual medium seems to do justice to the intensities crackling the written texts. However, because this is, at least, *meant* to be a review, I still would like to knit together, using the technique of what Lyotard calls elsewhere *dissertation* or *dissertion* (the carding of the wool), three pieces of the patchwork which appear to me to be of fundamental importance. A first episode expounds the Aristotelian model of the city, with the *meson* as the locus where all passions and goods are thrown together and the *chreia* guaranteed from excesses. This model, however, is soon deregulated by the introduction of a myth by Herodotus of Lydian men prostituting their daughters. A second episode, the most central, deals with the fiction of a Marxist theatrics made up with two Marxes pitted against one another. And a third episode expands on the second, where a critique of present day Capitalism, and specifically, of the 1929 crash and the more recent oil embargo, leads Lyotard to show how Marx's libidinal aspirations were ill-served by his theoretical, almost religious, convictions. Let us now take a closer look at each episode.

The Greek city manages to maintain a circulation of goods and work in a closed circuit, by using its *agora* as a *me-*

son where things are exchanged at the level of a reasonable *chreia* and with a small trade (the *kapelikon*) kept, at first, from overexpanding its profits. Let us notice in passing that Lyotard does not mention the whole body of slavery which is totally alienated from the citizenry. But the reason for this omission may be that traditional histories are wrong. Slaves are, indeed, a part of the libidinal compound of the city. While goods and work are thus exchanged, Lyotard claims that what is also exchanged is a restricted libido, in the sense that the prevailing homosexuality functions as a transformer and an annullator of differences within a circle where the men-citizens (the women are there only for reproductive purposes) are all equal and where no one can take advantage of an exchange. This is further illustrated by the famous anecdote of Socrates and Alcibiades: Alcibiades wanted to offer Socrates his body, so as to receive his wisdom in exchange; but Socrates refused and claimed Alcibiades had nothing to gain, since he, Socrates knew nothing. Lyotard safely concludes that this illustrates the first step in the regulation of the socio-political body. There cannot be a standard of exchange between Socrates (wisdom) and Alcibiades (sex), because Socrates has no knowledge to impart which might accrue to Alcibiades and make him richer. In other words, the exchange that takes place is simply for the sake of regulating the libido; it points to the triumph of the rational sign.

However, Herodotus's straight-faced anecdote that the Lydians were not only the richest men on earth (Croesus) owing to their invention of commerce, but that they also were the first to prostitute their daughters, helps Lyotard introduce into this well-balanced economy the seeds of deregulation, as prostitution, translating the libido into money, extends the exchange from a zero growth economy to one of, potentially, infinite growth, and the women, formerly used solely to produce children for the city, are now paid to fill the needs of citizens and strangers as well. One will notice, again, the fictional, a-historical flavor of the narrative as the ***Economie*** places Herodotus only *after* Aristotle and Socrates. This crab-like progression is typical of the Lyotardian patchwork: since the sweeps of the libido, and with it the incandescence of this or that fragment of the libidinal surface, are unpredictable, it is in the interest of the libidinal economist to spread his narrative across various removes of history (Herodotus) or theory (Aristotle). Most important, however, is that the libido has now been manifested *beyond* the circle of the *meson*. In the same crab-like manner which characterizes the whole book, this expansion, soon related to the expansion of a formerly modest and reasonable *kapelikon,* will be used later to account for the outrageous development of mercantilism under Louis XIV (history) and in Sade's libertine utopia (theory), where intensities of voracious pleasure are predicated on the starvation of the rest of Europe, indeed, of the rest of the world.

What the reader has learned so far, from the kind of libidinal song and dance he has been asked to participate in, Lyotard will now crystallize, one should say, *incandesce*

himself, by transferring the ambivalence/monovalence regulating and deregulating his libidinal theatre to the *locus,* the *center* of economic theory in the modern world: Marx and Marxism. Using his accoutrements of mask and fantasy, he transforms the complex named *Marx* into a dramatic spectacle. By doing this, he not only shows, again, the idea of the progress of History and Philosophy to be a myth, but he also uses this myth to show a thus discredited Marx as merely a part of a libidinal patchwork where the distinction between theoretical and non-theoretical texts is blurred. Not only is this mythification striking, since until the more recent *Nouveaux Philosophes*—whose bourgeois alignment and good old fashioned anti-Communism Lyotard immediately rejected—no self-respecting French intellectual would have enacted a Leftist political posture without paying some sort of homage to Marx's writing and Eastern Communism, but it also represents an attempt to plant the seed of libidinal economy at the rational root of the sign—of what Lyotard considers to be the most extravagant avatar of a libidinal theatrics: Marx and Marxism as sprung from the text of the *Capital.* Very simply then, we see how the rational/tensor sign ambivalence, applied to whatever is known as Marxism, yields a simulacrum of schizophrenia, uniting and dividing the naive, virginal *Petite Marx* (who pines away for regions unalienated, for pastoral Edens, for bodies organic and one with Nature) with/from the *Great Barbudo,* the Prosecutor of Capitalism, intent on showing the theory and the history of man's alienation from his work. Between these two, is established some sort of mercantile relationship, as the *Petite Marx* must pay for her dream-like visions of unalienation with the exorbitant saga of the economic historian at pains to finish a book which might bring him/them back to Eden—bring them back, that is, when the studying and the analyzing that make this return (to a classless society) possible are completed. But, as everyone knows, the *Capital* remains silent on the time after the revolution and the particulars of a Communist Eden: painfully open-ended. And the insatiable appetite for power of the *Prosecutor* is at odds with the uncontrollable desires of the *Petite Marx,* just as the strict rule of the *chreia* and the *meson* is at odds with Capitalism's insane desire to foster exchanges, literally, to Death (in the vain hope of finally securing, of possessing, in the instance of exchange itself, the ultimate good, the ultimate merchandise).

The example of the nineteen-twenties' financial debacles is only a further illustration of this paradox. Now that Marxism itself can be taken for an eidetic reduction of the libidinal struggle that it really is, world economic crises in general only demonstrate the libidinal potential of Capitalism.—An extraordinary potential, because, no longer dependent on referential value nor on predictions of this value (where is the Aristotelian *meson* today?) and simply appropriative of the value itself as the only reference, the system now operates on a largely fantasmatic exchange, where the institution of credit, originally conceived as a simple means to defray the costs of an expanded production, is now used in the form of a libidinal speculation on the eluded work value. Under the auspices of Capitalism, the libido creates new patches that can be monied, transferred, appropriated to the point of complete deregulation, as is clear from the history of economic crashes. The crashes are the inevitable manifestation of an exacerbated libido; and the only reassuring thing that could, perhaps, be said (but the *Economie* is not a *how-to* book) is that such disasters could possibly be avoided by the preventive practice of a libidinal economy. But could they? And wouldn't such a suggestion immediately throw us back into the circle of dominance and semiotics?—In the end (but is there an end?), the book is not into suggesting anything, because it wishes to escape everything, including suggestions:

> The interesting thing would be to stay where we are—but to grab without noise all opportunities to function as bodies and good conductors of intensities. No need of declarations, manifests, organizations; not even for exemplary actions. To let dissimulation play in favor of intensities. Safe plot, without leader, without core, without program or project, displaying through the bodies of signs the thousand cancers of tensors. We are not inventing anything; that's right, yes, yes, yes, yes. [p. 311]

But what must we think of Lyotard? Has he given us a new Gospel? The tone and the pace of the book, its *dissertions,* its pamphlets, as well as its sermons, could lead us to believe that Lyotard sees himself as the prophet of an unrestricted libido, presenting us with a rationale for psychic liberation which often sounds like the theoretical counterpart of works by Henry Miller, Timothy Leary or William Burroughs. Yet he has also constantly reminded us that he rejects theory as the product of a Western interpretive delirium. Is his *Economie* exceptionally radical because, instead of deconstructing Structuralism and semiotics, it disqualifies both by turning them into bags of tricks for his libidinal circus? But we must remember that Lyotard's intention in writing the *Economie* was not to privilege any part of a critical revolution whose effect, in the last ten years, has been mostly to give special status to the *text* and *textual analysis.* In fact, there is in the *Economie* hardly a reference to the *Structuralist Controversy,* as we are used to viewing it in America. Rather, it seems that Lyotard wanted to write on life and living, not writing itself—and that he did it in the fullest *eco-nomic* sense. Reflecting on the importance of the *nemos:* the sharing, the distribution of energies into specific loci, into patches to be consumed by readers and critics; but also pondering the weight of the *nomos:* the law, which sets limits between loci, making transgression from one to the next both a painful and pleasurable experience. That his quest led him to stage episodes, poems, monologues, dialogues along with diatribes and speeches only shows he remained aware all the while of the difficulties involved in his task.—Fully conscious that if it is indeed no longer possible to claim special exemption for a monadic subject possessed of history and knowledge, the duty of a true philosopher today can only be to experiment with the endless decomposition and recomposition of the *nemos* and the *nomos,* to seek the fragmentation of the subject, not simply as the symbol

of a new dis-order, but as a guarantee of infinite experience. The end of the *Economie,* which is not properly speaking an end—to the great dismay, perhaps, of readers steeped in the ideology of the well-written, the well-rounded book—only calls for more of the same. In this sense, the *Economie* reminds one of the *Satyricon:* a *satyra,* a basket of philosophical incongruities, celebrating desire in the context of eating and defecating, saving and spending, writing and acting, and using one's discourse to promote the one revolutionary mode par excellence: *decadence.* "'Why delay the start of the show then'?, said Eumolpus. 'Make me your master, if you think the idea is a good one.' No one dared condemn a scheme that would cost nothing" [*Satyricon,* 117].—But does it?

Alphonso Lingis (essay date 1979)

SOURCE: "A New Philosophical Interpretation of the Libido," in *Sub-Stance,* Vol. VIII, No. 4, 1979, pp. 87-97.

[*In the following essay, Lingis describes the process of the libidinal economy as Lyotard conceives it to function in the individual.*]

Working with new concepts of impulsive intensity—libidinal space, libidinal time, libidinal identity, Jean-François Lyotard's *Economie libidinale*[1] sets out to interpret in a coherent discourse the essential data of psychoanalysis, which had been formulated in a fragmented—physicalist, mechanist, hydraulic and mythical—language, or, in the phenomenological reworking, in mentalist, intentional, language. But Lyotard's book does not only devise a philosophically more coherent language for the findings of psychyanalysis; it also elaborates an interpretation of the data themselves. Assembling literary and theological texts along with certain Freudian texts given a new importance, Lyotard's book shows how theoretical activity and political economy reverberate with libidinal processes, and how the primary process libido continues even in its matured and sublimated forms. This new conceptual elaboration is principally due to a divesting of the Freudian conceptual apparatus of its phallocentric and reproductive normativity, and even of the idea of organism as a norm. If wholeness, organism, is the general form of any norm, then we can say that this philosophy presents a libido without norms.

Just what kind of theoretical work do we have here? It is not really an autonomous phenomenology of sexual experience, taken to be an exhibition of the pretheoretical, preconceptualized given experience. Phenomenology could pretend that it could, with its own vocabulary allegedly framed after immediate intuitions, elaborate a purely descriptive account of, among other things, sexual experience, which could then function as a criterion against which to judge the theoretical elaborations of science, because it thought it had found an autonomous locus of access to the primary and preconceptual experience itself. This locus was self-consciousness. It was originally all intuitive: an intuition of itself in its primary, that is, intuitive, acts or contacts with various zones of mundane reality.

Lyotard's work is, to be sure, philosophical and not empirical. In what sense? Not in this phenomenological sense. The "thing itself," the libidinal life, is not a succession of acts essentially intuitive. These sensuous sensations would not fit in, with minor adjustments, to the Husserlian concept of perceptions understood as objectifying the primary intuitions of the observer. And the phenomenological project is possible only if all the moments of the primary process, the pretheoretical experience, were accompanied by a possible "I think," were open to a structure of self-intuition. But sexual impulses are not reflexive structures in which an ego-identity is formed and maintained, but precisely processes in which the ego is dismembered and dissipated in discrete intensities, which discharge as soon as they form.

There is then no direct and autonomous access to the libidinal sphere through philosophical self-consciousness. Lyotard's work is rather in the direction of what Freud called "metapsychology," a reflective work on the concepts with which the empirical research was assembled and formulated. We know that Freud did not invent a new vocabulary for the psychoanalytic domain; its terms are borrowed from neurology, physics, chemistry, hydraulics and mythology. This was not due to some lack of inventive imagination or boldness or consistency; it expressed Freud's deep conviction that theoretical rigor would have to lead to a unified discourse encompassing the psychic phenomena into the physical universe. Freud's metapsychology is a provisional effort in the way of a metaphysics, in the Aristotelian and Whiteheadian sense, a universal and unified categorical system which could function to establish translatability between the data accounted for in physical terms and those accounted for in psychic terms.

Lyotard's work is in the direction of this same metapsychology, this metaphysics. But the physics of today is no longer the physics of Freud's time; the universal theory has to work with entirely different local theories. Thus, Deleuze and Guattari, in *Anti-Oedipus*,[2] actively attempt to construct a first project for such a theory, but following the paths in contemporary microbiology, where the differences but also continuities between microphysical and microbiological entities have to be formulated. Lyotard's work is not yet on that level. His book maintains a specifically psychic language, and is rather an effort to reformulate the concepts fixing psychic processes in more clear and more comprehensive ways. This effort is directed mainly against the two most important contemporary enterprises in the same direction: that of phenomenological intentionalism and of Lacanian neo-Hegelianism. It is then a regional theory preparatory for the universal metapsychology or metaphysics. But it also constantly extends itself into the socio-economic field; Lyotard frames his concepts in such a way that they would also function as the principle terms of political economics.

THE LIBIDINAL ZONE

In "the most obscure and inaccessible region,"[3] or in the beginning, or at the core, at the essence of life, there are excitations. Of themselves they are intensities, moments of potential that accumulate and discharge themselves, moments of feeling both pleasure and unpleasure.

They are surface effects in the sense that they occur at the point of conjuncture between a mouth and a breast, a thigh and the other thigh, lips and another's lips, lips and the pulp of fruit, toes and sands. They do not occur on a pregiven surface, but by occurring mark out a surface, make skin, down, vulva exist for itself and not for the sake of the interior or of the whole. Surface effects that do not express an inward or deep meaning or signify an exterior object or objective. Effects without causes—for that an excitation can be out of all proportion to the stimulus that preceded it is the most elementary datum of psychoanalysis.

Singularites and not auto-identifying syntheses, utterly affirmative but not ascribable to an underlying ego identity as its acts or as its accidents, intensities are anonymities.

And they are, Freud said, "in themselves 'timeless.' This means in the first place that they are not ordered temporally, that time does not change them in any way and that the idea of time cannot be applied to them."[4] An intensity is not a synthesizing process, surpassing but thereby retaining a past of itself, projecting or anticipating a future of itself. It is just passing, discharge of itself. It is a *tense*, Lyotard says—a singular tense. A movement, a moment, a passing, without memory and without expectations, ephemeral and useless, which can be surprised, and be as a surprise, a pleasure or an unpleasure.

Freud supposes that unpleasure corresponds to an increase in the quantity of the unbound excitation, and pleasure to a diminution. And that the organism endeavors to keep the quantity of excitation present in it as low as possible, or at least to keep it constant. The organism tends to stability, to return to the quiescence of the inorganic world. The most universal endeavor of all living substance is in reality a death drive. Of course an excessive excitation could achieve this by shattering definitively the stability of the organism, and making its reconstitution impossible. But the organism, by its organic constitution, endeavors to ward off any possible ways of returning to inorganic existence other than those which are immanent in the organism itself. If it endeavors to neutralize every excitation that occurs in it, that is only in order to be able to pursue the form of death immanent in itself.

But that means that there are two incidences of the death drive: inasmuch as it is predicated as intrinsic to the organism, and inasmuch as it is immanent to the excitation as such. The excitation is a 'solar' compulsion of an excess of potential to discharge itself. The pleasure is in the release, solar pleasure, Nietzsche said, that of the sun which as it descends to the earth, to its death, pours its gold on the seas, and, like the sun too, feels itself happiest when even the poorest fisherman rows with golden oars.[5] "We have all experienced how the greatest pleasure attainable by us, that of the sexual act," Freud wrote, "is associated with a momentary extinction of a highly intensified excitation."[6] The expenditure at a loss, the loss of force is not sadness here, and it occurs without regret and even without recall or memory. The pain involved in the libidinal excitation is that of the excess—not of force, but of incompossible figures being affirmed at once. It is the murmur or the disorder of the amorous nonsense that affirms and cries out that she open up, that he take me, that she resist, that he tighten his hold, that she give way, that he begin and stop, that she obey and command. It is the Bacchantes' frenzy, that of women bearing the masks of gods and of contradictory gods, goat-gods (but their civic womanhood is a figure, a mask, in exactly the same sense), bearing masks without having, being identities behind them, and whose contradictory speech intensifies into screams and explosions of laughter. It is the babbling of pleasure of the infant holding the teat between its lips, the warm pulp of the breast in its indexterous fingers, its neck cushioned in the female fat of the shoulder, dismembered eddies of surface excitations, the maternal eyes seeking oscillations of pleasure in the unfocused orbits. The specific pain of the intensity does not consist in sensing the incompossibility of all that the libido desires at once—that is, in sensing the lacking, missing totality, which is not yet conceived. It rather consists in the multiple, scissioning ways in which the intensity seeks to discharge and to disintegrate. This pain of the excess and this pleasure of the dying must not be separated; they are originally indecidable and constitutive of libidinal intensity. It will only *be ex post facto,* once the organism is constituted, that the pain of this excess is apprehended by the organism as a disturbance of its stability, and the pleasure of this discharge recorded in the remembering membrane of the organism as the maintenance of its own path to its immanent death. Originally one would have to conceive this excess as a pleasure in its discharge, and this dying as a pain in its very excess.

The libidinal excitations do not take place in a pregiven space, or invest a pregiven region; they extend a libidinal body, or, more exactly, a libidinal band, an erotogenic surface. This surface is not the surface of a depth, the contour enclosing an interior. When one enters the orifices of the libidinal body, one does not enter an inwardness, but extends the surface of pleasure. The libidinal movement discovers a continuity between the convexities and the concavities, the facial contours and the orifices, the swelling things and the mouths, everywhere glands surfacing, and what was protuberance and tumescence on last contact can now be fold, cavity, squeezed breasts, soles of feet forming still another mouth. Anything can be conjoined to anything to form an intensive contiguity: the libidinal band is a patchwork and not an organism. It is the discharge, the passage, the differential or the continuous displacement of the excitation that extends this surface.

The libidinous zone then is a Möbius band, where by following the outer face one finds oneself on the inner face, where one everywhere finds oneself on a surface and never in an inwardness. Or it is interminable, labyrinthian extension where there are no landmarks and no issue. Again, we should not say that the libidinal intensities occur in a labyrinthian space, but that they describe such a space by their very displacement and passage. There are indeed intersections and encounters, but the encounter is each time fled in terror or in gaiety, and this rebound traces out banks of transparent walls, secret thresholds, open fields and empty skies in which the encounter is fled, is diffused, is forgotten. The agitated caressing hand is not seeking an entry, nor a hold, nor a secret; it is only departing from the point of encounter, losing itself, describing a space in which it can lose itself.

There is a sort of exclusion and tautness involved in the excitation that has to be described for itself: each intensification that is produced as a *this,* a herenow, evokes "cries of jealousy" from the entourage, and thus extends an expanse where an other, an elsewhere, appeals and incites. The *this,* without lacking or craving anything, is revealed as a *non-that.* This exclusiveness of the intensity does not suppose a totality, an organic field first given, and thus the intensification of the this is not from the first a desire for, an intention aiming at, a lack of, the not-this. It is a surge of force arousing plenitudes about itself. This libidinous intensity and its spatiality is thus essentially different from the distance phenomenology accounted for in terms of an intentional and ecstatic ex-istence, anxious and needy, a lack or a care. It is not the Heideggerian *Ent-fernung.*

The force that intensifies at any point takes over surrounding forces, pumps off their energy, and tears from them "cries and exhalations of jealousy." Labyrinthian spaces are delineated by the appeals of other points for the libidinal intensity—by the jealousy of the vulva for the mouth, the jealousy of the nipple for the testicles, the jealousy of the woman over the book her lover is writing, the jealousy of the sun over the closed shutters behind which the reader reads that book.

The libidinal space is made both of the appeals of other sites and other expanses, and the displacement of the intensity made of the unstable affirmation of incompossible figures. Its displacement is both its expansion, describing an extension, and its dissipation, describing a space without verticality, the essentially supine libidinous zone. If the Nietzschean joy is the feeling of ever expanding, auto-affirming and auto-affecting, and elevating power, there is also a libidinal gaiety, whose incredulous and insolent laughter assents to nothing, posits nothing and awaits no one's recognition, and moves horizontally, through metamorphoses, whose buoyant and nervous agitations do not take pleasure in the dance-form they may be describing, but in this pointless and self-mocking turmoil.

THE ORGANISM

Life begins in the libidinal incandescences that circulate and describe an erotogenic zone, structured as a labyrinth without landmarks, points of outcome or issue, a Möbius band all surface. But it organizes itself into a functional and expressive apparatus—an organism. Lyotard refuses to see in the determinative factor in an organism an intentionality which would direct it teleologically to some end—and ultimately on ending as such—a movement that would take everything present as a reference, a sign, or a relay-point toward something absent, beyond, signified, and that, within the organism itself, would take every member or organ as a representative or substitute for another and thus for the whole. That is to interpret a body philosophically, metaphysically, as a system of functions where a part can figure functionally inasmuch as it can represent another and the whole, and as an expressive and desiring system which takes itself as reference to, an openness upon, a desire of, something beyond, exterior, the exterior world or the signified ideal reality, and finally exteriority or openness of nothingness itself.

Lyotard is working rather with the Freudian idea that the organism is the place where the freely mobile excitations can be bound, that is, fixed, determined, acquire identity, acquire position with respect to one another, and thus value. It is not their being directed upon an exteriority, absence or nothingness, that makes them significant and functional, but first their occurring in a field, a space of compossibility. For them to acquire sense, value, is for them to acquire identity and position, for each to be itself and not another—and be determined in its own identity by this not-being-another. This process is both the constitution of a register, a theatre, where they can be together, and, for each excitation, the scission of its ambivalent intensity.

The process is not to be conceived as an intentional arc traversing the field of excitations, movement of ex-istence which, for Goldstein and Merleau-Ponty, is the very essence of an organism. It is conceived by Lyotard as a slowing-down of the intensities. The tension in their inner incompossibilities disintensifies by disjunction: each becomes excitation of, affirmation of, this . . . and not that. This disjunction is a fixing of the this in its identity, and a synthetic exclusion of the non-this from it. The this and the non-this are both posited, but not at once: the differentiation is made in a movement of deferring, in a temporalizing that affirms the present and defers the absent, makes the past pass and the future to come. The constitution of the context, the field, a surface where traces are inscribed, is this very moment.

It occurs then as a slowing down of intensities, an internal deferring of the incompossibles converged in them, a temporal disjunctive synthesis. Temporalization is disintensification and disjunction. Now each this, each excitation is held, maintained in its identity, as it refers to, tends toward a non-this which is reserved, retained, absent, or deferred. An excitation becomes a sensation, by virtue of this tension toward what is deferred or temporarily removed from it, of which it is fixed as a trace. The inner space of an organism is constituted as this retentional field, the memory of the intensities, localization of their passages.

Freud supposes that the freely mobile excitations are thus fixed, bound, in order that they can be disposed of—that is, neutralized, such that an organism is the place where excitations are reduced, tranquillized, where the inorganic state, or death, is effected. Yet the organic structures that take form, if they can be read as issues toward death, are also accumulations of life force, and libidinal investments. If the organism as such is a stabilized structure, within which the excitations are fixed, consigned and conserved, the whole structure can in turn be the occasion of a libidinal excitation. A neurosis according to Freud is a compromise, a stabilization which both deadens and builds up excitation. The economic fixations which hold and stabilize excitations also block their circulation, and engender compulsive frustrations, disruptions, repetitions, malfunctionings, which are excitations in their turn. When on the body of a hysteric segments of the libidinal surface are bound, desensitized and excluded from the circulation of affects, partial systems are taking from and beginning to function on their own. The contracted, locked muscles, the tightened respiratory system become asthmatic, pit their bound forces as resistances to the analysis, and function as a sort of separately organized mechanism, in which psychoanalysis will be able to find its own logic, its own code, its own intelligibility. If its excitations are controlled, regulated, and the hysteric held in sterile repetitions, the partial organization is lethal inasmuch as it obstructs and disrupts the larger organism with which it is bound. But the very disorganization and malfunction produced in the larger organism also intensifies the excitations where they are blocked, such that they invest in this frozen channel or elude it in devious and ingenious ways. The partial system can be seen as a figure of the death drive, inasmuch as the bound configurations of intensity are rendered inert, inorganic, but also as a locus where excitations are composed and discharged, as a harrowing of Eros.

Freud first found the death drive as the meaning of systems of repetitive compulsions which make everything, even the most painful things, return—as in the dreams of traumatic neuroses. Yet the fixing of paths and the determining of operations that are produced in them also produce new itineraries for the circulation and discharge of excitations. Here the pleasure principle follows the death drive. But the accumulation of forces at the organic enclosure which will finally break through and break up the partial system and even threaten the survival of the organism as a whole, and which is the very force of the pleasure principle, also makes the Nirvana principle ensue from the pleasure principle.

Thus, repetition compulsions, neuroses, paranoic seizures, stabilized lethal disorders or the organic functioning, memory systems, all these partial organisms figure as the paths through which a zone of excitation and life pursues its own amortizement and death. They do so inasmuch as they inhibit the circulation of affects within the whole organism and block its functioning. But Freud sees the very constitution of an organism as a stabilization of a field of excitations, a binding process, a tranquillization and a relapse toward the inert. The organism as such is then itself wholly a work of death. If that is so, then the formation of these partial organisms by which the whole is dismembered is not only so many partial paths of a single-minded drive at work everywhere. For do not these partial organisms, these malfunctionings, neuroses and compulsive disorders, disrupt the general and immanent pursuit of death? These partial functionings which are organic malfunctionings ravage the organism—the crazed laughter that chokes and that asphyxiates the asthmatic, the local impotencies that drain off the force of those who shy away from the exercise of force, the obsessions that disintegrate the schizophrenic, the panic that dissipates the exuberant vigor of militants at a demonstration—and also, as unbindings, as releases, relieve and release the organism from the lethal system it itself represents—the orgasm that releases its seed, the drunkenness that releases its words, the dance that releases its musculature and its armor.

Thus, we no longer have two orders and two times, a primary process where the freely mobile libidinal excitations erupt and circulate as the very effervescence of life-force, and a secondary process where the organism takes form in a stabilization and a tranquillization, a deadening of these vital effervescences, and a return to the inorganic is intended. The primary process and the secondary process do not form fields of effects that would have to be read as composing two different systems, one of intensities, the other of functions or intentionalities. Or that would have to be read as forming two different networks or significant structures, or even as ambivalent or polysemic effects, connecting up as signs whose meaning would be eros and also thanatos. In reality the composition of an organism in the libidinal zone is the constitution of excitations into sensations, into signs; the organism is a semiotic field. A bound excitation makes sense by virtue of the divergency it marks and the opposition it fixes. In an organism the material of life functions as signs. Yet they also constitute intensities in their potential and singularity, as the partial systems of bound excitations, and the whole organism, constitute intensities.

Thus, Lyotard is committed to a new account of organic totalities as not only systems where an inner political economy is seated, but systems which have also their place in the libidinal economy. He is committed to detecting the organism itself in its libidinous use, an erotogenic zone, to detecting the discharge of libidinal intensities in its apparent functions and operations, the specific pleasure of libido in its very sufferings and lacks.

The negativist heritage in the thought of recent decades set out to show the constitution of an irremediable Absence in the auto-constitution of every spiritual, or intentional, system, set out, with Lacan, to exhibit the constitution of the Other that makes of an organism a desiring system, the opening up of the dimension of absence that makes a semiotic system possible, to thematize the differing-deferring behind the Ideal Presence that the Western metaphysical culture seems always to pursue, to exhibit the zone of ab-

solute nothingness which makes the ideal of absolute Being possible, the God that is dead or the death that is God. Lyotard means to consign the organism as a totality made wholly intentional by virtue of its teleological openness upon utter alterity, or alterity as such, to be part of the same metaphysics, the same religion or the same nihilism.

Where does the erotogenic zone start and where does it stop? Where do organisms start and where do they stop? For ultimately it is the same processes that take pleasure in constituting systems and organic totalities that are at work in thought, and in the organization of the body politic—at least that which, like that of the young Marx, depend on the idea of society as an organic totality. And the intensities of the primary process are excitations at the conjuncture of one's own surfaces with one another, of one's surfaces with those of another, of one's surfaces with those of the physical and social world. There is a libidinous economy at work in the very circulation of goods and services which constitute the political economy of capitalism. At every point of his book Lyotard follows the movements of the psyche writ large on the modern capitalist state. If his analyses are more than pure analyses, they are not so much also critical—where criticism would denounce the movements of the capitalist political economy in the name of a more rational, more coherent, finally more organic conception of the whole—as they are excited by certain events or happenings—the May '68 general strike in France, the Berkeley Free Speech movement, the Prague springtime—that belonged more to the order of events than of movements, to the order of potentials than to that of power, to the order of intensities rather than to that of actions, to that of uprisings rather than to that of revolutions, to the libidinal rather than the political economy.

THE PASSIONATE DEPERSONALIZATION

The libidinal relationship, according to Lyotard, is in no way an intersubjectivity, or even an intercorporeality. To become passionate is to become anonymous conductor of a circulation of libidinous effects, dismembered body where intensifications undergo their metamorphoses. "Make yourselves completely into conductors of heats and colds, bitternesses and sugarinesses, mutenesses and acutenesses, theorems and cries, let it travel over you, without ever knowing if it will work or not, if there will result an unheard-of, unseen, untasted, unthought-of, untested effect or not. And if in fact this passage does not add on a new piece to the beautiful and elusive libidinal patchwork, then, for example, weep, and your tears will be this fragment, since nothing is lost, and the most harsh deception can give place in turn to effects."[7]

This does not mean that Lyotard is ascribing to a sort of Spinozist or Nietzschean ethics, that his "lyse" involves some sort of valuation of the primary process over the secondary, of intensities over disintensifications, or potential over impotency, action over reaction. Eros and thanatos are undedicable, both in primary intensities and in the secondary organisms. His "lyse" finds meaning hidden in emotion, vertigo in reason itself. His discourse does not aim to be part of an ethics of the universal and of reactive force, as it does not aim to be part of an ethics of force, action, power, primary process over reactivity, secondary process fixations and reductions to inertia. It is not part of a project of organization and politics, as it is not part of a conspiracy of disorganization and anarchy. What there can be and is is a sort of *ars vitae* of which his own text would be an example: a patchwork or collage itself, traces of intensities that have passed. Traces and signs covering over punctual incandescences, there is a duplicity inherent in its composition. "In the 'theoretical order' one has to come to the point where one procedes that way, like this bar turning in duplicity, not out of concern for mimicry or *adaequatio,* but because thought is itself libidinous, and what counts is its force (its intensity), and that is what *has* to pass in the words, that interminable disquietude, that incandescent duplicity."[8]

Thus, the orgasmic will to become the pure conductor of libidinous intensities, although it is certainly a disinvestment of those channelling and excluding structures which are the ego, the person, the body as a closed volume, functional and expressive, as *corps propre* and organism, cannot be a will for a procedure of dismemberment, dictated by a theory of primary process libido. In fact the libidinal band is a labyrinth unchartable in advance, and the organism can itself be all incandescent. "One has to operate on the pricks, the vaginas, the assholes, the skins so as to make love be the condition for orgasm—that is what the lover, man or woman, dreams about, so as to escape the frightful duplicity of the surfaces traversed by impulses. But this operation would be an appropriation or, as Derrida says, a propriation, and finally a semiotics, in which the erections and discharges would infallibly signal impulsive movements. But there *must* not be such an infallibility—that is our ultimate and supreme recourse against the terror of power and the true. That fucking not be guaranteed in one way or another, neither as a proof of love nor as a gage of indifferent exchangability, that love, that is, intensity, slip in fortuitously, and that conversely intensities may withdraw from the skins of bodies (you didn't come?) and pass over upon the skins of words, sounds, colors, kitchen tastes, animal odors and perfumes, that is the dissimulation we will not escape, that's the anguish, and that is what we have to *want.* But this 'will' is itself something beyond the capabilities of any subjective freedom; we can meet this dissimulation only laterally, *neben,* as blind escapees, since it is unendurable and there is no question of making it lovable."[9]

Thus, we no longer have the idea of a *subject* of Eros structured as having, as being, an identity, seat of responsibility, agent of will and of power, lucid seer and foreseer. We have a libidinal band presenting itself as an anonymous and free conductor of intensities, polymorphous and feminine. What takes form in this band, partial organs produced by dismembering and deviation from their functioning in a whole self-maintaining organism, are personae,

masks behind which there is no personality or subjectivity or even causality. There is not *a libido* that would be behind all that, and that could be identified with the subject or the intentional arc that makes it exist. There are an indefinite multiplicity of singular intensities in those incandescences, those effects.

TOWARDS A METAPHYSICS WITHOUT NORMS

This theoretical formulation is in suspense; on the one hand, it is dependent on the findings yielded by the psychoanalytic techniques, which are external observations on processes essentially unconscious. (But it also importantly appeals to a certain literature—Artaud, Klossowski, Schreber, Augustine—which does not report on, but exhibits unconscious impulses.) On the other hand, it is provisional and awaits the universal theory, the metaphysics, which Lyotard would certainly rather call the universal materialism, which would be able to integrate it into the other regional sciences. Short of being able either to criticize the empirical data themselves which it intends to conceptualize—which would itself only be an empirical and not a conceptual task—or actually produce the universal categorial system—the philosopher's reaction is first to be struck with what this theory excludes, and which the other philosophical attempts to conceptualize the libidinous zone put forth.

Most obviously, the Lyotard concept of intensity excludes the intentional character phenomenology seen in sexual impulses. All phenomenology stands or falls on this issue. Undeniably the libidinal impulse is representational. For phenomenology this representational operation is not a production of "mental images," but a disclosure of being itself in the form of a phenomenon—object or objective. This Lyotard denies. The libidinous impulse does not "aim at" an entity in order to disclose it; it is not a verification of the world. And it is not a teleological movement. The phenomenological distinction between psychic and physical movements is entirely one of a distinction between a movement drawn to a telos and one produced by a cause. For Lyotard the libidinous effect is without aim as it is without cause. What would be required then is a positive theory of the libidinous phantasms. Lyotard criticizes the Klossowskian theory without really developing his own. The phantasm produced in libidinous impulses would have to be neither a true apparition of the beings themselves—would have to be false—nor an advance presentation of an objective—the libidinous impulses do not produce representations of either of their alleged objectives—the child for the race, the pleasure for the individual. They are obsessions with the impossible. The Lyotard metapsychology thus requires an epistemology of phantasms. It further requires—an enormously difficult task!—a theory that would stake out the production of true phenomena out of these false phantasms. That is, a passage from the pleasure principle to the reality principle. Unless one would want, like Nietzsche, to try to produce an artist metaphysics which has no place for the reality principle. . . .

We are not saying that such a metaphysics, which abandons the concept of *telos* and of true representation not only in the libidinal zone, but in all zones, is impossible or absurd. It was certainly the incredible project of Nietzsche. It is as a fragment of this stupendous effort that Lyotard's work belongs.

Notes

1. Paris: Les Editions de Minuit, 1974.

2. Transl. by Robert Hurley, Mark Seem and Helen R. Lane (New York: Viking, 1977).

3. Sigmund Freud, *Beyond the Pleasure Principle, Collected Works,* Vol. XVIII, transl. by James Strachey et al. (London: The Hogarth Press, 1955), p. 7.

4. *Ibid.,* p. 28.

5. Friedrich Nietzsche, *The Gay Science,* transl. by Walter Kaufmann (New York: Vintage, 1974), §337.

6. Sigmund Freud, *op. cit.,* p. 62.

7. Jean-François Lyotard, *op. cit.,* p. 307.

8. *Ibid.,* p. 42.

9. *Ibid.,* p. 304.

Seyla Benhabib (essay date 1984)

SOURCE: "Epistemologies of Postmodernism: A Rejoinder to Jean-François Lyotard," in *New German Critique,* No. 33, Fall, 1984, pp. 103-26.

[*In the following essay, Benhabib traces the history and development of Lyotard's philosophy of language, and argues that it tends to justify a retreat from critical social judgments.*]

In the recent, flourishing debate on the nature and significance of postmodernism, architecture appears to occupy a special place.[1] It is tempting to describe this situation through a Hegelianism: it is as if the *Zeitgeist* of an epoch approaching its end has reached self-consciousness in those monuments of modern architecture of steel, concrete, and glass. Contemplating itself in its objectifications, Spirit has not "recognized" and thus "returned to itself," but has recoiled in horror from its own products. The visible decay of our urban environment, the uncanniness of the modern megalopolis, and the general dehumanization of space appear to prove the Faustian dream to be a nightmare. The dream of an infinitely malleable world, serving as mere receptacle of the desires of an infinitely striving self, unfolding its powers in the process of conquering externality, is one from which we have awakened. Postmodernist architecture, whatever other sources it borrows its inspiration from, is undoubtedly the messenger of the end of this Faustian dream, which had accompanied the self-understanding of the moderns from the beginning.[2]

The end of the Faustian dream has brought with it a conceptual and semiotic shift in many domains of culture. This shift is not characterized by a moral or political critique of the Faustian aspects of modernity, but by the questioning of the very conceptual framework that made the Faustian dream possible in the first place. The following statement by Peter Eisenman, one of the key figures in the modernist/postmodernist constellation in architecture, captures the elements of this new critique quite precisely: "Architecture since the fifteenth century has been influenced by the assumption of a set of symbolic and referential functions. These can be collectively identified as the classical . . . 'Reason,' 'Representation' and 'History.' 'Reason' insists that objects be understood as rational transformations from a self-evident origin. 'Representation' demands that objects refer to values or images external to themselves . . . 'History' assumes that time is made up of isolatable historical moments whose essential characteristics can and should be abstracted and represented. If these classical assumptions are taken together as imperatives they force architecture to represent the spirit of its age through a rationally motivated and comprehensible sign system. . . . But if these 'imperatives' are simply 'fictions' then the classical can be suspended and options emerge which have been obscured by classical imperatives. . . ."[3]

Eisenman's statement describes rather accurately the conceptual self-understanding of postmodernism, not only in architecture, but in contemporary philosophy as well. In fact, if one were to substitute "philosophy" for "architecture" in the first paragraph of Eisenman's statement, it could serve as a pithy summary of Jean-François Lyotard's *The Postmodern Condition: A Report on Knowledge.*[4] For Lyotard as well the demise of the Faustian ideal signifies the end of the "grand narrative" of the moderns, and of the epistemology of representation on which it had been based. "I will use the term *modern* to designate any science that legitimates itself with reference to a metadiscourse of this kind making an explicit appeal to some grand narrative," writes Lyotard, "such as the dialectics of Spirit, the hermeneutics of meaning, the emancipation of the rational or working subject, or the creation of wealth" (xxiii). And like Eisenman, in the suspension of the classical, Lyotard sees the emergence of cognitive and social options which had been obscured by the "classical imperatives." He defines the new cognitive option variously as "paralogy" (60 ff.), "agonistics" (16), and "recognition of the heteromorphous nature of language games" (66). The new social option is described as a "temporary contract," supplanting permanent institutions in the professional, emotional, sexual, cultural, family, and international domains, as well as in political affairs (66).

Lyotard offers these cognitive and social options as alternatives that are authentic to the experience of post-industrial societies and to the role of knowledge within them. The hold of the classical episteme upon contemporary consciousness, however, tends to channel our cognitive as well as our practical imagination in two directions. In the first place, society is conceived of as a functional whole (11), and the condition of knowledge appropriate to it is judged as "performativity." Performativity is the view that knowledge is power, that modern science is to be legitimated through the increase in technological capacity, efficiency, control, and output it enables (47). The ideal of the theorists of performativity, from Hobbes to Luhmann, is to reduce the fragility intrinsic to the legitimation of power by minimizing risk, unpredictability, and complexity. Not only is knowledge power, but power generates access to knowledge, thus preparing for itself a self-perpetuating basis of legitimacy. "Power . . . legitimates science and the law on the basis of their efficiency, and legitimates this efficiency on the basis of science and law. . . . Thus the growth of power, and its self-legitimation, are now taking the route of data storage and accessibility, and the operativity of information" (47).

The second alternative is to view society as divided into two, as an alienated, bifurcated totality, in need of reunification. The corresponding epistemic vision is "critical" as opposed to "functional" knowledge. Critical knowledge is in the service of the subject; its goal is not the legitimation of power but the enabling of empowerment (12 ff.). It seeks not to enhance the efficiency of the apparatus but to further the self-formation of humanity; not to reduce complexity but to create a world in which a reconciled humanity recognizes itself. For Lyotard the contemporary representative of this 19th-century ideal, born out of the imagination of a German thinker, Wilhelm von Humboldt, is Jürgen Habermas (32). Had it been von Humboldt's ideal to have philosophy restore unity to learning via the development of a language game linking all the sciences together as moments in the becoming of Spirit (33), it is Habermas' purpose to formulate a meta-discourse which is "universally valid for language games" (65). The goal of such discourse is not so much the *Bildung* of the German nation, as it had been for von Humboldt, but the attainment of consensus, transparency, and reconciliation. Lyotard comments: "The cause is good, but the argument is not. Consensus has become an outmoded and suspect value. . . . We must . . . arrive at an idea and practice of justice that is not linked to that of consensus" (66).

Can Lyotard convince? Is his project to formulate the outlines of a postmodern episteme, beyond the dualism of functional and critical knowledge, beyond instrumental reason and critical theory, viable? What are the epistemological options opened by the demise of the classical episteme of representation?

THE CRISIS OF THE REPRESENTATIONAL EPISTEME

Modern Philosophy began with the loss of the world.[5] The decision of the autonomous bourgeois subject to take nothing and no authority for granted, whose content and strictures had not been subjected to rigorous examination, and that had not withstood the test of "clarity and distinctness," began with a withdrawal from the world. It was still possible for Descartes in the 17th century to describe this withdrawal in the language of Stoicism and Spanish Jesuit

philosophy as an ethical and religious gesture, either as a "suspension" of the involvement of the self with the world (Stoicism) or as the withdrawal of the soul to a communion with itself (Jesuit teaching of meditation). These were stages on the road to an equilibrium with the cosmos, or necessary for the purging of the soul in preparation for the truth of God. The future development of modern epistemology succeeded in repressing this ethical and cultural moment to the point where the typical reductions on which the classical episteme of representation rested could emerge. The corporeal, ethico-moral self was reduced to a pure subject of knowledge, to consciousness or to mind. The object of knowledge was reduced to "matters of fact" and "relations of ideas," or to "sensations" and "concepts." The question of classical epistemology from Descartes to Hume, from Locke to Kant was how to make congruous the order of representations in consciousness with the order of representations outside the self. Caught in the prison-house of its own consciousness, the modern epistemological subject tried to recover the world it had well lost.[6] The options were not many: either one reassured oneself that the world would be gained by the direct and immediate evidence of the senses (empiricism) or one insisted that the rationality of the creator or the harmony of mind and nature would guarantee the correspondence between the two orders of representations (rationalism).

Whether empiricist or rationalist, modern epistemologists agreed that the task of knowledge, whatever its origins, was to build an adequate representation of things. In knowledge, mind had to "mirror" nature.[7] As Charles Taylor points out, "When we hold that having X is having a (correct) representation of X, one of the things we establish is the neat separation of ideas, thoughts, descriptions and the like, on the one hand, and what these ideas, etc. are about on the other."[8] Actually modern epistemology operated with a threefold distinction: the order of representations in our consciousness (ideas or sensations); the signs through which these "private" orders were made public, namely words, and that of which our representations were representations, and to which they referred.[9] In this tradition, meaning was defined as "designation"; the meaning of a word was what it designates, while the primary function of language was denotative, namely to inform us about objectively existing states of affairs. The classical episteme of representation presupposed a spectator conception of the knowing self, a designative theory of meaning, and a denotative theory of language.

Already in the last century three directions of critique of the classical episteme, leading to its eventual rejection, formed themselves. Stylizing somewhat, the first can be described as the critique of the modern epistemic subject, the second as the critique of the modern epistemic object, and the third as the critique of the modern concept of the sign.

The critique of the Cartesian, spectator conception of the subject begins with German Idealism, and continues with Marx and Freud to Horkheimer in 1937, and to Habermas in *Knowledge and Human Interests.*[10] This tradition substitutes for the spectator model of the self the view of an active, producing, fabricating humanity, creating the conditions of objectivity confronting it through its own historical activity. The Hegelian and Marxist tradition also shows that the Cartesian ego is not a self-transparent entity that the epistemic self cannot reach full autonomy as long as the historical origin and social constitution of the "clear and distinct" ideas it contemplates remain a mystery. Here this critique joins hands with the Freudian one which likewise shows that the self is not "transparent" to itself, for it is not "master in its own house" (Herr im eigenen Haus). It is controlled by desires, needs, and forces whose effects upon it shape both the contents of its clear and distinct ideas, as well as its capacity to organize them. The historical and psychoanalytic critique of the Cartesian ego sees the task of reflection neither as the withdrawal from the world nor as access to clarity and distinctness, but as the rendering conscious of those unconscious forces of history, society and the psyche. Although generated by the subject, these necessarily escape its memory, control, and conduct. The goal of reflection is emancipation from self-incurred bondage.

The second line of criticism can be most closely associated with the names of Nietzsche, Heidegger, and Adorno and Horkheimer in *Dialectic of Enlightenment.* The modern episteme is viewed as an episteme of domination. For Nietzsche modern science universalizes Cartesian doubt. Modern knowledge divides the world into the realm of appearance on the one hand, and that of essence or things-in-themselves on the other.[11] This dualistic vision is internalized by the subject of knowledge who in turn is split into body and mind, the senses and the conceptual faculty. Nietzsche has no difficulty in showing that in this sense modern science signifies the triumph of Platonism. Heidegger drives the error underlying the modern episteme of representation further back than its Platonic origins, to a conception of being as presence, as what is available and present to the consciousness of the subject.[12] This conception of being as presence-to reduces the manyness of the appearances by making them available to a sovereign consciousness. By reducing appearances to what is present to it, this consciousness attains the option of controlling them. In a spirit that is quite akin to Heidegger's, in the *Dialectic of Enlightenment* Adorno and Horkheimer argue that it is the "concept," the very unit of thought in the Western tradition that imposes homogeneity and identity upon the heterogeneity of material. This drive for identity of conceptual thought culminates in the technical triumph of Western ratio, which can only know things in that it comes to dominate them. "The Enlightenment relates to things as the dictator to humans."[13]

The third tradition of criticism is initiated by Ferdinand de Saussure and Charles Sanders Peirce, and given sharper contours by Frege and Wittgenstein in our century. They argue that it is impossible to make sense of meaning, reference, and language in general when the view of linguistic signs as "private marks"[14] prevails. Instead, the public and shared character of language is a beginning point. Both de Saussure and Peirce point out that there is no *natural* relation between a sound, the word it represents in a language, and the content it refers to. For Peirce, the relation of the sign, of which words are but one species, to the signified is mediated by the interpretant.[15] For de Saussure, it is within a system of differential relations that certain sounds get arbitrarily frozen to stand for words.[16] Language is that sedimented set of relations which stands ideally behind the set of enunciations, called "parole." This move in the analysis of language from the private to the public, from consciousness to sign, from the individual word to a system of relations among linguistic signs, is followed by Frege and Wittgenstein, insofar as they too argue that the unit of reference is not the word but the sentence (Frege), and that meaning can only be understood by analyzing the multiple contexts of use (Wittgenstein).

The epistemological juncture at which Lyotard operates is characterized by the triumph of this third tradition. Whether in analytic philosophy, or in contemporary hermeneutics, or in French poststructuralism, the paradigm of language has replaced the paradigm of consciousness. This shift has meant that the focus is no longer on the epistemic subject and the private contents of its consciousness but on the public, signifying activities of a collection of subjects. Not only has there been a shift in the size of the interrogated epistemic unit from idea, sensation, and concept to the threefold character of the sign as signifier, signified, and interpretant (Peirce), to language and parole (Saussure) or to language games as "forms of life" (Wittgenstein). The identity of the epistemic subject has changed as well: the bearer of the sign cannot be an isolated self—there is no private language, as Wittgenstein has observed; either it is a community of selves whose identity extends as far as their horizon of interpretations (Gadamer) or it is a social community of actual language users (Wittgenstein). This enlargement of the relevant epistemic subject is one option. A second option, followed by French structuralism, is to deny that in order to make sense of the epistemic object, one need appeal to an epistemic subject at all. The subject is replaced by a system of structures, oppositions, and *différances* which, to be intelligible, need not be viewed as products of a living subjectivity at all.[17]

Lyotard wants to convince that the destruction of the episteme of representation allows only one option, namely, a recognition of the irreconcilability and incommensurability of language games, and the acceptance that only local and context-specific criteria of validity can be formulated. One must accept, in other words, an "agonistics" of language: ". . . to speak is to fight, in the sense of playing, and speech-acts fall within the domain of a general agonistics" (10). This cognitive option yields a "polytheism of values," and a politics of justice beyond consensus, characterized by Lyotard vaguely as the "temporary contract."

The shift in contemporary philosophy from consciousness to language, from the order of representations to that of speech-acts, from denotation to performance need not lead to a "polytheism" of values, and ultimately to Wittgenstein's dictum that "philosophy leaves everything as it is."[18] In order to see that the decline of the episteme of representation allows another alternative besides Lyotard's polytheism and agonistics of language, it is necessary to examine the self-contradictoriness of Lyotard's program more carefully. Lyotard wants to deny the choice between instrumental and critical reason, between performativity and emancipation. But his agonistic philosophy either leads to a "polytheism of values," from which standpoint the principle of performativity or of emancipation cannot be criticized, or this philosophy does not remain wholly polytheistic but privileges one domain of discourse and knowledge over others as a hidden criterion. The choice is still between an uncritical polytheism and a self-conscious recognition of the need for criteria of validity, and the attempt to reflexively ground them. Lyotard cannot escape the Scylla of uncritical polytheism nor the Charybdis of criteriological dogmatism.

TRUTH: THE FUTURE OF AN ILLUSION?

The differences between Lyotard's "agonistics" of language and the program of "universal" or "transcendental pragmatics," formulated by Apel and Habermas, serve as a good beginning point in developing this dilemma.[19] Insofar as both Lyotard's agonistics and the program of pragmatics reject the denotative function of language, they signal a turn to its performative aspects. This turn is accompanied by a redefinition of knowledge as argumentative, discursive practice. Whereas Habermas distinguishes between the "know-how" embedded in the pre-theoretical lifeworld, the implicit rules of communicative competence which guide each competent speaker of a language, Lyotard emphasizes the "narrativity" of a mode of knowledge repressed and marginalized by science. He defines this as a "know-how, knowing how to live, how to listen" (savoir-faire, savoir-vivre, savoir-écouter; 19). For Habermas discursive knowledge is *continuous* with everyday communicative practices; already everyday communication functions as its own reflexive medium through acts of interrogation, disagreement, questioning, and puzzling. In discourses we do not enter a Platonic heaven of ideas, but we "bracket" certain constraints of space and time, suspend belief in the truth of propositions, in the rightness of norms, and the truthfulness of our partners, and examine everyday convictions in which we have lost belief. For Lyotard, by contrast, "discourse" and "narrative knowledge" are radically discontinuous. Narrative knowledge appears to be in need of no legitimation. Lyotard describes the pragmatics of narrative knowledge such that it eo ipso seems to preclude the kind of questioning, puzzling, and disagreement which everyday communicative practices in fact always already allow (27).

Although Lyotard describes his philosophy of language as "pragmatics" as well—albeit an agonistic one—"rhetorics" would be a more adequate characterization of the view he develops. Both pragmatics and rhetorics emphasize the performative as opposed to denotative uses of language,

and both take as unit of analysis not the proposition but the speech-act. The pragmatic theory of speech-acts maintains that every act of communication is directed toward certain "validity claims" (Geltungsansprüche). Validity claims can be formulated with respect to the truth of statements, the rightness of norms, and the truthfulness of speaking subjects.[20] By contrast, the rhetorics of language Lyotard espouses does not distinguish between *raising a validity claim* and *forcing* someone to believe in something, between the coordination of action among participants on the basis of conviction generated through agreement, and the manipulative influencing of the behavior of others. Lyotard misses the boat when he accuses Habermas of reducing all language games to the meta-game of truth. In the theory of universal pragmatics truth-claims are one among two other validity claims, namely rightness and truthfulness, and are not privileged in any way.[21] The issue then is not whether Habermas privileges the meta-game of truth, but which view of language is more adequate: one that sees language as a *cognitive* medium through which norms of action coordination, patterns of interpretation of cultures, and frameworks for the exploration of our needs and desires are generated,[22] or a view that regards language as an *evocative* medium, in which validity and force, reasoned belief and manipulated opinion, can no longer be distinguished. Is this a fair charge against Lyotard? Let us look more closely. A long passage in which Lyotard explains his pragmatics of language is revealing in this regard: "A denotative utterance such as 'The university is sick,' made in the context of a conversation or an interview, positions its sender (the person who utters the statement), its addressee (the person who receives it), and its referent (what the statement deals with) in a specific way: the utterance places (and exposes) the sender in the position of 'knower' . . . (If we consider a declaration such as 'The university is open,' pronounced by a dean or rector at convocation, it is clear that the previous specifications no longer apply. . . . The distinctive feature of this second, 'performative' utterance is that *its effect upon the recipient coincided with its enunciation*. . . . That this is so is not subject to discussion or verification on the part of the addressee, who is immediately placed within the new context created by the utterance. As for the sender, he must be invested with the authority to make such a statement. Actually, we could say it the other way around: the sender is dean or rector—that is, *he is invested with the authority to make this kind of statement—only insofar as he can directly affect both the referent (the university) and the addressee (the university staff) in the manner I have indicated*" (9. My emphasis).

This lengthy passage in which Lyotard explicates the pragmatic dimension of language-games betrays that he no longer distinguishes between power and validity. The "sender" is defined as the one invested with the "authority" to make a certain kind of statement, but then this authority is said to be invested in him "only insofar as he can affect both the referent . . . and the addressee." But surely the *investment* of authority in someone or in an institution and the *effective exercise* of this authority are two different things. The first is a matter of *validity,* the second a matter of *power.* Just as the one invested with authority may not be effective in exercising it, there may be others effective in exercising authority but not invested with the right to exercise it. Lyotard seems to imply that only the one who effectively exercises authority is also invested with the title to it. If this is so, however, all authority would be charismatic, dependent, that is, upon the individual qualities and characteristics of a special individual, and not liable to justification through procedure, rules, and grounds. Power and validity, might and right would then be indistinguishable.

Lyotard writes: ". . . the utterance places (and exposes) the sender in the position of the 'knower' . . . the addressee is put in the position of having to give or refuse his assent . . ." (9). The difference between universal and transcendental pragmatics and Lyotard's agonistics turns around the question as to how this "giving" or "refusing" of assent is to be understood. Lyotard regards this to be a consequence of a language-game with many moves, and does not specify the process whereby assent is generated or refusal obtained. But surely there is a distinction between agreeing and giving in; consenting and being persuaded to do so; presenting reasons to convince and blackmailing; refusing and being obstinate. Lyotard actually does not eliminate these distinctions altogether, for he writes, "to speak is to fight, in the sense of playing, and speech acts fall within the domain of a general agonistics. *This does not necessarily mean that one plays in order to win*" (10. My emphasis). The question is, why not? Why isn't language simply a sphere through which the universal power-game is carried on? Why isn't all conversation seduction? all consensus conquest? all agreement the result of a delusion, of a "narcissisme à deux," as Lacan would have it?[23] Despite a certain ambivalence, Lyotard cannot escape these conclusions.

The line between truth and deception, consensus and coercion disappears in Lyotard's agonistics, for, to speak with J.L. Austin, Lyotard cannot differentiate between illocutionary and perlocutionary speech-acts. According to Austin, "the illocutionary act . . . has a certain *force* in saying something; the perlocutionary act . . . is the *achieving of* certain *effects* by saying something"[24] (my emphasis). For example, *in* saying I would shoot someone, I threaten them (illocutionary act); *by* saying I would shoot them, I alarm them (perlocutionary). The consequences attained by an illocutionary act can be stated at the beginning of a statement in the form of an *explicit* intention, "I threatened to shoot him"; in the case of a perlocutionary statement, however, the speaker can only attain the desired effect as long as his or her intentions are not explicitly made part of the speech-act.[25] If it is my goal to alarm someone, I do not begin a statement by saying "I want to alarm you that . . .". In this case my act would be illocutionary, and intended with the purpose of apprehending you about a certain state of affairs. This in turn leaves open the possibility that you may assent or refuse to respond in the way I desire you to. In perlocutionary acts, however, the speaker

wants to generate a certain effect upon the hearer *regardless* of the assent or dissent of the latter. In fact, it is necessary to achieve certain effects that the intentions of the speaker not be revealed. For Lyotard the primary use of speech is perlocutionary. The use of speech to affect and influence the hearer, for whatever purposes, is the paradigm. But then the agonistics of language can no longer distinguish between manipulative and non-manipulative uses of speech. The consequence of this position is that not truth alone, but all claims to validity are at best pious wishes, at worst illusions fabricated to deceive.

It is not difficult to show that any theory which denies the claims to truth, and the possibility of distinguishing between it and sheer manipulative rhetoric would be involved in a "performative self-contradiction."[26] This may not be terribly difficult, but it does not settle the issue either. For, from Nietzsche's aphorisms, to Heidegger's poetics, to Adorno's stylistic configurations, and to Derrida's deconstructions, we have examples of thinkers who accept this performative self-contradiction, and who self-consciously draw the consequences from it by seeking a new way of writing and communicating. That, following this tradition, Lyotard has not experimented with style in *The Postmodern Condition* may be more the result of accident than of conceptual consistency. We must seek to approach Lyotard's presuppositions through yet another route.

SCIENCE: THE SAME OLD DREAM

In a recent article on "Habermas and Lyotard on Postmodernity," Richard Rorty has described the impasse between Habermas and Lyotard as follows: "To put the opposition in another way, the French writers whom Habermas criticizes are willing to drop the opposition between 'true consensus' and 'false consensus,' or between 'validity' and 'power,' in order not to have to tell a metanarrative in order to explicate 'true' or 'valid.' But Habermas thinks that if we do drop the idea of the 'better argument' . . . we shall have only a 'context-dependent' sort of social criticism."[27] Rorty observes that Lyotard would respond to Habermas' claim that even the sciences are propelled beyond themselves towards self-reflection, by responding that "Habermas misunderstands the character of modern science."[28] Indeed, Lyotard's discussion of postmodern science is intended to accomplish a most peculiar function. This is also the point at which we see that Lyotard avoids the performative self-contradiction of stylistic self-deconstruction à la Derrida, by falling into dogmatism, i.e., by privileging a knowledge-practice above others to serve as their criterion, while failing to justify this explicitly.

Drawing from such diverse sources as Gödel's metamathematical research, quantum mechanics, microphysics, and catastrophe theories, in an obscure discussion, Lyotard attempts to show that the pragmatics of postmodern scientific knowledge has little to do with performativity or instrumental criteria (54).[29]

Lyotard writes: "Postmodern science . . . is theorizing its own evolution as discontinuous, catastrophic, nonrectifiable, and paradoxical. *It is changing the meaning of the word knowledge, while expressing how such a change can take place.* It is provoking not the known, but the unknown" (60. My emphasis). This epistemic privileging of mathematical and natural science is problematical. It avoids a series of questions which any serious epistemological theory would have to face. The distinction between the natural, social and human sciences (Geisteswissenschaften) is completely ignored. It remains to be shown that problems of concept formation, formulation of law-like generalities, procedures of verification, the interaction between pre-theoretical and theoretical cognition in the social and human sciences can be illuminated by the model of postmodern knowledge Lyotard proposes.[30] The privileging of developments in mathematical and natural science does not break with the tradition of modern sciences which simply ignores the knowledge claims and problems of the human and social sciences.

More significant is the question "What is the relationship between the antimodel of pragmatics of science, and society? Is it applicable to the vast clouds of language material constituting a society? . . . Is it an impossible ideal of an open community?" (64). Lyotard's answer to this question is incoherent. On the one hand he admits that social and scientific pragmatics are different, for social pragmatics is not as simple as scientific pragmatics, "but is a monster formed by the interweaving of heteromorphous classes of utterances" (65). On the other hand, the postmodern epistemology of science is said to approach the practice of narrativity (le petit récit). In other words, either Lyotard privileges natural and mathematical science, thus falling into traditional scientistic dogmatism, or there is a criterion of knowledge, transcending modern natural science, and with reference to which science itself is legitimized, and which, in turn, needs to be defended. It would appear that narrative knowledge is such a criterion.

Indeed, Rorty as well interprets Lyotard as wanting to diminish the distance between scientific and narrative knowledge.[31] In Lyotard's construction of narrativity, Rotry discovers affinities with his own contextual-pragmatism. Closing fronts with Lyotard, he writes that "the trouble with Habermas is not so much that he provides a metanarrative of emancipation as that he feels the need to legitimize, that he is not content to let the narratives which hold our culture together do their stuff. He is scratching where it does not itch."[32] Rorty's argument is revealing for two reasons: first, it indicates that epistemological questions flow into assessments of culture and society. Whether "the narratives which hold our culture together do their stuff" is an empirical question. Likewise, whether critical theory "scratches where it does not itch" depends upon our understanding of the problems, struggles, crises, conflicts and miseries of the present. Epistemological issues are indeed closely linked with moral and political ones.

In the second place, we must note that Lyotard himself is not as sanguine as Rorty about the vitality and continuing role of narrative in modern society and culture. Narrative knowledge, far from being an alternative to the modern scientific one, is sometimes described as if it were "premodern" knowledge, a historically lost mode of thought.[33] Yet, narrative knowledge is also viewed as the "other" of discursive knowledge—not its past historical but its contemporaneous other. Narrative knowledge, to use a phrase of Bloch's, is the "non-contemporaneous contemporary" of discursive knowledge. The scientist "classifies them as belonging to a different mentality: savage, primitive, underdeveloped, backward, alienated, composed of opinions, customs, authority, prejudice, ignorance, ideology. Narratives are fables, myths, legends, fit only for women and children" (27). Is the meaning of Lyotard's postmodernist epistemology then a gesture of solidarity with the oppressed? A gesture toward the recognition of the otherness of the other? This may seem so, but Lyotard constructs the epistemology of narrative knowledge in such a way that it can no longer challenge scientific knowledge, let alone provide a criterion transcending it. Narrative knowledge belongs to the ethnological museum of the past.

"Narrative knowledge," writes Lyotard, "does not give priority to the question of its own legitimation in that it certifies itself in the pragmatics of its own transmission without having recourse to argumentation and proof" (27). This global characterization of narrative knowledge as pre-reflexive, as a self-sustaining whole, flattens the internal contradictions and tensions which affect narrative no less than discursive practices.[34] It also implies that all change in this episteme must come from without, through violence. Such an episteme has no self-propelling or self-correcting mechanism. But, in fact, this is to condemn the subjects of this episteme to ahistoricity, to deny that they inhabit the same space with us. We do not interact with them as equals, we inhabit a space in which we observe them as ethnologists and anthropologists, we treat them with distance and indifference. But if this is not so, if indeed narrative knowledge is the "other" of *our* mode of knowledge, then Lyotard must admit that narrative and scientific knowledge are not merely incommensurable, but that they can and do clash, and that sometimes the outcome is less than certain.[35] To admit this possibility would amount to the admission that "narrative" and "discursive" practices occupy the same epistemic space, and that both raise claims to validity, and that an argumentative exchange between them is not only possible but desirable. You cannot respect the "otherness" of the other, if you deny the other the right to enter into a conversation with you, if you do not discard the objective indifference of an ethnologist, and engage with the other as an equal. Instead of reckoning with this dilemma of recognition and distance, acceptance and tolerance, Lyotard agrees with Wittgenstein that philosophy must leave everything as is. "It is therefore impossible to judge the existence or validity of narrative knowledge on the basis of scientific knowledge and vice versa: the relevant criteria are different. All we can do is gaze in wonderment at the diversity of discursive species, just as we do at the diversity of plant or animal species. Lamenting the 'loss of meaning' in postmodernity boils down to mourning the fact that knowledge is no longer principally narrative. Such a reaction does not necessarily follow. Neither does an attempt to derive or engender (using operators like development) scientific knowledge from narrative knowledge, as if the former contained the latter in an embryonic state" (26-27). If we cannot lament the passing away of narrative knowledge, nor indicate a possible line of transition from one knowledge type to another, then in fact narrative knowledge possesses no epistemic priority to scientific knowledge. Equipped with "undecidables, 'fracta,' catastrophes and pragmatic paradoxes," we can face the brave, new world of postmodernity.

Thus in the final analysis, Lyotard avoids performative self-contradiction, or simply incoherence, by privileging one practice of knowledge to serve as a criterion over others. This criterion is provided by the model of a discontinuous, fractured, and self-destabilizing epistemology, said to characterize modern mathematical and natural science. We may have woken from the Faustian dream but not from the scientistic one!

Let us return once more to the question, what are the options opened in the present by the demise of the episteme of representation?

The Politics of Postmodernism

As Fredric Jameson has remarked, "The problem of postmodernism . . . is at one and the same time an aesthetic and a political one. The various positions which can logically be taken on it, whatever terms they are couched in, can always be shown to articulate visions of history, in which the evaluation of the social moment in which we live today is the object of an essentially political affirmation or repudiation."[36] Jean-François Lyotard's political trajectory led him from the *Socialisme ou Barbarie* group to a farewell to Marx and Freud, and to the embracing of Nietzsche in **Economie Libidinale** (1974). Casting aside the mask of the social critic, as simply a disguise for clerical and Christian values, Lyotard put on "the mask of paganism, polytheism."[37] "So you would challenge Spinozist or Nietzschean ethics, which separates the movements of being-more and those of being-less, of action and reaction?—Yes, but let us be aware of an entire morality and an entire politics, with their sages, militants, courts and jails, taking advantage of these dichotomies to appear again . . . We do not speak as liberators of desire."[38]

Lyotard writes as a disillusioned Marxist, as one who has discovered that the grand metanarrative of history leads to an "entire morality and an entire politics." Lyotard prefers the Spinozist or Nietzschean conatus of being, the drive of the will to preserve itself, to the Republic of Virtue and Terror. In fact, for Lyotard this choice between a polytheism of desire and a republic of terror appears so compelling that no one who has ever spoken in the name of Humanity, History, Emancipation, and Unity can escape its curse. Terror did not begin with the citizens' committees

of the French Revolution, nor with the banning of the Mensheviks and Social Revolutionaries from the revolutionary Dumas. No, it is not Pol-Pot or Stalin, but Kant and Hegel who lie at its origin. This total loss of historical perspective in the rhetoric of disillusionment leads Lyotard to finish his essay **"What is Postmodernism?"** on the following note: "Finally, it must be clear that it is our business not to supply reality but to invent allusions to the conceivable which cannot be presented. And it is not to be expected that this task will effect the last reconciliation between language games . . . and that only the transcendental illusion (that of Hegel) can hope to totalize them into a real unity. But Kant also knew that the price to pay for such an illusion is terror. The nineteenth and twentieth centuries have given us as much terror as we can take. We have paid a high enough price for the nostalgia of the whole and the one, for the reconciliation of the concept and the sensible, of the transparent and communicable experience. Under the general demand for slackening and for appeasement, we can hear the mutterings of the desire for a return of terror, for the realization of the fantasy to seize reality. The answer is: Let us wage a war on totality; let us witness to the unpresentable, let us activate the differences and save the honor of the name" (82). Surely Lyotard knows that under the heading of "Absolute Freedom and Terror," Hegel in chapter six of the *Phenomenology* provided one of the most brilliant discussions of terror in the history of modern political thought.[39] Surely, he also knows (or should know) that Habermas and Wellmer, whom he accuses of propagating a "nostalgia for the whole and the one," are not German neo-Romantics, but thinkers who have insisted upon the need to revitalize whatever fragile tradition of participatory, civillibertarian democratic resources the Federal German Republic possesses. Why then this misunderstanding? What is at stake?

As with the crisis of the representational episteme, the demise of the metanarrative of traditional Marxism suggests diverse possibilities, among which the return to Nietzsche and Spinoza is one among many, and not the most compelling one. Whereas the demise of the episteme of representation initiated a shift from the philosophy of consciousness to the philosophy of language, from denotation to performance, from the proposition to the speech-act, the demise of the metanarrative of traditional Marxism opens the possibility of a post-Marxist radical, democratic politics. The issue is whether the conceptual polytheism and agonistics proposed by Lyotard aids in this project, or whether indeed under the guise of postmodernism, a "young conservatism"[40] is not establishing itself among the avant-garde of the 1980s.

Lyotard's project is ambivalent. His defense of the morally uncompromising gesture of the aesthetic avant-garde, his insistence upon the spirit of innovation, experimentation, play, and his call "to activate differences and save the honor of the name" (82), could be constituents of a post-Marxist radical, democratic politics. Indeed, **The Postmodern Condition** intends to sketch "the outline of a politics that would respect both the desire for justice and the desire for the unknown" (67). Yet insisting upon the incommensurability of language games, in the name of polytheism, may generate moral and political indifference; the call for innovation, experimentation and play may be completely dissociated from social reform and institutional practice, and the activation of differences may not amount to a democratic respect of the right of the "other" to be, but to a conservative plea to place the other, because of her otherness, outside the pale of our common humanity and mutual responsibility.

The moral debate between Lyotard and the tradition of critical theory concerns the nature of the *minimum cognitive and moral commitments* necessary to keep the fronts clear between a post-Marxist radical, democratic politics and a postmodernist, young conservatism. Critical social theory at the present defines these cognitive and moral criteria as the defense of a communicative, discursive concept of reason; the acceptance that knowledge should serve moral autonomy, and the recognition that intentions of the good life cannot be dissociated from the discursive practice of seeking understanding (Verständigung) among equals in a process of communication free from domination. Admittedly, whether a non-foundationalist justification of these commitments, which also avoids the metanarratives which Lyotard so effectively dismantles, is possible, needs to be investigated. This is surely Lyotard's challenge to the program of a critical social theory at the present. Only Lyotard's agonistic theory of language and paralogistic theory of legitimation cannot serve as a basis for a post-Marxian radical, democratic politics. The political alternatives that follow from Lyotard's epistemology are twofold: the first is a vaguely defined neo-liberal pluralism; the second, a contextual pragmatism.

Lyotard ends his essay on the postmodern condition with a plea to "give the public free access to memory and data banks" (67). This is justified on the grounds that it would prevent the total computerization of society, and supply groups "discussing metaprescriptives" with the information they need to make knowledgeable decisions. "Language games would then be games of perfect information at any moment. But they would also be non-zero sum games" (67). Despite Lyotard's caveat that his task is not to supply reality with models but "to invent allusions to the conceivable which cannot be presented" (81), the reader might well want to know who these groups discussing "metaprescriptives" are. Are they social movements, citizens' groups, institutions, interest groups or lobbies? How far would the demand "to give the public free access to memory and data banks" go? Can IBM or any other multinational corporation democratize its trade secrets and technical information? Is the military likely to democratize its procedures of acquiring, processing, and storing information? It is not incumbent upon Lyotard to provide a "blue-print" of the society of the future, but this image of a society with free access to data banks on the part of competing groups whose identity remains unclear, is hardly "the outline of a politics that would respect both the desire for justice and the desire for the unknown." Lyotard ends

up with a neo-liberal interest group pluralism plus the democratization of computers.[41]

Surely there is much in the traditional liberal conception of pluralism, tolerance, and the public competition of ideals that would need be incorporated into a post-Marxist radical, democratic politics. Yet the difficulty with political liberalism, old and new, is the neglect of the *structural* sources of inequality, influence, resource, and power among competing groups. In the absence of radical, democratic measures redressing economic, social, and cultural inequalities and forms of subordination, the pluralistic vision of groups Lyotard proposes remains naive. It would fail to redress the plight of those for whom the question of the democratization of information is a luxury, simply because, as marginalized groups in our societies, they fail even to have access to organizational let alone informational resources. At the present, these groups include increasing numbers of women, minorities, foreigners, unemployed youth, and the elderly.

Lyotard's neo-liberal interest group pluralism is naive in yet another way. The assumption that language games would be games of perfect information, suggests that language games do not compete, struggle with, or contradict one another, not in the sense of jousting in a tournament, but in the actual sense of struggling to delegitimize, overpower, and silence the language game of the other. To take a concrete example: surely Lyotard cannot maintain that the current attempt of conservative, pro-life groups to establish a "new reverence for life and creation," to deny the moral legitimacy of abortion, to even ask science to provide exact criteria as to when the fetus becomes a person, are "narratives" in our culture that point to a happy polytheism of language games. The polytheism of language games either assumes that culture and society are harmonious wholes, or that the struggles within them are plays only. But there are times when philosophy cannot afford to be a "gay science," for reality itself becomes deadly serious. To deny that the play of language games may not turn into a matter of life and death, and that the intellectual cannot remain the priest of many gods but must take a stance, is cynical.

The second political gesture which follows from Lyotard's agonistics of language games was described as "contextual-pragmatist." Actually, it is Richard Rorty who articulates this position most clearly. His view, however, is a perfectly logical consequence of Lyotard's claim that "narratives . . . thus define what has the right to be said and done in the culture in question, and since they are themselves a part of that culture, they are legitimated by the simple fact that they do what they do" (23). Rorty agrees with Lyotard that Habermas' difficulty is that "he scratches where it does not itch."[42] This means that neither our culture nor our societies need justification or criticism, adoration or reprimand. We have to satisfy ourselves with context-immanent criteria that the political practices of Western democracies provide us with.[43] Rorty further advocates the development of a "de-theoreticized sense of community," the growth of an "analogue of civil virtue—tolerance, irony, and a willingness to let spheres of culture flourish without worrying too much about their 'common ground,' their unification. . . ."[44] This admirable demand, to use an expression of another decade, "to let hundred flowers bloom," is motivated by a desire to depoliticize philosophy. "Then one might see," writes Rorty, "the canonical sequence of philosophers from Descartes to Nietzsche as a distraction from the history of concrete social engineering which made the North Atlantic culture what it is now, with all its glories and all its dangers."[45]

Perhaps one should admire the honesty of one of the leading philosophers of the Anglo-American culture in this sad avowal of the marginality to which the "glorious North Atlantic culture" reduces philosophical thought. Yet, Rorty's statement is sad in another way. It reveals the internalization by an intellectual of the distrust and disparagement of intellectuals, accompanying the modern temperament from Edmund Burke to Norman Podhoretz. In fact, it reveals the internalization of the charge that were it not for the "Weltschmerz" of a few "pessimistic and too exclusively German individuals"[46] and those influenced by them, we would not have an adversary culture in this country. Isn't there indeed a curious convergence between postmodernism and "young conservatism"?

Thus, the agonistics of language games leads to its own paralogisms. On the one hand, there is Lyotard's faith in the aesthetic avant-garde intellectuals as messengers of the "sublime," and harbingers of the way to the "unknown"; on the other hand, there is Rorty's advice to abandon the "illusion of the intellectuals as a revolutionary vanguard,"[47] and to return to a strange synthesis of Deweyian pragmatism and British conservatism.

Hence, the frustrating eclecticism of postmodernism in philosophy and elsewhere. Just as the postmodern architects of the "Chicago Seven" can cite classical, oriental and Renaissance themes and details, all in one breath, in their plans for Chicago town-houses,[48] contemporary philosophy, dazzled by the dissolution of the episteme of representation, is anxious to cite American pragmatism, French Nietzscheanism, British conservatism, and Heideggerian wisdom all in one breath. It is likely that we will have to live with this polytheism, and dazzling "play of surfaces," as Jameson has named them, for some time to come. Nor is it unwelcome that the frozen fronts of philosophy are becoming so fluid again. Only it is necessary that we think the epistemic alternatives created by the present also to their moral and political ends. For questions of truth, as Lyotard admits and Rorty denies, are still matters of justice as well.

The paradigm shift in contemporary philosophy from consciousness to language, from the denotative to the performative, from the proposition to the speech-act, need not lead to a self-contradictory polytheism and to a vision of politics incapable of justifying its own commitment to justice. This paradigm shift can also lead to an epistemology

and politics which recognizes the lack of metanarratives and foundational guarantees, but which nonetheless insists on formulating minimal criteria of validity for our discursive and political practices. The struggle over what lies beyond the classical imperative remains unresolved. In this sense, the definition of postmodernity may be that of a future which we would like to think of as our past.

Notes

1. Paolo Portoghesi, *After Modern Architecture* (New York: Rizzoli, 1982), p. 7 ff.

2. Cf. M. Berman, *All That Is Solid Melts Into Air* (New York: Simon and Schuster, 1982), pp. 37 ff.; 60-71.

3. Peter Eisenman, Accompanying text to exhibit piece, "Cite Unseen," in "Revision der Moderne," Deutsche Architekturmuseum, Summer 1984, Frankfurt am Main. For some of the difficulties in characterizing Eisenmann's work, cf. Charles A. Jencks, *Late-Modern Architecture and Other Essays* (New York: Rizzoli, 1980), pp. 13; 137 ff.

4. Jean-François Lyotard, *The Postmodern Condition: A Report on Knowledge,* trans. by Geoff Bennington and Brian Massouri, Foreword by F. Jameson (Minneapolis: University of Minnesota Press, 1984). All future references in the text are to this edition. Appended to the English translation is also the essay, "Answering the Question: What is Postmodernism," trans. by R. Durand, originally in *Critique,* No. 419 (April 1982).

5. Cf. H. Arendt's statement: "Descartes' philosophy is haunted by two nightmares which in a sense became the nightmares of the whole modern age, not because this age was so deeply influenced by Cartesian philosophy, but because their emergence was almost inescapable once the true implications of the modern world view were understood. These nightmares are very simple and very well-known. In the one, reality, the reality of the world as well as of human life, is doubted. . . . The other concerned . . . the impossibility for man to trust his senses and his reason." *The Human Condition* (Chicago: University of Chicago Press, 1973), eighth printing, p. 277.

6. I borrow the phrase from R. Rorty's well-known article, "The World Well Lost," which argues that the conclusion to be drawn from contemporary epistemological disputes about conceptual frameworks is that "The notion of the 'world' that is correlative with the notion of a 'conceptual framework' is simply the Kantian notion of a thing-in-itself. . . . " (originally in *Journal of Philosophy* [1972], reprinted in *Consequences of Pragmatism* (Minneapolis: University of Minnesota Press, 1982), p. 16.

7. Richard Rorty, *Philosophy and the Mirror of Nature* (Princeton: Princeton University Press, 1979), pp. 131 ff.

8. Charles Taylor, "Theories of Meaning," Daves Hickes Lecture, Proceedings of the British Academy (Oxford: University Press, 1982), p. 284.

9. Thomas Hobbes, *Leviathan,* ed. by C. B. McPherson (Baltimore: Penguin Books, 1971), p. 101 ff. Cf. M. Foucault, *The Order of Things: An Archaeology of the Human Sciences* (New York: Random House, 1973), First Vintage Books edition: "In its simple state as an idea, or an image, or a perception, associated with or substituted for another, the signifying element is not a sign. It can become a sign only on condition that it manifests, in addition, the relation that links it to what it signifies. It must represent, but that representation, in turn, must also be represented within it" (64).

10. The transition from "consciousness" to "self-consciousness," from representation to desire in ch. III of Hegel's *Phenomenology of Spirit* contains also a critique of the spectator conception of the knowing subject. Hegel's point is that an epistemological standpoint confined to the spectator conception of the self cannot solve the questions it raises; most notably, it cannot explain the genesis and becoming of the object of knowledge. It is only insofar as the knowing self is also an acting one that it can destroy the myth of the given in knowledge (Hegel, *Phenomenology of Spirit,* trans. with an analysis and Foreword by J.N. Findlay [Oxford: Clarendon Press, 1977], pp. 104-110). Cf. "He does not see how the sensuous world around him is not a given direct from all eternity, ever the same, but the product of industry and of the state of society, and indeed in the sense that it is an historical product, the result of the activity of a whole succession of generations," K. Marx and F. Engels, *The German Ideology,* ed. and introd. by R. Pascal (New York: International Publishers, 1969), p. 35. M. Horkheimer, "Traditional and Critical Theory," in *Critical Theory,* trans. by M.J. O'Connell and others (New York: Herder and Herder, 1972), pp. 188-244. J. Habermas, *Knowledge and Human Interests,* trans. by J. Shapiro (Boston: Beacon Press, 1972), pp. 1-65. S. Freud, "A Difficulty in the Path of Psychoanalysis" in the *Standard Edition* (London: Hogarth, 1953), vol. 17, pp. 137-144. For this reading of Freud, I am much indebted to Paul Ricoeur, *Freud and Philosophy: An Essay on Interpretation,* trans. by Denis Savage (New Haven: Yale University Press, 1977), pp. 419-459.

11. Friedrich Nietzsche, "The Genealogy of Morals," *The Birth of Tragedy and the Genealogy of Morals,* trans. by F. Golffing (New York: Doubleday, 1958), pp. 289 ff.

12. Martin Heidegger, *Being and Time,* trans. by John Macquarrie and Edward Robinson (New York: Harber and Row, 1962), pp. 47 ff.; "Die Frage nach der Technik?" *Vorträge und Aufsätze* (Stuttgart: Gunther Neske, 1974), fourth ed., pp. 27 ff.

13. M. Horkheimer and Th. Adorno, *Dialektik der Aufklärung* (Frankfurt am Main: Fischer Verlag, 1980), p. 12, originally published in Amsterdam 1947.

14. Cf. Wittgenstein's critique of the "naming" theory of meaning and of the impossibility of viewing language as a private game in *Philosophical Investigations,* trans. by G.E.M. Anscombe (The Macmillan Company: New York, 1965), tenth printing, pp. 27-32, 38, and 39; 180 and 199 ff.

15. Charles Sanders Peirce, "Some Consequences of Four Incapacities, in *Selected Writings,* ed. and with an Introd. and Notes by Philip Wiener (New York: Dover Publications, 1966), pp. 53-54; K.-O. Apel, "From Kant to Peirce: The Semiotical Transformation of Transcendental Logic," in *Toward a Transformation of Philosophy,* trans. by G. Adey and D. Frisby (London: RKP, 1980), pp. 77-93.

16. Ferdinand de Saussure, *Course in General Linguistics,* ed. by C. Bally and A. Sechehaye, trans. and introd. by Wade Baskin (New York: McGraw Hill, 1959), pp. 67 ff.

17. Cf. Manfred Frank, *Was ist Neostrukturalismus?* (Frankfurt am Main: Suhrkamp, 1984), pp. 71 ff.; 83 ff.; 259. Pierre Bourdieu and J.C. Passeron, "Sociology and Philosophy in France since 1945: Death and Resurrection of a Philosophy without the Subject," *Social Research,* 34:1 (Spring 1983), 162-212.

18. Wittgenstein, *Philosophical Investigations,* pp. 124, 49e.

19. K.-O. Apel, "Sprechakttheorie und transzendentale Sprachpragmatik zur Frage ethischer Normen," in *Sprachpragmatik und Philosophie,* ed. by K.-O. Apel (Frankfurt am Main: Suhrkamp, 1976), pp. 10-81; J. Habermas, "Was heisst Universalpragmatik?" *ibid.,* pp. 184-273, English translation by T. McCarthy, "What is Universal Pragmatics?" in *Communication and the Evolution of Society* (Boston: Beacon Press, 1979), pp. 1-69.

20. J. Habermas, "An Excursus on Theory of Argumentation," in *The Theory of Communicative Action,* v. 1, trans. by T. McCarthy (Boston: Beacon Press, 1984), pp. 23 ff.

21. One of Habermas' main purposes in developing a theory of discourse and argumentation was to formulate a concept of the validity of ethical norms, which avoided the dogmatism of natural law theories (that confuse moral validity and factual assertions) and the arbitrariness of emotivism (that reduced moral claims to statements of taste). Cf. "Zwei Bemerkungen zum praktischen Diskurs," in *Konstruktionen versus Positionen,* ed. by Kuno Lorenz (Berlin: Walter de Gruyter, 1979); "Wahrheitstheorien," in *Wirklichkeit und Reflexion,* ed. by H. Fahrenbach (Pfullingen: Neske, 1973), pp. 211-265.

22. Against Lyotard's reading, I want to emphasize that linguistically mediated communicative action serves *three* functions: first, the coordination of social action among individuals; second, the socialization and individuation of members of a human group, and third, the appropriation of cultural tradition, and the generation of meaning and symbolic patterns which define the hermeneutic horizon of a culture, cf. Habermas, *The Theory of Communicative Action,* pp. 100-101; 136 ff.

23. Quoted in Frank, *Was ist Neostrukturalismus?,* p. 111.

24. J.L. Austin, *How to do Things with Words* (Cambridge, Mass.: Harvard University Press, 1962), p. 120.

25. Admittedly, the interpretation of the distinction between "illocutionary" and "perlocutionary" acts is controversial (cf. Austin, *How to do Things with Words,* pp. 120 ff.). The difficulty with Lyotard's interpretation of Austin's thesis appears to be that he conflates the illocutionary force of an utterance with the producing of certain effects, intended or otherwise, by means of an utterance. Thus he describes a "performative utterance" as one whose "effect upon the recipient coincided with its enunciation" (*Postmodern Condition,* p. 9). Austin, however, identifies an illocutionary act as an act we perform *in* saying something (*How to do Things with Words,* p. 99), and the description of which can figure in the first person indicative as "I pronounce that," "I warn you that," "I inform you that," etc. In his valuable article, "Intention and Convention in Speech Acts," P.F. Strawson clarifies in fact how irrelevant the achieving of certain effects upon the hearer is to the identifying of illocutionary acts; he shifts the focus instead to the overt intention of the speaker and the recognition by his hearers of this intention, regardless of how they choose to respond to it; in *Philosophical Review,* No. 73 (1964), 439-460.

26. Habermas, "The Entwinement of Myth and Enlightenment: Rereading the *Dialectic of Enlightenment,*" *New German Critique,* 26 (Spring-Summer 1982).

27. R. Rorty, "Habermas and Lyotard on Postmodernity," *Praxis International,* 4:1 (April 1984), 33.

28. *Ibid.*

29. This argument is somewhat unconvincing because Lyotard does not distinguish between the internal *cognitive dynamics of science* and its *social* uses. Performativity, or what is known as "scientism" in the tradition of critical theory, is a view that legitimizes science by an appeal—although not exclusively—to its social-technological uses. That scientism is not an adequate theory of the natural sciences has been argued forcefully by others like

Mary Hesse, *Revolutions and Reconstructions in the Philosophy of Science* (Bloomington: Indiana University Press, 1980). However, in attacking this ideology, Lyotard ignores the social reality it expresses. The fact that postmodern natural science operates with a discontinuous epistemology of instabilities, does not decide the question of its social role. Lyotard emphasizes the internal, cognitive dynamics of modern science, while ignoring its social-technological aspects. For the distinction between the cognitive and social dynamics of science, cf. G. Bohme et al., *Finalization in Science,* ed. by W. Schaefer (Boston: D. Reidel Publishing, 1983), pp. 3-11.

30. For a recent statement of problems and issues, cf. R.J. Bernstein, *The Restructuring of Social and Political Theory* (Philadelphia: University of Pennsylvania Press, 1976).

31. Rorty, "Habermas and Lyotard on Postmodernity," 34.

32. *Ibid.*

33. Frank, *Was ist Neostrukturalismus?,* p. 106.

34. Cf. E. Gellner, "Concepts and Society," in *Rationality,* ed. by B.R. Wilson (New York: Harper and Row, Publishers, 1970), pp. 18-50; P. Bourdieu, *Outline of a Theory of Practice,* trans. by Richard Nice (Cambridge: Cambridge University Press, 1979), pp. 22-30.

35. In portraying this relationship, Lyotard adopts the *observer's* point, the standpoint of the curator of an ethnological museum of the past. Had he adopted the *participant's* perspective, he would have had to concede that "gazing in wonderment at the variety of discursive species" is hardly the attitude to take when confronted with the moral and epistemic problems that the coexistence of incompatible discursive modes pose for us qua children of the modern West. In this essay, I am only arguing that these modes of thought cannot harmoniously coexist in one epistemic space, that their very presence next to each other poses moral as well as cognitive problems, or that the question of validity inevitably confronts us, and that we cannot extricate ourselves from an answer by gazing in wonderment at the plurality of language games and life forms. For a recent statement of these thorny questions, cf. *Rationality and Relativism,* ed. by Steven Lukes and Martin Hollis (Cambridge: MIT Press, 1984).

36. Fredric Jameson, "The Politics of Theory: Ideological Positions in the Postmodernism Debate," *New German Critique* 33, (Fall 1984), 53.

37. I adopt this phrase from Vincent Descombes, *Modern French Philosophy* (New York: Cambridge University Press, 1980), p. 184.

38. Lyotard, *Économie Libidinale,* pp. 54-55, as cited by Descombes, p. 185.

39. *Hegel's Phenomenology of Spirit,* pp. 355-364. Indeed, it is this condemnation of the Terror that

leads Hegel "to conceptually legitimize the revolutionizing reality without the Revolution itself," Habermas, "Hegel's Critique of the French Revolution," in *Theory and Practice,* John Viertel, trans. (Boston: Beacon Press, 1971), pp. 123 and ff.

40. J. Habermas, "Modernity versus Postmodernity," *New German Critique,* 22 (Winter 1981), 13. In his "Questions and Counter-questions" (forthcoming *Praxis International*) Habermas has modified this charge somewhat, but it strikes me as being quite accurate for at least one possible implication of the postmodernist epistemological positions.

41. Albrecht Wellmer makes a similar point in his "Zur Dialektik von Moderne und Postmoderne," forthcoming, *Praxis International.*

42. Rorty, "Habermas and Lyotard on Postmodernity," 34.

43. *Ibid.,* 35.

44. *Ibid.,* 38.

45. *Ibid.,* 41.

46. *Ibid.,* 38.

47. *Ibid.,* 35. This is a curious demand, since the whole revival of critical theory in Europe as well as in this country, and certainly a main political impetus behind Habermas' and Wellmer's works, was the abandonment and critique by the Student Movement and of the New Left of the illusion of a revolutionary vanguard. It is as if some French and American intellectuals are suffering a lapse of memory in the 1980s, accusing the Student Movement and the New Left of attitudes that they did most to combat.

48. Cf. the works of the Chicago School (Stanley Tigerman, Frederick Read, Peter Pran, Stuart Cohen, Thomas Beeby, Anders Nerheim) exhibited at "Die Revision der Moderne," Deutsches Architekturmuseum, Frankfurt, Summer 1984.

Peter Dews (essay date 1984)

SOURCE: "The Letter and the Line: Discourse and Its Other in Lyotard," in *Diacritics,* Vol. 14, No. 3, Fall, 1984, pp. 40-9.

[*In the following discussion of* Discours, *Dews explains the distinction Lyotard draws between the significations of words and the significantions of figures.*]

There is a certain irony, but also an appropriateness, in the fact that Jean-François Lyotard should only recently have become more widely known in the English-speaking world for his work on the "postmodern condition," on the intersecting aesthetic, political, and ethical problems posed by modernity and its—supposed—exhaustion, and that this work has been presented as the latest contribution to a continuing poststructuralism. Irony, because if poststructuralism as a whole can be characterized by its avoidance of the moral dimension of politics, by its assumption—explicit in works such as Foucault's *Discipline and Punish*—that normative thought can only operate in the interests of power, then in *Au Juste,* and in subsequent works, Lyotard can be seen as initiating a reflection on the limitations of poststructuralism itself, limitations which he had himself revealed in an exacerbated form in *Économie libidinale.* Appropriateness, because this subtle but unmistakable exit from post-structuralism reveals something more general about Lyotard's relation to his philosophical milieu. Lyotard arrived late at the Nietzschean festivities of the sixties and seventies, and departed early. His central concern with the visual arts, in a period dominated by the theory of the text, his genuine feeling for political issues, evident even when his writing comes closest to the mere political posturing of the majority of his contemporaries, his early awareness of, and willingness to engage with, the arguments of the Frankfurt School, are sufficient to mark Lyotard out as something of an anomaly. Lyotard has, in a number of respects, remained on the margins of an orthodoxy which defined itself precisely in terms of its focus on, and celebration of, the marginal.

This heterodoxy is already apparent in the work with which Lyotard made his first major impact on French philosophical debate, *Discours, figure.* In direct opposition to the then-triumphant philosophies of the text (the book was first published in 1971), Lyotard here takes up the defense of the perceived world against the imperialism of language. "This book," he affirms on the opening page, "protests: that the given is not a text, that there is within it a density, or rather a constitutive difference, which is not to be read, but to be seen: and that this difference, and the immobile mobility which reveals it, is what is continually forgotten in the process of signification" [9]. Lyotard inverts the structuralist and poststructuralist denunciations of the naivety of "lived experience," and suggests that the mark of the Western intellectual tradition has been its occlusion, rather than its vain pursuit of the world of the senses. He declares his target to be the "penumbra which, after Plato, speech has thrown like a gray veil over the sensible, which has been constantly thematized as less-than-being, and whose side has very rarely truly been taken, taken in truth, since it was understood that this was the side of falsity, of skepticism, of the rhetorician, the painter, the condottiere, the libertine, the materialist . . . [11]." One succinct phrase summarizes the gulf between Lyotard's position and the accepted wisdom of the 1960s: "one does not at all break with metaphysics by putting language everywhere" [14].

In *Discours, figure* Lyotard's defense of perception is already acquiring the overtones of Nietzsche's denunciations of the philosophers' obliteration of the sensible world, but the roots of Lyotard's opposition to the "primacy of the symbolic" can be traced as far back as 1954, long before any significant Nietzschean influence, to his introductory monograph on phenomenology. Here, Lyotard argues that, because of its founding task of an intuitive capture of "the things themselves" prior to all predication, phenomenology may be described as "a combat of language with itself in its effort to attain the originary" [*La Phénoménologie* 43]. The phenomenological project is "fundamentally *contradictory*" the effort of language to capture a prelinguistic world is foredoomed, since "as the designation of a prelogical signified which is there in being itself, it is forever incomplete, because referred back dialectically from being to meaning via intentional analysis" [44]. For the mainstream of structuralism and poststructuralism this inherent dilemma of phenomenology points to a conclusion of which Derrida's work probably offers both the most extreme and the most coherent formulation: since, in any attempt to capture a world prior to and independent of language, language is always already presupposed; there cannot be "a truth or an origin escaping the play and the order of the sign" [Derrida, *L'Ecriture et la différence* 427]; indeed, there can be "nothing before the text . . . no pretext which is not already a text" [Derrida, *Dissemination* 328]. For Lyotard, however, there is an illicit jump in this argument: rather than demonstrating the ultimate illusoriness of any language-independent reality, why should not the impossibility of a linguistic grasping of the originary rather reveal the inherent limitations of language itself, its ultimate powerlessness when confronted with the nonlinguistic? If "the defeat of philosophy is certain," this is not because philosophy is inescapably mesmerized by an illusion of presence, but because it is unable to acknowledge the world of sense in which it is immersed and from which it emerges, because "the originary is no longer the originary in so far as it *is* described" [*La Phénoménologie* 43]. For Derrida, in other words, it is *différance,* as the principle of reflexivity, which cannot itself be reflexively grasped, whereas for Lyotard "there is always a prereflexive, an unreflected, an ante-predicative, upon which reflection science must lean, and which it conjures away every time it wishes to give an account of itself" [5].

However, these phenomenological origins of Lyotard's defense of the perceived world should not be taken to imply that, in **Discours, figure,** his understanding of language has remained at the phenomenological stage. Rather, Lyotard admits that structuralism has made a decisive advance in its account of language as a system of differential relations which precedes and makes possible the speech of the individual speaking subject. "Within the anonymous system," Lyotard suggests, "there are intervals which maintain the terms at a constant distance from each other, so that this 'absolute object' is—so to speak—full of holes, and encloses within itself a dialectic which is immobile, and yet generative, and which causes the definition and value of a term to pass via the other terms with which it is in correlation" [33]. For Lyotard the crucial point is that this anonymous system renders inadequate any phenomenological attempt to ground linguistic meaning in a logically prior intentionality or gesturality. Any "dialectical" account of language in the Sartrian sense—as "the inert depository of a power of speech which would be logically anterior to it"—is impossible, since it must be recognized

that "language precedes speech in as much as no speaker can claim, even modestly, to have founded the former, nor dream of instituting another, and . . . any attempt to reform language comes up against the circle that it is our tool, the only tool we possess, for the purpose of transforming it" [34].

For Lyotard, however, the structuralist acquisition that *parole* cannot be considered anterior to *langue,* as phenomenology in its diverse forms had always been tempted to claim, does not entitle us to dispense with a consideration of the impact of *parole,* and of the dimension specific to language in use. While the view of language as an autonomous system of purely internal relations may be accepted as the basis of a structuralism which confines itself to its strictly scientific tasks, it becomes misleading when presented as a characterization of language *tout court.* For what is omitted in the understanding of language as a closed system of signifiers representing signifieds is any sense of the referential dimension of language. "There is a fact," Lyotard suggests, "which our experience of speech does not permit us to deny, the fact that every discourse is cast in the direction of something which it seeks to seize hold of, that it is incomplete and open, somewhat as the visual field is partial, limited and extended by an horizon. How can we explain this almost visual property of speaking on the basis of this object closed in principle, shut up on itself in a self-sufficient totality, which is the system of *langue?*" [32]. In Lyotard's view such an explanation is impossible. He argues that, in order to account for the fact that "it is not signs which are given, but something to be signified" [31] we must consider language in use as characterized by two distinct forms of negativity. Saussure was undoubtedly correct to insist that, since the value of a linguistic term is constituted by its differences from other terms, since what a term *is* is defined solely by what it is not, in language there are only differences. But, at the same time, this negativity of difference must be set in relation to what Lyotard calls the "negativity of transcendence," the fact that "the speaker is torn away from that of which he speaks, or this is torn away from him, and he continues to hold it at a distance in speaking, as the object of his discourse, in a 'vision'" [118].

At this point it might appear open to a defender of a Derridean position to argue that Lyotard has misconstrued the deconstructionist case. Derrida does not deny that, in speaking, we experience the dimension of reference; he remarks, at one point in *Positions,* that we should avoid "an indispensable critique of a certain naive relation to the signified or to the referent, to meaning or to thing, becoming fixed in a suspension, or a pure and simple suppression of sense and reference" [90]. And yet the logic of Derrida's position pushes him inevitably toward the conclusion that the referential can possess only a secondary and derivative status, since he immediately goes on to suggest that "what is needed is to determine in *another way,* in accordance with a differential system, the *effects* of ideality, of signification, of meaning, of reference" [90]. Because Derrida is operating with a simple duality of identity and difference, and because he subordinates the former unequivocally to the latter, arguing that "nothing—no present and indifferent entity—precedes spacing and difference" [40], he is obliged to dismiss the perceived world as no more than a system of traces, or—alternatively—if the concept of perception is considered inseparable from the notion of a subject-centered and unmediated form of awareness, to suggest that "there is no perception."[1] Since, for Derrida, there is only the spacing of the text, he cannot accommodate the clash and interference between two forms of negativity, between vision and language, which is at the heart of Lyotard's concerns.

Nothing obliges us, however, to accept Derrida's initial dichotomy of identity and difference. It is possible to argue that the perceived world does not possess the structure of a text, without accepting that it could be flattened out into the immediacy of sensation or the pure presence of entities. Thus Lyotard points out that the perceived does not possess the reversible relativity of the linguistic, that the relation between here and there, above and below, in front and behind, to the right and to the left, is not assimilable to the diacritical relation between terms within a linguistic system:

> the place indicated, the *here,* is grasped in a sensible field, undoubtedly as its focus, but not in such a way that its surroundings are eliminated, as is the case with the choices made by a speaker; they remain there, with the uncertain, undeniable, curvilinear presence of that which lingers on the borders of vision, a reference absolutely essential to the indication of place . . . but whose nature marks a complete break with that of a linguistic operation: the latter refers back to a discontinuous inventory, sight to a topological space, the first is subordinated to the rule of the spoken chain which requires the uniqueness of the actual and the elimination of the virtual, the second determines a sensible field ruled by the quasi-actuality of the virtual, and the quasi-virtuality of the actual. [*Discours* 38]

If this distinction is accepted, then any attempt to absorb the exteriority of the perceived world into the interiority of language—Lyotard's target is Hegel, but the argument applies equally well to Derrida—must be seen as falling prey to a "logophiliac presupposition." "It is all very well," Lyotard writes, "to affirm that everything is sayable; this is true; but what is not true is that the signification of discourse can gather up all the sense of the sayable. One can say that the tree is green, but the colour will not have been put into the sentence": language may be considered as the phenomenological, but not as the ontological ground of the perceived world [52, 129].

Throughout *Discours, figure* this awareness of an "unsuppressible gap" between the sensible and the intelligible is expressed in terms of a contrast between the "letter" and the "line," between a graphic and a figural space. "The letter," Lyotard argues, "is the support of a conventional, immaterial signification, in every respect identical with the presence of the phoneme. And this support effaces itself behind what is supported: the letter only gives rise to rapid recognition, in the interests of signification" [211]. In Derrida's work the prioritization of the written over the spoken word, and the consequent inclusion of the latter in the former, is employed as a means of blocking this effacement. But since the letter is composed of a group of highly stereotyped traits which are indifferent to the space in which they are inscribed, and which therefore tend toward the suppression of their own materiality and plasticity, writing—no less than speech—is intrinsically oriented toward intelligibility. It is only the line, by contrast, which thwarts recognition and assimilation—which obstructs the eye and forces it to linger. "The manner in which meaning is present in the line (in any constituent of a figure)," affirms Lyotard, "is felt as an opacity by the mind habituated to language. An almost interminable effort is required in order for the eye to let itself be captured by the form, to receive the energy which it contains" [218]. In an interview dating from 1970, Lyotard turns this contrast explicitly against the idealism of the Derridean concept of "archiwriting," by means of a simple example drawn from one of the key artists discussed in *Discours, figure*: "one cannot at all say that the line which Klee's pencil traces on a sheet of paper is charged with effects of sense in the same way as the letters which he writes under this line, and which say simply: 'Fatal leap' . . ." [Lyotard, **"Sur la théorie,"** in *Dérive à partir de Marx et Freud* 229].

As Lyotard's phenomenological background would lead one to expect, the argument of these opening chapters of *Discours, figure* is heavily indebted to the work of Merleau-Ponty, and in particular to the later writings, where Merleau-Ponty attempts to move beyond the metaphysical categories of subject and object, not by a process of speculative *Aufhebung,* but by returning below the subject-object relation to uncover "our mute contact with things before they become things said" [Merleau-Ponty, *Le Visible et l'invisible* 61]. In Merleau-Ponty's late thought the key notions of "depth" and "opacity," applied to what is perceived and to the act of perceiving, are employed to suggest that perception can never entirely possess either its object or itself. The world upon which perception opens is not a domain of pure presences—and therefore, in poststructuralist terms, a domain of illusion—but an "ambiguous field of horizons and distances," an overlapping and intertwining of the visible and the invisible. Throughout his career Merleau-Ponty remained stubbornly opposed to the view that whatever meaning the world possesses must be bestowed by language, but—because of the rootedness of his thought in phenomenology—he also resists the notion that there might be an unbridgeable hiatus between language and the world. For Merleau-Ponty there are meanings concealed in the world's dimension of depth which language brings to light and consolidates, but does not produce, so that there is a spontaneous cooperation and affinity between perception and language. "To understand," he suggests, "is to translate into available significations a meaning initially captive in the thing and in the world itself" [58]. And again: "language realizes, in breaking the silence, that which silence wishes for, yet could not obtain" [230].

This "tenderness" toward the perceived world, a *parti pris* which lies at the heart of Merleau-Ponty's philosophy, is clearly irreconcilable with structuralist and early poststructuralist thought, where there can be no doubt that, even granted the coherence of the notion of a language-independent reality, it is language which segments and determines the meaning of the world. But significantly, it is also the point at which **Discours, figure,** which up till now could almost have been read as a phenomenological critique of structuralism, also begins to query the work of Merleau-Ponty, and therefore may be said to mark the decisive shift into a form of poststructuralism in Lyotard's thought. Lyotard, as we have seen, cannot accept the structuralist screening-out of reference, or the theorization of saying as purely determined by linguistic structure: language can neither speak itself, nor speak merely about itself. But neither can he accept Merleau-Ponty's attempt to "introduce the gesture, the mobility of the sensible directly into the invariance characteristic of the system of language, in order to say what is constitutive of saying, in order to restore the act which opens the possibility of speaking" [**Discours** 56]. If, as structuralism contends, the anonymous system of *langue* is irreducible to individual acts of speech, then neither the "horizontal" nor the "vertical" dimension of negativity can be reduced to its complement, and "the gesture of speech which is assumed to create signification can never be seized in its constitutive function" [56].

Yet to abandon Merleau-Ponty's thought, in this way, as the "last effort of a transcendental reflection" is not—for Lyotard—to dissolve the autonomy of the dimension of reference across which speech emerges. Lyotard's objection is principally to the notion that there exists a "connaturality" or elective affinity between language and the world. Perception is phenomenologically grounded in language, but the subject and object connected in perception must be seen as "fragments deriving from an initial deflagration of which language itself was the starting spark" [109]. After this rending of our original unity with the world, the perceived object is revealed as inherently ambiguous and opaque; it can never be grasped as it is "in itself." Thus language, far from articulating the implicit meaning of the world, perpetually excludes what it seeks to possess. It is in the gap left by this exclusion, Lyotard suggests, that there emerges what we call "desire": "reality and desire are born together with the entry into language" [125].

This argument marks the midstream transition in **Discours, figure** from a phenomenological to a psychoanalytical vocabulary. But it should not be taken to imply an identity between Lyotard's position and that of Lacan. For although **Discours, figure** is a consciously fragmented work, broken between a "before" and an "after of structuralism, there is nevertheless a deep continuity between its phenomenological and its Freudian argument. In his critique of the Hegelian (and not only Hegelian) absorption of seeing into saying, Lyotard had emphasized the contrast between the mobility of the referential "eye which maintains itself on

the edge of discourse," and the process of selection and combination in language, between the continuous and asymmetrical nature of the visual field, and articulated and differential nature of *langue*. But he goes on to point out that, in a certain sense, this set of contrasts also lies at the heart of Freud's work: "Freud's reflections are, from the beginning to the end of his career, from the *Traumdeutung* to *Moses*, centered on the relation of language and silence, of signification and sense, of articulation and the image, of the commentary which interprets or constructs and the desire which figures" [59]. From this standpoint, the nonarticulated, perpetually-shifting nature of the perceptual field may be taken as an analogue of that mobility of cathexis in the unconscious which Freud refers to as the "primary process." There is, Lyotard suggests, "a radical connivence between the figural and desire" [271]. But just as the phenomological argument of the first part of **Discours, figure** had brought Lyotard into conflict with both structuralism and the philosophy of writing, so his emphasis on the figurality of desire leads to a clash with the Lacanian conception of psychoanalysis as a "logic of the signifier." This confrontation becomes explicit in the chapter entitled **"Le Travail du Rêve ne Pense Pas,"** a detailed elucidation of Freud's accounts of the "dream-work" in *The Interpretation of Dreams*.

In order to appreciate the full import of Lyotard's argument, in a theoretical milieu largely dominated by the Lacanian account of the unconscious as "structured like a language," we must examine the manner in which Lacan himself reformulates the basic aspects of the dream-work—condensation, displacement, considerations of representability, and secondary elaboration—described by Freud in the sixth chapter of *The Interpretation of Dreams* Lacan begins his most systematic commentary on the nature of the dream-work by arguing that the similes of the "pictographic script," the "picture puzzle," and the "rebus," which Freud employs in the introduction to this chapter, establish definitively "the agency in the dream of that same literalizing (in other words, phonematic) structure in accordance with which the signifier is articulated and analyzed in discourse" [Lacan, "The Agency of the Letter in the Unconscious," in *Ecrits: A Selection* 159]. Within the dream, in other words, the images or components of images have no figurative function whatsoever: the dream is composed—to employ Lyotard's distinction—of "letters" rather than "lines." Lacan reinforces his point by an elaboration of Freud's reference to pictographic script, remarking that, in deciphering hieroglyphs, "it would be ludicrous to deduce from the frequency with which a vulture, which is an *aleph*, or a chicken, which is a *vau*, signify the form of the verb to be and the plural, that the text is in any way interested in these ornithological specimens" [159].

Having established that, despite its visual, pictorial form, the dream is essentially a kind of writing, an organization of signifiers, Lacan can present his reformulation of the dreamwork procedures discussed by Freud. The overall operation of "disguise, necessitated by the censorship," which Freud refers to as *Entstellung* (distortion), is translated by Lacan as "transposition," and is equated with the "sliding of the signified under the signifier," the semantic instability, overlooked by the ego in its inertia, which—for Lacan—is characteristic of all discourse. Within this general process of transposition Lacan aligns the operations of *Verdichtung* (condensation) and *Verschiebung* (displacement) with the two fundamental axes of language discerned by Roman Jakobson, the axis of selection and the axis of combination, which give rise to "metaphor" and "metonymy." Although there has been much puzzlement about the relation between Jakobson's theory and the use made of this theory by Lacan, the manner in which Lacan's formulations both extend and diverge from those of Jakobson can in fact be characterized fairly straightforwardly. Lacan continues the linguist's argument in so far as he views metaphor and metonymy as two fundamental processes of all discourse (rather than two specific rhetorical figures—although these figures provide the most vivid exemplifications of these processes); but he goes beyond Jakobson in viewing metaphor as the mark of the relation of discourse to the subject, and metonymy as the mark of its relation to the object. Thus Lacan employs poetic examples to illustrate his definition of metaphor as "the substitution of one signifier for another, by which is produced an effect of signification which is of poetry or creation" [164], but the creativity to which he refers is actually inherent in all discourse, since no appearance of a signifier can be deduced from the preceding signifiers in the chain. What this definition of metaphor points to, therefore, is Lacan's insistence that *langue* as a virtual system, the "treasure of the signifier," cannot actualize itself, that discourse requires a speaking subject. But although each successive signifier reveals the *existence* of a subject, the signifier which appears cannot be seen as an unambiguous representation of the subject: the bar between signifier and signified, on which Lacan lays so much stress, blocks any automatic determination of meaning, so that it is the emergence of a further interpreting signifier, a crossing of the bar in which the first signifier now becomes the signified, which may be "provisionally merged with the place of the subject" [164], since this reveals how the subject is revealed to itself. But since this second signifier appears under the same conditions as the first, there can be no absolute determination of the place of the subject: each signifier is a "metaphor of the subject," a representation of the subject mediated by another signifier.

Lacan's corresponding definition of metonymy is: "the connection from signifier to signifier, which permits the elision through which the signifier installs a lack-of-being in the object-relation, by making use of the reference-value of signification to invest this relation with a desire aimed at the lack which it supports" [164]. For Lacan, to attach a predicate to, or offer a description of, an object is always to present that object from a specific point of view. But since no single predicate or description can claim to exhaust the being of the object, and since there is a potential infinity of points of view, the attempt to grasp the object in language becomes an endless process, in which

each description points toward further possibilities of description, but in which no description can capture the object as it is "in itself." The relation between this account and the traditional definition of metonymy as a figure in which a part is taken for the whole is clear, as is the connection between the metonymic process and the Lacanian notion of desire: in Lacan desire is attached to a lost object which language permanently excludes. In metonymy, therefore, in contrast to metaphor, the bar between signifier and signified is not crossed: the object always appears "beyond" or "on the other side of" discourse, as the underlying coherence of the sequence of signifieds which cannot itself be signified. The *objet petit a* in Lacan, to which the subject entrusts its being at the "panic point" when the singularity of this being is threatened by absorption into the universal dimension of language, is the sole object which is presumed to elude these linguistic conditions for the representation of objects. But it is precisely the belief in the possibility of the absolute presence of the *objet petit a* which condemns it to a permanent absence, and marks the phantasy relation to the *objet a* as imaginary. Since, for Lacan, the dream is essentially a text like any other, no more than any other sequence of signifiers can it embody or portray this object.

For Lyotard, Lacan's linguistic version of condensation and displacement is fully in continuity with the denegation and subordination of the dimension of the visible in Western thought. If Merleau-Ponty was mistaken in assuming that language could be opened up to and capture what was already implicit in the domain of the sensible, Lacan is equally at fault for relegating the perceived object to the register of the imaginary, of an immediacy which can only be grasped as already-lost from the standpoint of the symbolic, and which can therefore have no independent *effect upon* the symbolic. Certainly, there is a relation between the entry of the subject into language and phantasy, but the object of phantasy does not function merely as the impossible, imaginary end-term of the metonymyic chain of any discourse. Rather, the entry into language is a genuinely traumatic event, a "primal repression" which establishes an irrecoverable phantasy in the unconscious: this phantasy will then seek to reveal itself through a disruption and overturning of the order of language, rather than through operations which are themselves merely linguistic. "The supposed doubling of the pre-world [by language]," Lyotard argues, "does not simply open up the distance in which the eye is installed on the edge of discourse. This tearing-away produces *in* discourse effects of distortion. A figure is installed in the depths of our speech, which operates as the matrix of these effects; which attacks our words in order to make them into forms and images. . . . By the *Entzweiung* the object is lost; by means of the phantasy it is re-presented" [*Discours* 129]. For Lyotard the work of the dream is the clearest example of such an irruption of the primary process into the secondary process, of the manner in which a "figure-matrix," by its twisting of the order of language, traces—through the very distortions which it imposes—a figuration of the unfigurable. "The dream," he suggests, "is not the speech of desire, but its work . . . it results from the application of a force to a text. Desire does not speak, it violates the order of speech" [238].

Clearly, such a standpoint imposes a very different understanding of what Freud means by "condensation" and "displacement" from that of Lacan. "Condensation," Lyotard argues, "should be understood as a physical process by which one or more objects occupying a given space are reduced to inhabiting a smaller volume. . . . To crush the signifying or signified unities against each other, to confuse them, is to neglect the stable gaps which separate the letters, the words of a text, to disregard the invariant distinctive graphemes of which they are composed, ultimately to be indifferent to the space of discourse" [244]. In support of this argument, Lyotard points to some of the "amusing and curious neologisms" which Freud reports in *The Interpretation of Dreams* (the adjective "*norekdal*," for example, is decomposed into a parody of German superlatives such as "*kolossal*" or "*pyramidal*," and the names of two Ibsen characters—"Nora" and "Ekdal" [Freud 4:296]), or to the tangle of associations attached to the "botanical monograph" in Freud's dream of the same name [Freud 4:169-76]. Lyotard is unquestionably closer to Freud than the Lacanian reformulation of condensation as the metaphorical relation between a latent and a patent signifier. Lacan explicitly excludes the view of metaphor as "the presentation of two images, that is, of two signifiers, equally actualized" [*Ecrits* 157], whereas in Freud's writings condensation frequently takes the form of an overlapping of disparate traits to form a single composite figure, as if—as Lyotard puts it—"the place where one dreams [were] narrower than the place where one thinks" [*Discours* 259].

The gulf between Lyotard and Lacan is equally wide in their respective understandings of displacement. In *The Interpretation of Dreams* this concept refers to the manner in which, in the course of the formation of a dream, "essential elements, charged, as they are, with intense interest, may be treated as though they were of small value, and their place taken in the dream by other elements, of whose small value in the dream thoughts there can be no question" [Freud 4:306]. In order to illustrate this aspect of the dream-work, Lyotard takes the example of a poster advertising a film of the Russian Revolution, on which the letters of the phrase "*Révolution D'Octobre*" are written in an undulating manner, suggesting a banner blowing in the wind. The process of displacement can then be represented as a reinforcement of certain areas of the text, so that, if the speed of the wind were to increase, only these strengthened sections would remain visible on the flapping standard. There could remain visible, for example, merely the letters: *Révon D'Or,* which can be read as "*Rêvons d'or*" ("let us dream of gold"). In this sense, displacement—as Freud suggests in his discussion of the topic—is a preliminary process which provides the conditions for condensation or overdetermination. Again, we are remote from Lacan's account of displacement as the metonymic circling of discourse around an object which it has itself ex-

communicated. For Lacan, the object of phantasy is merely the ungraspable coherence of the chain of signifiers, and desire itself is nothing other than this sequence, the "metonymy of a want-to-be." Desire cannot act as a force upon language, as the wind and the pattern of strengthening compress and transform the text of the banner.

This disagreement between Lacan and Lyotard focuses many of the most crucial questions about the nature of, and relation between, the conscious and the unconscious. In Lacan it is the conscious and the perceptual which is described in terms of the passivity and stasis of the imaginary, while the unconscious is equated with the instability of the symbolic, whereas Lyotard sees stasis in the fixed intervals of the linguistic system, and links the unconscious with the fluidity and mobility of the perceived world. These opposed interpretations clearly bear also on the problems of archaism and regression in the unconscious. For Lyotard, there *is* a primacy—or at least a primitiveness—of perception: the figural is in a sense both more rudimentary and more forceful than speech: "the first condition of discourse, which is discontinuity, the existence of *articuli,* is not satisfied by unconscious 'discourse.' Freud always characterizes the unconscious as *work,* as the other of discourse, and not as another discourse" [*Dérive* 225]. Lacan, by contrast, repudiates any equation of the unconscious with "the place of the divinities of night": there is nothing elementary about the unconscious except the elements of the signifier. This clash is most starkly illustrated by the differing interpretations of the third factor in Freud's account of the dream-work: *Rücksicht auf Darstellbarkeit.* Since Freud's theory of the dream is inseparable from his distinction between a secondary process—the process of logical, waking thought—and a primary process which tends toward a reckless, hallucinatory fulfillment, the value of the dream as the "royal road to the unconscious" appears to depend on its exemplification of the primary process, on its status as "a substitute for an infantile scene modified by being transferred onto a recent experience" [5:546]. However, if what Freud terms "the most striking psychological characteristic of the process of dreaming," the fact that "a thought, and as a rule a thought of something that is wished, is objectified in the dream, is represented in a scene, or, as it seems to us, experienced" [5:534] is as essential an aspect of the dream-work as condensation and displacement, then Lacan's argument for a purely "literal" understanding of dreams appears to be undermined.

Lacan parries this possible attack, in "*The Agency of the Letter in the Unconscious,*" by suggesting that what he terms "regard for the means of staging" is a condition which "constitutes a limitation operating *within* the system of writing." He compares the dream with a game of charades, and suggests that the very ingenuity with which "such logical articulations as causality, contradiction, hypothesis" are communicated despite this limitation, in both the dream and the game, demonstrates once again that "the dream-work follows the laws of the signifier" [*Ecrits* 161]. The attention of the analyst should be directed toward the proverb which the dumb-show is intended to convey, rather than toward the characteristic forms of mime and gesture by means of which the participants communicate their silent message. In so far as these forms have any interest, the questions which they raise are purely psychological. Elsewhere in the *Ecrits* Lacan offers a list of such questions—"little work of value has been done on space and time in the dream, on whether one dreams in colour or black and white, on whether smell, taste and touch occur, or the sense of vertigo, of the turgid and the heavy" [259]—but immediately goes on to suggest that these problems are remote from Freud's concern, which is with the "elaboration of the dream" in the sense of its "linguistic structure." Questions of interpretation are therefore, for Lacan, entirely distinct from psychological explanations of the material of the dream; and the "means of staging" are *not* part of the dream-work, in the sense of its linguistic elaboration. If the dream is the royal road to the unconscious, this is not because it operates in accordance with a primary process, but because it reveals the subject's possibilities, allowing the subject "to be in a state of perhaps" [*être à l'état de peut-être*] [Lacan, *"Radiophonie"* 69].

A similar relegation is apparent in Lacan's treatment of the fourth and final factor in the dream-work, secondary revision. Lacan pauses only to suggest that the phantasies or daydreams employed in secondary revision can be used either as signifying elements for the statement of unconscious thought, or in secondary revision in the true sense: this is a process which Lacan compares to the application of patches of whitewash to a stencil, in an effort to attenuate the rebarbative appearance of the rebus or hieroglyphs by transforming them into the semblance of a figurative painting. There are two important implications of this account. The first is that, although Lacan admits the "rebarbative" appearance of the stenciled forms, he cannot admit any connection between this appearance and the nature of the unconscious: secondary revision is not a means of concealing a threatening disorder, since the unconscious is itself simply a hidden order. The second is that Lacan affirms a strict disjunction (*"ou bien/ou bien"*) between the function of phantasy and daydream as a signifier of unconscious thought *within* the text of the dream, and the cosmetic operation of secondary revision carried out *on* the dream-text. For Lacan, the plastic transformation of a signifier cannot alter its function as a signifier, whereas for Freud—as Lyotard points out—no such disjunction can be said to apply. Lacan stresses a quotation in which Freud suggests that the activity of secondary revision is not to be distinguished from waking thought. But in his introductory essay "On Dreams" Freud argues that "one would be mistaken in seeing in the facade of the dream merely such actually uncomprehending and apparently arbitrary reworkings of the dream-content by the conscious agency of our psychic life" [5:667]. Since the wish-phantasies which are employed in the manufacture of this facade of illusory coherence are of the same kind as unconscious phantasy, it can be argued that "in many dreams the facade of the dream shows us directly the kernel of the dream, distorted through its mixture with other material" [5:667]. For Lyo-

tard this ambiguous status, midway between the center and the surface of the dream, torn between the discursive and the figural, is characteristic of phantasy.

Although, by this point, Lyotard's greater fidelity to Freud may seem assured, this fidelity in itself does not settle the difficulties, particularly since the dispute between Lyotard and Lacan has a significant political dimension. Since, for Lacan, desire is not a force, it cannot clash with any other force: desire may be the victim of a paradox, but not of a coercion. "Primal repression" consists simply in the fact that language both brings desire into being and permanently delays its satisfaction, and it is for this reason that Lacan exonerates the "symbolic order" by consistently portraying the *object petit a* as the result of an act of *self*-mutilation, a preemptive sacrifice.[2] By contrast, Lyotard in *Discours, figure* describes the phantasy as "a word lost in a hallucinatory scenography, an initial violence" [270]: *Discours, figure* is a critique of discourse in the name of its distorted and distorting others. Indeed what attracts Lyotard specifically to psychoanalysis at this point in his career is Freud's undialectical dualism, a dualism which is figured (rather than signified) in the very title *Discours, figure.* Since the primary process is not constitutive of the secondary process, but is revealed only privately through its disruptions of the secondary process, any philosophy, aesthetics, or politics of mediation and reconciliation—of the kind which Lyotard had formerly espoused during his career as a Marxist militant—is rendered impossible. Thus the Freudian investigations of *Discours, figure* form part of the elaboration of an aesthetic in which the work of art is seen as being constantly on the edge of its own rupture" [384], repudiating any reconciliation of Eros and Logos, phantasy and reality, as a betrayal of the radicality of the unconscious. And this aesthetics in turn becomes the model for the type of political practice in which Lyotard was engaged as a member of the *Mouvement du 22 Mars,* whose interventions were intended not to heal, but to exacerbate, the split between universal and particular, abstract and concrete, product and producer, characteristic of capitalism. Yet this rejection of any strategic political goals ultimately confronts Lyotard with the prospect of a "task of demystification" which would be "indefinite, inexhaustible" [*Dérive* 225] and therefore not so different from the Derridean deconstruction which Lyotard had initially repudiated in the name of the figural, nondiscursive nature of desire. The only escape from this situation appears to be to abandon the concept of critique altogether, to engage in a celebration of intensity over intention which finds its definitive expression in *Économie libidinale.*

Given that Lyotard himself has now admitted that "it is not true that the quest for intensities or for something of that kind can provide the content of a politics, because there is the problem of injustice" [*Au juste* 170-71], indeed that this reflection can be said to constitute the point of departure for the most recent phase of his work, should the imaginary nature of any conflict or discrepancy between language and its exterior be conceded? This is by no means a necessary conclusion. Lyotard's error, in *Dis-*

cours, figure, was not to protest against the imperialism of the signifier, but—in his haste to detach himself from Marxism—to abandon, even as a desirable aim, the transformation of discourse through the incorporation of its presently excluded others. It is this aim which the decline of poststructuralism has made it possible to rehabilitate. From the beginning Lyotard has focused his attention on, and has taken the side of, those "fragments of the soul at a loss for words" which *Discours, figure* evokes [346], and this concern has returned with renewed force in his latest work. What Lyotard now describes as *le différend* is precisely such a mute reality, no less real for being excluded from the world of language, and the difficulties which his most recent book explores are those which he had encountered in his own attempts to protest against the complacency of philosophies of the text. "In the *différend*," Lyotard writes, "something 'asks' to be put into sentences, and suffers the wrong of not being able to be at the moment." But he now concludes, recalling an earlier Merleau-Pontyan vein: "It is the concern of a literature, of a philosophy, perhaps of a politics, to testify to these *différends* by finding an idiom for them" [*Le différend* 30].

Notes

1. See the discussion following Derrida's "*Structure, Sign and Play in the Human Sciences*" in Macksey and Donato, eds., *The Structuralist Controversy* (Baltimore and London: Johns Hopkins Univ. Press, 1972).

2. See, for example, *The Four Fundamental Concepts of Psychoanalysis.* Trans. Alan Sheridan (New York: Norton, 1977) 103.

Works Cited

Derrida, Jacques. *L'Ecriture et la différence.* Paris: Seuil, 1967.

———. *Positions.* Paris: Seuil, 1972.

———. *Dissemination.* Tr. Barbara Johnson. Chicago: Univ. of Chicago Press, 1982.

Freud. *The Interpretation of Dreams* and *On Dreams. The Standard Edition of the Complete Psychological Writings of Freud.* Vol. 4-5. Tr. and Ed. James Strachey. London: The Hogarth Press, 1953-74.

Lacan, Jacques. *Ecrits:* A Selection. Trans. Alan Sheridan. New York: Norton, 1977.

———. "Radiophonie." In *Scilicet* 2/3 (1970).

Lyotard, Jean-François. *La Phénoménologie.* Paris: Presses Universitaires de France, 1954.

———. *Dérive à partir de Marx et Freud.* Paris: 10/18, 1973.

———. *Le différend.* Paris: Editions de Minuit, 1983.

———, and Jean-Loup Thebaud. *Au juste.* Paris: Christian Bourgois, 1979.

Merleau-Ponty, Maurice. *Le Visible et l'invisible.* Paris: Gallimard/TEL, 1981.

Cecile Lindsay (essay date 1984)

SOURCE: "Experiments in Postmodern Dialogue," in *Diacritics,* Vol. 14, No. 3, Fall, 1984, pp. 52-62.

[*In the following review of Lyotard's* Instructions païennes *and* Au juste, *Lindsay discusses Lyotard's use of the philosophical dialogue as a device for deconstructing the authority of a centralized, universalizing narrator.*]

> We possess a remarkable document that reflects the simultaneous birth of scientific thinking and of a new artistic-prose model for the novel. These are the Socratic dialogues.
>
>   M. M. Bakhtin, *The Dialogic Imagination*

1.

Near the beginning of Thomas Pynchon's *Gravity's Rainbow,* a group of allied scientists in World War II tries to come to terms with the German V-2, a sinister new rocket which, traveling faster than sound, arrives before the noise of its own approach. The V-bomb statistics chart an equation of probability on the map of London; an aging Pavlovian scientist is appalled by the nonchalance of a younger colleague, a statistician named Roger Mexico, toward the absurd pattern of doom he projects and logs daily. The Pavlovian discovers that statistical probability provides no clues for shelter, since, unlike dogs, bombs have no memory and no prior conditioning—not an easy lesson for a Pavlovian to learn:

> How can Mexico play, so at his ease, with these symbols of randomness and fright? Innocent as a child, perhaps unaware—perhaps—that in his play he wrecks the elegant rooms of history, threatens the idea of cause and effect itself. What if Mexico's whole generation have turned out like this? Will Postwar be nothing but "events" newly created one moment to the next? No links? Is it the end of history? [56]

The recent work of Jean-François Lyotard reflects on the Pavlovian's concern for the fate of causality and history, and has dwelt at length on just such a "post-" era, which Lyotard calls the postmodern, and which he characterizes as, in part, a generalized incredulity about precisely those grand explicating metanarratives, like the notion of cause and effect, that have served as the guiding lights of the Western past. In addition to the discourse of scientific determinism, Lyotard identifies in *La Condition postmoderne* other "grand Narratives" [*grands Récits*]: those of speculative philosophy, of universal emancipation, of Marxism. When causality no longer provides explanatory links, phenomenality dissociates into disjoined "events": the Pavlovian's nightmare constitutes for Lyotard a salutary new condition of human thought and praxis based on the refusal of any metanarrative which claims to subtend and explain phenomena. Lyotard cautions that his designation of a postmodernity must not be taken as a periodization, since its traits can also be identified in the discourse of the Sophists, in certain Pascalian texts, or in the pantheon of ancient Greek mythology. Rather, postmodernity implies a multitude of alternatives to the Idealist tradition that has dominated Western thought at least since Plato banished the poets from his Republic.

Lyotard's 1977 text **Instructions païennes** proposes a program of sorts for the "post-" generation. The program begins with the recognition that all talking, all discourse, is the recounting of narratives. All narratives take place in what **Instructions païennes** defines as a pragmatic context: ". . . the set of very complicated relations existing between the person who narrates and what he is talking about; between the person narrating and the person listening; and between this latter and the story discussed by the former" [16]. The referents of a narrative are never events or brute facts in themselves, but rather other narratives. A multitude of varying narratives can take their points of departure from any proffered narrative. The question of the greater or lesser "truth" of the various narratives thus has no general pertinence, just as the universality or omnitemporality of any narrative is undercut by its inscription within a given pragmatic context. For example, "pagan instructions" are not a set of laws or lessons to be applied universally, but rather local indications of what is appropriate for a certain pragmatic context; when that context disappears, the instructions no longer make sense. This relativized vision of discourse leads to the rejection of what Lyotard in this work calls the *pious* attitude of belief or conviction that had made the dominant response to the various "grand Narratives" of the past "a persistent piety for the Passion of the true throughout history" [14]. A sustained effort at *paganism* would level all narratives, denying to any one narrative the privilege of speaking, containing, or translating the others. Thus, theoretical narratives such as those proposed by Marxism, speculative philosophy, aesthetics, or capitalism fall from their place in the pious hierarchy and stand as equals among a virtually infinite set of competing, conflictual alternative narratives. The Pavlovian scientist of *Gravity's Rainbow* fears that history has come to an end; in the vision proposed by *Instructions païennes,* history as a metanarrative—as the story of the continual progression of the speculative Spirit or that of a dialectical process of struggle and emancipation of the oppressed—has indeed come to an end. In its place we find a teeming multitude of *historiettes* that are at once "insignificant and serious" [39].

Once the many narratives have been leveled, with none providing the justification for any other, certain troublesome questions are posed to a program of paganism: how is justice in human affairs to be determined and administered under such conditions? How is it possible to envision justice and to act justly in an era that no longer believes in Truth, God, universal emancipation, the liberation of the proletariat, cause and effect, or History? *Au juste*

takes up this interrogation concerning justice in terms of a notion of multiple language games [*jeux de langage*] that make up all discourse, all narratives. Lyotard finds in certain Aristotelian texts, as well as in Kant and most explicitly in Wittgenstein, the notion that language is not a unified whole, but is differentiated into separate *types* of enunciations: prescriptive, denotative, speculative, fictive, etc. Each category has its rules, which constitute the various contracts at work within given narratives and their pragmatic contexts. The idea of justice in social or political life has much to do with these language games, and *Au juste* argues for *experimentation* in language games as an aspect of postmodernity necessary to the achievement of a "pagan" justice. "Experiments" like non-Euclidean geometry, four-dimensional space, or avant-garde painting, and experimenters like Kurt Gödel, James Joyce, Marcel Duchamp, Gertrude Stein, or Michel Butor point, Lyotard argues, to a way of questioning certain pious notions that have maintained distinctions—and thus injustices—between various language games and various realms of narratives.

By raising the question of the *just* in these terms, **Instructions païennes** and **Au juste** situate their interrogations of and meditations on narratives both grand and experimental squarely in the field of the social, the historical, and the political. In **Au juste,** the link between the narrative, the political, and the just is made explicit: ". . . my excuse for writing has always been a political one; I've always considered that sufficient. Therefore it is quite evident that I accept entirely that there is a prescriptive function in the idea of paganism: it lies in the direction this idea indicates as necessary to follow" [34]. Both **Instructions païennes** and **Au juste,** then, connect two domains of discourse which much critical thought still today sees as not only distinct but hierarchized; that is, on the one hand, the field of playful experimentation in artistic or literary forms (for example, *Gravity's Rainbow* or *Glas*), and, on the other hand, the domain of the historicopolitical, the domain in which the serious question of justice arises.

The unusual juxtaposition, in Lyotard's work, of experimentation with justice thus provides an approach to a critical and social problem that still persists, defying any fin-de-siècle postmodernity, in the grand narratives of University discourse as well as in the contiguous narratives of economic and social priorities that impinge on the University. In many universities today, the discourses of science and technology have a larger and more respected voice than those of the humanities, which are equally divided among themselves as to their respective order in a hierarchy of value: philosophy often still sees itself as closer to the Truth than literature, and is not convinced that it shares with that fallen form any common motives or attributes. Further divisions and hierarchies are still in place within discourses such as literary criticism: for many, a definite literary canon exists and certain works or groups of works (especially experimental forms) fail to meet the entrance requirements. If the persistence of this kind of hierarchization of discourse makes one hesitant to claim a widespread penetration of the postmodern condition, it also points out the importance of Lyotard's work in a critical examination of the nature and consequences of our lingering assumptions. By articulating a postmodern condition of narrative linking justice to experimentation, Lyotard's work proposes a form of dialogue between narrative realms still very much considered different and unequal.

2.

What could be less experimental than a philosophical dialogue? Both *Instructions païennes* and *Au juste* are overtly structured like that most staple of Socratic items, the dialogue. The back cover of *Instructions païennes* informs us that in the book, a *provincial* and a *métèque* together address a situation acknowledged by both: that the "grand Narratives" of the political right and left have lost their credibility with the intelligentsia of the country in question. While the provincial finds cause for concern, the *métèque* rejoices and undertakes to instruct the addressee (although claiming theirs to be a collective instruction) in a program for a new politics of paganism. The first pages reveal that the "province" in question is France, with its general disillusionment on the part of the left and the recent prominence of its "new philosophers." The *métèque,* defined by the dictionary as a foreigner residing in Greece without rights of citizenship, serves a function familiar from other texts by Lyotard: that of the teacher, the imported "flying professor." In **"La Force des faibles,"** Lyotard's contribution to the 1976 edition of *L'Arc* devoted to his work, the term "flying professors" refers to those nomadic Sophists who went "from city to city selling their lessons and their lectures" [5-6]. In *Le Mur du Pacifique* it similarly and humorously refers to the current practice of academic exchange between universities.

The overtly pedagogical (albeit sometimes Sophistic) format of *Instructions païennes* finds a corollary in the dialogues presented by *Au juste,* whose subtitle is **"Conversations."** Here the speakers are identified by name on the back cover and by initials throughout the text: Jean-François Lyotard, we read, was approached by a younger man, Jean-Loup Thébaud, with questions about the former's books. Specifically, the younger man wants to know if Lyotard is still interested in the question of the political—of justice—when his recent books seem to indicate that communication, and thus social existence, is impossible. *Au juste* claims to be the record of seven days of discussion spread over seven months. The youth of one interlocutor and the academic record of the other points, if not precisely to the student-teacher relationship of the *Instructions païennes,* then at least to a structure of unequal experience and authority which is mirrored in the use of direct address pronouns: JFL uses the familiar *tu,* while JLT employs the formal *vous.* In each text, the questioning takes place on both sides, and while the provincial and JLT participate both oppositionally and affirmatively in the formulation of the various points made, the major roles are undeniably those of the *métèque* and JFL. The question

that arises is an obvious one: how to read such an apparently classical format whose own message is that old forms of authority and dominance must be opposed by new ways of viewing language games, genres of discourse, and narratives? An approach to this paradox is offered by the mixed reputation of the genre of philosophical dialogue, a reputation which, Lyotard reminds us, has long been a divergent one.

Aristotle opposed to the didactic wisdom of speculative discourse a lower form of discussion, the *dialéktikè,* which is considered frivolous, Lyotard notes, because "opinions challenge each other; ordinary little narratives compete with each other" [*Instructions* 41]. For Lyotard, the "lower" form of discussion is of great interest because it allows for the impious coexistence of a multitude of competing narratives. Pedagogical dialogues such as those conducted by Socrates really permit only one voice, the one pronouncing the narrative of wisdom. The addressee is reduced to silence even when given the ritual turn to speak: "If he is sometimes allowed to speak, that is, put in the place of the narrator, it is only in order to verify that he can correctly recite the lesson" [41]. Thus the Socratic "dialogue" is in effect simply a divided monologue, returning always to the unity of a singular discourse on knowledge: "The only listener tolerated by philosophy is the disciple" [*Au juste* 137]. In a late essay, Lyotard notes the same move on the part of Hegel, who similarly discredits *Konversation* in the Preface to *The Phenomenology of Mind.* Rather than leave the *dialéktike* outside the speculative system, however, Hegal subsumes it within that order: "Science in the Hegelian sense does not put the *dialéktikè* aside, as did Aristotle's didactics. Rather, Hegelian science includes it in its own genre, the speculative. In this genre, the *two* of the *dialéktikè,* which gives rise to paralogisms and aporia, is enrolled in the service of the didactic end, the *one.* There are no real discussions" [**"Discussions, ou: phraser après Auschwitz,"** *Les Fins de l'homme* 283]. Thus the genre that is "dialogue" can go in two directions whose consequences are radically divergent, as Bakhtin points out in the passage which serves as epigraph to this essay: Socrates' dialogues reflect "the simultaneous birth of scientific thinking and of a new artistic-prose model for the novel."[1] For Bakhtin, the term novel is intended in a very broad sense as a "dialogic" discourse, a discourse admitting of many voices and many narratives; novelization is effected by whatever forces operate within discourse to challenge the single-voicedness of authority or regulating ideals. Lyotard finds in the *dialéktikè* of discussion between many competing opinions exciting prospects for paralogisms, paradoxes, and aporia that, like Bakhtin's conception of novelization, challenge the single-voicedness of "grand Narratives," Socratic dialogues, and theories in general. One strategy for opening up unifying dialogue to heteroglossia is what Lyotard calls experimentation.

Experimentation is a term which belongs to the domains of both scientific and artistic discourse, just as, for Bakhtin, the Socratic dialogues gave rise to both scientific thinking and artistic forms. The conjunction and/or confusion of the "scientific" with the "artistic" is a significant one in both *Instructions païennes* and *Au juste;* the advent of the postmodern is heralded in part by a recognition of the similarity of their respective operations. It is science, Lyotard argues, which today fulfills the pious need to believe in a "truth" about "reality" in an era when overt belief in other transcendent explanations has succumbed to scepticism:

> Nietzsche saw quite clearly this restauration of faith in the trappings of scientificity. No one believes in anything any more, but something still remains: scientific asceticism. . . . Confidence, though masked by the critical spirit, nevertheless maintains activity and thought in the belief that the true is the most important thing. . . . This is the persistence of Platonism today: the prejudice that there is a reality to know. Everything is put into doubt except doubt itself. ["Petite mise en perspective de la décadence et de quelques combats minoritaires à y mener," *Politiques de la Philosophie* 126-27]

The self-application of doubt is the first step taken by discourses of art and science whose experimentation characterizes them, for Lyotard, as postmodern.

In *La Condition postmoderne,* the crisis of modern science is identified as a crisis of *determinism* faced with an increasing recognition of instability and undecidability, much like the conflict between the Pavlovian and the probability statistician in *Gravity's Rainbow.* Gödel's Incompleteness Theorem serves as the paradigm for a postmodern science of undecidability: translating the ancient and Sophist "liar's paradox" into mathematical terms, Godel's theorem subjects the discourse of theoretical mathematics to its own discourse of validation. The result is a paradoxical situation in which the axiomatic system of number theory is revealed to be incomplete: it winds up incapable of proving certain true statements. Unrestricted self-reference is the culprit in these mathematical paradoxes, as it is in the liar's paradox, and is the key to understanding Lyotard's notion of the experimental and the postmodern. Just as Bertrand Russell "solved" the liar's paradox by separating it into two types of enunciations that cannot be mutually applied (the statement "I am a liar" must not apply to the statement "I am telling you the truth when I say I am a liar"), any theoretical metanarrative, be it that of mathematical validation or that of Marxist theory of labor, must refrain from including itself in the realm of discourse about which it purports to tell the truth if it wishes to preserve its status as science or theory. The maddening thing about the Sophists and Rhetoricians was that they refused to respect the confines of established genres, situations, and roles within discourse: a student could be at the same time an adversary from whom one might demand payment on both accounts simultaneously.[2] In the pagan or postmodern optic, then, wisdom and rhetorical seduction are equated, and "theory" becomes merely "the most recent of the language arts, one literary genre among others" [*Instructions* 44]. The paradox of self-reference collapses

theory into literature and science into art, and leads above all to inventiveness and imagination in all realms: "Science is not the discourse of an efficacious knowledge which claims to find in its conformity to 'reality' the confirmation of its value; rather, science is the creator of realities, and its value resides in its ability [*puissance*] to redistribute perspectives, not in its power [*pouvoir*] to master objects. Science is in this respect comparable to the arts" [**"Petite mise en perspective"** 134]. Both *Instructions païennes* and *Au juste* place themselves deliberately under the aegis of a postmodern self-reference (the epigraph to *Au juste* cites Aristotle's *Nichomachean Ethics:* "The rule of indetermination is itself indeterminate"). Their ruminations on the nature of the experimental and on the question of their own experimentation range across the fields of politics, society, and justice as well as those of art and science.

In *Instructions païennes,* an inventive and experimental self-reference is opposed to the "auto- effect" [*l'effet auto-*] that results from the pragmatics of capitalism, as well as to the repression of narratives that results from the discourse of totalitarianism. According to the "pagan" vision, we recall, all of history, all of social existence is composed of millions of "wisps of narratives" [39] that disperse or gather together, with some coming to form major grids of power. The pagan vision recognizes that all narration situates us within a pragmatic context: "as the narrator, narratee, or narrated of a narrative which implicates you, you come under the jurisdiction of that narrative. In fact, we are always in the hands of some narrative or other: someone has always already said something to us, and we have already been spoken" [47]. Situated in narrative, we play all the roles—narrator, narratee, narrated—in turn, according to the pragmatic context that situates us. Whereas the pagan realizes that one is never the first to enunciate any narrative, that one is never the origin of one's narrative, the discourse of capitalism is based on just such a premise. Capitalism accords importance only to the position of the narrator, so that the revenues and profits of the narrative (i.e., the property) revert always to the narrating pole (the proprietor), which must never be seen as capable of passing to the positions of narrated or narratee: "Thus there exists in capitalism a devotion: the exclusive cult it devotes to the entrepreneur of narratives" [78]. While a totalitarian pragmatics legislates that all citizens must always occupy all three narrative poles, at once enunciating, receiving, and executing (only) the official narrative, a pragmatics of capital is founded on a belief in the autonomy and creativity of an author who is the prime mover (*premier moteur*) of the proffered narrative, which is viewed as something "new": "It is true that you cannot be an entrepreneur of narratives if you don't seem to have invented some new story, some different product" [80]. Capital maintains a cult of origins and originality, of self-creation, by repressing any recognition of the series of narratives that gives rise to any "new" story.

The effacement, in capitalist pragmatics, of the *series* of narrators and narratives that always situate any "new" narrative act is what the *métèque* of ***Instructions païennes*** terms the "auto- effect" and considers to be as nefarious to justice as the totalitarian practice of repressing unauthorized narratives. The question posed by the provincial is then: is there any alternative to, on the one hand, the repressive "originality" or autonomy of the "auto- effect" and, on the other hand, the single legislated voice of the totalitarian regime? In response, the dialogue between the *métèque* and the provincial begins to sketch a pagan pragmatics of narrative based on the paradoxes of self-reference. The *métèque* offers as an example the relations existing between the gods of Greek mythology and the humans who deal with them. Ruse, rhetoric, and seduction characterize these relations; recognizing that the gods, as incarnations of power, are always more protean and thus stronger than they, humans attempt to circumvent the gods' narratives and narrate the gods in whatever way possible. Possibilities always exist for turning the narrative tables to some degree, since narration is a question of ruse rather than of Truth: "Pagans don't worry themselves over the conformity of the narrative to its object. They know that the references are organized by the words, and that the gods are no guarantee, because their word is no more truthful than that of humans. Pagans are quite busy enough with rhetoric and hunting—where one never has the last word and there is no *coup de grâce*" [45]. When even the gods' narratives must submit to the rules of self-reference, in which no narratives have the last word, the possibility of minor, local victories gives the term "new" a new sense.

The conversations of ***Au juste*** continue to sketch out a "casuistics of imagination" (the designation given to the fourth day's discussion) in which the invention of ruses and variant moves (*coups*) within the language games that situate us allows for a measure of "play" in the sense of a certain freedom of movement within imposed limits:

> I think that pagans are artists. That is, they are able to move from one game to another, and in each of these games (this would be the optimum case), they try to come up with new moves. Moreover, they try to invent new games. What we call an "artist" in the current sense of the term is someone who, in relation to this or that medium—that of the canvas, the picta, for example—proposes new rules for the pictorial game. The same thing goes for what we call independent cinema. Or music. . . . Paganism would be precisely that. The point is not that the games are preserved, but that in each existing game people effect new moves; they open up the possibility of new efficacies in games as they are currently regulated. And, on the other hand, they change the rules. . . . [119-20]

Such a "newness" in language games is never the illusion of radical autonomy and initiative that has counted for so much in modern Western thought, but is rather a will and an ability to imagine new effects while never forgetting that one always resides within the realm of the already-recounted.

This pagan conception of newness is linked, in ***Au juste,*** to experimentation in all domains, and is seen as a sign of

the postmodern even when it occurs in works like Diderot's *Le Neveu de Rameau* and *Jacques le fataliste*. What is experimental and postmodern about these eighteenth-century dialogues is first of all that they comprise a narrative pragmatics full of substitutions and permutations: ". . . permutations between the author and the narrator, between the narratee and the speaker and the one spoken about . . . " [*Au juste* 26]. The effect of such chancy and frequent permutations is one of *humor,* a humor roused by the "denaturing" of whatever standard forms and structures of thought or sensibility typically comprise a regulating ideal for the particular language game in question. This humor is, for Lyotard, "the characteristic of the experimenter, of any experimenter" [*Au juste* 26]. A second way in which Diderot participates in the postmodern is the "evanescence of the addressee" [26] at work in certain of his texts. While the classical text was written with a specific group of readers and a given system of values in mind, the postmodern text is characterized by the *lack* of a known or knowable interlocutor. As a result, Lyotard argues, the artistic avant-garde is reproached for inventing works that no one can understand or appreciate. This avant-garde refuses the notion of a universal subject of history to whom and in whose name all artistic "messages" are communicated. The postmodernity of the avant-garde work consists instead in the paradoxical fact that out of its solitude it produces and situates its own narrator and narratee: "To experiment means, in a certain sense, solitude and celibacy. But on the other hand it also means that if what is produced is truly strong, it will wind up creating its own readers, viewers, listeners. In other words, the experimental work will have as its effect the constitution of a pragmatic situation that did not previously exist. It is the message itself, by its form, which will give rise to both its addressee and its addresser" [23]. The postmodern optic does not look to situate the innovations of an experimental work in respect to an originary and autonomous past that would be its author-proprietor; rather, it sees the "newness" of the avant-garde work as always qualified by its insertion within the seriality of whatever discourse(s) it takes as its point of departure. That newness then resides in the work's potential for *future* effects, for future moves calling forth addressers and addressees who did not exist as such before. In this way, the bogus novelty of the "auto-effect" is unmasked in favor of a cautious and casuistic experimentation and a qualified newness grounded in self-reference.

Perhaps it is time now to take up again the question posed at the beginning of this section; that is, how experimental can a philosophical dialogue be? In what way, if at all, do ***Instructions païennes*** and ***Au juste*** constitute experimental, postmodern dialogues? In at least one sense, the conversations these books present do claim to break with the didactic genre, for while the discussions comment on their own genre or, in the case of ***Au juste,*** on ***Instructions païennes*** as well as other texts by Lyotard, they claim *not* to comprise metadialogues or -narratives that would tell the truth about themselves or about the earlier works. Objecting to the way in which traditional pedagogical dialogue silences its interlocutor *Au juste* proposes to experiment, in its own format, with a permutation of roles in which the reader of earlier texts (in this case, JLT) now assumes a new function: "If he requires of the author of books that he leave that solitude and unresponsiveness in which he wrote, putting himself in such a position that he can be a partner who questions and answers . . . then it is true that this is an experimentation to be attempted" [20]. JFL goes on to claim in his segments of *Au juste* that if the reader of previous books becomes an interlocutor in the current conversations, then the author of the earlier books experiences a *démaîtrise,* a loss of the mastery and authority that are typically associated with an author, since the partner's questions have the ability to abruptly switch the discussion from one language game to another. Far from constituting a metacommentary on certain earlier books, then, *Au juste* would become merely one of the future effects of those books on two of their addressees, neither of whom possesses any particular privilege. In fact, JFL argues, since his interlocutor has begun asking questions and emitting new messages, *Au juste* will paradoxically become a book "of his" that he will not really have written, but which will have situated both him and his discussion partner.

The interlocutor JLT raises certain objections to this portrait of nonmastery, and his questions anticipate the perplexity of the reader of both *Instructions païennes* and *Au juste.* Specifically, JLT suspects that the dialogue genre simply provides the author with "an occasion for being the master differently" [*Au juste* 17], thus putting in doubt the claim that both partners are equally situated by the pragmatic context in which they participate. As an addressee of the two texts, the reader, too, must wonder to what degree these discussions are an orchestrated set of language games, or whether the question of orchestration versus spontaneity is relevant to a genre that has discredited the "auto-effect" of originality. How to judge whether the nonmasterful and anti-metanarrative claims made for this genre are indeed the case? According to what criteria can these works be judged experimental? It is precisely in respect to the realm of *judging* that *Instructions païennes* and *Au juste* make what are perhaps their strongest "moves." *Au juste* takes up, in respect to the experimental, a vision of judging and judgment that Lyotard began to develop in earlier texts, and which he sees as related to Aristotle's description of the prudent judge, the Kantian Idea, and Nietzsche's notion of perspective.

In works such as the *Rhetorics,* the *Politics,* or the *Nichomachean Ethics,* Aristotle proposes an atypical vision of the judge's activity. Lyotard points out that the judge described in these works is not the public official authorized to decide on individual cases in light of a given system of laws, but rather an authority whose decisions have no guiding formulations: ". . . the true nature of the judge is precisely to pronounce judgments, and therefore prescriptions, without criteria. What Aristotle calls *prudence* is finally nothing other than that. Prudence consists in practicing justice with no models" [*Au juste* 52-53]. In

weighing the situations of all parties in a litigation, the judge is actually dealing with enunciations or narratives which belong to the realm of opinion rather than that of truth, so that once again we are in the domain of *dialéktikè* or discussion, where opinions vie with each other. Thus the judge's prescriptive opinions are based only on other opinions; with the Aristotelian judge, Lyotard maintains, "we're dealing with a discourse which tries to establish the right *technè,* an art rather than knowledge, in matters where there can be no knowledge because we're immersed in opinion. Politics belong to this sphere, not to the sphere of knowledge" [56]. The judge is caught up in and situated by the same sphere of language as the judged; the only way to recognize a just judge is by his/her acts, which must be made one by one for each occasion, be it political, social, or aesthetic. A judge's proper *ethos* is not the cause or origin of his/her just judgments, but resides in a future effect: it is that which is manifested in just judgments.

Lyotard finds in Kant's *Critique of Judgment* a similar passage from knowledge to art. This Kant—"the Kant of the imagination, when he recovered from the malady of knowledge and rules and passed over to the paganism of art and nature" [*Instructions* 36]—provides the notion of an Idea which enables judgment. The Idea guiding judgment has no content and presents no law or system; rather, it provides for a maximization or anticipation, an *imagination* concerning the future ends of a certain judgment: "Whatever allows us to decide is not acquired, but remains to be acquired; it lies ahead of us, like an Idea" [*Au juste* 157]. Following the Idea of judgment thus proposed, we possess no criteria for deciding the question of the degree of experimentation evinced by *Instructions païennes* and *Au juste.* We can only judge, with no theory or checklist of the avant-garde as guide, according to our anticipation of the possible effects of the moves made by these texts. Judgments formulated in this way make for a justice of and among all language games, including the language game that is justice. What results is paganism, "a situation in which we judge, and we judge not only on questions of truth, but also on questions of beauty (aesthetic efficacy), and also on questions of justice, that is, of politics or ethics, without criteria" [*Au juste* 33]. By effacing the distinction between science (or knowledge) and art, and by focusing attention on anticipated effects, experimentation becomes a model for justice in all domains.

A justice of this kind constitutes a new perspective in the Nietzschean sense of a challenge or an alternative to whatever vision holds dominant sway in a particular culture. Such a challenge is actually comprised, for Lyotard, of a multitude of "insignificant and serious" heterogenous narratives; a just situation is one in which all potential narrators are able to exercise their ability to narrate from their own perspectives, and where none of the narrative poles holds privilege over any other. The directives for such a justice of narrative perspectives are enunciated at the end of *Instructions païennes:*

> Destroy narrative monopolies. . . . Strip the narrator of
> the privilege he grants himself. Valorize the equally

important power that lies on the side of reception as well as the power of execution, the narrated side. Struggle instead for the inclusion of metanarratives, theories, and doctrines, especially political ones, in the set of narratives. May the intelligentsia have as its function not to tell the truth and save the world, but to will the capacity to enact, hear, and tell stories. [86-87]

Justice, like experimentation, then lies always ahead of us, to be acquired, in the potential prospects of variant perspectives. Injustices in all domains are linked to an attitude of piety toward that *past* which is the human Subject of narration, a subject whose autonomy and priority in respect to narration must be subjected to the paradoxes of self-reference prescribed by these pagan instructions.

3.

The conversations in *Au juste* take place under the aegis of an unquiet ear: like the Londoner of World War II straining to hear the V-2 rocket—something that can only be heard if it is not addressed to you—the left ear pictured on the book's cover is paradoxically asking "eh?" in respect to some inaudible message or mumbling interlocutor. And the expression *au juste* can be used to talk about exactitude [*justesse*] as well as justice. The problematic nature of communication constitutes a silent subtext in these dialogues which, along with *Instructions païennes,* seem at first to make louder claims for conversation, for *dialéktikè.* In making their case for the permutation of poles of narration, of the exchange of initiative in question-and-answer encounters, of a perspective for compatibility and justice for the millions of minor "wisps of narration," these dialogues may give the impression that if the constraints of totalitarian or capitalist narrative pragmatics were to be successfully countered, then positive communication would be possible among the individuals and groups which shift in and out of the various narrative instances. The example of *Le Dit des hommes,* a public ritual of narration practiced by the Cashinahua Indians of South America, provides a paradigm for a pagan version of narrative communication and community between the individual and the social group. In this serial transmission of narratives, the narrator presents himself as someone to whom something has been narrated. The pagan narrator never sees himself as an "author" existing outside of his narrative, but as always implicated and positioned within it. Stating his name only at the end of his version of the story, the narrator situates himself for his listeners in an extremely precise familial network, pointing thereby to his having already been socially narrated. In this way, the poles of narratee and narrated, so discredited by the Western tradition, assume an importance fundamental to a justice of paganism. Such a model of narrative tradition may give the impression that this kind of social and narrative organization would provide for a communication of meaning which, if not immediate, at least takes place in a comfortable and familiar collective mediacy. These impressions of a positive, collective communicability would be at bottom mistaken in respect to Lyotard's texts, and it is important to make explicit the postmodern vision of "communication" at work there.

Another text dealing with a "post-" era, Jacques Derrida's *La Carte postale, de Socrate à Freud et au-delà,* suggests that communication can no longer be thought of in terms of integral subjects emitting and sending precise, intended messages to other autonomous subjects who effectively receive them. A postcard of Socrates and Plato provides the occasion for lengthy meditations on the fate of the model of communication—the Postal Era—inaugurated by that odd couple. Derrida finds in the postcard as an emblem of "communication" an immense potential for detours, delays, and dead letters. Dialogue between individuals is subject to the same difficulties: "This endless flow of words, these days and nights of explanations will not make us change or exchange places, although we constantly try to do so, to pass to the other side. . . . But there are the others, the others within us, I'll grant you, and we can't help it at all. There's a veritable crowd, and that's the truth" [51]. Exchanging places with another is as impossible as occupying one's own place fully or singularly: such is the fate of a Truth linked to a metaphysics of presence and uniqueness. In *Au juste* the inherent plurality of being is tied to language games: ". . . we can enter inside but not *play* these games, for it is the games that make us their players, and we are thus ourselves *several* beings (let us call 'beings' here those proper names which are positioned at the pragmatic instances of each of these games). Thus we are the *addressees* of obligations, *addressers* of artistic messages, and so on" [99]. Quotation marks charge the word *being* with equivocacy and irony in Lyotard's definition; "being" becomes a matter not of essence but of nomenclature. But if we are several beings because we occupy the different narrative poles, we are also, following Derrida, several beings even *when* we occupy each position.

Lyotard approaches this heterogeneity of the individual subject, again, from the perspective of the "narrative explosion" [*Instructions païennes* 26] that atomizes discourse into multiple and incommensurable language games, or phrases, as Lyotard later calls them. In a 1981 essay, **"Introduction à une étude du politique selon Kant,"** in *Rejouer le politique,* Lyotard characterizes postmodernity as a sense of the *fission* of heterogeneous language games, perspectives, and ends. This postmodern recognition goes well beyond Kant's perception of the abysses between categories of discourse and his explanation for the impulse, in human thought, to unite or subsume them:

> Kant reduces the idea of an impulse toward commerce among phrases to that of a subject who, without it, would fly to pieces and of a reason which, without it, would enter into conflict with itself and no longer deserve its name. We, today—and this is part of the Begebenheit of our time—sense that the fission which takes place there also extends to that subject and that reason. At least, after Marx, we have learned to recognize that what remains of the attraction between phrases in the postmodern Babel, and what seems to verify them . . . is precisely this impostor subject and this blindly calculating reason which is called capital, espe-

cially when it takes possession of phrases themselves in order to make them merchandise. . . . *[133]*

The illusion of a fullness or homogeneity of presence on the part of the subject participates in the same canonical myth as capitalism's "auto- effect" of enterpreneurial originality. A V-bomb, a noiseless fission of the subject, must be read as the subtext for the pagan pragmatics mapped out in *Instructions païennes* and *Au juste.*

If such a notion of the subject (and of the vision of "communication" it entails) must be taken as a given for the postmodern, it is by no means a foregone or even widespread conclusion in contemporary discourse, so that Lyotard is quite right to point out that the postmodern condition does not necessarily coincide with any historical periodization. A mainly unquestioned notion of the classical subject still subtends dominant modes of thought, and Derrida reminds us that the Postal Era is still very much in effect, with Socrates and Plato still sending out signals "to which we're all still tuned in" [Derrida 116]. Traditional models of communication still inform the domains of pedagogy and politics. What results is that in the discourse of the University, as in those of the capitalist or totalitarian states, certain narratives are elevated over others because they are seen as containing the truth of the others or as constituting merchandise for turning a profit. By meticulously unmasking the operations of the various types of metanarratives, by turning the conditions of any narrative back upon itself, Lyotard's work points to a powerful potential for a dialogic situation among genres of discourse that have been kept separate and hierarchized. This potential lies in the capacity of experimentation to produce possible future effects, one of which would be the "denaturing" of the human subject as it is traditionally conceived:

> Apollinaire used to say that contemporary artists have to make themselves inhuman. What they are testing out in their works is what Aristotle called *endechomenon:* the possible in the sense of what can be tolerated. Can a given genre, for example the theater, tolerate "cruelty" the way in which Artaud understands it? Can painting tolerate Malevitch's "supreme"? Can literature tolerate Butor's "book-object" or Gertrude Stein's "paragraph"? By breaking down the boundaries of different genres, these works engender their confusion. . . . In this way is constituted a universe of experimentation with forms, which can be termed satirical in the sense that the genres are mixed together (satura), and that the program for each is to saturate the tolerable.
> [**"Petite mise en perspective"** 125]

Lyotard's work points to the possibility of "moves" whose future effect would be the satirical *humor* of mixing together what dominant thought needs to separate in order to maintain its sober dominance: art and science; literature and philosophy; philosophy and autobiography; theory and its object; the canon and its excluded other. A postmodern saturation of the tolerable is not a head-on power struggle, but rather a series of skirmishes or "*combats minoritaires*" whose goal is the "insertion of a foreign, minor *historiette*" [*Instructions* 84] into a major, constituted narrative

apparatus. The Pavlovians of any theory or doctrine find this confusion of confines and categories intolerable, but even Pynchon's staunch Pavlovian eventually becomes the schizophrenic site of several heterogenous voices. Such a dialoguing between genres and within genres combats the injustice of discounting or discrediting discourses one is not yet ready to hear, for which ears have not yet been constituted. Bakhtin locates in Socrates' dialogues the simultaneity of the birth of art and science, those "elegant rooms of history"; it is the recognition of this simultaneity that experimentation makes possible and postmodern justice prescribes.

Notes

1. M. M. Bakhtin, *The Dialogic Imagination,* tr. Caryl Emerson and Michael Holquist (Austin: Texas, 1981), 24. For a discussion of Bakhtin's theory on language as dialogic or "many-voiced," see David Carroll, "The Alterity of Discourse: Form, History, and the Question of the Political in M. M. Bakhtin," Diacritics 13.2 (Summer 1983), 65-83.

2. In "La Force des faibles," *L'Arc* 64 (1976), 7-8, Lyotard analyzes the example of Protagorus, who includes the teacher-student conflict within the class of conflicts for which the teacher prepares the student. Protagorus demands payment from his student on the grounds that no matter which of them wins the dispute over payment that they are currently engaged in, the teacher has earned his payment.

Works Cited

Derrida, Jacques. *La Carte postale, de Socrate à Freud et au delà.* Paris: Aubier-Flammarion, 1980.

Lyotard, Jean-François. "La Force des faibles." *Arc* 64 (1976).

———. "Petite mise en perspective de la décadance et de quelques combats minoritaires à y mener." In *Politiques de la philosophie.* Paris: Grasset, 1976.

———. *La Condition postmoderne.* Paris: Editions de Minuit, 1979.

———. *Le Mur du Pacifique.* Paris: Galilée, 1979.

———. "Discussions, ou: phraser après Auschwitz." In *Les Fins de l'homme.* Paris: Galilée, 1981.

———. "Introduction à une étude du politique selon Kant." In *Rejouer la politique.* Paris: Galilée, 1981.

Pynchon, Thomas. *Gravity's Rainbow.* New York: Viking Press, 1973.

George Van Den Abbeele (essay date 1984)

SOURCE: An interview in *Diacritics,* Vol. 14, No. 3, Fall, 1984, pp. 16-20.

[In the following interview, Abbeele and Lyotard discuss Lyotard's attitude toward texts, contexts, language, names, and the use of philosophy as understood inside a postmodern framework.]

[Georges Van Den Abbeele]: *In reading your work, one cannot help but be struck by its heterogeneity, its diversity, its relentless questioning of previously advanced categories. What one could call the protean or nomadic quality of your thought inevitably places its critic in the position of feeling already passed by, of being dépassé by your work, such that a potential point of disagreement may turn out no longer to be current in your thinking. The question raised then is that of the "responsibility" of your writing. More pointedly, your long-held allegiance to avant-garde esthetics (evidenced by numerous books and articles on contemporary art from Duchamp to Monory) makes your work open to the charge of seeking the new for its own sake. In the political sphere, the charge would be that of pursuing a liberalist pluralism, if not anarchism. Can you respond to this criticism by clarifying the underlying concerns of your intellectual project as a whole?*

[Jean-François Lyotard]: If the heterogeneity of "my" work "passes by" [*dépasse*] the reader, it also "passes by" me, insofar as I am my first reader. However, I am also the supposed "author" of "my" work, and you ask about my responsibility in regard to it. Two defenses are possible. The first is that we never publish anything except rough drafts. Even *Le différend* (1984), which I spent nine years elaborating and writing, remains a sketch, whose master I have not been. And in this sense, I can without lying plead limited responsibility. That is to say: a reader cannot incorrectly locate in a piece of writing an aspect which, according to me, is not at all there. This is the matter for a litigation, perhaps for a *différend*.

The second defense, compatible with the first, is that I accept—in fact I seek—heterogeneity. All thought conceals something of the unthought. We must then take it up, be it at the price of self-contradiction. The interests of that which is to be thought must unhesitatingly prevail over the concern to make a good impression, to construct one's authorial identity. I here plead full and entire responsibility for the heterogeneity of the result. This result would be homogeneous if that which is to be thought presented itself as a unity and as a totality. But it happens, each time, now, like a singular event. Thinking only takes place by listening in attentively to the question: "is it happening that . . .?" [*arrive-t-il que . . .?*]. Theory, *stricto senso*, forthwith assigns to the question the answer it holds in reserve. Philosophy tries to make the question reverberate. Theory is by its principle outside of time; philosophy is immersed in the *kairos*. That philosophy, once transported into the political sphere, appears "liberal," "pluralist," or "anarchist" is quite possible. But politics is not a sphere; politics has to do with the way one phrase is linked to another; it is inscribed right onto being [*à même l'être*].

One way to describe your recent work is as a project to analyze sociopolitical problems of justice in terms of a problematics of language. This project is founded upon your supposition that "the observable social linkage is made out of 'moves' in language" [**La condition post-moderne** *24]. In what ways do you feel that this is an adequate (or useful) model of the relationship between language and society? And while an attentive reading of your work reveals that your concern is primarily with the contextual, pragmatic dimensions of language use, does not your use of linguistic terminology and of formulations like the above risk reducing the complexity of social phenomena to discourse, a reduction which in your early* **Discours, figure** *you denounce as endemic to Western metaphysics? How do you reconcile the language-game model of society with your manifest interest in alternative media and especially in the visual arts?*

First, the simplest of phrases presents a "universe" that is a society of instances: addresser, addressee, referent, meaning (and I am neglecting the *support* of the phrase and its code). These instances are or are not "occupied." But society and the explication of society always presuppose this elementary interaction at the heart of the language atom. This interaction is the social link. You can recount its foundation, deduce its economy from the purposiveness of interest, or of passion, etc. . . .: this link is presupposed in your act of recounting or deducing. It does not follow that you must not recount or deduce, but that in doing so you are making but a theory.

Secondly, one cannot enclose oneself in language; for that to occur it would have to be a closed totality. It's a linguist's idea that it is this totality, because he makes it into his domain of reference, his thing. The philosopher asks how to link one phrase *well* to the next. He is not in possession of the good rule; he is looking for it. He must reflect and judge, as Kant says. And through this he relates to language in the same way as the common person does: an infinite, or in any case an indefinite, number of phrases remains possible at each instant.

Thirdly, "language" has no exterior because it is not in space. But it can say space. It can say the body. It can say that the body "says" something, that silence speaks. Idiolects can certainly be imagined: the language of the unconscious, the language of classes, the language of nature. . . . But in order to assert that language is involved, it is necessary to say what they say, and they cease therefore to be idiolects. The "exterior" of language is the nothingness which slips between one phrase and the one which will link up with it. The exterior is imminence. But the latter is the intimacy of phrases among themselves.

Fourthly, I did not try in **Discours, figure** to oppose language and image. I was suggesting that a (discursive) principle of readability and a (figural) principle of unreadability shared one in the other. The book is certainly not exempt from a nostalgia for some extralinguistic entity. I believe, however, that it is legitimate to establish congruences between the "discourse" of back then and the "genre of discourse" brought to bear in **Le différend** and between the "figure" of the first book and the "is it happening that . . .?" of the last. All of which can in short answer the request for homogeneity. . . .

Could you explain your use and subsequent abandonment of the term "language game," which you borrow from Wittgenstein? What is gained in the move from the game model to one of "phrases"?

The answer to this question is given in **Le différend.** Briefly: I have schooled myself in the *Philosophische Untersuchungen* in order to purge myself of the metaphysics of the subject (still present, in my opinion, in the *Tractatus*). Little thought, since Spinoza, the Sophists, Dogen, and Kant(!), displays as much . . . divested. Desolating my culture fecundated me. Thereafter, it seemed to me that "language games" implied players that made use of language like a toolbox, thus repeating the constant arrogance of Western anthropocentrism. "Phrases" came to say that the so-called players were on the contrary situated by phrases in the universes those phrases present, "before" any intention. Intention is itself a phrase, which doubles the phrase it inhabits, and which doubles or redoubles the addresser of that phrase.

In your recent work, you insist very much upon the incommensurability (or untranslatability) of different phrase universes, as if to maintain their integrity. In **Au juste,** *for example, you argue extensively against the derivation of prescriptives from descriptives as metaphysical and dangerous. On the other hand, in* **"Introduction à une étude du politique selon Kant,"** *you describe the critical act in terms of the seeking of "passages" (übergänge) between phrase universes. Could you explain your view of the critical act, and what you mean by these "passages"? What is the urgency that underlies your casting the task of the intellectual in this way?*

First of all, the word "passage"—*übergänge*—is found in the Introduction to Kant's *Third Critique.* It designates the very task that Kant assigns himself in that book, a task already set in the discussion of the Third Antinomy of Reason, in the First *Critique.* Having, like no one before him, aggravated the incommensurability between the cognitive law (descriptive) and the moral law (prescriptive), Kant seeks to re-establish "over the abyss" a passage between the two domains. He believes this passage to be found in the esthetic judgment and in the idea of a purposiveness of nature in man. My reading is then the following: he in fact finds a faculty of "passing," that of the reflective judgment, the capacity to judge without criteria (already at work, in fact, although under diverse titles, in the two domains); but this faculty does not permit the reestablishment of a subject's unity nor of a system's architecture. This faculty is "only" critical, as Kant explains in the First Project for an Introduction to the Third *Critique;* it comes and goes between domains which remain incommensurable. A Hegelian outcome to this dispersion (the word is in Kant's anthropology) is thus refuted in advance as a "transcendental appearance."

Secondly, I believe that the ruin of subject-systems (which in *La condition postmoderne* I called "great narratives"), the liberal, the marxist, the capitalist, the Christian, the speculative, reveals to us today once again this condition of thought (and thus of action) when it must reflect and judge without letting its course be inflected by a purposiveness (anthropological, cosmological, or ontological) which would legitimate it.

In **La condition postmoderne,** *you speak of postmodernity as "ringing the deathknell of the era of the professor" [88]. Given the diversity of your own teaching experience (at Nanterre in 1968, at Vincennes, with the Institut Polytechnique de Philosophie, and with the Collège International de Philosophie), what do you feel to be the pedagogical responsibilities of those of us still engaged in "classical" university teaching? What alternatives can you propose to the great Enlightenment narrative of education as emancipation?*

Whether it be in the "classical" university or in the supplementary institutions to which you allude, the pedagogical task, once stripped of its trappings, that of the great narrative of emancipation, can be designated by one word: an apprenticeship in resistance. Resistance against the academic genres of discourse to the extent that they forbid the reception of the "is it happening that . . .?," against the great narratives themselves, against the way thought is treated in the new postmodern technologies insofar as they express the most recent application of capitalist rules to language, resistance against every object of thought which is given to be grasped through some "obvious" delimitation, method, or end. Pedagogical responsibility is not the responsibility to think, but to teach those to think who supposedly don't know how. And there are no good criteria (the successful passing of examinations is not a good criterion). We created the Institut and the Collège to get away from "good criteria." It does not follow from that that we have better criteria but that we dispose of a space-time wherein the endurance of thinking can be felt without extrinsic obstacles (especially in regard to objects which do not form part of the classical curricula of philosophy). I touched upon this question in **"Endurance and the Profession,"** *Yale French Studies* 63 (1982).

Your work often seems guided by an impious use of other texts (this is not a criticism). One is even tempted to describe as "wild" your use of terms from pragmatics, from the later Kant, from Lévinas, etc. Can you justify this practice of intellectual bricolage in terms of a more general reading strategy? The diversity of styles and genres which you draw upon in your writing also testifies to an explicit attempt on your part to reject traditional forms of writing philosophy. Can you speak then to the pragmatic occupations of your discourse?

First of all, I remain continually surprised by the surprise that my readings of works provoke in my readers. I can't seem to make myself feel guilty for any disrespect but I ought to feel that way out of incongruousness. I must be a bad reader, not sufficiently sensitive or "passive" in the greater sense of the word, too willful, "aggressive," not sufficiently espousing the supposed organic development of the other(?), in a rush to place it in the light of my own concerns. "Wild" if you wish (but my concerns are cultivated); "impious" certainly in the sense whereby Plato judges as impious the belief that the gods (here the works I read) are corruptible by petitions and gifts. Should I try to seduce what I read? (In any case, not "*bricoleur.*")— Rather I would say: one writes because one hears a request [*demande*] and in order to answer it; I read Kant or Adorno or Aristotle not in order to detect the request they themselves tried to answer by writing, but in order to hear what they are requesting from me while I write or so that I write. It seems to me that Diderot proceeded in this manner.

Secondly, as for the "traditional forms of writing philosophy," I know of none. The proper of philosophy is not to have a proper genre. Tragedy, novel, tale, journal, dialogue, conversation, apology, report, theses, study, research, inquiry, essay, manual, treatise—all genres are good for it. This is because philosophical discourse is in quest of its rule and does not have it from the start. Philosophy borrows it from a genre, in order to insert into that genre the reflective judgment through which the genre's rules are interrogated. And that suffices to turn the borrowed genre away from its generic purposiveness.

For some time now (at least since **Economie libidinale***), you have denounced the "terrorism of theory" in the name of the irreducibly particular, of the contextually specific. In* **Au juste,** *you are very careful to insist upon the possibility of justice and of making just judgments without, however, being willing to elaborate a "theory" of justice, which, if I understand you correctly, could not fail at some moment or other to be productive of specific injustices. I wonder, though, if theory can be so easily dispensed with. Is there not necessarily a theoretical (or speculative) moment in the very conceptualization of the particular? And if, as you also suggest, theory is merely one genre of discourse among others, is not the problem then less that of avoiding theory than of finding other ways to "phrase" theory?*

Theory is in effect a genre, a tough genre. Modern logic has elaborated the rules for this genre: consistency, completeness, decidability of the system of axioms, and independence of the axioms. I have no objection to formulate against this genre (genres are not subject to objection). And in this case, theory is a remarkable elaboration of the linkings between phrases, and first of all of their formation into "well-formed expressions" or propositions. It is not a question of "phrasing" theory otherwise (you might as well phrase tragedy otherwise). It is only a question of determining the cases in which the theoretical genre engenders paralogisms (which the Sophists, Russell, or Gödel did, each in his own way). One thus learns that these cases must not be accepted into theory such as it is, because they arise from another genre. It is necessary then to judge,

outside of all genres, what existing or inexistent genre is suitable for phrasing these cases (which cease then to be paralogisms). Although an amateur, I have always been attracted by formalism. It proceeds to a kind of mine-clearing of the potencies of language. There exists not only the sapper's light touch, but also an ironic and terrified respect for the imminence of the explosion. Terror through theory only begins when one also claims to axiomatize discourses that assume or even cultivate inconsistency, incompleteness, or indecidability. Contemporary "French thought" is often accused of irrationalism because it resists this extension. But it is this extension that is irrational.

Much of the difficulty in presenting your texts to an Anglo-American audience comes from their often admirable and very self-conscious grounding within the particular contexts in which they were written. **Instructions païennes** *is perhaps the most clearly marked of these texts. Do you not fear that the widespread distribution and translation of your writings, that is, of their abstraction from the particular times and places in which they were initially circulated, will allow for the most egregious attempts to apply your ideas in a uniform, universalizing manner? Is there not something illusory or nostalgic in the notion of a discourse rigorously situated in a particular context or scene of intervention?*

Every phrase links onto other phrases, be they explicit, presupposed, or implicitly understood. None of them is the first phrase. If there is illusion and nostalgia, it is in the expectation (Cartesian for example) of a first phrase, without precedent (or a last one, without rejoinder). It is more conformable to this condition to render explicit the "context" than to omit it. Universality is always a horizon to attain from the starting point of an immanent, singular situation. See Benjamin, the latter Adorno. This condition in effect generates difficulties when it is necessary not only to translate from one language into another, but to transfer from one "culture" (a complex agglomerate of contexts) to another. Misapprehensions are inevitable, especially if one claims to "apply ideas" thus elaborated from a singular situation. Ideas are not operators or categories, but horizons of thought. They are by no means applied. There would be much to say about their means of propagating themselves. In any case, I would rather be little read, if it is at least done in this spirit, than diffused like an article of intellectual commerce. A recent experience at Trinity College in Cambridge, England, reassures me moreover that if the resistances to propagation are multiplied at the institutional (university, editorial, journalistic) level, it is precisely on account of the fact that the intellectual "*petit peuple,*" young instructors, students, unregistered auditors, are working for the acclimatization of foreign ideas, and demand their propagation. There is something heroic in this will. I salute it here in your person as well as in the persons of all the young scholars who have resolved to propagate the singularity of my writings in the Germanophone, Italian, Brazilia, Hispanophone, or Japanese worlds.

Your notion of the différend allows for subtle and complex analyses of the relation between politics and language in specific cases of oppression. In the United States today, the most widespread and vital strand of criticism that deals with the literature of an oppressed group or with the problems of an oppressed discourse is no doubt feminist criticism. Is there a specifically feminine différend, an unlitigatable "injustice" done to women? In what ways might your work be of interest to (or at odds with) feminism?

First of all, not all oppressions signal *différends* (they can involve litigations), and I do not think that every *différend* gives rise to oppression. Secondly, is there a feminine idiom untranslatable into the masculine idiom to the same extent that the tragic idiom does not translate into the elegiac nor the mathematic into the epic nor the speculative into the cognitive? If this is the question, the answer requires that we look into what we mean then by idiom. Freud certainly busied himself trying to delineate a feminine idiom irreducible to the masculine. But at the same time he insistently indicates the bisexuality of men and women. He indicates. If an injustice has occurred in this affair, it is bisexuality that is the suffering party, as much for men as for women: an interdiction is passed forbidding the latter from assuming their virility, and the former from fulfilling their femininity. It would still be necessary, I repeat, to articulate what is meant by these entities. Are they anything other than modes in the musical sense? Men or women, we have the capacity for the major mode and the minor mode. It is in between them, in between these modes that incommensurability resides.

Finally, after reflecting upon it for a moment, I can count many texts relative to the question man/woman from ***Discours, figure*** up to a text on Valerio Adami, **"On dirait qu'une ligne . . ."** (1983), which is my most feminine text, I believe.

Your analysis of the proper name as a "quasi-deictic" leads you to an understanding of the political in terms of a kind of generalized agonistics of the proper name. The stakes involved in what meanings can or cannot be attributed to a proper name, in how that name can or cannot occur in certain phrases, become very high. But then the philosophical stakes in knowing what constitutes a proper name become just as high. Are there not certain common nouns which are also at issue in différends? In other words, how is the proper name as contested in a différend to be distinguished from debate over the meaning and usage of any word or concept?

Proper names have that property of attracting to themselves phrases belonging to different regimens and to heterogeneous genres of discourse: *Caesar, for pity's sake! Down with Caesar! Caesar was at that time consul. Was Caesar a great writer? Your Caesar annoys me.* It is for this reason that the *différend* flourishes in and around proper names. A "debate" over the signification of a common noun is a genre strictly regulated in its end (the establishment of a definition) and in its procedures

(dialogue). The difference between one and the other is the one noted by Aristotle at the beginning of the *Rhetoric,* shall we say: the difference between School and political life, which tears apart the man of knowledge or of litigation, at the tribune, at the tribunal or in the street, the agonistical places.

Mark Conroy (essay date 1985)

SOURCE: A review of *The Postmodern Condition: A Report on Knowledge,* in *Southern Humanities Review,* Vol. XIX, No. 4, Fall, 1985, pp. 874-77.

[*In the following review of* The Postmodern Condition, *Conroy outlines and evaluates the principal concepts of postmodernism.*]

Although there is considerable evidence that the phenomenon known as modernism has yet to be adequately grasped by those who would make cultural analysis their business, and that the current obsession with *fin-de-siècle* Vienna among other indices reveals an awareness of this inadequacy, nevertheless the pitiless onrush of events now deposits something called postmodernism for our consideration. The term thus far is as ill-defined as it is unaesthetic: a colleague vowed once that he would not become interested in postmodernism "until they decided to call it something else." This fact has not kept the problematic from assuming ever greater prominence; and the French philosopher Jean-François Lyotard, ever sensitive to seismic rumblings, has produced one of the first booklength treatments of the matter.

Actually, "book-length" may be stretching the term a bit; and in fact the structure of this book is that of two separate sections altogether, the first and major treating academic learning, the second discussing the arts and literature. This very split in the structure of the book is therefore symptomatic of what the postmodern condition itself displays; and much of the energy of the author goes toward demonstrating the reasons for this split.

Lyotard tells the reader a narrative as his means of explaining what has come about: a narrative which itself concerns narratives, specifically narratives of legitimation for knowledge at various points in Western history. We note in this connection the subtitle, **"A Report on Knowledge."** According to this construction, the stories that the learned class has told itself in order to legitimate its knowledge and provide it a context (Lyotard calls these the "grand narratives") have disintegrated, leaving only the criterion of "performativity," or maximum output for input, as a rationale for institutional learning. The older grand narratives were two: the speculative (where knowledge accumulates to enhance the reflective ability of self-consciousness) and the emancipatory (where knowledge renders to individuals the ability through democratic processes to govern themselves, and to realize their desires).

The first grand narrative assumes a kind of "metadiscourse" wherein all the great learning is collected, and springs from the University; the second puts knowledge in the service of democratic decision-making, facilitating the goals of the people (the "practical subject" who possesses knowledge). Both narratives are crumbling fast, however; what remains after the "delegitimation" of these narratives is "the only credible goal" of research in the new age: that of "power."

Lyotard brings to light the eerie circularity implicit in this form of legitimation. If a statement is made about "reality," it is more likely to be right if the one making it can alter that "reality" to suit the statement. Technology allows such increased mastery of "reality" and so can help legitimate truth claims. But scientific information is needed in order to manipulate "reality" technologically, so to that extent knowledge about "reality" is essential; and so forth. The intertwining of the arts of power and the arts of knowledge becomes thus almost complete. Systems theory is the only thing approaching a "metadiscourse" for a relation such as this, and that would be more description than prescription in any case. Such is Lyotard's picture.

The role of education in that picture is fairly cut and dried. It is "no longer . . . to train an elite capable of guiding the nation towards its emancipation but to supply the system with players capable of acceptably fulfilling their roles at the pragmatic posts required by its institutions." So, farewell, *École normale supérieure;* greetings, *École nationale d'administration:* managers, not moral examples, are what is needed. Ideals, virtue and Greek *paideia* are all irrelevant; but skills are key, and can in addition be taught "à la carte" (in Lyotard's telling cafeteria metaphor) without need of a larger discourse—either speculative or emancipatory—to sustain their transmission. The place for the humanities, value-laden and thus useless as they are, is marginal. As a suggestion of the shift, Lyotard dubs data banks "the Encyclopedia of tomorrow," which unlike that Enlightenment project are beyond "the capacity of each of their users. They are 'nature' for postmodern man."

In such a context, the point of having the humanities at all would seem to be very slight. But Lyotard manages to give with one hand what the other has taken. He argues that in the postmodern universe, the notion of "performativity," or maximum output for input, assumes a stable system. Such a premise smacks of determinism and it comes from the very nineteenth-century notions that flow from thermodynamics. Lyotard here uses Michael Serres' insights into the obsolescence of closed-system thermodynamics for twentieth-century epistemology, and he extends them. The problem with any closed system, for Lyotard, is that the totality of any given situation cannot be known by the actors who have to make their moves within that situation; and beyond that, at various crisis points the system itself becomes unstable, in a manner described most famously by catastrophe theorists such as mathematician René Thom. Lyotard's example of such a crisis situation is that of a dog that is challenged: the curves of both anger and fear will characteristically rise at the same time, so that the dog's impulses to flee or fight will shift from moment to moment.

This instability in any system becomes the means by which Lyotard may triumphantly extricate his argument from performativity and its determinism. As soon as the use of knowledge in a concrete situation is at issue, he contends, "systems theory and the kind of legitimation it proposes have no scientific basis whatsoever." He points out that science itself does not operate according to this criterion, and that it has advanced in large part by challenging the boundaries of previously guarded systems and methods. Hence, imagination—the ability to conceive and argue for departures from the existing norms and consensus notions—is reinstated. What Lyotard calls "legitimation by paralogism" is his formula for this renewed role of imagination.

In stressing this centrality of imagination, Lyotard goes against such contemporary theorists as Jürgen Habermas, heir to the Frankfurt School, whom he sees as trying to revive a discredited model of human emancipation, that leftover of *Aufklärung,* as a counterweight to the technocratic determinism of systems analysts. For both Habermas and Lyotard, the spokesman for such systems analysts is the German thinker Niklas Luhmann. While Luhmann is, for Lyotard as much as for the Habermas of *Legitimation Crisis,* the figure to be overcome, Lyotard does it, he feels, without recourse to a "grand narrative" from the nineteenth century. He sees "paralogism," a constant challenging of the given rules, as a way beyond the technocratic legitimation of knowledge; and he rejects Habermas's "search for universal consensus" because it is impossible to reach rules valid for all "language games" and also because consensus per se is not necessarily desirable.

What Lyotard seems to be saying—and what Fredric Jameson in turn chides him for in the introduction, albeit in the gentlest of terms—is that the communitarian urge behind the Enlightenment desire for emancipation of the collective will has dissipated, and is in fact archaic. He has prior to this point made it plain that Marxism is a relic of pre-postmodernism, with Stalinism corresponding to the "life of the Spirit" wing and the Frankfurt School the "emancipation" wing of those older narratives. This ash-can-of-history gesture allows Lyotard's paralogism to emerge as the only progressive possibility.

There are two problems with Lyotard's subtle, well-argued, and comprehensive thesis: (1) the *Aufklärung* is not really so dead after all, its essential dynamic being a bit different from Lyotard's description of it; and (2) Lyotard's breakthrough notion of paralogism as a new justification for non-technocratic learning (what used to be termed "the humanities") is scarcely a breakthrough at all.

On the first point, I would take issue with Lyotard's mode of treating the "grand narratives." The implication of his treatment of each of the two Enlightenment narratives as complementary of the other is that the two were synchronous; that the "life-of-the-reflective-Spirit" University story and the "emancipation" Civil Society story are part of identical historical circumstances. Yet the University structure, with the hierarchy of disciplines Lyotard describes, was the product not of the Enlightenment so much as of the late middle ages. The self-assertion of a secular populace comes rather later, as the eighteenth century turns to the nineteenth. In *The Legitimacy of the Modern Age,* Hans Blumenberg limns this process of self-assertion, and in taking it back to the Renaissance distinguishes it from medievalism. It is true that Lyotard goes to lengths to trace his notion of the life of the self-reflective spirit to "the founding, between 1807 and 1810, of the University of Berlin"; and he lays out the attendant German idealist rhetoric quite learnedly. Still, he fails to convince here; for this University structure, much like German idealism itself, is not exclusively a modern instance, but rather has sediment from medieval ideology as well. Thinking no doubt of Hegel's *Phenomenology of Mind,* Lyotard says: "The encyclopedia of German idealism is the narration of the '(hi)story' of this life-subject." The "life-subject" here is the knower whose spiritual journey is its own reward, and whose knowledge then only secondarily grounds state or society. But this is merely a secularization of the medieval clerisy, with its vision of harmonious, hierarchized disciplines, which is finally scholastic in origin, and not chiefly a feature of modernity as such.

From this point flows the conclusion that of the two narratives Lyotard invokes as "grand narratives"—and in that he is correct, incidentally: both are crucial—one may decline before the other, and independently of the other. I would argue, thus, that the German idealist speculative narrative is indeed dying, even if the University structure that once housed it, for all of Lyotard's optimistic predictions, is by no means slated for immediate demolition. However, and more importantly, the narrative of emancipation is still an active and vital part of an Enlightenment legacy; and the criterion of performativity, which Lyotard feels has displaced emancipatory legitimation, is closer to a twin rival of it, both products of a secular age of self-assertion. In this respect, the interesting division of Marxism, for example, would be less into "speculative" versus "emancipatory" camps than into those of scientistic determinism versus the liberation of will, as Alvin Gouldner has argued in his *Two Marxisms.* In any case, such a paradigm would make the idea of an appeal to some communitarian self-assertion, whether or not à la Habermas, a very live option. The alternative Lyotard apparently offers of accepting the degraded categories of the performativity principle and trying to work one's way out of that seems tolerable, at least to me, only if there is no other possibility.

This leads to my second objection, which is that Lyotard's paralogism is far too ill-defined to present much of a path beyond what we already have; at most, it designates the fact that paradigms do shift and that systems undergo shocks to their assumptions, and that therefore the ability

to generate theories that jar patterns of thought is legitimate. Although "imagination" is vaguely called forth in this connection, Lyotard's notion of paralogism is not a path out of performativity's maze so much as one way of keeping the system stabilized. With no alternative value to that of the system, parologism is inevitably folded back into the ongoing structure of that system, the only question being how quickly in any given case. It is significant, by the way, that Lyotard's formula for the proper role of the avant garde in the second section is similar to that of paralogism in the first. According to his view, that role is to present the "unpresentable," or sublime—to point to what cannot be figured. Presumably such works escape the reduction to predictable realistic forms, just as parologism is to resist reduction to technocratic system. But again, for lack of a determinate value apart from what it opposes, the sublime—like paralogism—risks being absorbed back into the categories it opposes.

Lyotard's specific recommendations are hard to object to. How to argue against the value of interdisciplinary studies, or opening computer banks to the generality? One cannot argue against them, but neither can one find them as radical as Lyotard seems to do. That "grand narrative" of emancipation, in a less Utopian key perhaps, may yet have some usefulness as a way of getting beyond what Lyotard rightly calls the "cynicism" of the performativity criterion of value. This book in many ways does an admirable job of charting the movements that led to this cynicism. Yet its tendency to view this cynicism as ineluctable, and even in some way desirable, along with a resultant reluctance to raise moral issues, make his text more reliable as an account of how we got into the postmodern condition than as a guide to how we get out of it.

Kate Linker (essay date 1985)

SOURCE: "A Reflection on Post-Modernism," in *Artforum,* Vol. XXIV, No. 1, September, 1985, pp. 104-05.

[*In the following excerpt, Linker reflects upon the significance of Lyotard's postmodern exhibition* Les immateriaux.]

In 1968, London's Institute of Contemporary Art organized "Cybernetic Serendipity," an exhibition intended to indicate the effects of technology on modern life. As its title suggests, this dizzying display of technology presented a paradisiacal vision of the capacity of the machine, and to this day it remains one of the central projections of a technological utopia based on the notion of modernization. Underlying it was the premise of "technoscience" as a prosthetic, or aid, to universal mastery; the cybernetic revolution appeared to accomplish man's aim of material transformation, of shaping the world in the image of himself. "Cybernetic Serendipity" was launched in the name of Modernity, an ideal that, since the time of Descartes, has focused on the will and creative powers of the human subject. But in two decades those terms have seemingly changed: in *Les Immatériaux* (Immaterials), an exhibition recently developed by the Centre de Création Industrielle of Paris' Centre Georges Pompidou,[1] the effects of advanced science were examined under the aegis of the post-Modern. And underlying the show, instead of optimism, was a sense of instability, the result of an assault on the Modern figure of the self.

Les Immatériaux is part of an ongoing polemic—a reflection on post-Modernism—by its organizer, Jean-François Lyotard. For Lyotard, as for certain other theorists, post-Modernism is not a style succeeding the dissolution of Modernism, but rather a cultural condition resulting from the erosion of Modern period ideals; it marks a historical moment, one of fairly slow germination, characterized by a shift in assumptions inherited from the Enlightenment. At the core of these assumptions is the humanist code as it converges on the "masterly" figure of man; inasmuch as post-Modernism emphasizes the regulating power of social forces, it can be said to describe the decentering of the self. For Lyotard, one of the crucial factors in this process has been the postwar development of technoscientific culture. The result is an exhibition that fetishized technology, using myriad display vitrines, computer consoles, and scientific products. It was a wax museum, computer center, and curiosity shop rolled into one. However, the implications of its perspective are rich in speculation.

The specific aim of *Les Immatériaux* was to examine the way in which the new immaterial" materials associated with the technological revolution have altered man's identity as maker; the exhibition comprised an inquiry into the changes effected by the demise of creation defined as material production. Since the implications of "creation" are both theological and juridical, the end of the concept of masterable reality has broad repercussions. Some 69 sites, developed with the aid of a group of researchers, were dispersed through the gallery so as to provoke questions in science, literature, art, and daily life—to define post-Modernism, in other words, within the complex of a moment in culture. The spectator moved among different "zones" equipped with headphones which transmitted a series of texts and musical arrangements. The sites were disposed along five interlocking routes with carefully chosen themes. Beginning from the Sanskrit root *"ma"* (to make by hand, to measure, to build) and using certain terms of linguistic "pragmatics," Lyotard conceived these paths so as to inquire into the origin (*maternité*), medium (*matériau*), equipment (*matériel*), subject matter (*matière*), and code (*matrice*) of contemporary reality. What emerged, then, was both a physical manifestation and a conceptual interrogation of the displacements of postindustrial society.

As presented in *Les Immatériaux,* the instability of post-Modernity is induced by the dislocation of cultural coordinates. For Lyotard, the waning of the Modern period is linked to the decline of objects, which can no longer be opposed, as before, to a shaping subject. The dissolution of the object into complexes of microelements, or interac-

tive energy states, marks the end of the dualisms that gave security to the Modern self. And it is in this manner, Lyotard suggests, that new technologies force us to reconsider the very notion of creative endeavor. For the loss of matter as a palpable medium subverts the Modern concept of production, which implies both an origin, or author, and a finality, or product. It involves an assault on expressive totalities: since man no longer defines himself through the appropriation of objects, the object cannot be seen, as in Hegelian esthetics, as the mirror of the subject. The plural "messages" that comprise reality do not converge on the self, nor can they (as Walter Benjamin commented) return man's gaze. Without the self as center all is interchangeable, for man is a part of, rather than apart from, the reality he once controlled. Indeed, such general interaction was a major theme of *Les Immatériaux,* one that Lyotard sketched in the exhibition prospectus:

> Whereas mechanical servants hitherto rendered services which were essentially "physical", automatons generated by computer science and electronics, can now carry out mental operations. Various activities of the mind have consequently been mastered. . . . But, in so doing, . . . the new technology forces this project to reflect on itself. . . . It shows that Man's mind, in its turn, is also part of the "matter" it intends to master; that . . . matter can be organized in machines which, in comparison, may have the edge on mind. Between mind and matter the relation is no longer one between an intelligent subject with a will of its own and an inert object. . . .

Which is to say that once-uncrossable boundaries are defied.

For Lyotard, the end of the model of production is part of general breakdown in the linear teleologies of the Modern. As he has written elsewhere, the current crisis in ideals pertains to the shift "from the ends of action to its means"[2] (i.e., to the medium or language) that becomes sensible toward the end of the '50s. The decline of the utopian projects of Marxism and of the Modern Movement in architecture, for example, are symptoms of a collapse in the idealist "master narratives" that provided legitimating discourses for society. These narratives, Lyotard's *"grands récits,"* offered meaning, expressing the human goal as either universal emancipation (as in the Marxist formulation) or the consolidation of mind (as in the Hegelian philosophy of knowledge). But what is at stake in post-Modernism is a state of dissension in which these unifying structures cannot maintain their claims to legitimacy. Such dissension is evident in current knowledge, which no longer retains the contours separating disciplines: deprived of narrative, boundaries dissolve, ". . . overlappings occur at the borders between sciences. . . . The speculative hierarchy of learning gives way to an immanent and, as it were, 'flat' network of areas of inquiry, the respective frontiers of which are in constant flux."[3] This dispersion is paralleled in politics by the atomization of the social, which breaks up into individual particles. In a way corresponding to the erosion of matter, the Modern representation of an organic whole gives way to multiple and heterogeneous domains.

Les Immatériaux contained many features invoking other aspects of post-Modernity. A series of key themes was brought forth and reiterated: the primacy of the model over the real, and of the conceived over the perceived. That we live in a world in which the relation between reality and representation is inverted was made clear by countless examples. Much attention was paid to the copy, to simulation, and to the artificiality of our culture. In fact, *Les Immatériaux* suggested nothing so much as our common fate in living with abstractions. But these ideas were unpersuasively presented; the exhibition banalized its central themes. The artistically primed viewer, for example, could only wonder why so much '60s conceptual art was trotted out, except to illustrate the moribund notion of art's dematerialization. Indeed, a '60s, McLuhanesque air ran throughout the show, hinting that the computer is a substitute for consciousness. There was too much mechanical hokum—too many light machines and holograms, too many buttons to push and atomizers to squeeze. In one section (*"Toutes les copies"* [All the copies]) a uniformed technician photocopied household objects, including gloves, candy, and cheese. In another, a machine registered the steady but imperceptible growth of plants (*"Irreprésentable"* [Unrepresentable]). Elsewhere, a color slide show on industrial materials made much of their spectacular, atomized beauty, showing that the world of special effects lies within our contemporary horizon. *Les Immatériaux* oversimplified, as if attributing change to a single variable; for example, Lyotard seemed to forget that ours is not only a technocratic society but also a mediacratic one, in which the construction of the subject through representation is linked with toppling its sovereign sway. The exhibition's problem was that despite the claims of its organizers ("the incontrovertible technoscience is present without occupying the scene"), technology occupied center stage. *Les Immatériaux* was very much a homage to the machine's effects, if not to its powers, as presumed by the industrial utopia. And the difficulty with deploying the effects of technology to make sensible our post-Modern condition of uncertainty is that it can end up applauding technology, and thus repeating the ideology of progress. It can illustrate the situation—hardly unknown to argument—of an example that threatens to negate, or subvert, the very idea it defines. Here technology was a source of fascination; it was the hero, in fact, of Lyotard's dramaturgy of the post-Modern. The entire installation staged an elaborate processional, moving from a semicircular mirrored "theater," one of the last holdouts of subject/object dualisms, to the vast Borgesian "labyrinth of language," a sort of parking lot for computers. It was a processional, then, from body to language, from matter to light. And it was a complex processional, with many interlocking paths and byways that pointed to intricate reticulations of thought. But it was one that inevitably valorized, and thereby mystified, the immanence of contemporary technology.

Les Immatériaux, however, may be an exhibition that looks better on paper and reads better in its accompanying literature than it did in its physical form. It raises the question of whether profound shifts of a philosophical nature can be represented through objects—whether the immaterial can be, as it were, materialized. For despite the privilege it granted to technology, *Les Immatériaux* was rich with suggestive speculation concerning the assault being made on the Western program of mastery. Above all, the show was an attack on the philosophy of being, grounded in experience, that Benjamin said atrophied with the entry of the machine. And it contained an important directive to historicize, not ontologize or perpetuate, objectification, abandoning it with other Enlightenment baggage. The multivolume publication that accompanied *Les Immatériaux* prompts inquiry into the changes wrought by the decline of the direct or transitive function of the author—to say nothing of the shifts thereby effected in claims to authority, to legitimacy and control. Such ideas resist trivializing illustration through computerized bric-a-brac. But, similarly, the idea of the installation transcends its realization, for, in a move that has bearing on esthetics, Lyotard suggests that the mastery Western culture accords the eye may be diminishing with the post-Modernist valorization of time. In an installation whose many sites were designed to resemble constellations, the geometry of domination transmitted through Renaissance perspective no longer informed the disposition of space. Space did not radiate from and return to the spectator who progressed through it, but was dispersed in zones, the diffusion of whose boundaries was extended by sound. Through this unstable configuration, which imposed no fixed itinerary, Lyotard would remind us that the gallery, in contrast, is a Modern institution, obeying a linear teleology: "Gallery: an establishment of culture, that is to say of acquisition and assimilation of heterogeneous data, within the unity of an experience which constitutes a subject."

Les Immatériaux marks an important event in France, where attention to post-Modernism has been impeded by a tradition that stresses manufacture. It is to Lyotard's credit that he presents post-Modernism both as a historical condition and as a philosophical relation. And it is also to his credit that he encourages us to "think" it as a problem, as the collective heritage of the late 20th century. Beneath *Les Immatériaux* is the sense that returns are impossible: that we are at a cultural crisis, or point of rupture—the end point of the humanist code. To attempt to revive that code through a return to the hand and to outmoded techniques of facture is nostalgic, an obliteration of historical reality. So if the viewer could see through the winking, blinking machines, the exhibition framed an astonishing perspective: things have changed. The center does not quite hold, and we must revise our outworn categories and assumptions to encompass our century's radical transformations.

Notes

1. *Les Immatériaux* ran from March 26 to July 15, 1985. Among others assisting chief organizer Jean-François Lyotard was organizer Thierry Chaput Unless otherwise noted, all quotations in this article are from the prospectus or press material for the exhibition.

2. Jean-François Lyotard. *The Postmodern Condition. A Report on Knowledge,* trans Geoff Bennington and Brian Massumi, Minneapolis: University of Minnesota Press, 1984, p. 37.

3. Ibid., p. 39.

Herman Rappaport (essay date 1986)

SOURCE: A review of *Le différend,* in *Sub-Stance,* Vol. 15, No. 1, November, 1986, pp. 83-6.

[*In the following review, Rappaport considers* Le différend, *its philosophical influences, its divergences from them, and an ethical looseness he finds in it.*]

Le différend by Jean-François Lyotard develops further the French post-structuralist engagement with analytic philosophy and is very sensitive to questions which concern speech acts in the broadest sense of the term. In large part I find that the book develops ideas central to Ludwig Wittgenstein's *On Certainty,* in which the issue of validating or proving propositions is considered from the perspective of judgment.

We recall that in the *Tractatus Logico-Philosophicus,* Wittgenstein offered as one of the tentative conclusions that if one has to say a proposition is identical to what it represents, then such a proposition is necessarily not identical. In short, identity is not constative but inherent in the performance of the proposition's logic. "In logic, process and result are equivalent," Wittgenstein writes.

But much later, after considering language games in the *Philosophical Investigations,* Wittgenstein, in the subtle volume entitled *On Certainty,* began an unsettling series of speculations stressing the constative—that is, assertions of fact. Very important is the idea that reference and naming depend, not on some innate congruity between logic and world, as in the *Tractatus,* but on someone's judgment or belief which necessarily places faith in rules, assumptions, evidence, agreements, consensus, examples. In a definite move away from the notion of a language game, Wittgenstein went so far as to write: "We do not learn the practice of making empirical judgments by learning rules: we are taught judgments and their connection with other judgments. A totality of judgments is made plausible to us." With respect to the "counting of evidence" upon which judgments are made, Wittgenstein admits that someone could discount such obvious evidence as that the earth existed a hundred years ago, for to count it means that one has to suspend doubt and accept or believe that the earth existed. Being reasonable in such contexts, Wittgenstein says, means not to have doubts about things upon which everyone agrees. Hence facticity depends upon social consensus.

In *Le différend,* Lyotard examines a situation in which a group of people develop a discursive body of knowledge

which chooses not to be "reasonable" in that it holds doubts about that which we believe to know for certain. This group consists of those revisionist historians who have chosen to doubt the status of the Holocaust and emphatically deny that six million Jews were liquidated by the Nazis during World War Two. Indeed, Lyotard himself takes it as fact that the Holocaust did happen. But he wants to interrogate a discursive situation in which a most "certain" historical event has difficulty in "presenting" or "presencing" itself as that which can be validated, proven, made manifest. He wants to interrogate how "philosophical" doubt can be used politically to expedite prejudice, and he wants to study to what degree all philosophizing in the Wittgensteinian sense is merely a matter of making prejudicial pacts, of learning "judgments" in whose connection victimage and its denial or erasure is effected.

Unlike Wittgenstein, Lyotard develops these thoughts in terms of the Jakobsonian poles of addressor/addressee and their relevance for speech act theory. His term, *le différend,* refers, specifically, to a performative speech act in which the addressee is a victim without redress. "I would like to call the *différend* the case where a defendant is stripped of the means to argue and because of this fact turns into a victim. If the addressee, the addressor, and the meaning of testimony are neutralized, all is as if no harm had been done." The *différend* is a difference which exists in a blatant manner but which is structured such that the victim cannot find a means by which to address it. This is precisely the case worked out at length by Franz Kafka in *The Trial,* and Lyotard sees it as crucial to an understanding of how the Holocaust could be put into practice by the Nazis. At issue here are those performative acts comdemning the victim to death—acts which, in their very performance, efface the articulation of that difference by means of which the victim could present himself or herself as an other who is wronged. The revisionist historians who today claim to doubt the veracity of the Holocaust merely perpetuate that speech act situation in which countless people were deported and gassed.

Le différend contains several chapters, each with lengthy intratexts set apart in small size fonts. The first chapter is entitled "Le différend" and digresses from its main concern with the Holocaust to issues concerning the dialogues of Plato. Some people may find this juxtaposition of Auschwitz/Plato rather curious, but close inspection of the text on Plato quickly reveals very pertinent connections in terms of "The Apology" of Socrates and the philosophic handling of the issue of "testimony" by the ancient Greeks. Lyotard notices that for the pre-Socratics the question of reference is subsumed in the site of the addressor, who is a god. Thus testimony consists of revelation. For Gorgias, on the contrary, reference is established between addressor and addressee and depends upon refutation. Thus "the word *logos* changes its meaning." Lyotard adds, "it is necessary for Plato to establish those rules of argumentation which prohibit the weaker argument from detracting from the stronger. . . ." Of course, in order to do this one must first have a preconception of what is right or just. Only from this can rules follow. But if this preconception is not already linked to the gods, how can it be asserted? This is the problem Lyotard explores with respect to the pre-Socratics. Of course, the sophistic and later Aristotelian rules of argument give way to the "administration of proofs." This entails what Lyotard calls the "metalepsis" of sequencing argumentative judgments by way of a chain of executors. The result is social consensus.

The next chapter, "The Referent, The Name," dwells on Wittgenstein's *Tractatus,* discussing the relation of propositions to the real. Not surprisingly, Lyotard argues that reality is inaccessible even in the case of deictic markers, since no deictic marker can be communicated without it shifting places in an addressor/addressee model. Thus even here there is displacement. Moreover, in the invocation of a deictic marker (i.e., *"here* I am") one finds a constative expression which, of course, Wittgenstein has explicitly demolished in *On Certainty.* At the end of this chapter, Lyotard returns to the question of Auschwitz in wondering about the testimony of its survivors, of the "here, look at what happened to me." Lyotard wonders implicitly about the validity of eye witness accounts, especially in the face of what he sees as the disappearance of evidence. And without this validity, what is the status of testimony, of the voices of the Holocaust?

In "Presentation," a chapter with digressions on Aristotle, Kant, and Gertrude Stein, Lyotard interrogates the categories that make up testifying structures, categories which mediate what is presented; and he interrogates the system of propositions in which these presentations are to be found. Following is a chapter entitled "The Result." Lyotard suggests that the Jews were prevented access to those categories through which their testimony could be recognized. Because of *le différend,* it appeared as if the Jews had no legitimate complaint. And because the addressor/addressee polarities were deconstituted, it was possible for the SS to murder people without taking responsibility for any crime, since the killing of the victim was not like passing sentence and carrying it out; rather, the killing was based on the presupposition that these people were already supposed to be dead and had no claim to be otherwise. Hence the judgment as both constative and performative is presupposed. The rest is merely mop up. It is precisely a reestablishment of communicative contact between addressor/addressee that the Nuremburg trials had to effect. And again the Eichmann trial in Israel was especially significant in the sense that it gave to the victim his or her voice, his or her right to redress.

The last three chapters of *Le différend* are "Obligation," "Genre and Norm," and "The Sign of History." Let me just remark on the digression about Emmanuel Lévinas's work in "Obligation." The digression is included perhaps because Lévinas was himself a survivor, but almost certainly because his view of obligation in terms of a deconstruction of the Greek rhetorical model of addressor/addressee produces many interesting counterpoints throughout *Le différend.* Lyotard notices that whereas the

suspension and deconstitution of an addressor/addressee relation leads to Holocaust within a National Socialist context, that within Hebrew tradition itself this addressor/addressee relation is also made asymmetrical. Levinas "places the accent upon the asymmetry of the relation I/you [je/tu]. The latter is not reversible; it imposes and maintains the destabilization of the knowledge where the I was an I (the oneself oneself, identity)." Lyotard continues, "the I understands [here] nothing more of the ethical; it can only believe that it understands." Clearly, the victim is situated in the Hebrew context with respect to God as Other, a position in which the victim's expression of redress is not heard, is, as Buber said, eclipsed. But for Levinas it is this eclipse, this occultation, this silence of the other which demands an obligation in which ethics is, in fact, established. Hence, *le différend* can be viewed from not only the perspective of criminality, but of holiness.

I am not sure that **Le différend** clarifies how one is supposed to relate sections such as those on Lévinas with those on the concentration camps. It may well be that Lyotard sees judgment as suspended, the ethical as that which evades decidability in terms of the presencing of a distinct moment in which something is determined. "Silences signal the interruption of self [Selbst], its fission." **Le différend**: is it a suspension, an interruption of silence, a moment of undecided decidability which invests itself in numerous moments in which the ethical is determined as the undetermined? If so, Lyotard may be viewing *le différend* in terms of an archipelago of contexts. "There is no moral diachrony," Lyotard writes. There is no homogeneity of law, he says also. And yet it is hard to read **Le différend** without linking and historicizing the relations between the fragments Lyotard presents, for the text suggests a collage which may be viewed as a unified schema. However, if one does view the text as a unity, one may well begin to have reservations about Lyotard's suturing of sections like that on Lévinas with those on Nazi persecution, since the linkage may suggest the difference between Jewish culture and Nazi culture is undecidable with respect to the question of ethics. A reader who may find such an inference may begin to wonder why the text of **Le différend** does so little to discourage one from making associations compatible with anti-Semitic ideology. Indeed, if one reads beyond **Le différend** into Lyotard's **Au juste** (the two books are closely related), one will notice passages such as those on the Hegelian conviction that Jews have developed a culture that resists direct confrontation, recognition, and engagement, passages which evoke rather than revoke the idea that Jewish culture is itself diffident. It may well be that we are not supposed to make the kinds of inferences which would give credence to anti-Semitic ideas, but given the way Lyotard's recent writings lend themselves to free association, it would have been reassuring to have had some sentences in the recent texts which might allay the suspicion that Lyotard is supporting the notion that the Holocaust is the consequence of a form of thought or logical principle that can be derived from Jewish ethics. Indeed, it is as if Lyotard's ethical philosophy were curiously uninhibited with respect to allowing for a transference with those very political resonances which have been so catastrophic for Jews in modern times. Indeed, this is an aspect of Lyotard's work that needs a fuller and perhaps much more thoughtful investigation than one can give in a review. Such a fuller treatment would include close inspection of **"Discussions, ou phrases 'après Auschwitz'"** in *Les fins de l'homme* (1981) and the more recent **"Judicieux dans le différend"** in *La faculté de juger* (1985). Given the elusiveness of these texts, it is perhaps prudent to give Lyotard the benefit of one's doubts; nevertheless, I find his recent work touching on the Holocaust deeply distressing and repellant. For me it marks a limit where certain modes of post-structuralist interpretation reveal major inadequacies as methods of philosophical reflection.

John Keane (essay date 1987)

SOURCE: "The Modern Democratic Revolution: Reflections on Jean-François Lyotard's *La condition postmoderne*," in *Chicago Review,* Vol. 35, No. 4, Spring, 1987, pp. 4-19.

[*In the following essay, Keane argues that Lyotard's postmodernism can be seen as a "political ally of the modern democratic project" described by Alexis de Tocqueville.*]

> No sooner do you set foot upon American soil then you are stunned by a type of tumult; a confused clamor is heard everywhere, and a thousand voices simultaneously demand the satisfaction of their social needs. Everything is in motion around you; here the people of one town district are meeting to decide upon the building of a church; there the election of a representative is taking place; a little farther on, the delegates of a district are hastening to town in order to consult about some local improvements; elsewhere, the laborers of a village quit their ploughs to deliberate upon a road or public school project. Citizens call meetings for the sole purpose of declaring their disapprobation of the conduct of government; while in other assemblies citizens salute the authorities of the day as the fathers of their country, or form societies which regard drunkenness as the principal cause of the evils of the state, and solemnly pledge themselves to the principle of temperance.
>
> Alexis de Tocqueville, *De la démocratie en Amérique*

1. The observation that modern societies are uniquely restless and self-revolutionizing because they invent and universalize democratic mechanisms for the interrogation and control of power has been familiar since Tocqueville's *De la démocratie en Amérique.*[1] According to Tocqueville's highly original thesis, which remains much neglected in theories of modernization, a 'great democratic revolution' (57, vol. 1) has begun to sweep through all spheres of modern life. In post-aristocratic societies, daily existence becomes agitated because democratic mechanisms awaken and foster a widespread passion for the equalization of

power, property and status within the spheres of state and civil society. In the political realm, Tocqueville observed, everything becomes disputed and uncertain. The convincing power of sentimental tradition, absolute morality and religious faith in other-worldly aims is shaken; in this skeptical, secular age of political democracy, the stars of mythical belief fall to earth, the light of faith grows dim, and the horizons of political action become worldly, and thus subject to argument, persuasion and practical judgment. Those who live in democratic nations consequently look upon political power with a jealous eye; they are prone to suspect or depise those who wield it, and are thereby impatient with arbitrary state regulation. The state and its laws lose their divinity, coming to be regarded as necessary and/or expedient, and as properly based on the voluntary consent of the citizens. The spell of absolute monarchic power is broken, political rights are extended gradually from the privileged political classes to the humblest citizens, and political regulations and laws are subjected constantly to redefinition and alteration.

Tocqueville emphasized that distinctions and privileges are eroded gradually not only in the field of politics, but also within the domain of civil society. Modern democracies are subject to a permanent "social revolution" (69, vol. 1). Naturalistic definitions of social life are replaced by avowed conventions (Tocqueville notes, for instance, that democracy gradually destroys or modifies "that great inequality of man and woman, which has appeared hitherto to be rooted eternally in nature" [263, vol. 2]); (hereditary) property is parceled out, social power is shared ever more widely, and the unequal capacities of classes tend to dissolve. This is not to say that democracies are without concentrations of wealth. Such concentrations of property persist, but Tocqueville saw them to be vulnerable, as subject constantly to redistribution through changes in fortune, competition, legal redefinition and social pressures from the property-less. Having subverted the systems of feudalism and absolute monarchy, the democratic revolution refuses to bow before the social power of notables, merchants and industrial capitalists. The fear of losing their privileges strikes at the heart of these social groups—which is also why they have a hearty dislike of democratic mechanisms. Tocqueville evidently exaggerated the momentum and extent of this leveling process, and yet the logic of his explanation remains compelling: once certain social claims (e.g., rights to property) are defended by one group, the pressure is greater for extending them to other social groups; and after each such concession, new demands from the socially less powerful force new concessions from the privileged, until the once restricted social claims become *universal* in scope. The dilemma of modern civil societies is that they must extend social rights to everyone or to nobody. Since the latter option is an open embarrassment to democracy, the process of social leveling tends to develop an irreversible momentum of its own. Democratic mechanisms, or so Tocqueville argued, stimulate a passion for social equality which they can never quite satisfy: "This complete equality slips from the hands of the people at the very moment when they think they have grasped it and flies, as Pascal says, an eternal flight" (285, vol. 1). The less powerful ranks of civil society are caught especially in the grip of this dynamic. Agitated by the fact of their subordination and by the possibility of overcoming it, they are also irritated by the uncertainty of achieving equality; their initial enthusiasm and hope gives way to disappointment and frustration, and to renewed commitment to the struggle for equality. This "perpetual movement of society" (261, vol. 1) fills the new world of modern democracy with radical skepticism and an impatient love of novelty. In this democratic maelstrom, nothing seems anymore to be fixed or inviolable, except the passionate, dizzying struggle for social equality and political freedom.

2. At first sight, Tocqueville's expectation that democracy would become a universal and irresistible principle of modern life seems completely unrelated to the subject of postmodernism. Two explanations might be offered for this doubt. First, most of the recent controversies about postmodernism have severed themselves from theories of the modernization process—a symptom of which is postmodernism's relative absence of interest in the disciplines of sociology, politics and economics. The objection to my interest in Tocqueville would be that the postmodernism discussion is concerned only with "cultural" phenomena and not with social and political life. I am not convinced by this objection, for what is most often presented as an "aesthetic" or "scientific" contribution to the modernism/postmodernism debate is saturated deeply with (often implicit) political judgments about the modernization process, which is either stigmatized as corrupt (Tafuri; Jameson) or saluted as culturally, economically or politically advanced (post-war social democracy; neo-conservatism). The centrality of the prefix *post*-modernism provides a second explanatory clue as to why it might be argued that Tocqueville's theory of the modern democratic revolution is irrelevant to the subject of postmodernism: among many advocates of postmodernism *stricto sensu,* all things modern, not only modern art and scientific inquiry, but modern socio-political structures as well, are seen to be deeply problematic. From this standpoint, the modern project as a whole is a lost cause and cannot be rescued or revived; it has become (or for a long time has been) canonical, deadly and stultifying and (it is argued) it must therefore be broken, repudiated and exceeded. The original objection would therefore remain: is not Tocqueville's theory of the modern democratic revolution merely of interest, say, to antiquarians who inhabit the dark corners of museums and archives, or to traditional political philosophers searching for certitudes under fluorescent lights, but quite irrelevant to the contemporary discussion of postmodernism?

The answer I wish to defend in this lecture is emphatically negative: the fundamental importance of Tocqueville's thesis is that it furnishes the (admittedly incomplete and, in places, unsatisfactory) outlines of a socio-political understanding which is both implied and (for reasons of self-consistency) required by the most advanced philosophical

defenses of postmodernism, among which I include Jean-François Lyotard's *La condition postmoderne.*[2] Expressed conversely, and much more paradoxically, the fundamental socio-political importance of philosophical essays such as Lyotard's lies in their *potential* call for the deepening of the democratic revolution first analyzed and defended by Tocqueville. Viewed from this paradoxical angle, philosophical postmodernism of the type defended by Lyotard is not a break with the modernization project but, potentially at least, its sociopolitical ally, a vigorous agent of the renewal and deepening of modernity's democratic potential.

In attempting to unravel and defend this potentially intimate, if paradoxical, relationship between philosophical postmodernism and modern democracy, I shall concentrate exclusively on Lyotard's *La condition postmoderne.* In so doing, I do not wish to make claims about its 'representativeness' of the postmodern movement as a whole. This movement is marked by a deeply protean quality; its breathtaking heterogeneity of questions and pursuits is to be expected and encouraged, not only because "modernism", its object of criticism, is itself highly differentiated (the architecture of Le Corbusier, Abstract Expressionist painting, and the neo-positivist science of Popper are evidently not isomorphic phenomena), but also and more specifically because philosophical postmodernism, to which I am in several ways deeply sympathetic, has a justified aversion to attempted totalizations of the world, a world which is seen in fact as an infinitely complex, dynamic and linguistically charged reality that can therefore only ever be interpreted from a multiplicity of perspectives.[3] This latter point explains not only why I am not concerned to point to the "representativeness" of *La condition postmoderne;* it also suggests why I am concerned neither to summarize it in its own terms nor to extract from it systematic generalizations and hard and fast conclusions. I should like to avoid these options, preferring instead to pursue a type of hermeneutic approach which attempts to reconstruct the deliberately organized arguments of *La condition postmoderne* in defense of postmodernism, in order to indicate the ways in which they carry the text away from the "positions" advocated by its author—more precisely, my aim is to foreground the adventures of argumentation which lead the text to both deny (in the name of *post*-modernism) *and* sanction sociopolitical claims compatible with the modern democratic project outlined and defended by Tocqueville.

3. The stated concern of *La condition postmoderne* is the altering status of science and technology within late capitalist—or, as Lyotard prefers, postmodern—societies. This concern functions, however, as a means of exploring a much broader variety of questions, such as the future of the university, social justice, the contemporary fetishism of efficiency and effectiveness, the crisis of metaphysics, systems theory, the structure and functions of narrative, the dangers of a fully computerized society, and the possibility of a postmodern science which places emphasis on discontinuity, catastrophe, non-rectifiability and paradox.

Of special interest to Lyotard is the problem of legitimacy, that is, the processes by which every particular language game seeks to authorize its "truth", "rightness" and (potential) efficacy—and therewith its superiority over other, rival language games—through utterances which specify, more or less explicitly to the "bearers" of a particular language game, rules concerning such matters as the need for narration, internal consistency, experimental verification, consensus obtained through discussion, and so on. These rules consist not only of guidelines concerning how to form denotative utterances (in which the true/false distinction is central); they pertain to notions of *savoir-entendre, savoir-dire, savoir-vivre*, that is, to the ability to form and understand 'good' evaluative and prescriptive statements and, thereby, to speak and interact with others in a normative way. It is precisely consensus about these pragmatic rules, or so Lyotard argues, that permits the participants within a language game to identify each other as interlocutors, as well as to circumscribe their language game, distinguishing it from other, possibly incommensurate language games.

From this (neo-Wittgensteinian) perspective, Lyotard emphasizes that every utterance within a particular language game should be understood as an activity, as a "move" with or against players of one's own or another language game. Utterances may in addition be understood as moves in opposition to the most formidable adversary of all: the prevailing language itself. This is Lyotard's 'first principle': to perform speech acts involves jousting, adopting agonistic or solidaristic postures toward other players or language itself. In this respect, players within language games are always embedded in relations of power—power here understood as the capacity of actors to wilfully block or effect changes in speech activities of others within the already existing framework of a language game which itself always prestructures the speech activities of individuals and groups.

This point about power and language games also implies—this is Lyotard's "second principle"—that language games must be considered as definite social practices: to perform rule-bound or rule-breaking utterances is at the same time to participate in the production, reproduction or transformation of forms of social life. Society can be understood neither as an organically arranged functional whole (Parsons) nor as a totality subject to dualistic fragmentation (Marx). Rather, the social bond resembles a complex labyrinth of different, sometimes hostile, slipping and sliding language games, which obey rules of an indeterminate variety and therefore cannot be apprehended or synthesized under the authority of any single meta-discourse. Lyotard quotes Wittgenstein (*Philosophical Investigations*, section 18) to drive home this point concerning the thousands of language games, trivial or not so trivial, that weave the fabric of our societies: "Our language can be seen as an ancient city: a maze of little streets and squares, of old and new houses, and of houses with additions from various periods; and this surrounded by a multitude of new boroughs with straight regular streets and uniform houses."

The aim of postmodernism, in Lyotard's view, is to accentuate this insight about the infinite and splintered character of the social. Practically speaking, this means that postmodernism is committed to the task of dissolving the dominant language games which have hitherto cemented together and "naturalized" a particular—modern—form of social bonding. The multiplicity of language games circulating in any society cannot be transcribed and evaluated in any totalizing metadiscourse; attempts to do precisely that must therefore be countered by the practice of paralogism *(la paralogie)*, that is, by attempts to defer consensus, to produce dissension and to permanently undermine the search for commensurability among nonidentical language games. In my view, Lyotard's text is at its finest and most insightful when interrogating and doubting various types of language games: the Platonic dialogue, with its patterns of argumentation oriented to reaching a consensus (*homologia*) between communicating partners; the popular narratives which define what may or may not be said and done in traditional societies; the crucial dependence of modern scientific discourse upon mainly post-narrative techniques, such as didacticism, denotation, argument- and proof-based methods of falsification and rules of diachronic rhythm; the concern of German Idealism to synthesize the various sub-branches of knowledge through a totalizing metanarrative that understood both this knowledge and itself as moments in the becoming of Spirit; the early modern theory of socio-political legitimacy, according to which the consensus of a deliberating people is a necessary condition of political liberty and justice; and recent technocratic proposals for abandoning the old ideals of liberal democratic humanism in favour of effectiveness and efficiency—*performativité*—as the sole criteria of legitimacy. These interrogations emphasize the heteromorphous and wholly conventional nature of language games, thereby raising doubts about their "imperialistic" claims to be absolute. Lyotard's interrogations do not necessarily lead (*pace* Seyla Benhabib[4]) to a privileging of one language game—a mathematical and natural science which emphasizes discontinuity and self-destabilization—over other possibly incommensurate language games. Lyotard is not caught in a performative contradiction. He covers himself against this outcome by rehabilitating the logic of occasion as it is found, say, within the writings of the Greek sophists. The curious feature of this logic is its claim to give the lie to the logic of the one universal truth, by signaling that the latter is only a particular case of the logic of the particular, of the special case, of the unique occasion. This procedure is not at all self-contradictory, since this logic of particularity is presented as neither a more universal logic nor a "truer truth". On the contrary, Lyotard's interrogations consistently depend upon the logic of particularism, and consequently they contribute decisively, or so I would argue, to a revised theory of the ideological functions of language games.[5]

Under pressure from the type of paralogism defended by Lyotard, ideology can no longer be understood, nor its riddles explained and criticized, within the classical Marxian mode. Contrary to the classical Marxian schema, Lyotard's interrogations suggest that ideology is not a form of posthumous misrepresentation of a prior ontological reality of class-divided material life processes, which function (as Marx thought) as both the pre-linguistic, Archimedean point of origin of ideological forms and as the point of truth that contradicts the 'false' dissimulations of ideology. Lyotard reminds us that there is nothing specifically social—not even the labor process itself—which is constituted from such an Archimedean point "outside" and "below" language games. Language games cannot be conceived as simply a "level" or "dimension" of any social formation: they are co-extensive with social and political life as such. Further, Lyotard's interrogations remind us not only that ideology is not simply (in the most vulgar Marxian sense) a veil-like substance draped over the surface of "real" social relations, but also that there can be no "end of ideology" in the sense of a future society finely tuned to a "reality" freed from the rules and effects of language games. His emphasis on the heteromorphous and wholly conventional character of language games implies a radically different, critical conception of ideology, one that abandons the search for foundations and totalizing truth and instead embraces the logic of particularity and context-dependent polytheism. From this revised, post-Marxian standpoint, ideology would be understood as a *grand récit,* as a particular type of (potentially) hegemonic language game which functions, not always successfully, to mask both the conditions of its own engendering as well as the pluralism of language games within the established socio-political order of which it is a vital aspect. In other words, the concept of ideology would be applicable to any and all particular language games which endeavor to represent and secure themselves as a general or universal interest, as unquestionable and therefore freed from the contingency of the present; ideological language games are those which demand their *general* adoption and, therefore, the exclusion and/or repression (the "terrorizing", as Lyotard would say) of every other *particular* language game. So understood, the *critique* of ideology would break decisively with the anti-modern political aim of the classical Marxian theory of ideology, namely, its attempt to devalue the false universality of an opponent's language game by presenting its own language game as universally true and ethically justified, hence unassailable. To criticize ideology in this revised way would be to emphasize that there is an inverse, but nevertheless intimate relationship between ideology and the modern democratic revolution: to tolerate ideology is to stifle and potentially undo the very plurality of language games which, as Tocqueville first argued, this revolution has greatly facilitated.

4. Here I admit to extending and "politicizing" a line of thought which is at most hinted at in *La condition postmoderne.* In general, this essay is deeply reticent about developing further its own political connotations. Lyotard may have donned "the mask of paganism, polytheism"[6], but social and political matters are choked off constantly in this essay by the resort to obscure formulas and shapeless suggestions. In this respect, *La condition postmoderne* resembles the bulk of postmodernist writing. One

could say that, often in spite of itself, most postmodernism remains pre-political. Its political credentials—its implications for the existing distribution and legitimacy of power crystallized in state and non-state institutions—remain wholly ambiguous. Postmodernism is said to involve the practice of resistance; challenging master narratives with the discourse of others; questioning rather than exploiting cultural codes; opening closed systems to the heterogeneity of texts; becoming more sensitive to difference; emphasizing discontinuity, incompleteness and paradoxes—and yet phrases such as these remain highly amorphous, thereby marginalizing or repressing outright further consideration of socio-political questions.

La condition postmoderne is similarly marked by a profound uncertainty and lack of clarity about its socio-political affiliations. Symptomatic of this is Lyotard's tantalizing summary description of his essay as an outline of "a politics that would equally respect the desire for justice and the desire for the unknown" (108). Equally tantalizing is his insistence (88-97) that postmodern knowledge aims to refine our sensitivity to the heterogeneity of the rules of language games, and to reinforce our ability to tolerate their incommensurability. More troubling still are those solipsistic, deeply apolitical moments in *La condition postmoderne* (e.g., 8; 63-8) in which Lyotard proposes that we are at last entering an age devoid of grand narratives, a period of postmodern austerity, it seems, in which individuals can only laugh cynically down their noses or smile happily into their own beards at every belief taught them. This is a preposterous suggestion, for not only does it suppose, falsely, that grand (or ideological) language games are everywhere dead, and, again falsely, that all individuals and groups presently living, say, in western and eastern European and North American systems already enjoy the full civil and political liberties necessary for defending themselves against the rise of future ideologies; Lyotard's suggestion also misleadingly supposes, by means of a lapse into a curious form of neo-romantic expressivism, that an age devoid of grand language games would lead to the withering away of power and conflict, as if the array of specifically modern democratic mechanisms for limiting serious conflicts as well as concentrations of power could be superseded, like water wheels, handicrafts and other historical curiosities, by a fully transparent and harmonious whole.

Lyotard argues persuasively that language games are intelligible and interpretable only in terms of their own or other language games' rules and that, lacking a privileged language game, there is no alternative but to recognize the *difference* among language games, the potential infinity of rules defining them. This is well and good, but if this postmodernist conclusion that language games may be non-identical is to have any political credibility; if it is to avoid sliding into an uncritical deference to the existing patterns of unfreedom and inequality of late capitalist societies (succumbing, that is, to the dangerous charms of Wittgenstein's maxim that philosophy must leave everything as it is); and if it is not to adopt a blasé, carefree attitude towards the achievements of modernization (evidenced in a recent essay by Lyotard, where he says, against Habermas, that "Auschwitz may be taken as a paradigm, as a name for the tragic unfinished of modernity"), then it must engage, or so I would argue, in a further questioning of its own tacitly presupposed conditions of possibility. In my view, there is potentially an intimate connection—and not a simple hiatus—between Lyotard's examination of the postmodern condition and the line of political argument defended in Tocqueville's examination of the modern condition. I am basing this claim not only on Lyotard's paradoxical (but self-consistent and highly plausible) defense of the dynamic, antirepresentational thrust of modernist aesthetics, which, as Lyotard says, is pregnant with the will to question reality as "unreal" and to invent new and different realities.[7] My thesis is broader: postmodernism of the type defended by Lyotard does not constitute a radical (or even mediated) break with the modernization process, but instead a dialectical intensification of its democratic impulses. Expressed paradoxically, Lyotard's postmodernism implies the need for a renewal and further development of the modern democratic tradition; that is, postmodernism is a call for ultra-modernism, a defense of the dynamic and future-oriented democratic revolution identified by Tocqueville. This paradoxical equation can be established and clarified, I believe, by asking after the sociopolitical presuppositions of Lyotard's postmodernism, that is, by reflecting counterfactually upon the socio-political conditions necessary for its institutionalization and preservation as such.

Consider the following line of argument, which can be considered as one possible response to Lyotard's unanswered question: "Where can legitimacy reside after the metanarratives?" (8) This question, concerning which of those gods who strive to gain power over our lives we can or should serve in an age of nihilism, is also raised (but again left unanswered) in Lyotard's earlier work, *L'économie libidinale.* It prompts the following response. To begin with, the postmodernist thesis that language games may be incommensurable, and that they are intelligible and interpretable only in terms of their difference from, or similarity with, other language games, *implies* an opposition to all claims and contexts which thwart or deny this thesis. A self-consistent postmodernism, that is to say, is compelled to devote itself to the philosophico-political project of questioning and disarticulating all essentialist or absolutist Truth claims or what I have called ideologies. Postmodernism therefore cannot rest content with prepolitical assertions about the need for tolerating the incommensurable, supporting our culture "conversationally" through the telling of stories[8] or, in Lyotard's version, "marvelling at the diversity of discursive species, just as we do at the diversity of plant and animal species" (47). And postmodernism certainly cannot cling naively to the complacent view—associated frequently with various forms of ethical and cognitive relativism—that "every belief about every matter is as good as every other". Postmodernism rather *implies* the need for democracy, for institutional arrangements which guarantee that protagonists

of similar or different forms of language games can openly and continuously articulate their respective forms of life.

Postmodernism further *implies,* no doubt, the need for *political* mechanisms (of conflict resolution and compromise) which *limit* and *reduce* the serious antagonisms that frequently issue from struggles among incompatible forms of life. Postmodernism does not imply anarchism, for active and strong political institutions, as Tocqueville pointed out against his contemporaries who dreamt of the withering away of the state, are a necessary condition of preserving the democratic revolution. Just as all speakers of a language (to appropriate Tocqueville's simile) must have recourse to definite grammatical rules in order to express themselves, so citizens living together under modern democratic conditions are obliged to submit themselves to a political authority, without which they would fall into confusion and disorder (and, it might be added with hindsight, into the peculiarly modern type of yearning for existential security and grand ideologies that is produced by the experience of temporal and institutional discontinuity unleashed by modern societies). According to Tocqueville, the need for political mechanisms is especially pressing within large and complex societies, whose common interest, such as the formulation and administration of positive law, and the conduct of foreign policy, cannot be taken care of effectively without a powerful and centralized administration.

If Lyotard's philosophical postmodernism implies the need for state mechanisms of conflict mediation, it also suggests the need for mechanisms capable of preventing absolute state power. Tocqueville's political theory, concerned as it is with simultaneously defending modern democracy and pointing to its dangerous consequences, again provides some useful hints in this respect. Tocqueville argued that, in order to prevent the yoke of administrative despotism (a popularly elected state despotism that institutes a "well-regulated, gentle and peaceful servitude") from descending upon the modern world and paralyzing its revolutionary momentum, mechanisms of several kinds are required for preventing the buildup of dangerous monopolies of power. Within the realm of *state* institutions, Tocqueville argued, the paralysis of the democratic revolution can be minimized by ensuring that political power is distributed into many and various hands. A legislative power subject to periodic elections, combined with a separate executive authority and an independent judiciary, for instance, minimize the risk of despotism by ensuring that political power frequently changes hands and adopts different courses of action, being therefore prevented from becoming excessively centralized and all-embracing. Tocqueville also stressed the very rich democratic consequences of citizens' action *within* state institutions, and saw the American jury system as exemplary of this principle of supplementing representative democratic mechanisms (e.g., citizens' election of representatives to the legislature) with *direct* citizen participation. The jury system, in his view, facilitates citizens' self-government as well as teaching them how to govern others prudently and fairly; they learn to be sensitive and respectful of otherness, better capable of judging their fellow citizens as they would wish to be judged themselves.

Tocqueville was certain that these kinds of *political* checks upon despotism must be reinforced by the growth and development of *civil* associations which lie beyond the control of state institutions. Tocqueville no doubt underestimated the scope and anti-democratic implications of the rise of capitalist manufacturing industry, as well as the democratic potential of workers' resistance to its grip on civil society. (In *De la démocratie en Amérique* Tocqueville does not consider workers as a separate social class but, rather, as a menial fragment of *la classe industrielle.* This point of view, defended by Hegel and criticized bitterly by Marx, was also evident among other French writers such as Saint-Simon, for whom workers and entrepreneurs comprised a single social class, *les industriels.* This partly explains why Tocqueville reacted in contradictory ways to the events of 1848; as François Furet and others have pointed out, Tocqueville both interpreted these events as a continuation of the democratic revolution and, spitefully, as a "most terrible civil war" threatening the very basis of "property, family and civilization".) Tocqueville failed to consider the possibility of a *socialist* civil society—a type of ultra-modern civil society no longer dominated by capitalist enterprises and patriarchal families.[9] He nonetheless saw correctly that forms of civil association such as scientific and literary circles, schools, publishers, inns, manufacturing enterprises, religious organizations, municipal associations and independent households—to which we could add self-managed enterprises, refuges for battered women, lesbian and gay collectives, housing cooperatives, independent recording studios, and neighborhood police monitoring associations—are crucial barriers against both social and political despotism. Tocqueville never tired of repeating the point that the "independent eye of society"—an eye comprising a plurality of interacting, self-organized and constantly vigilant civil associations—is necessary for consolidating the democratic revolution. In contrast to political forms of involvement (such as participation in elections or jury service) which are concerned with the wider, more general interests of the community, civil associations consist of combinations of citizens preoccupied with "small affairs". Civil associations no doubt enable citizens to negotiate wider undertakings of concern to the whole polity. But they do more than this: they also nurture and powerfully deepen the local and particular freedoms so necessary for maintaining democratic equality. Tocqueville acknowledged that civil associations in this sense always depend for their survival and coordination upon centralized state institutions. Yet freedom and equality among individuals and groups *also* depend upon preserving types of organizations which nurture local freedoms and provide for the active expression of particular interests. A pluralistic and self-organizing civil society independent of the state—a type of anti-politics—is an indispensible condition of democracy. Tocqueville anticipated, correctly in my view, that whoever promoted the unification of state and civil society would endanger the democratic revolution. State power without social obstacles, he concluded, is always hazardous and undesirable, a license for despotism.

5. This line of argument, which is so near and yet so far from Lyotard's, suggests that philosophical postmodernism is potentially a protagonist and potential political ally of the modern democratic project. The separation of civil society and the state, as well as the democratization of each—a socialist civil society and a democratic state—are implied or counterfactual conditions of postmodern endeavors. To defend philosophical postmodernism of Lyotard's type requires a political stance which is thoroughly modern; it implies the need for establishing or strengthening a democratic state and a civil society consisting of a plurality of public spheres, within which individuals and groups can openly express their solidarity with (or opposition to) others' ideals. Understood in this way, democracy could no longer stand accused of being a substantive ideological "ought", a Tenth Commandment, a type of heteronomous principle or grand narrative that seeks to foist itself upon other social and political actors in the name of some universal interest. As Hans Kelsen first hinted,[10] and as my interrogation of Lyotard's text suggests, sociopolitical democracy is an implied, counterfactual condition of the practice of paralogism, and not a type of normative (or, as Kant would have said, imperative) language game. The type of thinking with and against postmodernism employed here suggests, however, that democracy cannot be interpreted as merely one language game among others, as if particular groups struggling to defend or realize their particular language games could decide self-consistently to conform to democratic arrangements for a time, only later to abandon them. On the contrary, their rejection of democracy would constitute a lapse into ideology—it would evidently contradict the particularity of their language games. They would be forced to represent themselves to themselves and to others as bearers of a universal language game, and they would thereby cover up the wholly conventional social and political processes of conflict and solidarity through which all particular language games are practically established, maintained and altered.

From this perspective, finally, democracy could no longer be seen as synonymous with the withering away of social division and political conflict. In democratic societies, as Tocqueville recognized, the foundations of social and political order are permanently unstable. Having severely weakened the power of norms whose legitimacy depends upon either transcendental standards (such as God) or a naturally given order of things (such as cultural tradition), modern societies begin to sense the need to summon up their socio-political identity from within themselves. The processes of modernization bring about an end to the naturalistic determination of the means and ends of life; destroying the old reference points of ultimate certainty, modern social actors begin to sense that they are not in possession of any ultimates (based on knowledge, conviction or faith), and that they are continually, and forever, forced to define for themselves the ways in which they wish to live. Trotsky's remark that those persons desiring a quiet life had done badly to be born into the twentieth century in fact applies to the *whole* of the modern epoch. Modern democratic societies are historical societies *par excellence*. It becomes evident to modern social actors that theirs is a society marked by socio-political indeterminacy; they sense that so-called ultimate social and political means and ends do not correspond to an immutable and "real" origin or essence, and that their techniques and goals are therefore always subject to debate, conflict and resistance and, hence, to temporal and spatial variation.

This is why in modern societies institutions and decisions are never accepted fully—as if controversies concerning power, justice or law could somehow be resolved once and for all through the adoption of a universal metalanguage. Democratic societies recognize the necessity of relying always on judgment, for they know of their ignorance, which is to say (cf. the Socratic attitude) that they know that they do not know or control everything. Democratic societies cannot flatter themselves on assumptions about their capacity to grasp the whole directly, for they always consist of risky and often ambiguous action in the process of self-invention in all quarters of life. To defend democracy in this sense is to reject every ideology which seeks to stifle this indeterminacy by demanding the general adoption of particular forms of life that are clothed in the familiar repertoire of old and new metaphors: every woman needs a man, as the herd needs the shepherd, the ship's crew a captain, the proletariat the Party, and the nation a Moral Majority; the end justifies the means; doctors know best; mankind is the master and possessor of Nature; scientific evidence is the most rational criterion of knowledge; capitalism is the most effective and efficient (and therefore best) form of property system; and so on. To defend democracy against these and other ideologies is to welcome indeterminacy, controversy and uncertainty. It is to be prepared for the emergence of the unexpected, and for the possibility of creating the new. It is, contrary to the self-understanding of philosophical *post*modernism, to recognize the need for *continuing* the modern democratic revolution which is incomplete, highly vulnerable, and today threatened by a world heaving with an assortment of old and new antimodern trends.

Notes

1. *De la démocratie en Amérique,* preface by François Furet, 2 vols. (Paris, 1981 [1835-1840]). All translations from this edition are my own.

2. Jean-François Lyotard, *La condition postmoderne: Rapport sur le savoir* (Paris, 1979). All translations from this edition are my own.

3. This point remains curiously unaddressed in Frederic Jameson's writings on postmodernism. Driven by a desire for a unitary, totalizing standpoint constructed of monistic assumptions, Jameson acknowledges the protean quality of cultural postmodernism, but only in order to better criticize it as an expression of the logic of universal commodification of contemporary consumer capitalist societies. Cultural postmodernism is rejected as a blind accomplice of the (temporary) disappearance of a collectively shared sense of class-based History, as an agent of the capitalist societies' fetishism of symbolic representation and celebration of the fragmentation of the experience of time into a series of perpetual presents. See, for example, "Post modernism and Consumer Society", in Hal Foster ed., *Postmodern Culture* (London and Sydney, 1985), pp.111-125; "Postmodernism, Or, The Cultural Logic of Late Capitalism", *New Left Review,* 146 (July-August 1984), pp.53-92; and "The Politics of Theory: Ideological Positions in the Postmodernism Debate", *New German Critique* 33 (1984), 53-65.

4. Seyla Benhabib, "Epistemologies of Postmodernism: A Rejoinder to Jean-François Lyotard", *New German Critique* 33 (1984), 120.

5. Cf. my "Democracy and the Theory of Ideology", *Canadian Journal of Political and Social Theory/Revue canadienne de théorie politique et sociale 7, (1983), 5-17.*

6. *Vincent Descombes, Modern French Philosophy* (New York, 1980), p.184.

7. See his "Réponse à la question: qu'est-ce que le postmoderne?", in *Critique* (April 1982), pp.357-67, which is translated and included as an appendix to Jean-François Lyotard, *The Postmodern Condition: A Report on Knowledge* (Minneapolis, 1984). Lyotard here defends postmodern aesthetics not as that which lies beyond modernism, but as an immanent dynamic within modernism: "Modernity, in whatever age it appears, cannot exist without a shattering of belief and without discovery of the 'lack of reality' of reality, together with the invention of other realities" (77).

8. This view is presently associated with Richard Rorty's *Philosophy and the Mirror of Nature* (Oxford, 1980). Aside from its failure to deal with the type of non-foundational, counterfactual reasoning sketched in this essay, the conversational model fails to acknowledge the dangers of totalitarian language games, to which (as Claude Lefort has pointed out in his *L'Invention démocratique,* [Paris, 1982]) modern societies are prone constantly because of their self-revolutionizing, self-questioning character. More recently ("Habermas and Lyotard on Postmodernity", *Praxis International,* 4 [1984], 34), Rorty has argued for the reliance upon a potentially anti-democratic instruction ("let the narratives which hold our culture together do their stuff"), as if the fact of existence of certain narratives automatically implied their sacred right to an undisturbed future existence.

9. This argument is developed in two forthcoming volumes, *Socialism and Civil Society* (London and

New York, 1987), and *The Rediscovery of Civil Society* (London and New York, 1987).

10. Hans Kelsen, *Vom Wesen und Wert der Demokratie* (Tübingen, 1981 [1929]), pp.98-104.

David Ingram (essay date 1988)

SOURCE: "The Postmodern Kantianism of Arendt and Lyotard," in *The Review of Metaphysics,* Vol. XLII, No. 1, September, 1988, pp. 51-77.

[*In the following essay, Ingram compares how Hannah Arendt and Lyotard use Kant in their formulations of the basis for legitimate judgement.*]

> [O]nly a redeemed mankind receives the fullness of its past—which is to say, only for a redeemed mankind has its past become citable in all its moments. Each moment it has lived becomes a *citation à l'ordre du jour*—and that day is Judgment Day.[1]
>
> Walter Benjamin

The past decade has witnessed an extraordinary resurgence of interest in Kant's writings on aesthetics, politics, and history. On the Continent much of this interest has centered on the debate between modernism and postmodernism. Both sides of the debate are in agreement that Kant's differentiation of cognitive, practical, and aesthetic domains of rationality anticipated the fragmentation of modern society into competing if not, as Weber assumed, opposed lifestyles, activities, and value spheres, and that this has generated a crisis of *judgment*. Tradition is deprived of its authority as a common reference point for deliberation; judgment appears to be all but submerged in the dark void of relativism. Yet, having both accepted Kant's differentiation of reason as emblematic of the pluralism of modern life, modernists and postmodernists remain divided in their response to its implications. Modernists—Habermas and Arendt too, I believe, can be classified under this rubric— attempt to circumvent the relativism of cultural fragmentation by appealing to a universal ideal of community. This solution recalls Kant's own grounding of judgments of taste in the notion of a *sensus communis.* By contrast, postmodernists such as Lyotard embrace relativism. Whereas the modernist emphasizes the capacity of rational agents to rise above the parochial limits of local community in aspiring toward an autonomous perspective, the postmodernist denies the possibility of impartiality altogether, thus binding judgment to the traditional constraints of practice.

This way of viewing the debate, I shall argue, neglects the fact that the postmodernist, no less than the modernist, must acknowledge a higher community of discourse, and for two reasons: first, because the constant state of revolution endemic to the postmodern condition fosters an autonomous perspective oriented toward the idea of indeterminacy and conflict, in short, toward plurality for its own sake; second, because the affirmation of pluralism implies the idea of a community wherein everyone agrees to disagree. If this analysis is correct, the distinct advantage of the postmodernist position would reside in its capacity to combine—in however paradoxical a manner—both practical and aesthetic moments of judgment: both the Aristotelian notion of *phronsis,* or the application of general rules heteronomously determined by local habits of thought, and the Kantian notion of taste, or the free, reflexive discovery of rules in light of indeterminate, transcendent ideas of community.

Taking the philosophies of Hannah Arendt and Jean-François Lyotard as representative of modernist and postmodernist responses to the crisis of judgment respectively, I intend to show that neither adequately explains the possibility of truthful evaluation. Whereas the modernist approach escapes the dilemma of relativism only at the cost of aestheticizing or depoliticizing judgment, the postmodernist alternative affirms the political reality of judgment by delivering it to the vicissitudes of changing circumstance. I therefore concur with Jean-Luc Nancy that judgment must ultimately be located in the prediscursive nexus of habits and meanings that precedes propositionally differentiated language.

The first section reviews Kant's contribution to the debate, especially his resolution of the conflict between theoretical and practical reason in the third *Critique*. The mediation of nature and freedom in aesthetic judgment is of cardinal importance for Arendt and Lyotard since it provides them with a non-teleological model for reconciling the standpoints of actor and philosopher-spectator. In addition, the judgmental disclosure of analogical relationships between distinct fields of rationality suggests a possible grounding for philosophical rationality which, as we shall later see, is exploited to good advantage by Lyotard. Clearly, the delimitation of fields of rationality undertaken by the critical philosopher cannot be grounded exclusively in any particular field. Philosophical no less than aesthetic judgment must remain autonomous, or detached from particular theoretical and practical interests, since its aim is to regulate in as impartial a manner as possible the conflict arising from them. Such impartiality, however, can only be secured by invoking a universal community of discourse. The second section discusses Arendt's use of this principle in addressing the crisis of judgment besetting the modern age. She is less concerned with the problem of justifying global philosophical judgments about rightful boundaries and more interested in the meaning of history. In particular, she hopes to show how judgment can "redeem the past" without resorting to teleological interpretations that deny the autonomy of actor and spectator. The problem with this solution, which involves transferring the model of aesthetic judgment developed by Kant to the political and historical sphere, is that it ends up depoliticizing judgment. The postmodern alternative of Lyotard discussed in the third section seems to circumvent this difficulty in that it reinstates the practical dimension of judgment (*phronsis*) alongside the aesthetic. However, the tension between these two poles is once again resolved in favor of the aesthetic. Deprived of prescriptive force and decentered (or, if one prefers, centered on a wholly indeterminate ideal of community), judgment ceases to discriminate or discriminates in a manner that constantly vacillates depending on local circumstances. I conclude that this radical relativism can be mitigated and the truthfulness of judgment accounted for only if one acknowledges the continuity of effective history as an ontological ground supporting radical heterogeneity.

I

It is vexing to expositors of Kant that he left unclarified what is arguably the most important concept in his philosophy: judgment. Doubtless he meant many things by this term: a "faculty of thinking the particular as contained under the universal," common to cognitive, practical, and aesthetic modes of experience; a capacity for finding analogical passageways linking these disparate modalities; a distinct faculty of taste.[2] It suffices to note for our purposes that, notwithstanding its designated role within Kant's system, a species of judgment was identified by him that may be described as evaluative in the broadest sense of the term and one, moreover, that he himself thought to exercise in coming to grips with the political events of his day. The most detailed discussion of judgment occurs in the *Critique of Judgment,* where it is introduced in conjunction with two problems.[3] The former concerns the need to bridge the "immeasurable gulf" separating "the sensible realm of nature and the supersensible realm of the concept of reason." This "gulf" was a by-product of Kant's famed resolution of the problem of free will and determinism in the *Critique of Pure Reason.* Since understanding (the faculty of natural concepts responsible for causality) and reason (the faculty of supersensible ideas responsible for freedom) have their source in the subject, it is entirely possible, Kant concluded, that they exercise, "two distinct legislations on one and the same territory of experience without prejudice to each other" (*CJ,* 12). He later realized, however, that this resolution of the problem was not entirely satisfactory, for the categorical distinction between heterogeneous orders of reality, *phenomena* and *noumena,* belies the integral experience of the embodied moral agent for whom "the concept of freedom is meant to actualize in the world of sense the purpose proposed by its laws." Nature, Kant reasoned, "must be so thought that the conformity to law of its (causal) form at least harmonizes with the possibility of the purposes to be effected in it according to laws of freedom" (*CJ,* 11-12). Somehow we have to imagine the possibility of a supersensible ground of freely willed purposes producing causal effects in nature. Though such production is beyond our ken, Kant insisted that it is presupposed whenever we try to explain a complex event in terms of natural teleology or judge nature to be beautiful. As regards the latter case—of signal importance for understanding the possibility of a global judgment capable of delimiting the rightful boundaries of distinct domains of action and discourse—the underlying feeling of pleasure announces a kind of harmony between

understanding and reason arising from the non-cognizable purposiveness of nature with respect to our subjectivity.

As a solution to the conflict of faculties this appeal to taste seems at first highly disingenuous since evaluative judgments are one and all subjective. The tendency to conclude that judgments of this type are merely arbitrary opinions is nonetheless resisted by Kant, who follows Shaftesbury and Burke in defending their presumption of intersubjective validity. It would be folly, Kant notes, to reprove another person's judgment of what is gratifying in an immediate, non-reflective way, since "as regards the pleasant . . . the fundamental proposition is valid: everyone has his own taste (the taste of sense)." Thus "he is quite contented that if he says 'Canary wine is pleasant,' another man may correct his expression and remind him that he ought to say, 'It is pleasant to me.'" It is otherwise in the case of pure aesthetic judgments:

> Many things may have charm and pleasantness—no one troubles himself at that—but if he gives out anything as beautiful, he supposes in others the same satisfaction; he judges not merely for himself, but for everyone, and speaks of beauty as if it were a property of things. Hence he says, "The thing is beautiful," and he does not count on the agreement of others with this his judgment of satisfaction, because he has found this agreement several times before, but he *demands* it of them. (*CJ,* 46-47)

Judgments of taste, then, are at once evaluative and cognitive, that is, they refer a subjective feeling to an object in a manner conducive to bringing about an expectation of universal agreement. However, unlike judgments of the good, which produce similar expectations, the ground of aesthetic judgments cannot be conceptually represented and objectively demonstrated; one cannot show that a painting is beautiful in the same way that one can show that a saw is useful, a square perfect, an action worthy, or an end universalizable. For to say that something is beautiful is to say nothing at all about its possible utility, worthiness, perfection, or purposiveness with respect to any conceivable end.

But how can judgment lay claim to universal validity if its source is subjective pleasure? One might suppose that an appeal to transcendental grounds would help here, for on Kant's reading of the matter, transcendental judgments attributing categorical properties to objects have their origin in the subject too. The appeal can be made but not, Kant adds, without encountering difficulties arising from the peculiar reflexivity that distinguishes aesthetic from categorical judgments. The categorical properties predicated of objects of knowledge, such as causality and substance, can be proven to be universally and necessarily valid as *a priori* conditions for the possibility of objectivity. Ascriptions of this sort are instances of what Kant calls *determinant* judgment, or predication which subsumes a particular under a *pre-given* universal. Judgments of taste clearly do not determine their object in this way; one does not judge this diamond to be beautiful because it has been universally established in advance that all diamonds are beautiful. Rather, one judges it so only after associating its particular formal attributes with feelings of pleasure. Stated differently, such *reflective* judgments discover the universal (or the beautiful, or the sublime) which best captures our subjective response to a given particular.

For Kant, it is the *disinterested* contemplation of an object solely in regard to its *pure form* alone independent of any purpose it might serve (be it subjective gratification of the senses or objective conformity to some concept) that suggests a way out of the grounding dilemma. Might there not be *a priori* formal conditions of aesthetic pleasure analogous to the formal unity of cognitive faculties underlying the possibility of objective knowledge? The deduction of such a ground cannot, of course, aspire to rigorous demonstration in accordance with concepts or other determinate criteria, since we are here talking about the *exemplary* necessity and universality of certain subjective states of pleasure—our general feeling that all persons of disinterested mind ought to agree in matters of taste—not the apodeicticity of categories of possible objective knowledge. What is at issue here is the existence of a common sense (*sensus communis*) which enables feelings to be communicated as universally as cognitions. According to Kant, there would be no agreement in people's feelings or cognitions unless they shared the same cognitive faculties and the same "state of mind" affected by acts of judgment (*CJ,* 75-76). Now judgment involves the subsumption of a particular under a universal, a process bringing into play the imagination (the faculty of representing sensible intuitions) and the understanding (the faculty of concepts). As for logical judgments of cognition, or judgments which ascribe a universal property such as causality to a particular object, a sensible intuition is schematized by the faculty of imagination in prior conformity to the laws of the understanding. In the case of aesthetic judgments, however, the predicate ascribed to the object does not refer to an objective concept, but to a subjective feeling. Here the formal unity of understanding and imagination is not predetermined by understanding. Instead, the imagination, representing only the mere form of a particular intuition apart from any sensuous or conceptual content, harmonizes with the understanding spontaneously (*CJ,* 128-32).

The feeling of pleasure arising from the *free play* of cognitive faculties permits us to judge the subjective purposiveness, or beauty, of an object in a manner that leads Kant to formulate a new solution to the conflict of faculties. Not only is the imagination in its freedom harmonized with the understanding in its conformity to law, but as Kant later notes, beauty—especially natural beauty—can also be said to symbolize, and thereby harmonize with, morality. For Kant, symbols function as indirect representations and, more specifically, as concrete *analogues* of rational ideas to which no direct sensible intuition corresponds. In his opinion, nature in the wild, independent of any conceptual or utilitarian associations, excites those pure aesthetic feelings whose underlying formal structure—implicating, free, immediate, universal, and disinter-

ested pleasure—is analogous to the feeling of respect accompanying our fulfillment of moral duty. Hence there is a sense in which the symbolizing of moral ideas such as freedom and the kingdom of ends by means of aesthetic "ideas" implies a supersensible ground (sometimes referred to as *Geist*) identifiable with neither nature nor freedom taken singly (*CJ,* 196-99).

II

Those who have followed the discussion thus far may well wonder what Kant's aesthetics has got to do with postmodern political thought. To begin with, the conflict between theoretical and practical reason motivating much of Kant's discussion of judgment crops up again in the postmodernism debate. True, one no longer talks about reason *per se,* yet the issue of fragmentation and conflict—in this case involving domains of discourse and action—is the same. Two questions arise concerning this fragmentation: What place does philosophy occupy in this scheme? And to whom can the political actor appeal in deciding what is right? Lyotard is interested principally in the former, that is, he is concerned with the legitimacy of a discipline that aspires to the status of an impartial tribunal regulating the rightful boundaries of heterogeneous language games. In particular he wonders whether it makes sense to appeal to a transcendent (or transcendental) notion of reason, or community, in defending philosophy's right to judge in these matters. If the philosopher, like the aesthetician, must judge without claiming a privileged standpoint outside the relativity of language games and must discover at each moment the universal which best fits the particular case independent of determinate criteria, then whatever regulative idea he or she invokes must necessarily remain formal and empty. Perhaps a universal ideal of community is operational here, but if so, what kind? One conforming to the harmonistic model underwriting judgments of beauty or one conforming to the transgressional aesthetics of the sublime? Lyotard, as we shall see, hopes to avoid a politics of terror (or totalitarianism) by opting for the latter. The second question is of concern to both Lyotard and Arendt, though it is Arendt who initially formulated it. Given the unreliability of conventional authority and the constraints of action in the modern age, is it not wiser (*contra* Lyotard) to reserve judgment to the spectator whose aesthetic distance on life secures a semblance of impartiality? If so, then would such a notion not imply something like an ideal community of speakers capable of agreeing with one another?

I shall begin with Arendt's diagnosis of modernity, which focuses on the devastating impact the Industrial Revolution had on traditional societies "held together only by customs and traditions."[4] This impact was immediately registered in the degradation of cultural goods to the status of exchange values serving the social aspiration of philistine *parvenus.* With the advent of mass society, concern with cultural fabrication (work) gave way to the functional production of entertainment and other consumer goods (labor). Absorption of culture into the life process was not without political implications since the public sphere—the stage on which the drama of political life is acted out and recorded before an audience of spectator-judges—is itself constituted by the narratives, artistic images, and other cultural artifacts that lend it permanence:

> Culture indicates that art and politics, their conflicts and tensions notwithstanding, are interrelated and even mutually dependent. . . . [T]he fleeting greatness of word and deed can endure in the world to the extent that beauty is bestowed upon it. Without the beauty, that is, the radiant glory in which potential immortality is made manifest in the human world, all human life would be futile and no greatness could endure.[5]

Inasmuch as political action depends for its enduring appearance, its meaning and purpose, on the sound judgment and judicious understanding of a public, the "crisis in culture" is a political crisis as well. Gone is the man of action, replaced by a mass man whose "capacity for consumption [is] accompanied by inability to judge, or even to distinguish."[6]

Symptomatic, too, of the crisis in culture is the widespread dissemination of scientific and technological modes of thought. The rational questioning of cultural tradition and authority and the concomitant spread of what, since Nietzsche, has come to be known as nihilism—scepticism regarding the existence of absolutes, devaluation of values claiming universal assent, and resignation to a life devoid of meaning and purpose—has had the further consequence of depriving judgment of any reliable standards. In conjunction with the rise of state bureaucracy devoted to global economic management, the demise of community based on shared values and the attendant withering away of common sense also play important roles in Arendt's account of the emergence of totalitarianism. Having "clearly exploded our categories of political thought and our standards of moral judgment," totalitarianism challenges not only the capacity of the actor to discern right from wrong, but also the capacity of the historian to understand.[7]

The Eichmann trial in the sixties seemed to confirm her thesis. Not Eichmann's diabolical nature (if he possessed one) but his banal thoughtlessness, his failure to engage in responsible judgment by blindly obeying the orders of others, was the root cause of his evil. Consequently, Arendt felt that it was all the more imperative that we ascribe to each and everyone "an independent human faculty, unsupported by law and public opinion, that judges anew in full spontaneity every deed and interest whenever the occasion arises."[8] But how can one judge or understand the unprecedented inhumanity of totalitarianism? What gives the historian the right to judge actions whose circumstances are so novel as to defy comprehension? Is not the actor better qualified to judge than the historian? This question was raised by Gershom Scholem with regard to Arendt's harsh judgment of those Jewish Elders who had urged compliance with Nazi authorities. Had she not presumed first-hand knowledge of their plight? While conceding that it might be too early for a "balanced judgment," Arendt re-

plied that "the argument that we cannot judge if we were not present and involved ourselves seems to convince everyone, although it seems obvious that if it were true, neither the administration of justice nor the writing of history would be possible."[9] The moral of this story is that if the historian must judge, the actor must understand, or insert his or her own judgments into the broader framework of a community of persons united by common narratives, meanings, and goals. Eichmann was evil because he lacked the imagination to take into account other persons' interests save those of his own chosen company.[10] In the words of Arendt, "understanding becomes the other side of [political] action" engaged in making a new beginning, for one must "eventually come to terms with what irrevocably happened and to what unavoidably exists," including, one would think, the provenance of one's own identity and that of the community to which one belongs.[11]

A crisis of meaning and judgment likewise clouds political action aimed at initiating fundamental change. To appreciate the role of understanding in coming to terms with action of this sort one must turn to Arendt's transcription of Kant's system in *The Life of the Mind.* After treating the *vita activa*—the life of labor, work, and political action—in *The Human Condition,* Arendt returned to some of her earlier concerns pertaining to thinking, willing, and judgment—the triad comprising the *vita contemplativa,* or "life of mind," modeled on Kant's three *Critiques.* Kant's distinction between *Vernunft* and *Verstand* is preserved in her distinction between *thought,* which "deals with invisibles, with representations of things that are absent" (the combined capacities of abstraction, critical reflection, and imaginative reproduction and synthesis) and *intellect,* which involves the necessary conditions for cognition.[12] Thinking endows life with meaning by weaving experience into a coherent narrative; cognition, which depends on thinking, aims at demonstrable truth. The other, non-cognitive faculties of mental life—willing and judging—are also dependent on (but irreducible to) thinking.

Now Arendt no less than Kant must contend with the conflict of faculties. The freedom to initiate fundamental political change imposes a responsibility—the need to legitimate the new order—that can only be accomplished by situating the founding act within a historical narrative connecting it to a prior foundation in the past.[13] One is tempted to recount a story of progress in which the revolutionary event is justified as inevitable or necessary, but this cannot be done without denying freedom of the will. Two alternatives remain: one resigns oneself to nihilism or redeems the meaningfulness of the past (along with hope in the future) without any appeal to ultimate ends. Nietzsche, in Arendt's opinion, tried to do both and failed. According to Nietzsche, in order for the will to affirm nihilism as a positive expression of its freedom and power it would (so it seems) have to deny the past—that residue of congealed meaning weighing upon the present and future like a "stone." "Powerless against what has been done," the will, Nietzsche tells us, "is an angry spectator of all that is past."[14] Short of denying time itself (which would usher in the extinction of the will), Nietzsche can only affirm its inherent purposelessness—the "innocence of all Becoming"—in the doctrine of Eternal Recurrence.[15] A better solution—one which does not end up denying the temporal openness necessary for freedom—would require redeeming each moment of the past by disinterested judgment.

At this juncture Arendt turns to Kant. She here notes two ways in which he sought to apply the concept of judgment in order to retrieve meaning out of political chaos, each demarcating distinct philosophies of history. The first departs from the central tenets of the *Critique of Practical Reason:* we are enjoined by practical reason to strive for moral perfection; such a state presupposes the realization of a universal kingdom of self-legislating agents regarded as ends in themselves—an ideal condition that cannot be attained by imperfect, mortal beings; yet "ought" implies "can"—we can only be obligated to strive for what we have reasonable hope of attaining; hence, we must postulate as regulative ideas the immortality of the soul and divine providence. The pursuit of moral perfection on earth is taken up further in Kant's miscellaneous writings on history, where he argues that the achievement of a cosmopolitan federation of republics in a state of "perpetual peace" is a precondition for the free exercise of practical reason (*CJ,* 284). The question is posed whether we have any reason to hope that such a state can be brought about by a species naturally inclined to pursue its own selfish interests. For the moral agent caught up in the vicissitudes of action, the answer would appear to be negative.[16] However, from the vantage point of the spectator-judge surveying the totality of human history, the situation is quite different. The basis for this optimism (following the strategy outlined above) resides in the Idea of nature as a supersensible realm of final ends. In response to the question raised in the second half of the third *Critique*—Why is it necessary that man should exist at all?—Kant defends the view that humanity, like any other class of living things, must ultimately be accounted for in terms of teleology, since "absolutely no human reason . . . can hope to explain the production of even a blade of grass by mere mechanical causes" (*CJ,* 258). On this reading, our natural self-interestedness is judged to be so providentially designed as to force us out of a state of nature (which Kant, following Hobbes, conceives as a state of war) and into a political condition compelling lawful behavior culminating in "a moral predisposition." Man's natural "unsocial sociability" is here understood as causally effecting the progressive advent of an unnatural (i.e., moral) state of peace and harmony in accordance with an Idea of reason. It is this teleologically based interpretation of natural history, then, which perhaps explains how Kant could wax enthusiastic over the sublimity of the French Revolution as a symbol of eternal moral progress while yet condemning the lawlessness of its leaders.[17]

The appeal to reason notwithstanding, Arendt finds this use of teleological judgment in resolving the dilemma of nature and freedom, and explaining the superior insight of the philosopher-historian questionable, since it relegates moral agents to the undignified status of means in attaining prior ends.[18] Elsewhere, however, the aesthetic strain prevails in Kant's conceptualization of historical judgment, and it is here, she believes, that the core of Kant's political thought resides. The "wishful participation that borders closely on enthusiasm" which Kant detects in his positive judgment of the French Revolution is described as consisting in "simply the mode of thinking of the spectators which reveals itself publicly in this game of great transformations, and manifests such a general yet disinterested sympathy for the players on one side against those on the other, even at the risk that this partiality could become very disadvantageous for them if discovered."[19] Implicit in this description is an aesthetics of judgment which Arendt characterizes as essentially imaginative, dialogical, and communitarian.[20] To begin with, there is the idea that the aesthetic attitude of the spectator is superior to the moral attitude of the actor. From the standpoint of the actor revolution "is at all times unjust" since its success would involve violating the principle of publicity. As Kant puts it, a "maxim which I cannot divulge publicly without defeating my own purpose must be kept secret if it is to succeed; and, if I cannot publicly avow it without inevitably exciting general opposition to my project, the . . . opposition which can be foreseen *a priori* is due only to the injustice with which the maxim threatens everyone."[21] This perspective seems to clash with that of the spectator-judge for whom the sublimity of the ends takes precedence over the ignominity of the means—in this regard, at least, war is by no means a handmaiden to the "commercial spirit . . . low selfishness, cowardice, and effeminacy" wrought by a successful peace (*CJ,* 102). Arendt goes on to say, however, that insofar as "publicness is already the criterion of rightness in (Kant's) moral philosophy," the opposition between the practical and aesthetic standpoints and with it, "the conflict of politics with morality," is partially resolved.[22] The "political moralist," whom Kant sees as forging "a morality in such a way that it conforms to the statesman's advantage," is the one who takes the narrow view of history as a "mere mechanism of nature." The moral politician, by contrast, is capable of viewing history, if not as a natural process progressively striving to realize a final end, then at least as a theater of moral purposes in which his or her own freedom is tested and affirmed.[23] In this instance the possibility of taking up the moral standpoint, far from opposing the aesthetic distance of the spectator-judge, actually presupposes it. Publicity not only becomes the great regulator of moral action; it also anticipates an ideal public of spectators who transform their solitary perspectives by communicating with one another.

Arendt proceeds to unpack the meaning of this ideal in terms of the disinterestedness of the spectator. Of the three "maxims of common human understanding" mentioned by Kant—think for oneself; think from the standpoint of everyone else; and think consistently—it is the second, the maxim of "enlarged thought," that specifically applies to the disinterestedness of the spectator's judgment. A person of enlarged mind "detaches himself from subjective personal conditions of his judgment, which cramp the minds of so many others, and reflects upon his judgment from a universal standpoint (which he can only determine by shifting his ground to the standpoint of others)" (*CJ,* 136-37). The importance of enlarged thought for the problem of judgment hinges on the role of imagination. In her earlier essay, "Understanding and Politics" (1953), Arendt writes: "Imagination alone enables us to see things in their proper perspective, to put that which is too close at a certain distance so that we can see and understand it without bias or prejudice, to bridge abysses of remoteness until we can see and understand everything that is too far away from us as though it were our own affair."[24] Imagination enables one to "represent something to oneself that is no longer present"; thinking subjects the representation to the critical dialogue of the mind. Judging, by contrast, does not deal with representations (universal or otherwise) but "always concerns particulars and things close to hand." Nonetheless, it is "the by-product of the liberating effect of thinking" and "realizes thinking, makes it manifest in the world of appearances."[25] The thoughtful distancing of imagination "cannot arise unless we are in a position to forget ourselves, the cares and interests and urges of our lives, so that we will not seize what we admire but let it be as it is, in its appearance."[26] As Ernst Vollrath and Ronald Beiner have pointed out, the kind of impartiality intended here should not be confused with scientific objectivity.[27] If anything, it is more kindred to phenomenological openness; things are to be judged afresh in all their phenomenal richness and inexhaustible particularity without being subsumed in advance under conventional universals or habitual modes of classification. Still, without some mediation of universal and particular neither perception nor judgment would be possible. In the case of phenomenological description particular appearances are elevated to the rank of exemplary universals (essences) through a process of imaginative variation and eidetic intuition. Something similar happens to particular events when judged; brought into relief with the aid of narrative understanding and imaginatively interpreted with an ideal audience in mind, human actions come to exemplify what is best or worst in us, what should or should not be emulated. This is how "redemptive" judgment resolves the antinomy of freedom and necessity, willing and thinking; reconciliation with the past is made possible by endowing the contingent particular with intrinsic meaning and worth.

The work of imagination is captured further by Kant in terms of an ideal community, or audience of interpreters who are thought of as striving to reach impartial agreement and mutual understanding:

> [U]nder the *sensus communis* we must include the idea of a sense common to all, i.e., of a faculty of judgment which, in its reflection, takes into account (*a priori*) the mode of representation of all other men in thought, in order, as it were, to compare its judgment with the collective reason of humanity. . . . This is done by comparing our judgment with the possible rather than the actual judgments of others, and by putting ourselves in the place of any other man, by abstracting from the limitations which contingently attach to our own judgment. (*CJ,* 136)

Implicit reference is here made to the importance of publicity. In Kant's opinion, it is not enough to possess a right to the private use of one's reason, for even the most conscientious exercise of judgment will be biased unless it is exposed to public examination. Hence, the principle of aesthetic judgment has as its corollary freedom of speech and press.[28]

III

One wonders just how successful Arendt's reconstruction of Kant's "other" political philosophy is in dealing with the crisis of judgment symptomatic of the postmodern condition. If the postmodern condition renders reason and tradition equally suspect as authoritative reference points for judgment, then what can be the basis for saying that the standpoint of the spectator is any better than that of the actor? Can community still provide an "impartial" touchstone for judging our fragmented, alienated, and anomic condition? Before answering this question I would like to return again to Arendt's choice of Kant's aesthetics as a model of political judgment. This model, as we have seen, privileges the standpoint of the spectator over that of the actor. Although she herself would like to believe that the perspectives of actor and spectator coincide, it is clear from her own remarks that such is not really the case. Though both categorical imperative and *sensus communis* enjoin the universalizability of perspectives, the former compels the judgment of particular actions in isolation from unintended consequences, the latter does not. Interestingly, some of Arendt's earlier writings anticipate a way out of this dilemma in their fusion of Aristotelian and Kantian motifs. In "The Crisis in Culture," for example, Arendt discusses the role of *phronsis* in judgment:

> That the capacity to judge is a specifically political ability in exactly the sense denoted by Kant, namely the ability to see things not only from one's own point of view but in the perspective of all those who happen to be present, even that judgment may be one of the fundamental abilities of man as a political being insofar as it enables him to orient himself in the public realm, in the common world. . . . The Greeks called this ability *phronsis,* or insight, and they considered it the principal virtue or excellence of the statesman in distinction from the wisdom of the philosopher.[29]

The juxtaposition of Aristotelian and Kantian motifs is quite surprising given Kant's own conviction that prudence, or *prudentia* (following Aquinas's Latin translation of *phronsis*), ought to be excluded from the moral-political realm as a "heteronomous" exercise of will. This decision rests on narrowly interpreting the prudence of the "political moralist" as a purely theoretical (or technical-practical) skill involving the calculation of means for efficiently bringing about desired ends, such as "exercising an influence over men and their wills" for the sake of advancing interests of state (*CJ,* 8). Aristotle, however, was careful to distinguish *phronsis* from *techn* and *epistm,* and accorded it the title of practical wisdom, by which he meant deliberation over ends as well as means. This activity clearly has certain features in common with Kant's notion of reflective judgment; it is "concerned with particulars as well as universals," not simply in order to subsume the particular under the universal (application), but to discover the universal, or rather, the proper mean, appropriate to a given situation; and its exercise involves considering the good of the community as well as one's own.[30] One reflects on the particular situation and the opinion of one's fellow citizens in qualifying the universal, and in this regard, at least, prudence is more open to the particular and less rigidly determined by the universal than Kant's "law-testing" approach to moral judgment" (as Hegel referred to it). Still, it is quite opposed to Kant's notion of reflective judgment in its focus on the substantive qualifications of statesmanship—experience, cultivation of virtuous character, formation of sound habits, and so on—which, presupposing active membership within local political communities bound by common customs, cannot fulfill ideal conditions of impartiality, universalizability, and autonomy.[31]

One wonders why Arendt ever abandoned this classical conception of judgment, since it comports much better with the presumed truthfulness of political opinion—a presumption whose basis resides in the shared convictions of a community rather than in the demonstrations of moral theorists.[32] Yet for a civilization whose identity has become so abstract as to verge on total disintegration, the only community capable of serving as touchstone for judgment may well be that disinterested ideal mentioned by Kant. Despite formalistic shortcomings, the "aestheticization" and concomitant "depoliticization" of *sensus communis* for which Gadamer rebukes Kant is possibly a better gauge of how things really stand with us than he or any other neo-Aristotelian would care to admit.[33]

Now, no contemporary thinker of repute has capitalized on this aspect of Kant's thought to the extent that Lyotard has. The aestheticization of science and politics which his philosophy proclaims is clearly descended from that great fragmentation of value spheres animating German thought since Kant. Yet notwithstanding the somewhat cynical manner in which Lyotard embraces the debasement of value to exchange commodity, his otherwise positive, Nietzschean paean to iconoclasm and innovation is at least tempered by a strong moral proclivity which owes as much, perhaps, to the "pagan" notion of *phronsis* as it does to the modern deontological ethics of Kant. This postmodern disrespect for stylistic boundaries, whose very eclecticism mocks the rational demand for consistency, purity, and progress, would appear to put Lyotard on the side of relativism were it not for his retrieval—highly uncharacteristic of most poststructuralism—of universal notions of justice and judgment.

I will not bother repeating what I have said elsewhere about Lyotard's vision of postmodern society.[34] It suffices to note that the fragmentation of persons and institutions into so many atomic roles and incommensurable language games bears witness to a new legitimation crisis. According to Lyotard, the local nature of radically incommensurable language games essentially frustrates any attempt to uncover overarching rules of communication. Indeed the rules internally regulating any given language game are themselves continually contested; for in science as in daily life, conflicts between competing descriptive, prescriptive, and expressive language games go well beyond inducing the sorts of innovations generated within the rules of normal discourse.[35] Since the postmodern condition fosters an incessant search for the new, the unknown, the anomolous, the subversive, the eclectic—in short, dissent from dominant conventions and decentralization of subjectivity—Lyotard concludes that only a "legitimation by paralogy" can satisfy "both the desire for justice and the desire for the unknown."[36] Consequently, the democratic demand that social practices conform to a universally binding consensus as a condition of their legitimation—the modernist position defended by Habermas and Arendt—strikes him as nothing less than totalitarian.

What are the implications of this analysis for a theory of judgment? Because there is no overarching community of discourse Lyotard maintains that judgment is bound by conventional standards of taste possessing at most local validity. The accent here is on competencies related to *phronsis;* since standards are general—prescribing only the limits of possible judgment—their application in any given situation and, therewith, their specific meaning and validity, will also be undetermined, at least with respect to these limits. It is at this juncture, however, where practical (pagan) competencies for judgment and action lead to a more modern, aestheticized notion of the Kantian type. The heteronomy (habitualness) and parochiality (determinateness) of conventional judgment is itself permanently relativized vis-à-vis the judge's freedom to reinterpret the content of standards. As Lyotard puts it, "the veritable nature of the judge is just to pronounce judgments, *hence prescriptions,* without criteria."[37] In other words, the limits which immediately determine judgment are violated as soon as they are imaginatively reinterpreted in light of an indefinite horizon of possible situations. This spectatorial horizon is likened by Lyotard to a regulative idea which postulates neither the convergence of all possible judgments nor the universalizability of any standard, but only the autonomy of judgment—its capacity to "maximize opinions," or generate new possibilities.[38] If a communitarian ideal is implicated here it is that wherein the *plurality of voices* (or language games) would be preserved without the violence of hegemony.

Lyotard first hinted at combining Aristotelian and Kantian notions of judgment in his 1979 interview with Jean-Loup Thébaud. Shortly thereafter critics such as Jean-Luc Nancy pointed out the paradox inherent in this position. Defending an Aristotelian perspective, Lyotard denied any possibility of grounding judgments claiming universal validity. Yet his self-acknowledged willingness to play "the great prescriber" who judges the proper limits governing all language games from the detached perspective of the spectator clearly presupposed such a possibility, otherwise his own critique of scientism and discursive hegemony would have been without foundation. Moreover, by prescribing very determinate boundaries to the prescriptive and descriptive language games of morality and science respectively he may have confused (so Nancy argues) determinant and reflective judgment.[39] On this reading Lyotard over-stepped the boundaries of aesthetic judgment. The latter may well be guided by an indeterminate idea of community, but this universal is not of the order of something that can be prescribed as a definite purpose to be striven for. Having thus succumbed to a kind of transcendental illusion, Lyotard became entrapped in a totalitarian logic of his own making—that of absolute pluralism.

One need not accept Nancy's contention that Lyotard confused *phronsis* and reflective judgment to see the problem implicit in playing the "great prescriber." Even if, as Gadamer and other hermeneuticists have claimed, every valid application of a general rule to a concrete situation involves reinterpreting the rule in light of the peculiar circumstances of the situation while relativizing these same circumstances with respect to an indeterminate ideal of community, that is, even if every determinate judgment presupposes a reflective judgment and vice versa, such application does not always or necessarily entail prescription. This objection was finally acknowledged by Lyotard in **Le différend** (1983) where he once again returned to Kant in order to clarify the notion of a community of heterogeneous faculties "without which (the partisans of consensus, or beautiful harmony, or the partisans of conflict, or sublime incommensurability) would not even be able to *agree* that they are in *disagreement*."[40] Lyotard's preferred symbol for this new conception of community is an archipelago:

> The faculty of judging would be at least in part like a ship owner or an admiral who would launch from one island to another expeditions destined to present to the one what they have found (discovered in the old meaning of the term) in the other, and who could serve up to the first some "as-if" intuition in order to validate it. This force of intervention, war or commerce, hasn't any object, it has no island of its own, but it requires a milieu, the sea, the archipelago, the principal sea as the Aegean Sea was formerly named.[41]

The third *Critique* takes note of symbolic or analogical passages (*Übergänge*) linking what are otherwise heterogeneous moral, aesthetic, and cognitive faculties. Lyotard curiously finds in this "oceanic" simile something like a higher ground on which to base the critical judgment of the philosopher—a common place (the sea) in terms of which competing islands of discourse can be relativized (located) with respect to their particular domains of validity—though he characteristically interprets it in a manner that brings into relief an underlying tension. In *The Strife of the Faculties* (1798), Kant no longer conceived critical philosophy as a neutral tribunal that delivers final verdicts (prescriptions) without incurring new wrongs. We find instead the notion of a guardian who, while not a litigant in the dispute, intervenes indirectly on behalf of the weaker

party by judging what is "just," or conducive to an agreement to disagree. The dispute in question is the conflict of faculties—in the first instance, between the "higher" university faculties of theology, law, and medicine and the "lower" faculty of philosophy; and in the second, between opposed cognitive and practical mental faculties laying claim to the same territory, human nature. One cannot regulate the various injustices (or *différends,* as Lyotard prefers to call them) which arise when conflicting "discourses" range over the same territory; at most, one can expose them by defending the equally valid claim of the weaker party, the advocate of freedom, against the apparently stronger claim of the dogmatist. The basis for this peculiar judgment would thus appear to be that the conflict of mental faculties—indeed, the very sickness of the distracted subject—may yet be conductive to the health of the soul.

For Lyotard the kind of critical judgment exercised by the philosopher is reflective rather than determinate, aesthetic rather than teleological. It is not restricted to any given locale (or discursive regime) but ranges over an entire "archipelago." Nor is it guided in advance by any theoretical or practical notion of finality. What guides this judgment are aesthetic considerations pertaining to the integrity of a whole whose parts achieve harmonious equilibrium only through conflict. This is not a judgment of beauty in Kant's sense, but a judgment of the sublime. Whereas judgments of beauty reflect the imagination's success in discovering symbols which represent ideas of reason and attest to the unity of faculties—the unity of the cognitive and the practical in the supersensible Idea of nature being a case in point—judgments of the sublime articulate just the opposite—the incommensurablity of imagination and understanding, the presentation of the unpresentable. Sublime for Kant are those experiences of formlessness, boundlessness, and lack of finality such as political revolutions, which paradoxically arouse enthusiasm in us because they manage in spite of themselves to signal the finality and community they empirically deny.[42] Sublime, too, is the lack of finality evident in the *différend* since it symbolizes a community in which conflict is the basis for integrity, harmony, and justice. Lyotard's philosophy therefore testifies to a justice of judgment rather than of action and representation. As he puts it, "politics cannot have for its stake the good, but would have to have the least bad."[43] By contrast, justice demands only that one judge without prescribing, that one listen for the silences that betoken *différends* so as to finally let the suppressed voice find its proper idiom.[44]

Lyotard's refusal to grant judgment any prescriptive force follows from the postmodern standpoint he shares with Arendt. If Arendt and Lyotard do not exactly repudiate the finality of judgment, they certainly deny it any determinate content. In the absence of any final verdicts we are left with little consolation but the dignity that comes from judging responsibly. Arendt, of course, found hope in a purely formal idea of community—one, she believed, that might serve to regulate our search for mutual understanding and reconciliation. Although Lyotard also embraces a formal ideal of "community"—he like Arendt has long since abandoned the quest for global narratives in favor of recounting the *petit récits* of localizable collectivities—he more than she has been atuned to the pessimistic implications of the current crisis. Having resigned himself to the end of community *as a locus of consensus,* he urges acceptance of the sublimely indeterminate, yet painful, spectacle of never-ending conflict, disruption, and (it would seem) injustice. This solution seems paradoxical in light of Lyotard's insistence on politicizing art and philosophy; for if ideas of community and justice still find a niche in his philosophy it is in the depoliticized sense of a healthy equilibrium of heterogeneous discourses composed of discontinuous phrases—a justice, if you will, of mutually cancelling injustices. Once the sundering of the community of reason is accomplished, however, philosophical judgment is left curiously suspended in an oceanic void. Due to its extreme discrimination, judgment has deprived itself of any determinate ground on which to discriminate, thereby perhaps explaining Lyotard's curious opinion that the only appropriate response to linguistic fragmentation is silence. At least Arendt continued to regard the function of judgment as in some sense preserving a space for the disclosure of community and world. Lyotard's rejection of the ontological no less than the practical role of judgment, on the contrary, raises doubts about the normative basis underlying his own critical judgment.[45]

Viewed in this light, Nancy's critique of Lyotard is decisive:

> [Lyotard] posits "passages between 'areas' of legitimacy" such as "language (which, if you will, is Being without illusion) *in process (en train)* of establishing diverse families of legitimacy, critical language, without rules." Language—that is to say, if I understand correctly, the difference either of/between phrases—is defined "if you will" as "Being without illusion." That is to say that illusion is to speak of Being, but that speaking *is* Being "without illusion" . . . It is in process, it hasn't finished or begun, but it is in process *à la place* What is this place? Lyotard would doubtless say that this question is illegitimate. Let's say that he is right. But what is it to be right? Ultimately it is not a "play of phrases" which decides what is right. . . . If it is not "Being" it is at least that which happens to it, in fact the truth of an experience, the judgment of a (hi)story. It is not "phrases" that are "right" . . . Truth is not a phrase—and yet truth happens.[46]

In situating this difficult passage one must bear in mind Lyotard's insistence on the contextuality of all judgment. This would perhaps explain the inconsistency of many of his own judgments in the Thébaud interview about the rightful boundaries separating moral and scientific discourse. Depending on the context of his own reasoning, Lyotard argued both that prescription should be left out of science and that scientific discourse is and even should be impure and undecided. That the logical status of a scientific law or a rule of language hovers somewhere between the prescriptive and the descriptive is something to be at

once praised as "paralogical" and condemned as "terroristic." The resulting lack of centeredness and discrimination conveys precisely the impression of sophistry Lyotard seeks so assiduously to cultivate. Nancy's remark, I think, can be understood as a response to the indeterminacy and ungroundedness of this situation. Accepting much of Lyotard's thesis concerning the postmodern condition, Nancy still prefers to read Kant through the eyes of Arendt and Heidegger. Judgment is not an arbitrary game of reversal, but presupposes some relationship to the truth, however this is interpreted. Judging discloses Being—discriminates and brings to light what there is. At the same time, it remains firmly embedded in a form of life, or mode of being, that presupposes a deeper, pre-thematic understanding of a global nexus of meaningful relationships comprising the always implicit background against which one acts and experiences. This disclosure (or "truth" as Heidegger would say) is already centered (enclosed or located) within a linguistically determined horizon of possible meaning— what Gadamer would call the "effective history" of past precedent (tradition as a repository of possibilities)—and for that reason must be distinguished from the sort of cognitive truth expressed in propositional or categorical judgments. Kant, too, emphasized the centrality of judgment in bringing about the synthesis of intuition and concept necessary for the possibility of experience, but by this he meant a categorial determination. For Nancy, on the contrary, this synthesis presupposes a deeper disclosure of world, self and community involving reflective judgment, or the interpretative creation or discovery of new modes of action, feeling, and cognition. Though reflective judgment encompasses and even incorporates the differential structure of language encapsulated in the notion of the *différend,* it does not dissolve into "a play of phrases." For prior to all decentralization judgment is determined precategorially by the web of meanings comprising an ontological preunderstanding. If this is so, then the roots of reason reach further down into the ground than its discursive fragmentation would indicate. Can we accept the finality of this judgment? We can, I believe, so long as we remember that even in our postmodern condition—a condition in which tradition, now fragmented, has lost much of its authority—the indeterminacy of final ends and the determinacy of finite purposes, the aesthetics and pragmatics of judgment, are never absolutely opposed, but remain aspects of one and the same Being.

Notes

1. Walter Benjamin, "Theses on the Philosophy of History," in *Illuminations,* ed. Hannah Arendt, trans. H. Zohn (New York: Harcourt, Brace, and World, 1968), 256.

2. Immanuel Kant, *Critique of Judgment,* trans. J. H. Bernard (London: MacMillan, 1951), 15. Hereafter abbreviated as '*CJ*'.

3. Aside from occasional references to judgment in Kant's *Logic,* his essay "Theory and Practice," and his treatise, *Education,* a more detailed discussion of this faculty and its relationship to taste can be found in *Anthropology from a Pragmatic Point of View.*

4. Arendt, "Understanding and Politics," *Partisan Review* 20 (1953): 385. The reader is urged to consult Ronald Beiner, "Interpretative Essay" in Arendt, *Lectures on Kant's Political Philosophy,* ed. Ronald Beiner, (Chicago: Chicago University Press, 1982).

5. Arendt, "The Crisis in Culture," in *Between Past and Future* (New York: Viking Press, 1980), 218.

6. Ibid., 199.

7. Arendt, "Understanding and Politics," 379.

8. Arendt, "Personal Responsibility Under Dictatorship," *The Listener,* August 6, 1964, 185-87.

9. Arendt, *Eichmann in Jerusalem: A Report on the Banality of Evil* (New York: Viking Press, 1965), 295-96.

10. Arendt, "Basic Moral Propositions" (Course given at the University of Chicago, Seventeenth Session), Hannah Arendt Papers, Library of Congress, Container 41, p. 024560. Cited by Beiner in Arendt, *Lectures on Kant's Political Philosophy,* 112.

11. Arendt, "Understanding and Politics," 391.

12. Arendt, *Thinking,* vol. 1 of *The Life of the Mind,* ed. Mary McCarthy (New York: Harcourt, Brace, Jovanovich, 1978), 193.

13. Arendt's claim that the secular orders founded by the framers of the Declaration of Independence and the Declaration of the Rights of Man required legitimation vis-à-vis the civic ideals of classical antiquity lends credence to the view that the modern age is a continuation of the past by other means. This secularization thesis, which denies modernity any claim to legitimacy other than that bestowed upon it in virtue of its substantial identity with the paganism of antiquity and the Christianity of the Middle Ages, would appear to contradict Arendt's contention that the modern world constitutes a radical break with the past. However, as Hans Blumenberg notes, Arendt correctly saw that the worldliness of the modern age is no more a simple repetition of pagan antiquity than is the unworldliness of the scientific demythologization of nature a simple repetition of the otherworldliness of the Middle Ages. See Arendt, *On Revolution* (New York: Viking Press, 1962), 195-215; *The Human Condition* (Chicago: University of Chicago Press, 1958), 320; and Hans Blumenberg, *The Legitimacy of the Modern Age,* trans. Robert M. Wallace (Cambridge, Mass.: MIT Press, 1983), 8-9.

14. Frederick Nietzsche, *Thus Spoke Zarathustra,* in *The Portable Nietzsche,* trans. and ed. Walter Kaufmann (New York: Viking Press, 1968), 251.

15. Arendt, *Willing,* vol. 2 of *The Life of the Mind,* 170.

16. Kant, "Theory and Practice," in *Kant's Political Writings,* ed. H. Reiss, trans. H. B. Nisbet (Cambridge: Cambridge University Press, 1971), 91.

17. Kant, "An Old Question Raised Again: Is the Human Race Constantly Progressing?" part 2 of "The Strife of the Faculties," in *On History,* ed. Lewis White Beck (Indianapolis: Bobbs-Merrill, 1963), 144. For a more detailed account of Kant's condemnation of revolution in general and the French Revolution in particular, see Kant, *The Metaphysical Elements of Justice,* trans. John Ladd (Indianapolis: Bobbs-Merrill, 1965) 84-89, 113-14.

18. Arendt, *Lectures on Kant's Political Philosophy,* 18, 31.

19. Kant, *Strife of the Faculties,* 143.

20. Arendt, *Lectures on Kant's Political Philosophy,* 66-67.

21. Kant, *Perpetual Peace,* in *On History,* 129-30.

22. Arendt, *Lectures on Kant's Political Philosophy,* 19.

23. Kant, *Perpetual Peace,* 119.

24. Arendt, "Understanding and Politics," 392.

25. Arendt, *Thinking,* 192-93.

26. Arendt, *Between Past and Future,* 210.

27. Cf. Beiner, "Interpretive Essay," 111; and Ernst Vollrath, "Hannah Arendt and the Method of Political Thinking," *Social Research* 44 (1977): 163-64.

28. Arendt, *Lectures on Kant's Political Philosophy,* 74-75. Cf. Kant, "Was heißt: Sich im Denken orientieren?" in *Gesammelte Schriften,* Prussian Academy edition (Berlin: Reimer & de Gruyter, 1910-66), vol. 8, 131-47. Cf. Kant, *On History,* 89, 103-03.

29. Arendt, *Between Past and Future,* 221.

30. Aristotle, *Nicomachean Ethics* 6.2-4, 7-9.

31. Arendt, *Between Past and Future,* 220-21. Substantive considerations, however, do enter into the account of judgment and social taste presented in Kant's *Anthropology.* There, judgment ("the faculty of discovering the particular so far as it is an instance of a rule") is similar to Aristotle's golden mean in that it involves correct understanding, which "maintains the properness of concepts necessary for the purpose for which they are used" (Kant, *Anthropology,* 92). Such discrimination "cannot be taught, but only exercised," and "does not come for years" (ibid., 93). Elsewhere, Kant talks about the "goodness of soul . . . around which the judgment of taste assembles all its judgments" as the "pure form under which all purposes must be united." But "greatness of soul and strength of soul relate to the matter (the tools for certain purposes)" (ibid., 144). Finally, Kant remarks that "to be well-mannered, proper, polite, and polished (by disposing of crudeness)" is a condition of taste, albeit a negative one (ibid., 147).

32. Echoing Habermas's criticism of Arendt's contention that "practice rests on opinions that

cannot be true or false in the strict sense" (Jürgen Habermas, "Hannah Arendt's Communicative Concept of Power," *Social Research* 44 [1977]: 22), Beiner remarks that "it is not clear how we could make sense of opinions that did not involve any cognitive claims . . . or why we should be expected to take seriously opinions that assert no claims to truth (or do not at least claim more truth than is claimed by available alternative opinions)" ("Interpretive Essay," 137). Interestingly, in her essay, "What is Freedom," Arendt followed Kant very closely in speaking of "the judgment *of the intellect* which precedes action" (*Between Past and Future*, 156—emphasis added). However, in her unpublished lectures delivered in 1965 and 1966 she reversed herself, identifying judgment with the "arbitrating function" of the will. It was only after expressing doubts about the status of judgment that she eventually aligned it with the noncognitive *vita contemplativa*.

33. See Hans-Georg Gadamer, *Wahrheit und Methode* (Tübingen: J. C. B. Mohr, 1960), 39-77. For further discussion of the relevance of *phronsis* to the problem of hermeneutic application see pp. 295-307; and David Ingram, "Hermeneutics and Truth," *Journal of the British Society for Phenomenology* 15 (January 1984): 62-78.

34. See David Ingram, "Legitimacy and the Postmodern Condition: The Political Thought of Jean-François Lyotard," *Praxis International* (forthcoming). See also Lyotard, *The Postmodern Condition: A Report on Knowledge*, trans. G. Bennington and B. Massumi (Minneapolis: University of Minnesota Press, 1984); and Lyotard and Jean-Loup Thébaud, *Au juste* (Paris: Christian Bourgeois, 1979), 188.

35. Lyotard, *Postmodern Condition*, 20.

36. Ibid., 65-67.

37. Lyotard and Thébaud, *Au juste*, 52-53. Emphasis added.

38. Ibid., 146-53.

39. Jean-Luc Nancy, "Dies Irae," in *La faculte de juger* (Paris: Les Editions de Minuit, 1985), 13-14.

40. Lyotard, *Le différend* (Paris: Les Editions de Minuit, 1983), 24-25.

41. Ibid., 190.

42. Lyotard, *Le différend*, 240-43.

43. Ibid., 203.

44. Ibid., 30.

45. Habermas also has difficulty accounting for the normative basis of judgment, though for somewhat different reasons. He is inclined to distinguish judgment from practical reason, the application of general norms (*phronsis*), from their discursive justification. Although his understanding of judgment is informed by Gadamer's hermeneutics, which invests *phronsis* with a certain reflexivity and dialogical openness, he is not willing to see in it a different, perhaps aesthetic, conception of rationality at work. The notion of aesthetic rationality in Habermas's philosophy is unclear, but some of his recent essays have alluded to a kind of artistic rationality and "truth" which would be holistic and prediscursive, implying more than an ideal speech situation. See Habermas, "Questions and Counterquestions," in *Moralbewuβtsein und kommunikatives Handeln* (Frankfurt: Suhrkamp, 1983), 53-125; R. J. Bernstein, ed., *Habermas and Modernity* (Cambridge: M. I. T. Press, 1985); and David Ingram, *Habermas and the Dialectic of Reason* (New Haven: Yale University Press, 1987), 101-03, 177-88.

46. Jean-Luc Nancy, *L'imperatif categorique* (Paris: Flammarion, 1983), 60.

John Leo (essay date 1988)

SOURCE: "Postmodernity, Narratives, Sexual Politics: Reflections on Jean-François Lyotard," in *The Centennial Review*, Vol. XXXII, No. 4, Fall, 1988, pp. 336-50.

[*In the following essay, Leo explores Lyotard's postmodern critique of modernist doctrine.*]

I

Beginning in the 1960s a group of skeptical (and mainly gay) theorists emerged in Europe (mainly France) whose common stance has been the decolonization of just about everything administered by a white, straight, occidental patriarchy.[1] Figures such as Roland Barthes, Jean Baudrillard, Hélène Cixous, Jacques Derrida, Michel Foucault, Guy Hocquenghem, Julia Kristeva, Jean-François Lyotard, and Monique Wittig are just some of the thinkers who have changed irrevocably how we describe, understand, and participate in social formations. Their commentaries on sexuality, psychoanalysis, signs and codes, the pervasive power of the state and of institutions ("discourses"), economic exchange, and mass communications are today the core of European university curricula and the interpretive frameworks (and occasional inspirations) for work in the arts and literature. Theirs is not a thematic/semantic exposition on power but instead a practical anatomy of the secrets and interstices of its workings, a return of the repressed within and onto a modernist philosophy of *logical* language games in the name of *rules* and *effects*.

Even more influential today in Europe and the US, these poststructuralists are the most astute observers of our common postmodernity, if by that term we generally mean a crisis within and point of departure from the culture of modernism—its theological notions of "self" and subjectivity, its presumed universality of scientific procedures and epistemology, and its compartmentalization of the body and rhythmic organization of daily practices around work. In the United States the impact of these thinkers is to be found in the fields of art history and criticism (e.g. Lyotard's appearances in *Artforum* and *Art in America),* literature, film and television (including videoart), and increasingly in psychology, law, and the history of the family. Hal Foster, Stephen Greenblatt, Annette Kuhns, Frank Lentricchia, Mark Poster, Wendy Steiner, and Linda Williams are just some of the American critics whose work indicates the informational and intellectual redefinition now underway within the academy and other discourses. Not only is much of this activity of direct interest to many women, gays, and others politically disenfranchised, it is also of direct consequence in structuring the discursive terms defining us. What is at stake is a massive reorientation of the conceptual apparatus of the West and a practical intervention in contemporary power relations. As sweeping as this statement sounds, we have only to note the recent rifts within discourses and disciplines over the ligitimacy of critical objects or areas of inquiry—e.g. women's studies *and* pornography *and* Catholicism, the American Psychiatric Association *and* the Supreme Court *and* gays—to realize, in turn, that "difference" has inscribed *itself* and in opposition to structures of dominance. The resulting fissures, imbalances, and regroupings require different descriptive terms.

Poststructuralism, like the postmodern culture it evaluates, is not a movement; it is at once a recognition, a reaction, and a set of methods. By challenging traditionalist mystifications of sexuality—for example, its confusion with morality (by the church), with compulsory heterosexuality (or "normalcy," by psychiatry), or the confusion of sexism with "natural law" (by just about everybody)—poststructuralism announces entirely new versions of a radically pluralized human subject. The "self"—whatever it may otherwise be—is not a behaviorist entity, nor a surrogate for the "soul" nor missionary for some divine "higher state," nor is it "true" (as in the self-help library) and "centered." It is a delusion to invoke or to believe in a self which is unequivocal, unambiguous, which acts in a "whole" and "unified" way, and which speaks with one mind and voice; such a gesture falsifies the truly open-ended nature of the subject. Yet it is precisely this presumed "unitary subject" we find embedded within much language of philosophy, psychology, and literary criticism, say, as well as in much popular religion and national myth. It is a tacit but tenacious faith that, somehow, selfhood is either the final sum of, or completely explainable by, a range of empiricisms or positivist disciplines, genes, demographics, psychological thermodynamics, and even karmas. In Lyotard's sense this faith in selfhood is mediated by cultural narratives coming out of authoritative discourses such as religion, sociology, and psychiatry, and despite their differences they share some major assumptions. Surely one is that the "self" is equatable with the "individual," i.e. one-to-one in its relationships and at once the presumption behind, and the locus of innumerable discrete causalities. Selfhood, however—or rather the "subject"—is best described as the subject-in-process, at

once social and libidinal, and most importantly as "dissolved" into myriads of relations, con(dis)junctions, networks, structures of contradicting codes, and as Lyotard shows repeatedly, relations of power.

II

The "social bond" connecting us all, Lyotard argues trenchantly in ***The Postmodern Condition,***[2] is an energetic information field which by its nature neither creates nor ratifies archaic notions of the "self" or of the "individual" otherwise nostalgically invoked by dominant ideologies, religious myth, popular culture, and other narratives. Authority, power, groupings and alliances among people, access to information—these are the issues and also the structural characteristics ("poles of attraction") of postmodern society making it different from modernist traditions, hierarchies, hero-worship, and the like:

> A *self* does not amount to much, but no self is an island; each exists in a fabric of relations that is now more complex and mobile than ever before. Young or old, man or woman, rich or poor, a person is always located at "nodal points" of specific communication circuits, however tiny these may be. Or better: one is always located at a post through which various kinds of messages pass. No one, not even the least privileged among us, is ever entirely powerless over the messages that traverse and position him at the post of sender, addressee, or referent. One's mobility in relation to these language game effects (language games, of course, are what this is all about) is tolerable, at least within certain [vague] limits; it is even solicited by regulatory mechanisms, and in particular by the self-adjustments the system undertakes in order to improve its performance. . . . [T]here is no need to resort to some fiction of social origins to establish that language games are the minimum relation required for society to exist; even before he is born, if only by virtue of the name he is given, the human child is already positioned as the referent in the story recounted by those around him, in relation to which he will inevitably chart his course. Or more simply still, the question of the social bond, insofar as it is a question, is itself a language game, the game of inquiry. It immediately positions the person who asks, as well as the addressee and the referent asked about: it is already the social bond.

But if all is flux, energy, and nodal points, how does "order" occur in society? Why or how do I even have the impression of a "self"? The social bond and interiority are largely constructed by narratives which in Lyotard's usage are "language games" (or "linkings of phrases") having any number of "pragmatics" (actual effects): denotations, performatives, commands, prayers, the prescription of norms, the legitimation of various "authorities," and the maintenance of subject positions (9-11). In short society is mapped by narratives; more precisely, the social bond is the linguistic fabric made up of heterogenous narratives. It is already there in speaking and writing and positioning.

And social bonding as a form of power, as Lyotard demonstrates, is quite "straight" and propped by the circularity of modern discursive reasoning, i.e. language games or phrase linkages creating the conditions, rules, and results of "knowledge." He writes:

> But the fact remains that since performativity [i.e. optimal efficiency] increases the ability to produce proof, it also increases the ability to be right; the technical criterion, introduced on a massive scale into scientific knowledge, cannot fail to influence the truth criterion. . . . This procedure operates within the following framework: since "reality" is what provides the evidence used as proof in scientific argumentation, and also provides prescriptions and promises of a juridical, ethical, and political nature with results, one can master all of these games by mastering "reality." That is precisely what technology can do. By reinforcing technology, one "reinforces" reality, and one's chances of being just and right increase accordingly. . . . This is how legitimation by power takes shape. Power is not only good performativity but also effective verification and good verdicts. It legitimates science and the law on the basis of their efficiency, and legitimates this efficiency on the basis of science and law. It is self-legitimating. . . . (46-47)

Nietzsche might have said that Might Makes Right. *What works* is "true" not only because it is what finally has the power to install itself—what *is*, finally, is what *is there*—but precisely because it calls the shots, determines the rules, controls the criteria and "narratives of legitimation," and does so because performance *is* efficiency is optimal is measurement is the final court of appeal: (the technological base of) *information* and its retrieval and application. Thus the circularity of information and its social uses is both objective condition and subjective circuitry, both a set of constraints on subjectivity and the field for its contestation, i.e. the continuous (de)regulation of the subject. The postmodern condition "designates the state of our culture following the transformations which, since the end of the nineteenth century, have altered the game rules for science, literature, and the arts" (xxiii). Clearly poststructuralism as a set of diagnostic practices, and postmodernity as a set of material cultural conditions, are instrinsically at odds with any form of authority pretending to find its basis in the mind of God (or similar absolutes, e.g. "Nature") and not in the intersection of subjects, social conventions, discourses, and social narratives. We simply do not *really* believe in the transcendental, Lyotard argues, because "reality" is largely an agreement among parties in order to optimize the business of capitalism, its "performance" here and now. Clearly this is true in the universities, officially (i.e. "only in the context of the grand narratives of legitimation") the custodians of the best that has been thought and said and the production points of "truth." "But it is probable," Lyotard argues,

> that these narratives are already no longer the principal driving force behind interest in acquiring knowledge. . . . The question (overt or implied) now asked by the professionalist student, the State, or institutions of higher education is no longer "Is it true?" but "What use is it?" In the context of the merchantilization of knowledge, more often than not this question is equiva-

lent to: "Is it saleable?" And in the context of power-growth: "Is it efficient?" (51)

And similarly with religious thought (despite dogma). The culture of modernism has witnessed its secularization into something *other* than what its master religious narrative—the Judeo-Christian—claims. If the party line is that heaven and earth, like soul and body, are distinct, then modernism's culture of the market gradually subverts and delegitimizes the distinction on the basis of its activity—exchange and substitution, the endless production and consumption and assignment to oblivion of new intensities. What modernism brings forth is the huge surprise (for some) of the postmodern "sublime" of capitalism, its destruction of the familiar and its opening onto the anxiety, terror, pleasure and pain of indeterminancy. What Lyotard calls "hypercapitalism" erodes the idea that there is only *one* Rule, *one* Law, *one* Story overriding and grounding all the others.

III

One of the biggest transformations marking the disjunction between modernism and postmodernism is the collapse of the "master narratives" or "grand stories"—"the dialectics of Spirit . . . the emancipation of the rational or working subject, or the creation of wealth"—which earlier claimed our belief and assent. In a recent interview Lyotard refers to these "great narratives" as "the ruin of subject-systems . . . the liberal, the marxist, the capitalist, the christian, the speculative" (*Diacritics* 14 [Fall 1984]: 18). The narrative of "Spirit" is the syntax, grammar, emplotment, and disposition of character types by the churches, followed by the narrative of liberalism and socialism and by the narrative of enlightened self-interest or capitalism. They share a narrative purpose—to train subjects (narrative characters) in specific roles—and they share a narrative trajectory (plot)—to relate a "universal" history which manifests the "progressive" unfolding of the "Spirit" of "Man" or of the "People" in the form of "Emancipation" or "Freedom." These "master narratives" traditionally have been the very boundaries, the outlines, of what and how we believe and see and thus have seemed given and beyond question. In short the party lines of religion, marxism, and capitalism are dead. The allegorical and culturally cementing stories of the little baby Moses, little Jesus, the young Buddha, the young Marx, the middleaged Henry Ford, the late Lenin, and so on—all these prescriptions, culturally useful constructions of guilt, ancestral rites—are grand ghost stories, murmurings from the grave of modernism. What's left is the postmodern condition: the production and use of *information* and of multiple *micronarratives* (as opposed to "grand" or "master"). "In a sense," Lyotard remarks,

> the people are only that which actualizes the narratives; once again, they do this not only by recounting them, but also by listening to them and recounting themselves through them; in other words, by putting them into "play" in their institutions. . . . Narratives, as we have seen, determine criteria of competence and/or illustrate how they are to be applied. They thus define what has

the right to be said and done in the culture in question, and since they are themselves a part of that culture, they are legitimated by the simple fact that they do what they do. (23)

The Postmodern Condition is a slim but dense discussion of these changed game rules and dispersed "language clouds" (including media and images) which today float about institutions and operate their power. We plug into these "clouds" at all levels according to our desires, class positions, genders, and other changes and ratios we experience.

> Conveyed within each cloud are pragmatic valences specific to its kind. Each of us lives at the intersection of many of these. However, we do not necessarily establish stable language combinations, and the properties of the ones we do establish are not necessarily communicable. Thus the society of the future falls less within the province of a Newtonian anthropology (such as structuralism or systems theory) than a pragmatics of language particles. (xxiv)

But what of power and decision-making? Lyotard's comments are an incisive review of a remarkable heterogeneity controlled by managerial and administrative procedures unanimously predicated on power, legitimacy, and efficiency.

> The decision makers . . . attempt to manage these clouds of sociality [i.e. language clouds] according to input/output matrices, following a logic which implies that their elements are commensurable and that the whole is determinable. They allocate our lives for the growth of power. In matters of social justice and of scientific truth alike, the legitimation of that power is based on its optimizing the system's performance—efficiency. The application of this criterion to all of our games necessarily entails a certain level of terror, whether soft or hard: be operational (that is commensurable) or disappear. (xxiv)

Lyotard's analyses of applied and pure scientific research, and of universities and grantsmanship, are instructive for showing the economics of "disciplines," the limitations of their models and paradigms, and their power to configurate information and the rules ("legitimation narratives") for its interpretation. He gives the following example of narrativizing power and performance:

> What do scientists do when they appear on television or are interviewed in the newspapers after making a "discovery"? They recount an epic of knowledge that is in fact wholly unepic. They play by the rules of the narrative game; its influence remains considerable not only on the users of the media, but also on the scientist's sentiments. This fact is neither trivial nor accessory; it concerns the relationship of scientific knowledge to "popular" knowledge, or what is left of it. The state spends large amounts of money to enable science to pass itself off as an epic; the State's own credibility is based on that epic, which it uses to obtain the public consent its decision makers need. (27-28)

The notion of "realism" undergoes a similar debunking quite forceful in its opposition to what the universities

preach. Market conditions (or politically "correct" prescriptions) create an eclectic "mixing process" for the various avant-gardes; their cutting edges are continuously dulled and rechanneled less threateningly into more comfortable (familiar) genres and formats, which after all are language games (the asethetics of, say, "mimesis") pretending to be a substitute for "reality" (understood to be "Unity, simplicity, communicability, etc." [75]). The passage is worth quoting at length:

> But capitalism inherently possesses the power to derealize familiar objects, social roles, and institutions to such a degree that the socalled realistic representations can no longer evoke reality except as nostalgia or mockery, as an occasion for suffering rather than for satisfaction. Classicism seems to be ruled out in a world in which reality is so destabilized that it offers no occasion for experience but one for ratings and experimentation. . . . Photography did not appear as a challenge to painting from the outside, any more than industrial cinema did to narrative literature. The former was only putting the final touch to the program of ordering the visible elaborated by the quattrocento; while the latter was the last step in rounding off [passages of time] as organic wholes, which had been the ideal of the great novels of education since the eighteenth century. That the mechanical and the industrial should appear as substitutes for hand or craft was not in itself a disaster—except if one believes that art is in its essence the expression of an individuality of genius assisted by an elite craftsmanship. The challenge lay essentially in that photographic and cinematographic processes can accomplish better, faster, and with a circulation a hundred thousand times larger than narrative or pictorial realism [the assigned task of realism]: to preserve various consciousnesses from doubt. Industrial photography and cinema will be superior to painting and the novel whenever the object is to stabilize the referent, to arrange it according to a point of view which endows it with a recognizable meaning, to reproduce the syntax and vocabulary which enables the addressee to decipher images and sequences quickly, and so to arrive easily at the consciousness of his own identity as well as the approval which he thereby receives from others—since such structures of images and sequences constitute a communication code among all of them. This is the way the effects of reality, or if one prefers, the fantasies of realism, multiply. (74)

It is devastating for critical readers to apply these insights to the world of decision-making surrounding them. To "stabilize the referent" means that cultural artifacts will repeat—efficiently, "quickly" and "easily"—a "point of view" with "recognizable meaning." The cultural *effect* produces homogeneity rather than heterogeneity, ideological sameness at the expense of difference. One's social "identity" is caught up in a repetitive web of approval and a shared "communication code," a process of denial and compensation. It is difficult to imagine the function of an avant-garde in a society where the "effects of reality" are "the fantasies of realism" endlessly reproduced. If representations of gays and women as *different*, for example, are taken at all as potential indications of an avant-garde (in the sense of opening onto an unknown, the "unpresented"), then they are to be "mixed" (stereotyped, with diluted strength) the better to interface with the optimal growth of power—mainly patriarchal power. The resulting pastiche or representation is then a "realism." It is certainly apparent that certain groups knowingly manipulate media and information to enforce certain social identities and the meanings ("norms") attached to them; its equally clear how difficult it is for gay and feminist themes and subject matter to have credibility and legibility when there is no guarantee of a wide social audience literate ("competent") with the codes, signs, and narratives of sexual differences. What operates these exclusions are media "realisms" "as the appropriate remedy for the anxiety and depression that [the] public experiences" (75). "Realisms" then are "somewhere" between a hollowed out official "cultural policy" ("academicism"), mainly on the order of the National Endowment for the Arts, the museums and universities, and what's left ("kitsch"), or the banality of endless multiple forms and mishmashes of citation, pastiche, and collage. "Eclecticism is the degree zero of contemporary general culture," Lyotard elaborates, for kitsch simply is the culture and has become the de facto "realism of the 'anything goes'"—in short, the "realism . . . of money," whereby works are valued "according to the profits they yield" (76).

IV

Lyotard's writing consistently demonstrates an exacting intelligence with a surgical but elegant *logique*.[3] In earlier work—*Des Dispositifs pulsionnels* (1973; *Drive Devices*), *Dérive à partir de Marx et Freud* (1973; *Drifting Away from Marx and Freud*), and *Économie libidinale* (1974: *Libidinal Economy*)—he argues essentially that the libido "maps" itself onto whatever economic order it finds itself in: an "economic-libidinal mixing" as he says in his review essay of Gilles Deleuze and Felix Guattari's *Anti-Oedipus* ("**Energumen Capitalism**," *Semiotext(e)* 2 [1977]: 14). This is so because both the psychic apparatus and capitalism (as just one instance of an economic "configuration") are structures of exchange, i.e. "markets," and therefore embodiments of the Law of Exchange. For example, both "markets" (obviously an extendable notion) exchange and substitute one thing for another, whether we call this the production and circulation of goods and services or psychic condensation, displacement, "secondary elaboration" of primary impulses, and so on. Both markets are vast networks and configurations which tap, transform, and (re)circulate *energies*. Lyotard makes this clear in "**Energumen Capitalism**":

Configurations [i.e. social formations, markets] and vast networks dispute energies; the way to tap, transform and circulate them is completely different, depending on whether the configuration is capitalist or despotic. . . . [T]here is a kind of *overflowing* of force inside the same system that liberated it from the savage and barbaric markings; any object that can be exchanged (according to the law of value), what can be metamorphosed from money into machines, from merchandise into merchandise, from force into work, from

work into salary, from salary into work force, is an object for Kapital. And thus nothing is left but an enormous moving around, objects appear and disappear . . . and objectness gives way to sheer obsolescence, what is important is no longer the object, a concretion inherited from the codes, but metamorphosis, fluidity. . . . Not at all *another* instinct, another energy, but within the libidinal economy, an inaccessible "principle" of excess and disorder. (14-15, 25-26)

This notion of utter reterritorialization, of a market's capacity to continuously recode and decode everything it touches in its work of endless *production* and *consumption*, obviously has startling implications for traditionalist notions of the body, much less of what that body can do sexually. There is, finally, no finality; capitalism, socialism, other economic/administrative configurations, and the psychic apparatus are exchange structures without limits. They are processes and truly "mindless" moving circuits (in senses liberated from all traditionality). They are housings, itineraries, and "posts" for nomadic desire. "Another configuration is rising," Lyotard remarks in "**Energumen Capitalism**,"

the libido is withdrawing from the capitalist apparatus, and desire is finding other ways of spreading itself out, according to another configuration . . . a bastard in rags of this and that, in words of Marx and Jesus and Mohammed and Nietzsche and Mao, communal practices and job actions, occupation, boycott, squatting, kidnap and ransom, happenings and demusicalized music and sit-ins and sit-outs . . . liberation of gays and lesbians and the "madmen" and criminals. . . . What can capitalism possibly do against this unserviceability that is rising from within it . . . against this thing that is the new libidinal configuration? (24-25)

In this view there is no such thing as "identity," only positions, shifting categories, bureaucracies and of course procedural definitions and language games, such as those prescribed by bourgeois psychiatry in its benign reign of terror—in the name of optimal performance/standardization of behavior—against the utter self-production and atheism of the drive. Lyotard's dismantling of the very frameworks we think in and through, changes completely the definitions and identities of the things we think about, such as "homosexuality" and the "authorities" who feel compelled to "control" it and the conditions of its information and accessibility.

The Postmodern Condition extends these arguments in ways important to thinkers on difference, power, and sexuality. As a group of speakers and participants in language games with the dominant world around us, we exemplify the activity of postmodernism in challenging the culture of modernism while remaining a part of it. But it goes further. The labor of postmodernism is to show *the other side,* what Lyotard calls "the unpresentable" (i.e. that which lacks or is denied terms/power within the cultural ideology and sexism of dominant modernism). Postmodernism as a counterstatement, and gays and women as the culturally *sexual others,* put in question already thoroughly tired notions of the unity of the whole as both social meta-phor ("melting pot") or as aesthetic orthodoxy (the ideol-ogy of "organicism," literary reviews, English departments).

"The grammar and vocabulary of literary language are no longer accepted as given," Lyotard argues in *The Post-modern Condition,* but he could as well be describing het-erosexist norms; "rather, they appear as academic forms, as ritual originating in piety (as Nietzsche said) which pre-vent the unpresentable from being put forward" (80-81). The "unpresentable" is sought, but safely. It must undergo a preliminary truncating or trivialization at the level of idealized nostalgia: lace but not leather, *La Cage aux Folles* but not *Taxi zum Klo,* Betty Friedan but not Kathy Acker, Amber Hollibaugh, or the women's s/m collective SAM-OIS. The first term in these pairings participates in a language/power game which is *modern,* that is, one re-flecting "the consensus of a taste which would make it possible to share collectively the nostalgia for the unattain-able" (82); the opposing terms mark the postmodern which "denies itself the solace of good forms . . . in order to im-part a stronger sense of the unpresentable" (81). "Gay," for many straights and haberdashers, is chi chi and trendy, at the colonized level of style but surely not at the level of even a banal "realism" or in recognition of daily practices of sexual *difference.* As the admen make clear, homosexu-ality is a "lifestyle," i.e. a market term describing the com-modity form of lived experience and a "target group" for further consumption—all without representation of sexual difference and of the "targets." In most media today gay sexuality is capable only of nostalgic representation—the wishful gaze or straight fantasy—simply because there has never been a popular (i.e. straight) narrative "realism" por-traying—legitimating—its activity. Piety is still a determi-nant of the unpresentable, bounding it as unacceptable ex-teriority or utopian projection even while alluding to it as exotic kitsch.

Women and gays in particular become adept at the post-modernist gesture of inventing "allusions to the conceiv-able which cannot be presented" (81), but not because dif-ferences are reconcilable. Lyotard's conclusion to *The Postmodern Condition* is sobering:

> The nineteenth and twentieth centuries have given us as much terror as we can take. We have paid a high enough price for the nostalgia of the whole and the one, for the reconciliation of the concept and the sen-sible. . . . Let us wage a war on totality; let us be wit-nesses to the unpresentable; let us activate the differ-ences and save the honor of the name. (82)

Notes

1. The intellectual overhaul of the French university system in particular, and that of Europe in general, begins with the events of April-May 1968. Lyotard directed *Les Immatériaux,* a vast exhibition on postmodern culture, technology, and artifacts at the Beaubourg (28 March-25 July 1985); see John Rajchman's review, "The Postmodern Museum," *Art in America* 73 (October 1985): 110-17, 171.

2. *The Postmodern Condition: A Report on Knowledge* (Minneapolis: U of Minnesota P, 1984).

3. See Maureen Turim, comp., "Jean-François Lyotard: A Partial Bibliography," *Camera Obscura* 12 (1984): 107-09.

Ronald Bogue (essay date 1989)

SOURCE: A review of *Peregrinations: Law, Form, Event,* in *Philosophy and Literature,* Vol. 13, No. 1, April, 1989, pp. 209-10.

[*In the following review of* Peregrinations, *Bogue offers a lucid thumbnail sketch of that volume and of Lyotard's ca-reer.*]

Where to locate the elusive Lyotard? Over the years, many have asked this question about the protean poststructural-ist, and in 1986 the organizers of the Wellek Library Lec-tures at the University of California at Irvine invited Lyo-tard himself to respond. His answer, contained in the three lectures collected in this volume, is that he is not on any philosophical map, but off in the clouds—for "thoughts are clouds" (p. 5), fuzzy-edged, shifting, essentially tem-poral formations that summon us to their exploration. Lyo-tard calls that summons "law" and its proper response "probity": "Imagine the sky as a desert full of innumerable cumulus clouds slipping by and metamorphosing them-selves, and into whose flood your thinking can or rather must fall and make contact with this or that unexpected aspect. Probity is being accessible to the singular request coming from each of the different aspects" (p. 8). Lyotard sees law, form, and event as the three unavoidable themes that have infused his thought as it has drifted above the traditional domains of ethics, esthetics, and politics. In Chapter One, he describes thought and law; in Chapter Two, the event as the object of artistic and political judg-ment; and in Chapter Three, the divergent ends of esthetic and political thought. To respond to an event, he claims, is "to be able to endure occurrences as 'directly' as possible without the mediation or protection of a 'pre-text'" (p. 18). The artist seeks to confront the singular "thisness" within data, the politician the manifold contingency of the historical situation. The political and the esthetic differ, however, in that political disputes can further moral progress by spreading republican principles, whereas there can "be no such thing as esthetic progress toward the for-mation of a republic of taste" (p. 39). (Unless, Lyotard adds, the postmodern sublime that he has been delineating for the last few years allows reason rather than imagina-tion to be the faculty that responds to esthetic events.)

Most often in these essays Lyotard floats in clouds of Kant—as he does in such recent works as *Le Différend, Au Juste,* and *L'Enthousiasme*—making use of the Sec-ond and Third Critiques to depart from the First Critique's domain of cognition and determinant judgment. The re-sults are hardly Kantian, save in the frequent insistence on the moral fact of duty or law, and it is here that I find Lyotard least convincing. Must we answer the call of clouds, as Lyotard asserts? Can an ethics of responsiveness to singularity and contingency signal more than a personal preference? Or is not Lyotard simply making a profession of faith and himself issuing the summons to the law? And even if we should answer that summons, can an ethics of the form of thought keep from collapsing into an aestheticism capable of justifying anything?

It is a shame that in these lectures Lyotard does not choose to position himself in the field of current criticism, for it would be interesting to hear his assessment of his relation to such figures as Deleuze, Baudrillard, Foucault, and Derrida. But if he does not map today's critical terrain, he does provide an implicit narrative of his own peregrinations—from Marxist commitment through disillusionment and demonic descent (*Economie libidinale*) to ethical recovery (*Le Différend*)—that might serve as an exemplary history of a certain postwar destiny. These thoughtful and elegant essays are among Lyotard's finest productions, at once complex and informal, abstract, and personal. The afterword, a translation of a 1982 essay by Lyotard on his *différend* with Marxism, is a fitting complement to the three lectures. The volume's exhaustive bibliography of Lyotard's work is invaluable.

Avital Ronell (essay date 1989)

SOURCE: "The Differends of Man," in *Diacritics*, Vol. 19, Nos. 3-4, Fall-Winter, 1989, pp. 63-75.

[*In the following essay, Ronell discusses the meanings of the term "différend" as Lyotard applies it to connections and disconnections made in the exchange of language and "phrases."*]

1.

Lyotard has observed that Nazism, when it was "over," was let down like a rabid dog but never as such refuted. To be sure, a number of persuasive assertions have been made, analyses have been attempted, and an indisputable sense of justice has seemed to reinstall itself. Still, these do not provide philosophical proof or a rigorous guarantee of the intelligibility of the Nazi disaster. In fact, the recourse to the sublime, to modalities of the unthinkable and uncontrolled, suggest to us that Nazism continues to place us before what Walter Benjamin has called *Denkfaulheit:* a failure or falling off of thinking, a kind of lethargy that overwhelms language. Among other things, this means that the gas has not been entirely turned off but continues to leak and to spread its effects.

Yet it may be that the stunning toxicity is wearing off, and thinking is beginning to stir, to come to. This does not mean that the technologically constellated torture systems have been shut down, of course. But thanks to a number of courageous individuals—I think proper names are essential here: Jacques Derrida, Werner Hamacher, Philippe Lacoue-Labarthe, Jean-Luc Nancy, Sarah Kofman, Claude Lanzmann, Shoshana Felman, and others—the Holocaust, the break in any hope for naive historical continuity, has come into focus. I think it necessary to indicate at the outset, since this has strangely become a point of contention, that Derrida had been listening for the murmurs of the Holocaust long before this became, for intellectuals, somewhat of a journalistic imperative. I offer evidence in a footnote so that this can be set aside and we can get past the roadblocks that have been set up in order to stop a genuine thinking of that which has invaded us in this century.[1]

In France, as Jean-François Lyotard notes in *Heidegger et "les juifs,"* something has been happening, a scene has broken open that can be linked to a certain geophilosophy: "L'affaire Heidegger est une affaire 'française'" [16]. Whether the "French" can be made to communicate with the "Jews" under arrest in the quotation marks of the title is something we shall need to decide. The displacement to France of the Heidegger scandal, the suspension of the Jews, and the dislocation of a *différend* reflect the temporal discontinuity to which this book seems to owe its existence. Like the Heidegger disclosures which marked the end of a latency period—everyone knew Heidegger's Nazi seduction was there, but things were beginning to stir only now—*Heidegger et "les juifs"* seems to emerge from a latency period that I will call "Cerisy." This is not to diminish the immeasurable importance of the disasters under discussion but to include the frame that allows Lyotard to name this a French affair. Why the displacement to France? Which is another way of asking ourselves why "deconstruction"—this miserable orphan of a name—has become the living target range for shots against our Nazi past. It is not wrong to wrest Nazism from the deceptively secure space of a restricted national spasm. For the range and programming by metaphysics or Christianity, the major complicities shared by the most surprising parties, corporations, nations, and individuals, all fed the death machine—one, as we may soon learn, that was not, as we tend to say, out of intellectual cowardice, merely "irrational." It makes sense. Indeed, what needs to be considered is that the *project of making sense* or rather of making *one* sense is implicated in history's break-up with itself.

2.

There are two scenes that I wish to evoke, two prologues to Lyotard's book which exceeds itself and takes place elsewhere than between its covers (but what book ever takes place within its own site, letting itself be contained or bound by some simple determination?). Sometimes, however, the referential effects of elsewhere are less troubling than in this context.

DEBATE FOLLOWING *"DISCUSSIONS: OU, PHRASER 'APRES*

AUSCHWITZ.'"

Lyotard repeats, "Il faut enchaîner après Auschwitz, mais sans résultat speculatif" ("it is obligatory to connect phrases after Auschwitz but without trying to obtain a speculative result") [*Les fins de l'homme* 312]. In response to a question, he specifies: "*We* would be simply the hostages of: it is obligatory to connect phrases, *we* don't have the rule, we're looking for it, we are connecting phrases in searching for it. . . . The search for the rules of connectability is a search for the intelligible. Adorno speaks of the readable, Derrida of unreadability—which is a radical divergence, yet if *we* are the community of hostages held by 'Il faut enchaîner,' this is because we learn to read, thus we do not know how to read and, for *us,* to read is precisely to read the unreadable."[2] At one moment Lyotard reminds his interlocutors that he has not talked about Heidegger ("*Lyotard* fait observer qu'il n'a pas parlé de Heidegger") although it is clear that ontology is at stake in the idea of phrasing. . . .

[Shift of scene.] *Johnson* thinks that the most horrifying aspect of Auschwitz is not the phrasing "You must die" but that it is unutterable, that the act being committed could not be accounted for in an utterance (except a sadistic one). *Derrida* adds that, indeed, this sentence could be uttered only within the context of a reasoned legality (such as the verdict of a jury): through Auschwitz no statement can legitimate the phrasing "You must die." After some discussion, *Nancy* intervenes: "Thus there would be a specific difference between Auschwitz and other seemingly comparable situations." Now, *Derrida* and *Lyotard* appear to have come to an agreement: names other than that of Auschwitz, just as unconnectable, demand no less to be connected. *Lacoue-Labarthe* asks that one name them ("*Lacoue-Labarthe* demande qu'on dise lesquels"). *Nancy* sees the specificity of Auschwitz in that "the end of man was in itself its project, and it was not the outgrowth of another project." "Auschwitz initiates the project of the end of man, which means: extermination, the final solution." *Lyotard* doubts that this project would be exclusive to Nazism. It is Western, Christian: the work of the Churches of the New World in Africa, like that of Hegel on Judaism. . . . *Lyotard* thinks that there is also a Nazi discourse of reformation but concedes only that what distinguishes "Auschwitz" is the absence of a discourse deriving destruction from a project of reformation (in contrast to the Soviet camps, adds *De Gandillac,* where the latter exists). Indeed, but *Lyotard* wonders if this isn't a question of the addressee. For Nazism, certain men are not at all reformable (on racial principle). The "You must die" which is addressed to them is pure destruction. They wouldn't even understand the reformation discourse. CUT.

Anyone who has followed the works of those participating in this debate will recognize essential threads of a more sustained argument. We have selected and frozen this frame in order to splice it into the ongoing narrative, however frayed and complicated, in which the effects of Auschwitz are submitted to interminable analysis. It is necessary to jump-cut to these syncopations of thinking if we are at all to understand the major blank around which the Heidegger debate is being organized: Heidegger's silence over Auschwitz. The major default consists in Heidegger's refusal to enter the politics of connecting; as Lacoue-Labarthe sees it, Heidegger offered nothing but silence on the subject of Auschwitz. Thus, for both Lacoue-Labarthe and Lyotard, the mute but powerful interlocutor of Heidegger will have been Paul Celan. Heidegger's silence cut a wound into the name of Paul Celan, which is why Lyotard ends his book on this name and Lacoue-Labarthe never stops citing and reciting "Todtnauberg." In fact, Lyotard's book will end on a slippage of sorts, when the proper name "Celan" is traded in—we might say somewhat precipitously—for "the jews": "'Celan' n'est ni le commencement ni la fin de Heidegger, c'est son manque: ce qui lui manque, ce qu'il manque, et dont le manque lui manque" [152]. (Somehow, I find this kind of pairing of the *Dichter and Denker* more nostalgic and pious than the relentless readings the deconstructions tend to go after. Why the couple and its unbearable proliferation: *Heidegger et le nazisme, Heidegger et "les juifs," Heidegger und Celan,* Kant and Moses, Kant and Hegel, etc.? Why are we forced to attend some sort of Moonie marriage ceremony whenever something at once as singular and disseminated as Auschwitz demands that thinking strain itself?) Of course Heidegger misses the appointment and the point of Celan; but we still do not know what it is to get the point. Particularly when, in our sententious discourse on Auschwitz, we still subject this proper name to metonymic usury. There is nothing so abhorrent as a German who appropriates the suffering evoked by Auschwitz in a post-Nazi fit of insight and wins prizes for his efforts—a regular occurrence in the American university. The constant blare of moral loudmouths may be far more pernicious than a silence that we haven't yet learned to read. And what Heidegger has in fact written may be more disturbing than his silence. As for the American university, we must take a close look at what often passes for a "Germanist."

Reviewing the scene of Cerisy, we find markings of certain symptomatic mentions that ought not escape our screening devices. Lyotard's omission of Heidegger, Lacoue-Labarthe's probity, Derrida's precision of legality and context, Nancy's ability to generalize the project of Auschwitz will all reemerge in displaced but readable ways in Lyotard's **Heidegger et "les juifs"** where the missing Heidegger comes to name the *différend* that Lyotard will want to articulate with his interlocutors.

3.

Several of Lyotard's recent works have been concerned with the problem of rephrasing the political. His regard for justice has always put him on the side of Aristotle, Nietzsche, and Kant rather than that of Hegel and cognitive regimens of historical narration. While Aristotle produces a description of the prudent judge ("Prudence consists in practicing justice with no models" [*Au juste* 52-53]), Kant establishes the Idea of Justice, which, as David Carroll and Geoffrey Bennington have variously shown, prevents the hardening of justice into dogma or doctrine.[3] The "critical" faculty teaches one to judge without criteria and to negotiate incommensurable domains. Thus Kant aggravated the incommensurability between the cognitive law (descriptive) and the moral law (prescriptive). What interests Lyotard is precisely the unbridgeable gap between the cognitive and the ethical faculties. Because of Kant's "phrasing of the ethical, of obligation," he comes after Hegel, for Lyotard.[4] Kant's belief in obligation in the absence of any demonstrable proof of its existence is what engages Lyotard. His text, however, decidedly privileges Kant's *Third Critique,* because the problem of critical judgment is announced here in its most radical possibility and in terms of the "aesthetic."

4.

When Jean-François Lyotard showed up that day at the colloquium organized by Nancy and Lacoue-Labarthe, he had already begun his work on justice. It was a turning point. No one was absolutely sure that he was going to be there when the time to honor Derrida came around. There had been so much silence between them, a break that no one really talks about. Lyotard had begun to articulate his apparent disillusion with certain aspects of militant politics in **"A Memorial of Marxism: For Pierre Souyri."** By then, we were all getting despondent. Every revolution had submitted to the spectacle of failure. Maoism turned out to be a disaster, the so-called Third World, according to entirely readable power failures, could not be expected to offer a model for revolution; the Black Panthers had been wiped out. The sclerosal fix of dialectics was showing up on the scanner as a kind of paleo-marxism. Even the "sexual revolution," while complex as libidinal accounts go, largely ended up fucking with women. All these phrases needed to be filled out, studied, connected to explanatory discourses. I am merely trying to establish the mood, as Kant would say, for the day on which the debate took place. So Lyotard actually did come. It was maybe a kind of turning point. He had omitted to mention Heidegger. But on this eve of the retreat of politics, one was turning with Lyotard toward a more universal idiom of ethics and moral law. Kant in a way was the name of this retreat—Kant, whom Hölderlin had appreciated for his retreat from great revolutionary fervor, for democratizing in the mediated mode of reflective judgment. In any case, Kant, along with Levinas, offered the best means of exposing the "transcendental illusion" of revolutionary politics.

As for the retreat of the political, Nancy and Lacoue-Labarthe were addressing it in their critical project for the "Center for Philosophical Research on the Political." In the "Ouverture" to *Rejouer le politique,* they write:

> This double demand—the recognition of the closure of the political and the unsettling practice of philosophy

in terms of itself and its own authority—leads us to think in terms of the re-treat of the political. The word is to be taken in what is at least its double sense: retreat from the political in the sense of what is "well known," the evidence (the blinding evidence) of politics from the "everything is political" through which our imprisonment in the enclosure of politics can be described. But it is also to be taken in the sense of retracing the political, remarking it—that is, making appear what is for us a new question, the question of its essence. This could in no way constitute . . . a withdrawal into "apoliticism." . . . This is to say that the activity of retreat is itself a political activity—by which it is undoubtedly a question of exceeding something of the political, but absolutely not in the form of an "escape from the political."[5]

The move governed by the *Ent-zug* (*re-trait*) is decidedly Heideggerian, though to our knowledge Heidegger never made it or marked it politically. What is called the political? These people were submitting "the political" to a most watchful examination, trying to sort out ways in which the politics of horror might be retrieved from the domains of the unthinkable or unanalyzable. Lyotard phrased it somewhat differently but appears to have shared similar assumptions. His aim, at the time, was to "destroy narrative monopolies."[6]

5.

The *différend* as defined by Lyotard is an unlitigable injustice. Presented nonetheless like a philosophical brief, *The Differend: Phrases in Dispute* argues where argument as such has been suspended. *The Differend* takes up the defense where Faurisson's outrageous claims concerning the unproven existence of gas chambers situate him as plaintiff. It is henceforth up to the victims of extermination to prove that extermination, an impossible convening of a court of ghosts.

> As distinguished from a litigation, a differend (*différend*) would be a case of conflict, between (at least) two parties, that cannot be equitably resolved for lack of a rule of judgment applicable to both arguments. One side's legitimacy does not imply the other's lack of legitimacy. However, applying a single rule of judgment to both in order to settle their differend as though it were merely a litigation would wrong (at least) one of them (and both of them if neither side admits the rule). . . .
> The title of this book suggests (through the generic value of the definite article) that a universal rule of judgment between heterogeneous genres is lacking in general. [xi]

What follows assumes some familiarity with the further contents of *The Differend.* In a looser sense "différend" has come to mean unresolved differences between two parties who do not share the same rules of cognition. Thus philosophers can be seen to exhibit *différends*, often with the aim of undermining the legitimacy of the discourse of the other. When Jürgen Habermas, for instance, makes such outlandish claims as (1) "All denials notwithstanding,

Derrida remains close to mysticism" (a curious and symptomatic statement, for Derrida nowhere denies his affinities with Hebraic thought); (2) as a Jewish mystic, Derrida "degrades politics and contemporary history . . . so as to romp all the more freely, and with a greater wealth of associations, in the sphere of the ontological"; or (3) "[a] return to the Greeks, whenever it was attempted by Jews, always had about it something of a lack of power," these utterances (to put it politely), through the effects of irresponsible indictment, indicate a *différend*.[7]

The suspicious split between Hellenism and Judaism indicates, as Michael MacDonald has argued, an act of delegitimation toward the party identified—surprise—as Jewish. The question of lining up and identifying the Jew must remain undecided, MacDonald argues, and we should read this "must" as an effect of moral law: "Is Derrida a Greek or Jew? This must remain undecided. What should now be clear, however, is that Habermas characterizes Derrida as a Jewish mystic to disqualify deconstruction as a legitimate philosophical enterprise with its own set of premises and styles of argumentation" [9].

The Jewish station identification is, in fact, beamed back from Hegel, whom Lyotard will set against Kant precisely owing to Hegel's anti-Judaic swallowing machines, that is, to his reduction of the other to a stage in self-consciousness. One might graft onto Lyotard's passage on Hegel in **Heidegger et "les juifs"** a similar one from *Glas*, for the two together form a stereophonic blast. In this passage, Derrida locates the figure of the Jew within a dialectic, which is, as MacDonald has shown, above all a dialectic of master and slave "that ensures the sovereignty of the Christian by excluding the Jew from the realm of Spirit. For Hegel, the Jew is an uneconomic moment in this process, a moment of negativity, just as surely as Christianity is a dialectical transcendence of Judaism" [12]. Derrida puts it this way: "The Jew falls back again. He signifies that which does not let itself be raised up . . . to the level of the *Begriff*. He retains, draws down the *Aufhebung* toward the earth" [55].[8] MacDonald's reading of the passage is crucial here, for it shows how the reduction of difference and heterology to identity that characterizes Hegel's speculative logic persists, for Levinas, in Heidegger's fundamental ontology. This is where "il faut enchaîner" with Lyotard's reading of **Heidegger and "the jews,"** where Heidegger is seen to subordinate structures governing the relation with the Other to the relation with Being. The Hegelian infection is what the etiologists of philosophy's persistent anti-Semitic agency are rightly going after. Getting back to Hegel and Derrida, where the Jew falls back again, unable to be elevated to the level of concept, we discover a regressive coherency:

> This seems to remain true for Habermas, who determines the Jew as mystic to exclude him/her from the order of philosophy; the order of the *Begriff*. In forsaking the Spirit and Logos (ontotheology) in favor of the dead letter of scripture and inscription, the Jew, for Hegel as for Habermas, falls back into the irrationalism of mystical inspiration and frenzied cryptology. [MacDonald 11]

I think we have sufficiently brought into focus the injustice of Habermas's position—masked as it is by the pseudocoding of legitimate argumentation—to warrant the classification of *différend*. *Différend* carves out an abyss within interlocution; cables have not been set up to hear the other without static, warping, and constant interruption. Of course, the problem is not static, parasitism, and random noise but the published refusal, precisely, to show the minimal decency that consists in making a connection: *il faut enchaîner*. In this particular case, which has been metonymized by Habermas into the negativity of philosophical grandeur (to the extent that philosophy has kept its reputation for bludgeoning a persecuted other, call it women or Jews, call it South Africa, if you will), one can repeat and show, cite and argue that Derrida has said this or that; one can offer evidence of injustice and wrongdoing or probe the resistance, on the part of Habermas, to discerning the phantasm and violence of "the Jew" (Joyce, for his part, worked through to the jewgreek). But there is something like a broken connection dominating the thinking fields.

6. CERISY LA SALLE. TAKE TWO

Yet another form of the *différend* exists, one that strains beyond the politics of ressentimental phrasing. This version talks and negotiates; it listens and articulates itself responsively rather than reactively. In fact, to the extent that it explores the limits of *différend* in the mode of positivity, it is questionable whether it constitutes the *différend* as such, or whether the *différend* can indeed guarantee the conditions of co-legitimacy that it promises. What I would call the "affirmative *différend*" has been brought to bear by Philippe Lacoue-Labarthe in his address to Lyotard at a subsequent Cerisy colloquium, organized around the theme, "Comment juger?" Lacoue-Labarthe launches the "Differénd dans le judicieux" ("Talks") with the quasi-performative injunction: "Let's talk." But one of the *différends* that he puts in place as he begins negotiations with Lyotard is Lyotard's willingness to negotiate with Habermas: "Why take seriously a kind of dinosaur from the *Aufklärung*? And why go after him?" In other words, why encourage the degradation of *différend* into gang wars [25]?[9]

Two years after the debate cited in Cerisy I, then, Philippe Lacoue-Labarthe shows up to name "a real *différend*." Let's talk, he begins, because "that's why we are here, at least in principle. But let's talk also, and above all, because two years ago, right here, you came with this motive and on these grounds, not to claim this as your theme, but to respond to an address or to an injunction that already occupied us a great deal at the time" [24]. As I see it, Lacoue-Labarthe has come to the point where a summit meeting of sorts needs to be called. The stakes are political, as certain territorialities are going to be covered or divided up. They respond to what happened "two years ago, right here" by repeating the inaugural gesture: you came here with this motivation which I now affirm by repetition and irony. "In principle" we're here at Cerisy to talk. But to the extent that Lacoue-Labarthe names the motivation that he claims to be reproducing, he's calling the shots; he is the one to open talks, so to speak. He institutes the couple and draws up the contract whose terms we still have to figure.

> What does this mean: "Let's talk?" For us (I mean for the two of us, you and me) this means, and in a way it is very simple: let's continue talking. Or: let's take up the discussion again—in the manner of: where were we now? The discussion between us is not continuous, even less is it organic in nature. But it happens that for some time now, the mode of relation properly our own, with highs and lows (there have even been some pretty low lows), sometimes also without direct exchange, from a distance and in silence, is, more than anything else, discussion. And it is discussion because everything, despite the esteem and friendship, despite the affection, despite the pleasure of the times we have spent together,finally we are not in agreement, we have a real *différend.* I emphasize: finally. [24]

Now, the precise location of the *différend* creates some difficulties. Lacoue-Labarthe emphasizes "finally," which carries temporal implications as well as indicating the end of a logical sequence or spatial properties: given the distance and silence, despite the times we have spent, the modulations of affect, finally, beyond a certain Kantianism, we—now that I have established us as a "we" in our singularity ("properly our own" relation)—now find ourselves disjointed, in the predicament of a *différend.* My question would be addressed to both Lyotard and Lacoue-Labarthe: is the constitution of a "we" possible where there is a real *différend?* Or doesn't the *différend* precisely disarticulate the "we," undermining the stability of the other? Sure, to get a divorce means you were really tight at one point, but when the *différend* finally hits does it not dissolve the very conditions binding a "we" to itself? Put differently, the *différend* between Faurisson and the Jews (let us hope those who feel attacked by Faurisson are not limited to the Jews), between Habermas and Derrida, essentially aims to delegitimate the other, producing through the discourse of an indictment a second annihilation that is always in communication with the first project of annihilation.

There remains another possibility. The "finally" stressed by Lacoue-Labarthe may be referentially pointing toward the future: in the end we will have had a real *différend.* It is important to establish the precise terms of the document being drawn up here because Lacoue-Labarthe will serve in *Heidegger et "les juifs"* as a principal target area for the installment of a real *différend.* The bull's-eye has Derrida's face written all over it. However, this is not news. Here, at Cerisy II, Lacoue-Labarthe appears to be constructing what Lyotard elsewhere calls the *dispositif,* the device or set-up that prepares the ground for a breakdown in talks. Interestingly, when Lyotard deciphers, in a decidedly critical way, Lacoue-Labarthe's posture toward Heidegger, he reappropriates terms with which Lacoue-Labarthe identifies himself: notably, "pious," the word upon which he closes the address ("piety"), only to find it reanimated and transsvaluated some years later. For Lyo-

tard will find Lacoue-Labarthe, and most of deconstruction, too pious, that is to say he marks them as "encore trop pieux, de trop respectueusement nihiliste," a characterization that appears rhetorically to collapse and neutralize itself. The problem is, he wants to *deconstruct* what is still too pious, etc., in deconstruction. Or rather, he wants to deconstruct "la déconstruction derridienne." Now, seeing as he has just rejected Heidegger's deconstruction, I personally don't figure how he's going to cut it without "Derridean deconstruction." (Believe me, he's not about to go for "Paul de Man's deconstruction.") While the stakes are very high indeed, the complaint is so curious that it is difficult not to wonder whether Lyotard is proposing that we adopt some form of disrespectful nihilism to overcome the respect that still inundates deconstruction. This choice of idiom seems very odd for a Kantian.

At the same time, one understands why Lyotard would get p.o.'d at the Heidegger affair; one often shares his frustration and impatience with the slow-paced serenity that apparently rules these respectful types. The difficulty resides in the fact that the nature and feasibility of the *différend* are at stake.

It is Lacoue-Labarthe himself who aligns his sensibility in terms of piety. "I do not share the hatred you have for intellectuals," he starts.

> Reading you, my first reaction is to say to myself: there, it's very clear; I am on the side of the modern and he of the postmodern, that is what unites us (since the one does not go without the other) and what separates us (since there is a moment when the division is made, and must be made violently). And everything over which we diverge, over which we have come many times to argue, comes down to this: I regret, he experiments; I am in *melancholia,* he is in *novatio;* I am nostalgic, sad, elegiac, reactive, pious; he is affirmative, gay, satirical, active, pagan. A great separation of "values," and I don't exactly find myself on the best side. . . . [25]

While he offers the very terms of opposition around which Lyotard's critique of him years later will pivot, Lacoue-Labarthe, in a second movement of autodescription, retreats from such reactive posturing. He does not recognize himself in regret or melancholy, he now claims. What affects him, inscribes him as it were, is that the "epoch is given to mourning, but nothing prevents us from bearing it in an easy manner, or with discretion. One can even secretly rejoice" [25]. Lacoue-Labarthe will not sustain the oppositional logic with which the address has begun but reroutes this principle through Lyotard's modeling of tensions: "it is the very opposition of the modern and the postmodern that bothers me and seems questionable to me. . . . It is necessary, I believe, to put into question—or rather to thwart—oppositions. But not directly, nor, above all, by attacking the opposition . . . and to allow oneself to be enclosed within it" [25].

This would be the place to spot a certain unsettling of the *différend.* The affirmative *différend* has come to introduce a complication into the itinerary of differences viewed as sheer oppositionality or incommensurability. "Let's talk" at once involves a posturing of the *différend* Dasein while it challenges the unbridgeable gap imputed to the post-*différend* condition. "Let's talk" figures a kind of Heideggerian *Mitsein* (Being-with) asserting the irreducible precedence of the Other to the self. Indeed, "let's talk" means "let's listen," because talking always implies a prior listening. It is a mode of talking as listening that would mark our epoch—though ours is the end of epochality—as one of mourning. For listening regulates distance and alterity, the discontinuity of a dialogue with an other. It searches out the echo of freedom.[10]

7.

Perhaps the way I directed Cerisy I and II as successive stagings in the launching of **Heidegger et "les juifs"** will have seemed overly mediatic as narrative. The pervasive mood of irony and the cuts of screening are arguably incommensurate with the gravity of what is addressed when one is writing under the gun of "Heidegger-Art-and-Politics." Yet something has made itself felt, something that would turn the mechanical reproduction of the same rhetorical mood into a further instance of indecency. At times, our age of mourning unleashes a certain libidinal upsurge, the giddiness of terror. One wants to see again, according to the script of tonal modulation, Hölderlin's "Wechsel der Töne," which now gets fed through an entirely new technology of shredding and splicing.

Among those whose thinking has been perceptibly invaded by Auschwitz, Werner Hamacher offers a most persuasive statement:

> We do not just write "after Auschwitz." There is no historical or experiential "after" to an absolute trauma. The historical continuum being disrupted, any attempt to restore it would be a vain act of denegation. The "history" of Auschwitz, of what made it possible, supported it and still supports it in all its denials and displacements—this "history" cannot enter into any history of development or progress of enlightenment, knowledge, reflection, or meaning. This "history" cannot enter into history. It deranges all dates and destroys the ways to understand them. [459]

What does the disaster of a history have to do with the media? In the first place, the "*différend*" between Lyotard and "deconstruction" unravels around the event of *Shoah.* Second, Lyotard localizes the Heidegger affair as an affair of the media, underscoring, he suggests, the wholly impoverished encounter between art and politics. While the mediatic determination of *Shoah* as such is never submitted to critical discussion, the Heidegger story fades into an affair of the media, the single beneficiary, according to Lyotard, of philosophy's scandal. Third, the media has everything to do with the age of mourning, the pulverization of narrative monopoly, and the encrypting of unacknowledged loss. The media places us before the enigma of transference, which is to say, political hypnosis and the

fascisoid *jouissance* of the sensorium. The Nazis made a number of crucial decisions concerning the media, divesting television while colonizing the air with blasts of radio and promoting Riefenstahl. Since at least the critical intervention of Kraus, Benjamin, and Adorno, the media has become a place where the clear-cut distinction between art and politics no longer abides. Call it national aestheticism, call it transference machine and body invasion, the technologies of the media are coextensive with the German disaster. This is why Lacoue-Labarthe analyzes one film, and Lyotard another; this is why Friedrich Kittler analyzes gramophone, film, and the organization of the SS in his new military histories; this is why Laurence Rickels, writing on German crypts, analyzes film, radio, and the WWII bunker; this is why Werner Hamacher analyzes journalism and the breakdown, "after" Auschwitz, of historical narrative; this is why Alice Jaeger Kaplan analyzes radio transmission and fascism; and, if you will permit me, this is why I analyze the telephone and the narcissistic blowout of the terroristic state.[11] So the media, I think, ought not to surprise us when it starts blaring the news of its being whenever the political is at stake. (The Reagan years, which have juridically regressed and morally devastated America, cannot be thought without media and the autofeeding productions of the Presidency and the televisual metaphysic.) Still, Lyotard is perturbed. He names the media the principal beneficiary of the Heidegger affair.

This may be altogether wrongheaded, but it does little to explain the inexorable relatedness of Heidegger's involvement with the NSDAP, for which he momentarily became a loudspeaker, to the mediatic desire. Heidegger staged himself and the university when he became an amplifier of State-*schicksal* (Rectorate Speech of May 27, 1933); while he disdained television, he likened it at one point to his thinking and did not decline an invitation to appear on it (on Sundays, he'd hang out at his neighbor's to watch soccer). He talked, finally, through the organized space of *Gerede's* printout: the supplement to his thinking and politics appeared in his famous *Spiegel* interview, put into circulation after his death, like a black box surviving a crash. How are we to interpret the fact that Heidegger had an admission policy reserved for the press? What indeed does it mean for us that a Heidegger claims to tell the truth in a newspaper? It means, for one thing, that the media is not simply situated outside philosophy, running along parallel and aggressive tracks. Philosophy has always spilled into the streets, run diffusion campaigns, and made scratch noises on the public record. To accomplish these aims, it would travel on a different track, to be sure, at a greater speed. The media and philosophy are neither friends nor enemies; they're not even cutting it according to territorialized gang wars.

But something happened to us moderns, I think, when God got dead, and, crashing down, He slipped the microphone to Zarathustra. Zarathustra, remember, is Nietzsche's anchorman, announcing the death of God long before people were tuned in. The mediatechnic catastrophe should not be read in keeping with naive or merely technophobic command systems. What is "the media" that it can profit from Heidegger, the Nazis, and the general administration of sensational pain? Where is it to be located, mapped out, and stabilized? These questions are circuited through the works named above.

8.

The part of his book titled "Heidegger" begins with the fifteenth chapter. Lyotard, about to put down the media, opens with the tone of an emergency broadcast. Is the interruption of media a part of it? "Il y a urgence à penser l'affaire Heidegger." Nietzsche—once again returning—spoke of the emergency conditions under which philosophy grows. But Lyotard urges a different temporality of urgency, even though he is himself rather fast on the trigger, "postmodern," and pagan. Under the circumstances, I have often found it difficult to connect. One problem, admittedly, may be that Lyotard has gone for disconnectability in his text. Even the "et" of the title names a disjunction that refuses to connect. The violence and disconnection, the surprise attacks, too, may be rooted in the fact that Lyotard has himself gone for "tout déchainement":

> Ce n'est en effet pas "par hasard" que "les juifs" ont fait l'objet de la solution finale. . . . Cette absence de hasard ne signifie pas pour autant qu'on puisse "expliquer" Auschwitz, et je ne l'explique pas plus qu'un autre. Car de la Verdrängung originaire il n'y a pas d'explication. Elle ne se laisse pas enchaîner. Elle est au "principe" de tout déchainement. [130]

9.

It would be pointless to oppose connectability to disconnection; nowadays we are operating an entirely different switchboard. The ways in which we have been invaded by technology have only begun to affect thinking, though Heidegger saw it and called it, if only too late. *Shoah* connects the utterly disparate articulation of a Jewish person with a Nazi document that ends: "Submitted for decision to Gruppenleiter II D, SS-Obersturmbannführer Walter Rauff. Signed: Just." The Jewish person speaks of dreaming, survival, and the soul: "But I dreamed too that if I survive, I'll be the only one left in the world, not another soul." The Nazi document speaks that late spasm of metaphysics—technology:

> Berlin, June 5, 1942. Since December 1941, ninety-seven thousand have been processed by the three vehicles in service, with no major incidents. In the light of observations made so far, however, the following technical changes are needed: The vans' normal load is usually nine per square yard. In Saurer vehicles, which are very spacious. . . . [103]

The rhetorical disjunction between a dreaming self and the technological breach leaves the film speechless. Still, when film loses its voice, it's still on the job. The van has not vanished into this memo. On the contrary, Lanzmann shows the metaphysical metaphor rolling down the Autobahn.

Notes

1. Jacques Derrida's immense reading of the Holocaust and the metaphysics of race includes "White Mythology," "Of an Apocalyptic Tone Recently Adopted in Philosophy," "Two Words for Joyce," "Geschlecht I, II?" "Restitutions," "Feu la cendre," "Otobiographies," "Racism's Last Word," *Schibboleth: Pour Paul Celan, Glas, The Post Card, Of Spirit: Heidegger and the Question, Topoi:* "Interview with Jean-Luc Nancy," and so forth. Available at bookstores everywhere.

2. In what follows I translate and cite from pp. 312-13 of the "Débat."

3. See David Carroll, *Paraesthetics: Foucault, Lyotard, Derrida* (New York: Methuen, 1987), and Geoffrey Bennington, *Lyotard: Writing the Event* (New York: Columbia UP, 1988); "August: Double Justice" in *diacritics* 14.3 (1984): 64-71; here 69.

4. David Carroll, "Rephrasing the Political with Kant and Lyotard: From Aesthetic to Political Judgments," *diacritics* 14.3 (1984): 74-88; here 80.

5. Rejouer le politique (Paris: Galilée, 1981) 18. I have consulted David Carroll's translation of this passage.

6. See Cecile Lindsay's discussion of *Au juste* in "Experiments in Postmodern Dialogue," *diacritics* 14.3 (1984): 52-62; esp. 59.

7. In *Philosophical-Political Profiles* (Cambridge: MIT P, 1985) 1, 181. Consider also the waste product metaphors with which Habermas insults deconstruction, e.g., deconstruction lets the "refuse heap of interpretations, which it wants to clear away in order to get at the buried foundations, mount even higher" [183]. Beyond the indecency of metaphorical selection, the statement makes little sense.

8. Translation modified. See also Werner Hamacher's work on Hegel and Christianity. "pleroma—zu Genesis und Struktur einer dialektischen Hermeneutik bei Hegel," which appeared as the introduction to Georg Wilhelm Friedrich Hegel's »Der Geist des Christentums« Schriften 1796-1800 (Frankfurt: Ullstein, 1978) 7-333.

9. The talk was first delivered on August 1, 1982, at Cerisy-la-Salle during the colloquium honoring the works of Jean-François Lyotard.

10. Jean-Luc Nancy, "La liberté est l'in-fini de la pensée," *L'expérience de la liberté* (Paris: Galilée, 1988).

11. Philippe Lacoue-Labarthe, *La fiction du politique* (Heidegger, l'art et la politique) (Paris: Bourgois, 1989); Friedrich Kittler, *Gramaphon. Film. Typewriter* (Berlin: Brinkmann & Bose, 1987), and lectures on the SS, computers, military strategies (Siegen, Kassel, Bochum: 1989); Laurence A. Rickels, *Aberrations of Mourning: Writing on German Crypts* (Detroit: Wayne State UP, 1988);

Werner Hamacher, "Journals, Politics"; Alice Jaeger Kaplan, *Reproductions of Banality: Fascism, Literature and French Intellectual Life* (Minneapolis: U of Minnesota P, 1986), 135-37; Avital Ronell, *The Telephone Book: Technology, Schizophrenia, Electric Speech* (Lincoln: U of Nebraska P, 1989).

Works Cited

Derrida, Jacques. *Glas.* Trans. John P. Leavey, Jr., and Richard Rand. Lincoln: U of Nebraska P, 1986.

Hamacher, Werner. "Journals, Politics: Notes on Paul de Man's Wartime Journalism." Trans. Susan Bernstein, Peter Burgard, et al. *Responses: On Paul de Man's Wartime Journalism.* Ed. Werner Hamacher, Neil Hertz, and Thomas Keenan. Lincoln: U of Nebraska P, 1989.

Lacoue-Labarthe, Philippe. "Talks." Trans. Christopher Fynsk. *diacritics* 14.3 (1984): 24-40.

Lyotard, Jean-François. *The Differend: Phrases in Dispute.* Trans. Georges Van Den Abbeele. Minneapolis: U of Minnesota P, 1988.

———. "Discussions, ou, phraser 'après Auschwitz.'" *Les fins de l'homme: À partir du travail de Jacques Derrida, colloque de Cerisy.* Paris: Galilée, 1981.

———. "Pierre Souyri: Le marxisme qui n'a pas fini." *Esprit* 61.1 (1982): 11-31.

MacDonald, Michael. Unpublished essay, 1989. Rhetoric Dept., U of California, Berkeley.

Shoah: An Oral History of the Holocaust (The Complete Text of the Film). New York: Pantheon, 1985.

Kevin Paul Geiman (essay date 1990)

SOURCE: "Lyotard's 'Kantian Socialism'," in *Philosophy & Social Criticism,* Vol. 16, No. 1, 1990, pp. 23-37.

[*In the following essay, Geiman characterizes Lyotard's arrival at the idea of dissensus-as-authentic-consensus as the evolution of a Kantian socialism he sees at the root of Lyotard's politics.*]

The work of Jean-François Lyotard has been characterized as "an eclectic look at the overlapping boundaries between aesthetic, political and ethical territories."[1] This is not surprising. Like most French philosophers in the twentieth century—including Jean-Paul Sartre and Maurice Merleau-Ponty—Lyotard pursues his philosophical investigations with a great sensitivity to contemporary political and cultural developments. What separates him from many of his former and present compatriots, whose work has been often deemed "bereft of any moral orientation,"[2] is his active concern for the place and the character of ethics in this constellation. His more recent works, *Au juste*[3] and *Le Différend,*[4] reflect this concern. In them, Lyotard seeks to establish the outlines of a conception of justice that is not

linked to consensus-formation. The immediate reference is to Jürgen Habermas and Niklas Luhmann; the protracted reference is to any form of social criticism that proceeds from a model (Lyotard will call it a "metanarrative") setting out determinate conditions of rational social organization. In opposition to these, Lyotard advocates "dissensus," the search for incongruities and rifts in the social fabric. It is here, he maintains, that a viable yet critical understanding of justice can be found.

It is often difficult to appreciate the import of Lyotard's analyses. To begin with, his eclecticism often leaves one without fixed points of reference, and even *Le Différend* (his "philosophical book") is only partially helpful in this regard. The reader is invited to witness a series of remarks and observations grouped in loosely connected sections. The problem is compounded further by Lyotard's choice of philosophical dialogue partners; the text contains extended analyses of Hegel, Heraclitus, Marx and Kant, but offers very few references to contemporary thinkers.[5] Finally, his style is such that the reader is left in a position of either taking or leaving the stance; minimal effort is made to encourage assent.

Despite these difficulties, there is, I will maintain, an argument to be found amidst the clouds of analysis. It is an argument first put forth by Immanuel Kant, but brought to critical light only in the wake of the social transformations of the nineteenth century. In opposition to the rise of a deterministic and a-moral Marxism, Kant's doctrine of the "highest good," the union and harmony of human happiness and perfect morality, was appealed to as containing the rudimentary form of a socially transformative, critical ethics that did not result in a potentially oppressive doctrine. Lyotard's "search for dissensus" can be profitably viewed as a continuation of this "Kantian socialism" and specifically as a response to its greatest philosophical challenge, the antinomy of practical reason, the inability to reconcile, in a determinate fashion, the pursuit of human happiness and the demands of morality. Against the backdrop of "Kantian socialism," the urgency of Lyotard's efforts can be seen more clearly. More importantly, possible points of weakness in his argument might be detected and made subject to criticism, although I will not do so in this essay.

"Kantian socialism" has its origins primarily among certain German social theorists at the turn of the century.[6] It is associated with names such as Karl Vorländer and Conrad Schmidt, a member of the SPD, who invoked Kant against "Hegel's poetic metaphysics"[7] in an attempt to secure a rational foundation for Marx's social theory. Similarly, Eduard Bernstein pitted Kant against the "cant" of unreflective dogmatism surrounding the revisionism debate within Social Democracy.[8] Hermann Cohen, a Marburg Neo-Kantian, wrote that Kant "is the true and real originator of German socialism,"[9] a claim that, while ambitious, is not wholly removed from the truth. For while Kant himself was a liberal and maintained the right to private property, his practical philosophy could be interpreted as containing "moral and philosophical insights crucial to socialist thought"[10] as well as an implicit criticism of Marxist socialism.

Marxist socialism rests on the premise that all socially transformative action begins with the contradictions inherent in the material conditions of society. These contradictions are centered on the appropriation and control of the means of production necessary for satisfying needs. Any attempt at social transformation is to be evaluated based on the extent to which material conditions are altered as to end oppression and increase human potential. It is possible to speak of a normative moment in Marxist theory only on the condition that human happiness is understood as the implicit goal.

Kant's views on happiness in the *Grundlegung* are well known; there he is critical of basing morality on the principle of happiness because it is an heteronomous principle, one that undercuts the autonomy of rational agents. The problem of happiness has wider ramifications, and, in "Theory and Practice," Kant recognized the politically disastrous consequences of taking happiness as one's principle:

> [T]he principle of happiness . . . has an evil effect in regard to political right as it does in morals. . . . The sovereign wants to make people happy in accord with his own concept of happiness and becomes as despot; the people will not give up their universal human claim to their own happiness and become rebels.[11]

Kant is, of course, anticipating what Hegel analyzed in terms of the master/slave dialectic. As opposed to Hegelian Marxism, Kant refused to limit the conditions of human progress to this antagonism. The satisfaction of needs alone only touched upon one aspect of human existence; left to the side were the rational and, above all, moral development of the species.[12]

While the pursuit of happiness could be rejected as a pernicious principle of social organization, there is no political equivalent for the duty to follow the moral law at the possible expense of happiness. Perfect morality, bought in the coin of failing to work actively for the transformation of the material and social world, would fall short of creating a world fit for humans. Thus, in his reply to Garve, Kant insists that human morality alone cannot be the end of creation:

> Neither human morality alone nor happiness alone is the Creator's end; instead, that end is the highest good possible in the world, which consists of the union and harmony of the two.[13]

It would be inconsonant with Kant's thought to assume that the union of happiness and morality is to be found only in the individual. The concept of the highest good refers explicitly to the external, social conditions in which humanity as a whole progresses. "The need to assume a highest good in the world," Kant writes, "[derives] from a deficiency in those external conditions in which alone an object as an end in itself (as a morally ultimate end) can be produced."[14] A rational and satisfied humanity is the ultimate end, and the aim for the highest good involves the transformation of the conditions under which such a humanity could arise. The categorical imperative, then, could be taken to indicate that "there is a . . . [social] duty to strive with all one's abilities to insure *that* a world conforming to the highest moral end exists."[15] In accordance with the socialist spirit, it could be seen that the workers' cooperative would further the conditions under which human autonomy was possible, while the system of capitalist private enterprise would hinder it.[16] Further, by insisting that the highest good contains within itself an ethical principle, one could maintain (against certain forms of Marxist theory) that the revolutionary struggle ought at no time violate the moral character of human agents as ends in themselves; agents ought not be used merely as means toward the realization of the socialist society.

What is interesting at this point is the philosophical status of the concept of the highest good. For while the concept may invoke a sympathetic response from those otherwise disposed to the socialist agenda, it would need to be shown that this concept is indeed a requirement of reason if it were to command rational assent. Kant, it will be recalled, harbored no illusions concerning the indeterminate status of the concept:

> We cannot prove the concept of this good, as to whether it has objective reality, in any experience that is possible for us, and hence adequately for the theoretical use of reason.[17]

Kant's point is that no presently existing objective social conditions could be offered as a proof or confirmation of the existence of this highest good. This is in keeping with his constant concern to avoid holding up any material condition as an indication or incarnation of critical reason. But, if no objective proof could be found for the validity of the highest good, no solace could be found through reflection on one's conscious actions either:

> In the highest good which is practical for us, i.e. one which is to be made real by our will, virtue and happiness are thought of as necessarily combined, so that the one cannot be assumed by practical reason without the other belonging to it.[18]

It is this necessary connection that poses difficulties for a socialist ethic. Kant argues that the combination of the two cannot be analytic, because the principles of virtue and happiness differ from one another, i.e., one's moral uprightness cannot be equated with one's happiness and vice versa. Hence the combination must be a synthetic one, with the pursuit of virtue the efficient cause of happiness or vice versa. In the first case, this is impossible, for every effect in the world is brought about through our knowledge of natural laws and our physical ability to press them into the service of our ends. "[C]onsequently," Kant writes, "no necessary connection, sufficient to the highest good, between happiness and virtue in the world can be expected from the most meticulous observance of the moral law."[19] In the second case, the combination of virtue and happiness cannot be the result of the mere pursuit of happiness, for happiness can serve only as a heteronomous ground of the will, making true virtue (as well as a just social order) impossible. Kant's solution to the antinomy is that "[s]ince it is, indeed, within our power to approach this end from one though not from both directions at once, reason is for practical purposes to believe in a moral ruler of the world and in a future life."[20] God and immortality, then, become necessary rational assumptions if we are to set ourselves to the task of striving for the highest good.

Even if we assume that Kant's premises are sound, we can detect three difficulties this "solution" poses for critical social ethics. First, the assumption of a rational ruler of the world, a guarantor of the harmony of morality and happiness, can be only a rational hope. In its proper place, it can serve to fortify the will and increase perseverance. But, the belief in a God in whom all differences are reconciled might hide the truly tragic character of many of our actions under an ideological cloak. Second, the rational hope of a future life may make sense for a private ethics concerned with individual virtue and happiness, but not for a social ethics. Personal immortality is the hope that my moral efforts will be rewarded in a context removed from their historical occurrence. There is no social equivalent for personal immortality, unless one were to hold out for the possibility that history itself will be redeemed.[21] Third, both of these factors, taken together, could lead to a social quietism or conservatism that would run counter to the duty to pursue actively the highest good. Effectively, we are left in a situation in which all criteria for fashioning policy and proposing plans of action consonant with aiming at the highest good are denied us.

Kant never addressed the social difficulties connected with the solution to the antinomy. Because Kant himself never pursued these points, it could be (and was) concluded that "an adequate social ethics must at some point go beyond Kant."[22] The problem here concerns the form this "going beyond" should take. One of the greatest difficulties in appropriating Kant for the development of a social theory is that something approaching the "Critique of Political Reason" was never written. Whatever one might hope to fashion as the quintessentially Kantian position concerning the limits of social reason must be drawn not only from the relevant passages in the critical writings, but from the many socio-political texts scattered throughout Kant's work as well. What is clear is that any departure from Kant that is motivated by the search for a social ethics will have to be accountable to Kant's anthropology somehow, for it is human society and the character of (just) human association that is at issue.

Hannah Arendt suggests that it is possible to cull two pictures of humanity out of Kant's writings:

> Man = reasonable being, subject to the laws of practical reason which he gives to himself, autonomous, an

end in himself, belonging to a Gelsterrelch, realm of intelligible beings.

> Men = earthbound creatures, living in communities, endowed with common sense, *sensus communis,* a community sense; not autonomous, needing each other's company even for thinking.[23]

If one takes as a starting point the position that society does (or ought to) resemble a realm of intelligible beings, then it would appear to be possible to elucidate the conditions of reason that are (or would have to be) fulfilled if this society is to exist: just as there are, following Kant, transcendental conditions of possible understanding, there are transcendental conditions of rational association. If one takes as a starting point the position that society does (or ought to) resemble a community of common folk, then the task becomes that of analyzing those processes whereby these folk already are associated. The first conception, Arendt points out, leads one to the first two *Critiques;* the second to the third *Critique* and the socio-political tracts.

Recent attempts to pursue a contemporary Kantian social theory, such as Rawls's and Habermas's, tend toward the former. Here, the effort is made to elucidate the minimal conditions of rational association. In Rawls's case, this involves the development of two principles of justice drawn from the conditions in an "original position." For Habermas, this concerns setting out something of a transcendental argument from which to analyze the conditions for an ideal speech situation in which non-oppressive, communicative action can occur. Of course, these and other similar efforts are consonant with Kant's own theory of the development of constitutional right and the formation of a republican commonwealth out of a state of nature. Further, these programs are also consonant with the fundamental premises of a capitalist, liberal democracy. To this extent they go some distance to stipulate the conditions of formal rights, but the question concerning human happiness—here understood as the transformation of material social conditions with a view toward the well-being of all—is left to the side. Habermas clearly recognizes that this is the outcome of his position:

> [We] ought not be misled into inferring an idea of the good life from the formal concept of [communicative] reason which the decentering understanding of the world in the modern age has left us.[24]

Rawls, to my knowledge, does not address the problem. In short, it is not clear how, or to what extent, either Rawls's or Habermas's theories are able to address and account for the nature of actual processes of social action aimed at altering institutional and environmental conditions.

Lyotard's strategy follows the latter anthropological conception. In this social condition,

> We are always within opinion, and there is no possible discourse of truth on the situation. And there is no discourse because one is caught up in a story, and one cannot get out of this story to take up a metalinguistic

position from which the whole could be dominated. We are always immanent to stories in the making, even when we are the ones telling the story to the other.[25]

There is no overarching theoretical framework (what Lyotard calls a "grand Narrative") under which the diversity of opinion may be brought, for in any attempt to articulate this framework, the narrator would have to extract him or herself from the obtaining order and assume that this discourse could serve to function as an organizing principle of that order. But, even though we are in the realm of opinions, we need not surrender to anarchism, either in the political or intellectual spheres:

> [T]his breaking up of the grand Narratives . . . leads to what some authors analyze in terms of the dissolution of the social bond and the disintegration of social aggregates into a mass of individual atoms thrown into the absurdity of Brownian motion. Nothing of the kind is happening.[26]

Nothing of the kind is happening, according to Lyotard, because the nature of the social bond is not such that when the philosophical system of regulation breaks down, chaos results. Indeed, for Lyotard, there is no such system. This idea is at best a left-over from the nineteenth century, when it was felt that "society forms an organic whole in the absence of which it ceases to be a society."[27] The various modifications on this theme, be they of functionalist or systems-theoretic form, only recapture and heighten this fundamental tenet. And even the Marxist position that society is essentially a two-tiered reality (capitalist on the one side and proletarian on the other), does not shake itself loose from this conception. The view that "Brownian motion"—an orderless movement of social "particles"—results from the dismissal of these positions is, on Lyotard's account, "haunted by the paradisaic representation of a lost 'organic' society,"[28] which we are then counseled to regain.

Of course, there are certain advantages that follow from the model of "the social whole." Such a model carries with it a particular understanding of the character of socially transformative agency. Within the organic society, only certain of its members are capable of occupying a critical role. Marxism is here the clearest case; the proletarian "part" was saddled with the task of revolutionizing the entire capitalist system of production and association. But, it was precisely with reference to this understanding of social transformation that this "grand Narrative" was shown to be at its weakest:

> [W]e cannot conceal the fact that the critical model in the end lost its theoretical standing and was reduced to the status of a "utopia" or "hope," a token of protest raised in the name of man or reason or creativity, or again of some social category—such as the Third World or the students—on which is conferred *in extremis* the henceforth improbable function of critical subject.[29]

The supposition of a totality that would be altered on the basis of a determinate part led to the fact that no critical subjects worthy of the name could be found.

For his part, Lyotard attempts to avoid this impasse by appealing to a different understanding of social transformation. On this account, everyday persons exhibit the characteristics of critical subjects in that they participate in any number of linguistic interactions or, to use Wittgenstein's term, "language games:"

> Young or old, man or woman, rich or poor, a person is always located at "nodal points" of specific communication circuits, however tiny these may be. Or better: one is always located at a post through which various kinds of messages pass. No one, not even the least privileged among us, is ever entirely powerless over the messages that traverse and position him at the post of sender, addressee, or referent.[30]

Precisely because of one's poverty, one's sex or one's age, certain lines of communication and not others will pass one's way. A general theory of social communicative competence is only minimally of use here, Lyotard would maintain, for it does not take the specificity of the various "nodal points" into account. The fact is that "there are contingencies; the social web is made up of a multitude of encounters between interlocutors caught up in different pragmatics." And, as for the evaluation of any of these encounters, Lyotard continues, "[o]ne must judge case by case."[31]

Lyotard aligns the faculty of political or social judgment with the Kantian faculty of aesthetic/teleological judgment. What is at issue here is not the aestheticization of politics or the politicization of art, but rather, the form of judgment appropriate to both spheres: reflective judgment. For Kant, the faculty of reflective judgment is assigned the task of reflecting on, but not determining, situations presented to the intellect; it operates when "the particular is given and judgment has to find the universal [rule] for it."[32] A determinate judgment, by contrast, is made when a particular case can be brought under an already established universal rule. Further, reflective judgment itself cannot be guided by a rule, otherwise a second rule would be needed in order to apply the rule, *ad infinitum*. In the case of aesthetic beauty and nature's teleology, then, the ascription of progress toward beauty or perfection is made not on the conformity of the object to a determinate concept, but with reference to the feeling it stirs in the perceiving subject. Perfection and beauty are qualities for the perceiving subject and are not objective standards for evaluation. Because they are subject-relative evaluations, one can assume neither the necessity nor the continuation of occurrences that manifest the appearance of a beautiful work and the discernment of a teleology in nature. Following his conception of the social bond, Lyotard extends this faculty to the realm of the historical-political:

> Our faculty of reflective judgment is not based on a category or on an already given universal principle waiting to be applied; rather it has to judge, when faced with a singular instance or with an unexpected case, without a rule precisely in order to establish the rule. The activity of the artist, of the critical philosopher and the "republican statesman" proceeds from this use of

reflective judgment; this is also true of any inventive approach which, on the track of the unknown and the unacceptable, breaks with constituted norms, shatters consensus and revives the sense of the *différend*.[33]

The assumption here is that events in the social sphere are (for the purposes of cognition) similar to appearances of beautiful works of art. Just as a new work shatters previously held conceptions of beauty, so too a "move" in the network of language games can render useless heretofore held views on the character of social organization.

Difficulties emerge for Lyotard when this form of judgment is used to determine social or political progress. The purposiveness of nature is, on Kantian grounds, itself purposeless. Are we to draw from this the conclusion that social progress, too, is purposeless, random and without direction? In the "Dispute of the Faculties," the question was raised whether and, if so, how, it can be said that humanity is progressing toward the highest good. Kant submitted that, while no fact could indicate this progress, a judgment that progress had occurred was possible. What was necessary was to discover in the thick of events a *sign,* or indication, that humanity was capable of progress toward the highest good, because there could be no determinate *concept* of social perfection under which one could subsume a particular action or event. Lyotard follows this line of thought:

> We shall have to look in the experience of humanity, not for an intuitive *datum* (a *Gegebene*) . . . but for what Kant calls a *Begebenheit,* an event, a deal (in the card-playing sense)—a *Begebenheit* which would only indicate (*hinweisen*) and not prove (*beweisen*) that humanity is capable of being not only the cause (*Ursache*) but also the author (*Urheber*) of its progress.[34]

Kant had looked to the enthusiasm with which the world greeted the revolution of 1789; Lyotard refers to our collective disgust in the face of Auschwitz, the events in Budapest in 1956 and in Paris in 1968, all of which are instances of such "deals." What he finds particularly revealing about these three events is that there was at the time of their appearance no theoretical reason why they should have occurred. Or, to use the Hegelian formulation, it was with these *Begebenheiten* that the real showed itself not to be rational, i.e., in accordance with the prevailing rationalizations of the day. It would not be inconsistent with Lyotard's position to locate further *Begebenheiten* in the context of everyday life. They need not be as dramatic as the events to which he refers, but can function, nevertheless, by virtue of their reception among a reflective audience, as indicators of a locally specific progress.

On Lyotard's reading, the "solution" to the antinomy of practical reason is not to be found in the presuppositions of God and immortality, but through a conscious awareness of social events:

> With this *Begebenheit* we must get as close as possible to the abyss to be crossed between mechanism on the one hand and liberty or finality on the other, between

the domain of the sensory world and the field of the supersensible—and we should be able to leap across it without suppressing it, by fixing the status of the historico-political—a status which may be inconsistent and indeterminate, but which can be spoken and which is, even, irrefutable.[35]

Interestingly enough, Kant himself had discovered this other solution in his minor works and had prepared the critical groundwork for it in the third *Critique*. With each occurrence of a *Begebenheit,* the mind is provoked and previously accepted interpretive patterns are shattered. As Kant had put it in the *Critique of Judgment,* these occurrences do not conform to a pattern; rather they provoke "an unspeakable wealth of thought." In this way, Lyotard writes,

> [H]istory, because it is never achieved—that is to say human(e) *[humaine]* is not an assignable object; but because it is also human(e), history is not without sense. In this way the . . . thesis of a philosophy that is never finished with the question of a "radical beginning" is justified anew.[36]

Reflective judgment does not determine objective validity once and for all, but brings the sense of the world to expression. In principle, then, one must be a perpetual beginner in the task of historical-political evaluation by rejecting the consolation of an established interpretive framework and by being open to the possibility that "dissolution" is, at certain times and in certain contexts, a "solution."

The requirement constantly to reapproach the social-political realm indicates, for Lyotard, its own conception of justice. Against the model of the autonomous agent who legislates for all, Lyotard locates the first moment of justice in listening. "[T]here are," he writes, "language games in which the important thing is to listen, in which the rule deals with audition. Such a game is the game of the just."[37] The move is to link justice with obligation and these with listening. The first moment of any obligation expressed in a command consists of setting up the relationship between the speaker and hearer in such a way that the hearer finds him or herself compelled to listen to the forthcoming prescriptive content. The pragmatics of obligation are such that the hearer places him or herself in a passive position with respect to the speaker. Implicitly, there is a recognition of the other as one worthy of respect, the respect due by the observance of the moral law. We do not, of course, know in a determinate fashion what the content of this respect will require of us. Nevertheless, failure to observe this posture of respect can be viewed straightaway as a form of injustice:

> Absolute injustice would occur if the pragmatics of obligation, that is the possibility of continuing to play the game of the just, were excluded. That is what is unjust. Not the opposite of the just, but that which prohibits that the question of the just and the unjust be, and remain, raised.[38]

In the absence of grand Narratives of universal reconciliation, the question of justice is opened, and it is through dissent that it remains so. "This sketches," according to Lyotard, "the outline of a politics that would respect both the desire for justice and the desire for the unknown."[39]

I have suggested that Lyotard's recent work can be read as a further development and refinement of the problems bequeathed by Kantian ethical socialism. Lyotard himself never uses the phrase, however, and the alignment of his work with Kantian socialism might appear forced. Still, he openly aligns his recent **Le Différend,** in which Kant occupies a central place, with his involvement in the French leftist group, *Socialisme ou Barbarie,* during the 1950's and 1960's. This peregrination that led to Kant, he writes,

> [B]egan for me around 1950 and followed the just mentioned group for fifteen years. One cannot correctly understand the book when one does not have in view this horizon of sorts—one that is both distant and close—out of which the book emerges and which it perhaps still approaches.[40]

Lyotard broke with the group in a dispute over the ability of Marxist categories and interpretive strategies to function as adequate tools for the analysis of postwar society.[41] In the light of Stalinism, the question was raised whether Marxism did not contain already within itself a justification of the trials and the gulag due to its failure to address the role of morality and justice in the context of class struggle. Similar questions concerning the political ramifications of Marxism already had been raised by the Kantian socialists well before the establishment of the Soviet Union. It comes as no surprise that Lyotard should follow a similar path.

Socialisme ou Barbarie never achieved a status greater than that of a small, relatively isolated, group at the margins of the French Left. Evaluating its practical contribution to social transformation, one commentator writes:

> As a practical revolutionary organization the *Socialisme ou Barbarie* group proved to be a dismal failure. But as a journal representing a certain tendency of thought it proved to be surprisingly successful. . . . Ironically their success as social theorists derived directly from their practical understanding of social processes which they acquired in their political organizing experiences.[42]

Lyotard himself draws attention to the practical inefficacy of the group: "For fifteen years Socialisme ou Barbarie was ridiculed and defamed as a . . . group of inconsistent intellectuals cut off from the masses. . . . And in fact, we did not have any *efficacy,* thank God."[43] For Lyotard, this apparent "failure" of the group was actually a sign of its "success." Rather than becoming *the* voice of the masses and propounding *the* organizing principle of a new revolutionary class, *S ou B* found itself to be in a position critical of any development in the social field. It would not be unwarranted to make the claim that this, too, was the fate of the Kantian socialists; with the exception of Kurt Eisner, who led the Munich Revolution in its initial stages, none of them assumed positions of political authority. This

is not to say they were apolitical, but that they tended to steer clear of direct political involvement.[44] Beyond this historical similarity, Lyotard shares with Kantian socialism the view that "the ethical approach is basically relevant, although not sufficient, to deal with everything we call the political,"[45] for "[e]thics is born of suffering; the political is born of the supplement history adds to this suffering."[46] Lyotard's search for "dissensus," then, affirms an ethical social theory and practice that does not rely on doctrine or dogma, but that is itself a *modus vivendi,* an active involvement in the living present of our (post)modern condition where history is perpetually in the making.

Notes

1. Jean-François Lyotard, *Peregrinations: Law, Form, Event.* (New York: Columbia University Press, 1988), p. 5.

2. Peter Dews, *Logics of Distintegration: Post Structuralist Thought and the Claims of Critical Theory.* (London Verso Press, 1987), p. 138.

3. Jean-François Lyotard and Jean-Loup Thébaud, *Just Gaming,* trans., W. Godzich (Minneapolis: University of Minnesota Press, 1985).

4. Jean-François Lyotard, *Le Différend* (Paris: Editions de Minuit, 1983). English translation: *The Différend* (University of Minnesota Press, 1988).

5. The most notable exception is the frequent mention of Jürgen Habermas in *The Postmodern Condition.*

6. For an historical overview of Kantian socialism, see Harry van der Linden, *Kantian Ethics and Socialism* (Indianapolis: Hackett, 1988), pp. 291-307.

7. Conrad Schmidt; cited in Van der Linden, p. 291.

8. Eduard Bernstein, *Evolutionary Socialism* (New York: Schocken Books, 1961), p. 201.

9. Hermann Cohen, *"Einleitung mit kritischem Nachtrag zu Langes Geschichte des Materialismus,"* in Co- hen, *Schriften zur Philosophie und Zeltgeschichte,* Vol. II (Berlin: Akademie Verlag, 1928), p. 98; cited in Van der Linden, p. vii.

10. *Ibid.*

11. Immanuel Kant, "On the Proverb: That May be True in Theory, but is of No Practical Use," *Perpetual Peace and Other Essays* (Indianapolis: Hackett, 1983), p. 81.

12. See Kant's remark in "What is Enlightenment?": "Perhaps a revolution can overthrow autocratic despotism and profiteering or powergrabbing oppression, but it can never truly reform a manner of thinking. . . . " *Perpetual Peace and Other Essays,* p. 42.

13. Kant, "On the Proverb . . .," p. 64.

14. *Ibid.*

15. *Ibid.*

16. See Van der Linden, p. 225.

17. Immanuel Kant, *Critique of Judgment*, trans., W.S. Pluhar (Indianapolis: Hackett, 1987), Ak. 469; p. 362.

18. Immanuel Kant, *Critique of Practical Reason*, trans., Lewis White Beck (New York: MacMillan, 1988), p. 117.

19. *Ibid.*, p. 118.

20. Kant, "On the Proverb . . .," p. 64.

21. This is an idea to be found in Benjamin's work.

22. Van der Linden, p. 38.

23. Hannah Arendt, *Lectures on Kant's Political Philosophy* (Chicago: University of Chicago Press, 1982), p. 27.

24. Jürgen Habermas, "A Reply to My Critics," in J.B. Thompson and D. Held, eds. *Habermas: Critical Debates* (Cambridge, MA: MIT Press, 1982), p. 262.

25. Lyotard, *Just Gaming*, p. 43.

26. Lyotard, *The Postmodern Condition*, p. 15.

27. *Ibid.*, p. 11.

28. *Ibid.*, p. 15.

29. *Ibid.*, p. 13.

30. *Ibid.*, p. 15.

31. Lyotard, *Just Gaming*, pp. 73-4.

32. Kant, *Critique of Judgment*, AK. 179, pp. 18-9.

33. Lyotard, cited in Claude Piché, "Lyotard's Reassessment of the Kantian Critique," *MS*, 1988.

34. Jean-François Lyotard, "The Sign of History," in D. Attridge, G. Bennington and R. Young, eds., *Poststructuralism and the Question of History* (Cambridge: Cambridge University Press, 1987), p. 169.

35. *Ibid.*, p. 170.

36. Jean-François Lyotard, *La Phénoménologie* (Paris: Presses Universitaires de France, 1954), p. 121.

37. *Just Gaming*, pp. 71-2.

38. *Ibid*, pp. 66-7.

39. Lyotard, *The Postmodern Condition*, p. 67.

40. Jean-François Lyotard, *Immaterialität und Postmoderne*, trans., Marianne Karbe (Berlin: Merve Verlag, 1985), pp. 36-7; [My translation.]

41. See Jean-François, "Pierre Souyri: Le marxisme qui n'a pas fini," *Esprit* 61 (1982), pp. 11-31; English. Pierre Souyri: A Memorial for Marxism," in *Peregrinations*, pp. 45-75.

42. Arthur Hirsch, *The French New Left: An Intellectual History from Sartre to Gorz* (Boston: South End Press, 1981), p. 115.

43. Jean-François Lyotard, *Dérive à partir de Marx et Freud* (Paris: Union Générale d'Editions, 10/18, 1973), pp. 11-2.

44. Of course, conditions in Wilhelmian Germany were not particularly conducive to direct political involvement on the part of many of the Kantian socialists, many of whom were Jewish.

45. Lyotard, *Peregrinations*, p. 35.

46. *Ibid.*, p. 60.

Todd G. May (essay date 1990)

SOURCE: "Kant the Liberal, Kant the Anarchist: Rawls and Lyotard on Kantian Justice," in *The Southern Journal of Philosophy*, Vol. XXVIII, No. 4, Winter, 1990, pp. 525-38.

[*In the following essay, May compares how Lyotard and the philosopher John Rawls use Kant's work in their formulations of justice.*]

The current crisis of Marxist thought is certain to provoke renewed investigations by political philosophers of their field. Radical philosophers will cast about for a viable alternative, while liberal philosophers will turn back to their tradition either to account for its seeming success or to deepen it. In both cases, the question of justice will become central, since it is especially this dimension of social life that appears to be vitiated under communist rule. For Marxists, justice has always devolved upon an equitable economic order; thus the demand, particularly among East Europeans, for an irreducible political sphere—a sphere seeking just social relations—has raised fundamental questions about the viability of Marxist practice.

Liberal thinkers have long realized the necessity for a vital concept of justice. As the discussions from Rawls, Walzer and Gauthier show, the question of the nature of justice dominates their investigations. Radical thinkers, however, are beginning to discuss justice as well. Among these, Jean-François Lyotard has spent much of his recent work elucidating a radical notion of justice. What is perhaps surprising is that, in the case of Rawls and Lyotard, attempts to articulate diametrically opposed conceptions of justice—the one unitary and liberal, the other multiple and anarchist—have turned for their historical inspiration (and at times philosophical justification) to the same figure: Kant. Kant has, in short, been claimed as the father of the two traditions currently competing with Marxist political theory: liberalism and post-structuralist anarchism.[1]

This paper will examine the return to Kant by both Rawls and Lyotard, focussing upon their major discussions of justice, *A Theory of Justice* and ***The Differend***, respectively. It will be seen that, in order to account for the Kantian inspiration, these philosophers turn two different works of Kant, and use those works differently. I will argue that although it is Rawls that gets the Kantian intention right—to articulate a unitary conception of justice—it is Lyotard's investigations into Kant's multiple and irreducible ontological territories that gets the Kantian achievement right. Kant's attempt to be a liberal landed him instead squarely within the current anarchist tradition.

Kant's own reflections on justice occur in a text cited neither by Rawls nor Lyotard. In *The Metaphysical Elements of Justice,*[2] he delineated the sphere of justice and marked it off from the sphere of the ethical, with which it might be confused. All forms of legislation, he argued, whether ethical or juridical, consist both in a law and an incentive to follow that law. Without the law, there is nothing for the will to follow; without the incentive, there is no connection between the law and the will. What differentiates the ethical from the juridical lies in this:

> If legislation makes an action a duty and at the same time makes this duty the incentive, it is *ethical*. If it does not include this latter condition in the law and therefore admits an incentive other than the Idea of duty itself, it is *juridical*.[3]

Justice, then, does not carry its incentive within it; unlike ethics, its laws do not move the will to act in accordance with them merely through their existence. An external motive is required,[4] and external codification as well (since the laws of justice do not present themselves immediately to the will).

Following this distinction, Kant sees three parameters defining the sphere of justice. First, justice applies only in situations of external relationships between people. Second, it applies only in relationships between wills, not between wishes and desires (wills being not only the representation of a desire or a desired object, but also the recognition of a capacity to realize that desire[5]). Last, since justice must apply to all wills, it cannot found itself on specific desires or desired objects, but must be founded solely on "the form of the relationship between the wills insofar as they are regarded as free."[6] He concludes that "[j]ustice is therefore the aggregate of those conditions under which the will of one person can be conjoined with the will of another in accordance with a universal law of freedom."[7] In short, justice is a matter of balancing the multiplicity of wills in a given society by recourse to the unitary concept of freedom. Freedom—for Kant the ability to act in accordance with reason, apart from animal impulses[8]—becomes the standard by which to judge the justice of an action, yielding a single principle of justice for all actions:

> Every action is just [right] that in itself or in its maxim is such that the freedom of the will of each can coexist together with the freedom of everyone in accordance with a universal law.[9]

Given this conception of justice, it is clear why an external motive is required in order to promote justice. In the ethical situation, the will places itself under the legislation of reason alone; thus duty and desire are united. Justice, however, must arise within a context in which first the wills are divergent and second, since those wills have not placed themselves solely under the legislation of reason,

there is no internal motive to act in accordance with the principle of justice. An external motive—coercion—is therefore a necessary component of justice, and not just a limitation imposed from the outside. Were coercion to be a part of ethics, the limitation would be external; but because of the multiplicity and heteronomy of wills, coercion is required in order for freedom to be attained. As Kant says:

> if a certain use of freedom is itself a hindrance to freedom according to universal laws (that is, unjust), then the use of coercion to counteract it, inasmuch as it is the prevention of a hindrance to freedom, is consistent with freedom according to universal laws; in other words, this use of coercion is just.[10]

Kant concludes, then, that "the concept of justice [or a right] can be held to consist immediately of the possibility of the conjunction of universal reciprocal coercion with the freedom of everyone."[11]

Justice, for Kant, is a matter of discovering unity in the midst of two related multiplicities, a multiplicity of the desires of wills and a multiplicity of sources—animal impulse as well as reason—for those wills. The unity he finds, freedom, is derived not from ethical laws but from a balancing of allowance and restriction on the basis of self-interest and reason. Reason enters in at the level of freedom because it is the *possibility* of acting freely—that is, in accordance with reason—that is protected; self-interested action is not *per se* rejected however.

John Rawls retains the notion of self-interest as a foundation for his theory of justice, but attempts to unite ethics and justice in seeking to articulate a Kantian theory of justice. The heart of Rawls' self-comparison with Kant occurs in Chapter 4 of *A Theory of Justice*. Before that, however, Rawls indicates his general view of Kantian ethics by way of a contrast with utilitarianism. Unlike utilitarianism, Kantian ethics (which Rawls calls a "social contract" theory[12]) refuses to accept lower standards of treatment for some people, whether or not this will contribute to the general welfare. Rawls sees this refusal in his own difference principle, roughly that inequalities are permissible only inasmuch as they serve the least favored. The difference principle, arising from the original contractual situation under the veil of ignorance, is a way of realizing the Kantian imperative to "treat humanity, whether in your own person or in the person of any other, never simply as a means, but always at the same time as an end."[13] Rawls' contract theory provides in this way "a sense in which men are to be treated as ends and not as means only."[14]

In order to draw this conclusion, Rawls must collapse the distinction, crucial to Kant, between the heteronomous and the autonomous. Heteronomy arises when "the will seeks the law that is to determine it *anywhere else* than in the fitness of its maxims for its own making of universal law."[15] Heteronomy implies acting in accordance with the law from motives other than the duty the law implies; thus, heteronomy can offer only hypothetical imperatives, never categorical ones. That Rawls collapses the two provides the key for his attempt to unify justice and ethics under the name of Kant. It will be recalled that for Kant, what differentiates ethics from justice is the matter of whether motivation is internal or external: i.e., categorical or hypothetical. One commits an action for its own sake or for the sake of something else. In the Kantian view, the former is ethics and the latter justice. For Rawls, however, since self-interest and morality are bound together by the decision issuing from the original position, the distinction between ethics and justice is moot.

With this gloss upon Kant's own view, Rawls places his own social contract theory squarely within the Kantian tradition. In Chapter 4, Rawls cites five central points of convergence with Kant.[16] First, he sees his two principles as the object of rational choice, and as being the most rational principles that could be chosen. Second, the principles provide for a kingdom of ends. Third, they characterize people as free and rational. Fourth, the veil of ignorance behind which they are chosen prevents what Rawls calls "heteronomy", and which he characterizes as influence emanating from "social position or natural endowments, or in view of the particular kind of society in which he lives or the specific things that he happens to want."[17] (It has already been shown that he does not exclude from heteronomy, as Kant does, general self-interest.) Fifth, and related to this, the two principles coverge with Kant's idea of the categorical imperative, in then sense that each of them is "a principle of conduct that applies to a person in virtue of his nature as a free and equal rational being."[18]

These five points of convergence with Kantian thought are all drawn from the ethical writings, particularly the *Groundwork* and the second critique. By trying to unite justice and ethics through an introduction of self-interest into the ethical sphere, Rawls saw his project as one less of modifying Kant than of offering a substantive deepening of Kantian ethics. This deepening occurs by means of the original position, which is "a procedural interpretation of Kant's conception of autonomy and the categorical imperative."[19] Questions about the accuracy of the interpretation aside, two points must be stressed. First, Rawls' appropriation of Kant concerns itself solely with what Kant calls in the third critique "the supersensible realm of the concept of freedom."[20] Second, because of this, Rawls' "Kantian solution" to the problem of justice is necessarily a liberal one.

The *Critique of Judgement* attempts to bridge the "immeasurable gulf"[21] between the realms of freedom and nature, and it is upon the recognition of such a gulf that Lyotard will found his own interpretation of Kantian justice. For Rawls, however, the question of justice does not devolve upon the relationship between the two realms, but rather solely upon the realm of freedom. Justice is a question of ethics, not of judgment; as such, its proper realm is the noumenal, the supersensible realm of freedom. This is what gives Rawls' thought its unity. It is precisely because Rawls assimilates self-interest into ethics that he can avoid

the heteronomy that Kant himself finds in his discussion of justice. Therefore, to speak of justice is not to relate concepts that are different in kind, but rather to find the proper articulation of a certain realm of experience: that of free, rational beings. Rawls emphasizes that in the original position specific interests—interests belonging to the realm of nature—are excluded, leaving the task of a theory of justice to be solely the articulation of ethical principles derived from pure, practical reason.

It is the formal nature of Rawls' method that renders his appropriation of Kant a liberal one. By absorbing justice into Kantian ethics, Rawls offers a theory of justice that explicitly avoids concern with the material circumstances of people. What is just derives not from a consideration of the relation of social conditions at a certain time and place to a given set of ethical beliefs, but from a formal method that assumes people to be free, rational beings. Both the assumption and the formality of the method based on that assumption are legacies of the liberal tradition that starts with Locke. Rawls' theory of justice, as a contractarian one, grounds its substantive principles upon a procedure that itself relies on one of Kant's realms—the realm of freedom and its corresponding faculty of pure, practical reason—as an interpretation of human beings. Thus for Rawls the unity and formality found in Kant's ethical writings form the basis of an appropriation of Kant as a liberal political theorist.

Jean-François Lyotard has often found himself inhabiting the outer edge of the French radical political scene. In recent years, however, he has turned from the more freewheeling style of such works as *Economie Libidinale*[22] toward the question of justice and how it is to be realized in a society that no longer believes in a "grand narrative"[23] of the type offered by liberalism or Marxism. His major discussion of justice, *The Differend,* relies on an appropriation of Kant that becomes increasingly clear as the text progresses. To grasp this appropriation, however, one must be clear on what is meant by a "differend."

For Lyotard:

> A case of differend between two parties takes place when the 'regulation' of the conflict that opposes them is done in the idiom of one of the parties while the wrong suffered by the other is not signified in that idiom.[24]

The differend Lyotard opens with is that of the denial by Robert Faurisson that the Holocaust ever took place (because he could find no one who could testify to the existence of the gas chambers). From the idea of the differend, Lyotard develops a theory of language that views it less in terms of communication than in terms of strategies of competing genres vying for dominance. Between genres there are no assimilations, only differends. Thus the capitalist genre and the Marxist genre are in a relation of differend, because the exploitation of labor cannot be formulated in capitalist terms; and there is a differend between narrative knowledge of traditional cultures and scientific knowledge of contemporary culture, because the latter cannot be formulated in the genre of the former.

Injustice, on this model, is the violence that one genre commits upon another through its exclusion of that other by means of a differend. Lyotard does not say whether this is the only type of injustice that can occur, but he makes it clear that inasmuch as language creates our world (specifically, phrases of language create "phrase universes"[25] for which genres compete in comprising our world), the injustice that arises through differends is a central one, from which many if not all others flow.

It is in this context that Lyotard's interpretation of Kant takes root, the bulk of which appears in four "Kant Notices" distributed throughout the text. In the first, Lyotard notes that in Kant's first critique, there is a differend between the sensory apparatus and the sensed. The sensed is not so much rendered by the faculty of intuition as it is suppressed by it in being subjected to intuition's constraints: "the subject cannot have presentations, but only representations."[26] The second "Kant Notice" brings out another differend, that between the descriptive and the prescriptive, between which there is an "abyss."[27] The existence of this abyss entails that no event in the world can bring a sense of obligation with it: ethical obligation is irreducible to any phenomenal event or situation. That is why, Lyotard notes, Kant sees freedom as derived from obligation and not from empirical observation. Freedom is the condition of the possibility of acting morally, not an implication from the phenomenal world, within which there can only be causes.

The question Lyotard raises for Kant in the third "Kant Notice," then, is how it will be possible to move between the genres of the descriptive and the prescriptive (as well as the aesthetic) without doing an injustice to either—that is, without reducing one to the other and thereby committing a violence upon it. Here Kant's third critique assumes its importance for Lyotard. Judgment, which cannot create a realm of its own, moves among the different realms in order to create "passages"[28] that are irreducible to any one realm. Lyotard offers a picture of judgment as the vessel navigating the archipelago of realms. The passages cannot reconcile the various realms or faculties; they can only arrange them or put them in perspective. This occurs by way of analogy, as when the beautiful is analyzed as a symbol of the good or the moral law is conceived on analogy with natural law.

This perspective would seem to preclude any hope for a community within which justice would find its realization. If justice is the respect accorded to the heterogeneity of various genres—with all the implications that respect has for the victims of differends, for instance those of the Holocaust—then it would seem to preclude any unifying principle that would define a communal space. However, Lyotard claims, in the fourth "Kant Notice," that Kant's political writings, viewed from the perspective of the third critique, do offer such a community. This community is not an empirical one, but instead a community created by a specific experience of the sublime.

Lyotard defines the Kantian concept of the sublime as the "finality of a nonfinality and the pleasure of a displeasure."[29] For Kant, the sublime, like the beautiful, is aesthetic in the sense that its object provokes a pleasure by means of the imagination which cannot be accounted for conceptually. However, unlike the beautiful, the feeling of the sublime does not arise from a free agreement of faculties—"the imagination's *free conformity to law.*"[30] Rather, it is in the discordance among faculties that the sublime arises. The object that induces the feeling of the sublime hints at an overpowering greatness that seems, according to Kant, "to violate purpose in respect of the judgment, to be unsuited to our presentative faculty, and as it were to do violence to the imagination."[31] The sublime is the wholly other whose monumental stature can only be hinted at in experience, and whose hint brings a pleasure only through overwhelming feeling of discordance that it provokes. Thus, unlike the beautiful, the sublime, while aesthetic, provokes heterogeneity rather than harmony. That heterogeneity consists both in the relation of the sublime to experience and in the relation of faculties to one another in the feeling of the sublime.

The community created by an audience to an event, for example the storming of the Bastille, in which the enthusiasm of the audience appropriates the event as a sign of humanity's progress, is the type of community created by the sublime. The progress of humanity—both the fact that humanity does progress and that the storming of the Bastille expresses this progress—is the experience of the sublime that creates a community out of the audience to the event. Viewed from the perspective of the descriptive regimen, history—the unfolding of events—is chaos and the idea of a community is illusory. It is only from the aesthetic perspective of the sublime that a community can arise, as what Lyotard calls a "sentimental anticipation of the republic."[32] What binds such a community is neither a descriptive nor a prescriptive regimen, but rather a feeling of that which is other to both and which does not seek to establish a harmony between them.[33]

Lyotard argues that a community that is the product of an aesthetic experience of the sublime introduces heterogeneity into the heart of Kantian thought. "With the sublime, Kant advances far into heterogeneity."[34] What overcomes the injustice of the differend, then, is not an empirical community that agrees on fundamental ethical principles (this would not only be impossible, it would recreate the differend between the ethical and the descriptive), but an aesthetically realized community that preserves the heterogeneity of realms and faculties while constructing passages between them. Thus, for Lyotard, it is the judgment of the third critique rather than the ethics of the second that forms the lynchpin of interpretation for a Kantian approach to justice, an approach characterized by respect for different genres rather than their erasure or assimilation.

The theory of justice arising from this interpretation is one on which the anarchist and post-structuralist traditions converge. What it resists above all is a reduction of genres to a single, dominant genre, preferring to seek justice in multiplicity and heterogeneity rather than in unity, in passages across genres rather than in the victory of a certain genre. In another text, Lyotard writes:

> The purposiveness that the twentieth century has witnessed has not consisted, as Kant had hoped, of securing fragile passages above abysses. Rather, it has consisted of filling up those abysses at the cost of the destruction of whole worlds of names.[35]

What is just is not to find the principle or set of principles that will allow for a proper social balance, but instead to preserve the multiplicity of different genres that can allow for the fullest articulation of experience. Lyotard establishes his notion of justice in direct opposition to both liberal and Marxist conceptions, viewing them as totalitarian in their attempt to reduce various phrasings to a single genre.

It follows from Lyotard's analysis that justice, like the aesthetic community that hopes for it, must remain an Idea in the Kantian sense, a "concept formed from notions and transcending the possibility of experience."[36] Because there are always conflicts of genres, and because language occurs by means of linking one phrase to another, and because while "to link is necessary; how to link is contingent,"[37] there will always be the threat of one genre's attaining dominance. The project of creating justice is both to realize that injustice is inevitable—it occurs every time a genre takes hold of a set of phrasings—and to struggle against the wholescale domination or suppression of genres. In this sense, Lyotard's conception of justice is, as one critic has noted, a "negative dialectic,"[38] offering constant criticism without the possibility of achieving a final synthesis, at least at the empirical level. The foundation for this negative dialectic is to be found in Kant's separation of realms, a separation that offers possibilities of passage but precludes the justice of capture. For Lyotard, then, Kant, rightly interpreted, is the founder of a post-structuralist, anarchist theory of justice.

Rawls and Lyotard engage in diametrically opposed appropriations of Kant in arguing their conceptions of justice. For Rawls, there is a unity of form that can be had even across realms that Kant held separate. For Lyotard, it is precisely the holding separate of realms that lays the groundwork for the possibility of an adequate conception of justice. It remains only to ask whether Kant should be seen more legitimately as the liberal Rawls finds in him or as the radical post-structuralist Lyotard would have him be.

Kant must certainly have intended his theory of justice to be seen in a more nearly Rawlsian light. Although, unlike Rawls, Kant distinguished ethics from justice, he tried to lay a single principle of justice[39] that relied on a single concept—freedom—at the base of all reflection about justice. Moreover, this single principle, like Rawls' two principles, was a formal one, relying not upon the specific ob-

jects of competing wills (because they are too divergent to offer the possibility of drawing a unitary conception of justice), but upon the form of willing alone. Such a reliance assumes that human willing, and thus that human nature, is essentially free and rational. Thus, Kant's own reflections about justice conform to the criteria for liberal political thinking—followed also by Rawls—of formal principles based upon a common assumption about the nature of human beings.

There is also a deeper reason to believe that Kant intended a unitary conception of justice. It is to be found in the project of the third critique, which is to try to reconcile the realm of nature and the realm of freedom delineated in the first two critiques. That such a reconciliation is crucial for Kant's philosophy follows from the fact that human beings are considered to be subject to both realms. As Kant points out in the *Logic,* the question "What is man?" underlies the three questions of what can I know, what ought I to do, and what can I hope?[40] Thus a conception of human being as a whole requires a reconciliation of the realms of nature and of freedom. As Kant writes in the second introduction to the *Critique of Judgement:*

> The concept of freedom is meant to actualize in the world of sense the purpose proposed by its laws, and consequently nature must be so thought that the conformity to law of its form at least harmonizes with the possibility of the purposes to be effected in it according to laws of freedom.[41]

That harmonizing is the purpose of the third critique, especially the second division on teleological judgment, with its attempted reconciliation between determinant and reflective judgment. In order to give a coherent answer to the question "What is man?", Kant had to do precisely what Lyotard argued he could not do: give a final unity to his thought. He had to find a way not merely to pass across but to bridge permanently the gulf between the realm of nature and that of freedom, the descriptive and the prescriptive.

Thus, even if there is a distinction to be made between the ethical and the political at the level of legislating action, that distinction would be transcended at a deeper level in the harmonization of the realms of nature and freedom. Rawls, if perhaps misguided in introducing self-interest into the ethical at the level of the theory of justice, would be vindicated at the level of the final reconciliation of Kantian thought, when the realm of nature and the realm of freedom would find a common "territory"[42] by means of the intervention of judgment.

The Kantian intention, then, both specifically in the question of justice and generally at the level of the entire architectonic, conforms more closely with the Rawlsian interpretation. Lyotard's argument, if it is to be vindicated, must point not to Kant's intention, but rather to his achievement. Lyotard must argue that what Kant actually constructed was a theory with passages but no permanent bridges. Such an argument would be correct.

In order to understand why this is so, it is necessary to turn back to the *Critique of Judgement*. In the resolution to the antinomy of teleological judgment, Kant argues that determinant and reflective judgment do not converge onto a common territory. Instead, the resolution finds that the relationship between determinant and reflective judgment is asymptotic: what cannot be accounted for in nature by the advance of determinant judgment can still be accounted for by reflective judgment. At the end of the Dialectic of Teleological Judgement, Kant writes:

> We should explain all products and occurences in nature, even the most purposive, by mechanism as far as is in our power . . . those things which we cannot even state for investigation, except under the concept of a purpose of reason, must . . . be subordinated by us finally to causality in accordance with purposes.[43]

The consequences of this asymptotic relationship between determinant and reflective judgment are far-reaching. If there is to be no final reconciliation—no common territory on which reflective and determinant judgment are to converge—then the realm of nature, accounted for through determinant judgment, and the realm of freedom, accounted for through reflective judgment, must remain separate. There is an abyss between them.[44] And thus there can be no final unity of human being, and no unified answer to the question "What is man?" If this is so, then the reconciliation of self-interest and ethics which Rawls sought cannot be achieved within the Kantian framework. The solution to the antinomy of teleological judgment moves us no further than the *Critique of Pure Reason*. Nature and freedom are not to be reconciled; their relationship is one of differend, not harmony.

This conclusion also has effects upon Kant's text on justice. Seen from Lyotard's perspective of separate and irreducible realms, the text on justice is of restricted scope. It applies not to a general conception of what is just, but solely to the realm of legally permissible behavior. Although there is a unity to be found within this limited scope, and although it is a formal unity, it remains bound to the context in which it is articulated. To apply it elsewhere would be to create an injustice in Lyotard's sense. The juridical, in *The Metaphysical Elements of Justice*, must be understood in the restricted sense of legally just, not in the wider sense—as Rawls and others have understood it—as morally or socially just. That the formal unity of the juridical is based upon the conception of human beings as free and rational does not create any permanent bridges, any convergences, among realms. The only possible convergence arising from this basis is between the ethical and the juridical inasmuch as they apply to free beings; and this is a convergence Kant did not deny.

In the end, it is because Lyotard takes seriously the differences among the various parts of the Kantian whole that he discovers the heterogeneity that inhabits it. By moving in the opposite direction from Rawls, Lyotard has been more loyal to what Kant actually achieved, notwithstanding Rawls' fidelity to the Kantian search for a principle of unity. If one must move from a restricted sense of the term "justice" to a wider sense in order to account for its application to a relation between realms, this does not seem controversial, given the breadth of scope that both Rawls and Lyotard are trying to achieve.

It seems jarring at first to view Kant as a political radical. However, the movement of his entire philosophy, and the care he took not to mix realms or to reduce one to another (even when it was his intention to unify them) conforms with the principles of multiplicity and irreducibility that have characterized post-structuralist political thought. Lyotard, it seems, has captured that movement in his attempt to conceive of a justice not subject to the "grand narratives" of the past. In the search for justice, then, it appears that—despite his own intentions—Kant's brethren are to be found more in the camp of the anarchists than in that of the liberals.

Notes

1. I use the term anarchism here to denote a thought which attempts to criticize liberalism from a perspective that denies an Archimedean point from which all radical change could issue, thus counting the tasks of political interventions to be multiple, de-centered, and irreducible. This perspective occurs in the works of Michel Foucault and Gilles Deleuze as well as Lyotard. For more on this, see my "Is Post-structuralist Political Theory Anarchist?" in *Philosophy and Social Criticism*, Vol. 15, 2, pp. 167-182.

2. tr. John Ladd, Indianapolis, Bobbs-Merrill, 1965.

3. *Ibid.*, p. 19.

4. Here we can see why Rawls would turn to Kant's second critique rather than this work to ground his own thought. For Kant, justice involves the distinction between the will's interest and the will's obligation, which is precisely the distinction Rawls methodology is trying to overcome. For a criticism of Rawls on this point, see Robert Paul Wolff's *Understanding Rawls* (New Jersey, Princeton University Press, 1977), pp. 113-115. Also, see the discussion on Rawls below.

5. Cf., *Ibid.*, p. 12; *Critique of Practical Reason*, Indianapolis, Bobbs-Merrill, 1956, p. 15.

6. *Ibid.*

7. *Ibid.*

8. Cf. *Ibid.*, p. 13; *Critique of Practical Reason, op. cit.*, p. 28.

9. *Ibid.*, p. 35.

10. *Ibid.*, p. 36.

11. *Ibid.*

12. *A Theory of Justice*, Cambridge, Harvard University Press, 1971, p. 11.

13. *Groundwork of the Metaphysic of Morals*, tr. H. J. Paton, New York, Harper and Row, 1964, p. 96.

14. Rawls, *op. cit.*, p. 180.

15. *Groundwork of the Metaphysic of Morals, op. cit.*, p. 108.

16. The following analysis is drawn from pp. 251-257.

17. *Ibid.*, p. 252.

18. *Ibid.*, p. 253.

19. *Ibid.*, p. 256.

20. *Critique of Judgement*, tr. J. H. Bernard, New York, Hafner Press, 1951, p. 12.

21. *Ibid.*

22. Paris, Editions de Minuit, 1974.

23. *The Postmodern Condition: A Report on Knowledge*, tr. Geoff Bennington and Brian Massumi, Minneapolis, University of Minnesota Press, 1984 (or. pub. 1979), p. xxiii.

24. *The Differend*, tr. Georges Van Den Abbeele, Minneapolis, University of Minnesota Press, 1988 (or. pub. 1983), p. 9.

25. *Ibid.*, pp. 70-71.

26. *Ibid.*, p. 64.

27. *Ibid.*, p. 123.

28. *Ibid.*, p. 130. Lyotard borrows the idea of a "passage" (Uebergange) from the second introduction to the *Critique of Judgement, op. cit.*, pp. 12 and 33 (translated there as "transition").

29. *Ibid.*, p. 165. Note Kant's own definition of the feeling of the sublime as "a feeling of pain arising from the want of accordance between the aesthetical estimation of magnitude formed by the imagination and the estimation of the same formed by reason. There is at the same time a pleasure thus excited, arising from the correspondence with rational ideas of this very judgment of the inadequacy of our greatest faculty of sense, in so far as it is a law for us to strive after these ideas." *Critique of Judgement, op. cit.*, p. 96.

30. *Critique of Judgement, op. cit.*, p. 77.

31. *Ibid.*, p. 83.

32. Lyotard, *op. cit.*, p. 168.

33. It is in this context, perhaps, that we may understand Kant's claim that there is a bond between the beautiful and the good which does not hold for the sublime. Cf. *Critique of Judgement, op. cit.*, pp. 199-200.

34. *Ibid.*, p. 169.

35. "Judiciousness in Dispute, Or Kant After Marx," tr. Cecile Lindsay, in Murray Krieger (ed.), *The Aims of Representation*, New York, Columbia University Press, 1987, p. 64.

36. *Critique of Pure Reason*, tr. Norman Kemp Smith, New York, St. Martin's, 1965, p. 314 (A320/B377). Here we must understand an Idea as an end that is

regulative without being teleological. The hetergeneous community that Lyotard appropriates from Kant is one that cannot arise empirically but can guide us in our political choices.

37. *The Differend, op. cit.*, p. 29.

38. Ingram, David, "Legitimacy and the Postmodern Condition: The Political Thought of Jean-François Lyotard," *Praxis International*, Vol. 7, #3-4 (1987-88), p. 297.

39. See above, p. 3.

40. *Logic*, tr. Robert S. Hartman and Wolfgang Schwartz, New York, Bobbs-Merrill, 1974, p. 29.

41. *Critique of Judgement, op. cit.*, p. 12.

42. *Ibid.*, p. 13.

43. *Ibid.*, p. 264.

44. J. D. McFarland argues that Kant attempts his final reconciliation not in the Dialectic of Teleological Judgement but in the Methodology. This seems to me to be incorrect, but his final judgment, that Kant fails to achieve his sought after unity, agrees with my own. See his article, "The Bogus Unity of the Kantian Philosophy," in P. Laberge, F. Duchesneau, and B. Morrisey (ed.), *Proceedings of the Ottawa Congress on Kant in the Anglo-American and Continental Traditions, Held October 10-14, 1974*, Ottawa, University of Ottawa Press, 1976, pp. 280-296.

Gayle L. Ormiston (essay date 1990)

SOURCE: A review of *Peregrinations: Law, Form, Event*, in *The Journal of Aesthetics and Art Criticism*, Vol. 48, No. 1, Winter, 1990, pp. 88-90.

[*In the following review of* Peregrinations, *Ormiston outlines the meaning of thinking according to Lyotard.*]

Peregrinations presents Lyotard's Wellek Library Lectures in Critical Theory delivered at the University of California at Irvine (May 1986). Titled **"Clouds," "Touches,"** and **"Gaps,"** these lectures recount the thoughts, borrowed idioms, phrasic connections, "reflective judgments," and desires (the Kantian Ideas) that have led him on certain textual and narrative paths in the pursuit of "new artistic clouds and new clouds of thought" (p. 43). **Peregrinations** also includes a paper published originally in French, **"A Memorial of Marxism: for Pierre Souyri,"** which chronicles Lyotard's relation to the French Marxist Pierre Souyri, Lyotard's own involvement with Marxism (1954-1966), and his work with Souyri on the journal *Socialisme ou Barbarie* and the newspaper *Pouvoir Ouvrier*. The last section of the book is a "Checklist of Writings by and about Jean-François Lyotard: A Selected Bibliography" compiled by Eddie Yeghiayan.

Each part of this text narrates the very rich, complex and often contradictory and fragmentary positions that constitute Lyotard's intellectual and practical *wanderings*. As a whole, *Peregrinations* provides a necessary propaedeutic to the broader issues and questions addressed in Lyotard's other works such as *Discours, figure* (1971), *Des Dispostifs pulsionnels* (1973), *Economie libidinale* (1974), *La Condition postmoderne: Rapport sur le savoir* (1979; *The Postmodern Condition: A Report on Knowledge* [1984]); *Au Juste* (1979; *Just Gaming* [1985]), and more recently *Le Différend* (1983; *The Differend: Phrases in Dispute* [1989]). It will whet the appetites of those readers familiar with the breadth and depth of Lyotard's writings and it will satisfy the desire of those readers who are looking for a brief and accessible yet sound and rigorous introduction to his work and the question of postmodernity.

To call Lyotard's peregrinations "wanderings" is not to say the journeys on which he has embarked over some forty odd years of philosophical, ethical, and aesthetic writing and political and artistic activity are aimless, meandering excursions. Lyotard's peregrinations are clearly defined *interrogations* of the boundaries that traditionally separate specific fields of inquiry into the real estate of academic disciplines and literary or political genres according to what he calls "narrative monopolies."

Lyotard's writings have consistently pursued the complicity of ethical-political law, aesthetic form, and historical event, and *Peregrinations,* as its subtitle suggests, is no exception in this regard. In fact, it is this complicity or this "phrasic network" of law, form, and event, as it pertains to the totalitarian *use* of language, traditions, and texts in philosophy, art, literary criticism, ethics and politics, and history that Lyotard pursues here in a fresh, unencumbered, and non-technical fashion. "[A]ll three entities [law, form, and event]," writes Lyotard, "are active, unavoidable, in the three fields [ethics-politics, aesthetics, and history] with the same force, even if not present in the same way. . . . Sometimes one of these poles is predominant, sometimes another" (pp. 5-6). With this announcement, Lyotard obviates the demand (the ostensible assumption behind Murray Krieger and David Carroll's invitation to Lyotard to present the Wellek Lectures) to define his "'position' in the field of criticism and *the* path which led [him] to this position" (p. 4, emphasis added).

Rather than presenting a "position" as such, or building "a system of total knowledge about clouds of thoughts by passing from one site to another and accumulating the views it produces at each site" (p. 6), Lyotard's *Peregrinations* describes "the condition of thinking insofar as it takes into account the principle of relativity it is affected by" (p. 7). For Lyotard, such a description of the condition of thinking, and what might otherwise be phrased as the condition of acting and judging, "does not induce any skepticism, even if the defenders of rationality try to persuade us that it does. It inspires only the principle of the endless pursuit of the task of discussing clouds" (p. 7). In other words, thinking does not present a "rational," "coherent" system where the gap between "thought" and its "object" is bridged. Nor does thinking present ideas as op-

erators or Kantian categories. Thinking presents and pursues "clouds" or "horizons" of thought.

Furthermore, thinking remains interminably episodic. Always beginning in the "middle of things" (p. 2) or the "middle of time" (p. 8), thinking "consists in a re-thinking" [*anámnesis*] where "there is nothing the presentation of which could be said to be the 'premiere.' The emergence of something reiterates something else, every occurrence is a recurrence, not at all in the sense that it could repeat the same thing or be the rehearsal of the same play, but in the sense of the Freudian notion of *Nachträglich* . . . " (pp. 8-9). The condition of thinking, acting, and judging, then, is a condition of internal dissension, cleavages, rifts, gaps, and fragmentation; it is a condition of the incessant generation of multiple positions, situations, "selves," and stories *we* tell ourselves about our*selves*. It is this condition that Lyotard has tried to articulate with the notion of *le différend.*

The *différend* is or presents "the unstable state and instant of language wherein something must be able to be put in phrases cannot yet be" (Jean-François Lyotard, *Le Différend* [Les Éditions Minuit, 1983], paragraph 22). The *différend* signals the condition and the possibility of thinking: it signals the possibility of reiteration, re-phrasing and creating new links between language, thought, and reality. To be sure, it is *the postmodern condition.* Furthermore, the *différend* indicates the possibility for the conflict of faculties, the generation of discordant idioms, vocabularies, and desires. And yet the *différend* indicates the impossibility of conceptualizing the condition of thinking except in terms of the phrase and the breach or the gap that makes each phrase necessary. As Lyotard remarks in *Peregrinations,* "The gap separating one phrase from another is the 'condition' of both presentation and occurrences, but such a 'condition' remains ungraspable in itself except by a new phrase, which in turn presupposes the first phrase. This is something like the condition of Being, as it is always escaping determination and arriving both too soon and too late" (p. 32).

And finally, for Lyotard, the *différend* signifies that it is not the indeterminate character of thought that threatens the "work of thinking (or writing)" or inquiry but, rather, that any form of thinking "pretends to be complete" (p. 6). So instead of concerning himself with the establishment of boundaries or with a project of substantiating a conception of community and consensus grounded in classical theories of communication, as evidenced in the writings of Habermas, Apel, and Rorty, Lyotard pursues the *différend.* A community—aesthetic, ethical, or political—based on a theory of language remains, for Lyotard, "only an Idea, . . . a horizon for an expected consensus" (p. 38). It is a community that remains in a constant state of transfiguration—it "must always be in the process of doing *and* undoing itself, . . . combining both life and death, . . . always keeping open the issue of whether or not it actually exits" (p. 38). Thus, Lyotard writes at the end of the lecture entitled **"Gaps"**: "It seems to me that the only consensus we ought to be worrying about is one that would encourage this heterogeneity or 'dissensus'" (p. 44).

Peregrinations reiterates the significance of these conditions as they are expressed throughout Lyotard's writings and activities. It is a text maintaining Lyotard's conviction that today and always the "philosopher," the "artist," the "writer" works without rules; any rules and categories that are to be employed remain to be articulated within specific pragmatic contexts (see ***The Postmodern Condition*** [University of Minnesota Press, 1984], pp. 82-83).

Alexander Weber (essay date 1990)

SOURCE: "Lyotard's Combative Theory of Discourse," in *Telos,* No. 83, Spring, 1990, pp. 141-50.

[*In the following essay, Weber argues that, in his assertion of language as a means by which incommensurates challenge each other for dominance, Lyotard is assuming a position similar to nineteenth century Social Darwinism.*]

"Parler, c'est agir" is an old rhetorical commonplace.[1] Speech is generally regarded as an instrument of communication and understanding. Lyotard, however, wants to replace communication with *agon;* to him speech is a contest: *"parler est combattre."*[2] He emphatically rejects the humanist notion that language is in a state of harmony disrupted only by the speakers' opposing interests. For Lyotard, the idea that individuals control language is an anthropocentric illusion. The internal structure of language necessarily places it in a condition of *bellum omnium contra omnes.*

Lyotard finds this civil war in the heterogeneity of language. According to him, all phrases are formed according to certain rules—*"régimes de phrases"* (to reason, to know, to describe, to narrate, to ask etc.). Phrases pertaining to different *"régimes de phrases"* are incompatible. They can, however, be linked by different *"genres de discours"* so as to reach particular aims such as to know, to teach, to maintain, to mislead or to justify. The genres of discourse are heteromorphic and are not covered by a universal metadiscourse. (Although Lyotard is a keen defender of "innovative" contradictions and paralogisms,[3] he repeatedly attempts to show that a metadiscourse is untenable because logically contradictory). Any idiom which strives to step out of the insular genres of discourse is an attempt at fraudulent inclusiveness: it is an act of terrorism, because it suppresses the irreducible plurality of genres of discourse. The principle of universal rationality is an instrument of repression. There can be no "final grounding" of philosophy because all genres of discourse can claim equal legitimacy. Hence, any distinction between ideology and critical reflection is impossible. In view of the equal validity of conflicting claims, there remains only self-conscious equivocation.

The problem is that the heterogeneous genres of discourse mutually hinder their development. This premise is crucial for Lyotard's theory of combat: he postulates that there is a necessary superfluity of genres which is suppressed by the limited number of idioms that can survive. Whenever we utter a phrase there are always more phrases which demand to be connected to it than there are available possibilities of linkage. The process of linking phrases is never interrupted (Lyotard even defines keeping quiet as a phrase); phrases *must* be linked, but no rule determines *how* phrases should be linked. Consequently, a structural conflict between the innumerable heteromorphic phrases is unavoidable. The context in which the winning phrase proves stronger is merely contingent. The same phrase might well lose if it occurred in another idiom; it can be both strong and weak if it occurs in two different genres.[4] (The Sophists were therefore right to maintain that they can make the stronger argument the weaker). Phrases could only be strong or weak in themselves if language were a unified whole. Only if this false premise were granted would the agonistic process of selection be teleological. Each genre has its own aim, but there is no universal *telos* which would link all genres of discourse to an organic unity. These are like monads which know only their own destination; and as these destinations differ, language is in a condition of permanent civil war.

Lyotard works from another important premise. He states that genres of discourse are heterogeneous, but does not really prove it; the same problem occurs when he postulates that the phrases which demand to be linked vary. How is this variation initiated? Why are the genres heterogeneous? If these premises cannot be borne out, Lyotard's central theory of combat between genres, in its acute agonistic form, collapses. And there do seem to be reasons why this heterogeneity and variability cannot be linguistically expressed at all. The difficulty is that one can only perceive the harmless kind of conflict Lyotard calls *"litige."* In this case, it is possible to find an idiom which can solve the conflict because it covers both parties and provides a *"régle de jugement."* A *"différend,"* by contrast, is a conflict which for structural reasons cannot be resolved equitably; in this case, there is no idiom applicable to both parties. Only force decides which genre of discourse comes out on top. The stronger genre suppresses all possible variants pertaining to another genre; these become victims unable to express the violence ("tort") they have suffered. Should they find an idiom to voice this violence, the conflict ceases to be what it was: a *"différend."* It is fundamental that only one aspect of a *"différend"*—the self-contained, successful idiom—can be perceived. The variants remain beneath the surface, and hence cannot be expressed, or even proved to exist, without coercing and forcibly reducing the *"différend"* to a *"litige."* The heterogeneity of language, the most important premise of the *"différend,"* can therefore not be established. Lyotard makes two assertions about suppressed varying phrases which both claim to be valid even though they are contradictory: 1) we cannot have knowledge of suppressed variants; 2) we have knowledge of suppressed variants because we know that they exist. A linguistic analysis of the *"différend"* being impossible, Lyotard proposes another epistemological approach: feeling. According to him only feeling can perceive the mass of suppressed phrases. But the problem of how to *speak* about a "*différend*," without neutralizing it, remains unsolved.

How can we describe a "*différend*" at all? Lyotard claims that, because he deals with phrases, his approach is metalinguistic in a linguistic rather than a logical sense.[5] It is not quite clear how this approach can ever lead to any description of a "*différend*," without implicitly subscribing to the possibility of a metadiscourse. Simplifying this somewhat, one could say: if language were in the condition Lyotard claims, he could never have written a book like *Le différend* without doing it violence. How can Lyotard speak in the sense of a linguist if his description of language is true? Linguistics is nothing if not speaking about language and hence must be affected by the relativity of idioms. Yet Lyotard's theory of "*différend*" wants to be more than one among an unlimited number of possible ways of speaking about language. If it is hard to describe the radical heterogeneity of language, it is made no easier by the authority Lyotard must claim for his absolute description.

We can see how distorted Lyotard's agonistic concept of language is if we examine his interpretation of Wittgenstein's language games. In *Le différend* Lyotard emphasizes not rule-following, but solely the aspect of winning or losing. (Like most post-structuralists, he views the playing subjects as mere epiphenomena of a spontaneous language). He uses the term "game" as a near-synonym for competition or rivalry. Wittgenstein, in contrast, states: ". . . is there always winning and losing or competition between players? Think of patience. In ball games there is winning and losing; but when a child throws his ball at the wall and catches it again, this feature has disappeared."[6] Lyotard stresses that language games are incommensurable and that they fail to translate, whereas Wittgenstein is interested in both the alteration *and* the continuity of language games. "A main source of our failure to understand is that we do not *command a comprehensive view* of the use of outwords. Our grammar is lacking in this sort of comprehensiveness. A comprehensive view produces just that understanding which consists in 'seeing connexions'. Hence the importance of finding and inventing *intermediate cases*. The concept of a perspicuous representation is of fundamental significance for us. It determines the form of account we give, the way we look at things."[7] This is not to find fault with Lyotard's interpretation of Wittgenstein. The question is whether we should prefer his tendentious interpretation to Wittgenstein himself. There are two important assumptions in Lyotard's interpretation of language games: the heterogeneity of the different genres of discourse and the rivalry between them. As we have seen, however, he is unable to prove these assumptions.

Lyotard shares this problem with some of his 19th century precursors. It is illuminating to establish the genealogy of his combative style and theory. Lyotard is aware of part of this agonistic tradition. He alludes explicitly to Nietzsche's essay, "Homer's Contest,"[8] in *The Postmodern Condition.*[9] Nietzsche attributes the triumph of Greece to the presence of competition at every level of political and cultural life. The *agon* is motivated by an aversion to undivided sovereignty and centralized power. A second strong man is promoted to counter the overarching ambition of the tyrant. To combat the conservatism and paralysis of absolutism, Lyotard and Nietzsche favor a decentralized dynamic of power. "That is the kernel of the Hellenic concept of *agon:* it abominates autocracy, and fears its dangers; as a *safeguard* against genius it calls for—a second genius."[10] Nietzsche, however, is only one of many 19th century philosophers who follow the agonistic paradigm. His theory of combat is not too original.

The 19th century is dominated by different types of agonistic theory, such as Malthus' principle of population, Spencer's evolutionism, Marx' class struggle, Darwin's natural selection, Nietzsche's perspectivism and Social Darwinism. This line of competitive theory was initiated by Malthus. He maintained: "First, That food is necessary to the existence of man. Secondly, That the passion between the sexes is necessary, and will remain nearly in its present state. These two laws ever since we have had any knowledge of mankind, appear to have been fixed laws of our nature. . . . Assuming then, my postulata as granted, I say that the power of population is indefinitely greater than the power in the earth to produce subsistence for man. Population, when unchecked, increases in a geometrical ratio. Subsistence increases only in an arithmetical ratio."[11]

The influence of this "principle" on the 19th century cannot be overestimated. From these premises it follows that there is always an excess population which cannot survive because nature cannot feed it. Hence there are structural reasons why rivalry and combat in nature and in human society are inevitable. Too many guests must fight for a limited number of seats at the table of life.

Later, Spencer concluded that the better and stronger pass this selection whereas the weak and inferior perish. According to his evolutionism, the mechanism of competitive selection leads to social and cultural progress. Therefore, only politically underdeveloped societies are ruled by absolute power. Subsequently, societies must initiate a competitive "survival of the fittest" in order to succeed. Governmental interference hinders progress; conscious "*laissez-faire*" allows a strong competitive evolution.

Both Malthus and Spencer were interested primarily in human society; it was Darwin who applied their theories to nature. He explained the evolution of species by combining Malthus' theory of selection with his scientific observation of modified descent. In contrast to the evolutionist Spencer, Darwin is a pure selectionist. Nature has no *telos;* since strength or weakness are dependent on accidental circumstance, we lack a criterion for progress.

Ernst Haeckel and the Social Darwinists—Alfred Ploetz, Ludwig Gumplowicz, Wilhelm Schallmayer, Alexander

Tille and others—in turn applied Darwin's agonistic theory to society and culture.[12] Thanks to Darwin, competitive selection had come to be regarded as unassailable scientific knowledge. In order to understand the rise of Social Darwinism it is crucial to follow how the paradigm of competitive selection is transposed from society to nature and then back to society. Two positions emerge from the reception of Darwin. One school maintained that the sciences should be used as an instrument in order to change the world. Most scholars, from Engels to Bebel, who pleaded for this position were evolutionists and saw social conflict as teleological. On the other hand, Social Darwinists like Tille, Ploetz and de Lapouge, were pure selectionists who denied a *telos,* and held that, for structural reasons, similar conflicts would be perpetuated infinitely. They declared that science should only create the conditions for an *agon,* but must not interfere in it. Schallmayer demanded: "All cultural achievements, all social institutions, the law and customs of sexuality (including the composition of the family), the ordering of property and the economy, political organizations, religious institutions, the quality of ethical and scientific education, the development of technology, the administration of justice etc., must be viewed as equipment for the life-struggle."[13] Lyotard's position is similar; he wants to tear down all barriers which hinder the struggle between genres of discourse. All attempts at outside intervention in the structurally inevitable conflict are forbidden. Like most Social Darwinists, Lyotard is a pure selectionist. (The "*différend*" is undirected because language is not a homogeneous organism which follows a single *telos.*) Hence Lyotard has to face the same problem as the selectionists. They were able to describe the mechanism of selection very well, but could never explain why variations occur at all—a decisive weakness which Darwin himself openly acknowledged. The evolutionists, in contrast, could provide a teleological vindication for variability, because they attributed ends to natural selection. As we saw above, Lyotard cannot demonstrate the multiformity and variability of language. It is symptomatic that he must confess in **The Postmodern Condition** that one can only marvel at the diversity of narrative and of scientific knowledge, as at the diversity of plants or animals.[14]

Lyotard shares other important assumptions with the Social Darwinists. Superfluity and variability cause an agonistic selection which allows only a few strong variants to survive and suppresses a great number of weaker ones. Both Lyotard and the Social Darwinists take the same attitude of neutrality towards conflicts, which can be observed and analysed, at best promoted, but in no circumstances evaluated or interfered in. Criticism is ruled out because any tenable position must itself have been won in struggle and can command only limited assent as it is always, quite literally, open to attack.

Apart from these general parallels, it is striking that the Social Darwinists even anticipated Lyotard's concept of language. The principle of *agon* is extended to all cultural phenomena. It is important to see that cultural rivalry does not depend only on the physiological struggle for life of its combatants. There are combats within culture itself which are not controlled by individuals. Some 19th century linguists tried to apply Darwinism to language.[15] This school saw language as consisting of dissimilar spontaneous organisms which compete with each other. Darmesteter, for example, stated that there is a "*concurrence vitale*" between the words of a language,[16] and Schleicher compared the pedigree of the Indo-European languages to that of animals and plants.[17] He concluded that, in language as in nature, there is a struggle for life between different species, some of which decline while others flourish. This school of linguists also found it very hard to give reasons for the heterogeneity and competitive structure of language. They put forward the thesis that the history of language was initiated by a great number of ambitious and antagonistic primitive languages. This thesis was also used to strengthen polygenesis in anthropology. The Social Darwinists believed that mankind is not descended from a single primitive race (or one couple as in biblical history) but from several conflicting races. Ludwig Gumplowicz stated: "Today polygenesis is regarded as less controversial in linguistics than its counterpart, polygenesis in anthropology."[18] In an interesting chapter on the multiple origins of primitive languages and cults, Gumplowicz comes to the following conclusion: "We have shown that in all likelihood mankind is descended from countless primitive tribes, and that as a result of increasing commerce and intercourse of a largely inimical and mutually exploitative character, more and more tribes are forced out of the arena, which they did not have the strength to defend, while others expand and maintain their hold on the blood-drenched earthly battlefield. Languages present us with an analogous drama. Men start to express their ideas in countless primitive languages. With increasing commerce and intercourse some languages disappear without a trace or are written off as 'dead,' while others survive and expand their territory ever wider and achieve ever greater power."[19] This struggle is not limited to the interrelation among different languages. The conflict is no less prevalent within individual languages. "As seen by linguists, the events which take place for men on the historical stage at large, and obtrusively determine the relation between languages are enacted within the microcosm of every single language. Each primitive language is a struggle for life among roots and forms. Most are defeated, while the survivors grow stronger in spirit and meaning."[20]

The terminology may be outmoded, but Lyotard's theory of "*parler est combattre*" is here in all its essentials.[21] Schleicher stated that language consists of living organisms which are autonomous. There is in Lyotard's writings a similar tendency to give language an ontological status. Welsch has recently deplored this tendency and criticized Lyotard for regarding even a shower of rain as a linguistic phenomenon.[22] Just as Lyotard applies linguistic attributes to nature, linguists influenced by Darwin described language in terms of nature. Schleicher grounds this explicitly in a monism which treats thought and matter as a unity.[23] Darmesteter, Haeckel and most Social Darwinists used monism in order to justify their applying natural selection to society, culture and language. Lyotard's position might also be called monistic. In contrast to the Social Darwinists, he starts with linguistics: the nameless conflicting forces which work through language shape the world as a whole. But, for both, the concept of language as a medium for reflection and communication between individuals is exposed as an anthropocentric fiction, while the self is seen as an epiphenomenon. Language should be dehumanized. The self is governed by the presiding principle of struggle, to which it also owes everything which in its vanity it believes that it creates. Man is convicted of a hubristic belief that nature and language are at his service, dethroned from the summit of creation, and for his law is substituted the eternal law of the *agon* which demotes him to what Tille calls *"eine Welle im Daseinsstrom,"* a ripple in the current of being.

Lyotard, Nietzsche and the Social Darwinists try to escape a cultural situation they regard as decadent by affirming life as struggle. Man must be liberated from the chains of the old order—Christianity, humanism, enlightenment rationality—which restrain the agonistic imperative. (Without war the world stagnates; on this Lyotard and his predecessors agree.) Even the memory of such obsolete faiths should be eradicated and a new skepticism cultivated. Paganism is lauded in ardent tones. The old narratives, *"grands récits"* like the biblical genesis, have to be deconstructed: Haeckel wrote an alternative natural history of creation in which the omnipotent creator is replaced by anonymous forces of nature.[24]

Legitimacy in state, the sciences and law, can be attached only to what promotes unrestricted dissension. For Lyotard, prevailing "narratives" like Christianity or the enlightenment myth of the emancipation of mankind have lost all power to legislate; such *"grands récits"* disintegrate into descriptive, prescriptive, denotative, narrative and other elements which issue an immediate declaration of war. Consensus cannot provide legitimacy because it violates the diversity of genres of discourse. In the postmodern condition, radical dissension and paralogism are the only legitimate maneuvers: i.e., in the academy, those moves which most successfully subvert the hegemony of the experts. They respond by ignoring the threat of innovation. Consensus forms a bulwark of the weak majority in the defense of their institutional hierarchy against the strength of minority assault.

We now can clarify to which agonistic tradition Lyotard adheres. He explicitly criticizes the Marxist class struggle, the most important 19th century theory of conflict, because it subscribes to the enlightenment myth of emancipation. In its speculative discourse it postulates one unified human subject—which both Lyotard and Social Darwinists like Gumplowicz think impossible.[25] Furthermore, in Marxism the struggle has a historical *telos,* it is not necessarily perpetuated infinitely. This was also the position of the evolutionist interpreters of Darwin. They—as much as the Marxists—insisted that philosophers must not only interpret the world but change it. The right-wing interpreters of Darwin, in contrast, maintained that the life-struggle never reaches conclusion and that any intervention in the mechanism of selection is pernicious. The post-modern "anything goes" becomes a re-encounter with the Social Darwinists' *"laissez faire."* The Social Darwinists found themselves in a compromising dialectic of liberalism and coercion when they sought to establish the social conditions for unrestricted competition. The post-modernist repudiation of all limitation, even the accepted limits of argument, can take the open road to totalitarianism; Lyotard's equality of all discourses, whether rational or racist, cannot be politically institutionalized without transformation into terror. A philosophy whose sincere aim is to combat terror would then have failed.

Notes

1. See Wilfried Barner, *Barockrhetorik. Untersuchungen zu ihren geschichtlichen Grundlagen* Tubingen: M. Niemeyer Verlag, 1970), p. 89.

2. Jean-François Lyotard, *The Postmodern Condition: A Report on Knowledge,* trans. by Geoff Bennington and Brian Massumi (Minneapolis: University of Minnesota Press, 1984), p. 10.

3. *Ibid.,* pp. 60-61.

4. See Jean-François Lyotard, *The differend: Phrases in Dispute,* trans. by Georges Van Den Abbeele (Minneapolis: University of Minnesota Press, 1988).

5. *Ibid.,* p. 12.

6. Ludwig Wittgenstein, *Philosophical Investigations,* trans. by G.E.M. Anscombe (Oxford: Blackwell, 1958), p. 32e (translation modified).

7. *Ibid,* p. 49e.

8. Friedrich Nietzsche, "Homer's Contest. Preface to an Unwritten Book," in *Early Greek Philosophy and Other Essays,* trans. by Maximilian A. Mügge (London: Allen & Unwin.1911), pp. 49-62.

9. Lyotard, *The Postmodern Condition, op. cit.,* p. 10.

10. Nietzsche ("Homer's Contest," trans. by Maximilian A. Mügge in *Complete Works* Vol. 2 [London: T.N. Fowlis, 1911]), quoted in Lyotard, *The Postmodern Condition, op cit.,* p 10.

11. Thomas Robert Malthus, *First Essay on Population 1798* (London: Macmillan, 1966), pp. 11-14.

12. My outline of the development of Social Darwinism is based on the following literature: Günter Altner, ed., *Der Darwinismus. Die Geschichte einer Theorie* (Darmstadt: Wissenschaftliche Buchgesellschaft, 1981). Peter J. Bowler, "Malthus, Darwin, and the Concept of Struggle," *Journal of the History of Ideas,* Vol. 37 (1976), pp. 631-50. Hedwig Conrad Martius, *Utopien der Menschenzüchtung. Der Sozialdarwinismus und seine Folgen* (Munich: Kosel Verlag, 1955). Yvette Conry, *L'introduction du Darwinisme en France au XIXe siècle* (Paris: J. Vrin, 1974). Gertrude Himmelfarb, *Victorian Minds*

(New York: Knopf, 1968), pp. 314-32. Hannsjoachim W. Koch, *Der Sozialdarwinismus. Seine Genese und sein Einfluβ auf das imperialistische Denken* (Munich: Beck Verlag, 1973). Georg Lukács, *The Destruction of Reason,* trans. by Peter Palmer (London: Merlin, 1980). Günter Mann, ed., *Biologismus im 19. Jahrhundert* (Stuttgart: Enke, 1973). James Allen Rogers, "Darwinism and Social Darwinism," *Journal of the History of Ideas,* Vo. 33 (1972), pp. 265-80. Michael Ruse, "Social Darwinism: The Two Sources," *Rivista di Filosofia,* Vol. 73 (1982), pp. 36-52. Hans Günter Zmarzlik, "Der Sozialdarwinismus in Deutschland als geschichtliches Problem," *Vierteljahreshefte für Zeitgeschichte,* Vol. 11 (1963), pp. 246-73.

13. Wilhelm Schallmayer, "Traditionswerte. Übertragung des Selektionsgedankens auf nicht vererbbare und nur traditionsfähige Errungenschaften," *Der Darwinismus,* ed. G. Altner, p. 110 (English translation from German original by A. Weber and M. Pedroz).

14. Lyotard, *The Postmodern Condition, op. cit.,* p. 26.

15. Very little has been written on this school of linguistics. The best introduction is Yvette Conry, *L'introduction du Darwinisme en France, op. cit.,* pp. 91-107.

16. Arsène Darmesteter, *La vie des mots étudiée dans leurs significations* (Paris: Delagrave, 1889), pp. 134ff.

17. August Schleicher, "The Darwinian Theory and the Science of Language," in *Linguistics and Evolutionary Theory: Three Essays,* trans. by Alex V.W. Bikkers, ed. by Konrad Koerner (Philadelphia: John Benjamins Publishing Co., 1983), pp. 1-69.

18. Ludwig Gumplowicz, *Der Rassenkampf. Soziologische Untersuchungen* (Innsbruck Wagner'sche Universität, 1883), p. 87f.

19. *Ibid.,* p. 136.

20. *Ibid.*

21. Nietzsche chooses a similar decentralized viewpoint: "Even in the domain of the inorganic an atom of force is concerned only with its neighborhood: distant forces balance one another. Here is the kernel of the perspective view and why a living creature is 'egocentric' through and through." Nietzsche, *The Will to Power,* trans. by Walter Kaufmann and R.J. Hollingdale (New York: Vintage Books, 1968), p. 340.

22. Wolfgang Welsch, *Unsere postmoderne Moderne* (Weinheim: Acta Humaniora, 1987), p. 253; see Lyotard, *Le différend, op cit.,* p. 203.

23. August Schleicher, "The Darwinian Theory," *op. cit.,* pp. 20-21.

24. Ernst Haeckel, *Natürliche Schöpfungsgeschichte* (Berlin: G. Reimer, 1902).

25. See Ludwig Gumplowicz, *Grundriβ der Soziologie* (Vienna: Manzsche k.u.k. Hof-Verlags-u. Universitäts-Buchhandlung, 1885), p. 217: "Whatever we have learned about social development has invariably been partial, local and transient; we have already stated that if we have no concept of the development of mankind as a unified whole it is because we cannot have a coherent and complete notion of its subject."

Julian Pefanis (essay date 1991)

SOURCE: "Lyotard and the Jouissance of Practical Reason," in *Heterology and the Postmodern: Bataille, Baudrillard, and Lyotard,* Duke University Press, 1991, pp. 85-101.

[*In the following excerpt, Pefanis traces Lyotard's career from Marxism to Postmodernism with an emphasis of his deconstruction of Marx and his valorization of libidinal intensities in* Économie libidinale.]

The enemy and accomplice of writing, its Big Brother (or rather its O'Brien), is language (langue), by which I mean not only the mother tongue, but the entire heritage of words, of the feats and works of what is called the literary culture. One writes against language, but necessarily with it. To say what it already knows how to say is not writing. One wants to say what it does not know how to say, and what it should be able to say. One violates it, one seduces it, one introduces into it an idiom which it had not known. But when that same desire to be able to say something other than what has been already said—has disappeared, and when language is experienced as impenetrable and inert rendering vain all writing, then it is called Newspeak.

—Jean-François Lyotard, *Le Postmoderne expliqué aux enfants*

The struggle against totalitarianism—against totalitarianisms—has taken and takes many forms. The forms of this resistance are contingent upon the techniques and forces deployed by the despotic organizations, the big brothers. As political totalitarianism gives way to complex new forms—technoscientific, commercial, and lingusitic dominance of modes of life and everyday life—so new means of combating them must be invented and thought. For Jean-François Lyotard they are conditions that preclude a recourse to common sense and everyday language,[1] since the events of the twentieth century, for which Auschwitz and Hiroshima stand out as horrifying beacons, have done something more than delay the progress of emancipation set in train by the Enlightenment: they have clouded its very ideals. For Lyotard it is not a case of abandoning the project of modernism—which is the charge leveled by Habermas against him[2]—but of the project having been liquidated by such events. The postmodern (or postmodernity) is instituted and initiated by a new species of historical crime, that of "populocide."[3]

Lyotard is, therefore, skeptical and resistant toward simplifications and "simplifying slogans," resistant too toward the call and desire for "the restoration of sure values,"[4] by which he means the call to renew the project of modernism (*le project moderne*). Slogans and simplifications are the product of doctrine and the doctrinaire mind which is incapable, and unwilling, to accept the singularity of the event which irrupts into the order of "fixed meaning." And yet the experience of art and writing in modernism is antidoctrinal, and, for Lyotard, has borne witness to the irruption of meaning, to the irruption of the event, no matter how lowly or earth-shattering. Thus Lyotard affirms writing which, like Winston Smith's journal, bears witness to the infamy of bureaucratic Newspeak; he affirms that we must be "guerrillas of love" against the code of feelings: "The labor of writing is akin to the work of love, since it inscribes the trace of an initiatory event in language, and thus offers to share it—and if not a share of knowledge, then a share of the feeling which it can and must hold as communal."[5]

By way of introduction, . . . let us say that the problematic of writing is by no means surpassed in Lyotard's theoretical propositions, and occupies a central, even metacritical position in his oeuvre (his Text). It is a position that might be described as an aesthetic which, in correlating the practices of art and writing as resistance, defines his postmodernism as a direct continuation of the radical hypotheses of modernism.[6] The purpose of this chapter is threefold; to contextualize Lyotard's discourse on the postmodern; to place Lyotard's thought in relation to the tradition of discourse that we have examined thus far in this book, and particularly in relation to the transgressive text; and to specify, via the analysis of a particular text, Lyotard's relationship to the thought of Jean Baudrillard. In the opening chapter use was made of Lyotard's well-known and often repeated discussion of the crisis of the meta-narratives[7] in order to initiate a discourse on the fate of history in the post-Hegelian era in French theory. Against this historical horizon of crisis several themes have been outlined. In the interest of a certain reciprocity, it is now necessary to return to that crisis and to place it in the context of Lyotard's own theoretical development.

Such a contextualization will, perforce, demonstrate both deep continuities within Lyotard's work, and equally, in the most recent texts,[8] the tendency toward a style that results in an aphoristic discontinuity reminiscent of Nietzsche's writings. The rapid dissemination of Lyotard's later texts in English also provides a historical contingency; since his interventions are being recognized on questions concerning postmodernism, desire theory, language theory, and post-Marxism—including an exchange with the Habermasian version of critical theory.[9] (This exchange itself attests to the condition of transnationalization of contemporary theoretical discourse.)

In light of this complex field of debate, the aim of this present chapter is not to engage in a close analysis of the positions which have been ranged for and against the work

of Lyotard in English language criticism. The reader familiar with the reception of Lyotard's work (and the reception of French post-structuralism generally) will be aware that some of the finest theoretical minds in the anglophone world have turned their pens and energy to the critical examination of these texts. Some of this response and reaction is extremely provocative and significant in its own right; postmodernism is the object of a fairly intense contestation, and sometimes the locus for the desire for revenge, vilification, and vindication.[10] The confession here is that, while a comparative analysis of the relative merits of competing epistemological systems is an important continuing project, its appearance here would be premature, and in a sense dangerous, even vaguely pompous. Rather my aim is to continue the narration of the heterodoxical tradition of French thought, this cartography of a ruptured and abyssal territory.

We have, throughout this work, noted certain features of the landscape and the tracks connecting them; these features would be those writers and theorists, the "thinking heads" and intellectual capitals invested in the conceptual labor of producing new figures, of discourse, for which the gift economy, transgression, the general economy, and symbolic exchange serve as representatives. These figures have been discussed in the context of several themes—the anthropological critique, the theories of writing (écriture), and the theories of representation. In addition to an examination of Lyotard's crisis with the metanarratives, the desire now is to situate his thought without fixing it within this ensemble, in order to grant it a measure of free play.

Bataille's thought provides a context for this situation. When Foucault imagined a new era of transgression he suggested that its hopeful beginnings were readable in the "calcinated roots" of Bataille's thought. Transgression, and the thought for which it was a rhetorical figure, would ultimately come to replace the dialectical thought of contradiction. Transgression is the game of limits: a play at the conventional frames of language, at the border of disciplines, and across the line of taboo; in writing, transgression involves the sacrifice of signs, for Bataille a potlatch of the genres of writing and the forms of authorial sovereignty. Bataille wrote, "*il faut le système Et il faut l'excés,*"[11] in an expressive formula which indicates the line of taboo which the transgression seeks to cross and then to recross. Transgression maintains the taboo, since without it it would lose its fundamental violence. A society without taboos would be outside human society. And the taboo also maintains transgression, since the concept of a limit, such as a taboo, is only possible on the condition of its infringement: an unpassable limit would require no social constraint to prevent its crossing. Transgression is very close, therefore, to the figure of the Aufhebung, in which the contradiction which is surpassed is sublated as a trace and readable in the new structural arrangement of the dialectic. There is an irony in Foucault's prediction.

It is hardly a large conceptual leap to suggest that what Lyotard calls "impiety" can be related to the "method of obstinacy" described by Klossowski apropos Bataille, and that Lyotard's attempts to subvert and to intervene in the systems of thought, theoretical discourse, and belief systems owe something to the example of Bataille.[12] Now if Bataille, in following the example of Nietzsche and de Sade, exulted in the profanation of religious beliefs and bourgeois morality, even if this was to remain ultimately religious, then it might be said that Lyotard's transgression is directed at that sphere which is held to be an heir of religion: political faith. Perhaps in this sense Lyotard's text remains political.

In the preceding chapter we noted the outlines of Baudrillard's vehement anti-productivism. In a sense, Lyotard's thought might be opposed to Baudrillard's as a nonpositive affirmation of the productive system. It is important to be clear about this, since when they are lumped together under the rubric of postmodernism (see Guattari, "The Postmodern Dead End"),[13] a level of violence is delivered to their texts. Whilst linked at a thematic level, in terms of a "critique" of criticism (and in this way post-Marxist), the texts of the two writers, particularly those produced in the 1970s, are, nonetheless, opposed in several respects. The most important of these is over this question of production, expressible in terms of a contest between the concept of "symbolic exchange" and the "analytic of desire" employed by Lyotard under the title of the "libidinal economy." But before we turn to this arena, let us first examine the context of Lyotard's development as a theorist.

Trained as a philosopher, Lyotard published his first book, *Phénoménologie* in 1954; it was not until 1971 that he published his next book, *Discours, figure,* being a version of his *doctorat d'état* on the subject of psychoanalysis and art. Since 1971 a very large number of books have been published over a spectrum of theoretical concerns: art theory, psychoanalysis, philosophy, and political and social theory. A glance at the bibliography explains something here; in the seventeen years separating the first two books Lyotard's output is in the form of journal articles which are largely concerned with the Algerian struggle for independence from colonial rule, (predominantly published in the review *Socialisme ou barbarie*); there are also several critical pieces in *L'Art vivant,* passing reference to Marxist and psychoanalytic theory, and a critique of Lévi-Straussian structuralism ("The Indians don't cook flowers").[14] But what seems to dominate in this period is the connection with *Socialisme ou barbarie,* a militant Trotskyist tendency which represented, along with other splinter groups, a tradition of non-PCF Marxism and socialism in France. The group was committed to militancy and to workers' power, committed thus to theoretical practice defined as praxis philosophy. Lyotard wrote in this period, in a deeply productivist formula: "Man is the work of his works."[15]

In this context we can assert that the incredulity which Lyotard expresses toward the narrative of Marx, the emancipation of the subject of history, and the historical accomplishment of socialism, was by no means so sublime as

The Postmodern Condition might suggest. After two decades of praxis philosophy, Lyotard had, in a manner, lost his belief in the revolutionary program represented by *Socialisme ou barbarie.* Why?

This is a complex question, since in part we must consider Lyotard's militancy against the background of a countervailing tendency toward Nietzsche which had taken hold in contemporary philosophy—in the work of Foucault and Klossowski, but perhaps above all, in the work of Deleuze.[16] But as Lyotard himself avers, he is not above fashion; he is a philosopher *dans le vent:* phenomenology, praxis philosophy, Nietzscheanism, postmodernism, language games, desire theory—Lyotard is an opportunist, in a way a *promiscuous* thinker.

Vincent Descombes, in *Modern French Philosophy,* argues that the militant Lyotard had availed himself of revolutionary theory that recounted the story of the contradiction of the mode of production; a contradiction which would lead either to war (or generalized fascism) or—through the mobilization of a latent revolutionary potential at the point of capital's crisis—to socialism. But, according to Descombes,[17] Lyotard made two discoveries: first, that the truth which he thought himself to be speaking was in fact "no more than a moral ideal. . . . It was therefore not *the truth* at all, but only the expression of a *desire for truth.*"[18] Second, that this collapse of the truth referent of revolutionary Marxism was not the result of a movement in a philosophical game, but rather the result of an analysis of concrete historical conditions.

These discoveries can, however, still be generally related to the critique of Soviet state socialism generated by the *Socialisme ou barbarie* group.[19] The major thrust of their analysis developed from a perception that the character of Stalinism was counterrevolutionary because it subverted the Bolshevik ideal of world socialism. Therefore, it followed that the Communist parties in the West which followed the Moscow line participated in the travesty. The perception was itself grounded in Cornelius Castoriadis's critical analysis of the mode of production in the putatively socialist economy of the USSR.[20] In a complex argument Castoriadis claimed to demonstrate that this socialist state, which acted as a concrete reference for socialists throughout the world, was in fact involved in a betrayal. Far from following Marx's formulae for the equitable redistribution of the surplus, the state was, in effect, still involved in the construction of new forms of exploitation and domination in the sphere of political economy. The mechanism, and beneficiary, of this domination was, of course, the Stalinist bureaucracy. In Lyotard's terms this organization incanted the narrative of emancipation while at the same time setting itself above the terms which it narrated, above the worker-citizens, above the idea of the people from which it drew its legitimation. Alas, was Althusser tragically correct in asserting the existence of ideology in socialism? This narrative of emancipation was ruthlessly enforced by a paranoiac organization which could brook no counter-chant, no counter-narrative. The evidence of this, for Lyotard, was the historical suppression of what he had come to consider as a vital sphere of liberationist thought: art and literature.

For the disenchanted militant who had regarded theoretical practice as an important source of the critique of capitalist totality, it was an intolerable and hypocritical situation. For Lyotard it revealed a pious morality which inherited the Stalinist condemnation of art and literature as elitist practices. It was a morality which authorized a search for the *salvation* and a *revenge* on the guilty. In this sense, the morality of militant Marxism began to represent, for Lyotard, a thoroughly messianic religious metaphor. And as though this was not a bitter enough pill to swallow, it had to be washed down by the experience of the events of May 1968. These events, to a certain way of thinking, demonstrated the near-total failure of the organized militant left to participate in the ludic insurrection of the May Days. These organizations had failed to anticipate the sectors of contemporary society from which the rebellious urge would spring, and were unprepared for the scenodramatic effects of the critique of the spectacle. The situationists had been altogether closer to the mark. All in all, it was a very bad month for theoretical practice.

In 1964 Lyotard had split with *Socialisme ou barbarie* on questions of theory and practice. This break, combined with a similar break from Freudian psychoanalysis, conspired to set Lyotard adrift, hence the title of the collection of essays of 1973: *Dérive à partir de Marx et Freud (Adrift from Marx and Freud).*[21] In this work Lyotard attempts to specify his relationship to the central practice and methodology of Marxist theory: the critique. Lyotard writes: "If reason, which has been handed over to the air-conditioned totalitarianism of the very disputatious end of this century, is not to be relied upon, then its great tool, its very mainspring, its provision of infinite progress, its fertile negativity, its pains and toiling i.e. critique—should not be given any credit either."[22] Reason, critique, power—they are all one to Lyotard. To criticize is to know better—but this critical relationship can only operate in the sphere of knowledge, and hence in the sphere of power. We have come across this critical crisis before, though not in identical terms, in the theory of the heterogeneous as expounded by Bataille. His mystical *expérience* of thinking and exceeding thought at the same time, lurching at the edge of the abyss of *unreason* by activating the heterogeneous elements, stands outside the critical relation. The rejection of the critical relation is also found in Baudrillard's critique of the critical mirror—the reflection of capital in Marxism as the formal accomplishment of identity in the thought of production.

When the name Lyotard becomes hitched up to an idea and an entire problematic of the postmodern (a term which avoids the specificity of postmoder*nity* or postmoder*nism*), it becomes possible to suggest that the "crisis of the meta-narratives" can be read as a narration of Lyotard's own crisis with the meta-narratives of Freud and Marx, and a type of loss of political faith. The major text on postmod-

ernism, *The Postmodern Condition,* is in many ways atypical in relation to Lyotard's other works. Published under commission from the Council of Universities of Quebec in 1979, and subtitled **"Report on Knowledge,"**[23] the work is a sustained analysis, among other things, of the conditions of the legitimation of knowledge in contemporary science, a discourse thus following in the wake of the new physics, and indeterminacy. This analysis focuses, and even exaggerates, the relationship between the narrative and knowledge, and Lyotard devotes much energy to the analysis of the pragmatics of speech acts, since it is within their structure that conditions of authority of modern science are to be found in the philosophical meta-narratives such as Kant's transcendental idea of freedom and the potential perfectability of the rational, purposive subject of the enlightenment, or in Hegel's culmination of world history, and Marx's inversion of the same. The legitimacy of science is thus based on the deferred idea of the "promised community."[24] Perhaps above all others, it is this narrative of the promised community, which "remains beyond reach like an horizon," which is fractured and liquidated by the irruption of the event—for which Auschwitz serves as such a potent sign. "Reason" in the service of the idea of humanity, in the service of its achievable end through history, stands crossed and double-crossed at the threshold of *post-history* by the signs of its historical failure. Lyotard writes:

> The enthusiasm aroused by the French Revolution represented for Kant an eminent example of the unforeseen opportunities which such an event can grant us. In it he discovered the "historical sign" of a moral disposition in humanity, and the index of a progress towards an ultimate goal for the species. If our feelings are not the same as Kant's it is because we are confronted by a multiplicity of historical signs—in which the names of Auschwitz and Kolyma, Budapest 1956 and such as it is, May 68, are evoked in their heterogeneity—each emphasizing in their way the dispersion of ends and the decline of Ideas established in the Enlightenment.[25]

The critique of "semiological reason" thus rejects the positivities of science and the enlightenment ushered in by Kant's thought, and stands, before the collapse of their ideas, in the condition of incredulity. One is in the postmodern if and when one is incredulous; to be reductive, to be incredulous is the condition of the postmodernist.

Lyotard got it drifting—from philosophy to militancy into art via psychoanalysis, back through Wittgenstein on his way to the Greeks, ethics, and paganism. Lyotard revels in a heterogeneous experience of knowledge—leading him to privilege the little narrative which proliferate in the space of the fallen idols, in the demise of transhistorical and transcendental values. Thus also a Nietzscheanism which reaches quite a fervor:

> Here is a course of action: harden, worsen and accelerate decadence. Adopt the perspective of active nihilism, exceed the mere recognition—be it depressive or admiring—of the destruction of all values. Become more and more incredulous. Push decadence further still and

accept, for instance, to destroy the belief in truth under all its forms.[26]

The situationist, Raoul Vaneigem, in *The Revolution of Everyday Life,* repeats Nietzsche's description of the difference between active and passive nihilism. The passive nihilist believes simply in nothing, and passive nihilism is an overture to conformism. On the other hand, the active nihilist "criticises the causes of disintegration by speeding up the process. *Active nihilism is pre-revolutionary: passive nihilism is counter-revolutionary.* And most people waltz tragi-comically between the two."[27] Lyotard would, in this sense, have to be classified as a pre-revolutionary thinker.

The game of drifting, however, dissimulated certain intensities in Lyotard's text—up to the point of their violent eruption in the work of 1974, *Economie libidinale,* a work which Lyotard later describes as a "scandal" and "devoid" of dialectics in the Aristotlean sense of the term, "because it is all rhetoric, working entirely at the level of persuasion."[28]

A difficult and refractory text, *Economie libidinale* nonetheless represents a crucial text to the unfolding of Lyotard's own narrative. (The relative absence of reference to this work in English-speaking discourse is understandable and regrettable; taken as a whole it is an enormous work and written in a highly idiomatic style, and thus not easily rendered into English. It is, if you like, a Deleuzian text in the sense of being schizophrenic and nonnegotiable in a poetic way: the reader is left little room to move except in the direction of the flow. What it lacks in the clarity of its outcome is replaced by the intensity of its expression, its irrepressible antagonism and agonism.[29]) Lyotard does allow, however, that the work can be taken as a series of theses whilst admitting their inconsistency, eschewing the manipulation of the reader in the Platonic dialogue. These would rather be the ends of reason, making sense at the expense of experience, in the sense of *expérience,* in this instance in the name of the *intense* sign read at the surface of the social, *la grande pellicule.*[30] (*Pellicule* read here in both its senses: as a membrane capable of transferring here and obstructing there the flows and investments of a *desire* which is of the order of production, the libidinal economy; and as a photographic film surface, a screen or gel, a thick holographic plate capable of registering the multiple traces of this movement of desire as a *phantasm.*)[31]

What we have here, in the framework of a polemic and contestation is a fusion of a Freudian theory of drives with a Marxist political economy—applied as an "analytic of desire," a deconstruction of the intense sign lodged in the text of desire, or the desiring text. What I would now like to do is to present, to re-present, an example of this operation—bearing in mind Lyotard's own caution in terms of the articulation of theses. While the libidinal economy is primarily concerned with texts, both as a theory of writing and as an analytic of texts, it can also be applied to any psychic apparatus, be it a written text or a work of art. In this respect, the libidinal economy has an aesthetic dimension, since it evolved in Lyotard's thought (writing) in relation to his early studies of psychoanalysis and art.[32]

Before we turn to the analysis of Marx's text in the ***Economie libidinale***—chosen for its thematic and methodological content—we need to turn briefly to Freud's general theory of the libido, which he characterizes as the sexual drive. This meaning, as the sexual drive, is always present in Freud both in the noun and the adjectival "libidinal." However, there is a second sense expressed by the difference and *différance* of the terms libido and *libidinal relations.* For the child, as Freud tells us in *Group Psychology and the Analysis of the Ego,*[33] the sexual drive is initially directed at one or the other parent. When eventually it becomes obvious to the child that this drive will lead nowhere, because it transgresses that fundamental prohibition and the symbolic code of the father, then the child will produce affection instead. "Libidinal" thus refers to the affection which is produced in the inhibition of the sexual instincts. This theory is, however, more interesting in terms of its dysfunctional aspects, in terms of a theory of perversion in which the abnormal arrangement is one in which sexual attraction is expressed for those who are despised, while affection is reserved for those who are (merely) respected. This dysfunctional sense of the libidinal is, as I presently argue, of some consequence for Lyotard. In the same text, Freud remarks on the lack of criticism which is directed toward the loved one, and which he calls *idealization.*[34] This is particularly developed in terms of the psychoanalysis of the leader: the affection which the members of a group express toward a leader, and the feelings the leader has toward her or himself (the narcissistic type) or, more rarely, the feelings of the leader for the group (Jesus), are all likewise libidinal.

Therefore, when the analytic of desire is applied to the Text of Marx, we can see that for the militant Lyotard there will be powerful effects to witness, particularly in terms of the dysfunctional psychoanalytic arrangement of libidinal relations. But we must not stop here without an idea of what animates the model, of what gives it a pretension to the economic. This is another Freudian motion found in the later theory of drives in the "Metapsychological Essays."[35] For Lyotard these works, which introduced the death-drive and the Nirvana principle, permitted Freud's theory of a libido "to escape from thermodynamism and mechanism": his theory of the unconscious would avoid closing in on itself as a theoretical system. The Nirvana principle remained an expression of the undecidability of the dualism of the principle of life and the principle of death. "Freud brilliantly said that the death drive works silently in the rumor of Eros."[36]

Once again, in order to grasp Lyotard's understanding of an economic psychic function, we need to refer to his work on psychoanalysis and art—which will demonstrate the way in which he plays the later Freud against the young Freud in the grip of the representational model. From this analysis will arise the replacement of the metaphor by the metonym, which is a legacy of the Saussurian theory of communication. The sign becomes, in Lyotard's analysis, a metonym of substitution, rather than a screen on which the subjective reference is simulated and dissimulated, and for which the sign serves as a substitute. This is very close to the way that Lyotard conceives exchange in the discourse of political economy; signification is deferred, interminable, "meaning is never present in flesh and blood"—so that even the materiality of the sign is insignificant and not valuable in itself. Lyotard calls this process dematerialization and relates it to Adorno's work on serialism. Material in serialism is not valuable in itself, but in the relationship of one term to the next. The rejection of the Port-Royal semiology—a "Platonism of the theory of ideas"—is thus related to the privilege of the libidinal relations and libidinal economy over the libido and the theory of sexual drives, and to the condition of this dematerialization. This is a fundamentally modern phenomenon, and is not simply the equivalent of capital in the realm of sensibility; it is the fragmentation and abstraction of signs and the fabrication of new ones. Recurrence and repetition are installed as basic traits within the system, and a new region, "a pulsional strip"[37] is colonized: the sculptural, political, erotic, linguistic—"offering the libido new occasions for intensifications."

The problem with Freud's aesthetic theory, explains Lyotard in the essay, **"Psychanalyse et peinture,"**[38] was that he (Freud) had privileged the subject of the work of art over its plastic support which, in the process of mimesis, is rendered transparent to the inaccessible scene behind it. In a further process, one discovers a latent content dissimulated in the object represented: the trace or silhouette of a form which is determinant in the painter's unconscious. Put simply, for Lyotard, Freud's schema made it impossible to analyze anything but the representational painting or work of art. Impossible, therefore, the analysis of the nonrepresentational painting in which "the traditions and space of the QuattroCento tumbled into ruins" and in which the function of representation, so crucial to Freud's theory, is rendered insignificant. To address the lacuna in Freud, Lyotard decides to "read Freud against himself," by availing himself of the theory of drives and the libidinal economy. Lyotard expresses great hope for the new analytic arrangement, for it might free the object from a dubious psychoanalysis without a subject. It might also free aesthetic theory from its Platonism in which the object takes the form of a mimetic representation in the unconscious modeled as a screen or palimpsest and interpreted according to the law of the father and his symbolic code. The object, which is now free to be itself, can become the locus "of libidinal operations engendering an inexhausible polymorphy." Lyotard muses "maybe the hypothesis should be extended to other objects, objects to produce and consume, ones to sing and to listen to, objects to love."[39]

So it is in this context of a disengagement from Freud, from the Freud of the Leonardo studies at any rate, that the discussion can now turn to an aspect of the *Economie libidinale,* itself a vast psychic arrangement where Lyotard gives rein to his affections and disaffections. Specifically, I would like to turn to what for my purposes is the central piece of the work; **"The Desire named Marx."** Three reasons can be advanced: the essay gathers up, in an intensely rhetorical way, Lyotard's orientation in respect to Marx and the militant legacy he left behind; the essay serves to highlight Lyotard's own deconstructive practice of writing the impious by applying the analytic of desire, with its *topoi* of repetition, delay, and ambivalence to the text of Marx, thereby giving form to his incredulity before the latter's meta-narration; the essay establishes Lyotard's negative relation to (actually another nonpositive affirmation of) the thought of Jean Baudrillard.

The intention, declares Lyotard, is to "take Marx as though he were an author" full of affects, to take "his text as a folly and not as a theory," but without hate or devotion, to activate Marx's desire in the complex libidinal volume called his text. This desire is to be found not simply in the major theoretical works but equally in the margin "at the edge of the continent," in notes and letters, in *lapsi* and in the figures of repetition and delay in the machinery of theoretical analysis. To uncover this desire is also, in a sense, to uncover Lyotard's—the militant's desire to unmask the process of capital, the desire to bring an end to its reign. It is additionally thus the desire of the idealist to bring about a harmony of people in nature, the love of people for others, of men for women and vice versa. All very well and proper these desires we might say; what is the problem? The problem is that these are not the only figures of desire at play in the militant idealist.

To awaken these closeted desires, Lyotard caresses a metonym borrowed from Bataille—Marx's beard—a partial object in a Lacanian sense,[40] eroticized as a channel for the transference and counter-transference of libidinal energies, which is to say the object of a desire which is never directed toward the genital figure of *jouissance,* but toward a prolongation, through repetition and substitution, of an endless *deferral* of accomplishment.

The libidinal Marx is a polymorphous creature, a hermaphrodite with the "huge head of a warlike and quarrelsome man of thought" set atop the soft feminine contours of a "young Rhenish lover." So it is a strange bi-sexuated arrangement giving rise to a sort of ambivalence: the old man and the young woman, a monster in which femininity and virility exchange indiscernibly, "thus putting a stop to the reassuring difference of the sexes."[41]

Now the young woman Marx, who is called Alice (of Wonderland fame), is obfuscated by the perverse body of capital because it simultaneously occasions in her a revulsion and a strange fascination. She is the epicurean Marx, the Marx of the doctoral thesis, the aesthetic Marx. She claims a great love for this man of thought who offers to act as the Great Prosecutor of the crimes of capital. He is "assigned to the accusation of the perverts" and entrusted with the invention of a suitable lover, the proletariat, for the little Alice. The bi-sexed Marx is composed of stereotypes; the chaste young woman is a dreamer, dreaming of a reconciliation with her lover, while the man of thought is irascible and domineering. All the better to underline Lyotard's sentiment: this theoretical practice is really a very *male* thing,[42] as it concerns the formulation and the handing down of laws. Thus the beard is a metonym for the desire for law, the desire of the patriarch (Abraham, Moses, Marx, and Freud). And so Lyotard is led to say that theoretical practice is also about power, and not simply or not at all the power of the narrated proletariat, but the power which the militant assumes when the kid gloves are removed or, in default of the revolution, the power which is capitalized on behalf of the oppressed, which is also Alice's desire for something different and better.

So the beard belongs to the man of law, the prosecutor of the crimes of capital in the court of history. And yes, we agree, this is a great and important undertaking. Like a permanent crimes commission the lawyer works overtime in the British Museum, methodically considering every instantiation of capital's infamy. And it is a very beautiful thing, this dossier on the accused, and it attests to an admirable force of intellect and invention, itself passably libidinal. But lodged in the massive machinery of theoretical elaboration is a figure of delay. For here there is an aesthetic figure which delays the appearance of the text on capital: sentences become paragraphs, and paragraphs become chapters in the cancerous process of theoretical articulation. The *non finito* of the text is evidence, for Lyotard, that what is being produced is a work of art, in this case a text. A psychic apparatus.

But Alice is restless, and she wonders why it takes so long for the intellectual head to produce the healthy body of socialism in the obstetrics of capital. Why does the prosecutor take so long to sum up? What is it about theoretical discourse that makes it so interminable? It is, for Lyotard, because the result of this investment of time and grey matter can also be considered a *jouissance différé*, a jouissance of the same order as the jouissance of capital—which is as a channel for libidinal intensities in its prostitutive arrangement. What is more, capital will never give birth to the healthy infant of socialism because its body is barren, and Lyotard's (or is it Marx's?) task is phenomenological, to bear witness to the stillborn birth of socialism. Alice will be forever condemned to dream of that reconciliation, when she and her lover will meet in a different time and place.

Put another way, when something approaching the desired reality of the socialist body suddenly appeared on the scene, at the International of 1871, Marx was to write to his Russian translator, Danielson:

> It is doubtless useless to wait for the revision of the first chapter, as my time, for quite a time now, has been so taken up (and there is little prospect for amelioration) that I can no longer pursue my theoretical works. It is certain that one beautiful morning I will put a stop to it, but there are circumstances when one is morally obliged to be concerned with things much less attractive than study and theoretical research.

And Lyotard translates into the libidinal: "'Not very attractive,' says the equivocal prosecutor, 'your beautiful proleratian body, let us return our gaze once again to the unspeakable prostitute of capital.'"[43] So here is the reason for the delay and the cause of Alice's unhappiness. The old man is cheating on her, besotted as he is by the object which he loves to hate.

We could recall Alice's complaint: "Jam yesterday, jam tomorrow, never jam today!" And this too can be translated: "There was communism in the undivided social body of the 'primitive,' there will be a reunification of the alienated body in 'advanced' communism, but today there is only alienation from the memory and dream, the alienation which marks my body." Everybody is going to pay for this, Alice with her eternal misery, the prosecutor in a mass of words, articulations, and organized arguments—a theoretical torture with which he will martyr himself for Christ the proletariat, whose suffering will be the price of its redemption.[44]

Lyotard admits that it would be possible to use this religious metaphor in a critique of what is religious in Marx and in militancy; guilt, resentment, and morality. But he argues that this reunified body, which is to act as the reference for the sacrifice of the martyrs or the agony of the proletariat, has never and will never exist. In any event, what would be the use of another critique, even if it was to be an atheist one, and apart from the fact that there are already a hundred thousand of them? It would be to reinstall himself "armed with bi-focal lenses, like some sort of Lilliput . . . on a small piece of the giant's posterior."[45] Lyotard has something else in mind, "something beyond religion and atheism, something like the Roman parody."[46] He would rather evoke the pagan in all its heterogeneity, including the Clastrian idea of pagan society as primitive society, as society against the state, dialectically sublated in the parody—a joyous science of the social . . ."[47] So we come to the central propositions of the text: that all political economy is libidinal economy, and the symbolic exchange is likewise a libidinal economy. Lyotard argues that, in referring to a "prostitutive" arrangement of labor/capital, Marx presents a libidinal figure of the proletariat. Capital, the pimp, extracts value by alienating the erogenous zones of the prostitute, labor. In the analogy, the disconnected fragments of the body are linked to the fluid transformations and exchanges of intensities and signs in an endless account of in-comings and out-goings. Lyotard understands that while such a regime gives rise to exploitation, to the domination and regulation of the body, it also involves another species of jouissance, to what I have referred, in the title, as the jouissance of practical reason.

The ancient formula of Hegel—work or die, which means also die or die *in* or *of* work—is refuted by Lyotard:

> And if one does *this* [work], if one becomes a slave of the machine, the machine of the machine, the screwer

screwed by it, eight hours a day, twelve in the last century, is it because one is forced to do it, constrained because one clings to life? Death is not an alternative to *that,* it is part of it, it attests that there is a *jouissance* in it. The workless English did not become workers in order to survive, they were—buckle up tightly and spit on me later—delighted [*joui*] by the hysterical exhaustion, masochism, who knows, of *staying* in the mines, in the foundries and workshops, in hell. They were delighted in and by the insane destruction of their inorganic body which was of course imposed on them, delighted by the decomposition of their personal identity which the peasant tradition had constructed for them, delighted by the dissolution of families and villages and delighted by the new and monstrous anonymity of the suburbs and the pubs in the morning and evening.[48]

In the libidinal economy there is thus an affection for the prostitutive arrangement imposed by capital. To claim that this is perversity changes nothing, because, according to Lyotard, it was always so—and hence the impossibility of speaking of alienation; there never was and never will be a productive, artistic, or poetic metamorphosis without the dissolution of the body. There will never be a resolution of the hermaphroditic text. Alienation itself springs out of the fantasy of such a body, a strange combination of the erotic, hygienic Greek body and the erotic, supernatural Christian body.[49] For Lyotard, the militant's resentment (*ressentiment*) derives from a desire for the return of the whole body, the reunification of the "(in)organic body" of the earth with the body without organs of the socius and the body with organs of the worker. Nor is alienation related to castration, nor to the "foreclosure" of castration as Baudrillard's symbolic exchange might have it. Castration has no part in the fundamental schema which, as Baudrillard himself will point out, is deeply economistic, deeply exchangist. The fear of alienation is not the fear of loss, but the fear of not being able to give, of not being able to enter into the flux of exchanges and the investment of energies, even the deferred, strange, and partial jouissance of partial bodies: the autonomization and metamorphoses of the fragmented body in production, their investment in the labor-time of the system. The metaphor of the unified body, whether in mythic communism or the "pre-economy," is ultimately religious, since "the only way of not being alienated since Hegel, and no doubt Jesus, is to be God."[50]

Lyotard directed this last remark at Castoriadis who, "justly tired of rehashing the problems of historical materialism," proposed replacing it with a theory of generalized creativity. Giving full rein to his disaffections, Lyotard reserves for this theory a parenthesis of hate. Because, when Castoriadis, the militant, renounced militancy, he became a "valet" of the people—still secretly and ambivalently continuing with the adultery of knowledge and power.

> Finally it was not necessary to say: let us restart the revolution, rather . . . it was necessary to say: let us eliminate the idea as well, since it has become and perhaps has always been a little idea about nothing, the idea of a reversal of position in the sphere of economic

and political power and thus the idea of the preservation of this sphere. . . ."Thinking heads are always connected by invisible threads to the body of the people," wrote a delighted Marx to Meyer (1871).[51]

The parenthesis occurs in a general discussion of the thought of Baudrillard, for whom Lyotard reserves some fraternal criticism. From our point of view **"The Desire Named Marx"** is a significant text because it is one of the few places in contemporary French literature where Baudrillard's thought is examined in any detail, and it is especially significant in that it occurs in the context of Lyotard's rendezvous with desire in Marx.[52]

Lyotard describes his relationship with Baudrillard as copolarized and synchronized, but claims that the latter's thought is burdened by theoretical and critical hypotheses—even though Baudrillard's denunciation of "the critical" and "the theoretical" (in *The Mirror of Production*) are made in formulae which Lyotard would "joyfully countersign." The problem for Lyotard is that Baudrillard still aims at the "true" when he reproaches Marxism for censuring or debarring social relationships commanded by the symbolic exchange—relationships centered on the exhaustion of libidinal energies "of love and death." Lyotard's critique amounts to a sort of critique of Baudrillard's anthropological critique. For Lyotard it is a fantasy to imagine a society without political economy and without the unconscious, or to imagine that political economy or the unconscious appeared, *sponte sua,* from thin air and then to be imposed on the social body which had not known them; or to imagine that political economy was not present "in filigree, in embryo" in archaic society. Just like the commodity in Marx, Bataille's potlatch is emphatically as much a figure of order as the former: they both compose the semiotic surface of the social. Mauss understood this in terms of the interest which accrues in the cycles of the exchange of gifts. That the symbolic exchange is charged with powerful effect changes nothing for, as Lyotard tells us, to have a "lack" is the same thing as having any other sort of "have." In this way, Lyotard distances himself from the alibi and lost reference of the gift-economy:

> Why can't he [Baudrillard] see that the whole problematic of the gift and symbolic exchange, as he receives it from Mauss, with or without the deflections of Bataille, Caillois and Lacan, pertain completely to imperialism and Western racism—that it is the good savage of ethnology, slightly libidinalized, who he inherits with the concept.[53]

Just as there is no time, neither is there space or place for the reference of the symbolic exchange—which will amount to no more than an enactment of representation in the theater of the sign—the setting aside of an ideal reference. It is a similar fantasy, for Lyotard, as believing there is a human nature which is good to the degree that it is rebellious, the same dream as Plato's when he sought "a source for his Atlantic Utopia among the ancient savages of Egypt"; the same dream as Marx's when he invents the proletariat as the negation of negation and the place of the absence of contradiction and alienation; the same as Baudrillard's when he discovers, positively, the subversive reference in today's "marginals." The dream is one of a non-alienated region which would be able to escape the law of capital. But there is no region which can escape the regimes of power, "regime and reign, sign and apparatus." To have faith in one recommences religion, and this will assure us of being desperate: "Perhaps," writes Lyotard, "in terms of politics, our desire is to be, and always remain, desperate.[54]

Let us conclude here on a note of the co-polarity in the thought of the two postmodernists. It's possible, if in the circumstances parodic, to call this thought dialectically opposed, a dialectic in, and of, postmodernism. Lyotard's ironic affirmation of the system of production and exchange which champions the inventive moves it enables in technology, science, and the realm of sensibility, the potentiality of artistic and linguistic expression in cultures of the avant-grade is momentarily mirrored in Baudrillard's denunciation of the same, in his fascination with the "perverse polymorphy" of signification. But in spite of their rejection of critique and dialectical thought, they carry on the critique by other means. The continuity of their thought on writing—instituted by Bataille—can be instructively compared. In ***Just Gaming***, Lyotard remarks: "The difference between what I write and poetry and literature is that, in principle, what I write is not fiction. But I do wonder more and more: is there a real difference between theory and a fiction? After all, don't we have the right to present theoretical statements under the form of fictions? Not *under* the form, but *in* the form."[55] In an interview on the publication of his book, *L'Amérique*, Baudrillard says something similar: "I do not really think of myself as a philosopher. Criticism [*critique*] has come to me through a movement of radicality which has a poetic, as opposed to philosophical, origin. It is not a function of distantiation or I know not what dialectical critique of phenomena: it would rather be the attempt to seek in the object a path of disappearance, a disappearance of the object and the subject itself at the same time."[56]

In proposing a relationship between theory and fiction—between philosophy and poetry—the postmodernists have underlined, in a way, the continuity of their thought and writing with the thought and writing of Bataille. They are simultaneously witnesses (no doubt phemomenological) and participants in an aesthetic movement, instituted by the critical surrealism of Bataille, which introduces into the "philosophically serious" the figures of the game: an indeterminacy and a disintegration of the certainties and positivities of so-called theoretical thought—radically questioning the function of criticism and the role of writing and art, and the very position of the other in Western thought. . . .

Notes

1. See Lyotard and Rogozinski, "La police de la pensée."

2. See Jürgen Habermas "Modernity versus Postmodernity," in *New German Critique* 22, 1981.

Lyotard's reply, such as it is, is in *The Postmodern Condition*, "Answering the Question: What is Postmodernism." See also Richard Rorty, "Habermas and Lyotard on Postmodernity," in Richard J. Bernstein (ed.), *Habermas and Modernity*.

3. Lyotard, *Le Postmoderne expliqué aux enfants*, p. 40. After the execution of Louis XVI, the people became the sovereign source of legitimation: "modern war between nations is always a civil war: me, the government of the people, contest the legitimacy of *your* government. With 'Auschwitz,' one has physically destroyed a modern sovereign: an entire people. One has tried to destroy it. It is the crime which opens postmodernity, the crime of lese-sovereignty, no longer regicide, but populocide (as distinct from ethnocide)" (pp. 39-40).

4. Ibid., p. 133. "Billet pour un nouveau décor."

5. Ibid., p. 150.

6. Therefore also a confirmation of the avant-gardes of history and a "politics by other means." It suffices to recall, lest we doubt the historical-political significance of the avant-gardes, "the fate meted out to the so-called historical 'avant-gardes' by political totalitarianisms. Or to observe in the alleged 'surpassing' [*dépassement*] by today's avantgardism, armed with the pretext of returning to a communication with the public, a scorn towards the responsibility of resisting and bearing witness, a responsibility the avant-gardes assumed for over a century." Ibid., p. 150.

7. Lyotard, *La Condition postmoderne*, p. 7ff.

8. Specifically, in Jean-François Lyotard, *Le Différend*. *Le différend*, which translates as the "disagreement" or the difference of opinion, also means a conflict of irreconcilable frames of reference or discourses. It is a trait of the aesthetic judgment in Kant. Matters of taste "cannot be demonstrated by the means of 'determinate concepts'; it is necessary to make the rules on the basis of a given singularity."

9. In addition to the piece by Guattari, "the Postmodern Dead End," Lyotard's thought and writing has attracted considerable attention in the global sphere of contemporary theory. At random, consider the French *L'Arc* issue devoted to his reception in France, primarily concerned with the "aesthetic of desire" set into play by Lyotard in *Economie libidinale*. Hubert Damisch, "Dynamique libidinale," remarks that Lyotard's enterprise is one of "theoretical licentiousness" which has started to "bear some fruits," in terms of the analysis of the economic functioning of a psychic apparatus, giving it precedence over its *topical* (Freud) and *structural* levels (*L'Arc* 64, 1976). From England one might refer to the publication in 1986 of *Postmodernism* in the ICA Documents series, based on a two-day conference held in 1985 devoted, largely, to

questions raised in the reception of Lyotard's *The Postmodern Condition.* In addition, one might refer to articles in the *New Left Review:* Peter Dews, "Adorno, Post-Structuralism and the Critique of Identity" (*New Left Review* 157, May/June 1986), which involves an examination of the figure of Adorno in the post-structuralists' encounter with Nietzsche, and the critique of identity as expounded by Lyotard; and on a more polemical note refer to Terry Eagleton's "Capitalism, Modernism and Postmodernism" (*New Left Review* 152, July/August 1985), lamenting the wrong turn which postmodernism took by crossing its avant-gardism (as though this was not a modernism) "with the *unpolitical* impulses of modernism." This is going to forestall the development of "an authentically political art." (Reproduced in Terry Eagleton, *Against the Grain: Selected Essays.*) In particular, these two articles, along with Fredric Jameson, "Postmodernism, or the Cultural Logic of Late Capitalism" (*New Left Review* 146, July/August 1984), indicate the contours of a political response to post-structuralism emerging in Anglo-American criticism. The post-structuralist reception in Germany has likewise produced a dialogue with the post-Frankfurt school theorists—for example, Albrecht Wellmer refers to Lyotard's philosophy as the most "pregnant expression" of the "search" for postmodernist thought, in which *"aesthetic"* postmodernism appears as radical aesthetic *modernism,* "as the self-consciousness as it were of modernism." (In Albrecht Wellmer, "On the Dialectic of Modernism and Postmodernism," *Praxis International* 4, no. 4, January 1985.) However, in my opinion Wellmer mistakenly reads the "pluralism" of language games (cf. Lyotard, *The Postmodern Condition*) as the "horizon" of Lyotard's political thought and reduces it too quickly to a "limp ideology of consensus," in Lyotard's terms, inherent in the Habermasian theory of communicative action, in order to rethink, in Wellmer's words, "the moral-political universalism of the Enlightenment, the ideas of individual and collective self-determination, reason and history in a new fashion" (Wellmer, "On the Dialectic of Modernism and Postmodernism," p. 360).

10. Cf. Lyotard, "La police de la pensée," accusing the neo-Kantians of waging a bitter and vengeful campaign against the most radical advances of modernism, which include the work of Lacan, Foucault, and Derrida. The thought of Kant, however, is too important to leave to the neo-Kantians, among whom Lyotard numbers L. Ferry and A. Renaut (*La Pensée '68*), and J. Bouveresse (*La Philosophie chez les autophages,* and *Rationalité et cynicisme*). This last writer is one of the rare French philosophers to specifically place himself in relation to the British analytic tradition of philosophy. There are many interesting parallels between the work of the neo-Kantians, in their calls for "a return of the subject," "ordinary language," and "common (linguistic) sense," and the recent work of Anthony Giddens in his Wittgensteinian turn (Giddens in a public lecture, "Recent Social Theory," Melbourne, 1986.)

11. Georges Bataille quoted in Arnaud and Excoffon-Lafarge, *Bataille,* p. 67.

12. Translator Allan Stoekl writes in the introduction to Bataille's *Visions of Excess* (p. xi), that *heterogeneous* matter was "matter so repulsive that it resisted not only the idealism of Christians, Hegelians and surrealists, but even the conceptual edifice-building of traditional materialists. It was indeed an all-out assault on dignity."

13. Guattari, "The Postmodern Dead End." The impulse toward inclusivity in the construction of a discursive totality is one which post-structuralism both disavows and implicitly engages in. It is the paradox of making general statements about discontinuous phenomena. Fredric Jameson does something similar in *The Political Unconscious: Narrative as a Socially Symbolic Act,* when he suggests that post-structuralism—in the forms of Deleuze and Guattari's schizo-analysis, Foucault's archeology and political-technology of the body, Derrida's grammatology and deconstruction, Lyotard's libidinal economy, Baudrillard's symbolic exchange, and Kristeva's *sémanalyse*—can be grasped as a "new hermeneutic in its own right." These practices amount to "an *anti*-interpretive method" and "a demand for the construction of a new and more adequate, immanent or anti-transcendent hermeneutic model" (p. 23).

14. In Raymond Bellour and Catherine Clement (eds.), *Claude Lévi-Strauss.*

15. In Descombes, *Modern French Philosophy,* p. 180.

16. In particular, Gilles Deleuze, *Nietzsche et la philosophie.*

17. Descombes, *Modern French Philosophy,* p. 181.

18. Ibid.

19. The prime movers of this group were Cornelius Castoriadis and Claude Lefort. Arthur Hirsh, in his historical analysis of the review *Socialisme ou barbarie,* argues that at the end of a long engagement with the theoretico-practice, Castoriadis came to reject the moves to existentilize or revise and no doubt to structuralize Marx in the light of what is at least inconsistent in the theoretical system of Marxism. Questioning the nature of theory per se, Castoriadis viewed the return to Marx "as inconsistent with Marx's own contention that a theory should be judged by what it has become in practice." (In Hirsh, *The French New Left: An Intellectual History from Sartre to Gorz,* "The Gauchist Rejection." To judge from Lyotard's own evidence in *Economie libidinale,* the split in 1964 was a bitter experience. Lyotard's split from the

group—and the splinter review, *Pouvoir ouvrier*—occasioned some rancour, which Lyotard expresses in both *Dérive à partir de Marx et Freud*, and *Economie libidinale*.

20. Developed in the pages of *Socialisme ou barbarie* between 1949-1965, and brought together in Cornelius Castoriadis, *La Société bureaucratique: les rapports de production en Russie*.

21. Several of the essays in this work are included in the collection by Lyotard, *Driftworks*. On a vaguely textual note about the translations: be warned. For unacknowledged reasons, sections of the opening essay, "Adrift," as well as other essays in the collection, have been excised. These sections include a discussion of the events surrounding the split with *Socialisme ou barbarie*, and thus address the political significance of drifting. One gains the impression that the editors wished to present, cut and pasted, an aestheticized Lyotard. In any event, to edit the text is one thing. . . .

22. Ibid., p. 11.

23. Lyotard, *La Condition postmoderne*. In an interview Lyotard has spoken about this work: "I told stories in the book, I referred to a quantity of books I'd never read, apparently it impressed people, it's all a bit of a parody. . . . I remember an Italian architect who bawled me out because he said it was a pointlessly sophisticated, complicated book, and the whole thing could have been done much more simply. . . . I wanted to say first that it's simply the worst of my books, they're almost all bad, but that one's the worst . . . really that book is related to a specific circumstance, it belongs to the satirical genre." Interviewed and translated by Arias-Mission for *Lotta Poetica*, republished in *Eyeline*, November 1987, p. 17.

24. The idea of such a community is a major figure in Lyotard's meditations on Kant, particularly in relation to the ethics pursued in *Le différend* ("Le Signe d'histoire"). Lyotard writes, in "Notice Kant 4, 5," that "The *sensus communis* forms . . . part of aesthetics as the total of all reasonable practices in ethics. It is an appeal to the community which is made a priori, and which judges without a rule of direct presentation; simply, the community is necessary as a moral obligation for the mediation of a concept of reason, the Idea of liberty, whereas the community of senders and receivers of statements about the beautiful are invoked immediately, without mediation of any concept, by feeling alone for whatever can be shared *a priori*. It already exists as taste, but does not yet exist as rational consensus" (p. 243). In the aesthetic antinomy, continues Lyotard, the antinomy of the *sublime* is the most extreme because it involves both a finality and an anti-finality, "a pleasure for pain," whereas in the beautiful there is a finality without end, based on the free accord of the faculties. "With the sublime Kant advanced a long way into a sort of heterogeneity in which the solution to the aesthetic antinomy appears more difficult for the sublime than for the beautiful" (p. 243).

25. Lyotard and Rogozinski, "La police de la pensée," p. 34.

26. Lyotard, *Driftworks*, endnotes.

27. Vaneigem, *The Revolution of Everyday Life*, p. 136. The passive nihilist "compromises with his own lucidity" about the collapse of values: "He makes one final nihilistic gesture: throws [the] dice to decide his 'cause,' and becomes a devoted slave, for Art's sake, and for the sake of a little bread. . . . Nothing is true, so a few gestures become hip. Joe Soap intellectuals, pataphysicians, crypto-fascists, aesthetes of the *acte gratuit*, mercenaries, Kim Philbys, pop-artists, psychedelic impresarios—bandwagon after bandwagon works out its own version of the *credo quia absurdum est*: you don't believe in it, but you do it anyway; you get used to it and you even get to like it in the end" (p. 136).

28. Jean-François Lyotard and Jean-Loup Thébaud, *Au juste: conversations*, pp. 11-17.

29. Nonnegotiable in the sense that the poet does not concern him or herself with whether the reader or listener has understood the poem.

30. In Lyotard, *Economie libidinale*, part 1, "La grande pellicule éphémère."

31. Allen Weiss, in "A Logic of the Simulacrum or the Anti-Roberte" (*Art and Text* 18 July 1985) writes that: "Phantasms may be considered to represent the solution of an enigma. According to psychoanalytic theory, phantasmic fabulations reveal the origins of subjectivity: the phantasm of a primal seduction is at the origin of sexuality; the phantasm of castration is at the origin of sexual differentiation; the phantasm of the primal scene is at the origin of individuality" (p. 115). Weiss points to the fundamental opposition in the thought of Klossowski's *Roberte Ce Soir and the Revocation of the Edict of Nantes*, and *Sade mon prochain*, between the simulacrum of the unique sign—"monstrous, perverse, transgressive" and the system of exchangeable signs—it is "always recuperated within the general system of exchange by means of the simulacra which expresses it. Such a misappropriation may well explain the confusion of the stereotype with reality and the rational with the real, a confusion which is at the very center of Western metaphysics" (p. 119). Such a conception may be compared with Lyotard's distinction, in *Economie libidinale*, between the intense sign and the intelligible sign, proposed in relation to Klossowski's *Monnaie vivante*.

32. In addition to Lyotard, *Discours, figure*, see his "Par delà la représentation," in the introduction to Anton Ehrenzweig, *L'Ordre caché de l'art*, and Lyotard's

"Contribution des tableaux de Jacques Monory à l'intelligence de l'économie politique libidinale du capital dans son rapport avec le dispositif pictural," in Collectif, *Figurations*.

33. Sigmund Freud, *Group Psychology and the Analysis of the Ego*, chapter 7.

34. Ibid., p. 56.

35. Sigmund Freud, *On Metapsychology: The Theory of Psychoanalysis*, in particular, "The Economic Problem of Masochism."

36. Lyotard, *Economie libidinale*, p. 27. Freud in *On Metapsychology*, "The Economic Problem of Masochism," writes that the pleasure principle can no longer be considered solely as the lowering of tension due to stimulus, since pleasure may be obtained in the heightening of excitation. The Nirvana principle, which Freud calls a case of Fechner's tendency toward stability, would represent the pleasure principle in the service of the death instincts which seek to return "the restlessness of life into the stability of the inorganic state." (This latter theme is developed in his *Beyond the Pleasure Principle*.) Freud further writes, in a passage critical to the concept of the libidinal economy: "The *Nirvana* principle expresses the trend of the death instinct; the *pleasure* principle represents the demands of the libido; and the modification of the latter principle, the *reality* principle, represents the influence of the external world. . . . None of these three principles is actually put out of action by one another. As a rule they are able to tolerate one another, although conflicts are bound to arise occasionally from the fact of the differing aims that are set for each—in one case a quantitative reduction of the load of the stimulus, in another a qualitative characteristic of the stimulus, and, lastly [in the third case], a postponement of the discharge of the stimulus and a temporary acquiescence in the unpleasure due to tension" (pp. 413-15).

37. Lyotard, *Economie libidinale*, pp. 58-59.

38. In Jean-François Lyotard, "Psychanalyse et la peinture," *Encyclopaedia universalis*.

39. Ibid., pp. 745-49.

40. Lacan, *Ecrits*, p. 25.

41. Lyotard, *Economie libidinale*, p. 119.

42. Also known *as le surmâle* (the supermale), the title of Jarry's novel of 1902 about a future (1920s) man, super in every way. In "The Tears of the Supermale," Nigey Lennon writes that "Marcueil, although he is far superior to everyone else, feels that he must disguise his superiority from the prying eyes of the world by pretending to be thoroughly average and mundane, a man who 'embodied so absolutely the average man that his very ordinariness became extraordinary,'" in Lennon, *Alfred Jarry: The Man with the Axe*. Lyotard uses *super-mâle* to describe Castoriadis's concept of "generalized creativity" in a "parenthesis of hate" in the *Economie libidinale*, pp. 142-46.

43. Ibid., p. 122.

44. Ibid.

45. Ibid., p. 127.

46. Ibid.

47. A related theme is addressed, among other things, in *Instructions païennes*. Lyotard argues, in the form of a dialogue, for the justice of impiety. This manifests itself as disrespect for political institutions of the left and right, and a generalized shortcircuiting of the meta-narratives by the impious, heterogeneous (i.e., unassimilable) genre of the *petit récit*.

48. Lyotard, *Economie libidinale*, p. 136.

49. Ibid., p. 137.

50. Ibid., p. 144.

51. Ibid., pp. 144-45.

52. One might recall, to recall something which does not exist, the absence of the sought-after response from Foucault solicited by Baudrillard's "Oublier Foucault," in Peter Botsman (ed), *Theoretical Strategies*.

53. Lyotard, *Economie libidinale*, p. 132.

54. Ibid., p. 133.

55. Jean-François Lyotard and Jean-Loup Thébaud, *Just Gaming*, p. 5. (Originally published as *Au juste: conversations*.)

56. "America," continues Baudrillard, "is hell, after a fashion; I loathe it, but there is something infernal in its seduction over me. So I don't criticize, but expel at the same time as intensely absorb. In all of this there is hardly room for the critical subject, it's banal to say it." Baudrillard in an interview with Jacques Henric and Guy Scarpetta, "L'amérique comme fiction," *Art press* 103 (May 1986): 40-42.

John Rajchman (essay date 1991)

SOURCE: "The Postmodern Museum," in *Philosophical Events: Essays of the '80s*, Columbia University Press, 1991, pp. 105-17.

[*In the following essay, originally published in 1985, Rajchman describes* Les Immatériaux, *and discusses the nature of postmodernism and its relation to language, technoscience and modernism.*]

Les Immatériaux (March 28-July 25, 1985) was the most expensive exhibition in the Beaubourg museum to date. A collective effort of more than fifty people working over two years under the auspices of the Centre de Création Industrielle, it was directed by the French philosopher Jean-

François Lyotard. Lyotard and company transformed the fifth floor of the museum into a gigantic metallic maze, divided by gray gauze screens into sixty-one "sites"; these sites were arranged consecutively along five adjacent pathways. For the most part the sites consisted of small installations of various cultural artifacts; technological representations and electronic devices, and were titled by the ideas or conditions that they were intended to represent or demonstrate.

The visitor entered the maze equipped with headphones that furnished a sound track synchronized with the sites—a selection of dramatically recited classics mostly from French theory (Blanchot, Baudrillard, Barthes) and modern writing (Beckett, Artaud, Mallarmé, Proust, Zola, Kleist). In this manner one confronted an extraordinary array of things taken from hospitals, factories, research centers, libraries, and museums of all sorts—from Paris' Musée national d'art moderne to the Center of Creative Photography at the University of Arizona. IBM and astrophysics laboratories were credited along with well-known artists. Most European countries were represented, as well as Japan, the United States, and Australia; there was little, however, from the third world.

There were video, film, slides and photographs—commercial and artistic, anonymous and signed, old and recent. There were robots, an elaborate photocopier, the first display of a holographic movie, and, of course, computers—lots of them. There were examples of rugosymmetric reproduction, electromicroscopy, spectrography, holography, Doppler effects, and Fourier series; displays of astrophysics, genetics, and statistics. There was even a Japanese sleeping cell from the Kotobuki Seating Co.

Works of art—traditional, modernist, and Conceptual— were juxtaposed with technological displays or ludic devices to make music or compose poems. Among the artists and authors variously represented in the sites were Hans Christian Andersen and Jacques Derrida, Georges Seurat and Elvis Costello, Joseph Kosuth and Edgar Allan Poe, Malevich and Muybridge, Moholy-Nagy and Saul Steinberg, Robert Ryman and Peter Eisenman, Duchamp and Warhol, Yves Klein and Irving Penn. At several computer consoles positioned throughout the show one could read the meditations of thirty illustrious Parisian intellectuals and writers on fifty alphabetized and cross-referenced words such as Author, Desire, Meaning, Mutation, Simulation, Voice, and Speed. *Les Immatériaux* boasted many great names; but not only were things not classfied by such proper names, one was told (explicitly by Derrida in a text set near the beginning of the show) that "authorship" itself was in question.

Yet while all these heteroclite objects figured in sites titled by the concepts they were supposed to illustrate, the aim of the show was not the didactic one of presenting new art work or new technical devices to the public. Rather, the objective was to induce a state of uncertainty, an inability to name what it is that all these sites might refer to. "That

we know not how to name what awaits us is the sure sign that it awaits us,"[1] says Lyotard darkly to French *Vogue*. *Les Immatériaux* was intended not to be futurological, but to frustrate the demand to say what the future is—a future which surrounds us without our being able to name it, which is "ours," without our knowing how or why.

Two notions seemed to govern the conception of the show: "immateriality," implicit in the title, and "postmodernism," a particular concern of Lyotard the philosopher. How did these neologisms relate to this singular assemblage of objects? Was the show about a great reclassification, a new "order of things," that of postmodernism? Or is the postmodern condition rather like a Borgesian encyclopedia, a purposeless or random accumulation, a vast, overwhelming *bricolage?* These are like the questions of the Sphinx: who are you among all this? The show produced a plethora of supporting materials, explanations, and interviews, plus an international colloquium and an elaborate bibliography. And yet, when asked (in a *Flash Art* interview) what on earth postmodernism is, Lyotard responds with cunning modesty: "My work is, in fact, directed to finding out what it is, but I still don't know."[2]

THE INVERTED MUSEUM

Les Immatériaux was a singular museological exercise— the movement of an influential strand of current French thought into a museum space, a great public or popular display of what that thought takes to be our condition. We have seen "theoretical" artifacts, and art for theory's sake. Here it was the museum itself which was turned into a theoretical object.

Museums contextualize things. Not so many years back, pre-Beaubourg Cultural Minister André Malraux was talking about the "museum without walls." Today, any artifact becomes a putative museum object, something that might be acquired or appropriated by a museum without regard for its source or context. This museological process reached a sort of inverted apotheosis in *Les Immatériaux*. The show included many "anti-aesthetic" artworks (e.g. Raoul Hausmann's *Spirit of Our Time, Mechanical Head*, 1919) once intended to challenge the spread of museological representation, and many readymade bits of "reality" once supposed to interrupt representation and so question "art." But today readymades are often considered high art, and it is "reality" which is questioned by a groundless multiplication of images. If our world is basically populated less by things than by simulacra, if everything exists only to be endlessly recomposed, the distinction between representation and reality seems to become irrelevant or "immaterial." *Les Immatériaux* addressed this state of affairs by suggesting a new continuity between what is inside and outside the museum: the museum became no longer a space or sanctuary apart from things, but a mirror of their infinite reiteration.

It is to the French sociologist Jean Baudrillard that we owe the vision of a culture of simulacra, a culture of empty recycling of past contents. And it is precisely in the Beaubourg museum that he thinks this culture finds its monument and instrument. For Baudrillard, the postmodern condition is the Beaubourgeois condition. It is paradoxical to ask what to put into the museum, for the museum "functions as an incinerator absorbing and devouring all cultural energy"; to put nothing in it would be a Romantic gesture. Rather, one should accelerate the processes of simulation by turning the place into a "labyrinth, the infinite combinatory library . . . in short, the universe of Borges."[3] *Les Immatériaux* made this sardonic suggestion good; it even had the recorded voice of Baudrillard telling of the advent of the Age of the Simulacrum.

The modern museum recontextualizes things in a formal or aesthetic space. The postmodern museum, as intimated by the show, foregrounds the condition in which real and simulated things seem equivalent—an environment in which aesthetic, non-aesthetic, and even anti-aesthetic objects coexist. The museum of "Les Immatériaux" might be the first postmodern museum: it not only collected readymades from the most diverse sources; it set them within a universe of museological nominalism—there existed no fixed, general classification of things, no cultural division tied down by "Reality" or "Human Nature"; things were not compartmentalized into art and technology, high and mass cultures, esthetic and nonesthetic forms.

One inferred: "postmodern" culture does not affirm itself through a dominant art; it is not the sort of thing a cultural ministry can administrate. Its "ism" does not refer to a school with specific aesthetic principles; it has no manifesto or slogan or formal program. It does not justify itself with a progressive scheme; it sees the very idea of "advanced art" as one more arbitrary classification. In short, it has no "metanarrative" to tell about itself. "Postmodern" refers instead to a condition, and *Les Immatériaux* was an attempt to dramatize that condition. What sort of drama was it? It was not narrative; it was not even disruptive in a Brechtian sense. It was electronic. The headphoned masses milling through the maze were part of it. When they made music with the motion of their bodies or composed poetry on a computer, there was no effect of "distance" or "alienation." One could not "participate" in this theater because one was already part of it.

The master trope of *Les Immatériaux* derived from the Borges fable about the library that contains, in all conceivable languages, everything that can be said. Lyotard says the show was "a reduced monograph of the Library of Babel (that is, of the universe). . . ."[4] Everywhere in its electronic maze were words—heard, seen, projected, and photographed, in neon lights and on computer screens. But the notion that the show, like Borges' story, was about the infinite library is more than a metaphor; it is also the best way to think about the show: to see it as a book and to ask, what sort of book about our postmodern condition was it?

The sixty-one sites of *Les Immatériaux* fell into five sequences; the principal pathways that ran throughout the

maze, they were the "chapters" of this book. As one entered the introductory site, called "The Theater of the Nonbody," the sound track played a fragment from Beckett's *The Unnameable,* which narrates the predicament of an "I" who cannot speak yet cannot remain silent. The site, a mirrored vestibule, then opened onto the five paths, each of which was announced by a window display prepared by Beckett's set designer, Jean-Claude Fall.

Essentially, each path was to demonstrate a different kind of artificial extension or replacement of the body (e.g., the way in which scientific instruments exceed the senses in the apprehension of atomic particles). One was also advised in the catalogue that the five paths or chapters had two sorts of linguistic structure, corresponding, on the one hand, to aspects of communication (from where, to where, how, by means of what, and concerning what messages are sent) and, on the other, to five keywords with the prefix *mat-* (matter, material, maternal, and so forth); these abstract rubrics governed the allocation of sites along the pathways. Thus, all the disparate immaterial things in the show were classified at the start within a *table des matières* (table of contents), and they all concluded in a site called "The Labyrinth of Language"—a world of word-processing, of language stored, analyzed, composed, recomposed, and otherwise manipulated by electronic devices. In the world of *Les Immatériaux,* everything starts in the body and ends in language.

Ambulating through the maze became a form of reading. At different points along the way the postmodern reader-*flâneur* passed computer consoles with handy didactic summaries of the sites and, as he entered and exited, a computerized index of the concepts of the show; there was also a bibliography of related readings in the form of a little bookstore. Thus the show, itself a monograph of Babel, led to other books. Apparently, the book—its linguistic order—survives in the electronic world, but altered in its form so that it may simulate this world even as it diagnoses it.

According to Lyotard, language theory not only survives the electronic revolution, but also provides it with its order. "In essence," he explains, "the new technologies concern language" (primarily the language of artificial intelligence). Further, as language determines our "whole social bond *(lien social),*"[5] the new technologies also concern our "being-together." This reasoning provided the show with its project: to illuminate how the electronic world is rooted in language, and how we are bound to one another within it.

And yet how seriously are we to take Lyotard's suggestion that this world can be analyzed through the etymology of the root *mat-* in French words (which has no single function and for which there exists no exact English equivalent), or in terms of structuralist theory about the parameters through which messages can be sent? Are not such linguistic categorizations in reality less a deep hermeneutical fact about our being-together in language than a piece of modernist writing in the manner of Brisset, Borges, or Roussel?

The trope of the Library is hardly new or postmodern; in the '60s Foucault saw it as a central metaphor of the modernity initiated by Flaubert and Manet:

> Flaubert is to the library what Manet is to the museum. They both produce works in a self-conscious relationship to earlier paintings or texts . . . [They] are responsible for books and paintings within works of art.[6]

It is through the metaphor of the Library that *Les Immatériaux* managed to infuse the electronic world with modernist meaning. Thus we arrive at the fabulous premise of this demonstration, with its foreground of electronic gadgetry and its background of modernist textuality: that the "book" on or of our postmodern electronic condition is in fact a modernist one!

Baudelaire announced "modernity" within a still Romantic vocabulary; here Lyotard announces "postmodernity" in a modernist idiom. "Thus he goes, he runs, he searches . . . what is he seeking? . . . something we might call *modernity*," said Baudelaire, 122 years ago, of the Painter of Modern Life. Now we have the philosopher Lyotard running in search of what we might call postmodernity "for no better word is at hand to express the idea in question."[7] There is still the modernist quest, the uncertainty, the confrontation with the "unnameable." But now, like the worried jogger with his Walkman, the postmodern *flâneur* carries with him the tape of modernist textuality. It comes to him in defamiliarized form like the voice of a bygone era, like the beautiful relics of modernist "nontheater" which are the signposts of his quest. Thus, for all its immaterial electronics, over the entire show hung the shadow of what in his analysis of Pop, Barthes called "this old thing called art."[8]

MELANCHOLY AND MANIA

For Lyotard, *Les Immatériaux* was involved in "a kind of grieving or a melancholy with respect to the ideas of the modern era, a sense of disarray."[9] And in the show (or at least in its conception), a sort of oscillation between melancholy and mania replaced high-modernist anxiety. For the art melancholic, nothing seems intellectually at stake in "advanced art" any more, and theory becomes a space of mourning for this loss. (Lyotard finds this melancholy in the "negative," "almost cynical" approach of Theodor Adorno, "which is the measure of the breadth of his despair.")[10]

"Mania" meanwhile is the opposite reaction to this lost object of art: a plunge into the mad, groundless reproduction of things. In *this* state one gets the sort of hysteria of electronic culture which Paul Virilio calls "speed," a catastrophic panic before an endlessly future-shocking condition;[11] one also gets the consumerist thrills or "intensities" which Fredric Jameson describes as "free-floating and im-

personal . . . dominated by a curious form of euphoria."[12] Along with its "latent or implicit . . . melancholy,"[13] *Les Immatériaux* manifested this mania in its frantic multiplication of images and in its mad electronic exuberance—its jumble of installations and profusion of computers. *Les Immatériaux* was itself manic-depressive.

Jameson is impressed by the "waning of affect" in postmodern culture—the affect of high-modernist anxiety or alienation. Such angst has its formal apotheosis in absolute abstraction: white monochromes, the blank page, the hours-long fixed camera, in which representation is pushed to its limits—extinction. Anxiety is the affect associated with the end of representation: the heroic encounter of the artist with the strange object that dispossesses him or divides him from himself. Now the end of representation has become a general feature of our world or condition, of the endless recomposition of things; it is not only a matter of art. So, instead of anxiety, we have melancholy and mania, tropes of a postmodern condition, "subjectivity" in a culture which can no longer place the human subject at its center. We also have one sense of "immateriality": in formalist modernism, the end of representation assumed the form of a purification of the basic "materials" of art. Now the criterion of the specificity of medium or material can no longer be used to separate "art" from the decadent "kitsch" culture it was meant to save us from. The great question of modernism was: what is art? Now it is replaced by the postmodern question: who are we in all of this?

DISLOCATIONS

In his writings Lyotard's answer to this question starts with "technoscience." Technoscience transforms the State and economic production; it alters the nature of knowledge; it redefines the very ideas of "art" and "culture." Philosophically, it causes the questions "What is Enlightenment?" and "What is Revolution?" to be replaced with the questions "What is technoscience?" and "Who are we in it?" The postmodern condition is a technoscientific one.

One difference between the industrial revolution and the electronic one is the central place of abstract science in it: to build a steam engine no advanced physics is required. The interlocking of science and technology, today symbolized by Silicon Valley, is of recent origin. But as science and technology become a single thing, it becomes increasingly implausible to think of them in terms of the progressive, optimistic values of the Enlightenment: the I. G. Farben chemical complex ends in the death camps. Thus, Lyotard thinks that what is at issue in technoscience is not the enlightened values it might embody, or the consensus about the nature of the physical world it might make possible, but its singular new place in society, and the deadly reach of its consequences.[14]

These controversial views of Lyotard supplied the philosophical framework for the notion of "immateriality" which gave the show its title. To understand this conception and its connection with our postmodern condition, it is useful to distinguish two sorts of technoscientific "immateriality."

First, there is the electronic dispossession of the human body. *Les Immatériaux* was a phenomenologist's nightmare; everywhere one was shown the replacement of the material activities of the "lived body" with artificial ones, or with formal or immaterial languages. One entered a world of simulation of the body: eating and sleeping (represented by a fast-food display and the Japanese sleeping cell), but also thinking and seeing (the computers and scientific instruments). There were filmic and video simulations of movements and memories, and even a display in which "human" skin was fabricated.

In short, the show suggested that life and death are subject to technoscientific intervention and redefinition. For example, in the site "Vain Nakedness," photographs of Muybridge's 1887 *Animal Locomotion* were juxtaposed with stills from Joseph Losey's film *Monsieur Klein* of anatomical dissection in the Nazi death camps. And in the site "Angel," different photomontages displayed the possibilities of transsexualism and hermaphroditism, while on the sound track a feminine voice (that of Dolores Rogozinski, who arranged all the writings) mused on mythologies of sexual difference. Apparently, even gender succumbs to technoscientific manipulation, as transsexual operations open up the specter of a "third sex." Finally, in the site "The Small Invisibles," it was demonstrated that bodily senses no longer supply the empirical court of appeal for scientific theories. Today, space and time, once thought to be the "forms of intuition" of the world that the body experiences and science studies, exist largely as complex theoretical constructs from which is created the artificial world in which we live.

Second, there is the dematerialization of space. It is not just that we no longer build solely from the materials of our earth. (One site, "Forgotten Soil," presented fragments of brick, wood, and ceramic from buildings of Frank Lloyd Wright and Alvar Aalto as if they were ruins of a lost age.) It is not just that we have elevated the architectural representation to an importance all but equal to that of the building itself. (In the site "Plane Architecture," one was shown how pictorial and architectural codes seem to coalesce in certain works of Malevich and Piet Zwart and, in "Inverted Reference," how the architectural models of Peter Eisenman are so abstract as to become autonomous works.) The sort of civilization technoscience brings with it is endlessly transportable; it goes anywhere. It does not collect people into urban centers; it spreads them out into an atopic anywhere from which they are connected to everywhere by cable: from one's Japanese sleeping cell one tunes into the world. The key image of our immaterial civilization is not the industrial or Saint-Simonian city, but the placeless shopping-center complex.[15]

Les Immatériaux simulated our "immaterial" anywhere. The show was not a center around which (industrial) objects were arrayed, but an "implosion" of (postindustrial) things from all over. In this sense, one might say that *Les Immatériaux* is to electronic civilization what the great nineteenth-century universal expositions were to industrial civilization. But this immaterial culture of technoscience was not presented in horrified fascination (à la the humanist vision of a dystopian technology). The aim of the show was not ideological critique, and Lyotard has no use for the category of "alienation" (it is a piece of outmoded theology, he says).[16] Contemporary dislocations of body and place, or the impossibility today of continuous narrative, are not simply the evils of commodification or kitsch; again, these postmodern conditions are already announced in the modernist texts of Beckett.

Technoscience, then, should not provoke a Romantic nightmare. Lyotard wants us to think of it instead as a modernist text in which we can continue the war of heterogeneous invention—once the province of advanced art—by other means. The danger he sees in technoscience is not an alienation of our supposedly natural identity; it is the "totalitarian" possibility that there exists only *one* artificial identity; it is the "totalitarian" possibility that there exists only *one* artificial identity that submits us to centralized control. It is the danger of a homogeneous unity of languages reflected in the informationalist vision of controlled communication. The question "Who are we in all of this?" need not have a single answer; "we" are not a single entity which technoscience alienates or realizes. Rather, in inventing new heterogeneous languages, we constantly reinvent ourselves—that is what modernism has to tell us about our postmodern condition. Thus, Lyotard's "map" is not intended to provide a path out of the postmodern condition, but to accelerate and complicate incommensurable diversity from within, to insure that technoscience be a "heterotopia" of the babbling of languages rather than a utopia of a single world for a single people.

THE AMERICAN VIDEO GAME

"Postmodern" is a label coined in America. It refers, says Lyotard, to "a subject the French don't know very well, since they're always turned so completely in upon themselves."[17] And yet, in America, following Hal Foster's useful distinction, we already distinguish between two forms of "postmodernism," one of which is French-inspired or poststructuralist.[18]

There is a curious aspect of the current debate over postmodernism. It is the confrontation of the advanced French thought of the last twenty years with American mass culture. (One saw this in the audiovisual juxtapositions of the show: a text by Artaud near an image of Elvis Costello, etc. Indeed, an American, making his way through the sixty-one sites, listening in his headset to the ponderous intonation of such "fast" metaphysics as "the world is a video game," might have had a wearied impression of déjà vu.) Jameson thinks that at bottom postmodernism is the name of the strange sort of culture America spreads throughout the globe and into the heavens: "this whole global, yet American, postmodern culture" is carried forth by a "whole new wave of American military and economic domination throughout the world."[19] According to Jameson, the ironies of international capital would have it that the great flourishing of modernist writing and theory in Paris, in which the self-centered linguistic text was cut free from all moorings in the world, finds its sorry realization in the delirious theater of commodities and signs that is the contemporary American shopping mall.

Perhaps never since Adorno blamed the Enlightenment for Los Angeles has there been such a monumental effort to find a place for "Americanism" in the history and philosophy of Europe as in the postmodern debate. Indeed, Lyotard, referring to Virilio's vision of the "overexposed" city, remarks that "Les Immatériaux" is a miniature simulation of what it is like for a French intellectual to travel somewhere between San Diego and L.A. with nothing but his car radio to mark the changes.[20]

The period of high modernism was a period of the "American in Paris," of the cosmopolitan pilgrimage to the "capital of the nineteenth century." In America, where a diasporic modernism was once greeted as a preservation of the "value" of art in the face of the decadence of "kitsch," modernism became the official ideology of a new wave of museological proliferation. Now it is Paris which looks into a future dominated by American-Japanese electronic culture, and attempts to put that culture into *its* museum.

The entrance of advanced French theory into the museum comes at a time in which, in an international philosophical debate, that theory is under attack as "irrationalist" or "relativist." For such opponents the extravagant dilemmas the show dramatized will no doubt seem less a diagnosis of our condition than a predictable product of a misguided philosophy. In its broad terms the international debate over "French Theory" has assumed the form of a debate over the reevaluation of the European Enlightenment in a non-Eurocentric age.[21] It is no wonder that America has a capital place in this debate; we have invented the great "postcolonial" kind of "modernization" or "Westernization" seen in Japan.

The great irruption of a cosmopolitan artistic modernism in pre-Stalinist Russia and prewar Europe, with its fitful manifestoes and radical proclamations, has become an ambiguous piece of cultural heritage, both in the Soviet Union and in the West, at least since the cold war set in. And yet, between here and there, modernism may survive in "French Theory," with all its claims to radicality and celebrations of heterogeneity. This survival of modernism in the very thought on and of our postmodern condition was the final, perhaps unintended, implication of *Les Immatériaux.*

Notes

1. Quoted in French *Vogue,* June-July 1985, p. 476.

2. "A Conversation with Jean-François Lyotard," *Flash Art,* March 1985, p. 35.

3. Jean Baudrillard, *Simulacres et simulation* (Paris: Galilée, 1981), pp. 93 and 99.

4. Quoted in *Le Monde,* May 3, 1985.

5. Jean-François Lyotard, *Tombeau de l'intellectuel et autres papiers* (Paris: Galilée, 1984) pp. 48 and 83.

6. Michel Foucault, "Fantasia of the Library," in *Language, Counter-Memory, Practice,* trans. Donald F. Bouchard and Sherry Simon (Ithaca; Cornell University Press, 1977) pp. 92-93. For Foucault, the metaphor of the Library represents the break between the classical art of rhetoric and the modernist writing of a "heterogeneity of languages," a heterogeneity which insures that there can be no fixed vocabulary or master discourse. This condition, which Lyotard elsewhere terms postmodern, may thus have a modernist basis.

7. Charles Baudelaire, *Oeuvres complètes* (Paris: Gallimard, 1961), p. 1163.

8. Roland Barthes, *L'Obvie et l'obtus,* (Paris: Seuil, 1982), pp. 189.

9. "A Conversation," p. 33.

10. Ibid.

11. Paul Virilio, *L'Espace critique,* (Paris: Bourgois, 1984).

12. Fredric Jameson, "Postmodernism, or the Cultural Logic of Late Capitalism," *New Left Review* (July-August 1984), 146:58.

13. "A Conversation," p. 33.

14. The "new science" of the seventeenth and eighteenth centuries grew up within the ideology of the Enlightenment; but this ideology is no longer required to support it. It can be transplanted anywhere; it is compatible with many different sorts of political regimes; it is used by philanthropist and terrorist, democratic consumer and religious fanatic alike. Its universality lies not in its principles of discussion but in the scope of its technical consequences and in the sort of culture it brings about. Far from carrying enlightened ideas with it, it seems to work without a single ideology or legitimizing narrative. It brings rather the crisis of ideologies in its wake. The war of industrial ideologies is replaced by the wars of postindustrial technosciences.

15. The show was not at all an endorsement of what is known as "postmodern" architecture. Postmodern "historicism" is rather a symptom of a loss of public monumental history in a culture dominated by instantaneous transmission; it is a way of avoiding what Virilio calls "the 'transhistorical' temporality that issues from the technological ecosystems" (*L'Espace Critique,* p. 14). Historicist allusion in postmodern architecture is not simply a stylistic departure from the austerities of the International Style; it may also be a reaction to the

"immaterialization of place" that technoscience injects into our world.

16. Lyotard, *Tombeau de l'intellectuel,* pp. 83-84.

17. "A Conversation," p. 33.

18. Hal Foster, "(Post)Modern Polemics," *New German Critique* (Fall 1984), no. 33.

19. Jameson, "Postmodernism," p. 57.

20. Quoted in Lyotard, *Les Immatériaux* (Paris: Album, 1985), p. 19.

21. "Postmodernism" has become the rubric for a philosophical debate about French theory. For example, Jürgen Habermas defends a Weberian conception of modernity and sees in French theory its irrationalist denial. Lyotard challenges Habermas' obsession with "communication" and "consensus" with the values of the incommensurability or heterogeneity of languages. And, while Richard Rorty sides with Lyotard against Habermas' foundationalism, he nevertheless finds in (American) pragmatism a way of maintaining solidarity with enlightened modernity.

Robert John Sheffler Manning (essay date 1991)

SOURCE: A review of *The Differend: Phrases in Dispute,* in *The Journal of Religion,* Vol. 71, No. 2, April, 1991, pp. 282-83.

[*In the following review of* Le différend, *Manning places the work in the context of Lyotard's previous philosophical investigations and praises Lyotard for centering his inquiries inside the historical fact of the Holocaust.*]

The Differend: Phrases in Dispute clearly illustrates two essential reasons why Lyotard should be considered one of the most important philosophers writing today. First, it shows (again) that Lyotard is one of those very rare philosophers whose work bridges the gulf between analytic and Continental philosophy. Second, although *The Differend* continues the discussion of language games and of justice begun in his two earlier works—*The Postmodern Condition* (Minneapolis: University of Minnesota Press, 1984) and *Just Gaming* (Minneapolis: University of Minnesota Press, 1985)—it also shows that Lyotard is not one who merely rehashes old themes but is unusually open to being challenged. In *The Differend,* the terror of history forces him to rethink the issue of justice in order to further his quest to write a philosophy that is thoroughly enmeshed in the political.

This book obviously owes much to the later Wittgenstein. With its numbered paragraphs, it even looks like the *Philosophical Investigations* (New York: Macmillan, 1953). Appearances, however, can deceive. *The Differend* does not untie the knots in our language but stubbornly insists on "the impossibility of avoiding conflicts" (p. xii) because each genre of discourse is governed by its own rules. Hence, the title: "The title of this book suggests . . . that a universal rule of judgment between heterogeneous genres is lacking in general" (p. xi). Lyotard's insistence on the chasm between genres of discourse indicates that he borrows from Wittgenstein, but only as a Kantian. His appeal to Kant and Wittgenstein as "the two thoughts which beckon to the A" (p. xiii) expresses well the breadth of Lyotard's philosophical inheritance.

Those familiar with Lyotard's work will see that his discussion in *The Differend* of the heterogeneity of genres of discourse and of justice is nothing new. In *Just Gaming,* he insisted that each language game is played by its own rules and that it is not possible to judge one language game, such as the descriptive, from the point of view of another language game, such as the prescriptive (*Just Gaming,* p. 96). Similarly, in *The Postmodern Condition* he insisted that recognizing the heterogeneity of language games is the first step toward "an idea and practice of justice that is not linked to that of consensus" (*The Postmodern Condition,* p. 66).

If *The Differend* is also about language games and justice, what is different about it is the recognition of the stakes involved. *The Postmodern Condition* ended with Lyotard's triumphal rallying cry (so similar in tone to the conclusion of Jacques Derrida's "Structure, Sign, and Play" in *Writing and Difference* [Chicago: University of Chicago Press, 1978]) to "actuate the differences" (*The Postmodern Condition,* p. 82). At the conclusion of *Just Gaming,* Lyotard stated that the idea of justice consists in preserving the purity of each language game. To Lyotard's conversation partner in this work, Jean-Loup Theboud, this sounded like a prescriptive and made Lyotard "the great prescriber himself" (*Just Gaming,* p. 100). At this, *Just Gaming* ended in laughter. *The Differend,* however, begins where laughter ends, for in this work the issue of justice is a much more dangerous game than the philosophical issue involving heterogeneous language games. Justice is always discussed in *The Differend* in terms of a harsh historical reality, the Holocaust. Justice consists not merely in preserving the purity of language games but also in the necessity to link phrases together justly and to find rules for that linkage. Just gaming, justice as respecting the rules of each language game, gives way to justice as finding a phrase that links justly onto, does justice to, the phrase that comes before it. *The Differend*'s initial phrase—Auschwitz—testifies to the fact that Lyotard has accepted the onus of subjecting his reflections on language games and justice to the harsh reality of history. With this phrase, justice cannot consist merely in observing the rules of the language game of historical inquiry (p. 57). Auschwitz is the phrase that raises the central question of what genre of discourse can link onto it.

The Differend, then, driven by this question and this phrase, accepts the challenge of history and thereby carries Lyotard's discussion of language games and of justice to much more profound levels. It also carries him further along in his goal to philosophize at a level at which thinking is politics, making **The Differend** a significant contribution to the work of this unusual and important philosopher.

Betty McGraw (essay date 1992)

SOURCE: "Jean-François Lyotard's Postmodernism: Feminism, History, and the Question of Justice," in *Women's Studies: An Interdisciplinary Journal,* Vol. 20, Nos. 3-4, March, 1992, pp. 259-72.

[*In the following essay, McGraw discusses the importance of Lyotard's theory and critique of narrative for feminists in the pursuit of justice and reconstructing history.*]

> "Lorsque l'Un est pulvérisé et l'identité disloquée, et que règne le polémos, c'est alors . . . qu'il n'est plus question de faire n'importe quoi et qu'il est urgent d'être juste." Ph. Lacoue-Labarthe. (*La Faculté de Juger*)

BALANCE-SHEET

The capitalist game of competition waged between the Anglo-American type of feminist pragmatics and the various forms of French theoretical imports has resulted in a net loss: eight years of Reaganomics, prolonged by the present laissez-faire attitude, has just about cancelled any socio-economic advances made in the sixties and seventies by cultural feminists. Unmistakably echoic, an anxious literary establishment, scrambling for ever-diminishing funds, and perceiving theoretical investment negatively has rejuvenated the myth of a universal canonical truth to regain control over experimental forms of literary productions. Clearly, growing incidences of intellectual schizophrenia,[1] coupled with the reality of ever-diminishing funds, have brought reactionary politics back to the forefront of the social and academic scene. Following a brief historical over-view of recent forms of feminist criticism which, at some point, held emancipatory appeal for women, this article will suggest a different configuration where thinking the feminine is invested with new and innovative possibilities. In so doing, it will borrow from Jean-François Lyotard's postmodernist vision of a reality which redistributes power on the basis of the tolerant[2] *concurrence* rather than a harmful competition. Also under consideration will be Lyotard's concept of "pagan" justice which sets a prescriptive tone for a rewriting of (women's) history with an end to abolishing future inequities.

RE/PRESENTING/AESTHECIZING

Modern[3] feminism was launched when, back in 1970, Kate Millett set a historical milestone with the publication of her *Sexual Politics.*[4] Aligned with Hegel's theory of the subject's existence, Millett's manifesto agitated for the creation of an autonomous entity—Woman—and de-

manded reparation for the violence done to it and for the silence it had to endure throughout the history of Western civilization. Her spirited course charted a long and unfinished struggle in which Millett and other pragmatist feminists mandated economic and social autonomy. In Academia, the desire for self-determination translated into a belief that women were writing from within a particular biological, political and historical configuration.[5] Requests to supplement the "core curriculum"—i.e. the male canon—with courses on women immediately followed. Little if anything was said, then, about the fact that women have been perceiving "their" history through a male model of reality whose mode of thinking is based on a normative order of discourse. As theorists have since argued, any "objective" explanation of the "facts" of women's repression is part of a Man's history whose "factual" method—reason's crowning achievement—not only become irrelevant to women but, to use Lyotard's phrase, is fundamentally *injust.*[6]

The move to situate women's experience within the neo-positivist tradition of an empiricism which assumes a specific female consciousness was categorically denounced in 1977 by Luce Irigaray in *Ce sexe qui n'en est pas un.* Irigaray argued that the Anglo-American feminists' attempt to devise a model of perception that is woman's alone is a militant gesture in reverse, one which simply turns the male hierarchy on its head. In positing a universal category of women, a homogeneous essence with no link to the male counterpart, cultural feminists resort to a mysogynist activity in reverse and turn history into another form of phallocratism.[7] The pragmatic corrective which aims at replacing the self-effaced woman with the superwoman, in effect only succeeds in rewriting history as destiny—that of an oppression.[8] And to accept a reification of history is to reduce, even to artificially end its conflicts.

Contesting the above celebration of one sex, another "gynetic"[9] configuration emerged from the poststructuralist theories of Michel Fourcault, Jacques Lacan and Jacques Derrida. Foucault's radical critique of the perceptual subject puts into doubt the notion of a specific womanhood, while Lacan denounces the concept of a universal Woman (with a capital letter) whose essentialism rejects the diversity among women themselves: "Woman cannot *be,* and cannot be *described* discursively," says Lacan. "Her place is there, but it is empty. The 'la' of '*la* femme' is a signifier which must be marked, but as *trace* only. Thus the woman "is not all. Which does not permit us to speak of Woman with a capital W."[10] Finally, in Derrida's grammatological project, which associates voice to *logos* and specifically opposes it to a positive use of *Écriture,*[11] practioners of feminine writing believe they have discovered a means to write against the traditional language of power, i.e. man's language.

Thus animated by the added discovery of the Lacanian Symbolic Order, which discloses that experience is what structures the subject and not the other way around, *l'écriture féminine* (feminine writing) has rejected the no-tion of experience altogether. Inasmuch as experiential perspectives are informed by a metaphysical tradition which has historically excluded women's representation, practioners of feminine writing have abjured the phallo-cratic model of historical narrative, and have determined that any attempt to restructure the subject's experience must begin with a restructuring of the power relation within language. Simply put, the aesthetics of feminine writing prescribes a reformulation of the subject as a becoming-woman (or a becoming-man) via pre-linguistic, pre-semantic models of language, and in terms which em-phasize the body's kinetic rhythm, not the "facts" or the "truth" of such and such experiences, for subjects are nei-ther "true" nor "false." In a rather oxymoronic mode then, it is aligned with the above theoretical *masters* whose pos-tulates have served as a launch pad for experimental forms of writing. Informed by the Derridian notion of *différance,* these feminists seek to neutralize the effects of the phallo-cratic model of discourse whose logic evolves from a rec-ognition of the symbolic presence of the Law of the Father (the *nom du père*)—a recognition paired with the discov-ery of women's nonrepresentation.[12]

But while French feminists have pointed to the myth which governs a pragmatic feminist practice which hopes to posi-tively impact the Sociopolitical with an experiential belief in the woman's subject, cultural feminists argue that theo-rists of the feminine are nurturing an illusion of their own (the very nurturing that men, in their supposed wisdom, have often attributed to women), in that a prescription[13] for a feminine critique which consists in writing the body and its kinetic rhythm has no practical future effects. To be sure, when discursivity is placed at the service of the "body of the mother," as is the case in much of Hélène Cixous's writing, for example,[14] it redefines the "mother" as a sort of deity, a gesture which amounts to nothing more than an aesthetics informed by a return to essentialist values. While the point has been made that this type of idealism "seeks to transcend . . . the deadly asperities of male violence and destruction,"[15] writing the body nevertheless under-scores the dangers of glorifying the subversive effect of style in an entirely dehistoricized fashion.

Feminist criticism has thus become an issue *sans issue,* splintered by quarrels among devotees of competing criti-cal denominations. The dispute between "real life politics" and "poetic politics"[16] is turning into a *discours de sourds* with devastating effects on the human community. To be sure, cultural feminists are less interested in defining the Woman (the Lacanian *La* Femme) than in furthering the political agenda of women ("Ce que *les* femmes veulent). They demand the right to be heard, not to be written across a text as narrative destinies. At the same time, they ques-tion whether or not theorizing or aestheticizing life's situa-tions can produce a writing that is progressive, virulent and at the same time usable, in a social sense. Preferring action to theoretical games, cultural feminists perceive socio-political expediency as essential for a feminist *praxis,* and yearn to vindicate a historical subject victimized by a

tradition of male-dominated capitalist repression. To the extent that they denounce capital injustice and work from the premise of an emancipated self, their struggle reso-nates within the writings of several Marxist critics[17] for whom victimization can be explained and, therefore, rem-edied through an understanding of the historical process. For what would progress be without an understanding of history? Isn't history a contingency which significantly in-forms our cultural and artistic heritage, and which, they reason, has been left out of Lacanian theories which dehis-toricize the subject?

The recent call to history emerges from Michel Foucault's studies of the relation between knowledge and power, and his analyses of institutionally situated discursive practices. Rejecting the Derridian statement "there is no outside-the-text" ("il n'y a pas de hors texte"), Foucault moves away from a textual hermeneutics to investigate the formation rules for a variety of discourses within a given period. In-deed, Foucault appears to be encouraging us to move be-yond the text: "we must not go from discourse towards its interior, hidden nucleus, towards the heart of a thought or signification supposed to be manifested in it; but, on the basis of discourse itself, its appearance and its regularity, go towards its external conditions of possibility."[18] But, as Jonathan Culler astutely points out, Foucault's archeologi-cal project does not give us history, that is, not in the sense of an explanation of what "the 'real' conditions were at a particular moment."[19] What Foucault's brilliant analy-ses do give us are *"histories* of the terms, categories and techniques through which certain things become at certain times the focus of a whole configuration of discussion and procedure."[20] Inasmuch as these analyses clearly do not expose history's participation in the silencing of women, some other form of historical knowledge—the kind that begins to think itself *obliquely,* i.e., outside its sphere of influence—is called for. Now, against the back-drop of a metaphysical specular identity that mistakes logic for real-ity, and opposing the repressiveness of a performance-driven capitalist identity supported by the techno-sciences, Jean-François Lyotard proposes a "new historicism" where social phenomena are wrenched from reason's confusion. More specifically, what Lyotard is suggesting is a reading of history against the grain, i.e., not according to its facts but by "respossessing" those "signs" which have been cast away to the junkpile of History. In the pages which follow, I will now investigate just how this radical criticism holds a promise of hope for a feminist critique.

REWRITING

In an complex argument, Lyotard modifies Foucault's analyses of institutionally situated discursive practices to include the "great narratives" (*les grands récits*) of his-tory; those of cause and effect, scientific determinism, uni-versal Marxist emancipation, and others which have served as the guiding lights of our western past. But in keeping with the logophobia of our "post" age, Lyotard angles into history with a belief in the multiple and heteronomous ex-perimentation of "paganism." In so doing, he succeeds in breaching in the traditional historical method of validating research, borrowed from the positivist scientific disciplines. More specifically, Lyotard questions history's retroactive and synthesizing method of containing past states and events within discourse for the purpose of "recording, reproducing and representing them."[21] For what is it that we are representing? Lyotard asks. The Latin etymology warns that the prefix RE means to *re*turn, that it is a becoming after in the closed circle of the metaphysical tautology.

Here, Lyotard would come down especially hard on a feminism whose knowledge of the "facts" of women's history and their experiential perspective evolve from an established linear syntax, i.e., from man's language of power and exclusion. He could suggest that the problem of *re*presenting a history that is nothing more than a recollecting of past events whose outcome is already known, even with the intent of denouncing it, is that it creates a situation wherein the subject who writes the facts of women's repression becomes an unwilling accomplice of history's hegemonic discourse. In fact, Lyotard compares the normative order of phrases involved in the process of writing *about* and therefore repeating women's repression to the oracle of the Oedipus tale: "woman's destiny"[22] becomes a narrative paradigm whose fate is outlined in its own telling. In other words, it is already inscribed in whatever "projection, proposal or program"[23] feminism proclaims.

But Lyotard would equally chastise practioners of feminine writing precisely for postulating that a *re*turn to presemantic, pre-male linguistic models is a re/pro/gression to a time/place prior to the piling up of a prejudicial process. As far as he is concerned, returning to a pre-logical writing model is not unlike repeating (also understood as *répéter, répétition,* i.e. in the sense of a dramatic rehearsal) that very metaphysical gesture feminine writers hope to dismantle. The cultural philosopher indeed believes that returning amounts to nothing more than producing "already uttered judgments taken for granted without reconsideration."[24] Thus Lyotard's undeniable attraction to a certain reading of Kant stimulates his desire for establishing an ethical underpinning based on a "deaestheticizing" of the aesthetic, something which is not necessarily achieved when writing *au féminin.*

What Lyotard envisions, therefore, is an altogether different type of writing, one that is not given to its English definition, i.e., a "putting down." For what is it that has been "put down," and for too long a time? To be sure, it is not just historical events but the woman. Amplifying his critique of the complicity between history *re*presenting itself and the normative order of phrases involved in recording the "facts" of women's repression, Lyotard concentrates on the analysis of a specific term—*re*membering. In the aftermath of Proust's *Recherche,* Lyotard argues that in remembering we want to grasp past events or states, we want to overcome the nostalgia of the lost, the initial moment, the guilt or anxiety. Remembering also implies the phenomenological bracketing gesture which isolates the subject's experience and desires, and thus facilitates the distinction between (feminine) difference and (masculine) sameness. Aligned with Foucault's discovery of the will to overtake others, either socially or epistemologically, remembering involves a metaphysical process whose *Weltanschauungen* is to produce the "great narratives" which perpetrate the repressive positioning of the female subject within an *archè* and a *telos.* Thus remembering may raise the question of women's past repression, but it does so in a manner which only insures its repressive idiom.

To counter the *logos*'s ability to neutralize all disruptions, past and anticipated, Lyotard dreams of a writing which would not be a remembering, but "a working through," in the sense Freud uses the term to describe an "equally floating attention."[25] As is well known, by focusing on the *logos*'s irreducible otherness, the Freudian rule equalizes all available experiences and shows "no prejudices, but suspension of judgments, responsiveness, and equal attention to all occurrences as they occur."[26] In Lyotard's view, this operation could produce a counter reading of history (social, political, literary) which would insure that chaotic and contradictory events are not merely subsumed in some major scheme of historical development, but are allowed to co-exist equally with recognized historical events. The status of mere "incidents," what are now called women's issues, could then be raised to the level of "events" and subjected to a reading which would challenge the status quo. Once *a-priori* judgment is suspended, whatever has been forced into silence can be heard. And the feminine idiom which has not had its day in court can acquire the means to establish its claim.[27]

HER/STORIES = HIS/STORIES

Lyotard's ambition is to replace the "pious" devotion we give to the great narratives with mini-stories depicting *combats minoritaires*—those minorities' struggles of the type women have had to wage throughout their history. To achieve his goal, Lyotard devises the notion of a "pagan" justice, and raises the question of the *just*[28] in term of postmodern experimentations with language games, for "pagans don't worry themselves over the conformity of the narrative to its object. They know that the references are organized by the words, and that the gods are no guarantee, because their word is no more truthful than that of humans. They are quite busy with rhetoric and hunting—where one never has the last word and there is no *coup de grâce.*"[29]

Influenced by Kant—the Kant of critical judgment[30]—and by Wittgenstein's language-game theories, Lyotard's experimentation with language is based on the *concurrence* of separate types of enunciations (prescriptive, denotative, speculative, fictive, etc.) and not on the subordination of one to the others. "Different but equal" is congruent with Lyotard's belief in replacing a univocal rationalism with a plurivocal and conflictive practice where invention comes before signification, happening (Lyotard's famous "qu'arrive-t-il?") before knowledge. His postmodern vision extends to a historico-cultural pragmatic context which incorporates and dialectizes different mediatic experiments and proposes a dialogue between the varying narrative realms that are still considered unequal today.[31] Not only does this radical critical politics of nonresolvable heterogeneity keep in abeyance speculative, totalizing modes of thought, and challenge the authoritative single voice of the great narratives (*Les grands récits*), but by the same token it destroys the myth of liberation under which these narratives (and one can't help but be reminded here of the promises of Marxist emancipation) have been operating throughout the history of our Western past.

Paralleling the need to change emphasis from the great narratives to the "incidents" of history (from *l'Histoire* to *les histoires*) is Lyotard's desire to phrase the political in a more diversified, less monolythic way, i.e., to treat events as if they were sentences. This strategy pursues the (Kantian) Idea of justice that arises out of the need to respect the plural and the heterogeneous. It combines a neo-Kantian problematics of passage between the aesthetics and the political with the constitutive instances of discourse—addressee, addresser, referent and meaning—to arrive at a variety of possible worlds. Each discursive instance is situated in terms of the other in a manner that creates new and unpredictable signification. Theorizing that phrasing is a political question—the one which asks what occurs next after the occurrence of any phrase—, Lyotard poses the problem strategically: if to link is necessary, "how to link is not."[32] Here, Lyotard prescribes a series of moves activating passage from the constative to the performative function of language. For Lyotard argues that normative sentences are always vying for a position of jurisdiction, whereas performatives have an admonitory connotation which denounces unquestioned authoritative domains.[33]

Clearly, Lyotard's model of "phrases"[34] and discourse, which he subsequently relates to human beings with an end to the "judicious," is a significant departure from the earlier Wittgensteinian language-game theory, for it makes possible "manipulating the concept of game without implying a subject-player who is outside the game."[35] For this "postmodern Descartes" refuses to accept the evidence of the cogito and fall into the trap of a kind of scientific linguistics which supports the notion of a controlling subject. As far as he is concerned, "a philosophy of phrases can be considered critical . . . only insofar as it situates the subject, makes the subject a position within the universe of phrases, and thus only as it undermines the notion of a subject posited as existing prior to or outside the universe of phrases."[36]

What is significant about emphasizing positionality from *within* the universe of phrases is that it relates to the question of marginality, as enunciated by Julia Kristeva. For "what is perceived as marginal at any given time depends on the position one occupies"[37] on the symbolic register. The marginal becomes aware of his/her painful relationship to a dominant linguistic idiom and, by extension, to

economic and social repression. But, in demonstrating that a sentence can be formed to represent several differing domains concomitantly and unexpectedly, what Lyotard advocates is a heterogeneous and multiple universe which gives all subjects the right to be heard equally. The result is that the formerly dominant subject experiences a *démaîtrise;* no longer a controlling master, the subject becomes a nomenclature which may or may not "occupy" phrase instances such as addressee, addresser, referent, meaning, etc. As part of an ongoing narrative organization, the addresser is positioned in a collective production and does not know who the addressee will be, nor does he know the nature of the address. All that is known is that, like body and shadow, both addresser and addressee occupy the same space. The upshot is the possibility of collapsing the masculine into the feminine, for there is no masculine or feminine writing per se, but only codes and systems used by writers. The way a writer avails him/herself of these rules is a matter of positionality, i.e., the subject's position on the symbolic spectrum of Law, language and society. Thus what Lyotard calls phrases in dispute (the *Différend*) is a refusal to determine, *in advance,* the nature of the Social and the Law, and an invitation to imagining new and unheard-of effects.[38]

The drive to redefine the Social in terms of the subject's positionality parallels the ambition to change the status of aesthetic experimentations to reflect something other than judgments of taste. But while Lyotard authorizes an aestheticism grounded in the political and allows for experimentation to reflect the need to "explore an historical situation of life,"[39] he nevertheless refuses to work from within the speculative philosophy which governs even the most "effective" of liberating discourses. Thus it would be wrong to view his writing as moving towards the direction of cultural feminists. For he argues for a "judicial" plurality and not for a plurality of justices, for a nonresolvable heterogeneity which is aligned with Habermas' position that experimentation should be "brought into relation with problems of existence."[40] The result is—*pace* the feminists—that there is nothing in Lyotard's phrasing of the political that can be construed as a means to flee from the real, the "authentic" ground of political engagement. In fact, Lyotard describes his own philosophical gesture as "a project to analyze sociopolitical problems of justice in terms of a problematics of language,"[41] and goes to great length not to evacuate the political from the aesthetic notion of performance mentioned above, nor to let himself fall into the trap of speech act theory. In fact, by suggesting that the political and the social have something to do with "the way one phrase is linked to another"[42] Lyotard renders the real problematical.

SIGNS

While Lyotard comes down especially hard on any attempt to posit the ethical in terms of an Ideal Community, a knowable entity to be imposed on society at large, he does not deny the prescriptive overtone of his alliance between discursive experiments and serious questions of justice.

That he views this relationship as necessary is evoked in *Au juste*[43], for example, when he addresses the "responsibility" of his writings in general, and of the performatives within the larger context of pagan pragmatics: "my excuse for writing," he states, "has always been a political one; I've always considered that sufficient. Therefore it is quite evident that I accept entirely that there is a prescriptive function in the ideal of paganism: it lies in the direction this idea indicates as necessary to follow"[44]

In order to illustrate his preference for a prescriptive pagan injustice over the cognitive phrases of history, Lyotard uses a specific case of "injustice"—the denial of the existence of victims in Auschwitz as narratively validated by the historian Faurisson.[45] Lyotard's intention is thus to agitate for a history that would not rely on pseudo facts but that would make room for an interpretation sensitive to what he calls, after Kant, the "*sign*" of history. Practicing a radicalized political history such as this means that the historian "must break with the monopoly granted to the cognitive order of phrases over history and dare to lend an ear to what is not presentable in the rules of knowledge. Every reality carries within this demand insomuch as it carries within it the possibilities of unknown meanings."[46] Obviously, listening to the "sign of history" demands a response other than a quantitative one, and the risk of sentimentalism and/or irrationalism is great. But in disclosing different historico-political modes of thinking based on a variety of discursive universes, Lyotard in fact offers a powerful critical instrument which precludes subjectivism. Insisting on an "ethics of feeling" that is rigorous, without being limited to what can be proved by logic and reasoning, does not have to berate our intellectual ideals. To the contrary. Lyotard's ethics of feeling is enhanced by the thought that it encompasses the silent injustices which have been forgotten through the traditional methods of validation.

The commitment to being sensitive to the *sign* of history differs from the feminists' assessment of prescriptive criticism, for it endorses a rewriting[47] (rereading) of the entire historical field. This prescriptive gesture is not a simple reformulation of a *modus operandi,* and must not be mistaken for another historical periodization since similar gestures have been made—only to be repressed—by the Sophists, by the Greek mythological pantheon, by Pascal, and closer to us, by Nietszche who, "in spite of himself," Lyotard notes, was guilty of repeating "the fault of his predecessors, rewriting from within the *Grund* he sought to destroy, repeating the process of metaphysics he attempted to denouce."[48] Lyotard's vigilant strategy hopes to avoid the faults of our predecessors by respecting "the desire for justice and the desire for the unknown."[49] In so doing, Lyotard redistributes the perspectives in the interpretative field, not in its power to seek out the "facts" but, rather, in its ability to present that which cannot be articulated, that which is not presentable under any rule of knowledge whatsoever.

REINVESTING

Lyotard's critical operation via Kant and his elaboration of a "pagan justice" based on the idea of experimentation in language games open a new area of research for both the feminist and the practioner of feminine writing. To be sure, by focusing on phrases in dispute, Lyotard reaffirms the primary of language in interpretation, communication, and even in the admonition to "be fair." But unlike aesthetic feminism, there is in Lyotard's own brand of postmodernism an unwavering desire to expose and adamantly resist all totalizing rhetorical manoeuvres. By the same token, unlike most emancipatory appeals made by a consciously politicized engagement which rarely questions the superiority of privileged forms of discourse, Lyotard's pagan experimentation gives us a radical politics of heterogeneity which reflects the desire "to practice a justice in terms of the non-resolution of *différends*"[50] without falling back into the trap of competitive pluralism.

Undoubtedly, Lyotard's "adjoining" criticism facilitates the passage between feminine aesthetics and feminist politics by bringing the universe of phrases into the sociopolitical arena. But, most of all, his disengagement from the totalizing operation of a traditional historical narrative represents a significant means to reconfigure gynesis in terms of what History has overlooked. Of course, any strategy which advocates thinking History's exclusion by listening to the "wisps of narratives"[51] also encourages wrecking "the elegant room of History" (Bakhtin). But no matter, for rewriting History from its *footnotes* may keep us from repeating it, once more.[52]

Notes

Excerpts from this article were presented at the *Midwest Modern Language Association,* in Minneapolis (Nov. 1989) during a session entitled "Romancing the Throne."

1. I am using the term, here, not in its clinical sense but as a metaphor to depict an intellectual disorder. Nevertheless, following Annette Kolodny's address, "The Feminist as Literary Critic," the discussion printed in *Critical Inquiry* 2:4 (Summer 1976) in which William Morgan accused Annette Kolodny of advocating a "separatist" attitude which was, of course, contrary to the best tradition of Western thought is highly disturbing insofar as Morgan mistook the object of his phobia.

2. Actually, "writing" and "love" are the two terms upon which Lyotard bases his active resistance to universal homogeneisation, for both demonstrate a marvelous potential for switching perspective from "mine" to "thine." "Writing, like loving, necessarily implies a surrendering of one's field of mastery." See *Au Juste* (Paris, 1979), p. 18, (transl. mine). Lyotard relates/these two terms to a "moral" law which affects but cannot be determined. To be "receptive" seems to be the guiding term of this ethical situation whose emphasis has been switched from sender to

receiver; "passivity" (in Lévinas's sense), receptiveness and openness to the other are demanded, rather than knowledge of the law. See David Carroll's "Rephrasing the Political with Kant and Lyotard: From Aesthetic to Political judgments." *Diacritics* (Fall 1984). See also, Francis Guibal's "Penser avec Jean-François Lyotard): Le temps du risque," in *Témoigner du différend.* Presented by Pierre-Jean Labarrière. (Paris: Editions Osiris, 1989) pp. 11-58.

3. Defined, here, as a certain historical period whereby the subject is viewed as the maker of his/her society.

4. New York: Doubleday, 1970.

5. See Alica A. Jardine, *Gynesis: Configurations of Women and Modernity,* (Ithaca: Cornell University Press, 1985) p. 55.

6. I explain the choice of this term later in this article.

7. Irigaray in *Ce sexe qui n'en est pas un:* "history . . . boil[s] back down to the same of phallocratism." (Paris: Editions de Minuit, 1977), p. 32.

8. Susan Suleiman has raised similar objections in an astute discussion of Monique Wittig's *Les Guerrillères* which she characterizes as a feminist's stronghold featuring an antagonistic relation between the two sexes, stressing their mutually exclusive division. Cf. her article entitled "(Re)Writing the Body," *Poetics Today.* Vol. 6: 1-2 (1985), pp. 43-65.

9. The term is borrowed from Alice A. Jardine's *Gynesis. Configurations of Women and Modernity.* (Ithaca: Cornell University Press, 1985).

10. Lacan, *Encore, 1972-73,* Vol. 20 of *Le Séminaire de Jacques Lacan* (Paris: Editions du Seuil, 1975), p. 68. The more complete quotation is as follows: "Il n'y pas *La* femme, article défini pour désigner l'universel. Il n'y a pas *La* femme puisque . . . de son essence elle n'est pas toute" ("Woman with a capital W, in the sense that Woman designates a universal, because . . . it is her essence to be not all."

11. One is here reminded of the Barthesian distinction between *écrivain* i.e., the one who writes autoreferentially, and *écrivant* i.e., the writer of messages based on thematics rather than significance.

12. While aesthetic feminists search for a model outside the field of representation, Julia Kristeva has pointed to the possibility of articulating women's own space around the symbolic order with her own definition of the semiotic *chora.* See Julia Kristeva's *Revolution in Poetic Language,* trans. Margaret Waller (New York: Columbia University Press, 1986), p. 13.

13. Prescriptive criticism has become offensive in some feminist quarters. Thus Kolodny states: ". . . I am suspicious of wanting to influence the future of creative expression . . . in feminist criticism, as in all literary critical endeavor, I would rather have the literature give rise to the critical rules than have the critical rules formulate the literature." op. cited, p. 828. Meanwhile, Jane Gallop dismisses it altogether in a recent paper entitled *"The Scandal of Prescriptive Criticism,"* read at the *Midwest Modern Language Association,* Minneapolis, November 1989. Needless to say that Lyotard's brand of prescription for justice in the critical realm is altogether different from the accepted norm of what prescriptive criticism is according to both Kolodny and Gallop.

14. Other examples would include the writings of Xavière Gauthier and Marie Cardinale.

15. It is Naomi Schor who makes this beautiful point while discussing the concrete, everyday, homey woman world of the detail. Schor believes that there is a femininity to woman that lies in a certain form of idealism "one that seeks to transcend not the sticky feminine world of prosaic details, but rather that deadly asperities of male violence and destruction." *Reading in Detail,* (New York an London: Methuen, 1987), p. 97.

16. This is the description Susan Suleiman gives of the dispute in the article cited above.

17. Those include Fredric Jameson, Dominick La Capra and Terry Eagleton, to name the most prominent. However, the privileged position given to Marxist criticism, notably in Terry Eagleton's *Literary Theory* (Oxford: Blackwell, 1983), is refuted by Foucault's analyses of power discourse [cf., in particular Foucault's concept of the "repressive hypothesis" in *Power/Knowledge,* Ed. Colin Gordon (New York: Pantheon, 1980).

18. Michel Foucault, *L'Ordre du discours* (Paris: Gallimard, 1971), p. 55. Cited in Jonathan Culler's *Framing the Sign: Criticism and Its Institution* (Norman & London: University of Oklahoma Press, 1988), p. 62.

19. Culler *Framing the Sign,* p. 63.

20. John Rajchman *Michel Foucault and the Freedom of philosophy* (New York: Columbia University Press, 1985), p. 51. Cited in Culler, p. 63. My emphasis.

21. Jean-François Lyotard. "Re-writing Modernity," *SubStance,* Vol. XVI, Number 3 (1987), p. 4.

22. It might be useful to remember, here, that the expression "woman's destiny" cannot be considered without its male counterpart in our binary system of thought.

23. Lyotard. "Re-writing Modernity," p. 4.

24. Lyotard. "Re-writing Modernity," p. 4. In this article, Lyotard also notes a curious correlation between the historical representation of events and states, and theory: By virtue of being outside of time, both produce a similar result, for both methods

merely imply a simple return to a question which has been held in abeyance. Both modes of thought complacently assign to the question they raise the answer that had been held in reserve.

25. See "Remembering, Repeating and Working-Through," in *The Complete Works of Sigmund Freud.* Vol. XII (1911-13), tr. J. Strackey, Standard Edition.

26. Lyotard. "Re-writing Modernity," p. 7. In this same article, Lyotard explains the significant distinction Freud makes between remembering, *Erinnerung,* and working through, *Durcharbeitung.* In remembering we want to grasp past events or states (Proust), we want to overcome the nostalgia of the lost, the initial moment—the guilt or anxiety. We want to objectify so that we may separate, bracket our experiences, our desires. To this extent, remembering comes with a purpose, and end (hence the ambiguity of the French word *fin*—both an end and a purpose—in pursuing this end, desire fills its purpose). But then, remembering becomes the *repetition* of the wish to fulfill itself in enacting one's present life. The pursuit of this psychic device—neurosis of psychosis—re-memorates and transforms.

27. To echo woman's predicament, Lyotard suggests the existence of a silence, something left unsaid within the destiny of history and theory concerning its relationship to humanism. "All thought conceals something of the unthought," says Lyotard in an interview conducted by Georges Van Den Abbeelee and reprinted in *Diacritics.* Vol. 14, Number 3 (Fall 1984), p. 16. This could explain its languishing, its lack of effectiveness (its lack of effective praxis) in the socio-political sphere. Antoine Compagnon makes a similar claim with regards to literary history. See "The Two Barthes," in *Signs of Culture. Roland Barthes Today,* edited by Steve Ungar and Betty R. McGraw, (Iowa City: University of Iowa Press, 1989).

28. It may be interesting to note the plurivocity of the term "just" which can be understood as *justice* and as *justesse* i.e., something that fits closely like a garment, or that is exact, but also *justesse* in the sense of a close call.

29. Lyotard. *Instructions païennes.* (Paris: Editions Galilée, 1981), p. 45.

30. That is the Kant of the Third and Fourth Critiques, the "the critical watchman." See the article entitled "Rephrasing the Political with Kant and Lyotard: From Aesthetics to Political Judgment," by David Carroll in *Diacritics.* Vol. 14, Number 3 (Fall 1984), p. 79.

31. Included in those are the sciences before literature, the canon before experimental writing, and corporate profits before the need to upgrade the minimum wage.

32. Lyotard. *Le Différend* (Paris: Editions de Minuit, 1983), p. 103.

33. Lyotard discusses the function of the performative speech acts, such as the admonition to "be fair," in an extended essay entitled *Au juste.* Opus Cited.

34. See "Introduction à une étude du Politique selon Kant," in *Rejouer la politique* (Paris: Galilée, 1981), in which Lyotard describes the critical act in terms of the seeking of "passages" (übergänge) between phrase universes.

35. Carroll, "Rephrasing the Political with Kant and Lyotard, p. 77.

36. Carroll, "Rephrasing the Political with Kant and Lyotard, p. 77.

37. Toril Moi, *Sexual/Textual Politics: Feminist Literary Theory* (London: Routledge, 1985), p. 166.

38. Obviously, Lyotard does not forget Derrida's belief that we are always-already in the situation of the already-recounted.

39. This is Lyotard citing Harbermas in an article by Philippe Lacoue-Labarthe entitled "Talk," in *Diacritics.* Vol. 14, Number 3 (Fall 1984), p. 25.

40. Habermas, cited by Lyotard in Lacoue-Labarthe's article. Opus cited, p. 25.

41. To a question raised by Van Den Abbeele. Opus cited, p. 16.

42. Lyotard. Interview with Van Den Abbeele. Opus cited, p. 16. See also how, in this respect, Lyotard discusses the Faurisson case as an example of how faulty rules used to establish historical reality can be. See *Le différend,* pp. 16-7. See also David Carroll's account of *Le différend* along similar lines: "Lyotard's philosophy of phrases does not flee or retreat from . . . claim to reality but confronts it head-on in an attempt to render it problematical." In "Rephrasing the Political with Kant and Lyotard," p. 77.

43. Opus cited, p. 34.

44. Interview with Van Den Abbeele. Opus cited, p. 16.

45. See *Le différend* which puts into practice the political philosophy elaborated in *Au Juste.*

46. Lyotard *Le différend,* p. 92.

47. This is Lyotard's term who prefers to use the expression "re-writing" (as hyphenated construction) to that of "post-modern" believing that "the improvement lies in a double displacement: a lexical commutation from 'post-' to 're-'; and a syntactical one dealing with the transfer of the prefix which is now connected with 'writing' rather than with 'modernity.'" See Lyotard, "Re-writing Modernity." Opus cited, p. 3.

48. Ibid., p. 6.

49. Lyotard. *La Condition postmoderne.* (Paris: Minuit, 1979), p. 108.

50. Carroll. "Rephrasing the Political with Kant and Lyotard." Opus cited, p. 78.

51. Cecile Lindsay, "Experiments in Postmodern Dialogue," *Diacritics.* Vol. 14, No 2, (Fall 1984), p. 56.

52. Jonathan Culler makes an interesting observation along these lines. As far as he is concerned, there is a compelling reason for loosening our grip over our Western cultural heritage. It resides in the fact that, in light of current demographic projections, it will be "hard seriously to imagine the establishment of a common culture based on the Greeks and other classics." *Framing the Sign: Criticism and Its Institution,* p. 49.

Susan E. Shapiro (essay date 1994)

SOURCE: "Ecriture judaique: Where Are the Jews in Western Discourse?" in *Displacements: Cultural Identities in Question,* edited by Angelika Bammer, Indiana University Press, 1994, pp. 182-201.

[*In the following essay, Shapiro argues that, in "Heidegger and 'the Jews,'" Lyotard replaces "actual Jews" with a universal category.*]

In the dominant discourse(s) of the Christian/West[1] the Jew has been located in a place that defines and fixes "his"[2] identity stereotypically.[3] Both in explicitly Christian discourse and in discourses derived from and influenced by it, the Jew has been figured in negative terms as that which lacks legitimacy or value.[4] This negative figure (the Jew as the "Other" of the Christian/West) has been embodied in the trope of "the Jew," and it is through this tropic lens that actual Jews have been seen. For example, the figure of the wandering Jew represented the punishment of the Jew exiled from home, condemned to diasporic suffering until the second coming (see Anderson; and Dundes and Hasan-Rokem). The perceived carnality of the "Old Testament" corresponded to the view of the Jew as overly or deviantly sexual.[5] Taking circumcision as a sign of exclusivity, Jews were seen as intransigent, stubbornly particular, and particularistic.[6] For continuing to identify and live as Jews, they[7] were represented as refusing to embrace the "universal" spirituality of Christianity. By extension, this meant failing to become fully assimilated to the universal citizenry of Man in allegiance to the Nation.[8]

Confined to this trope of "the Jew" as to a ghetto, the ongoing and diverse histories of Jews and Judaism(s) (not only) in the West have been effaced.[9] This absence or invisibility has been operative not only in the writing of religious or "world" history, but in other discourses and disciplines, such as literature and philosophy, as well. In poststructuralist or postmodern theory, the figure of the Jew appears in numerous guises. Indeed, as compared, say, to the rather notable absence of Jews as subjects in postcolonial writing,[10] postmodern discourses would initially seem to better or more adequately provide resources for articulating Jewish (post-Holocaust) identities.[11]

Postmodern discourse has been read as occasioned by, and as identical with, post-Holocaust writing. Its form of ruptured and displaced writing has been regarded as representing, or as being a consequence of, the Shoah and its shattering of the telos and coherence of the Western subject.[12] While this "disaster" is interpreted as an effect of the Shoah, the Shoah is interpreted as a symptom of a disaster within writing [*écriture*] itself (Blanchot; Jabès). In this way, the subject(s) of postmodernism and post-Holocaust writing are identified and the Holocaust is subsumed under the discourse of postmodernism.[13] The question of the identity of the Jew after the Holocaust, thus, figures consistently in postmodern discourses.

There is yet another way in which Jewish and deconstructive writing have been associated. The undecidability of discourse as evidenced in postmodern writing has been interpreted as midrashic in character (see Handleman; and Hartman and Budick) and Midrash, in turn, has been interpreted through the resources of postmodern theories (see Daniel Boyarin, *Intertextuality*). The term "Midrash" has become a trope that, emptied of its historical and cultural specificity, has come to represent the undecidability of meaning itself.[14] Midrash, thus, has been taken as exemplifying, indeed as identical with, deconstruction, while postmodern discourse has been considered a form of what I here term *écriture judaïque.* The displaced, exiled, catastrophic writing of postmodernism is troped by the Jews as other and vice versa; writing and Jew(daism) have become metonyms of one another.

A third point of contact between Jewish and postmodern discourses is occasioned by the association of post-Holocaust writing and *écriture judaïque.* If the previous two affiliations are considered positive, this last one has often been read negatively. As Sander Gilman has demonstrated, the "damaged" language of the Jews has been troped as evidence of their diseased, pathological nature (*Jewish Self-Hatred* 309-92; *Jew's Body* 10-37). Similarly, the critique of deconstructive writing within the academy has increasingly been framed in terms of health and disease: it is seen as dangerous to the hygiene of Western discourse. While in the early stages of its reception deconstruction was often read as culturally Jewish (by both its adherents and critics), after the de Man and Heidegger controversies, the purported "Jewishness" of this writing has been further complicated and put in question.[15]

While there are several thinkers whose writings bear on this inquiry into contemporary critical resources for articulating Jewish identity/ies, I will focus primarily on the work of Jean-François Lyotard, especially his ***Heidegger and "the jews."*** Framed in the context of historical anti-Judaism in the West, it is an attempt to write against it. Moreover, written specifically in the context of the controversy over Heidegger's Nazism, Lyotard's work asks how to read (and not read) Heidegger in light of the question of how to represent Jews.[16] Lyotard introduces something new and important into this debate. For he calls attention not only to the fate of actual Jews, but to the tropological construction of "the jews" within the rhetoric and logic of Western discourse(s). According to Lyotard, the problem of "the jews" is the problem of originary or primary repression: the desire of the West to forget the unforgettable, or what he calls the "immemorial."[17]

"Primary repression" refers to the belief that all that is present(ed) to both the unconscious and the conscious mind is already pre-encoded. This means that there is an epistemological limit to what can be known of the self. Because what cannot be known, by definition, can be neither represented nor forgotten, there is also that which cannot be remembered because it cannot, in this sense, be forgotten. It can only be "remembered" as the immemorial, or (as it is also sometimes termed in Lyotard's text, so as to signify its difference from the known/forgotten) the "Forgotten."

Secondary repression is the process by which the forgotten past (however indirectly) is re-presented, for example, in dreams. It makes use of two strategies: effacing and representing. The first—effacing—is an attempt to hide or disguise the particulars of a case; it is not a forgetting. Representing, on the other hand, does not hide or disguise, but puts forth an assertion as fact. In so doing, it "forgets" that this "fact" is both partial and constructed. The denial of this amnesia within representation does not allow for anamnesis, for a "remembering" of the Forgotten. Primary repression is, thus, forgotten in representation, and it is this lack of memory, this silence, of which Lyotard seeks to remind us in the name of "the jews" and Heidegger, both of whom are taken as differently witnessing the immemorial (see Lyotard, *Heidegger* 11-12, 15, 17-20).

In remembering the Forgotten, then, Lyotard must especially be wary of the dangers of amnesia lurking in every representation. He can do so by an *écriture* that writes against representation, a writing that questions representation by a perpetual dismantling and displacing of its subject. Such a writing is evident in the figure of the *différend*, a shifting term Lyotard treats more extensively in his text of that title.[18] In *Heidegger and "the jews,"* the shifting term, the displaced *écriture*, is "the jews."[19] "The jews" in this text, like primary repression, are figured in terms of an "unsettling strangeness" (13) a "stranger in the house" (17). They are, thus, figured as the *unheimlich*, the "uncanny," the "un-homey."[20]

> *"The jews" are the irremissible in the West's movement of remission and pardon. They are what cannot be domesticated in the obsession to dominate, in the compulsion to control domain, in the passion for empire, recurrent ever since Hellenistic Greece and Christian Rome. "The jews," never at home wherever they are, cannot be integrated, converted, or expelled. They are also always away from home when they are at home, in their so-called own tradition, because it includes exodus as its beginning, excision, impropriety, and respect for the forgotten. . . . (22; emphasis mine)*

The anti-Semitism of the Occident should not be confused with its xenophobia; rather, anti-Semitism is one of the means of the apparatus of its culture to bind and represent as much as possible—to protect against—the originary terror, actively to forget it. It is the defensive side of its attack mechanisms—Greek science, Roman law and politics, Christian spirituality, and the Enlightenment, the "underside" of Knowledge, of having, of wanting, of hope. One converts the Jews in the Middle Ages, they resist by mental restriction. One expels them during the classical age, they return. One integrates them in the modern era, they persist in their difference. One exterminates them in the twentieth century. (23)

What is most real about real Jews is that Europe, in any case, does not know what to do with them. . . ."The jews" are the object of a dismissal with which Jews, in particular, are afflicted in reality. (3)[21]

"The jews" are "never at home wherever they are. . . . [T]hey are also always away from home when they are at home." They are the *unheimlich*, the trope or figuration of otherness, of primary repression.[22] Thus, the slippage in the text between the two terms, "the jews" and the *real Jews*,[23] marks the movement for Lyotard between primary and secondary repression, between the immemorial and the representation (and thus forgetting) of the Forgotten.

How can we account for this double negation of Jews in Lyotard's text? Is the European writer necessarily an agent of primary repression in which the *unheimlich* Other is made to disappear? Is the attempt not to forget forgetting always doomed to be figured through repression, that is, forgotten in the end? If so, is it not of some consequence how primary repression is figured?

THE RHETORICS AND POLITICS OF IDENTIFICATION

One way of approaching the question of who are "the jews" and the *real Jews* in Lyotard's text is to trace out its rhetorics of identification. For the question of identification *is* the "Jewish Question."

A figuring of "the jews" frames *Heidegger and "the jews."* Its opening paragraphs establish "the jews" as a construct. It is a construct, however, that is first defined negatively, in terms of what it is not. The quotation marks signify and secure the borders between the rhetorical trope of "the jews" and the historically marked *real Jews*. However, as Lyotard emphasizes, it is *real Jews* who are "afflicted in reality" with the "dismissal" to which "the jews" are subject (3).

In order to further address this "Jewish" question, consider first what Lyotard says in the end-frame of his text, a final meditation on forgetting and its consequences:

> Granel reintroduces today, half a century after the Holocaust, the forgetting of what has tried to forget itself through it. He thus seriously misses the debt that is *our* only lot—the lot of forgetting neither that there is the Forgotten nor what horror the spirit is capable of in its headlong madness to make us forget that fact. "Our"

lot? Whose lot? It is the lot of this nonpeople of survivors, Jews and non-Jews, called here "the jews," whose Being-together depends not on the authenticity of any primary roots but on that singular debt of interminable anamnesis. . . . The West is thinkable under the order of *mimesis* only if one forgets that a "people" survives within that is not a nation (a nature). Amorphous, indignant, clumsy, involuntary, this people tries to listen to the Forgotten. (94)

It is with this shifting, displaced trope of "the jews" that Lyotard identifies. He throws in his lot with "the jews," this "nonpeople of survivors, Jews and non-Jews." He refers to their lot as "our lot." This is the point in his text where Lyotard's own identification is most in evidence. "The jews" are a "people" (albeit "an amorphous nonpeople") within the West, "not a nation (a nature)."[24]

Lyotard's identification of/with "the jews" becomes evident in his rhetorics of identification, in his shifting use of "us," "they," "we," "them," "I," and "one." *Heidegger and "the jews"* opens with an "I" that defines Lyotard's use of "the jews." They, like the *real Jews,* are referred to as "they" and "them" in the opening paragraphs and chapters.

A telling use of "us" is introduced as well in the first chapter: "How could this [Heidegger's] thought forget and ignore 'the jews' to the point of suppressing and foreclosing to the very end the horrifying (and inane) attempt at exterminating, at making *us* forget forever what, in Europe, reminds *us,* ever since the beginning, that 'there is' the Forgotten?" (4; emphasis mine).

Who is this "us"? It is the European (Christian/Western) subject: the one who must be reminded of the Other, the Forgotten, that which the West would forget, that which has resisted empire "ever since the beginning." This "us" initially is not "the jews," although through the work of anamnesis, the "us" may throw in their lot with "the jews." It may then become "our lot." The "they" and "them" of "the jews" in the beginning of the text may become "our lot" in the end through the work of remembering the immemorial.

Who, then, is the "one" in this text that we find in sentences like: "Here, to fight against forgetting means to fight to remember that *one* forgets as soon as *one* believes, draws conclusions, and holds for certain"? (10; emphasis mine). "One" marks an ambiguous and distanced form of identification. It is a "them/they" that does not become "ours," that will have to be resisted by the "us," that is, Europeans who increasingly remember the Forgotten and, thus, increasingly identify with/as "the jews."

ÉCRITURE JUDAÏQUE AND THE WRITING OF EMPIRE

In this rhetoric of identification, where are the actual Jews? They/we[25] cannot be found, although the "conversion" of Europeans to "the jews" can be traced. It finally becomes clear that it is the putting in place of the European, Western subject (Lyotard's "us") as it remembers the immemo-

rial that is the subject of *Heidegger and "the jews."* The terms of identification differently (differingly?) name the split European subject: split between the "one" that forgets the Forgotten and the "us" that remembers it. It is the imperial subject that is Lyotard's subject. "The jews" are European.

But, as I have already suggested, "the jews" are still subject to, as well as subjects of, the West. In some ways, the double or split European subject of "the jews" seems to resemble what Homi Bhabha terms "the 'splitting' of the national subject."[26] However, in contrast to Bhabha's national subject, the category of "the jews" is not a site of resistance, of a "mimicry" that unmasks the imperial subject of the West from *within* its own terms. Bhabha's observation that the national subject refers not only to the "master" but also to the "slave," making the dialectics of power not a matter of reversal, but of hybridity, is an important shift. The participation of the "slave" in the construction of the "master" gives agency to the colonized and oppressed. But in the case of "the jews," there is another masquerade being performed, another form of mimicry and reversal.

The West produces "the jews" as the other side of empire: They are figured as that which is (those who are) outside, even if physically inside, the West. "The jews" thus metonymically refers to all the Others the West created in its multiple acts of making and building empire. As such, the figure of "the jews" seems ready-to-hand for figuring the colonial and postcolonial subject. But at a cost.

> I write "the jews" this way neither out of prudence nor lack of something better. I use lower case to indicate that I am not thinking of a nation. I make it plural to signify that it is neither a figure nor a political (Zionism), religious (Judaism), or philosophical (Jewish philosophy) subject that I put forward under this name. I use quotation marks to avoid confusing these "jews" with real Jews. What is most real about real Jews is that Europe, in any case, does not know what to do with them; Christians demand their conversion; monarchs expel them; republics assimilate them; Nazis exterminate them. "The jews" are the object of a dismissal with which Jews, in particular, are afflicted in reality. (Lyotard, *Heidegger* 3)[27]

In order for the figure of "the jews" to be useful for Lyotard, it must first be purged of its Jewish "particularity." The category of "the jews" need not necessarily contain Jews.[28] Indeed, the nonintrinsically Jewish character of the category of "the jews" is essential for Lyotard (and not only for him).[29] For the symbol or mark of particularity, of exclusivity, in the West has been predominantly the Jews.[30] Displacing Jewish identity, thus, becomes a way of deconstructing particularity as such.

What should be clear from this polarity between "the jews" and the *real Jews* is that in neither case are the lives, experiences, beliefs, and discourses of Jews themselves expressed. So, for Jews, there is no difference in identifying with either "the jews" or the *real Jews.* Not only are the images of, descriptions of, and attitudes toward "the jews" drawn from the situation of the Jew in (and from the perspective of) the European, Christian/West, but the prevailing understanding of the *real Jews* is informed by these same, negatively defined, images, descriptions, and attitudes.

The problem here is twofold. First, by excluding as particularistic the *real Jews* from the term, "the jews," Lyotard represses and effaces an important aspect of the trope of the Jew(s) in the West that has figured them as stubbornly Other and inassimilable. Second, by representing the *real Jews* as particular(istic) and excluding them from the category of "the jews," Lyotard is purifying that category and, in so doing, ironically and terribly repeating the gesture with which the Jews have historically been separated from the West: marginalized, oppressed, excluded. He is forgetting the Forgotten (through effacement and representation) as he claims Heidegger did in maintaining silence about the Jews and the Shoah, even after 1945. As in the dialectics of emancipation in France after 1778 and in Germany in the nineteenth century where the Jews could be citizens only as "men" but not as Jews, so too in Lyotard's text they could be accepted into the category of "the jews" only on the condition that no traces of their particularity as Jews (as opposed to as "jews") remain:

> And the Jews (without quotation marks) are not less, but rather more exposed than others (they are "stiff necked") to forgetting the unnameable. Every Jew is a bad "jew," a bad witness to what cannot be represented, just like all texts fail to reinscribe what has not been inscribed. (81)

The *real Jew* is here figured as the opposite of "the jew," a "bad witness to what cannot be represented." The Jews, in other words, themselves forget "the jews"; they are "stiff necked" and, thus, "more exposed than others . . . to forgetting the unnameable." This splitting between good "jews" and bad "jews" (that is, *real Jews*) perniciously repeats the negative tropology of Jews in the West. In Lyotard's categories, Jews are the worst representations and representatives of "the jews," just as the stiff-necked Jews of the Old Testament, in their literalistic, carnal hermeneutics, were not the truest interpreters of the book they had inherited. Instead, the Jews, in Christian tropology and political practices, were superseded and replaced by the new chosen people, the Christians, who could interpret the spirit of the Hebrew Bible, the Torah, properly as the "Old Testament." "Christians" (like "the jews") are nonparticularistic, defined as such by their putative "universal" inclusiveness.

This universalism, however, may be regarded as a manifestation of empire. Indeed, the very category of "the jews," instead of including the marginal(ized), constructs its categories by repeating a very ancient dialectic of empire in the West. For the Jews (like Lyotard's *real Jews*) are precisely those who must be excluded from the "new covenant" of Christianity and the "social contract" of

emancipation. Thus, Jews (like *real Jews*) bear the negative weight of the West's imperial repression of "the particular," whereas "the jews" (predicated upon the exclusion of the "particularistic") represents the putatively "inclusive" category of the Others of the West.

Thus, while Lyotard's project seems to be an unmasking of the dialectics of empire in the troping of "the jews" as the Other of/in the West, it in fact continues the negative process of forgetting and silencing the Jews through the double strategies of effacement/representation. In Lyotard's text, the work of empire continues. Certain negative situations and experiences of the Jews in the West—diaspora, marginalization, oppression, exclusion, nonrepresentation—are attached to "the jews" and valorized. However, these newly positive figurations are then dialectically opposed in Lyotard's text to many of the old negative stereotypes of the *real Jews:* stiff-necked, particularistic, exclusivistic, badly representing the unrepresentable.

The Jewish question, the "problem" of the situation of the Jews in the West, thus, is reinstated in **Heidegger and "the jews"** through the splitting between "the jews" and *real Jews*. The trope of "the jews" takes the place of the universal Christian, the latest incarnation of the regulative (if not legislative) subject of the West. For it is not the Jew who writes *écriture judaïque* in Lyotard's text but, rather, the European subject who writes this form of post-identity as "the jews."

WHO SPEAKS FOR/AS THE JEWS?

Bhabha suggests that "that boundary that secures the *cohesive* limits of the western nation may imperceptibly turn into a contentious *internal* liminality that provides a place from which to speak both of, and as, the minority, the exilic, the marginal, and the emergent."[31] He is not, however, suggesting that the European subject is the one who not only "speak(s) both of, and as" (DissemiNation 300), but also *for* the minority; rather, he proposes it is the exilic, the marginal, the minority, and the emergent who find through this internal liminality a place from which to speak *within* the West in a (post)colonial situation. Within Lyotard's text, there is no place for Jews to speak. The "location" of the Jews in his dialectic of "the jews"/*real Jews* is neither to be found in either one of the terms, nor on the boundary between them. The Jews' absence (an old story, indeed) is a necessary condition of Lyotard's very construction of "the jews" as a category. Indeed, as Bhabha notes,

> What does need to be questioned, however, is the *mode of representation of otherness,* which depends crucially on *how* the "west" is deployed within these discourses. . . . Paradoxically, then, cultural otherness functions as the moment of *presence* in a theory of *difference.* The "destiny of non-satisfaction" is fulfilled in the recognition of otherness as a *symbol* (not sign) of the presence of *significance* or *difference.* . . . What is denied is any knowledge of cultural otherness as a differential *sign,* implicated in specific historical and discursive condi-

tions, requiring construction in different practices of reading. The place of otherness is fixed in the west as a subversion of western metaphysics and is finally appropriated by the west as its limit-text, anti-west [in a] . . . process by which forms of racial/cultural/historical otherness have been marginalized in theoretical texts committed to the articulation of *différance, significance*. . . . ("Other" 72-73)

"The jews" becomes a way for the European subject both to critique the (logo)center and identify with/as the margins of the West without changing its terms. It maintains the logic of the West by reducing otherness to a symbol of the limits of the West, its limit-text. As a trope of otherness, "the jews," like exilic figures of diaspora, ironically *contains* the rupturing of Western discourse. This form of writing the Other, *écriture judaïque,* does not signify difference but *différance* within a system opened endlessly (nomadically) internally. It is not ruptured from within or without, opening it to another, an outside; indeed such differences are deferred, erased, effaced. While such strategies of *différance* may certainly be performed in a tone of humility, of epistemological finitude, this *écriture* is also susceptible to a borderless expansion that looks much like another version of empire.

While it is clear that "the jews" is a constructed trope, the constructedness of the category of the *real Jews* is effaced or forgotten. In Lyotard's text, the *real Jews* stand for (re)present) the "real." "The jews" now provides the basis for specifically *European* identification with the margin(al) in the West inasmuch as traditionally negative stereotypes of, for example, the wandering, exiled, diasporic (Jew) are now valorized.

The forgetting in this representation of *real Jews,* Lyotard's failure to place this term as well in quotes, is no mere strategy of marginalization or displacement. Between the positive figuration of "the jews" and the negative figuration of *real Jews* (except insofar as they become "jews," that is, "convert" or assimilate), there is no space left in the West for the intervention of actual Jews in their multiple and conflicting identities. That these are specifically Christian and Western ways of representing Jews, creating "the Jewish problem" or "the question of the Jews," is always/already effaced. The European is never represented to him/herself as specific, located; specificity is only represented as the sign of the parochialism of the *real Jews.*

While Lyotard, certainly, attempts always to deconstruct and displace identity in such a way as to undo the rule of "master narratives" and the oppositional dialectics of identity and difference in the West, he ironically repeats this very dialectic (and one of the West's primary and foundational master narratives) in his rhetoric of identification of/with "the jews." It is always the Jews, as "particularistic," in the dialectics of Christian/Western identity who must be split (Old Testament/New Testament, Old Chosen people/New Chosen people) in the construction of specifically Christian/Western identity. Had Lyotard better been able not to "forget" the historical construction of the Jew(s) in and by the West, he would not, perhaps, have repeated its tropology.

It seems at first that this recognition of the cultural construction of the Jew(s) in the West is precisely what Lyotard is writing. But, instead, he seeks to write his own *écriture judaïque,* his own (re)use of the trope of the Jew as "the jews," now plural, lower case and in quotes. It is a Jewish writing without Jews, much like *écriture feminine* is a writing without women.[32] These strategies of *différance,* however, do not shatter the dialectics of identity in the West or even help us to remember what is forgotten. The Jews are always already "Forgotten." They disappear in, and between, the terms of "the jews"/*real Jews.* The saving grace of "the other within" is an anthem sung by a chorus of post-identity theorists.[33] While there are people relegated to and regulated at the margins of the West, and while there are those who suffer exile and displacement, this European "confession" of *différance* is not adequate; in some ways, it perpetuates and is part of the problem. As Edward Said notes in discussing the massive exiles of this century,

> [A]t most the literature about exile objectifies an anguish and a predicament most people rarely experience at first hand; but to think of the exile informing the literature as beneficially humanistic is to banalize its mutilations, the losses it inflicts on those who suffer them, the muteness with which it responds to any attempt to understand it as "good for us." Is it not true that the views of exile in literature and, moreover, in religion obscure what is truly horrendous: that exile is irredeemably secular and unbearably historical; that it is produced by human beings for other human beings; and that, like death but without death's ultimate mercy, it has torn millions of people from the nourishment of tradition, family and geography? ("Reflections" 357-58)

What, then, are the implications of the treatment of the Jew(s) as the "selected" site of exile and of split, displaced identity in the Christian/West and, more specifically, in Lyotard's postmodern text? What is being "forgotten" here? Is it not the pain, the violence, the irredeemable loss that are effaced in the construction of the category of "the jews"? Who must suffer the dialectics of Christian/Western identity so that it may become "universal" or, in its most recent incarnation, inclusively "post-identified"? Is there a time or space for Jewish identity/ies in this Western tropology of "the jews"/*real Jews?* Lyotard's postmodern discourse may, thus, preserve the ancient economy of identity/difference of the West, now in a more sophisticated form, but with a strangely familiar result: the disappearance, the "forgetting" of the Jews.

When the Jews' exile is taken as a trope—the "wandering Jew" functions as a sign of unredemption and "the jews" as an *unheimlich* symbol of displaced Western identity—a kind of amnesia, a forgetting of pain and violence is "accomplished." A discourse which preserves the always exilic figure of the diasporic Jew in the West further anesthetizes both discourse and memory.[34] The *real Jews,* always already frozen in past time as "Old Testamental" (in Christian time marked as either "B.C." or "A.D."), are treated as fossils or relics. "The jews," however, like "the Other," do not exist in the West and will not, as such, suffer history. The Christian/West has repeatedly made the (for Jews) fatal misidentification of the figure of the Old Testament Jew and actual Jews (obscuring, in the process, the fact that "the Jew" is a specifically *Christian* trope). In this case, too, the West has literalized its tropes of the Jew, whether capitalized,[35] lower cased, pluralized, or put in quotes. Lyotard would do better to deconstruct these terms in their historical specificity than to create again an amorphous, catch-all category on the bodies of dead Jews. For it is the figure of the dead or, at least, persecuted Jew(s) with which Lyotard (and Europe) is most comfortable. One can piously mourn and "remember" dead Jews as the unrepresentable, the immemorial. But actual, living Jews in their/our[36] complex and contradictory identities *as Jews,* still have no place in the Europe of Lyotard's text.

The "Jewish Question" cannot be "solved" until we realize that what is in question is *not* the Jews and never has been. In question and at stake is the power of empire and the imperial subject as Christian/Western. The category of "the jews" as a "solution" to the Jewish Question (which is itself a particularistic way of naming the question of *Western* identity) is an effacing of its true subject: the European Christian. Jews are not *in* these discourses of the West, despite their figurative inclusion.

Indeed, Jew(s) are no more present in Lyotard's **Heidegger and "the jews"** than they/we are in Augustine's hermeneutics of the "Old Testament." "The jews" in Lyotard's text is a mirage. It distracts us from attending to the actual differences of/among Jews within/outside the West and it effaces, as well, the actual history of cultural, religious, and so-called "racial" differences of others.

To get *beyond* the disappearance (indeed, the absence) of the Jews in the discourse(s) of Western identity requires more than a new (and improved?) category of "the jews." These Western discourses must be ruptured by the voices of those who have been made invisible through their/our erasure and objectification.[37] Jews must speak for them/ourselves—and be heard—in/outside of Western discourses. But a discourse, such as Lyotard's, that purports to remember the Jews as "the jews" does not allow a time[38] or space for such speaking or hearing.

Notes

1. I use the term "Christian/West" to signal the intrinsic connection between these identities. The West has been understood as shaped by the "Judeo-Christian tradition," a term which already constitutes a displacement/appropriation of both Judaism and the Torah. When I use the term "Western subject," therefore, I am referring to this Christian, imperial construction of the West, even in its secularized forms.

2. The Jew is figured as male, even if feminized, in the history of Western anti-Judaism. In my treatment of this trope, I maintain this male gendering to make clear that it is a trope and not Jews or Jewish identities that is at issue. This male gendering even informs postmodern discussions of Jews such as Jean-François Lyotard's *Heidegger and "the jews,"* which is the focus of my essay.

3. See Gilman, *Difference and Pathology:*

   Stereotypes are a crude set of mental representations of the world. They are palimpsests on which the initial bipolar representations are still vaguely legible. They perpetuate a needed sense of difference between the "self" and the "object," which becomes the "Other." Because there is no real line between self and the Other, an imaginary line must be drawn; and so that the illusion of an absolute difference between self and Other is never troubled, this line is as dynamic in its ability to alter itself as it the self. . . . The most negative stereotype always has an overtly positive counterweight. As any image is shifted, all stereotypes shift. Thus stereotypes are inherently protean rather than rigid. (18)

4. In this brief exposition, I can only allude to the typologies, stereotypes, and dynamics of the history of anti-Judaism in the West. I mention instances and figures of this projection of otherness as/onto Jews to set the scene for the later reappearance of some of these tropes within recent critical theory.

5. In this light, male Jews were also demasculinized, carnally feminized. See Gilman, *Difference and Pathology* chapter 9, 191-216; and also Gilman, *The Jew's Body.*

6. For an explication of Paul's views on circumcision, see Daniel Boyarin, "'This We Know to Be the Carnal Israel'"; see also Gilman, *The Jew's Body* 91-95; Eilberg-Schwartz 141-76; and Josef Stern.

7. I use the term "they" to refer to these constructions of Jewish identity as the Other. Part of the burden of my argument here is that the tropology of the Jew and Judaism in/outside of the West is not to be literalized or entitized, but rather recognized precisely as figurative.

8. This slippage between Christianity and Nation can be traced throughout the purportedly secular discourse of the late eighteenth/early nineteenth-century period of Emancipation/Enlighten- ment. For a discussion of the Napoleonic code and its history of effects, see Chazan and Raphael; and Hyman. That entrance into the liberal social contract was offered to Jewish men only, and then only as individual members of society, not as Jews, is important to note here. As Clermont- Tonnure remarked at the National Assembly in 1789, "To the Jews as individuals— everything; to the Jews as a group—nothing. They must constitute neither a body politic nor an order; they must be citizens individually" (Hyman 5). For a consideration of the impact of this gendered character of liberalism on Jewish women's identities, see Levitt chapter 2. I

am indebted to Laura Levitt for the critical use of the term "identity/ies." For the modernization of the Jew in Germany, see Meyer.

9. Again, it is important to differentiate the trope of the Jew from the multiple, complex, even conflicting identities of Jews. The failure to see Jews is fundamentally related to their confusion with the trope of the Jew. As James E. Young suggests in his treatment of John Berryman's "The Imaginary Jew,"

[A]s becomes painfully clear to [Berryman], it is precisely the point at which a figurative Jew is reified that the danger begins. For as he concludes, it is always only the figurative Jew that antisemites hate—i.e., the imaginary Jew of their minds—but once acted upon, the figure is reified, and real blood flows. (115-16)

10. In "'Race,' Writing and Culture," Tzvetan Todorov notes the absence of any discussion of Jewish history and the Shoah in Gates, *"Race," Writing, and Difference,* the volume to which this letter is a response:

I [Todorov] was surprised, not to say shocked, by the lack of any reference to one of the most odious forms of racism: anti-Semitism. Given the fact that the Nazis' "final solution" to the "Jewish problem" led to the greatest racial massacre in the history of humankind, its absence from the volume suggests that the authors chose to "actively ignore" it, to borrow an expression used by Hazel V. Carby in a different context. . . . (377)

His implied question, however, was not addressed in the editor's response. Indeed, "Jews" only appear in the text (as even a glance at its index will indicate) as first-world Zionist oppressors of third-world Palestinians. The most troubling reference, however, appears in Houston Baker's critique of Edward Said's binary opposition between Israelis and Palestinians:

Said presents a case for the Palestinians by summoning all the texts of Jewish defense, apology, invective, and disparagement. It is difficult to hear a Palestinian voice separate from the world of Jewish discourse. (Of course, Jews are not likely to feel this way, and will probably call for Said's head on a platter. But that is the necessary reaction of well-financed client states.) (388-89)

Not only does Baker confuse Israelis with Jews, using these terms interchangeably, but the association of Jewish Israelis with money, as "well-financed" by the first-world, not only repeats a Christian anti-Jewish trope but constructs all Israelis as first-world, ignoring the fact that many Jewish Israelis are either from Palestine or originate from Arab countries.

This "identification" of Jews and Israelis with whiteness, Europe, and the first-world marks postcolonial feminism as well. Consider, for example, the absence of any writings by Israeli or Mizrahi Jewish women in an anthology as important as *Third World Women and the Politics of Feminism.* Jewish women, on the other hand, are also often considered white in first-world feminism and are assimilated into the "Judeo-Christian" West. Despite the light skin of some Jewish women (which in our racist society offers privilege), our specific ethnicities and histories both "in" and "out" of the West make Jewish women's experiences more like those of women of color than those of white, first-world women. Like postcolonial writing more generally, however, recent feminist discourse is beginning to make some more inclusive gestures toward Jews. While Audre Lorde, for example, still refers to Jews as part of the white community (and it is the case that some Jews can "pass" and become part of this community), she makes the point that Jews, like blacks, share in histories of racist oppression that affect gender-relations within our particular (Jewish or black) communities (284). Recently, as well, Henry Louis Gates importantly addressed the problem of black anti-Semitism in "Black Demagogues and Pseudo-Scholars" (15).

11. It is precisely these initial presumptions that will be examined and questioned here. (Indeed, postcolonial writings will be found, in the body of this paper, to offer many important resources for the critique of postmodern discourses.) While I distinguish postmodern and postcolonial theories, I recognize that some postcolonial theorists draw upon and reinterpret postmodern theories. I also find persuasive Edward W. Said's argument in "Representing the Colonized" that the crises of postmodern discourse and theory are significantly occasioned by the emergence of postcoloniality. Thus, while there are important differences of positionality between postmodern and postcolonial discourses, I do not seek to mark this difference as a simple either/or. Nor do I wish to elide them under a single "post." To this problematic, I also raise the question of the status of post-Holocaust writing between these two other "posts"—postmodernism and postcolonialism.

12. I alternate between the two terms, "Holocaust" and "Shoah," because different individuals and communities name and, thus, interpret the event differently and because, juxtaposed, each term may call attention to the problems and limits of the other. There are, of course, other terms that have been used to name this event(s): for example, *Churban* and *Tremendum.*

13. See my "Failing Speech." In this essay, I was also concerned with a certain aestheticization and abstraction of the Shoah in postmodern discourse, a concern that is expressed as well by Santner. See, in this regard, note 28 below.

14. This has occurred more through its reception by a general audience not acquainted with specific

midrashim than because the writers (cited in the note above) have juxtaposed these interpretive resources. See David Stern, "Midrash and Indeterminacy"; and his *Parables in Midrash.*

15. In an attempt to disavow the Jewishness of deconstruction, David Hirsch goes to the extreme of identifying it with Nazism.

16. I will not attend to the details of the Heidegger controversy here as I am, rather, focusing on the question of the construction of Jewish identity/ies in Lyotard's text.

17. The immemorial is

    that which can neither be remembered (represented to consciousness) nor forgotten (consigned to oblivion). It is that which returns, uncannily [*unheimlich*]. As such, the immemorial acts as a kind of *figure* for consciousness and its attempts at representing itself historically. The prime example is Auschwitz [and "the jews"], which obliges us to speak so that this event remains an event, so that its *singularity* is not lost in historical representation, so that it does not become something that happened, among other things. The task of not forgetting, of anamnesis, is the task of the avant-garde, which struggles to keep events from sinking into the oblivion of either representation (voice) or silence. (Readings xxxii)

    In the paragraphs that follow, I interpret Lyotard's use of the terms "originary [or primary] repression" and "secondary repression."

18. See Lyotard, *The Differend.* This text is, in my opinion, more nuanced than *Heidegger and "the jews."* Much depends on how one interprets the term, "differend": through a logic that undercuts all metanarrative grounding or through a rhetoric that identifies with, and speaks from, the position of the excluded. Is injustice an abstract and necessary character of the system of reason or is it something that can be ameliorated through a utopic identification with, and listening to, that which cannot be expressed? Both strands seem to be present in Lyotard's text. It is the second, rhetorical attitude of attentiveness to the differend that I find both helpful and important. The logical insight about metanarratives (while accurate) risks the abstract thinking that Eric Santner critiques. See note 28 below.

19. This writing that I am calling "*écriture judaïque*" has been treated in different ways by Edmond Jabès and Jacques Derrida (see, for example, notes 29 and 30 below).

    The suggestion was made that instead of writing "the jews" I should write "the lower case" so as to feature this character(istic) and to minimize the confusion between what I and Lyotard refer to as Jews. (I thank Laura Levitt for this suggestion and for reading an earlier draft of this essay.) While I

didn't in the end follow this suggestion, it remains an intriguing one. Keeping these terms clearly distinct will require of readers close attention to diacritical marks.

20. I use the term "un-homey" instead of the more usual translation of *unheimlich,* "un-homely," because its connotations seem less problematic.

21. While anti-Semitism is a matter of primary repression, xenophobia pertains, rather, to secondary repression. In understanding Jewishness as a function of anti-Semitism, Lyotard's views seem to be in the "tradition" of Sartre.

22. For a similar description of the Jews in the West, see Pinsker:

    The World saw in this people [the Jews] the uncanny form of one of the dead walking among the living. The ghostlike apparition of a living corpse, of a people without unity or organization, without land or other bonds of unity, no longer alive, and yet walking among the living—this spectral form without precedence in history, unlike anything that preceded or followed it, could but strangely affect the imagination of the nations. (163)

    Compare this description with that of the "incarnation," the terrible literalizing of this figure of the *unheimlich,* living dead in the concentration camps:

    Their life is short, but their number is endless; they, the *Muselmänner,* the drowned, form the backbone of the camp, an anonymous mass, continually renewed and always identical, of non-men who march and labour in silence, the divine spark dead within them, already too empty to really suffer. One hesitates to call them living: one hesitates to call their death death, in the face of which they have no fear, as they are too tired to understand. (Levi 82).

23. I have italicized the term *real Jews* to make note of its constructedness despite its lack of diacritical markings in Lyotard's text.

24. The figuration of "the jews" as a "people" (lower case and in quotes to signify that the term does not refer to a historical people), signals the unwelcoming of the Jews (as *unheimlich*) in the West. Lyotard's discourse resonates with the Zionist Leo Pinsker's diagnosis of the situation of the Jew in the West: "[The Jews are at] home everywhere, but are nowhere at home. The nations have *never* to deal with a Jewish nation but always with mere *Jews.* The Jews are not a nation . . . the Jews seem rather to have lost all remembrance of their former home" (162).

    In his essay "*Heidegger and 'the jews':* A Conference in Vienna and Freiberg (1989)," Lyotard further refines some of the terms he employs in the book of that title. He amends his use of the terms "nation" and "people," only to a certain extent ameliorating their problematic usage in the book.

(See, especially, p. 143 of his essay.) However, Lyotard's qualifying commentary, while clarifying and making more explicit some of the terms of his book—for example, the figuration of "the jews" in terms of primary repression (as explicated on pp. 141-143)—does not erase the troubling inscription of his thought within the very dynamics and discourses of the West which he criticizes. In his essay, for example, Lyotard clearly states the problem of representing "the Jewish condition" in the West: "it alone is the impossible witness, always improper (there are only bad jews), to this unconscious affect" (p. 143); yet, as I delineate below, Lyotard appears irresistibly to repeat this problematic equation of the *real Jew* and "bad jews."

25. The dilemma of how to refer to actual Jews, as opposed to Lyotard's "the jews" or *real Jews,* informs and resonates throughout my entire text. I mark this problem of reference here as "they/we" to draw attention to the difference between this question of identification and that referred to in note 7 above. In the pages that follow, however, I do not further mark this difference until the last few paragraphs of this essay.

26. See Bhabha:

How do we conceive of the "splitting" of the national subject? How do we articulate cultural differences within this vacillation of ideology in which the national discourse also participates, sliding ambivalently from one enunciatory position to another? . . . What might be the cultural and political effects of the liminality of the nation, the margins of modernity, which cannot be signified without the narrative temporalities of splitting, ambivalence and vacillation? ("DissemiNation" 298)

27. While, as I have suggested (in note 21), Lyotard's figuration of "the jews"/*real Jews* (as *unheimlich* others of the West) seems to repeat Sartre's views, Sartre seems to resemble Bhabha when Sartre writes:

[The democrat] has no eyes for the concrete syntheses with which history confronts him. He recognizes neither Jew, nor Arab, nor Negro, nor bourgeois, nor worker, but only man. . . . He resolves all collectivities into individual elements. . . . This means that he wants to separate the Jew from his religion, from his family, from his ethnic community, in order to plunge him into the democratic crucible whence he will emerge naked and alone, an individual and solitary particle like all the other particles. . . . [The democrat is thus] hostile to the Jew to the extent that the latter thinks of himself as a Jew. (55-57)

28. It may well be that it is the very figuration of "the jews"/*real Jews* as primary repression that is integral to their invisibility, even for Lyotard: 1) They are the products of Western identity and are necessarily,

always already, silence(d); 2) With such an identification of Jews/"the jews" and primary repression, a mourning, a "working through," or an undoing of its repetition/return in anti-Semitism would seem impossible. My concerns here resonate with those of Santner (8-30). Like Santner, I am exploring the possibilities of thinking "the 'postwar' under the double sign of the postmodern and the post-Holocaust" (8). As Santner notes,

To return to Lyotard's remark regarding the relation between amnesia with respect to Auschwitz and the repression of the failures of European modernity more generally to deal with difference, one must wonder whether the elaboration of those failures, which is an essential aspect of so much postmodern critical practice, can also be understood as a gesture of genuine anamnesis and mourning toward the Holocaust and its victims. Insofar as deconstruction as practiced by de Man and others privileges a heroism of an abstract mode of bereavement—let me call it a heroism of the elegiac loop—it cannot be considered an adequate response to an earlier complicity, however "abstract" it may have been, in German fascism's hegemony over Europe and all that that entailed. . . . The more difficult labour would have been, of course, openly and explicitly to *sediment* these tasks of mourning to explore the ways in which they might, in the long run, mutually enlighten one another. (13-30)

29. In a way, Lyotard's distinction between "the jews" and *real Jews* resembles Derrida's characterization of Edmond Jabès as "more and less Jewish than the Jew" (75). As Derrida goes on to remark,

[T]he Jew's identification with himself [note the male gendering] does not exist. The Jew is split, and split first of all between the two dimensions of the letter: allegory and literality. His history would be but one empirical history among others if he established or nationalized himself within difference and literality. He would have no history at all if he let himself be attenuated within the algebra of an abstract universalism. ("Edmond Jabès" 75)

The split in the identity of the Jew is written by Derrida as a difference between two modes of interpretation: the rabbi and the poet (67). I refer to other forms of splitting (Jewish) identity below.

30. Derrida also treats the question of marks of identity and the displacement of exclusivity in his reflections on circumcision [note again the male figuration of the Jew and Jewish membership] in "Shibboleth." Of course, women, like Jews, are also marked and marginalized as particular, although not necessarily as particularistic.

31. This internal liminality is figured by Bhabha in terms of the *unheimlich:*

I am attempting to discover the uncanny moment of cultural difference. . . . At this point I must give way to the *vox populi:* to . . . [the] wandering peoples who will not be contained within the *Heim* of the national culture . . . but are themselves marks of the shifting boundary that alienates the frontiers of the modern nation. ("DissemiNation" 312, 315)

The use of the uncanny to question national culture, not to re-present it (as in Lyotard's use of "the jews"), offers an epistemological/political reading of the *unheimlich* that differs significantly from its use by Lyotard criticized here.

32. See Tania Modleski, *Feminism without Men;* and "Feminism and the Power of Interpretation." *Écriture judaïque* resembles *écriture feminine* in that, just as the latter is not necessarily produced by women (and, indeed, the category of "woman/women" is contingent), so the former does not require (and in some cases, does not allow) Jews.

33. For example, in a section entitled, "The Stranger within Us" In *Strangers to Ourselves* (169-92), Julia Kristeva writes:

Freud teaches us how to detect foreignness in ourselves. . . . Freud brings us the courage to call ourselves disintegrated in order not to integrate foreigners and even less so to hunt them down, but rather to welcome them to that *uncanny strangeness,* which is as much theirs as it is ours. (191-92; emphasis mine)

Notice the domestication of the *unheimlich* as already (as it were, uncannily) present in the term *heimlich.* Freud's gesture in this regard may be read as his attempt to read the *unheimlich* Jews (and, thus, himself) into the universal (and, thus, *heimlich*) condition of humankind itself.

34. The problem is that in signifying certain results of the practices of empire as positive, even if in elegiac terms, some postmodern discourses (including that of Lyotard in *Heidegger and "the jews"*) repeat, rather than get beyond, these practices. Under the guise of identifying with the exiled, the *unheimlich* others, then, these practices are further institutionalized, rather than critiqued.

35. See Derrida, *The Other Heading* 16-28:

Perhaps identification in general . . . always has a capital form, the figurehead . . . of the advanced point, and of capitalizing reserve. . . . By selection, I will deduce the form of all my propositions from a grammar and syntax of the heading, of the *cap,* from a difference in kind and gender [*genre*], that is, from *capital* and *capitale.* (26-27, 16)

36. Because the subject here is explicitly about Jewish identity, I use the term "their/our" (and, in the paragraphs that follow, the terms "they/we" and "them/ourselves" as well) to further dramatize the dilemma of reference referred to in note 25. As this text is about to go to press in December 1992, I must register my outrage and disgust at Europe's "failure" again to find a safe place within its borders for its *unheimlich* others: once again, "foreigners" and refugees (for example, Africans, Asians, Arabs), gypsies, the handicapped, and Jews among them.

37. This would include the speaking of those Jews that Lyotard excludes from the category of "the jews": the figure of "the political (Zionism), religious (Judaism), or philosophical (Jewish philosophy)" identity/ies of Jews (*Heidegger* 3).

38. For a consideration of Jewish habitation of time instead of space, see Jonathan Boyarin. See also Horowitz for consideration of the situation of Jewish Studies in the "New Academy." I thank Sara Horowitz for her generous reading of an earlier version of this essay.

Works Cited

Anderson, George K. *The Legend of the Wandering Jew.* Hanover: UP of New England, 1966, 1991.

Baker, Houston. "Caliban's Triple Play." Gates, *"Race," Writing, and Difference* 381-95.

Berryman, John. "The Imaginary Jew." *The Kenyon Review* 7 (1945): 529-39.

Bhabha, Homi. "DissemiNation." *Nation and Narration.* Ed. Homi Bhabha. London: Routledge, 1990. 291-322.

———. "The Other Question: Difference, Discrimination and the Discourse of Colonialism." Ferguson 71-87.

Blanchot, Maurice. *The Writing of the Disaster.* Trans. Ann Smock. Lincoln: U of Nebraska P, 1986.

Boyarin, Daniel. *Intertextuality and the Reading of Midrash.* Bloomington: Indiana UP, 1990.

———. "'This We Know to Be the Carnal Israel': Circumcision and the Erotic Life of God and Israel." *Critical Inquiry* 18.3 (1992): 474-505.

Boyarin, Jonathan. *Storm from Paradise: the Politics of Jewish Memory.* Minneapolis: U of Minnesota P, 1992.

Chazan, Robert, and Marc L. Raphael, eds. *Modern Jewish History: A Source Book.* New York: Schocken, 1969.

Derrida, Jacques. "Edmond Jabès and the Question of the Book." *Writing and Difference.* Trans. Alan Bass. Chicago: U of Chicago P, 1978. 64-78.

———. *The Other Heading: Reflections on Today's Europe.* Trans. Pascale-Anne Brault and Michael B. Naas. Bloomington: Indiana UP, 1992.

———. "Shibboleth." *Midrash and Literature.* Hartman and Budick 340-47.

Dundes, Alan, and Galit Hasan-Rokem, eds. *The Wandering Jew: Essays in the Interpretation of a Christian Legend.* Bloomington: Indiana UP, 1986.

Eilberg-Schwartz, Howard. *The Savage in Judaism: Anthropology of Israelite Religion and Ancient Judaism.* Bloomington: Indiana UP, 1990.

Ferguson, Russell et al., eds. *Out There: Marginalization and Contemporary Cultures.* Cambridge: MIT P, 1990.

Gates, Henry Louis, Jr. "Black Demagogues and Pseudo-Scholars." *New York Times* 20 Jul. 1992: A15.

———, ed. *"Race," Writing, and Difference.* Chicago: U of Chicago P, 1985.

Gilman, Sander L. *Difference and Pathology: Stereotypes of Sexuality, Race, and Madness.* Ithaca: Cornell UP, 1985.

———. *Jewish Self-Hatred: Anti-Semitism and the Hidden Language of the Jews.* Baltimore: Johns Hopkins UP, 1986.

———. *The Jew's Body.* New York: Routledge, 1991.

Handleman, Susan. *Slayers of Moses: The Emergence of Rabbinic Interpretation in Modern Literary Theory.* Albany: SUNY P, 1982.

Hartman, Geoffrey H., and Sanford Budick, eds. *Midrash and Literature.* New Haven: Yale UP, 1986.

Hirsch, David H. *The Deconstruction of Literature: Criticism after Auschwitz.* Hanover: Brown UP, 1991.

Horowitz, Sara. "Jewish Studies as Oppositional? or Gettin' Mighty Lonely Out Here." *Styles of Cultural Activism: From Theory and Pedagogy to Women, Indians, and Communism.* Ed. Philip Goldstein. Newark: U of Delaware P, 1994.

Hyman, Paula. *From Dreyfus to Vichy: The Remaking of French Jewry, 1906-1939.* New York: Columbia UP, 1979.

Jabès, Edmond. *The Book of Questions.* Trans. Rosmarie Waldrop. Middlebury: Wesleyan UP, 1972. Trans. of *Le Livre des Questions.* Paris: Gallimard, 1963.

Kristeva, Julia. *Strangers to Ourselves.* New York: Columbia UP, 1991.

Levi, Primo. *Survival in Auschwitz.* New York: Macmillan, 1961.

Levitt, Laura. *Reconfiguring Home: Jewish Feminist Identitylies.* Emory University, Ph.D. dissertation, 1993.

Lorde, Audre. "Age, Race, Class, and Sex: Women Redefining Difference." Ferguson 281-88.

Lyotard, Jean-François. *The Differend: Phrases in Dispute.* Trans. Georges Van Den Abbeele. Minneapolis: U of Minnesota P, 1988.

———. *Heidegger and "the jews."* Trans. Andreas Michel and Mark Roberts. Minneapolis: U of Minnesota P, 1990. Trans. of *Heidegger et "le juifs."* Paris: Galilée, 1988.

———. "*Heidegger and 'the jews':* A Conference in Vienna and Freiberg (1989)." Trans. Bill Readings and Kevin Paul Geiman. Minneapolis: U of Minnesota P, 1993.

Meyer, Michael A. *The Origins of the Modern Jew: Jewish Identity and European Culture in Germany, 1749-1824.* Detroit: Wayne State UP, 1979.

Modleski, Tania. "Feminism and the Power of Interpretation: Some Critical Readings." *Feminist Studies/Critical Studies.* Ed. Teresa de Lauretis. Bloomington: Indiana UP, 1986. 121-38.

———. *Feminism without Men: Culture and Criticism in a "Postfeminist" Age.* New York: Routledge, 1991.

Pinsker, Leo. "Auto-Emancipation: An Appeal to His People by a Russian Jew." Chazan and Raphael 161-74.

Readings, Bill. *Introducing Lyotard: Art and Politics.* London: Routledge, 1991.

Said, Edward. "Reflections on Exile." Ferguson 357-66.

———. "Representing the Colonized: Anthropology's Interlocutors." *Critical Inquiry* 15.2 (1989): 205-26.

Santner, Eric. *Stranded Objects: Mourning, Memory, and Film in Postwar Germany.* Ithaca: Cornell UP, 1990.

Sartre, Jean-Paul. *Anti-Semite and Jew.* New York: Schocken, 1948.

Shapiro, Susan. "Failing Speech: Post-Holocaust Writing and the Discourse of Postmodernism." *Semeia* 40 (1987): 65-91.

Stern, David. "Midrash and Indeterminacy." *Critical Inquiry* 14.1 (1988): 133-61.

———. *Parables in Midrash: Narrative and Exegesis in Rabbinic Literature.* Cambridge: Harvard UP, 1991.

Stern, Josef. "Maimonides' Parable of Circumcision." *S'vara: A Journal of Philosophy, Law, and Judaism* 2.2 (1991): 35-48.

Third World Women and the Politics of Feminism. Ed. Chandra Talpade Mohanty, Ann Russo, and Lourdes Torres. Bloomington: Indiana UP, 1991.

Todorow, Tzvetan. "'Race,' Writing and Culture." Gates, *Race, Writing, and Difference* 370-80.

Young, James E. *Writing and Rewriting the Holocaust: Narrative and the Consequences of Interpretation.* Bloomington: Indiana UP, 1990.

Anne Tomiche (essay date 1994)

SOURCE: "Rephrasing the Freudian Unconscious: Lyotard's Affect-Phrase," in *Diacritics*, Vol. 24, No. 1, Spring, 1994, pp. 43-62.

[In the following essay, referring to Freud and Lacan, Tomiche explores Lyotard's psychology of irreconcilables, unrepresentables, and irreducibles.]

In the foreword of ***The Inhuman,*** Lyotard notes: "The irreconcilable is what, belatedly, I realize I have always tried to preserve—under various headings: work, figurality, heterogeneity, dissensus, event, thing" [12]. From ***Discours, figure*** (1971), Lyotard's first major work, up to his most recent one, ***Lectures d'enfance*** (1991), the irreconcilable has indeed been, at different levels, at the heart of his work. At the historico-political level, the critical goal of such works as ***The Postmodern Condition, Just Gaming,*** and ***The Differend*** was to make it possible to phrase that which "reality," a politics rooted in it, and political theory have not allowed to be phrased, have always attempted to reduce, suppress, or resolve. At the aesthetic level, Lyotard's valorization of the avant-garde in twentieth-century art stems from his interest in its use of pictorial, musical, or linguistic *matter,* an interest, that is, in what cannot be reduced by representation (and Lyotard links this aesthetic tradition to the Kantian sublime as the experience of a radical irreconcilability between Imagination and Reason). Not only is the irreconcilable at the heart of Lyotard's rephrasing of the historico-political and of the aesthetic, but it is also in terms of such an irreconcilable that Lyotard wants to think and rephrase "psychical reality"—the unconscious. In fact, for Lyotard there is a continuity of stakes in thinking the political, the aesthetic, and the psychic apparatus: to "defend" the radically heterogeneous. A text such as ***Heidegger and the "jews"*** suggests that there is a link between the irreducible in the psychic apparatus (the unconscious affect or affect-phrase) and the immemorial in history: in Lyotard's rephrasing, the historico-political and the psychical function analogically. Lyotard has been criticized precisely for the way such an analogy between the historical and the psychical might entail a loss of the specificity of the historical.[1] My point here is not to enter this debate but instead to focus on Lyotard's work that is directly concerned with a rephrasing of "psychical reality," and more precisely on the texts written after the elaboration of what Lyotard refers to as a "philosophy of phrases" or a "phrastics" in ***The Differend: The Inhuman*** (1988), ***Heidegger and "the jews"*** (1988), **"Emma,"** in *Nouvelle revue de psychanalyse* (1989), and ***Lectures d'enfance*** (1991).[2] In other words, my point is to investigate the relation of Lyotard's recent work to the psychoanalytic field.

The first step of my reading will be to analyze how Lyotard raises and answers the question: what about the unconscious in terms of phrases? Then, since Lyotard himself stresses that preserving the irreconcilable is at the heart of his work, in a second step of analysis the question will become: what about the irreconcilable in the unconscious conceived in terms of phrases? As we shall see, the aim is to articulate, in terms of phrases and through an elaboration of the specificity of what Lyotard calls the affect-phrase, the question of primal repression. Finally, given that from his earliest work on Freud in ***Discours,*** *figure* until his latest "return to Freud" Lyotard's most direct and explicit interlocutor in the field of psychoanalysis has been Lacan, my reading will trace both the divergence between Lacan and Lyotard and their convergence. Although Lyotard's early work (***Discours, figure, Economie libidinale, Dispositifs pulsionnels***) constituted an explicit attempt to resist the Lacanian emphasis on the signifier and communication (as exemplified in "The Agency of the Letter") by foregrounding energetics and forces as the other of linguistic communication, and although we shall see that Lyotard's formulation of the unconscious (as phrase) diverges significantly from Lacan's (as signifier), I would like to show that Lyotard's emphasis on the irreconcilability and irreducibility of the affect-phrase brings him close to the Lacanian emphasis, developed in the '60s and '70s, on the irreducibility of the Thing.

THE UNCONSCIOUS AS PHRASE

The "phrase" is what Lyotard, in ***The Differend,*** offers as the elemental unit of analysis. Although the French term *phrase* evokes grammar and linguistics, Lyotard's phrase is not the linguist's sentence: it is not a minimal unit of signification or the expression of thought. A word as well as a sentence can be considered a phrase: nonlinguistic units such as gestures, silences, signals, notes of music also constitute phrases. A phrase is not defined in terms of meaning and signification: it is a pragmatic entity that is defined by—and defines—the situating of its instances with regard to one another. This constellation of instances is what Lyotard calls a "universe," which consists of four poles: a referent (the case), a meaning (what is signified of the case), an addressee (that to which or to whom something is signified of the case), and an addressor (that "by" which or in whose name something is signified of the case). These four poles organize two axes: the semantico-referential axis (reference and meaning) and the axis of address (addressee and addressor). Rather than conceiving of individuals speaking sentences, Lyotard conceives of phrases as *events* taking place. As they happen, these phrases-events present universes: they present individuals situated as addressors or addressees, they present a referent, they present a meaning. The "subjects" (addressors and addressees) thus do not preexist the phrase universe: they do not exist outside or independently of it; they are positions *within* the universe presented by the phrase. Similarly, meaning, referentiality, and reality are effects of certain kinds of phrases or groupings of phrases. The phrase thus interests Lyotard insofar as it is a pure occurrence, "before" representation, signification, and the subject: it is what merely "happens," the *presentation of the universe,* before the question can even be raised of what has happened, before the question of the *universe presented* can be raised. The status of this pure occurrence is complex, however: it happens *now,* but taking that now as the referent of other phrases inevitably loses it as event. From this perspective of the phrase as event, even silence makes a phrase, since the refusal to phrase is itself an occurrence that "happens": it happens that one refuses to phrase. Silences, but also gestures, feelings, and *affects* have to be analyzed as phrases. There is therefore nothing before phrases, and there is no such thing as an absence of phrase.

It is within the framework of this "philosophy of phrases" that, since **The Differend,** Lyotard has pursued his rephrasing both of the historico-political and of the aesthetic. It is also within the framework of the "philosophy of phrases" that Lyotard extends the rephrasing of historico-political "reality" to a rephrasing of "psychical reality" through his "return to Freud." To the question "what about the unconscious in terms of phrases?" Lyotard answers: "The unconscious 'happens' in phrases, hence as phrase, but as *inarticulate phrase*" ["**Emma**" 48-49; my emphasis]. The concept of (in)articulation is crucial to Lyotard's "phrastics." It is, however, important to understand that, by articulation, Lyotard means neither what structural linguists usually refer to as the "double articulation of language" (that is, its organization in morphemes and phonemes) nor what logicians understand as articulation (well-structured expressions and their combinations). In Lyotard's analysis, a phrase is articulate insofar as it presents a universe, that is, insofar as it is polarized along the axes of referentiality and address. Polarization is more a transcendental condition necessary for articulation than an empirical fact: a phrase can be more or less articulate, its poles can be more or less marked, and indeed, a lot of observable phrases fail to mark all the instances of their universe. That a phrase is *inarticulate,* on the other hand, means that it does not present a universe: the inarticulate phrase "lacks the instances which articulate a phrase universe; it is therefore impossible to say that it presents a universe" ["**Emma**" 56]. It can therefore not be related to any referent; it does not issue from any sender and is not addressed to any receiver. The inarticulate phrase is thus a nonsignifying, nonaddressing, and nonreferenced phrase. However, it points to a meaning that is only of one type: a feeling (of pleasure and/or pain: anxiety, fear, and so on). The inarticulate phrase thus does not "speak of" anything but "says" (without articulating) that there is something, without signification, reference or address: the inarticulate phrase "'says' that there is something, as *da,* here and now, insofar as this something is *not anything,* neither meaning, nor reference, nor address . . . the something that it [the inarticulate phrase] 'presents' is its own 'presence,' its being-there now" ["**Emma**" 56]. To say that "the unconscious happens as inarticulate phrase" thus means that it happens as a pure "it happens," a pure presentation without anything being presented.

To say that the unconscious "happens as inarticulate phrase" does not mean that the distinction between the articulate and the inarticulate corresponds to Freud's opposition between the conscious and the unconscious. Rather it seems to correspond to the distinction between the order of *Vorstellung* (representation) and that of the affect (which is *not* a representation and which Lyotard associates with the order of *Darstellung,* presentation). For Freud, the unconscious, insofar as it is a *repressed* unconscious (that is, insofar as it is repression that constitutes the unconscious) is made of "thoughts" and "wishes," which belong to the

order of representation. In the essay "Repression," Freud elaborates how a drive (*Trieb*) manifests itself by means of representatives (*Triebrepräsentanten*), that consist, on the one hand, of an ideational content (*Vorstellung,* the order of word and thing representations) and, on the other hand, of a charge of affect (*Affektbetrag*) detached from the idea. While the idea belongs to the order of representation (*Vorstellung*), the affect is a representative of the drive (*Triebrepräsentanz*) detached from the idea, a representative that is therefore not a representation. The affect is the qualitative expression of the quantity of libidinal energy and of its fluctuations. The affect thus belongs to an order radically different from that of the word and thing representations. And indeed, in "The Unconscious," published the same year as "Repression," Freud notes that the radical difference between these two orders is attested to by the fact that repression does not bear directly on the drive or on its non representational *Repräsentanz* (the affect) but on its *Vorstellungrepräsentanz:* only representations can be repressed into the unconscious.

After having asserted that the contents of the unconscious can only be representational, however, Freud raises the question of what he paradoxically calls "unconscious affect and unconscious emotion." One would think, Freud notes, that the very essence of an emotion is to be perceived, hence to belong to consciousness. Moreover, if repression bears only on representations, there could not be any unconscious affect or emotion. In fact, things work differently. An affect can be perceived yet remain unrecognized or misconstrued because its own ideational representative has been repressed and the affect has attached itself to another representation of which, as far as consciousness can tell, it is the manifestation. As Freud writes, "in every instance where repression has succeeded in inhibiting the development of affects, we term those affects . . . 'unconscious'" [*SE* 14: 178]. The difference between unconscious affects and unconscious ideas is crucial: "Unconscious ideas continue to exist after repression as actual structures in the system Ucs, whereas all that corresponds in that system to unconscious affects is a potential beginning which is prevented from developing" [*SE* 14: 178]. Topologically the status of the unconscious affect in the system Ucs/Cs is thus paradoxical: the unconscious affect belongs to consciousness (insofar as the affect is *perceived*) while at the same time it is outside consciousness, since the representation of the original affect has been repressed and lies in the unconscious.

Lyotard's inarticulate phrase and the inarticulate/articulate opposition correspond to Freud's unconscious affect and the *Affekt/Vorstellung* opposition. From a topical point of view, both the unconscious affect and the inarticulate phrase are simultaneously inside and outside consciousness. Both manifest themselves to consciousness: the affect is *perceived,* and the inarticulate phrase *happens* (as symptom or feeling of fear, for example). But both are also outside consciousness, since the unconscious affect remains unrecognized or misconstrued and the inarticulate phrase does not speak of anything and is not addressed to anyone. What makes this paradoxical position possible is the fact that neither the unconscious affect nor the inarticulate phrase belongs to the order of representation. Through the notion of "unconscious affects," as opposed to *Vorstellungrepräsentanten*, Freud had opened up the possibility of a nonrepresentational unconscious. Lyotard's inarticulate phrase thus constitutes a "return" to Freud's "unconscious affect": indeed Lyotard also calls the inarticulate phrase an affect-phrase and the two expressions function interchangeably in his texts considered here. A crucial consequence of Lyotard's approach to the unconscious as inarticulate phrase and in his distinction between inarticulate and articulate phrases is precisely to stress the nonrepresentational status of the unconscious. But what is furthermore at stake in Lyotard's approach is the *nonrepresentative* status of the unconscious: not only does the affect not belong to the order of representation, but it does not belong to the order of address and destination, hence of delegation, either. The affect-phrase is there, present, but it is a presence that is neither representational (representing something) nor representative (standing for something). It "is there, but it is not there for something else than itself. That is what makes at the same time its irrefutability and its insufficiency as a witness. It only 'says' one thing: that it is there, but it does not say for what or of what it bears witness. Neither does it say from when or from where" ["**Emma**" 55]. The status of the affect is thus that of a "pure" presence (*Darstellung*), that is, without representation (*Vorstellung*).

While Lyotard's inarticulate phrase constitutes a "return to Freud"'s unconscious affect in order to stress both the nonrepresentational and the nonrepresentative status of the unconscious, it also constitutes a turn away from the Lacanian "return to Freud," precisely on the issue of the nonrepresentative component of the drive (*Trieb*). For Lacan there is no drive that is not always already represented in *Vorstellungrepräsentanten,* that is, in signifiers. The signifier for Lacan is not, as it is in Saussure, a "representation" of a mental concept or the "impression" the sound makes upon the senses, which belongs to the order of perceptions. Interpreting unconscious thoughts as elements of language that do not reveal their meaning, Lacan does not call them signs but instead signifiers detached from their signifieds. As Mikkel Borch-Jacobsen has shown, Lacan's systematic reduction of the Saussurian sign to the signifier intends to empty the linguistic sign of its representational function [see chap. 6, *Lacan le maître absolu*]. Indeed, for Lacan it is precisely because there is nothing in the unconscious but signifiers (*Vorstellungrepräsentanten*) that the drive and desire cannot be represented or articulated, that they are *indicibles*. For if the *Vorstellung* belongs to the order of representation and signification, the *Repräsentanz* (*représentant*) does not. As Lacan explains in *The Four Fundamental Concepts:*

> We mean by representatives (*représentants*) what we understand when we use the phrase, for example, the representative of France. What do diplomats do when they address one another? They simply exercise, in relation to one another, that function of being pure repre-

sentatives and, above all, their own signification must not intervene. . . . In the very exchange of views, each must record only what the other transmits in his pure function as signifier. . . . The term *Repräsentanz* is to be taken in this sense. The signifier has to be understood in this way, it is at the opposite pole from signification. [220]

The representative is not a representation (which Lacan calls a *représentant représentatif*): it is a delegate that takes the place of a representation (hence Lacan's expression *tenantlieu de la représentation*). What is repressed in the unconscious is thus not the represented of desire (the signification, the representation) but the representative which takes the place of a representation. This representative is a delegate, that is, a substitute: it is there for something else.

The Lacanian signifier (unconscious) is thus at the same time exclusively representative (only *Vorstellungrepräsentanten,* that is, delegates) and strictly nonrepresentational (it only stands for a representation) although still directed toward communication (hence Lacan's emphasis on a communicational dialogue between diplomats). On the other hand, Lyotard's inarticulate phrase (unconscious) is nonrepresentative (*Affekt* and *Darstellung* rather than *Vorstellungrepräsentanten*), nonrepresentational, and noncommunicational. The affect is a nondelegate: it is a *représentant sans label de représentance* ["**Emma**" 51], that is, a substitute that does not let itself be recognized as substitute, a substitute that does not give any sign of its origin and does not allow for any localization. Insofar as it is neither a representation nor a delegate, the inarticulate phrase has neither finality nor address and cannot be approached by a pragmatics of communicational destination or delegation.

Lyotard's turn away from Lacan's communicational model bears not only on the issue of the nonrepresentative status of the unconscious but also on the question of the *subject,* introduced in Lacan's discussion of the *Vorstellungrepräsentanten* in the form of the *diplomats* addressing one another. Of course, for Lacan, it is not a question of a preexisting subject representing an idea or a signified by means of a signifier for another subject: the signifier is not the product of a subject, and it is not addressed to a preexisting subject. However, what is nevertheless instituted, in and through the signifier, is the subject: as Lacan repeats, "the signifier represents the subject for another signifier" ["Subversion du sujet," *Écrits* 819; "Position de l'inconscient," *Écrits* 835; *Four Fundamental Concepts* 198-99]. And as Jean-Luc Nancy and Philippe Lacoue-Labarthe have shown, "caught in the separation between the subject of the *énoncé* and the subject of the *énonciation,* the Lacanian subject poses itself or imposes itself as a pure signifier—or as that which a signifier "represents" in a "representation" which is not a reference" [72]. In their discussions each subject-diplomat thus imposes himself "in his pure function as signifier." Whereas Lacan's signifier represents (manifests) the subject, Lyotard's inarticulate phrase, insofar as it is a pure occurrence, comes "before" not only representation or signification but also the subject. The inarticulate manifests a "presubject," what Lyotard calls the *infant*. What is involved is obviously not an evolutionary development leading from a "presubject" to a subject, from the *infant* (etymologically, he who does not speak) to the adult: *infantia* is not a stage of life but that which adulthood (that is, discourse, signification, reason) cannot reconcile or appropriate. The *infant* is, within the adult, that which the adult, the subject of reason, cannot reduce. *Infantia* is the latest name of the irreconcilable, inscribed in the title of Lyotard's most recent book, ***Lectures d'enfance.***

In fact, Lyotard began resisting the Lacanian privilege granted, through a theory of the signifier, both to a communicational model and to a theory of the subject as early as ***Discours, figure.*** Lyotard's resistance in ***Discours, figure*** and his resistance after the elaboration of the philosophy of phrases in ***The Differend,*** differ, however, in his reliance, in ***Discours, figure,*** on energetics, hence on a physicist model of the unconscious. In particular, in the chapter of ***Discours, figure*** entitled "The Dream-Work Does Not Think," Lyotard's reading of the *Traumarbeit* as described by Freud sought to oppose Lacan's interpretation of the dream operations elaborated in "*The Agency of the Letter or Reason since Freud*" [*Écrits*]. As the title indicates, Lacan's interpretation privileged the letter, the signifier, and tended to support his thesis that "the unconscious is structured like a language." On the contrary, Lyotard's reading emphasizes the work of forces that, through the four operations of condensation, displacement, considerations of representability, and secondary revision, deconstruct articulated and communicational discourse.[3] As Lyotard concludes: "the dream work is not a language; it is the effect on language of the force exerted by the figural" [***Discours, figure*** 270]. Throughout ***Discours, figure*** the figural is the name of an unspeakable other necessarily at work *within* and *against* discourse. It is not opposed to discourse but is the point at which the oppositions by which discourse works are opened to a radical heterogeneity. Against Lacan's "linguisterie," Lyotard thus promoted forces and energetics. As Geoffrey Bennington notes in *Lyotard: Writing the Event,* for the Lyotard of the ***Discours, figure*** and ***Economie libidinale*** period (that is, of the early '70s), "force or energy as libido can be struggling with the theatre of representation but also accounting for its constitution" [15]. Insofar as the "figure" is unrepresentable, heterogeneous to the order of discourse, and inarticulate, insofar as it "inhabits" discourse while being outside of it at the same time, the figure has the same relation to discourse as the inarticulate phrase has to articulation.[4]

The shift from the figural (and its corollaries: force, work) to the phrase constitutes a move away from Lyotard's own earlier emphasis on energetics and physics, which is a move away from Freud's physicist model. The Freudian concept of *Affekt* presupposes a quantitative theory of cathexis: the affect is defined as the subjective transposition of the quantity of energy attached to the drive. Freud makes a clear distinction between the subjective aspect of the affect and the energy processes that determine it. Indeed, he uses the expression "quota of affect" (*Affektbetrag*) when wanting to place emphasis on the economic aspect. Whereas Freud's "unconscious affect," conceived from a dynamic and economic point of view and defined as a "quantum of energy," relies on a prequantic and prerelativistic physicist model, Lyotard's phrase conceived as occurrence is defined without recourse to energetics and physics. The phrase has the merit of being less metaphysical than the force/figure, conveying no naturalistic notions of energy.

THE RADICAL DIFFEREND BETWEEN THE INARTICULATE PHRASE AND ARTICULATION

Since there is no such thing as an absence of phrase and since it is impossible not to phrase, it is therefore necessary that a phrase be linked to another phrase: another phrase cannot not happen. A phrase is, constitutively, linked to other phrases. After a phrase another is inevitable (even if that phrase is a silence). Insofar as linking means that a phrase comes *after* another one which comes *after* another one and so on, the question of linkage is a temporal one. And Lyotard's shift from the figural to the phrase is not only a shift away from energetics but also a shift from an emphasis on space (the figural as space) to an emphasis on time (the linkage of phrases). Compare, for example, the focus of Lyotard's account of what Freud calls "polymorphous sexuality," that is, infantile sexuality, in ***Economie libidinale*** and in **"Emma."** In ***Economie libidinale*** he writes: "So-called infantile perverse (really simply diverse) polymorphousness is in endless displacement on a *surface* without holes. . . . Diverse polymorphousness knows that there are no holes, no inside, so sanctuary to respect. That there is only *skin.* 'The infant,' that phantasy of the West, the infant, i.e., desire, is energetical, economical, not representational" [31-32; my emphases]. Whereas in ***Economie libidinale*** the emphasis on energetics and forces as the other of representation is accompanied by an emphasis on space (surface, skin), in **"Emma"** the emphasis shifts to phrases and, with them, to time: "polymorphous sexuality' is the name given by the adult to infantia as affectivity" [68], that is, as "pure" affect-phrase, which Lyotard examines from a temporal perspective as he focuses on the analysis of *Nachträglichkeit.* The movement from ***Discours, figure*** and ***Economie libidinale*** to ***The Inhuman, Heidegger and "the jews", "Emma,"*** and ***Lectures d'enfance*** is thus the movement not only from an "energetical infant" to a "phrastic infant" but also from an emphasis on space to an emphasis on time, that is, on the linkage of phrases.

While to link is a necessity (it "is not an obligation, a *Sollen,* but a necessity, a *Müssen*" [***The Differend*** 66], *how* to link is a contingency. There are many ways of making linkage, many modes of organization: Lyotard calls these *genres.* Any phrase that "happens" may enter into a conflict of possible linkages, a conflict that stems from the heterogeneity and incommensurability of the different genres of discourse governing the different possible linkages. This conflict among genres of discourse as to how to link is a *differend,* that is, "a case of conflict between (at least) two parties that cannot be equitably resolved for lack of a rule of judgment applicable to both arguments. One side's legitimacy does not imply the other's lack of legitimacy. However, applying a single rule of judgment to both in order to settle their differend as though it were merely a litigation would wrong (at least) one of them" [xi]. What such a radical conflict calls into question is the very possibility of linkage (no arbitration is possible): in the differend something "asks" to be phrased and suffers the wrong of not being able to be phrased. Lyotard thus defines the differend as a dispute, without possibility of linkage, between two parties. The notion, however, is equally pertinent for him when a single party is involved: the aesthetic experience of the sublime (which is the one that interests Lyotard) produces a differend—"a radical division or cleavage within the subject between what can be conceived and what can be imagined" [**"Le sublime et l'avant-garde,"** *The Inhuman* 109]. And the notion of differend is suitable not only for describing a historico-political "reality" or the aesthetic experience of the sublime but also for describing "psychical reality," what "happens" in the origination of the unconscious: an unresolvable conflict and an impossibility of linkage between the inarticulate phrase and articulation.

Lyotard explicitly elaborates this original differend between the affect-phrase and articulation in a reading of a section of Freud's *Project for a Scientific Psychology* that deals with the case history of Emma [*SE* 1:353-56]. It is in the *Project* that Freud develops most elaborately an energetic and mechanistic model of the unconscious, described in terms of forces, excitations, and traces of the application of these forces of excitation leading to facilitations (*Bahnungen*). It is thus interesting that Lyotard chooses the most physicist of Freud's texts to rephrase the case of Emma without recourse to physics and in terms of phrases.

Emma's symptom is a fear of going in stores alone. She links this fear with the memory of a scene that took place when she was twelve, shortly after puberty: she went in a store and felt frightened because the two shop assistants, one of whom she remembers having found sexually attractive, were laughing at her clothes (Freud calls this memory scene 1). The memories aroused, however, explained neither Emma's compulsion (being laughed at because of her clothes and finding a shop assistant attractive are not sufficient reasons to explain the compulsive fear of going in stores alone) nor the nature of the symptom (whether she is accompanied or not makes no difference to her clothes or to the fact that she found the shop-assistant attractive). Further associations led back from scene 1 to another scene that had taken place when she was eight: she had gone in a store and had been sexually aggressed by the grinning shopkeeper, who had grabbed at her genitals through her dress (scene 2, four years before scene 1). In spite of this experience, she had gone back to the shop a

second time. The "aggression" had therefore not caused any affect of fear. However, she now (that is, during her analysis by Freud) reproached herself for having gone to the store a second time, as though she had wanted to provoke the assault. Freud concludes that scene 1 is the deferred response to the aggression of scene 2. Scene 2 did not affect Emma (scene 2 did not produce any affect of fear). However, the "memory" of scene 2, although not conscious, has been activated by scene 1 because of the elements linking the two scenes (shopkeeper/shop assistants; grin/laughter).

Freud adds that such a "memory" of scene 2 at the moment of scene 1 "aroused what it was certainly not able to at the time, a *sexual release,* which was transformed into anxiety" [*SE* 1: 354]. The "sexual release" in scene 1 (the fact that Emma found the shop assistant attractive), transformed into fear, is thus linked to the unconscious memory of the assault. But this sexual release and the subsequent fear were not linked to the assault when it was experienced: "Here we have the case of a memory arousing an affect which it did not arouse as an experience because in the meantime the change brought about in puberty had made possible a different understanding of what was remembered" [*SE* 1: 356]. The affect, absent in scene 2, appeared only in scene 1. And Freud links this delay in the emergence of the affect to a latency in genital development. Emma was not affected during scene 2 (at age 8) because she had not reached puberty yet. However, the memory of scene 2 activated by scene 1, at a time when she had reached puberty, provoked the affect: "Although it does not usually happen in psychical life that a memory arouses an affect which it did not give rise to as an experience, this is nevertheless something quite usual in the case of a sexual idea, precisely because the retardation of puberty is a general characteristic of the organization" [*SE* 1: 356]. The intervention of puberty thus introduces an inversion between the two scenes. Scene 2 has a sexual content ("aggression") for an external spectator and in the shopkeeper's intention, but for the child, for whom the scene cannot fully have this signification, it produces no immediate sexual effect. On the other hand, during scene 1 there is no sexual aggression. However, it is scene 1 that, through its connections with scene 2, provokes a sexual reaction (the "sexual release" transformed into anxiety).

What is interesting about the case of Emma is that it provides all the elements of Freud's seduction theory as it was elaborated, until September 1897, in order to delineate the etiology of hysterical neurosis: the case provides both the elements that remained after the seduction theory collapsed and the elements that were responsible for that collapse. Although, in a famous letter addressed to Fliess and dated 21 September 1897, Freud announced that he had abandoned the idea of the reality of the seduction scenes, the temporal aspect of the theory—that is, the notion of "deferred action" of a trauma, a notion on which the case of Emma relies—remained central to Freudian (and also to Lacanian) theory.[5] The trauma does not take place in one scene but through several scenes that are linked together.

It is not in itself that the scene of "sexual aggression" (scene 2) is traumatic. In fact the subject does not react at all at the time when the scene is experienced. He/she reacts when another, later scene brings back the memory of the original scene. It is the memory, not the new scene, that functions as a source of traumatic energy. The seduction theory thus relies on the specific temporal structure of deferred action (*Nachträglichkeit*) linking scene 2 (the most remote and repressed one) and all its subsequent repetitions. It is this temporal structure that explains, in the case of Emma for example, the process of repression by which scene 2 can have no effect when it happens but only deferred effects at the time of scene 1. Although neither scene is traumatic in itself (scene 2 does not produce any affect, and scene 1 does not contain any sexual aggression), the trauma is in the sequence of the two scenes and in their linkage.

Analysis thus reveals that behind the most recent scene lies another one and from one scene to the other, one is led to an "originary scene" of seduction. In the case of Emma, which exemplifies Freud's theory of infantile seduction before 1897, a child, fundamentally unprepared for what happens to him/her, *hilflos,* is passively confronted with adult sexuality in the form of the shopkeeper's aggression. Soon after the *Project,* Freud, in his quest for the "originary scene" of seduction, questioned the possibility of situating this scene as late as it occurs in the case of Emma (when she is eight). But what matters here much more than the age at which the scenes took place is that scene 2 is paradigmatic of an "originary seduction." As Lyotard notes: "under the name of the shopkeeper I am talking about all the 'seductors' and 'seductresses' (including the mother)" [**"Emma"** 67]. The case of Emma relies on Freud's view that originary seduction consists in the child's passive confrontation with a "perverse" adult.

In fact, if the seduction theory in its early form crumbled, it is because Freud stumbled on the nature of the phenomenon of seduction which he did not understand in terms other than psychopathological, relying on a clinical conception of perversion (and more precisely of the perverse father). From that point of view Freud had to wonder about the reality of the seduction scene in statistical terms, and the theory collapsed because it could not account for the fact that not all fathers, not even all hysterics' fathers, are perverse. Discarding the seduction theory meant giving up the belief in the *actual* reality of the seduction scene and discovering its *psychical* reality. However, in spite of the fact that he abandoned the idea that the sole cause of psychoneurosis was the *actual* reality of seduction, Freud never ceased to assert that sometimes it is the repression of a real trauma that underlies the formation of symptoms, and sometimes it is the repression of phantasy.[6] Indeed, Freud never completely abandoned the idea of an actual seduction: the description, much later, of the preoedipal attachment to the mother led him to speak of an actual seduction by the mother, in the form of the bodily attentions bestowed upon the infant at the breast—a real seduction taken as the prototype for the subsequent phantasies: "the phantasy touches the ground of reality for it was really the mother who by her activities over the child's bodily hygiene inevitably stimulated, and perhaps even roused for the first time, pleasurable sensations in her genitals" ["New Introductory Lectures on Psychoanalysis," *SE* 22: 120]. From the *Project to the New Introductory Lectures,* the seductor has thus shifted from the perverse father to the mother, but the *fact* of seduction remains. As Jean Laplanche and Jean-Bernard Pontalis note,

> Apparently Freud could never resign himself to treating phantasy as the pure and simple outgrowth of the spontaneous sexual life of the child. He is forever searching, behind the phantasy, for whatever has founded it in its reality: perceived evidence of the primal scene, . . . the seduction of the infant by its mother, and even more fundamentally the notion that phantasies are based in the last reckoning on 'primal phantasies'—on a mnemic residue transmitted hereditarily from actual experiences in the history of the human species. [407]

Finally, the crisis of the seduction theory, which originated in the order of facts (the actuality of the scenes), also revealed a crisis on the level of the theory itself: what the emphasis on a psychopathological conception of seduction left unquestioned was the idea that the unconscious was psychopathological, that is, that it could be completely reduced and that such was precisely the goal of psychoanalysis (in his 21 September 1897 letter to Fliess, Freud talks about the possibility "of the unconscious being completely tamed by the conscious"). The idea of a "normal," irreducible unconscious—that is, the idea of primal repression—was still absent at that point. However obscure the notion of primal repression is in Freud it nonetheless became a cardinal element in his theory of repression, and it recurs in his work from the *Case of Schreber* (1911) onward. There would be no repression, Freud notes, if the repressed term did not connect up with elements of the unconscious that were already there and that exert on it a real attraction. But for that attraction to operate, there must already be an unconscious system, and this is why Freud has recourse to the concept of primal repression in order to account for the originary presence of some formations in the unconscious, formations that cannot have been drawn there by other ones: "we have reason to assume that there is a *primal repression,* a first phase of repression, which consists in the psychical (ideational) representative of the instinct being denied entrance into the conscious" ["Repression," *SE* 14: 148]. According to this definition, then, the object of primal repression was never conscious; but neither was it unconscious before being repressed, since primal repression accounts for the presence of *originary* formations in the unconscious. Although the concept of primal repression was not yet articulated in 1897 in the *Project,* if one considers scene 2 as the prototype of an *originary* seduction, one is also led to see it as the prototype of an *originary* repression through which the unconscious constitutes itself.

> was still scanty, and it happened by chance to include a disproportionately large number of cases in which sexual seduction by an adult or by older children played

the chief part in the patient's childhood. I thus over-estimated the frequency of such events. . . . Moreover, I was at that point unable to distinguish with certainty between falsifications made by hysterics in their memories of childhood and traces of real events. ["My Views komon the Part Played by Sexuality in the Aetiology of Neuroses," *SE* 7: 174]

Indeed, in **"Emma"** Lyotard repeats several times that what is at stake in his reading of the case is the question of primal repression. Lyotard transcribes Freud's account of the case into his language of phrases in order to use that transcription to rephrase the Freudian concept of *Nachträglichkeit* in terms of the linkage of phrases and to rephrase the concept of *primal repression* via an extension of the seduction theory: he links primal repression, phrased as original differend, to an *originary seduction* phrased not as an actual or phantasied aggression passively experienced by the child, but as the infant's passibility, a pure affectedness.

In his rephrasing of the concept of deferred action (*après-coup* in the French translation of *Nachträglichkeit,* and the question of *coup,* literally "blow" or "shock," is crucial to Lyotard's rephrasing), Lyotard calls t2 the time when scene 2 took place, t1 the time of scene 1, and t0 the time of the analytic scene (Emma on Freud's couch). What is at stake in the temporal structure of the case, Lyotard argues, is not, as Freud claims, the production at t1 of an affect (the fear of going in shops) that was previously absent at t2 and that would have been produced by a mnemic representation. Indeed, Freud himself notes that at t2, when she was 8, Emma went back to the shop after the aggression. This repetition, which structures scene 2, indicates that, while there was a sexual aggression on the part of the shopkeeper, there was also a temptation (to seduce or be seduced) on Emma's part since she went back to the shop. At t2 Emma had thus been affected, and Lyotard cannot follow Freud when he says that the affect appeared at t1. Although it did not produce any representation, scene 2 produced an affect. Insofar as scene 2 produces an affect but no representation, it testifies to a "pure" possibility of being affected, "pure" in the sense that the possibility of being affected by an event is independent from the (im)possibility of representing the event. Such a "pure" possibility of being affected is what Lyotard calls *passibility.* And it is important not to confuse passibility, the fact that one is affected without there being any representation of what has produced the affect, with passivity. Whereas passivity is opposed to activity, passibility is not: in fact, the active/passive opposition presupposes passibility. Between t2 (when Emma's passibility has been excited, that is, when she has been affected) and t1 and until t0, scene 2 has been forgotten, which means that Emma has no representation of the scene and of the affect (temptation) it involved. What is at stake in the structure of *Nachträglichkeit* is thus not to explain the production of an affect (in t1) that was previously absent, but to explain why, having been affected at t1, Emma has forgotten that she had been.

The affect produced by scene 2 is a phrase but a specific kind of phrase, since it is an inarticulate phrase, which, as we have seen, is radically nonsignifying, nonaddressing, and nonreferenced and which points to only one type of meaning: pleasure and/or pain. Because the inarticulate phrase is without object, reference, and destination, no linkage to Emma's affect-phrase is possible: something has happened in scene 2 but has not been registered, could not have been (registering would entail linking), and there has been no determination of *what* happened (since the affect-phrase has no object). The affect-phrase is present in t2, present but not represented, and since it lacks the agencies that articulate a universe and that are needed for another phrase to link to it, the affect-phrase remains unlinked, or, as Lyotard says, "pure." The affect-phrase can therefore not be the referent of another later phrase, which means that the affect-phrase cannot be remembered; "it inscribes effects without the inscription being 'memorized' in the form of recollection" [*The Inhuman* 21], and this is why Emma cannot remember scene 2. The temporality of the inarticulate phrase is thus exclusively the present of the here and now. The affect-phrase is outside diachronic time. As Lyotard says, "the time of feeling is *now.* . . . At the moment when it occurs, it points to itself, it is tautegoric. . . . One could say that a feeling appears and disappears entirely at every instant, that it is ageless" [**"The Inarticulate"** 5]. Rather than the appearance in t1 of an affect absent in t2, what is thus at stake in *Nachträglichkeit* is the modification of the "pure affect-phrase," which "touched" Emma in scene 2 and which the articulate phrase retroactively tries to assimilate in t1.

Scene 2 can therefore be described as the scene of an encounter between two kinds of phrases: an articulate phrase (the shopkeeper's "sexual aggression") on the one hand and Emma's inarticulate affect-phrase on the other. The affect-phrase and articulation can meet but cannot link up, since Emma's inarticulate phrase does not allow for any kind of linkage. That encounter is thus a clash, a shock, a *coup* between the affect-phrase—the inarticulate infantile phrase (*in-fans* since the affect does not speak)—and the articulate, addressed, and referenced phrase. Such a clash is produced by the radical and insolvable heterogeneity between the two sets of phrases—it is a radical differend produced by the encounter between the affect-phrase and articulation: "between this affectivity and articulation, the differend is inescapable" [**"Emma"** 69]. Not only is such a differend irreducible but, Lyotard says, it is also ineluctable, "one could not avoid it. The adult articulate phrase always comes to awaken (excite) passibility" [**"Emma"** 70]. Lyotard's description of the case of Emma in terms of phrases thus constitutes a "rephrasing" of originary repression in terms of a radical differend that stems from the incommensurability between infantile and adult phrases.

Such a differend cannot be reduced to a "confusion of tongues," as Sandor Ferenczi elaborated it. Ferenczi emphasizes that there is an opposition between the universe of the child—characterized by what he calls "tenderness," that is, "the playful gratifications" of infantile sexuality—and that of the adult governed by "passion," that is, genital sexuality. The encounter, in the child, of the language of tenderness with that of passion produces a "confusion of tongues," which in Ferenczi's analysis is at the source of the originary psychical trauma. However, not only does Ferenczi leave unanswered the question of the actual nature of the difference between infantile eroticism and adult sexuality, but furthermore he suggests that such a difference can be reduced by paying attention to the "very critical way of thinking and speaking to your children . . . [so as] to loosen, as it were, their tongues" ["Confusion of Tongues" 166]. In other words, the "confusion of tongues" designates the confrontation of two languages, which are different but are nevertheless languages, which implies that there are a certain number of correspondences between them. In Lyotard's analysis, on the other hand, the infantile phrase is not a tongue, not a language, since it lacks the articulations that would be required for it to be translatable. The differend between the infantile affect-phrase and the adult articulate phrase is not a litigation and cannot be dealt with through discussion or compromise because the heterogeneity between affectivity and articulation is absolutely irreducible.

I have focused on **"Emma"** in order to analyze Lyotard's rephrasing of primal repression in terms of an "originary" differend between the affect-phrase and articulation. But this is not the only text where Lyotard addresses the question of the unconscious in terms of phrases. In *Heidegger and "the jews,"* what Lyotard calls "the jews," a name that is always plural, in quotation marks, and in lower case, refers neither to a nation nor to a political, philosophical, or religious figure or subject. It is neither a concept nor a representation of any specific people as such. What "the jews" designates is an otherness that Western thought cannot think but cannot not think, either. "The jews" functions in its relation to Western thinking as the affect, the inarticulate, infancy function in relation to articulation, adulthood. In fact, "the jews" *is* the unconscious affect whose paradoxical temporal status Lyotard analyzes in the opening section of the book, a section devoted to an analysis of *Nachträglichkeit* that echoes that of **"Emma."** In *The Inhuman,* the term "inhuman" designates the irreducible infancy that lies in each of us adults. And in *Lectures d'enfance* (**"Voix"**), analyzing the different ways in which the voice is inscribed in and by psychoanalysis, Lyotard distinguishes between articulated voice, which he calls *lexis* (and which "goes from a sender to a receiver and communicates to the receiver a signification concerning its referent" [132]), and the voice as timber, which, following Aristotle, he calls *phônè*. *Phônè* is not articulated; "it does not refer to an object whose signification it would communicate to a receiver on behalf of a sender" [133]. *Phônè* and *lexis* relate to each other in exactly the same way as inarticulation (affect-phrase) and articulation do in **"Emma."** Whereas *lexis* communicates, tells stories, *phônè* communicates nothing, has no stories to tell, but manifests itself. *Phônè* is nonreferenced (it does not refer to anything) and nonaddressed (it has neither sender nor receiver, which means that it does not function on the axis of destination), but this does not mean that it is meaningless noise: "it is meaning itself insofar as

meaning signals itself. . . . *Phônè* is the affect insofar as it is the signal of itself" [134]. *Phônè* is thus "pure manifestation"; that is, *phônè* manifests an *affectedness,* the possibility of being affected, passibility. Furthermore, whereas temporality is inscribed in the very structure of *lexis* (the linkage of one articulated phrase *after* another implies temporalization), *phônè* is not temporal: it is a pure singularity whose time is that of the here and now—"the now of the affect is not framed by a *before* and an *after.* It is not the now of temporalization and historization" [136-37]. And Lyotard's analysis of *lexis* and *phônè* in *Lectures d'enfance* reaches a conclusion very similar to that of **"Emma"**: "the encounter between *phônè* and *lexis* is inevitably traumatic, seductive" [138].

What Lyotard's rephrasing of primal repression thus suggests, beyond the contingencies of an actual traumatic scene (real or phantasied seduction), is the principle of an originary, ontological "seduction" that consists less in a physical aggression to which a passive child is being subjected than in the intrusion of articulation into the child's universe of inarticulation and affects, a seduction that is thus the awakening of passibility. Insofar as it founds the unconscious in an originary moment that is *both* seductive and traumatic, Lyotard's concept of an originary differend meets Laplanche's theory of "originary seduction." In fact, it is interesting to note that, like Lyotard, Laplanche uses the case of Emma described by Freud in the *Project* in order to articulate his theory of originary and generalized seduction.[7] The case of Emma interests Laplanche insofar as he sees it as the structural paradigm of something more originary than the events described by Freud and Emma as taking place when Emma was eight and twelve years old. Moving the scenes backward toward early infancy does not change their (temporal) structure, and what Laplanche is interested in analyzing through the case of Emma is "the birth of the unconscious in and through the first repressions" [*Problématiques IV* 126]. For Laplanche, as for Lyotard, the originary situation is the confrontation between the child and the adult world; this world is not something objective that the child would have to learn and discover but "is characterized by messages in the most general sense of the term (linguistic, . . . prelinguistic or paralinguistic) which interrogate the child before he can understand them" [*Nouveaux fondements* 123-24]. Through these messages (Lyotard's phrases) something is signified to the child, something is *signified to the subject,* but remains nonunderstood and nonunderstandable: although the message conveys a content in itself, it has no content *for the subject* (in the case of Emma, scene 2 has a sexual content—aggression—in itself and in the mind of the shopkeeper but not for Emma, who cannot understand, that is, represent the scene as sexual aggression). Hence Laplanche's reformulation of the case of Emma:

> We have to understand that what is described, in a schematic and almost caricatural way, as an *event* in the Freudian theory of the *proton pseudos* is something like the implantation of adult sexuality in the child. We think that it must be reinterpreted, no longer as an event, as an actual and datable trauma but as a fact

more diffuse and more structural, a fact more originary too. [*Vie et mort* 75]

The originary situation—the implantation of adult sexuality in the child—is thus the situation whereby the child is sent messages that he cannot understand. Laplanche calls enigmatic signifiers these messages which interrogate the child but to which he cannot respond. Signifiers, Laplanche notes, function on two distinct levels: as signifiers of something (signifiers of signifieds; this level correponds to what Lyotard calls the semantico-referential axis) and as signifiers to someone (Lyotard's axis of address). What characterizes the enigmatic signifier is that it signifies to someone (the shopkeeper's sexual aggression is addressed to Emma) but it is a designified signifier, a signifier that has no signification for the subject to whom it is signified.[8] Laplanche's enigmatic signifier can thus be compared to what Lyotard has described as the encounter between the adult phrase and the infantile phrase: the articulate phrase can only "touch" or "affect" the inarticulate child (and thus "interrogate" him in Laplanche's terms) without placing him on the axis of referentiality or of address (that is, without allowing him to represent and respond). In this possibility to "interrogate," "touch", or "affect" lie both the originary trauma and the originary seduction. Indeed, for Laplanche the seduction lies in the enigma (in the interrogation) itself: "The enigma . . . is *seduction in itself,* and it is not in vain that the female Sphinx is posted at the doors of Thebes even before the drama of Oedipus" [*Nouveaux Fondements* 126]. Whether the seduction scene is the scene of the "mother's" care for the baby, the scene of the "father's" perversion, or the "primal scene," what makes each of them scenes of seduction is their enigmatic nature (in each case something is signified *to* the child but has no signification *for* the child). And the trauma stems from the fact that the enigmatic signifier is de-signified (it is not the signifier of any signified). It conveys no signification: "the enigmatic message . . . conveys nothing except its energy. . . . [T]he message is necessarily traumatic because it tends to transform itself into pure energy, into pure excitation" [*Problématiques IV* 128]. What makes seduction is the enigma; what makes the message an enigma and makes the enigma traumatic is that it is "pure energy."

Lyotard also emphasizes the originarily traumatic and seductive nature of the "touch" (the differend). But, in his terms, what makes the encounter traumatic is the impossibility of linkage—the shock stems from the incommensurability between the two types of phrases—and what reveals that the encounter is seductive is that it awakens the infant's passibility and produces a "pure affect." Whereas Laplanche's originary seduction/trauma relies on an energetic model ("the pure energy" of the enigmatic signifier), Lyotard's "pure affectivity" is the nonphysicist name of excitability. It signals a passibility that is irreducible to articulation.

LYOTARD'S ORIGINARY DIFFEREND AND LACAN'S MISSED ENCOUNTER

In spite of the difference, analyzed above, between Lyotard's phrase and Lacan's signifier, Lyotard's rephrasing of primal repression as originary and inescapable differend enters into dialogue with Lacan's elaboration of primal repression around the concepts of the Thing and of the Real as missed encounter. In the mid-'50s, based on his reading of Freud's "Verneinung," Lacan elaborated a theory of originary repression (*Urverdrängt*) as structural *Verwerfung* by the speaking subject.[9] In these texts the concept of *Verwerfung* (which Lacan translates as foreclosure) was intended to account for the specificity of psychosis (as opposed to neurosis) and for the psychotic's inability to symbolize (hence Lacan's formulation: what has been *verworfen* "appears in the Real" in the form of the psychotic's hallucinations). In the later texts, however, foreclosure becomes the characteristic of the signifying order as such: every symbolic structure is structured around a gap, around the foreclosure of a key signifier. Such a movement entailed two shifts: one from the subjective (the impossibility of the Real as the psychotic's inability to symbolize) to the objective (the impossibility of the Real as the impossibility of the Thing); and one from foreclosure as originary expulsion to the encounter with the Thing as missed encounter. It is precisely the Lacanian concepts of the Thing and of the missed encounter that can be compared to Lyotard's affect-phrase and differend. That Lacan is a direct interlocutor for Lyotard throughout his own "return to Freud" and his rephrasing of the unconscious is attested to by the recurring, though passing, references Lyotard makes to Lacan. In ***The Inhuman,*** for example, Lyotard explicitly links the irreducible discussed in the context of aesthetics to the Lacanian Thing: "Under the name of matter, I mean *the Thing*"—Matter, another name for the heterogeneous and the irreconcilable, has to do with the Thing [154].[10]

Lacan introduces The Thing in his seminar VII on the ethics of psychoanalysis, as he returns to Freud's essay "Verneinung." Whereas in the mid-'50s ("Réponse à Jean Hyppolite" and *Les psychoses*) Freud's "Verneinung" had been the starting point of Lacan's elaboration of the notion of *Verwerfung*, defined as foreclosure of the primordial signifier (castration in the case of the Wolf Man) by the psychotic subject, Lacan returns to Freud's essay in *L'éthique de la psychanalyse* in order to elaborate the distinction marked by the German terms *die Sache* and *das Ding*, a distinction that Freud never explicitly exploited. The Freudian context of Lacan's argument is the distinction between thing presentations (*Sachvorstellungen*) and word presentations (*Wortvorstellungen*). Lacan stresses the link between *Sachvorstellungen* and *Wortvorstellungen*: "*Sache* and *Wort* are thus tightly linked; they make a couple" [*Éthique* 58]. On the other hand, *das Ding* "is situated elsewhere" [58]. The Thing has nothing to do with the object, which belongs to the world, temporality and language: "the object—insofar as it specifies man's directions

. . . in his world . . . —this object is precisely not the Thing insofar as it is at the heart of the libidinal economy" [133]. The Thing stands beyond all human objects as the "outside-the-signified" (*hors-signifié*) in relation to which "the subject keeps his distance and is constituted in a mode of relation, of primary affect, prior to any repression" [67-68]. The Thing therefore does not belong to the order of representation: "at the level of the *Vorstellungen,* it is not that the Thing is nothing, but literally that the Thing is not—its specificity is to be absent, foreign" [*Éthique* 78]. Whereas *Sachvorstellungen* and *Wortvorstellungen* belong to the order of *Vorstellung,* the Thing does not.

The Thing, which belongs neither to the realm of the imaginary objects of desire nor to the order of representations, belongs to the field of the Real. Returning to the distinction between the two kinds of judgment made by Freud in "Verneinung,"[11] Lacan argues that *die Sache* ultimately refers to particular qualities whose possession in the human world can be affirmed or denied. In contrast, *das Ding* ultimately refers to the very existence of a thing, which can be affirmed or denied independently of the attribution to the thing of various qualities. Insofar as the distinction between attributive judgment and judgment of existence is a distinction between symbolic properties predicated to an object (the *quid* of the object) and the object as a "this" before any symbolic determination (the object as *quod*), Lacan's Thing emerges as the pure "this" of the object without properties—a *quod* without any *quid.* Moreover, inasmuch as Freud's distinction between the two kinds of judgment occurs in an analysis of the primordial distinction between what is "inside" and what is "outside" the subject,[12] Lacan's Thing emerges as the excluded interior, that which is excluded inside: "*das Ding* is precisely at the center (of the subjective world of the unconscious organized in signifying relations) insofar as it is excluded" [*Éthique* 87].

Just like the Thing, Lyotard's pure affect-phrase is *not* a tangible and material object. Discussing the affect Lyotard says: "we are talking about . . . a 'this' which is not at all a thing, but the occasion of a feeling and of a 'pure feeling' . . . insofar as it is not motivated," that is, not addressed and not referenced [***Lectures d'enfance*** 125]. The "pure affect-phrase" is an occurrence as such: it is the mere fact *that* something happens, before all determination of the "*what* happens," it is a *quod* before any *quid:* "it is the essence of the event that *there is* 'before' *what* there is" [***Heidegger et "les juifs"*** 35]. The eventhood of the affect-phrase is the radical singularity of the happening, the "it happens" empty of content: the eventhood of the affect-phrase is what makes it "outside-the-signified" and links it to the Lacanian Thing. Moreover, the affect is both inside and outside articulation. Like Lacan's Thing, which constitutes a primordial exclusion at the center of the subject's unconscious (the Thing is at the heart of the unconscious but is there as excluded, as a hole, a cut around which the signifier structures reality), Lyotard's affect is excluded inside: it inhabits articulated discourse while being its radical other. The Thing and the affect-phrase thus come to name an otherness that can never be assimilated, an irreducible otherness that eludes symbolization and representation while at the same time structuring it. It is the otherness of "something" that has no other content than a pure "there is" before any determination of *what* there is.

Moreover, after the mid-'60s Lacan comes to describe the encounter with the Thing and with the Real as a missed encounter[13] and as the untying of a knot.[14] The "discovery of psychoanalysis," Lacan says in *The Four Fundamental Concepts of Psychoanalysis,* is that of an essential encounter, "an appointment to which we are called with the Real which eludes us" [53]. Borrowing the term *tuché* from Aristotle, Lacan translates it as "the encounter with the Real"—"the encounter insofar as it may be missed, insofar as it is essentially the missed encounter" [55]. The encounter with the Real is always a missed encounter on several accounts. First, "missed" characterizes the primordial object: not only because the primordial object (the Thing) can never be reached and is always missed (*raté,* Lacan says) but also because of the impossibility of the Thing, that is, because the essence of the Thing is to be missed and missing ("the essence of the Thing," Lacan says in *Encore,* "is the *ratage*" [55]). Furthermore, the encounter with the Real is always a missed encounter because the signifier comes to hide, to cover up what is missed (the impossibility of the Thing): the Real as hole disappears without ever having appeared, only leaving traces (hallucinations, phantasies, symptoms). The impossibility of the Real is that the signifier comes to occupy its hole. Even as hole the Real thus has no positivity. Its logical consistency is only that of a construct that eludes the structure, although it is only through its effects in the structure that it can be perceived. The impossibility of the Real is thus the impossibility of its inscription (hence Lacan's recurrent statement that the Real is "that which never stops not being written"[15]). This does not mean, however, that the Real acquires the status of an inaccessible transcendental: although the inscription of the Real is impossible, this very impossibility can be inscribed, so that the Real coincides with the impossibility of its own inscription.

In seminars XXII and XXIII, Lacan elaborates, through various forms of the Borromean knot, how to inscribe the impossibility of inscribing the Real. The Real emerges only through the idea of the knot; it is characterized by being knotted (*se nouer*) because the Borromean knot is made of three rings of string that interlock in such a way that when any one of the rings is cut the entire interlocking system falls apart. It is thus impossible to undo one of the rings without undoing the two other rings. The moment of untying, when a single cut disperses the rings, is nothing but the advent of the Real as such. The Real as such is thus (imaginarily) figured as the breaking of the knot, the interruption of linkages: "the mark of the Real, as such, is that it does not link to anything" [*Le sinthome* 36]. In *Les noms indistincts,* Jean-Claude Milner translates the topology of the Borromean knot and of the three orders of the Real, the Symbolic, and the Imaginary into three suppositions: the Real coincides with the supposition that "there is," the mere gesture of a cut without content (the cut that undoes the knot); the Symbolic coincides with the supposition that "there is something of One" (*il y a de l'Un*); and the Imaginary with the supposition that "there is something of the Same" (*il y a du Même*).[16] What characterizes the pure supposition "there is" is the fact that from it nothing can be logically and reciprocally deduced; no linkage is possible. As opposed to the Symbolic, which institutes distinctions, and to the Imaginary, which institutes linkages, the Real is the indistinct and the unbound as such.

For Lyotard too the encounter between the affect-phrase and the articulated phrase can only be a missed encounter. First, because insofar as it is inarticulate, the affect-phrase does not allow for linkages according to the rules of any genres of discourse but only suspends or interrupts linkages. The affect-phrase disrupts any preexisting referential frame within which it might be represented or understood; it is always in excess of such a frame. And it is precisely because of the radical impossibility of their linkage that the encounter between the affect-phrase and the articulate phrase can only be a *ratage*: an affect-phrase and an articulate phrase can only meet by missing each other. Second, it is also because of its temporal structure, which is that of *Nachträglichkeit,* that the encounter can only be a missed encounter. The affect "stemming" from the first shock cannot be identified at the time of the first shock because the event (affect-phrase) cannot be understood *at the time* (its singularity is alien to the language or structure of understanding that it affects). And when the affect later reappears, it is not recognized but takes place as a new feeling each time that it happens. Nevertheless the affect of fear testifies to the fact that the infantile affect-phrase did "happen": while "the first blow (*premier coup*) strikes the psychic apparatus without observable internal effect . . . with the second blow an affect takes place without shock . . . and . . . informs consciousness *that* there is something there, without consciousness being able to tell *what* it is" [**Heidegger and "the jews"** 34-35]. The affect constitutes a warning of the *quod*, but not of the *quid*. Ultimately, what governs the logic, or rather the phrastic, of the deferred effects of this originary *differend* is the complex dialectic between the "too soon" and the "too late" that structures human development: "too late" because genital sexuality, articulation comes too late for the infant (Emma) to be able to "understand" (that is, latch onto, represent) the adult phrase (the shopkeeper's sexual aggression) when it happens; and at the same time "too soon" because sexuality, articulation, comes from the outside and from the adult world too soon for the infant to "understand" it. What thus emerges is "nothing else than the unpreparedness of the psychic apparatus for the 'first blow'; a prematuration or immaturation, as one says, pretending to know what maturity is; an 'infancy,' thus, which would not be a period of the life cycle, but an incapacity to represent and bind a certain something" [**Heidegger and "the jews"** 17]. The first shock, which constitutes a "pure"

event, paradoxically always happens too soon (to be understood) and too late (to be recovered), and the moment of passage between the "too soon" and the "too late" is always impossible to determine, always missed.

Although Lacan and Lyotard think the unconscious from different perspectives (one as a psychoanalyst, the other as a philosopher), they share a basic assumption about the construction of "psychical reality": beyond, beneath, and in "psychical reality" there is something that cannot be reduced, something around which "reality" is constructed. Whether phrased in terms of signifiers or in terms of phrases, this "something" is the irreducibility of a pure *there is*: a thetic proposition that has no other content than its position, the position of a cut without which there is not anything. The cut of the empty "there is" is the *béance* of the Lacanian Real as well as the eventhood of Lyotard's affectphrase. The construction of reality, however, involves precisely reducing or resolving this irreducible. This is where, for both Lacan and Lyotard, the sense of an obligation toward the irreducible comes into play. For Lacan, the ethics of psychoanalytic theory emerges as a relation to *das Ding* that takes the Real as a kind of limit. And, for Lyotard, what is at stake in the aesthetic avant-gardes as well as in critical thinking is doing justice to the event, the pure happening of the affect-phrase. Being attentive to the Real, doing justice to the event necessarily entails a reduction, a betrayal of the nature of the Real, an injustice: such is the paradox of the obligation toward the irreducible.

Notes

1. See for example Avital Ronell's review of *Heidegger et "les juifs"* in *Diacritics* 19.3-4 (1989): 63-75; also David Carroll's foreword to the English translation of *Heidegger and "the jews."*

2. All translations of untranslated texts are my own; when a published translation exists I have consulted it and modified it when necessary.

3. For an analysis of Lyotard's resistance in *Discours, figure* to the Lacanian emphasis on the letter, see Peter Dews, "The Letter and the Line: Discourse and Its Other in Lyotard," *Diacritics* 14.1 (1984): 40-49.

4. I am aware that *Discours, figure* was written long before *The Differend*, before Lyotard elaborated the notion of phrase. What I am suggesting is that while the "philosophy of phrases" allowed Lyotard to rephrase the figural, there is nevertheless a continuity between the figure and the inarticulate phrase.

5. Indeed, Freud applies the concept of *Nachträglichkeit*, beyond the psychoanalysis of the individual, to the history of culture: in *Moses and Monotheism* his analysis of the history of the Jewish people relies on an analogy drawn between Jewish monotheism and neurosis, based on the similar structure of latency and deferred effects: "it must strike us that, in spite of the fundamental difference

between the two cases—the problem of traumatic neurosis and that of Jewish monotheism—there is nevertheless one point of agreement: namely, in the characteristic that might be described as 'latency'" [*SE* 23: 68].

6. In his first published revision of the seduction theory, Freud wrote that his case material at the time he formulated the seduction theory The abandonment of the seduction theory does not so much discount the accounts based upon "real events" as it emphasizes that phantasies of seduction have effects similar to those of real events.

7. *Laplanche discusses the case of Emma in detail in* Vie et mort en psychanalyse *[64-76];* Problématiques IV: L'inconscient et le ça *[124-28];* Nouveaux fondements de la psychanalyse *[109-11].*

8. Furthermore, in Laplanche's analysis, the *enigmatic* signifier is enigmatic not only for the child but also for the adult himself: the enigmatic signifier conveys meanings that remain nonunderstood and nonunderstandable for the adult. In other words, the enigmatic signifier manifests the parental unconscious.

9. The texts in question are: "Réponse au commentaire de Jean Hyppolite sur la 'Verneinung' de Freud," *Écrits;* "D'une question préliminaire à tout traitement de la psychose," *Écrits;* Séminaire III: Les psychoses. In all these texts, Lacan discusses *Verwerfung* as an originary expulsion from the subject. Since *Verneinung,* as a discursive process, only happens as a result of *Verwerfung* (*Verneinung* is the "derivative of expulsion," Freud stated), *Verwerfung* is therefore more originary than repression, which takes place after verbalization. As Lacan says in *Les psychoses:* "In the unconscious, it is not that everything is repressed, that is, misrecognized by the subject after having been verbalized, but one also has to acknowledge that there is, behind the process of verbalization, an admission into symbolic meaning, which can be missing" [21].

10. For similar associations, see *The Inhuman* [42]; *Heidegger and "the jews"* [17]; and *Lectures d'enfance* [136]: "the temporal paradox . . . of the affect and of *phônè* is analyzed by Lacan as *the Thing.*"

11. In "Verneinung" Freud distinguishes two sorts of judgments: attributive judgments (asserting or denying that a thing has a particular property) and judgments of existence (affirming or disputing that a *Vorstellung* exists in reality).

12. Behind both kinds of judgment lies the opposition between introjection ("I should like to eat that") and expulsion ("I should like to spit it out"). Both types of judgment are therefore connected to the inside vs. outside duality upon which the ego constitutes itself—what is inside the ego and constitutes it and what is outside of it and alien to it.

13. *Séminaire XI: Les quatre concepts fondamentaux de la psychanalyse* and *Séminaire XX: Encore.*

14. *Séminaire XXII: R. S. I.* and *Séminaire XXIII: Le sinthome.*

15. See, for example, *Encore* [87] and the seminar of 17 May 1977, *Ornicar?* 17/18 (1979): 23.

16. Jean-Claude Milner, *Les noms indistincts,* especially the first two chapters, "R, S, I" and "Les mêmes et les autres."

Works Cited

Bennington, Geoffrey. *Lyotard: Writing the Event.* Manchester: Manchester UP, 1988.

Borch-Jacobsen, Mikkel. *Lacan le maître absolu.* Paris: Flammarion, 1990.

Ferenczi, Sandor. "Confusion of Tongues between Adults and the Child." *Final Contributions to the Problems and Methods of Psycho-Analysis.* London: Hogarth, 1955. 156-67.

Freud, Sigmund. *The Standard Edition of the Complete Psychological Works of Sigmund Freud.* Trans. James Strachey. London: Hogarth, 1957. [*SE*]

Lacan, Jacques. "The Agency of the Letter or Reason since Freud.". Trans. A. Sheridan. New York: Norton, 1977. Trans. of "L'instance de la lettre dans l'inconscient ou la raison depuis Freud." *Écrits.* Paris: Seuil, 1966.

———. "D'une question préliminaire à tout traitement de la psychose." *Écrits* 531-84.

———. "Réponse au commentaire de Jean Hyppolite sur la 'Verneinung' de Freud." *Écrits* 381-400.

———. *Séminaire III: Les psychoses.* Paris: Seuil, 1981.

———. *Séminaire VII: L'éthique de la psychanalyse.* Paris: Seuil, 1986.

———. *Séminaire XI: Les quatre concepts fondamentaux de la psychanalyse.* Paris: Seuil, 1973. [*Seminar XI: The Four Fundamental Concepts of Psychoanalysis.* Trans. Alan Sheridan. New York: Norton, 1978.]

———. *Séminaire XX: Encore.* Paris: Seuil, 1975.

———. *Séminaire XXII: R. S. I. Ornicar?* 2, 3, 4, 5 (1975).

———. *Séminaire XXIII: Le sinthome. Ornicar?* 6, 7, 8, 9, 10, 11 (1976-77).

Laplanche, Jean. *Nouveaux fondements de la psychanalyse.* Paris: PUF, 1987.

———. *Problématiques IV: L'inconscient et le ça.* Paris: PUF, 1981.

———. *Vie et mort en psychanalyse.* Paris: Flammarion, 1970.

Laplanche, Jean, and Jean-Bernard Pontalis. *The Language of Psycho-Analysis.* Trans. Donald Nicholson-Smith. New York: Norton, 1973.

Lyotard, Jean-François. *The Differend: Phrases in Dispute.* Trans. George van den Abbeele. Minneapolis: University of Minnesota P, 1988. Trans. of *Le différend.* Paris: Minuit, 1983.

———. *Discours, figure.* Paris: Klincksieck, 1971.

———. *Economie libidinale.* Paris: Minuit, 1974.

———. "The Inarticulate or the Differend Itself." Lecture. State University of New York at Buffalo, March 1992.

Milner, Jean-Claude. *Les noms indistincts.* Paris: Seuil, 1983.

Nancy, Jean-Luc, and Philippe Lacoue-Labarthe. *Le titre de la lettre.* Paris: Galilée, 1973.

Kevin Porter (essay date 1996)

SOURCE: "'Games of Perfect Information': Computers and the Metanarratives of Emancipation and Progress," in *Sub-Stance,* Vol. XXV, No. 79, November, 1996, pp. 24-45.

[*In the following essay, Porter contests the feasibility and the desirability of Lyotard's idea that a complete computerization of information would supply a democratically available resource, arguing—aside from the resulting information overload—that the language needed for such an enterprise would be the sort of "totalizing" grand narrative Lyotard condemns.*]

In *The Postmodern Condition,* Jean-François Lyotard argues that "knowledge has become the principle force of production" in the modern world. Because information is indispensable to productive power, it "will continue to be . . . a major—perhaps *the* major—stake in the worldwide competition for power." Consequently, "it is conceivable that the nation-states will one day fight for control of information . . . and afterwards for control of access to and exploitation of raw materials and cheap labor" (5, original emphasis). Of course, knowledge can empower or enslave individuals as well as nation-states. Those who are "in the know" hold an advantage over those who are not. To avoid an ever-widening gap between "developed and developing countries," or, as I suggest, developed and developing individuals, Lyotard calls for providing the public "free access to the memory and data banks" of the world's computers, in order to "aid groups discussing metaprescriptives by supplying them with the information they usually lack for making knowledgeable decisions. . . . Language games would then be games of perfect information at any given moment" (67). Everyone would possess the same information, and thus no individual or group could hold the dominant position created by superior knowledge.

Lyotard's position is shared by a number of theorists who view *access* as a critical issue. While these other scholars do not refer to "games of perfect information," the spirit of the proposal lives in their efforts to give everyone access to data. In place of "games of perfection information," these universalists use terms like "democracy" or "democratization."[1] Graham Murdock and Peter Golding assert that citizenship in a democracy now includes "the rights of universal access to communications and information facilities" (182); this will "ensure the exercise of citizenship regardless of income or area of residence" (184). Mass media magazines also repeat the refrain: "access to the information may determine the basic ability to function in a democratic culture" (Ratan 25). Preventing this egalitarian society is a conspiracy of "a few dominating computer and telecommunications industries . . . multinational companies and banks" (Qvortrup 144), "private economic interests" (Hills 18), "old monopolies of information and the political and economic power structures dependent upon them" (Gillespie and Robins 12), and those who desire the "privatization of information which is of *public relevance*" (Dahlgren 28, original emphasis).

Since businesses cannot be trusted to share their data, information must be controlled by a State and dispensed equally among its citizens.[2] Jill Hills posits that governments have been working to increase citizen "penetration" into data banks (194). But if Murdock and Golding are correct that government is a partner with corporate interests (192), then it is difficult to trust government to dispense information. The same State that the universalists hope will make public all data is, ironically, a major holder of "private" information—military, diplomatic, surveillance—that gives it great power.

Critics have raised practical objections to this proposal. Though advocating universal access, Douglas W. Johnson admits that the logistical demands "have not been adequately explored" (85). And Seyla Benhabib, critiquing Lyotard, questions "how far would the demand 'to give the public free access to memory and data banks' go? Can IBM or any other multinational corporation democratize its trade secrets and technical information?" (123).[3] Benhabib's objection is duly noted, but is not an obstacle for the universalists; such an objection would disappear if there were a radical shift in politics away from capitalism and property rights. This alteration in society is *theoretically* feasible. And, as Benhabib concedes to Lyotard, it is not necessary for universalists to provide the detailed "'blue-print' of the society of the future" as long as the general outline could *possibly* work (123).

But could it theoretically operate? Underlying the universalist position are several unquestioned assumptions: (1) that data banks actually contain all the data necessary to provide "perfection information," and that a bibliographic system could be devised to sift through the massive amounts of information generated by modern society;[4] (2) that access to data is equal to understanding the data;[5] (3) that individuals and groups can learn to comprehend the information, discounting any limitations on learning and understanding; and (4) that "games of perfect information" suggests each side views the data in the same way, the "perfect way," which disregards the unstable nature of language. (If each side views the information differently, in what way can they be said to have the same knowledge?)

THE "PERFECT" DATA BANK?

For "perfect information," we need access to a "perfect" data bank. Naturally, any use of the word "perfect" is suspect, and this suspicion is justified. As Patrick Wilson states, "the complete encyclopedia could not be written" (24). This results from the inescapable condition of published material: limited in scope but maddeningly cumbersome in quantity. These reasons may seem contradictory, but "a world view based only on published documents would leave out too much of what is known in the world" (7). For example, the scholarly books and articles rejected for publication alone could fill warehouses. And oral forms of knowledge are ignored if one relies solely on printed material. As Lyotard says, "scientific knowledge does not represent the totality of knowledge; it has always existed in addition to, and in competition and conflict with, another kind of knowledge, which I call narrative" (*Postmodern Condition* 7).[6]

The second condition, the amount of information, has led to "information overload." Academic and commercial publications describe how people are "swamped with information" (Byrne 25).[7] For example, the number of periodical titles has increased three-fold from 1965 to 1990, and the annual number of books has doubled during the same period (Olevnik 2-3). Orrin E. Klapp sadly notes that "every year thousands of pages of books, reports, and theses stack up in libraries without being read" (98). Experts estimate that "the production of knowledge is growing three times as fast as consumption" (Ekecrantz 82); looking ahead, we are warned that information will "double every 4 to 5 years" (Keyes 7).

But if the complete data bank could be created, bibliographers would bear the Herculean task of organizing the information so it could be retrieved. Finding the data requires access to properly designed and continuously updated bibliographic tools. Confronted with an impersonal computer terminal, data-bank users "must be able to calculate how the bibliographer would label documents" (P. Wilson 90). This is no easy task, as anyone who has struggled with card catalogues and the newer computerized systems will attest. Yet without the perfect bibliography, "most of the complete library [would be] . . . simply in the way" (P. Wilson 89).

Because of the complexity of data-banks and information retrieval, users often find themselves lost (Caragata 61) or "frustrated" (McDonald and Micikas 111). To meet the demands of data-retrieval, a whole new occupation, the "information professional," is being created. These "information professionals" take (or are projected to take) on a variety of functions and forms, some not even human: they will be teachers with "information expertise" who can guide students to proper materials (McDonald and Micikas 117); they may be hybrids of "part person and part computer program" that "gather and digest information, then disseminate it to their clients just as high-priced consultants do today" (Snider 17); or, ultimately, they may be data-retrieval programs that use artificial intelligence to find desired information and even "draw conclusions" for the client (Hawkins 38). Of course, if the data-bank user must rely on "information professionals" to find information for him or her, isn't the user caught in yet another power relationship? And computerized "information professionals" are only as good as their programming, hardly an encouraging thought.

The "perfect" data bank and bibliographic system are necessary planks for the universalists' goal of "perfect information." Unfortunately, the universalists have fallen victim to the illusion/delusion of futurist technology—that technology can provide the solution to any problem. Such claims are commonplace, from the prediction that "the computer era . . . promises to lead to a society of abundance and widespread leisure" (Cordell 14) to the limitless promise of progress: "in the next few years, we will see the appearance and spread of data base management systems of power and flexibility that are inconceivable now. They will hold everything you know. . . . This new generation of super-DBMS is not here yet, but stay tuned" (Byrne 29). But the future never arrives, and we are always asked to "stay tuned" for the latest and best development (until another comes along that will "revolutionize" society). As Andrew Gillespie and Kevin Robins wryly state, "despite the fact that this promise has never been fulfilled and that stark disparities still persist, the belief in the potential of technological deliverance paradoxically remains undimmed" (15). But why does it remain undimmed? Is it wishful thinking or mere blindness? According to Jerry L. Salvaggio, the myth of technology is perpetuated by the information industry itself, which is "investing billions of dollars into manufacturing an image as a guarantee that the information age is not a futuristic illusion" (154). If this is true, then the universalists are the dupes of the very controllers of information whom they think technology can replace.

The technical difficulties of designing a global (or even national) data bank are far beyond those encountered in current systems, yet the hardware and software for even these complex but limited networks are error prone. Tom Forester and Perry Morrison describe a bleak world where "failures in computer system development and use are not just commonplace. More often than not they are the rule" (69). System failures occur because computer scientists are unable to account for "the behavior of existing complex systems" (77). Yet the computer system required by the universalists is not even an "existing complex system." Another cause of system failure is the impossibility of finding and removing all program errors ("bugs"). For instance, the verification of a software program that monitors only 100 binary (on/off or yes/no) signals, using a "debugging" program "far beyond present capabilities," would require "some 4×10^{24} years to test the array of possible states that this piece of software might conceivably take. Unfortunately, such a figure is many times the life of the universe" (Forester and Morrison 78).

COMMUNICATION AND "EXPERT" KNOWLEDGE

Successful communication requires the understanding of the listener; such a statement is banal. But what is "understanding"? Maeve Cooke summarizes Jürgen Habermas's definition: the success of "communicative action . . . depends on the hearer's responding 'Yes' or 'No' to the validity claim raised with a given utterance" (29). Thus, a speech-act succeeds only if the participants "share the pre-understandings of the language game in question and can be said to agree in a common form of life" (115). The hearer who cannot form "Yes" or "No" answers and the accompanying reasons concedes a "lack of understanding" (114).

What applies to speech applies to writing: the data-bank user who cannot respond "Yes" or "No" does not understand the text. Yet this problem will affect the universalists' data-bank users whenever they encounter unfamiliar expert or specialized knowledge.[8] The proliferation of micro-specialities, terminology, and jargon will force information-seekers into uneasy, confusing situations.[9] Even skilled and knowledgeable data-bank users will find themselves weighed under "a heavy burden of decoding" these "exogenous" documents (Klapp 88). Such technical language creates the "expert representation" of scholars and the "naive representation" of everyone else, changing reading and writing into "arcane practices restricted to just a few" (Geisler xi-xii).

Opening the data banks will not alone achieve the universalists' goal of "games of perfect information," because availability of information is not a guarantee of understanding it. As Patrick Wilson explains, "in all cases, acquiring knowledge involves more than coming to have in one's possession a representation of knowledge; it involves the development of an ability" (9). Such ability is not inborn, but learned. Since the universalists cannot assume that all knowledge is readily comprehensible to a data-bank user, perhaps they believe any information can be learned eventually. But here, the universalists would run into additional problems.

LIMITATIONS OF LEARNING AND UNDERSTANDING

There are three basic observations about learning: it develops through stages; time from ignorance to mastery depends upon the complexity of the information; this time also depends upon the learner's aptitude. James F. Brulé and Alexander Blount discuss a four-stage model of learning. "Learning 0" is an organism's simple reflex actions. "Learning I" is "a change of responses within the same set of alternatives," such as learning the rules and movement patterns of chess pieces (32). After mastering Learning I, the student can advance to "Learning II," which means he or she "sees general patterns in the alignment of the pieces, patterns that are generalizations" of gaming experiences (33). The final stage is "Learning III," which Brulé and Blount discuss only abstractly; it is an unteachable leap in perception and application of information—a flash of intuition or insight.

Brulé and Blount's learning stages may be arbitrary, but learning is undeniably a process. Lyotard agrees; he speaks of learning as a process where "the alterity of the master, the strangeness of another logic is, in silence, imposed. He takes me hostage in order to make me hear and say what I do not know" (**"Other's,"** 142). Whether or not learning is as violent as Lyotard suggests, he believes it is a temporal process.

The process is difficult and requires hard work. Data-bank users will be confronted with expert knowledge beyond their comprehension, knowledge that "can only be acquired through specialized training and practice" (Geisler 53). During this training and practice, the learner mentally develops by "switch[ing] to more abstract representations" (Geisler 61). But since expert knowledge is abstract knowledge, it presents a problem for learning: "things written in one's native language but employing an unfamiliar conceptual vocabulary are more work to read than those employing a familiar one" (P. Wilson 54). So where does this leave the universalists' data-bank user confronted by expert knowledge? Reading the text won't suffice; to understand the information, the user must *learn* the information.

This is easier said than done, because what an individual may learn has limitations. First, prior knowledge often constrains learning: "past history limits future history, and those who already know the most are best able to find out more" (P. Wilson 55).[10] Citing research on student learning, Cheryl Geisler notes "the only information that these students appeared to acquire from texts was that which matched or did not contradict their prior knowledge" (43). Thus, an ardent capitalist studying economics would likely not be able to master the subtleties of Marx's writings, just as an average Marxist would not absorb Adam Smith. It is important to note that prior knowledge operates as a trend; not all students will be so limited—but many will be.

A second (and distasteful) limitation is the aptitude constraint of an individual. Some expert knowledge will remain beyond the data-bank user's comprehension: "not everyone will get it [expert knowledge], even among those who try" (Geisler 53). Such thoughts are unpleasant, but, like Patrick Wilson, we must acknowledge that while no sharp line divides the sources difficult to master from those "impossible to use because we cannot understand them no matter how hard we work," some subjects will remain "permanently unintelligible" (55).

While universalists may object to this line of reasoning, with few exceptions the case to the contrary has not been presented, but merely assumed, because such limitations are "unfair."[11] However, Pierre Bourdieu and Jean-Claude Passeron offer one counter-argument; improved pedagogy could overcome these limitations "even without changing vocabulary or syntax—were there a concern at every moment with difinition and with verifying the real comprehension needs of a real public" (22). Here, the authors are discussing classroom discourse between professor and student. But could this idea translate into the texts of a data bank? Can texts continuously layer definitions, explaining one concept after another until the user finally has the prerequisite knowledge? How recursive would texts have to be, especially considering the difficulty of defining abstract words? (Gilson 33). Wouldn't this concept, if applied, prohibit texts written for other experts with assumed knowledge of a subject?

The futurists hold out the technological dream that computerized texts will have "stylistic levels" that will be "reader-selectable rather than permanently dumbed down" (Lanham 10). Supposedly, a student could begin with the "novice level" of St. Augustine's *Confessions* and eventually reach the actual text itself. But isn't something lost in the process of "dumbing down," as Lanham says? Wouldn't the novice still be in an inferior position to the expert? And, given the problems with computer hardware and software, how reliable will these "stylistic levels" be?

Even if any data is theoretically comprehensible, certainly the data-bank user cannot master all forms of knowledge. As Jesse H. Shera notes, "the increasing magnitude and specialization of recorded information has ended, probably forever, the day of the polyhistor. No longer is it possible for a single mind to grasp the sum of human knowledge as did Aristotle, Leonardo, and Goethe of their respective ages" (5). But even these intellects did not "grasp the sum" of information, because human knowledge cannot be accounted for absolutely. Such totalization is unthinkable.

The physical process of reading also is an inescapable constraint on learning; time is an "absolute limit" (Ekecrantz 82). Gilson asserts that

> the modern reader has too many books to read; he is too hurried. . . . There are those who are "stupefied by reading." Not without danger does one put oneself in a state of voluntary passivity, sought after as a resignation of the intellect, leaving it to another to think for one. (134)[12]

Many reading-shocked graduate students have collapsed under the pressures of a relentless semester. No doubt faculty, too, under deadlines for publishing and conferences, feel the same displeasure and staleness of reading, at times. Lyotard indicts capitalism, arguing that "in the next century there will be no books. It takes too long to read, when success comes from gaining time" (*Differend* xv). Rather, it simply takes too long to learn.

Another absolute limit is the capacity of the human brain. Evidence suggests that "we may be actually pushing the physical limits of our ability to process information" (Keyes 7). Neuropsychologists have observed differences in the "functions and channel capacities" of the left and right hemispheres of the brain (Klapp 100). When its information-handling ability is overloaded, the brain cannot evaluate and store data; it may be processed incorrectly or omitted entirely (Klapp 101). Again, the futurists promise a technological fix; William O. Baker, who adjures us to "celebrate joyfully the union of science and engineering with humanism in thought and action," and promises that "through machine processing of words, letters, and their displays, we can select and develop stimuli for optimal recognition and memory" (64-65). Baker is grimly behavioristic, and one wonders how much "stimuli" will be necessary to keep pace with the information explosion.

These temporal and neurological constraints are exacerbated by the corrosive effects of outdated or simply erroneous information; as Patrick Wilson argues, "Our heads are full of nonsense, mistakes, wild conjectures, and outmoded and superseded opinions; so are the documents" (4). How is a data-bank user to determine what information is outdated, except by extensive research that includes foreign sources? If experts have difficulty maintaining their command of the field—monitoring shifts in theoretical perspectives, advances—how much more so the data-bank user, whose career is not related to that field? And as for erroneous knowledge, consider how much of what we read contains a composite of other sources we have not read. We trust in the veracity and ability of the author (the author of this article included) in summarizing other books and articles. To verify each source, a data-bank user would need Olympian determination and abundant free time. But the reader who accepts these sources at face value subordinates his or her own interpretation to the author's.

The universalists' solution to the problematic mass and specialization of knowledge is an interdisciplinary education, as if the barriers to "games of perfect information" were only the artificial boundaries of academia. For instance, Lyotard insists that education should train students to "connect fields jealously guarded from one another by the traditional organization of knowledge" because "an interdisciplinary approach is specific to the age of delegitimation" (*Postmodern Condition* 52). And Lyotard practices his idea of interdisciplinarity; in *The Postmodern Condition,* for instance, he uses "such diverse sources as Gödel's metamathematical research, quantum mechanics, microphysics, and catastrophe theories" (Benhabib 117).

But the question remains: what use are these references for a data-bank user unaware of the intricacies of these disciplines? When Lyotard writes, "the metamathematical research that lead to Gödel's theorem is a veritable paradigm of how this change in nature takes place," how can the text be appreciated if the data-bank user does not have the requisite knowledge? (*Postmodern Condition* 55). Lyotard assumes the data-bank user knows (1) the term "metamathematical," (2) a person named "Gödel," (3)

Gödel's theorem, and (4) the term "paradigm." Lyotard's footnote on Gödel's theorem cites the source but does not even provide a sketch of its meaning—so unless one has a handy copy of "Über formal unentscheidbare Sätze der Principia Mathematica und verwandter Systeme," the reference will remain obscure (95, 99). Lyotard's tour de force amply demonstrates the mental effort required to succeed with an interdisciplinary study.

Interdisciplinarity has its dangers, such as "distortion and misunderstanding of borrowed material," the "use of data, methods, concepts, and theories out of context," and the "use of borrowings out of favor in their original context" (Klein 88). Though he cites examples only from literary criticism, Richard Levin argues that many supposed interdisciplinarians do not try to "master" the other fields or "even try to acquire an overall sense of the other discipline, of the sort that could be derived from a few good introductory courses" (14-15). Of course, non-interdisciplinary work has the same difficulties—misread sources, distorted quotations, outmoded but recycled ideas—yet the intellectual demands of interdisciplinary work exacerbate the errors.

In a reflection on the specialization of knowledge and its attendant creation of isolated language games, Lyotard admits that "we may form a pessimistic impression of this splintering: nobody speaks all of those languages, they have no universal metalanguage . . . the diminished tasks of research have become compartmentalized and no one can master them all" (*Postmodern Condition* 41). Lyotard does not view this situation pessimistically, but as a positive sign of the erosion of the metanarrative, the hope of a totalized system. The multiplicity of language games does not make society "barbarous," but frees it from language games of "performativity" (*Postmodern Condition* 41). What is puzzling here is Lyotard's apparently contradictory positions: that we can educate people to cross disciplinary borders and that the multiplicity of language games cannot be mastered by a single individual. Which should we believe?

TERMINISTIC SCREENS

We have touched on the constraints on learning caused by prior knowledge. I would like to explore this further, because prior knowledge also contains a linguistic element identified by Kenneth Burke: the terministic screen. Burke contends that "even if any given terminology is a reflection of reality, by its very nature as a terminology it must be a selection of reality; and to this extent it must function as a deflection of reality" (45). Terms "affect the nature of our observations," which are *but implications of the particular terminology in terms of which the observations are made*" (46, original emphasis). Thus, what we see is generally what we expect to see: "much that we take as observations of 'reality' may be the spinning out of possibilities implicit in our particular choice of terms" (46). Our terministic screens affect our perception, but we cannot do without them "since we can't say anything without the use of terms" (50).

Terministic screens affect discourses in academia, where various disciplines and specialties (with their own terministic screens) seem alien to each other and often clash. Critics like Newton Garver comment on the hostility between British and American philosophers and those on the European continent (ix). Much has been made of Jacques Derrida and John Searle's antagonism over speech-act theory: "Searle and Derrida seemed like two ships in the night, passing in opposite directions and not even sharing a common language in which to exchange signals" (Dasenbrock 7). And Lyotard begins the second section of *Libidinal Economy* with an admonition emphasizing terministic screens: "Let's take up this business of signs once more, you have not understood, you have remained rationalists, semioticians, Westerners, let's emphasize it again" (43).

Terministic screens may be cultural as well as academic, and Lyotard is aware of this fact, at least indirectly. The Cashinahua, whom Lyotard frequently mentions, best exemplify how cultural screens work. The Cashinahua construct their society through narratives (which is why Lyotard repeatedly cites them). Their narratives define the society. These stories are not without rules; they have strict conditions set upon them. As Lyotard explains, "To *hear* a Cashinahua narrative, one has to be an adult male or a girl prior to puberty. To *recount* a narrative, one has to be a man and have a Cashinahua name. Finally, every Cashinahua without exception can *form the object* of one of these narratives" (**"Memorandum"** 44, original italics). The narrative act is a ritual that is "handed down in initiation ceremonies, in absolutely fixed form" (*Postmodern Condition* 21).

Lyotard does not mention what might occur if someone violated these rules, but a curious passage suggests such an event might be inconceivable within the Cashinahua system: "Whatever stands outside this tradition—any event, natural or human, for which there is no name—is *not*, for it is not authorized (not 'true')" (**"Memorandum"** 46). In short, a word for the false telling of a narrative wouldn't exist, because it wouldn't be part of the Cashinahua society. But whether a false narrative is possible, the larger concept remains that whatever does not fit into the Cashinahua narratives does not exist *because it is outside the culture's terministic screens*. Just as the Cashinahua deny foreign knowledge, so too might single-culture users reject a significant part of a multicultural data bank. The universalists promise, once more, a technological solution, including "all kinds of reading assistance—spoken accompaniments, language glossing embedded hypertextually, dynamically interactive bilingual texts" (Lanham 10).

LANGUAGE: OTHER IMPOSITIONS AND LIMITATIONS

The way we define terms has several problematic implications in language: the multiple contexts of words, the rhetoric of a work, and the problems of translation (to name a few). These categories all impose limitations on knowledge acquisition. First, the data-bank user must understand the context of the words in the document. This idea is not astonishing: "everyone knows that the meaning of a word depends on its context" (Gilson 26). Expanding on this, Stanley Fish affirms that "it is impossible even to think of a sentence independently of a context, and when we are asked to consider a sentence for which no context has been specified, we will automatically hear it in the context in which it has been most often encountered" (310). Such "automatic contextualization" obviously is not infallible, but we cannot blame the words themselves for the data-bank user's confusion; words may be misinterpreted (using an inappropriate "but otherwise acceptable definition of a word") (Gilson 26).

Data-bank users will face the problem of misinterpretations. And the more unfamiliar the information, the less likely that they would have even the false confidence of an "automatic contextualization"; the information would have no connotations for them. This definition-defying slipperiness of language, well-documented by Derrida and Lyotard, among others, prohibits the acquisition of "perfect information."

Rhetoric, or style, also forms terministic screens that powerfully affect contextualization. The author's method of presentation and use of language may complicate texts and exclude potential data-bank users. Patrick Wilson argues that "stylistic features influence readability" and that the "complex syntax and hard words" form a barrier that may cause readers to avoid otherwise valuable sources of information (54). Readers of Derrida, whose name seems widely known but whose texts are, I suspect, less widely read, are confused by his style because it "is full of metaphors, of plays upon words that often do not survive translation, of florid language that sometimes leaves one mystified as to Derrida's intent and of verbal contradictions or absurdities" (Garver xxvi). Garver concedes that "we cannot complain because Derrida is often obscure, for the problems are exceedingly difficult, and a demand for pedestrian prose would be misplaced. But clarity is more than just pedestrian" (xxvi).

If establishing a context is as difficult as I suggest, imagine doing so for a foreign language. Beyond grasping the word's context, the translator also must attempt to breach cultural terministic screens. This is the daunting challenge of translation, which cannot be ignored, because "games of perfect information" require a global data bank. Lyotard's position on translation is, frankly, muddled. He insists that texts may be shifted between cultures "because languages are, hypothetically, translatable" (*Reader* ix). Lyotard believes that cultural differences (i.e. terministic screens) cause confusion and struggle "since the names and narratives of one community are exclusive of the other" (*Differend* 157).[13] While allowing that "linguistic difference" may aggravate group conflicts, Lyotard maintains that "every language is translatable" (*Differend* 157). He fails to see that terministic (or cultural) screens are an intrinsic part of language. He also shrugs off the objections to his (first) position on translation: "I do not wish to

take up here the difficulties and enigmas of translation. The theoretical possibility of translation is quite sufficient. . . ." ("**Other's**" 139). But what does Lyotard mean by "theoretical"? Does he mean that he has established or is aware of a "theory of translation" that proves why languages are translatable? Or does his claim rest on the old cliché that "anything is theoretically possible"?

Besides making an unconvincing case for universal translation, Lyotard also suggests, at times, that the opposite is true. On the very same page on which he contends that "languages are, hypothetically, translatable," he later muses, "it is also possible that two different languages may not offer the same range of styles of accommodation, or at least that the range of styles they offer may not overlap. Hard to tell" (*Reader* ix). Or, more precisely, languages may have "blind spots" where the meanings of one cannot be directly transcribed into another.

Other scholars have more sanguine hopes for overcoming translation difficulties. Roman Jakobson believes that "languages differ essentially in what they *must* convey, and not in what they *may* convey" (149). He also asserts that "no lack of grammatical device in the language translated into makes impossible a literal translation of the entire conceptual information contained in the original" (147). Mutability of grammatical forms, such as gender or mood, may exist, but can we equate "literal translation" with "conceptual information"? A more recent work by Roger T. Bell attempts to map out a theory of translation (267), but even his enthusiasm is tempered by the realization that "the ideal of total equivalence [between languages] is a chimera" (6). And he overturns Jakobson's argument: "[languages] are different in form, having distinct codes and rules regulating the construction of grammatical stretches of languages and these forms have different meanings" (6).

Set against Lyotard's wavering position and these optimistic scholars are the theoretical perspectives and the very real problems of translators who, unlike Lyotard or Jakobson, cannot achieve perfect translation.[14] Gilson remarks that while "the desire for precision [in translation] could not affirm itself with greater force," its attainment is "uncertain"; we may "reason" what a word means to a native-speaker, but this proves "nothing" (106). Lawrence Venuti, discussing his efforts at translating the poetry of Milo De Angelis, speaks of "irreducible differences between the source and target languages" (11). And the less conventional a work is (particularly in literature), the more difficult is the translation.[15] How much information would be excluded from the users of the universalists' data bank for lack of a translation? Or, if the "best" translation is only a poor approximation, is it possible to have "games of perfect information" between two groups where one can read a seminal work in its native tongue and the other group cannot?

UNIVERSAL LANGUAGES AND ARTIFICIAL LANGUAGES

The universalists desire "games of perfect information," but what do they offer to overcome learning limitations, terministic screens, multiple contexts, stylistic difficulties, and translation problems? To hold the universalists' position, we must assume (1) all information can be learned/taught, (2) terministic screens can be overcome, (3) contexts can be settled, and (4) languages are universally translatable. But underlying these is a critical assumption: the existence of a universal language. This does not mean that we all speak English or French or Russian; but if "every language is translatable" as Lyotard or Jakobson suggest, then languages would be equivalents: English equaling French equaling Russian.

Since this isn't true, the universalists' plan would require a "real," universally applicable artificial language, a language all humans would understand equally, a language of "perfect information." Universal languages have failed several times: William the Conqueror, Catholicism, and Marxism did not succeed (K. Wilson, 78-79). Modern "attempts to develop artificial natural languages as means to cultivate international and community understanding," such as Esperanto, have been famous but also ineffectual.[16] Kenneth Wilson's curious oxymoron, "artificial natural languages," suggests the hopelessness of the task: how can a "natural" language be synthesized?

Etienne Gilson discusses the old dream of an artificial language and its dilemma. He argues that artificial languages are "dead" languages because "it is natural . . . that words should be born, mature, flourish, mutually fecundate each other, grow old and die as all living things do. This is why every artificial language, be its inspiration mathematical or logical, is a language born dead" (42). Gilson later quotes the linguist J. Vendryès, who argues that artificial languages would "immediately deteriorate" if they became "living" languages because "there would be set up between the forms differences of value; certain forms would dominate others, the law of analogy would come into play, and disorder would succeed to the initial good order. . . . Ideal, logical language is only a dream" (42).

Vendryès's scholarly position is echoed in literature by Václav Havel's "dramatic-satirical invention of the perfectly cybernetic yet depersonalized language called 'ptydepe'" (Matustík 248), which is found in Havel's play, *The Memorandum*. Ptydepe is a synthetic language supposedly "built on a strictly scientific basis" (Havel 65). The creators justify Ptydepe by claiming that natural language is too imprecise, too unstable for it to be efficient; therefore, Ptydepe's goal is "to guarantee to every statement, by purposefully limiting all similarities between individual words, a degree of precision, reliability and lack of equivocation quite unattainable in any natural language" (66). But Ptydepe requires rules too complicated and a vocabulary too vast for its promising pupils and even its creators to master.

Because Ptydepe attempts to contain all possible expression, all shades of meaning, it is a totalizing system (as any universal language would be). Every sentiment falls within its domain; nothing exists outside of it. The language is whole. However, the effort fails, as we know it must from the beginning. Many of the scenes, particularly Mark Lear's Ptydepe lecture to an empty classroom, wittily illustrate how the language collapses under its onerous weight.

Havel also critiques the political nature of language. In the play, anyone who does not have a command of Ptydepe is at the mercy of those who do. Although referring to Havel's *Temptation*, Marketa Goetz-Stankiewicz could easily be discussing Ptydepe when she states that "while seeming to inform, it mystifies; while apparently communicating, it sets up a barrier totally preventing communication" (97). And a person's power or freedom depends upon which side of the barrier he or she is located. For example, the Managing Director, Josef Gross, is vulnerable to blackmail because he cannot translate the memorandum proving his innocence.

Esperanto and Ptydepe are dead languages; no one speaks them. But the languages of academic discourse have been labeled "artificial languages, *par excellence*" by Bourdieu and Passeron (8). Academic discourse is a "dead language" because it is "no one's mother tongue" (8). And like the students of Ptydepe who cannot handle its complexity, "many university students are unable to cope with the technical and scholastic demands made on their use of language as students" (4). As a result, "they cannot define the terms which they hear in lectures or which they themselves use" and "are remarkably tolerant of words lifted from the language of ideas but applied inappropriately or irrelevantly" (4). Bourdieu and Passeron argue that academic discourse is intentionally used for the "eminent function of keeping the pupil at a distance" (3). Or, as Marjorie Reeves echoes, academic discourse is improperly used as "a means of staking out a claim to a particular territory" (123). To close the gap between teacher and learner (or data bank and data-bank user), Bourdieu and Passeron advocate "pedagogical" communication, which occurs only when "every effort is made to eliminate the faulty 'signals' inherent in an incomplete knowledge of code and to transmit the code in the most efficient way" (5).[17]

However admirable the goal, confusion cannot be "eliminated" by fiat. Knowledge acquisition and language itself have limitations that prohibit it. Still, the universalists call for "games of perfect information." How can these games exist if John cannot have the quality of information Sally has? Sally would always be in the superior position. If John *cannot* be brought up to Sally's level, then Sally must be reduced to John's level, through censorship. Patrick Wilson agrees: "If we required of public knowledge that it be made public in a form intelligible to everyone, we would limit it to what is available to the most limited intelligence" (9). Knowledge and language would be distorted along Orwellian lines, shrinking instead of expanding, until, finally, each person would be a polyhistor—made realizable by the infantile simplicity of the information.

One can imagine the terror of such a system. A world where all knowledge must be universally comprehensible would be in ruins: diseases that could not be cured, scientific discoveries that could not be made, artistic works that could not be created, et cetera. People would not or could not think what could not also be thought by everyone else. This Orwellian world would violate one of Lyotard's cardinal positions: "The law says: Thou shalt not kill. Which means: you shall not refuse to others the role of interlocutor" (**"Other's"** 147). Yet the implications of "games of perfect information" would work forcibly in the opposite direction, by limiting the interlocutory range of people who would normally be able to surpass the "least common denominator" language that the universalists' proposal would necessitate.

Metanarratives of Emancipation and Progress?

Lyotard defines the term "postmodern" as "incredulity toward metanarratives" (**Postmodern Condition** xxiv), those "great codes which in their abstraction necessarily deny the specificity of the local and traduce it in the interests of a global homogeneity, a universal history" (Docherty 11). Lyotard and others have usefully critiqued the "sutured understanding of society by which they refer to theories that totalize from one level, reduce multiplicity into unity, or organize discourse toward an end or telos which is usually utopian" (Poster, "Postmodernity" 573); however, the universalist position is a metanarrative of emancipation and progress: emancipation, because perfect data banks will give all people "perfect information," freeing them from the metaprescriptivists; progress, because these data banks can be created by technology, and all people can learn from them.

It is noteworthy that the term "enlightenment," which Lyotard critiques, has been applied to the universalists' dream of "perfect information." For example, Fred Fejes and James Schwoch observe that the "concept of the information age as social salvation" has appeared in "each and every age, from the Egyptians, Greeks, through the age of enlightenment, age of reason, and the industrial age" (159). And Bill Readings states the idea "that knowledge would make mankind free" is "part of the long narrative of education that the Enlightenment, above all in France, inculcated" (200). Finally, while valuing many of Lyotard's ideas, Barry Kanpol warns that "we must take pains to avoid this democratic possibility's becoming another master narrative, sovereign truth, or essentialist reconstruction" (152). Lyotard and the other universalists offer utopian visions worthy of high modernism.

And utopian—unattainable—visions they will remain. The universalists are struggling, however nobly, against the inescapable conditions of language (or any other form of knowledge) and learning. The universalists' "games of perfect information" become ironically named because the gain of complete, equal knowledge on both sides necessitates a destruction, a negation of knowledge. Perfect parity of information can be achieved only by "dumbing down," not by advancing, learning. If applied, the universalists' plan would make all language-game players equal—in their ignorance.

Notes

1. For convenience, I use the term "universalists" to categorize those scholars who propose universal access.

2. Attempts have been made in the US to blunt public perception that information access is restricted or that private companies have sinister designs to control data. Lynn Forester, the president of an unnamed company that owns wireless telecommunications companies, argues that "we must not create an information underclass" (17). And for Richard A. Lanham, the financial interests of early computer pioneers dissolve into a myth of noble selflessness: "The people who developed the personal computer considered it a device of radical democratization from its inception" (108). While I do not doubt the motives of individual scientists and technicians, can we speak of IBM or Apple as philanthropic organizations?

3. For other concerns about the rights of privacy, see Haynes B. Johnson (108) and Douglas W. Johnson (87). And as the July 18, 1994 *Newsweek* reports, corporations and the United States government want to strengthen copyright laws for computerized data (Kantrowitz, Cohen, and Liu 54).

4. Were this data bank possible (it isn't), it would be the kind of totalizing system Lyotard and other postmodernists oppose.

5. That is, what causes an imbalance in knowledge is merely physical access to the documents: one side has them and the other does not. If this is not the universalists' assumption, then how can we connect data access to "games of perfect information"? Of what use is information the individual or group cannot understand?

6. Mark Poster argues against the idea that the information society will "herald an era of *perfect* communications" because its advocates assume that "the entire printed corpus" can be "digitally encoded and stored" and that "nothing significant is lost in the process of digital encoding, storage, retrieval, transmission, and reproduction" (*Modes* 70, my emphasis). But Poster also agrees with Lyotard's demand to open the data banks (ibid. 98). Since the goal of "games of perfect information" seems contradictory to his observation on "perfect communication," Poster tries to solve the conflict by labeling Lyotard's plan "an oppositional strategy" (ibid. 98). Simply put, we should follow Lyotard's plan not because it will work but because it opposes the status quo.

7. I add to my "short" list of those who refer to information overload Eugene F. Bedell (7), Haynes B. Johnson (108), and Paul Saffo (213).

8. I will use "data-bank user" where "reader" might seem warranted for the sake of clarity (by not shifting between terms) and because printed material is, in a real sense, a data-bank.

9. Lyotard has been criticized for his own complex writing: Benhabib accuses him of engaging in "obscure discussion" (117), and Honi Fern Haber labels him an "obscurantist" (9).

10. See also Robert A. White, 155.

11. Lyotard would have problems making such a case. For example, he concedes in *The Differend* that "despite every effort to make his thought communicable, the A. knows that he has failed, that this is too voluminous, too long, and too difficult" (xv).

12. Contrast Gilson's quote to the "information professionals" who will evaluate data (i.e. do the thinking) for the client.

13. The "exclusive" nature of cultural narratives is a concept quite applicable to the Cashinahua's rejection of anything outside of their narratives.

14. Cooke describes the frustration of translating the "notoriously difficult word 'Verständigung'" (9). And Iain Hamilton Grant, the translator of Lyotard's *Libidinal Economy,* states that the text's style forced him to choose "stylistically insensitive but comprehensible English," or a "vain" effort to "convey the rhythms and distortions of the original" (viii).

15. Julian Pefanis contends that Georges Bataille has suffered from relative obscurity because translating his works would be "a formidable task" (41). And Michael Riffaterre asserts that translating literary texts is problematic because "in most cases it is not possible to find a comparable intertext in the target language" (212)

16. Wilson offers an unapologetically Christian theological language to provide a common discourse (81-85).

17. Yet Bourdieu and Passeron use, without explanation, such words as "milieu," "pedagogical," "Socratic," and "mnemonic" (9, 10, 13, 15). Is their own writing accessible to the underprivileged students they champion?

Works Cited

Baker, William O. "Modern Techniques Linking Knowledge to Action." *Libraries and Information Science in the Electronic Age.* Ed. Hendrik Edelman. Philadelphia: ISI Press, 1986. 57-65.

Barnett, Ronald, ed. *Academic Community: Discourse or Discord?* Higher Education Policy Series 20. London: Jessica Kingsley Publishers, 1994.

Bedell, Eugene F. *The Computer Solution: Strategies for Success in the Information Age.* Homewood: Dow-Jones-Irwin, 1985.

Bell, Roger T. *Translation and Translating: Theory and Practice.* London: Longman, 1991.

Benhabib, Seyla. "Epistemologies of Postmodernism: A Rejoinder to Jean-François Lyotard." *New German Critique* 33 (1984): 103-126.

Bourdieu, Pierre, and Jean-Claude Passeron. "Introduction: Language and Relationship to Language in the Teaching Situation." *Academic Discourse: Linguistic Misunderstanding and Professorial Power.* By Pierre Bourdieu, et al. Trans. Richard Teese. Stanford: Stanford University Press, 1994.

Brulé, James F., and Alexander Blount. *Knowledge Acquisition.* New York: McGraw-Hill, 1989.

Burke, Kenneth. *Language as Symbolic Action: Essays on Life, Literature, and Method.* Berkeley: University of California Press, 1966.

Byrne, Richard B. "The Well-Managed Data Base." *Personal Computing* October 1985: 25-29.

Caragata, Wayne. "Information Overload." *Maclean's* 19 September 1994: 60-61.

Cooke, Maeve. *Language and Reason: A Study of Habermas's Pragmatics.* Cambridge: MIT Press, 1994.

Cordell, Arthur J. "Work in the Information Age." *The Futurist* December 1985: 12-14.

Dahlgren, Peter. "Ideology and Information in the Public Sphere." Slack and Fejes 24-46.

Dasenbrock, Reed Way. "Redrawing the Lines: An Introduction." *Redrawing the Lines: Analytic Philosophy, Deconstruction, and Literary Theory.* Ed. Reed Way Dasenbrock. Minneapolis: University of Minnesota Press, 1989. 3-26.

Docherty, Thomas. "Postmodernism: An Introduction." *Postmodernism: A Reader.* Ed. Thomas Docherty. New York: Columbia University Press, 1993. 1-31.

Ekecrantz, Jan. "The Sociological Order of the New Information Society." Slack and Fejes 78-94.

Fejes, Fred, and James Schwoch. "A Competing Ideology for the Information Age: A Two-Sector Model for the New Information Society." Slack and Fejes 158-169.

Fish, Stanley. *Is There a Text in This Class? The Authority of Interpretive Communities.* Cambridge: Harvard University Press, 1980.

Forester, Lynn. "Protect the Information Underclass." Editorial. *New York Times* 27 December 1993, late ed., sec. A: 17.

Forester, Tom, and Perry Morrison. *Computer Ethics: Cautionary Tales and Ethical Dilemmas in Computing.* Cambridge: MIT Press, 1990.

Garver, Newton. Preface. *Speech and Phenomena and Other Essays on Husserl's Theory of Signs.* By Jacques Derrida. Trans. David B. Allison. Northwestern University Studies in Phenomenology and Existential Philosophy. Evanston: Northwestern University Press, 1973.

Geisler, Cheryl. *Academic Literacy and the Nature of Expertise: Reading, Writing, and Knowing in Academic Philosophy.* Hillsdale: Lawrence Erlbaum Associates, 1994.

Gillespie, Andrew, and Kevin Robins. "Geographical Inequalities: The Spatial Bias of the New Communications Technologies." *Journal of Communication* 39.3 (Summer 1989): 7-18.

Gilson, Etienne. *Linguistics and Philosophy: An Essay on the Philosophical Constants of Language.* Trans. John Lyon. Notre Dame: University of Notre Dame Press, 1988.

Goetz-Stankiewicz, Marketa. "Variations of Temptation—Václav Havel's Politics of Language." *Modern Drama* 33 (1990): 93-105.

Haber, Honi Fern. *Beyond Postmodern Politics: Lyotard, Rorty, Foucault.* New York: Routledge, 1994.

Havel, Václav. *The Memorandum.* Trans. Vera Blackwell. *The Garden Party and Other Plays.* New York: Grove Press, 1993. 53-130.

Hawkins, William J. "Information Overload." *Popular Science* January 1990: 38.

Hills, Jill, with Stylianos Papathanassopoulos. *The Democracy Gap: The Politics of Information and Communication Technologies in the United States and Europe.* Contributions to the Study of Mass Media and Communications 30. New York: Greenwood Press, 1991.

Jakobson, Roman. "On Linguistic Aspects of Translation." *On Translation.* Ed. Reuben Brower. Cambridge: Harvard University Press, 1959. Rpt. in Schulte and Biguenet 144-151.

Johnson, Douglas W. *Computer Ethics: A Guide for the New Age.* Elgin: Brethren Press, 1984.

Johnson, Haynes B. "Social and Human Factors in the Information Age." *Critical Issues in the Information Age.* Ed. Robert Lee Chartrand. Metuchen: Scarecrow Press, 1991. 105-109.

Kanpol, Barry. "Is Education at the End of a Sovereign Story or at the Beginning of Another? Cultural-Political Possibilities and Lyotard." Peters 147-165.

Kantrowitz, Barbara, Andrew Cohen, and Melinda Liu. "My Info is Not Your Info." *Newsweek* 18 July, 1994: 54.

Keyes, Jessica. *Solving the Productivity Paradox: TQM for Computer Professionals.* New York: McGraw-Hill, 1995.

Klapp, Orrin E. *Overload and Boredom: Essays on the Quality of Life in the Information Society.* Contributions in Sociology 57. New York: Greenwood Press, 1986.

Klein, Julie Thompson. *Interdisciplinarity: History, Theory, and Practice.* Detroit: Wayne State University Press, 1990.

Lanham, Richard A. *The Electronic Word: Democracy, Technology, and the Arts.* Chicago: University of Chicago Press, 1993.

Levin, Richard. "The New Interdisciplinarity in Literary Criticism." *After Poststructuralism: Interdisciplinarity and Literary Theory.* Eds. Nancy Easterlin and Barbara Riebling. Evanston: Northwestern University Press, 1993. 13-43.

Lyotard, Jean-François. *The Differend: Phrases in Dispute.* Trans. Georges Van Den Abbeele. Theory and History of Literature 46. Minneapolis: University of Minnesota Press, 1988.

———. *Libidinal Economy.* Trans. Iain Hamilton Grant. Bloomington: Indiana University Press, 1993.

———. *The Lyotard Reader.* Ed. Andrew Benjamin. Oxford: Basil Blackwell, 1989.

———. "Memorandum on Legitimation." *The Postmodern Explained: Correspondence, 1982-1985.* Trans. Don Barry. Minneapolis: University of Minnesota Press, 1993. 39-59.

———. "The Other's Rights." Trans. Chris Miller and Robert Smith. *On Human Rights.* Eds. Stephen Shute and Susan Hurley. The Oxford Amnesty Lectures Series 1993. N.p.: Harper Collins, 1993. 135-147.

———. *The Postmodern Condition: A Report on Knowledge.* Trans. Geoff Bennington and Brian Massumi. Theory and History of Literature 10. Minneapolis: University of Minnesota Press, 1993.

Matustík, Martin J. *Postnational Identity: Critical Theory and Existential Philosophy in Habermas, Kierkegaard, and Havel.* New York: Guilford Press, 1993.

McDonald, Joseph A., and Lynda Basney Micikas. *Academic Libraries: The Dimensions of Their Effectiveness.* New Directions in Information Management 32. Westport: Greenwood Press, 1994.

Murdock, Graham, and Peter Golding. "Information Poverty and Political Inequality: Citizenship in the Age of Privatized Communications." *Journal of Communication* 19.3 (Summer 1989): 180-195.

Olevnik, Peter P. "Information Literacy and the Library." ERIC, 1991. ED 338 238.

Pefanis, Julian. *Heterology and the Postmodern: Bataille, Baudrillard, and Lyotard.* Durham: Duke University Press, 1991.

Peters, Michael, ed. *Education and the Postmodern Condition.* Critical Studies in Education and Culture Series. Westport: Bergin and Garvey, 1995.

Poster, Mark. *The Modes of Information: Poststructuralism and Social Context.* Chicago: University of Chicago Press, 1990.

———. "Postmodernity and the Politics of Multiculturalism: The Lyotard-Habermas Debate over Social Theory." *Modern Fiction Studies* 38.3 (Autumn 1992): 567-580.

Qvortrup, Lars. "The Information Age: Ideal and Reality." Slack and Fejes 133-145.

Ratan, Suneel. "A New Divide Between Haves and Have-Nots?" *Time* Special Issue (Spring, 1995): 25-26.

Readings, Bill. "From Emancipation to Obligation: Sketch for a Heteronomous Politics of Education." Peters 193-207.

Reeves, Marjorie. "The Power of Language." Barnett 122-132.

Riffaterre, Michael. "Transposing Presuppositions on the Semiotics of Literary Translation." *Texte: Revue de critique et théorie* 4 (1985). Rpt. in Schulte and Biguenet 204-217.

Saffo, Paul. "Surfing for Information." *Personal Computing* July 1989: 213-214.

Salvaggio, Jerry L. "Projecting a Positive Image of the Information Society." Slack and Fejes 146-157.

Schulte, Rainer, and John Biguenet. *Theories of Translation: An Anthology of Essays from Dryden to Derrida.* Chicago: University of Chicago Press, 1992.

Shera, Jesse H. *Libraries and the Organization of Knowledge.* Hamden: Archon Books, 1965.

Slack, Jennifer Daryl, and Fred Fejes, eds. *The Ideology of the Information Age.* Communication and Information Science. Norwood: Ablex Publishing Corporation, 1987.

Snider, James H. "Democracy On-Line: Tomorrow's Electronic Electorate." *The Futurist* September-October 1994: 15-19.

Venuti, Lawrence. "Simpatico." *SubStance* 65 (1991): 3-20.

White, Robert A. "Democratization of Communication: Normative Theory and Sociopolitical Process." *Conversations on Communication Ethics.* Ed. Karen Joy Greenberg. Norwood: Ablex Publishing Corporation, 1991. 141-164.

Wilson, Kenneth. "Towards a Common/Universal Language." Barnett 72-85.

Wilson, Patrick. *Public Knowledge and Private Ignorance: Toward a Library and Information Policy.* Contributions in Librarianship and Information Science 10. Westport: Greenwood Press, 1977.

FURTHER READING

Bibliography

Nordquist, Joan. *Jean-François Lyotard: A Bibliography.* Santa Cruz: Reference and Research Services, 1991, 60 p.
    A comprehensive listing of Lyotard's work and work about his work.

Criticism

Atwill, Janet M. "Contingencies of Historical Representation." In *Writing Histories of Rhetoric,* edited by Victor J. Vitanza, pp. 98-111. Carbondale: Southern Illinois University Press, 1994.
    Applies Lyotard's conception of the *différend* to a study of historiographical method.

Bennington, Geoffrey. *Lyotard: Writing the Event.* New York: Columbia University Press, 1988, 189 p.
    Provides a clear and thorough explanation of Lyotard's philosophy, by one of Lyotard's English translators.

Brons, H. R. "Philosophy under Fire: J. F. Lyotard: Transcending the Trenches of Postmodernity." *History of European Ideas* 20, No. 4-6 (February 1995): 785-90.
    Discusses Lyotard's strategy for enabling discourse in the face of disagreement.

Jay, Martin. "The Ethics of Blindness and the Postmodern Sublime: Levinas and Lyotard." In *Downcast Eyes: The Denigration of Vision in Twentieth Century French Thought,* pp. 543-86. Berkeley: University of California Press, 1993.
    Analyzes the role of vision and "the politics of the eye" in the formulation and expression of Lyotard's postmodernism.

Poster, Mark. *Existential Marxism in Postwar France: From Sartre to Althusser.* New Jersey: Princeton University Press, 1975, 415 p.
    Presents an overview of the intellectual context in which Lyotard's political philosophy developed.

Readings, Bill. *Introducing Lyotard: Art and Politics.* London: Routledge, 1991, 184 p.
    An introduction to Lyotard's thought and works written in Lyotard's manner.

Rojek, Chris, and Turner, Brian, eds. *The Politics of Jean-François Lyotard: Justice and Political Theory.* London: Routledge, 1998, 168 p.
    A collection of essays that explain and evaluate Lyotard's political thought and examine his influence in shaping the political thought of others.

Roof, Judith. "Lesbians and Lyotard: Legitimation and the Politics of the Name." In *The Lesbian Postmodern,* edited by Laura Doan, pp. 47-66. New York: Columbia University Press, 1994, 267 p.
    Discusses Lyotard's stance on the validity of categorical meanings.

Sim, Stuart. *Jean-François Lyotard.* London: Prentice Hall/Harvester Wheatsheaf, 1996, 159 p.
    Surveys Lyotard's major works and explains his primary concepts.

Williams, James. *Lyotard: Towards a Postmodern Philosophy.* Cambridge: Polity Press, 1998, 150 p.
    Examines Lyotard's works with an emphasis on exploring his ideas and methodology.

Maria Montessori
1870-1952

Italian educator and physician.

INTRODUCTION

Montessori developed a revolutionary method of early childhood education that continues to influence many school programs around the world. The first woman in Italy to earn a medical degree, Montessori was a practicing physician working with developmentally disabled children when she discovered that these children were educable—a discovery that was in direct contrast to the prevailing notion that mentally retarded children should be confined to institutions for life. Further research with nondisabled children showed that Montessori's theories were applicable across the curriculum. A well-known pacifist, Montessori believed that a link existed between world peace and proper childhood education and regularly addressed international organizations on the subject. Her work in this area led to nominations for the Nobel Peace Prize in 1949, 1950, and 1951.

BIOGRAPHICAL INFORMATION

Montessori was born in Chiaravalle, Ancona, Italy, in 1870. She graduated from Regia Scuola Tecnica Michelangelo Buonarroti in 1886 and Regia istituto tecnico Leonardo da Vinci in 1890. The first woman ever admitted to the school of medicine at the University of Rome, in 1896 Montessori became the first woman in Italy to graduate with a medical degree. She practiced medicine from 1896 to 1910, at the same time lecturing regularly at the Regio istituto superiore di Magistero Femminile, the Scuola magistrale Ortofrenica, and the University of Rome. An early feminist, Montessori began representing Italian women at women's conferences around the world shortly after obtaining her medical degree. She also began to treat mentally retarded children. She soon came to believe that, with proper instruction, they could be successfully educated according to their individual abilities, rather than spending their entire lives committed to mental institutions, as was the standard of the time. As she further developed her theories, Montessori decided to test her method on nondisabled children. Focusing on the children of the poor, she opened her Case dei Bambini ("children's houses") in Rome—nursery schools in which "self education" was the central approach. By 1907 Montessori's schools were considered so successful that educators around the world began to adopt her methods and open Montessori-style schools in their own countries. Montessori societies arose,

and Montessori herself led congresses throughout Europe, India, and the United States to teach her method. Already an internationally respected figure, Montessori earned further acclaim in the 1930s, when she began to address organizations such as the League of Nations, the International Peace Congress, the World Fellowship of Faiths, and UNESCO about the connection between education that focused on individual social and psychological needs and the development of a society based on peace and justice. For her work in the peace movement, Montessori was nominated for the Nobel Peace Prize three times. She died in the Netherlands in 1952, while at a conference teaching her method.

MAJOR WORKS

Montessori's theories about child education are most thoroughly detailed in her book *Metodo della pedagogica scientifica applicata all' educazione infantile nelle case dei bambini* (*The Montessori Method*; 1909), in which she discussed the teaching method used first at her Case dei Bambini and later at Montessori schools around the world. The Montessori method is based on the notion that the "work" of children is not to behave as small versions of adults, but to learn through the sensory exploration of their environments. Accordingly, Montessori advocated classrooms with child-sized furniture and teachers who provided the basic tools for learning and little discipline, with the goal of encouraging children to be self-guiding and self-disciplined. In 1917 and 1918 Montessori published the two-volume *The Advanced Montessori Method,* based on her further research into the subject. *The Secret of Childhood* (1936) is a practical guidebook to understanding the educational needs of children aimed primarily at parents. *La mente del bambino* (*The Absorbent Mind*; 1949) is a collection of lectures Montessori delivered at a conference in Ahmedabad, India, exploring her theory that children move through certain periods where they are particularly open to learning certain things. *Educazione e Pace* (*Education and Peace*; 1949) is a collection of Montessori's lectures on the "science of peace," which held that world peace and justice were possible through education, starting at birth, aimed at fostering each individual's potential for spiritual liberation.

CRITICAL RECEPTION

By the time she published *The Montessori Method,* Montessori had become a revered figure in the field of education, and her theories are still employed at Montessori schools around the world. She was not, however, without detractors. On her first visit to the United States in 1913, she was very well received. But interest in her method diminished after a few years and was not revived until the 1960s. Some critics speculate that, in the United States, Montessori and her ideas fell victim to the then-popular eugenics movement, which held that certain qualities such as mental illness and criminality were dependent on genetic rather than environmental factors, and that undesirable traits were far more common in certain ethnic groups, particularly southern Europeans. As an Italian—and an unmarried professional woman with a child—Montessori, commentators charge, may have appeared to pose a threat to the established belief that most women, immigrants, and especially the disabled could not and should not be educated. But as attitudes evolved, the Montessori method was increasingly adopted in the United States, and, although debate over its efficacy continues, it is widely considered a valid and successful educational theory.

PRINCIPAL WORKS

Metodo della pedagogica scientifica applicata all' educazione infantile nelle case dei bambini [*The Montessori Method*] (essay) 1909

Antropologia pedagogica [*Pedagogical Antropology*] (essay) 1910

Dr. Maria Montessori's Own Handbook (essay) 1914

The Advanced Montessori Method. 2 vols. (essay) 1917-1918

Peace in Education (essay) 1932

The Secret of Childhood (essay) 1936

Education for a New World (essay) 1946

Educazione e Pace [*Education and Peace*] (essay) 1949

La mente del bambino [*The Absorbent Mind*] (essay) 1949

CRITICISM

John Edgar (essay date 1914)

SOURCE: A review of *Pedagogical Anthropology,* in *Mind,* No. 91, July, 1914, pp. 433-34.

[*In the following essay, Edgar reviews Montessori's* Pedagogical Anthropology, *noting that although there is little new in the collection of lectures, Montessori's enthusiasm for her subject is admirable.*]

This volume [*Pedagogical Anthropology*] comprises the lectures delivered by Dr. Montessori during a period of four years in the Pedagogic School of the University of Rome.

In view of the great fame which her method of educating young children has won for the author, we opened the book with high expectations which have only partly been fulfilled. There is really little that is new in the volume, yet it glows with the enthusiasm of a teacher whose aim is not merely truth, but the betterment of society through its influence. Detailed technical discussions of such subjects as the principles of General Biology, Craniology, the Thorax, etc., are interspersed with digressions in which some social or pedagogical moral is pointed. Perhaps this is natural considering the fact that the lectures were intended to show the bearings of anthropology upon pedagogy. The plan at any rate was deliberately chosen. "The first chapter," writes the author in the preface, "contains an outline of general biology, and at the same time biological and social generalisations concerning man considered from our point of view as educators."

She would have education based upon and guided by the anatomical or anthropological characteristics of each child, and so safeguard and allow free development for individuality.

By this means she hopes on the one hand to deliver normal individuals from the blight and curse of uniformity and conventional commonplaceness, and on the other largely to do away with the need for prisons and hospitals. Schools for the abnormal and the subnormal, who would be early recognised from their family records and biometric charts, would be so multiplied and perfected that in time prisons and hospitals would practically cease to be required.

"If criminal anthropology has been able to *revolutionise the penalty* in modern civilisation, it is our duty to undertake, in the school of the future, to *revolutionise the individual*" (p. 18).

Pedagogical Anthropology, according to Dr. Montessori, studies man from two different points of view: his development and his variations. The variations, however, constitute the most important subject of inquiry because through the help of variable characteristics we may be able to "discover a way for the future perfectionment of the human species and the individual" (p. 35). Pedagogical anthropology seeks for a more scientific and accurate knowledge of the normal human being, and so differs from criminal anthropology which pays special attention to the abnormal. The child in the school environment must become the subject of the most careful research, and innumerable biographic charts must be drawn and studied. The school therefore must be looked upon as a great "pedagogical clinic."

Much of this has been urged by medical men before, and already we have in this country and elsewhere medical inspection, and biometric charts for the guidance of teachers—and special schools for the feeble minded, the blind, the deaf and dumb and other exceptional classes.

The title *Pedagogical Anthropology* suggests not only a science, but the application of a science in a particular social direction. It aims at "the possible amelioration of man" through "the positive knowledge of the laws of human life." But surely "the laws of human life" are much wider than anthropology;—men are good or bad in spite of the shape of their nose or ears, or the measurements of their cranium. There are saints whom anthropological characteristics would brand as sinners, and there are human brutes with the faces of angels. Hence when Madame Montessori defines the science as "a method that systematises the positive study of the pupil for pedagogic purposes and with a view to *establishing philosophic principles of education*," we must insist that anthropology alone can never establish such principles.

Even granting that the individuality of any child or person has its basis in the anatomical structure of the child or person, and that every psychical phenomenon or characteristic has its physical or anatomical counterpart, we cannot admit that anthropology can provide anything more than an anthropological (*i.e.* physical) outlook upon the problems of education. Education has to deal with individuals possessing, to start with, many minute anatomical differences, but, while leaving some room for individuality, it aims at producing a social or civic type and on the whole succeeds.

Modern education takes individuals with different heredities, different peculiarities, different capacities, brings them together in the school, gives them, within certain limits, a similar training, similar activities, a similar environment; it rubs individuality against individuality,—mind against mind—and, in the long run, produces in all of them some share of that desirable common quality or synthesis of qualities which we call national character. They leave school inspired to some extent by national ideals, possessing some desirable national characteristics, endowed with a little of that necessary civic acquirement—a national common sense.

On broad lines it *does* consider the individualities marked out by anthropological conditions. It deals with the feeble minded and the imbecile apart, with the precocious criminal apart, with the normal or approximately normal, who constitute the majority, in the ordinary schools—and from them it selects the supernormal—the specially able and capable—and gives them a higher culture suited to their natural abilities.

Education really succeeds because it does *not* leave the individual, as Madame Montessori would apparently do, to work out his life on the lines that heredity or anthropology would in every case prescribe for him.

Intellectual and ethical ideals, and high social purposes count in modern education no less than the tendencies which are bred in the bone.

Robert John Fynne (essay date 1924)

SOURCE: "Maria Montessori (1870-)," in *Montessori and Her Inspirers,* Longmans, Green and Co., 1924, pp. 213-85.

[*In the following essay, Fynne provides a detailed explanation of Montessori's theories and methods and traces major influences in the development of her thought.*]

"The Montessori Method" is now so well known to students of education, and so many excellent works have already been written in detailed exposition and criticism of its principles and practice, that for the purposes of this chapter it will suffice to consider in broad outline its history, fundamental conceptions, didactic apparatus and procedure, in order that its relations to, and the degree of its dependence upon, the work of Pereira, Itard, and Séguin may become clear.

Maria Montessori was born in the year preceding the consummation of Italian independence and unity under the constitutional monarchy of Victor Emmanuel. The only child of middle-class parents who were not very well-to-do, the thoughtful girl grew up amid the new social, political and economic conditions that were rapidly developing with the expanding national life of the free and united people. The modest rank and financial resources of her family brought to her studious mind direct personal knowledge of many of the pressing problems of life, and to possible solutions for these she devoted much thought even before she reached the age of womanhood. She played a notable part in the great movement for the emancipation of women from the thraldom of prejudice and convention and for the extension of their spheres of interest and activity. In defiance of one very strong prejudice of the time she became a student in the medical school of the University of Rome, and was the first woman in Italy to take the degree of Doctor of Medicine.

Upon the completion of her medical course she was appointed assistant doctor of the Psychiatric Clinic of the University. But while devoting herself assiduously to the various duties of this post she had visions of a greater work awaiting her. The study of the thyroid gland and the various abnormalities due to its defects was then developing, and as a consequence the attention of many physicians was being directed to defective children. Dr. Montessori had early begun to specialise in children's diseases, more particularly those of a mental nature; and she soon perceived that for the cure of the latter education could offer more potent means than medicine. "The fact that pedagogy must join with medicine in the treatment of disease was," she writes, "the practical outcome of the thought of the time. And because of this tendency the method of treating disease by gymnastics became widely popular. I, however, differed from my colleagues in that I felt that mental deficiency presented chiefly a pedagogical, rather than mainly a medical, problem."[1]

Part of her duty consisted in frequently visiting the insane asylums of the city to study the patients and select from among them suitable subjects for the clinic. During these visits she became interested in the idiot children whom she found at the asylums, for at that time all such children were housed along with the insane. Interest led to inquiry and she soon "became conversant with the special method of education devised for these unhappy little ones by Edward Séguin."[2] The latter's work confirmed her belief that the amelioration of the sad lot of the idiot child must be achieved by educational rather than by medical means. To this belief she gave public expression at the Pedagogical Congress at Turin in 1898. "I believe," she says, "that I touched a chord already vibrant, because the idea, making its way among the physicians and elementary teachers, spread in a flash as presenting a question of lively interest to the school."[3] As a result of this address on **"Moral Education"** the Minister of Education requested her to give a course of lectures to the teachers of Rome on the education of the feeble-minded child. From this lecture course there soon developed the State Orthophrenic School of which she was in charge for more than two years during 1898 to 1900. To this institution were transferred such pupils of the public elementary schools as were considered hopelessly deficient. Later through the assistance of a philanthropic association it was found possible to add to these all the idiot children from the insane asylums of the city. During the two years she directed this school Dr. Montessori not only took the chief part in the training of special teachers in the observation and education of the defective

pupils, but was also engaged many hours daily in teaching the children herself. Nor did she rely entirely upon her own knowledge and experience. She visited during this period both London and Paris for the purpose of studying in a practical way the best methods in use in these cities for the education of the mentally deficient, and on her return she devoted almost all her school hours to the actual teaching of her pupils, being present from eight in the morning till seven in the evening.

From the beginning of her practical teaching at the Orthophrenic School Dr. Montessori felt that the methods she employed, which were, as we shall see, mainly those of Séguin, had nothing in them to limit their application to the development of idiots. She felt, indeed, that the principles upon which they were based were *more rational* than those underlying the usual practice of the ordinary schools—"so much more so, indeed, that through their means an inferior mentality would be able to grow and develop. This feeling, so deep as to be in the nature of an intuition, became my controlling idea after I had left the school for deficients, and, little by little, I became convinced that similar methods applied to normal children would develop or set free their personality in a marvellous and surprising way."[4] Her later and more thorough study of Séguin's work revealed to her that her great inspirer had himself realised not only the possibility but the great desirability of applying his principles and methods in the education of the normal child. Dr. Montessori was also influenced in this direction by the works of famous Italian anthropologists and chiefly by those of Giuseppe Sergi. Following the methods of Lombroso, who applied the principles of anthropology to the study of criminology, and of De Giovanni, who employed them in the practice of medicine, Sergi sought to found upon them a scientific education. "To-day in the social world," says Sergi, "an imperative need makes itself felt—the reconstruction of educational methods; and he who fights for this cause, fights for human regeneration." In his pedagogical writings collected in a volume under the title of *Educazione ed Instruzione* (Pensieri),[5] he gives a *résumé* of the lectures in which he encouraged this new movement, and says that he believes the way to this desired regeneration lies in a methodical study of the one to be educated, carried on under the guidance of pedagogical anthropology and experimental psychology.[6]

Completely convinced at last of the soundness of her own and Séguin's views as to the value of the physiological method in the education of normal children, Dr. Montessori abandoned for a time her personal teaching of defectives and the training of their teachers and devoted her energies to further observation, experiment and thought. Not only did she enter upon what she calls "a genuine and thorough study" of remedial pedagogy, but also registered as a student of philosophy at the University of Rome in order that she might undertake an advanced study of normal education and its fundamental principles. "At this time," she writes, "I was registered at the University as a student of philosophy, and followed the course in experimental psychology, which had only recently been established in Italian universities, namely, at Turin, Rome and Naples. At the same time I made researches in Pedagogic Anthropology in the elementary schools, studying in this way the methods in organisation used for the education of normal children. This work led to the teaching of Pedagogic Anthropology in the University of Rome."[7]

Her "genuine and thorough study" of remedial education was mainly concerned with the work of Séguin and of her other great inspirer, Dr. Itard. In the work of the latter she finds the origin of the methods for the education of deficients. "He was," she says, "the first to attempt a methodical education of the sense of hearing. He made these experiments in the institute for deaf-mutes. . . . Later on, having in charge for eight years the idiot boy known as 'the wild boy of Aveyron,' he extended to the treatment of all the senses those educational methods which had already given such excellent results in the treatment of the sense of hearing. A student of Pinel, Itard was the first educator to practise the *observation* of the pupil in the way in which the sick are observed in the hospitals, especially those suffering from diseases of the nervous system."[8] In our chapter on Pereira we have seen that the education of defectives has a very much earlier origin than that assigned to it in the above passage. And in our introductory chapter we have seen that Dr. Montessori does not show in her writings any direct knowledge of Pereira's work, and is consequently unaware of his practice of scientifically observing and examining his deaf-mute pupils, and of his pioneer work in the education of the senses. She is wrong too in assuming that Itard's work with deaf-mutes prepared the way for his education of the wild boy. The fact is, as we have already noted, that while endeavouring to train this boy's sense of hearing he made observations and experiments that were of great value in his subsequent education of the deaf. The wild boy's education too did not continue for eight, but only for about four years. "The pedagogic writings of Itard," she adds, "are most interesting and minute descriptions of educational efforts and experiences, and anyone reading them to-day must admit that they were practically the first attempts at experimental psychology."[9] We shall find evidence later that she was profoundly impressed as well as guided and helped by Itard's inspiring pamphlets.

On the connexion between Séguin and Itard she writes: "But the merit of having completed a genuine educational system for deficient children was due to Edward Séguin, first a teacher and then a physician. He took the experiments of Itard as his starting point, applying these methods, modifying and completing them during a period of ten years' experience with children taken from the insane asylums and placed in a little school in Rue Pigalle in Paris."[10] Dr. Montessori is unaware of the inspiration derived by Séguin from the wonderful work of Pereira.

Very shortly after her graduation she had begun the close study of Séguin's first great work, *Traitement Moral, Hygiène et Education des Idiots,* published in French in 1846.

For a long time, however, she was unable to obtain a copy of his later work, *Idiocy: and its Treatment by the Physiological Method,* published in English in America in 1866. This great book was unknown to or forgotten by those of her acquaintance who ought to have been thoroughly conversant with its contents, and the consequences were deplorable. She made a vain quest for it, going, as she says, from house to house of nearly all the English physicians who were known to be specially interested in deficient children, or who were superintendents of special schools. The fact that this book was unknown in England although it had been published in the English language, made her think that Séguin's system had never been understood. In fact although Séguin was constantly quoted in all the publications dealing with institutions for deficients, the educational applications described, were, she found, quite different from the applications of Séguin's system. Almost everywhere the methods employed in the education of deficients were more or less similar to those in use in ordinary schools. German educators, she found, maintained as a principle the use of the same methods for defective and normal pupils. She spent some time at Bicêtre, and even there, where the educators had the French text in their hands, it was the didactic apparatus far more than the method of the master that was in use. She says that the teaching there was merely mechanical, each teacher following the rules in a merely literal manner. "After this study of the methods in use throughout Europe," she writes, "I concluded my experiments upon the deficients of Rome, and taught them throughout two years. I followed Séguin's book, and also derived much help from the remarkable experiments of Itard."[11] She perceived and was deeply impressed by the *spiritual* nature of the thought and work of the former. One day a directress in the Institution for Deficients drew her attention to the thirty-seventh chapter of the book of *Ezekiel* in which he prophesies the revival of the dead hope of Israel; and the words of the prophet recalled to her the spirit and work of her great master.

The following passage reveals the thoroughness of her study of the works of the two men who did so much to inspire and guide her. "Having through actual experience justified my faith in Séguin's method, I withdrew from active work among deficients, and began a more thorough study of the works of Itard and Séguin. I felt the need of meditation. I did a thing which I had not done before, and which perhaps few students have been willing to do,—I translated into Italian and copied out with my own hand, the writings of these men, from beginning to end, making for myself books as the old Benedictines used to do before the diffusion of printing. I chose to do this by hand, in order that I might have time to weigh the sense of each word, and to read, in truth, the spirit of the author. I had just finished copying the 600 pages of Séguin's French volume when I received from New York a copy of the English book published in 1866. The old volume had been found among the books discarded from the private library of a New York physician. I translated it with the help of an English friend. This volume did not add much in the way of new pedagogical experiments, but dealt with the philosophy of the experiments described in the first volume. The man who had studied abnormal children for thirty years expressed the idea that the physiological method, which has as its base the individual study of the pupil and which forms its educative methods upon the analysis of physiological and psychological phenomena, must come also to be applied to normal children. This step, he believed, would show the way to a complete human regeneration. The voice of Séguin seemed to be like the voice of the forerunner crying in the wilderness, and my thoughts were filled with the immensity and importance of a work which should be able to reform the school and education."[12]

Having through this thorough mode of study become intimately acquainted with her forerunners' educational principles and with the details of their experiments and expedients, and imbued with their noble spirit, Dr. Montessori resumed the teaching of deficient children and arranged some original experiments. Of this work, she writes: "This is not the place for a report of these experiments, and I will only note that at this time I attempted an original method for the teaching of reading and writing, a part of the education of the child which was most imperfectly treated in the works of both Itard and Séguin. I succeeded in teaching a number of the idiots from the asylums both to read and to write so well that I was able to present them at a public school for an examination together with normal children. And they passed the examination successfully."[13] To those who saw this result of her work the success appeared almost miraculous. The teacher herself realised, however, that nothing in the nature of a miracle had been achieved: her idiot pupils had been able to compete with normal children simply because they had been taught scientifically. "They had been helped in their psychic development, and the normal children had, instead, been suffocated, held back." To her the result of that examination afforded conclusive proof that the methods of education in use in ordinary schools were not only based upon unscientific principles which were not in accord with child nature and its developmental needs, but were also applied without regard to that nature and its needs. It ought not to have been possible to raise the attainments of her idiot pupils in reading and writing so close to the level usually reached by the ordinary pupil. She found herself thinking, she says, that if some day, the special education which had developed these idiot children in such a marvellous fashion, could be applied to the development of normal children, the 'miracle' of which her friends talked would no longer be possible. The abyss between the inferior mentality of the idiot and that of the normal brain, she points out, can never be bridged if the normal child has reached his full development. While everyone was admiring the progress of her idiot pupils, she was searching for the reasons which could keep the happy, healthy children of the common schools on so low a plane that they could be equalled in tests of intelligence by her unfortunate pupils.

So far Dr. Montessori had not had an opportunity of personally applying her methods in the education of normal

children, and very curiously she had not thought of seeking such opportunity in the various institutions where very young children were cared for. In January, 1907, however, her great chance came unsought. Signor Eduardo Talamo, the director of a philanthropic society called the Roman Association for Good Building, had conceived the novel and happy idea of providing in every tenement erected and controlled by his Association a large room in which it would be possible to gather together and educate all the children of the tenement who were between the ages of three and seven. The play and work of these little ones were to be supervised by a special teacher who would reside in the tenement. Dr. Montessori was invited to organise these "schools within the house," and eagerly undertook the task. For this new kind of school her friend Signora Olga Lodi, suggested the happy name of *Casa dei Bambini, The Babies' House,* and under that name the first was opened in the Via dei Marsi on January 6th, 1907. Others soon followed both in the poorer and middle-class areas, and all proved successful.

As justifying the application of her methods to the work in these schools, Dr. Montessori found a parallel between the deficient and the normal child who is very young: *"the child who has not the force to develop* and *he who has not yet developed are in some ways alike."* The latter has not yet developed the power of co-ordinated muscular movements, and so walks and performs other ordinary acts of life in an imperfect manner: he has, for example, no skill in the fastening and unfastening of garments. His organs of sense are not completely developed, as may be seen, for instance, in the weak power of accommodation of the eye. His language is primitive and is marked by many characteristic defects. The normal infant and the deficient child are alike in their general instability and in their feeble power of fixing their attention. She points out, further, that Preyer, in his psychological study of children, illustrates the parallel between pathological linguistic defects and those of the normal child in the process of developing. From all this it should follow that methods of education which made possible the considerable mental development of the idiot ought to aid the development of the ordinary child, "and should be so adapted as to constitute a hygienic education of the entire personality of a normal human being."

Towards the end of her brief history of her method Dr. Montessori again expresses her indebtedness to Itard and Séguin in these terms: "Here lies the significance of my pedagogical experiment in the 'Children's Houses.' It represents the result of a series of trials made by me, in the education of young children, with methods already used with deficients. My work has not been made in any way an application, pure and simple, of the methods of Séguin to young children, as anyone who will consult the works of the author will readily see. But it is none the less true that, underlying these two years of trial, there is a basis of experiment which goes back to the days of the French Revolution, and which represents the earnest work of the lives of Itard and Séguin. As for me, thirty years after the publication of Séguin's second book, I took up again the ideas and, I may even say, the work of this great man, with the same freshness of spirit with which he received the inheritance of the work and ideas of his master Itard. For *ten years* I not only made practical experiments according to their methods, but through reverent meditation absorbed the works of those noble and consecrated men, who have left to humanity most vital proof of their obscure heroism.

Thus my ten years of work may in a sense be considered as a summing up of the forty years of work done by Itard and Séguin. Viewed in this light, fifty years of active work preceded and prepared for this apparently brief trial of only two years, and I feel that I am not wrong in saying that these experiments represent the successive work of three physicians, who from Itard to me show in a greater or less degree the first steps along the path of psychiatry."[14] Thus she pays generous tribute to her two great inspirers. As we have seen in our introductory chapter, Dr. Montessori in these passages definitely groups herself with Itard and Séguin, acknowledges once again the inspiration which she received from them, and clearly concatenates her work with theirs.

Her direct personal association with the Children's Houses continued for about four years. During that period she trained the teachers and superintended and guided their efforts, while continuing her own observational, experimental, and teaching work. In the light of her growing experience in the education of normal children she was able to modify and extend the methods originally based on the study of idiots and other mentally deficient children. Gradually the knowledge of her principles and practice spread through Italy and other countries. *McClure's Magazine, The World's Work,* and the *Fortnightly Review* did much to inform the English-speaking educational world of the work that was being done in the Children's Houses at Rome. And when satisfied with the approach her system had made towards completion Dr. Montessori published her own *Il Metodo della Pedagogia Scientifica applicato all' educazione infantile nelle Case dei Bambini,* which appeared in English in 1912 under the unsatisfactory title of *The Montessori Method.* The English edition contains two chapters which were not included in the original Italian work, and these treat more fully of discipline and obedience and discuss some further conclusions and impressions.

Since 1911, Dr. Montessori has not been associated personally with the Children's Houses or very intimately with the actual work of any school in which her methods are employed. She has made it very clear that a great deal remains to be achieved along the lines suggested by her work; and this being true, it is, as Dr. Boyd points out, "unfortunate . . . there is no longer any institution in which her method is at work under her personal direction."[15] The intervening years have been devoted to efforts to promote the adoption of her method in many countries and to further study and experiment with a view to its ap-

plication to the education of older children. The results of this further study were given to the world in a large work, in two volumes, which was translated into English and published in 1917 under the title of *The Advanced Montessori Method.* The first volume treats of "Spontaneous Activity in Education," and the second of "The Montessori Elementary Education." There has also appeared a practical treatise entitled *Dr. Montessori's Own Handbook: A Manual for Teachers and Parents.* In this country the Montessori Society has been formed for the following objects: "to help the diffusion of the Montessori Method by all possible means; to encourage the foundation of Montessori Schools either private or in connection with public schools; to guarantee, as far as possible, the integrity of its application; to defend it from misrepresentations and falsifications."

It is to be sincerely hoped that the Society, Dr. Montessori herself, and the increasing body of her disciples will not seek the achievement of the third object above in a narrow and jealous spirit. If the system of educational theory and practice in which they are all so deeply interested is to become permanent it must be allowed to grow and develop like the child to whose unfolding life it is sought to relate it so intimately. Especially must they avoid the danger of stunting or retarding its growth and development by a too rigorous insistence upon the continued use of the didactic apparatus as it is today. In regard to this last point Dr. Boyd has well said: "They (*i.e.,* "those who have accepted the system as a great new discovery") see the principles becoming effective through the apparatus and the apparatus getting its significance from the principles, and they regard them in their conjunction as an organic whole. But if the history of thought makes one thing clearer than another, it is that principles of any kind only become a permanent factor in the advance of the human spirit by shedding the forms in which they first gained recognition."[16]

FUNDAMENTAL CONCEPTIONS

The most fundamental of all Dr. Montessori's educational conceptions is this: That the child is an organism capable of *spontaneous* development, having inherent in him not only the tendency to develop all his potentialities, but also the power of using to that end the means to be found in his environment. Her whole body of educational doctrine and procedure is founded ultimately upon this conception of organic spontaneity. The tendency referred to is a definite, active, purposive "drive" or "urge," impelling the organism to engage in such activities as have developmental value. These activities are always either actions upon or reactions to the environment, which though of great importance is, according to Dr. Montessori, but a secondary factor in the existence and development of the vital processes. *"Environment,"* she writes, "is undoubtedly a *secondary* factor in the phenomena of life; it can modify in that it can help or hinder, but it can never create. The modern theories of evolution, from Naegeli to De Vries, consider throughout the development of the two biological branches, animal and vegetable, this interior factor as the essential force in the transformation of the species and in the transformation of the individual. The origins of the *development,* both in the species and in the individual, *lie within.* The child does not grow *because* he is nourished, *because* he breathes, *because* he is placed in conditions of temperature to which he is adapted, he grows because the potential life within him develops, making itself visible, because the fruitful germ from which his life has come develops itself according to the biological destiny which was fixed for it by heredity. Adolescence does not come *because* the child laughs, or dances or does gymnastic exercises, or is well nourished; but because he has arrived at that particular physiological state. Life makes itself manifest—life creates, life gives; and is in its turn held within certain limits and bound by certain laws which are insuperable. The fixed characteristics of the species do not change—they can only vary.

This concept, so brilliantly set forth by De Vries in his Mutation Theory, illustrates also the limits of education. We can act on the *variations* which are in relation to the environment, and whose limits vary slightly in the species and in the individual, but we cannot act upon the *mutations.* The mutations are bound by some mysterious tie to the very font of life itself, and their power rises superior to the modifying elements of the environment."[17]

Now, if the fruitful germ from which the child gets his life develops spontaneously according to fixed biological laws, what is the function of education? Dr. Montessori's answer is in effect that its function is to encourage the manifestations of spontaneity at their period of incipiency and to facilitate their fulfilment in such activities as will make for "a harmonious innate development." The greatest care must be taken lest in tendering help we interfere with spontaneity. Spontaneous acts, unless they are useless or dangerous, must never be suppressed: "We cannot know the consequence of suffocating a *spontaneous* action at the time when the child is just beginning to be active: perhaps we suffocate *life itself.* . . . If any educational act is to be efficacious, it will be only that which tends to *help* toward the complete unfolding of this life. To be thus helpful it is necessary rigorously to avoid the *arrest of spontaneous movements and the imposition of arbitrary tasks.*"[18] Again and again throughout the pages of **The Montessori Method** we find this doctrine repeated in one form or another. Thus: "By education must be understood the active help given to the normal expansion of the life of the child. The child is a body which grows, and a soul which develops,—these two forms, physiological and psychic, have one eternal font, life itself. We must neither mar nor stifle the mysterious powers which lie within these two forms of growth, but we must *await from them* the manifestations which we know will succeed one another."[19] The greatest triumph of our educational method should always be this: *"to bring about the spontaneous progress of the child."*[20] And again: "So the spontaneous psychic development of the child continues indefinitely and is in direct relation to the psychic potentiality of the child himself, and not with the work of the teacher."[21]

Now, implicit in all this is Dr. Montessori's second basic principle—that there must be formulated a scientific pedagogy, an exact science of childhood. For, in order that the educator may *help* the spontaneous development of the child and avoid retarding, marring, misdirecting or suppressing it, he must understand the laws which it has to obey and the organic needs and impulses with which it is intimately associated. Every effort must be made to ascertain and systematise all the facts of child life, growth, and development. The scientific student of childhood must seek assistance from biology, anthropology, physiology, hygiene, and psychology, and utilise also the lore of the physician. But while all these sciences may greatly help in education by revealing and explaining many facts and aspects of child life, the educator must remember the essential unity of the child. The knowledge of greatest direct service is that obtained by observation of the pupil during the hours when he is spontaneously living his life. Dr. Montessori does not place much reliance upon the results of experimental investigations in psychological laboratories; for during the experiment the subject finds himself in an unnatural environment where he is tormented by instruments, circumscribed in his action and reaction, and prevented from spontaneously manifesting his psychic needs and modes of expression. In her introductory lecture to her first International Training Course, held in Rome in 1913, she said: "For the adequate study of man we require not a method precisely similar to methods formerly used by science, but a method analogous to them. When for instance it is desired to study the insects . . . what does the scientist do? He goes where the insects live naturally, taking care not to disturb them, so as to see exactly all their doings. What does the man who would study plants do? He goes where the plants grow naturally. To study the peronospera (a vine blight), the scientist seeks the affected vines. The bacteriologist tries to place the microbes in their natural environment. And in studying for the purposes of hygiene those pathological germs which are found in man, it is endeavoured to give the microbes conditions of life as similar as possible to those of their normal environment; soups and gelatins are prepared and kept at the temperature of the human body. Why should we do otherwise in studying man? Why, peculiarly in the case of man must he be taken from his natural surroundings? Why put him in a laboratory and torment him with instruments? Why circumscribe his existence and submit him to the test of a second? Man, the great builder of civilisation?

Let us do only what we did when studying all other living beings. Let us observe him in his natural state. What do we do, however, when we wish to study living organisms? We give them the best conditions of life. We need to found a laboratory for the experimental study of man, which will give a group of human beings the best conditions of existence. . . . Give the best conditions of life, and then?—as is done with all other living organisms leave them free, and see what they do; disturbing them not at all, or as little as possible, though certainly helping them by every means in their development. Thus it is not enough to give the best living conditions but freedom must also be given

. . . the place which is best adapted for real scientific research is undoubtedly the school."[22]

According to Dr. Montessori an environment is *natural* to an organism when it provides the best possible conditions of life: and the best possible conditions of life are those in which the individual organism finds "all that is necessary for his development." And she claims that for the child of modern civilised life the school may be made such an environment: and when it is made so it becomes the ideal laboratory for the scientific study of childhood.

Implied in the foregoing are three other fundamental principles of the Montessori system which call for discussion in turn. They are, first, the principle requiring the scientific determination of the pupil's environment; second, the biological principle of liberty; and third, the principle that scientific pedagogy must be grounded upon the direct study of the *individual* and that individuality, personality, must be afforded full opportunity to reveal its characteristics and provided with all necessary means for organising and developing itself.

In her later and larger work, **The Advanced Montessori Method,**[23] she writes thus in regard to the first of these principles while assuming the second: "In order to expand, the child, left at liberty to exercise his activities, ought to find in his surroundings something *organised* in direct relation to his internal organisation which is developing itself by natural laws just as the free insect finds in the form and qualities of flowers a direct correspondence between form and sustenance. The insect is undoubtedly free when, seeking the nectar which nourishes it, it is in reality helping the reproduction of the plant. There is nothing more marvellous in nature than the correspondence between the organs of these two orders of being destined to such a providential co-operation.

The secret of the free development of the child consists, therefore, in organising for him the means necessary for his internal nourishment, means corresponding to a primitive impulse of the child, comparable to that which makes the newborn infant capable of sucking milk from the breast, which by its external form and elaborated sustenance, corresponds perfectly to the requirements of the infant. It is in the satisfaction of this primitive impulse, this internal hunger that the child's personality begins to organise itself and reveal its characteristics. We must not therefore set ourselves the educational problem of seeking means whereby to organise the internal personality of the child and develop his characteristics; the sole problem is that of offering the child the necessary nourishment. It is by this means that the child develops an organised and complex activity which, while it responds to a primitive impulse exercises the intelligence and develops qualities we consider lofty and which we supposed were foreign to the nature of the young child, such as patience and perseverance in work, and in the moral order, obedience, gentleness, affection, politeness, serenity; qualities we are accustomed to divide into different categories and as to which,

hitherto, we have cherished the illusion that it was our task to develop them gradually by our direct interposition, although in practice we have never known by what means to do so successfully."

Here the sole problem of education is reduced to its simplest terms: to provide the child with the best means for spontaneous development, for *auto-education*. These means are to form part of his specially arranged environment. And two obvious points for criticism are already met. First, the environment so prepared is not artificial for the child of modern society; it is natural in that it contains the best possible conditions for his physical, mental and moral development. Secondly, in such a definitely organised environment he is not deprived of his freedom any more than is the wild bee which finds its sustenance in the highly organised flower. And just as the structure and properties of the flower correspond with the bee's organic structure and needs, so must the means provided for the auto-education of the child correspond, as closely as science can determine, with his organic constitution and developmental needs. Dr. Montessori claims that her scientific study of childhood has enabled her to decide with a considerable approach to exactitude what these means should be and how they should be used; that her science of education, formulated on the results of direct observation, has determined not only the general organisation of the school environment in regard to spacing, hygienic conditions, furniture, decoration, and so on, but has also determined the nature, construction, grading, and use of her didactic apparatus. While leaving questions of the apparatus for later discussion it must be repeated that the scientific determination of the school environment is an essential basic principle of the Montessori system. Without such determination there can be no real laboratory and therefore no direct observation, under natural conditions, of the child's manifestations of spontaneity.

Much has been written concerning the Montessori principle of freedom. The majority of teachers and students of education appear to regard this as the one great fundamental principle by the acceptance or rejection of which by the educational world the system must stand or fall. In reality it is not so. As we have seen above the first essential basic principle is auto-education, the spontaneous development of the child; the second is that which declares absolutely necessary the formulation of a science of pedagogy based on observation; and the third is that which demands a natural environment in which spontaneity may manifest itself and in which its manifestations may be observed under the best conditions. Now, all these principles require as an essential *condition* that the child shall have freedom—freedom to act spontaneously and to have interrelations with the *prepared* environment. Unless his activities are free our observation of them cannot possibly procure trustworthy data for a science of education. This is the real significance of what Dr. Montessori calls "the biological concept of liberty in pedagogy." "From the biological point of view the concept of *liberty* in the education of the child in his earliest years must be understood as demanding those conditions adapted to the most favourable *development* of his entire individuality. So from the physiological side as well as from the mental side, this includes the free development of the brain. The educator must be as one inspired by a deep *worship of life,* and must, through this reverence, *respect,* while he observes with human interest, the *development* of the child life."[24] And in her later and fuller work in which she treats in greater detail of many matters incompletely dealt with in her first book, she says: "The contribution I have made to the education of young children tends, in fact, to *specify* by means of the revelations due to experiment the form of liberty in internal development; it would not be possible to conceive liberty of development if, by its very nature the child were not capable of a spontaneous organic development, if the tendency to develop his energies (expansion of latent powers), the conquest of the means necessary to a harmonious innate development, did not already exist. . . . In order that the phenomenon should come to pass it is *necessary* that the spontaneous development of the child should be accorded *perfect liberty*; that is to say that its calm and peaceful expansion should not be disturbed by the intervention of an untimely and disturbing influence; just as the body of the newborn infant should be left in peace to assimilate its nourishment and grow properly. In such an attitude ought we to await the *miracles* of the inner life, its expansions and also its unforeseen and surprising explosions. . . . But to ensure the psychical phenomena of growth, we must prepare the 'environment' in a definite manner and from this environment offer the child the external means directly necessary for him. This is the *positive* fact which my experiment has rendered concrete. Hitherto the liberty of the child has been vaguely discussed, no clearly defined limit has been established between liberty and abandonment. We were told: 'liberty has its limits,' 'liberty must be properly understood.' But a special method indicating how liberty should be interpreted and what is the intuitive *quid* which ought to co-exist with it had not been determined. The establishment of such a method should open up a new path to all education. It is therefore necessary that the environment should contain the means of auto-education."[25]

In order to understand clearly Dr. Montessori's principle of freedom it is of the first importance to grasp the essential fact that it is only for such spontaneous activities as have direct relationship with her *prepared* environment that she insists upon the granting of *perfect liberty*. She claims that her school environment, the most vitally important—even dominating—part of which is the special didactic apparatus, can be so scientifically prepared in strict accordance with the nature and needs of the child that it will be intrinsically attractive and satisfying to him, and that only on exceedingly rare occasions will he manifest any tendency to enter into other than desirable relationships with it. To the ordinary child the really interesting apparatus makes an irresistible appeal, absorbing attention, inciting to educative activity, and thus pleasantly but effectively preventing useless and dangerous conduct. Once the child comes under the pleasant, helpful, and alluring influence of this prepared environment no question as to the advisability of allowing him perfect freedom can arise. But if he has not yet come under that influence or if for any reason it is temporarily inoperative, and the child as a consequence is guilty of useless or dangerous acts, they are immediately *"suppressed, destroyed."*

On the moral side there is gradual definite development through the same outlet of spontaneity guided and controlled in and by the prepared environment. Gradually the moral personality arises through the constant exercise and consequent growth of the will. "When the child chooses from among a considerable number of objects the one he prefers, when he moves to go and take it from the sideboard, and then replaces it, or consents to give it up to a companion; when he waits until one of the pieces of the apparatus he wishes to use is laid aside by the child who has it in his hand at the moment; when he persists for a long time and with earnest attention in the same exercise, correcting the mistakes which the didactic material reveals to him; when, in the silence-exercise, he restrains all his impulses, all his movements and then rising when his name is called, controls these movements carefully to avoid making a noise with his feet or knocking against the furniture he performs so many acts of the 'will.' It may be said that in him the exercise of the will is continuous; nay, that the factor which really acts and persists among his aptitudes is the will, which is built up on the internal fundamental fact of a prolonged attention."[26] In this connexion Professor Nunn points out that there can be no "training of the will" apart from the general process by which the sentiments are built up, and adds: "Hence Dr. Montessori is right in maintaining that to train a child's will we must begin by leaving him free to work out his own impulses. For if he is constantly checked or constantly acts only on the directions of another, there can be no building up of strong sentiments to be the basis of effective and well-regulated conduct."[27]

In regard to the social aspects of freedom her general position is stated thus: "The liberty of the child should have as its *limit* the collective interest, as its *form,* what we universally consider good breeding. We must, therefore, check in the child whatever offends or annoys others or whatever tends towards rough or ill-bred acts. But all the rest,— every manifestation having a useful scope—whatever it be, and under whatever form it expresses itself, must not only be permitted but must be *observed,* by the teacher."[28] The carefully prepared environment in which the child is free to enter into numerous and varied relations with his fellows, affords ample opportunity, encouragement, incentive to the building up of social sentiments.

The fifth fundamental Montessori principle is that which insists upon the vital importance of the pupil's individuality. Always for her "the child" means the individual child. The spontaneity, the needs, the observation, the freedom, are always those of the individual. Child-life, all its manifestations, conduct, will, attention, intelligence, imagination—every topic discussed in her great study—are considered ultimately in their relation to the individual. "Now, child-life," she asserts, "is not an abstraction; *it is the life of individual children*. There exists only one real biological manifestation: *the living individual*; and toward single individuals, one by one observed, education must direct itself."[29] So the individual child is allowed to come and go freely, to use the apparatus when and how he chooses, to help others or seek help from them, and generally to manifest the strong and the weak powers of his mind, the traits of his character, and his likes and dislikes: and all this provided he does not exceed the *limit* or mar the *form* referred to above. While he is thus living his individual life and his personality is asserting and revealing itself he is being carefully observed by the educator so that she may be enabled to give wisely on occasion that help which is education as far as she is concerned. But the education which is alone of vital value is auto-education: "Each one of them perfects himself through his own powers and goes forward guided by that inner force which distinguishes him as an individual."[30] A sixth principle—that education must be through the senses, can be more conveniently considered in the section following.

There are many points in connexion with Dr. Montessori's principles and her own exposition of them which invite critical consideration. Such criticism, however, to be just and of value, would involve a discussion too full for inclusion within the limits of this chapter. Nor would it, indeed, be germane to our purpose here which is, as we have indicated, to give in broad outline an account of her principles and practice with a view to establishing their relationship to those of her inspirers. The next chapter will be devoted to criticism.

We have already considered her generous acknowledgment of the general inspiration and guidance she received from Itard and Séguin. In the tenth chapter of ***The Montessori Method*** she devotes several pages to an account of the former's great achievement in the education of the Savage of Aveyron, and points out that when he came to realise the idiocy of his pupil, "his philosophical theories gave place to the most admirable, tentative, experimental pedagogy." As she herself did a century later, Itard observed and experimented, prepared an environment, allowed all the freedom that was possible in the case of such a wild creature, and spent *whole hours* in close watching for the spontaneous manifestations of his pupil, more especially as they were operative in the freedom of the garden, during Nature's more active and expressive moments of storm, or when left at liberty in his room or at the Observatory. In the nature of the case, of course, his whole attention was devoted to an *individual,* whom he studied from all points of view in a manner most thorough and detailed. "To this child," she says, "are due the first steps of positive pedagogy." His fears, perplexities, pains, pleasures; his looks, grimaces, gestures; his likes and dislikes; his needs, and his defects of all kinds were studied with almost incredible patience. "Here is a sample of the admirably patient work of Itard as *observer of the spontaneous expressions* of his pupil: it can most truly give teachers,

who are to prepare for the experimental method, an idea of the patience and the self-abnegation necessary in dealing with a phenomenon which is to be observed": and she quotes at length Itard's account of his observations with which we dealt fully in our second chapter. She concludes her account of his work in these terms: "In the education of little children Itard's educative drama is repeated: we must prepare man, who is one among the living creatures and therefore belongs to nature, for social life, because social life, being his own peculiar work, must also correspond to the manifestation of his natural activity."[31] In Itard's poignant and eloquent pages she found very clearly implied, often, indeed, expressed, the great fundamental principles of her own educational system.

It will be clear from the detailed account in the previous chapter of Séguin's thought and practice that Dr. Montessori must have found during her long and close study of his work both inspiration and guidance in regard to her six fundamental principles. It must be remembered, however, that all Séguin's practical educational work was concerned with idiots, that he had to begin with "the rather immovable or ungovernable mass called an idiot," a mass with which it was impossible to associate the ideas of spontaneity, freedom, and individuality in the large sense in which we have hitherto discussed them. And yet these three great ideas animated all his magnificent work! They were, in truth, *ideals* to the realisation of which all his best educative efforts were patiently directed, being in some cases sustained for several years. To render his poor idiot pupils capable of spontaneous manifestations and activities, to enable them to appreciate and make use of their physical, mental and moral freedom, and to *create,* we must almost say, or to deliver from its bondage and develop the feeble individuality of each idiot child—these were among the great objects he ever sought to achieve. He endeavoured always to elevate his idiot pupils towards the high level of the normal child, of whom he thought as living his individual life spontaneously and freely. And always he aimed at developing in them the power of spontaneously desiring, choosing, and acting; at producing in them "the echoing spontaneity which is the completely free man"; of restoring to them, "in spontaneous will, the synergic faculty of the race." We have already quoted a passage[32] in which he expressly states that individuality must be secured, and that the first test of fitness in a teacher is respect for the individuality of the pupil. A close study of his educational views and aims makes it abundantly clear that had he had the opportunity of educating normal children he would, like his great follower, have included these three principles among the fundamentals of his system. Dr. Montessori found in his pages expressions of reverence for the spontaneous manifestations of normal childhood. He strongly condemned their suppression, the denial of liberty to the child, all oppression, and the setting up of "fatal antagonisms." He would, indeed, allow greater freedom for spontaneous activity than she would. Thus he writes: "One of the earliest and most fatal antagonisms taught to a child is the forbidding of using his hands to ascertain the qualities of surrounding objects, of which his sight gives him but an imperfect notion, if it be not aided by the touch; and of breaking many things as well, to acquire the proper idea of solidity. The imbecility of parents in these matters has too often favoured the growth of the evil spirit. The youngest child, when he begins to totter on his arched legs, goes about, touching, handling, breaking everything. It is our duty to foster and direct that beautiful curiosity, to make it the regular channel for the acquisition of correct perceptions and tactile accuracy; as for breaking, it must be turned into the desire of preservation and the power of holding with the will; nothing is so simple, as the following example will demonstrate":—[33]

He goes on to relate the story of a very excitable child, eighteen months old, "touching, breaking, throwing everything he could," whom he allowed to throw away and break unmatched Bohemian glasses and *Sèvres* cups. The child was not prevented from thus acting spontaneously; his freedom was not interfered with; no anger was turned upon him—"only the composure and accent of pity for the child who could willingly incur such a loss." Later this baby spontaneously developed the power of taking care of still finer cups and glasses: he taught his little fingers how to embrace with security the thin neck of one, the large body, or the diminutive handle of others. "In practising these so varied handlings, his mind became saving and his hands a model of accuracy."

As to Séguin's position in regard to the two remaining Montessori principles, which insist upon a scientific system and a prepared environment, little need be said. His whole system was soundly based on science. And his observation and experiments had definite reference to each individual child. Every pupil was examined with most minute care, and throughout his education his special needs received the most delicate observation and attention. Science determined every observation, experiment, and mode of treatment. Séguin brought to his work a first-class mind, highly trained in the general principles and methods of science, and possessing a profound knowledge of the physiology and psychology of his time. He had, as we have seen, made a long and careful study of Pereira's work, which also had a definite scientific basis, and which, indeed, revealed to him the marvellous potentialities of the human organism. As a student under Itard and a diligent and eager reader of the latter's two educational pamphlets, he was, of course, impressed by the value of the detailed scientific study of the individual to be educated. Our study of his methods in the previous chapter has shown how elaborately he prepared the environment and how scientifically he adapted it to the needs of each pupil. His room of silence and darkness, with its many kaleidoscopic and other contrivances, and his skilfully arranged floor may be referred to again as illustrating his realisation of the value of this principle. He refers to his prepared environment as being *artificial,* while Dr. Montessori speaks of hers as being *natural*: but there is no difference in their points of view. Both advocate the preparation to suit the nature and needs of the child, and he calls his artificial for the literal reason that it is arranged by human agency.

MUSCULAR AND SENSE TRAINING.

The influence of Séguin is plainly seen in the importance which Dr. Montessori attaches to the training of the muscles, as well as in the nature of the apparatus and methods she uses for this purpose. But she apparently fails to appreciate, as he so clearly did, the great psychical significance of muscular development. He realised that the education of the muscles had a definite effect on that of the intellect. He also perceived clearly the close connexion between the muscular and sensorial systems and the influence which the educational development of one of them had upon that of the other. For her, on the other hand, the training of the muscles has merely physiological significance, and she appears to regard the muscle and sense systems as being mutually independent in work and development. It is possible that she has understood Séguin's emphasis on these interrelations and influences as having its full significance in regard only to "the immovable or ungovernable mass" of an idiot. She thus states her very narrow view of the education of the muscles: "We must understand by *gymnastics* and in general by muscular education a series of exercises tending to *aid* the normal development of physiological movements (such as walking, breathing, speech), to protect this development, when the child shows himself backward or abnormal in any way, and to encourage in the children those movements which are useful in achievement of the most ordinary acts of life; such as dressing, undressing, buttoning their clothes and lacing their shoes, carrying such objects as balls, cubes, etc."[34] Throughout the chapter she devotes to this subject there is no reference to mental or moral effects. She treats in some detail of the physical proportions, morphological differences, and bodily defects to be considered, but nowhere escapes from the physiological level. She has forgotten or failed to appreciate Séguin's conception of the unity of the educable organism.

For the physiological development of the child through muscular training she makes use of special apparatus, partly chosen from Séguin's sets and partly invented by herself. The principle determining its selection, invention, and employment is that it must provide exercises corresponding to those bodily movements which the child *needs to make* in order to develop, and must allow him a proper outlet for his individual activities. In this connexion she learned much through closely observing the children's tendencies and habits. Thus she noticed that some of the pupils engaged in marching exercises occasionally left the ranks through fatigue; but instead of resting on the ground or available seats they climbed on to a wire fence and pulled themselves sideways along the wires. They had found a way of enjoying considerable movement without throwing their whole weight on to their legs, and thus had solved one of the observer's problems. The wire fence, which she recommends for general use, was adapted for indoor use, wooden bars being substituted for the wires. Among other pieces of apparatus she includes Séguin's ingenious swing or "trampolino," rubber balls attached to a cord and used in a game called "The Pendulum," a little wooden spiral staircase, a low wooden platform, with painted lines, used for long jumping, and rope ladders. The movements involved in the child's use of all these contrivances are useful, she claims, because they help him to acquire first of all equilibrium and then the muscular co-ordination which is necessary to him.

Dr. Montessori also makes use of free gymnastics for which no apparatus is required. These exercises are of two kinds: prescribed, such as marching; and free games with balls, hoops, bean bags, or kites. In the prescribed class she also includes many of Froebel's games which are accompanied by songs. The object of the marching is poise only, and not rhythm. Dr. Boyd's short criticism[35] of this exclusion of rhythm may seem to imply that Dr. Montessori always excludes it. She does not, however; it receives due consideration in her musical exercises, and special marching in which the chief object is rhythm is often practised.[36] Her point here is apparently that in marching intended for muscular development poise is more important than rhythm. Here the march should be accompanied by the singing of little songs, "because this furnishes a breathing exercise very helpful in strengthening the lungs." She also uses exercises which she calls "respiratory gymnastics." Their purpose is to regulate the respiratory movements, "to teach the art of breathing." Allied to them are exercises to encourage the formation of correct speech habits. In these the correct use of lips, tongue and teeth is carefully practised. Every effort is made to secure good articulation, the pupils being tested and helped individually and all defects and difficulties being carefully noted by the directress.

The greater part of Dr. Montessori's practice is concerned with the education of the senses, and it is for this special purpose that almost all her didactic material has primarily been selected or invented. She thus states the object of this part of her work: "The education of the senses has, as its aim, the refinement of the differential perception of stimuli by means of repeated exercises."[37] A careful study of her three chapters on sense training will reveal the fact that she realises that it has higher aims than this. Towards the close of the third of these chapters she takes a higher view. She declares that from the physiological point of view, the importance of the education of the senses is evident from an observation of the scheme of the diagrammatic arc which represents the functions of the nervous system. The external stimulus acts upon the organ of sense, and the impression is transmitted along the centripetal way to the nerve centre; the corresponding motor impulse is elaborated, and is transmitted along the centrifugal path to the organ of motion, provoking a movement. She shows that although the arc represents diagrammatically the mechanism of reflex spinal actions, it may still be considered as a fundamental key explaining the phenomena of the more complex nervous mechanisms. Man, by means of his peripheral sensory system, gathers various stimuli from his environment, putting himself thus in direct communication with his surroundings. "The psychic life develops, therefore, in relation to the system of nerve centres; and

human activity, which is eminently social activity, manifests itself through acts of the individual—manual work, writing, spoken language, etc.—by means of the psychomotor organs."[38] References to the nervous system in her writings are few.

In this chapter she affirms very definitely too that "All education of little children must be governed by this principle—to help the natural *psychic* and *physical development* of the child"[39]; and although she does not elaborate the theme it is evident that she sees in the training of the senses the best means of intellectual, moral, and aesthetic development. For her the aim of education in general is twofold, biological and social. From the point of view of the first we must help the natural development of the individual, while from that of the second we must prepare him for his environment. For both these purposes the training of the senses is of the greatest importance. Biologically considered, it must precede all superior intellectual development, and it should therefore receive our closest attention and be our chief care during the formative period of childhood—from three to seven. This is the period during which adapted and graduated sense stimuli produce their greatest developmental effects. Socially viewed, the training of the senses enables the pupil to enter more effectively into relations with his environment. His perceptive powers will become more exact and discriminating in their operations and he will thus be more efficient in his life's work. The child so trained will be a better cook or a more skilful physician than would otherwise be possible. Critics have said that there is necessarily involved in all this the idea of formal training. This idea is not discussed by Dr. Montessori, but unconsciously she supplies an answer to such critics when she assumes that the result of sense training is the establishment of physiological habits; and these may, without any question arising as to the possible transfer of sensory capacity, have influence in most numerous and varied relations of life.

The education of the senses is necessarily auto-education. A teacher cannot give a child sensory powers any more than she can give him gymnastic agility. This is true, indeed, of all education, but is strikingly so in the case of the senses. It is true also that much more help can be given in some parts of intellectual education, by a process of clear arrangement or simplification, for example: but for his sensory education the child himself must do everything. Unless he sees, touches, hears, tastes and smells, sense education is impossible for him. The only work for the teacher here is to induce the pupil to use the material necessary for his self-education, and to observe and record his progress or retardation.

A very important point in Dr. Montessori's technique is the isolation of the particular sense being educated. In the case of every sense except sight the child is blindfolded. Here again she is following Itard and Séguin. She finds that normal children greatly enjoy and are deeply interested in the tests and exercises for which they are blindfolded. Freed from the innumerable distractions of sight they take part in various exercises of great value in the training of the other senses. Thus after a solemn silence has been secured they have to listen for the gentle whisper of their names at varying distances. Or they have games in which they have to recognise various weights or distinguish various materials by touch. In another important particular of her technique she also follows Itard and Séguin. This is her use of wide differences and strong contrasts in the objects or qualities presented to the senses. Thus the longest and the shortest rods are presented together, or the thinnest and thickest: in colours, blue and red are shown. Gradually the differences are lessened until the most delicately differing tints or the slightest differences in length or thickness can be distinguished. The principle is to proceed from few stimuli strongly contrasting to many stimuli in gradual differentiation, always more fine and imperceptible.

In all this work the primary aim is "sensory culture": that must come first. But though not directly aimed at, knowledge will also come. Both concrete and abstract ideas will be acquired through the spontaneous development of the senses. In due course will come, too, the desire and the ability to express knowledge and thought in language. Here the teacher's function as helper comes into play; and the method she is to use is once again inspired by Séguin. "However desirable it may be to furnish a sense education as a basis for intellectual ideas, it is nevertheless advisable at the same time to associate the *language* with these *perceptions*. In this connection I have found excellent for use with normal children the *three periods* of which the lesson according to Séguin consists: *First Period,.*—The association of the sensory perception with the name. For example, we present to the child two colours, red and blue. Presenting the red, we say simply, 'This is red,' and presenting the blue, 'This is blue.' Then, we lay the spools upon the table under the eyes of the child. *Second Period.*—Recognition of the object corresponding to the name. We say to the child, 'Give me the red,' and then, 'Give me the blue.' *Third Period.*—The remembering of the name corresponding to the object. We ask the child, showing him the object, 'What is this?' and he should respond, 'Red.' Séguin insists strongly upon these three periods and urges that the colours be left for several instants under the eyes of the child. He also advises us never to present the colours singly, but always two at a time, since the contrast helps the chromatic memory."[40] She says she has proved that there is no better method of teaching deficients; but points out that for normal children there is a period preceding those of Séguin, and that it is then that true sense education takes place. This is the period in which the child acquires "a fineness of differential perception, which can be obtained *only* through *auto-education*." To Itard, "this pioneer in pedagogy," as she names him, she also acknowledges her indebtedness in this matter of associating perceptions and language. She quotes *in extenso* three sections from his second Report on the education of the Savage of Aveyron, and her concluding comment is: "Here also is demonstrated the great educative superiority of scientific pedagogy for normal children."

Sensory auto-education "leads to a perfecting of the child's psychosensory processes" and so achieves intellectual development. Dr. Montessori heads her short chapter on intellectual education with a quotation expressing Séguin's aim—"To lead the child from the education of the senses to ideas." And this is one of her own ultimate aims. The great means is the concentration of attention during such lessons after Séguin as that briefly outlined above and others more advanced. Just as the sense to be trained is isolated, and with it the pupil's objective attention, so must the "inner attention" be isolated on occasion by the process of concentration. The way leads from sensations to ideas—first concrete, then abstract—on to association of ideas. "The movement, or the *spontaneous psychic activity* starts in our case from the education of the senses and is maintained by the observing intelligence." She claims that moral and aesthetic education is closely related to sensory education; that as we multiply the sensations and develop the capacity of appreciating delicate differences in stimuli we refine the sensibility, and increase the number while elevating the nature of man's pleasures. To the man with coarse senses the essential harmonies of nature and life do not appeal: the world to him is narrow and barren. Only the strongest stimuli, which seldom have moral sources or outlets, are perceived by such a man. Thus his pleasures are necessarily gross and his moral nature remains crude.

THE TEACHING OF WRITING AND READING

Though Dr. Montessori expresses no keen appreciation of the fact, the finer muscular powers are trained and developed during the process of sensory education. Their development, together with that of the senses, facilitates the acquisition of the art of writing, which is taught before reading. Writing and reading found no place in her original scheme for the work of the Children's Houses. But the sense training developed her pupils intellectually in such a surprising way that it soon appeared necessary to provide some definite *conclusion* of the exercises. A number of the children went to her and "frankly demanded to be taught to read and write"; and their parents also requested that she should undertake this work. She had, as we have seen above, already succeeded in teaching defectives to read and write, and found no difficulty in adapting her method to the teaching of normal pupils. Moreover, her experience with one idiot girl of eleven led her to the discovery of a most important principle. This girl, though possessed of normal strength and motor power in her hands, could not learn to sew, or even to darn. She was set to practising weaving with the familiar Froebel mats in which strips of paper are threaded transversely in and out among vertical strips. The movements required for this being similar to those for darning and sewing, but on a larger scale, practice in them *prepared* for the latter, and when the girl was brought back to darning it was found that her difficulties had vanished. "I saw," says Dr. Montessori, "that the necessary movements of the hand in sewing *had been prepared without having the child sew,* and that we should really find the way to *teach* the child *how,* before *making him execute* a task. I saw especially that preparatory movements could be carried on, and reduced to a mechanism, by means of repeated exercises not in the work itself but in that which prepares for it. Pupils could then come to the real work, able to perform it without ever having directly set their hands to it before."[41]

Her normal pupils had already had much experience in touching the contours of her geometric insets and it was easy to extend this to the forms of script letters. The letters were cut in sandpaper, 8 cm. high and ½ cm. broad, and glued on cardboard. The children pass their fingers over these letters, guided by the roughness, and practise the larger movements required in writing. But it is also necessary to prepare for the use of pen or pencil, which involves a different set of muscular movements. This is done by getting the child to trace designs of the geometric insets and fill in the space by drawing lines with coloured pencils. Progress in this exercise is rapid, the short and indefinite lines soon giving place to longer lines nearly parallel, and these in their turn being replaced by quite regular strokes. Exercises are next introduced which aim at associating the visual and muscular—tactile sensations with the sound of letters. Two of the sandpaper letters are given to the pupil and he is told their names. He is shown, if necessary, the direction in which to trace them and is then allowed to pass his index finger over them repeatedly. He finds pleasure in doing this with his eyes closed. Lessons based on Séguin's three periods then help to associate definitely the sounds of the letters with the sensations of sight, touch and muscles. At the conclusion of such a lesson the child should be able to answer correctly the question, "What is this?" In teaching the consonants only the *sounds* are given and they are united with vowels at once. It is not necessary to teach all the vowels before beginning with consonants. In addition to the cards containing single letters, larger cards are used, each containing several letters grouped according to contrasted or analogous forms.

By learning each consonant in association with vowels the child, has, of course, learned syllables, and when he knows a few letters of each kind he is ready for exercises in the composition of words. He is now provided with a box containing four copies of the alphabet, the letters being of the same form and size as those already used, but cut out of cardboard and not mounted: they can thus be more usefully handled and more easily placed together. The box contains a special compartment for the four copies of each letter, so that the pupil can readily find those he requires. It is his duty to replace them correctly at the end of the lesson. The directress pronounces very clearly, several times, such a word as *mama,* emphasising the *m* sound. Almost always the child, with an impulsive movement, seizes the *m* and lays it on the table. *Ma-ma* is then repeated, and the child places an *a* near the *m*: and similarly for the second syllable. He has composed a word, but there remains the greater difficulty of reading it. The directress sits beside him "urging him to read, and reading the word with him once or twice, always pronouncing very distinctly." Her function as helper is here very strongly op-

erative. Soon the child triumphs over this difficulty, other words are taught similarly and progress is rapid. The importance of these exercises, Dr. Montessori points out, is very complex. The child analyses, perfects, fixes his own spoken language, placing an object in correspondence to every sound which he utters. The composition of the word furnishes him with substantial proof of the necessity for clear and forceful enunciation. The exercise, thus followed, associates the sound which is heard with the graphic sign which represents it, and lays a most solid foundation for accurate and perfect spelling.[42] As soon as one word is learned the letters used are returned by the child to their respective compartments. Dr. Montessori points out that each lesson supplies three sets of exercises which help to fix the desired associations: first, there are those of the comparison and selection of the required letters, secondly those during which the word is composed, and thirdly those involved in correctly replacing the letters in their compartments. In all this the intellectual powers are clearly being developed. The child *thinks* about the problems involved, and though helped a good deal his spontaneity is not interfered with unduly. One day a little boy of four was found running about on the terrace saying repeatedly, "To make Zaira, I must have z-a-i-r-a."

So far the child has not written, though he has learned the two sets of movements necessary—those actually involved in forming the letters and those required in the manipulation of the pen or pencil. Usually no effort is made, or is necessary, to induce him to write. The average child will "come into his full power by way of a spontaneous explosion into writing." Indeed, it is often necessary to arrange judiciously that this "explosion" shall not be too violent: and Dr. Montessori gives some guiding hints in regard to this important matter. She writes very eloquently of the children's glowing joy in their new-found powers. After the first spontaneous burst their progress is very rapid and they can very soon write all the words they know. Some of her pupils have learned to write their first words at the early age of three-and-a-half years. The period that elapses between the first preparatory exercises and the writing of the first word ranges for the average child of four, from four to six weeks; and for the child of five it is shorter. The form of the writing is beautifully round and flowing, resembling very closely the carefully made cardboard script letters with which they performed their preparatory exercises.

The child, as we have seen, pronounces or "reads" the word he composes. This process must not, however, be confused with reading proper. In the first case he is simply *verifying* the word he has formed, is translating signs into sounds as he had previously translated sounds into signs. Reading proper is "the interpretation of an idea from the written signs." The child first *reads* in the true sense when, not having heard a word pronounced, he recognises it when formed from the cardboard letters, pronounces it, and knows its meaning. He must recognise the word as a whole and associate it with what it represents. "The intervention of a superior work of the intellect is necessary if he is to read": and hence she claims that reading must be taught after writing. Moreover, it is clear that the method of teaching writing greatly facilitates the task of learning to read. For the teaching of reading in the proper sense of the term Dr. Montessori writes in large clear script on cards or slips of writing paper some well-known words which have been frequently pronounced by the children. Usually they are names of toys or other objects in the room. At first the object is placed near the child to help his interpretation of the word to be read. No question arises as to the difficulty of the words first used, as the child has learned through his composition of words to name the sounds composing all those of ordinary difficulty. One word is presented to the pupil who slowly names its component sounds. If all are correctly named he is urged to pronounce them more rapidly, and still more rapidly, until in his phonetic language he finds himself pronouncing the whole word, and its meaning bursts upon his consciousness: he assumes an air of great satisfaction as if he had recognised a friend. He then places the card bearing the word under the object whose name it is, and the lesson is finished. Numerous words are learned in this way in a surprisingly short time. Later they play a most interesting game. The names of the many toys are written on cards which are folded and placed in a basket. The pupils then select folded cards in turn and take them to their seats where they read them mentally. Then each goes to the directress in turn, presents his card, pronounces the name upon it, and if correct he is allowed to have the corresponding toy to play with as long as he pleases. After a time, however, Dr. Montessori's pupils refused to accept the toys, preferring to continue the choosing and reading of the folded cards! Their desire for knowledge of words was amazing. So the toys were put away and *hundreds* of written slips containing names of persons, places, things, colours and qualities were placed in open boxes from which the children could take them when they wished. No mere childish inconstancy was displayed here: each child read right through the contents of a box before proceeding to another. Later she was about to teach them to read ordinary print, but they had forestalled her! They had learned to read both plain and Gothic print on a wall calendar. Friends who had noted the children's ability to read print presented them with beautifully illustrated books containing simple fairy stories. But although they could read them they did not understand them, as Dr. Montessori proved by tests. She stopped the reading from books and waited until the real meaning of words, of language, of composition came spontaneously. One day four children rose at the same time and joyously wrote phrases on the blackboard expressing their gladness that the garden had begun to bloom. She then realised it was time to begin the reading of phrases. Following the clue afforded by the four pupils, she wrote on the blackboard, "Do you love me?" The children read it aloud slowly, remained silent a moment as if thinking, and then cried out, "Yes! Yes!" Many other phrases and sentences were written on the board and were all understood. Later she wrote somewhat long directions on cards and handed them to the pupils, who were soon

able to understand and carry out the orders. In this way intelligent reading was taught in a remarkably short time.

In the first of her two chapters on the teaching of writing and reading Dr. Montessori discusses at considerable length the theory and practice of Itard and Séguin. Her adverse criticism of the latter's ideas is based on the account of his work given in his earlier book written in 1846. Through misunderstanding or carelessness she misrepresents him in at least one essential matter. "We have Séguin," she says, "teaching geometry in order to teach a child to write, and making the child's mind exert itself to follow geometrical abstractions only to come down to the simple effort of drawing a printed *D*."[43] Here she is quite wrong. Séguin did not teach geometry or devote any attention to its abstractions before the formation of letters *evolved.* He taught *form,* which he analysed into certain basic types, among these being circles, squares, triangles, and other geometrical figures. He taught his idiots to *draw* these forms. Later he taught them to draw various combinations of straight and curved lines, and from this the *drawing* of letters was evolved, and hence writing. He came no nearer to teaching geometry for this purpose than does Dr. Montessori, whose pupils have considerable practice in touching and placing geometrical insets before they proceed to learn writing.

Aided by her long scientific observation and teaching of normal children, she has, in regard alike to principle and technique, progressed considerably beyond the position reached by the great pioneer who inspired her. But there are some matters of both theory and practice in regard to which her indebtedness to him is obvious. Her important principle of preparing for writing or other work "by means of repeated exercises not in the work itself" was also Séguin's principle. According to him, before we begin the teaching of drawing and writing "we have given to their hands the firmness and the precision necessary to draw and to write."[44] Again he says, "Contrarily to school practice, and agreeably to nature, our letters are to be written before being read."[45] Almost an echo is her "Contrary to the usually accepted idea, writing precedes reading."[46] Séguin used letters cut out of cardboard as she does, and "small cards, bearers of a single syllable or word; the large cards showing whole series of the same," for reading. Like her, he grouped letters according to contrasts and analogies and taught reading by whole words. Finally her method of associating sounds with visual, tactile and muscular sensations is admittedly based upon his.

THE DIDACTIC APPARATUS

The Montessori didactic apparatus, which provides for the training of all the senses except taste and smell,[47] consists of twenty-six sets varying considerably in purpose and construction. She began her work in the Children's Houses by allowing the pupils to practise "contemporaneously with the most varied exercises": but experience showed that there were five grades or stages for the proper presentation of the material. In all these grades training, apart from the special apparatus, is given through "exercises of practical life." In the first grade this consists in teaching the child to move little chairs silently. Two sets of the apparatus are found especially suitable at this stage. The first consists of ten frames to each of which are attached two pieces of cloth or leather which can be fastened down the middle by means of buttons, hooks, laces, ribbons, or automatic fasteners. By the use of these the child develops muscular power and learns the movements necessary for dressing and undressing. The second set used now consists of three solid blocks of wood, each containing ten wooden cylinders fitting exactly into holes in the block, and provided with brass or wooden tops for holding with the fingers. Each piece resembles a chemist's set of weights. In the first block the cylinders are all of equal height but differ in diameter; in the second the diameters are equal while the heights vary; in the third both height and diameter vary. The child takes all the cylinders out of the block, scatters them on the table, and then replaces them. The blocks are not all of the same difficulty and should be used in the above order unless a child clearly desires to use them in another order. By playing with these insets the pupil acquires experience of size and learns to distinguish objects according to height and thickness. All errors are revealed by the apparatus.

In the second grade the exercises in practical life include rising and being seated in silence and walking on a chalk line. The special apparatus consists of the set of cubes, the Big or Broad Stair and the Long Stair. There are ten rose-coloured cubes varying from 10 cm. to 1 cm. side, and the child has to build these regularly into a tower, beginning with the largest. Here he has to distinguish larger and smaller objects as they lie about at different distances. The Big Stair is built up by the child with ten rectangular prisms, 20 cm. long and with bases ranging from 10 cm. to 1 cm. This exercise teaches him to distinguish thickness and thinness. The Long Stair is constructed with ten rectangular rods, each 3 cm. thick, varying in length from a metre to a decimetre. The decimetre lengths on all rods are painted alternately red and blue. Beginning with the longest, and arranging corresponding colours together, the rods have to be built up to make a stair. This difficult exercise leads to an appreciation of length and is also of use in teaching arithmetic. In these exercises more difficult movements and greater muscular effort are involved; and as the apparatus does not so readily indicate errors the eye has to do more work than in the first grade. At this stage the child is capable of fixing his attention upon and of being interested in the tactile and thermic stimuli. Dr. Montessori is fully aware that biologically touch precedes sight, but she found that tactile stimuli did not *attract attention* as early as the visual. She therefore does not present the former until the education of attention begins. Training the thermic sense makes touch more acute. The hands are placed in basins of water of widely differing temperatures, thus using the principle of contrast. Later the differences of temperature are graded, a set of bowls being used. There follows practice in the correct method of touching surfaces with the finger tips, and materials of many kinds are used.

In all the touch exercises the eyes are closed. Two pieces of special apparatus are also used; one being a rectangular board half of which is polished or covered with smooth paper and half covered with sandpaper. At this period also a beginning is made in the training of the colour sense. Sometimes pieces of stuff or wool balls are used for this purpose; but formal didactic material has been arranged, consisting of sixty-four tablets wound with wool or silk, and having raised ends to keep the coloured stuff off the table. The children are taught to handle the tablets at the ends only. There are eight gradations of tint for each of the eight colours, black (ranging through greys to white), red, orange, yellow, green, blue, violet and brown. A beginning is made by the child arranging strongly contrasting colours like red, blue, and yellow in corresponding pairs, Itard's and Séguin's principle of proceeding from wide to narrow differences being followed. The contrasts gradually become less striking as more colours and shades are introduced, until at last the child can distinguish delicate differences. Later he learns to grade the tints of all the colours and acquires the power of going some distance to obtain a tablet of corresponding shade to one shown him.

In the third grade the lessons in practical life enable the children to wash, dress and undress themselves, dust tables and handle various objects. They are also exercised in the discrimination of more delicate gradations in the stimuli already experienced, their spontaneity being allowed free play. Stimuli for the sense of hearing and for the baric sense are now presented. In the training of the former sense the principle of spontaneity cannot be relied upon: the teacher has to do a great deal for the children. As in Séguin's practice, the first essential here is the securing of silence and immobility before the lessons begin. Exercises are then arranged to enable the pupils to distinguish *noise* from *sound* and to discern the differences among noises and among sounds. For the former small boxes containing pebbles, sand, and other substances are used, the boxes being shaken and differences distinguished: for the latter Pizzoli's series of little whistles can be used. A double series of thirteen bells gave no valuable results, as the children could not strike the corresponding bells with equal force. "I believe," confesses Dr. Montessori, "that the best results can be obtained with the primitive means employed by Itard in 1805. He used the drum and the bell."[48] Here again the principle of progress from wide to narrow differences rules. The apparatus for the training of the sense of weight consists of three tablets of the same size made of wistaria, walnut, and pine, and weighing 24, 18 and 12 grammes respectively. They are perfectly smooth so as to produce no distraction through touch. The child places one in each palm at the base of the fingers, and moving his hands gently up and down while the eyes are closed, decides which is heavier: the third is similarly compared with the lighter. After a time the up-and-down movement of the hand should become hardly noticeable. There follows the training of the stereognostic sense which "leads to the recognition of objects through feeling, that is through the simultaneous help of the tactile and muscular sense." For this Froebel's bricks and cubes are first used. By handling without the aid of sight the pupil has to arrange the cubes on one side and the bricks on the other. Various other objects, including toys, balls and coins are used later. During this stage the child is being trained to appreciate form, and for this purpose the apparatus is elaborate. It consists of a large number of geometrical shapes which can be fitted exactly into corresponding slots or spaces. "The idea of these insets goes back to Itard and was also applied by Séguin."[49] These insets are contained in frames which are kept in rectangular trays. They are taken from their frames and scattered on a table. They are carefully examined by sight, touch and muscular sense, and then have to be placed correctly in their frames. The pupil passes his index finger along the edges of the contrasting shapes and their spaces, and thus visual, tactual and muscular impressions are associated. Later three sets of cards are used: on the first are pasted geometrical figures in blue paper corresponding exactly with the insets; on the second are outlines of the same figures in blue paper a centimetre wide; on the third their outlines in thin lines. The child has to learn to recognise the correspondence between these three sets of figures and the insets and to prove his having done so by placing an inset over each figure correctly. Thus he gradually becomes able to recognise the representation of form by simple lines.

In the fourth grade the children learn to perform various domestic duties and to attend to the more minute details of personal toilet. Through rhythmic exercises they learn to walk with perfect freedom and balance, and they practise spontaneously all the exercises referred to above. Prominence is given to music at this stage, both voice and instruments being used to teach them to distinguish notes. The bells already referred to are used here, but Dr. Montessori believes that "simple and primitive instruments are the ones best adapted to the awakening of music in the soul of the little child," and she notes the valuable "educational disciplinary effect" of rhythmical tunes. It is at this period as a rule that the child practises tracing and filling in with pencil the geometrical outlines preparatory to writing, and that he learns to recognise the sandpaper letters by touch. Now also he learns to count the pieces of apparatus and to arrange the insets to make interesting designs. Séguin's plan is here used for associating numbers with figures by placing the correct number of coloured counters under the figures on the table.

In the fifth and last stage of the child's stay in a Montessori school he continues spontaneously all the foregoing exercises, many of which may be made more complex as he grows in proficiency. The various rhythmic exercises increase considerably in complexity. In design he is introduced to the use of water colours, and free drawing from nature is also practised. During this stage he progresses in writing, reading and simple arithmetic. "The children at this stage present most interesting differences of development. They fairly *run* towards instruction, and order their *intellectual growth* in a way that is remarkable." It must be noted that these five grades or stages represent no definite divisions of time, nor do they involve any classifica-

tion of the children. It is simply an observed fact that as a rule the child in relation to the didactic materials passes through such stages.

When Dr. Montessori began her educational work with idiots she made use of much of the apparatus described by Itard and Séguin, while most of that she devised herself was based on theirs. "Guided by the work of these two men, I had manufactured a great variety of didactic material,"[50] she writes; and later, "This belief that we must act upon the spirit served as a sort of *secret key,* opening to me the long series of didactic experiments so wonderfully analysed by Edward Séguin."[51] When, however, she commenced to teach normal children she found that modifications and extensions were necessary, and she began to think about the principles which should determine these. As often in her career, her close and sympathetic observation of children led her to the discovery of such important principles. She observed that they became so completely absorbed in their spontaneous exercises with certain pieces of apparatus that they did not notice very deliberate attempts—made as experiments—to distract their attention. They continued to repeat the exercises as often as forty times. This did not happen with other apparatus, some of which, indeed, was not often spontaneously used. This polarisation of attention and repetition of the exercise obviously offered means of judging the value of didactic material. On this principle Dr. Montessori discarded several items (which are now kept in a museum cupboard), modified others, and added new pieces that could pass the great test. A valuable secondary principle is closely allied to the first: the polarisation and repetition do not as a rule take place unless the didactic apparatus controls errors: unless it either automatically reveals the child's errors, as in the case of the cylindrical solid insets and the geometrical forms; or by its exact and symmetrical completed structure helps the eye to perceive mistakes, as in the case of the tower of cubes. Through prolonged and close study and observation, guided by these principles, she has gradually organised her "prepared environment" in harmony with the spontaneous manifestations of childhood. She believes that still more suitable apparatus will be evolved in time through the use of more detailed experiment than her own. Of the latter she says: "This long, occult experiment—suggested to me, as I have already said, by Itard and Séguin—is, in fact, my initial contribution to education. All this preparatory work has served for the determination of the method now well known, but it is also the key to its continuation."[52] Educators will await with interest the results of this continuation, more especially in its application to the education of older children.

. . . . .

In all that has been said in the foregoing pages in regard to the inspiration and guidance which Dr. Montessori has received from Itard and Séguin there has been no intention of detracting from the value of her original contribution to the theory and practice of education. It is a very great contribution. It has attracted the attention of educators in all parts of the world, bringing a challenge to some, an incentive to others, inspiration to many and suggestion to all. Experience and experiment may later prove that much of her work, as of that of all other pioneers of education, possesses only transitory significance. But it may well be that her fundamental principles will stand the tests of all time.

Notes

1. *The Montessori Method*, p. 31.

2. *Ibid.*

3. *Ibid.*, p. 32.

4. *Op. cit.*, p. 33.

5. *Trevisini*, 1892

6. *Montessori, op. cit.*, pp. 2 and 3.

7. *Ibid.*, p. 42.

8. *Ibid.*, pp. 33 and 34.

9. *Op. cit.*, p. 34.

10. *Ibid.*

11. *Op. cit.*, p. 36.

12. *Op. cit.*, pp. 41 and 42.

13. *Op. cit.*, p. 38.

14. *Op. cit.*, pp. 45 and 46.

15. *From Locke to Montessori*, 1917, p. 134.

16. *From Locke to Montessori*, 1917, p. 180.

17. *The Montessori Method*, pp. 105 and 106. In all our quotations from Dr. Montessori, the *italics* are hers.

18. *Ibid.*, 87 and 88.

19. *The Montessori Method*, pp. 104 and 105.

20. *Ibid*, p. 228.

21. *Ibid*, p. 230.

22. Quoted by C. A. Claremont, "Has Dr. Montessori made a true contribution to science?" Essay published 1920.

23. Pp. 70 and 71.

24. *The Montessori Method*, p. 104.

25. *The Advanced Montessori Method*, Vol. I., pp. 70 and 72.

26. *The Advanced Montessori Method*, Vol. I., p. 170.

27. *Education: Its Data and First Principles*, 1920, p. 174.

28. *The Montessori Method*, p. 87.

29. *The Montessori Method*, p. 104.

30. *Ibid*, p. 374.

31. *The Montessori Method*, p. 153.

32. Chapter III., p. 146.

33. *Idiocy*, etc., p. 143.

34. *The Montessori Method*, p. 138.

35. *From Locke to Montessori*, p. 157.

36. Vide *The Montessori Method*, pp. 207, 208 and 342. On page 208 she clearly expresses her appreciation of the educational value of rhythm. A whole chapter of *The Advanced Montessori Method* is devoted to this subject—Chapter IV., Vol. II.

37. *The Montessori Method*, p. 173.

38. *The Montessori Method*, pp. 222 and 223. On the former page there is a simple diagram illustrating centripetal and centrifugal transmission.

39. *Ibid*, p. 216.

40. *The Montessori Method*, pp. 178 and 179.

41. *The Montessori Method*, p. 263.

42. *The Montessori Method*, pp. 283 and 284. It will be remembered that the Italian language is almost purely phonetic.

43. *The Montessori Method*, p. 256.

44. *Idiocy*, etc., p. 121.

45. *Ibid*, p. 123.

46. *The Montessori Method*, p. 296.

47. With regard to these two senses she says: "This phase of sense education is most difficult, and I have not as yet had any satisfactory results to record." *Op. cit.*, p. 190.

48. *The Montessori Method*, p. 205.

49. *Ibid*, p. 196.

50. *The Montessori Method*, p. 36.

51. *Ibid*, p. 37.

52. *The Advanced Montessori Method*, p. 81.

Mandel Sherman (essay date 1940)

SOURCE: A review of *The Secret of Childhood*, in *The American Journal of Sociology*, Vol. XLVI, No. 1, July, 1940, pp. 117-18.

[In the following essay, Sherman reviews Montessori's The Secret of Childhood, *noting that the book presents "many good, common-sense deductions and suggestions" and is recommended reading for parents but may be rather simplistic for educators and theorists.]*

This book [*The Secret of Childhood*] presents an extremely well-written, clear description of those educational problems of the young child which have always been of interest to Miss Montessori. Although the material is not new and might well have been written years ago, the book contains many good, common-sense deductions and suggestions. The author continually emphasizes the need for the consideration of children as individuals who have definite psychological functions which can be studied only by sympathetic observers. She makes an interesting point when she states that most adults study children in accordance with their own viewpoints and consider children merely as miniature reflections of adults. Instead, she considers adults as reflections of children. She emphasizes especially the importance of genetic psychology.

There is one inherent difficulty in evaluating a book which is translated, namely, the difficulty of understanding the peculiar terms which are employed. For example, the author mentions many times that adults should be careful in studying the spiritual development of the child and his soul. Whether this reflects the author's archaic knowledge of psychology or whether it is merely an idiomatic expression employed in Italian, the reviewer does not know. She employs many religious ideas and symbols in her explanation of child behavior, and this again may be due to expressions of the culture in which the author lives rather than an indication of her psychological viewpoints. On page 131 she states, "That which the teacher must seek is to be able to see the child as Jesus saw him. It is with this endeavor, thus defined and delimited, that we wish to deal." The reviewer knows of books written sometime during the middle of the nineteenth century in which ideas and attitudes of this type were used, but they would not be considered as scientific treatises.

In general, the book will make excellent reading for many parents, especially those who have little knowledge of the recent work in the fields of psychology and child development. The serious student or research worker in the fields of psychology and education will be rather intolerant of the author because of the elementary way in which the material is presented and because of the peculiar expressions which she uses.

J. McV. Hunt (essay date 1964)

SOURCE: An introduction to *The Montessori Method,* by Maria Montessori, Schocken Books, 1964, pp. xi-xxxix.

[*In the following introduction to a later English translation of Montessori's* The Montessori Method, *Hunt remarks on the relevance of Montessori's theories in schools of the second half of the twentieth century and reviews her elemental beliefs.*]

The enlightened self-interest that provided the first *Casa dei Bambini* in the slum tenements of Rome will find a responsive note today. Modern administrators and educators are faced with vandalism and aimless violence among economically and culturally deprived children who reject and are rejected by the traditional school system. In offering Dr. Montessori space for the new enterprise, the director of the Roman Association for Good Building and the owners of the buildings in the San Lorenzo district were motivated in large part by the hope that keeping the unruly young children, usually left alone during the day by their working parents, in something like a school would prevent vandalism and save damage to their property.

It is 70 years since Montessori became interested, while yet a medical student serving as an intern in the psychiatric clinic of Rome, in the "idiot children" then housed in the insane asylums. It is 66 years since she began the work with mentally deficient children that led her to examine Jean Itard's (1801) attempts at educating the "wild boy of Aveyron" and to utilize the materials and methods devised by Edouard Séguin (1844, 1866) for educating the mentally deficient children. It is 57 years since she extended her modified Séguin-approach in education of retarded children to the education of normal young children in the first *Casa dei Bambini,* or "Homes of Children" as Dorothy Canfield Fisher translated the term.

According to the reports (Fisher 1912, Stevens 1913), Montessori's success far surpassed her sponsors' fondest hopes, if not also hers. Not only was vandalism prevented, but these children, three to seven years old, became avid pupils. Not only did they learn "cleanliness," "manners," "some grace in action," and "something about proper diet," but they became acquainted with animals and plants and with the manual arts. They got both sensory and motor training with the didactic apparatus and even learned the basic symbolic skills of counting, reading, and writing, often before they were five years old. People were impressed. When, in 1909, Montessori published her **Scientific Pedagogy as Applied to Child Education in the Children's Houses,** people from all over the world beat Emersonian paths to her door and pressed her to communicate her methods to others.

Americans were among the first to become interested, and their interest rapidly exploded into a social movement. Perhaps the explosion of interest and its waning is best illustrated by rates of publication about Montessori's work. Jenny Merrill first described Montessori's work in the December, 1909, and March, 1910, issues of the *Kindergarten Primary Magazine.* The year 1911 brought six reports of Montessori's work. The number rose to 54 in 1912, and then jumped to a maximum of 76 in 1913. Then the explosion appears to have rapidly subsided: in 1914 the number of publications declined to 55; they dwindled to 15 in 1915, to eight in 1917, and amounted to less than five a year thereafter.

Why this sudden explosion of interest? Why the equally sudden fall? Why revisit today what may appear from such evidence to have been a mere fad in American education? What concerns does such a revisit arouse? These are the issues I would like to discuss in introducing this new edition of **The Montessori Method.**

WHY THE EXPLOSION OF INTEREST

A definitive accounting for this explosion of interest in Montessori's work is hardly possible, but certain factors help to explain it. Americans had been primed to hope for progress with all kinds of problems. Winning the West had encouraged such hope. The "muck-rakers" had been uncovering, in article after article on "the shame of the cities" in *McClure's Magazine,* the seamy side of the human urban condition. American excitement about reform, recently fostered by the progressive Republicanism of Theodore Roosevelt, was still high. Many people, moreover, had become accustomed to see in children the chief hope of fundamental reform. This hope had been fostered by a half-century of activity of the Froebel Society, by nearly a quarter-century of G. Stanley Hall's child-study movement, and by John Dewey's (1900, 1902) attempts—inspired chiefly by the "reform Darwinism" of Lester F. Ward and Albion Small (Cremin, 1962)—to make that age-old institution the school an instrument of progress and social reform.

Reports of Montessori's success in the "Houses of Children" made her pedagogic methods look to many of the most progressive-minded like the way to a new day, or like the most rapid route yet uncovered to fundamental reform. Many of these progressive-minded people who visited Montessori or became interested in her work had, like Alexander Graham Bell, tremendous prestige; some of them, like McClure, controlled major sources of mass communication; others, like Dorothy Canfield Fisher (1912) and Ellen Yale Stevens (1913), had facile pens. They got the news out fast, and they spread it wide. These factors help explain the explosion of interest.

But why did the interest subside almost as rapidly as it exploded? Perhaps it failed, at least in part, because the Dottoressa rejected McClure's offer in 1913 to build her an institution in America. On the other hand, her rejection may merely have saved her a painful defeat.

Conceptions of nature and of how to deal with any problem may fail either because they run counter to the facts of empirical observation or because they run counter to other conceptions which are somehow better anchored in the beliefs of men at a given time, or because of some combination of these two. On the side of empirical observation, the impressions of Montessori's great educational success reported by American writers lent support to the validity of her conceptions. Some of these people should have been good observers; they included, for instance, such psychologists as Dorothy Canfield Fisher (who is better known for her novels), Arnold and Beatrice Gesell, Joseph Peterson, Howard C. Warren, and Lightner Witmer (see Donahue, 1962, for their publications). However, various conceptions of Montessori ran into almost head-on dissonance with conceptions which, from a variety of communicative influences, were becoming dominant in the minds of those Americans who became most influential. Most of Montessori's support had come from the elite of the political and educational progressives and through popular magazines; it had not come from those formulating the new psychological theories nor from those formulating the philosophy of education. Although Montessori got support from Howard C. Warren (1912), then president of the American Psychological Association, and from Lightner Witmer (1914), founder of the first Psychological Clinic at the University of Pennsylvania, she failed to get support from those psychologists of the functional school or of the emerging behavioristic school whose conceptions were shortly to become dominant. With such emerging theories, with the conceptions of the intelligence-testing movement, and with the psychoanalytic theory of psychosexual development, then just beginning to get a foothold in America following Freud's visit of 1909 at the invitation of G. Stanley Hall, Montessori's notions were too dissonant to hold their own.

CONCEPTIONS DISSONANT WITH MONTESSORI'S

These dissonant conceptions need to be stated because it is in them that we have been seeing radical changes since World War II. Some of them were still relatively inexplicit at the time; they did not figure in the published criticisms of Montessori's pedagogy. Others were explicit; they did figure in the criticisms.

First, the notion that school experience for three- and four-year-olds could be significantly important for later development was deprecated. For those who thought behavior controlled by conscious intentions, the fact that such early experiences would seldom be recalled seemed to mean that they could have no influence. For those who followed the conservative Darwinism of Herbert Spencer and William Graham Sumner, the development of the individual organism was supposed to be predetermined by heredity. I shall return to give this belief special attention. For those giving credence to the new psychoanalytic theory of psychosexual development, it was the fate of the instinctual modes of pleasure-striving that was supposed to matter, not cognitive development. Moreover, for tax-payers the notion of extending the age for schooling down to three years looked like a highly unnecessary addition to the burden of school taxes. Worse, it looked to some like an infringement on the functions and rights of the family.

Second, the belief in fixed intelligence, later a basic assumption of the intelligence-testing movement, was among those little noted at the time. This notion has roots in Darwin's theory of evolution by natural selection (see Hunt, 1961, pp. 10ff). Americans had absorbed the notion of natural selection about a decade after the Civil War from John Fiske's *Outlines of Cosmic Philosophy* and from Herbert Spencer's *Synthetic Philosophy.* Although this conception of evolution was optimistic about progress, the characteristics of an individual organism or person were seen as fixed by his heredity. The assumption of fixed intelligence is but a special case of this more general view. This assumption came into American psychological thought via J. McKeen Cattell, who was a student of Darwin's younger cousin, Francis Galton, and via G. Stanley Hall, whose students at Clark University established the mental-testing movement. The notion was widely disseminated among educators as "the constant I.Q." (see Hunt, 1961, ch. 2). Montessori's conception of mental retardation as a defect calling for pedagogical treatment was basically dissonant with this notion. Thus, with her intellectual roots in the work of Itard and Séguin, she was definitely out of step with one of the central notions rapidly becoming dominant in the educational psychology of America.

Third, the belief in predetermined development. This also figured but slightly in the published criticisms of Montessori's method. This belief, like the belief in fixed intelligence, has roots in Darwin's theory of evolution by natural selection. It was also implicit in the notion that "ontogeny recapitulates phylogeny," that is, that each individual in its development goes through the same stages that the species goes through in its evolution. Belief in recapitulation was at the heart of G. Stanley Hall's developmental psychology. He apparently communicated it to all of his students but John Dewey, and these included such important figures in the testing movement as Goddard, Kuhlmann, and Terman, as well as Arnold Gesell, who gave the developmental psychology of the 1920's and 1930's its normative character. Just as Montessori was making her first trip to America, the earliest studies showing the evanescence of the effects of practice were coming out. They appeared to imply that teaching children reading, writing, and counting before they were about eight years old was, at best, a waste of time and, as Kilpatrick (1914) noted, might possibly be harmful. Here again, Montessori was out of step with the conceptual movements in psychology.

Fourth, the belief that *all* behavior is motivated by instincts or by painful stimuli, homeostatic needs, and sex, or by acquired drives based on these. When Montessori was opening the Houses of Children, William McDougall (1908) was writing the *Social Psychology* that disseminated in America the English vogue of attributing behavior to inborn instincts. It rapidly became popular, and many educational psychologists advocated that teachers arrange to associate the content of each lesson with one of the instincts listed by McDougall. At very nearly the same time, the students of animal learning, following C. Lloyd Morgan (1894) in Britain and Edward L. Thorndike (1898) in the United States, were discovering that to elicit specified activities from animal subjects, it was helpful, if not necessary, to induce these activities with painful stimulation or such homeostatic needs as hunger or thirst. The animal then acted to eliminate these distressing drive-stimuli. In Austria, during the same period, Freud (1900) was developing his drive theory and popularizing the statement that "all behavior is motivated." In this statement, Freud commonly left implicit: "by wishes originating in physiological stimuli or homeostatic needs or pain" (see Freud, 1915). According to this doctrine, the aim of all behavior is to reduce or to eliminate excitement from such sources, and implicit in it is the point that animals and children will become quiescent in the absence of such motivation (see Hunt, 1963a). These conceptions of motivation were just emerging as the dominant view when popular interest in Montessori's work exploded. To those who held any version of such a view of motivation, Montessori's notion of basing her method of education upon "children's spontaneous interest in learning" must have appeared to be as nonsensical as perpetual motion. Moreover, for these people Montessori's claim that her materials were intrinsically interesting to children must have seemed too obviously false to be worth empirical investigation.

Fifth, the belief that the response side of the reflex arc is the one essential in education. This notion had roots in the psychological theorizing of the past. G. Stanley Hall had popularized his aphorism that, "the mind of man is handmade." In Britain, C. Lloyd Morgan (1894) had almost eliminated mind as a concept by showing how loose was the analogical reasoning in imputing to animal subjects the same conscious processes human beings can report. Morgan's work, which is a part of a stream of European mechanistic thought about living organisms that can be traced back to Descartes, set the stage for E. L. Thorndike's (1898) studies of problem-solving in animals. Thorndike's interpretation replaced *mind* with connections between stimuli and responses. The stream flowed on into the behavioristic revolt, led by John B. Watson (1914), which replaced *consciousness* with *behavior* as the subject-matter of psychology. Methodologically, of course, the observables *are limited to* the situation and the organism's activities. These were dubbed stimuli and responses. Stimulus-response theory, however, went further to limit the function of the brain to essentially static connections between stimuli and responses after an analogy with that dramatic new invention, the telephone switchboard. Moreover, it was the response side which supplied the evidence of learning. As a consequence, interest in perception and central processes suffered. With such a view emerging into dominance, it is hardly surprising that Montessori's emphasis on sensory training met all too often with contempt. It is not surprising that Montessori was characterized by Kilpatrick (1914), her most articulate critic, as representing theory more than half-a-century behind the times. Furthermore, Montessori described her "education of the senses" with the graded "didactic materials" as having, "as its aim, the refinement of differential perception of stimuli." This is the language of the faculty psychology which Thorndike and Woodworth (1901) had discredited by their epochal experiments on the transfer of training. Here again, Montessori was out of step with the *Zeitgeist.*

Sixth—and this is not a theoretical conception—there is the traditional desire of teachers for an orderly classroom and for control of the educational process. The influence of Rousseau, Pestalozzi, and Froebel had already helped to call into question this traditional desire for control. Pestalozzi had compared children to plants unfolding from within and requiring only a favorable and cultivated environment for their growth. Froebel wrote in similar fashion. In Froebel's kindergartens, however, the teacher continued to be at the center of the stage (see Fisher, 1912). In the Houses of Children, on the other hand, the lock-step of education was almost completely broken. Each individual child had a stage of his own where the didactic materials were at the center of his attention. The role of the teacher was limited to that of observer-helper of the children in their spontaneous efforts to cope with the didactic materials. One gleans that this demotion was irritating to many teachers with other than Montessori training and indoctrination, and I believe this irritation persists among teachers today.

Perhaps Montessori was unfortunate to have as her chief critic William Heard Kilpatrick (1914). Kilpatrick was an eloquent lecturer at Teachers College, where he was known as the "million-dollar professor." In 1913, at the height of the enthusiasm for Montessori's work, it was Kilpatrick who appeared before the annual meeting of the International Kindergarten Union to point out that, except for her Houses of Children, Montessori's ideas about education were not new. Further, he considered her to belong in the Rousseau-Pestalozzi-Froebel tradition with beliefs in the educational process as an unfolding of what was present at birth, and in liberty as a necessary condition for this unfolding in faculties of the mind and in sense-training. Since these beliefs had had to be "strictly revised to square with modern conceptions," he felt "compelled to say that in the content of her doctrine, she belongs to the midnineteenth century, some fifty years behind the present development of educational theory" (Kilpatrick, 1914, pp. 62-63).

Kilpatrick also compared Montessori with his guiding light, John Dewey. He wrote: "The two have many things in common. Both have organized experimental schools; both have emphasized the freedom, self-activity, and self-education of the child; both have made large use of 'practical life' activities. . . . There are however wide differences. For the earliest education, Madame Montessori provides a set of mechanically simple devices. These in large measure do the teaching. A simple procedure embodied in definite, tangible apparatus is a powerful incentive to popular interest. Professor Dewey could not secure the education which he sought in so simple a fashion. Madame Montessori was able to do so only because she had a much narrower conception of education, and because she could hold to an untenable theory as to the value of formal and systematic sense-training. Madame Montessori centered much of her effort upon devising more satisfactory methods of teaching reading and writing, utilizing thereto in masterly fashion the phonetic character of the Italian language. Professor Dewey, while recognizing the duty of the school to teach these arts, feels that early emphasis should rather be placed upon activities more vital to child-life which should at the same time lead toward the mastery of our complex social environment. . . . Madame Montessori hoped to remake pedagogy; but her idea of pedagogy is much narrower than is Professor Dewey's idea of education. His conception of the nature of the thinking process, together with his doctrines of interest and of education as life—not simply a preparation for life—include all that is valid in Madame Montessori's doctrines of liberty and sense-training, afford the criteria for correcting her errors, and besides, go vastly further in the construction of the educational method" (Kilpatrick, 1914, pp. 63-66).

One can make this comparison in another way. Montessori was reforming pedagogy and basing her innovations on her own clinical observations of children, first those mentally retarded and then those culturally deprived who participated in the Houses of Children. Dewey (1897), on the other hand, was attempting to foster social reform in the schools, and he based his attempt, as already noted, on the reformed Darwinism of Lester F. Ward and Albion Small, to be contrasted with the conservative Darwinism of Herbert Spencer and Herbert Graham Sumner. Dewey's approach was part of that progressive movement in post-Civil War America that reached its peak during the 1890's. Kilpatrick's comparison was effective. His little book circulated widely among teachers and educators. It was a wet blanket on the fire of enthusiasm for Montessori's work.

WHY REVISIT MONTESSORI TODAY

All this was a half-century ago, when the beliefs of Stimulus-response theory, the intelligence testers, and psychoanalysis were becoming dominant. They remained dominant for the period between the two World Wars and through World War II. Stimulus-response methodology was highly productive of observational evidence. Ironically, it is this evidence from S-R methodology which has been the undoing of the beliefs dominant in psychological theory, even some of those central to S-R theory. Moreover, it is this evidence from S-R methodologies which suggests that Montessori built pedagogically better than her critics knew, even though the language of her constructs may seem even more quaint today than Kilpatrick found it in 1912. Consider in turn the various beliefs synopsized.

BELIEF IN THE UNIMPORTANCE OF EARLY EXPERIENCE

It was Freud's (1905) observation that the free associations of his patients led back to infancy, and his imaginative interpretation in the theory of psychosexual development, that began to lend force to the notion that very early experience, even preverbal experience, might be important for the development of adult characteristics. Freud's theory, however, put the emphasis on the fate of instinctive modes of infantile pleasure-striving, *i.e.*, sucking, elimination, and genitality. To a substantial degree, objective studies of the effects of these factors explicitly concerned in early psychosexual development have generally tended to depreciate their importance (see Child, 1954; Hunt, 1945; Orlansky, 1949; Sears, 1943).[1] On the other hand, studies of the effects of various kinds of early infantile experience in animal subjects have left very little room for doubt that early experience is a factor in behavioral development. Ready-made infantile responses, like the sucking of the calf—as any farmer knows—or of the human infant (Sears & Wise, 1950), the pecking response in chicks (Padilla, 1935), or the flying response of young birds (Spalding, 1873), will wane if these patterns go unused for too long a time. Similarly, such presumably instinctive patterns as mothering fail to develop in female rats that have been deprived of licking themselves by means of Elizabethan collars worn from weaning to adulthood (Birch, 1956). Even certain aspects of the anatomical maturation itself appear to depend upon experience. Chimpanzees (Riesen, 1958), kittens (Weiskrantz, 1958), rabbits (Brattgård, 1952), and rats (Liberman, 1962) that are reared in darkness develop anomalous retinae which are deficient in Müller fibers and show deficient RNA production in the retinal ganglion cells (Brattgård, 1952; Liberman, 1962; Rasch, Swift, Riesen, & Chow, 1961). Moreover, rats deprived of vision for the 10 days immediately after the eyes open are not as quickly responsive to visual cues in adulthood as are litter-mates which were deprived of hearing for 10 days after their ears opened, and vice versa (Wolf, 1943; Gauron & Becker, 1959). (That is, the rats deprived of hearing are not as quickly responsive to aural cues as are rats deprived of vision.) Although there is still much confusion concerning this issue, rats petted, shook, or submitted to electric shock and to marked drops in temperature have shown repeatedly, as adults, a reduction in the tendency to defecate and urinate in a strange open field, increased readiness to enter strange places, and more rapid learning to avoid shock than controls left unmolested in the maternal nest (see Denenberg, 1962; Levine, 1961). These are but a sample of the various kinds of effects of infantile experience on the adult behavior of animal subjects (see also Beach & Jaynes, 1954). Still others will be noted in connection with other beliefs. Clearly, Montessori's concern with the experience of three- and four-year-olds need be no will-o'-the-wisp.

BELIEF IN FIXED INTELLIGENCE

The belief in fixed intelligence was based in considerable part upon the notion that the genes which carry the heredity of the individual fix his intellectual capacity. It is probably true that the genes determine an individual's potential to develop intellectual capacity, but they do not guarantee that the individual will achieve his potential capacity. Elsewhere (Hunt, 1961), I have summarized the evidence (a) that scores from tests administered in the preschool years predict very poorly scores for tests administered at adolescence, (b) that substantial differences in the I.Q. have been found for identical twins reared apart and that the degree of difference of I.Q. is related to the degree of difference between the sets of circumstances under which the twins have developed, and (c) that the commonly predicted drop in intelligence to be expected from the fact that the majority of each new generation comes from the lower half of the population intellectually has failed to occur and that, instead, rather substantial increases have been found.

It is especially interesting to note that Harold Skeels has recently followed up those individuals in the study by Skeels & Dye (1939). In this study, a group of 13 infants with a mean I.Q. of 64.3 and a range between 36 and 89 and with chronological ages ranging from seven to 30 months, was transferred from an orphanage to a school for the mentally retarded. There they were placed on a ward where the older and brighter girls became very much attached to them and would play with them during most of the infants' waking hours. After being on this ward for periods ranging between six months, for the seven-month-old youngster, and 52 months, for the 30-month-old youngster, they were retested. Each of the 13 showed a gain in I.Q.: the minimum gain was seven points, the maximum was 58 points, and all but four showed gains of more than 20 points. In the same study, for purposes of contrast, were 12 other orphanage inmates, this group having a mean I.Q. of 87, an I.Q. range from 50 to 103, and an age range from 12 to 22 months. These infants were left in the orphanage. When they were retested after periods varying from 21 to 43 months, they all showed a decrease in I.Q. One decrease was only eight points, but for the remaining 11 children, the decreases varied between 18 and 45 points, with five exceeding 35 points. In the follow-up study, all of these cases were located after a lapse of 21 years. The findings are startling. Of the 13 in the group transferred from the orphanage to the school for the mentally retarded: all are self-supporting; none is a ward of any institution, public or private; 11 of the 13 are married, and nine of these have had children. On the other hand, of the 12 children, originally higher in I.Q., who were kept in the orphanage: one died in adolescence following continuous residence in a state institution for the mentally retarded; five are still wards of state institutions, one in a mental hospital and the other four in institutions for the mentally retarded; of the six no longer wards of state institutions, only two have been married and one of these is divorced. In education, the disparity between the two groups is similarly great. For the 13 transferred from the orphanage to the school for the mentally retarded, the median grade completed is the twelfth (*i.e.,* graduation from high school); four have gone on for one or more years of college work, with one of the boys having received a bachelor's degree from a big state university. Occupationally, the range is from professional and semi-professional to semi-skilled laborers or domestics. For the 12 who remained in the orphanage, half failed to complete the third grade, and none got to high school. Only three of the six not now in state institutions are now employed (Skeels, personal communication, 1964). Clearly there is a difference here that counts. The superiority of the foster home, where the child receives a variety of experience and stimulation, over the old orphanage is relevant here (see Goldfarb, 1963).

Evidence that early experience influences adult problem-solving capacity comes also from studies with animal subjects. This work stems from the neuropsychological theorizing of Donald Hebb (1949). Hebb was concerned with the facts of attention and thought. For him, the switchboard conception of brain-function could not be true, for these facts imply that semi-autonomous processes must be operating within the brain. He also found evidence for these in neurophysiology, and he termed them *cell assemblies*, based upon early learning involving perceptual experiences, and *phase sequences*, based upon the sequential organizations of later learning. The electronic computer has replaced the telephone switchboard as the mechanical model of brain function. On the assumption that problem-solving would be a function of the richness of these semi-autonomous central processes, Hebb (1947) compared the problem-solving ability of rats reared in cages in the laboratory with that of rats reared as pets in his home. The problem-solving ability was measured by the Hebb-Williams (1946) test of animal intelligence. The pet-reared animals were superior to their cage-reared litter-mates. Thompson & Heron (1954), also at McGill, have done a similar experiment with dogs as subjects. Some were reared under isolation in laboratory cages from weaning to eight months of age. Their litter-mates were reared for this same period in homes as pets. The cage-reared and the pet-reared dogs were put together in a dog-pasture for 10 months; then, at 18 months of age, their problem-solving ability was assessed in the Hebb-Williams mazes. The pet-reared dogs were superior to their cage-reared litter-mates. In fact, the superiority of the pet-reared dogs over the cage-reared dogs appears to have been even more marked than the superiority of the pet-reared rats over the cage-reared rats. This suggests that the degree of effect of infantile experience on adult problem-solving capacity may well be a function of the proportion of the brain not directly connected with either receptor inputs or motor outputs. This proportion, termed the A/S ratio by Hebb (1949) increases up the phylogenetic scale.

There is a good possibility that the cultural deprivation involved in being reared under slum conditions may be somewhat analogous to cage-rearing while being reared in a family of the educated middle class most resembles pet-rearing. This possibility suggests that an enrichment of early experience during the preschool years might well serve as an antidote for this cultural deprivation, if it comes early enough (see Hunt, 1964). It might thereby give those children whose lot it has been to be born to parents living in slums a more nearly even opportunity to hold their own in the competitive culture of the public school once they get there. The "Houses of Children" established by Montessori in the San Lorenzo district of Rome and the methods of teaching that she developed there provide a splendid beginning precisely adapted for this purpose of counteracting cultural deprivation.

Belief in Predetermined Development

The notions that psychological development is predetermined by the genes and that the response repertoire emerges automatically as a function of anatomic maturation are no longer tenable. The early evidence appearing to support such a conception of development was either based on investigations with such lowly organisms as Amblystoma and frogs (see Hunt, 1961, pp. 49ff), or it was based upon the effects of practicing a given kind of skill. Such lower organisms as these amphibia used as subjects by Carmichael (1926) and Coghill (1929) differ from mammals, and especially from human beings in two very fundamental ways. They have substantially greater regenerative capacity, and this fact suggests that biochemical determiners may well be considerably more prepotent in determining their development than such factors are in determining the development of mammals. They also have a

much lower proportion of the brain not directly connected with receptor inputs or motor outputs (in Hebb's terms, a lower A/S ratio). This fact suggests that semi-autonomous central processes deriving from experience must have a much smaller role in determining their behavior than it has in mammals, and especially in man. Moreover, the evidence concerning the effects of very early experience both on the anatomical development of the retinae and on adult behavior in animal subjects is clearly dissonant with this notion of predetermined development.

Those studies showing that practice has but evanescent effects on such early abilities as tower-building, ladder-climbing, buttoning, and cutting with scissors (see Gesell & Thompson, 1929; Hilgard, 1932) missed the point that abilities appear to be hierarchically organized, that the experiences governing the age at which such abilities appear do not constitute exercise in those abilities themselves. Rather, they constitute encounters with quite different circumstances important in establishing abilities lower in the hierarchy. At the level of school subjects, this can be illustrated by noting how useless practice in long division is if the child has not learned to add and subtract. More to the point, however, is such evidence from animal studies as Birch's (1956) finding that female rats do not mother their young properly if they have been deprived of licking themselves by means of Elizabethan collars. Still more to the point, at the level of human beings, is that dramatic finding of Dennis (1960) that children being reared in a Teheran orphanage where visual and auditory inputs are relatively homogeneous are markedly delayed in their *locomotor* development. Of these children, 60% were still not sitting up alone at two years of age, and 85% were still not walking at four years of age. Variations of visual and auditory input would appear in terms of our conceptions of practice to have little to do with locomotor skills. Thus, while the genotype does set limits on an individual's potential, it does not guarantee that this potential in capacity will be reached. The achievement of genotypic potential appears to be a function of a continuous interaction between the organism and its environment. It has long been obvious that there must be a biochemical interaction manifested in the processes of food and water intake and elimination, but it now appears that psychological development is also highly dependent upon what one may characterize as the organism's informational interaction with the environment.

One more factor relevant to the role of early experience in psychological development. During the earliest phases, the longer a developing organism is deprived of a given sort of experience, or, to put it another way, the longer an organism is deprived of a given kind of informational interaction with the environment, the more likely is the effect of that deprivation to become permanent. For instance, in the work of Cruze (1935, 1938) chicks reared in darkness for only five days quickly developed their expected accuracy in pecking, but chicks allowed only some 15 minutes out of darkness for pecking each day for 20 days not only failed to improve but also appeared to be permanently deficient in pecking accuracy. Moreover, when Padilla (1935) kept newly-hatched chicks from pecking for eight consecutive days or longer, the chicks lost completely their inclination or capacity to peck. Such relationships are still inadequately understood, but they have a clear implication for childhood education. They imply that the longer cultural deprivation lasts, the greater and the more permanent will be its effects. Such considerations make it important to consider ways to enrich preschool experience as an antidote for such cultural deprivation, and the earlier the better (see Hunt, 1964). Moreover, from the observations of Americans who visited Montessori's Houses of Children, one gathers they were successful at precisely this business of counteracting the effects of cultural deprivation on those symbolic skills required for success in school and in an increasingly technological culture. Here, having based her pedagogy on earlier attempts to educate the mentally retarded was probably a highly pertinent advantage.

BELIEF THAT "ALL BEHAVIOR IS MOTIVATED"

The proposition that all behavior is motivated by painful stimulation, homeostatic needs, or sex, or by acquired drives based upon these, has run into an accumulation of dissonant evidence. One of the most obvious implications of this commonly-believed proposition is that organisms will become quiescent in the absence of such motivation. They do not. For instance, play in animals is most likely to occur in the absence of such motivating conditions (Buhler, 1928; Beach, 1945). Similarly, manipulative behavior in chimpanzees (Harlow, Harlow & Meyer, 1950), spatial exploration in rats (Berlyne, 1960; Nissen, 1930), spontaneous alternation in rats (Montgomery, 1953, 1955), and visual and auditory exploration in monkeys (Butler, 1953, 1958) have all been found to occur repeatedly in the absence of such motivation (see Hunt, 1963a).

Such evidence has recently been given theoretical recognition in the postulation of a variety of new drives and needs. Such drives and needs, however, are no more than descriptions of the behavior they propose to explain. Moreover, in motive-naming we are merely revisiting the instinct-naming popularized by McDougall (1908) early in this century and rejected immediately after World War I. We should know better. This evidence has also been unfortunately recognized in motives named in terms of their telic significance, such as the "urge of mastery" of Ives Hendrick (1943) and the "competence motivation" of White (1959), and in terms of spontaneous activity by such people as Hunt (1960). I say unfortunately recognized because such conceptual approaches provide no means of developing hypotheses about testable antecedent-consequent relationships.

Elsewhere I have proposed a mechanism for motivation inherent in information processing and action (Hunt, 1963a) or, if you will, within the organism's informational interaction with the environment. The nature of this mechanism has been suggested by the recent radical change in our conception of the functional unit of the nervous system from that of reflex arc to that of feedback loop. From the standpoint of the feedback loop, activity is instigated, not merely by the onset of some kind of stimulation, but by the occurence of a discrepancy between the input of the moment and some standard existing within the organism. This discrepancy I have termed, following the lead of Miller, Galanter, & Pribram (1960), *incongruity*. As I see it, some standards, like those for homeostatic needs, are built into the organism, but some standards are established through experience as coded residues of encounters with the environment which are stored within the nervous system. In the language of common sense, they are expectations. Probably these residues are stored within those intrinsic portions of the brain not directly connected with receptor inputs and motor outlets. Incongruity is typically accompanied by emotional arousal, but emotional arousal does not appear to be, by itself, a sufficient determiner of whether the organism will approach or withdraw from a source of stimulation (see Haywood & Hunt, 1963). The determiners of approach and withdrawal, presumably associated with the hedonic value of the source of input, appear to inhere within the organism's informational interaction with circumstances. If there is too little incongruity, the organism approaches sources of incongruity, but if there is too much incongruity, the organism withdraws from sources of incongruous inputs (see Hebb, 1949). The former condition is illustrated in the study of Bexton, Heron, & Scott (1954). There, McGill students refused to remain within a situation where variation in receptor inputs was minimized even though they were paid $20 a day. On the other hand, withdrawal from too much incongruity is illustrated in Hebb's (1946) studies of fear. There, chimpanzees encountering various familiar situations in an unfamiliar guise retreated with distressed vocalizing and pupils wide open. Such withdrawal appeared in a young pet chimpanzee when the highly-familiar and much-loved experimenter appeared in a halloween mask or even merely in the coat of the animal keeper. These facts appear to mean that there is an optimum incongruity which is continually sought (Hunt, 1963a). It is a basis for continuous cognitive growth with joy. It also justifies the older notions that children have a spontaneous interest in learning. In basing her pedagogy on such motivation, I now believe Montessori was on solid ground.

The notion of an optimum of incongruity, coupled with the notion that the standard upon which incongruity is based derives from experience, gives rise to what I have termed "the problem of the match" (Hunt, 1961, pp. 267ff). This "problem of the match" implies that if the circumstances encountered are to be attractive and interesting and are yet to be challenging enough to call forth those accommodative changes, within the structure of central processes, that presumably constitute learning, they must be properly matched to those "standards" which the child has already developed in the course of his past experience. The status of our knowledge about these matters is entirely inadequate for us to arrange such matches entirely from the outside. It would appear that the child must have some opportunity to follow his own bent. Thus, we come to the importance of that liberty emphasized by the Rousseau-Pestalozzi-Froebel tradition and by Montessori.

It was this "problem of the match" that prompted my interest in Montessori's work. When I wrote *Intelligence and Experience,* this problem of the match loomed as a large obstacle in the way of maximizing intellectual potential. I deserve no credit for discovery, however, because as recently as two years ago, the name of Montessori would have meant to me only one of those educational "faddists" who came along shortly after the turn of the century. It was after a day-long discussion of such matters with Lee Cronbach and Jan Smedslund at Boulder in the summer of 1962, that Jan Smedslund asked me if I knew of Montessori and her work. When I claimed no such knowledge, he advised me to look her up, because, and I quote his words as I remember them, "she has a solution to your problem of the match—not a theoretical solution, but a practical one." I believe Smedslund is correct, for in arranging a variety of materials in graded fashion, in putting together children ranging in age from three to seven, and in breaking the lock-step in infant education, Montessori went a long way toward a practical solution. Grading the materials permits the child to grow as his interests lead him from one level of complexity to another. Having children aged from three to seven years together should permit the younger children a graded series of models for imitation and the older ones an opportunity to learn by teaching. Breaking the lock-step provides that opportunity for the child to make his own selection of materials and models. In the present state of our knowledge about the match, I believe only the child can make an appropriate selection. Thus, I believe there is an important psychological basis for Montessori's practice.

BELIEF IN THE RELATIVE IMPORTANCE OF MOTOR RESPONSE AND
RECEPTOR INPUT

The belief that it is the motor response that is all-important in learning is less tenable than it was half a century ago. Although the issue is still far from settled, recent evidence appears to indicate that the role of the eyes and the ears, and perhaps the tactile organs, may be much more important in the organism's on-going informational interaction with the environment than are the motor outlets. In this connection, it is exceedingly interesting to recall that Hopi children reared on cradleboards walked as soon as did Hopi children reared with the free use of their arms and legs. Tying of the arms and legs to the cradleboard inhibits movement almost completely during the waking hours. Dennis & Dennis (1940) found that the distributions of ages of walking for the cradleboard-reared Hopi children and those allowed free movement could be superimposed, one on the other. The average age for both conditions of rearing was about 15 months. Consider, in this same connection, the finding by Dennis (1960) that 60% of the Teheran-orphanage children are not yet sitting up alone at two years of age and that 85% are not walking at four years of age. The children in this orphanage have free use

of their arms and legs, but the variety of visual and auditory inputs encountered is highly restricted. Note too that those Hopi children reared on cradleboards were often carried about on their mothers' backs. Thus, while their arms and legs might be restricted, their eyes and ears could feast upon a rich variety of inputs. From such considerations and from the evidence assembled by Fiske & Maddi (1961), it would appear that variations in the circumstances with which an infant has informational interaction is an exceedingly important determiner of his rate of early development and of his achieving his genotypic potential in ability.

Still another line of suggestive evidence comes from the work of O. K. Moore. This concerns what he calls "responsive environments." In teaching nursery-school children to read, he has them strike the keys of an electric typewriter so arranged that, as each key is struck, the child sees the letter struck and hears the name of the letter. Nursery-school children are introduced to the apparatus by a child who explains that "we take turns." Each day a child is asked if he wishes his turn. Given this opportunity, each child nearly always does. After a period of free exploration of the keyboard, the speaker in the apparatus can be used to tell the child what letter to strike. By keeping all keys but the named one fixed, the child can gradually be taught the keyboard. By means of further programmed changes in the experience, children can fairly rapidly be led to the point where they are typing from dictation. While this program concerns reading, it minimizes the motor side and is based on visual and auditory responses from the typing on the apparatus. When children with several months of such experience are provided with a blackboard, Moore reports that after noting that some of their marks resemble the letters they have learned on the typewriter, they quickly explore making all those letters with chalk. Moreover, the motor dexterity and the control of these four- and five-year-olds, as it appears in their writing, has been judged by experts to be like that typical of seven- and eight-year-olds (Moore, personal communication). Such observations suggest that motor control may be less a matter of educating the child's muscles than it is of his having clear images of what he is trying to make with his hands. On the basis of such evidence, perhaps Montessori's pedagogical emphasis on "sensory learning," based as it was on careful clinical observation of the learning of mentally retarded children was closer to reality than the theories of those who held such emphasis in contempt. Her theoretical attribution of the effects of "sensory learning" to increased power of a discriminative faculty may have been logically circular, but it was no more wrong than the emphasis on the response side.

In view of the various lines of recent evidence that I have been synopsizing, Montessori's pedagogy appears to fall into step with what may well be a new *Zeitgeist.* Moreover, developments in technology are putting a new premium on the ability to solve problems in linguistic and mathematical terms. Those lacking these skills are finding less and less opportunity to participate in the culture, even to the degree that they can make a living. Furthermore, those children born to parents without these skills suffer that cultural deprivation associated with poverty and slums which makes them retarded in the underlying capacities required to succeed in the public schools. It would appear from the evidence cited that enrichment of preschool experience would be a promising antidote to such cultural deprivation. Montessori's Houses of Children in the San Lorenzo district of Rome supply an apt model with which to start. Thus, these changing beliefs about child development and the problem of coping with cultural deprivation in a culture where technology is playing an increasingly important role are reasons sufficient for revisiting Montessori's approach to child pedagogy.

Words Of Caution

On the other hand, there are dangers in revisiting Montessori's approach. While her practice is no longer out of step with the conceptions emerging from recent evidence, her theory was never the kind that supplies a good guide to the observation and investigation required to settle the various issues that are still highly problematical. Those who turn to Montessori's approach to pedagogy should simultaneously examine the changes in the conception of psychological development now being formulated. One hopes that these changes are more than another one of those swings in the pendulum of opinion that have so commonly characterized our notions of education and child-rearing. But, like the new conceptions of half a century ago, these of today may be wrong in substantial part, and it is highly important to confront them with evidence that will correct them.

In revisiting Montessori's pedagogical practice, there may be the danger of developing a cult which will restrict innovation and evaluation. Let me be concrete. Interesting and valuable as the didactic apparatus assembled and invented by Montessori is, there should be nothing sacrosanct about it. What has become the standard assembly of didactic materials may be too rich for a start with children who are severely deprived culturally. This may be true even though the children in the original San Lorenzo houses were indeed culturally deprived. From conversations with teachers, I have gathered that some of these culturally deprived children become uncontrollably excited when confronted with this standard assembly. These children remind one of the cage-reared dogs of Thompson & Heron (1954) when they are first released from their cages into a laboratory room filled with objects. On the other hand, with children of upper-middle-class families, the standard assembly may already be "old stuff." Of the same order is the dissatisfaction with kindergarten commonly shown by children who have already been in nursery school for a year or two (see Simmons, 1960). This dissatisfaction can be attributed to boredom. It may be seen as a consequence of too little variation in the match between the circumstances available to such children and the information and skills they have already assimilated (see Hunt, 1961, 1963a). Children of

the middle class who have encountered a rich variety of situations and things become "I-do-myself-ers" very early. They may become avidly interested, even at only three years of age, in learning to read, to write, to count, and to experience quantity in its various aspects. Unless someone is making approval and affection contingent upon a child's show of such interest, no one need fear for overstimulation. Gratifying their interest in acquiring such skills can be a source of exhilaration. Gratifying their interest in reading may be facilitated by means of new kinds of didactic apparatus. Electronics make feasible what O. K. Moore calls "responsive environments." These were outside the ken of Montessori. Even now no one can anticipate their full pedagogical potential. The point is that the standard assembly should be viewed only as a starting point, and those revisiting Montessori should imitate her resourcefulness in inventing pedagogical apparatus and in adapting it to the use of individual children.

There may be another aspect to this danger of cultishness. This is the danger of standardizing the ways in which each child is supposed to utilize the various didactic materials. In response to my recommendation that Montessori's pedagogy be reexamined, various people have complained about Montessori teachers who insist that each child must pass through each of a set of prescribed steps of work with each kind of material. Such insistence obviously misses the meaning of what I call the "problem of the match" and ruins the practical solution of it that Jan Smedslund found in Montessori pedagogy. It loses the basic advantage of breaking the lock-step of having all children doing the same thing at the same time by demanding that all children do the same series of things with each kind of didactic material. Either way, the basic pedagogical implication of individual differences is missed, and children lose the growth-fostering pleasure of following their own predilections in their informational interaction with the environment.

In revisiting Montessori's pedagogy, there may also be dangers of underemphasis, first, on the role and importance of interpersonal relationships, and, second, on the importance of the affective and aesthetic aspects of life concerned with art and music. In recent years, emphasis on social and emotional adjustment has tended to overstress social and affective matters at the expense of cognitive development, but this does not justify an overcorrection and neglect of these matters. Even though the traditional three "R"s are important channels for the enrichment of a child's future informational interaction with the environment, and even though learning them is fun under proper circumstances, they are not all of life. Montessori teacher-training might well borrow some of the social and disciplinary skills so much emphasized recently in the education of nursery-school teachers. Moreover, Montessori schools might well increase the variety of sensory materials; they might well supply opportunities for children to encounter more in the way of art and music, to make music, and to learn musical technique.

Perhaps one of the most important things to be gained by revisiting Montessori's pedagogy is her willingness and ability to observe children working with the didactic apparatus, and from observation to invent, on the spot, modifications of the situation that will foster a child's psychological development. She referred to this variously as "scientific pedagogy," as "pedagogical anthropology," and even as "experimental psychology." When she considered Itard's work with the "wild boy of Aveyron" as "practically the first of attempts at experimental psychology" (Montessori, 1909, p. 34), however, she confused experimentation with clinical observation, as indicated by the fact that she notes further, that "Itard was perhaps the first educator to practice the observation of the pupil in the way in which the sick are observed in hospitals" (1909, p. 34). Careful clinical observation is needed in pedagogy, but it is not easy to teach this to teachers. Those who have attempted to do so have commonly fallen back upon metaphors and similes for their communication. I would now guess that the cutting edge of psychological development resides chiefly in the individual's attention and intention or plan. If a teacher can discern what a child is trying to do in his informational interaction with the environment, and if that teacher can have on hand materials relevant to that intention, if he can impose a relevant challenge with which the child can cope, supply a relevant model for imitation, or pose a relevant question that the child can answer, that teacher can call forth the kind of accommodative change that constitutes psychological development or growth. This sort of thing was apparently the genius of Maria Montessori.

Another of the most important things to be gained from revisiting Montessori's pedagogy is a scheme of preschool education nicely adapted by its origins to contribute toward the solution of one of the major educational challenges of our day. Children from the homes of many parents of the lower class come to the first grade, and even to kindergarten, unprepared to profit from regular school experience. In the light of the evidence which has become available largely since World War II, we can no longer rest upon the assumption that their lack of preparation is predetermined by the genes received from their parents of lower-class status. Regular schooling, moreover, may come too late. We must try to help these children overcome their handicap by enriching their experience during their preschool years. Montessori has provided a model. According to the impressionistic reports of observers, her "Houses of Children" worked quite well. We can well emulate Montessori's model, but we should not stop with it. Moreover, in the future those who become concerned with the question of the effectiveness of Montessori's model, and of revisions to come, should have more than the impressionistic reports of observers to go on. They should have demonstrations employing the experimental method and the best techniques available for educational and psychological assessment.[2]

Notes

1. I must except here a growing variety of factors in parent-child relationships which are being shown to be quite important (see Becker, 1962). These studies stem in large part from the psychoanalytic conception of the Oedipal relationship as that conception has been elaborated in the learning theory of Dollard & Miller (1950).

2. Prepared with the support of USPHS Grant No. MH—K6-18,567. The writer also wishes to acknowledge with gratitude grants from the Carnegie Corporation, from the Commonwealth Fund, and from the Russell Sage Foundation.

References

The references cited in the text are identified by the name of the author and a date following the name. This date is that of original publication. Page references are given for the edition available to the writer, and this edition, if it is not the original, is identified by the date given at the end of a reference.

Beach, F. A. 1945. Current concepts of play in animals. *American Naturalist, 79,* 523-541.

Beach, F. A., & Jaynes, J. 1954. Effects of early experience upon the behavior of animals. *Psychological Bulletin, 51,* 239-263.

Becker, W. C. 1962. Developmental psychology. *Annual Review of Psychology, 13,* 1-34.

Berlyne, D. E. 1960. *Conflict, arousal, and curiosity.* New York: McGraw-Hill.

Bexton, W. H., Heron, W., & Scott, T. H. 1954. Effects of decreased variation in the sensory environment. *Canadian Journal of Psychology, 8,* 70-76.

Birch, H. G. 1956. Sources of order in maternal behavior of animals. *American Journal of Orthopsychiatry, 26,* 279-284.

Brattgård, S. 1952. The importance of adequate stimulation for the chemical composition of retinal ganglion cells during early post-natal development. *Acta Radiology,* Suppl. *96.*

Buhler, K. 1928. Displeasure and pleasure in relation to activity. In M. L. Reymert (Ed.), *Feelings and emotions: the Wittenberg symposium.* Worcester, Mass.: Clark University Press. Ch. 14.

Butler, R. A. 1953. Discrimination learning by rhesus monkeys to visual exploration motivation. *Journal of comparative and physiological Psychology, 46,* 95-98.

Butler, R. A. 1958. The differential effect of visual and auditory incentives on the performance of monkeys. *American Journal of Psychology, 71,* 591-593.

Carmichael, L. 1926. The development of behavior in vertebrates experimentally removed from influence of external stimulation. *Psychological Review, 34,* 253-260.

Child, I. L. 1954. Socialization. In G. Lindzey (Ed.), *Handbook of social psychology.* Cambridge, Mass.: Addison-Wesley. Ch. 18.

Coghill, G. E. 1929. *Anatomy and the problem of behavior.* Cambridge: Cambridge University Press.

Cremin, L. A. 1962. *The transformation of the school: Progressivism in American education, 1876-1957.* New York: Knopf.

Cruze, W. W. 1935. Maturation and learning in chicks. *Journal of comparative Psychology, 20,* 371-409.

Cruze, W. W. 1938. Maturation and learning ability. *Psychological Monographs, 50,* No. 5.

Denenberg, V. H. 1962. The effects of early experience. In E. S. E. Hafez (Ed.), *The behaviour of domestic animals.* London: Baillière, Tindall & Cox. Ch. 6.

Dennis, W. 1960. Causes of retardation among institutional children. *Journal of genetic Psychology, 96,* 47-59.

Dennis, W., & Dennis, Marsena G. 1940. The effect of cradling practice upon the onset of walking in Hopi children. *Journal of genetic Psychology, 56,* 77-86.

Dewey, J. 1897. *My pedagogic creed.* Washington, D.C.: Progressive Education Association of America.

Dewey, J. 1900. *The school and society.* Chicago: University of Chicago Press, Phoenix Books P3, 1960.

Dewey, J. 1902. *The child and the curriculum.* Chicago: University of Chicago Press, Phoenix Books P3, 1960.

Dollard, J., & Miller, N. E. 1950. *Personality and psychotherapy.* New York: McGraw-Hill.

Donahue, G. E. 1962. Dr. Maria Montessori and the Montessori Movement: A general bibliography of materials in the English language, 1909-1961. In: Nancy M. Rambusch, *Learning how to learn.* Baltimore, Md.: Helicon Press.

Fisher, Dorothy Canfield. 1912. *A Montessori mother.* New York: Holt.

Fiske, J. 1869. *Outlines of cosmic philosophy.* New York: Appleton.

Fiske, D. W., & Maddi, S. R. 1961. *Functions of varied experience.* Homewood, Ill.: Dorsey Press.

Freud, S. 1900. The interpretation of dreams. In: A. A. Brill (Trans. & Ed.), *The basic writings of Sigmund Freud.* New York: Modern Library, 1938.

Freud, S. 1905. Three contributions to the theory of sex. In: A. A. Brill (Trans. & Ed.), *The basic writings of Sigmund Freud.* New York: Modern Library, 1938.

Freud, S. 1915. Instincts and their vicissitudes. *Collected papers.* Paper no. 4 in Vol. 4. London: Hogarth, 1950.

Gauron, E. F., & Becker, W. C. 1959. The effects of early sensory deprivation on adult rat behavior under competition stress: An attempt at replication of a study by Alexander Wolf. *Journal of comparative and physiological Psychology, 52,* 689-693.

Gesell, A., & Thompson, Helen. 1929. Learning and growth in identical twin infants. *Genetic Psychology Monographs, 6,* 1-124.

Goldfarb, W. 1953. The effects of early institutional care on adolescent personality. *Journal of experimental Education, 12,* 106-129.

Harlow, H. F., Harlow, M. K., & Meyer, D. R. 1950. Learning motivated by a manipulation drive. *Journal of experimental Psychology, 40,* 228-234.

Haywood, H. C., & Hunt, J. McV. 1963. Effects of epinephrine upon novelty preference and arousal. *Journal of abnormal and social psychology, 67,* 206-213.

Hebb, D. O. 1946. On the nature of fear. *Psychol. Rev., 53,* 259-276.

Hebb, D. O. 1947. The effects of early experience on problem-solving at maturity. *American Psychologist, 2,* 306-307.

Hebb, D. O. 1949. *The organization of behavior.* New York: Wiley.

Hebb, D. O., & Williams, K. 1946. A method of rating animal intelligence. *Journal of genetic Psychology, 34,* 59-65.

Hendrik, I. 1943. The discussion of the 'instinct to master.' *Psychoanalytic Quarterly, 12,* 561-565.

Hilgard, Josephine R. 1932. Learning and maturation in preschool children. *Journal of genetic Psychology, 41,* 36-56.

Holmes, H. W. 1912. Introduction. To *The Montessori Method,* as translated from the first Italian edition of *Scientific pedagogy as applied to child education in the Children's Houses.* New York: Frederick A. Stokes.

Hunt, J. McV. 1945. Experimental psychoanalysis. In P. L. Harriman (Ed.), *Encyclopedia of psychology.* New York: Philosophical Library. Pp. 140-156.

Hunt, J. McV. 1960. Experience and the development of motivation: Some reinterpretations. *Child Development, 31,* 489-504.

Hunt, J. McV. 1961. *Intelligence and experience.* New York: Ronald.

Hunt, J. McV. 1963a. Motivation inherent in information processing and action. In: O. J. Harvey (Ed.), *Motivation and social interaction: Cognitive determinants.* New York: Ronald. Ch. 3.

Hunt, J. McV. 1963b. Piaget's observations as a source of hypotheses concerning motivation. *Merrill-Palmer Quarterly, 9,* 263-275.

Hunt, J. McV. 1964. How children develop intellectually. *Children, 11* (No. 3), 83-91.

Itard, J. M. G. 1801. *The wild boy of Aveyron.* (Trans. by George and Muriel Humphrey). New York: Appleton-Century, 1932.

Kilpatrick, W. H. 1914. *The Montessori system examined.* Boston: Houghton Mifflin.

Levine, S. 1961. Psychophysiological effects of early stimulation. In: E. Bliss (Ed.), *Roots of behavior.* New York: Hoeber.

Liberman, R. 1962. Retinal cholinesterase and glycolysis in rats raised in darkness. *Science, 135,* 372-373.

McDougall, W. 1908. *An introduction to social psychology.* Boston: Luce.

Merrill, Jenny B. 1909. New method in kindergarten education. *Kindergarten Primary Magazine, 22,* 106-107, 142-144, 211-212, 297-298.

Miller, G. A., Galanter, E., & Pribram, K. H. 1960. *Plans and the structure of behavior.* New York: Holt.

Montessori, Maria. 1909. *The Montessori method: Scientific pedagogy as applied to child education in "The Children's Houses": with additions and revisions.* (Trans. by Anne E. George, with introduction by H. W. Holmes.) New York: Frederick A. Stokes, 1912.

Montessori, Maria. 1929. *The discovery of the child.* (Translated from the third Italian edition of *The method of scientific pedagogy applied to child education in the Children's Houses.*) Madras, India: Kalakshetra Publications (sold by The Theosophical Press, Wheaton, Ill.), 1962.

Montgomery, K. C. 1953. Exploratory behavior as a function of "similarity" of stimulus situations. *Journal of comparative and physiological Psychology, 46,* 129-133.

Montgomery, K. C. 1955. The relation between fear induced by novel stimulation and exploratory behavior. *Journal of comparative and physiological Psychology, 48,* 254-260.

Moore, O. K. 1960. Automated responsive environments. (Motion picture, Parts 1 & 2) Hamden, Conn.: Basic Education, Inc.

Morgan, C. L. 1894. *An introduction to comparative psychology.* (2nd ed.) London: Scott, 1909.

Nissen, H. W. 1930. A study of exploratory behavior in the white rat by means of the obstruction method. *Journal of genetic Psychology, 37,* 361-376.

Orlansky, H. 1949. Infant care and personality. *Psychological Bulletin, 46,* 1-48.

Padilla, S. G. 1935. Further studies on the delayed pecking of chicks. *Journal of comparative Psychology, 20,* 413-433.

Rasch, E., Swift, H., Riesen, A. H., & Chow, K. L. 1961. Altered structure and composition of retinal cells in dark-reared mammals. *Experimental Cell Research, 25,* 348-363.

Riesen, A. J. 1958. Plasticity of behavior: Psychological aspects. In: H. F. Harlow & C. N. Woolsey (Eds.), *Biological and biochemical bases of behavior.* Pp. 425-450.

Riess, B. F. 1954. The effect of altered environment and of age on mother-young relationships among animals. *Annals of the New York Academy of Science, 51* (6), 1093-1103.

Sears, R. R. 1943. Survey of objective studies of psychoanalytic concepts. *Bulletin of the Social Science Research Council,* No. 51.

Sears, R. R., & Wise, G. W. 1950. Relation of cup feeding in infancy to thumb-sucking and oral drive. *American Journal of Orthopsychiatry, 20,* 123-138.

Séguin, E. 1846. *Traitement Moral, Hygiène et Education des Idiots.* Paris: Bibliotheque d'education speciale, 1906.

Séguin, E. 1866. *Idiocy: and its treatment by the physiological method.* Albany: Columbia University Teachers College Educational Reprints, 1907.

Simmons, Virginia C. 1960. Why waste our five-year-olds? *Harper's Magazine,* 220, No. 1319, 71ff.

Skeels, H. M., & Dye, H. B. 1939. A study of the effects of differential stimulation of mentally retarded children. *Proceedings of the American Association on Mental Deficiency, 44,* 114-136.

Spalding, D. A. 1873. Instinct. *Macmillan's Magazine, 27,* 282-293.

Stevens, Ellen Yale. 1913. *A guide to the Montessori method.* New York: Frederick A. Stokes.

Thompson, W. R., & Heron, W. 1954. The effects of restricting early experience on the problem-solving capacity of dogs. *Canadian Journal of Psychology, 8,* 17-31.

Thorndike, E. L. 1898. Animal intelligence. *Psychological Review Monograph Supplement, 2,* No. 8.

Thorndike, E. L., & Woodworth, R. S. 1901. The influence of improvement in one mental function upon the efficiency of other functions. *Psychological Review, 8,* 247-261, 384-395, 553-564.

Warren, H. C. 1912. The "House of Childhood": A new primary system. *Journal of educational Psychology, 3,* 121-132.

Watson, J. B. 1914. *Behavior, an introduction to comparative psychology.* New York: Holt.

Weiskrantz L. 1958. Sensory deprivation and the cat's optic nervous system. *Nature, 181,* 1047-1050.

White, R. W. 1959. Motivation reconsidered: The concept of competence. *Psychological Review, 66,* 297-333.

Witmer, L. 1914. The Montessori method. *Psychological Clinic, 8,* 1-5.

Wolf, A. 1943. The dynamics of the selective inhibition of specific functions in neuroses. *Psychosomatic Medicine, 5,* 27-38.

Joan N. Burstyn (essay date 1979)

SOURCE: A review of *Maria Montessori,* in *History of Education Quarterly,* Vol. 19, No. 1, Spring, 1979, pp. 143-49.

[*In the following essay, Burstyn reviews Rita Kramer's biography* Maria Montessori, *finding that while Kramer provides a thorough account of her life, she fails to fully study or evaluate Montessori's career in its historical context, ultimately failing to address Montessori's revolutionary lifestyle and work in late-nineteenth-century Italy.*]

The Montessori movement is thriving in the United States today. The local public library has a shelf of books on Montessori education, and within a five mile radius of my house are more than five Montessori schools. What does a Montessori education offer to young children? It offers a prepared environment with child-size furniture (a Montessori innovation now copied by nursery schools the world over), sequenced educational materials designed for children to work on alone once they have been shown how to use them, the opportunity to learn to read and write by touching letters and literally putting them into words and sentences, the opportunity to categorize things by their size, shape, smell, taste and color. The freedom to find out things for oneself, under the guidance of a directress who is not a conventional teacher but who introduces materials to children when they have reached the "sensitive period" for absorbing them. Montessori said that children are as different from adults as caterpillars are from butterflies. One does not expect a caterpillar to fly, that is not its work. Caterpillars eat; so likewise, children learn in order to prepare themselves to become adults. Many adults call children's work play: "Don't play with that!" they shout as a child takes to pieces the telephone. Montessori taught that taking things apart is children's work. They learn through their senses. Their tasks are not those of adults, but adults should respect children's work just as they respect the work of other adults.

Maria Montessori, the founder of the Montessori method, was a virtuoso in the field of education. Her life is a challenge to any biographer, and perhaps that is why so few have attempted to write her biography. Born in 1870, and still teaching when she died at the age of eighty-one, she brought to education the skills of clinical observation she had learned as a physician. Her stamina was magnificent. For that reason alone she achieved much, but what she achieved was unusually varied. She was a successful physician, the first woman in Italy to receive a medical degree, and in her twenties she was known for her work in the hospitals of Rome and for her interest in the mentally retarded. She was a feminist who, at the turn of the century, represented Italian women at international women's congresses. She was an educational philosopher who, in her thirties and forties, developed her own theory and method of education. She was the designer of educational materials and a new learning environment for young children. For over forty years, at the end of her long life, she was a teacher-educator who personally trained thousands of teachers. She was a business woman who controlled a world-wide organization for the spread of Montessori education. And lastly, an attribute which characterized all her work, she was a teacher whose charisma attracted young and old, whose faith in children formed the basis for her educational, religious, and political actions.

Any biographer of Montessori should grapple with what it meant for her to be an Italian woman interested in medicine and education during the last years of the nineteenth century, a time of ferment in Europe over women's political and professional roles, and how far the structure of her career was influenced by the fact that she was not a man, but a woman. Alas, E. M. Standing in his 1957 biographical sketch and outline of Montessori's educational philosophy did not touch these issues.[1] Montessori's latest biographer, Rita Kramer, copes with them peripherally. Unlike Standing, Kramer has chosen to deal briefly with Montessori's philosophy and to concentrate instead on an historical account of her life. Hence, she does throw light on the personal choices Montessori made, and she deals skillfully with the role that Montessori's illegitimate son, Mario, had in her life. But much of her interpretation of the early years is similar to Standing's, and she does not explore the ways Montessori's choices were made for her by the male establishment, nor does she ask whether Montessori's routes for self-expression were dictated by the fact that she was a woman. No one has yet examined Montessori's impact on the women she trained from the perspective of their aspirations and achievements as women.

In Kramer's biography Montessori becomes an intensely human character, with a strain of arrogance in defending her ideas and her didactic materials. She became more regal, more aloof from criticism as she grew older. One cannot deny that Montessori acquired these characteristics. What virtuoso does not? Yet, by explaining them in terms of Montessori's personality, and by emphasising them at the expense of her ideas, Kramer has unwittingly reduced Montessori's stature and masked both the phenomenal success she achieved in her lifetime and the significance of her psychological insights into individual cognitive and emotional development.

A question that bemuses academics when discussing Montessori's work is why she insisted on keeping control of her methods and teaching materials. Until 1916 Montessori had an academic appointment at the Istituto Superiore di Magistero Femminile in Rome, and one might have expected her to behave as other academics, publishing her method in pedagogical journals and encouraging the free use of the didactic materials she had designed. (One has to pause here, however, to wonder how many of her colleagues at the teacher training institute had anything like her training or her record of publications, and to ask why she never became fully established on the faculty of the University of Rome in the years after 1900.) Kramer is particularly exercised by Montessori's persistent defense of her method and she implies that Montessori's decision to leave academia to head a private movement for spreading her ideas narrowed her vision. It gave her financial incentive for keeping control of the rights to teach her method and manufacture her materials, which in turn kept her intellectually from accepting criticism and befriending those who would develop her ideas further. Instead, Montessori became accustomed to a life of adulation. Those who attended her lectures saw her as a teacher rather than a colleague. Over the years she became insulated from criticism. There were always enough new worlds to conquer to make it unnecessary for her to reassess her work in the light of new developments in psychology and pedagogy.

Montessori cannot be judged, however, solely as a scientist and a scholar. In the first decades of the twentieth century she faced a unique problem. She had developed a philosophy for teaching children of all ages. According to Montessori, it was worthless to use her methods and materials without understanding and believing in their rationale. Her task was to give to as many people as possible that understanding. Her problem was one of strategy: How could she, a woman and an academic, best do that?

The model Montessori chose for publicizing her ideas was not that of the scholar, although she maintained close ties with the universities in many countries. Rather than follow the academic model, Montessori chose to build upon another strand of her experience, her involvement with the worldwide women's movement. She represented Italian women first at an International Congress of Women in Berlin in 1896, and later at another Congress in London. In Berlin she captivated her audience, as she later captivated audiences around the world; from that time on she could have had no doubt of her power to influence large groups. The political style of an international conference, the exhilaration of meeting people from many countries, the generation of commitment among those present, of faith that they could return home to effect change, these were the characteristics that Montessori recreated in the Montessori movement. Through her international training sessions she sought, and achieved, a social impact far broader than she could ever have had as a lecturer, or, had she received such an appointment, as a professor at the University of Rome.

Montessori's biographers mention in passing that most people attending her courses were women. And yet that, in itself, was part of the Montessori revolution. The women who attended Montessori's training sessions returned home to *organize* and *administer* Montessori schools and societies, undertaking tasks they had previously ascribed to men. Sometimes Montessori misjudged people's abilities, but what she did superbly was to place her trust in young women and expect from them mature organizational skills. This is not to imply that the Montessori movement was exclusively female; it was not. But, within the movement, women found room to share with men the roles of organizer and educational administrator which outside the movement were often closed to them.

Women supporters, however, do not bring to an organization the ready access to capital provided by men, and a major problem for Montessori was how to raise enough money to keep the various Montessori societies in operation. Though Montessori schools brought in fees, capital endowment was needed for them, for the societies, and for teacher training institutes. Montessori seems never to have allowed the need for money to blind her to the terms on which it was granted. She preferred to see Montessori societies wither than be subverted from her aims. She persuaded a number of governments to give financial and political recognition to her schools. Her program was adopted in Catalonia for a number of years, in Italy under Mussolini until Montessori realized that political interference was affecting the curriculum, and in Holland. In England a number of school districts adopted the Montessori method, and in India, after 1940, her method gained wide acclaim.

In the United States Montessori met a complex situation politically and intellectually. She was given a triumphant reception when she first visited the United States in 1913, but enthusiasm for her method collapsed within a few years, and not until the 1960s did the Montessori movement in the United States revive. Then, concern with the rights of each individual led educators to turn to the welfare of the handicapped, the poor, and the child who was discriminated against for whatever reason. Montessori had provided a scheme and a set of materials for educating such children; she had shown that early education was essential to combat environmental deprivation. She was rediscovered by American educators. According to R. E. Orem, writing in 1969: "The developmental needs of the huge population of special children, and all other children for that matter, can be met only by an individualized education, of which the Montessori approach provides an outstanding example."[2] The history of the Montessori movement in the United States is therefore intriguing. Why did the method's popularity rise and fall so precipitately? Kramer disentangles many of the influences that were at work, but she leaves several others untouched.

Maria Montessori was an unmarried professional woman. In 1913 tempers ran high in the United States over women's suffrage and the broader issue of women's participation in the professions. There were many who opposed women's professional aspirations, fearing, among other things, that women with careers would be unlikely to marry and have children. To them, Montessori must have personified the new woman. She was also Italian and a practicing Catholic. She saw moral education as closely bound to her secular method. In the United States, and especially in California where Montessori gave an international course in 1915, there was a strong nativist movement that was both anti-southern European and anti-Catholic. The nativist movement found a language of respectability in eugenics, which had been hailed at an international conference in London in 1912. Eugenicists postulated a hierarchy of intelligence among the races in which northern Europeans held predominance over southern Europeans. In the United States, those who opposed large scale immigration pointed to the dangers inherent in populating the country with inferior races. They felt the influx of immigrants from southern Europe, combined with the reluctance of college educated American women to reproduce, presented a crisis for society. Among the greatest dangers was the likelihood that the number of criminal types in the society would increase. Scientists suggested that there were criminal types, with criminal germ plasmas. Politicians hinted that these personalities could be prevented from multiplying only by compulsory sterilization laws. In all these discussions, Italians, of whom Montessori was a proud representative, were among the groups claimed to be inferior. Montessori was herself trained in anthropometrics, but she did not maintain that certain types of humans were inherently criminal, incorrigible or inferior. She held that to prevent the development of criminal tendencies one had to train a child from birth. Hence, she told a reporter on her arrival in the United States there were no bad children, only bad methods for rearing them.

Montessori's ideas, therefore, did not jibe with those of the eugenicists. Yet among her first sponsors in this country was Alexander Graham Bell who became Honorary President of the second International Eugenics Conference. Bell's son-in-law decried Montessori later for not knowing who her friends were in the United States when she broke with the group who had first sponsored her, and Kramer echoes his dismay. Did Montessori, perhaps, understand the price of accepting their support?

Least hospitable to Montessori was the American academic community. Kramer discusses the intellectual disagreements over Montessori's method, but the most acute analysis still seems to be that of J. Mc V. Hunt in his 1964 introduction to *The Montessori Method*.[3] Hunt shows how Montessori's ideas were at odds with fundamental beliefs held by intellectuals at the time she visited the United States: that early life experiences were unimportant; that each individual had a fixed intelligence; and that development was predetermined by one's genes. Each of these beliefs had been abandoned by the 1960s, hence the reawakening of interest in Montessori's work at that time.

There was a crucial difference also between the terminology that Montessori and American educators used to define children's activities. American educators urged parents to understand the importance of *play* to children. There was strong political pressure for children to be given legal privileges in the form of compulsory schooling, and juvenile courts where they were not to be held responsible for their actions in the same way as adults. Montessori spoke of children's activities as their *work* and claimed that even young children could and should accept a shared responsibility for maintaining the integrity of their prepared environment. Only by examining the words, work and play, in the cultural contexts that were understood by Montessori and educators in the United States can we visualize how their vocabulary served to magnify their differences in philosophy.

Despite our interest in Montessori's impact on education in the United States, she gave her work a global setting. No-one has yet assessed it in terms of the revolutionary goals she set for it. Her first Casa dei Bambini was in the slums of Rome. She achieved startling results there with the children of the poorest families in urban society. Her

pupils acquired self-confidence and academic skills. Montessori recognized the revolutionary potential of this achievement and believed that by spreading it to children in all countries she could effect a change in the nature of human society. She envisaged a new kind of person who would be self-directed and confident, who would function well at work and in the community, who was opposed to war and worked actively for peace. How can we measure whether Montessori's aims have been achieved?

Kramer has provided a stimulating historical account of Montessori's life and an impressionistic evaluation of her work. However, as David Elkind pointed out in a brief essay comparing Piaget and Montessori, we have still to wait for definitive research on the effectiveness of her method.[4] This evaluation necessitates discrete studies that will differentiate her method's influence upon various social classes, and nationalities, in different decades. (Ironically in the United States at least, her method has been adopted most eagerly by privileged members of society, not the poor, so that its revolutionary character has been subverted.) We have to separate and measure Montessori's success as a teacher of children, her success as a teacher of adults, and the success of those whom she trained to be teachers. Montessori claimed that the method and the didactic materials, not the directress, were the crucial parts of her learning environment, but there were those who knew her who claimed she underestimated her power as a directress. Research by Pedersen, Faucher, and Eaton on "the effects of first-grade teachers on children's subsequent adult status" suggests that it may be possible to ascertain how correct Montessori was, and that by using longitudinal studies of children educated in different Montessori schools we will be able to assess the influence of her method upon their lives as adults.[5] At the same time we could gather information on simpler questions such as: how many people who have won the Nobel Peace Prize since 1910 have had a Montessori education? How many of those who have been leaders in the United Nations, and in various peace organizations? How many of those who have designed programs for worker participation in running industries? How many of the leaders of the present day women's movement? The task for scholars is formidable, not only to find the information but to assess how causal links can be established. Even with adults who went on from their studies with Montessori to develop their own theories, such as Helen Parkhurst, the founder of the Dalton Plan for education, or Jean Piaget, for several years head of the Swiss Montessori Society, a researcher can indicate only the probable influence of Montessori's ideas. There is much work still to be done before a definitive biography of Montessori can be written.

Notes

1. E. M. Standing, *Maria Montessori: Her Life and Work* (Fresno, California. Academy Library Guild, 1957).

2. R. C. Orem, *Montessori and the Special Child* (New York, 1969), p. xiv. Since the revival of interest in Montessori's work in the United States, Orem has

written and edited books on Montessori's method for teachers and the general public.

3. J. McV. Hunt, "Introduction: Revisiting Montessori", in Maria Montessori, *The Montessori Method* (New York, 1964) pp. xi-xxxix. Hunt's essay contains many references to research studies which confirm the insightfulness of Montessori's theories.

4. David Elkind, *Children and Adolescents: Interpretive Essays on Jean Piaget* (New York, 1974), pp. 128-138.

5. Eigil Pedersen, Therese Annette Faucher, with William W. Eaton, "A New Perspective on the Effects of First-grade Teachers on Children's Subsequent Adult Status", *Harvard Educational Review,* v. 48, no. 1 (February 1978): 1-31.

Stelio Cro (essay date 1987)

SOURCE: "Education and Utopia in Maria Montessori," in *Canadian Journal of Italian Studies,* Vol. 10, No. 34, 1987, pp. 23-42.

[*In the following essay, Cro analyzes the place of Montessori's* Absorbent Mind *in the philosophical notion of utopia, from the ideal of the Renaissance Man to the dystopic visions of George Orwell and Aldous Huxley.*]

Sforzinda by Filarte, Leonardo's project for Milan in the sixteenth-century and the other architectural projects of the Renaissance belong, for chronological reasons as well as for philosophical ones, to a traditional, classical view of education. That view, which prevailed until the end of the Second World War, states that, given the proper environment, the ideal man, the Renaissance man, will be able to develop to his fullest potential.[1]

But after Sigmund Freud's theories on the subconscious the exploration of the potential of the human mind has opened new perspectives for a better understanding of the relation between the child and the environment.

Let us review briefly the special relationship that education has always enjoyed with the utopian genre, before we analyze this relationship in Maria Montessori's writings, especially her **Absorbent Mind,** first published in Italian as **La mente del bambino,** 1960, and translated into English the following year. But the content was already well known in the late 40's and early 50's since it was made up of a series of lectures delivered in India where she was a refugee during the war.[2]

First of all it is necessary to take into account the different views on education and on utopia, conceived during the last fifty years, since these views not only differ radically, but have a direct bearing on our current views on education as well as Montessori's views on education.[3]

We can safely say that since the end of the Second World War education has undergone a revolutionary process consisting of the implementation of a utopian concept—democracy—to education. American education was caught in the change following the first Soviet Sputnik in 1957 when the American public perceived "progressivism," the current trend at the time, as being too soft on the child. But the reform has never been carried out systematically and "Progressivism" and "Perennialism" have coexisted. I believe that the American experience is still at the heart of most western public schools' reformist trends. Let me summarize briefly these trends:

I a) 1) Already in 1916, John Dewey in his *Democracy and Education* formulated the school known as *Progressivism:* "We thus reach a technical definition of education: it is that reconstruction or reorganization of experience which adds to the meaning of experience, and which increases the ability to direct the course of subsequent experience."[4] Dewey believes that the only method is the experimental one: "The most direct blow at the traditional separation of doing and knowing and at the traditional prestige of purely 'intellectual' studies, however, has been given by the progress of experimental science. If this progress has demonstrated anything, it is that there is no such thing as genuine knowledge and fruitful understanding except as the offspring of *doing* (. . .) Men have *to do* something to the tings when they wish to find out something; they have to alter conditions. This is the lesson of the laboratory method, and the lesson which all education has to learn" (pp. 321-322). Furthermore, in Dewey's opinion only democracy permits, indeed encourages, the free interplay of ideas and personalities that is a necessary condition of true growth. In the progressivist view democracy and cooperation are said to imply each other. Ideally, democracy is "shared experience." As Dewey puts it, "A democracy is more than a form of government; it is primarily a mode of associated living, of conjoint communicated experience" (p. 101). In order to teach democracy, the school itself must be democratic. It should promote student government, the free discussion of ideas, joint pupil-staff planning, and the full participation of all in the educative experience. Dewey warns that schools however should not indoctrinate students in the tenets of a new social order. To instruct them in a specific program of social and political action would be to adopt an authoritarianism that progressivism specifically rejects.

2) Freud influenced decisively progressivism. The child, according to this theory, was to be freed—freed *from* the restraints of the traditional teacher and the shackles of the authoritarian school, freed *by* art and Freud. If a new educational system could be introduced, one in which children are encouraged to develop their personalities, then the world would be saved by this new, free, generation. Freud's work was applied to education by a group of disciplines in psychology, in social work, and especially, in the mental hygiene movement. The pattern for the new education can be found in the writings of the latter. In this pattern the following are key strands. Maladjustment, anti-

social behavior, and mental illness could be prevented or ameliorated. The emotional life of the individual was the key behavior. The emotions could be molded or trained or controlled if the right environment were supplied in childhood. Finally, the public school was the strategic agency for the training of the emotions. Certain consequences follow from these assumptions. In the etiology of maladjustment and neurosis, failure and retardation in schools ranked high. Failure and retardation would be eliminated by abandoning or minimizing formal courses of instruction, abandoning or minimizing academic subjects, and abandoning or minimizing competition and achievement. In their place would be substituted projects and other group activities, play, and especially creative self-expression through art and other aesthetic activities. For the ethic of psychoanalysis and that of creative self-expression were joined in the mental hygiene movement. Among the foremost values of mental health, creativity is prominent. For some the absence of creativity is not just a symptom of neurosis, but the very essence of it. Conversely the release of creativity becomes close to being identical with mental health. The concern of many progressivists for creative activities, such as art, music, theatre and dance, was not so much to make education as rich and rounded as possible, but to treat it as a form of therapy. In conclusion, the child coming from a "normal home" would be treated as a potential patient of an experimental brainwashing institute.

b) *Perennialism*'s philosophic foundations are embedded in classical realism; the philosophers most quoted are Aristotle and Aquinas. Among its leading spokesmen are Robert Maynard Hutchins, Mortimer L. Adler, and Sir Richard Livingstone, an English classicist who has won an appreciable following in the United States. Although some perennialist ideas are in practice nearly everywhere, they have been applied most consistently at St. John's College, Annapolis, Maryland. Perennialism believes in the permanent values of "great books".[5] Perennialism reacted to Progressivism. The launching of the first Sputnik by the Soviet Union in 1957 marked the end of this American educational theory, because the public perceived it as too soft on the child.[6]

Still progressivism continues today in George Axtelle, William O. Stanley, Ernest Bayles, Lawrence G. Thomas and Frederic C. Neff. The *pragmatist* view is that change, and not permanence, is the essence of reality. Progressivism adheres totally to the pragmatic view,[7] and believes that education is always in the process of development. The special quality of education is not to be determined by applying perennial standards of goodness, truth and beauty, but by construing education as a continual reconstruction of experience. Its social aim is well defined by Kneller: "Progressivism acknowledges no absolute goal, unless it is social progress attained through individual freedom."[8] The student should engage in projects that spring from his natural curiosity to learn and acquire significance as they are worked out in cooperation with other members of the class and under guidance of the teacher. Thus, all projects should be both personally and socially significant.[9] Ac-

cording to this the teacher's role is not to direct, but to endorse.[10] Also, school should encourage cooperation rather than competition. Progressivism rejects the social Darwinist view developed by Herbert Spencer, that society should imitate nature and encourage competition. Life in the jungle does indeed appear "in tooth and claw," but only when animals are hungry, angered, or mating. Because they are unable to control their condition, animals cannot improve it; man, who is able to control his condition, can.[11]

Foster McMurray, in "The Present Status of Pragmatism in Education" believes that "the intent of Dewey's theory was to stimulate more and better learning of arts, sciences and technologies. There was in this program no concern for immediate practical or directly utilitarian bits of information and technique, nor any process of choosing and organizing information around characteristic activities of daily life. On the contrary, in Dewey's version of pragmatism, characteristic activities of daily life were psychologically useful starting points, for moving the learner to a consideration of meaning increasingly remote, abstract, and related to one another in impersonal systems rather than to practical daily use."[12]

Progressivism left many questions on education unanswered: for example, to what extent can the self-discipline necessary to learning be self-taught? How can one balance the individual versus the group, the single-mind versus the mass-mind and how can forced cooperation and conformism be avoided?

c) One of the leading studies which has attempted to assess the state of education in the United States is *Reform of Undergraduate Education* by Arthur Levine and John Weingart.[13] The authors survey the state of current undergraduate education and reforms under way to modify and improve the curriculum of the typical four year college. The authors, at the beginning of their study, confess that they had supported the notion of a "free," or "open" curriculum one which might encourage students' participation in the pursuit of a more meaningful education.[14] But they had to realize later on that their predictions "were a disaster" (p. 8). They in fact discovered that "students do not participate in programs that permit them to plan their own education" (p. 8). The authors feel that too many colleges show an "incestuous," "ivory tower" nature. Their conclusion is that "with the increasing technological need for greater specialization, general education is increasingly important to provide a basis for common humanity among people. Specialization isolates people, underlines their differences, and is, in this sense, divisive. General education is capable of providing a commonality sufficient to surmount the differences in vocation" (p. 50). They also say, that it is almost impossible to find a college, which provides that kind of education (p. 50). The reason for this, they say, is the lack of "general educationists" (p. 51). They conclude, that "Scholarship forces scholars so far apart that they can no longer understand each other" (p. 51).

This brief survey of current trends in education indicates two major areas which have either been ignored or where the situation has worsened. First, little emphasis is placed on the child at the pre-school age and, second, increased specialization leads to an increased sense of divisiveness. To both these issues Montessori provided answers in her work **The Absorbent Mind.** In so doing she has conceived education, not as an end in itself, but as a means to achieve a greater understanding among both individuals and nations. It is this universal aim that brings Montessori's theory on education within the borders of the Utopian genre.

The word utopia itself needs a previous clarification. This word, which has been in use since 1516, the date of More's *Utopia,* the title of which would eventually characterize a genre, has come to have a popular meaning and in this semantic connotation is taken to mean something unattainable, an impossible dream, or description of a fictitious place with no relationship whatsoever to the real world. As such, it has often been considered something of an odd genre, outside of history or literature, or even philosophy.

However, in the last fifty years, due perhaps to the nuclear threat to our civilization, more and more attention is being paid to this genre. Attempts to classify it have so far all failed because each criterion has been motivated and conditioned by the content and intention of the works ascribed to the genre, regardless of the profound difference of philosophical depth which often separates one from the other. Let us say immediately that, contrarily to the popular meaning referred to above, the best utopian works always had a potential for real progress and a real-life application. After all, Leonardo's flying machines came true, even though it took over four centuries to do so. The same can be said of Bacon's movie houses, sound reproducing machines, light beams which make one think of the laser beam, and a form of energy which is inexhaustible and makes one think of nuclear energy.[15] Most utopian technological projects have been fulfilled in the twentieth- century. But there is one, the most important one, which has so far eluded us; this is the dream of a united and peaceful world. It is perhaps because of the extraordinary technological advances achieved in the twentieth-century that utopia has gained interest for us, because of the frustration of our troubled world seemingly unable to find peace. This is where the interest for the genre and Montessori's message come full circle.

Let us review some of the criteria with which this genre has been classified in order to place Montessori's contribution in relation to it:

II a) In 1929 Karl Mannheim published his *Ideologie und Utopie.*[16] According to him "ideology" is a political idea inspired and supported by a system—the "establishment"—in power, while "utopia" is the idea which opposes this particular ideology currently in power. Therefore in Mannheim the definition of "utopia" means progress and revolution, whereas that of "ideology" is static and reactionary. According to Mannheim there are four types of utopia:

1) The religious utopia of the sixteenth-century, where he places the origin of modern utopia.

2) The humanitarian-liberal utopia of the enlightenment bourgeoisie of the eighteenth-century.

3) The pious utopia, which flourished in the eighteenth and nineteenth-century and revived the first religious utopia.

4) The communist utopia which he considers "the new definition of utopia in terms of reality".[17]

It is important to underline this last category because for Mannheim utopia is not only possible but, in this last case, is the reality of a certain geopolitical area of the world.

b) The opposite of Mannheim is Etienne Gilson's criterium as explained in his work *Les metamorphoses de la Cité de Dieu,* published in 1952. After reviewing the origin and development of what he calls the "universal society," referring to utopian conceptions, Gilson concludes that man has not yet succeeded in founding a utopian organization on a world scale. The French historian believes that the reason for this failure is the lack of an amalgamating principle, that is Christian faith. "Il peut y avoir une cité des hommes, et elle ne se fera pas sans les politiciens, les juristes, les savants ni les philosophes, mais elle se fera moins encore sans l'Eglise et les theologiens."[18] Gilson believes that Christianity is the highest value for a nation. His definition implies that definition of nation provided by Saint Augustine, based on Cicero: "Populus est coetus multitudinis rationalis rerum quas diligit concordi ratione sociatus."[19] Gilson rejects Marxism because he does not consider it spiritually attractive.

c) In several of his studies Eugenio Garin has elaborated a view of utopia which is different from both Mannheim and Gilson. Garin identifies utopia as the ideal city which in the fifteenth-century Italian humanists such as Leonardo Bruni and Leon Battista Alberti identified with Florence, Venice or Milan.[20] Garin believes that the fifteenth-century conceived the terrestrial ideal city by renouncing the ideal Christian heavenly one: "La città ideale di tante scritture del secolo XV è una città razionale: è una città reale portata a compimento, svolta secondo la sua natura; è un piano o un progetto attuabile; è Firenze, è Venezia, è Milano, quando sian perfezionate le loro leggi e finite le loro fabbriche (. . .). La città ideale del Quattrocento è in terra, e non si confonde nè si confronta con la città celeste."[21] This city, however, never became a reality. Already in the fifteenth-century, after the loss of political freedom and the fall of the Republican state, Garin sees, as a reaction, the apocalyptic state of Savonarola and the tyranny of Machiavelli: "Nello sconforto savonaroliano come nell'amarezza di Machiavelli si esprimeva la catastrofe di una civiltà (. . .) tra delusioni e sconfitte nascono profezie, previsioni apocalittiche, evocazioni di paradisi originari e sogni di soluzioni al di fuori di ogni realtà. Non piu Sforzinda, ma città solari e repubbliche immaginarie."[22]

Garin's schema presents a duality consisting of the opposition between a layman's pagan humanism—in which Garin sees the elaboration of the fifteenth-century utopia—and the religious theological reaction, insensitive to that elaboration, the clearest example of which, according to Garin, would be Dante, whom he contrasts with Dante's biographer Leonardo Bruni.[23] Besides Dante, Garin considers Savonarola hostile to that elaboration and Campanella opposed to it.[24] This duality is taken to its most extreme consequences by Garin who proceeds to identify the layman's city as the new one, that in which one can find progress and reform, whereas its opposite, the theological and apocalyptical, would be represented by the political thinking of Dante, Savonarola and Campanella. However, modern utopia was born within the boundaries of Christian Humanism, whose influence on the genre is considered by Garin non-existent or utterly counterproductive.

d) Raymond Trousson in *Voyages aux pays de nulle part*[25] considers the utopian genre as fiction. According to him the author of a utopia conceives an artistic work in which reality has an important part. In other words, we have a utopia when this has a plot in which an ideal state is described which is totally different from the existing states but which could represent a possible society. However, contrary to Mannheim and Gilson, Trousson does not see any practical or moral meaning in the utopian genre. Trousson differentiates this genre from those which he calls the "genres apparentés," the similar genres as those of the golden age and the Arcadia, considered by Trousson only as the expression of a nostalgia for a mythical past or as an evasion or refusal to accept a social organization. In conclusion, Trousson's definition of utopia is a negative one: utopia is not a political or moral treatise, it is not the myth of the golden age or the Arcadia, nor the adventures modelled on Robinson Crusoe. In his definition Trousson includes also those works which satirize utopia, such as Huxley's *Brave New World*, Orwell's *1984* and *Animal Farm*. Trousson excludes from his definition those experimental utopias whose purpose is to establish an ideal state.

e) In my last book on the subject of utopia I have proposed the following definition: "Modern utopia is a genre which represents the theoretical elaboration of the experience of the discovery and conquest of America and which aims at the assimilation of this experience and its historical connotations within the boundaries of a Western Medieval Christian tradition with the purpose of providing as a political solution the temporal and spiritual unity of mankind."[26] According to this definition, I believe that the true reformers were the Christian utopists, because of the moral component of their projects: More, Campanella, Bacon and the anonymous author of *Sinapia*. Education is a vital component of their utopian conception.

III Montessori's theory of education shares a utopian element with these Christian utopists. In fact the gap between

these Renaissance thinkers and Montessori was filled by Rousseau, who in his *Emile* has two passages which must have exercised a powerful influence over Montessori. In his "Preface" to *Emile*, Rousseau says that his book's subject matter is good education for the child, whom he presents, as Montessori does, as a "little man": "On ne connait point l'enfance: sur les fausses idées qu'on en a, plus on va, plus on s'égare. Les plus sages s'attachent à ce qu'il importe aux hommes de savoir, sans considerer que les enfants sont en ètat d'apprendre. Ils cherchent toujours l'homme dans l'enfant, sans penser à ce qu'il est avant que d'être homme. Voilà l'étude à laquelle je me suis le plus appliquée."[27]

And the following intuition of Rousseau clearly anticipates the essence of Montessori's theory and the basic assumption of **The Absorbent Mind,** concerning the learning ability of the child in his first few years of life: "Je le répète, l'éducation de l'homme commence à sa naissance; avant de parler, avant que d'entendre, il s'instruit dejà. L'experience previent les leçons; au moment qu'il connait sa nourrice, il a dejà beaucoup acquis (. . .). Mais nous ne songeons guère aux acquisitions generales, parce qu'elles se font sans qu'on y pense et même avant l'age de raison."[28]

Montessori propounds a method of education which has many utopian elements. In fact, it could be thought of as a sort of "scientific utopia."

She starts with a descriptive approach, accurately defining the different stages of conception, the evolution of the embryo, the gestation period, birth and the stages in the development of the growing child: from birth to six years (subdivided in birth to three years and three to six years), from six to twelve years (the happy state), and from twelve to eighteen years (subdivided in twelve to fifteen years and fifteen to eighteen years), after which, according to Montessori, man only grows in age.

Even her psychological exploration, which acknowledges Freudian theories and recent contributions from Boring, Langfeld, Weld, Katz, McDougall, Watson, Child, and behaviorist theories from Watson, Child, and other psychologists and behaviorists has a sound scientific foundation.

However, from this scientific data emerges a double thesis. One which proposes a mechanical functioning of the mind of the child, accurately described as the "absorbent mind," and another which appeals to a spiritual growth, to a unifying social concept of education based on love.

It is this second stage of Montessori's thesis where her educational theories can be termed utopian. By this I mean a general, universal aim which is based on value judgments, generally religious values, a belief in divine law and divine grace, love for mankind, an unshakable certitude in the goodness of natural law, a rejection of authority and tradition and, above all, a conviction that, given the proper environment, the children will grow up loving each other and this will somehow solve the grave conflicts which have plagued civilized man since time immemorial, and in the end, this "natural child," this perfect human being, will unite mankind.

I do not intend to argue the scientific value of Montessori's theory as far as the mechanism of the absorbent mind. It is in a sense a fascinating theory, quite ingenious and articulate and it does offer a method to approach that still unknown period of the first three years of the child's mental life. What I would like to point out is that within the scope of her scientific theories Montessori leaves room for scientific fiction. A few examples:

1) *Eugenics*: Montessori speaks of a new science which can select the best human types. This is a classic topic in the utopian genre.[29] In Campanella's *City of the Sun,* the Genovese pilot who describes the habits and values of the Solarians, tells how the Solarians laughed at the thought that, while the Europeans spent much time and effort in trying to improve the race of horses and dogs, they did nothing to improve the human race.

2) Under the general heading of *genetic engineering,* a topic common to both Campanella's *City of the Sun* and Bacon's *New Atlantis,* Montessori suggests a further step: psychic engineering. "If, by an effort of imagination, we visualize mental development as following similar paths, it would be natural to suppose that man, who today can act on life to create new types of a higher order, must be able, also, to help and control man's mental formation" (p. 50). This is also a topic of the most recent utopian tradition exemplified in Orwell's *1984* and A. Huxley's *Brave New World.* However, both these works belong to that branch of the utopian genre which some scholars have classified as dystopias or anti-utopias, in which the perfect state has become a hellish nightmare, devoid of any spiritual human value. This, of course, is quite the opposite of what Montessori wants, since her aim is a richly spiritual world united in love and peace and not controlled by robot-like machines.

3) *Language*: Montessori describes the process by which the child absorbs language. This is possible through the interaction of different forces. One, which Montessori calls *Mneme,* could be explained as unconscious memory and is much stronger than conscious memory because it acts on the subconscious with the child's active knowledge. Therefore, whatever is absorbed by the Mneme stays with the child forever: "With our conscious memory we forget, but the unconscious, although it seems to feel nothing and not to remember, does something worse, for impressions made at this level are handed over to the Mneme. They become graven on the personality itself" (p. 77). From the Mneme orginates an energy, which Montessori calls the *nebula*: "The child receives from the nebula of language suitable stimuli and guidance for the formation in himself of his mother tongue, which is not inborn in him, but something he finds in his environment and absorbs according to immutable laws. Thanks to the nebular energy of language,

the child is able to distinguish the sounds of spoken language from the sounds and noises which reach him, all mixed together. Thanks to this, he can incarnate the language he hears just as perfectly as if it were a racial characteristic. In the same way, he takes on the social character and customs which make him a man belonging to his particular part of the world" (p. 79). And again Montessori emphasizes how the child always learns language through an unconscious process: "The child inherits the power of constructing a language by an unconscious activity of absorption. This potentiality is what we have called the *nebula of language*" (p. 80).

A third element guides the unconscious activity of the child toward his goal. This is what Montessori calls *Horme*: "A vital force is active within the child and this guides his efforts towards their goal. It is the force called *horme* by Sir Percy Nunn. This term resembles Bergson's *e`lan vital* and Freud's *libido,* and it is the source of all evolution. This allows him his natural development and ultimately his conquest of independence" (p. 84).

A) THE EXPOSITION OF MONTESSORI'S THEORY OF LANGUAGE.

Montessori distinguishes two stages in the child's psychic mechanism of learning a language:

Stage I. According to this the *first* stage begins in the deepest shadows of the unconscious mind; there it is developed and the product becomes fixed. Only then does it appear in the open. The mechanism at work causes all this to happen. The quantity of inner work may be immense, yet the outer signs of it are often small. This means there is a great disproportion between the powers of expression and the inner work the child is doing. It is also found that visible progress does not take place gradually, but by leaps. At a certain time, for example, the power to pronounce syllables appears, and then for months the child utters only syllables. Externally, he seems to be making no progress, but all of a sudden, he says a word. Then, for a long time, he uses only one or two words, and his progress seems discouragingly slow. Nevertheless, other forms of activity show that his inner life is undergoing a steady and remarkable expansion. There is no smooth, slow advance, word by word, but here also we find explosive phenomena—as psychologists call them—which are not provoked by any teacher's action, but occur of themselves for no apparent reason. Every child, at a particular period of his life, bursts out with a number of words all perfectly pronounced. Within a space of three months, the child who was almost mute, learns to use easily all the varied forms of the noun, suffixes, prefixes, and verbs. And, in every child, all this occurs at the end of the second year of his life (pp. 113-114). This is a treasure prepared in the unconscious, which is then handed over to consciousness, and the child, in full possession of his new power, talks and talks without cessation (p. 114).

Stage II. At about the age of two and a half, which marks a border line in man's mental formation, a new period begins in the organization of language, which continues to develop without explosions, but with a great deal of liveliness and spontaneity. This second period lasts till somewhere around the fifth or sixth year, and during that period the child learns many new words and perfects his sentence formation. It is true that if the child's circumstances are such that he hears very few words, or nothing but dialect, he will come to speak like this. But if he lives among cultured people with a wide vocabulary, he takes it all in equally well. Circumstances, therefore, are very important, yet the child's language, at this time, becomes richer no matter what his surroundings. Belgian psychologists, Montessori tells us, have found that the child of two and a half has only two or three hundred words, but at six he knows thousands. And this all happens without a teacher. We must be careful to bear in mind the double path which is always followed. There is an unconscious activity that prepares speech, succeeded by a conscious process which slowly awakens and takes from the unconsciousness what it has to offer (pp. 114-115).

b) Scientific hypothesis for language.

Montessori explains that since the last century the brain cortex were shown to be connected with language. These are areas of nerve cells, or "centers." Two of these are primarily involved, one being concerned with the *hearing* of speech (an auditory receptive center), and the other with the *production* of speech, of the movements required for vocalizing words. One of these is therefore a sensorial center, the other a motor center (p. 116).

Montessori supposes that the hearing organs are connected to the mysterious seat of mental life, where the child's language is evolved in the depths of his unconscious mind. As for the motor side, its activities can be inferred from the astonishing complexity and precision of the movements needed to produce spoken words.

It is clear, she says, that when the child is born, he has neither hearing nor speech. Some psychologists tend to believe that children are born deaf, but Montessori suggests another possibility: that the child's hearing organs are so disposed that they block out all sounds except those of speech (pp. 117-119). "It is only because nature has constructed and isolated these centers for the purpose of language, that the child ever learns to speak at all" (p. 119).

Montessori believes that "a special mechanism exists for language. Not the possession of language in itself, but the possession of this mechanism which enables men to make language of their own, is what distinguishes the human species. Words, therefore, are a kind of fabrication which the child produces, thanks to the machinery which he finds at his disposal. In the mysterious period which immediately follows birth, the child—who is a psychic entity endowed with a specially refined form of sensitiveness—might be regarded as an *ego* asleep. But all of a sudden he wakes up and hears delicious music; all his fibers begin to vibrate. The baby might think that no other sound had ever reached his ears, but really it was because his soul was not responsive to other sounds. Only human speech had any power to stir him" (pp. 119-120).

Montessori says that it is as if inside the child there were a tiny teacher who tells the child what to do at the right time. The child first fixes the sounds and then the syllables, following a gradual process as logical as the language itself. Words follow and finally we enter the field of grammar. Here, the first words to be learned are the names of things, substantives. We see how greatly nature's teaching illuminates our own thought. Nature is the teacher, and at her behest the child learns what to us adults seem the dullest parts of language. Yet, according to Montessori, the child shows the keenest interest, and this lasts well into the next period of his development, from three to five years of age. Methodically, Nature teaches nouns and adjectives, conjunctions and adverbs, verbs in the infinitive, then the conjugation of verbs and the declension of nouns; prefixes and suffixes, and all the exceptions. It is like a school, and we have at the end an examination, in which the child shows in practice that he can use every part of speech (pp. 120-121).

Montessori is also of the opinion that children learn grammar easily between the ages of four and six by repeating the same sequence observed in the first period (birth to three years): "If, then, we give him some grammatical help when he is four years old, while he is perfecting his language mechanisms and enriching his vocabulary, we provide conditions favorable to his work. By teaching grammar, we help him to master perfectly the spoken language that he is absorbing. Experience has shown us that little children take the liveliest interest in grammar, and that this is the right time to put them in touch with it. In the first period (from 0 to 3) the acquisition of grammatical form was unconscious; now it can be perfected consciously. And we notice something else; that the child of his age learns many new words. He has a special sensitiveness for words; they attract his interest, and he spontaneously accumulates a very great number" (pp. 173-174).

The utopian dimension of this theory is that there is in the child a universal, preordained, pre-established mechanism which conceives language, creates it by absorbing the sounds of human speech—something which could be termed a "philosophical" language which enables children to adopt the different languages of the world. An example could be drawn from the software of the computer, the language of which is built in so that it permits the machine to receive orders and respond. This universal or philosophical language, which is far more advanced than anything we know, is the aim of Montessori's method, when she talks about "the discovery of the human soul" (p. 172). This discovery would allow one of the earliest utopian dreams to come true; a philosophical language which does not require explanations because it is so clear and concise. This is the language of More's Utopians and Campanella's Solarians.

4) *Environment*. Montessori's method is based on a drastic change of environment. She rejects the current environ-

ment of the schools because it is artificial, anti-pedagogical and harmful for the child. The children who come out of this system are all more or less abnormal, she says. Instead only the right environment can produce the perfect normal child: "We cannot make a genius. We can only give to each individual the chance to fulfill his potential possibilities. But if we are to speak of a process of biological maturation we must also be prepared to recognize a process of psychological maturation. *Maturation* is far more important than the net sum of the gene effects operating in a self-limited time-cycle, for besides the effects of the genes there are also the effects of the environment on which they act. This environment has a dominant part to play in the process of maturation" (pp. 94-95). Montessori's idea of education is based on a rearrangement of the environment which implies a radical change of values concering adults who must change their mental and physical habits in order to allow the child's growth and its beneficial effects on earth. Montessori believes that her experiments with preparing a special world for three to six year olds with furnishings the size of children were entirely positive: "The social life that these children then came to lead brought out in them unexpected tendencies and tastes. It was the children themselves who showed that they preferred one another's company to dolls, and the small 'real life' utensils to toys" (p. 169).

Montessori believes that when the attraction of the new environment exerts its spell, offering motives for constructive activity, then all these energies combine and the deviations can be dispersed. A unique type of child appears, a "new child," but it is really the child's true personality, set free to develop normally (p. 203). Montessori believes that the child's mind requires constant attention, because it "starves easily." Today, after so many years and much experimentation, the truth of this is established. In the *Child Guidance Clinics* which are being widely founded for the treatment of "difficult children," the child is offered an environment rich in motives for activity, in which he can choose what he will take and use. In making this choice he is free from the control of any teacher or indeed from adult control in general (pp. 204-205). Montessori also believes that the mind of the child needs to work continuously. Spiritual development only occurs if the mind is always busy in healthy occupations. The devil enters the idle mind. The indolent man cannot be spiritual. Montessori agrees with the words of Gibran in the *Prophet*: "Work is love made visible." (The work ethic is a common element in most utopias.)

Montessori believes that by the time the child is six years old he can no longer be taught anything. The only thing we can do is to put education on a scientific footing so that children can work effectively, without being disturbed or impeded (p. 208).

She also believes that children, in such an environment, enjoy learning. They become cultured by means of spontaneous activity, but, she adds, this joyful experience has a limited time span: "By the age of five and a half or six,

this sensitivity has ceased to exist; so it is clear that writing can be learned with joy and enthusiasm only before that age. Children older than this have lost the special opportunity which nature grants them of learning to write without making special and conscious efforts of application and will" (p. 173).

The change of the environment is perhaps the most obvious utopian aspect of Montessori's method. All utopias are located in isolated regions, more often than not they are islands or peninsulas, far away from the center of corruption in Europe. Their city planning with spacious squares, luminous buildings, temples and harbours, are conceived to shelter a society of almost perfect individuals. Utopists, like Montessori, believe that the environment is an essential and vital element of their utopias. Campanella describes how the children, guided by their teacher, visit the several walls and adjoining museums of the City of the Sun and in this way he claims that the children of the Solarians learn all things easily and without effort.

5) *Peace and unity of the world.* Many utopists have made it clear that the whole purpose of their work was to make either a direct or an indirect reference to present conditions in their country or the world and that their system was proposed either as an alternative or as a speculative hypothesis capable of bringing into focus those social, political and moral issues which, by their absence in the society of the time, made it possible in their view for war, injustice and violence to prevail.

In this Montessori behaves like a true utopist, with the same concern for the conditions of the world, the same awareness of the social, political and moral issues at stake, and an unshakable faith in the virtues of science to bring solutions to a troubled world. Whereas for most utopists science embraces many disciplines, they all distinguish education as that branch of knowledge which achieves the highest goal, that of forming the ideal citizen for the ideal state. This is the same model followed by Montessori.

After having made references to the Second World War and the dictatorships of Hitler and Mussolini, Montessori makes an appeal for Christian love for the children, a kind of love which will unite the world. She states that this unity will happen if we pay sufficient attention to the absorbent mind of the child.

Children are capable of spontaneous action because they are directed by an unconscious power and vitalized by a social spirit. This phenomenon is what Montessori calls a *cohesion in the social unit.* It is a sense of solidarity which is a gift of nature, one capable of great personal sacrifices for the honor of the group. This would allow "the whole human family to be reborn" (p. 234). Montessori recommends that "This integration of the individual with his group must be cultivated in the school, because it is just this that we lack, and the failure and ruin of our civilization is due to this lack" (p. 234). The children can bring back that cohesion which Europe once had in the Middle

Ages, due to its religious faith: "The Middle Ages of European history saw something that in our own days, lacerated by war, all our leaders try in vain to reach: real union of the European nations. How was it done? The secret of this triumph lay in the religious faith which had captured all the people who lived in the various empires and European kingdoms, uniting them by its tremendous force of cohesion. Those days really saw all kings and emperors (each of whom governed in his own fashion) subject to Christianity, and dependent on its strength" (p. 237).

One could add that this desire for medieval unity was felt immediately at the dawn of modern times by those few who had realized that only a profound change in society could bring back that unity. These are the Christian utopists of the Renaissance, especially those like More, Campanella, Las Casas, Quiroga, and the author of *Sinapia,* who perceived the potential of the New World and the new man as the foundation for a new beginning in a spirit of unity and peace.

Therein lies Montessori's thesis that only education can bring back that unity. Even the exceptionally gifted leader must count on an educated populace. The hope for a new Messiah who can lead the world out of its present predicament must be accompanied by a program of education for the masses: "It is the masses themselves who are totally unprepared for social life in our civilization. Hence the problem is to educate the masses (. . .). The great task of education must be to secure and to preserve a normality which, of its own nature, gravitates toward the center of perfection" (p. 239). But this renewal of spiritual unity will not happen according to Montessori if we continue to ignore the child, the gift which God has given mankind to allow it to reunite: "Without knowing it, we are ignoring the creation of man, and trampling on the treasures which God himself has placed in every child. Yet here lies the source of those moral and intellectual values which could bring the whole world on to a higher plane" (p. 239).

There are strong Biblical overtones when Montessori claims that "Not the fear of death, but the knowledge of our lost paradise should be our tribulation" (p. 240).

As a concluding proof of how the absorbent mind of the child works according to divine law and love, Montessori quotes a text from St. Paul, in which the Apostle says, "Charity is slow to anger, is kind: charity envieth not, dealeth not perversely; is not puffed up. Is not ambitious, seeketh not its own, provoketh not opposition, plans no evil. Rejoiceth not in injustice, but delighteth in the truth; beareth all things, believeth all things, hopeth all things, endureth all things" (*Corinthians,* I, XIII) (p. 291). Montessori remarks that these words of St. Paul seem to describe the **Absorbent Mind** of the child, a mind which receives, does not judge, does not refuse, does not react. She concludes that "grownups and children must join their forces. In order to become great, the grownup must become humble and learn from the child. Strange, is it not, that among all the wonders man has worked, and the dis-

coveries he has made, there is only one field to which he has paid no attention; it is that of the miracle that God has worked from the first: the miracle of our children" (p. 293). In short, this method is inspired by a Christian feeling of love which must reveal itself through the absorbent mind of the child: "This is the path that man must follow in his anguish and his cares if, as his aspirations direct, he wishes to reach salvation and the union of mankind" (p. 296).

It is clear then that Montessori's discovery of the ability of the child to learn language, coupled with her description of the child's unconscious process of becoming a member of a given social order, constitute conditions for a scientific utopia. Montessori's method resembles that of the Christian utopists, but it incorporates the scientific thinking of modern man. Therefore, in that evolution which the utopian thought seems to reveal, Montessori's contribution stands out as a clear alternative to the impossibly elitist theories of Renaissance man and the dire predictions of Orwell and Huxley.

Notes

1. For a general view of Renaissance utopia vis-à-vis the limitations of a humanistic tradition see Stelio Cro, "L'utopia rinascimentale: conformismo e riforma", *Il Rinascimento. Aspetti e problemi attuali,* a cura di Vittore Branca, Claudio Griggio, Marco e Elisanna Pecoraro, Gilberto Pizzamiglio, Eros Sequi, Firenze, Olschki, 1982, pp. 325-345. For a general view of the modern theories on education see note 3 below.

2. See Maria Montessori, *La mente del bambino* (Milano: Garzanti, 1960). Published in English as *The Absorbent Mind,* translated by C. A. Claremont, Adyar, Madras, India: The Theosophical Publishing House, 1961.

3. In George F. Kneller's *Foundations of Education* (New York: Wiley, 1971), a work which studies the major current theories on education, the name of Mussolini is mentioned three times whereas that of Montessori is never mentioned. Furthermore, the discussion of Fascist theories on education are given the same relevance as those of the Communist and Soviet educational systems, making one wonder how a now defunct system can be given the same treatment as one which has been in power for seventy years. By the way, Kneller believes that Marcuse's "new left" has produced "valuable reforms" in the American political as well as educational system. See George F. Kneller, "Political Ideologies", in *Foundations of Education, op. cit.,* pp. 136-144. The same excessive preoccupation with political process and comparative downplay of actual educational experiments and/or experimental educational environments is evident in the otherwise informative and lucid survey of Howard Ozmon, *Utopias and Education* (Minneapolis, Burgess Publishing Co., 1969), in which the name of

Montessori is never mentioned. The author aptly points out that "most utopian writers not only have a high regard for education but are educationists themselves" (p. x).

4. *Cf.* John Dewey, *Democracy and Education* (New York: McMillan, 1916), pp. 89-90. From now on I will quote page numbers of this work in the body of the text. For a general view on current trends on education see G. F. Kneller, *Foundations of Education, op. cit.* I will refer often to this work in this paper, especially in regard to its general survey of educational theories.

5. G. F. Kneller, "Contemporary Educational Theories," *Foundations of Education, op. cit.*, p. 234.

6. John I. Goodland, "Elementary Education," in G. F. Kneller, *Foundations of Education, op. cit.*, p. 500.

7. George F. Kneller, "Contemporary Educational Theories," *Foundations of Education, op. cit.*, p. 236.

8. *Ibidem*, p. 237.

9. *Ibidem*, p. 239.

10. *Ibidem*, p. 239.

11. *Ibidem*, p. 240.

12. In *School and Society*, LXXXVII [2145], January 17, 1959, pp. 14-15.

13. San Francisco, Washington, London: Jossey-Bass Publishers, 1974.

14. Pp. 7-8.

15. These, and other inventions can be found in Sir Francis Bacon's *New Atlantis*, written in 1626.

16. I have read the English version: *Ideology and Utopia*, New York, Harvest Book, 1936, reprinted, n.d.

17. *Ideology and Utopia, op. cit.*, p. 245.

18. *Les metamorphoses de la Cite` de Dieu*, Paris, Presses Universitaires de France, 1952, p. 268.

19. *De Civitate Dei*, XIX, 24.

20. Cf. E. Garin, "La città ideale," in *Scienza e vita civile nel Rinascimento italiano*, Roma-Bari, Universale Laterza, 1975, pp. 33-56; *L'Educazione in Europa; 1400-1600*; Roma-Bari, Universale Laterza, 1976, p. 316; *l'Umanesimo italiano. Filosofia e vita civile nel Rinascimento*, 6a ed., Roma-Bari, Universale Laterza, 1975, p. 276; *La Renaissance histoire d'une revolution culturelle* (Marabout Universite` Verviers, Des Presses de Gerard & Co., 1970), pp. 9, passim.

21. "La città ideale," *op. cit.*, pp. 52-53.

22. "La città ideale," *op. cit.*, pp. 52-54.

23. "La città ideale," *op. cit.*, pp. 42-45.

24. "La città ideale," *op. cit.*, p. 54.

25. Brussels, Editions de l'université de Bruxelles, 1975.

26. Cf. Stelio Cro, *Realidad y utopía en el descubrimiento y conquista de la América Hispana (1492-1682)*, Troy, International Book Publishers, 1983, pp. 224-225.

27. Cf. Jean-Jacques Rousseau, *Emile*, Tome I, Classiques Larousse, 1972, p. 28.

28. *Emile, op. cit.*, "Libre Premier," p. 41.

29. This and the other scientific ideas of Montessori are discussed in her study *The Absorbent Mind*, quoted in note 2; page numbers given in parenthesis in the body of the text refer to this edition.

David Gettman (essay date 1987)

SOURCE: "Montessori and Her Theories," in *Basic Montessori: Learning Activities for Under-Fives*, St. Martin's Press, 1987, pp. 1-35.

[*In the following essay, Gettman provides an overview of Montessori's theories and methods.*]

INTRODUCTION

Maria Montessori, who lived from 1870 to 1952, was a brilliant and original educator, scientist, healer, humanitarian and philosopher.

In Montessori's time, a woman in Italy was not given the same educational opportunities as a man. But even as a child, Maria won special opportunities because of her intellect. She attended an all-boys' technical school, and there expressed an ambition to pursue a career in engineering. When she was not given professional encouragement in this, she developed an interest in biology, and settled on becoming a doctor instead. At university, Maria, the only girl, was shunned by her colleagues, and she spent many months pent up in a room to study by herself—until, near the end of her first year, when she was called to deliver a paper to the class, the other students found themselves cheering and applauding her brilliance and insight. After becoming the first woman to graduate in medicine from the University of Rome, Montessori practised surgical medicine for the next ten years. During this period, when she could have gloated over her unusual place of honour among women, she instead helped other women through their own higher education, and campaigned heartily for equal rights for all women.

Soon after graduating, stimulated by her further studies in psychology, and having begun to teach in the psychiatric clinic at the university, Montessori became involved in visiting the patients in the nearby mental institution. Believing instinctively that mental deficiency was more of an educational than a medical problem, she arranged to remove the younger children from the institution and work with them separately. Every day for two years, Montessori did her best to help these disturbed and handicapped children learn and develop, basing her teaching methods on the principles of two prominent French physicians whose research she had read and admired: Jean Itard—teacher of the famous 'Savage of Aveyron'—and Edouard Sequin. Remarkably, a number of the children progressed so quickly that Montessori signed them up for ordinary school examinations, which they passed without difficulty. But she was not impressed by her accomplishment. Instead, she wondered what was wrong with the schools who gave such examinations if two short years of her improvised methods could bring seriously disturbed and handicapped children to the same standard of education as that expected of ordinary children.

Montessori then turned her thoughts to the education of the ordinary child. She returned to the University of Rome for further academic work in educational philosophy, psychology and anthropology—which she undertook with such distinction that in 1904 she was appointed Professor of Anthropology. At the same time, she continued to study childhood nervous conditions, and to publish her findings in medical journals.

In 1907, an opportunity came for her to begin to work with ordinary children. In a reconstructed tenement in San Lorenzo, an impoverished quarter of Rome, a children's day nursery was set up by the housing authorities, and it needed a director—someone to be in charge of about fifty wretchedly poor three-to-six year olds, mainly to keep them from playing on the stairs and dirtying the newly painted walls. Little did the tenement's authorities suspect that this humble nursery, which Montessori called her 'Casa dei Bambini', or Children's House, would become a place of great discovery for the shy, tearful children who came there, and for Montessori herself.

Montessori began by attempting to use in the Children's House some of the same teaching techniques she had used at the mental institution. She found that the children enjoyed the exercises, but that they preferred to do them independently, without her help. As Montessori introduced more and different materials for the children to work with, some materials were accepted enthusiastically, while others were left untouched. She did not force anything on the children, but offered and presented each new activity like a gift, to be taken up at will by any interested child.

Some time into this process, Montessori began to notice something very strange and wonderful about some of the children. Those who freely participated in the activities began to reveal a facet of childhood which Montessori had never seen before. Some of the more experienced children began to evidence a kind of inner calmness, and they were able to concentrate contentedly for very long periods of time. Not only did they quickly absorb complex skills and sophisticated knowledge, they also developed a self-discipline which relieved any need for external authority. In their dealings with adults and other children, they began to show great thoughtfulness, compassion and understanding. It was as if their work at the Children's House lifted some great weight off their minds, freeing them to focus on their own inner thoughts and purposes. Montessori herself scarcely believed what she was seeing, but the pattern persisted. She continued to introduce new self-teaching materials that built upon the principles of the earlier ones, carefully observed the children's use of them, and if the children were not spontaneously and repeatedly drawn to the activities, those materials were taken away and not offered again. Montessori's method developed and grew purely on the basis of what the children showed her about themselves.

It was not until much later, after two decades of working with young children and sensitively observing them, that Montessori began to tie her observations together in the form of theories. This chapter aims to summarise Montessori's basic ideas about development and learning, and about why children in Montessori classes all over the world exhibit that remarkable sense of self-assurance and contentment in their work. Throughout Montessori's own writings, she repeatedly reminds us that she did not just sit back in an armchair and dream up these theories. Montessori wanted us to remember that it was the children themselves who, by their free and natural inclinations, revealed to her the true nature of their growth and development.

The Young Child's Special Mind

The most basic principle in Montessori's theory of education is that the learning capacity of a young child is fundamentally different from that of an adult. To realise this ourselves, we need only think of one learning task attempted by both adults and young children—learning to speak a new language.

We know from adult experience that learning to speak a new language is an enormously complex and difficult task, requiring prolonged concentration, a well-developed memory, and a strong sense of grammatical logic. How is it possible that a very young child is able to master his or her first language, having only a very temporary attention span, a weak ability to recognise people and objects, and no apparent sense of logic at all? When an adult undertakes the task, the vocabulary and grammar of the new language are systematically related to those of the adult's native language; the native language serves as the vehicle that gives meaning to the new words and phrases. But the young child starts with no language whatsoever. In what world of meaning does the child interpret its new language? Also, the adult who learns a foreign language rarely speaks it well enough to pass as a native; most travellers or immigrants have accents and tendencies to misuse local syntax which betray their own native languages. How does the young child learning its first language invariably speak it so perfectly, utilising the exact portions of the mouth, tongue and throat necessary to reproduce the language's sounds, and acquiring a precise national accent, a regional dialect, all the local idioms, and even neighbourhood or family idiosyncrasies? No one but a one-to-three year old can accomplish this remarkable feat.

Clearly, the young child has a unique and extremely powerful capacity for learning such skills as language, a capacity which is mysteriously lost, or perhaps buried, somewhere on the way to adulthood. The difference between the adult and the young child is not merely in the quantity that can be learned; unlike the adult, the child appears able simply to absorb, through activity, but without effort, certain complete and precise abilities and skills, with a completeness and preciseness that an adult cannot even conceive of. Montessori called this unique early learning capacity the young child's 'absorbent mind'.

The absorbent mind makes possible the transformation of a helpless, gurgling infant into a young personality with all the basic physical and mental abilities needed for daily human existence: feeding, cleaning and dressing oneself; sitting, climbing, grasping and a wide range of fine motor skills; as well as language, recognition, memory, will, grace, courtesy, cultural customs, and a self-identity. This feat of self-creation is accomplished by the child's simply living in and 'absorbing' the surrounding cultural environment.

Montessori used the term 'absorb', not in the sense of 'take in' as a dry sponge absorbs water, but rather in the sense of 'combining into itself'. One imprecise but useful analogy is a crystal growing in a saturated solution. Like a growing crystal, the child's absorbent mind dwells in a rich environment, and as it absorbs impressions of its surroundings, new behaviours and thoughts become incorporated additions that alter the mind's pattern or direction, and increase its surface area for further growth. In contrast with the child's absorbent mind, the adult mind maintains its basic form and capacity, and acquires knowledge not by absorption but by intentionally testing hypotheses and logically synthesising conclusions. This is why a child, unlike an adult, enjoys and seeks the repetition of the same stimuli many times over. Each impression slightly alters the child's perspective, so that even the same stimulus appears slightly different each time. The adult, who laboriously draws inductions from experience, and draws deductions from inductions, but whose perception remains essentially unchanged, finds the repetition of previously assessed stimuli to be boring and tedious.

In Montessori's experience, the young child's absorbent mind usually lasts about six years, a period which she observed to be divided into two three-year phases. Its mode of action subtly changes between the first phase and the second phase.

The first phase of the absorbent mind's activity, from birth to three years, is the most formative in childhood. During this phase, the child absorbs almost all available impressions in full detail, and each impression is instantly incarnated into and superimposed on all previous ones. The absorbent mind acquires nearly any impression, simple or complex, with equal ease and accuracy. It primarily responds to human stimuli, especially the human voice, but within the full range of human activity it is impartial and non-selective, using every sense to perceive the child's entire emotional as well as behavioural and cultural environment. For example, a baby in the living room of its home will absorb the complete and detailed actions and attitudes of mother reading, father tinkering, and brother and sister playing a game, even if all these activities are going on at once. Because the absorbent mind in this first phase does not have to be awakened by any exercise of the child's will, Montessori called its operation 'unconscious'. However, despite its effortless operation, the early absorbent mind is active and not passive, involving the child in imitation, movement and manipulative play, to capture, vary and augment the available field for experience.

Utilising the surrounding cultural environment as substance to absorb, the early absorbent mind helps create, in about three years, the child's basic human abilities. These creations do not appear gradually, but seem to be formed by an inner development that is only occasionally manifested in quantum leaps of ability. This creative transformation becomes readily apparent when you compare the behaviour of a newborn infant with that of a speaking three year old.

In the second phase of the young child's development, from ages three to six, the absorbent mind continues to function, but it now appears more specifically focused on certain impressions gained through intentional interaction with the material as well as human environment. These new experiences solidify, further develop and, most importantly, integrate the abilities earlier created. While the first phase of the absorbent mind consisted mostly of a quiet inner development that occasionally surfaced in surprising gains, the second phase appears busy and the maturation of skills is open and continuous. Also, whereas previous activity in the environment had been largely unconscious and spontaneous, the three-to-six year old interacts with the environment consciously and intentionally, strongly preferring certain experiences to others. These special impressions pursued and captured by the three-to-six year old, like the largely accidental experiences of the nought-to-three year old, continue to be acquired by the absorbent mind without effort or strain, no matter how complex they appear to us.

AN ORDERED GROWTH

Having been born with an 'absorbent mind', a young child simply 'absorbs' most of the various goings on in its immediate human environment. But to say that 'the child has an absorbent mind' isn't really enough to explain how a baby uses what it absorbs to create all the various human characteristics possessed by a child of six. Obviously, the child does not just reproduce, like a video and sound recorder, everything that the absorbent mind perceives. Even if we take into account the cumulative metamorphosis of the absorbent mind, a young child's human nature still consists of something more than just a highly superimposed image of the surrounding human environment. We need to ask how the absorbent mind goes about turning its accumulated impressions of a culture into an intelligence which will later participate in and contribute to the culture being absorbed.

Montessori's answer was that the child's absorbent mind indeed receives impressions, but it also processes, categorises and otherwise interprets them, filtering bits of impressions through, and fitting them into, an inherited intellectual structure. She also deduced that this structure is not static, but gradually changes and unfolds as the child grows. The structure and its pattern of unfolding appear to be basically the same for all children everywhere. What makes each child's intellectual development different are the varying experiences that the absorbent mind has been exposed to at each stage of the structure's unfolding.

So although the absorbent mind's first phase is unconscious, it is not undirected. At any one time, the child's unfolding intellectual structure makes special use of certain aspects of the impressions it absorbs. It is the effect of absorbed experience on the underlying structure that actually creates the child's intellectual abilities. By the second phase of the absorbent mind, starting around age three, the structure's developmental work has progressed sufficiently to give the child enough mental faculties to express interest consciously in the particular experiences that will henceforth most benefit the evolving structure. So, from ages three to six, the child feels and shows preferences for the types of stimuli needed to refine and integrate the basic abilities created from ages nought to three.

This may be illustrated by use of a simple analogy. Consider how one would go about building a house. It isn't enough just to gather together the various materials which go into a house. All you'd have then is a pile of bricks, wood, metal and glass. It also wouldn't do simply to re-create disjointed impressions of a finished house—to build the stone facade there, the interior of the bedroom over here, the patio up there. One really needs three things to build a house: first, a detailed structural blueprint of the finished house; second, a building schedule, to tell us that the foundation must be laid first, then the frame, then the plumbing, then the outer walls, then the electrical work, and so on; and third, sufficient labour and materials to build the house with. But as the house is actually being built, there comes a time when the builders no longer need to refer constantly to the blueprints and the schedule. The house itself begins to take on a definite shape, and what needs to be done next presents itself very clearly to the builders.

When Nature constructs a young human being from a helpless infant, its blueprint is that underlying, inherited intellectual structure, its building schedule is the pre-determined unfolding of this structure over time, and the labour and materials are the many experiences and impressions received by the absorbent mind. When the work is well under way, Nature makes self-evident what needs doing next by awakening and exercising the child's will.

In her many years of observing children, Montessori was able to work out a very general outline of the 'building schedule', that is, what kinds of faculties are being developed at various points in the first six years of life. She was able to deduce this rough order of development by noting which sorts of activities and experiences seemed to benefit, and for the older ones, seemed to appeal to, the children most. The general order of the hidden construction work going on within the young children was thus suggested by special, transient sensitivities to certain categories of stimuli. Montessori called these broad, but distinct and temporary sensitivities, the 'sensitive periods'.

In all, Montessori noted six of these sensitive periods.

The first one, a sensitive period for the development of 'sensory perception', begins at birth and continues all the way through age five. During this sensitive period, the child needs to exercise all the sense faculties as fully as possible. A great deal of frustration in many young children is caused by parents' constant admonitions not to touch anything, and by plasticised, deodorised and highly sheltered surroundings.

The second sensitive period, which is for 'language', doesn't begin until age three months, but it too lasts to about age five or five-and-a-half. The many stages of this sensitive period, which Montessori traced in some detail, include for example an early sensitivity to the sound of the human voice and the sight of the human mouth speaking. It may seem obvious that a baby will begin to imitate the speaking sounds it hears. But a baby hears many sounds, including for instance musical melodies, dogs barking, and kitchen noises. The fact that these sounds are not imitated or incorporated into the child's communicative behaviour supports the theory that the baby has a special sensitivity to, and can unconsciously select from all the varied sounds in the environment, just human conversation.

A sensitive period for 'order' usually starts around the child's first birthday, peaks at about age two, and subsides when the child is three. This sensitivity is rarely recognised by parents and is probably the cause of much of that inconsolable crying and fretfulness long associated with the 'terrible two's'. At this time in the child's development, the construction of the intellect appears to be going through a vital organisational phase. Impressions and experiences are being placed in ordered patterns that will form the basis for the child's emerging world view, which is in turn beginning to make possible the ordered expression, in language, of ideas about the world. If order in daily experience is constant, this allows the child to build an understanding of life on the foundations of the patterns perceived. External order will facilitate the child's development of an internal sense of order.

This means that the child aged one and two will greatly benefit, and be happiest, when the world all around appears constant in its patterns and arrangements. External order would include such constancies as: keeping most material objects, like furniture, toys, and clothing, in the same location from day to day; following the same daily routines, such as where and when meals are taken, how and when family chores are done, and when family members depart and arrive; and using the same procedures in doing things with the child, such as how the child is picked up and held, how meals are fed, and how baths are given. When a child of two seems unduly upset for no apparent reason, it is often because some small thing has been inadvertently changed—something which may be totally unimportant to the adult, but which is a vital cornerstone of consistency in the child's understanding of how life is conducted. When some disorder is necessary in the young child's surroundings, we should be sympathetic and supportive, and should stress the things that haven't changed.

A brief but important sensitive period, which occurs right around age two, is the sensitive period for 'small detail'. Now it is rather easy to see how sensitivities to sensory perception, language and order can help the unfolding inner structure, in combination with the absorbent mind, to create a human intellect. But the creative value of a transient sensitivity to 'small detail' is not immediately apparent.

First of all, what did Montessori mean by 'small detail'? During this sensitive period, the toddler will, for example, be strolling slowly along with you on a hillside path that permits a breathtaking view of the town below. But instead of standing with feet wide apart gazing out upon the edifying panorama, as you had intended, the child will be on all fours following with great interest the zig-zag crawl of a little black ant. Or later, with the two-year-old on your lap, you are leafing through a big colourful picture book with scenes of the zoo, and you are naming the animals featured on each page. But instead of taking note of the bright orange, roaring tiger, the child will be asking you about the "lolly", and you will notice that in the bottom left corner of the picture, there is a small drawing of a little girl, standing away from the tiger's cage, holding a tiny orange ice lolly in one hand. Why should the child be preoccupied with these insignificant details?

Consider Sherlock Holmes, the fictional detective. Holmes was always being clever for two reasons: first, he gave equal weight to all evidence, no matter how insignificant it seemed; and second, he had a special ability to concentrate very deeply on one specific problem at a time. Sherlock's friend Watson was invariably drawn to only the most obvious of clues, and always tried to solve the whole mystery, with its many unanswered questions, at one fell swoop. The Sherlock Holmes stories point up two vital components of human intelligence: we must be capable of widening our powers of observation to include all phenomena, since the meaning of a situation is not always to be found in the most obvious phenomena; and second, we must be able to concentrate our intellectual powers on specific problems. It is also essential to early development that a child be able to broaden the field of observation available to the absorbent mind, and to tighten the concentration of the inner intellectual structure in processing what is absorbed. This is the purpose of the sensitive period for

'small detail': to awaken the mind's control over the child's attention. The sensitivity to small detail draws the child to the tiniest objects, the separated fragments, the faintest noises, the hidden corners—all the phenomena previously overshadowed by the brightest, biggest objects, the fastest moving or the loudest. Also, when the child is drawn to a small thing, the sensitivity holds the child's attention there for an extended period, fostering the ability to focus on that one small stimulus to the exclusion of all else.

Just as that sensitive period is completing its work, at around age two-and-a-half, the child enters the sensitive period for 'co-ordination of movement', and this lasts until about age four. Co-ordination of movement essentially means bringing the body under the control of the will: being able to use one's fingers, hands, legs, feet, mouth and so on, precisely the way one wishes to. This does not mean that a child of this age can more easily acquire complex physical skills—in other words, this is not necessarily the ideal age for becoming a violin virtuoso or a prima ballerina. Having a sensitive period for co-ordination of movement only means that there is an involuntary inclination to perform and repeat movements purely for the sake of gaining greater and more precise control. For example, a child aged about three loves washing hands, not for the sake of getting them clean, but simply to be able to work on the manipulative skills involved: turning taps, holding slippery soap, rubbing to make lather, rinsing, and finger-drying. By contrast, children aged four or older will normally only wash their hands to get them clean (if you can get them to do it at all). The importance of this sensitive period is that it helps the child become physically capable of pursuing activities that—in the absorbent mind's second phase—are consciously selected to provide the greatest benefit to the unfolding intellectual structure.

The last sensitive period in the life of the absorbent mind is a sensitivity to 'social relations', which starts around two-and-a-half, and persists through age five. This helps to orient the child towards intellectual development after age six, which occurs mostly in a social setting, and consists largely of the acquisition of social and cultural knowledge. In this sensitive period, the young child pays special attention to the effect of one's behaviour on the feelings and actions of others, and how one's behaviour is in turn affected by the judgements and tendencies of a group of children. Whereas the under-three year olds tend to play alone or just 'alongside' one another, the work of this sensitive period enables recognisable affections and friendships to develop, allows play to be somewhat co-operative, and makes mischief begin to appear conspiratorial. The two-and-a-half to five year old is also quite interested in, and readily absorbs, the basic rules of social relations, such as manners, mealtime customs, graceful movement, and showing consideration for others.

LEARNING BY CONNECTING

The 'absorbent mind' is Montessori's answer to the mystery of how a baby is dramatically transformed into a thinking being. And 'sensitive periods' are the essence of Montessori's theory about how basic human skills are systematically developed. But one should now ask: given a basic intellect and certain general abilities, what equips the child to then acquire specific information and know-how? We've discussed how the absorbent mind feeds an unfolding, inherited structure, and how the sensitive periods help provide the right materials for the building of particular skills. But when and how are these general skills integrated, expanded and filled out with the knowledge and understanding that makes them useful in the real world?

You will recall that by age two-and-a-half or three, the special sensitivities to certain impressions needed by the absorbent mind's inherited inner structure, in each phase of its unfolding, start to be expressed consciously. They begin to appear in the child as purposeful activity and explicit expressions of curiosity and interest. For example, the child wants to be shown how to place blocks in a row, to see what we're doing in the kitchen, to hear what noises come out of the telephone receiver, and to discover where the water in the bath goes when it disappears down the drain. This age marks the onset of what we usually think of as 'learning'.

'Learning' is one of those words we use without really knowing what we mean by it. When a person lacks an ability one moment and then displays the ability the next moment, we say that the person has 'learned' it, and by the word 'learn' we imply that some sort of operation has taken place that installs the new ability in the person. But what sort of operation accomplishes this and how does it work? We know that repetition often leads to learning, but we wouldn't want to say that learning consists entirely of repetition. Even when we are the ones learning, we are hard pressed to describe what actually goes on in our heads at that moment of realisation, if there is one, or over that long period of practice. All we know is, suddenly we are able to do or think what we could not do before.

In Montessori's view, the act of learning does not involve the acquisition of anything new. Simply being awake to the world, the absorbent mind is constantly acquiring the substance of whatever will be learned by the young child. The 'learning' itself is the act of joining or connecting these previous acquisitions in such a way that they are bound together by use or meaning, and so that they have a place in a larger system of uses or meanings. Whatever is thereby learned then becomes, like each earlier acquisition, a piece of knowledge that can be further bound to other pieces, in some later act of learning.

Educators have long observed that learning, this binding together of what was earlier absorbed, occurs in three basic stages. In terms of Montessori's theories, these stages can be described as follows.

The first stage is absorbing, via the absorbent mind, a full impression of all the various separate components that will later be joined. This can occur naturally, over many

months, or it can be intentionally provided in a few minutes. Because of the child's propensity for movement, this is always a participatory event on the child's part, rather than a passive reception. Also, in order for full absorption to take place, an effort of concentration is required; it will not work if the child is at all distracted. In this first stage, whatever is being absorbed, because it is being processed through that inherited inner structure, is already starting to become loosely associated in the back of the child's mind. Consequently, the child senses a motivation to strengthen and complete these associations. In brief, this first stage is the absorption of certain component phenomena, which if complete, creates a motivation for learning.

The second stage of learning consists of repeatedly acting out connections between the absorbed phenomena, which for the young child again usually involves physical activity. This firmly bridges the absorbed phenomena that were only loosely associated in the first stage. Through repetition, the child explores and establishes all the different ways that the component phenomena fit together, so that in the end they are irrevocably joined. In order to make the connections, such as between a verbal sound and a letter of the alphabet, the child must clearly perceive what is being connected and what is being left unconnected. Similarly, the primary aspect of any intentional activity, such as hammering a nail, is accurate control over what is being acted upon, distinguished in the actor's mind from what is not to be acted upon. In essence, then, this second stage of learning solidly binds, through repeated and carefully controlled activity, certain previously absorbed phenomena, and thereby draws clear distinctions around them, making of them a unified concept.

The third stage of learning is the conscious application of the now bound and circumscribed concept to tasks and situations that will give it a meaningful place in the child's world. This could mean, for example, using the new sound-letter combination to write a word in a story the child is composing, or using the hammer and nail to help build a 'Wendy House' in the child's garden. When a concept, such as an abstract mathematical relation, has no obvious practical application, the child may create an application by inventing a game that makes use of the new concept. Sometimes, putting the concept into language is enough to give it a meaningful place in the child's mind. Alternatively, the child may give application to the new concept by trying to teach it to someone else. However it is done, the object of this last stage is to make the concept meaningful for the child, by giving it a purpose in the child's daily life, and a relationship to other concepts the child has learned.

So learning is essentially connecting—a set of related perceptions motivating connective activity that is in turn given application. Going back to Montessori's larger view of the child's development, we can now explain how the child, in the second phase of the absorbent mind, is able to integrate and expand the skills and abilities created in the first phase—and so starts to acquire real knowledge and skills.

As we've noted, the three year old's activities begin to be more purposeful, because the child's development has progressed to a point which awakens the will. Purposeful activity starts to integrate the child's abilities by bringing them into a personally managed relation with the world. Also at this age, the child is first made capable, partly by the sensitive period for small detail, of giving concentrated attention to any activity intentionally selected. At the same time, the sensitive period for co-ordination of movement is developing the physical skills needed to pursue those activities.

So at this point, three–stage learning can begin to operate: the child's new powers of concentration support the first stage; repetition and striving for control, which are characteristic of the sensitive period for co-ordination, help drive the second stage; and purposeful activity, guided by the will, becomes the basis for the third stage. Together, these enable the child to perform 'learning by connecting'—the three stage process which fills out early basic skills with knowledge and understanding.

THE CHILD'S WORK PLACE

Because of the importance, especially in the second phase of the child's absorbent mind, of having particular stimuli and experiences available at critical periods of the intellectual structure's unfolding, early development may be greatly assisted if the three-to-six year old is in an environment that makes these stimuli and experiences likely.

In accordance with the principles we've been discussing, such an environment would ideally offer purposeful experiences that permit the exercise and integration of the abilities newly created in the child's first few years. These experiences would make clear, tangible and accessible to the child's absorbent mind the basic patterns of the culture's customs, practices, beliefs and perceptions. The experiences would be generated largely through physical activities, each of which would be presented to the child in accordance with the principle of three stage learning. And the experiences would be made accessible only when they were required at each point in the child's inner construction, but thereafter they would be freely available for the child to seek out at will.

Purposeful physical activities, reflecting the culture, presented by three stage learning at critical periods, and later available for use by the child at will—this is precisely the sort of environment that Montessori, in response to the expressed desires of the children, developed at her Children's House in San Lorenzo.

The Montessori environment is a place that fully satisfies the requirements of the absorbent mind, the sensitive periods, and the three stage learning process. Montessori called this place the 'prepared environment', since it is specially prepared to meet all the child's developmental needs. The 'prepared environment' is the ideal work place for the young child's vocational pursuit of self-construction, to create from a baby an independent, thinking human being.

Most parents consider the home to be the ideal environment for their young child. Montessori agreed that in the first stage of the absorbent mind when basic human abilities, feelings and attitudes are being unconsciously created by close and constant exposure to people, the secure and direct effect of parental love and attention is most conducive to early growth. But in the second stage of the absorbent mind, which requires true freedom, purposeful activity, and cultural involvement in order to function, the child can greatly benefit from additional exposure to an environment specially prepared to meet these needs.

The main distinguishing features of Montessori's 'prepared environment', in contrast with an ordinary nursery school, are the many specially selected learning and cultural activities, each of which is introduced precisely when the child is ready, and is thereafter freely available for the child to conduct independently. Most of the remainder of this book details the basic activities and how to present them. But there are other aspects of the Montessori environment which should be discussed first, since their absence could lessen the activities' effectiveness. Although it is easiest to appreciate the importance of the activities themselves, the whole Montessori environment is designed to complement the activities and the children's participation in them. Remember that all aspects of the 'prepared environment' were originally included by Montessori because they were repeatedly favoured by the children she worked with, and not because they seemed desirable by adult standards.

A Montessori environment can be created in a home, a school building, a church hall, or a community centre, or even in an empty shop, the ground floor of an office block, or any place that child-minding would be permitted. Nothing fancy is required; the very first Montessori environment was a room in a working-class tenement building. The site need not be luxurious, but like any area for children it must be clean, warm, secure, pleasant in appearance, brightly lit, and isolated from dangers like building work or busy roads. You do not need a lot of space: one separated half of a playroom would do fine for one or two children at home; for a group of children, one large room or two smaller rooms, with ready access to a WC and a fenced outdoor play area, would be best. If you're thinking about opening a Montessori school for children other than your own, you probably also need to ask local authorities about planning, licensing, fire safety, and building regulations—including rules about the amount of space required per child.

The room or rooms should be furnished very simply, with child-size furnishings. You'll need a child-size table and chair for each child, and some child-size open shelving. By 'child-size' I mean comfortable for the child to be working at: for the chair, the child's feet should rest flat on floor; for the table, a seated child should be able to rest elbows on the surface; for shelves, the child should be able to see the contents of a bowl on the top shelf. The tables, chairs and shelves should have water-resistant surfaces for easy cleaning, and should of course be free of splinters and sharp corners or edges. The only other essential furnishings are 'table mats', each made of a two-foot-square piece of felt, and also, even if the space is carpeted, 'floor mats' of stiff, thick felt, each about three feet by four feet, rolled and stored upright in a low bin. Optional furnishings might include: a child-size easel for painting; two large plastic buckets, one as a water source (with a ladle) and the other to put used water in; a well-lit reading corner with a small bookcase and a soft child-size chair or fluffy pillow; interesting pictures to hang on the wall at the child's eye level; and for each table, a vase to put flowers in. For yourself, you might want a lockable cabinet for supplies, and a low but comfortable stool to sit on when you are working with a child at a table. With the exception of these two last items, everything in the Montessori environment is designed for use by children.

The most notable elements of the 'prepared environment' are the specially-constructed materials used by the child to conduct the Montessori activities. In principle, you should try to get professionally-made Montessori materials for as many of the activities as possible. However, there are only a few manufacturers in the world who produce them commercially. The largest and best of these companies, 'Nienhuis Montessori', is based in Holland, and has a mail-order catalogue obtainable from the following address: Nienhuis Montessori International B.V., PO Box 16, 7020 AA, Zelhem (Gld.), Holland. The professionally-made materials are best because they will last longer, and their lasting beauty and perfection make them more enticing for children to use. Also, a number of the materials would be difficult for anyone but a master craftsperson to make—if you want to provide these materials, you will probably have to buy them.

However, professionally-made Montessori materials can be expensive, and you may need to make do with some home-made materials. A handy adult will be able to make many of them from readily available household items, supplemented by modest purchases from a sewing supplies shop and a hardware or DIY shop. For those Montessori materials which are easiest to make, a few 'DIY hints' are included with the activities descriptions in this book. (Incidentally, the glossy, full-colour Nienhuis Montessori catalogue would be a very useful visual aid to anyone trying to make their own materials.) Finally, there are some Montessori materials which cannot be bought at all, and for these I provide detailed suggestions on how to make them.

Many adults are surprised and delighted when they see Montessori materials for the first time. The objects are simple, basic shapes in pure, wholesome materials—small wooden cabinets and containers with neat, enamel-painted elemental forms inside, squares of wool and cotton fabric, plain ceramic jugs and basins, and other similarly uncomplicated artefacts. To some adults, the materials may seem a bit too elemental, or even old fashioned. But Montessori discovered that young children actually prefer this simplicity, and seek it out in their environment.

There is a recent trend in nursery and primary schools to conduct lessons for young children with computers, calculators and other implements of high technology. The rationale is that these are the tools of modern times, and that every child should become comfortable with their use and operation. Montessori would have agreed that because these machines are an important part of modern society—like cars, say—their presence should be a natural occurrence in the child's general environment, and their identity and purpose should be known to young children. But Montessori would no more have suggested that four year olds use a computer than that they drive on a motorway.

The successful and creative use of high technology, such as computers, requires a complete understanding of what the automated operation would consist of, if it were performed by hand. Young children do not have this understanding. Rather than leap into advanced techniques, the Montessori method always starts with the concrete and gradually builds up to the abstract—for example, grouping and counting beads to understand in a literal, material sense what is meant by adding quantities, before proceeding to work with numbers in themselves as abstractions. Montessori's hands-on activities give a solid grounding for later abstractions, which are thereby more fully understood, and are not carried out as mere rote operations.

All Montessori materials which the children may wish to use, and to which the children have been properly introduced, should be kept out and available on the child-size open shelves. Also, each piece of material should have an assigned place and position on these shelves. Although it is not necessary, you may wish to group the materials on the shelves by subject matter (e.g. Mathematics, Language, Sensorial). It is essential, however, that the children be able to see and retrieve, without any adult assistance, all the materials and supplies needed to conduct any activity which has been presented to them. Unless these materials are being used by someone else, the children must always find them in precisely the same place and position on the shelves every time they look for them. This will help the children become independent, and will help them understand what is expected when putting the materials away.

The 'prepared environment' is ideally open every day throughout the child's waking hours, as the child is then able to work and learn whenever the urge strikes. This is quite possible in the home, by simply leaving open, all day long, the room with the Montessori materials, and occasionally devoting a half-hour or so to introducing new activities or observing the child's work. But with groups of children not living under the same roof, some compromise is usually necessary.

All-day nursery facilities, which may run from early morning to early evening, often find that they and the children only have sufficient energy to devote part of their long day to Montessori work. Some all-day nursery schools concentrate on Montessori presentations from 9.00 to 12.00 in the morning, interrupted only by snack time, and then the materials are left out for free access throughout the afternoon. I've also seen day nurseries that focus on Montessori work for two separate one-hour-and-a-half sessions: one session in the morning, say from about 10.00 to 11.30, and the other in the afternoon, from about 2.00 to 3.30. I would not suggest restricting Montessori work much more than this, since different children reach their peak concentration times at different hours of the day. Short Montessori sessions tend to end just as a child is getting involved, and may cause some children to flit superficially from one activity to another in order to pass the time until the end of the session is announced. Nursery schools or play groups which are open only in the morning or in the afternoon for a few hours, sometimes only a few days a week, are obviously able to maintain the Montessori environment for only a limited time period, but they can more easily offer it without interruption.

The time arrangement you settle upon will obviously depend upon what is practical and possible in your situation. The main points to remember here are: the Montessori environment is intended only as an aid to the child's self-development; it is no use forcing the activities on any child at a particular time; no harm whatsoever is done if a child does not wish to participate at a particular time, or indeed at all; and whatever exposure a child has to the Montessori environment, no matter how small or temporary, cannot hurt, but will only help.

HOW THE ADULT CAN HELP

The bright room, the furniture, and the Montessori materials together constitute only half of the 'prepared environment'. The other half is you, the adult.

The adult in the Montessori environment can serve the child in three ways: as the main 'caretaker' and guardian of the work space, its furnishings, and the materials; as a 'facilitator' of the child's interaction with the materials; and as an 'observer' of the child's work and development. You can be all three of these things at once, but never the child's teacher in the traditional sense, since in the Montessori environment the child learns through active discovery, rather than through passive reception. Montessori called the adult who assumes the above three roles the environment's 'director'.

The director's 'caretaker' role is a more important one than it sounds. Because the child accomplishes self-development by independent work with the materials in the environment, these objects and the way they are arranged must be sufficiently pleasing and attractive to draw the child to them, so to speak. Although as an adult you will tend to think of your own tastes and needs, always try to consider how the environment could be more pleasant and more convenient for the child.

To start, the materials must always be complete, with no parts or pieces missing, and with any supplies such as paper or pencils ready to use and available in plentiful amounts. All materials and associated supplies should be nicely arranged on the shelves, perfectly aligned in their designated places, and easy to take off the shelves without disturbing other things. The materials should be in perfect repair, that is, any scratch or scrape should soon after be touched up with matching paint and any broken or chipped parts replaced as quickly as possible. The materials, the shelves and the work tables should also be immaculately clean, which means dusting them every day, and removing grime and fingerprints with a moist cloth about once a week.

These tasks should not only be performed as a matter of routine, but also in light of the child's responsiveness to the materials. For example, if a certain material has been ignored, perhaps it is because it is too difficult to get at, in which case you should announce its move to a more accessible spot, or perhaps it is ignored because it is damaged, in which case it should be repaired or replaced. Incidentally, if you are carrying out these caretaker duties in the presence of any child, you must do your work in precisely the same manner that you would want the child to do Montessori work. For instance, even if you are in a hurry, do not carry more than one object at a time, do not move about hastily or carelessly, and do not handle your working materials roughly, because you will find the child absorbing these bad habits and reproducing them.

The 'facilitator' role is what will take up most of the director's time and attention. In this role, the director actually presents the Montessori activities to the child. The activities are presented one at a time, usually to only one child at a time. In conducting these presentations, the director has three distinct responsibilities.

First, each activity should be presented at precisely the right moment in a particular child's development, so that it will challenge the child's intellectual and physical abilities, and tie together certain of the child's previous experiences, thereby stimulating the child to observe the presentation closely and later to attempt the activity independently. To help create a challenge, the director doing the presentation must conduct the activity as perfectly as humanly possible, with a strong sense of confidence and an appearance of facility and grace. Rather than put the child off, this vision of perfection will be absorbed by the absorbent mind, and will lead the child to repeat the activity many times in pursuit of that perfection. The director must perceive when the initial challenge has been met in the child's daily attempts, and then introduce the additional exercises that build on the activity and its principles.

Second, after an activity has been presented to a child whose curiosity was sufficiently stimulated by it, the director must have the restraint to allow the child voluntarily to select and independently attempt the activity, and to attempt it many times without interference, comments or assistance. In other words, you must resist your sentimental impulse to help, and the child must be permitted to explore the new material freely and to struggle towards reproducing your presentation. However, if for some reason the child did not fully grasp the whole presentation, or seems hung up by the lack of an important step or technique, then sometime in the near future the director should repeat the presentation.

When repeating a presentation, the director chooses a time that the child will not relate to any failed attempt, and simply says, 'I would like to show you this material again', without reference to the child's previous attempts or to the earlier presentation. In the repeated presentation, the director makes especially obvious the points in the activity which the child previously missed.

There is a fine line between difficulties that the child, through practice, will gradually be able to overcome, and difficulties which indicate that something in the presentation was missed; it is up to the director to recognise the difference. If a child has missed something important in the presentation, and this is not soon after corrected by repeating the presentation, the child is very likely to begin misusing the materials—that is, giving up the activity's original goal, which seemed impossible to achieve, and inventing a different, more achievable way to use the materials. For example, in the PINK TOWER activity, ten cubes of different sizes are built into a tower of cubes of consistently decreasing sizes. Without having absorbed the point in the presentation where you locate the next smaller cube to put on the tower, the child will be unable to build it properly. If the director does not note this difficulty and its reason, and does not repeat the presentation, the child will eventually abandon the idea of a diminishing tower, and may decide to arrange the cubes in the shape of a house or castle, or to pretend they are train cars, since these would be more achievable goals.

Third, when a child, after much practice, is finally conducting an activity and its related exercises with proficiency, the director must help the child realise that something has been learned in the process. This is done by placing the principles disclosed by the activity, and the skills and knowledge gained by the child in doing it, in a wider context of meaning and application. Often the next Montessori activity in the sequence accomplishes this purpose, by building on the concepts of previous activities. But the director should also provide other opportunities for applying new skills, by making up and playing little games, or by asking the child's help in some small job that needs doing around the environment. For example, a child experienced in building the Pink Tower might be invited to stack a scattered set of books from largest to smallest. The Sensorial Activities are especially easy to adapt as game-playing, when the child is ready.

The director's responsibilities in presenting Montessori activities are clearly related to the theoretical concepts we were discussing earlier. The director's presentation depends for its success upon the workings of the absorbent mind. The child's responsiveness is dependent upon the readiness of the unfolding intellectual structure, broadly manifested in the sensitive periods, for the particular challenge the presentation poses. Lastly, the three resposibilities of the director as a facilitator—creating a challenge, allowing the child to practise, and placing what was learned in a wider context—are based on the three stages of learning—absorption, connection and application.

The purpose of the director's third role, that of an 'observer', is mainly to assist the director's work as a facilitator. As we've noted, to be sure that a presentation will pose a challenge to the child, the director must know precisely when to offer it. This sense of timing is based on the director's long-term observation of the child's development, which has shown that the child is far enough along in the appropriate sensitive periods and that the child has had sufficient experience with preparatory activities. Also, when giving a presentation, the director must closely observe the child's level of interest, and provide sufficient opportunities for involvement to maintain the child's attention. When the child is attempting an activity independently, the director must observe from a distance where difficulties arise in these attempts, to determine whether another presentation is needed, and if it is needed, what special points to emphasise. These observations will also suggest when a child has mastered an activity, and therefore needs the further challenge of the next exercise, the next activity in the scheme, or practical application through simple games and tasks.

More generally, the director must constantly observe all the activities selected by the child each day, to see where the child's natural interests lie. These overall observations of the child's work are vital because the several schemes of activities described in this book are not intended to be followed like a syllabus; decisions on what new presentations to offer should follow the child's natural inclinations. For instance, if the child is selecting a lot of physical activities, the director should offer activities that involve much movement; if the child seems particularly interested in reading and printed material, the director should offer activities that use charts or tags or books. Also, special interests shown by a child in particular subjects, like boats or rocks or clothes, should be incorporated into the activities whenever possible—for example, by providing 'rocks' to count in the MEMORY PLAY activity in Mathematics. In brief, if the director is successfully to direct the environment on the child's behalf, then the child must be allowed to direct the director.

If it is helpful, all these daily observations may be recorded in a diary. If a director is working with a number of children, a summary may be drawn up for each child at the end of each day, indicating what presentations were given, what presentations were repeated, what presentations should be given again with what points to emphasise, what work the child did, and what special tendencies the child displayed. At the end of each week, the director should review these records to understand each child's needs and inclinations better.

The three roles of a Montessori director—taking care of an environment specially for a child, facilitating a child's independent activities, and patiently observing progress—are difficult and somewhat unnatural roles for most of us to play. For example, if the facilitator role were left to our instincts, we would probably want to fumble a presentation to make it fun and humorous, so as not to intimidate the child. We would later want to give constant suggestions to aid the child's attempts at the activities, and to do part of the work for the child if it seemed too hard or slow. And we would be endlessly overlooking imperfect work, never repeating a presentation, attributing a child's mistakes to laziness or naughtiness, and in the face of difficulty, always pushing the child on to the next activity in the scheme rather than dwelling on the difficulties. But the Montessori activities, as remarkable an educational aid as they can be, would do the child little good if conducted in this manner. Because the adult behaviour which is most beneficial to a child's development is so unnatural to us, we all need to prepare ourselves to be Montessori directors, emotionally and in our attitudes, if all of those carefully prepared activities are to derive any benefit for children.

Our over-riding attitude should be that we do not wish to teach the child, or in any other way dominate the child, but only to help provide the child's natural development with the best environment in which to unfold freely. Second, we should realise that although the use of the Montessori materials will generate cultural and intellectual matter for the child's mind to absorb, it is up to us to provide the absorbent mind with emotional, moral and spiritual substance. In this respect, we should strive to be compassionate in our emotions, tolerant in our ethics, and humble in spirit. Third, when we present the child with our emotional, moral and spiritual substance, we need to know our weaknesses, to be alert to our preconceptions and prejudices, to reassess our motives constantly, and to acknowledge and learn from our mistakes. In a word, we must be honest. Children will absorb what we do, and then compare it to what we say. We should never put on an act with children, for not only are they sure to see through it, but we may risk permanently losing their trust. Finally, we should believe in the innate potential for goodness in every child, so that even when we don't see an angel before us, we know there is one in there somewhere, and that by providing the right freedoms and opportunities, we can help the goodness to surface.

Montessori believed that we adults, as part of the child's world, will necessarily either be a hindrance or a help to the child's development. As Montessori directors, our goal is to understand the child sufficiently that we will only ever be a help.

THE ACTIVITIES

THE FIVE SUBJECTS

Over her many years of directing Children's Houses, Montessori developed a great number of fun and interesting activities for young children to engage in. These activities provide the child with stimuli and experiences that, in terms of our theory discussions, nourish the absorbent mind, fulfil the needs of the sensitive periods and the child's unfolding inner intellectual structure, and follow the process of three stage learning. To help the director know the order in which to present the activities, so that the availability of new experiences will correspond to the changing needs of the unfolding inner structure, Montessori organised her activities into five disciplines or subjects, and within each subject worked out a general sequence for presenting the activities. From the child's point of view, the distinctions between these subjects are blurred and unimportant, and indeed most of the activities create experiences that give benefits in more than one subject area. It is therefore not useful for the director to stress to the child the purely rhetorical distinctions between the subject areas. The five subjects are themselves not sequenced; they are conducted more or less in parallel. But as shown in the lists below, certain activities in one subject area are best conducted before, at about the same time as, or after certain activities in the other subject areas.

One subject area consists of the Practical Activities, which develop basic personal and social skills used in daily living, like dressing oneself, cleaning things, and being polite. Another subject area is represented by the Sensorial Activities, which serve to enhance and enlarge the child's sense perceptions of the world. Another two subject areas are the Language Activities, which start the child reading and writing, and the Mathematics Activities, which introduce counting and arithmetic. The last subject area, called Culture Activities, exposes the child to such fields of inquiry as physical science, history, geography, anthropology and biology.

AN OVERVIEW OF THE SEQUENCE

The main reason for presenting the Montessori activities to the child is to provide appropriate experiences that satisfy the child's changing developmental needs. Each activity, in itself, provides some such experience to aid some particular stage of development. Taken together, the activities also build on one another to create an inter-related web of experience that helps integrate the individual abilities developed along the way.

In this web of Montessori experience, everything the child does is preparation for something the child will do later. This principle of 'indirect preparation' is incorporated into the design of each and every Montessori activity, and is reflected in the sequence for presenting the activities. Indirect preparation occurs in the Montessori environment in three ways: first, by the separate introduction, in two or three activities, of the component parts of a later activity; second, by the training of the child in specific, often physical, skills that build in stages toward a more complex skill; and third, by the creation of broad abilities or sensitivities that will generally be important in later work.

An example of the first form of indirect preparation is how the analysis of word sounds in the I SPY activity, and the association of sounds with letter shapes in the SANDPAPER LETTERS activity, are combined in the later MOVABLE ALPHABET activity to become the expression of words by arranging letters. An example of the second form of indirect preparation is how the small wooden knobs on the CYLINDER BLOCKS prepare the child's fingers for small grasping, which is further refined through the SORTING GRAINS activity, is given motor control through the METAL INSETS activity, is given lightness of touch in the SANDPAPER LETTERS activity, and is finally applied to handwriting in the WRITING INDIVIDUAL LETTERS activity. An example of the third form of indirect preparation is how the Practical Activities generally help develop the child's sense of order, through the organisation of the materials used in one's work. This is a skill that becomes crucial to successfully conducting many of the Mathematics Activities and the later Sensorial Activities.

Every Montessori activity, then, has a special place in the sequence, because it satisfies some transitory need that will arise at a particular point in the child's development, and because it provides at least one form of indirect preparation for an activity that will come later.

The following lists indicate the general sequence in which the Montessori activities may initially be offered to the child. For simplicity, I have divided the overall Montessori nursery programme into seven time 'Periods', under each of which is listed activities in the five subject areas. A child just starting out in the Montessori environment should be presented with activities in Period One, and thereafter the child may progress, at an individual pace, numerically through the other Periods. (The names of activities which are fully described in this book are printed in CAPITALS. Although there are seven Periods, this book mainly covers activities through Period Four, and some in Period Five; hence the title, *Basic Montessori.*) Usually, a child working within a particular Period in one subject area will also be working in the same Period in other subject areas. Note that these lists only indicate when an activity is first presented; the activity and its derivative exercises will continue to be conducted by the child in later Periods.

While the Periods tell you the proper sequence of the activities, you should, as has been mentioned before, only follow a particular series of activities when the child has shown an interest in pursuing such directions. This is an important qualification to the use of these lists: your overriding responsibility is to follow the child's inclinations. Within the scope of the child's inclinations, these lists will help you know what doors to open next. To expand on this metaphor, you should not lead the child down these corridors, but rather follow closely behind the child, so that whichever direction the child turns, you can reach out and open a door.

Period One

(Early Practical Activities, introductory Sensorial, Culture, and Language Activities, no Mathematics.)

Practical: POURING BEANS BETWEEN TWO JUGS; opening and closing containers; BUTTONING; buckling; other simple Dressing Frames; carrying and laying floor mats and table mats; SAYING 'THANK YOU'; other early grace and courtesy work; carrying a tray; lifting, carrying and putting down a chair; sitting down on and getting up from a chair at a table; climbing and descending stairs; WALKING ON THE LINE; folding; hanging clothes on a hook; brushing hair; dusting.

Sensorial: CYLINDER BLOCKS; PINK TOWER; box 1 of the COLOUR TABLETS; presentation tray of the GEOMETRIC CABINET; SENSITISING THE FINGERS; TOUCH BOARDS; presentation (1) of GEOMETRIC SOLIDS; STEREOGNOSTIC BAGS presentation.

Language: CLASSIFIED PICTURES exercises (1) and (2); SPEECH; stages (1), (2) and (3) of I SPY; BOOK CORNER AND LIBRARY.

Mathematics: none.

Culture: LAND AND WATER presentation.

Period Two

(Building fundamental skills in all subject areas except Mathematics, concentrating on sight and touch in Sensorial work.)

Practical: pouring water from a jug; medium difficulty Dressing Frames; simple braiding of rope or yarn; laying a table for a meal; polishing brass, glass surfaces, shoes or furniture; washing hands; washing cloths; scrubbing a table top; SWEEPING SAWDUST; brushing clothes; folding clothes; hanging clothes on a hanger; HANDLING A BOOK; asking for and receiving scissors; greeting people; kindness to visitors; BEING SILENT.

Sensorial: advanced CYLINDER BLOCKS exercises; BROWN STAIR; RED RODS; boxes 2 and 3 of COLOUR TABLETS; GEOMETIRC CABINET exercises (1) through (4); BINOMIAL CUBE; BLINDFOLD; TACTILE TABLETS; later GEOMETRIC SOLIDS presentations; STEREOGNOSTIC BAGS exercises; SORTING GRAINS; SOUND BOXES; preliminary presentations of BELLS; Three Stage Lessons on the names of Sensorial qualities.

Language: CLASSIFIED PICTURES exercises (3) and (4); stage (4) of I SPY; exercise (1) with the single-letter SANDPAPER LETTERS; METAL INSETS; frequent SPEECH 'Questioning'.

Mathematics: none.

Culture: LAND AND WATER exercises; first MAPS; PLACES classified pictures; preliminary work for CLASSIFICATION BY LEAF.

Period Three

(Developing more advanced Practical skills, concentrating on other senses in Sensorial work, completing preparatory work in Language, fully entering Culture work, starting Mathematics.)

Practical: pouring water from a jug, also through a funnel; bows, laces and other difficult Dressing Frames; advanced braiding, then plaiting hair; tying a tie; simple cooking chores; ironing; making beds.

Sensorial: GEOMETRIC CABINET exercises (5) through (8); CONSTRUCTIVE TRIANGLES; SQUARE OF PYTHAGORAS; TRINOMIAL CUBE; FABRICS; THERMIC BOTTLES; BARIC TABLETS; presentations of BELLS.

Language: exercise (1) with the double-letter SANDPAPER LETTERS; stages (5) and (6) of I SPY, frequently; exercise (2) with all SANDPAPER LETTERS.

Mathematics: NUMBER RODS exercise (1).

Culture: all MAPS; PLACES picture folders; PAST AND PRESENT; STORIES ABOUT THE PAST; AIR; WATER; MAGNETISM; CLASSIFYING ANIMALS; CLASSIFICATION BY LEAF; PARTS OF ANIMALS; PARTS OF PLANTS.

Period Four

(Advanced Sensorial Activities, early Language reading and writing, Mathematics Group 1 and starting Group 2.)

Practical: responsibility for certain daily Care of the Environment duties; helping and advising younger ones in a group.

Sensorial: GEOMETRIC CABINET exercises (9) and (10); THERMIC TABLETS; MYSTERY BAG; VISUAL WORK WITH BLINDFOLD; BELLS exercises (1), (2), and (3); TASTING CUPS; SMELLING BOXES.

Language: MOVABLE ALPHABET; WRITING INDIVIDUAL LETTERS; WRITING FAMILIES OF LETTERS; POSITIONING LETTERS ON LINES; SANDPAPER CAPITALS; BOX 1 of OBJECT BOXES; ACTION CARDS; BOX 2 of OBJECT BOXES; READING FOLDERS exercise (1).

Mathematics: NUMBER RODS exercise (2); SANDPAPER NUMBERS; NUMBER TABLETS (with the Number Rods); SPINDLES; NUMBERS AND COUNTERS; MEMORY PLAY; LIMITED BEAD MATERIAL; NUMBER CARDS; FUNCTION OF THE DECIMAL SYSTEM; FRACTIONS.

Culture: GRAVITY; SOUND; OPTICS; PLACES artefacts.

Period Five

(Further development in Language reading and writing, essence of counting, adding, subtracting and multiplying in Mathematics.)

Practical: assisting with group activities; attending to visitors; comforting other children.

Sensorial: Knobless Cylinders; BELLS exercises (4), (5), and (6).

Language: Matching and Writing Capitals; The Alphabetic Sequence; Writing Copies; PUZZLE WORDS; READING FOLDERS exercise (2); Classified Reading; Environment Cards; Articles; Adjectives; Conjunctions; Prepositions; Verbs.

Mathematics: FORMATION OF COMPLEX NUMBERS; INTRODUCTION TO TEENS; INTRODUCTION TO TENS; Unlimited Bead Material (ADDITION, Subtraction and Multiplication); Counting; Stamps (Addition, Subtraction and Multiplication); Dots; Fractions exercises.

Culture: PLANT LIFE CYCLES; TIME LINE.

Period Six

(Advanced Language work, basic division and arithmetic memory work in Mathematics.)

Practical: serving snacks and meals; subtle etiquette.

Sensorial: advanced Bells work.

Language: Margins; Punctuation Cards; READING FOLDERS exercises (3) and (4); Adjective Matching; Detective Adjective Game; Adverbs; Command Cards; Adverb Matching; Verb Games; Plurals; Feminine and Masculine; Root Word Charts.

Mathematics: Unlimited Bead Material (Division); Stamps (Division); Addition and Subtraction Snake Games; Addition and Subtraction Strip Boards; Multiplication Tables; Multiplication Bead Board; Addition, Subtraction and Multiplication Charts; advanced work with Fractions.

Culture: reading 'Classified Cards' in Geography, Nature Studies and History; fact books from the library.

Period Seven

(Application activities in Language, abstraction in Mathematics.)

Practical: helping the director prepare the environment; presenting Practical Activities to younger children.

Sensorial: presenting early Sensorial Activities to younger children.

Language: Written Questioning; Free Writing; READING FOLDERS exercise (5); Reading Analysis.

Mathematics: Unit Division Board; Division Charts; Short Bead Frame; Hierarchies; Long Bead Frame; Simple Division.

Culture: definition stages of 'Classified Cards' in Geography, Nature Studies and History; field nature observation work.

PRESENTING AN ACTIVITY

When a child has been enthusiastically pursuing a subject area and has gained experience that would appear to provide the requisite preparation for a particular new activity, then the director needs to respond at the earliest convenient time with a 'presentation' of the new activity. Unobtrusively place out the activity's materials in the spots you have set aside for them on the shelves, privately tell the child, with evident excitement, 'I have something new to show you . . .', and proceed to present the new activity.

For each Montessori activity in this book, you will find: a statement of the activity's *Aim* or purpose in the Montessori programme, which explains how the child can benefit from it; a list and description of the *Material* needed for the presentation and the ensuing exercises; in some cases, 'D*IY* hints' or suggestions on *How to Make the Material*; a discussion of any *Preliminary Activities* or *Preliminary Presentations* or any special *Preparation* to be done by the director; a full step-by-step guide to giving the actual *Presentation* or *Presentations*; and complete descriptions of ensuing *Exercises* and how to present them. 'Exercises' are the work that the child does independently, after the presentation. The first exercise is usually simply the child independently trying to reproduce what you did so perfectly in the presentation. You later briefly present each of the other exercises, one at a time, when and if the child has mastered what's been presented so far. Although it is not always part of the description, every presentation and exercise concludes with the child putting all the materials back in their places in the Montessori environment, perfectly ready for another child to use.

As you will see, the step-by-step course of a presentation usually follows the process of three stage 'learning by connecting', described earlier. First, you simply show the material—naming it, showing where it is kept, identifying the scope of experience it provides, and inviting the child to handle it and otherwise become familiar with it. Second, you demonstrate the 'connection' or concept embodied in the material, and distinguish the material's purpose from that of other materials, by showing precisely how to use it and how best to observe and experience the 'connection'. Third, you give application and context to the concept, by immediately inviting the child to attempt what you have shown, and to try it again later, independently. Occasionally, the presentation is simply a Three Stage Lesson, which is a special method, based on the process of three stage learning, for helping the child memorise terms or other abstract associations.

Similarly, the overall structure of an activity parallels the process of three stage learning: the presentation is simply providing the activity to the absorbent mind; early exercises enable the child to act out the connections and concepts embodied in the activity; and later exercises—such as the memory exercises in the Sensorial Activities—allow application of the concept in a meaningful context.

When you are first teaching yourself an activity, you may follow the step-wise instructions given in this book, in the same way you would follow a recipe. But never give a presentation to a child while reading the directions for the first time. All the materials and supplies you will need for the presentation must be complete and in their designated places in the environment before you begin, and you will obviously have to work out in advance what you'll need and where to keep it. Also, before giving any presentation, you must fully understand its process and purpose, and have a great deal of experience in conducting the activity yourself. This means that you must practise it, and practise it often enough to keep yourself well trained, so that whenever you need to present a material you will be ready to give a flawless demonstration of how it's used.

Each presentation you give must be absolutely perfect, for three reasons. First, the child will benefit most by repeating and repeating an activity, and only the image of perfection created by your presentation will draw the child on to repeat the activity in pursuit of that perfection. Second, the child's absorbent mind will pick up every single little error you make, no matter how subtle it is or how quickly you correct yourself, and these errors may later frustrate or prevent the success of the child's independent attempts at the activity. Third, you must be able to conduct the activity with complete ease and familiarity, so that rather than concentrating on getting it right, you can concentrate on keeping the child's interest and attention.

You may often think that a presentation sounds so simple—'after all, a three-year old can do it'—that practice on your part seems unnecessary. Although many of the activities are indeed based on comparatively simple procedures, without a lot of practice you will find it nearly impossible to conduct an activity without hesitation or mistake, while exuding absolute confidence, and while simultaneously trying to keep the child more interested in what you're doing than in what's going on across the room.

Keeping a young child's attention, while not diverging unnecessarily from the main flow of the presentation, is a subtle art that is best learned by experience. If you're working with a group of children, you will find that different children respond best to different techniques. For some children, an atmosphere of fun will keep their attention, while others are more fascinated by a sense of wonder and magic. During your presentation, you can occasionally invite the child to do some small physical task, like handing you something or putting something back in its box. Also, you can make the child's observation of what you're doing involve some activity; for example, invite the child to re-count the beads you've just counted, or to feel the cloth you've just felt. If nothing seems to be working, and the child is simply not absorbing the presentation, then gracefully conclude it in the middle, and wait until another day to try it again from the beginning. Never, in desperation, conduct the activity jointly with the child—you doing some, and the child doing some—since unlike an adult, it is difficult for a young child to grasp the essence of an activity by alternately taking directions and observing. More generally, a presentation to a young child should never consist, in whole or in part, of verbal instructions. Remember that the young child's mind does not analyse nearly as well as it absorbs. Therefore, the essence of a good presentation is that you don't explain the activity to the child—you show it.

Whether a presentation is successful depends partly on the director's skills in conducting it, and partly on the child's readiness to respond to it. If a child, when later working independently, has continuous difficulty with an activity or appears to be manipulating the materials aimlessly, then either another presentation is needed, or the child is not yet ready for the challenges which the activity presents. If the child makes no errors at all when first attempting the activity, it is likely that the child is already too advanced and may lose interest in the activity before benefiting from it. When the child has grasped the purpose of the activity from the presentation, but there are occasional errors in judgement and technique, then the child is at just the appropriate stage of development. The challenge to perfect the activity will induce repetition and concentration, resulting in that remarkable self-directed, self-motivated learning that Montessori first witnessed in her Children's House.

THE CHILD FREELY AT WORK

Imagine that the child has recently been given a number of very high quality presentations, the cleaned and polished materials are neatly stored in their designated places in the carefully ordered Montessori environment, you are sitting expectantly in the corner waiting to observe some of that remarkable Montessori self-teaching, and what is the child doing? Playing with the cat.

Sounds frustrating? Well, it shouldn't. We must be very careful not to get in the frame of mind that there is anything whatsoever wrong with the child's playing with the cat, nor indeed with any typically childlike behaviour. The point cannot be emphasised too strongly that the Montessori environment is only there to help the child. Forcing it on the child, making evident our expectations of the wonders that Montessori's method can work, or in any way coercing the child to give up behaviour that comes naturally, will only cause harm and distress. If the Montessori environment is to help and not harm, it must be offered like a loving gift, without expectations or conditions, as a place for the child to be absolutely free—free to observe presentations or not observe them, to work or not work, to join in activities or just mess about, to be active or to rest.

Montessori observed that if she prepared the environment and presented it to the child properly, and allowed the child sufficient freedom to respond to those presentations at an individual pace, then a kind of space for natural growing is opened in the child's life.

The young child starting off in the Montessori environment is usually quite incapable of working on anything for very long, and typically flits from one activity to another, acting either in a frenzied manner or withdrawn. Then gradually the director's presentations begin to arouse the child's interest, focusing attention on a small number of activities. This aroused interest is delicate, and when it is exhibited it should be nurtured and protected from distractions. One day, when the child is attempting one of the

simpler activities, the attempt will go on a lot longer than usual for no obvious reason, and then abruptly end, with the child looking around, as though just awakened from a daydream. Later in the same day, this experience of prolonged work may be repeated, perhaps several times, separated by distinct periods of restlessness. In the next stage, these extended work periods occur more often, and the times of restlessness between the work periods become shorter and less frequent. Also, a daily pattern evolves, wherein the child engages in a number of activities, not delving into any of them too deeply, before coming to the 'main activity' of the day, on which the child focuses quite intensely for a considerable period of time. Now, rather than end in a state of restlessness, each activity ends in a state of repose, during which the child contemplates and digests the work just experienced. This newfound ability to 'concentrate', as Montessori formally termed it, and the ensuing periods of tranquil contemplation, apparently fulfil a deep inner need, and this fulfilment begins to be expressed as a subtle increase in gentleness, kindness and thoughtfulness towards others. In the last phase, concentration continues, and spreads to other activities of the day, so that there are many focused activities rather than just one 'main activity'. Perseverance becomes a habit, and calmness and serenity a permanent aspect of the child's personality.

This is, of course, the ideal, but we can look for signs of it as we work with the child each day. Again, we cannot force the child to awaken into 'concentration'. It is in large part an awakening of the child's conscious will, which can only flourish in an atmosphere where it is fully free and respected.

DIRECTING A GROUP OF CHILDREN

The original Children's House had a considerable number of children, at various ages and stages of development, all working simultaneously, and this is the way all Montessori classes have been organised since.

One would suppose that putting together children of different abilities, who are all working at different stages, would create jealousies and competition among them. However, the truth is precisely the opposite. It is the grouping of children who are all at roughly the same stage of development that invites comparisons and breeds jealousies. In a mixed-age group, each child, at any one moment, is working on something different and unique, and comparisons in 'performance' are not possible.

When we are uncertain of something, we often have as our first impulse the desire to seek help, or simply a vote of confidence, from another person who we believe to be more experienced. It is also a child's natural impulse to consult the more experienced. In a group of children of mixed ages, this older, more experienced person need not be the director—it can be another child.

Having a mixed-age group, and directing a child, who needs minor help, to another child more experienced, has a number of distinct advantages. First, for materials like the SOUND BOXES, which provide no inherent feedback that an error has been made, the director can ask an uncertain child to consult another more experienced child. This approach suggests to the first child that there are no absolute or final answers to certain questions, but only people working together to improve their perception and understanding. A second advantage is that a child who lacks self-esteem can be greatly encouraged by having someone else come to him or her for help. All children are good at something, and if the director keeps in mind several things that each child is good at, then whenever children want a check on one of those activities, they may be sent to the 'resident expert' for help. Another advantage of this approach is that having to show or explain something to someone else forces a child to organise it mentally, and so deepens the child's own understanding of it. Also, new children in the group can be given certain simple presentations by older children, especially of the Practical Activities and early Sensorial Activities, which helps welcome the new ones into the group, and incidentally, frees up a little time for the director.

A mixed-age group working together provides indirect preparation for younger children, who watch and begin to absorb the activities they will be doing later, and it helps the older children realise their progress when they see the younger ones attempting things that they themselves mastered some time ago. The general social atmosphere of the group benefits from children helping one another, as it becomes a fact of life that some people are more experienced in some things, but that everyone needs a little help from others.

The Montessori environment is thus a lively, social place, in which the children are free to work together if they like, and in which they often observe and discuss one another's work. Montessori children are encouraged to look to one another for answers and ideas as much as they look to adults.

Although the original Children's House had a large group of children, there is no reason that most of Montessori's principles and activities cannot be put to use in a private home, with just one or a few children. You will find that some of the activities discussed in this book are described as though they will be conducted with a small group of children. But with a little imagination, and where necessary, by assuming the roles of the other children yourself, you can readily adapt all the activities to a single child working alone.

GROWTH TOWARDS INDEPENDENCE

In devising her method, Maria Montessori had but one aim: to assist the child's natural development. Because the endpoint of a child's development is, one hopes, a self-sufficient, well-adjusted adult, any assistance we offer to 'development' must by definition foster independence and self-sufficiency. Our reason for practising the Montessori method is thus to aid the child's growth towards independence.

The Montessori method fosters independence in two ways: first, in the short term, it provides freedom and independence in learning; second, in the long run, it helps the child acquire tools for living, that is, the skills and abilities which give a person greater choices in life, and which make one free from dependence on others.

Let's first consider freedom in learning. We have all heard about educational methods that are based on 'freedom', in that they permit any activity or non-activity that strikes the child's fancy, provided it doesn't hurt or disturb anyone. Freedom in the Montessori environment is different from this. The Montessori method is not a licence for the child to act out momentary whims; instead, it introduces and upholds the child's right to make thoughtful choices. Although 'acting out whims' feels like freedom at first, a person eventually finds it quite limiting. Following our every whim, we would incur consequences we didn't want, we would make no progress towards fulfilling our deeper desires and, unable to make serious decisions, we would repeatedly find that our long-range choices had been made for us. True freedom, in Montessori's view, is control over one's own destiny, and that means controlling our whims, working towards long-range goals, and making conscious choices about our actions and their consequences. In other words, every act of truly 'free' choice is preceded by an act of judgement. This is a kind of freedom that must be learned, and to which we must lead a child, little by little.

When the child is new in the Montessori environment, we verbally offer very simple choices between clearly contrasting experiences, for example, a choice between a quiet activity like working with a 'Dressing Frame', and an energetic activity like dusting all the table tops in the room. To help the child grasp the idea that thoughtful choosing requires self-evaluation, it is important that these early choices be between genuinely different activities, presenting a contrast that a young child can readily appreciate. Later, after we have presented many activities to the child, we give a greater number of choices, say four or five, any of which would pose the right level of challenge to inspire practice and stimulate growth. As has been stressed before, we must pay attention to and follow the interests demonstrated by the child in making these choices, and then create new opportunities in directions suggested by the child's natural inclinations. Gradually, the child's choices need not be pointed out as often by the director, since they become self-evident in the wide range of interesting materials that we have presented to the child and which are waiting attractively on their shelves.

Corollaries to the child's freedom in choosing activities are the freedoms to conduct those activities when, where, as long as, as often as, and at whatever pace the child likes. For example, the child in a home Montessori environment can set to work with an activity at dusk or daybreak, can set it up under the piano bench or in the bed-room, can work on it for ten minutes or for eight hours straight, can set it up just once or twelve days in a row, and can work intensively at great speed or intermittently between roaming around and daydreaming. In a group environment, in addition to the above sorts of freedom, the child can also share an activity with another child, provided they have both been properly presented with the material. These freedoms aren't so much a matter of liberty, as they are a matter of respecting the child's dignity as an individual. Respecting children teaches children to respect themselves; it builds their trust in their own judgement, and so supports their basic freedom to make thoughtful choices.

The second type of independence fostered by the Montessori environment is the cultivation of certain skills and knowledge, like reading, writing, maths, geography, social courtesy, physical grace and household skills, all of which help a person live competently. This sort of competence in daily living frees us from dependence upon others, it often frees us from manipulation by others, and by enabling us to deal efficiently with mundane matters, it frees our minds for more profound and rewarding pursuits. The world in general, and human society in particular, have forces and pressures which are larger and more powerful than any one of us. If we do not understand these forces, they will forever drag us along in their wake. But if we can acquire insight into these forces, and learn to adapt to them, we can use their momentum to propel us in our own creative directions.

Montessori characterised the child's gradual growth towards independence as a continual emergence, or liberation, into ever-larger spaces to adapt to. Birth is the first liberation, freeing the baby from containment by the womb, but leaving the baby vulnerable to the changeable environment outside. A second emergence, which comes in the first month or two, is a deliberate facing of the world and its sensory impressions, which the baby's absorbent mind begins to incarnate. A third liberation is weaning, making the baby independent of its mother's body, but also making it responsible for the complex set of actions necessary to feeding one's self and expressing needs. With the onset of speech, the baby emerges into social life, and is liberated from the isolation of the solitary thinker, but must also begin to cope with social expectations and judgements. At about one year of age, the child begins to learn to walk, emerging into a greater field for exploration, but also becoming responsible for knowing when and where not to explore. With each emergence into a greater space come new freedoms and new responsibilities.

In the Montessori environment, it may be useful for us to think of the child's progress in just this way. It implies that we, as directors, can help equip the child for each adaptation to a given intellectual space, and can then gradually lead the child to emerge from it, to face a wider space, with exciting new opportunities and challenges. The free-dom to work at these adaptations at an individual pace solidly grounds the new skills that are gained in the process of adapting. These new skills become new freedoms, which collectively open the gate to the next larger space for the child to grow into. The process continues, and when the child eventually emerges into the space usually called society, and becomes self-sufficient in that space, the child starts to be called an adult.

PEACE THROUGH SELF-FULFILMENT

Maria Montessori lived through the two most terrible wars in the history of mankind, and the causes of war were very much on her mind, especially in the years after the Second World War. She came to believe that the widespread application of her method of education could help lead the world towards peace.

Montessori believed that her method enables children to satisfy fully their instinctual and personal developmental needs, and so helps to create fulfilled and well-balanced adults, whose innate goodness can shine forth unimpeded by neurotic ambitions and desires. If her method would spread sufficiently throughout the world, she hoped, millions of adults raised by it would be free from such tendencies as greed and aggression. Then, with the passing of the old generations, threats to world peace would gradually subside and disappear.

The Montessori method may also help promote peace by its study and support of the work of the absorbent mind. If we consider the action of the absorbent mind—that children fully accept, without critique or prejudice, the behaviour and traits of those around them, that children transform themselves by incarnating these ways, and that children place complete faith in the goodness and benevolence of others—we see more than a mechanism for learning, but also children's saint-like charity or spiritual love for people. This love emanates unconsciously from each and every child in each and every family and community in the world. If the Montessori method were widely applied, this love, as embodied in the absorbent mind, would be studied and cultivated rather than ignored and distracted. Perhaps the child's innate spirit of love would also carry over from childhood to adulthood, and eventually affect the way in which adults behaved towards one another.

Lastly, Montessori may have helped promote peace by awakening us to the importance of childhood to society. Children's absorbent minds, by assimilating the language, ideas, customs and manners of society, allow the cultural adaptations of each community to be continuous and built upon, from one generation to the next. In this sense, the absorbent mind makes possible all civilisation and its progress, and provides an ever-recurring bond that holds society together. Whatever their differences, most societies share a reverence for children's innocent affections, trust and generosity. Montessori had great hopes that the study of the child would bring together the world's societies in a common and universally beneficial cause. Indeed, Montessori lived to see her method being followed and pursued, at least to some extent, on every continent on the globe.

Deborah L. Cohen (essay date 1990)

SOURCE: "Montessori Methods in Public Schools," in *The Education Digest,* Vol. 56, No. 1, September, 1990, pp. 63-6.

[*In the following essay, Cohen discusses reasons for the failure of American public schools to adopt Montessori methods.*]

Although private schools remain the primary settings for Montessori instruction in the United States, the philosophy and methods identified with the movement have spread rapidly in the public system in the 1980s. First embraced by public educators in the mid-1970s as a theme for magnet programs designed to spur desegregation, the approach is now being used in about 110 public schools in 60 districts. Some 14,000 pupils were enrolled as of last year.

Many districts are expanding their programs into additional classrooms and schools, and five to seven new districts begin programs each year, according to the North American Montessori Teachers Association. Proponents say the "renaissance" is helping extend Montessori's benefits to a broader mix of students, and they argue that public schools can supplement those benefits with distinctive resources and programs of their own.

But some educators, particularly in private schools, worry that bureaucratic constraints and a lack of Montessori-trained teachers will mean public schools adopt "Montessori in name," without fully adhering to the movement's principles. Tim Seldin, headmaster of the Barrie School, a private Montessori school in Washington, D.C., maintains that many public school programs "are being run by people who are very sincere in what they are trying to do. But they are being asked to compromise to such an extent that my fear is that when they are finished compromising, what they are doing is not going to look very much like Montessori." What Montessori should look like, however, is subject to debate even among Montessorians.

The two major professional groups in the field differ on the extent to which Montessori methods should be adapted to today's society, and dozens of different associations provide teacher training. Association leaders say they are working separately and together to promote the movement's spread into the public sector. But they concede that their efforts are relatively recent.

"The Montessori community has done a less than admirable job of promoting itself," said Paul Epstein, coordinator of the Montessori magnet program in Prince George's County, Maryland. "It's probably the most incredibly well-kept secret of education."

The "secret" is based on the work of Maria Montessori, an Italian physician and biologist born in 1870 who first worked with children labeled retarded and then with the children of poor families in inner-city Rome. Her observations led her to conclude that children learn best in environments that respect and support their individual development.

Maintaining that children's first six years are the most critical for learning, Montessori promoted a holistic approach that would begin children's education at an early age. She envisioned such education fostering social and emotional growth as well as cognitive competence.

She proposed a "prepared environment" of multi-sensory materials laid out in an ordered sequence that would allow children to both enjoy and succeed at learning. The method relies heavily on practical skills and hands-on learning; it incorporates activities ranging from simple tasks, such as sorting beads and learning to work buckles and buttons, to complex arithmetic and cultural studies.

The materials are designed to help children gain an understanding of whole processes, rather than piecemeal concepts, and allow teachers to assess their progress and diagnose problems by observation without formal tests. The model groups children not by grades, but in multi-age clusters that correspond to developmental stages and allow interaction and modeling among younger and older children. The methods are designed to stimulate children's independence and self-directed learning, with teachers serving as guides.

In the eighties, the emphasis on early childhood education and the emergence of the school choice movement have further bolstered the popularity of Montessori ideas among school-savvy parents. Educators estimate that there may be as many as 4,000 schools bearing the Montessori name in the United States, ranging from programs in church basements to college-preparatory schools. Although the method is most commonly practiced in preschool and the early grades, some schools have extended it to the junior and senior high levels.

The American Montessori Society (AMS) represents more than 700 schools. The U.S. branch of the Association Montessori Internationale (AMI)—an international association based in Holland—represents 130 schools. The AMS generally supports efforts to adapt and update Montessori methods, while the AMI has sought to preserve the original model as closely as possible.

While only about two dozen public schools are officially recognized by either the AMS or the AMI, many public school teachers have been trained in programs accredited by those groups. Some of the more established public programs hire only Montessori-trained staff members. But some schools are instituting programs too rapidly to ensure that teachers and administrators receive proper training first, experts warn.

"The most important crisis we are facing is that the programs may expand in advance of our community's ability to maintain the supply of Montessori teachers," says David Kahn, executive director of the North American Montessori Teachers Association. While the training formats of the major associations differ, both require extensive preservice training beyond traditional teacher certification.

Apart from the issue of training, Virginia A. McHugh, executive director of the AMI-U.S.A., raises the concern that public school programs may be "diluted just by having to go through the bureaucracies." While the Montessori model calls for grouping 3- to 6-year-olds, for example, many public schools are able to enroll 3- and 4-year-olds only on a tuition or part-day basis, and others begin the programs at age 5—practices some contend can compromise the Montessori "dynamic." Others argue that public school programs may be hampered by curriculum and testing requirements, political pressures, and constraints in choosing pupils and teachers well suited to the method.

Many educators involved in the movement say public schools face no greater risk of diluting Montessori methods than do private schools. The AMS, stressed Bretta Weiss, its national director and president of the Council for American Private Education, advises parents to "look at a school, its materials, and the training of teachers" before enrolling a child in a Montessori program. "That wouldn't relate just to public schools," she observed.

Because the AMI failed in a 1960s attempt to patent the Montessori name, "anybody can create an early childhood center and call it Montessori," noted Paula Biwer of the Denver district, a Montessori-trained public school principal who has worked in the private sector. Many private programs face "problems of training and erroneous personal interpretations" and "sacrifice Montessori principles in order to attract or keep tuition-paying students," said Jean K. Miller, implementor of a Montessori program at the Greenfield School in Milwaukee, Wisconsin.

"In spite of the fact that the overwhelming majority of private Montessori schools practice [it] in a form that is hardly recognizable," she wrote, "good Montessori practice has survived. . . . The same is possible in public schools."

Others argue that even with their shortcomings, public schools are making important contributions. "Even though they may not start out with the total training Montessorians see as necessary, the things they have tried have been valuable, and many of them are asking for further training," said Sylvia Cooper, principal of the Palm Academy, a magnet public school in Lorain, Ohio, that offers a "Montessori-like" program.

While many public programs "do not come close to the standards" demanded by critics, "their test scores are still the best in the city, and kids are doing well and are happy," noted Dennis Schapiro, editor of *The Public School Montessorian*. "For a lot of parents, that's enough."

Rather than undermining Montessori principles, advocates argue, public schools are helping spread them. "Having a good public school program only enhances the work of private schools," said Biwer, who noted that the publicity—and long waiting lists—drawn by public school programs has boosted private schools' business.

Public schools, argued Cooper, also have increased access to the method, not just for "people who can afford it," but for "the urban child" who was the focus of Montessori's initial work. Public educators also maintain that state and local standards can be successfully integrated with Montessori methods—and that computer education, arts programs, and other public school resources can be an asset to Montessori goals.

Although Montessori methods embody many principles of "developmentally appropriate" education espoused by national authorities on early childhood, the model has not been widely promoted because "there is no one body that says this is what Montessori is," said Barbara A. Willer of the National Association for the Education of Young Children. Some also say the movement's factionalism has undercut efforts to validate the method through research and to ensure adequate training. The professional groups "ought to get together and decide on how they can best serve the needs of the students," said Cooper.

While denying that differences among the groups have "hindered the spread of Montessori," Weiss conceded that backers of the method "haven't been good salespeople." But last year, she noted, the board of the AMS made it a priority to extend Montessori to pupils in a range of settings, including public schools.

Dennis Schapiro (essay date 1993)

SOURCE: "What if Montessori Education Is Part of the Answer?" in *The Education Digest*, Vol. 58, No. 7, March, 1993, pp. 40-3.

[*In the following essay, Schapiro argues that Montessori's methods should be carefully reviewed and considered valid educational options for children in the United States.*]

You need not think the Montessori Method holds the cure for all that ails American education to regret it has never been given a fair chance to prove just how much it can do.

We talk about needing systematic rather than piecemeal reform. The Montessori approach is integrated across the curriculum and through the ages from preschool through elementary. The benefit may be greatest for children from chaotic homes. By creating respectful, stable, and integrated learning environments for children from early preschool through the elementary years and beyond, Montessori schools can provide a sense of order in an otherwise disordered world.

We talk about reforms that meet the test of the market-place. Montessori education has succeeded in the market-place with almost no governmental support and almost no support from this country's educational establishment. To-day about 3,000 independent schools and 130 public schools—some starting with preschools, some reaching eighth grade—describe themselves as Montessori schools.

Where Montessori education has been accepted in the pub-lic sector, it often has been as a desegregation tool. The "Montessori Method" developed by Maria Montessori in the early years of this century was built on the needs of the neediest children. It is the advocacy of white, middle-class women that revived the movement and kept it alive in the United States. Thus, for city school systems like those in Buffalo, Cincinnati, Dallas, Denver, Kansas City, and Milwaukee, Montessori schools become an obvious strategy: Montessori magnets, if done well, are effective with the neediest and draw children of the middle class.

Nearly everywhere it has been implemented in the public sector, the waiting lists are long and the signs of parents' approval are clear. Is it out of line to ask if there is some larger contribution this approach could make?

Expansion of programs is limited by several factors, in-cluding the shortage of trained Montessori teachers, the upfront costs of starting a program, and, most important, the discomfort key players—both Montessorians and those in the public sector—have in making the leap of faith nec-essary to move forward.

Montessori, born in 1870 and the first female physician in Italy, focused her attention on the way young children learn. Her approach was scientific and inductive. She watched and developed materials and procedures that built on children's capacities and proclivities. She looked to de-velop an approach that worked on a given day and pro-vided a basis of continuity that would work with children years later.

In the implementations I have seen and admired most, teachers create a structured environment for learning, mak-ing extensive use of standardized didactic materials. Mate-rials are designed to be self-correcting, emphasizing chil-dren's contact with learning rather than judgments or interventions of teachers. The entire curriculum is linked in many ways—including materials used at different levels of sophistication as the children grow. The experience is built on the intellectual and spiritual potential of the chil-dren and their connections to other people and the natural world.

Montessori was not a compromiser. Her distrust of others to carry on or interpret her work may have preserved her method's purity, but it undermined its effectiveness in the United States. Then, in the early 1960s, Nancy Rambusch, now a professor of early-childhood education at the State University of New York at New Paltz, and a band of other

mothers led a revival. In essence, they countered a major objection to Montessori's method—Montessori herself.

They were committed to adapting the principles of the ap-proach to the American experience. Montessori had died in 1952, but those who had risen to protect her work and, some would say elevated her to the status of a cult figure, no longer had a monopoly. The principles she espoused—not simply her personality and extrapolations of her archi-val material—would play a vital role in the Montessori movement in the United States.

Sexism?

Even in revived form, the approach could not penetrate mainstream educational policy, although policy-makers did take to shipping their children off to private Montessori schools. Some observers question the relationship between this lack of acceptance and the fact that the movement was initiated by a woman and revived by a grassroots cam-paign made up almost entirely of women.

Over the past 30 years, the movement has become frac-tionated in the United States. The Holland-based Associa-tion Montessori-International, established by Montessori to protect her vision, has a branch in the United States. Al-though it resists Americanization, the AMI is significant in this country, and at least four successful public school sys-tems follow its lead closely.

The American Montessori Society, founded by Rambusch, is the largest Montessori organization in the United States and most active with public schools. Dozens of smaller groups and individuals provide Montessori training. Al-though a new, voluntary organization was founded in 1991 to accredit teacher-training programs and provide some agreed-upon standards, there is today no single nationally accepted model of a Montessori school or a Montessori training regimen.

Given the difficulty in standardizing Montessori-based education, and the outsider status to which it has been rel-egated, one thing must be said: If done with any reason-able amount of integrity, it works. Satisfied parents and young people are the basis for the judgment. Unfortu-nately, traditional research is not.

Some conventional research has been done, but the best of it is only suggestive. Lacking a standard definition of a Montessori school or classroom, there is no reliability of measurement. Each study of Montessori programs begins with a different set of classroom conditions, making gener-alizations impossible.

More Trouble

Research problems go beyond that. Children in good Mon-tessori classrooms have usually done quite well on stan-dardized tests, but it appears that they show even greater advantages over their peers when measured years later. This suggests that these children may be building a strong base for later learning, whether or not they reach the year's districtwide learning objectives. For that reason, research would need to be long-term. Also, the goals of a Montessori-based education go beyond the easily measurable. How do you measure the uneven evolution of children who grow into adults who respond creatively to new challenges, resolve conflicts effectively, understand their relatedness to others, and take responsibility for their own lives?

The university-based research community has shied away from Montessori education. By now it is a vicious cycle: Few university researchers study it, and without research, we have no proof it is effective, no way to justify its place in higher education.

STANDARD FARE

Without formal acceptance, bits and pieces of Montessori's method have become standard fare in schools—manipulatives for math, a literature-based approach to reading, multi-age grouping, a world-view social science curriculum, emphasis on developmental levels of children, and structured observation by the teacher.

What is missing in this piecemeal borrowing is the integrated whole. This integration of all the pieces carries much of the approach's potential—especially for young people in disintegrating families. It is our unwillingness to try a total package that has made so limited the potential of Montessori-based education.

Are these times when—for investigation purposes if no other—we ought to consider giving the approach a fair test? To make it work, several things would need to happen:

• *Educational leaders and reformers must pledge to give the approach a fair trial.* If a public Montessori magnet exists only to provide good desegregation numbers, that is one thing. If it is there to do a remarkable job of educating children, it needs support in terms of funding, admission policies, teacher training, student assessment, preschool components, etc. The integrity of the total approach must be respected.

• *Researchers must make a commitment not only to study the phenomenon, but to understand it.* That means not only agreement on a definition of a Montessori school, but a willingness to respect its aims that goes beyond simple measures of academic achievement.

• *Concerned educators must forge a common definition of a Montessori education experience.* Ideally, the definition would be the work of Montessori teachers and trainers, but given the fractionation, it may require incentives that can be provided only by other educators and foundations.

• *Montessori teacher-trainers must expand their scope.* These educators, now working almost entirely outside major colleges and universities, must bring their work into traditional teacher-training institutions and find a way to expand the number of people qualified to train.

It may not be easy. But why not give an idea that has endured and thrived through decades of challenges the chance to contribute to the solutions we all seek?

FURTHER READING

Biographies

Kramer, Rita. *Maria Montessori: A Biography.* Oxford, England: Basil Blackwell, 1976, 410 p.

>Biography that seeks to dispel myths about Montessori and centers on concrete facts about her life, work, and achievements. The volume includes a foreword by Anna Freud.

Standing, E. M. *Maria Montessori: Her Life and Work.* Fresno, Calif.: Academy Library Guild, 1957, 354 p.

>Focuses on Montessori's career and her major influences.

Criticism

Baber, Ray E. A review of *The Secret of Childhood,* by Maria Montessori. *American Sociological Review* 5, No. 4 (August 1940): 656-58.

>Finds *The Secret of Childhood* full of "keen insight into child nature" but at times overly "mystical."

Meyer, Judith Wangerin. *Diffusion of an American Montessori Education.* Chicago: University of Chicago Press, 1975, 97 p.

>Examines the introduction and wide acceptance of the Montessori method in the United States.

Montessori, Mario M. Jr., *Education for Human Development: Understanding Montessori.* Edited by Paula Polk Lillard. New York: Schocken Books, 1976, 119 p.

>Collection of essays by Montessori's grandson examining her methods which includes an appreciation by Buckminster Fuller.

Orem, R. C., ed. *Montessori: Her Method and the Movement. What You Need to Know.* New York: G. P. Putnam's Sons, 1974, 263 p.

>Collection of commentaries on the Montessori method, including a compendium of questions and answers and a biographical sketch.

Rambusch, Nancy McCormick. *Learning How to Learn: An American Approach to Montessori.* Baltimore: Helicon Press, 1962, 180 p.

Overview of Montessori's method as it is applied in the United States; includes a secondary bibliography.

Additional coverage of Montessori's life and career is contained in the following source published by the Gale Group: *Contemporary Authors,* **Vols. 115, 147.**

How to Use This Index

Literary Criticism Series
Cumulative Author Index

Andersen, Hans Christian 1805-1875
.. **NCLC 7, 79; DA; DAB; DAC; DAM MST, POP; SSC 6; WLC**
See also CLR 6; DA3; MAICYA; SATA 100; YABC 1

Anderson, C. Farley
See Mencken, H(enry) L(ouis); Nathan, George Jean

Anderson, Jessica (Margaret) Queale 1916-
.... **CLC 37**
See also CA 9-12R; CANR 4, 62

Anderson, Jon (Victor) 1940- . **CLC 9; DAM POET**
See also CA 25-28R; CANR 20

Anderson, Lindsay (Gordon) 1923-1994
.... **CLC 20**
See also CA 125; 128; 146; CANR 77

Anderson, Maxwell 1888-1959 ...... **TCLC 2; DAM DRAM**
See also CA 105; 152; DLB 7, 228; MTCW 2

Anderson, Poul (William) 1926- ..... **CLC 15**
See also AAYA 5, 34; CA 1-4R, 181; CAAE 181; CAAS 2; CANR 2, 15, 34, 64; CLR 58; DLB 8; INT CANR-15; MTCW 1, 2; SATA 90; SATA-Brief 39; SATA-Essay 106

Anderson, Robert (Woodruff) 1917-
.... **CLC 23; DAM DRAM**
See also AITN 1; CA 21-24R; CANR 32; DLB 7

Anderson, Sherwood 1876-1941 .... **TCLC 1, 10, 24; DA; DAB; DAC; DAM MST, NOV; SSC 1; WLC**
See also AAYA 30; CA 104; 121; CANR 61; CDALB 1917-1929; DA3; DLB 4, 9, 86; DLBD 1; MTCW 1, 2

Andier, Pierre
See Desnos, Robert

Andouard
See Giraudoux, (Hippolyte) Jean

Andrade, Carlos Drummond de ..... **CLC 18**
See also Drummond de Andrade, Carlos

Andrade, Mario de 1893-1945 ...... **TCLC 43**

Andreae, Johann V(alentin) 1586-1654
.... **LC 32**
See also DLB 164

Andreas-Salome, Lou 1861-1937 .. **TCLC 56**
See also CA 178; DLB 66

Andress, Lesley
See Sanders, Lawrence

Andrewes, Lancelot 1555-1626 .... **LC 5**
See also DLB 151, 172

Andrews, Cicily Fairfield
See West, Rebecca

Andrews, Elton V.
See Pohl, Frederik

Andreyev, Leonid (Nikolaevich) 1871-1919
.... **TCLC 3**
See also CA 104; 185

Andric, Ivo 1892-1975 .... **CLC 8; SSC 36**
See also CA 81-84; 57-60; CANR 43, 60; DLB 147; MTCW 1

Androvar
See Prado (Calvo), Pedro

Angelique, Pierre
See Bataille, Georges

Angell, Roger 1920- .... **CLC 26**
See also CA 57-60; CANR 13, 44, 70; DLB 171, 185

Angelou, Maya 1928- ... **CLC 12, 35, 64, 77; BLC 1; DA; DAB; DAC; DAM MST, MULT, POET, POP; PC 32; WLCS**
See also AAYA 7, 20; BW 2, 3; CA 65-68; CANR 19, 42, 65; CDALBS; CLR 53; DA3; DLB 38; MTCW 1, 2; SATA 49

Anna Comnena 1083-1153 .... **CMLC 25**

Annensky, Innokenty (Fyodorovich) 1856-1909 .... **TCLC 14**

See also CA 110; 155

Annunzio, Gabriele d'
See D'Annunzio, Gabriele

Anodos
See Coleridge, Mary E(lizabeth)

Anon, Charles Robert
See Pessoa, Fernando (Antonio Nogueira)

Anouilh, Jean (Marie Lucien Pierre) 1910-1987 .... **CLC 1, 3, 8, 13, 40, 50; DAM DRAM; DC 8**
See also CA 17-20R; 123; CANR 32; MTCW 1, 2

Anthony, Florence
See Ai

Anthony, John
See Ciardi, John (Anthony)

Anthony, Peter
See Shaffer, Anthony (Joshua); Shaffer, Peter (Levin)

Anthony, Piers 1934- ... **CLC 35; DAM POP**
See also AAYA 11; CA 21-24R; CANR 28, 56, 73; DLB 8; MTCW 1, 2; SAAS 22; SATA 84

Anthony, Susan B(rownell) 1916-1991
.... **TCLC 84**
See also CA 89-92; 134

Antoine, Marc
See Proust, (Valentin-Louis-George-Eugene-) Marcel

Antoninus, Brother
See Everson, William (Oliver)

Antonioni, Michelangelo 1912- .... **CLC 20**
See also CA 73-76; CANR 45, 77

Antschel, Paul 1920-1970
See Celan, Paul
See also CA 85-88; CANR 33, 61; MTCW 1

Anwar, Chairil 1922-1949 .... **TCLC 22**
See also CA 121

Anzaldua, Gloria (Evanjelina) 1942-
See also CA 175; DLB 122; HLCS 1

Apess, William 1798-1839(?) .... **NCLC 73; DAM MULT**
See also DLB 175; NNAL

Apollinaire, Guillaume 1880-1918 . **TCLC 3, 8, 51; DAM POET; PC 7**
See also CA 152; MTCW 1

Appelfeld, Aharon 1932- .. **CLC 23, 47; SSC 42**
See also CA 112; 133; CANR 86

Apple, Max (Isaac) 1941- .... **CLC 9, 33**
See also CA 81-84; CANR 19, 54; DLB 130

Appleman, Philip (Dean) 1926- .... **CLC 51**
See also CA 13-16R; CAAS 18; CANR 6, 29, 56

Appleton, Lawrence
See Lovecraft, H(oward) P(hillips)

Apteryx
See Eliot, T(homas) S(tearns)

Apuleius, (Lucius Madaurensis) 125(?)-175(?) .... **CMLC 1**
See also DLB 211

Aquin, Hubert 1929-1977 .... **CLC 15**
See also CA 105; DLB 53

Aquinas, Thomas 1224(?)-1274 ... **CMLC 33**
See also DLB 115

Aragon, Louis 1897-1982 . **CLC 3, 22; DAM NOV, POET**
See also CA 69-72; 108; CANR 28, 71; DLB 72; MTCW 1, 2

Arany, Janos 1817-1882 .... **NCLC 34**

Aranyos, Kakay
See Mikszath, Kalman

Arbuthnot, John 1667-1735 .... **LC 1**
See also DLB 101

Archer, Herbert Winslow
See Mencken, H(enry) L(ouis)

Archer, Jeffrey (Howard) 1940- ..... **CLC 28; DAM POP**
See also AAYA 16; BEST 89:3; CA 77-80; CANR 22, 52; DA3; INT CANR-22

Archer, Jules 1915- .... **CLC 12**
See also CA 9-12R; CANR 6, 69; SAAS 5; SATA 4, 85

Archer, Lee
See Ellison, Harlan (Jay)

Arden, John 1930- ..... **CLC 6, 13, 15; DAM DRAM**
See also CA 13-16R; CAAS 4; CANR 31, 65, 67; DLB 13; MTCW 1

Arenas, Reinaldo 1943-1990 . **CLC 41; DAM MULT; HLC 1**
See also CA 124; 128; 133; CANR 73; DLB 145; HW 1; MTCW 1

Arendt, Hannah 1906-1975 .... **CLC 66, 98**
See also CA 17-20R; 61-64; CANR 26, 60; MTCW 1, 2

Aretino, Pietro 1492-1556 .... **LC 12**

Arghezi, Tudor 1880-1967 .... **CLC 80**
See also Theodorescu, Ion N.
See also CA 167; DLB 220

Arguedas, Jose Maria 1911-1969 ... **CLC 10, 18; HLCS 1**
See also CA 89-92; CANR 73; DLB 113; HW 1

Argueta, Manlio 1936- .... **CLC 31**
See also CA 131; CANR 73; DLB 145; HW 1

Arias, Ron(ald Francis) 1941-
See also CA 131; CANR 81; DAM MULT; DLB 82; HLC 1; HW 1, 2; MTCW 2

Ariosto, Ludovico 1474-1533 .... **LC 6**

Aristides
See Epstein, Joseph

Aristophanes 450B.C.-385B.C. ..... **CMLC 4; DA; DAB; DAC; DAM DRAM, MST; DC 2; WLCS**
See also DA3; DLB 176

Aristotle 384B.C.-322B.C. ... **CMLC 31; DA; DAB; DAC; DAM MST; WLCS**
See also DA3; DLB 176

Arlt, Roberto (Godofredo Christophersen) 1900-1942 ..... **TCLC 29; DAM MULT; HLC 1**
See also CA 123; 131; CANR 67; HW 1, 2

Armah, Ayi Kwei 1939- ..... **CLC 5, 33, 136; BLC 1; DAM MULT, POET**
See also BW 1; CA 61-64; CANR 21, 64; DLB 117; MTCW 1

Armatrading, Joan 1950- .... **CLC 17**
See also CA 114; 186

Arnette, Robert
See Silverberg, Robert

Arnim, Achim von (Ludwig Joachim von Arnim) 1781-1831 .... **NCLC 5; SSC 29**
See also DLB 90

Arnim, Bettina von 1785-1859 ..... **NCLC 38**
See also DLB 90

Arnold, Matthew 1822-1888 .... **NCLC 6, 29, 89; DA; DAB; DAC; DAM MST, POET; PC 5; WLC**
See also CDBLB 1832-1890; DLB 32, 57

Arnold, Thomas 1795-1842 .... **NCLC 18**
See also DLB 55

Arnow, Harriette (Louisa) Simpson 1908-1986 .... **CLC 2, 7, 18**
See also CA 9-12R; 118; CANR 14; DLB 6; MTCW 1, 2; SATA 42; SATA-Obit 47

Arouet, Francois-Marie
See Voltaire

Arp, Hans
See Arp, Jean

Arp, Jean 1887-1966 .... **CLC 5**
See also CA 81-84; 25-28R; CANR 42, 77

See also BEST 89:4; CA 57-60; CANR 11, 41, 59; MTCW 1, 2

Bakhtin, M.
See Bakhtin, Mikhail Mikhailovich

Bakhtin, M. M.
See Bakhtin, Mikhail Mikhailovich

Bakhtin, Mikhail
See Bakhtin, Mikhail Mikhailovich

Bakhtin, Mikhail Mikhailovich 1895-1975
.... **CLC 83**
See also CA 128; 113

Bakshi, Ralph 1938(?)- .... **CLC 26**
See also CA 112; 138

Bakunin, Mikhail (Alexandrovich)
1814-1876 .... **NCLC 25, 58**

Baldwin, James (Arthur) 1924-1987 . **CLC 1, 2, 3, 4, 5, 8, 13, 15, 17, 42, 50, 67, 90, 127; BLC 1; DA; DAB; DAC; DAM MST, MULT, NOV, POP; DC 1; SSC 10, 33; WLC**
See also AAYA 4, 34; BW 1; CA 1-4R; 124; CABS 1; CANR 3, 24; CDALB 1941-1968; DA3; DLB 2, 7, 33; DLBY 87; MTCW 1, 2; SATA 9; SATA-Obit 54

Bale, John 1495-1563 .... **LC 62**
See also DLB 132

Ballard, J(ames) G(raham) 1930- ... **CLC 3, 6, 14, 36, 137; DAM NOV, POP; SSC 1**
See also AAYA 3; CA 5-8R; CANR 15, 39, 65; DA3; DLB 14, 207; MTCW 1, 2; SATA 93

Balmont, Konstantin (Dmitriyevich)
1867-1943 .... **TCLC 11**
See also CA 109; 155

Baltausis, Vincas
See Mikszath, Kalman

Balzac, Honore de 1799-1850 .. **NCLC 5, 35, 53; DA; DAB; DAC; DAM MST, NOV; SSC 5; WLC**
See also DA3; DLB 119

Bambara, Toni Cade 1939-1995 ..... **CLC 19, 88; BLC 1; DA; DAC; DAM MST, MULT; SSC 35; WLCS**
See also AAYA 5; BW 2, 3; CA 29-32R; 150; CANR 24, 49, 81; CDALBS; DA3; DLB 38; MTCW 1, 2; SATA 112

Bamdad, A.
See Shamlu, Ahmad

Banat, D. R.
See Bradbury, Ray (Douglas)

Bancroft, Laura
See Baum, L(yman) Frank

Banim, John 1798-1842 .... **NCLC 13**
See also DLB 116, 158, 159

Banim, Michael 1796-1874 .... **NCLC 13**
See also DLB 158, 159

Banjo, The
See Paterson, A(ndrew) B(arton)

Banks, Iain
See Banks, Iain M(enzies)

Banks, Iain M(enzies) 1954- .... **CLC 34**
See also CA 123; 128; CANR 61; DLB 194; INT 128

Banks, Lynne Reid .... **CLC 23**
See also Reid Banks, Lynne
See also AAYA 6

Banks, Russell 1940- ... **CLC 37, 72; SSC 42**
See also CA 65-68; CAAS 15; CANR 19, 52, 73; DLB 130

Banville, John 1945- .... **CLC 46, 118**
See also CA 117; 128; DLB 14; INT 128

Banville, Theodore (Faullain) de 1832-1891
.... **NCLC 9**

Baraka, Amiri 1934- . **CLC 1, 2, 3, 5, 10, 14, 33, 115; BLC 1; DA; DAC; DAM MST, MULT, POET, POP; DC 6; PC 4; WLCS**
See also Jones, LeRoi

See also BW 2, 3; CA 21-24R; CABS 3; CANR 27, 38, 61; CDALB 1941-1968; DA3; DLB 5, 7, 16, 38; DLBD 8; MTCW 1, 2

Barbauld, Anna Laetitia 1743-1825
.... **NCLC 50**
See also DLB 107, 109, 142, 158

Barbellion, W. N. P. .... **TCLC 24**
See also Cummings, Bruce F(rederick)

Barbera, Jack (Vincent) 1945- .... **CLC 44**
See also CA 110; CANR 45

Barbey d'Aurevilly, Jules Amedee 1808-1889
.... **NCLC 1; SSC 17**
See also DLB 119

Barbour, John c. 1316-1395 .... **CMLC 33**
See also DLB 146

Barbusse, Henri 1873-1935 .... **TCLC 5**
See also CA 105; 154; DLB 65

Barclay, Bill
See Moorcock, Michael (John)

Barclay, William Ewert
See Moorcock, Michael (John)

Barea, Arturo 1897-1957 .... **TCLC 14**
See also CA 111

Barfoot, Joan 1946- .... **CLC 18**
See also CA 105

Barham, Richard Harris 1788-1845
.... **NCLC 77**
See also DLB 159

Baring, Maurice 1874-1945 .... **TCLC 8**
See also CA 105; 168; DLB 34

Baring-Gould, Sabine 1834-1924 . **TCLC 88**
See also DLB 156, 190

Barker, Clive 1952- ..... **CLC 52; DAM POP**
See also AAYA 10; BEST 90:3; CA 121; 129; CANR 71; DA3; INT 129; MTCW 1, 2

Barker, George Granville 1913-1991
.... **CLC 8, 48; DAM POET**
See also CA 9-12R; 135; CANR 7, 38; DLB 20; MTCW 1

Barker, Harley Granville
See Granville-Barker, Harley
See also DLB 10

Barker, Howard 1946- .... **CLC 37**
See also CA 102; DLB 13, 233

Barker, Jane 1652-1732 .... **LC 42**

Barker, Pat(ricia) 1943- .... **CLC 32, 94**
See also CA 117; 122; CANR 50; INT 122

Barlach, Ernst (Heinrich) 1870-1938
.... **TCLC 84**
See also CA 178; DLB 56, 118

Barlow, Joel 1754-1812 .... **NCLC 23**
See also DLB 37

Barnard, Mary (Ethel) 1909- .... **CLC 48**
See also CA 21-22; CAP 2

Barnes, Djuna 1892-1982 ... **CLC 3, 4, 8, 11, 29, 127; SSC 3**
See also CA 9-12R; 107; CANR 16, 55; DLB 4, 9, 45; MTCW 1, 2

Barnes, Julian (Patrick) 1946- .... **CLC 42; DAB**
See also CA 102; CANR 19, 54; DLB 194; DLBY 93; MTCW 1

Barnes, Peter 1931- .... **CLC 5, 56**
See also CA 65-68; CAAS 12; CANR 33, 34, 64; DLB 13, 233; MTCW 1

Barnes, William 1801-1886 .... **NCLC 75**
See also DLB 32

Baroja (y Nessi), Pio 1872-1956 .... **TCLC 8; HLC 1**
See also CA 104

Baron, David
See Pinter, Harold

Baron Corvo
See Rolfe, Frederick (William Serafino Austin Lewis Mary)

Barondess, Sue K(aufman) 1926-1977
.... **CLC 8**
See also Kaufman, Sue
See also CA 1-4R; 69-72; CANR 1

Baron de Teive
See Pessoa, Fernando (Antonio Nogueira)

Baroness Von S.
See Zangwill, Israel

Barres, (Auguste-) Maurice 1862-1923
.... **TCLC 47**
See also CA 164; DLB 123

Barreto, Afonso Henrique de Lima
See Lima Barreto, Afonso Henrique de

Barrett, (Roger) Syd 1946- .... **CLC 35**

Barrett, William (Christopher) 1913-1992
.... **CLC 27**
See also CA 13-16R; 139; CANR 11, 67; INT CANR-11

Barrie, J(ames) M(atthew) 1860-1937
.... **TCLC 2; DAB; DAM DRAM**
See also CA 104; 136; CANR 77; CDBLB 1890-1914; CLR 16; DA3; DLB 10, 141, 156; MAICYA; MTCW 1; SATA 100; YABC 1

Barrington, Michael
See Moorcock, Michael (John)

Barrol, Grady
See Bograd, Larry

Barry, Mike
See Malzberg, Barry N(athaniel)

Barry, Philip 1896-1949 .... **TCLC 11**
See also CA 109; DLB 7, 228

Bart, Andre Schwarz
See Schwarz-Bart, Andre

Barth, John (Simmons) 1930- .. **CLC 1, 2, 3, 5, 7, 9, 10, 14, 27, 51, 89; DAM NOV; SSC 10**
See also AITN 1, 2; CA 1-4R; CABS 1; CANR 5, 23, 49, 64; DLB 2, 227; MTCW 1

Barthelme, Donald 1931-1989 . **CLC 1, 2, 3, 5, 6, 8, 13, 23, 46, 59, 115; DAM NOV; SSC 2**
See also CA 21-24R; 129; CANR 20, 58; DA3; DLB 2, 234; DLBY 80, 89; MTCW 1, 2; SATA 7; SATA-Obit 62

Barthelme, Frederick 1943- .... **CLC 36, 117**
See also CA 114; 122; CANR 77; DLBY 85; INT 122

Barthes, Roland (Gerard) 1915-1980
.... **CLC 24, 83**
See also CA 130; 97-100; CANR 66; MTCW 1, 2

Barzun, Jacques (Martin) 1907- ..... **CLC 51**
See also CA 61-64; CANR 22

Bashevis, Isaac
See Singer, Isaac Bashevis

Bashkirtseff, Marie 1859-1884 ..... **NCLC 27**

Basho
See Matsuo Basho

Basil of Caesaria c. 330-379 .... **CMLC 35**

Bass, Kingsley B., Jr.
See Bullins, Ed

Bass, Rick 1958- .... **CLC 79**
See also CA 126; CANR 53, 93; DLB 212

Bassani, Giorgio 1916- .... **CLC 9**
See also CA 65-68; CANR 33; DLB 128, 177; MTCW 1

Bastos, Augusto (Antonio) Roa
See Roa Bastos, Augusto (Antonio)

Bataille, Georges 1897-1962 .... **CLC 29**
See also CA 101; 89-92

Bates, H(erbert) E(rnest) 1905-1974
..... **CLC 46; DAB; DAM POP; SSC 10**
See also CA 93-96; 45-48; CANR 34; DA3; DLB 162, 191; MTCW 1, 2

See also CA 170
Benjamin, David
See Slavitt, David R(ytman)
Benjamin, Lois
See Gould, Lois
Benjamin, Walter 1892-1940 .... **TCLC 39**
See also CA 164
Benn, Gottfried 1886-1956 .... **TCLC 3**
See also CA 106; 153; DLB 56
Bennett, Alan 1934- .... **CLC 45, 77; DAB; DAM MST**
See also CA 103; CANR 35, 55; MTCW 1, 2
Bennett, (Enoch) Arnold 1867-1931
.... **TCLC 5, 20**
See also CA 106; 155; CDBLB 1890-1914; DLB 10, 34, 98, 135; MTCW 2
Bennett, Elizabeth
See Mitchell, Margaret (Munnerlyn)
Bennett, George Harold 1930-
See Bennett, Hal
See also BW 1; CA 97-100; CANR 87
Bennett, Hal .... **CLC 5**
See also Bennett, George Harold
See also DLB 33
Bennett, Jay 1912- .... **CLC 35**
See also AAYA 10; CA 69-72; CANR 11, 42, 79; JRDA; SAAS 4; SATA 41, 87; SATA-Brief 27
Bennett, Louise (Simone) 1919- ..... **CLC 28; BLC 1; DAM MULT**
See also BW 2, 3; CA 151; DLB 117
Benson, E(dward) F(rederic) 1867-1940
.... **TCLC 27**
See also CA 114; 157; DLB 135, 153
Benson, Jackson J. 1930- .... **CLC 34**
See also CA 25-28R; DLB 111
Benson, Sally 1900-1972 .... **CLC 17**
See also CA 19-20; 37-40R; CAP 1; SATA 1, 35; SATA-Obit 27
Benson, Stella 1892-1933 .... **TCLC 17**
See also CA 117; 155; DLB 36, 162
Bentham, Jeremy 1748-1832 .... **NCLC 38**
See also DLB 107, 158
Bentley, E(dmund) C(lerihew) 1875-1956
.... **TCLC 12**
See also CA 108; DLB 70
Bentley, Eric (Russell) 1916- .... **CLC 24**
See also CA 5-8R; CANR 6, 67; INT CANR-6
Beranger, Pierre Jean de 1780-1857
.... **NCLC 34**
Berdyaev, Nicolas
See Berdyaev, Nikolai (Aleksandrovich)
Berdyaev, Nikolai (Aleksandrovich)
1874-1948 .... **TCLC 67**
See also CA 120; 157
Berdyayev, Nikolai (Aleksandrovich)
See Berdyaev, Nikolai (Aleksandrovich)
Berendt, John (Lawrence) 1939- .... **CLC 86**
See also CA 146; CANR 75, 93; DA3; MTCW 1
Beresford, J(ohn) D(avys) 1873-1947
.... **TCLC 81**
See also CA 112; 155; DLB 162, 178, 197
Bergelson, David 1884-1952 .... **TCLC 81**
Berger, Colonel
See Malraux, (Georges-)Andre
Berger, John (Peter) 1926- .... **CLC 2, 19**
See also CA 81-84; CANR 51, 78; DLB 14, 207
Berger, Melvin H. 1927- .... **CLC 12**
See also CA 5-8R; CANR 4; CLR 32; SAAS 2; SATA 5, 88
Berger, Thomas (Louis) 1924- . **CLC 3, 5, 8, 11, 18, 38; DAM NOV**
See also CA 1-4R; CANR 5, 28, 51; DLB 2; DLBY 80; INT CANR-28; MTCW 1, 2

Bergman, (Ernst) Ingmar 1918- .... **CLC 16, 72**
See also CA 81-84; CANR 33, 70; MTCW 2
Bergson, Henri(-Louis) 1859-1941 . **TCLC 32**
See also CA 164
Bergstein, Eleanor 1938- .... **CLC 4**
See also CA 53-56; CANR 5
Berkoff, Steven 1937- .... **CLC 56**
See also CA 104; CANR 72
Bermant, Chaim (Icyk) 1929- .... **CLC 40**
See also CA 57-60; CANR 6, 31, 57
Bern, Victoria
See Fisher, M(ary) F(rances) K(ennedy)
Bernanos, (Paul Louis) Georges 1888-1948
.... **TCLC 3**
See also CA 104; 130; DLB 72
Bernard, April 1956- .... **CLC 59**
See also CA 131
Berne, Victoria
See Fisher, M(ary) F(rances) K(ennedy)
Bernhard, Thomas 1931-1989 .... **CLC 3, 32, 61**
See also CA 85-88; 127; CANR 32, 57; DLB 85, 124; MTCW 1
Bernhardt, Sarah (Henriette Rosine)
1844-1923 .... **TCLC 75**
See also CA 157
Berriault, Gina 1926-1999 ...... **CLC 54, 109; SSC 30**
See also CA 116; 129; 185; CANR 66; DLB 130
Berrigan, Daniel 1921- .... **CLC 4**
See also CA 33-36R; CAAE 187; CAAS 1; CANR 11, 43, 78; DLB 5
Berrigan, Edmund Joseph Michael, Jr.
1934-1983
See Berrigan, Ted
See also CA 61-64; 110; CANR 14
Berrigan, Ted .... **CLC 37**
See also Berrigan, Edmund Joseph Michael, Jr.
See also DLB 5, 169
Berry, Charles Edward Anderson 1931-
See Berry, Chuck
See also CA 115
Berry, Chuck .... **CLC 17**
See also Berry, Charles Edward Anderson
Berry, Jonas
See Ashbery, John (Lawrence)
Berry, Wendell (Erdman) 1934- .. **CLC 4, 6, 8, 27, 46; DAM POET; PC 28**
See also AITN 1; CA 73-76; CANR 50, 73; DLB 5, 6, 234; MTCW 1
Berryman, John 1914-1972 . **CLC 1, 2, 3, 4, 6, 8, 10, 13, 25, 62; DAM POET**
See also CA 13-16; 33-36R; CABS 2; CANR 35; CAP 1; CDALB 1941-1968; DLB 48; MTCW 1, 2
Bertolucci, Bernardo 1940- .... **CLC 16**
See also CA 106
Berton, Pierre (Francis Demarigny) 1920-
.... **CLC 104**
See also CA 1-4R; CANR 2, 56; DLB 68; SATA 99
Bertrand, Aloysius 1807-1841 .... **NCLC 31**
Bertran de Born c. 1140-1215 .... **CMLC 5**
Besant, Annie (Wood) 1847-1933 ... **TCLC 9**
See also CA 105; 185
Bessie, Alvah 1904-1985 .... **CLC 23**
See also CA 5-8R; 116; CANR 2, 80; DLB 26
Bethlen, T. D.
See Silverberg, Robert
Beti, Mongo . **CLC 27; BLC 1; DAM MULT**
See also Biyidi, Alexandre
See also CANR 79
Betjeman, John 1906-1984 ..... **CLC 2, 6, 10, 34, 43; DAB; DAM MST, POET**

See also CA 9-12R; 112; CANR 33, 56; CDBLB 1945-1960; DA3; DLB 20; DLBY 84; MTCW 1, 2
Bettelheim, Bruno 1903-1990 .... **CLC 79**
See also CA 81-84; 131; CANR 23, 61; DA3; MTCW 1, 2
Betti, Ugo 1892-1953 .... **TCLC 5**
See also CA 104; 155
Betts, Doris (Waugh) 1932- ..... **CLC 3, 6, 28**
See also CA 13-16R; CANR 9, 66, 77; DLBY 82; INT CANR-9
Bevan, Alistair
See Roberts, Keith (John Kingston)
Bey, Pilaff
See Douglas, (George) Norman
Bialik, Chaim Nachman 1873-1934
.... **TCLC 25**
See also CA 170
Bickerstaff, Isaac
See Swift, Jonathan
Bidart, Frank 1939- .... **CLC 33**
See also CA 140
Bienek, Horst 1930- .... **CLC 7, 11**
See also CA 73-76; DLB 75
Bierce, Ambrose (Gwinett) 1842-1914(?)
.... **TCLC 1, 7, 44; DA; DAC; DAM MST; SSC 9; WLC**
See also CA 104; 139; CANR 78; CDALB 1865-1917; DA3; DLB 11, 12, 23, 71, 74, 186
Biggers, Earl Derr 1884-1933 .... **TCLC 65**
See also CA 108; 153
Billings, Josh
See Shaw, Henry Wheeler
Billington, (Lady) Rachel (Mary) 1942-
.... **CLC 43**
See also AITN 2; CA 33-36R; CANR 44
Binyon, T(imothy) J(ohn) 1936- ..... **CLC 34**
See also CA 111; CANR 28
Bion 335B.C.-245B.C. .... **CMLC 39**
Bioy Casares, Adolfo 1914-1999 .. **CLC 4, 8, 13, 88; DAM MULT; HLC 1; SSC 17**
See also CA 29-32R; 177; CANR 19, 43, 66; DLB 113; HW 1, 2; MTCW 1, 2
Bird, Cordwainer
See Ellison, Harlan (Jay)
Bird, Robert Montgomery 1806-1854
.... **NCLC 1**
See also DLB 202
Birkerts, Sven 1951- .... **CLC 116**
See also CA 128; 133; 176; CAAE 176; CAAS 29; INT 133
Birney, (Alfred) Earle 1904-1995 . **CLC 1, 4, 6, 11; DAC; DAM MST, POET**
See also CA 1-4R; CANR 5, 20; DLB 88; MTCW 1
Biruni, al 973-1048(?) .... **CMLC 28**
Bishop, Elizabeth 1911-1979 .... **CLC 1, 4, 9, 13, 15, 32; DA; DAC; DAM MST, POET; PC 3**
See also CA 5-8R; 89-92; CABS 2; CANR 26, 61; CDALB 1968-1988; DA3; DLB 5, 169; MTCW 1, 2; SATA-Obit 24
Bishop, John 1935- .... **CLC 10**
See also CA 105
Bishop, John Peale 1892-1944 .... **TCLC 103**
See also CA 107; 155; DLB 4, 9, 45
Bissett, Bill 1939- .... **CLC 18; PC 14**
See also CA 69-72; CAAS 19; CANR 15; DLB 53; MTCW 1
Bissoondath, Neil (Devindra) 1955-
.... **CLC 120; DAC**
See also CA 136
Bitov, Andrei (Georgievich) 1937- .. **CLC 57**
See also CA 142
Biyidi, Alexandre 1932-
See Beti, Mongo
See also BW 1, 3; CA 114; 124; CANR 81; DA3; MTCW 1, 2

Bjarme, Brynjolf
See Ibsen, Henrik (Johan)

Bjoernson, Bjoernstjerne (Martinius)
1832-1910 .... **TCLC 7, 37**
See also CA 104

Black, Robert
See Holdstock, Robert P.

Blackburn, Paul 1926-1971 .... **CLC 9, 43**
See also CA 81-84; 33-36R; CANR 34;
DLB 16; DLBY 81

Black Elk 1863-1950 .... **TCLC 33; DAM MULT**
See also CA 144; MTCW 1; NNAL

Black Hobart
See Sanders, (James) Ed(ward)

Blacklin, Malcolm
See Chambers, Aidan

Blackmore, R(ichard) D(oddridge)
1825-1900 .... **TCLC 27**
See also CA 120; DLB 18

Blackmur, R(ichard) P(almer) 1904-1965
.... **CLC 2, 24**
See also CA 11-12; 25-28R; CANR 71;
CAP 1; DLB 63

Black Tarantula
See Acker, Kathy

Blackwood, Algernon (Henry) 1869-1951
.... **TCLC 5**
See also CA 105; 150; DLB 153, 156, 178

Blackwood, Caroline 1931-1996 .. **CLC 6, 9, 100**
See also CA 85-88; 151; CANR 32, 61, 65;
DLB 14, 207; MTCW 1

Blade, Alexander
See Hamilton, Edmond; Silverberg, Robert

Blaga, Lucian 1895-1961 .... **CLC 75**
See also CA 157; DLB 220

Blair, Eric (Arthur) 1903-1950
See Orwell, George
See also CA 104; 132; DA; DAB; DAC;
DAM MST, NOV; DA3; MTCW 1, 2;
SATA 29

Blair, Hugh 1718-1800 .... **NCLC 75**

Blais, Marie-Claire 1939- ... **CLC 2, 4, 6, 13, 22; DAC; DAM MST**
See also CA 21-24R; CAAS 4; CANR 38,
75, 93; DLB 53; MTCW 1, 2

Blaise, Clark 1940- .... **CLC 29**
See also AITN 2; CA 53-56; CAAS 3;
CANR 5, 66; DLB 53

Blake, Fairley
See De Voto, Bernard (Augustine)

Blake, Nicholas
See Day Lewis, C(ecil)
See also DLB 77

Blake, William 1757-1827 ...... **NCLC 13, 37, 57; DA; DAB; DAC; DAM MST, POET; PC 12; WLC**
See also CDBLB 1789-1832; CLR 52;
DA3; DLB 93, 163; MAICYA; SATA 30

Blanchot, Maurice 1907- .... **CLC 135**
See also CA 117; 144; DLB 72

Blasco Ibanez, Vicente 1867-1928
.... **TCLC 12; DAM NOV**
See also CA 110; 131; CANR 81; DA3; HW
1, 2; MTCW 1

Blatty, William Peter 1928- ... **CLC 2; DAM POP**
See also CA 5-8R; CANR 9

Bleeck, Oliver
See Thomas, Ross (Elmore)

Blessing, Lee 1949- .... **CLC 54**

Blight, Rose
See Greer, Germaine

Blish, James (Benjamin) 1921-1975 . **CLC 14**
See also CA 1-4R; 57-60; CANR 3; DLB
8; MTCW 1; SATA 66

Bliss, Reginald
See Wells, H(erbert) G(eorge)

Blixen, Karen (Christentze Dinesen)
1885-1962
See Dinesen, Isak
See also CA 25-28; CANR 22, 50; CAP 2;
DA3; MTCW 1, 2; SATA 44

Bloch, Robert (Albert) 1917-1994 ... **CLC 33**
See also AAYA 29; CA 5-8R, 179; 146;
CAAE 179; CAAS 20; CANR 5, 78;
DA3; DLB 44; INT CANR-5; MTCW 1;
SATA 12; SATA-Obit 82

Blok, Alexander (Alexandrovich) 1880-1921
.... **TCLC 5; PC 21**
See also CA 104; 183

Blom, Jan
See Breytenbach, Breyten

Bloom, Harold 1930- .... **CLC 24, 103**
See also CA 13-16R; CANR 39, 75, 92;
DLB 67; MTCW 1

Bloomfield, Aurelius
See Bourne, Randolph S(illiman)

Blount, Roy (Alton), Jr. 1941- .... **CLC 38**
See also CA 53-56; CANR 10, 28, 61; INT
CANR-28; MTCW 1, 2

Bloy, Leon 1846-1917 .... **TCLC 22**
See also CA 121; 183; DLB 123

Blume, Judy (Sussman) 1938- . **CLC 12, 30; DAM NOV, POP**
See also AAYA 3, 26; CA 29-32R; CANR
13, 37, 66; CLR 2, 15; DA3; DLB 52;
JRDA; MAICYA; MTCW 1, 2; SATA 2,
31, 79

Blunden, Edmund (Charles) 1896-1974
.... **CLC 2, 56**
See also CA 17-18; 45-48; CANR 54; CAP
2; DLB 20, 100, 155; MTCW 1

Bly, Robert (Elwood) 1926- ..... **CLC 1, 2, 5, 10, 15, 38, 128; DAM POET**
See also CA 5-8R; CANR 41, 73; DA3;
DLB 5; MTCW 1, 2

Boas, Franz 1858-1942 .... **TCLC 56**
See also CA 115; 181

Bobette
See Simenon, Georges (Jacques Christian)

Boccaccio, Giovanni 1313-1375 .. **CMLC 13; SSC 10**

Bochco, Steven 1943- .... **CLC 35**
See also AAYA 11; CA 124; 138

Bodel, Jean 1167(?)-1210 .... **CMLC 28**

Bodenheim, Maxwell 1892-1954 ... **TCLC 44**
See also CA 110; 187; DLB 9, 45

Bodker, Cecil 1927- .... **CLC 21**
See also CA 73-76; CANR 13, 44; CLR 23;
MAICYA; SATA 14

Boell, Heinrich (Theodor) 1917-1985
. **CLC 2, 3, 6, 9, 11, 15, 27, 32, 72; DA; DAB; DAC; DAM MST, NOV; SSC 23; WLC**
See also CA 21-24R; 116; CANR 24; DA3;
DLB 69; DLBY 85; MTCW 1, 2

Boerne, Alfred
See Doeblin, Alfred

Boethius 480(?)-524(?) .... **CMLC 15**
See also DLB 115

Boff, Leonardo (Genezio Darci) 1938-
See also CA 150; DAM MULT; HLC 1;
HW 2

Bogan, Louise 1897-1970 ...... **CLC 4, 39, 46, 93; DAM POET; PC 12**
See also CA 73-76; 25-28R; CANR 33, 82;
DLB 45, 169; MTCW 1, 2

Bogarde, Dirk 1921-1999
See Van Den Bogarde, Derek Jules Gaspard
Ulric Niven

Bogosian, Eric 1953- .... **CLC 45**
See also CA 138

Bograd, Larry 1953- .... **CLC 35**
See also CA 93-96; CANR 57; SAAS 21;
SATA 33, 89

Boiardo, Matteo Maria 1441-1494 ...... **LC 6**

Boileau-Despreaux, Nicolas 1636-1711 . **LC 3**

Bojer, Johan 1872-1959 .... **TCLC 64**

Bok, Edward W. 1863-1930 .... **TCLC 101**
See also DLB 91; DLBD 16

Boland, Eavan (Aisling) 1944- . **CLC 40, 67, 113; DAM POET**
See also CA 143; CANR 61; DLB 40;
MTCW 2

Boll, Heinrich
See Boell, Heinrich (Theodor)

Bolt, Lee
See Faust, Frederick (Schiller)

Bolt, Robert (Oxton) 1924-1995 .... **CLC 14; DAM DRAM**
See also CA 17-20R; 147; CANR 35, 67;
DLB 13, 233; MTCW 1

Bombal, Maria Luisa 1910-1980 .... **SSC 37; HLCS 1**
See also CA 127; CANR 72; HW 1

Bombet, Louis-Alexandre-Cesar
See Stendhal

Bomkauf
See Kaufman, Bob (Garnell)

Bonaventura .... **NCLC 35**
See also DLB 90

Bond, Edward 1934- .... **CLC 4, 6, 13, 23; DAM DRAM**
See also CA 25-28R; CANR 38, 67; DLB
13; MTCW 1

Bonham, Frank 1914-1989 .... **CLC 12**
See also AAYA 1; CA 9-12R; CANR 4, 36;
JRDA; MAICYA; SAAS 3; SATA 1, 49;
SATA-Obit 62

Bonnefoy, Yves 1923- . **CLC 9, 15, 58; DAM MST, POET**
See also CA 85-88; CANR 33, 75; MTCW
1, 2

Bontemps, Arna(ud Wendell) 1902-1973
.... **CLC 1, 18; BLC 1; DAM MULT, NOV, POET**
See also BW 1; CA 1-4R; 41-44R; CANR
4, 35; CLR 6; DA3; DLB 48, 51; JRDA;
MAICYA; MTCW 1, 2; SATA 2, 44;
SATA-Obit 24

Booth, Martin 1944- .... **CLC 13**
See also CA 93-96; CAAS 2; CANR 92

Booth, Philip 1925- .... **CLC 23**
See also CA 5-8R; CANR 5, 88; DLBY 82

Booth, Wayne C(layson) 1921- .... **CLC 24**
See also CA 1-4R; CAAS 5; CANR 3, 43;
DLB 67

Borchert, Wolfgang 1921-1947 .... **TCLC 5**
See also CA 104; DLB 69, 124

Borel, Petrus 1809-1859 .... **NCLC 41**

Borges, Jorge Luis 1899-1986 ... **CLC 1, 2, 3, 4, 6, 8, 9, 10, 13, 19, 44, 48, 83; DA; DAB; DAC; DAM MST, MULT; HLC 1; PC 22, 32; SSC 4, 41; WLC**
See also AAYA 26; CA 21-24R; CANR 19,
33, 75; DA3; DLB 113; DLBY 86; HW 1,
2; MTCW 1, 2

Borowski, Tadeusz 1922-1951 .... **TCLC 9**
See also CA 106; 154

Borrow, George (Henry) 1803-1881
.... **NCLC 9**
See also DLB 21, 55, 166

Bosch (Gavino), Juan 1909-
See also CA 151; DAM MST, MULT; DLB
145; HLCS 1; HW 1, 2

Bosman, Herman Charles 1905-1951
.... **TCLC 49**
See also Malan, Herman
See also CA 160; DLB 225

Bosschere, Jean de 1878(?)-1953 .. **TCLC 19**
See also CA 115; 186

Boswell, James 1740-1795 ..... **LC 4, 50; DA; DAB; DAC; DAM MST; WLC**
See also CDBLB 1660-1789; DLB 104, 142

Bottoms, David 1949- .... **CLC 53**

See also CA 105; CANR 22; DLB 120; DLBY 83

Boucicault, Dion 1820-1890 .... **NCLC 41**

Bourget, Paul (Charles Joseph) 1852-1935
.... **TCLC 12**
See also CA 107; DLB 123

Bourjaily, Vance (Nye) 1922- ...... **CLC 8, 62**
See also CA 1-4R; CAAS 1; CANR 2, 72; DLB 2, 143

Bourne, Randolph S(illiman) 1886-1918
.... **TCLC 16**
See also CA 117; 155; DLB 63

Bova, Ben(jamin William) 1932- .... **CLC 45**
See also AAYA 16; CA 5-8R; CAAS 18; CANR 11, 56; CLR 3; DLBY 81; INT CANR-11; MAICYA; MTCW 1; SATA 6, 68

Bowen, Elizabeth (Dorothea Cole) 1899-1973
...... **CLC 1, 3, 6, 11, 15, 22, 118; DAM NOV; SSC 3, 28**
See also CA 17-18; 41-44R; CANR 35; CAP 2; CDBLB 1945-1960; DA3; DLB 15, 162; MTCW 1, 2

Bowering, George 1935- .... **CLC 15, 47**
See also CA 21-24R; CAAS 16; CANR 10; DLB 53

Bowering, Marilyn R(uthe) 1949- ... **CLC 32**
See also CA 101; CANR 49

Bowers, Edgar 1924-2000 .... **CLC 9**
See also CA 5-8R; CANR 24; DLB 5

Bowie, David .... **CLC 17**
See also Jones, David Robert

Bowles, Jane (Sydney) 1917-1973 .... **CLC 3, 68**
See also CA 19-20; 41-44R; CAP 2

Bowles, Paul (Frederick) 1910-1999 . **CLC 1, 2, 19, 53; SSC 3**
See also CA 1-4R; 186; CAAS 1; CANR 1, 19, 50, 75; DA3; DLB 5, 6; MTCW 1, 2

Box, Edgar
See Vidal, Gore

Boyd, Nancy
See Millay, Edna St. Vincent

Boyd, William 1952- .... **CLC 28, 53, 70**
See also CA 114; 120; CANR 51, 71; DLB 231

Boyle, Kay 1902-1992 .... **CLC 1, 5, 19, 58, 121; SSC 5**
See also CA 13-16R; 140; CAAS 1; CANR 29, 61; DLB 4, 9, 48, 86; DLBY 93; MTCW 1, 2

Boyle, Mark
See Kienzle, William X(avier)

Boyle, Patrick 1905-1982 .... **CLC 19**
See also CA 127

Boyle, T. C. 1948-
See Boyle, T(homas) Coraghessan

Boyle, T(homas) Coraghessan 1948-
... **CLC 36, 55, 90; DAM POP; SSC 16**
See also BEST 90:4; CA 120; CANR 44, 76, 89; DA3; DLBY 86; MTCW 2

Boz
See Dickens, Charles (John Huffam)

Brackenridge, Hugh Henry 1748-1816
.... **NCLC 7**
See also DLB 11, 37

Bradbury, Edward P.
See Moorcock, Michael (John)
See also MTCW 2

Bradbury, Malcolm (Stanley) 1932-
.... **CLC 32, 61; DAM NOV**
See also CA 1-4R; CANR 1, 33, 91; DA3; DLB 14, 207; MTCW 1, 2

Bradbury, Ray (Douglas) 1920- ... **CLC 1, 3, 10, 15, 42, 98; DA; DAB; DAC; DAM MST, NOV, POP; SSC 29; WLC**

See also AAYA 15; AITN 1, 2; CA 1-4R; CANR 2, 30, 75; CDALB 1968-1988; DA3; DLB 2, 8; MTCW 1, 2; SATA 11, 64

Bradford, Gamaliel 1863-1932 ..... **TCLC 36**
See also CA 160; DLB 17

Bradley, David (Henry), Jr. 1950- . **CLC 23, 118; BLC 1; DAM MULT**
See also BW 1, 3; CA 104; CANR 26, 81; DLB 33

Bradley, John Ed(mund, Jr.) 1958- . **CLC 55**
See also CA 139

Bradley, Marion Zimmer 1930-1999
.... **CLC 30; DAM POP**
See also AAYA 9; CA 57-60; 185; CAAS 10; CANR 7, 31, 51, 75; DA3; DLB 8; MTCW 1, 2; SATA 90; SATA-Obit 116

Bradstreet, Anne 1612(?)-1672 ..... **LC 4, 30; DA; DAC; DAM MST, POET; PC 10**
See also CDALB 1640-1865; DA3; DLB 24

Brady, Joan 1939- .... **CLC 86**
See also CA 141

Bragg, Melvyn 1939- .... **CLC 10**
See also BEST 89:3; CA 57-60; CANR 10, 48, 89; DLB 14

Brahe, Tycho 1546-1601 .... **LC 45**

Braine, John (Gerard) 1922-1986 .... **CLC 1, 3, 41**
See also CA 1-4R; 120; CANR 1, 33; CDBLB 1945-1960; DLB 15; DLBY 86; MTCW 1

Bramah, Ernest 1868-1942 .... **TCLC 72**
See also CA 156; DLB 70

Brammer, William 1930(?)-1978 ..... **CLC 31**
See also CA 77-80

Brancati, Vitaliano 1907-1954 ...... **TCLC 12**
See also CA 109

Brancato, Robin F(idler) 1936- .... **CLC 35**
See also AAYA 9; CA 69-72; CANR 11, 45; CLR 32; JRDA; SAAS 9; SATA 97

Brand, Max
See Faust, Frederick (Schiller)

Brand, Millen 1906-1980 .... **CLC 7**
See also CA 21-24R; 97-100; CANR 72

Branden, Barbara .... **CLC 44**
See also CA 148

Brandes, Georg (Morris Cohen) 1842-1927
.... **TCLC 10**
See also CA 105

Brandys, Kazimierz 1916- .... **CLC 62**

Branley, Franklyn M(ansfield) 1915-
.... **CLC 21**
See also CA 33-36R; CANR 14, 39; CLR 13; MAICYA; SAAS 16; SATA 4, 68

Brathwaite, Edward (Kamau) 1930-
.... **CLC 11; BLCS; DAM POET**
See also BW 2, 3; CA 25-28R; CANR 11, 26, 47; DLB 125

Brautigan, Richard (Gary) 1935-1984
. **CLC 1, 3, 5, 9, 12, 34, 42; DAM NOV**
See also CA 53-56; 113; CANR 34; DA3; DLB 2, 5, 206; DLBY 80, 84; MTCW 1; SATA 56

Brave Bird, Mary 1953-
See Crow Dog, Mary (Ellen)
See also NNAL

Braverman, Kate 1950- .... **CLC 67**
See also CA 89-92

Brecht, (Eugen) Bertolt (Friedrich) 1898-1956 .... **TCLC 1, 6, 13, 35; DA; DAB; DAC; DAM DRAM, MST; DC 3; WLC**
See also CA 104; 133; CANR 62; DA3; DLB 56, 124; MTCW 1, 2

Brecht, Eugen Berthold Friedrich
See Brecht, (Eugen) Bertolt (Friedrich)

Bremer, Fredrika 1801-1865 .... **NCLC 11**

Brennan, Christopher (John) 1870-1932
.... **TCLC 17**
See also CA 117; DLB 230

Brennan, Maeve 1917-1993 .... **CLC 5**
See also CA 81-84; CANR 72

Brent, Linda
See Jacobs, Harriet A(nn)

Brentano, Clemens (Maria) 1778-1842
.... **NCLC 1**
See also DLB 90

Brent of Bin Bin
See Franklin, (Stella Maria Sarah) Miles (Lampe)

Brenton, Howard 1942- .... **CLC 31**
See also CA 69-72; CANR 33, 67; DLB 13; MTCW 1

Breslin, James 1930-
See Breslin, Jimmy
See also CA 73-76; CANR 31, 75; DAM NOV; MTCW 1, 2

Breslin, Jimmy .... **CLC 4, 43**
See also Breslin, James
See also AITN 1; DLB 185; MTCW 2

Bresson, Robert 1901(?)-1999 .... **CLC 16**
See also CA 110; 187; CANR 49

Breton, Andre 1896-1966 . **CLC 2, 9, 15, 54; PC 15**
See also CA 19-20; 25-28R; CANR 40, 60; CAP 2; DLB 65; MTCW 1, 2

Breytenbach, Breyten 1939(?)- . **CLC 23, 37, 126; DAM POET**
See also CA 113; 129; CANR 61; DLB 225

Bridgers, Sue Ellen 1942- .... **CLC 26**
See also AAYA 8; CA 65-68; CANR 11, 36; CLR 18; DLB 52; JRDA; MAICYA; SAAS 1; SATA 22, 90; SATA-Essay 109

Bridges, Robert (Seymour) 1844-1930
.... **TCLC 1; DAM POET; PC 28**
See also CA 104; 152; CDBLB 1890-1914; DLB 19, 98

Bridie, James .... **TCLC 3**
See also Mavor, Osborne Henry
See also DLB 10

Brin, David 1950- .... **CLC 34**
See also AAYA 21; CA 102; CANR 24, 70; INT CANR-24; SATA 65

Brink, Andre (Philippus) 1935- ...... **CLC 18, 36, 106**
See also CA 104; CANR 39, 62; DLB 225; INT 103; MTCW 1, 2

Brinsmead, H(esba) F(ay) 1922- ..... **CLC 21**
See also CA 21-24R; CANR 10; CLR 47; MAICYA; SAAS 5; SATA 18, 78

Brittain, Vera (Mary) 1893(?)-1970 . **CLC 23**
See also CA 13-16; 25-28R; CANR 58; CAP 1; DLB 191; MTCW 1, 2

Broch, Hermann 1886-1951 .... **TCLC 20**
See also CA 117; DLB 85, 124

Brock, Rose
See Hansen, Joseph

Brodkey, Harold (Roy) 1930-1996 .. **CLC 56**
See also CA 111; 151; CANR 71; DLB 130

Brodsky, Iosif Alexandrovich 1940-1996
See Brodsky, Joseph
See also AITN 1; CA 41-44R; 151; CANR 37; DAM POET; DA3; MTCW 1, 2

Brodsky, Joseph 1940-1996 .... **CLC 4, 6, 13, 36, 100; PC 9**
See also Brodsky, Iosif Alexandrovich
See also MTCW 1

Brodsky, Michael (Mark) 1948- ...... **CLC 19**
See also CA 102; CANR 18, 41, 58

Brome, Richard 1590(?)-1652 .... **LC 61**
See also DLB 58

Bromell, Henry 1947- .... **CLC 5**
See also CA 53-56; CANR 9

Bromfield, Louis (Brucker) 1896-1956
.... **TCLC 11**
See also CA 107; 155; DLB 4, 9, 86

See also CA 104; 155; DLB 20, 225; MTCW 2

Campbell, Thomas 1777-1844 ...... NCLC 19
See also DLB 93; 144

Campbell, Wilfred .... TCLC 9
See also Campbell, William

Campbell, William 1858(?)-1918
See Campbell, Wilfred
See also CA 106; DLB 92

Campion, Jane .... CLC 95
See also AAYA 33; CA 138; CANR 87

Camus, Albert 1913-1960 ..... CLC 1, 2, 4, 9, 11, 14, 32, 63, 69, 124; DA; DAB; DAC; DAM DRAM, MST, NOV; DC 2; SSC 9; WLC
See also CA 89-92; DA3; DLB 72; MTCW 1, 2

Canby, Vincent 1924- .... CLC 13
See also CA 81-84

Cancale
See Desnos, Robert

Canetti, Elias 1905-1994 . CLC 3, 14, 25, 75, 86
See also CA 21-24R; 146; CANR 23, 61, 79; DA3; DLB 85, 124; MTCW 1, 2

Canfield, Dorothea F.
See Fisher, Dorothy (Frances) Canfield

Canfield, Dorothea Frances
See Fisher, Dorothy (Frances) Canfield

Canfield, Dorothy
See Fisher, Dorothy (Frances) Canfield

Canin, Ethan 1960- .... CLC 55
See also CA 131; 135

Cannon, Curt
See Hunter, Evan

Cao, Lan 1961- .... CLC 109
See also CA 165

Cape, Judith
See Page, P(atricia) K(athleen)

Capek, Karel 1890-1938 .. TCLC 6, 37; DA; DAB; DAC; DAM DRAM, MST, NOV; DC 1; SSC 36; WLC
See also CA 104; 140; DA3; MTCW 1

Capote, Truman 1924-1984 ...... CLC 1, 3, 8, 13, 19, 34, 38, 58; DA; DAB; DAC; DAM MST, NOV, POP; SSC 2; WLC
See also CA 5-8R; 113; CANR 18, 62; CDALB 1941-1968; DA3; DLB 2, 185, 227; DLBY 80, 84; MTCW 1, 2; SATA 91

Capra, Frank 1897-1991 .... CLC 16
See also CA 61-64; 135

Caputo, Philip 1941- .... CLC 32
See also CA 73-76; CANR 40

Caragiale, Ion Luca 1852-1912 .... TCLC 76
See also CA 157

Card, Orson Scott 1951- .... CLC 44, 47, 50; DAM POP
See also AAYA 11; CA 102; CANR 27, 47, 73; DA3; INT CANR-27; MTCW 1, 2; SATA 83

Cardenal, Ernesto 1925- ...... CLC 31; DAM MULT, POET; HLC 1; PC 22
See also CA 49-52; CANR 2, 32, 66; HW 1, 2; MTCW 1, 2

Cardozo, Benjamin N(athan) 1870-1938
.... TCLC 65
See also CA 117; 164

Carducci, Giosue (Alessandro Giuseppe) 1835-1907 .... TCLC 32
See also CA 163

Carew, Thomas 1595(?)-1640 . LC 13; PC 29
See also DLB 126

Carey, Ernestine Gilbreth 1908- ..... CLC 17
See also CA 5-8R; CANR 71; SATA 2

Carey, Peter 1943- .... CLC 40, 55, 96
See also CA 123; 127; CANR 53, 76; INT 127; MTCW 1, 2; SATA 94

Carleton, William 1794-1869 .... NCLC 3

See also DLB 159

Carlisle, Henry (Coffin) 1926- .... CLC 33
See also CA 13-16R; CANR 15, 85

Carlsen, Chris
See Holdstock, Robert P.

Carlson, Ron(ald F.) 1947- .... CLC 54
See also CA 105; CANR 27

Carlyle, Thomas 1795-1881 . NCLC 70; DA; DAB; DAC; DAM MST
See also CDBLB 1789-1832; DLB 55; 144

Carman, (William) Bliss 1861-1929
.... TCLC 7; DAC
See also CA 104; 152; DLB 92

Carnegie, Dale 1888-1955 .... TCLC 53

Carossa, Hans 1878-1956 .... TCLC 48
See also CA 170; DLB 66

Carpenter, Don(ald Richard) 1931-1995
.... CLC 41
See also CA 45-48; 149; CANR 1, 71

Carpenter, Edward 1844-1929 ...... TCLC 88
See also CA 163

Carpentier (y Valmont), Alejo 1904-1980
.... CLC 8, 11, 38, 110; DAM MULT; HLC 1; SSC 35
See also CA 65-68; 97-100; CANR 11, 70; DLB 113; HW 1, 2

Carr, Caleb 1955(?)- .... CLC 86
See also CA 147; CANR 73; DA3

Carr, Emily 1871-1945 .... TCLC 32
See also CA 159; DLB 68

Carr, John Dickson 1906-1977 .... CLC 3
See also Fairbairn, Roger
See also CA 49-52; 69-72; CANR 3, 33, 60; MTCW 1, 2

Carr, Philippa
See Hibbert, Eleanor Alice Burford

Carr, Virginia Spencer 1929- .... CLC 34
See also CA 61-64; DLB 111

Carrere, Emmanuel 1957- .... CLC 89

Carrier, Roch 1937- .... CLC 13, 78; DAC; DAM MST
See also CA 130; CANR 61; DLB 53; SATA 105

Carroll, James P. 1943(?)- .... CLC 38
See also CA 81-84; CANR 73; MTCW 1

Carroll, Jim 1951- .... CLC 35
See also AAYA 17; CA 45-48; CANR 42

Carroll, Lewis -1898 ... NCLC 2, 53; PC 18; WLC
See also Dodgson, Charles Lutwidge
See also CDBLB 1832-1890; CLR 2, 18; DLB 18, 163, 178; DLBY 98; JRDA

Carroll, Paul Vincent 1900-1968 ..... CLC 10
See also CA 9-12R; 25-28R; DLB 10

Carruth, Hayden 1921- .... CLC 4, 7, 10, 18, 84; PC 10
See also CA 9-12R; CANR 4, 38, 59; DLB 5, 165; INT CANR-4; MTCW 1, 2; SATA 47

Carson, Rachel Louise 1907-1964 . CLC 71; DAM POP
See also CA 77-80; CANR 35; DA3; MTCW 1, 2; SATA 23

Carter, Angela (Olive) 1940-1992 .... CLC 5, 41, 76; SSC 13
See also CA 53-56; 136; CANR 12, 36, 61; DA3; DLB 14, 207; MTCW 1, 2; SATA 66; SATA-Obit 70

Carter, Nick
See Smith, Martin Cruz

Carver, Raymond 1938-1988 .... CLC 22, 36, 53, 55, 126; DAM NOV; SSC 8
See also CA 33-36R; 126; CANR 17, 34, 61; DA3; DLB 130; DLBY 84, 88; MTCW 1, 2

Cary, Elizabeth, Lady Falkland 1585-1639
.... LC 30

Cary, (Arthur) Joyce (Lunel) 1888-1957
.... TCLC 1, 29

See also CA 104; 164; CDBLB 1914-1945; DLB 15, 100; MTCW 2

Casanova de Seingalt, Giovanni Jacopo 1725-1798 .... LC 13

Casares, Adolfo Bioy
See Bioy Casares, Adolfo

Casely-Hayford, J(oseph) E(phraim) 1866-1930 ..... TCLC 24; BLC 1; DAM MULT
See also BW 2; CA 123; 152

Casey, John (Dudley) 1939- .... CLC 59
See also BEST 90:2; CA 69-72; CANR 23

Casey, Michael 1947- .... CLC 2
See also CA 65-68; DLB 5

Casey, Patrick
See Thurman, Wallace (Henry)

Casey, Warren (Peter) 1935-1988 ... CLC 12
See also CA 101; 127; INT 101

Casona, Alejandro .... CLC 49
See also Alvarez, Alejandro Rodriguez

Cassavetes, John 1929-1989 .... CLC 20
See also CA 85-88; 127; CANR 82

Cassian, Nina 1924- .... PC 17

Cassill, R(onald) V(erlin) 1919- .. CLC 4, 23
See also CA 9-12R; CAAS 1; CANR 7, 45; DLB 6

Cassiodorus, Flavius Magnus c. 490(?)-c. 583(?) .... CMLC 43

Cassirer, Ernst 1874-1945 .... TCLC 61
See also CA 157

Cassity, (Allen) Turner 1929- ...... CLC 6, 42
See also CA 17-20R; CAAS 8; CANR 11; DLB 105

Castaneda, Carlos (Cesar Aranha) 1931(?)-1998 .... CLC 12, 119
See also CA 25-28R; CANR 32, 66; HW 1; MTCW 1

Castedo, Elena 1937- .... CLC 65
See also CA 132

Castedo-Ellerman, Elena
See Castedo, Elena

Castellanos, Rosario 1925-1974 ..... CLC 66; DAM MULT; HLC 1; SSC 39
See also CA 131; 53-56; CANR 58; DLB 113; HW 1; MTCW 1

Castelvetro, Lodovico 1505-1571 .... LC 12

Castiglione, Baldassare 1478-1529 ..... LC 12

Castle, Robert
See Hamilton, Edmond

Castro (Ruz), Fidel 1926(?)-
See also CA 110; 129; CANR 81; DAM MULT; HLC 1; HW 2

Castro, Guillen de 1569-1631 .... LC 19

Castro, Rosalia de 1837-1885 . NCLC 3, 78; DAM MULT

Cather, Willa -1947
See Cather, Willa Sibert

Cather, Willa Sibert 1873-1947 ..... TCLC 1, 11, 31, 99; DA; DAB; DAC; DAM MST, NOV; SSC 2; WLC
See also Cather, Willa
See also AAYA 24; CA 104; 128; CDALB 1865-1917; DA3; DLB 9, 54, 78; DLBD 1; MTCW 1, 2; SATA 30

Catherine, Saint 1347-1380 .... CMLC 27

Cato, Marcus Porcius 234B.C.-149B.C.
.... CMLC 21
See also DLB 211

Catton, (Charles) Bruce 1899-1978 . CLC 35
See also AITN 1; CA 5-8R; 81-84; CANR 7, 74; DLB 17; SATA 2; SATA-Obit 24

Catullus c. 84B.C.-c. 54B.C. .... CMLC 18
See also DLB 211

Cauldwell, Frank
See King, Francis (Henry)

Caunitz, William J. 1933-1996 .... CLC 34
See also BEST 89:3; CA 125; 130; 152; CANR 73; INT 130

Author Index

DAC; DAM MST, POET; PC 5; WLC
See also CA 73-76; CANR 31; CDALB 1929-1941; DA3; DLB 4, 48; MTCW 1, 2

Cunha, Euclides (Rodrigues Pimenta) da 1866-1909 .... **TCLC 24**
See also CA 123

Cunningham, E. V.
See Fast, Howard (Melvin)

Cunningham, J(ames) V(incent) 1911-1985 .... **CLC 3, 31**
See also CA 1-4R; 115; CANR 1, 72; DLB 5

Cunningham, Julia (Woolfolk) 1916- .... **CLC 12**
See also CA 9-12R; CANR 4, 19, 36; JRDA; MAICYA; SAAS 2; SATA 1, 26

Cunningham, Michael 1952- .... **CLC 34**
See also CA 136

Cunninghame Graham, R. B.
See Cunninghame Graham, Robert (Gallnigad) Bontine

Cunninghame Graham, Robert (Gallnigad) Bontine 1852-1936 .... **TCLC 19**
See also Graham, R(obert) B(ontine) Cunninghame
See also CA 119; 184; DLB 98

Currie, Ellen 19(?)- .... **CLC 44**

Curtin, Philip
See Lowndes, Marie Adelaide (Belloc)

Curtis, Price
See Ellison, Harlan (Jay)

Cutrate, Joe
See Spiegelman, Art

Cynewulf c. 770-c. 840 .... **CMLC 23**

Czaczkes, Shmuel Yosef
See Agnon, S(hmuel) Y(osef Halevi)

Dabrowska, Maria (Szumska) 1889-1965 .... **CLC 15**
See also CA 106

Dabydeen, David 1955- .... **CLC 34**
See also BW 1; CA 125; CANR 56, 92

Dacey, Philip 1939- .... **CLC 51**
See also CA 37-40R; CAAS 17; CANR 14, 32, 64; DLB 105

Dagerman, Stig (Halvard) 1923-1954 .... **TCLC 17**
See also CA 117; 155

Dahl, Roald 1916-1990 ..... **CLC 1, 6, 18, 79; DAB; DAC; DAM MST, NOV, POP**
See also AAYA 15; CA 1-4R; 133; CANR 6, 32, 37, 62; CLR 1, 7, 41; DA3; DLB 139; JRDA; MAICYA; MTCW 1, 2; SATA 1, 26, 73; SATA-Obit 65

Dahlberg, Edward 1900-1977 . **CLC 1, 7, 14**
See also CA 9-12R; 69-72; CANR 31, 62; DLB 48; MTCW 1

Daitch, Susan 1954- .... **CLC 103**
See also CA 161

Dale, Colin .... **TCLC 18**
See also Lawrence, T(homas) E(dward)

Dale, George E.
See Asimov, Isaac

Dalton, Roque 1935-1975
See also HLCS 1; HW 2

Daly, Elizabeth 1878-1967 .... **CLC 52**
See also CA 23-24; 25-28R; CANR 60; CAP 2

Daly, Maureen 1921-1983 .... **CLC 17**
See also AAYA 5; CANR 37, 83; JRDA; MAICYA; SAAS 1; SATA 2

Damas, Leon-Gontran 1912-1978 ... **CLC 84**
See also BW 1; CA 125; 73-76

Dana, Richard Henry Sr. 1787-1879 .... **NCLC 53**

Daniel, Samuel 1562(?)-1619 .... **LC 24**
See also DLB 62

Daniels, Brett
See Adler, Renata

Dannay, Frederic 1905-1982 . **CLC 11; DAM POP**
See also Queen, Ellery
See also CA 1-4R; 107; CANR 1, 39; DLB 137; MTCW 1

D'Annunzio, Gabriele 1863-1938 .. **TCLC 6, 40**
See also CA 104; 155

Danois, N. le
See Gourmont, Remy (-Marie-Charles) de

Dante 1265-1321 .... **CMLC 3, 18, 39; DA; DAB; DAC; DAM MST, POET; PC 21; WLCS**
See also Alighieri, Dante
See also DA3

d'Antibes, Germain
See Simenon, Georges (Jacques Christian)

Danticat, Edwidge 1969- .... **CLC 94**
See also AAYA 29; CA 152; CANR 73; MTCW 1

Danvers, Dennis 1947- .... **CLC 70**

Danziger, Paula 1944- .... **CLC 21**
See also AAYA 4; CA 112; 115; CANR 37; CLR 20; JRDA; MAICYA; SATA 36, 63, 102; SATA-Brief 30

Da Ponte, Lorenzo 1749-1838 ...... **NCLC 50**

Dario, Ruben 1867-1916 ..... **TCLC 4; DAM MULT; HLC 1; PC 15**
See also CA 131; CANR 81; HW 1, 2; MTCW 1, 2

Darley, George 1795-1846 .... **NCLC 2**
See also DLB 96

Darrow, Clarence (Seward) 1857-1938 .... **TCLC 81**
See also CA 164

Darwin, Charles 1809-1882 .... **NCLC 57**
See also DLB 57, 166

Daryush, Elizabeth 1887-1977 .... **CLC 6, 19**
See also CA 49-52; CANR 3, 81; DLB 20

Dasgupta, Surendranath 1887-1952 .... **TCLC 81**
See also CA 157

Dashwood, Edmee Elizabeth Monica de la Pasture 1890-1943
See Delafield, E. M.
See also CA 119; 154

Daudet, (Louis Marie) Alphonse 1840-1897 .... **NCLC 1**
See also DLB 123

Daumal, Rene 1908-1944 .... **TCLC 14**
See also CA 114

Davenant, William 1606-1668 .... **LC 13**
See also DLB 58, 126

Davenport, Guy (Mattison, Jr.) 1927- .... **CLC 6, 14, 38; SSC 16**
See also CA 33-36R; CANR 23, 73; DLB 130

Davidson, Avram (James) 1923-1993
See Queen, Ellery
See also CA 101; 171; CANR 26; DLB 8

Davidson, Donald (Grady) 1893-1968 .... **CLC 2, 13, 19**
See also CA 5-8R; 25-28R; CANR 4, 84; DLB 45

Davidson, Hugh
See Hamilton, Edmond

Davidson, John 1857-1909 .... **TCLC 24**
See also CA 118; DLB 19

Davidson, Sara 1943- .... **CLC 9**
See also CA 81-84; CANR 44, 68; DLB 185

Davie, Donald (Alfred) 1922-1995 ... **CLC 5, 8, 10, 31; PC 29**
See also CA 1-4R; 149; CAAS 3; CANR 1, 44; DLB 27; MTCW 1

Davies, Ray(mond Douglas) 1944- .. **CLC 21**
See also CA 116; 146; CANR 92

Davies, Rhys 1901-1978 .... **CLC 23**
See also CA 9-12R; 81-84; CANR 4; DLB 139, 191

Davies, (William) Robertson 1913-1995 .... **CLC 2, 7, 13, 25, 42, 75, 91; DA; DAB; DAC; DAM MST, NOV, POP; WLC**
See also BEST 89:2; CA 33-36R; 150; CANR 17, 42; DA3; DLB 68; INT CANR-17; MTCW 1, 2

Davies, Walter C.
See Kornbluth, C(yril) M.

Davies, William Henry 1871-1940 .. **TCLC 5**
See also CA 104; 179; DLB 19, 174

Da Vinci, Leonardo 1452-1519 ... **LC 12, 57, 60**

Davis, Angela (Yvonne) 1944- .... **CLC 77; DAM MULT**
See also BW 2, 3; CA 57-60; CANR 10, 81; DA3

Davis, B. Lynch
See Bioy Casares, Adolfo; Borges, Jorge Luis

Davis, B. Lynch
See Bioy Casares, Adolfo

Davis, H(arold) L(enoir) 1894-1960 . **CLC 49**
See also CA 178; 89-92; DLB 9, 206; SATA 114

Davis, Rebecca (Blaine) Harding 1831-1910 .... **TCLC 6; SSC 38**
See also CA 104; 179; DLB 74

Davis, Richard Harding 1864-1916 .... **TCLC 24**
See also CA 114; 179; DLB 12, 23, 78, 79, 189; DLBD 13

Davison, Frank Dalby 1893-1970 ... **CLC 15**
See also CA 116

Davison, Lawrence H.
See Lawrence, D(avid) H(erbert Richards)

Davison, Peter (Hubert) 1928- .... **CLC 28**
See also CA 9-12R; CAAS 4; CANR 3, 43, 84; DLB 5

Davys, Mary 1674-1732 .... **LC 1, 46**
See also DLB 39

Dawson, Fielding 1930- .... **CLC 6**
See also CA 85-88; DLB 130

Dawson, Peter
See Faust, Frederick (Schiller)

Day, Clarence (Shepard, Jr.) 1874-1935 .... **TCLC 25**
See also CA 108; DLB 11

Day, Thomas 1748-1789 .... **LC 1**
See also DLB 39; YABC 1

Day Lewis, C(ecil) 1904-1972 . **CLC 1, 6, 10; DAM POET; PC 11**
See also Blake, Nicholas
See also CA 13-16; 33-36R; CANR 34; CAP 1; DLB 15, 20; MTCW 1, 2

Dazai Osamu 1909-1948 . **TCLC 11; SSC 41**
See also Tsushima, Shuji
See also CA 164; DLB 182

de Andrade, Carlos Drummond 1892-1945
See Drummond de Andrade, Carlos

Deane, Norman
See Creasey, John

Deane, Seamus (Francis) 1940- ..... **CLC 122**
See also CA 118; CANR 42

de Beauvoir, Simone (Lucie Ernestine Marie Bertrand)
See Beauvoir, Simone (Lucie Ernestine Marie Bertrand) de

de Beer, P.
See Bosman, Herman Charles

de Brissac, Malcolm
See Dickinson, Peter (Malcolm)

de Campos, Alvaro
See Pessoa, Fernando (Antonio Nogueira)

See also AAYA 23; CDBLB 1832-1890; DA3; DLB 21, 55, 70, 159, 166; JRDA; MAICYA; SATA 15

Dickey, James (Lafayette) 1923-1997 .. **CLC 1, 2, 4, 7, 10, 15, 47, 109; DAM NOV, POET, POP**
See also AITN 1, 2; CA 9-12R; 156; CABS 2; CANR 10, 48, 61; CDALB 1968-1988; DA3; DLB 5, 193; DLBD 7; DLBY 82, 93, 96, 97, 98; INT CANR-10; MTCW 1, 2

Dickey, William 1928-1994 .... **CLC 3, 28**
See also CA 9-12R; 145; CANR 24, 79; DLB 5

Dickinson, Charles 1951- .... **CLC 49**
See also CA 128

Dickinson, Emily (Elizabeth) 1830-1886 . **NCLC 21, 77; DA; DAB; DAC; DAM MST, POET; PC 1; WLC**
See also AAYA 22; CDALB 1865-1917; DA3; DLB 1; SATA 29

Dickinson, Peter (Malcolm) 1927- . **CLC 12, 35**
See also AAYA 9; CA 41-44R; CANR 31, 58, 88; CLR 29; DLB 87, 161; JRDA; MAICYA; SATA 5, 62, 95

Dickson, Carr
See Carr, John Dickson

Dickson, Carter
See Carr, John Dickson

Diderot, Denis 1713-1784 .... **LC 26**

Didion, Joan 1934- . **CLC 1, 3, 8, 14, 32, 129; DAM NOV**
See also AITN 1; CA 5-8R; CANR 14, 52, 76; CDALB 1968-1988; DA3; DLB 2, 173, 185; DLBY 81, 86; MTCW 1, 2

Dietrich, Robert
See Hunt, E(verette) Howard, (Jr.)

Difusa, Pati
See Almodovar, Pedro

Dillard, Annie 1945- . **CLC 9, 60, 115; DAM NOV**
See also AAYA 6; CA 49-52; CANR 3, 43, 62, 90; DA3; DLBY 80; MTCW 1, 2; SATA 10

Dillard, R(ichard) H(enry) W(ilde) 1937- .... **CLC 5**
See also CA 21-24R; CAAS 7; CANR 10; DLB 5

Dillon, Eilis 1920-1994 .... **CLC 17**
See also CA 9-12R, 182; 147; CAAE 182; CAAS 3; CANR 4, 38, 78; CLR 26; MAICYA; SATA 2, 74; SATA-Essay 105; SATA-Obit 83

Dimont, Penelope
See Mortimer, Penelope (Ruth)

Dinesen, Isak -1962 . **CLC 10, 29, 95; SSC 7**
See also Blixen, Karen (Christentze Dinesen)
See also MTCW 1

Ding Ling .... **CLC 68**
See also Chiang, Pin-chin

Diphusa, Patty
See Almodovar, Pedro

Disch, Thomas M(ichael) 1940- .. **CLC 7, 36**
See also AAYA 17; CA 21-24R; CAAS 4; CANR 17, 36, 54, 89; CLR 18; DA3; DLB 8; MAICYA; MTCW 1, 2; SAAS 15; SATA 92

Disch, Tom
See Disch, Thomas M(ichael)

d'Isly, Georges
See Simenon, Georges (Jacques Christian)

Disraeli, Benjamin 1804-1881 . **NCLC 2, 39, 79**
See also DLB 21, 55

Ditcum, Steve
See Crumb, R(obert)

Dixon, Paige
See Corcoran, Barbara

Dixon, Stephen 1936- .... **CLC 52; SSC 16**
See also CA 89-92; CANR 17, 40, 54, 91; DLB 130

Doak, Annie
See Dillard, Annie

Dobell, Sydney Thompson 1824-1874 .... **NCLC 43**
See also DLB 32

Doblin, Alfred .... **TCLC 13**
See also Doeblin, Alfred

Dobrolyubov, Nikolai Alexandrovich 1836-1861 .... **NCLC 5**

Dobson, Austin 1840-1921 .... **TCLC 79**
See also DLB 35; 144

Dobyns, Stephen 1941- .... **CLC 37**
See also CA 45-48; CANR 2, 18

Doctorow, E(dgar) L(aurence) 1931- .... **CLC 6, 11, 15, 18, 37, 44, 65, 113; DAM NOV, POP**
See also AAYA 22; AITN 2; BEST 89:3; CA 45-48; CANR 2, 33, 51, 76; CDALB 1968-1988; DA3; DLB 2, 28, 173; DLBY 80; MTCW 1, 2

Dodgson, Charles Lutwidge 1832-1898
See Carroll, Lewis
See also CLR 2; DA; DAB; DAC; DAM MST, NOV, POET; DA3; MAICYA; SATA 100; YABC 2

Dodson, Owen (Vincent) 1914-1983 .... **CLC 79; BLC 1; DAM MULT**
See also BW 1; CA 65-68; 110; CANR 24; DLB 76

Doeblin, Alfred 1878-1957 .... **TCLC 13**
See also Doblin, Alfred
See also CA 110; 141; DLB 66

Doerr, Harriet 1910- .... **CLC 34**
See also CA 117; 122; CANR 47; INT 122

Domecq, H(onorio Bustos)
See Bioy Casares, Adolfo

Domecq, H(onorio) Bustos
See Bioy Casares, Adolfo; Borges, Jorge Luis

Domini, Rey
See Lorde, Audre (Geraldine)

Dominique
See Proust, (Valentin-Louis-George-Eugene-) Marcel

Don, A
See Stephen, SirLeslie

Donaldson, Stephen R. 1947- . **CLC 46, 138; DAM POP**
See also CA 89-92; CANR 13, 55; INT CANR-13

Donleavy, J(ames) P(atrick) 1926- ... **CLC 1, 4, 6, 10, 45**
See also AITN 2; CA 9-12R; CANR 24, 49, 62, 80; DLB 6, 173; INT CANR-24; MTCW 1, 2

Donne, John 1572-1631 .... **LC 10, 24; DA; DAB; DAC; DAM MST, POET; PC 1; WLC**
See also CDBLB Before 1660; DLB 121, 151

Donnell, David 1939(?)- .... **CLC 34**

Donoghue, P. S.
See Hunt, E(verette) Howard, (Jr.)

Donoso (Yanez), Jose 1924-1996 .. **CLC 4, 8, 11, 32, 99; DAM MULT; HLC 1; SSC 34**
See also CA 81-84; 155; CANR 32, 73; DLB 113; HW 1, 2; MTCW 1, 2

Donovan, John 1928-1992 .... **CLC 35**
See also AAYA 20; CA 97-100; 137; CLR 3; MAICYA; SATA 72; SATA-Brief 29

Don Roberto
See Cunninghame Graham, Robert (Gallnigad) Bontine

Doolittle, Hilda 1886-1961 ...... **CLC 3, 8, 14, 31, 34, 73; DA; DAC; DAM MST, POET; PC 5; WLC**
See also H. D.
See also CA 97-100; CANR 35; DLB 4, 45; MTCW 1, 2

Dorfman, Ariel 1942- ..... **CLC 48, 77; DAM MULT; HLC 1**
See also CA 124; 130; CANR 67, 70; HW 1, 2; INT 130

Dorn, Edward (Merton) 1929-1999 . **CLC 10, 18**
See also CA 93-96; 187; CANR 42, 79; DLB 5; INT 93-96

Dorris, Michael (Anthony) 1945-1997 .... **CLC 109; DAM MULT, NOV**
See also AAYA 20; BEST 90:1; CA 102; 157; CANR 19, 46, 75; CLR 58; DA3; DLB 175; MTCW 2; NNAL; SATA 75; SATA-Obit 94

Dorris, Michael A.
See Dorris, Michael (Anthony)

Dorsan, Luc
See Simenon, Georges (Jacques Christian)

Dorsange, Jean
See Simenon, Georges (Jacques Christian)

Dos Passos, John (Roderigo) 1896-1970 ..... **CLC 1, 4, 8, 11, 15, 25, 34, 82; DA; DAB; DAC; DAM MST, NOV; WLC**
See also CA 1-4R; 29-32R; CANR 3; CDALB 1929-1941; DA3; DLB 4, 9; DLBD 1, 15; DLBY 96; MTCW 1, 2

Dossage, Jean
See Simenon, Georges (Jacques Christian)

Dostoevsky, Fedor Mikhailovich 1821-1881 .... **NCLC 2, 7, 21, 33, 43; DA; DAB; DAC; DAM MST, NOV; SSC 2, 33; WLC**
See also DA3

Doughty, Charles M(ontagu) 1843-1926 .... **TCLC 27**
See also CA 115; 178; DLB 19, 57, 174

Douglas, Ellen .... **CLC 73**
See also Haxton, Josephine Ayres; Williamson, Ellen Douglas

Douglas, Gavin 1475(?)-1522 .... **LC 20**
See also DLB 132

Douglas, George
See Brown, George Douglas

Douglas, Keith (Castellain) 1920-1944 .... **TCLC 40**
See also CA 160; DLB 27

Douglas, Leonard
See Bradbury, Ray (Douglas)

Douglas, Michael
See Crichton, (John) Michael

Douglas, (George) Norman 1868-1952 .... **TCLC 68**
See also CA 119; 157; DLB 34, 195

Douglas, William
See Brown, George Douglas

Douglass, Frederick 1817(?)-1895 . **NCLC 7, 55; BLC 1; DA; DAC; DAM MST, MULT; WLC**
See also CDALB 1640-1865; DA3; DLB 1, 43, 50, 79; SATA 29

Dourado, (Waldomiro Freitas) Autran 1926- .... **CLC 23, 60**
See also CA 25-28R; 179; CANR 34, 81; DLB 145; HW 2

Dourado, Waldomiro Autran 1926-
See Dourado, (Waldomiro Freitas) Autran
See also CA 179

Dove, Rita (Frances) 1952- ...... **CLC 50, 81; BLCS; DAM MULT, POET; PC 6**
See also BW 2; CA 109; CAAS 19; CANR 27, 42, 68, 76; CDALBS; DA3; DLB 120; MTCW 1

Dye, Richard
    See De Voto, Bernard (Augustine)
Dylan, Bob 1941- .... **CLC 3, 4, 6, 12, 77**
    See also CA 41-44R; DLB 16
E. V. L.
    See Lucas, E(dward) V(errall)
Eagleton, Terence (Francis) 1943- . **CLC 63, 132**
    See also CA 57-60; CANR 7, 23, 68; MTCW 1, 2
Eagleton, Terry
    See Eagleton, Terence (Francis)
Early, Jack
    See Scoppettone, Sandra
East, Michael
    See West, Morris L(anglo)
Eastaway, Edward
    See Thomas, (Philip) Edward
Eastlake, William (Derry) 1917-1997 . **CLC 8**
    See also CA 5-8R; 158; CAAS 1; CANR 5, 63; DLB 6, 206; INT CANR-5
Eastman, Charles A(lexander) 1858-1939
    .... **TCLC 55; DAM MULT**
    See also CA 179; CANR 91; DLB 175; NNAL; YABC 1
Eberhart, Richard (Ghormley) 1904-
    .... **CLC 3, 11, 19, 56; DAM POET**
    See also CA 1-4R; CANR 2; CDALB 1941-1968; DLB 48; MTCW 1
Eberstadt, Fernanda 1960- .... **CLC 39**
    See also CA 136; CANR 69
Echegaray (y Eizaguirre), Jose (Maria Waldo) 1832-1916 ... **TCLC 4; HLCS 1**
    See also CA 104; CANR 32; HW 1; MTCW 1
Echeverria, (Jose) Esteban (Antonino) 1805-1851 .... **NCLC 18**
Echo
    See Proust, (Valentin-Louis-George-Eugene-) Marcel
Eckert, Allan W. 1931- .... **CLC 17**
    See also AAYA 18; CA 13-16R; CANR 14, 45; INT CANR-14; SAAS 21; SATA 29, 91; SATA-Brief 27
Eckhart, Meister 1260(?)-1328(?) ..**CMLC 9**
    See also DLB 115
Eckmar, F. R.
    See de Hartog, Jan
Eco, Umberto 1932- .... **CLC 28, 60; DAM NOV, POP**
    See also BEST 90:1; CA 77-80; CANR 12, 33, 55; DA3; DLB 196; MTCW 1, 2
Eddison, E(ric) R(ucker) 1882-1945
    .... **TCLC 15**
    See also CA 109; 156
Eddy, Mary (Ann Morse) Baker 1821-1910
    .... **TCLC 71**
    See also CA 113; 174
Edel, (Joseph) Leon 1907-1997 . **CLC 29, 34**
    See also CA 1-4R; 161; CANR 1, 22; DLB 103; INT CANR-22
Eden, Emily 1797-1869 .... **NCLC 10**
Edgar, David 1948- . **CLC 42; DAM DRAM**
    See also CA 57-60; CANR 12, 61; DLB 13, 233; MTCW 1
Edgerton, Clyde (Carlyle) 1944- ..... **CLC 39**
    See also AAYA 17; CA 118; 134; CANR 64; INT 134
Edgeworth, Maria 1768-1849 ... **NCLC 1, 51**
    See also DLB 116, 159, 163; SATA 21
Edmonds, Paul
    See Kuttner, Henry
Edmonds, Walter D(umaux) 1903-1998
    .... **CLC 35**
    See also CA 5-8R; CANR 2; DLB 9; MAICYA; SAAS 4; SATA 1, 27; SATA-Obit 99

Edmondson, Wallace
    See Ellison, Harlan (Jay)
Edson, Russell .... **CLC 13**
    See also CA 33-36R
Edwards, Bronwen Elizabeth
    See Rose, Wendy
Edwards, G(erald) B(asil) 1899-1976
    .... **CLC 25**
    See also CA 110
Edwards, Gus 1939- .... **CLC 43**
    See also CA 108; INT 108
Edwards, Jonathan 1703-1758 ..... **LC 7, 54; DA; DAC; DAM MST**
    See also DLB 24
Efron, Marina Ivanovna Tsvetaeva
    See Tsvetaeva (Efron), Marina (Ivanovna)
Ehle, John (Marsden, Jr.) 1925- ..... **CLC 27**
    See also CA 9-12R
Ehrenbourg, Ilya (Grigoryevich)
    See Ehrenburg, Ilya (Grigoryevich)
Ehrenburg, Ilya (Grigoryevich) 1891-1967
    .... **CLC 18, 34, 62**
    See also CA 102; 25-28R
Ehrenburg, Ilyo (Grigoryevich)
    See Ehrenburg, Ilya (Grigoryevich)
Ehrenreich, Barbara 1941- .... **CLC 110**
    See also BEST 90:4; CA 73-76; CANR 16, 37, 62; MTCW 1, 2
Eich, Guenter 1907-1972 .... **CLC 15**
    See also CA 111; 93-96; DLB 69, 124
Eichendorff, Joseph Freiherr von 1788-1857
    .... **NCLC 8**
    See also DLB 90
Eigner, Larry .... **CLC 9**
    See also Eigner, Laurence (Joel)
    See also CAAS 23; DLB 5
Eigner, Laurence (Joel) 1927-1996
    See Eigner, Larry
    See also CA 9-12R; 151; CANR 6, 84; DLB 193
Einstein, Albert 1879-1955 .... **TCLC 65**
    See also CA 121; 133; MTCW 1, 2
Eiseley, Loren Corey 1907-1977 .... **CLC 7**
    See also AAYA 5; CA 1-4R; 73-76; CANR 6; DLBD 17
Eisenstadt, Jill 1963- .... **CLC 50**
    See also CA 140
Eisenstein, Sergei (Mikhailovich) 1898-1948
    .... **TCLC 57**
    See also CA 114; 149
Eisner, Simon
    See Kornbluth, C(yril) M.
Ekeloef, (Bengt) Gunnar 1907-1968
    .... **CLC 27; DAM POET; PC 23**
    See also CA 123; 25-28R
Ekelof, (Bengt) Gunnar
    See Ekeloef, (Bengt) Gunnar
Ekelund, Vilhelm 1880-1949 .... **TCLC 75**
Ekwensi, C. O. D.
    See Ekwensi, Cyprian (Odiatu Duaka)
Ekwensi, Cyprian (Odiatu Duaka) 1921-
    .... **CLC 4; BLC 1; DAM MULT**
    See also BW 2, 3; CA 29-32R; CANR 18, 42, 74; DLB 117; MTCW 1, 2; SATA 66
Elaine .... **TCLC 18**
    See also Leverson, Ada
El Crummo
    See Crumb, R(obert)
Elder, Lonne III 1931-1996 .... **DC 8**
    See also BLC 1; BW 1, 3; CA 81-84; 152; CANR 25; DAM MULT; DLB 7, 38, 44
Eleanor of Aquitaine 1122-1204 .. **CMLC 39**
Elia
    See Lamb, Charles
Eliade, Mircea 1907-1986 .... **CLC 19**
    See also CA 65-68; 119; CANR 30, 62; DLB 220; MTCW 1

Eliot, A. D.
    See Jewett, (Theodora) Sarah Orne
Eliot, Alice
    See Jewett, (Theodora) Sarah Orne
Eliot, Dan
    See Silverberg, Robert
Eliot, George 1819- . **NCLC 4, 13, 23, 41, 49, 89; DA; DAB; DAC; DAM MST, NOV; PC 20; WLC**
    See also CDBLB 1832-1890; DA3; DLB 21, 35, 55
Eliot, John 1604-1690 .... **LC 5**
    See also DLB 24
Eliot, T(homas) S(tearns) 1888-1965 . **CLC 1, 2, 3, 6, 9, 10, 13, 15, 24, 34, 41, 55, 57, 113; DA; DAB; DAC; DAM DRAM, MST, POET; PC 5, 31; WLC**
    See also AAYA 28; CA 5-8R; 25-28R; CANR 41; CDALB 1929-1941; DA3; DLB 7, 10, 45, 63; DLBY 88; MTCW 1, 2
Elizabeth 1866-1941 .... **TCLC 41**
Elkin, Stanley L(awrence) 1930-1995
    .... **CLC 4, 6, 9, 14, 27, 51, 91; DAM NOV, POP; SSC 12**
    See also CA 9-12R; 148; CANR 8, 46; DLB 2, 28; DLBY 80; INT CANR-8; MTCW 1, 2
Elledge, Scott .... **CLC 34**
Elliot, Don
    See Silverberg, Robert
Elliott, Don
    See Silverberg, Robert
Elliott, George P(aul) 1918-1980 .... **CLC 2**
    See also CA 1-4R; 97-100; CANR 2
Elliott, Janice 1931-1995 .... **CLC 47**
    See also CA 13-16R; CANR 8, 29, 84; DLB 14; SATA 119
Elliott, Sumner Locke 1917-1991 ... **CLC 38**
    See also CA 5-8R; 134; CANR 2, 21
Elliott, William
    See Bradbury, Ray (Douglas)
Ellis, A. E. .... **CLC 7**
Ellis, Alice Thomas .... **CLC 40**
    See also Haycraft, Anna (Margaret)
    See also DLB 194; MTCW 1
Ellis, Bret Easton 1964- ... **CLC 39, 71, 117; DAM POP**
    See also AAYA 2; CA 118; 123; CANR 51, 74; DA3; INT 123; MTCW 1
Ellis, (Henry) Havelock 1859-1939
    .... **TCLC 14**
    See also CA 109; 169; DLB 190
Ellis, Landon
    See Ellison, Harlan (Jay)
Ellis, Trey 1962- .... **CLC 55**
    See also CA 146; CANR 92
Ellison, Harlan (Jay) 1934- . **CLC 1, 13, 42; DAM POP; SSC 14**
    See also AAYA 29; CA 5-8R; CANR 5, 46; DLB 8; INT CANR-5; MTCW 1, 2
Ellison, Ralph (Waldo) 1914-1994 ... **CLC 1, 3, 11, 54, 86, 114; BLC 1; DA; DAB; DAC; DAM MST, MULT, NOV; SSC 26; WLC**
    See also AAYA 19; BW 1, 3; CA 9-12R; 145; CANR 24, 53; CDALB 1941-1968; DA3; DLB 2, 76, 227; DLBY 94; MTCW 1, 2
Ellmann, Lucy (Elizabeth) 1956- .... **CLC 61**
    See also CA 128
Ellmann, Richard (David) 1918-1987
    .... **CLC 50**
    See also BEST 89:2; CA 1-4R; 122; CANR 2, 28, 61; DLB 103; DLBY 87; MTCW 1, 2
Elman, Richard (Martin) 1934-1997
    .... **CLC 19**

See also CA 17-20R; 163; CAAS 3; CANR 47

Elron
See Hubbard, L(afayette) Ron(ald)

Eluard, Paul .... TCLC 7, 41
See also Grindel, Eugene

Elyot, Sir Thomas 1490(?)-1546 .... LC 11

Elytis, Odysseus 1911-1996 ...... CLC 15, 49, 100; DAM POET; PC 21
See also CA 102; 151; MTCW 1, 2

Emecheta, (Florence Onye) Buchi 1944- . CLC 14, 48, 128; BLC 2; DAM MULT
See also BW 2, 3; CA 81-84; CANR 27, 81; DA3; DLB 117; MTCW 1, 2; SATA 66

Emerson, Mary Moody 1774-1863
.... NCLC 66

Emerson, Ralph Waldo 1803-1882 . NCLC 1, 38; DA; DAB; DAC; DAM MST, POET; PC 18; WLC
See also CDALB 1640-1865; DA3; DLB 1, 59, 73, 223

Eminescu, Mihail 1850-1889 .... NCLC 33

Empson, William 1906-1984 .. CLC 3, 8, 19, 33, 34
See also CA 17-20R; 112; CANR 31, 61; DLB 20; MTCW 1, 2

Enchi, Fumiko (Ueda) 1905-1986 ... CLC 31
See also CA 129; 121; DLB 182

Ende, Michael (Andreas Helmuth) 1929-1995 .... CLC 31
See also CA 118; 124; 149; CANR 36; CLR 14; DLB 75; MAICYA; SATA 61; SATA-Brief 42; SATA-Obit 86

Endo, Shusaku 1923-1996 .... CLC 7, 14, 19, 54, 99; DAM NOV
See also CA 29-32R; 153; CANR 21, 54; DA3; DLB 182; MTCW 1, 2

Engel, Marian 1933-1985 .... CLC 36
See also CA 25-28R; CANR 12; DLB 53; INT CANR-12

Engelhardt, Frederick
See Hubbard, L(afayette) Ron(ald)

Engels, Friedrich 1820-1895 .... NCLC 85
See also DLB 129

Enright, D(ennis) J(oseph) 1920- . CLC 4, 8, 31
See also CA 1-4R; CANR 1, 42, 83; DLB 27; SATA 25

Enzensberger, Hans Magnus 1929- . CLC 43; PC 28
See also CA 116; 119

Ephron, Nora 1941- .... CLC 17, 31
See also AITN 2; CA 65-68; CANR 12, 39, 83

Epicurus 341B.C.-270B.C. .... CMLC 21
See also DLB 176

Epsilon
See Betjeman, John

Epstein, Daniel Mark 1948- .... CLC 7
See also CA 49-52; CANR 2, 53, 90

Epstein, Jacob 1956- .... CLC 19
See also CA 114

Epstein, Jean 1897-1953 .... TCLC 92

Epstein, Joseph 1937- .... CLC 39
See also CA 112; 119; CANR 50, 65

Epstein, Leslie 1938- .... CLC 27
See also CA 73-76; CAAS 12; CANR 23, 69

Equiano, Olaudah 1745(?)-1797 .... LC 16; BLC 2; DAM MULT
See also DLB 37, 50

ER .... TCLC 33
See also CA 160; DLB 85

Erasmus, Desiderius 1469(?)-1536 ..... LC 16

Erdman, Paul E(mil) 1932- .... CLC 25
See also AITN 1; CA 61-64; CANR 13, 43, 84

Erdrich, Louise 1954- .... CLC 39, 54, 120; DAM MULT, NOV, POP
See also AAYA 10; BEST 89:1; CA 114; CANR 41, 62; CDALBS; DA3; DLB 152, 175, 206; MTCW 1; NNAL; SATA 94

Erenburg, Ilya (Grigoryevich)
See Ehrenburg, Ilya (Grigoryevich)

Erickson, Stephen Michael 1950-
See Erickson, Steve
See also CA 129

Erickson, Steve 1950- .... CLC 64
See also Erickson, Stephen Michael
See also CANR 60, 68

Ericson, Walter
See Fast, Howard (Melvin)

Eriksson, Buntel
See Bergman, (Ernst) Ingmar

Ernaux, Annie 1940- .... CLC 88
See also CA 147; CANR 93

Erskine, John 1879-1951 .... TCLC 84
See also CA 112; 159; DLB 9, 102

Eschenbach, Wolfram von
See Wolfram von Eschenbach

Eseki, Bruno
See Mphahlele, Ezekiel

Esenin, Sergei (Alexandrovich) 1895-1925
.... TCLC 4
See also CA 104

Eshleman, Clayton 1935- .... CLC 7
See also CA 33-36R; CAAS 6; CANR 93; DLB 5

Espriella, Don Manuel Alvarez
See Southey, Robert

Espriu, Salvador 1913-1985 .... CLC 9
See also CA 154; 115; DLB 134

Espronceda, Jose de 1808-1842 .... NCLC 39

Esquivel, Laura 1951(?)-
See also AAYA 29; CA 143; CANR 68; DA3; HLCS 1; MTCW 1

Esse, James
See Stephens, James

Esterbrook, Tom
See Hubbard, L(afayette) Ron(ald)

Estleman, Loren D. 1952- .... CLC 48; DAM NOV, POP
See also AAYA 27; CA 85-88; CANR 27, 74; DA3; DLB 226; INT CANR-27; MTCW 1, 2

Euclid 306B.C.-283B.C. .... CMLC 25

Eugenides, Jeffrey 1960(?)- .... CLC 81
See also CA 144

Euripides c. 485B.C.-406B.C. ..... CMLC 23; DA; DAB; DAC; DAM DRAM, MST; DC 4; WLCS
See also DA3; DLB 176

Evan, Evin
See Faust, Frederick (Schiller)

Evans, Caradoc 1878-1945 .... TCLC 85

Evans, Evan
See Faust, Frederick (Schiller)

Evans, Marian
See Eliot, George

Evans, Mary Ann
See Eliot, George

Evarts, Esther
See Benson, Sally

Everett, Percival 1956-
See Everett, Percival L.

Everett, Percival L. 1956- .... CLC 57
See also Everett, Percival
See also BW 2; CA 129

Everson, R(onald) G(ilmour) 1903- . CLC 27
See also CA 17-20R; DLB 88

Everson, William (Oliver) 1912-1994
.... CLC 1, 5, 14
See also CA 9-12R; 145; CANR 20; DLB 212; MTCW 1

Evtushenko, Evgenii Aleksandrovich
See Yevtushenko, Yevgeny (Alexandrovich)

Ewart, Gavin (Buchanan) 1916-1995
.... CLC 13, 46
See also CA 89-92; 150; CANR 17, 46; DLB 40; MTCW 1

Ewers, Hanns Heinz 1871-1943 .... TCLC 12
See also CA 109; 149

Ewing, Frederick R.
See Sturgeon, Theodore (Hamilton)

Exley, Frederick (Earl) 1929-1992 ... CLC 6, 11
See also AITN 2; CA 81-84; 138; DLB 143; DLBY 81

Eynhardt, Guillermo
See Quiroga, Horacio (Sylvestre)

Ezekiel, Nissim 1924- .... CLC 61
See also CA 61-64

Ezekiel, Tish O'Dowd 1943- .... CLC 34
See also CA 129

Fadeyev, A.
See Bulgya, Alexander Alexandrovich

Fadeyev, Alexander .... TCLC 53
See also Bulgya, Alexander Alexandrovich

Fagen, Donald 1948- .... CLC 26

Fainzilberg, Ilya Arnoldovich 1897-1937
See Ilf, Ilya
See also CA 120; 165

Fair, Ronald L. 1932- .... CLC 18
See also BW 1; CA 69-72; CANR 25; DLB 33

Fairbairn, Roger
See Carr, John Dickson

Fairbairns, Zoe (Ann) 1948- .... CLC 32
See also CA 103; CANR 21, 85

Fairman, Paul W. 1916-1977
See Queen, Ellery
See also CA 114

Falco, Gian
See Papini, Giovanni

Falconer, James
See Kirkup, James

Falconer, Kenneth
See Kornbluth, C(yril) M.

Falkland, Samuel
See Heijermans, Herman

Fallaci, Oriana 1930- .... CLC 11, 110
See also CA 77-80; CANR 15, 58; MTCW 1

Faludy, George 1913- .... CLC 42
See also CA 21-24R

Faludy, Gyoergy
See Faludy, George

Fanon, Frantz 1925-1961 . CLC 74; BLC 2; DAM MULT
See also BW 1; CA 116; 89-92

Fanshawe, Ann 1625-1680 .... LC 11

Fante, John (Thomas) 1911-1983 .... CLC 60
See also CA 69-72; 109; CANR 23; DLB 130; DLBY 83

Farah, Nuruddin 1945- . CLC 53, 137; BLC 2; DAM MULT
See also BW 2, 3; CA 106; CANR 81; DLB 125

Fargue, Leon-Paul 1876(?)-1947 ... TCLC 11
See also CA 109

Farigoule, Louis
See Romains, Jules

Farina, Richard 1936(?)-1966 .... CLC 9
See also CA 81-84; 25-28R

Farley, Walter (Lorimer) 1915-1989
.... CLC 17
See also CA 17-20R; CANR 8, 29, 84; DLB 22; JRDA; MAICYA; SATA 2, 43

Farmer, Philip Jose 1918- .... CLC 1, 19
See also AAYA 28; CA 1-4R; CANR 4, 35; DLB 8; MTCW 1; SATA 93

Farquhar, George 1677-1707 . **LC 21; DAM DRAM**
See also DLB 84

Farrell, J(ames) G(ordon) 1935-1979 . **CLC 6**
See also CA 73-76; 89-92; CANR 36; DLB 14; MTCW 1

Farrell, James T(homas) 1904-1979 . **CLC 1, 4, 8, 11, 66; SSC 28**
See also CA 5-8R; 89-92; CANR 9, 61; DLB 4, 9, 86; DLBD 2; MTCW 1, 2

Farren, Richard J.
See Betjeman, John

Farren, Richard M.
See Betjeman, John

Fassbinder, Rainer Werner 1946-1982
.... **CLC 20**
See also CA 93-96; 106; CANR 31

Fast, Howard (Melvin) 1914- . **CLC 23, 131; DAM NOV**
See also AAYA 16; CA 1-4R, 181; CAAE 181; CAAS 18; CANR 1, 33, 54, 75; DLB 9; INT CANR-33; MTCW 1; SATA 7; SATA-Essay 107

Faulcon, Robert
See Holdstock, Robert P.

Faulkner, William (Cuthbert) 1897-1962
..... **CLC 1, 3, 6, 8, 9, 11, 14, 18, 28, 52, 68; DA; DAB; DAC; DAM MST, NOV; SSC 1, 35, 42; WLC**
See also AAYA 7; CA 81-84; CANR 33; CDALB 1929-1941; DA3; DLB 9, 11, 44, 102; DLBD 2; DLBY 86, 97; MTCW 1, 2

Fauset, Jessie Redmon 1884(?)-1961
.... **CLC 19, 54; BLC 2; DAM MULT**
See also BW 1; CA 109; CANR 83; DLB 51

Faust, Frederick (Schiller) 1892-1944(?)
.... **TCLC 49; DAM POP**
See also CA 108; 152

Faust, Irvin 1924- .... **CLC 8**
See also CA 33-36R; CANR 28, 67; DLB 2, 28; DLBY 80

Fawkes, Guy
See Benchley, Robert (Charles)

Fearing, Kenneth (Flexner) 1902-1961
.... **CLC 51**
See also CA 93-96; CANR 59; DLB 9

Fecamps, Elise
See Creasey, John

Federman, Raymond 1928- .... **CLC 6, 47**
See also CA 17-20R; CAAS 8; CANR 10, 43, 83; DLBY 80

Federspiel, J(uerg) F. 1931- .... **CLC 42**
See also CA 146

Feiffer, Jules (Ralph) 1929- ... **CLC 2, 8, 64; DAM DRAM**
See also AAYA 3; CA 17-20R; CANR 30, 59; DLB 7, 44; INT CANR-30; MTCW 1; SATA 8, 61, 111

Feige, Hermann Albert Otto Maximilian
See Traven, B.

Feinberg, David B. 1956-1994 .... **CLC 59**
See also CA 135; 147

Feinstein, Elaine 1930- .... **CLC 36**
See also CA 69-72; CAAS 1; CANR 31, 68; DLB 14, 40; MTCW 1

Feldman, Irving (Mordecai) 1928- ... **CLC 7**
See also CA 1-4R; CANR 1; DLB 169

Felix-Tchicaya, Gerald
See Tchicaya, Gerald Felix

Fellini, Federico 1920-1993 .... **CLC 16, 85**
See also CA 65-68; 143; CANR 33

Felsen, Henry Gregor 1916-1995 .... **CLC 17**
See also CA 1-4R; 180; CANR 1; SAAS 2; SATA 1

Fenno, Jack
See Calisher, Hortense

Fenollosa, Ernest (Francisco) 1853-1908
.... **TCLC 91**

Fenton, James Martin 1949- .... **CLC 32**
See also CA 102; DLB 40

Ferber, Edna 1887-1968 .... **CLC 18, 93**
See also AITN 1; CA 5-8R; 25-28R; CANR 68; DLB 9, 28, 86; MTCW 1, 2; SATA 7

Ferdowsi, Abu'l Qasem 940-1020 . **CMLC 43**

Ferguson, Helen
See Kavan, Anna

Ferguson, Niall 1967- .... **CLC 134**

Ferguson, Samuel 1810-1886 .... **NCLC 33**
See also DLB 32

Fergusson, Robert 1750-1774 .... **LC 29**
See also DLB 109

Ferling, Lawrence
See Ferlinghetti, Lawrence (Monsanto)

Ferlinghetti, Lawrence (Monsanto) 1919(?)-
.... **CLC 2, 6, 10, 27, 111; DAM POET; PC 1**
See also CA 5-8R; CANR 3, 41, 73; CDALB 1941-1968; DA3; DLB 5, 16; MTCW 1, 2

Fern, Fanny 1811-1872
See Parton, Sara Payson Willis

Fernandez, Vicente Garcia Huidobro
See Huidobro Fernandez, Vicente Garcia

Ferre, Rosario 1942- .... **SSC 36; HLCS 1**
See also CA 131; CANR 55, 81; DLB 145; HW 1, 2; MTCW 1

Ferrer, Gabriel (Francisco Victor) Miro
See Miro (Ferrer), Gabriel (Francisco Victor)

Ferrier, Susan (Edmonstone) 1782-1854
.... **NCLC 8**
See also DLB 116

Ferrigno, Robert 1948(?)- .... **CLC 65**
See also CA 140

Ferron, Jacques 1921-1985 ... **CLC 94; DAC**
See also CA 117; 129; DLB 60

Feuchtwanger, Lion 1884-1958 .... **TCLC 3**
See also CA 104; 187; DLB 66

Feuillet, Octave 1821-1890 .... **NCLC 45**
See also DLB 192

Feydeau, Georges (Leon Jules Marie)
1862-1921 ..... **TCLC 22; DAM DRAM**
See also CA 113; 152; CANR 84; DLB 192

Fichte, Johann Gottlieb 1762-1814
.... **NCLC 62**
See also DLB 90

Ficino, Marsilio 1433-1499 .... **LC 12**

Fiedeler, Hans
See Doeblin, Alfred

Fiedler, Leslie A(aron) 1917- . **CLC 4, 13, 24**
See also CA 9-12R; CANR 7, 63; DLB 28, 67; MTCW 1, 2

Field, Andrew 1938- .... **CLC 44**
See also CA 97-100; CANR 25

Field, Eugene 1850-1895 .... **NCLC 3**
See also DLB 23, 42, 140; DLBD 13; MAI-CYA; SATA 16

Field, Gans T.
See Wellman, Manly Wade

Field, Michael 1915-1971 .... **TCLC 43**
See also CA 29-32R

Field, Peter
See Hobson, Laura Z(ametkin)

Fielding, Henry 1707-1754 ... **LC 1, 46; DA; DAB; DAC; DAM DRAM, MST, NOV; WLC**
See also CDBLB 1660-1789; DA3; DLB 39, 84, 101

Fielding, Sarah 1710-1768 .... **LC 1, 44**
See also DLB 39

Fields, W. C. 1880-1946 .... **TCLC 80**
See also DLB 44

Fierstein, Harvey (Forbes) 1954- ... **CLC 33; DAM DRAM, POP**
See also CA 123; 129; DA3

Figes, Eva 1932- .... **CLC 31**

See also CA 53-56; CANR 4, 44, 83; DLB 14

Finch, Anne 1661-1720 .... **LC 3; PC 21**
See also DLB 95

Finch, Robert (Duer Claydon) 1900-
.... **CLC 18**
See also CA 57-60; CANR 9, 24, 49; DLB 88

Findley, Timothy 1930- . **CLC 27, 102; DAC; DAM MST**
See also CA 25-28R; CANR 12, 42, 69; DLB 53

Fink, William
See Mencken, H(enry) L(ouis)

Firbank, Louis 1942-
See Reed, Lou
See also CA 117

Firbank, (Arthur Annesley) Ronald
1886-1926 .... **TCLC 1**
See also CA 104; 177; DLB 36

Fisher, Dorothy (Frances) Canfield
1879-1958 .... **TCLC 87**
See also CA 114; 136; CANR 80; DLB 9, 102; MAICYA; YABC 1

Fisher, M(ary) F(rances) K(ennedy)
1908-1992 .... **CLC 76, 87**
See also CA 77-80; 138; CANR 44; MTCW 1

Fisher, Roy 1930- .... **CLC 25**
See also CA 81-84; CAAS 10; CANR 16; DLB 40

Fisher, Rudolph 1897-1934 . **TCLC 11; BLC 2; DAM MULT; SSC 25**
See also BW 1, 3; CA 107; 124; CANR 80; DLB 51, 102

Fisher, Vardis (Alvero) 1895-1968 .... **CLC 7**
See also CA 5-8R; 25-28R; CANR 68; DLB 9, 206

Fiske, Tarleton
See Bloch, Robert (Albert)

Fitch, Clarke
See Sinclair, Upton (Beall)

Fitch, John IV
See Cormier, Robert (Edmund)

Fitzgerald, Captain Hugh
See Baum, L(yman) Frank

FitzGerald, Edward 1809-1883 ...... **NCLC 9**
See also DLB 32

Fitzgerald, F(rancis) Scott (Key) 1896-1940
.... **TCLC 1, 6, 14, 28, 55; DA; DAB; DAC; DAM MST, NOV; SSC 6, 31; WLC**
See also AAYA 24; AITN 1; CA 110; 123; CDALB 1917-1929; DA3; DLB 4, 9, 86; DLBD 1, 15, 16; DLBY 81, 96; MTCW 1, 2

Fitzgerald, Penelope 1916- .. **CLC 19, 51, 61**
See also CA 85-88; CAAS 10; CANR 56, 86; DLB 14, 194; MTCW 2

Fitzgerald, Robert (Stuart) 1910-1985
.... **CLC 39**
See also CA 1-4R; 114; CANR 1; DLBY 80

FitzGerald, Robert D(avid) 1902-1987
.... **CLC 19**
See also CA 17-20R

Fitzgerald, Zelda (Sayre) 1900-1948
.... **TCLC 52**
See also CA 117; 126; DLBY 84

Flanagan, Thomas (James Bonner) 1923-
.... **CLC 25, 52**
See also CA 108; CANR 55; DLBY 80; INT 108; MTCW 1

Flaubert, Gustave 1821-1880 .. **NCLC 2, 10, 19, 62, 66; DA; DAB; DAC; DAM MST, NOV; SSC 11; WLC**
See also DA3; DLB 119

Flecker, Herman Elroy
See Flecker, (Herman) James Elroy

See also CA 115; 133; CANR 69; MTCW 1, 2

Friedan, Betty (Naomi) 1921- .... **CLC 74**
See also CA 65-68; CANR 18, 45, 74; MTCW 1, 2

Friedlander, Saul 1932- .... **CLC 90**
See also CA 117; 130; CANR 72

Friedman, B(ernard) H(arper) 1926- .... **CLC 7**
See also CA 1-4R; CANR 3, 48

Friedman, Bruce Jay 1930- .... **CLC 3, 5, 56**
See also CA 9-12R; CANR 25, 52; DLB 2, 28; INT CANR-25

Friel, Brian 1929- .. **CLC 5, 42, 59, 115; DC 8**
See also CA 21-24R; CANR 33, 69; DLB 13; MTCW 1

Friis-Baastad, Babbis Ellinor 1921-1970 .... **CLC 12**
See also CA 17-20R; 134; SATA 7

Frisch, Max (Rudolf) 1911-1991 .. **CLC 3, 9, 14, 18, 32, 44; DAM DRAM, NOV**
See also CA 85-88; 134; CANR 32, 74; DLB 69, 124; MTCW 1, 2

Fromentin, Eugene (Samuel Auguste) 1820-1876 .... **NCLC 10**
See also DLB 123

Frost, Frederick
See Faust, Frederick (Schiller)

Frost, Robert (Lee) 1874-1963 . **CLC 1, 3, 4, 9, 10, 13, 15, 26, 34, 44; DA; DAB; DAC; DAM MST, POET; PC 1; WLC**
See also AAYA 21; CA 89-92; CANR 33; CDALB 1917-1929; CLR 67; DA3; DLB 54; DLBD 7; MTCW 1, 2; SATA 14

Froude, James Anthony 1818-1894 .... **NCLC 43**
See also DLB 18, 57, 144

Froy, Herald
See Waterhouse, Keith (Spencer)

Fry, Christopher 1907- .... **CLC 2, 10, 14; DAM DRAM**
See also CA 17-20R; CAAS 23; CANR 9, 30, 74; DLB 13; MTCW 1, 2; SATA 66

Frye, (Herman) Northrop 1912-1991 .... **CLC 24, 70**
See also CA 5-8R; 133; CANR 8, 37; DLB 67, 68; MTCW 1, 2

Fuchs, Daniel 1909-1993 .... **CLC 8, 22**
See also CA 81-84; 142; CAAS 5; CANR 40; DLB 9, 26, 28; DLBY 93

Fuchs, Daniel 1934- .... **CLC 34**
See also CA 37-40R; CANR 14, 48

Fuentes, Carlos 1928- . **CLC 3, 8, 10, 13, 22, 41, 60, 113; DA; DAB; DAC; DAM MST, MULT, NOV; HLC 1; SSC 24; WLC**
See also AAYA 4; AITN 2; CA 69-72; CANR 10, 32, 68; DA3; DLB 113; HW 1, 2; MTCW 1, 2

Fuentes, Gregorio Lopez y
See Lopez y Fuentes, Gregorio

Fuertes, Gloria 1918- .... **PC 27**
See also CA 178, 180; DLB 108; HW 2; SATA 115

Fugard, (Harold) Athol 1932- . **CLC 5, 9, 14, 25, 40, 80; DAM DRAM; DC 3**
See also AAYA 17; CA 85-88; CANR 32, 54; DLB 225; MTCW 1

Fugard, Sheila 1932- .... **CLC 48**
See also CA 125

Fukuyama, Francis 1952- .... **CLC 131**
See also CA 140; CANR 72

Fuller, Charles (H., Jr.) 1939- .... **CLC 25; BLC 2; DAM DRAM, MULT; DC 1**
See also BW 2; CA 108; 112; CANR 87; DLB 38; INT 112; MTCW 1

Fuller, Henry Blake 1857-1929 ... **TCLC 103**
See also CA 108; 177; DLB 12

Fuller, John (Leopold) 1937- .... **CLC 62**
See also CA 21-24R; CANR 9, 44; DLB 40

Fuller, Margaret
See Ossoli, Sarah Margaret (Fuller marchesa d')

Fuller, Roy (Broadbent) 1912-1991 . **CLC 4, 28**
See also CA 5-8R; 135; CAAS 10; CANR 53, 83; DLB 15, 20; SATA 87

Fuller, Sarah Margaret 1810-1850
See Ossoli, Sarah Margaret (Fuller marchesa d')

Fulton, Alice 1952- .... **CLC 52**
See also CA 116; CANR 57, 88; DLB 193

Furphy, Joseph 1843-1912 .... **TCLC 25**
See also CA 163; DLB 230

Fussell, Paul 1924- .... **CLC 74**
See also BEST 90:1; CA 17-20R; CANR 8, 21, 35, 69; INT CANR-21; MTCW 1, 2

Futabatei, Shimei 1864-1909 .... **TCLC 44**
See also CA 162; DLB 180

Futrelle, Jacques 1875-1912 .... **TCLC 19**
See also CA 113; 155

Gaboriau, Emile 1835-1873 .... **NCLC 14**

Gadda, Carlo Emilio 1893-1973 ...... **CLC 11**
See also CA 89-92; DLB 177

Gaddis, William 1922-1998 .. **CLC 1, 3, 6, 8, 10, 19, 43, 86**
See also CA 17-20R; 172; CANR 21, 48; DLB 2; MTCW 1, 2

Gage, Walter
See Inge, William (Motter)

Gaines, Ernest J(ames) 1933- ..... **CLC 3, 11, 18, 86; BLC 2; DAM MULT**
See also AAYA 18; AITN 1; BW 2, 3; CA 9-12R; CANR 6, 24, 42, 75; CDALB 1968-1988; CLR 62; DA3; DLB 2, 33, 152; DLBY 80; MTCW 1, 2; SATA 86

Gaitskill, Mary 1954- .... **CLC 69**
See also CA 128; CANR 61

Galdos, Benito Perez
See Perez Galdos, Benito

Gale, Zona 1874-1938 .... **TCLC 7; DAM DRAM**
See also CA 105; 153; CANR 84; DLB 9, 78, 228

Galeano, Eduardo (Hughes) 1940- . **CLC 72; HLCS 1**
See also CA 29-32R; CANR 13, 32; HW 1

Galiano, Juan Valera y Alcala
See Valera y Alcala-Galiano, Juan

Galilei, Galileo 1546-1642 .... **LC 45**

Gallagher, Tess 1943- ..... **CLC 18, 63; DAM POET; PC 9**
See also CA 106; DLB 212

Gallant, Mavis 1922- . **CLC 7, 18, 38; DAC; DAM MST; SSC 5**
See also CA 69-72; CANR 29, 69; DLB 53; MTCW 1, 2

Gallant, Roy A(rthur) 1924- .... **CLC 17**
See also CA 5-8R; CANR 4, 29, 54; CLR 30; MAICYA; SATA 4, 68, 110

Gallico, Paul (William) 1897-1976 .... **CLC 2**
See also AITN 1; CA 5-8R; 69-72; CANR 23; DLB 9, 171; MAICYA; SATA 13

Gallo, Max Louis 1932- .... **CLC 95**
See also CA 85-88

Gallois, Lucien
See Desnos, Robert

Gallup, Ralph
See Whitemore, Hugh (John)

Galsworthy, John 1867-1933 ... **TCLC 1, 45; DA; DAB; DAC; DAM DRAM, MST, NOV; SSC 22; WLC**
See also CA 104; 141; CANR 75; CDBLB 1890-1914; DA3; DLB 10, 34, 98, 162; DLBD 16; MTCW 1

Galt, John 1779-1839 .... **NCLC 1**
See also DLB 99, 116, 159

Galvin, James 1951- .... **CLC 38**
See also CA 108; CANR 26

Gamboa, Federico 1864-1939 .... **TCLC 36**
See also CA 167; HW 2

Gandhi, M. K.
See Gandhi, Mohandas Karamchand

Gandhi, Mahatma
See Gandhi, Mohandas Karamchand

Gandhi, Mohandas Karamchand 1869-1948 .... **TCLC 59; DAM MULT**
See also CA 121; 132; DA3; MTCW 1, 2

Gann, Ernest Kellogg 1910-1991 .... **CLC 23**
See also AITN 1; CA 1-4R; 136; CANR 1, 83

Garber, Eric 1943(?)-
See Holleran, Andrew
See also CANR 89

Garcia, Cristina 1958- .... **CLC 76**
See also CA 141; CANR 73; HW 2

Garcia Lorca, Federico 1898-1936 . **TCLC 1, 7, 49; DA; DAB; DAC; DAM DRAM, MST, MULT, POET; DC 2; HLC 2; PC 3; WLC**
See also Lorca, Federico Garcia
See also CA 104; 131; CANR 81; DA3; DLB 108; HW 1, 2; MTCW 1, 2

Garcia Marquez, Gabriel (Jose) 1928- ...... **CLC 2, 3, 8, 10, 15, 27, 47, 55, 68; DA; DAB; DAC; DAM MST, MULT, NOV, POP; HLC 1; SSC 8; WLC**
See also AAYA 3, 33; BEST 89:1, 90:4; CA 33-36R; CANR 10, 28, 50, 75, 82; DA3; DLB 113; HW 1, 2; MTCW 1, 2

Garcilaso de la Vega, El Inca 1503-1536
See also HLCS 1

Gard, Janice
See Latham, Jean Lee

Gard, Roger Martin du
See Martin du Gard, Roger

Gardam, Jane 1928- .... **CLC 43**
See also CA 49-52; CANR 2, 18, 33, 54; CLR 12; DLB 14, 161, 231; MAICYA; MTCW 1; SAAS 9; SATA 39, 76; SATA-Brief 28

Gardner, Herb(ert) 1934- .... **CLC 44**
See also CA 149

Gardner, John (Champlin), Jr. 1933-1982 . **CLC 2, 3, 5, 7, 8, 10, 18, 28, 34; DAM NOV, POP; SSC 7**
See also AITN 1; CA 65-68; 107; CANR 33, 73; CDALBS; DA3; DLB 2; DLBY 82; MTCW 1; SATA 40; SATA-Obit 31

Gardner, John (Edmund) 1926- .... **CLC 30; DAM POP**
See also CA 103; CANR 15, 69; MTCW 1

Gardner, Miriam
See Bradley, Marion Zimmer

Gardner, Noel
See Kuttner, Henry

Gardons, S. S.
See Snodgrass, W(illiam) D(e Witt)

Garfield, Leon 1921-1996 .... **CLC 12**
See also AAYA 8; CA 17-20R; 152; CANR 38, 41, 78; CLR 21; DLB 161; JRDA; MAICYA; SATA 1, 32, 76; SATA-Obit 90

Garland, (Hannibal) Hamlin 1860-1940 .... **TCLC 3; SSC 18**
See also CA 104; DLB 12, 71, 78, 186

Garneau, (Hector de) Saint-Denys 1912-1943 .... **TCLC 13**
See also CA 111; DLB 88

Garner, Alan 1934- .... **CLC 17; DAB; DAM POP**
See also AAYA 18; CA 73-76, 178; CAAE 178; CANR 15, 64; CLR 20; DLB 161; MAICYA; MTCW 1, 2; SATA 18, 69; SATA-Essay 108

Garner, Hugh 1913-1979 .... **CLC 13**
See also CA 69-72; CANR 31; DLB 68

Garnett, David 1892-1981 .... **CLC 3**
See also CA 5-8R; 103; CANR 17, 79; DLB 34; MTCW 2
Garos, Stephanie
See Katz, Steve
Garrett, George (Palmer) 1929- . **CLC 3, 11, 51; SSC 30**
See also CA 1-4R; CAAS 5; CANR 1, 42, 67; DLB 2, 5, 130, 152; DLBY 83
Garrick, David 1717-1779 ...... **LC 15; DAM DRAM**
See also DLB 84
Garrigue, Jean 1914-1972 .... **CLC 2, 8**
See also CA 5-8R; 37-40R; CANR 20
Garrison, Frederick
See Sinclair, Upton (Beall)
Garro, Elena 1920(?)-1998
See also CA 131; 169; DLB 145; HLCS 1; HW 1
Garth, Will
See Hamilton, Edmond; Kuttner, Henry
Garvey, Marcus (Moziah, Jr.) 1887-1940 .... **TCLC 41; BLC 2; DAM MULT**
See also BW 1; CA 120; 124; CANR 79
Gary, Romain .... **CLC 25**
See also Kacew, Romain
See also DLB 83
Gascar, Pierre .... **CLC 11**
See also Fournier, Pierre
Gascoyne, David (Emery) 1916- ..... **CLC 45**
See also CA 65-68; CANR 10, 28, 54; DLB 20; MTCW 1
Gaskell, Elizabeth Cleghorn 1810-1865 .. **NCLC 70; DAB; DAM MST; SSC 25**
See also CDBLB 1832-1890; DLB 21, 144, 159
Gass, William H(oward) 1924- . **CLC 1, 2, 8, 11, 15, 39, 132; SSC 12**
See also CA 17-20R; CANR 30, 71; DLB 2, 227; MTCW 1, 2
Gassendi, Pierre 1592-1655 .... **LC 54**
Gasset, Jose Ortega y
See Ortega y Gasset, Jose
Gates, Henry Louis, Jr. 1950- .... **CLC 65; BLCS; DAM MULT**
See also BW 2, 3; CA 109; CANR 25, 53, 75; DA3; DLB 67; MTCW 1
Gautier, Theophile 1811-1872 . **NCLC 1, 59; DAM POET; PC 18; SSC 20**
See also DLB 119
Gawsworth, John
See Bates, H(erbert) E(rnest)
Gay, John 1685-1732 . **LC 49; DAM DRAM**
See also DLB 84, 95
Gay, Oliver
See Gogarty, Oliver St. John
Gaye, Marvin (Penze) 1939-1984 .... **CLC 26**
See also CA 112
Gebler, Carlo (Ernest) 1954- .... **CLC 39**
See also CA 119; 133
Gee, Maggie (Mary) 1948- .... **CLC 57**
See also CA 130; DLB 207
Gee, Maurice (Gough) 1931- .... **CLC 29**
See also CA 97-100; CANR 67; CLR 56; SATA 46, 101
Gelbart, Larry (Simon) 1928- ... **CLC 21, 61**
See also Gelbart, Larry
See also CA 73-76; CANR 45
Gelbart, Larry 1928-
See Gelbart, Larry (Simon)
Gelber, Jack 1932- .... **CLC 1, 6, 14, 79**
See also CA 1-4R; CANR 2; DLB 7, 228
Gellhorn, Martha (Ellis) 1908-1998 .... **CLC 14, 60**
See also CA 77-80; 164; CANR 44; DLBY 82, 98
Genet, Jean 1910-1986 . **CLC 1, 2, 5, 10, 14, 44, 46; DAM DRAM**

See also CA 13-16R; CANR 18; DA3; DLB 72; DLBY 86; MTCW 1, 2
Gent, Peter 1942- .... **CLC 29**
See also AITN 1; CA 89-92; DLBY 82
Gentile, Giovanni 1875-1944 .... **TCLC 96**
See also CA 119
Gentlewoman in New England, A
See Bradstreet, Anne
Gentlewoman in Those Parts, A
See Bradstreet, Anne
George, Jean Craighead 1919- .... **CLC 35**
See also AAYA 8; CA 5-8R; CANR 25; CLR 1; DLB 52; JRDA; MAICYA; SATA 2, 68
George, Stefan (Anton) 1868-1933 . **TCLC 2, 14**
See also CA 104
Georges, Georges Martin
See Simenon, Georges (Jacques Christian)
Gerhardi, William Alexander
See Gerhardie, William Alexander
Gerhardie, William Alexander 1895-1977 .... **CLC 5**
See also CA 25-28R; 73-76; CANR 18; DLB 36
Gerstler, Amy 1956- .... **CLC 70**
See also CA 146
Gertler, T. .... **CLC 134**
See also CA 116; 121
Ghalib .... **NCLC 39, 78**
See also Ghalib, Hsadullah Khan
Ghalib, Hsadullah Khan 1797-1869
See Ghalib
See also DAM POET
Ghelderode, Michel de 1898-1962 ... **CLC 6, 11; DAM DRAM**
See also CA 85-88; CANR 40, 77
Ghiselin, Brewster 1903- .... **CLC 23**
See also CA 13-16R; CAAS 10; CANR 13
Ghose, Aurabinda 1872-1950 .... **TCLC 63**
See also CA 163
Ghose, Zulfikar 1935- .... **CLC 42**
See also CA 65-68; CANR 67
Ghosh, Amitav 1956- .... **CLC 44**
See also CA 147; CANR 80
Giacosa, Giuseppe 1847-1906 .... **TCLC 7**
See also CA 104
Gibb, Lee
See Waterhouse, Keith (Spencer)
Gibbon, Lewis Grassic 1901-1935 .. **TCLC 4**
See also Mitchell, James Leslie
Gibbons, Kaye 1960- ...... **CLC 50, 88; DAM POP**
See also AAYA 34; CA 151; CANR 75; DA3; MTCW 1; SATA 117
Gibran, Kahlil 1883-1931 . **TCLC 1, 9; DAM POET, POP; PC 9**
See also CA 104; 150; DA3; MTCW 2
Gibran, Khalil
See Gibran, Kahlil
Gibson, William 1914- . **CLC 23; DA; DAB; DAC; DAM DRAM, MST**
See also CA 9-12R; CANR 9, 42, 75; DLB 7; MTCW 1; SATA 66
Gibson, William (Ford) 1948- . **CLC 39, 63; DAM POP**
See also AAYA 12; CA 126; 133; CANR 52, 90; DA3; MTCW 1
Gide, Andre (Paul Guillaume) 1869-1951 .... **TCLC 5, 12, 36; DA; DAB; DAC; DAM MST, NOV; SSC 13; WLC**
See also CA 104; 124; DA3; DLB 65; MTCW 1, 2
Gifford, Barry (Colby) 1946- .... **CLC 34**
See also CA 65-68; CANR 9, 30, 40, 90
Gilbert, Frank
See De Voto, Bernard (Augustine)

Gilbert, W(illiam) S(chwenck) 1836-1911 .... **TCLC 3; DAM DRAM, POET**
See also CA 104; 173; SATA 36
Gilbreth, Frank B., Jr. 1911- .... **CLC 17**
See also CA 9-12R; SATA 2
Gilchrist, Ellen 1935- ..... **CLC 34, 48; DAM POP; SSC 14**
See also CA 113; 116; CANR 41, 61; DLB 130; MTCW 1, 2
Giles, Molly 1942- .... **CLC 39**
See also CA 126
Gill, Eric 1882-1940 .... **TCLC 85**
Gill, Patrick
See Creasey, John
Gilliam, Terry (Vance) 1940- .... **CLC 21**
See also Monty Python
See also AAYA 19; CA 108; 113; CANR 35; INT 113
Gillian, Jerry
See Gilliam, Terry (Vance)
Gilliatt, Penelope (Ann Douglass) 1932-1993 .... **CLC 2, 10, 13, 53**
See also AITN 2; CA 13-16R; 141; CANR 49; DLB 14
Gilman, Charlotte (Anna) Perkins (Stetson) 1860-1935 .... **TCLC 9, 37; SSC 13**
See also CA 106; 150; DLB 221; MTCW 1
Gilmour, David 1949- .... **CLC 35**
See also CA 138; 147
Gilpin, William 1724-1804 .... **NCLC 30**
Gilray, J. D.
See Mencken, H(enry) L(ouis)
Gilroy, Frank D(aniel) 1925- .... **CLC 2**
See also CA 81-84; CANR 32, 64, 86; DLB 7
Gilstrap, John 1957(?)- .... **CLC 99**
See also CA 160
Ginsberg, Allen 1926-1997 ... **CLC 1, 2, 3, 4, 6, 13, 36, 69, 109; DA; DAB; DAC; DAM MST, POET; PC 4; WLC**
See also AAYA 33; AITN 1; CA 1-4R; 157; CANR 2, 41, 63; CDALB 1941-1968; DA3; DLB 5, 16, 169; MTCW 1, 2
Ginzburg, Natalia 1916-1991 ..... **CLC 5, 11, 54, 70**
See also CA 85-88; 135; CANR 33; DLB 177; MTCW 1, 2
Giono, Jean 1895-1970 .... **CLC 4, 11**
See also CA 45-48; 29-32R; CANR 2, 35; DLB 72; MTCW 1
Giovanni, Nikki 1943- ...... **CLC 2, 4, 19, 64, 117; BLC 2; DA; DAB; DAC; DAM MST, MULT, POET; PC 19; WLCS**
See also AAYA 22; AITN 1; BW 2, 3; CA 29-32R; CAAS 6; CANR 18, 41, 60, 91; CDALBS; CLR 6; DA3; DLB 5, 41; INT CANR-18; MAICYA; MTCW 1, 2; SATA 24, 107
Giovene, Andrea 1904- .... **CLC 7**
See also CA 85-88
Gippius, Zinaida (Nikolayevna) 1869-1945
See Hippius, Zinaida
See also CA 106
Giraudoux, (Hippolyte) Jean 1882-1944 .... **TCLC 2, 7; DAM DRAM**
See also CA 104; DLB 65
Gironella, Jose Maria 1917- .... **CLC 11**
See also CA 101
Gissing, George (Robert) 1857-1903 .... **TCLC 3, 24, 47; SSC 37**
See also CA 105; 167; DLB 18, 135, 184
Giurlani, Aldo
See Palazzeschi, Aldo
Gladkov, Fyodor (Vasilyevich) 1883-1958 .... **TCLC 27**
See also CA 170
Glanville, Brian (Lester) 1931- .... **CLC 6**
See also CA 5-8R; CAAS 9; CANR 3, 70; DLB 15, 139; SATA 42**

Graham, Winston (Mawdsley) 1910-
.... **CLC 23**
See also CA 49-52; CANR 2, 22, 45, 66;
DLB 77

Grahame, Kenneth 1859-1932 ..... **TCLC 64;**
DAB
See also CA 108; 136; CANR 80; CLR 5;
DA3; DLB 34, 141, 178; MAICYA;
MTCW 2; SATA 100; YABC 1

Granovsky, Timofei Nikolaevich 1813-1855
.... **NCLC 75**
See also DLB 198

Grant, Skeeter
See Spiegelman, Art

Granville-Barker, Harley 1877-1946
.... **TCLC 2; DAM DRAM**
See also Barker, Harley Granville
See also CA 104

Grass, Guenter (Wilhelm) 1927- . **CLC 1, 2,**
4, 6, 11, 15, 22, 32, 49, 88; DA; DAB;
DAC; DAM MST, NOV; WLC
See also CA 13-16R; CANR 20, 75, 93;
DA3; DLB 75, 124; MTCW 1, 2

Gratton, Thomas
See Hulme, T(homas) E(rnest)

Grau, Shirley Ann 1929- . **CLC 4, 9; SSC 15**
See also CA 89-92; CANR 22, 69; DLB 2;
INT CANR-22; MTCW 1

Gravel, Fern
See Hall, James Norman

Graver, Elizabeth 1964- .... **CLC 70**
See also CA 135; CANR 71

Graves, Richard Perceval 1945- ..... **CLC 44**
See also CA 65-68; CANR 9, 26, 51

Graves, Robert (von Ranke) 1895-1985
.... **CLC 1, 2, 6, 11, 39, 44, 45; DAB;**
DAC; DAM MST, POET; PC 6
See also CA 5-8R; 117; CANR 5, 36; CD-
BLB 1914-1945; DA3; DLB 20, 100, 191;
DLBD 18; DLBY 85; MTCW 1, 2; SATA
45

Graves, Valerie
See Bradley, Marion Zimmer

Gray, Alasdair (James) 1934- .... **CLC 41**
See also CA 126; CANR 47, 69; DLB 194;
INT 126; MTCW 1, 2

Gray, Amlin 1946- .... **CLC 29**
See also CA 138

Gray, Francine du Plessix 1930- ... **CLC 22;**
DAM NOV
See also BEST 90:3; CA 61-64; CAAS 2;
CANR 11, 33, 75, 81; INT CANR-11;
MTCW 1, 2

Gray, John (Henry) 1866-1934 ..... **TCLC 19**
See also CA 119; 162

Gray, Simon (James Holliday) 1936-
.... **CLC 9, 14, 36**
See also AITN 1; CA 21-24R; CAAS 3;
CANR 32, 69; DLB 13; MTCW 1

Gray, Spalding 1941- ... **CLC 49, 112; DAM**
POP; DC 7
See also CA 128; CANR 74; MTCW 2

Gray, Thomas 1716-1771 ...... **LC 4, 40; DA;**
DAB; DAC; DAM MST; PC 2; WLC
See also CDBLB 1660-1789; DA3; DLB
109

Grayson, David
See Baker, Ray Stannard

Grayson, Richard (A.) 1951- .... **CLC 38**
See also CA 85-88; CANR 14, 31, 57; DLB
234

Greeley, Andrew M(oran) 1928- .... **CLC 28;**
DAM POP
See also CA 5-8R; CAAS 7; CANR 7, 43,
69; DA3; MTCW 1, 2

Green, Anna Katharine 1846-1935
.... **TCLC 63**
See also CA 112; 159; DLB 202, 221

Green, Brian
See Card, Orson Scott

Green, Hannah
See Greenberg, Joanne (Goldenberg)

Green, Hannah 1927(?)-1996 .... **CLC 3**
See also CA 73-76; CANR 59, 93

Green, Henry 1905-1973 .... **CLC 2, 13, 97**
See also Yorke, Henry Vincent
See also CA 175; DLB 15

Green, Julian (Hartridge) 1900-1998
See Green, Julien
See also CA 21-24R; 169; CANR 33, 87;
DLB 4, 72; MTCW 1

Green, Julien .... **CLC 3, 11, 77**
See also Green, Julian (Hartridge)
See also MTCW 2

Green, Paul (Eliot) 1894-1981 .... **CLC 25;**
DAM DRAM
See also AITN 1; CA 5-8R; 103; CANR 3;
DLB 7, 9; DLBY 81

Greenberg, Ivan 1908-1973
See Rahv, Philip
See also CA 85-88

Greenberg, Joanne (Goldenberg) 1932-
.... **CLC 7, 30**
See also AAYA 12; CA 5-8R; CANR 14,
32, 69; SATA 25

Greenberg, Richard 1959(?)- .... **CLC 57**
See also CA 138

Greene, Bette 1934- .... **CLC 30**
See also AAYA 7; CA 53-56; CANR 4; CLR
2; JRDA; MAICYA; SAAS 16; SATA 8,
102

Greene, Gael .... **CLC 8**
See also CA 13-16R; CANR 10

Greene, Graham (Henry) 1904-1991
... **CLC 1, 3, 6, 9, 14, 18, 27, 37, 70, 72,**
125; DA; DAB; DAC; DAM MST, NOV;
SSC 29; WLC
See also AITN 2; CA 13-16R; 133; CANR
35, 61; CDBLB 1945-1960; DA3; DLB
13, 15, 77, 100, 162, 201, 204; DLBY 91;
MTCW 1, 2; SATA 20

Greene, Robert 1558-1592 .... **LC 41**
See also DLB 62, 167

Greer, Germaine 1939- .... **CLC 131**
See also AITN 1; CA 81-84; CANR 33, 70;
MTCW 1, 2

Greer, Richard
See Silverberg, Robert

Gregor, Arthur 1923- .... **CLC 9**
See also CA 25-28R; CAAS 10; CANR 11;
SATA 36

Gregor, Lee
See Pohl, Frederik

Gregory, Isabella Augusta (Persse)
1852-1932 .... **TCLC 1**
See also CA 104; 184; DLB 10

Gregory, J. Dennis
See Williams, John A(lfred)

Grendon, Stephen
See Derleth, August (William)

Grenville, Kate 1950- .... **CLC 61**
See also CA 118; CANR 53, 93

Grenville, Pelham
See Wodehouse, P(elham) G(renville)

Greve, Felix Paul (Berthold Friedrich)
1879-1948
See Grove, Frederick Philip
See also CA 104; 141, 175; CANR 79;
DAC; DAM MST

Grey, Zane 1872-1939 . **TCLC 6; DAM POP**
See also CA 104; 132; DA3; DLB 212;
MTCW 1, 2

Grieg, (Johan) Nordahl (Brun) 1902-1943
.... **TCLC 10**
See also CA 107

Grieve, C(hristopher) M(urray) 1892-1978
.... **CLC 11, 19; DAM POET**

See also MacDiarmid, Hugh; Pteleon
See also CA 5-8R; 85-88; CANR 33;
MTCW 1

Griffin, Gerald 1803-1840 .... **NCLC 7**
See also DLB 159

Griffin, John Howard 1920-1980 .... **CLC 68**
See also AITN 1; CA 1-4R; 101; CANR 2

Griffin, Peter 1942- .... **CLC 39**
See also CA 136

Griffith, D(avid Lewelyn) W(ark)
1875(?)-1948 .... **TCLC 68**
See also CA 119; 150; CANR 80

Griffith, Lawrence
See Griffith, D(avid Lewelyn) W(ark)

Griffiths, Trevor 1935- .... **CLC 13, 52**
See also CA 97-100; CANR 45; DLB 13

Griggs, Sutton (Elbert) 1872-1930 . **TCLC 77**
See also CA 123; 186; DLB 50

Grigson, Geoffrey (Edward Harvey)
1905-1985 .... **CLC 7, 39**
See also CA 25-28R; 118; CANR 20, 33;
DLB 27; MTCW 1, 2

Grillparzer, Franz 1791-1872 . **NCLC 1; DC**
14; SSC 37
See also DLB 133

Grimble, Reverend Charles James
See Eliot, T(homas) S(tearns)

Grimke, Charlotte L(ottie) Forten
1837(?)-1914
See Forten, Charlotte L.
See also BW 1; CA 117; 124; DAM MULT,
POET

Grimm, Jacob Ludwig Karl 1785-1863
.... **NCLC 3, 77; SSC 36**
See also DLB 90; MAICYA; SATA 22

Grimm, Wilhelm Karl 1786-1859 . **NCLC 3,**
77; SSC 36
See also DLB 90; MAICYA; SATA 22

Grimmelshausen, Johann Jakob Christoffel
von 1621-1676 .... **LC 6**
See also DLB 168

Grindel, Eugene 1895-1952
See Eluard, Paul
See also CA 104

Grisham, John 1955- .. **CLC 84; DAM POP**
See also AAYA 14; CA 138; CANR 47, 69;
DA3; MTCW 2

Grossman, David 1954- .... **CLC 67**
See also CA 138

Grossman, Vasily (Semenovich) 1905-1964
.... **CLC 41**
See also CA 124; 130; MTCW 1

Grove, Frederick Philip .... **TCLC 4**
See also Greve, Felix Paul (Berthold
Friedrich)
See also DLB 92

Grubb
See Crumb, R(obert)

Grumbach, Doris (Isaac) 1918- ...... **CLC 13,**
22, 64
See also CA 5-8R; CAAS 2; CANR 9, 42,
70; INT CANR-9; MTCW 2

Grundtvig, Nicolai Frederik Severin
1783-1872 .... **NCLC 1**

Grunge
See Crumb, R(obert)

Grunwald, Lisa 1959- .... **CLC 44**
See also CA 120

Guare, John 1938- . **CLC 8, 14, 29, 67; DAM**
DRAM
See also CA 73-76; CANR 21, 69; DLB 7;
MTCW 1, 2

Gudjonsson, Halldor Kiljan 1902-1998
See Laxness, Halldor
See also CA 103; 164

Guenter, Erich
See Eich, Guenter

Guest, Barbara 1920- .... **CLC 34**

See also CA 25-28R; CANR 11, 44, 84;
DLB 5, 193

Guest, Edgar A(lbert) 1881-1959 . **TCLC 95**
See also CA 112; 168

Guest, Judith (Ann) 1936- .... **CLC 8, 30;
DAM NOV, POP**
See also AAYA 7; CA 77-80; CANR 15,
75; DA3; INT CANR-15; MTCW 1, 2

Guevara, Che .... **CLC 87; HLC 1**
See also Guevara (Serna), Ernesto

Guevara (Serna), Ernesto 1928-1967
.... **CLC 87; DAM MULT; HLC 1**
See also Guevara, Che
See also CA 127; 111; CANR 56; HW 1

Guicciardini, Francesco 1483-1540 ... **LC 49**

Guild, Nicholas M. 1944- .... **CLC 33**
See also CA 93-96

Guillemin, Jacques
See Sartre, Jean-Paul

Guillen, Jorge 1893-1984 ..... **CLC 11; DAM
MULT, POET; HLCS 1**
See also CA 89-92; 112; DLB 108; HW 1

Guillen, Nicolas (Cristobal) 1902-1989
.... **CLC 48, 79; BLC 2; DAM MST,
MULT, POET; HLC 1; PC 23**
See also BW 2; CA 116; 125; 129; CANR
84; HW 1

Guillevic, (Eugene) 1907- .... **CLC 33**
See also CA 93-96

Guillois
See Desnos, Robert

Guillois, Valentin
See Desnos, Robert

Guimaraes Rosa, Joao 1908-1967
See also CA 175; HLCS 2

Guiney, Louise Imogen 1861-1920 . **TCLC 41**
See also CA 160; DLB 54

Guiraldes, Ricardo (Guillermo) 1886-1927
.... **TCLC 39**
See also CA 131; HW 1; MTCW 1

Gumilev, Nikolai (Stepanovich) 1886-1921
.... **TCLC 60**
See also CA 165

Gunesekera, Romesh 1954- .... **CLC 91**
See also CA 159

Gunn, Bill .... **CLC 5**
See also Gunn, William Harrison
See also DLB 38

Gunn, Thom(son William) 1929- . **CLC 3, 6,
18, 32, 81; DAM POET; PC 26**
See also CA 17-20R; CANR 9, 33; CDBLB
1960 to Present; DLB 27; INT CANR-33;
MTCW 1

Gunn, William Harrison 1934(?)-1989
See Gunn, Bill
See also AITN 1; BW 1, 3; CA 13-16R;
128; CANR 12, 25, 76

Gunnars, Kristjana 1948- .... **CLC 69**
See also CA 113; DLB 60

Gurdjieff, G(eorgei) I(vanovich)
1877(?)-1949 .... **TCLC 71**
See also CA 157

Gurganus, Allan 1947- . **CLC 70; DAM POP**
See also BEST 90:1; CA 135

Gurney, A(lbert) R(amsdell), Jr. 1930-
.... **CLC 32, 50, 54; DAM DRAM**
See also CA 77-80; CANR 32, 64

Gurney, Ivor (Bertie) 1890-1937 .. **TCLC 33**
See also CA 167

Gurney, Peter
See Gurney, A(lbert) R(amsdell), Jr.

Guro, Elena 1877-1913 .... **TCLC 56**

Gustafson, James M(oody) 1925- . **CLC 100**
See also CA 25-28R; CANR 37

Gustafson, Ralph (Barker) 1909- ... **CLC 36**
See also CA 21-24R; CANR 8, 45, 84; DLB
88

Gut, Gom
See Simenon, Georges (Jacques Christian)

Guterson, David 1956- .... **CLC 91**
See also CA 132; CANR 73; MTCW 2

Guthrie, A(lfred) B(ertram), Jr. 1901-1991
.... **CLC 23**
See also CA 57-60; 134; CANR 24; DLB
212; SATA 62; SATA-Obit 67

Guthrie, Isobel
See Grieve, C(hristopher) M(urray)

Guthrie, Woodrow Wilson 1912-1967
See Guthrie, Woody
See also CA 113; 93-96

Guthrie, Woody .... **CLC 35**
See also Guthrie, Woodrow Wilson

Gutierrez Najera, Manuel 1859-1895
See also HLCS 2

Guy, Rosa (Cuthbert) 1928- .... **CLC 26**
See also AAYA 4; BW 2; CA 17-20R;
CANR 14, 34, 83; CLR 13; DLB 33;
JRDA; MAICYA; SATA 14, 62

Gwendolyn
See Bennett, (Enoch) Arnold

H. D. .... **CLC 3, 8, 14, 31, 34, 73; PC 5**
See also Doolittle, Hilda

H. de V.
See Buchan, John

Haavikko, Paavo Juhani 1931- . **CLC 18, 34**
See also CA 106

Habbema, Koos
See Heijermans, Herman

Habermas, Juergen 1929- .... **CLC 104**
See also CA 109; CANR 85

Habermas, Jurgen
See Habermas, Juergen

Hacker, Marilyn 1942- ..... **CLC 5, 9, 23, 72,
91; DAM POET**
See also CA 77-80; CANR 68; DLB 120

Haeckel, Ernst Heinrich (Philipp August)
1834-1919 .... **TCLC 83**
See also CA 157

Hafiz c. 1326-1389(?) .... **CMLC 34**

Hafiz c. 1326-1389 .... **CMLC 34**

Haggard, H(enry) Rider 1856-1925
.... **TCLC 11**
See also CA 108; 148; DLB 70, 156, 174,
178; MTCW 2; SATA 16

Hagiosy, L.
See Larbaud, Valery (Nicolas)

Hagiwara Sakutaro 1886-1942 .... **TCLC 60;
PC 18**

Haig, Fenil
See Ford, Ford Madox

Haig-Brown, Roderick (Langmere)
1908-1976 .... **CLC 21**
See also CA 5-8R; 69-72; CANR 4, 38, 83;
CLR 31; DLB 88; MAICYA; SATA 12

Hailey, Arthur 1920- .... **CLC 5; DAM NOV,
POP**
See also AITN 2; BEST 90:3; CA 1-4R;
CANR 2, 36, 75; DLB 88; DLBY 82;
MTCW 1, 2

Hailey, Elizabeth Forsythe 1938- .... **CLC 40**
See also CA 93-96; CAAS 1; CANR 15,
48; INT CANR-15

Haines, John (Meade) 1924- .... **CLC 58**
See also CA 17-20R; CANR 13, 34; DLB
212

Hakluyt, Richard 1552-1616 .... **LC 31**

Haldeman, Joe (William) 1943- ...... **CLC 61**
See also Graham, Robert
See also CA 53-56, 179; CAAE 179; CAAS
25; CANR 6, 70, 72; DLB 8; INT
CANR-6

Hale, Sarah Josepha (Buell) 1788-1879
.... **NCLC 75**
See also DLB 1, 42, 73

Haley, Alex(ander Murray Palmer)
1921-1992 . **CLC 8, 12, 76; BLC 2; DA;
DAB; DAC; DAM MST, MULT, POP**
See also AAYA 26; BW 2, 3; CA 77-80;
136; CANR 61; CDALBS; DA3; DLB 38;
MTCW 1, 2

Haliburton, Thomas Chandler 1796-1865
.... **NCLC 15**
See also DLB 11, 99

Hall, Donald (Andrew, Jr.) 1928- .... **CLC 1,
13, 37, 59; DAM POET**
See also CA 5-8R; CAAS 7; CANR 2, 44,
64; DLB 5; MTCW 1; SATA 23, 97

Hall, Frederic Sauser
See Sauser-Hall, Frederic

Hall, James
See Kuttner, Henry

Hall, James Norman 1887-1951 ... **TCLC 23**
See also CA 123; 173; SATA 21

Hall, Radclyffe -1943
See Hall, (Marguerite) Radclyffe
See also MTCW 2

Hall, (Marguerite) Radclyffe 1886-1943
.... **TCLC 12**
See also CA 110; 150; CANR 83; DLB 191

Hall, Rodney 1935- .... **CLC 51**
See also CA 109; CANR 69

Halleck, Fitz-Greene 1790-1867 ... **NCLC 47**
See also DLB 3

Halliday, Michael
See Creasey, John

Halpern, Daniel 1945- .... **CLC 14**
See also CA 33-36R; CANR 93

Hamburger, Michael (Peter Leopold) 1924-
.... **CLC 5, 14**
See also CA 5-8R; CAAS 4; CANR 2, 47;
DLB 27

Hamill, Pete 1935- .... **CLC 10**
See also CA 25-28R; CANR 18, 71

Hamilton, Alexander 1755(?)-1804
.... **NCLC 49**
See also DLB 37

Hamilton, Clive
See Lewis, C(live) S(taples)

Hamilton, Edmond 1904-1977 .... **CLC 1**
See also CA 1-4R; CANR 3, 84; DLB 8;
SATA 118

Hamilton, Eugene (Jacob) Lee
See Lee-Hamilton, Eugene (Jacob)

Hamilton, Franklin
See Silverberg, Robert

Hamilton, Gail
See Corcoran, Barbara

Hamilton, Mollie
See Kaye, M(ary) M(argaret)

Hamilton, (Anthony Walter) Patrick
1904-1962 .... **CLC 51**
See also CA 176; 113; DLB 191

Hamilton, Virginia 1936- ..... **CLC 26; DAM
MULT**
See also AAYA 2, 21; BW 2, 3; CA 25-28R;
CANR 20, 37, 73; CLR 1, 11, 40; DLB
33, 52; INT CANR-20; JRDA; MAICYA;
MTCW 1, 2; SATA 4, 56, 79

Hammett, (Samuel) Dashiell 1894-1961
.... **CLC 3, 5, 10, 19, 47; SSC 17**
See also AITN 1; CA 81-84; CANR 42;
CDALB 1929-1941; DA3; DLB 226;
DLBD 6; DLBY 96; MTCW 1, 2

Hammon, Jupiter 1711(?)-1800(?) . **NCLC 5;
BLC 2; DAM MULT, POET; PC 16**
See also DLB 31, 50

Hammond, Keith
See Kuttner, Henry

Hamner, Earl (Henry), Jr. 1923- .... **CLC 12**
See also AITN 2; CA 73-76; DLB 6

Hampton, Christopher (James) 1946-
.... **CLC 4**
See also CA 25-28R; DLB 13; MTCW 1

Higgins, George V(incent) 1939-1999
.... **CLC 4, 7, 10, 18**
See also CA 77-80; 186; CAAS 5; CANR
17, 51, 89; DLB 2; DLBY 81, 98; INT
CANR-17; MTCW 1

Higginson, Thomas Wentworth 1823-1911
.... **TCLC 36**
See also CA 162; DLB 1, 64

Highet, Helen
See MacInnes, Helen (Clark)

Highsmith, (Mary) Patricia 1921-1995
...... **CLC 2, 4, 14, 42, 102; DAM NOV,
POP**
See also CA 1-4R; 147; CANR 1, 20, 48,
62; DA3; MTCW 1, 2

Highwater, Jamake (Mamake) 1942(?)-
.... **CLC 12**
See also AAYA 7; CA 65-68; CAAS 7;
CANR 10, 34, 84; CLR 17; DLB 52;
DLBY 85; JRDA; MAICYA; SATA 32,
69; SATA-Brief 30

Highway, Tomson 1951- ...... **CLC 92; DAC;
DAM MULT**
See also CA 151; CANR 75; MTCW 2;
NNAL

Hijuelos, Oscar 1951- .... **CLC 65; DAM
MULT, POP; HLC 1**
See also AAYA 25; BEST 90:1; CA 123;
CANR 50, 75; DA3; DLB 145; HW 1, 2;
MTCW 2

Hikmet, Nazim 1902(?)-1963 .... **CLC 40**
See also CA 141; 93-96

Hildegard von Bingen 1098-1179 . **CMLC 20**
See also DLB 148

Hildesheimer, Wolfgang 1916-1991 . **CLC 49**
See also CA 101; 135; DLB 69, 124

Hill, Geoffrey (William) 1932- ..... **CLC 5, 8,
18, 45; DAM POET**
See also CA 81-84; CANR 21, 89; CDBLB
1960 to Present; DLB 40; MTCW 1

Hill, George Roy 1921- .... **CLC 26**
See also CA 110; 122

Hill, John
See Koontz, Dean R(ay)

Hill, Susan (Elizabeth) 1942- ... **CLC 4, 113;
DAB; DAM MST, NOV**
See also CA 33-36R; CANR 29, 69; DLB
14, 139; MTCW 1

Hillerman, Tony 1925- . **CLC 62; DAM POP**
See also AAYA 6; BEST 89:1; CA 29-32R;
CANR 21, 42, 65; DA3; DLB 206; SATA
6

Hillesum, Etty 1914-1943 .... **TCLC 49**
See also CA 137

Hilliard, Noel (Harvey) 1929- .... **CLC 15**
See also CA 9-12R; CANR 7, 69

Hillis, Rick 1956- .... **CLC 66**
See also CA 134

Hilton, James 1900-1954 .... **TCLC 21**
See also CA 108; 169; DLB 34, 77; SATA
34

Himes, Chester (Bomar) 1909-1984 . **CLC 2,
4, 7, 18, 58, 108; BLC 2; DAM MULT**
See also BW 2; CA 25-28R; 114; CANR
22, 89; DLB 2, 76, 143, 226; MTCW 1, 2

Hinde, Thomas .... **CLC 6, 11**
See also Chitty, Thomas Willes

Hine, (William) Daryl 1936- .... **CLC 15**
See also CA 1-4R; CAAS 15; CANR 1, 20;
DLB 60

Hinkson, Katharine Tynan
See Tynan, Katharine

Hinojosa(-Smith), Rolando (R.) 1929-
See also CA 131; CAAS 16; CANR 62;
DAM MULT; DLB 82; HLC 1; HW 1, 2;
MTCW 2

Hinton, S(usan) E(loise) 1950- . **CLC 30, 111;
DA; DAB; DAC; DAM MST, NOV**

See also AAYA 2, 33; CA 81-84; CANR
32, 62, 92; CDALBS; CLR 3, 23; DA3;
JRDA; MAICYA; MTCW 1, 2; SATA 19,
58, 115

Hippius, Zinaida .... **TCLC 9**
See also Gippius, Zinaida (Nikolayevna)

Hiraoka, Kimitake 1925-1970
See Mishima, Yukio
See also CA 97-100; 29-32R; DAM DRAM;
DA3; MTCW 1, 2

Hirsch, E(ric) D(onald), Jr. 1928- ... **CLC 79**
See also CA 25-28R; CANR 27, 51; DLB
67; INT CANR-27; MTCW 1

Hirsch, Edward 1950- .... **CLC 31, 50**
See also CA 104; CANR 20, 42; DLB 120

Hitchcock, Alfred (Joseph) 1899-1980
.... **CLC 16**
See also AAYA 22; CA 159; 97-100; SATA
27; SATA-Obit 24

Hitler, Adolf 1889-1945 .... **TCLC 53**
See also CA 117; 147

Hoagland, Edward 1932- .... **CLC 28**
See also CA 1-4R; CANR 2, 31, 57; DLB
6; SATA 51

Hoban, Russell (Conwell) 1925- . **CLC 7, 25;
DAM NOV**
See also CA 5-8R; CANR 23, 37, 66; CLR
3; DLB 52; MAICYA; MTCW 1, 2; SATA
1, 40, 78

Hobbes, Thomas 1588-1679 .... **LC 36**
See also DLB 151

Hobbs, Perry
See Blackmur, R(ichard) P(almer)

Hobson, Laura Z(ametkin) 1900-1986
.... **CLC 7, 25**
See also CA 17-20R; 118; CANR 55; DLB
28; SATA 52

Hoch, Edward D(entinger) 1930-
See Queen, Ellery
See also CA 29-32R; CANR 11, 27, 51

Hochhuth, Rolf 1931- . **CLC 4, 11, 18; DAM
DRAM**
See also CA 5-8R; CANR 33, 75; DLB 124;
MTCW 1, 2

Hochman, Sandra 1936- .... **CLC 3, 8**
See also CA 5-8R; DLB 5

Hochwaelder, Fritz 1911-1986 .... **CLC 36;
DAM DRAM**
See also CA 29-32R; 120; CANR 42;
MTCW 1

Hochwalder, Fritz
See Hochwaelder, Fritz

Hocking, Mary (Eunice) 1921- .... **CLC 13**
See also CA 101; CANR 18, 40

Hodgins, Jack 1938- .... **CLC 23**
See also CA 93-96; DLB 60

Hodgson, William Hope 1877(?)-1918
.... **TCLC 13**
See also CA 111; 164; DLB 70, 153, 156,
178; MTCW 2

Hoeg, Peter 1957- .... **CLC 95**
See also CA 151; CANR 75; DA3; MTCW
2

Hoffman, Alice 1952- . **CLC 51; DAM NOV**
See also CA 77-80; CANR 34, 66; MTCW
1, 2

Hoffman, Daniel (Gerard) 1923- ...... **CLC 6,
13, 23**
See also CA 1-4R; CANR 4; DLB 5

Hoffman, Stanley 1944- .... **CLC 5**
See also CA 77-80

Hoffman, William M(oses) 1939- .... **CLC 40**
See also CA 57-60; CANR 11, 71

Hoffmann, E(rnst) T(heodor) A(madeus)
1776-1822 .... **NCLC 2; SSC 13**
See also DLB 90; SATA 27

Hofmann, Gert 1931- .... **CLC 54**
See also CA 128

Hofmannsthal, Hugo von 1874-1929
.... **TCLC 11; DAM DRAM; DC 4**
See also CA 106; 153; DLB 81, 118

Hogan, Linda 1947- . **CLC 73; DAM MULT**
See also CA 120; CANR 45, 73; DLB 175;
NNAL

Hogarth, Charles
See Creasey, John

Hogarth, Emmett
See Polonsky, Abraham (Lincoln)

Hogg, James 1770-1835 .... **NCLC 4**
See also DLB 93, 116, 159

Holbach, Paul Henri Thiry Baron 1723-1789
.... **LC 14**

Holberg, Ludvig 1684-1754 .... **LC 6**

Holcroft, Thomas 1745-1809 .... **NCLC 85**
See also DLB 39, 89, 158

Holden, Ursula 1921- .... **CLC 18**
See also CA 101; CAAS 8; CANR 22

Holderlin, (Johann Christian) Friedrich
1770-1843 .... **NCLC 16; PC 4**

Holdstock, Robert
See Holdstock, Robert P.

Holdstock, Robert P. 1948- .... **CLC 39**
See also CA 131; CANR 81

Holland, Isabelle 1920- .... **CLC 21**
See also AAYA 11; CA 21-24R; 181; CAAE
181; CANR 10, 25, 47; CLR 57; JRDA;
MAICYA; SATA 8, 70; SATA-Essay 103

Holland, Marcus
See Caldwell, (Janet Miriam) Taylor
(Holland)

Hollander, John 1929- .... **CLC 2, 5, 8, 14**
See also CA 1-4R; CANR 1, 52; DLB 5;
SATA 13

Hollander, Paul
See Silverberg, Robert

Holleran, Andrew 1943(?)- .... **CLC 38**
See Garber, Eric
See also CA 144

Holley, Marietta 1836(?)-1926 ...... **TCLC 99**
See also CA 118; DLB 11

Hollinghurst, Alan 1954- .... **CLC 55, 91**
See also CA 114; DLB 207

Hollis, Jim
See Summers, Hollis (Spurgeon, Jr.)

Holly, Buddy 1936-1959 .... **TCLC 65**

Holmes, Gordon
See Shiel, M(atthew) P(hipps)

Holmes, John
See Souster, (Holmes) Raymond

Holmes, John Clellon 1926-1988 ..... **CLC 56**
See also CA 9-12R; 125; CANR 4; DLB 16

Holmes, Oliver Wendell, Jr. 1841-1935
.... **TCLC 77**
See also CA 114; 186

Holmes, Oliver Wendell 1809-1894
.... **NCLC 14, 81**
See also CDALB 1640-1865; DLB 1, 189,
235; SATA 34

Holmes, Raymond
See Souster, (Holmes) Raymond

Holt, Victoria
See Hibbert, Eleanor Alice Burford

Holub, Miroslav 1923-1998 .... **CLC 4**
See also CA 21-24R; 169; CANR 10; DLB
232

Homer c. 8th cent. B.C.- . **CMLC 1, 16; DA;
DAB; DAC; DAM MST, POET; PC 23;
WLCS**
See also DA3; DLB 176

Hongo, Garrett Kaoru 1951- .... **PC 23**
See also CA 133; CAAS 22; DLB 120

Honig, Edwin 1919- .... **CLC 33**
See also CA 5-8R; CAAS 8; CANR 4, 45;
DLB 5

Hood, Hugh (John Blagdon) 1928- . **CLC 15,
28; SSC 42**

Jakes, John (William) 1932- . **CLC 29; DAM NOV, POP**
See also AAYA 32; BEST 89:4; CA 57-60; CANR 10, 43, 66; DA3; DLBY 83; INT CANR-10; MTCW 1, 2; SATA 62

James, Andrew
See Kirkup, James

James, C(yril) L(ionel) R(obert) 1901-1989 .... **CLC 33; BLCS**
See also BW 2; CA 117; 125; 128; CANR 62; DLB 125; MTCW 1

James, Daniel (Lewis) 1911-1988
See Santiago, Danny
See also CA 174; 125

James, Dynely
See Mayne, William (James Carter)

James, Henry Sr. 1811-1882 .... **NCLC 53**

James, Henry 1843-1916 .... **TCLC 2, 11, 24, 40, 47, 64; DA; DAB; DAC; DAM MST, NOV; SSC 8, 32; WLC**
See also CA 104; 132; CDALB 1865-1917; DA3; DLB 12, 71, 74, 189; DLBD 13; MTCW 1, 2

James, M. R.
See James, Montague (Rhodes)
See also DLB 156

James, Montague (Rhodes) 1862-1936 .... **TCLC 6; SSC 16**
See also CA 104; DLB 201

James, P. D. 1920- .... **CLC 18, 46, 122**
See also White, Phyllis Dorothy James
See also BEST 90:2; CDBLB 1960 to Present; DLB 87; DLBD 17

James, Philip
See Moorcock, Michael (John)

James, William 1842-1910 ...... **TCLC 15, 32**
See also CA 109

James I 1394-1437 .... **LC 20**

Jameson, Anna 1794-1860 .... **NCLC 43**
See also DLB 99, 166

Jami, Nur al-Din 'Abd al-Rahman 1414-1492 .... **LC 9**

Jammes, Francis 1868-1938 .... **TCLC 75**

Jandl, Ernst 1925- .... **CLC 34**

Janowitz, Tama 1957- . **CLC 43; DAM POP**
See also CA 106; CANR 52, 89

Japrisot, Sebastien 1931- .... **CLC 90**

Jarrell, Randall 1914-1965 .. **CLC 1, 2, 6, 9, 13, 49; DAM POET**
See also CA 5-8R; 25-28R; CABS 2; CANR 6, 34; CDALB 1941-1968; CLR 6; DLB 48, 52; MAICYA; MTCW 1, 2; SATA 7

Jarry, Alfred 1873-1907 . **TCLC 2, 14; DAM DRAM; SSC 20**
See also CA 104; 153; DA3; DLB 192

Jawien, Andrzej
See John Paul II, Pope

Jaynes, Roderick
See Coen, Ethan

Jeake, Samuel, Jr.
See Aiken, Conrad (Potter)

Jean Paul 1763-1825 .... **NCLC 7**

Jefferies, (John) Richard 1848-1887 .... **NCLC 47**
See also DLB 98, 141; SATA 16

Jeffers, (John) Robinson 1887-1962 . **CLC 2, 3, 11, 15, 54; DA; DAC; DAM MST, POET; PC 17; WLC**
See also CA 85-88; CANR 35; CDALB 1917-1929; DLB 45, 212; MTCW 1, 2

Jefferson, Janet
See Mencken, H(enry) L(ouis)

Jefferson, Thomas 1743-1826 .... **NCLC 11**
See also CDALB 1640-1865; DA3; DLB 31

Jeffrey, Francis 1773-1850 .... **NCLC 33**
See also DLB 107

Jelakowitch, Ivan
See Heijermans, Herman

Jellicoe, (Patricia) Ann 1927- .... **CLC 27**
See also CA 85-88; DLB 13, 233

Jemyma
See Holley, Marietta

Jen, Gish .... **CLC 70**
See also Jen, Lillian

Jen, Lillian 1956(?)-
See Jen, Gish
See also CA 135; CANR 89

Jenkins, (John) Robin 1912- .... **CLC 52**
See also CA 1-4R; CANR 1; DLB 14

Jennings, Elizabeth (Joan) 1926- ..... **CLC 5, 14, 131**
See also CA 61-64; CAAS 5; CANR 8, 39, 66; DLB 27; MTCW 1; SATA 66

Jennings, Waylon 1937- .... **CLC 21**

Jensen, Johannes V. 1873-1950 ..... **TCLC 41**
See also CA 170

Jensen, Laura (Linnea) 1948- .... **CLC 37**
See also CA 103

Jerome, Jerome K(lapka) 1859-1927 .... **TCLC 23**
See also CA 119; 177; DLB 10, 34, 135

Jerrold, Douglas William 1803-1857 .... **NCLC 2**
See also DLB 158, 159

Jewett, (Theodora) Sarah Orne 1849-1909 .... **TCLC 1, 22; SSC 6**
See also CA 108; 127; CANR 71; DLB 12, 74, 221; SATA 15

Jewsbury, Geraldine (Endsor) 1812-1880 .... **NCLC 22**
See also DLB 21

Jhabvala, Ruth Prawer 1927- . **CLC 4, 8, 29, 94, 138; DAB; DAM NOV**
See also CA 1-4R; CANR 2, 29, 51, 74, 91; DLB 139, 194; INT CANR-29; MTCW 1, 2

Jibran, Kahlil
See Gibran, Kahlil

Jibran, Khalil
See Gibran, Kahlil

Jiles, Paulette 1943- .... **CLC 13, 58**
See also CA 101; CANR 70

Jimenez (Mantecon), Juan Ramon 1881-1958 .... **TCLC 4; DAM MULT, POET; HLC 1; PC 7**
See also CA 104; 131; CANR 74; DLB 134; HW 1; MTCW 1, 2

Jimenez, Ramon
See Jimenez (Mantecon), Juan Ramon

Jimenez Mantecon, Juan
See Jimenez (Mantecon), Juan Ramon

Jin, Ha
See Jin, Xuefei

Jin, Xuefei 1956- .... **CLC 109**
See also CA 152; CANR 91

Joel, Billy .... **CLC 26**
See also Joel, William Martin

Joel, William Martin 1949-
See Joel, Billy
See also CA 108

John, Saint 7th cent. - .... **CMLC 27**

John of the Cross, St. 1542-1591 .... **LC 18**

John Paul II, Pope 1920- .... **CLC 128**
See also CA 106; 133

Johnson, B(ryan) S(tanley William) 1933-1973 .... **CLC 6, 9**
See also CA 9-12R; 53-56; CANR 9; DLB 14, 40

Johnson, Benj. F. of Boo
See Riley, James Whitcomb

Johnson, Benjamin F. of Boo
See Riley, James Whitcomb

Johnson, Charles (Richard) 1948- ... **CLC 7, 51, 65; BLC 2; DAM MULT**
See also BW 2, 3; CA 116; CAAS 18; CANR 42, 66, 82; DLB 33; MTCW 2

Johnson, Denis 1949- .... **CLC 52**
See also CA 117; 121; CANR 71; DLB 120

Johnson, Diane 1934- .... **CLC 5, 13, 48**
See also CA 41-44R; CANR 17, 40, 62; DLBY 80; INT CANR-17; MTCW 1

Johnson, Eyvind (Olof Verner) 1900-1976 .... **CLC 14**
See also CA 73-76; 69-72; CANR 34

Johnson, J. R.
See James, C(yril) L(ionel) R(obert)

Johnson, James Weldon 1871-1938 ...... **TCLC 3, 19; BLC 2; DAM MULT, POET; PC 24**
See also BW 1, 3; CA 104; 125; CANR 82; CDALB 1917-1929; CLR 32; DA3; DLB 51; MTCW 1, 2; SATA 31

Johnson, Joyce 1935- .... **CLC 58**
See also CA 125; 129

Johnson, Judith (Emlyn) 1936- .. **CLC 7, 15**
See also Sherwin, Judith Johnson
See also CA 25-28R, 153; CANR 34

Johnson, Lionel (Pigot) 1867-1902 .... **TCLC 19**
See also CA 117; DLB 19

Johnson, Marguerite (Annie)
See Angelou, Maya

Johnson, Mel
See Malzberg, Barry N(athaniel)

Johnson, Pamela Hansford 1912-1981 .... **CLC 1, 7, 27**
See also CA 1-4R; 104; CANR 2, 28; DLB 15; MTCW 1, 2

Johnson, Robert 1911(?)-1938 ...... **TCLC 69**
See also BW 3; CA 174

Johnson, Samuel 1709-1784 . **LC 15, 52; DA; DAB; DAC; DAM MST; WLC**
See also CDBLB 1660-1789; DLB 39, 95, 104, 142

Johnson, Uwe 1934-1984 . **CLC 5, 10, 15, 40**
See also CA 1-4R; 112; CANR 1, 39; DLB 75; MTCW 1

Johnston, George (Benson) 1913- ... **CLC 51**
See also CA 1-4R; CANR 5, 20; DLB 88

Johnston, Jennifer (Prudence) 1930- . **CLC 7**
See also CA 85-88; CANR 92; DLB 14

Joinville, Jean de 1224(?)-1317 ... **CMLC 38**

Jolley, (Monica) Elizabeth 1923- ... **CLC 46; SSC 19**
See also CA 127; CAAS 13; CANR 59

Jones, Arthur Llewellyn 1863-1947
See Machen, Arthur
See also CA 104; 179

Jones, D(ouglas) G(ordon) 1929- .... **CLC 10**
See also CA 29-32R; CANR 13, 90; DLB 53

Jones, David (Michael) 1895-1974 ... **CLC 2, 4, 7, 13, 42**
See also CA 9-12R; 53-56; CANR 28; CD-BLB 1945-1960; DLB 20, 100; MTCW 1

Jones, David Robert 1947-
See Bowie, David
See also CA 103

Jones, Diana Wynne 1934- .... **CLC 26**
See also AAYA 12; CA 49-52; CANR 4, 26, 56; CLR 23; DLB 161; JRDA; MAICYA; SAAS 7; SATA 9, 70, 108

Jones, Edward P. 1950- .... **CLC 76**
See also BW 2, 3; CA 142; CANR 79

Jones, Gayl 1949- ... **CLC 6, 9, 131; BLC 2; DAM MULT**
See also BW 2, 3; CA 77-80; CANR 27, 66; DA3; DLB 33; MTCW 1, 2

Jones, James 1921-1977 .... **CLC 1, 3, 10, 39**
See also AITN 1, 2; CA 1-4R; 69-72; CANR 6; DLB 2, 143; DLBD 17; DLBY 98; MTCW 1

Keates, Jonathan 1946(?)- .... **CLC 34**
See also CA 163
Keaton, Buster 1895-1966 .... **CLC 20**
Keats, John 1795-1821 .... **NCLC 8, 73; DA;
DAB; DAC; DAM MST, POET; PC 1;
WLC**
See also CDBLB 1789-1832; DA3; DLB
96, 110
Keble, John 1792-1866 .... **NCLC 87**
See also DLB 32, 55
Keene, Donald 1922- .... **CLC 34**
See also CA 1-4R; CANR 5
Keillor, Garrison .... **CLC 40, 115**
See also Keillor, Gary (Edward)
See also AAYA 2; BEST 89:3; DLBY 87;
SATA 58
Keillor, Gary (Edward) 1942-
See Keillor, Garrison
See also CA 111; 117; CANR 36, 59; DAM
POP; DA3; MTCW 1, 2
Keith, Michael
See Hubbard, L(afayette) Ron(ald)
Keller, Gottfried 1819-1890 .. **NCLC 2; SSC
26**
See also DLB 129
Keller, Nora Okja 1965- .... **CLC 109**
See also CA 187
Kellerman, Jonathan 1949- . **CLC 44; DAM
POP**
See also BEST 90:1; CA 106; CANR 29,
51; DA3; INT CANR-29
Kelley, William Melvin 1937- .... **CLC 22**
See also BW 1; CA 77-80; CANR 27, 83;
DLB 33
Kellogg, Marjorie 1922- .... **CLC 2**
See also CA 81-84
Kellow, Kathleen
See Hibbert, Eleanor Alice Burford
Kelly, M(ilton) T(errence) 1947- ..... **CLC 55**
See also CA 97-100; CAAS 22; CANR 19,
43, 84
Kelman, James 1946- .... **CLC 58, 86**
See also CA 148; CANR 85; DLB 194
Kemal, Yashar 1923- .... **CLC 14, 29**
See also CA 89-92; CANR 44
Kemble, Fanny 1809-1893 .... **NCLC 18**
See also DLB 32
Kemelman, Harry 1908-1996 .... **CLC 2**
See also AITN 1; CA 9-12R; 155; CANR 6,
71; DLB 28
Kempe, Margery 1373(?)-1440(?) .. **LC 6, 56**
See also DLB 146
Kempis, Thomas a 1380-1471 .... **LC 11**
Kendall, Henry 1839-1882 .... **NCLC 12**
See also DLB 230
Keneally, Thomas (Michael) 1935- .. **CLC 5,
8, 10, 14, 19, 27, 43, 117; DAM NOV**
See also CA 85-88; CANR 10, 50, 74; DA3;
MTCW 1, 2
Kennedy, Adrienne (Lita) 1931- .... **CLC 66;
BLC 2; DAM MULT; DC 5**
See also BW 2, 3; CA 103; CAAS 20;
CABS 3; CANR 26, 53, 82; DLB 38
Kennedy, John Pendleton 1795-1870
.... **NCLC 2**
See also DLB 3
Kennedy, Joseph Charles 1929-
See Kennedy, X. J.
See also CA 1-4R; CANR 4, 30, 40; SATA
14, 86
Kennedy, William 1928- . **CLC 6, 28, 34, 53;
DAM NOV**
See also AAYA 1; CA 85-88; CANR 14,
31, 76; DA3; DLB 143; DLBY 85; INT
CANR-31; MTCW 1, 2; SATA 57
Kennedy, X. J. .... **CLC 8, 42**
See also Kennedy, Joseph Charles
See also CAAS 9; CLR 27; DLB 5; SAAS
22

Kenny, Maurice (Francis) 1929- .... **CLC 87;
DAM MULT**
See also CA 144; CAAS 22; DLB 175;
NNAL
Kent, Kelvin
See Kuttner, Henry
Kenton, Maxwell
See Southern, Terry
Kenyon, Robert O.
See Kuttner, Henry
Kepler, Johannes 1571-1630 .... **LC 45**
Kerouac, Jack ..... **CLC 1, 2, 3, 5, 14, 29, 61**
See also Kerouac, Jean-Louis Lebris de
See also AAYA 25; CDALB 1941-1968;
DLB 2, 16; DLBD 3; DLBY 95; MTCW
2
Kerouac, Jean-Louis Lebris de 1922-1969
See Kerouac, Jack
See also AITN 1; CA 5-8R; 25-28R; CANR
26, 54; DA; DAB; DAC; DAM MST,
NOV, POET, POP; DA3; MTCW 1, 2;
WLC
Kerr, Jean 1923- .... **CLC 22**
See also CA 5-8R; CANR 7; INT CANR-7
Kerr, M. E. .... **CLC 12, 35**
See also Meaker, Marijane (Agnes)
See also AAYA 2, 23; CLR 29; SAAS 1
Kerr, Robert .... **CLC 55**
Kerrigan, (Thomas) Anthony 1918- . **CLC 4,
6**
See also CA 49-52; CAAS 11; CANR 4
Kerry, Lois
See Duncan, Lois
Kesey, Ken (Elton) 1935- ... **CLC 1, 3, 6, 11,
46, 64; DA; DAB; DAC; DAM MST,
NOV, POP; WLC**
See also AAYA 25; CA 1-4R; CANR 22,
38, 66; CDALB 1968-1988; DA3; DLB
2, 16, 206; MTCW 1, 2; SATA 66
Kesselring, Joseph (Otto) 1902-1967
.... **CLC 45; DAM DRAM, MST**
See also CA 150
Kessler, Jascha (Frederick) 1929- ..... **CLC 4**
See also CA 17-20R; CANR 8, 48
Kettelkamp, Larry (Dale) 1933- ...... **CLC 12**
See also CA 29-32R; CANR 16; SAAS 3;
SATA 2
Key, Ellen (Karolina Sofia) 1849-1926
.... **TCLC 65**
Keyber, Conny
See Fielding, Henry
Keyes, Daniel 1927- ..... **CLC 80; DA; DAC;
DAM MST, NOV**
See also AAYA 23; CA 17-20R, 181; CAAE
181; CANR 10, 26, 54, 74; DA3; MTCW
2; SATA 37
Keynes, John Maynard 1883-1946
.... **TCLC 64**
See also CA 114; 162, 163; DLBD 10;
MTCW 2
Khanshendel, Chiron
See Rose, Wendy
Khayyam, Omar 1048-1131 .... **CMLC 11;
DAM POET; PC 8**
See also DA3
Kherdian, David 1931- .... **CLC 6, 9**
See also CA 21-24R; CAAS 2; CANR 39,
78; CLR 24; JRDA; MAICYA; SATA 16,
74
Khlebnikov, Velimir .... **TCLC 20**
See also Khlebnikov, Viktor Vladimirovich
Khlebnikov, Viktor Vladimirovich 1885-1922
See Khlebnikov, Velimir
See also CA 117
Khodasevich, Vladislav (Felitsianovich)
1886-1939 .... **TCLC 15**
See also CA 115
Kielland, Alexander Lange 1849-1906
.... **TCLC 5**

See also CA 104
Kiely, Benedict 1919- .... **CLC 23, 43**
See also CA 1-4R; CANR 2, 84; DLB 15
Kienzle, William X(avier) 1928- .... **CLC 25;
DAM POP**
See also CA 93-96; CAAS 1; CANR 9, 31,
59; DA3; INT CANR-31; MTCW 1, 2
Kierkegaard, Soren 1813-1855 .... **NCLC 34,
78**
Kieslowski, Krzysztof 1941-1996 .. **CLC 120**
See also CA 147; 151
Killens, John Oliver 1916-1987 .... **CLC 10**
See also BW 2; CA 77-80; 123; CAAS 2;
CANR 26; DLB 33
Killigrew, Anne 1660-1685 .... **LC 4**
See also DLB 131
Killigrew, Thomas 1612-1683 .... **LC 57**
See also DLB 58
Kim
See Simenon, Georges (Jacques Christian)
Kincaid, Jamaica 1949- .... **CLC 43, 68, 137;
BLC 2; DAM MULT, NOV**
See also AAYA 13; BW 2, 3; CA 125;
CANR 47, 59; CDALBS; CLR 63; DA3;
DLB 157, 227; MTCW 2
King, Francis (Henry) 1923- ...... **CLC 8, 53;
DAM NOV**
See also CA 1-4R; CANR 1, 33, 86; DLB
15, 139; MTCW 1
King, Kennedy
See Brown, George Douglas
King, Martin Luther, Jr. 1929-1968
...... **CLC 83; BLC 2; DA; DAB; DAC;
DAM MST, MULT; WLCS**
See also BW 2, 3; CA 25-28; CANR 27,
44; CAP 2; DA3; MTCW 1, 2; SATA 14
King, Stephen (Edwin) 1947- ... **CLC 12, 26,
37, 61, 113; DAM NOV, POP; SSC 17**
See also AAYA 1, 17; BEST 90:1; CA 61-
64; CANR 1, 30, 52, 76; DA3; DLB 143;
DLBY 80; JRDA; MTCW 1, 2; SATA 9,
55
King, Steve
See King, Stephen (Edwin)
King, Thomas 1943- .. **CLC 89; DAC; DAM
MULT**
See also CA 144; DLB 175; NNAL; SATA
96
Kingman, Lee .... **CLC 17**
See also Natti, (Mary) Lee
See also SAAS 3; SATA 1, 67
Kingsley, Charles 1819-1875 .... **NCLC 35**
See also DLB 21, 32, 163, 190; YABC 2
Kingsley, Sidney 1906-1995 .... **CLC 44**
See also CA 85-88; 147; DLB 7
Kingsolver, Barbara 1955- .... **CLC 55, 81,
130; DAM POP**
See also AAYA 15; CA 129; 134; CANR
60; CDALBS; DA3; DLB 206; INT 134;
MTCW 2
Kingston, Maxine (Ting Ting) Hong 1940-
...... **CLC 12, 19, 58, 121; DAM MULT,
NOV; WLCS**
See also AAYA 8; CA 69-72; CANR 13,
38, 74, 87; CDALBS; DA3; DLB 173,
212; DLBY 80; INT CANR-13; MTCW
1, 2; SATA 53
Kinnell, Galway 1927- ... **CLC 1, 2, 3, 5, 13,
29, 129; PC 26**
See also CA 9-12R; CANR 10, 34, 66; DLB
5; DLBY 87; INT CANR-34; MTCW 1, 2
Kinsella, Thomas 1928- .... **CLC 4, 19, 138**
See also CA 17-20R; CANR 15; DLB 27;
MTCW 1, 2
Kinsella, W(illiam) P(atrick) 1935- . **CLC 27,
43; DAC; DAM NOV, POP**
See also AAYA 7; CA 97-100; CAAS 7;
CANR 21, 35, 66, 75; INT CANR-21;
MTCW 1, 2

Llewellyn Lloyd, Richard Dafydd Vivian
1906-1983 .... **CLC 7, 80**
See also Llewellyn, Richard
See also CA 53-56; 111; CANR 7, 71;
SATA 11; SATA-Obit 37

Llosa, (Jorge) Mario (Pedro) Vargas
See Vargas Llosa, (Jorge) Mario (Pedro)

Lloyd, Manda
See Mander, (Mary) Jane

Lloyd Webber, Andrew 1948-
See Webber, Andrew Lloyd
See also AAYA 1; CA 116; 149; DAM
DRAM; SATA 56

Llull, Ramon c. 1235-c. 1316 .... **CMLC 12**

Lobb, Ebenezer
See Upward, Allen

Locke, Alain (Le Roy) 1886-1954 . **TCLC 43;**
BLCS
See also BW 1, 3; CA 106; 124; CANR 79;
DLB 51

Locke, John 1632-1704 .... **LC 7, 35**
See also DLB 101

Locke-Elliott, Sumner
See Elliott, Sumner Locke

Lockhart, John Gibson 1794-1854 . **NCLC 6**
See also DLB 110, 116, 144

Lodge, David (John) 1935- .. **CLC 36; DAM**
POP
See also BEST 90:1; CA 17-20R; CANR
19, 53, 92; DLB 14, 194; INT CANR-19;
MTCW 1, 2

Lodge, Thomas 1558-1625 .... **LC 41**

Lodge, Thomas 1558-1625 .... **LC 41**
See also DLB 172

Loennbohm, Armas Eino Leopold 1878-1926
See Leino, Eino
See also CA 123

Loewinsohn, Ron(ald William) 1937-
.... **CLC 52**
See also CA 25-28R; CANR 71

Logan, Jake
See Smith, Martin Cruz

Logan, John (Burton) 1923-1987 ...... **CLC 5**
See also CA 77-80; 124; CANR 45; DLB 5

Lo Kuan-chung 1330(?)-1400(?) .... **LC 12**

Lombard, Nap
See Johnson, Pamela Hansford

London, Jack .... **TCLC 9, 15, 39; SSC 4;**
WLC
See also London, John Griffith
See also AAYA 13; AITN 2; CDALB 1865-
1917; DLB 8, 12, 78, 212; SATA 18

London, John Griffith 1876-1916
See London, Jack
See also CA 110; 119; CANR 73; DA;
DAB; DAC; DAM MST, NOV; DA3;
JRDA; MAICYA; MTCW 1, 2

Long, Emmett
See Leonard, Elmore (John, Jr.)

Longbaugh, Harry
See Goldman, William (W.)

Longfellow, Henry Wadsworth 1807-1882
.. **NCLC 2, 45; DA; DAB; DAC; DAM**
MST, POET; PC 30; WLCS
See also CDALB 1640-1865; DA3; DLB 1,
59, 235; SATA 19

Longinus c. 1st cent. - .... **CMLC 27**
See also DLB 176

Longley, Michael 1939- .... **CLC 29**
See also CA 102; DLB 40

Longus fl. c. 2nd cent. - .... **CMLC 7**

Longway, A. Hugh
See Lang, Andrew

Lonnrot, Elias 1802-1884 .... **NCLC 53**

Lopate, Phillip 1943- .... **CLC 29**
See also CA 97-100; CANR 88; DLBY 80;
INT 97-100

Lopez Portillo (y Pacheco), Jose 1920-
.... **CLC 46**
See also CA 129; HW 1

Lopez y Fuentes, Gregorio 1897(?)-1966
.... **CLC 32**
See also CA 131; HW 1

Lorca, Federico Garcia
See Garcia Lorca, Federico

Lord, Bette Bao 1938- .... **CLC 23**
See also BEST 90:3; CA 107; CANR 41,
79; INT 107; SATA 58

Lord Auch
See Bataille, Georges

Lord Byron
See Byron, George Gordon (Noel)

Lorde, Audre (Geraldine) 1934-1992
...... **CLC 18, 71; BLC 2; DAM MULT,**
POET; PC 12
See also BW 1, 3; CA 25-28R; 142; CANR
16, 26, 46, 82; DA3; DLB 41; MTCW 1,
2

Lord Houghton
See Milnes, Richard Monckton

Lord Jeffrey
See Jeffrey, Francis

Lorenzini, Carlo 1826-1890
See Collodi, Carlo
See also MAICYA; SATA 29, 100

Lorenzo, Heberto Padilla
See Padilla (Lorenzo), Heberto

Loris
See Hofmannsthal, Hugo von

Loti, Pierre .... **TCLC 11**
See also Viaud, (Louis Marie) Julien
See also DLB 123

Lou, Henri
See Andreas-Salome, Lou

Louie, David Wong 1954- .... **CLC 70**
See also CA 139

Louis, Father M.
See Merton, Thomas

Lovecraft, H(oward) P(hillips) 1890-1937
.... **TCLC 4, 22; DAM POP; SSC 3**
See also AAYA 14; CA 104; 133; DA3;
MTCW 1, 2

Lovelace, Earl 1935- .... **CLC 51**
See also BW 2; CA 77-80; CANR 41, 72;
DLB 125; MTCW 1

Lovelace, Richard 1618-1657 .... **LC 24**
See also DLB 131

Lowell, Amy 1874-1925 ... **TCLC 1, 8; DAM**
POET; PC 13
See also CA 104; 151; DLB 54, 140;
MTCW 2

Lowell, James Russell 1819-1891 .. **NCLC 2,**
90
See also CDALB 1640-1865; DLB 1, 11,
64, 79, 189, 235

Lowell, Robert (Traill Spence, Jr.)
1917-1977 ... **CLC 1, 2, 3, 4, 5, 8, 9, 11,**
15, 37, 124; DA; DAB; DAC; DAM
MST, NOV; PC 3; WLC
See also CA 9-12R; 73-76; CABS 2; CANR
26, 60; CDALBS; DA3; DLB 5, 169;
MTCW 1, 2

Lowenthal, Michael (Francis) 1969-
.... **CLC 119**
See also CA 150

Lowndes, Marie Adelaide (Belloc) 1868-1947
.... **TCLC 12**
See also CA 107; DLB 70

Lowry, (Clarence) Malcolm 1909-1957
.... **TCLC 6, 40; SSC 31**
See also CA 105; 131; CANR 62; CDBLB
1945-1960; DLB 15; MTCW 1, 2

Lowry, Mina Gertrude 1882-1966
See Loy, Mina
See also CA 113

Loxsmith, John
See Brunner, John (Kilian Houston)

Loy, Mina ..... **CLC 28; DAM POET; PC 16**
See also Lowry, Mina Gertrude
See also DLB 4, 54

Loyson-Bridet
See Schwob, Marcel (Mayer Andre)

Lucan 39-65 .... **CMLC 33**
See also DLB 211

Lucas, Craig 1951- .... **CLC 64**
See also CA 137; CANR 71

Lucas, E(dward) V(errall) 1868-1938
.... **TCLC 73**
See also CA 176; DLB 98, 149, 153; SATA
20

Lucas, George 1944- .... **CLC 16**
See also AAYA 1, 23; CA 77-80; CANR
30; SATA 56

Lucas, Hans
See Godard, Jean-Luc

Lucas, Victoria
See Plath, Sylvia

Lucian c. 120-c. 180 .... **CMLC 32**
See also DLB 176

Ludlam, Charles 1943-1987 ...... **CLC 46, 50**
See also CA 85-88; 122; CANR 72, 86

Ludlum, Robert 1927- ... **CLC 22, 43; DAM**
NOV, POP
See also AAYA 10; BEST 89:1, 90:3; CA
33-36R; CANR 25, 41, 68; DA3; DLBY
82; MTCW 1, 2

Ludwig, Ken .... **CLC 60**

Ludwig, Otto 1813-1865 .... **NCLC 4**
See also DLB 129

Lugones, Leopoldo 1874-1938 ..... **TCLC 15;**
HLCS 2
See also CA 116; 131; HW 1

Lu Hsun 1881-1936 .... **TCLC 3; SSC 20**
See also Shu-Jen, Chou

Lukacs, George .... **CLC 24**
See also Lukacs, Gyorgy (Szegeny von)

Lukacs, Gyorgy (Szegeny von) 1885-1971
See Lukacs, George
See also CA 101; 29-32R; CANR 62;
MTCW 2

Luke, Peter (Ambrose Cyprian) 1919-1995
.... **CLC 38**
See also CA 81-84; 147; CANR 72; DLB
13

Lunar, Dennis
See Mungo, Raymond

Lurie, Alison 1926- .... **CLC 4, 5, 18, 39**
See also CA 1-4R; CANR 2, 17, 50, 88;
DLB 2; MTCW 1; SATA 46, 112

Lustig, Arnost 1926- .... **CLC 56**
See also AAYA 3; CA 69-72; CANR 47;
DLB 232; SATA 56

Luther, Martin 1483-1546 .... **LC 9, 37**
See also DLB 179

Luxemburg, Rosa 1870(?)-1919 .... **TCLC 63**
See also CA 118

Luzi, Mario 1914- .... **CLC 13**
See also CA 61-64; CANR 9, 70; DLB 128

Lyly, John 1554(?)-1606 .... **LC 41; DAM**
DRAM; DC 7
See also DLB 62, 167

L'Ymagier
See Gourmont, Remy (-Marie-Charles) de

Lynch, B. Suarez
See Bioy Casares, Adolfo; Borges, Jorge
Luis

Lynch, B. Suarez
See Bioy Casares, Adolfo

Lynch, David (K.) 1946- .... **CLC 66**
See also CA 124; 129

Lynch, James
See Andreyev, Leonid (Nikolaevich)

See also CA 77-80; CANR 14, 32, 57

Malory, (Sir) Thomas 1410(?)-1471(?)
.. **LC 11; DA; DAB; DAC; DAM MST;
WLCS**
See also CDBLB Before 1660; DLB 146;
SATA 59; SATA-Brief 33

Malouf, (George Joseph) David 1934-
.... **CLC 28, 86**
See also CA 124; CANR 50, 76; MTCW 2

Malraux, (Georges-)Andre 1901-1976
..... **CLC 1, 4, 9, 13, 15, 57; DAM NOV**
See also CA 21-22; 69-72; CANR 34, 58;
CAP 2; DLB 72; MTCW 1, 2

Malzberg, Barry N(athaniel) 1939- .. **CLC 7**
See also CA 61-64; CAAS 4; CANR 16;
DLB 8

Mamet, David (Alan) 1947- . **CLC 9, 15, 34,
46, 91; DAM DRAM; DC 4**
See also AAYA 3; CA 81-84; CABS 3;
CANR 15, 41, 67, 72; DA3; DLB 7;
MTCW 1, 2

Mamoulian, Rouben (Zachary) 1897-1987
.... **CLC 16**
See also CA 25-28R; 124; CANR 85

Mandelstam, Osip (Emilievich)
1891(?)-1938(?) .... **TCLC 2, 6; PC 14**
See also CA 104; 150; MTCW 2

Mander, (Mary) Jane 1877-1949 .. **TCLC 31**
See also CA 162

Mandeville, John fl. 1350- .... **CMLC 19**
See also DLB 146

Mandiargues, Andre Pieyre de .... **CLC 41**
See also Pieyre de Mandiargues, Andre
See also DLB 83

Mandrake, Ethel Belle
See Thurman, Wallace (Henry)

Mangan, James Clarence 1803-1849
.... **NCLC 27**

Maniere, J.-E.
See Giraudoux, (Hippolyte) Jean

Mankiewicz, Herman (Jacob) 1897-1953
.... **TCLC 85**
See also CA 120; 169; DLB 26

Manley, (Mary) Delariviere 1672(?)-1724
.... **LC 1, 42**
See also DLB 39, 80

Mann, Abel
See Creasey, John

Mann, Emily 1952- .... **DC 7**
See also CA 130; CANR 55

Mann, (Luiz) Heinrich 1871-1950 .. **TCLC 9**
See also CA 106; 164, 181; DLB 66, 118

Mann, (Paul) Thomas 1875-1955 .. **TCLC 2,
8, 14, 21, 35, 44, 60; DA; DAB; DAC;
DAM MST, NOV; SSC 5; WLC**
See also CA 104; 128; DA3; DLB 66;
MTCW 1, 2

Mannheim, Karl 1893-1947 .... **TCLC 65**

Manning, David
See Faust, Frederick (Schiller)

Manning, Frederic 1887(?)-1935 .. **TCLC 25**
See also CA 124

Manning, Olivia 1915-1980 .... **CLC 5, 19**
See also CA 5-8R; 101; CANR 29; MTCW
1

Mano, D. Keith 1942- .... **CLC 2, 10**
See also CA 25-28R; CAAS 6; CANR 26,
57; DLB 6

Mansfield, Katherine -1923 . **TCLC 2, 8, 39;
DAB; SSC 9, 23, 38; WLC**
See also Beauchamp, Kathleen Mansfield
See also DLB 162

Manso, Peter 1940- .... **CLC 39**
See also CA 29-32R; CANR 44

Mantecon, Juan Jimenez
See Jimenez (Mantecon), Juan Ramon

Manton, Peter
See Creasey, John

Man Without a Spleen, A
See Chekhov, Anton (Pavlovich)

Manzoni, Alessandro 1785-1873 ... **NCLC 29**

Map, Walter 1140-1209 .... **CMLC 32**

Mapu, Abraham (ben Jekutiel) 1808-1867
.... **NCLC 18**

Mara, Sally
See Queneau, Raymond

Marat, Jean Paul 1743-1793 .... **LC 10**

Marcel, Gabriel Honore 1889-1973 . **CLC 15**
See also CA 102; 45-48; MTCW 1, 2

March, William 1893-1954 .... **TCLC 96**

Marchbanks, Samuel
See Davies, (William) Robertson

Marchi, Giacomo
See Bassani, Giorgio

Margulies, Donald .... **CLC 76**
See also DLB 228

Marie de France c. 12th cent. - .... **CMLC 8;
PC 22**
See also DLB 208

Marie de l'Incarnation 1599-1672 ..... **LC 10**

Marier, Captain Victor
See Griffith, D(avid Lewelyn) W(ark)

Mariner, Scott
See Pohl, Frederik

Marinetti, Filippo Tommaso 1876-1944
.... **TCLC 10**
See also CA 107; DLB 114

Marivaux, Pierre Carlet de Chamblain de
1688-1763 .... **LC 4; DC 7**

Markandaya, Kamala .... **CLC 8, 38**
See also Taylor, Kamala (Purnaiya)

Markfield, Wallace 1926- .... **CLC 8**
See also CA 69-72; CAAS 3; DLB 2, 28

Markham, Edwin 1852-1940 .... **TCLC 47**
See also CA 160; DLB 54, 186

Markham, Robert
See Amis, Kingsley (William)

Marks, J
See Highwater, Jamake (Mamake)

Marks-Highwater, J
See Highwater, Jamake (Mamake)

Markson, David M(errill) 1927- ..... **CLC 67**
See also CA 49-52; CANR 1, 91

Marley, Bob .... **CLC 17**
See also Marley, Robert Nesta

Marley, Robert Nesta 1945-1981
See Marley, Bob
See also CA 107; 103

Marlowe, Christopher 1564-1593 ..... **LC 22,
47; DA; DAB; DAC; DAM DRAM,
MST; DC 1; WLC**
See also CDBLB Before 1660; DA3; DLB
62

Marlowe, Stephen 1928-
See Queen, Ellery
See also CA 13-16R; CANR 6, 55

Marmontel, Jean-Francois 1723-1799 . **LC 2**

Marquand, John P(hillips) 1893-1960
.... **CLC 2, 10**
See also CA 85-88; CANR 73; DLB 9, 102;
MTCW 2

Marques, Rene 1919-1979 ... **CLC 96; DAM
MULT; HLC 2**
See also CA 97-100; 85-88; CANR 78;
DLB 113; HW 1, 2

Marquez, Gabriel (Jose) Garcia
See Garcia Marquez, Gabriel (Jose)

Marquis, Don(ald Robert Perry) 1878-1937
.... **TCLC 7**
See also CA 104; 166; DLB 11, 25

Marric, J. J.
See Creasey, John

Marryat, Frederick 1792-1848 .... **NCLC 3**
See also DLB 21, 163

Marsden, James
See Creasey, John

Marsh, Edward 1872-1953 .... **TCLC 99**

Marsh, (Edith) Ngaio 1899-1982 ...... **CLC 7,
53; DAM POP**
See also CA 9-12R; CANR 6, 58; DLB 77;
MTCW 1, 2

Marshall, Garry 1934- .... **CLC 17**
See also AAYA 3; CA 111; SATA 60

Marshall, Paule 1929- . **CLC 27, 72; BLC 3;
DAM MULT; SSC 3**
See also BW 2, 3; CA 77-80; CANR 25,
73; DA3; DLB 33, 157, 227; MTCW 1, 2

Marshallik
See Zangwill, Israel

Marsten, Richard
See Hunter, Evan

Marston, John 1576-1634 .... **LC 33; DAM
DRAM**
See also DLB 58, 172

Martha, Henry
See Harris, Mark

Marti (y Perez), Jose (Julian) 1853-1895
.... **NCLC 63; DAM MULT; HLC 2**
See also HW 2

Martial c. 40-c. 104 .... **CMLC 35; PC 10**
See also DLB 211

Martin, Ken
See Hubbard, L(afayette) Ron(ald)

Martin, Richard
See Creasey, John

Martin, Steve 1945- .... **CLC 30**
See also CA 97-100; CANR 30; MTCW 1

Martin, Valerie 1948- .... **CLC 89**
See also BEST 90:2; CA 85-88; CANR 49,
89

Martin, Violet Florence 1862-1915
.... **TCLC 51**

Martin, Webber
See Silverberg, Robert

Martindale, Patrick Victor
See White, Patrick (Victor Martindale)

Martin du Gard, Roger 1881-1958
.... **TCLC 24**
See also CA 118; DLB 65

Martineau, Harriet 1802-1876 ..... **NCLC 26**
See also DLB 21, 55, 159, 163, 166, 190;
YABC 2

Martines, Julia
See O'Faolain, Julia

Martinez, Enrique Gonzalez
See Gonzalez Martinez, Enrique

Martinez, Jacinto Benavente y
See Benavente (y Martinez), Jacinto

Martinez Ruiz, Jose 1873-1967
See Azorin; Ruiz, Jose Martinez
See also CA 93-96; HW 1

Martinez Sierra, Gregorio 1881-1947
.... **TCLC 6**
See also CA 115

Martinez Sierra, Maria (de la O'LeJarraga)
1874-1974 .... **TCLC 6**
See also CA 115

Martinsen, Martin
See Follett, Ken(neth Martin)

Martinson, Harry (Edmund) 1904-1978
.... **CLC 14**
See also CA 77-80; CANR 34

Marut, Ret
See Traven, B.

Marut, Robert
See Traven, B.

Marvell, Andrew 1621-1678 . **LC 4, 43; DA;
DAB; DAC; DAM MST, POET; PC 10;
WLC**
See also CDBLB 1660-1789; DLB 131

Marx, Karl (Heinrich) 1818-1883 . **NCLC 17**
See also DLB 129

Masaoka Shiki .... **TCLC 18**
   See also Masaoka Tsunenori
Masaoka Tsunenori 1867-1902
   See Masaoka Shiki
   See also CA 117
Masefield, John (Edward) 1878-1967
   .... **CLC 11, 47; DAM POET**
   See also CA 19-20; 25-28R; CANR 33;
   CAP 2; CDBLB 1890-1914; DLB 10, 19,
   153, 160; MTCW 1, 2; SATA 19
Maso, Carole 19(?)- .... **CLC 44**
   See also CA 170
Mason, Bobbie Ann 1940- . **CLC 28, 43, 82;
   SSC 4**
   See also AAYA 5; CA 53-56; CANR 11, 31,
   58, 83; CDALBS; DA3; DLB 173; DLBY
   87; INT CANR-31; MTCW 1, 2
Mason, Ernst
   See Pohl, Frederik
Mason, Lee W.
   See Malzberg, Barry N(athaniel)
Mason, Nick 1945- .... **CLC 35**
Mason, Tally
   See Derleth, August (William)
Mass, William
   See Gibson, William
Master Lao
   See Lao Tzu
Masters, Edgar Lee 1868-1950 ...... **TCLC 2,
   25; DA; DAC; DAM MST, POET; PC
   1; WLCS**
   See also CA 104; 133; CDALB 1865-1917;
   DLB 54; MTCW 1, 2
Masters, Hilary 1928- .... **CLC 48**
   See also CA 25-28R; CANR 13, 47
Mastrosimone, William 19(?)- .... **CLC 36**
   See also CA 186
Mathe, Albert
   See Camus, Albert
Mather, Cotton 1663-1728 .... **LC 38**
   See also CDALB 1640-1865; DLB 24, 30,
   140
Mather, Increase 1639-1723 .... **LC 38**
   See also DLB 24
Matheson, Richard Burton 1926- ... **CLC 37**
   See also AAYA 31; CA 97-100; CANR 88;
   DLB 8, 44; INT 97-100
Mathews, Harry 1930- .... **CLC 6, 52**
   See also CA 21-24R; CAAS 6; CANR 18,
   40
Mathews, John Joseph 1894-1979 . **CLC 84;
   DAM MULT**
   See also CA 19-20; 142; CANR 45; CAP 2;
   DLB 175; NNAL
Mathias, Roland (Glyn) 1915- .... **CLC 45**
   See also CA 97-100; CANR 19, 41; DLB
   27
Matsuo Basho 1644-1694 .... **LC 62; DAM
   POET; PC 3**
Mattheson, Rodney
   See Creasey, John
Matthews, (James) Brander 1852-1929
   .... **TCLC 95**
   See also DLB 71, 78; DLBD 13
Matthews, Greg 1949- .... **CLC 45**
   See also CA 135
Matthews, William (Procter, III) 1942-1997
   .... **CLC 40**
   See also CA 29-32R; 162; CAAS 18; CANR
   12, 57; DLB 5
Matthias, John (Edward) 1941- .... **CLC 9**
   See also CA 33-36R; CANR 56
Matthiessen, F(rancis) O(tto) 1902-1950
   .... **TCLC 100**
   See also CA 185; DLB 63
Matthiessen, Peter 1927- .. **CLC 5, 7, 11, 32,
   64; DAM NOV**

   See also AAYA 6; BEST 90:4; CA 9-12R;
   CANR 21, 50, 73; DA3; DLB 6, 173;
   MTCW 1, 2; SATA 27
Maturin, Charles Robert 1780(?)-1824
   .... **NCLC 6**
   See also DLB 178
Matute (Ausejo), Ana Maria 1925- . **CLC 11**
   See also CA 89-92; MTCW 1
Maugham, W. S.
   See Maugham, W(illiam) Somerset
Maugham, W(illiam) Somerset 1874-1965
   .... **CLC 1, 11, 15, 67, 93; DA; DAB;
   DAC; DAM DRAM, MST, NOV; SSC
   8; WLC**
   See also CA 5-8R; 25-28R; CANR 40; CD-
   BLB 1914-1945; DA3; DLB 10, 36, 77,
   100, 162, 195; MTCW 1, 2; SATA 54
Maugham, William Somerset
   See Maugham, W(illiam) Somerset
Maupassant, (Henri Rene Albert) Guy de
   1850-1893 . **NCLC 1, 42, 83; DA; DAB;
   DAC; DAM MST; SSC 1; WLC**
   See also DA3; DLB 123
Maupin, Armistead 1944- .... **CLC 95; DAM
   POP**
   See also CA 125; 130; CANR 58; DA3;
   INT 130; MTCW 2
Maurhut, Richard
   See Traven, B.
Mauriac, Claude 1914-1996 .... **CLC 9**
   See also CA 89-92; 152; DLB 83
Mauriac, Francois (Charles) 1885-1970
   .... **CLC 4, 9, 56; SSC 24**
   See also CA 25-28; CAP 2; DLB 65;
   MTCW 1, 2
Mavor, Osborne Henry 1888-1951
   See Bridie, James
   See also CA 104
Maxwell, William (Keepers, Jr.) 1908-
   .... **CLC 19**
   See also CA 93-96; CANR 54; DLBY 80;
   INT 93-96
May, Elaine 1932- .... **CLC 16**
   See also CA 124; 142; DLB 44
Mayakovski, Vladimir (Vladimirovich)
   1893-1930 .... **TCLC 4, 18**
   See also CA 104; 158; MTCW 2
Mayhew, Henry 1812-1887 .... **NCLC 31**
   See also DLB 18, 55, 190
Mayle, Peter 1939(?)- .... **CLC 89**
   See also CA 139; CANR 64
Maynard, Joyce 1953- .... **CLC 23**
   See also CA 111; 129; CANR 64
Mayne, William (James Carter) 1928-
   .... **CLC 12**
   See also AAYA 20; CA 9-12R; CANR 37,
   80; CLR 25; JRDA; MAICYA; SAAS 11;
   SATA 6, 68
Mayo, Jim
   See L'Amour, Louis (Dearborn)
Maysles, Albert 1926- .... **CLC 16**
   See also CA 29-32R
Maysles, David 1932- .... **CLC 16**
Mazer, Norma Fox 1931- .... **CLC 26**
   See also AAYA 5; CA 69-72; CANR 12,
   32, 66; CLR 23; JRDA; MAICYA; SAAS
   1; SATA 24, 67, 105
Mazzini, Guiseppe 1805-1872 .... **NCLC 34**
McAlmon, Robert (Menzies) 1895-1956
   .... **TCLC 97**
   See also CA 107; 168; DLB 4, 45; DLBD
   15
McAuley, James Phillip 1917-1976 . **CLC 45**
   See also CA 97-100
McBain, Ed
   See Hunter, Evan
McBrien, William (Augustine) 1930-
   .... **CLC 44**
   See also CA 107; CANR 90

McCabe, Patrick 1955- .... **CLC 133**
   See also CA 130; CANR 50, 90; DLB 194
McCaffrey, Anne (Inez) 1926- .... **CLC 17;
   DAM NOV, POP**
   See also AAYA 6, 34; AITN 2; BEST 89:2;
   CA 25-28R; CANR 15, 35, 55; CLR 49;
   DA3; DLB 8; JRDA; MAICYA; MTCW
   1, 2; SAAS 11; SATA 8, 70, 116
McCall, Nathan 1955(?)- .... **CLC 86**
   See also BW 3; CA 146; CANR 88
McCann, Arthur
   See Campbell, John W(ood, Jr.)
McCann, Edson
   See Pohl, Frederik
McCarthy, Charles, Jr. 1933-
   See McCarthy, Cormac
   See also CANR 42, 69; DAM POP; DA3;
   MTCW 2
McCarthy, Cormac 1933- .... **CLC 4, 57, 59,
   101**
   See also McCarthy, Charles, Jr.
   See also DLB 6, 143; MTCW 2
McCarthy, Mary (Therese) 1912-1989
   ..... **CLC 1, 3, 5, 14, 24, 39, 59; SSC 24**
   See also CA 5-8R; 129; CANR 16, 50, 64;
   DA3; DLB 2; DLBY 81; INT CANR-16;
   MTCW 1, 2
McCartney, (James) Paul 1942- ..... **CLC 12,
   35**
   See also CA 146
McCauley, Stephen (D.) 1955- .... **CLC 50**
   See also CA 141
McClure, Michael (Thomas) 1932- .. **CLC 6,
   10**
   See also CA 21-24R; CANR 17, 46, 77;
   DLB 16
McCorkle, Jill (Collins) 1958- .... **CLC 51**
   See also CA 121; DLB 234; DLBY 87
McCourt, Frank 1930- .... **CLC 109**
   See also CA 157
McCourt, James 1941- .... **CLC 5**
   See also CA 57-60
McCourt, Malachy 1932- .... **CLC 119**
McCoy, Horace (Stanley) 1897-1955
   .... **TCLC 28**
   See also CA 108; 155; DLB 9
McCrae, John 1872-1918 .... **TCLC 12**
   See also CA 109; DLB 92
McCreigh, James
   See Pohl, Frederik
McCullers, (Lula) Carson (Smith) 1917-1967
   .. **CLC 1, 4, 10, 12, 48, 100; DA; DAB;
   DAC; DAM MST, NOV; SSC 9, 24;
   WLC**
   See also AAYA 21; CA 5-8R; 25-28R;
   CABS 1, 3; CANR 18; CDALB 1941-
   1968; DA3; DLB 2, 7, 173, 228; MTCW
   1, 2; SATA 27
McCulloch, John Tyler
   See Burroughs, Edgar Rice
McCullough, Colleen 1938(?)- .... **CLC 27,
   107; DAM NOV, POP**
   See also CA 81-84; CANR 17, 46, 67; DA3;
   MTCW 1, 2
McDermott, Alice 1953- .... **CLC 90**
   See also CA 109; CANR 40, 90
McElroy, Joseph 1930- .... **CLC 5, 47**
   See also CA 17-20R
McEwan, Ian (Russell) 1948- .. **CLC 13, 66;
   DAM NOV**
   See also BEST 90:4; CA 61-64; CANR 14,
   41, 69, 87; DLB 14, 194; MTCW 1, 2
McFadden, David 1940- .... **CLC 48**
   See also CA 104; DLB 60; INT 104
McFarland, Dennis 1950- .... **CLC 65**
   See also CA 165
McGahern, John 1934- . **CLC 5, 9, 48; SSC
   17**

Middleton, Christopher 1926- .... **CLC 13**
See also CA 13-16R; CANR 29, 54; DLB 40

Middleton, Richard (Barham) 1882-1911
.... **TCLC 56**
See also CA 187; DLB 156

Middleton, Stanley 1919- .... **CLC 7, 38**
See also CA 25-28R; CAAS 23; CANR 21, 46, 81; DLB 14

Middleton, Thomas 1580-1627 .... **LC 33; DAM DRAM, MST; DC 5**
See also DLB 58

Migueis, Jose Rodrigues 1901- .... **CLC 10**

Mikszath, Kalman 1847-1910 .... **TCLC 31**
See also CA 170

Miles, Jack .... **CLC 100**

Miles, Josephine (Louise) 1911-1985 . **CLC 1, 2, 14, 34, 39; DAM POET**
See also CA 1-4R; 116; CANR 2, 55; DLB 48

Militant
See Sandburg, Carl (August)

Mill, John Stuart 1806-1873 ... **NCLC 11, 58**
See also CDBLB 1832-1890; DLB 55, 190

Millar, Kenneth 1915-1983 .. **CLC 14; DAM POP**
See also Macdonald, Ross
See also CA 9-12R; 110; CANR 16, 63; DA3; DLB 2, 226; DLBD 6; DLBY 83; MTCW 1, 2

Millay, E. Vincent
See Millay, Edna St. Vincent

Millay, Edna St. Vincent 1892-1950
... **TCLC 4, 49; DA; DAB; DAC; DAM MST, POET; PC 6; WLCS**
See also CA 104; 130; CDALB 1917-1929; DA3; DLB 45; MTCW 1, 2

Miller, Arthur 1915- ..... **CLC 1, 2, 6, 10, 15, 26, 47, 78; DA; DAB; DAC; DAM DRAM, MST; DC 1; WLC**
See also AAYA 15; AITN 1; CA 1-4R; CABS 3; CANR 2, 30, 54, 76; CDALB 1941-1968; DA3; DLB 7; MTCW 1, 2

Miller, Henry (Valentine) 1891-1980 . **CLC 1, 2, 4, 9, 14, 43, 84; DA; DAB; DAC; DAM MST, NOV; WLC**
See also CA 9-12R; 97-100; CANR 33, 64; CDALB 1929-1941; DA3; DLB 4, 9; DLBY 80; MTCW 1, 2

Miller, Jason 1939(?)- .... **CLC 2**
See also AITN 1; CA 73-76; DLB 7

Miller, Sue 1943- .... **CLC 44; DAM POP**
See also BEST 90:3; CA 139; CANR 59, 91; DA3; DLB 143

Miller, Walter M(ichael, Jr.) 1923- .. **CLC 4, 30**
See also CA 85-88; DLB 8

Millett, Kate 1934- .... **CLC 67**
See also AITN 1; CA 73-76; CANR 32, 53, 76; DA3; MTCW 1, 2

Millhauser, Steven (Lewis) 1943- ... **CLC 21, 54, 109**
See also CA 110; 111; CANR 63; DA3; DLB 2; INT 111; MTCW 2

Millin, Sarah Gertrude 1889-1968 . **CLC 49**
See also CA 102; 93-96; DLB 225

Milne, A(lan) A(lexander) 1882-1956
. **TCLC 6, 88; DAB; DAC; DAM MST**
See also CA 104; 133; CLR 1, 26; DA3; DLB 10, 77, 100, 160; MAICYA; MTCW 1, 2; SATA 100; YABC 1

Milner, Ron(ald) 1938- ..... **CLC 56; BLC 3; DAM MULT**
See also AITN 1; BW 1; CA 73-76; CANR 24, 81; DLB 38; MTCW 1

Milnes, Richard Monckton 1809-1885
.... **NCLC 61**
See also DLB 32, 184

Milosz, Czeslaw 1911- .... **CLC 5, 11, 22, 31, 56, 82; DAM MST, POET; PC 8; WLCS**
See also CA 81-84; CANR 23, 51, 91; DA3; MTCW 1, 2

Milton, John 1608-1674 .... **LC 9, 43; DA; DAB; DAC; DAM MST, POET; PC 19, 29; WLC**
See also CDBLB 1660-1789; DA3; DLB 131, 151

Min, Anchee 1957- .... **CLC 86**
See also CA 146

Minehaha, Cornelius
See Wedekind, (Benjamin) Frank(lin)

Miner, Valerie 1947- .... **CLC 40**
See also CA 97-100; CANR 59

Minimo, Duca
See D'Annunzio, Gabriele

Minot, Susan 1956- .... **CLC 44**
See also CA 134

Minus, Ed 1938- .... **CLC 39**
See also CA 185

Miranda, Javier
See Bioy Casares, Adolfo

Miranda, Javier
See Bioy Casares, Adolfo

Mirbeau, Octave 1848-1917 .... **TCLC 55**
See also DLB 123, 192

Miro (Ferrer), Gabriel (Francisco Victor) 1879-1930 .... **TCLC 5**
See also CA 104; 185

Mishima, Yukio 1925-1970 .. **CLC 2, 4, 6, 9, 27; DC 1; SSC 4**
See also Hiraoka, Kimitake
See also DLB 182; MTCW 2

Mistral, Frederic 1830-1914 .... **TCLC 51**
See also CA 122

Mistral, Gabriela
See Godoy Alcayaga, Lucila

Mistry, Rohinton 1952- .... **CLC 71; DAC**
See also CA 141; CANR 86

Mitchell, Clyde
See Ellison, Harlan (Jay); Silverberg, Robert

Mitchell, James Leslie 1901-1935
See Gibbon, Lewis Grassic
See also CA 104; DLB 15

Mitchell, Joni 1943- .... **CLC 12**
See also CA 112

Mitchell, Joseph (Quincy) 1908-1996
.... **CLC 98**
See also CA 77-80; 152; CANR 69; DLB 185; DLBY 96

Mitchell, Margaret (Munnerlyn) 1900-1949
.... **TCLC 11; DAM NOV, POP**
See also AAYA 23; CA 109; 125; CANR 55; CDALBS; DA3; DLB 9; MTCW 1, 2

Mitchell, Peggy
See Mitchell, Margaret (Munnerlyn)

Mitchell, S(ilas) Weir 1829-1914 .. **TCLC 36**
See also CA 165; DLB 202

Mitchell, W(illiam) O(rmond) 1914-1998
.... **CLC 25; DAC; DAM MST**
See also CA 77-80; 165; CANR 15, 43; DLB 88

Mitchell, William 1879-1936 .... **TCLC 81**

Mitford, Mary Russell 1787-1855 .. **NCLC 4**
See also DLB 110, 116

Mitford, Nancy 1904-1973 .... **CLC 44**
See also CA 9-12R; DLB 191

Miyamoto, (Chujo) Yuriko 1899-1951
.... **TCLC 37**
See also CA 170, 174; DLB 180

Miyazawa, Kenji 1896-1933 .... **TCLC 76**
See also CA 157

Mizoguchi, Kenji 1898-1956 .... **TCLC 72**
See also CA 167

Mo, Timothy (Peter) 1950(?)- . **CLC 46, 134**
See also CA 117; DLB 194; MTCW 1

Modarressi, Taghi (M.) 1931- .... **CLC 44**

See also CA 121; 134; INT 134

Modiano, Patrick (Jean) 1945- .... **CLC 18**
See also CA 85-88; CANR 17, 40; DLB 83

Moerck, Paal
See Roelvaag, O(le) E(dvart)

Mofolo, Thomas (Mokopu) 1875(?)-1948
.... **TCLC 22; BLC 3; DAM MULT**
See also CA 121; 153; CANR 83; DLB 225; MTCW 2

Mohr, Nicholasa 1938- .... **CLC 12; DAM MULT; HLC 2**
See also AAYA 8; CA 49-52; CANR 1, 32, 64; CLR 22; DLB 145; HW 1, 2; JRDA; SAAS 8; SATA 8, 97; SATA-Essay 113

Mojtabai, A(nn) G(race) 1938- .... **CLC 5, 9, 15, 29**
See also CA 85-88; CANR 88

Moliere 1622-1673 .... **LC 10, 28; DA; DAB; DAC; DAM DRAM, MST; DC 13; WLC**
See also DA3

Molin, Charles
See Mayne, William (James Carter)

Molnar, Ferenc 1878-1952 . **TCLC 20; DAM DRAM**
See also CA 109; 153; CANR 83

Momaday, N(avarre) Scott 1934- .... **CLC 2, 19, 85, 95; DA; DAB; DAC; DAM MST, MULT, NOV, POP; PC 25; WLCS**
See also AAYA 11; CA 25-28R; CANR 14, 34, 68; CDALBS; DA3; DLB 143, 175; INT CANR-14; MTCW 1, 2; NNAL; SATA 48; SATA-Brief 30

Monette, Paul 1945-1995 .... **CLC 82**
See also CA 139; 147

Monroe, Harriet 1860-1936 .... **TCLC 12**
See also CA 109; DLB 54, 91

Monroe, Lyle
See Heinlein, Robert A(nson)

Montagu, Elizabeth 1720-1800 .... **NCLC 7**

Montagu, Mary (Pierrepont) Wortley 1689-1762 .... **LC 9, 57; PC 16**
See also DLB 95, 101

Montagu, W. H.
See Coleridge, Samuel Taylor

Montague, John (Patrick) 1929- .... **CLC 13, 46**
See also CA 9-12R; CANR 9, 69; DLB 40; MTCW 1

Montaigne, Michel (Eyquem) de 1533-1592
.... **LC 8; DA; DAB; DAC; DAM MST; WLC**

Montale, Eugenio 1896-1981 . **CLC 7, 9, 18; PC 13**
See also CA 17-20R; 104; CANR 30; DLB 114; MTCW 1

Montesquieu, Charles-Louis de Secondat 1689-1755 .... **LC 7**

Montessori, Maria 1870-1952 ..... **TCLC 103**
See also CA 115; 147

Montgomery, (Robert) Bruce 1921(?)-1978
See Crispin, Edmund
See also CA 179; 104

Montgomery, L(ucy) M(aud) 1874-1942
.... **TCLC 51; DAC; DAM MST**
See also AAYA 12; CA 108; 137; CLR 8; DA3; DLB 92; DLBD 14; JRDA; MAICYA; MTCW 2; SATA 100; YABC 1

Montgomery, Marion H., Jr. 1925- .. **CLC 7**
See also AITN 1; CA 1-4R; CANR 3, 48; DLB 6

Montgomery, Max
See Davenport, Guy (Mattison, Jr.)

Montherlant, Henry (Milon) de 1896-1972
.... **CLC 8, 19; DAM DRAM**
See also CA 85-88; 37-40R; DLB 72; MTCW 1

Perelman, S(idney) J(oseph) 1904-1979
.... **CLC 3, 5, 9, 15, 23, 44, 49; DAM DRAM; SSC 32**
See also AITN 1, 2; CA 73-76; 89-92; CANR 18; DLB 11, 44; MTCW 1, 2

Peret, Benjamin 1899-1959 .... **TCLC 20**
See also CA 117; 186

Peretz, Isaac Loeb 1851(?)-1915 . **TCLC 16; SSC 26**
See also CA 109

Peretz, Yitzkhok Leibush
See Peretz, Isaac Loeb

Perez Galdos, Benito 1843-1920 . **TCLC 27; HLCS 2**
See also CA 125; 153; HW 1

Peri Rossi, Cristina 1941-
See also CA 131; CANR 59, 81; DLB 145; HLCS 2; HW 1, 2

Perlata
See Peret, Benjamin

Perloff, Marjorie G(abrielle) 1931-
.... **CLC 137**
See also CA 57-60; CANR 7, 22, 49

Perrault, Charles 1628-1703 .. **LC 3, 52; DC 12**
See also MAICYA; SATA 25

Perry, Anne 1938- .... **CLC 126**
See also CA 101; CANR 22, 50, 84

Perry, Brighton
See Sherwood, Robert E(mmet)

Perse, St.-John
See Leger, (Marie-Rene Auguste) Alexis Saint-Leger

Perutz, Leo(pold) 1882-1957 .... **TCLC 60**
See also CA 147; DLB 81

Peseenz, Tulio F.
See Lopez y Fuentes, Gregorio

Pesetsky, Bette 1932- .... **CLC 28**
See also CA 133; DLB 130

Peshkov, Alexei Maximovich 1868-1936
See Gorky, Maxim
See also CA 105; 141; CANR 83; DA; DAC; DAM DRAM, MST, NOV; MTCW 2

Pessoa, Fernando (Antonio Nogueira) 1888-1935 ..... **TCLC 27; DAM MULT; HLC 2; PC 20**
See also CA 125; 183

Peterkin, Julia Mood 1880-1961 ..... **CLC 31**
See also CA 102; DLB 9

Peters, Joan K(aren) 1945- .... **CLC 39**
See also CA 158

Peters, Robert L(ouis) 1924- .... **CLC 7**
See also CA 13-16R; CAAS 8; DLB 105

Petofi, Sandor 1823-1849 .... **NCLC 21**

Petrakis, Harry Mark 1923- .... **CLC 3**
See also CA 9-12R; CANR 4, 30, 85

Petrarch 1304-1374 .... **CMLC 20; DAM POET; PC 8**
See also DA3

Petronius c. 20-66 .... **CMLC 34**
See also DLB 211

Petrov, Evgeny .... **TCLC 21**
See also Kataev, Evgeny Petrovich

Petry, Ann (Lane) 1908-1997 .. **CLC 1, 7, 18**
See also BW 1, 3; CA 5-8R; 157; CAAS 6; CANR 4, 46; CLR 12; DLB 76; JRDA; MAICYA; MTCW 1; SATA 5; SATA-Obit 94

Petursson, Halligrimur 1614-1674 .... **LC 8**

Peychinovich
See Vazov, Ivan (Minchov)

Phaedrus c. 18B.C.-c. 50 .... **CMLC 25**
See also DLB 211

Philips, Katherine 1632-1664 .... **LC 30**
See also DLB 131

Philipson, Morris H. 1926- .... **CLC 53**
See also CA 1-4R; CANR 4

Phillips, Caryl 1958- . **CLC 96; BLCS; DAM MULT**
See also BW 2; CA 141; CANR 63; DA3; DLB 157; MTCW 2

Phillips, David Graham 1867-1911
.... **TCLC 44**
See also CA 108; 176; DLB 9, 12

Phillips, Jack
See Sandburg, Carl (August)

Phillips, Jayne Anne 1952- .... **CLC 15, 33; SSC 16**
See also CA 101; CANR 24, 50; DLBY 80; INT CANR-24; MTCW 1, 2

Phillips, Richard
See Dick, Philip K(indred)

Phillips, Robert (Schaeffer) 1938- ... **CLC 28**
See also CA 17-20R; CAAS 13; CANR 8; DLB 105

Phillips, Ward
See Lovecraft, H(oward) P(hillips)

Piccolo, Lucio 1901-1969 .... **CLC 13**
See also CA 97-100; DLB 114

Pickthall, Marjorie L(owry) C(hristie) 1883-1922 .... **TCLC 21**
See also CA 107; DLB 92

Pico della Mirandola, Giovanni 1463-1494
.... **LC 15**

Piercy, Marge 1936- ... **CLC 3, 6, 14, 18, 27, 62, 128; PC 29**
See also CA 21-24R; CAAE 187; CAAS 1; CANR 13, 43, 66; DLB 120, 227; MTCW 1, 2

Piers, Robert
See Anthony, Piers

Pieyre de Mandiargues, Andre 1909-1991
See Mandiargues, Andre Pieyre de
See also CA 103; 136; CANR 22, 82

Pilnyak, Boris .... **TCLC 23**
See also Vogau, Boris Andreyevich

Pincherle, Alberto 1907-1990 ... **CLC 11, 18; DAM NOV**
See also Moravia, Alberto
See also CA 25-28R; 132; CANR 33, 63; MTCW 1

Pinckney, Darryl 1953- .... **CLC 76**
See also BW 2, 3; CA 143; CANR 79

Pindar 518B.C.-446B.C. .. **CMLC 12; PC 19**
See also DLB 176

Pineda, Cecile 1942- .... **CLC 39**
See also CA 118

Pinero, Arthur Wing 1855-1934 .. **TCLC 32; DAM DRAM**
See also CA 110; 153; DLB 10

Pinero, Miguel (Antonio Gomez) 1946-1988
.... **CLC 4, 55**
See also CA 61-64; 125; CANR 29, 90; HW 1

Pinget, Robert 1919-1997 ...... **CLC 7, 13, 37**
See also CA 85-88; 160; DLB 83

Pink Floyd
See Barrett, (Roger) Syd; Gilmour, David; Mason, Nick; Waters, Roger; Wright, Rick

Pinkney, Edward 1802-1828 .... **NCLC 31**

Pinkwater, Daniel Manus 1941- ...... **CLC 35**
See also Pinkwater, Manus
See also AAYA 1; CA 29-32R; CANR 12, 38, 89; CLR 4; JRDA; MAICYA; SAAS 3; SATA 46, 76, 114

Pinkwater, Manus
See Pinkwater, Daniel Manus
See also SATA 8

Pinsky, Robert 1940- ...... **CLC 9, 19, 38, 94, 121; DAM POET; PC 27**
See also CA 29-32R; CAAS 4; CANR 58; DA3; DLBY 82, 98; MTCW 2

Pinta, Harold
See Pinter, Harold

Pinter, Harold 1930- . **CLC 1, 3, 6, 9, 11, 15, 27, 58, 73; DA; DAB; DAC; DAM DRAM, MST; WLC**
See also CA 5-8R; CANR 33, 65; CDBLB 1960 to Present; DA3; DLB 13; MTCW 1, 2

Piozzi, Hester Lynch (Thrale) 1741-1821
.... **NCLC 57**
See also DLB 104, 142

Pirandello, Luigi 1867-1936 .... **TCLC 4, 29; DA; DAB; DAC; DAM DRAM, MST, DC 5; SSC 22; WLC**
See also CA 104; 153; DA3; MTCW 2

Pirsig, Robert M(aynard) 1928- .. **CLC 4, 6, 73; DAM POP**
See also CA 53-56; CANR 42, 74; DA3; MTCW 1, 2; SATA 39

Pisarev, Dmitry Ivanovich 1840-1868
.... **NCLC 25**

Pix, Mary (Griffith) 1666-1709 .... **LC 8**
See also DLB 80

Pixerecourt, (Rene Charles) Guilbert de 1773-1844 .... **NCLC 39**
See also DLB 192

Plaatje, Sol(omon) T(shekisho) 1876-1932
.... **TCLC 73; BLCS**
See also BW 2, 3; CA 141; CANR 79; DLB 225

Plaidy, Jean
See Hibbert, Eleanor Alice Burford

Planche, James Robinson 1796-1880
.... **NCLC 42**

Plant, Robert 1948- .... **CLC 12**

Plante, David (Robert) 1940- ..... **CLC 7, 23, 38; DAM NOV**
See also CA 37-40R; CANR 12, 36, 58, 82; DLBY 83; INT CANR-12; MTCW 1

Plath, Sylvia 1932-1963 .... **CLC 1, 2, 3, 5, 9, 11, 14, 17, 50, 51, 62, 111; DA; DAB; DAC; DAM MST, POET; PC 1; WLC**
See also AAYA 13; CA 19-20; CANR 34; CAP 2; CDALB 1941-1968; DA3; DLB 5, 6, 152; MTCW 1, 2; SATA 96

Plato 428(?)B.C.-348(?)B.C. .. **CMLC 8; DA; DAB; DAC; DAM MST; WLCS**
See also DA3; DLB 176

Platonov, Andrei
See Klimentov, Andrei Platonovich

Platt, Kin 1911- .... **CLC 26**
See also AAYA 11; CA 17-20R; CANR 11; JRDA; SAAS 17; SATA 21, 86

Plautus c. 251B.C.-184B.C. .. **CMLC 24; DC 6**
See also DLB 211

Plick et Plock
See Simenon, Georges (Jacques Christian)

Plieksans, Janis 1865-1929
See Rainis, Janis
See also CA 170; DLB 220

Plimpton, George (Ames) 1927- ...... **CLC 36**
See also AITN 1; CA 21-24R; CANR 32, 70; DLB 185; MTCW 1, 2; SATA 10

Pliny the Elder c. 23-79 .... **CMLC 23**
See also DLB 211

Plomer, William Charles Franklin 1903-1973
.... **CLC 4, 8**
See also CA 21-22; CANR 34; CAP 2; DLB 20, 162, 191, 225; MTCW 1; SATA 24

Plowman, Piers
See Kavanagh, Patrick (Joseph)

Plum, J.
See Wodehouse, P(elham) G(renville)

Plumly, Stanley (Ross) 1939- .... **CLC 33**
See also CA 108; 110; DLB 5, 193; INT 110

Plumpe, Friedrich Wilhelm 1888-1931
.... **TCLC 53**
See also CA 112

Po Chu-i 772-846 .... **CMLC 24**

Poe, Edgar Allan 1809-1849 .... **NCLC 1, 16, 55, 78, 94; DA; DAB; DAC; DAM MST,**

See also CA 45-48; CANR 2, 32, 63; DA3; DLB 113; HW 1, 2; MTCW 1, 2

Pulitzer, Joseph 1847-1911 .... **TCLC 76**
See also CA 114; DLB 23

Purdy, A(lfred) W(ellington) 1918- .. **CLC 3, 6, 14, 50; DAC; DAM MST, POET**
See also CA 81-84; CAAS 17; CANR 42, 66; DLB 88

Purdy, James (Amos) 1923- ... **CLC 2, 4, 10, 28, 52**
See also CA 33-36R; CAAS 1; CANR 19, 51; DLB 2; INT CANR-19; MTCW 1

Pure, Simon
See Swinnerton, Frank Arthur

Pushkin, Alexander (Sergeyevich) 1799-1837 .... **NCLC 3, 27, 83; DA; DAB; DAC; DAM DRAM, MST, POET; PC 10; SSC 27; WLC**
See also DA3; DLB 205; SATA 61

P'u Sung-ling 1640-1715 ...... **LC 49; SSC 31**

Putnam, Arthur Lee
See Alger, Horatio Jr., Jr.

Puzo, Mario 1920-1999 ..... **CLC 1, 2, 6, 36, 107; DAM NOV, POP**
See also CA 65-68; 185; CANR 4, 42, 65; DA3; DLB 6; MTCW 1, 2

Pygge, Edward
See Barnes, Julian (Patrick)

Pyle, Ernest Taylor 1900-1945
See Pyle, Ernie
See also CA 115; 160

Pyle, Ernie 1900-1945 .... **TCLC 75**
See also Pyle, Ernest Taylor
See also DLB 29; MTCW 2

Pyle, Howard 1853-1911 .... **TCLC 81**
See also CA 109; 137; CLR 22; DLB 42, 188; DLBD 13; MAICYA; SATA 16, 100

Pym, Barbara (Mary Crampton) 1913-1980 .... **CLC 13, 19, 37, 111**
See also CA 13-14; 97-100; CANR 13, 34; CAP 1; DLB 14, 207; DLBY 87; MTCW 1, 2

Pynchon, Thomas (Ruggles, Jr.) 1937- . **CLC 2, 3, 6, 9, 11, 18, 33, 62, 72, 123; DA; DAB; DAC; DAM MST, NOV, POP; SSC 14; WLC**
See also BEST 90:2; CA 17-20R; CANR 22, 46, 73; DA3; DLB 2, 173; MTCW 1, 2

Pythagoras c. 570B.C.-c. 500B.C. . **CMLC 22**
See also DLB 176

Q
See Quiller-Couch, SirArthur (Thomas)

Qian Zhongshu
See Ch'ien Chung-shu

Qroll
See Dagerman, Stig (Halvard)

Quarrington, Paul (Lewis) 1953- .... **CLC 65**
See also CA 129; CANR 62

Quasimodo, Salvatore 1901-1968 .... **CLC 10**
See also CA 13-16; 25-28R; CAP 1; DLB 114; MTCW 1

Quay, Stephen 1947- .... **CLC 95**
Quay, Timothy 1947- .... **CLC 95**
Queen, Ellery .... **CLC 3, 11**
See also Dannay, Frederic; Davidson, Avram (James); Deming, Richard; Fairman, Paul W.; Flora, Fletcher; Hoch, Edward D(entinger); Kane, Henry; Lee, Manfred B(ennington); Marlowe, Stephen; Powell, Talmage; Sheldon, Walter J.; Sturgeon, Theodore (Hamilton); Tracy, Don(ald Fiske); Vance, John Holbrook

Queen, Ellery, Jr.
See Dannay, Frederic; Lee, Manfred B(ennington)

Queneau, Raymond 1903-1976 .... **CLC 2, 5, 10, 42**

See also CA 77-80; 69-72; CANR 32; DLB 72; MTCW 1, 2

Quevedo, Francisco de 1580-1645 ..... **LC 23**

Quiller-Couch, SirArthur (Thomas) 1863-1944 .... **TCLC 53**
See also CA 118; 166; DLB 135, 153, 190

Quin, Ann (Marie) 1936-1973 .... **CLC 6**
See also CA 9-12R; 45-48; DLB 14, 231

Quinn, Martin
See Smith, Martin Cruz

Quinn, Peter 1947- .... **CLC 91**

Quinn, Simon
See Smith, Martin Cruz

Quintana, Leroy V. 1944-
See also CA 131; CANR 65; DAM MULT; DLB 82; HLC 2; HW 1, 2

Quiroga, Horacio (Sylvestre) 1878-1937 .... **TCLC 20; DAM MULT; HLC 2**
See also CA 117; 131; HW 1; MTCW 1

Quoirez, Francoise 1935- .... **CLC 9**
See also Sagan, Francoise
See also CA 49-52; CANR 6, 39, 73; MTCW 1, 2

Raabe, Wilhelm (Karl) 1831-1910 . **TCLC 45**
See also CA 167; DLB 129

Rabe, David (William) 1940- . **CLC 4, 8, 33; DAM DRAM**
See also CA 85-88; CABS 3; CANR 59; DLB 7, 228

Rabelais, Francois 1483-1553 .... **LC 5, 60; DA; DAB; DAC; DAM MST; WLC**

Rabinovitch, Sholem 1859-1916
See Aleichem, Sholom
See also CA 104

Rabinyan, Dorit 1972- .... **CLC 119**
See also CA 170

Rachilde
See Vallette, Marguerite Eymery

Racine, Jean 1639-1699 . **LC 28; DAB; DAM MST**
See also DA3

Radcliffe, Ann (Ward) 1764-1823 . **NCLC 6, 55**
See also DLB 39, 178

Radiguet, Raymond 1903-1923 ..... **TCLC 29**
See also CA 162; DLB 65

Radnoti, Miklos 1909-1944 .... **TCLC 16**
See also CA 118

Rado, James 1939- .... **CLC 17**
See also CA 105

Radvanyi, Netty 1900-1983
See Seghers, Anna
See also CA 85-88; 110; CANR 82

Rae, Ben
See Griffiths, Trevor

Raeburn, John (Hay) 1941- .... **CLC 34**
See also CA 57-60

Ragni, Gerome 1942-1991 .... **CLC 17**
See also CA 105; 134

Rahv, Philip 1908-1973 .... **CLC 24**
See also Greenberg, Ivan
See also DLB 137

Raimund, Ferdinand Jakob 1790-1836 .... **NCLC 69**
See also DLB 90

Raine, Craig 1944- .... **CLC 32, 103**
See also CA 108; CANR 29, 51; DLB 40

Raine, Kathleen (Jessie) 1908- .... **CLC 7, 45**
See also CA 85-88; CANR 46; DLB 20; MTCW 1

Rainis, Janis 1865-1929 .... **TCLC 29**
See also Plieksans, Janis
See also CA 170; DLB 220

Rakosi, Carl 1903- .... **CLC 47**
See also Rawley, Callman
See also CAAS 5; DLB 193

Raleigh, Richard
See Lovecraft, H(oward) P(hillips)

Raleigh, Sir Walter 1554(?)-1618 ...... **LC 31, 39; PC 31**
See also CDBLB Before 1660; DLB 172

Rallentando, H. P.
See Sayers, Dorothy L(eigh)

Ramal, Walter
See de la Mare, Walter (John)

Ramana Maharshi 1879-1950 .... **TCLC 84**

Ramoacn y Cajal, Santiago 1852-1934 .... **TCLC 93**

Ramon, Juan
See Jimenez (Mantecon), Juan Ramon

Ramos, Graciliano 1892-1953 .... **TCLC 32**
See also CA 167; HW 2

Rampersad, Arnold 1941- .... **CLC 44**
See also BW 2, 3; CA 127; 133; CANR 81; DLB 111; INT 133

Rampling, Anne
See Rice, Anne

Ramsay, Allan 1684(?)-1758 .... **LC 29**
See also DLB 95

Ramuz, Charles-Ferdinand 1878-1947 .... **TCLC 33**
See also CA 165

Rand, Ayn 1905-1982 ..... **CLC 3, 30, 44, 79; DA; DAC; DAM MST, NOV, POP; WLC**
See also AAYA 10; CA 13-16R; 105; CANR 27, 73; CDALBS; DA3; DLB 227; MTCW 1, 2

Randall, Dudley (Felker) 1914-2000 . **CLC 1, 135; BLC 3; DAM MULT**
See also BW 1, 3; CA 25-28R; CANR 23, 82; DLB 41

Randall, Robert
See Silverberg, Robert

Ranger, Ken
See Creasey, John

Ransom, John Crowe 1888-1974 . **CLC 2, 4, 5, 11, 24; DAM POET**
See also CA 5-8R; 49-52; CANR 6, 34; CDALBS; DA3; DLB 45, 63; MTCW 1, 2

Rao, Raja 1909- .... **CLC 25, 56; DAM NOV**
See also CA 73-76; CANR 51; MTCW 1, 2

Raphael, Frederic (Michael) 1931- .. **CLC 2, 14**
See also CA 1-4R; CANR 1, 86; DLB 14

Ratcliffe, James P.
See Mencken, H(enry) L(ouis)

Rathbone, Julian 1935- .... **CLC 41**
See also CA 101; CANR 34, 73

Rattigan, Terence (Mervyn) 1911-1977 .... **CLC 7; DAM DRAM**
See also CA 85-88; 73-76; CDBLB 1945-1960; DLB 13; MTCW 1, 2

Ratushinskaya, Irina 1954- .... **CLC 54**
See also CA 129; CANR 68

Raven, Simon (Arthur Noel) 1927- . **CLC 14**
See also CA 81-84; CANR 86

Ravenna, Michael
See Welty, Eudora

Rawley, Callman 1903-
See Rakosi, Carl
See also CA 21-24R; CANR 12, 32, 91

Rawlings, Marjorie Kinnan 1896-1953 .... **TCLC 4**
See also AAYA 20; CA 104; 137; CANR 74; CLR 63; DLB 9, 22, 102; DLBD 17; JRDA; MAICYA; MTCW 2; SATA 100; YABC 1

Ray, Satyajit 1921-1992 . **CLC 16, 76; DAM MULT**
See also CA 114; 137

Read, Herbert Edward 1893-1968 .... **CLC 4**
See also CA 85-88; 25-28R; DLB 20, 149

See also DA3

Rinehart, Mary Roberts 1876-1958
.... **TCLC 52**
See also CA 108; 166

Ringmaster, The
See Mencken, H(enry) L(ouis)

Ringwood, Gwen(dolyn Margaret) Pharis
1910-1984 .... **CLC 48**
See also CA 148; 112; DLB 88

Rio, Michel 19(?)- .... **CLC 43**

Ritsos, Giannes
See Ritsos, Yannis

Ritsos, Yannis 1909-1990 .... **CLC 6, 13, 31**
See also CA 77-80; 133; CANR 39, 61;
MTCW 1

Ritter, Erika 1948(?)- .... **CLC 52**

Rivera, Jose Eustasio 1889-1928 .. **TCLC 35**
See also CA 162; HW 1, 2

Rivera, Tomas 1935-1984
See also CA 49-52; CANR 32; DLB 82;
HLCS 2; HW 1

Rivers, Conrad Kent 1933-1968 .... **CLC 1**
See also BW 1; CA 85-88; DLB 41

Rivers, Elfrida
See Bradley, Marion Zimmer

Riverside, John
See Heinlein, Robert A(nson)

Rizal, Jose 1861-1896 .... **NCLC 27**

Roa Bastos, Augusto (Antonio) 1917-
.... **CLC 45; DAM MULT; HLC 2**
See also CA 131; DLB 113; HW 1

Robbe-Grillet, Alain 1922- ... **CLC 1, 2, 4, 6,
8, 10, 14, 43, 128**
See also CA 9-12R; CANR 33, 65; DLB
83; MTCW 1, 2

Robbins, Harold 1916-1997 ... **CLC 5; DAM
NOV**
See also CA 73-76; 162; CANR 26, 54;
DA3; MTCW 1, 2

Robbins, Thomas Eugene 1936-
See Robbins, Tom
See also CA 81-84; CANR 29, 59; DAM
NOV, POP; DA3; MTCW 1, 2

Robbins, Tom .... **CLC 9, 32, 64**
See also Robbins, Thomas Eugene
See also AAYA 32; BEST 90:3; DLBY 80;
MTCW 2

Robbins, Trina 1938- .... **CLC 21**
See also CA 128

Roberts, Charles G(eorge) D(ouglas)
1860-1943 .... **TCLC 8**
See also CA 105; CLR 33; DLB 92; SATA
88; SATA-Brief 29

Roberts, Elizabeth Madox 1886-1941
.... **TCLC 68**
See also CA 111; 166; DLB 9, 54, 102;
SATA 33; SATA-Brief 27

Roberts, Kate 1891-1985 .... **CLC 15**
See also CA 107; 116

Roberts, Keith (John Kingston) 1935-
.... **CLC 14**
See also CA 25-28R; CANR 46

Roberts, Kenneth (Lewis) 1885-1957
.... **TCLC 23**
See also CA 109; DLB 9

Roberts, Michele (B.) 1949- .... **CLC 48**
See also CA 115; CANR 58; DLB 231

Robertson, Ellis
See Ellison, Harlan (Jay); Silverberg, Robert

Robertson, Thomas William 1829-1871
.... **NCLC 35; DAM DRAM**

Robeson, Kenneth
See Dent, Lester

Robinson, Edwin Arlington 1869-1935
. **TCLC 5, 101; DA; DAC; DAM MST,
POET; PC 1**

See also CA 104; 133; CDALB 1865-1917;
DLB 54; MTCW 1, 2

Robinson, Henry Crabb 1775-1867
.... **NCLC 15**
See also DLB 107

Robinson, Jill 1936- .... **CLC 10**
See also CA 102; INT 102

Robinson, Kim Stanley 1952- .... **CLC 34**
See also AAYA 26; CA 126; SATA 109

Robinson, Lloyd
See Silverberg, Robert

Robinson, Marilynne 1944- .... **CLC 25**
See also CA 116; CANR 80; DLB 206

Robinson, Smokey .... **CLC 21**
See also Robinson, William, Jr.

Robinson, William, Jr. 1940-
See Robinson, Smokey
See also CA 116

Robison, Mary 1949- .... **CLC 42, 98**
See also CA 113; 116; CANR 87; DLB 130;
INT 116

Rod, Edouard 1857-1910 .... **TCLC 52**

Roddenberry, Eugene Wesley 1921-1991
See Roddenberry, Gene
See also CA 110; 135; CANR 37; SATA 45;
SATA-Obit 69

Roddenberry, Gene .... **CLC 17**
See also Roddenberry, Eugene Wesley
See also AAYA 5; SATA-Obit 69

Rodgers, Mary 1931- .... **CLC 12**
See also CA 49-52; CANR 8, 55, 90; CLR
20; INT CANR-8; JRDA; MAICYA;
SATA 8

Rodgers, W(illiam) R(obert) 1909-1969
.... **CLC 7**
See also CA 85-88; DLB 20

Rodman, Eric
See Silverberg, Robert

Rodman, Howard 1920(?)-1985 ...... **CLC 65**
See also CA 118

Rodman, Maia
See Wojciechowska, Maia (Teresa)

Rodo, Jose Enrique 1872(?)-1917
See also CA 178; HLCS 2; HW 2

Rodriguez, Claudio 1934- .... **CLC 10**
See also DLB 134

Rodriguez, Richard 1944-
See also CA 110; CANR 66; DAM MULT;
DLB 82; HLC 2; HW 1, 2

Roelvaag, O(le) E(dvart) 1876-1931
.... **TCLC 17**
See also Rolvaag, O(le) E(dvart)
See also CA 117; 171; DLB 9

Roethke, Theodore (Huebner) 1908-1963
.... **CLC 1, 3, 8, 11, 19, 46, 101; DAM
POET; PC 15**
See also CA 81-84; CABS 2; CDALB 1941-
1968; DA3; DLB 5, 206; MTCW 1, 2

Rogers, Samuel 1763-1855 .... **NCLC 69**
See also DLB 93

Rogers, Thomas Hunton 1927- .... **CLC 57**
See also CA 89-92; INT 89-92

Rogers, Will(iam Penn Adair) 1879-1935
.... **TCLC 8, 71; DAM MULT**
See also CA 105; 144; DA3; DLB 11;
MTCW 2; NNAL

Rogin, Gilbert 1929- .... **CLC 18**
See also CA 65-68; CANR 15

Rohan, Koda
See Koda Shigeyuki

Rohlfs, Anna Katharine Green
See Green, Anna Katharine

Rohmer, Eric .... **CLC 16**
See also Scherer, Jean-Marie Maurice

Rohmer, Sax .... **TCLC 28**
See also Ward, Arthur Henry Sarsfield
See also DLB 70

Roiphe, Anne (Richardson) 1935- . **CLC 3, 9**

See also CA 89-92; CANR 45, 73; DLBY
80; INT 89-92

Rojas, Fernando de 1465-1541 .... **LC 23;
HLCS 1**

Rojas, Gonzalo 1917-
See also HLCS 2; HW 2

Rojas, Gonzalo 1917-
See also CA 178; HLCS 2

**Rolfe, Frederick (William Serafino Austin
Lewis Mary)** 1860-1913 .... **TCLC 12**
See also CA 107; DLB 34, 156

Rolland, Romain 1866-1944 .... **TCLC 23**
See also CA 118; DLB 65

Rolle, Richard c. 1300-c. 1349 ..... **CMLC 21**
See also DLB 146

Rolvaag, O(le) E(dvart)
See Roelvaag, O(le) E(dvart)

Romain Arnaud, Saint
See Aragon, Louis

Romains, Jules 1885-1972 .... **CLC 7**
See also CA 85-88; CANR 34; DLB 65;
MTCW 1

Romero, Jose Ruben 1890-1952 ... **TCLC 14**
See also CA 114; 131; HW 1

Ronsard, Pierre de 1524-1585 ...... **LC 6, 54;
PC 11**

Rooke, Leon 1934- . **CLC 25, 34; DAM POP**
See also CA 25-28R; CANR 23, 53

Roosevelt, Franklin Delano 1882-1945
.... **TCLC 93**
See also CA 116; 173

Roosevelt, Theodore 1858-1919 .... **TCLC 69**
See also CA 115; 170; DLB 47, 186

Roper, William 1498-1578 .... **LC 10**

Roquelaure, A. N.
See Rice, Anne

Rosa, Joao Guimaraes 1908-1967 . **CLC 23;
HLCS 1**
See also CA 89-92; DLB 113

Rose, Wendy 1948- . **CLC 85; DAM MULT;
PC 13**
See also CA 53-56; CANR 5, 51; DLB 175;
NNAL; SATA 12

Rosen, R. D.
See Rosen, Richard (Dean)

Rosen, Richard (Dean) 1949- .... **CLC 39**
See also CA 77-80; CANR 62; INT
CANR-30

Rosenberg, Isaac 1890-1918 .... **TCLC 12**
See also CA 107; DLB 20

Rosenblatt, Joe .... **CLC 15**
See also Rosenblatt, Joseph

Rosenblatt, Joseph 1933-
See Rosenblatt, Joe
See also CA 89-92; INT 89-92

Rosenfeld, Samuel
See Tzara, Tristan

Rosenstock, Sami
See Tzara, Tristan

Rosenstock, Samuel
See Tzara, Tristan

Rosenthal, M(acha) L(ouis) 1917-1996
.... **CLC 28**
See also CA 1-4R; 152; CAAS 6; CANR 4,
51; DLB 5; SATA 59

Ross, Barnaby
See Dannay, Frederic

Ross, Bernard L.
See Follett, Ken(neth Martin)

Ross, J. H.
See Lawrence, T(homas) E(dward)

Ross, John Hume
See Lawrence, T(homas) E(dward)

Ross, Martin
See Martin, Violet Florence
See also DLB 135

Ross, (James) Sinclair 1908-1996 .. **CLC 13;
DAC; DAM MST; SSC 24**

Salamanca, J(ack) R(ichard) 1922- . **CLC 4, 15**
See also CA 25-28R

Salas, Floyd Francis 1931-
See also CA 119; CAAS 27; CANR 44, 75, 93; DAM MULT; DLB 82; HLC 2; HW 1, 2; MTCW 2

Sale, J. Kirkpatrick
See Sale, Kirkpatrick

Sale, Kirkpatrick 1937- .... **CLC 68**
See also CA 13-16R; CANR 10

Salinas, Luis Omar 1937- .... **CLC 90; DAM MULT; HLC 2**
See also CA 131; CANR 81; DLB 82; HW 1, 2

Salinas (y Serrano), Pedro 1891(?)-1951
.... **TCLC 17**
See also CA 117; DLB 134

Salinger, J(erome) D(avid) 1919- . **CLC 1, 3, 8, 12, 55, 56, 138; DA; DAB; DAC; DAM MST, NOV, POP; SSC 2, 28; WLC**
See also AAYA 2; CA 5-8R; CANR 39; CDALB 1941-1968; CLR 18; DA3; DLB 2, 102, 173; MAICYA; MTCW 1, 2; SATA 67

Salisbury, John
See Caute, (John) David

Salter, James 1925- .... **CLC 7, 52, 59**
See also CA 73-76; DLB 130

Saltus, Edgar (Everton) 1855-1921 . **TCLC 8**
See also CA 105; DLB 202

Saltykov, Mikhail Evgrafovich 1826-1889
.... **NCLC 16**

Samarakis, Antonis 1919- .... **CLC 5**
See also CA 25-28R; CAAS 16; CANR 36

Sanchez, Florencio 1875-1910 .... **TCLC 37**
See also CA 153; HW 1

Sanchez, Luis Rafael 1936- .... **CLC 23**
See also CA 128; DLB 145; HW 1

Sanchez, Sonia 1934- .. **CLC 5, 116; BLC 3; DAM MULT; PC 9**
See also BW 2, 3; CA 33-36R; CANR 24, 49, 74; CLR 18; DA3; DLB 41; DLBD 8; MAICYA; MTCW 1, 2; SATA 22

Sand, George 1804-1876 ... **NCLC 2, 42, 57; DA; DAB; DAC; DAM MST, NOV; WLC**
See also DA3; DLB 119, 192

Sandburg, Carl (August) 1878-1967 . **CLC 1, 4, 10, 15, 35; DA; DAB; DAC; DAM MST, POET; PC 2; WLC**
See also AAYA 24; CA 5-8R; 25-28R; CANR 35; CDALB 1865-1917; CLR 67; DA3; DLB 17, 54; MAICYA; MTCW 1, 2; SATA 8

Sandburg, Charles
See Sandburg, Carl (August)

Sandburg, Charles A.
See Sandburg, Carl (August)

Sanders, (James) Ed(ward) 1939- . **CLC 53; DAM POET**
See also CA 13-16R; CAAS 21; CANR 13, 44, 78; DLB 16

Sanders, Lawrence 1920-1998 .... **CLC 41; DAM POP**
See also BEST 89:4; CA 81-84; 165; CANR 33, 62; DA3; MTCW 1

Sanders, Noah
See Blount, Roy (Alton), Jr.

Sanders, Winston P.
See Anderson, Poul (William)

Sandoz, Mari(e Susette) 1896-1966 . **CLC 28**
See also CA 1-4R; 25-28R; CANR 17, 64; DLB 9, 212; MTCW 1, 2; SATA 5

Saner, Reg(inald Anthony) 1931- ...... **CLC 9**
See also CA 65-68

Sankara 788-820 .... **CMLC 32**

Sannazaro, Jacopo 1456(?)-1530 .... **LC 8**

Sansom, William 1912-1976 .... **CLC 2, 6; DAM NOV; SSC 21**
See also CA 5-8R; 65-68; CANR 42; DLB 139; MTCW 1

Santayana, George 1863-1952 ...... **TCLC 40**
See also CA 115; DLB 54, 71; DLBD 13

Santiago, Danny .... **CLC 33**
See also James, Daniel (Lewis)
See also DLB 122

Santmyer, Helen Hoover 1895-1986 . **CLC 33**
See also CA 1-4R; 118; CANR 15, 33; DLBY 84; MTCW 1

Santoka, Taneda 1882-1940 .... **TCLC 72**

Santos, Bienvenido N(uqui) 1911-1996
.... **CLC 22; DAM MULT**
See also CA 101; 151; CANR 19, 46

Sapper .... **TCLC 44**
See also McNeile, Herman Cyril

Sapphire
See Sapphire, Brenda

Sapphire, Brenda 1950- .... **CLC 99**

Sappho fl. 6th cent. B.C.- ... **CMLC 3; DAM POET; PC 5**
See also DA3; DLB 176

Saramago, Jose 1922- .... **CLC 119; HLCS 1**
See also CA 153

Sarduy, Severo 1937-1993 .... **CLC 6, 97; HLCS 1**
See also CA 89-92; 142; CANR 58, 81; DLB 113; HW 1, 2

Sargeson, Frank 1903-1982 .... **CLC 31**
See also CA 25-28R; 106; CANR 38, 79

Sarmiento, Domingo Faustino 1811-1888
See also HLCS 2

Sarmiento, Felix Ruben Garcia
See Dario, Ruben

Saro-Wiwa, Ken(ule Beeson) 1941-1995
.... **CLC 114**
See also BW 2; CA 142; 150; CANR 60; DLB 157

Saroyan, William 1908-1981 .. **CLC 1, 8, 10, 29, 34, 56; DA; DAB; DAC; DAM DRAM, MST, NOV; SSC 21; WLC**
See also CA 5-8R; 103; CANR 30; CDALBS; DA3; DLB 7, 9, 86; DLBY 81; MTCW 1, 2; SATA 23; SATA-Obit 24

Sarraute, Nathalie 1900-1999 .. **CLC 1, 2, 4, 8, 10, 31, 80**
See also CA 9-12R; 187; CANR 23, 66; DLB 83; MTCW 1, 2

Sarton, (Eleanor) May 1912-1995 .... **CLC 4, 14, 49, 91; DAM POET**
See also CA 1-4R; 149; CANR 1, 34, 55; DLB 48; DLBY 81; INT CANR-34; MTCW 1, 2; SATA 36; SATA-Obit 86

Sartre, Jean-Paul 1905-1980 .... **CLC 1, 4, 7, 9, 13, 18, 24, 44, 50, 52; DA; DAB; DAC; DAM DRAM, MST, NOV; DC 3; SSC 32; WLC**
See also CA 9-12R; 97-100; CANR 21; DA3; DLB 72; MTCW 1, 2

Sassoon, Siegfried (Lorraine) 1886-1967
. **CLC 36, 130; DAB; DAM MST, NOV, POET; PC 12**
See also CA 104; 25-28R; CANR 36; DLB 20, 191; DLBD 18; MTCW 1, 2

Satterfield, Charles
See Pohl, Frederik

Satyremont
See Peret, Benjamin

Saul, John (W. III) 1942- ..... **CLC 46; DAM NOV, POP**
See also AAYA 10; BEST 90:4; CA 81-84; CANR 16, 40, 81; SATA 98

Saunders, Caleb
See Heinlein, Robert A(nson)

Saura (Atares), Carlos 1932- .... **CLC 20**
See also CA 114; 131; CANR 79; HW 1

Sauser-Hall, Frederic 1887-1961 ..... **CLC 18**
See also Cendrars, Blaise
See also CA 102; 93-96; CANR 36, 62; MTCW 1

Saussure, Ferdinand de 1857-1913
.... **TCLC 49**

Savage, Catharine
See Brosman, Catharine Savage

Savage, Thomas 1915- .... **CLC 40**
See also CA 126; 132; CAAS 15; INT 132

Savan, Glenn 19(?)- .... **CLC 50**

Sayers, Dorothy L(eigh) 1893-1957
.... **TCLC 2, 15; DAM POP**
See also CA 104; 119; CANR 60; CDBLB 1914-1945; DLB 10, 36, 77, 100; MTCW 1, 2

Sayers, Valerie 1952- .... **CLC 50, 122**
See also CA 134; CANR 61

Sayles, John (Thomas) 1950- . **CLC 7, 10, 14**
See also CA 57-60; CANR 41, 84; DLB 44

Scammell, Michael 1935- .... **CLC 34**
See also CA 156

Scannell, Vernon 1922- .... **CLC 49**
See also CA 5-8R; CANR 8, 24, 57; DLB 27; SATA 59

Scarlett, Susan
See Streatfeild, (Mary) Noel

Scarron
See Mikszath, Kalman

Schaeffer, Susan Fromberg 1941- .... **CLC 6, 11, 22**
See also CA 49-52; CANR 18, 65; DLB 28; MTCW 1, 2; SATA 22

Schary, Jill
See Robinson, Jill

Schell, Jonathan 1943- .... **CLC 35**
See also CA 73-76; CANR 12

Schelling, Friedrich Wilhelm Joseph von 1775-1854 .... **NCLC 30**
See also DLB 90

Schendel, Arthur van 1874-1946 .. **TCLC 56**

Scherer, Jean-Marie Maurice 1920-
See Rohmer, Eric
See also CA 110

Schevill, James (Erwin) 1920- .... **CLC 7**
See also CA 5-8R; CAAS 12

Schiller, Friedrich 1759-1805 . **NCLC 39, 69; DAM DRAM; DC 12**
See also DLB 94

Schisgal, Murray (Joseph) 1926- ...... **CLC 6**
See also CA 21-24R; CANR 48, 86

Schlee, Ann 1934- .... **CLC 35**
See also CA 101; CANR 29, 88; SATA 44; SATA-Brief 36

Schlegel, August Wilhelm von 1767-1845
.... **NCLC 15**
See also DLB 94

Schlegel, Friedrich 1772-1829 ...... **NCLC 45**
See also DLB 90

Schlegel, Johann Elias (von) 1719(?)-1749
.... **LC 5**

Schlesinger, Arthur M(eier), Jr. 1917-
.... **CLC 84**
See also AITN 1; CA 1-4R; CANR 1, 28, 58; DLB 17; INT CANR-28; MTCW 1, 2; SATA 61

Schmidt, Arno (Otto) 1914-1979 ..... **CLC 56**
See also CA 128; 109; DLB 69

Schmitz, Aron Hector 1861-1928
See Svevo, Italo
See also CA 104; 122; MTCW 1

Schnackenberg, Gjertrud 1953- ...... **CLC 40**
See also CA 116; DLB 120

Schneider, Leonard Alfred 1925-1966
See Bruce, Lenny
See also CA 89-92

Schnitzler, Arthur 1862-1931 . **TCLC 4; SSC 15**
See also CA 104; DLB 81, 118

37, 60; DAB; DAM DRAM, MST; DC 7
 See also CA 25-28R; CANR 25, 47, 74;
 CDBLB 1960 to Present; DA3; DLB 13,
 233; MTCW 1, 2

Shakey, Bernard
 See Young, Neil

Shalamov, Varlam (Tikhonovich)
 1907(?)-1982 .... **CLC 18**
 See also CA 129; 105

Shamlu, Ahmad 1925- .... **CLC 10**

Shammas, Anton 1951- .... **CLC 55**

Shandling, Arline
 See Berriault, Gina

Shange, Ntozake 1948- ... **CLC 8, 25, 38, 74, 126; BLC 3; DAM DRAM, MULT; DC 3**
 See also AAYA 9; BW 2; CA 85-88; CABS
 3; CANR 27, 48, 74; DA3; DLB 38;
 MTCW 1, 2

Shanley, John Patrick 1950- .... **CLC 75**
 See also CA 128; 133; CANR 83

Shapcott, Thomas W(illiam) 1935- . **CLC 38**
 See also CA 69-72; CANR 49, 83

Shapiro, Jane .... **CLC 76**

Shapiro, Karl (Jay) 1913- . **CLC 4, 8, 15, 53; PC 25**
 See also CA 1-4R; CAAS 6; CANR 1, 36,
 66; DLB 48; MTCW 1, 2

Sharp, William 1855-1905 .... **TCLC 39**
 See also CA 160; DLB 156

Sharpe, Thomas Ridley 1928-
 See Sharpe, Tom
 See also CA 114; 122; CANR 85; DLB 231;
 INT 122

Sharpe, Tom .... **CLC 36**
 See also Sharpe, Thomas Ridley
 See also DLB 14

Shaw, Bernard
 See Shaw, George Bernard
 See also BW 1; MTCW 2

Shaw, G. Bernard
 See Shaw, George Bernard

Shaw, George Bernard 1856-1950 . **TCLC 3, 9, 21, 45; DA; DAB; DAC; DAM DRAM, MST; WLC**
 See also Shaw, Bernard
 See also CA 104; 128; CDBLB 1914-1945;
 DA3; DLB 10, 57, 190; MTCW 1, 2

Shaw, Henry Wheeler 1818-1885 . **NCLC 15**
 See also DLB 11

Shaw, Irwin 1913-1984 .... **CLC 7, 23, 34; DAM DRAM, POP**
 See also AITN 1; CA 13-16R; 112; CANR
 21; CDALB 1941-1968; DLB 6, 102;
 DLBY 84; MTCW 1, 21

Shaw, Robert 1927-1978 .... **CLC 5**
 See also AITN 1; CA 1-4R; 81-84; CANR
 4; DLB 13, 14

Shaw, T. E.
 See Lawrence, T(homas) E(dward)

Shawn, Wallace 1943- .... **CLC 41**
 See also CA 112

Shea, Lisa 1953- .... **CLC 86**
 See also CA 147

Sheed, Wilfrid (John Joseph) 1930- . **CLC 2, 4, 10, 53**
 See also CA 65-68; CANR 30, 66; DLB 6;
 MTCW 1, 2

Sheldon, Alice Hastings Bradley
 1915(?)-1987
 See Tiptree, James, Jr.
 See also CA 108; 122; CANR 34; INT 108;
 MTCW 1

Sheldon, John
 See Bloch, Robert (Albert)

Sheldon, Walter J. 1917-
 See Queen, Ellery
 See also AITN 1; CA 25-28R; CANR 10

Shelley, Mary Wollstonecraft (Godwin)
 1797-1851 .... **NCLC 14, 59; DA; DAB; DAC; DAM MST, NOV; WLC**
 See also AAYA 20; CDBLB 1789-1832;
 DA3; DLB 110, 116, 159, 178; SATA 29

Shelley, Percy Bysshe 1792-1822 . **NCLC 18, 93; DA; DAB; DAC; DAM MST, POET; PC 14; WLC**
 See also CDBLB 1789-1832; DA3; DLB
 96, 110, 158

Shepard, Jim 1956- .... **CLC 36**
 See also CA 137; CANR 59; SATA 90

Shepard, Lucius 1947- .... **CLC 34**
 See also CA 128; 141; CANR 81

Shepard, Sam 1943- ... **CLC 4, 6, 17, 34, 41, 44; DAM DRAM; DC 5**
 See also AAYA 1; CA 69-72; CABS 3;
 CANR 22; DA3; DLB 7, 212; MTCW 1,
 2

Shepherd, Michael
 See Ludlum, Robert

Sherburne, Zoa (Lillian Morin) 1912-1995
 .... **CLC 30**
 See also AAYA 13; CA 1-4R; 176; CANR
 3, 37; MAICYA; SAAS 18; SATA 3

Sheridan, Frances 1724-1766 .... **LC 7**
 See also DLB 39, 84

Sheridan, Richard Brinsley 1751-1816
 .. **NCLC 5, 91; DA; DAB; DAC; DAM DRAM, MST; DC 1; WLC**
 See also CDBLB 1660-1789; DLB 89

Sherman, Jonathan Marc .... **CLC 55**

Sherman, Martin 1941(?)- .... **CLC 19**
 See also CA 116; 123; CANR 86

Sherwin, Judith Johnson 1936-
 See Johnson, Judith (Emlyn)
 See also CANR 85

Sherwood, Frances 1940- .... **CLC 81**
 See also CA 146

Sherwood, Robert E(mmet) 1896-1955
 .... **TCLC 3; DAM DRAM**
 See also CA 104; 153; CANR 86; DLB 7,
 26

Shestov, Lev 1866-1938 .... **TCLC 56**

Shevchenko, Taras 1814-1861 .... **NCLC 54**

Shiel, M(atthew) P(hipps) 1865-1947
 .... **TCLC 8**
 See also Holmes, Gordon
 See also CA 106; 160; DLB 153; MTCW 2

Shields, Carol 1935- ...... **CLC 91, 113; DAC**
 See also CA 81-84; CANR 51, 74; DA3;
 MTCW 2

Shields, David 1956- .... **CLC 97**
 See also CA 124; CANR 48

Shiga, Naoya 1883-1971 .... **CLC 33; SSC 23**
 See also CA 101; 33-36R; DLB 180

Shikibu, Murasaki c. 978-c. 1014 . **CMLC 1**

Shilts, Randy 1951-1994 .... **CLC 85**
 See also AAYA 19; CA 115; 127; 144;
 CANR 45; DA3; INT 127; MTCW 2

Shimazaki, Haruki 1872-1943
 See Shimazaki Toson
 See also CA 105; 134; CANR 84

Shimazaki Toson 1872-1943 .... **TCLC 5**
 See also Shimazaki, Haruki
 See also DLB 180

Sholokhov, Mikhail (Aleksandrovich)
 1905-1984 .... **CLC 7, 15**
 See also CA 101; 112; MTCW 1, 2; SATA-
 Obit 36

Shone, Patric
 See Hanley, James

Shreve, Susan Richards 1939- .... **CLC 23**
 See also CA 49-52; CAAS 5; CANR 5, 38,
 69; MAICYA; SATA 46, 95; SATA-Brief
 41

Shue, Larry 1946-1985 .... **CLC 52; DAM DRAM**
 See also CA 145; 117

Shu-Jen, Chou 1881-1936
 See Lu Hsun
 See also CA 104

Shulman, Alix Kates 1932- .... **CLC 2, 10**
 See also CA 29-32R; CANR 43; SATA 7

Shuster, Joe 1914- .... **CLC 21**

Shute, Nevil .... **CLC 30**
 See also Norway, Nevil Shute
 See also MTCW 2

Shuttle, Penelope (Diane) 1947- .... **CLC 7**
 See also CA 93-96; CANR 39, 84, 92; DLB
 14, 40

Sidney, Mary 1561-1621 .... **LC 19, 39**

Sidney, SirPhilip 1554-1586 . **LC 19, 39; DA; DAB; DAC; DAM MST, POET; PC 32**
 See also CDBLB Before 1660; DA3; DLB
 167

Siegel, Jerome 1914-1996 .... **CLC 21**
 See also CA 116; 169; 151

Siegel, Jerry
 See Siegel, Jerome

Sienkiewicz, Henryk (Adam Alexander Pius)
 1846-1916 .... **TCLC 3**
 See also CA 104; 134; CANR 84

Sierra, Gregorio Martinez
 See Martinez Sierra, Gregorio

Sierra, Maria (de la O'LeJarraga) Martinez
 See Martinez Sierra, Maria (de la
 O'LeJarraga)

Sigal, Clancy 1926- .... **CLC 7**
 See also CA 1-4R; CANR 85

Sigourney, Lydia Howard (Huntley)
 1791-1865 .... **NCLC 21, 87**
 See also DLB 1, 42, 73

Siguenza y Gongora, Carlos de 1645-1700
 .... **LC 8; HLCS 2**

Sigurjonsson, Johann 1880-1919 .. **TCLC 27**
 See also CA 170

Sikelianos, Angelos 1884-1951 ..... **TCLC 39; PC 29**

Silkin, Jon 1930- .... **CLC 2, 6, 43**
 See also CA 5-8R; CAAS 5; CANR 89;
 DLB 27

Silko, Leslie (Marmon) 1948- . **CLC 23, 74, 114; DA; DAC; DAM MST, MULT, POP; SSC 37; WLCS**
 See also AAYA 14; CA 115; 122; CANR
 45, 65; DA3; DLB 143, 175; MTCW 2;
 NNAL

Sillanpaa, Frans Eemil 1888-1964 .. **CLC 19**
 See also CA 129; 93-96; MTCW 1

Sillitoe, Alan 1928- .. **CLC 1, 3, 6, 10, 19, 57**
 See also AITN 1; CA 9-12R; CAAS 2;
 CANR 8, 26, 55; CDBLB 1960 to Present;
 DLB 14, 139; MTCW 1, 2; SATA 61

Silone, Ignazio 1900-1978 .... **CLC 4**
 See also CA 25-28; 81-84; CANR 34; CAP
 2; MTCW 1

Silver, Joan Micklin 1935- .... **CLC 20**
 See also CA 114; 121; INT 121

Silver, Nicholas
 See Faust, Frederick (Schiller)

Silverberg, Robert 1935- .... **CLC 7; DAM POP**
 See also AAYA 24; CA 1-4R; 186; CAAE
 186; CAAS 3; CANR 1, 20, 36, 85; CLR
 59; DLB 8; INT CANR-20; MAICYA;
 MTCW 1, 2; SATA 13, 91; SATA-Essay
 104

Silverstein, Alvin 1933- .... **CLC 17**
 See also CA 49-52; CANR 2; CLR 25;
 JRDA; MAICYA; SATA 8, 69

Silverstein, Virginia B(arbara Opshelor)
 1937- .... **CLC 17**
 See also CA 49-52; CANR 2; CLR 25;
 JRDA; MAICYA; SATA 8, 69

4, 18, 37, 44, 50, 71; SSC 10
  See also CA 13-16R; 147; CANR 9, 50;
  DLBY 81, 94; INT CANR-9; MTCW 1, 2
Taylor, Robert Lewis 1912-1998 ..... **CLC 14**
  See also CA 1-4R; 170; CANR 3, 64; SATA
  10
Tchekhov, Anton
  See Chekhov, Anton (Pavlovich)
Tchicaya, Gerald Felix 1931-1988 . **CLC 101**
  See also CA 129; 125; CANR 81
Tchicaya U Tam'si
  See Tchicaya, Gerald Felix
Teasdale, Sara 1884-1933 ... **TCLC 4; PC 31**
  See also CA 104; 163; DLB 45; SATA 32
Tegner, Esaias 1782-1846 .... **NCLC 2**
Teilhard de Chardin, (Marie Joseph) Pierre
  1881-1955 .... **TCLC 9**
  See also CA 105
Temple, Ann
  See Mortimer, Penelope (Ruth)
Tennant, Emma (Christina) 1937- . **CLC 13,**
  52
  See also CA 65-68; CAAS 9; CANR 10,
  38, 59, 88; DLB 14
Tenneshaw, S. M.
  See Silverberg, Robert
Tennyson, Alfred 1809-1892 .. **NCLC 30, 65;**
  DA; DAB; DAC; DAM MST, POET;
  PC 6; WLC
  See also CDBLB 1832-1890; DA3; DLB
  32
Teran, Lisa St. Aubin de .... **CLC 36**
  See also St. Aubin de Teran, Lisa
Terence c. 184B.C.-c. 159B.C. .... **CMLC 14;**
  DC 7
  See also DLB 211
Teresa de Jesus, St. 1515-1582 .... **LC 18**
Terkel, Louis 1912-
  See Terkel, Studs
  See also CA 57-60; CANR 18, 45, 67; DA3;
  MTCW 1, 2
Terkel, Studs .... **CLC 38**
  See also Terkel, Louis
  See also AAYA 32; AITN 1; MTCW 2
Terry, C. V.
  See Slaughter, Frank G(ill)
Terry, Megan 1932- .... **CLC 19; DC 13**
  See also CA 77-80; CABS 3; CANR 43;
  DLB 7
Tertullian c. 155-c. 245 .... **CMLC 29**
Tertz, Abram
  See Sinyavsky, Andrei (Donatevich)
Tesich, Steve 1943(?)-1996 .... **CLC 40, 69**
  See also CA 105; 152; DLBY 83
Tesla, Nikola 1856-1943 .... **TCLC 88**
Teternikov, Fyodor Kuzmich 1863-1927
  See Sologub, Fyodor
  See also CA 104
Tevis, Walter 1928-1984 .... **CLC 42**
  See also CA 113
Tey, Josephine .... **TCLC 14**
  See also Mackintosh, Elizabeth
  See also DLB 77
Thackeray, William Makepeace 1811-1863
  . **NCLC 5, 14, 22, 43; DA; DAB; DAC;**
  DAM MST, NOV; WLC
  See also CDBLB 1832-1890; DA3; DLB
  21, 55, 159, 163; SATA 23
Thakura, Ravindranatha
  See Tagore, Rabindranath
Tharoor, Shashi 1956- .... **CLC 70**
  See also CA 141; CANR 91
Thelwell, Michael Miles 1939- .... **CLC 22**
  See also BW 2; CA 101
Theobald, Lewis, Jr.
  See Lovecraft, H(oward) P(hillips)

Theodorescu, Ion N. 1880-1967
  See Arghezi, Tudor
  See also CA 116; DLB 220
Theriault, Yves 1915-1983 ... **CLC 79; DAC;**
  DAM MST
  See also CA 102; DLB 88
Theroux, Alexander (Louis) 1939- ... **CLC 2,**
  25
  See also CA 85-88; CANR 20, 63
Theroux, Paul (Edward) 1941- .... **CLC 5, 8,**
  11, 15, 28, 46; DAM POP
  See also AAYA 28; BEST 89:4; CA 33-36R;
  CANR 20, 45, 74; CDALBS; DA3; DLB
  2; MTCW 1, 2; SATA 44, 109
Thesen, Sharon 1946- .... **CLC 56**
  See also CA 163
Thevenin, Denis
  See Duhamel, Georges
Thibault, Jacques Anatole Francois
  1844-1924
  See France, Anatole
  See also CA 106; 127; DAM NOV; DA3;
  MTCW 1, 2
Thiele, Colin (Milton) 1920- .... **CLC 17**
  See also CA 29-32R; CANR 12, 28, 53;
  CLR 27; MAICYA; SAAS 2; SATA 14,
  72
Thomas, Audrey (Callahan) 1935- .. **CLC 7,**
  13, 37, 107; SSC 20
  See also AITN 2; CA 21-24R; CAAS 19;
  CANR 36, 58; DLB 60; MTCW 1
Thomas, Augustus 1857-1934 .... **TCLC 97**
Thomas, D(onald) M(ichael) 1935- . **CLC 13,**
  22, 31, 132
  See also CA 61-64; CAAS 11; CANR 17,
  45, 75; CDBLB 1960 to Present; DA3;
  DLB 40, 207; INT CANR-17; MTCW 1,
  2
Thomas, Dylan (Marlais) 1914-1953
  .... **TCLC 1, 8, 45; DA; DAB; DAC;**
  DAM DRAM, MST, POET; PC 2; SSC
  3; WLC
  See also CA 104; 120; CANR 65; CDBLB
  1945-1960; DA3; DLB 13, 20, 139;
  MTCW 1, 2; SATA 60
Thomas, (Philip) Edward 1878-1917
  .... **TCLC 10; DAM POET**
  See also CA 106; 153; DLB 98
Thomas, Joyce Carol 1938- .... **CLC 35**
  See also AAYA 12; BW 2, 3; CA 113; 116;
  CANR 48; CLR 19; DLB 33; INT 116;
  JRDA; MAICYA; MTCW 1, 2; SAAS 7;
  SATA 40, 78
Thomas, Lewis 1913-1993 .... **CLC 35**
  See also CA 85-88; 143; CANR 38, 60;
  MTCW 1, 2
Thomas, M. Carey 1857-1935 ...... **TCLC 89**
Thomas, Paul
  See Mann, (Paul) Thomas
Thomas, Piri 1928- .... **CLC 17; HLCS 2**
  See also CA 73-76; HW 1
Thomas, R(onald) S(tuart) 1913- ..... **CLC 6,**
  13, 48; DAB; DAM POET
  See also CA 89-92; CAAS 4; CANR 30;
  CDBLB 1960 to Present; DLB 27; MTCW
  1
Thomas, Ross (Elmore) 1926-1995 . **CLC 39**
  See also CA 33-36R; 150; CANR 22, 63
Thompson, Francis Clegg
  See Mencken, H(enry) L(ouis)
Thompson, Francis Joseph 1859-1907
  .... **TCLC 4**
  See also CA 104; CDBLB 1890-1914; DLB
  19
Thompson, Hunter S(tockton) 1939-
  .... **CLC 9, 17, 40, 104; DAM POP**
  See also BEST 89:1; CA 17-20R; CANR
  23, 46, 74, 77; DA3; DLB 185; MTCW
  1, 2

Thompson, James Myers
  See Thompson, Jim (Myers)
Thompson, Jim (Myers) 1906-1977(?)
  .... **CLC 69**
  See also CA 140; DLB 226
Thompson, Judith .... **CLC 39**
Thomson, James 1700-1748 .. **LC 16, 29, 40;**
  DAM POET
  See also DLB 95
Thomson, James 1834-1882 .... **NCLC 18;**
  DAM POET
  See also DLB 35
Thoreau, Henry David 1817-1862 . **NCLC 7,**
  21, 61; DA; DAB; DAC; DAM MST;
  PC 30; WLC
  See also CDALB 1640-1865; DA3; DLB 1,
  223
Thornton, Hall
  See Silverberg, Robert
Thucydides c. 455B.C.-399B.C. ... **CMLC 17**
  See also DLB 176
Thumboo, Edwin 1933- .... **PC 30**
Thurber, James (Grover) 1894-1961 . **CLC 5,**
  11, 25, 125; DA; DAB; DAC; DAM
  DRAM, MST, NOV; SSC 1
  See also CA 73-76; CANR 17, 39; CDALB
  1929-1941; DA3; DLB 4, 11, 22, 102;
  MAICYA; MTCW 1, 2; SATA 13
Thurman, Wallace (Henry) 1902-1934
  .... **TCLC 6; BLC 3; DAM MULT**
  See also BW 1, 3; CA 104; 124; CANR 81;
  DLB 51
Tibullus, Albius c. 54B.C.-c. 19B.C.
  .... **CMLC 36**
  See also DLB 211
Ticheburn, Cheviot
  See Ainsworth, William Harrison
Tieck, (Johann) Ludwig 1773-1853
  .... **NCLC 5, 46; SSC 31**
  See also DLB 90
Tiger, Derry
  See Ellison, Harlan (Jay)
Tilghman, Christopher 1948(?)- ...... **CLC 65**
  See also CA 159
Tillich, Paul (Johannes) 1886-1965
  .... **CLC 131**
  See also CA 5-8R; 25-28R; CANR 33;
  MTCW 1, 2
Tillinghast, Richard (Williford) 1940-
  .... **CLC 29**
  See also CA 29-32R; CAAS 23; CANR 26,
  51
Timrod, Henry 1828-1867 .... **NCLC 25**
  See also DLB 3
Tindall, Gillian (Elizabeth) 1938- ..... **CLC 7**
  See also CA 21-24R; CANR 11, 65
Tiptree, James, Jr. .... **CLC 48, 50**
  See also Sheldon, Alice Hastings Bradley
  See also DLB 8
Titmarsh, Michael Angelo
  See Thackeray, William Makepeace
Tocqueville, Alexis (Charles Henri Maurice
  Clerel, Comte) de 1805-1859 . **NCLC 7,**
  63
Tolkien, J(ohn) R(onald) R(euel) 1892-1973
  .... **CLC 1, 2, 3, 8, 12, 38; DA; DAB;**
  DAC; DAM MST, NOV, POP; WLC
  See also AAYA 10; AITN 1; CA 17-18; 45-
  48; CANR 36; CAP 2; CDBLB 1914-
  1945; CLR 56; DA3; DLB 15, 160;
  JRDA; MAICYA; MTCW 1, 2; SATA 2,
  32, 100; SATA-Obit 24
Toller, Ernst 1893-1939 .... **TCLC 10**
  See also CA 107; 186; DLB 124
Tolson, M. B.
  See Tolson, Melvin B(eaunorus)
Tolson, Melvin B(eaunorus) 1898(?)-1966
  .... **CLC 36, 105; BLC 3; DAM MULT,**
  POET

See also BW 1, 3; CA 124; 89-92; CANR 80; DLB 48, 76

Tolstoi, Aleksei Nikolaevich
See Tolstoy, Alexey Nikolaevich

Tolstoy, Alexey Nikolaevich 1882-1945
.... **TCLC 18**
See also CA 107; 158

Tolstoy, Count Leo
See Tolstoy, Leo (Nikolaevich)

Tolstoy, Leo (Nikolaevich) 1828-1910
. **TCLC 4, 11, 17, 28, 44, 79; DA; DAB; DAC; DAM MST, NOV; SSC 9, 30; WLC**
See also CA 104; 123; DA3; SATA 26

Tomasi di Lampedusa, Giuseppe 1896-1957
See Lampedusa, Giuseppe (Tomasi) di
See also CA 111

Tomlin, Lily .... **CLC 17**
See also Tomlin, Mary Jean

Tomlin, Mary Jean 1939(?)-
See Tomlin, Lily
See also CA 117

Tomlinson, (Alfred) Charles 1927- .. **CLC 2, 4, 6, 13, 45; DAM POET; PC 17**
See also CA 5-8R; CANR 33; DLB 40

Tomlinson, H(enry) M(ajor) 1873-1958
.... **TCLC 71**
See also CA 118; 161; DLB 36, 100, 195

Tonson, Jacob
See Bennett, (Enoch) Arnold

Toole, John Kennedy 1937-1969 .... **CLC 19, 64**
See also CA 104; DLBY 81; MTCW 2

Toomer, Jean 1894-1967 .. **CLC 1, 4, 13, 22; BLC 3; DAM MULT; PC 7; SSC 1; WLCS**
See also Pinchback, Eugene; Toomer, Eugene; Toomer, Eugene Pinchback; Toomer, Nathan Jean; Toomer, Nathan Pinchback
See also BW 1; CA 85-88; CDALB 1917-1929; DA3; DLB 45, 51; MTCW 1, 2

Torley, Luke
See Blish, James (Benjamin)

Tornimparte, Alessandra
See Ginzburg, Natalia

Torre, Raoul della
See Mencken, H(enry) L(ouis)

Torrence, Ridgely 1874-1950 .... **TCLC 97**
See also DLB 54

Torrey, E(dwin) Fuller 1937- .... **CLC 34**
See also CA 119; CANR 71

Torsvan, Ben Traven
See Traven, B.

Torsvan, Benno Traven
See Traven, B.

Torsvan, Berick Traven
See Traven, B.

Torsvan, Berwick Traven
See Traven, B.

Torsvan, Bruno Traven
See Traven, B.

Torsvan, Traven
See Traven, B.

Tournier, Michel (Edouard) 1924- ... **CLC 6, 23, 36, 95**
See also CA 49-52; CANR 3, 36, 74; DLB 83; MTCW 1, 2; SATA 23

Tournimparte, Alessandra
See Ginzburg, Natalia

Towers, Ivar
See Kornbluth, C(yril) M.

Towne, Robert (Burton) 1936(?)- .... **CLC 87**
See also CA 108; DLB 44

Townsend, Sue .... **CLC 61**
See also Townsend, Susan Elaine
See also AAYA 28; SATA 55, 93; SATA-Brief 48

Townsend, Susan Elaine 1946-
See Townsend, Sue
See also CA 119; 127; CANR 65; DAB; DAC; DAM MST; INT 127

Townshend, Peter (Dennis Blandford) 1945-
.... **CLC 17, 42**
See also CA 107

Tozzi, Federigo 1883-1920 .... **TCLC 31**
See also CA 160

Tracy, Don(ald Fiske) 1905-1976(?)
See Queen, Ellery
See also CA 1-4R; 176; CANR 2

Traill, Catharine Parr 1802-1899 . **NCLC 31**
See also DLB 99

Trakl, Georg 1887-1914 ..... **TCLC 5; PC 20**
See also CA 104; 165; MTCW 1

Transtroemer, Tomas (Goesta) 1931-
.... **CLC 52, 65; DAM POET**
See also CA 117; 129; CAAS 17

Transtromer, Tomas Gosta
See Transtroemer, Tomas (Goesta)

Traven, B. (?)-1969 .... **CLC 8, 11**
See also CA 19-20; 25-28R; CAP 2; DLB 9, 56; MTCW 1

Treitel, Jonathan 1959- .... **CLC 70**

Trelawny, Edward John 1792-1881
.... **NCLC 85**
See also DLB 110, 116, 144

Tremain, Rose 1943- .... **CLC 42**
See also CA 97-100; CANR 44; DLB 14

Tremblay, Michel 1942- .... **CLC 29, 102; DAC; DAM MST**
See also CA 116; 128; DLB 60; MTCW 1, 2

Trevanian .... **CLC 29**
See also Whitaker, Rod(ney)

Trevor, Glen
See Hilton, James

Trevor, William 1928- . **CLC 7, 9, 14, 25, 71, 116; SSC 21**
See also Cox, William Trevor
See also DLB 14, 139; MTCW 2

Trifonov, Yuri (Valentinovich) 1925-1981
.... **CLC 45**
See also CA 126; 103; MTCW 1

Trilling, Diana (Rubin) 1905-1996 . **CLC 129**
See also CA 5-8R; 154; CANR 10, 46; INT CANR-10; MTCW 1, 2

Trilling, Lionel 1905-1975 ..... **CLC 9, 11, 24**
See also CA 9-12R; 61-64; CANR 10; DLB 28, 63; INT CANR-10; MTCW 1, 2

Trimball, W. H.
See Mencken, H(enry) L(ouis)

Tristan
See Gomez de la Serna, Ramon

Tristram
See Housman, A(lfred) E(dward)

Trogdon, William (Lewis) 1939-
See Heat-Moon, William Least
See also CA 115; 119; CANR 47, 89; INT 119

Trollope, Anthony 1815-1882 .. **NCLC 6, 33; DA; DAB; DAC; DAM MST, NOV; SSC 28; WLC**
See also CDBLB 1832-1890; DA3; DLB 21, 57, 159; SATA 22

Trollope, Frances 1779-1863 .... **NCLC 30**
See also DLB 21, 166

Trotsky, Leon 1879-1940 .... **TCLC 22**
See also CA 118; 167

Trotter (Cockburn), Catharine 1679-1749
.... **LC 8**
See also DLB 84

Trotter, Wilfred 1872-1939 .... **TCLC 97**

Trout, Kilgore
See Farmer, Philip Jose

Trow, George W. S. 1943- .... **CLC 52**
See also CA 126; CANR 91

Troyat, Henri 1911- .... **CLC 23**
See also CA 45-48; CANR 2, 33, 67; MTCW 1

Trudeau, G(arretson) B(eekman) 1948-
See Trudeau, Garry B.
See also CA 81-84; CANR 31; SATA 35

Trudeau, Garry B. .... **CLC 12**
See also Trudeau, G(arretson) B(eekman)
See also AAYA 10; AITN 2

Truffaut, Francois 1932-1984 .. **CLC 20, 101**
See also CA 81-84; 113; CANR 34

Trumbo, Dalton 1905-1976 .... **CLC 19**
See also CA 21-24R; 69-72; CANR 10; DLB 26

Trumbull, John 1750-1831 .... **NCLC 30**
See also DLB 31

Trundlett, Helen B.
See Eliot, T(homas) S(tearns)

Truth, Sojourner 1797(?)-1883 ..... **NCLC 94**

Tryon, Thomas 1926-1991 . **CLC 3, 11; DAM POP**
See also AITN 1; CA 29-32R; 135; CANR 32, 77; DA3; MTCW 1

Tryon, Tom
See Tryon, Thomas

Ts'ao Hsueh-ch'in 1715(?)-1763 .... **LC 1**

Tsushima, Shuji 1909-1948
See Dazai Osamu
See also CA 107

Tsvetaeva (Efron), Marina (Ivanovna) 1892-1941 .... **TCLC 7, 35; PC 14**
See also CA 104; 128; CANR 73; MTCW 1, 2

Tuck, Lily 1938- .... **CLC 70**
See also CA 139; CANR 90

Tu Fu 712-770 .... **PC 9**
See also DAM MULT

Tunis, John R(oberts) 1889-1975 .... **CLC 12**
See also CA 61-64; CANR 62; DLB 22, 171; JRDA; MAICYA; SATA 37; SATA-Brief 30

Tuohy, Frank .... **CLC 37**
See also Tuohy, John Francis
See also DLB 14, 139

Tuohy, John Francis 1925-
See Tuohy, Frank
See also CA 5-8R; 178; CANR 3, 47

Turco, Lewis (Putnam) 1934- .... **CLC 11, 63**
See also CA 13-16R; CAAS 22; CANR 24, 51; DLBY 84

Turgenev, Ivan 1818-1883 ..... **NCLC 21, 37; DA; DAB; DAC; DAM MST, NOV; DC 7; SSC 7; WLC**

Turgot, Anne-Robert-Jacques 1727-1781
.... **LC 26**

Turner, Frederick 1943- .... **CLC 48**
See also CA 73-76; CAAS 10; CANR 12, 30, 56; DLB 40

Tutu, Desmond M(pilo) 1931- .... **CLC 80; BLC 3; DAM MULT**
See also BW 1, 3; CA 125; CANR 67, 81

Tutuola, Amos 1920-1997 ..... **CLC 5, 14, 29; BLC 3; DAM MULT**
See also BW 2, 3; CA 9-12R; 159; CANR 27, 66; DA3; DLB 125; MTCW 1, 2

Twain, Mark 1835-1910 ..... **TCLC 6, 12, 19, 36, 48, 59; SSC 34; WLC**
See also Clemens, Samuel Langhorne
See also AAYA 20; CLR 58, 60, 66; DLB 11, 12, 23, 64, 74

Tyler, Anne 1941- . **CLC 7, 11, 18, 28, 44, 59, 103; DAM NOV, POP**
See also AAYA 18; BEST 89:1; CA 9-12R; CANR 11, 33, 53; CDALBS; DLB 6, 143; DLBY 82; MTCW 1, 2; SATA 7, 90

Tyler, Royall 1757-1826 .... **NCLC 3**
See also DLB 37

Tynan, Katharine 1861-1931 .... **TCLC 3**
See also CA 104; 167; DLB 153

See also CA 29-32R

Vialis, Gaston
See Simenon, Georges (Jacques Christian)

Vian, Boris 1920-1959 .... **TCLC 9**
See also CA 106; 164; DLB 72; MTCW 2

Viaud, (Louis Marie) Julien 1850-1923
See Loti, Pierre
See also CA 107

Vicar, Henry
See Felsen, Henry Gregor

Vicker, Angus
See Felsen, Henry Gregor

Vidal, Gore 1925- ..... **CLC 2, 4, 6, 8, 10, 22, 33, 72; DAM NOV, POP**
See also AITN 1; BEST 90:2; CA 5-8R; CANR 13, 45, 65; CDALBS; DA3; DLB 6, 152; INT CANR-13; MTCW 1, 2

Viereck, Peter (Robert Edwin) 1916- .... **CLC 4; PC 27**
See also CA 1-4R; CANR 1, 47; DLB 5

Vigny, Alfred (Victor) de 1797-1863 .... **NCLC 7; DAM POET; PC 26**
See also DLB 119, 192

Vilakazi, Benedict Wallet 1906-1947 .... **TCLC 37**
See also CA 168

Villa, Jose Garcia 1904-1997 .... **PC 22**
See also CA 25-28R; CANR 12

Villarreal, Jose Antonio 1924-
See also CA 133; CANR 93; DAM MULT; DLB 82; HLC 2; HW 1

Villaurrutia, Xavier 1903-1950 ..... **TCLC 80**
See also HW 1

Villehardouin 1150(?)-1218(?) ...... **CMLC 38**

Villiers de l'Isle Adam, Jean Marie Mathias Philippe Auguste, Comte de 1838-1889 .... **NCLC 3; SSC 14**
See also DLB 123

Villon, Francois 1431-1463(?) ..... **LC 62; PC 13**
See also DLB 208

Vine, Barbara .... **CLC 50**
See also Rendell, Ruth (Barbara)
See also BEST 90:4

Vinge, Joan (Carol) D(ennison) 1948- .... **CLC 30; SSC 24**
See also AAYA 32; CA 93-96; CANR 72; SATA 36, 113

Violis, G.
See Simenon, Georges (Jacques Christian)

Viramontes, Helena Maria 1954-
See also CA 159; DLB 122; HLCS 2; HW 2

Virgil 70B.C.-19B.C.
See Vergil

Visconti, Luchino 1906-1976 .... **CLC 16**
See also CA 81-84; 65-68; CANR 39

Vittorini, Elio 1908-1966 .... **CLC 6, 9, 14**
See also CA 133; 25-28R

Vivekananda, Swami 1863-1902 ... **TCLC 88**

Vizenor, Gerald Robert 1934- ...... **CLC 103; DAM MULT**
See also CA 13-16R; CAAS 22; CANR 5, 21, 44, 67; DLB 175, 227; MTCW 2; NNAL

Vizinczey, Stephen 1933- .... **CLC 40**
See also CA 128; INT 128

Vliet, R(ussell) G(ordon) 1929-1984 . **CLC 22**
See also CA 37-40R; 112; CANR 18

Vogau, Boris Andreyevich 1894-1937(?)
See Pilnyak, Boris
See also CA 123

Vogel, Paula A(nne) 1951- .... **CLC 76**
See also CA 108

Voigt, Cynthia 1942- .... **CLC 30**

See also AAYA 3, 30; CA 106; CANR 18, 37, 40; CLR 13, 48; INT CANR-18; JRDA; MAICYA; SATA 48, 79, 116; SATA-Brief 33

Voigt, Ellen Bryant 1943- .... **CLC 54**
See also CA 69-72; CANR 11, 29, 55; DLB 120

Voinovich, Vladimir (Nikolaevich) 1932- .... **CLC 10, 49**
See also CA 81-84; CAAS 12; CANR 33, 67; MTCW 1

Vollmann, William T. 1959- . **CLC 89; DAM NOV, POP**
See also CA 134; CANR 67; DA3; MTCW 2

Voloshinov, V. N.
See Bakhtin, Mikhail Mikhailovich

Voltaire 1694-1778 .... **LC 14; DA; DAB; DAC; DAM DRAM, MST; SSC 12; WLC**
See also DA3

von Aschendrof, BaronIgnatz
See Ford, Ford Madox

von Daeniken, Erich 1935- .... **CLC 30**
See also AITN 1; CA 37-40R; CANR 17, 44

von Daniken, Erich
See von Daeniken, Erich

von Hartmann, Eduard 1842-1906 .... **TCLC 96**

von Heidenstam, (Carl Gustaf) Verner
See Heidenstam, (Carl Gustaf) Verner von

von Heyse, Paul (Johann Ludwig)
See Heyse, Paul (Johann Ludwig von)

von Hofmannsthal, Hugo
See Hofmannsthal, Hugo von

von Horvath, Odon
See Horvath, Oedoen von

von Horvath, Oedoen -1938
See Horvath, Oedoen von
See also CA 184

von Liliencron, (Friedrich Adolf Axel) Detlev
See Liliencron, (Friedrich Adolf Axel) Detlev von

Vonnegut, Kurt, Jr. 1922- . **CLC 1, 2, 3, 4, 5, 8, 12, 22, 40, 60, 111; DA; DAB; DAC; DAM MST, NOV, POP; SSC 8; WLC**
See also AAYA 6; AITN 1; BEST 90:4; CA 1-4R; CANR 1, 25, 49, 75, 92; CDALB 1968-1988; DA3; DLB 2, 8, 152; DLBD 3; DLBY 80; MTCW 1, 2

Von Rachen, Kurt
See Hubbard, L(afayette) Ron(ald)

von Rezzori (d'Arezzo), Gregor
See Rezzori (d'Arezzo), Gregor von

von Sternberg, Josef
See Sternberg, Josef von

Vorster, Gordon 1924- .... **CLC 34**
See also CA 133

Vosce, Trudie
See Ozick, Cynthia

Voznesensky, Andrei (Andreievich) 1933- .... **CLC 1, 15, 57; DAM POET**
See also CA 89-92; CANR 37; MTCW 1

Waddington, Miriam 1917- .... **CLC 28**
See also CA 21-24R; CANR 12, 30; DLB 68

Wagman, Fredrica 1937- .... **CLC 7**
See also CA 97-100; INT 97-100

Wagner, Linda W.
See Wagner-Martin, Linda (C.)

Wagner, Linda Welshimer
See Wagner-Martin, Linda (C.)

Wagner, Richard 1813-1883 .... **NCLC 9**
See also DLB 129

Wagner-Martin, Linda (C.) 1936- .. **CLC 50**
See also CA 159

Wagoner, David (Russell) 1926- .. **CLC 3, 5, 15**
See also CA 1-4R; CAAS 3; CANR 2, 71; DLB 5; SATA 14

Wah, Fred(erick James) 1939- .... **CLC 44**
See also CA 107; 141; DLB 60

Wahloo, Per 1926- .... **CLC 7**
See also CA 61-64; CANR 73

Wahloo, Peter
See Wahloo, Per

Wain, John (Barrington) 1925-1994 . **CLC 2, 11, 15, 46**
See also CA 5-8R; 145; CAAS 4; CANR 23, 54; CDBLB 1960 to Present; DLB 15, 27, 139, 155; MTCW 1, 2

Wajda, Andrzej 1926- .... **CLC 16**
See also CA 102

Wakefield, Dan 1932- .... **CLC 7**
See also CA 21-24R; CAAS 7

Wakoski, Diane 1937- .... **CLC 2, 4, 7, 9, 11, 40; DAM POET; PC 15**
See also CA 13-16R; CAAS 1; CANR 9, 60; DLB 5; INT CANR-9; MTCW 2

Wakoski-Sherbell, Diane
See Wakoski, Diane

Walcott, Derek (Alton) 1930- ... **CLC 2, 4, 9, 14, 25, 42, 67, 76; BLC 3; DAB; DAC; DAM MST, MULT, POET; DC 7**
See also BW 2; CA 89-92; CANR 26, 47, 75, 80; DA3; DLB 117; DLBY 81; MTCW 1, 2

Waldman, Anne (Lesley) 1945- .... **CLC 7**
See also CA 37-40R; CAAS 17; CANR 34, 69; DLB 16

Waldo, E. Hunter
See Sturgeon, Theodore (Hamilton)

Waldo, Edward Hamilton
See Sturgeon, Theodore (Hamilton)

Walker, Alice (Malsenior) 1944- .. **CLC 5, 6, 9, 19, 27, 46, 58, 103; BLC 3; DA; DAB; DAC; DAM MST, MULT, NOV, POET, POP; PC 30; SSC 5; WLCS**
See also AAYA 3, 33; BEST 89:4; BW 2, 3; CA 37-40R; CANR 9, 27, 49, 66, 82; CDALB 1968-1988; DA3; DLB 6, 33, 143; INT CANR-27; MTCW 1, 2; SATA 31

Walker, David Harry 1911-1992 ..... **CLC 14**
See also CA 1-4R; 137; CANR 1; SATA 8; SATA-Obit 71

Walker, Edward Joseph 1934-
See Walker, Ted
See also CA 21-24R; CANR 12, 28, 53

Walker, George F. 1947- . **CLC 44, 61; DAB; DAC; DAM MST**
See also CA 103; CANR 21, 43, 59; DLB 60

Walker, Joseph A. 1935- ...... **CLC 19; DAM DRAM, MST**
See also BW 1, 3; CA 89-92; CANR 26; DLB 38

Walker, Margaret (Abigail) 1915-1998 . **CLC 1, 6; BLC; DAM MULT; PC 20**
See also BW 2, 3; CA 73-76; 172; CANR 26, 54, 76; DLB 76, 152; MTCW 1, 2

Walker, Ted .... **CLC 13**
See also Walker, Edward Joseph
See also DLB 40

Wallace, David Foster 1962- ... **CLC 50, 114**
See also CA 132; CANR 59; DA3; MTCW 2

Wallace, Dexter
See Masters, Edgar Lee

Wallace, (Richard Horatio) Edgar 1875-1932 .... **TCLC 57**
See also CA 115; DLB 70

Wallace, Irving 1916-1990 .... **CLC 7, 13; DAM NOV, POP**

See also CA 104; 132; CDALB 1929-1941;
DA3; DLB 9, 102; DLBD 2, 16; DLBY
85, 97; MTCW 1, 2

Wolfe, Thomas Kennerly, Jr. 1930-
See Wolfe, Tom
See also CA 13-16R; CANR 9, 33, 70;
DAM POP; DA3; DLB 185; INT
CANR-9; MTCW 1, 2

Wolfe, Tom .... **CLC 1, 2, 9, 15, 35, 51**
See also Wolfe, Thomas Kennerly, Jr.
See also AAYA 8; AITN 2; BEST 89:1;
DLB 152

Wolff, Geoffrey (Ansell) 1937- .... **CLC 41**
See also CA 29-32R; CANR 29, 43, 78

Wolff, Sonia
See Levitin, Sonia (Wolff)

Wolff, Tobias (Jonathan Ansell) 1945-
.... **CLC 39, 64**
See also AAYA 16; BEST 90:2; CA 114;
117; CAAS 22; CANR 54, 76; DA3; DLB
130; INT 117; MTCW 2

Wolfram von Eschenbach c. 1170-c. 1220
.... **CMLC 5**
See also DLB 138

Wolitzer, Hilma 1930- .... **CLC 17**
See also CA 65-68; CANR 18, 40; INT
CANR-18; SATA 31

Wollstonecraft, Mary 1759-1797 ... **LC 5, 50**
See also CDBLB 1789-1832; DLB 39, 104,
158

Wonder, Stevie .... **CLC 12**
See also Morris, Steveland Judkins

Wong, Jade Snow 1922- .... **CLC 17**
See also CA 109; CANR 91; SATA 112

Woodberry, George Edward 1855-1930
.... **TCLC 73**
See also CA 165; DLB 71, 103

Woodcott, Keith
See Brunner, John (Kilian Houston)

Woodruff, Robert W.
See Mencken, H(enry) L(ouis)

Woolf, (Adeline) Virginia 1882-1941
. **TCLC 1, 5, 20, 43, 56, 101; DA; DAB;**
DAC; DAM MST, NOV; SSC 7; WLC
See also Woolf, Virginia Adeline
See also CA 104; 130; CANR 64; CDBLB
1914-1945; DA3; DLB 36, 100, 162;
DLBD 10; MTCW 1

Woolf, Virginia Adeline
See Woolf, (Adeline) Virginia
See also MTCW 2

Woollcott, Alexander (Humphreys)
1887-1943 .... **TCLC 5**
See also CA 105; 161; DLB 29

Woolrich, Cornell 1903-1968 .... **CLC 77**
See also Hopley-Woolrich, Cornell George

Woolson, Constance Fenimore 1840-1894
.... **NCLC 82**
See also DLB 12, 74, 189, 221

Wordsworth, Dorothy 1771-1855 . **NCLC 25**
See also DLB 107

Wordsworth, William 1770-1850 . **NCLC 12,**
38; DA; DAB; DAC; DAM MST,
POET; PC 4; WLC
See also CDBLB 1789-1832; DA3; DLB
93, 107

Wouk, Herman 1915- .. **CLC 1, 9, 38; DAM**
NOV, POP
See also CA 5-8R; CANR 6, 33, 67;
CDALBS; DA3; DLBY 82; INT CANR-6;
MTCW 1, 2

Wright, Charles (Penzel, Jr.) 1935- . **CLC 6,**
13, 28, 119
See also CA 29-32R; CAAS 7; CANR 23,
36, 62, 88; DLB 165; DLBY 82; MTCW
1, 2

Wright, Charles Stevenson 1932- .. **CLC 49;**
BLC 3; DAM MULT, POET

See also BW 1; CA 9-12R; CANR 26; DLB
33

Wright, Frances 1795-1852 .... **NCLC 74**
See also DLB 73

Wright, Frank Lloyd 1867-1959 .. **TCLC 95**
See also AAYA 33; CA 174

Wright, Jack R.
See Harris, Mark

Wright, James (Arlington) 1927-1980
.... **CLC 3, 5, 10, 28; DAM POET**
See also AITN 2; CA 49-52; 97-100; CANR
4, 34, 64; CDALBS; DLB 5, 169; MTCW
1, 2

Wright, Judith (Arundell) 1915-2000
.... **CLC 11, 53; PC 14**
See also CA 13-16R; CANR 31, 76, 93;
MTCW 1, 2; SATA 14

Wright, L(aurali) R. 1939- .... **CLC 44**
See also CA 138

Wright, Richard (Nathaniel) 1908-1960
. **CLC 1, 3, 4, 9, 14, 21, 48, 74; BLC 3;**
DA; DAB; DAC; DAM MST, MULT,
NOV; SSC 2; WLC
See also AAYA 5; BW 1; CA 108; CANR
64; CDALB 1929-1941; DA3; DLB 76,
102; DLBD 2; MTCW 1, 2

Wright, Richard B(ruce) 1937- .... **CLC 6**
See also CA 85-88; DLB 53

Wright, Rick 1945- .... **CLC 35**

Wright, Rowland
See Wells, Carolyn

Wright, Stephen 1946- .... **CLC 33**

Wright, Willard Huntington 1888-1939
See Van Dine, S. S.
See also CA 115; DLBD 16

Wright, William 1930- .... **CLC 44**
See also CA 53-56; CANR 7, 23

Wroth, LadyMary 1587-1653(?) .... **LC 30**
See also DLB 121

Wu Ch'eng-en 1500(?)-1582(?) .... **LC 7**

Wu Ching-tzu 1701-1754 .... **LC 2**

Wurlitzer, Rudolph 1938(?)- ... **CLC 2, 4, 15**
See also CA 85-88; DLB 173

Wyatt, Thomas c. 1503-1542 .... **PC 27**
See also DLB 132

Wycherley, William 1641-1715 ..... **LC 8, 21;**
DAM DRAM
See also CDBLB 1660-1789; DLB 80

Wylie, Elinor (Morton Hoyt) 1885-1928
.... **TCLC 8; PC 23**
See also CA 105; 162; DLB 9, 45

Wylie, Philip (Gordon) 1902-1971 .. **CLC 43**
See also CA 21-22; 33-36R; CAP 2; DLB 9

Wyndham, John .... **CLC 19**
See also Harris, John (Wyndham Parkes
Lucas) Beynon

Wyss, Johann David Von 1743-1818
.... **NCLC 10**
See also JRDA; MAICYA; SATA 29; SATA-
Brief 27

Xenophon c. 430B.C.-c. 354B.C. .. **CMLC 17**
See also DLB 176

Yakumo Koizumi
See Hearn, (Patricio) Lafcadio (Tessima
Carlos)

Yamamoto, Hisaye 1921- ...... **SSC 34; DAM**
MULT

Yanez, Jose Donoso
See Donoso (Yanez), Jose

Yanovsky, Basile S.
See Yanovsky, V(assily) S(emenovich)

Yanovsky, V(assily) S(emenovich) 1906-1989
.... **CLC 2, 18**
See also CA 97-100; 129

Yates, Richard 1926-1992 .... **CLC 7, 8, 23**
See also CA 5-8R; 139; CANR 10, 43; DLB
2, 234; DLBY 81, 92; INT CANR-10

Yeats, W. B.
See Yeats, William Butler

Yeats, William Butler 1865-1939 ... **TCLC 1,**
11, 18, 31, 93; DA; DAB; DAC; DAM
DRAM, MST, POET; PC 20; WLC
See also CA 104; 127; CANR 45; CDBLB
1890-1914; DA3; DLB 10, 19, 98, 156;
MTCW 1, 2

Yehoshua, A(braham) B. 1936- . **CLC 13, 31**
See also CA 33-36R; CANR 43, 90

Yellow Bird
See Ridge, John Rollin

Yep, Laurence Michael 1948- .... **CLC 35**
See also AAYA 5, 31; CA 49-52; CANR 1,
46, 92; CLR 3, 17, 54; DLB 52; JRDA;
MAICYA; SATA 7, 69

Yerby, Frank G(arvin) 1916-1991 .... **CLC 1,**
7, 22; BLC 3; DAM MULT
See also BW 1, 3; CA 9-12R; 136; CANR
16, 52; DLB 76; INT CANR-16; MTCW
1

Yesenin, Sergei Alexandrovich
See Esenin, Sergei (Alexandrovich)

Yevtushenko, Yevgeny (Alexandrovich) 1933-
. **CLC 1, 3, 13, 26, 51, 126; DAM POET**
See also CA 81-84; CANR 33, 54; MTCW
1

Yezierska, Anzia 1885(?)-1970 .... **CLC 46**
See also CA 126; 89-92; DLB 28, 221;
MTCW 1

Yglesias, Helen 1915- .... **CLC 7, 22**
See also CA 37-40R; CAAS 20; CANR 15,
65; INT CANR-15; MTCW 1

Yokomitsu, Riichi 1898-1947 .... **TCLC 47**
See also CA 170

Yonge, Charlotte (Mary) 1823-1901
.... **TCLC 48**
See also CA 109; 163; DLB 18, 163; SATA
17

York, Jeremy
See Creasey, John

York, Simon
See Heinlein, Robert A(nson)

Yorke, Henry Vincent 1905-1974 .... **CLC 13**
See also Green, Henry
See also CA 85-88; 49-52

Yosano Akiko 1878-1942 .. **TCLC 59; PC 11**
See also CA 161

Yoshimoto, Banana .... **CLC 84**
See also Yoshimoto, Mahoko

Yoshimoto, Mahoko 1964-
See Yoshimoto, Banana
See also CA 144

Young, Al(bert James) 1939- . **CLC 19; BLC**
3; DAM MULT
See also BW 2, 3; CA 29-32R; CANR 26,
65; DLB 33

Young, Andrew (John) 1885-1971 ..... **CLC 5**
See also CA 5-8R; CANR 7, 29

Young, Collier
See Bloch, Robert (Albert)

Young, Edward 1683-1765 .... **LC 3, 40**
See also DLB 95

Young, Marguerite (Vivian) 1909-1995
.... **CLC 82**
See also CA 13-16; 150; CAP 1

Young, Neil 1945- .... **CLC 17**
See also CA 110

Young Bear, Ray A. 1950- ... **CLC 94; DAM**
MULT
See also CA 146; DLB 175; NNAL

Yourcenar, Marguerite 1903-1987 . **CLC 19,**
38, 50, 87; DAM NOV
See also CA 69-72; CANR 23, 60, 93; DLB
72; DLBY 88; MTCW 1, 2

Yuan, Chu 340(?)B.C.-278(?)B.C. . **CMLC 36**

Yurick, Sol 1925- .... **CLC 6**
See also CA 13-16R; CANR 25

Zabolotsky, Nikolai Alekseevich 1903-1958
.... **TCLC 52**
   See also CA 116; 164
Zagajewski, Adam 1945- .... **PC 27**
   See also CA 186; DLB 232
Zamiatin, Yevgenii
   See Zamyatin, Evgeny Ivanovich
Zamora, Bernice (B. Ortiz) 1938- . **CLC 89;**
   DAM MULT; HLC 2
   See also CA 151; CANR 80; DLB 82; HW
   1, 2
Zamyatin, Evgeny Ivanovich 1884-1937
.... **TCLC 8, 37**
   See also CA 105; 166
Zangwill, Israel 1864-1926 .... **TCLC 16**
   See also CA 109; 167; DLB 10, 135, 197
Zappa, Francis Vincent, Jr. 1940-1993
   See Zappa, Frank
   See also CA 108; 143; CANR 57
Zappa, Frank .... **CLC 17**
   See also Zappa, Francis Vincent, Jr.
Zaturenska, Marya 1902-1982 .... **CLC 6, 11**
   See also CA 13-16R; 105; CANR 22
Zeami 1363-1443 .... **DC 7**
Zelazny, Roger (Joseph) 1937-1995 . **CLC 21**
   See also AAYA 7; CA 21-24R; 148; CANR
   26, 60; DLB 8; MTCW 1, 2; SATA 57;
   SATA-Brief 39

Zhdanov, Andrei Alexandrovich 1896-1948
.... **TCLC 18**
   See also CA 117; 167
Zhukovsky, Vasily (Andreevich) 1783-1852
.... **NCLC 35**
   See also DLB 205
Ziegenhagen, Eric .... **CLC 55**
Zimmer, Jill Schary
   See Robinson, Jill
Zimmerman, Robert
   See Dylan, Bob
Zindel, Paul 1936- ... **CLC 6, 26; DA; DAB;**
   DAC; DAM DRAM, MST, NOV; DC 5
   See also AAYA 2; CA 73-76; CANR 31,
   65; CDALBS; CLR 3, 45; DA3; DLB 7,
   52; JRDA; MAICYA; MTCW 1, 2; SATA
   16, 58, 102
Zinov'Ev, A. A.
   See Zinoviev, Alexander (Aleksandrovich)
Zinoviev, Alexander (Aleksandrovich) 1922-
.... **CLC 19**
   See also CA 116; 133; CAAS 10
Zoilus
   See Lovecraft, H(oward) P(hillips)
Zola, Emile (Edouard Charles Antoine)
   1840-1902 .... **TCLC 1, 6, 21, 41; DA;**

   DAB; DAC; DAM MST, NOV; WLC
   See also CA 104; 138; DA3; DLB 123
Zoline, Pamela 1941- .... **CLC 62**
   See also CA 161
Zoroaster 628(?)B.C.-551(?)B.C. .. **CMLC 40**
Zorrilla y Moral, Jose 1817-1893 .. **NCLC 6**
Zoshchenko, Mikhail (Mikhailovich)
   1895-1958 .... **TCLC 15; SSC 15**
   See also CA 115; 160
Zuckmayer, Carl 1896-1977 .... **CLC 18**
   See also CA 69-72; DLB 56, 124
Zuk, Georges
   See Skelton, Robin
Zukofsky, Louis 1904-1978 .. **CLC 1, 2, 4, 7,**
   11, 18; DAM POET; PC 11
   See also CA 9-12R; 77-80; CANR 39; DLB
   5, 165; MTCW 1
Zweig, Paul 1935-1984 .... **CLC 34, 42**
   See also CA 85-88; 113
Zweig, Stefan 1881-1942 .... **TCLC 17**
   See also CA 112; 170; DLB 81, 118
Zwingli, Huldreich 1484-1531 .... **LC 37**
   See also DLB 179

Literary Criticism Series
Cumulative Topic Index

This index lists all topic entries in Gale's *Classical and Medieval Literature Criticism, Contemporary Literary Criticism, Literature Criticism from 1400 to 1800, Nineteenth-Century Literature Criticism,* and *Twentieth-Century Literary Criticism.*

Topic Index

Topic Index

TCLC Cumulative Nationality Index

AMERICAN

Adams, Andy **56**
Adams, Brooks **80**
Adams, Henry (Brooks) **4, 52**
Addams, Jane **76**
Agee, James (Rufus) **1, 19**
Allen, Fred **87**
Anderson, Maxwell **2**
Anderson, Sherwood **1, 10, 24**
Anthony, Susan B(rownell) **84**
Atherton, Gertrude (Franklin Horn) **2**
Austin, Mary (Hunter) **25**
Baker, Ray Stannard **47**
Barry, Philip **11**
Baum, L(yman) Frank **7**
Beard, Charles A(ustin) **15**
Becker, Carl (Lotus) **63**
Belasco, David **3**
Bell, James Madison **43**
Benchley, Robert (Charles) **1, 55**
Benedict, Ruth (Fulton) **60**
Benet, Stephen Vincent **7**
Benet, William Rose **28**
Bierce, Ambrose (Gwinett) **1, 7, 44**
Biggers, Earl Derr **65**
Bishop, John Peale **103**
Black Elk **33**
Boas, Franz **56**
Bodenheim, Maxwell **44**
Bok, Edward W. **101**
Bourne, Randolph S(illiman) **16**
Bradford, Gamaliel **36**
Brennan, Christopher John **17**
Bromfield, Louis (Brucker) **11**
Bryan, William Jennings **99**
Burroughs, Edgar Rice **2, 32**
Cabell, James Branch **6**
Cable, George Washington **4**
Cahan, Abraham **71**
Cardozo, Benjamin N(athan) **65**
Carnegie, Dale **53**
Cather, Willa Sibert **1, 11, 31, 99**
Chambers, Robert W(illiam) **41**
Chandler, Raymond (Thornton) **1, 7**
Chapman, John Jay **7**
Chesnutt, Charles W(addell) **5, 39**
Chopin, Kate **5, 14**
Cobb, Irvin S(hrewsbury) **77**
Coffin, Robert P(eter) Tristram **95**
Cohan, George M(ichael) **60**
Comstock, Anthony **13**
Cotter, Joseph Seamon Sr. **28**
Cram, Ralph Adams **45**
Crane, (Harold) Hart **2, 5, 80**
Crane, Stephen (Townley) **11, 17, 32**
Crawford, F(rancis) Marion **10**
Crothers, Rachel **19**
Cullen, Countee **4, 37**
Darrow, Clarence (Seward) **81**
Davis, Rebecca (Blaine) Harding **6**
Davis, Richard Harding **24**
Day, Clarence (Shepard Jr.) **25**

Dent, Lester **72**
De Voto, Bernard (Augustine) **29**
Dewey, John **95**
Dreiser, Theodore (Herman Albert) **10, 18, 35, 83**
Dulles, John Foster **72**
Dunbar, Paul Laurence **2, 12**
Duncan, Isadora **68**
Dunne, Finley Peter **28**
Eastman, Charles A(lexander) **55**
Eddy, Mary (Ann Morse) Baker **71**
Einstein, Albert **65**
Erskine, John **84**
Faust, Frederick (Schiller) **49**
Fenollosa, Ernest (Francisco) **91**
Fields, W. C. **80**
Fisher, Dorothy (Frances) Canfield **87**
Fisher, Rudolph **11**
Fitzgerald, F(rancis) Scott (Key) **1, 6, 14, 28, 55**
Fitzgerald, Zelda (Sayre) **52**
Flecker, (Herman) James Elroy **43**
Fletcher, John Gould **35**
Ford, Henry **73**
Forten, Charlotte L. **16**
Freeman, Douglas Southall **11**
Freeman, Mary E(leanor) Wilkins **9**
Fuller, Henry Blake **103**
Futrelle, Jacques **19**
Gale, Zona **7**
Garland, (Hannibal) Hamlin **3**
Gilman, Charlotte (Anna) Perkins (Stetson) **9, 37**
Glasgow, Ellen (Anderson Gholson) **2, 7**
Glaspell, Susan **55**
Goldman, Emma **13**
Green, Anna Katharine **63**
Grey, Zane **6**
Griffith, D(avid Lewelyn) W(ark) **68**
Griggs, Sutton (Elbert) **77**
Guest, Edgar A(lbert) **95**
Guiney, Louise Imogen **41**
Hall, James Norman **23**
Handy, W(illiam) C(hristopher) **97**
Harper, Frances Ellen Watkins **14**
Harris, Joel Chandler **2**
Harte, (Francis) Bret(t) **1, 25**
Hartmann, Sadakichi **73**
Hatteras, Owen **18**
Hawthorne, Julian **25**
Hearn, (Patricio) Lafcadio (Tessima Carlos) **9**
Hecht, Ben **101**
Henry, O. **1, 19**
Hergesheimer, Joseph **11**
Higginson, Thomas Wentworth **36**
Holley, Marietta **99**
Holly, Buddy **65**
Holmes, Oliver Wendell Jr. **77**
Hopkins, Pauline Elizabeth **28**
Horney, Karen (Clementine Theodore Danielsen) **71**
Howard, Robert E(rvin) **8**

Howe, Julia Ward **21**
Howells, William Dean **7, 17, 41**
Huneker, James Gibbons **65**
Ince, Thomas H. **89**
James, Henry **2, 11, 24, 40, 47, 64**
James, William **15, 32**
Jewett, (Theodora) Sarah Orne **1, 22**
Johnson, James Weldon **3, 19**
Johnson, Robert **69**
Kinsey, Alfred C(harles) **91**
Kornbluth, C(yril) M. **8**
Korzybski, Alfred (Habdank Skarbek) **61**
Kuttner, Henry **10**
Lardner, Ring(gold) W(ilmer) **2, 14**
Lewis, (Harry) Sinclair **4, 13, 23, 39**
Lewisohn, Ludwig **19**
Lewton, Val **76**
Lindsay, (Nicholas) Vachel **17**
Locke, Alain (Le Roy) **43**
London, Jack **9, 15, 39**
Lovecraft, H(oward) P(hillips) **4, 22**
Lowell, Amy **1, 8**
Mankiewicz, Herman (Jacob) **85**
March, William **96**
Markham, Edwin **47**
Marquis, Don(ald Robert Perry) **7**
Masters, Edgar Lee **2, 25**
Matthews, (James) Brander **95**
Matthiessen, F(rancis) O(tto) **100**
McAlmon, Robert (Menzies) **97**
McCoy, Horace (Stanley) **28**
McKay, Claude **7, 41**
Mead, George Herbert **89**
Mencken, H(enry) L(ouis) **13**
Micheaux, Oscar (Devereaux) **76**
Millay, Edna St. Vincent **4, 49**
Mitchell, Margaret (Munnerlyn) **11**
Mitchell, S(ilas) Weir **36**
Mitchell, William **81**
Monroe, Harriet **12**
Morley, Christopher (Darlington) **87**
Muir, John **28**
Nathan, George Jean **18**
Neumann, Alfred **100**
Nordhoff, Charles (Bernard) **23**
Norris, (Benjamin) Frank(lin Jr.) **24**
O'Neill, Eugene (Gladstone) **1, 6, 27, 49**
Osbourne, Lloyd **93**
Oskison, John Milton **35**
Park, Robert E(zra) **73**
Patton, George S. **79**
Peirce, Charles Sanders **81**
Percy, William Alexander **84**
Phillips, David Graham **44**
Porter, Gene(va Grace) Stratton **21**
Post, Melville Davisson **39**
Pulitzer, Joseph **76**
Pyle, Ernie **75**
Pyle, Howard **81**
Rawlings, Marjorie Kinnan **4**
Reed, John (Silas) **9**
Reich, Wilhelm **57**
Remington, Frederic **89**

Nationality Index

Nationality Index

TCLC-103 **Title Index**

ISBN 0-7876-4563-X

90000

9 780787 645632